MAINE
RULES OF COURT:
KEYRULES

VOLUME IIA - FEDERAL

2021

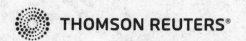

Mat #42690430

ISBN: 978-1-539-21781-7

PREFACE

Maine Rules of Court: KeyRules provides the practitioner with a comprehensive "single source" procedural guide for civil practice in the United States District Court for the District of Maine, combining applicable provisions of the Federal Rules of Civil Procedure, United States Code, local rules of practice, and analytical materials.

This book consists of outlines of the applicable rules of practice, timing requirements, filing and service requirements, hearing requirements, checklists, and other pertinent documents related to pleadings, motions, and discovery requests in United States District Courts.

THE PUBLISHER

August 2021

CONTACT US

For additional information or research assistance call our reference attorneys at 1-800-REF-ATTY (1-800-733-2889). Contact our U.S. legal editorial department directly with your questions and suggestions by email at editors.us-legal@tr.com.

ADDITIONAL KEYRULES COVERAGE ON WESTLAW

Documents for additional jurisdictions are available on Thomson Reuters Westlaw.

Table of Contents

DISTRICT OF MAINE

TABLE OF CONTENTS

VIII

UNITED STATES DISTRICT COURT

DISTRICT OF MAINE

Pleadings
Complaint

Document Last Updated July 2021

A. Checklist

(I) ❑ Matters to be considered by plaintiff

    (a) ❑ Required documents

        (1) ❑ Civil cover sheet

        (2) ❑ Complaint

        (3) ❑ Summons

        (4) ❑ Filing fee

        (5) ❑ Affidavit proving service

    (b) ❑ Supplemental documents

        (1) ❑ Notice and request for waiver of service

        (2) ❑ Notice of constitutional question

        (3) ❑ Notice of issue concerning foreign law

        (4) ❑ Nongovernmental corporate disclosure statement

        (5) ❑ DISTRICT OF MAINE: Additional supplemental documents

            (i) ❑ Motion for leave to proceed in forma pauperis and supporting affidavit

    (c) ❑ Timing

        (1) ❑ A civil action is commenced by filing a complaint with the court

        (2) ❑ If a defendant is not served within ninety (90) days after the complaint is filed, the court—on motion or on its own after notice to the plaintiff—must dismiss the action without prejudice against that defendant or order that service be made within a specified time

(II) ❑ Matters to be considered by defendant

    (a) ❑ Required documents

        (1) ❑ Answer

    (b) ❑ Supplemental documents

        (1) ❑ Waiver of the service of summons

        (2) ❑ Notice of constitutional question

        (3) ❑ Notice of issue concerning foreign law

        (4) ❑ Nongovernmental corporate disclosure statement

    (c) ❑ Timing

        (1) ❑ A defendant must serve an answer: (i) within twenty-one (21) days after being served with the summons and complaint; or (ii) if it has timely waived service under FRCP 4(d), within sixty (60) days after the request for a waiver was sent, or within ninety (90) days after it was sent to the defendant outside any judicial district of the United States

        (2) ❑ The United States, a United States agency, or a United States officer or employee sued only in an official

capacity must serve an answer to a complaint, counterclaim, or crossclaim within sixty (60) days after service on the United States attorney

(3) ❑ A United States officer or employee sued in an individual capacity for an act or omission occurring in connection with duties performed on the United States' behalf must serve an answer to a complaint, counterclaim, or crossclaim within sixty (60) days after service on the officer or employee or service on the United States attorney, whichever is later

(4) ❑ Unless the court sets a different time, serving a motion under FRCP 12 alters the periods in FRCP 12(a) as follows: (A) if the court denies the motion or postpones its disposition until trial, the responsive pleading must be served within fourteen (14) days after notice of the court's action; or (B) if the court grants a motion for a more definite statement, the responsive pleading must be served within fourteen (14) days after the more definite statement is served

(5) ❑ The notice and request for waiver must give the defendant a reasonable time of at least thirty (30) days after the request was sent—or at least sixty (60) days if sent to the defendant outside any judicial district of the United States—to return the waiver; a defendant who, before being served with process, timely returns a waiver need not serve an answer to the complaint until sixty (60) days after the request was sent—or until ninety (90) days after it was sent to the defendant outside any judicial district of the United States

B. Timing

1. *Commencing an action.* A civil action is commenced by filing a complaint with the court. FRCP 3.

   a. *Statute of limitations.* An action will be barred if it is not commenced within the period set forth in the applicable statute of limitations. Under the Federal Rules of Civil Procedure (FRCP), an action is commenced by filing a complaint with the court. Thus, in a suit on a right created by federal law, filing a complaint suffices to satisfy the statute of limitations. FEDPROF § 61:2.

      i. *Federal question cases.* Absent a specific statutory provision for tolling the statute of limitations, in federal question cases, the filing of the complaint will toll the statute, even if not all filing fees have been paid, although some courts have added the requirement of reasonable diligence in effecting service. FEDPROF § 61:2.

      ii. *Diversity cases.* In diversity actions the matter is less clear. In the landmark Ragan case, the Supreme Court held in construing FRCP 3 that if, under local law, an action is not commenced until the defendant has been served, the statute is not tolled until service has been accomplished. FEDPROF § 61:2; Ragan v. Merchants Transfer & Warehouse Co., 337 U.S. 530, 69 S. Ct. 1233, 93 L. Ed. 1520 (1949). However, in a subsequent case, the Supreme Court distinguished Ragan in holding that the provision of FRCP 4 governing methods of service prevails over a conflicting state rule requiring personal service. FEDPROF § 61:2; Hanna v. Plumer, 380 U.S. 460, 85 S. Ct. 1136, 14 L. Ed. 2d 8 (1965). The [Supreme Court] reaffirmed Ragan and held that (1) a state law mandating actual service of a summons to toll the statute of limitations must be followed in a diversity case, and (2) FRCP 3 only governs other timing requirements in the Federal Rules of Civil Procedure. FEDPROF § 61:2; Walker v. Armco Steel Corp., 446 U.S. 740, 100 S. Ct. 1978, 64 L. Ed. 2d 659 (1980).

      iii. *Mailbox rule for pro se incarcerated litigants.* Individuals who are incarcerated and are filing their legal documents pro se may benefit from a special "mailbox rule," which fixes the time of commencement of an action at the point when the complaint enters the prison mail system, rather than when it reaches the court clerk. FPP § 1052; Houston v. Lack, 487 U.S. 266, 276, 108 S. Ct. 2379, 2385, 101 L. Ed. 2d 245 (1988). For non-prisoners, however, placing a complaint in the mail for delivery to the court is generally not sufficient to commence an action for purposes of FRCP 3. FPP § 1052.

2. *Service of summons and complaint.* If a defendant is not served within ninety (90) days after the complaint is filed, the court—on motion or on its own after notice to the plaintiff—must dismiss the action without prejudice against that defendant or order that service be made within a specified time. But if the plaintiff shows good cause for the failure, the court must extend the time for service for an appropriate period. FRCP 4(m) does not apply to service in a foreign country under FRCP 4(f), FRCP 4(h)(2), or FRCP 4(j)(1), or to service of a notice under FRCP 71.1(d)(3)(A). FRCP 4(m).

3. *Computation of time*

   a. *Computing time.* FRCP 6 applies in computing any time period specified in the Federal Rules of Civil Procedure, in any local rule or court order, or in any statute that does not specify a method of computing time. FRCP 6(a).

      i. *Period stated in days or a longer unit.* When the period is stated in days or a longer unit of time: (A) exclude the day of the event that triggers the period; (B) count every day, including intermediate Saturdays, Sundays, and legal holidays; and (C) include the last day of the period, but if the last day is a Saturday, Sunday, or legal holiday,

2

the period continues to run until the end of the next day that is not a Saturday, Sunday, or legal holiday. FRCP 6(a)(1).

ii. *Period stated in hours.* When the period is stated in hours: (A) begin counting immediately on the occurrence of the event that triggers the period; (B) count every hour, including hours during intermediate Saturdays, Sundays, and legal holidays; and (C) if the period would end on a Saturday, Sunday, or legal holiday, the period continues to run until the same time on the next day that is not a Saturday, Sunday, or legal holiday. FRCP 6(a)(2).

iii. *Inaccessibility of the clerk's office.* Unless the court orders otherwise, if the clerk's office is inaccessible: (A) on the last day for filing under FRCP 6(a)(1), then the time for filing is extended to the first accessible day that is not a Saturday, Sunday, or legal holiday; or (B) during the last hour for filing under FRCP 6(a)(2), then the time for filing is extended to the same time on the first accessible day that is not a Saturday, Sunday, or legal holiday. FRCP 6(a)(3).

iv. *"Last day" defined.* Unless a different time is set by a statute, local rule, or court order, the last day ends: (A) for electronic filing, at midnight in the court's time zone; and (B) for filing by other means, when the clerk's office is scheduled to close. FRCP 6(a)(4).

v. *"Next day" defined.* The "next day" is determined by continuing to count forward when the period is measured after an event and backward when measured before an event. FRCP 6(a)(5).

vi. *"Legal holiday" defined.* "Legal holiday" means: (A) the day set aside by statute for observing New Year's Day, Martin Luther King Jr.'s Birthday, Washington's Birthday, Memorial Day, Independence Day, Labor Day, Columbus Day, Veterans' Day, Thanksgiving Day, or Christmas Day; (B) any day declared a holiday by the President or Congress; and (C) for periods that are measured after an event, any other day declared a holiday by the state where the district court is located. FRCP 6(a)(6).

vii. *DISTRICT OF MAINE: Applicability of FRCP 6.* FRCP 6 applies when computing any period of time stated in the Local Rules of the United States District Court for the District of Maine. ME R USDCT Rule 6(a).

b. *DISTRICT OF MAINE: Computation of electronic filing deadlines.* Filing documents electronically does not in any way alter any filing deadlines. All electronic transmissions of documents must be completed prior to midnight, Eastern Time, in order to be considered timely filed that day. Where a specific time of day deadline is set by court order or stipulation, the electronic filing must be completed by that time. ME R USDCT App. 4(f). A document filed electronically shall be deemed filed at the time and date stated on the Notice of Electronic Filing received from the court. ME R USDCT App. 4(d)(2).

i. *Technical failures.* A filing user whose filing is made untimely as the result of a technical failure may seek appropriate relief from the court. ME R USDCT App. 4(n). A technical failure of the court's ECF system is deemed to have occurred when the court's ECF site cannot accept filings continuously or intermittently over the course of any period of time greater than one (1) hour. Known system outages will be posted on the court's website along with guidance on how to proceed, if applicable. ME R USDCT App. 4(n).

c. *Extending time.* When an act may or must be done within a specified time, the court may, for good cause, extend the time: (A) with or without motion or notice if the court acts, or if a request is made, before the original time or its extension expires; or (B) on motion made after the time has expired if the party failed to act because of excusable neglect. FRCP 6(b)(1). A court must not extend the time to act under FRCP 50(b), FRCP 50(d), FRCP 52(b), FRCP 59(b), FRCP 59(d), FRCP 59(e), and FRCP 60(b). FRCP 6(b)(2). Refer to the United States District Court for the District of Maine KeyRules Motion for Continuance/Extension of Time document for more information on extending time.

C. General Requirements

1. *Pleading, generally*

   a. *Pleadings allowed.* Only these pleadings are allowed: (1) a complaint; (2) an answer to a complaint; (3) an answer to a counterclaim designated as a counterclaim; (4) an answer to a crossclaim; (5) a third-party complaint; (6) an answer to a third-party complaint; and (7) if the court orders one, a reply to an answer. FRCP 7(a).

   b. *Pleading to be concise and direct.* Each allegation must be simple, concise, and direct. No technical form is required. FRCP 8(d)(1).

   c. *Alternative statements of a claim or defense.* A party may set out 2 or more statements of a claim or defense alternatively or hypothetically, either in a single count or defense or in separate ones. If a party makes alternative statements, the pleading is sufficient if any one of them is sufficient. FRCP 8(d)(2).

   d. *Inconsistent claims or defenses.* A party may state as many separate claims or defenses as it has, regardless of consistency. FRCP 8(d)(3).

3

e. *Construing pleadings.* Pleadings must be construed so as to do justice. FRCP 8(e).

2. *Pleading special matters*

    a. *Capacity or authority to sue; Legal existence.* Except when required to show that the court has jurisdiction, a pleading need not allege: (A) a party's capacity to sue or be sued; (B) a party's authority to sue or be sued in a representative capacity; or (C) the legal existence of an organized association of persons that is made a party. FRCP 9(a)(1).

        i. *Raising those issues.* To raise any of those issues, a party must do so by a specific denial, which must state any supporting facts that are peculiarly within the party's knowledge. FRCP 9(a)(2).

    b. *Fraud or mistake; Conditions of mind.* In alleging fraud or mistake, a party must state with particularity the circumstances constituting fraud or mistake. Malice, intent, knowledge, and other conditions of a person's mind may be alleged generally. FRCP 9(b).

    c. *Conditions precedent.* In pleading conditions precedent, it suffices to allege generally that all conditions precedent have occurred or been performed. But when denying that a condition precedent has occurred or been performed, a party must do so with particularity. FRCP 9(c).

    d. *Official document or act.* In pleading an official document or official act, it suffices to allege that the document was legally issued or the act legally done. FRCP 9(d).

    e. *Judgment.* In pleading a judgment or decision of a domestic or foreign court, a judicial or quasi-judicial tribunal, or a board or officer, it suffices to plead the judgment or decision without showing jurisdiction to render it. FRCP 9(e).

    f. *Time and place.* An allegation of time or place is material when testing the sufficiency of a pleading. FRCP 9(f).

    g. *Special damages.* If an item of special damage is claimed, it must be specifically stated. FRCP 9(g).

    h. *Admiralty or maritime claim*

        i. *How designated.* If a claim for relief is within the admiralty or maritime jurisdiction and also within the court's subject-matter jurisdiction on some other ground, the pleading may designate the claim as an admiralty or maritime claim for purposes of FRCP 14(c), FRCP 38(e), and FRCP 82 and the Supplemental Rules for Admiralty or Maritime Claims and Asset Forfeiture Actions. A claim cognizable only in the admiralty or maritime jurisdiction is an admiralty or maritime claim for those purposes, whether or not so designated. FRCP 9(h)(1).

        ii. *Designation for appeal.* A case that includes an admiralty or maritime claim within FRCP 9(h) is an admiralty case within 28 U.S.C.A. § 1292(a)(3). FRCP 9(h)(2).

3. *Complaint.* A pleading that states a claim for relief must contain: (1) a short and plain statement of the grounds for the court's jurisdiction, unless the court already has jurisdiction and the claim needs no new jurisdictional support; (2) a short and plain statement of the claim showing that the pleader is entitled to relief; and (3) a demand for the relief sought, which may include relief in the alternative or different types of relief. FRCP 8(a).

    a. *Statement of jurisdiction.* Federal courts are courts of limited jurisdiction, and it is presumed that they are without jurisdiction unless the contrary affirmatively appears. FEDPROC § 62:38; Kirkland Masonry, Inc. v. Comm'r, 614 F.2d 532 (5th Cir. 1980). Therefore, in order for a complaint to comply with the requirement that it contain a short and plain statement of the grounds upon which the court's jurisdiction depends, unless the court already has jurisdiction and the claim needs no new jurisdictional support, the jurisdictional basis must be alleged affirmatively and distinctly on the face of the complaint. FEDPROC § 62:38; Spain v. U.S. Through Atomic Nuclear Regulatory Comm'n Through U.S. Atomic Safety & Licensing Bd., 397 F. Supp. 15 (M.D. La. 1975).

        i. *Sufficiency of statement.* Although it has been said that the jurisdictional statement requirement contemplates reference to a federal statute, a sufficient jurisdictional statement is not made by simply citing a federal statute without alleging facts which bring the plaintiff within the purview of the statute. FEDPROC § 62:38; Atkins v. Sch. Bd. of Halifax Cty., 379 F. Supp. 1060 (W.D. Va. 1974); Sims v. Mercy Hosp. of Monroe, 451 F.2d 171 (6th Cir. 1971).

        ii. *Allegations showing proper venue not necessary.* Improper venue is an affirmative defense, and a complaint need not include allegations showing venue to be proper. FEDPROC § 62:38; Ripperger v. A.C. Allyn & Co., 113 F.2d 332 (2d Cir. 1940).

    b. *Statement of claim*

        i. *Notice pleading.* Because the only function left exclusively to the pleadings by the Federal Rules of Civil Procedure is that of giving notice, federal courts frequently have said that the Federal Rules of Civil Procedure

4

have adopted a system of "notice pleading." FPP § 1202; Swierkiewicz v. Sorema N.A., 534 U.S. 506, 122 S. Ct. 992, 152 L. Ed. 2d 1 (2002). To comply with the requirement that a complaint contain a short and plain statement of the claim, a pleading must give the opposing party fair notice of the nature of a claim and of the basis or grounds for it, so that the defendant will at least be notified as to which of its actions gave rise to the claim upon which the complaint is based. FEDPROC § 62:45.

- *Plausibility standard.* Bell Atlantic Corporation v. Twombly and Ashcroft v. Iqbal have paved the way for a heightened "plausibility" pleading standard that requires plaintiffs to provide greater factual development in their complaints in order to survive an FRCP 12(b)(6) motion to dismiss. FPP § 1202; Bell Atl. Corp. v. Twombly, 550 U.S. 544, 127 S. Ct. 1955, 167 L. Ed. 2d 929 (2007); Ashcroft v. Iqbal, 556 U.S. 662, 129 S. Ct. 1937, 173 L. Ed. 2d 868 (2009). In discussing what appears to be the new plausibility standard, the [Supreme Court in Bell Atlantic Corp. v. Twombly] stated: "While a complaint attacked by a Rule 12(b)(6) motion to dismiss does not need detailed factual allegations. . .a plaintiff's obligation to provide the 'grounds' of his 'entitle[ment] to relief' requires more than labels and conclusions, and a formulaic recitation of the elements of a cause of action will not do. . .Factual allegations must be enough to raise a right to relief above the speculative level." FPP § 1216; Bell Atl. Corp. v. Twombly, 550 U.S. 544, 127 S. Ct. 1955, 167 L. Ed. 2d 929 (2007).

ii.   *Facts and evidence.* The complaint need only state enough facts to raise a reasonable expectation that discovery will reveal evidence of the necessary elements. FEDPROC § 62:52; Phillips v. Cty. of Allegheny, 515 F.3d 224 (3d Cir. 2008). A complaint is not intended to formulate issues or fully summarize the facts involved. FEDPROC § 62:52; Hill v. MCI WorldCom Commc'ns, Inc., 141 F. Supp. 2d 1205 (S.D. Iowa 2001). Under notice pleading, the full development of the facts and the narrowing of contested issues are accomplished through discovery and other pretrial procedures. FEDPROC § 62:52.

iii.   *Particularity.* The claim should be particularized sufficiently for the defendant to prepare an adequate defense, file a responsive pleading, determine whether the defense of res judicata is appropriate, and commence discovery. FEDPROC § 62:45; Kelly v. Schmidberger, 806 F.2d 44 (2d Cir. 1986); Frank v. Mracek, 58 F.R.D. 365 (M.D. Ala. 1973); Barlow v. Pep Boys, Inc., 625 F. Supp. 130 (E.D. Pa. 1985). The statement should be sufficient to [ensure] that the court is sufficiently informed to determine the issue presented and to decide whether the complaint states a claim upon which relief can be had. FEDPROC § 62:45; Philadelphia Dressed Beef Co. v. Wilson & Co., 19 F.R.D. 198 (E.D. Pa. 1956); Luckett v. Cohen, 145 F. Supp. 155 (S.D.N.Y. 1956).

c.   *Demand for relief sought.* FRCP 8(a)(3) does not require a party to frame the demand for judgment according to a prescribed form or set of particular words; any concise statement identifying the remedies and the parties against whom relief is sought will be sufficient. FPP § 1255; Chandler v. McKee Foods Corp., 2009 WL 210858 (W.D.Va. Jan. 28, 2009). Moreover, the pleader need only make one demand for relief regardless of the number of claims that are asserted. FPP § 1255; Liberty Mut. Ins. Co. v. Wetzel, 424 U.S. 737, 96 S. Ct. 1202, 47 L. Ed. 2d 435 (1976). Relief must be requested as to each defendant. FEDPROC § 62:58; RKO-Stanley Warner Theatres, Inc. v. Mellon Nat. Bank & Trust Co., 436 F.2d 1297 (3d Cir. 1970).

4.   *Joinder*

a.   *Joinder of claims.* A party asserting a claim, counterclaim, crossclaim, or third-party claim may join, as independent or alternative claims, as many claims as it has against an opposing party. FRCP 18(a).

i.   *Joinder of contingent claims.* A party may join two claims even though one of them is contingent on the disposition of the other; but the court may grant relief only in accordance with the parties' relative substantive rights. In particular, a plaintiff may state a claim for money and a claim to set aside a conveyance that is fraudulent as to that plaintiff, without first obtaining a judgment for the money. FRCP 18(b).

b.   *Joinder of parties; Required*

i.   *Persons required to be joined if feasible; Required party.* A person who is subject to service of process and whose joinder will not deprive the court of subject-matter jurisdiction must be joined as a party if: (A) in that person's absence, the court cannot accord complete relief among existing parties; or (B) that person claims an interest relating to the subject of the action and is so situated that disposing of the action in the person's absence may: (i) as a practical matter impair or impede the person's ability to protect the interest; or (ii) leave an existing party subject to a substantial risk of incurring double, multiple, or otherwise inconsistent obligations because of the interest. FRCP 19(a)(1).

ii.   *Joinder of parties by court order.* If a person has not been joined as required, the court must order that the person be made a party. A person who refuses to join as a plaintiff may be made either a defendant or, in a proper case, an involuntary plaintiff. FRCP 19(a)(2).

      iii.   *Venue.* If a joined party objects to venue and the joinder would make venue improper, the court must dismiss that party. FRCP 19(a)(3).

      iv.   *When joinder of parties is not feasible.* If a person who is required to be joined if feasible cannot be joined, the court must determine whether, in equity and good conscience, the action should proceed among the existing parties or should be dismissed. FRCP 19(b). For a list of the factors for the court to consider in determining whether joinder of parties is feasible, refer to FRCP 19(b)(1) through FRCP 19(b)(4).

      v.   *Pleading the reasons for nonjoinder.* When asserting a claim for relief, a party must state: (1) the name, if known, of any person who is required to be joined if feasible but is not joined; and (2) the reasons for not joining that person. FRCP 19(c).

      vi.   *Exception for class actions.* FRCP 19 is subject to FRCP 23. FRCP 19(d). For information on class actions, refer to FRCP 23.

   c.   *Joinder of parties; Permissible*

      i.   *Persons who may join or be joined*

- *Plaintiffs.* Persons may join in one action as plaintiffs if: (A) they assert any right to relief jointly, severally, or in the alternative with respect to or arising out of the same transaction, occurrence, or series of transactions or occurrences; and (B) any question of law or fact common to all plaintiffs will arise in the action. FRCP 20(a)(1).

- *Defendants.* Persons—as well as a vessel, cargo, or other property subject to admiralty process in rem—may be joined in one action as defendants if: (A) any right to relief is asserted against them jointly, severally, or in the alternative with respect to or arising out of the same transaction, occurrence, or series of transactions or occurrences; and (B) any question of law or fact common to all defendants will arise in the action. FRCP 20(a)(2).

- *Extent of relief.* Neither a plaintiff nor a defendant need be interested in obtaining or defending against all the relief demanded. The court may grant judgment to one or more plaintiffs according to their rights, and against one or more defendants according to their liabilities. FRCP 20(a)(3).

      ii.   *Protective measures.* The court may issue orders—including an order for separate trials—to protect a party against embarrassment, delay, expense, or other prejudice that arises from including a person against whom the party asserts no claim and who asserts no claim against the party. FRCP 20(b).

   d.   *Misjoinder and nonjoinder of parties.* Misjoinder of parties is not a ground for dismissing an action. On motion or on its own, the court may at any time, on just terms, add or drop a party. The court may also sever any claim against a party. FRCP 21.

5.   *Right to a jury trial; Demand*

   a.   *Right preserved.* The right of trial by jury as declared by U.S.C.A. Const. Amend. VII, or as provided by a federal statute, is preserved to the parties inviolate. FRCP 38(a).

   b.   *Demand.* On any issue triable of right by a jury, a party may demand a jury trial by: (1) serving the other parties with a written demand—which may be included in a pleading—no later than fourteen (14) days after the last pleading directed to the issue is served; and (2) filing the demand in accordance with FRCP 5(d). FRCP 38(b).

      i.   *DISTRICT OF MAINE: Removed actions.* A demand for jury trial in actions removed to the United States District Court for the District of Maine from the state courts shall be filed in accordance with the provisions of FRCP 81(c). ME R USDCT Rule 38.

   c.   *Specifying issues.* In its demand, a party may specify the issues that it wishes to have tried by a jury; otherwise, it is considered to have demanded a jury trial on all the issues so triable. If the party has demanded a jury trial on only some issues, any other party may—within fourteen (14) days after being served with the demand or within a shorter time ordered by the court—serve a demand for a jury trial on any other or all factual issues triable by jury. FRCP 38(c).

   d.   *Waiver; Withdrawal.* A party waives a jury trial unless its demand is properly served and filed. A proper demand may be withdrawn only if the parties consent. FRCP 38(d).

   e.   *Admiralty and maritime claims.* The rules in FRCP 38 do not create a right to a jury trial on issues in a claim that is an admiralty or maritime claim under FRCP 9(h). FRCP 38(e).

6.   *DISTRICT OF MAINE: Appearances.* An attorney's signature to a pleading shall constitute an appearance for the party filing the pleading. Otherwise, an attorney who wishes to participate in any manner in any action must file a formal written

appearance identifying the party represented. An appearance whether by pleading or formal written appearance shall be signed by an attorney in his/her individual name and shall state his/her office address. ME R USDCT Rule 83.2(a). For more information, refer to ME R USDCT Rule 83.2.

7. *DISTRICT OF MAINE: Alternative dispute resolution (ADR)*. Litigants are authorized and encouraged to employ, at their own expense, any available ADR process on which they can agree, including early neutral evaluation, settlement conferences, mediation, non-binding summary jury trial, corporate mini-trial, and arbitration proceedings. ME R USDCT Rule 83.11(a). For more information on ADR, refer to ME R USDCT Rule 83.11.

D. Documents

1. *Required documents*

   a. *Civil cover sheet.* A civil cover sheet is submitted with each civil complaint filed in the district court. Copies of the cover sheet may be obtained from the clerk of the court. Each district may have different instructions for filling out the form. Counsel should always check with the pertinent local rules. FEDPROF § 1A:252(Practice Notes).

      i. *DISTRICT OF MAINE.* All complaints shall be accompanied by a properly completed Civil Cover Sheet (Form JS-44) which is available from the clerk. ME R USDCT Rule 3(a).

   b. *Complaint.* Refer to the "C. General Requirements" section of this KeyRules document for information on the complaint.

   c. *Summons.* A summons must be served with a copy of the complaint. FRCP 4(c)(1).

      i. *Form and content.* A summons must: (A) name the court and the parties; (B) be directed to the defendant; (C) state the name and address of the plaintiff's attorney or—if unrepresented—of the plaintiff; (D) state the time within which the defendant must appear and defend; (E) notify the defendant that a failure to appear and defend will result in a default judgment against the defendant for the relief demanded in the complaint; (F) be signed by the clerk; and (G) bear the court's seal. FRCP 4(a)(1).

   d. *Filing fee.* The clerk of each district court shall require the parties instituting any civil action, suit or proceeding in such court, whether by original process, removal or otherwise, to pay a filing fee. 28 U.S.C.A. § 1914(a).

      i. *DISTRICT OF MAINE.* The filing fee shall be paid to the clerk upon filing the complaint. ME R USDCT Rule 3(a).

      ii. *Advance payment of fees.* Each district court by rule or standing order may require advance payment of fees. 28 U.S.C.A. § 1914(c).

      iii. *Fee schedule.* For information on filing fees and the District Court Miscellaneous Fee Schedule, refer to 28 U.S.C.A. § 1914.

   e. *Affidavit proving service.* Unless service is waived, proof of service must be made to the court. Except for service by a United States Marshal or deputy marshal, proof must be by the server's affidavit. FRCP 4(l)(1). Refer to the "F. Filing and Service Requirements" section of this KeyRules document for more information.

2. *Supplemental documents*

   a. *Notice and request for waiver of service.* An individual, corporation, or association that is subject to service under FRCP 4(e), FRCP 4(f), or FRCP 4(h) has a duty to avoid unnecessary expenses of serving the summons. The plaintiff may notify such a defendant that an action has been commenced and request that the defendant waive service of a summons. FRCP 4(d)(1).

      i. *Form and content.* The notice and request must: (A) be in writing and be addressed: (i) to the individual defendant; or (ii) for a defendant subject to service under FRCP 4(h), to an officer, a managing or general agent, or any other agent authorized by appointment or by law to receive service of process; (B) name the court where the complaint was filed; (C) be accompanied by a copy of the complaint, two (2) copies of a waiver form appended to FRCP 4, and a prepaid means for returning the form; (D) inform the defendant, using the form appended to FRCP 4, of the consequences of waiving and not waiving service; (E) state the date when the request is sent; (F) give the defendant a reasonable time of at least thirty (30) days after the request was sent—or at least sixty (60) days if sent to the defendant outside any judicial district of the United States—to return the waiver; and (G) be sent by first-class mail or other reliable means. FRCP 4(d)(1).

   b. *Notice of constitutional question.* A party that files a pleading, written motion, or other paper drawing into question the constitutionality of a federal or state statute must promptly: (1) file a notice of constitutional question stating the question and identifying the paper that raises it, if: (A) a federal statute is questioned and the parties do not include the United States, one of its agencies, or one of its officers or employees in an official capacity; or (B) a state statute is questioned and the parties do not include the state, one of its agencies, or one of its officers or employees in an official capacity; and (2) serve the notice and paper on the Attorney General of the United States if a federal statute is questioned—or on the state attorney general if a state statute is questioned—either by certified or registered mail or by sending it to an electronic address designated by the attorney general for this purpose. FRCP 5.1(a).

    i. *DISTRICT OF MAINE.* To enable the court to comply with the provisions of 28 U.S.C.A. § 2403 and FRCP 24(c), in any action, suit or proceeding to which the United States or any agency, officer or employee thereof is not a party, any party who shall draw into question the constitutionality of any Act of Congress affecting the public interest shall forthwith so notify the clerk in writing, stating the title of the action, its docket number if any, and the Act of Congress in question. ME R USDCT Rule 5.1. To enable the court to comply with the provisions of 28 U.S.C.A. § 2403, in any action, suit or proceeding to which a state or any agency, officer or employee thereof is not a party, any party who shall draw in question the constitutionality of any statute of that state affecting the public interest shall forthwith so notify the clerk in writing, stating the title of the action, its docket number if any, and the statute of the state in question. ME R USDCT Rule 5.1.

    ii. *No forfeiture.* A party's failure to file and serve the notice, or the court's failure to certify, does not forfeit a constitutional claim or defense that is otherwise timely asserted. FRCP 5.1(d).

  c. *Notice of issue concerning foreign law.* A party who intends to raise an issue about a foreign country's law must give notice by a pleading or other writing. In determining foreign law, the court may consider any relevant material or source, including testimony, whether or not submitted by a party or admissible under the Federal Rules of Evidence. The court's determination must be treated as a ruling on a question of law. FRCP 44.1.

  d. *Nongovernmental corporate disclosure statement.* A nongovernmental corporate party must file two (2) copies of a disclosure statement that: (1) identifies any parent corporation and any publicly held corporation owning ten percent (10%) or more of its stock; or (2) states that there is no such corporation. FRCP 7.1(a). A party must: (1) file the disclosure statement with its first appearance, pleading, petition, motion, response, or other request addressed to the court; and (2) promptly file a supplemental statement if any required information changes. FRCP 7.1(b).

    i. *DISTRICT OF MAINE: Notice of interested parties.* To enable the court to evaluate possible disqualification or recusal, counsel for all non-governmental parties shall file with their first appearance a Notice of Interested Parties, which shall list all persons, associations of persons, firms, partnerships, limited liability companies, joint ventures, corporations (including parent or affiliated corporations, clearly identified as such), or any similar entities, owning ten percent (10%) or more of the named party. Counsel shall be under a continuing obligation to file an amended Notice if any material change occurs in the status of an Interested Party, such as through merger, acquisition, or new/additional membership. ME R USDCT Rule 7.1.

  e. *DISTRICT OF MAINE: Additional supplemental documents*

    i. *Motion for leave to proceed in forma pauperis and supporting affidavit.* A party who desires to proceed in forma pauperis pursuant to 28 U.S.C.A. § 1915 shall file with the complaint a motion for leave to proceed in forma pauperis together with an affidavit showing in detail the party's inability to pay fees and costs and that the party is entitled to redress. ME R USDCT Rule 3(a).

E. Format

1. *Form of documents*

  a. *DISTRICT OF MAINE: Font size, line spacing, and paper size.* All such documents shall be typed in a font of no less than size twelve (12) point, and shall be double-spaced or printed on eight and one-half by eleven (8-1/2 x 11) inch paper. Footnotes shall be in a font of no less than size ten (10) point, and may be single spaced. ME R USDCT Rule 10.

  b. *Caption.* Every pleading must have a caption with the court's name, a title, a file number, and an FRCP 7(a) designation. FRCP 10(a).

    i. *Names of parties.* The title of the complaint must name all the parties; the title of other pleadings, after naming the first party on each side, may refer generally to other parties. FRCP 10(a).

    ii. *DISTRICT OF MAINE: Additional caption requirements.* All pleadings, motions and other papers filed with the clerk or otherwise submitted to the court, except exhibits, shall bear the proper case number and shall contain on the first page a caption as described by FRCP 10(a) and immediately thereunder a designation of what the document is and the name of the party in whose behalf it is submitted. ME R USDCT Rule 10.

    iii. *DISTRICT OF MAINE: Three-judge district court.* To enable the court to comply with the provisions of 28

U.S.C.A. § 2284, in any action or proceeding which a party believes is required to be heard by a three-judge district court, the words "THREE-JUDGE DISTRICT COURT REQUESTED" or the equivalent shall be included directly beneath the designation of the pleadings. ME R USDCT Rule 9(a).

    iv. *DISTRICT OF MAINE: Injunctive relief.* If a pleading or motion seeks injunctive relief, in addition to the prayer for such relief, the words "INJUNCTIVE RELIEF SOUGHT" or the equivalent shall be included on the first page. ME R USDCT Rule 9(b).

    v. *DISTRICT OF MAINE: Demand for jury trial.* If a demand for jury trial is endorsed upon a pleading pursuant to FRCP 38(b), in addition to said endorsement the designation of the pleading shall include the words "AND DEMAND FOR JURY TRIAL" or the equivalent on the first page. ME R USDCT Rule 38.

c. *Claims or defenses*

    i. *Numbered paragraphs.* A party must state its claims or defenses in numbered paragraphs, each limited as far as practicable to a single set of circumstances. A later pleading may refer by number to a paragraph in an earlier pleading. FRCP 10(b).

    ii. *Separate statements.* If doing so would promote clarity, each claim founded on a separate transaction or occurrence—and each defense other than a denial—must be stated in a separate count or defense. FRCP 10(b).

d. *Adoption by reference.* A statement in a pleading may be adopted by reference elsewhere in the same pleading or in any other pleading or motion. FRCP 10(c).

    i. *Exhibits.* A copy of a written instrument that is an exhibit to a pleading is a part of the pleading for all purposes. FRCP 10(c).

e. *DISTRICT OF MAINE: Page numbering.* All pages shall be numbered at the bottom. ME R USDCT Rule 10.

f. *DISTRICT OF MAINE: Attachment of ancillary papers.* Ancillary papers shall be attached at the end of the document to which they relate. ME R USDCT Rule 10.

g. *Acceptance by the clerk.* The clerk must not refuse to file a paper solely because it is not in the form prescribed by the Federal Rules of Civil Procedure or by a local rule or practice. FRCP 5(d)(4).

2. *Form of electronic documents.* A paper filed electronically is a written paper for purposes of the Federal Rules of Civil Procedure. FRCP 5(d)(3)(D).

a. *DISTRICT OF MAINE: Document format.* The ECF system only accepts documents in a portable document format (PDF). Although there are two types of PDF documents—electronically converted PDF's and scanned PDF's—only electronically converted PDF's may be filed with the court using the ECF system, unless otherwise authorized by local rule or order. ME R USDCT App. 4. Any document or exhibit to be filed or submitted to the court shall not be password-protected or encrypted. ME R USDCT App. 4(g)(12).

    i. *Electronically converted PDFs.* Electronically converted PDF's are created from word processing documents (MS Word, WordPerfect, etc.) using Adobe Acrobat or similar software. They are text searchable and their file size is small. ME R USDCT App. 4. Software used to electronically convert documents to PDF which includes proprietary or advertisement information within the PDF document is prohibited. ME R USDCT App. 4.

    ii. *Scanned PDFs.* Scanned PDF's are created from paper documents run through an optical scanner. Scanned PDF's are not searchable and have a large file size. ME R USDCT App. 4.

b. *DISTRICT OF MAINE: Title.* All pleadings filed electronically shall be titled in accordance with the approved dictionary of civil or criminal events of the ECF system of the United States District Court for the District of Maine. ME R USDCT App. 4(d)(3).

c. *DISTRICT OF MAINE: Attachments.* Attachments to filings and exhibits must be filed in accordance with the court's ECF User Manual, unless otherwise ordered by the court. ME R USDCT App. 4(j). When there are fifty (50) or fewer attachments to a pleading, the attachments must be filed by counsel electronically using ECF. When there are more than fifty (50) attachments, the attachments must be filed in one of the following ways: (A) using ECF, simply attach them to the pleading being filed; (B) using ECF, use the "Additional Attachments" menu item; (C) on paper; or (D) on a properly labeled three and one-half (3-1/2) inch floppy disk, CD or DVD. ME R USDCT App. 4(j)(2). Attachments filed on paper or on disk must contain a comprehensive index that clearly describes each document. ME R USDCT App. 4(j)(2).

    i. A filing user must submit as attachments only those excerpts of the referenced documents that are directly germane to the matter under consideration by the court. Excerpted material must be clearly and prominently identified as such. Users who file excerpts of documents do so without prejudice to their right to timely file additional excerpts or the complete document, as may be allowed by the court. Responding parties may timely file additional excerpts or the complete document that they believe are directly germane. ME R USDCT App. 4(j)(3).

 ii. Filers shall not attach as an exhibit any pleading or other paper already on file with the court in that case, but shall merely refer to that document. ME R USDCT App. 4(j)(4).

 d. *DISTRICT OF MAINE: Compliance with technical standards.* All documents filed by electronic means must comply with technical standards, if any, established by the Judicial Conference of the United States or by the United States District Court for the District of Maine. ME R USDCT App. 4(a)(3).

3. *Signing of pleadings, motions and other papers*

 a. *Signature.* Every pleading, written motion, and other paper must be signed by at least one attorney of record in the attorney's name—or by a party personally if the party is unrepresented. The paper must state the signer's address, e-mail address, and telephone number. FRCP 11(a).

  i. *No verification or accompanying affidavit required for pleadings.* Unless a rule or statute specifically states otherwise, a pleading need not be verified or accompanied by an affidavit. FRCP 11(a).

  ii. *Unsigned papers.* The court must strike an unsigned paper unless the omission is promptly corrected after being called to the attorney's or party's attention. FRCP 11(a).

 b. *Electronic signing.* A filing made through a person's electronic-filing account and authorized by that person, together with that person's name on a signature block, constitutes the person's signature. FRCP 5(d)(3)(C).

  i. *DISTRICT OF MAINE: Attorneys.* The user log-in and password together with a user's name on the signature block constitutes the attorney's signature pursuant to the Federal Rules of Civil Procedure and the Local Rules of the United States District Court for the District of Maine. All electronically filed documents must include a signature block and must set forth the attorney's name, address, telephone number and e-mail address. The name of the ECF user under whose log-in and password the document is submitted must be preceded by a "/s/" in the space where the signature would otherwise appear. ME R USDCT App. 4(h)(1).

  ii. *DISTRICT OF MAINE: Multiple signatures.* The filer of any document requiring more than one signature (e.g., pleadings filed by visiting lawyers, stipulations, joint status reports) must list thereon all the names of other signatories, preceded by a "/s/" in the space where the signatures would otherwise appear. By submitting such a document, the filing attorney certifies that each of the other signatories has expressly agreed to the form and substance of the document and that the filing attorney has their actual authority to submit the document electronically. ME R USDCT App. 4(h)(2). For more information, refer to ME R USDCT App. 4(h)(2).

  iii. *DISTRICT OF MAINE: Documents signed under oath.* Affidavits, declarations, verified complaints, or any other document signed under oath shall be filed electronically. The electronically filed version shall contain the typed name of the signatory, preceded by a "/s/" in the space where the signature would otherwise appear indicating that the paper document bears an original signature. ME R USDCT Rule 10; ME R USDCT App. 4(h)(3). For more information, refer to ME R USDCT Rule 10.

 c. *Representations to the court.* By presenting to the court a pleading, written motion, or other paper—whether by signing, filing, submitting, or later advocating it—an attorney or unrepresented party certifies that to the best of the person's knowledge, information, and belief, formed after an inquiry reasonable under the circumstances: (1) it is not being presented for any improper purpose, such as to harass, cause unnecessary delay, or needlessly increase the cost of litigation; (2) the claims, defenses, and other legal contentions are warranted by existing law or by a nonfrivolous argument for extending, modifying, or reversing existing law or for establishing new law; (3) the factual contentions have evidentiary support or, if specifically so identified, will likely have evidentiary support after a reasonable opportunity for further investigation or discovery; and (4) the denials of factual contentions are warranted on the evidence or, if specifically so identified, are reasonably based on belief or a lack of information. FRCP 11(b).

 d. *Sanctions.* If, after notice and a reasonable opportunity to respond, the court determines that FRCP 11(b) has been violated, the court may impose an appropriate sanction on any attorney, law firm, or party that violated FRCP 11(b) or is responsible for the violation. FRCP 11(c)(1). Refer to the United States District Court for the District of Maine KeyRules Motion for Sanctions document for more information.

4. *Privacy protection for filings made with the court*

 a. *Redacted filings.* Unless the court orders otherwise, in an electronic or paper filing with the court that contains an individual's Social Security number, taxpayer-identification number, or birth date, the name of an individual known to be a minor, or a financial-account number, a party or nonparty making the filing may include only: (1) the last four (4) digits of the Social Security number and taxpayer-identification number; (2) the year of the individual's birth; (3) the minor's initials; and (4) the last four (4) digits of the financial-account number. FRCP 5.2(a).

    i. *DISTRICT OF MAINE.* To address the privacy concerns created by the Internet access to court papers, unless otherwise ordered by the court, counsel shall modify certain personal data identifiers in pleadings and other papers as follows: (1) minors' names: use of the minors' initials only; (2) Social Security numbers: use of the last four (4) numbers only; (3) dates of birth: use of the year of birth only; [and] (4) financial account numbers: identify the type of account and the financial institution, but use only the last four (4) numbers of the account number. ME R USDCT Redacting Pleadings. Counsel should also use caution when filing papers that contain a person's medical records, employment history; financial information; and any proprietary or trade secret information. ME R USDCT Redacting Pleadings.

b. *Exemptions from the redaction requirement.* The redaction requirement does not apply to the following: (1) a financial-account number that identifies the property allegedly subject to forfeiture in a forfeiture proceeding; (2) the record of an administrative or agency proceeding; (3) the official record of a state-court proceeding; (4) the record of a court or tribunal, if that record was not subject to the redaction requirement when originally filed; (5) a filing covered by FRCP 5.2(c) or FRCP 5.2(d); and (6) a pro se filing in an action brought under 28 U.S.C.A. § 2241, 28 U.S.C.A. § 2254, or 28 U.S.C.A. § 2255. FRCP 5.2(b).

c. *Limitations on remote access to electronic files; Social Security appeals and immigration cases.* Unless the court orders otherwise, in an action for benefits under the Social Security Act, and in an action or proceeding relating to an order of removal, to relief from removal, or to immigration benefits or detention, access to an electronic file is authorized as follows: (1) the parties and their attorneys may have remote electronic access to any part of the case file, including the administrative record; (2) any other person may have electronic access to the full record at the courthouse, but may have remote electronic access only to: (A) the docket maintained by the court; and (B) an opinion, order, judgment, or other disposition of the court, but not any other part of the case file or the administrative record. FRCP 5.2(c).

d. *Filings made under seal.* The court may order that a filing be made under seal without redaction. The court may later unseal the filing or order the person who made the filing to file a redacted version for the public record. FRCP 5.2(d).

    i. *DISTRICT OF MAINE.* For information on filing sealed documents in the District of Maine, refer to ME R USDCT Rule 7A, ME R USDCT App. 4(p)(2), and ME R USDCT Sealed Filings.

e. *Protective orders.* For good cause, the court may by order in a case: (1) require redaction of additional information; or (2) limit or prohibit a nonparty's remote electronic access to a document filed with the court. FRCP 5.2(e).

f. *Option for additional unredacted filing under seal.* A person making a redacted filing may also file an unredacted copy under seal. The court must retain the unredacted copy as part of the record. FRCP 5.2(f).

    i. *DISTRICT OF MAINE.* A party wishing to file a document containing the personal data identifiers specified above may. . .file an unredacted document under seal. This document will be retained by the clerk's office as part of the record. ME R USDCT Redacting Pleadings. The court may, however, still require the party to file a redacted copy for the public file. ME R USDCT Redacting Pleadings.

g. *Option for filing a reference list.* A filing that contains redacted information may be filed together with a reference list that identifies each item of redacted information and specifies an appropriate identifier that uniquely corresponds to each item listed. The list must be filed under seal and may be amended as of right. Any reference in the case to a listed identifier will be construed to refer to the corresponding item of information. FRCP 5.2(g).

    i. *DISTRICT OF MAINE.* A party wishing to file a document containing the personal data identifiers specified above may. . .file a reference list under seal. The reference list shall contain the complete personal data identifier(s) and the redacted identifier(s) used in its (their) place in the filing. All references in the case to the redacted identifiers included in the reference list will be construed to refer to the corresponding complete identifier. The reference list must be filed under seal, and may be amended as of right. It shall be retained by the clerk's office as part of the record. ME R USDCT Redacting Pleadings. The court may, however, still require the party to file a redacted copy for the public file. ME R USDCT Redacting Pleadings.

h. *DISTRICT OF MAINE: Responsibility for redaction.* The clerk is not required to review documents filed with the court for compliance with FRCP 5.2. The responsibility to redact filings rests with counsel and the party or nonparty making the filing. ME R USDCT App. 4(i); ME R USDCT Redacting Pleadings. For guidelines for filing confidential information in civil cases in the District of Maine, refer to ME R USDCT Confidentiality.

i. *Waiver of protection of identifiers.* A person waives the protection of FRCP 5.2(a) as to the person's own information by filing it without redaction and not under seal. FRCP 5.2(h).

F. Filing and Service Requirements

1. *Filing requirements.* A civil action is commenced by filing a complaint with the court. FRCP 3. The first step in a civil action in a United States district court is the filing of the complaint with the clerk or the judge. FPP § 1052. Filing a complaint requires nothing more than delivery of the document to a court officer authorized to receive it. FPP § 1052; Cent. States, Se. & Sw. Areas Pension Fund v. Paramount Liquor Co., 34 F. Supp. 2d 1092 (N.D. Ill. 1999).

   a. *DISTRICT OF MAINE: Place of filing.* The filing party shall file each new action in Bangor or Portland, and the latter shall ordinarily be tried in Bangor or Portland, by reference to the county in which a substantial part of the events or omissions giving rise to the claim occurred or in which a substantial part of the property that is the subject of the action is situated. Cases arising in the counties of Aroostook, Franklin, Hancock, Kennebec, Penobscot, Piscataquis, Somerset, Waldo and Washington shall be filed and ordinarily tried at Bangor. Cases arising in the counties of Androscoggin, Cumberland, Knox, Lincoln, Oxford, Sagadahoc and York shall be filed and ordinarily tried at Portland. ME R USDCT Rule 3(b). For more information, refer to ME R USDCT Rule 3(b).

   b. *Nonelectronic filing.* A paper not filed electronically is filed by delivering it: (A) to the clerk; or (B) to a judge who agrees to accept it for filing, and who must then note the filing date on the paper and promptly send it to the clerk. FRCP 5(d)(2).

      i. *DISTRICT OF MAINE: Documents to be filed in paper.* The following documents shall be filed in paper, which may also be scanned into ECF by the clerk's office: (A) all handwritten pleadings; and (B) all pleadings and documents filed by pro se litigants who are incarcerated or who are not registered filing users in ECF. ME R USDCT App. 4(g)(8). Non-prisoner pro se litigants in civil actions may register with ECF or may file (and serve) all pleadings and other documents in paper. The clerk's office will scan into ECF any pleadings and documents filed on paper in accordance with ME R USDCT App. 4(g). ME R USDCT App. 4(o). For more information, refer to ME R USDCT App. 4(g).

   c. *Electronic filing*

      i. *DISTRICT OF MAINE: Authorization.* Unless exempt or otherwise ordered by the court, papers shall be filed and served electronically as required by the court's Administrative Procedures Governing the Filing and Service by Electronic Means, which is set forth in ME R USDCT App. 4. The provisions of the court's Administrative Procedures Governing the Filing and Service by Electronic Means (ME R USDCT App. 4) shall be applied and enforced as part of the Local Rules of the United States District Court for the District of Maine. ME R USDCT Rule 5(c).

      ii. *Filing by represented persons.* A person represented by an attorney must file electronically, unless nonelectronic filing is allowed by the court for good cause or is allowed or required by local rule. FRCP 5(d)(3)(A).

         • *DISTRICT OF MAINE.* An attorney may apply to the court for permission to file paper documents. ME R USDCT App. 4(a)(5).

      iii. *Filing by unrepresented persons.* A person not represented by an attorney: (i) may file electronically only if allowed by court order or by local rule; and (ii) may be required to file electronically only by court order, or by a local rule that includes reasonable exceptions. FRCP 5(d)(3)(B).

         • *DISTRICT OF MAINE.* Non-prisoner pro se litigants in civil actions may register with ECF or may file (and serve) all pleadings and other documents in paper. ME R USDCT App. 4(o). A non-prisoner who is a party to a civil action and who is not represented by an attorney may register to receive service electronically and to electronically transmit their documents to the court for filing in the ECF system. If during the course of the action the person retains an attorney who appears on the person's behalf, the clerk shall terminate the person's registration upon the attorney's appearance. ME R USDCT App. 4(b)(2).

      iv. *DISTRICT OF MAINE: Scope of electronic filing.* All documents submitted for filing in civil and criminal cases, regardless of case commencement date, except those documents specifically exempted in ME R USDCT App. 4(g), shall be filed electronically using the electronic case filing system (ECF). ME R USDCT App. 4(a)(1). For special filing requirements and exceptions, refer to ME R USDCT App. 4(g).

      v. *DISTRICT OF MAINE: Consequences of electronic filing.* Electronic transmission of a document to the ECF system, together with the transmission of a Notice of Electronic Filing (NEF) from the court, constitutes filing of the document for all purposes of the Federal Rules of Civil Procedure. ME R USDCT App. 4(d)(1).

      vi. *DISTRICT OF MAINE: Review of documents.* Documents filed with the clerk's office will normally be reviewed no later than the close of the next business day. It is the responsibility of the filing party to promptly notify the clerk's office via telephone of a matter that requires the immediate attention of a judicial officer. ME R USDCT App. 4(a)(4).

d. *DISTRICT OF MAINE: Facsimile filing.* No papers shall be submitted to the court by means of a facsimile machine without prior leave of the court. ME R USDCT Rule 5(c); ME R USDCT App. 4(m).

e. *DISTRICT OF MAINE: Civil case opening documents filed via e-mail.* Civil case opening documents, such as a complaint, petition, or notice of removal, together with a properly completed summons and civil cover sheet, shall be filed by e-mail in PDF, so that the documents can be added to ECF. ME R USDCT App. 4(c)(1).

2. *Issuance of summons.* On or after filing the complaint, the plaintiff may present a summons to the clerk for signature and seal. If the summons is properly completed, the clerk must sign, seal, and issue it to the plaintiff for service on the defendant. A summons—or a copy of a summons that is addressed to multiple defendants—must be issued for each defendant to be served. FRCP 4(b).

   a. *DISTRICT OF MAINE: Electronic issuance.* The clerk's office will imprint the seal of the court and the clerk's signature on the summons and issue the summons electronically to counsel. ME R USDCT App. 4(c)(2).

   b. *Amendments.* The court may permit a summons to be amended. FRCP 4(a)(2).

3. *Service requirements.* A summons must be served with a copy of the complaint. The plaintiff is responsible for having the summons and complaint served within the time allowed by FRCP 4(m) and must furnish the necessary copies to the person who makes service. FRCP 4(c)(1).

   a. *By whom served.* Any person who is at least 18 years old and not a party may serve a summons and complaint. FRCP 4(c)(2).

      i. *By a marshal or someone specially appointed.* At the plaintiff's request, the court may order that service be made by a United States Marshal or deputy marshal or by a person specially appointed by the court. The court must so order if the plaintiff is authorized to proceed in forma pauperis under 28 U.S.C.A. § 1915 or as a seaman under 28 U.S.C.A. § 1916. FRCP 4(c)(3).

      ii. *DISTRICT OF MAINE: Agreement on acceptance of service.* When service documents are issued in any civil case where a plaintiff has been granted in forma pauperis status in an action involving the State of Maine or its employees, and in all cases where a petitioner has filed a habeas corpus petition under 28 U.S.C.A. § 2254, regardless of whether or not the filing fee has been paid, procedures for service will be pursuant to the agreement between the Attorney General of Maine and the court set forth in ME R USDCT App. 3. ME R USDCT Rule 4. For more information, refer to ME R USDCT App. 3.

   b. *Serving an individual within a judicial district of the United States.* Unless federal law provides otherwise, an individual—other than a minor, an incompetent person, or a person whose waiver has been filed—may be served in a judicial district of the United States by: (1) following state law for serving a summons in an action brought in courts of general jurisdiction in the state where the district court is located or where service is made; or (2) doing any of the following: (A) delivering a copy of the summons and of the complaint to the individual personally; (B) leaving a copy of each at the individual's dwelling or usual place of abode with someone of suitable age and discretion who resides there; or (C) delivering a copy of each to an agent authorized by appointment or by law to receive service of process. FRCP 4(e).

   c. *Serving an individual in a foreign country.* Unless federal law provides otherwise, an individual—other than a minor, an incompetent person, or a person whose waiver has been filed—may be served at a place not within any judicial district of the United States: (1) by any internationally agreed means of service that is reasonably calculated to give notice, such as those authorized by the Hague Convention on the Service Abroad of Judicial and Extrajudicial Documents; (2) if there is no internationally agreed means, or if an international agreement allows but does not specify other means, by a method that is reasonably calculated to give notice: (A) as prescribed by the foreign country's law for service in that country in an action in its courts of general jurisdiction; (B) as the foreign authority directs in response to a letter rogatory or letter of request; or (C) unless prohibited by the foreign country's law, by: (i) delivering a copy of the summons and of the complaint to the individual personally; or (ii) using any form of mail that the clerk addresses and sends to the individual and that requires a signed receipt; or (D) by other means not prohibited by international agreement, as the court orders. FRCP 4(f).

   d. *Serving a minor or an incompetent person.* A minor or an incompetent person in a judicial district of the United States must be served by following state law for serving a summons or like process on such a defendant in an action brought in the courts of general jurisdiction of the state where service is made. A minor or an incompetent person who is not within any judicial district of the United States must be served in the manner prescribed by FRCP 4(f)(2)(A), FRCP 4(f)(2)(B), or FRCP 4(f)(3). FRCP 4(g).

   e. *Serving a corporation, partnership, or association.* Unless federal law provides otherwise or the defendant's waiver

13

has been filed, a domestic or foreign corporation, or a partnership or other unincorporated association that is subject to suit under a common name, must be served: (1) in a judicial district of the United States: (A) in the manner prescribed by FRCP 4(e)(1) for serving an individual; or (B) by delivering a copy of the summons and of the complaint to an officer, a managing or general agent, or any other agent authorized by appointment or by law to receive service of process and—if the agent is one authorized by statute and the statute so requires—by also mailing a copy of each to the defendant; or (2) at a place not within any judicial district of the United States, in any manner prescribed by FRCP 4(f) for serving an individual, except personal delivery under FRCP 4(f)(2)(C)(i). FRCP 4(h).

f. *Serving the United States and its agencies, corporations, officers, or employees*

  i. *United States.* To serve the United States, a party must: (A) (i) deliver a copy of the summons and of the complaint to the United States attorney for the district where the action is brought—or to an assistant United States attorney or clerical employee whom the United States attorney designates in a writing filed with the court clerk—or (ii) send a copy of each by registered or certified mail to the civil-process clerk at the United States attorney's office; (B) send a copy of each by registered or certified mail to the Attorney General of the United States at Washington, D.C.; and (C) if the action challenges an order of a nonparty agency or officer of the United States, send a copy of each by registered or certified mail to the agency or officer. FRCP 4(i)(1).

  ii. *Agency; Corporation; Officer or employee sued in an official capacity.* To serve a United States agency or corporation, or a United States officer or employee sued only in an official capacity, a party must serve the United States and also send a copy of the summons and of the complaint by registered or certified mail to the agency, corporation, officer, or employee. FRCP 4(i)(2).

  iii. *Officer or employee sued individually.* To serve a United States officer or employee sued in an individual capacity for an act or omission occurring in connection with duties performed on the United States' behalf (whether or not the officer or employee is also sued in an official capacity), a party must serve the United States and also serve the officer or employee under FRCP 4(e), FRCP 4(f), or FRCP 4(g). FRCP 4(i)(3).

  iv. *Extending time.* The court must allow a party a reasonable time to cure its failure to: (A) serve a person required to be served under FRCP 4(i)(2), if the party has served either the United States attorney or the Attorney General of the United States; or (B) serve the United States under FRCP 4(i)(3), if the party has served the United States officer or employee. FRCP 4(i)(4).

g. *Serving a foreign, state, or local government*

  i. *Foreign state.* A foreign state or its political subdivision, agency, or instrumentality must be served in accordance with 28 U.S.C.A. § 1608. FRCP 4(j)(1).

  ii. *State or local government.* A state, a municipal corporation, or any other state-created governmental organization that is subject to suit must be served by: (A) delivering a copy of the summons and of the complaint to its chief executive officer; or (B) serving a copy of each in the manner prescribed by that state's law for serving a summons or like process on such a defendant. FRCP 4(j)(2).

h. *Territorial limits of effective service.* Serving a summons or filing a waiver of service establishes personal jurisdiction over a defendant: (A) who is subject to the jurisdiction of a court of general jurisdiction in the state where the district court is located; (B) who is a party joined under FRCP 14 or FRCP 19 and is served within a judicial district of the United States and not more than 100 miles from where the summons was issued; or (C) when authorized by a federal statute. FRCP 4(k)(1).

  i. *Federal claim outside state-court jurisdiction.* For a claim that arises under federal law, serving a summons or filing a waiver of service establishes personal jurisdiction over a defendant if: (A) the defendant is not subject to jurisdiction in any state's courts of general jurisdiction; and (B) exercising jurisdiction is consistent with the United States Constitution and laws. FRCP 4(k)(2).

i. *Asserting jurisdiction over property or assets*

  i. *Federal law.* The court may assert jurisdiction over property if authorized by a federal statute. Notice to claimants of the property must be given as provided in the statute or by serving a summons under FRCP 4. FRCP 4(n)(1).

  ii. *State law.* On a showing that personal jurisdiction over a defendant cannot be obtained in the district where the action is brought by reasonable efforts to serve a summons under FRCP 4, the court may assert jurisdiction over the defendant's assets found in the district. Jurisdiction is acquired by seizing the assets under the circumstances and in the manner provided by state law in that district. FRCP 4(n)(2).

j. *DISTRICT OF MAINE: Electronic service not allowed.* A party may not electronically serve a civil complaint but shall print the embossed summons and effect service in the manner in accordance with FRCP 4. ME R USDCT App. 4(c)(2).

   k. *Proving service*

      i. *Affidavit required.* Unless service is waived, proof of service must be made to the court. Except for service by a United States Marshal or deputy marshal, proof must be by the server's affidavit. FRCP 4(l)(1).

      ii. *Service outside the United States.* Service not within any judicial district of the United States must be proved as follows: (A) if made under FRCP 4(f)(1), as provided in the applicable treaty or convention; or (B) if made under FRCP 4(f)(2) or FRCP 4(f)(3), by a receipt signed by the addressee, or by other evidence satisfying the court that the summons and complaint were delivered to the addressee. FRCP 4(l)(2).

      iii. *Validity of service; Amending proof.* Failure to prove service does not affect the validity of service. The court may permit proof of service to be amended. FRCP 4(l)(3).

      iv. *Results of filing a waiver of service.* When the plaintiff files a waiver, proof of service is not required and FRCP 4 applies as if a summons and complaint had been served at the time of filing the waiver. FRCP 4(d)(4).

   l. *Service of other process.* For information on service of other process, refer to FRCP 4.1.

4. *DISTRICT OF MAINE: Filing and service of highly sensitive documents (HSDs).* For information on filing and serving highly sensitive documents (HSDs) in the District of Maine, refer to ME R USDCT General Order 21-5.

G. Hearings

1. There is no hearing contemplated in the federal statutes or rules for the complaint and summons.

H. Forms

1. Official Federal Complaint and Summons Forms

   a. Notice of a lawsuit and request to waive service of summons. FRCP 4.

   b. Duty to avoid unnecessary expenses of serving a summons. FRCP 4.

2. Federal Complaint and Summons Forms

   a. Summons. 2 FEDFORMS § 3:23.

   b. Proof of service by U.S. Marshal. 2 FEDFORMS § 3:24.

   c. Summons; Suit against officers of the United States. 2 FEDFORMS § 3:26.

   d. Request for summons. 2 FEDFORMS § 3:27.

   e. Civil cover sheet. 2 FEDFORMS § 3:29.

   f. Motion for appointment of person to serve process. 2 FEDFORMS § 3:30.

   g. Motion for appointment of United States Marshal to serve process. 2 FEDFORMS § 3:34.

   h. Notice of lawsuit and request for waiver of service of summons and waiver of summons. 2 FEDFORMS § 3:36.

   i. Motion for payment of costs of personal service. 2 FEDFORMS § 3:37.

   j. Affidavit of personal service; Delivery to individual. 2 FEDFORMS § 3:54.

   k. Declaration of service; Delivery to individual. 2 FEDFORMS § 3:55.

   l. Declaration of service; Delivery at usual place of abode or residence. 2 FEDFORMS § 3:56.

   m. Declaration of service; Service on corporation; Delivery to officer. 2 FEDFORMS § 3:57.

   n. Declaration of service; Service on United States. 2 FEDFORMS § 3:69.

   o. Declaration of service; Service on officer of United States. 2 FEDFORMS § 3:71.

   p. Complaint. 2 FEDFORMS § 7:14.

   q. Pro se complaint for a civil case. 2 FEDFORMS § 7:14.30.

   r. Pro se complaint and request for injunction. 2 FEDFORMS § 7:14.50.

   s. Introductory clause; Single claim stated. 2 FEDFORMS § 7:16.

   t. Introductory clause; Several claims stated in separate counts. 2 FEDFORMS § 7:18.

   u. Allegations on information and belief. 2 FEDFORMS § 7:19.

    v.   General prayer for relief. 2 FEDFORMS § 7:21.

    w.   Complaint; Single count. FEDPROF § 1A:171.

    x.   Complaint; Multiple counts; With same jurisdictional basis. FEDPROF § 1A:172.

    y.   Complaint; Multiple counts; With different jurisdictional basis for each. FEDPROF § 1A:173.

    z.   Civil cover sheet; General form (form JS-44). FEDPROF § 1A:252.

I. Applicable Rules

1. *Federal rules*

    a.   District court; Filing and miscellaneous fees; Rules of court. 28 U.S.C.A. § 1914.

    b.   Commencing an action. FRCP 3.

    c.   Summons. FRCP 4.

    d.   Serving and filing pleadings and other papers. FRCP 5.

    e.   Constitutional challenge to a statute; Notice, certification, and intervention. FRCP 5.1.

    f.   Privacy protection for filings made with the court. FRCP 5.2.

    g.   Computing and extending time; Time for motion papers. FRCP 6.

    h.   Pleadings allowed; Form of motions and other papers. FRCP 7.

    i.   Disclosure statement. FRCP 7.1.

    j.   General rules of pleading. FRCP 8.

    k.   Pleading special matters. FRCP 9.

    l.   Form of pleadings. FRCP 10.

    m.   Signing pleadings, motions, and other papers; Representations to the court; Sanctions. FRCP 11.

    n.   Joinder of claims. FRCP 18.

    o.   Required joinder of parties. FRCP 19.

    p.   Permissive joinder of parties. FRCP 20.

    q.   Misjoinder and nonjoinder of parties. FRCP 21.

    r.   Right to a jury trial; Demand. FRCP 38.

    s.   Determining foreign law. FRCP 44.1.

2. *Local rules*

    a.   *DISTRICT OF MAINE*

       i.   Commencement of action. ME R USDCT Rule 3.

      ii.   Service of process. ME R USDCT Rule 4.

     iii.   Service and filing of pleadings and other papers. ME R USDCT Rule 5.

     iv.   Notice of constitutional question. ME R USDCT Rule 5.1.

      v.   Time. ME R USDCT Rule 6.

     vi.   Corporate disclosure. ME R USDCT Rule 7.1.

     vii.   Pleading special matters. ME R USDCT Rule 9.

    viii.   Form of pleadings, motions and other papers. ME R USDCT Rule 10.

     ix.   Demand for jury trial. ME R USDCT Rule 38.

      x.   Attorneys; Appearances and withdrawals. ME R USDCT Rule 83.2.

     xi.   Alternative dispute resolution (ADR). ME R USDCT Rule 83.11.

     xii.   Administrative procedures governing the filing and service by electronic means. ME R USDCT App. 4.

    xiii.   Redacting pleadings. ME R USDCT Redacting Pleadings.

Pleadings
Answer

Document Last Updated July 2021

A. Checklist

(I) ❑ Matters to be considered by plaintiff

   (a) ❑ Required documents

      (1) ❑ Civil cover sheet

      (2) ❑ Complaint

      (3) ❑ Summons

      (4) ❑ Filing fee

      (5) ❑ Affidavit proving service

   (b) ❑ Supplemental documents

      (1) ❑ Notice and request for waiver of service

      (2) ❑ Notice of constitutional question

      (3) ❑ Notice of issue concerning foreign law

      (4) ❑ Nongovernmental corporate disclosure statement

      (5) ❑ DISTRICT OF MAINE: Additional supplemental documents

         (i) ❑ Motion for leave to proceed in forma pauperis and supporting affidavit

   (c) ❑ Timing

      (1) ❑ A civil action is commenced by filing a complaint with the court

      (2) ❑ If a defendant is not served within ninety (90) days after the complaint is filed, the court—on motion or on its own after notice to the plaintiff—must dismiss the action without prejudice against that defendant or order that service be made within a specified time

(II) ❑ Matters to be considered by defendant

   (a) ❑ Required documents

      (1) ❑ Answer

   (b) ❑ Supplemental documents

      (1) ❑ Waiver of the service of summons

      (2) ❑ Notice of constitutional question

      (3) ❑ Notice of issue concerning foreign law

      (4) ❑ Nongovernmental corporate disclosure statement

   (c) ❑ Timing

      (1) ❑ A defendant must serve an answer: (i) within twenty-one (21) days after being served with the summons and complaint; or (ii) if it has timely waived service under FRCP 4(d), within sixty (60) days after the request for a waiver was sent, or within ninety (90) days after it was sent to the defendant outside any judicial district of the United States

      (2) ❑ The United States, a United States agency, or a United States officer or employee sued only in an official capacity must serve an answer to a complaint, counterclaim, or crossclaim within sixty (60) days after service on the United States attorney

      (3) ❑ A United States officer or employee sued in an individual capacity for an act or omission occurring in connection with duties performed on the United States' behalf must serve an answer to a complaint, counterclaim, or crossclaim within sixty (60) days after service on the officer or employee or service on the United States attorney, whichever is later

      (4) ❑ Unless the court sets a different time, serving a motion under FRCP 12 alters the periods in FRCP 12(a) as

follows: (A) if the court denies the motion or postpones its disposition until trial, the responsive pleading must be served within fourteen (14) days after notice of the court's action; or (B) if the court grants a motion for a more definite statement, the responsive pleading must be served within fourteen (14) days after the more definite statement is served

(5) ❑ The notice and request for waiver must give the defendant a reasonable time of at least thirty (30) days after the request was sent—or at least sixty (60) days if sent to the defendant outside any judicial district of the United States—to return the waiver; a defendant who, before being served with process, timely returns a waiver need not serve an answer to the complaint until sixty (60) days after the request was sent—or until ninety (90) days after it was sent to the defendant outside any judicial district of the United States

B. Timing

1. *Answer.* Unless another time is specified by FRCP 12 or a federal statute. . .a defendant must serve an answer: (i) within twenty-one (21) days after being served with the summons and complaint; or (ii) if it has timely waived service under FRCP 4(d), within sixty (60) days after the request for a waiver was sent, or within ninety (90) days after it was sent to the defendant outside any judicial district of the United States. FRCP 12(a)(1)(A).

   a. *Time to serve other responsive pleadings.* Unless another time is specified by FRCP 12 or a federal statute, the time for serving a responsive pleading is as follows:

      i. *Answer to counterclaim or crossclaim.* A party must serve an answer to a counterclaim or crossclaim within twenty-one (21) days after being served with the pleading that states the counterclaim or crossclaim. FRCP 12(a)(1)(B).

      ii. *Reply to an answer.* A party must serve a reply to an answer within twenty-one (21) days after being served with an order to reply, unless the order specifies a different time. FRCP 12(a)(1)(C).

   b. *United States and its agencies, officers, or employees sued in an official capacity.* The United States, a United States agency, or a United States officer or employee sued only in an official capacity must serve an answer to a complaint, counterclaim, or crossclaim within sixty (60) days after service on the United States attorney. FRCP 12(a)(2).

   c. *United States officers or employees sued in an individual capacity.* A United States officer or employee sued in an individual capacity for an act or omission occurring in connection with duties performed on the United States' behalf must serve an answer to a complaint, counterclaim, or crossclaim within sixty (60) days after service on the officer or employee or service on the United States attorney, whichever is later. FRCP 12(a)(3).

   d. *Effect of FRCP 12 motion on the time to serve a responsive pleading.* Unless the court sets a different time, serving a motion under FRCP 12 alters the periods in FRCP 12(a) as follows: (A) if the court denies the motion or postpones its disposition until trial, the responsive pleading must be served within fourteen (14) days after notice of the court's action; or (B) if the court grants a motion for a more definite statement, the responsive pleading must be served within fourteen (14) days after the more definite statement is served. FRCP 12(a)(4).

2. *Waiver of service.* The notice and request for waiver must give the defendant a reasonable time of at least thirty (30) days after the request was sent—or at least sixty (60) days if sent to the defendant outside any judicial district of the United States—to return the waiver. FRCP 4(d)(1)(F).

   a. *Time to answer after a waiver.* A defendant who, before being served with process, timely returns a waiver need not serve an answer to the complaint until sixty (60) days after the request was sent—or until ninety (90) days after it was sent to the defendant outside any judicial district of the United States. FRCP 4(d)(3).

3. *Computation of time*

   a. *Computing time.* FRCP 6 applies in computing any time period specified in the Federal Rules of Civil Procedure, in any local rule or court order, or in any statute that does not specify a method of computing time. FRCP 6(a).

      i. *Period stated in days or a longer unit.* When the period is stated in days or a longer unit of time: (A) exclude the day of the event that triggers the period; (B) count every day, including intermediate Saturdays, Sundays, and legal holidays; and (C) include the last day of the period, but if the last day is a Saturday, Sunday, or legal holiday, the period continues to run until the end of the next day that is not a Saturday, Sunday, or legal holiday. FRCP 6(a)(1).

      ii. *Period stated in hours.* When the period is stated in hours: (A) begin counting immediately on the occurrence of the event that triggers the period; (B) count every hour, including hours during intermediate Saturdays, Sundays, and legal holidays; and (C) if the period would end on a Saturday, Sunday, or legal holiday, the period continues to run until the same time on the next day that is not a Saturday, Sunday, or legal holiday. FRCP 6(a)(2).

iii. *Inaccessibility of the clerk's office.* Unless the court orders otherwise, if the clerk's office is inaccessible: (A) on the last day for filing under FRCP 6(a)(1), then the time for filing is extended to the first accessible day that is not a Saturday, Sunday, or legal holiday; or (B) during the last hour for filing under FRCP 6(a)(2), then the time for filing is extended to the same time on the first accessible day that is not a Saturday, Sunday, or legal holiday. FRCP 6(a)(3).

iv. *"Last day" defined.* Unless a different time is set by a statute, local rule, or court order, the last day ends: (A) for electronic filing, at midnight in the court's time zone; and (B) for filing by other means, when the clerk's office is scheduled to close. FRCP 6(a)(4).

v. *"Next day" defined.* The "next day" is determined by continuing to count forward when the period is measured after an event and backward when measured before an event. FRCP 6(a)(5).

vi. *"Legal holiday" defined.* "Legal holiday" means: (A) the day set aside by statute for observing New Year's Day, Martin Luther King Jr.'s Birthday, Washington's Birthday, Memorial Day, Independence Day, Labor Day, Columbus Day, Veterans' Day, Thanksgiving Day, or Christmas Day; (B) any day declared a holiday by the President or Congress; and (C) for periods that are measured after an event, any other day declared a holiday by the state where the district court is located. FRCP 6(a)(6).

vii. *DISTRICT OF MAINE: Applicability of FRCP 6.* FRCP 6 applies when computing any period of time stated in the Local Rules of the United States District Court for the District of Maine. ME R USDCT Rule 6(a).

b. *DISTRICT OF MAINE: Computation of electronic filing deadlines.* Filing documents electronically does not in any way alter any filing deadlines. All electronic transmissions of documents must be completed prior to midnight, Eastern Time, in order to be considered timely filed that day. Where a specific time of day deadline is set by court order or stipulation, the electronic filing must be completed by that time. ME R USDCT App. 4(f). A document filed electronically shall be deemed filed at the time and date stated on the Notice of Electronic Filing received from the court. ME R USDCT App. 4(d)(2).

i. *Technical failures.* A filing user whose filing is made untimely as the result of a technical failure may seek appropriate relief from the court. ME R USDCT App. 4(n). A technical failure of the court's ECF system is deemed to have occurred when the court's ECF site cannot accept filings continuously or intermittently over the course of any period of time greater than one (1) hour. Known system outages will be posted on the court's website along with guidance on how to proceed, if applicable. ME R USDCT App. 4(n).

c. *Extending time.* When an act may or must be done within a specified time, the court may, for good cause, extend the time: (A) with or without motion or notice if the court acts, or if a request is made, before the original time or its extension expires; or (B) on motion made after the time has expired if the party failed to act because of excusable neglect. FRCP 6(b)(1). A court must not extend the time to act under FRCP 50(b), FRCP 50(d), FRCP 52(b), FRCP 59(b), FRCP 59(d), FRCP 59(e), and FRCP 60(b). FRCP 6(b)(2). Refer to the United States District Court for the District of Maine KeyRules Motion for Continuance/Extension of Time document for more information on extending time.

d. *Additional time after certain kinds of service.* When a party may or must act within a specified time after being served and service is made under FRCP 5(b)(2)(C) (by mail), FRCP 5(b)(2)(D) (by leaving with the clerk), or FRCP 5(b)(2)(F) (by other means consented to), three (3) days are added after the period would otherwise expire under FRCP 6(a). FRCP 6(d).

C. General Requirements

1. *Pleading, generally*

a. *Pleadings allowed.* Only these pleadings are allowed: (1) a complaint; (2) an answer to a complaint; (3) an answer to a counterclaim designated as a counterclaim; (4) an answer to a crossclaim; (5) a third-party complaint; (6) an answer to a third-party complaint; and (7) if the court orders one, a reply to an answer. FRCP 7(a).

b. *Pleading to be concise and direct.* Each allegation must be simple, concise, and direct. No technical form is required. FRCP 8(d)(1).

c. *Alternative statements of a claim or defense.* A party may set out 2 or more statements of a claim or defense alternatively or hypothetically, either in a single count or defense or in separate ones. If a party makes alternative statements, the pleading is sufficient if any one of them is sufficient. FRCP 8(d)(2).

d. *Inconsistent claims or defenses.* A party may state as many separate claims or defenses as it has, regardless of consistency. FRCP 8(d)(3).

e. *Construing pleadings.* Pleadings must be construed so as to do justice. FRCP 8(e).

2. *Pleading special matters*

   a. *Capacity or authority to sue; Legal existence.* Except when required to show that the court has jurisdiction, a pleading need not allege: (A) a party's capacity to sue or be sued; (B) a party's authority to sue or be sued in a representative capacity; or (C) the legal existence of an organized association of persons that is made a party. FRCP 9(a)(1).

      i. *Raising those issues.* To raise any of those issues, a party must do so by a specific denial, which must state any supporting facts that are peculiarly within the party's knowledge. FRCP 9(a)(2).

   b. *Fraud or mistake; Conditions of mind.* In alleging fraud or mistake, a party must state with particularity the circumstances constituting fraud or mistake. Malice, intent, knowledge, and other conditions of a person's mind may be alleged generally. FRCP 9(b).

   c. *Conditions precedent.* In pleading conditions precedent, it suffices to allege generally that all conditions precedent have occurred or been performed. But when denying that a condition precedent has occurred or been performed, a party must do so with particularity. FRCP 9(c).

   d. *Official document or act.* In pleading an official document or official act, it suffices to allege that the document was legally issued or the act legally done. FRCP 9(d).

   e. *Judgment.* In pleading a judgment or decision of a domestic or foreign court, a judicial or quasi-judicial tribunal, or a board or officer, it suffices to plead the judgment or decision without showing jurisdiction to render it. FRCP 9(e).

   f. *Time and place.* An allegation of time or place is material when testing the sufficiency of a pleading. FRCP 9(f).

   g. *Special damages.* If an item of special damage is claimed, it must be specifically stated. FRCP 9(g).

   h. *Admiralty or maritime claim.*

      i. *How designated.* If a claim for relief is within the admiralty or maritime jurisdiction and also within the court's subject-matter jurisdiction on some other ground, the pleading may designate the claim as an admiralty or maritime claim for purposes of FRCP 14(c), FRCP 38(e), and FRCP 82 and the Supplemental Rules for Admiralty or Maritime Claims and Asset Forfeiture Actions. A claim cognizable only in the admiralty or maritime jurisdiction is an admiralty or maritime claim for those purposes, whether or not so designated. FRCP 9(h)(1).

      ii. *Designation for appeal.* A case that includes an admiralty or maritime claim within FRCP 9(h) is an admiralty case within 28 U.S.C.A. § 1292(a)(3). FRCP 9(h)(2).

3. *Answer.* In responding to a pleading, a party must: (A) state in short and plain terms its defenses to each claim asserted against it; and (B) admit or deny the allegations asserted against it by an opposing party. FRCP 8(b)(1). The purpose of an answer is to formulate issues by means of defenses addressed to the allegations of the complaint, and to give the plaintiff notice of the defenses the plaintiff will be called upon to meet. FEDPROC § 62:70; Lopez v. U.S. Fid. & Guar. Co., 15 Alaska 633 (D. Alaska 1955); Moriarty v. Curran, 18 F.R.D. 461 (S.D.N.Y. 1956). An answer is adequate where it accomplishes these purposes, even if it contains general and specific denials and at the same time asserts additional facts by way of justification or explanation, and even if it sets forth conclusions of law. FEDPROC § 62:70; Johnston v. Jones, 178 F.2d 481 (3d Cir. 1949); Burke v. Mesta Mach. Co., 5 F.R.D. 134 (W.D. Pa. 1946).

   a. *Denials.* A denial must fairly respond to the substance of the allegation. FRCP 8(b)(2).

      i. *General and specific denials.* A party that intends in good faith to deny all the allegations of a pleading—including the jurisdictional grounds—may do so by a general denial. A party that does not intend to deny all the allegations must either specifically deny designated allegations or generally deny all except those specifically admitted. FRCP 8(b)(3).

      ii. *Denying part of an allegation.* A party that intends in good faith to deny only part of an allegation must admit the part that is true and deny the rest. FRCP 8(b)(4).

      iii. *Lacking knowledge or information.* A party that lacks knowledge or information sufficient to form a belief about the truth of an allegation must so state, and the statement has the effect of a denial. FRCP 8(b)(5). An answer merely stating that the defendant lacks knowledge to form a belief as to the plaintiff's allegations, and making no statement as to the defendant's lack of information, has been held to be insufficient, the court suggesting that the phrase might be used in an attempt to mask the defendant's inability to make a good-faith denial of the allegations. FEDPROC § 62:73; Gilbert v. Johnston, 127 F.R.D. 145 (N.D. Ill. 1989).

      iv. *Effect of failing to deny.* An allegation—other than one relating to the amount of damages—is admitted if a responsive pleading is required and the allegation is not denied. If a responsive pleading is not required, an allegation is considered denied or avoided. FRCP 8(b)(6).

b. *Affirmative defenses.* In responding to a pleading, a party must affirmatively state any avoidance or affirmative defense, including: (1) accord and satisfaction; (2) arbitration and award; (3) assumption of risk; (4) contributory negligence; (5) duress; (6) estoppel; (7) failure of consideration; (8) fraud; (9) illegality; (10) injury by fellow servant; (11) laches; (12) license; (13) payment; (14) release; (15) res judicata; (16) statute of frauds; (17) statute of limitations; and (18) waiver. FRCP 8(c)(1).

    i. *Mistaken designation.* If a party mistakenly designates a defense as a counterclaim, or a counterclaim as a defense, the court must, if justice requires, treat the pleading as though it were correctly designated, and may impose terms for doing so. FRCP 8(c)(2).

c. *How to present defenses.* Every defense to a claim for relief in any pleading must be asserted in the responsive pleading if one is required. But a party may assert the following defenses by motion: (1) lack of subject-matter jurisdiction; (2) lack of personal jurisdiction; (3) improper venue; (4) insufficient process; (5) insufficient service of process; (6) failure to state a claim upon which relief can be granted; and (7) failure to join a party under FRCP 19. FRCP 12(b).

    i. A motion asserting any of these defenses must be made before pleading if a responsive pleading is allowed. If a pleading sets out a claim for relief that does not require a responsive pleading, an opposing party may assert at trial any defense to that claim. FRCP 12(b).

    ii. Refer to the United States District Court for the District of Maine KeyRules Motion to Dismiss for Lack of Subject Matter Jurisdiction, Motion to Dismiss for Lack of Personal Jurisdiction, Motion to Dismiss for Improper Venue, and Motion to Dismiss for Failure to State a Claim documents for more information on motions under FRCP 12(b)(1), FRCP 12(b)(2), FRCP 12(b)(3), and FRCP 12(b)(6).

d. *Waiving and preserving certain defenses.* No defense or objection is waived by joining it with one or more other defenses or objections in a responsive pleading or in a motion. FRCP 12(b).

    i. *When some are waived.* A party waives any defense listed in FRCP 12(b)(2) through FRCP 12(b)(5) by:

       • Omitting it from a motion in the circumstances described in FRCP 12(g)(2); or

       • Failing to either: (i) make it by motion under FRCP 12; or (ii) include it in a responsive pleading or in an amendment allowed by FRCP 15(a)(1) as a matter of course. FRCP 12(h)(1).

    ii. *When to raise others.* Failure to state a claim upon which relief can be granted, to join a person required by FRCP 19(b), or to state a legal defense to a claim may be raised:

       • In any pleading allowed or ordered under FRCP 7(a);

       • By a motion under FRCP 12(c); or

       • At trial. FRCP 12(h)(2).

    iii. *Lack of subject matter jurisdiction.* If the court determines at any time that it lacks subject-matter jurisdiction, the court must dismiss the action. FRCP 12(h)(3).

4. *Counterclaim and crossclaim*

a. *Compulsory counterclaim.* A pleading must state as a counterclaim any claim that—at the time of its service—the pleader has against an opposing party if the claim: (A) arises out of the transaction or occurrence that is the subject matter of the opposing party's claim; and (B) does not require adding another party over whom the court cannot acquire jurisdiction. FRCP 13(a)(1).

    i. *Exceptions.* The pleader need not state the claim if: (A) when the action was commenced, the claim was the subject of another pending action; or (B) the opposing party sued on its claim by attachment or other process that did not establish personal jurisdiction over the pleader on that claim, and the pleader does not assert any counterclaim under FRCP 13. FRCP 13(a)(2).

b. *Permissive counterclaim.* A pleading may state as a counterclaim against an opposing party any claim that is not compulsory. FRCP 13(b).

c. *Relief sought in a counterclaim.* A counterclaim need not diminish or defeat the recovery sought by the opposing party. It may request relief that exceeds in amount or differs in kind from the relief sought by the opposing party. FRCP 13(c).

d. *Counterclaim against the United States.* The Federal Rules of Civil Procedure do not expand the right to assert a counterclaim—or to claim a credit—against the United States or a United States officer or agency. FRCP 13(d).

e. *Counterclaim maturing or acquired after pleading.* The court may permit a party to file a supplemental pleading asserting a counterclaim that matured or was acquired by the party after serving an earlier pleading. FRCP 13(e).

f. *Crossclaim against a coparty.* A pleading may state as a crossclaim any claim by one party against a coparty if the claim arises out of the transaction or occurrence that is the subject matter of the original action or of a counterclaim, or if the claim relates to any property that is the subject matter of the original action. The crossclaim may include a claim that the coparty is or may be liable to the cross-claimant for all or part of a claim asserted in the action against the cross-claimant. FRCP 13(g).

g. *Joining additional parties.* FRCP 19 and FRCP 20 govern the addition of a person as a party to a counterclaim or crossclaim. FRCP 13(h).

h. *Separate trials; Separate judgments.* If the court orders separate trials under FRCP 42(b), it may enter judgment on a counterclaim or crossclaim under FRCP 54(b) when it has jurisdiction to do so, even if the opposing party's claims have been dismissed or otherwise resolved. FRCP 13(i).

5. *Third-party practice*

a. *Timing of the summons and complaint.* A defending party may, as third-party plaintiff, serve a summons and complaint on a nonparty who is or may be liable to it for all or part of the claim against it. But the third-party plaintiff must, by motion, obtain the court's leave if it files the third-party complaint more than fourteen (14) days after serving its original answer. FRCP 14(a)(1).

b. *Third-party defendant's claims and defenses.* The person served with the summons and third-party complaint—the "third-party defendant": (A) must assert any defense against the third-party plaintiff's claim under FRCP 12; (B) must assert any counterclaim against the third-party plaintiff under FRCP 13(a), and may assert any counterclaim against the third-party plaintiff under FRCP 13(b) or any crossclaim against another third-party defendant under FRCP 13(g); (C) may assert against the plaintiff any defense that the third-party plaintiff has to the plaintiff's claim; and (D) may also assert against the plaintiff any claim arising out of the transaction or occurrence that is the subject matter of the plaintiff's claim against the third-party plaintiff. FRCP 14(a)(2).

c. For more information on third-party practice, refer to FRCP 14.

6. *Joinder*

a. *Joinder of claims.* A party asserting a claim, counterclaim, crossclaim, or third-party claim may join, as independent or alternative claims, as many claims as it has against an opposing party. FRCP 18(a).

   i. *Joinder of contingent claims.* A party may join two claims even though one of them is contingent on the disposition of the other; but the court may grant relief only in accordance with the parties' relative substantive rights. In particular, a plaintiff may state a claim for money and a claim to set aside a conveyance that is fraudulent as to that plaintiff, without first obtaining a judgment for the money. FRCP 18(b).

b. *Joinder of parties; Required*

   i. *Persons required to be joined if feasible; Required party.* A person who is subject to service of process and whose joinder will not deprive the court of subject-matter jurisdiction must be joined as a party if: (A) in that person's absence, the court cannot accord complete relief among existing parties; or (B) that person claims an interest relating to the subject of the action and is so situated that disposing of the action in the person's absence may: (i) as a practical matter impair or impede the person's ability to protect the interest; or (ii) leave an existing party subject to a substantial risk of incurring double, multiple, or otherwise inconsistent obligations because of the interest. FRCP 19(a)(1).

   ii. *Joinder of parties by court order.* If a person has not been joined as required, the court must order that the person be made a party. A person who refuses to join as a plaintiff may be made either a defendant or, in a proper case, an involuntary plaintiff. FRCP 19(a)(2).

   iii. *Venue.* If a joined party objects to venue and the joinder would make venue improper, the court must dismiss that party. FRCP 19(a)(3).

   iv. *When joinder of parties is not feasible.* If a person who is required to be joined if feasible cannot be joined, the court must determine whether, in equity and good conscience, the action should proceed among the existing parties or should be dismissed. FRCP 19(b). For a list of the factors for the court to consider in determining whether joinder of parties is feasible, refer to FRCP 19(b)(1) through FRCP 19(b)(4).

   v. *Pleading the reasons for nonjoinder.* When asserting a claim for relief, a party must state: (1) the name, if known, of any person who is required to be joined if feasible but is not joined; and (2) the reasons for not joining that person. FRCP 19(c).

   vi. *Exception for class actions.* FRCP 19 is subject to FRCP 23. FRCP 19(d). For information on class actions, refer to FRCP 23.

    c. *Joinder of parties; Permissible*

        i. *Persons who may join or be joined*

- *Plaintiffs.* Persons may join in one action as plaintiffs if: (A) they assert any right to relief jointly, severally, or in the alternative with respect to or arising out of the same transaction, occurrence, or series of transactions or occurrences; and (B) any question of law or fact common to all plaintiffs will arise in the action. FRCP 20(a)(1).

- *Defendants.* Persons—as well as a vessel, cargo, or other property subject to admiralty process in rem—may be joined in one action as defendants if: (A) any right to relief is asserted against them jointly, severally, or in the alternative with respect to or arising out of the same transaction, occurrence, or series of transactions or occurrences; and (B) any question of law or fact common to all defendants will arise in the action. FRCP 20(a)(2).

- *Extent of relief.* Neither a plaintiff nor a defendant need be interested in obtaining or defending against all the relief demanded. The court may grant judgment to one or more plaintiffs according to their rights, and against one or more defendants according to their liabilities. FRCP 20(a)(3).

        ii. *Protective measures.* The court may issue orders—including an order for separate trials—to protect a party against embarrassment, delay, expense, or other prejudice that arises from including a person against whom the party asserts no claim and who asserts no claim against the party. FRCP 20(b).

    d. *Misjoinder and nonjoinder of parties.* Misjoinder of parties is not a ground for dismissing an action. On motion or on its own, the court may at any time, on just terms, add or drop a party. The court may also sever any claim against a party. FRCP 21.

7. *Right to a jury trial; Demand*

    a. *Right preserved.* The right of trial by jury as declared by U.S.C.A. Const. Amend. VII, or as provided by a federal statute, is preserved to the parties inviolate. FRCP 38(a).

    b. *Demand.* On any issue triable of right by a jury, a party may demand a jury trial by: (1) serving the other parties with a written demand—which may be included in a pleading—no later than fourteen (14) days after the last pleading directed to the issue is served; and (2) filing the demand in accordance with FRCP 5(d). FRCP 38(b).

        i. *DISTRICT OF MAINE: Removed actions.* A demand for jury trial in actions removed to the United States District Court for the District of Maine from the state courts shall be filed in accordance with the provisions of FRCP 81(c). ME R USDCT Rule 38.

    c. *Specifying issues.* In its demand, a party may specify the issues that it wishes to have tried by a jury; otherwise, it is considered to have demanded a jury trial on all the issues so triable. If the party has demanded a jury trial on only some issues, any other party may—within fourteen (14) days after being served with the demand or within a shorter time ordered by the court—serve a demand for a jury trial on any other or all factual issues triable by jury. FRCP 38(c).

    d. *Waiver; Withdrawal.* A party waives a jury trial unless its demand is properly served and filed. A proper demand may be withdrawn only if the parties consent. FRCP 38(d).

    e. *Admiralty and maritime claims.* The rules in FRCP 38 do not create a right to a jury trial on issues in a claim that is an admiralty or maritime claim under FRCP 9(h). FRCP 38(e).

8. *DISTRICT OF MAINE: Appearances.* An attorney's signature to a pleading shall constitute an appearance for the party filing the pleading. Otherwise, an attorney who wishes to participate in any manner in any action must file a formal written appearance identifying the party represented. An appearance whether by pleading or formal written appearance shall be signed by an attorney in his/her individual name and shall state his/her office address. ME R USDCT Rule 83.2(a). For more information, refer to ME R USDCT Rule 83.2.

9. *DISTRICT OF MAINE: Alternative dispute resolution (ADR).* Litigants are authorized and encouraged to employ, at their own expense, any available ADR process on which they can agree, including early neutral evaluation, settlement conferences, mediation, non-binding summary jury trial, corporate mini-trial, and arbitration proceedings. ME R USDCT Rule 83.11(a). For more information on ADR, refer to ME R USDCT Rule 83.11.

D. Documents

1. *Required documents*

    a. *Answer.* Refer to the "C. General Requirements" section of this KeyRules document for information on the answer.

        i. *Certificate of service.* No certificate of service is required when a paper is served by filing it with the court's electronic-filing system. When a paper that is required to be served is served by other means: (i) if the paper is filed, a certificate of service must be filed with it or within a reasonable time after service; and (ii) if the paper is not filed, a certificate of service need not be filed unless filing is required by court order or by local rule. FRCP 5(d)(1)(B).

2. *Supplemental documents*

    a. *Waiver of the service of summons.* An individual, corporation, or association that is subject to service under FRCP 4(e), FRCP 4(f), or FRCP 4(h) has a duty to avoid unnecessary expenses of serving the summons. FRCP 4(d)(1). Waiving service of a summons does not waive any objection to personal jurisdiction or to venue. FRCP 4(d)(5).

        i. *Failure to return; Expenses.* If a defendant located within the United States fails, without good cause, to sign and return a waiver requested by a plaintiff located within the United States, the court must impose on the defendant: (A) the expenses later incurred in making service; and (B) the reasonable expenses, including attorney's fees, of any motion required to collect those service expenses. FRCP 4(d)(2).

    b. *Notice of constitutional question.* A party that files a pleading, written motion, or other paper drawing into question the constitutionality of a federal or state statute must promptly: (1) file a notice of constitutional question stating the question and identifying the paper that raises it, if: (A) a federal statute is questioned and the parties do not include the United States, one of its agencies, or one of its officers or employees in an official capacity; or (B) a state statute is questioned and the parties do not include the state, one of its agencies, or one of its officers or employees in an official capacity; and (2) serve the notice and paper on the Attorney General of the United States if a federal statute is questioned—or on the state attorney general if a state statute is questioned—either by certified or registered mail or by sending it to an electronic address designated by the attorney general for this purpose. FRCP 5.1(a).

        i. *DISTRICT OF MAINE.* To enable the court to comply with the provisions of 28 U.S.C.A. § 2403 and FRCP 24(c), in any action, suit or proceeding to which the United States or any agency, officer or employee thereof is not a party, any party who shall draw into question the constitutionality of any Act of Congress affecting the public interest shall forthwith so notify the clerk in writing, stating the title of the action, its docket number if any, and the Act of Congress in question. ME R USDCT Rule 5.1. To enable the court to comply with the provisions of 28 U.S.C.A. § 2403, in any action, suit or proceeding to which a state or any agency, officer or employee thereof is not a party, any party who shall draw in question the constitutionality of any statute of that state affecting the public interest shall forthwith so notify the clerk in writing, stating the title of the action, its docket number if any, and the statute of the state in question. ME R USDCT Rule 5.1.

        ii. *No forfeiture.* A party's failure to file and serve the notice, or the court's failure to certify, does not forfeit a constitutional claim or defense that is otherwise timely asserted. FRCP 5.1(d).

    c. *Notice of issue concerning foreign law.* A party who intends to raise an issue about a foreign country's law must give notice by a pleading or other writing. In determining foreign law, the court may consider any relevant material or source, including testimony, whether or not submitted by a party or admissible under the Federal Rules of Evidence. The court's determination must be treated as a ruling on a question of law. FRCP 44.1.

    d. *Nongovernmental corporate disclosure statement.* A nongovernmental corporate party must file two (2) copies of a disclosure statement that: (1) identifies any parent corporation and any publicly held corporation owning ten percent (10%) or more of its stock; or (2) states that there is no such corporation. FRCP 7.1(a). A party must: (1) file the disclosure statement with its first appearance, pleading, petition, motion, response, or other request addressed to the court; and (2) promptly file a supplemental statement if any required information changes. FRCP 7.1(b).

        i. *DISTRICT OF MAINE: Notice of interested parties.* To enable the court to evaluate possible disqualification or recusal, counsel for all non-governmental parties shall file with their first appearance a Notice of Interested Parties, which shall list all persons, associations of persons, firms, partnerships, limited liability companies, joint ventures, corporations (including parent or affiliated corporations, clearly identified as such), or any similar entities, owning ten percent (10%) or more of the named party. Counsel shall be under a continuing obligation to file an amended Notice if any material change occurs in the status of an Interested Party, such as through merger, acquisition, or new/additional membership. ME R USDCT Rule 7.1.

E. Format

1. *Form of documents*

    a. *DISTRICT OF MAINE: Font size, line spacing, and paper size.* All such documents shall be typed in a font of no less than size twelve (12) point, and shall be double-spaced or printed on eight and one-half by eleven (8-1/2 x 11) inch paper. Footnotes shall be in a font of no less than size ten (10) point, and may be single spaced. ME R USDCT Rule 10.

b. *Caption.* Every pleading must have a caption with the court's name, a title, a file number, and an FRCP 7(a) designation. FRCP 10(a).

    i. *Names of parties.* The title of the complaint must name all the parties; the title of other pleadings, after naming the first party on each side, may refer generally to other parties. FRCP 10(a).

    ii. *DISTRICT OF MAINE: Additional caption requirements.* All pleadings, motions and other papers filed with the clerk or otherwise submitted to the court, except exhibits, shall bear the proper case number and shall contain on the first page a caption as described by FRCP 10(a) and immediately thereunder a designation of what the document is and the name of the party in whose behalf it is submitted. ME R USDCT Rule 10.

    iii. *DISTRICT OF MAINE: Three-judge district court.* To enable the court to comply with the provisions of 28 U.S.C.A. § 2284, in any action or proceeding which a party believes is required to be heard by a three-judge district court, the words "THREE-JUDGE DISTRICT COURT REQUESTED" or the equivalent shall be included directly beneath the designation of the pleadings. ME R USDCT Rule 9(a).

    iv. *DISTRICT OF MAINE: Injunctive relief.* If a pleading or motion seeks injunctive relief, in addition to the prayer for such relief, the words "INJUNCTIVE RELIEF SOUGHT" or the equivalent shall be included on the first page. ME R USDCT Rule 9(b).

    v. *DISTRICT OF MAINE: Demand for jury trial.* If a demand for jury trial is endorsed upon a pleading pursuant to FRCP 38(b), in addition to said endorsement the designation of the pleading shall include the words "AND DEMAND FOR JURY TRIAL" or the equivalent on the first page. ME R USDCT Rule 38.

c. *Claims or defenses*

    i. *Numbered paragraphs.* A party must state its claims or defenses in numbered paragraphs, each limited as far as practicable to a single set of circumstances. A later pleading may refer by number to a paragraph in an earlier pleading. FRCP 10(b).

    ii. *Separate statements.* If doing so would promote clarity, each claim founded on a separate transaction or occurrence—and each defense other than a denial—must be stated in a separate count or defense. FRCP 10(b).

d. *Adoption by reference.* A statement in a pleading may be adopted by reference elsewhere in the same pleading or in any other pleading or motion. FRCP 10(c).

    i. *Exhibits.* A copy of a written instrument that is an exhibit to a pleading is a part of the pleading for all purposes. FRCP 10(c).

e. *DISTRICT OF MAINE: Page numbering.* All pages shall be numbered at the bottom. ME R USDCT Rule 10.

f. *DISTRICT OF MAINE: Attachment of ancillary papers.* Ancillary papers shall be attached at the end of the document to which they relate. ME R USDCT Rule 10.

g. *Acceptance by the clerk.* The clerk must not refuse to file a paper solely because it is not in the form prescribed by the Federal Rules of Civil Procedure or by a local rule or practice. FRCP 5(d)(4).

2. *Form of electronic documents.* A paper filed electronically is a written paper for purposes of the Federal Rules of Civil Procedure. FRCP 5(d)(3)(D).

a. *DISTRICT OF MAINE: Document format.* The ECF system only accepts documents in a portable document format (PDF). Although there are two types of PDF documents—electronically converted PDF's and scanned PDF's—only electronically converted PDF's may be filed with the court using the ECF system, unless otherwise authorized by local rule or order. ME R USDCT App. 4. Any document or exhibit to be filed or submitted to the court shall not be password-protected or encrypted. ME R USDCT App. 4(g)(12).

    i. *Electronically converted PDFs.* Electronically converted PDF's are created from word processing documents (MS Word, WordPerfect, etc.) using Adobe Acrobat or similar software. They are text searchable and their file size is small. ME R USDCT App. 4. Software used to electronically convert documents to PDF which includes proprietary or advertisement information within the PDF document is prohibited. ME R USDCT App. 4.

    ii. *Scanned PDFs.* Scanned PDF's are created from paper documents run through an optical scanner. Scanned PDF's are not searchable and have a large file size. ME R USDCT App. 4.

b. *DISTRICT OF MAINE: Title.* All pleadings filed electronically shall be titled in accordance with the approved dictionary of civil or criminal events of the ECF system of the United States District Court for the District of Maine. ME R USDCT App. 4(d)(3).

c. *DISTRICT OF MAINE: Attachments.* Attachments to filings and exhibits must be filed in accordance with the court's

ECF User Manual, unless otherwise ordered by the court. ME R USDCT App. 4(j). When there are fifty (50) or fewer attachments to a pleading, the attachments must be filed by counsel electronically using ECF. When there are more than fifty (50) attachments, the attachments must be filed in one of the following ways: (A) using ECF, simply attach them to the pleading being filed; (B) using ECF, use the "Additional Attachments" menu item; (C) on paper; or (D) on a properly labeled three and one-half (3-1/2) inch floppy disk, CD or DVD. ME R USDCT App. 4(j)(2). Attachments filed on paper or on disk must contain a comprehensive index that clearly describes each document. ME R USDCT App. 4(j)(2).

   i. A filing user must submit as attachments only those excerpts of the referenced documents that are directly germane to the matter under consideration by the court. Excerpted material must be clearly and prominently identified as such. Users who file excerpts of documents do so without prejudice to their right to timely file additional excerpts or the complete document, as may be allowed by the court. Responding parties may timely file additional excerpts or the complete document that they believe are directly germane. ME R USDCT App. 4(j)(3).

   ii. Filers shall not attach as an exhibit any pleading or other paper already on file with the court in that case, but shall merely refer to that document. ME R USDCT App. 4(j)(4).

  d. *DISTRICT OF MAINE: Compliance with technical standards.* All documents filed by electronic means must comply with technical standards, if any, established by the Judicial Conference of the United States or by the United States District Court for the District of Maine. ME R USDCT App. 4(a)(3).

3. *Signing of pleadings, motions and other papers*

  a. *Signature.* Every pleading, written motion, and other paper must be signed by at least one attorney of record in the attorney's name—or by a party personally if the party is unrepresented. The paper must state the signer's address, e-mail address, and telephone number. FRCP 11(a).

   i. *No verification or accompanying affidavit required for pleadings.* Unless a rule or statute specifically states otherwise, a pleading need not be verified or accompanied by an affidavit. FRCP 11(a).

   ii. *Unsigned papers.* The court must strike an unsigned paper unless the omission is promptly corrected after being called to the attorney's or party's attention. FRCP 11(a).

  b. *Electronic signing.* A filing made through a person's electronic-filing account and authorized by that person, together with that person's name on a signature block, constitutes the person's signature. FRCP 5(d)(3)(C).

   i. *DISTRICT OF MAINE: Attorneys.* The user log-in and password together with a user's name on the signature block constitutes the attorney's signature pursuant to the Federal Rules of Civil Procedure and the Local Rules of the United States District Court for the District of Maine. All electronically filed documents must include a signature block and must set forth the attorney's name, address, telephone number and e-mail address. The name of the ECF user under whose log-in and password the document is submitted must be preceded by a "/s/" in the space where the signature would otherwise appear. ME R USDCT App. 4(h)(1).

   ii. *DISTRICT OF MAINE: Multiple signatures.* The filer of any document requiring more than one signature (e.g., pleadings filed by visiting lawyers, stipulations, joint status reports) must list thereon all the names of other signatories, preceded by a "/s/" in the space where the signatures would otherwise appear. By submitting such a document, the filing attorney certifies that each of the other signatories has expressly agreed to the form and substance of the document and that the filing attorney has their actual authority to submit the document electronically. ME R USDCT App. 4(h)(2). For more information, refer to ME R USDCT App. 4(h)(2).

   iii. *DISTRICT OF MAINE: Documents signed under oath.* Affidavits, declarations, verified complaints, or any other document signed under oath shall be filed electronically. The electronically filed version shall contain the typed name of the signatory, preceded by a "/s/" in the space where the signature would otherwise appear indicating that the paper document bears an original signature. ME R USDCT Rule 10; ME R USDCT App. 4(h)(3). For more information, refer to ME R USDCT Rule 10.

  c. *Representations to the court.* By presenting to the court a pleading, written motion, or other paper—whether by signing, filing, submitting, or later advocating it—an attorney or unrepresented party certifies that to the best of the person's knowledge, information, and belief, formed after an inquiry reasonable under the circumstances: (1) it is not being presented for any improper purpose, such as to harass, cause unnecessary delay, or needlessly increase the cost of litigation; (2) the claims, defenses, and other legal contentions are warranted by existing law or by a nonfrivolous argument for extending, modifying, or reversing existing law or for establishing new law; (3) the factual contentions have evidentiary support or, if specifically so identified, will likely have evidentiary support after a reasonable opportunity for further investigation or discovery; and (4) the denials of factual contentions are warranted on the evidence or, if specifically so identified, are reasonably based on belief or a lack of information. FRCP 11(b).

d. *Sanctions.* If, after notice and a reasonable opportunity to respond, the court determines that FRCP 11(b) has been violated, the court may impose an appropriate sanction on any attorney, law firm, or party that violated FRCP 11(b) or is responsible for the violation. FRCP 11(c)(1). Refer to the United States District Court for the District of Maine KeyRules Motion for Sanctions document for more information.

4. *Privacy protection for filings made with the court*

a. *Redacted filings.* Unless the court orders otherwise, in an electronic or paper filing with the court that contains an individual's Social Security number, taxpayer-identification number, or birth date, the name of an individual known to be a minor, or a financial-account number, a party or nonparty making the filing may include only: (1) the last four (4) digits of the Social Security number and taxpayer-identification number; (2) the year of the individual's birth; (3) the minor's initials; and (4) the last four (4) digits of the financial-account number. FRCP 5.2(a).

   i. *DISTRICT OF MAINE.* To address the privacy concerns created by the Internet access to court papers, unless otherwise ordered by the court, counsel shall modify certain personal data identifiers in pleadings and other papers as follows: (1) minors' names: use of the minors' initials only; (2) Social Security numbers: use of the last four (4) numbers only; (3) dates of birth: use of the year of birth only; [and] (4) financial account numbers: identify the type of account and the financial institution, but use only the last four (4) numbers of the account number. ME R USDCT Redacting Pleadings. Counsel should also use caution when filing papers that contain a person's medical records, employment history; financial information; and any proprietary or trade secret information. ME R USDCT Redacting Pleadings.

b. *Exemptions from the redaction requirement.* The redaction requirement does not apply to the following: (1) a financial-account number that identifies the property allegedly subject to forfeiture in a forfeiture proceeding; (2) the record of an administrative or agency proceeding; (3) the official record of a state-court proceeding; (4) the record of a court or tribunal, if that record was not subject to the redaction requirement when originally filed; (5) a filing covered by FRCP 5.2(c) or FRCP 5.2(d); and (6) a pro se filing in an action brought under 28 U.S.C.A. § 2241, 28 U.S.C.A. § 2254, or 28 U.S.C.A. § 2255. FRCP 5.2(b).

c. *Limitations on remote access to electronic files; Social Security appeals and immigration cases.* Unless the court orders otherwise, in an action for benefits under the Social Security Act, and in an action or proceeding relating to an order of removal, to relief from removal, or to immigration benefits or detention, access to an electronic file is authorized as follows: (1) the parties and their attorneys may have remote electronic access to any part of the case file, including the administrative record; (2) any other person may have electronic access to the full record at the courthouse, but may have remote electronic access only to: (A) the docket maintained by the court; and (B) an opinion, order, judgment, or other disposition of the court, but not any other part of the case file or the administrative record. FRCP 5.2(c).

d. *Filings made under seal.* The court may order that a filing be made under seal without redaction. The court may later unseal the filing or order the person who made the filing to file a redacted version for the public record. FRCP 5.2(d).

   i. *DISTRICT OF MAINE.* For information on filing sealed documents in the District of Maine, refer to ME R USDCT Rule 7A, ME R USDCT App. 4(p)(2), and ME R USDCT Sealed Filings.

e. *Protective orders.* For good cause, the court may by order in a case: (1) require redaction of additional information; or (2) limit or prohibit a nonparty's remote electronic access to a document filed with the court. FRCP 5.2(e).

f. *Option for additional unredacted filing under seal.* A person making a redacted filing may also file an unredacted copy under seal. The court must retain the unredacted copy as part of the record. FRCP 5.2(f).

   i. *DISTRICT OF MAINE.* A party wishing to file a document containing the personal data identifiers specified above may. . .file an unredacted document under seal. This document will be retained by the clerk's office as part of the record. ME R USDCT Redacting Pleadings. The court may, however, still require the party to file a redacted copy for the public file. ME R USDCT Redacting Pleadings.

g. *Option for filing a reference list.* A filing that contains redacted information may be filed together with a reference list that identifies each item of redacted information and specifies an appropriate identifier that uniquely corresponds to each item listed. The list must be filed under seal and may be amended as of right. Any reference in the case to a listed identifier will be construed to refer to the corresponding item of information. FRCP 5.2(g).

   i. *DISTRICT OF MAINE.* A party wishing to file a document containing the personal data identifiers specified above may. . .file a reference list under seal. The reference list shall contain the complete personal data identifier(s) and the redacted identifier(s) used in its (their) place in the filing. All references in the case to the redacted identifiers included in the reference list will be construed to refer to the corresponding complete identifier. The reference list must be filed under seal, and may be amended as of right. It shall be retained by the clerk's office as part of the record. ME R USDCT Redacting Pleadings. The court may, however, still require the party to file a redacted copy for the public file. ME R USDCT Redacting Pleadings.

h. *DISTRICT OF MAINE: Responsibility for redaction.* The clerk is not required to review documents filed with the court for compliance with FRCP 5.2. The responsibility to redact filings rests with counsel and the party or nonparty making the filing. ME R USDCT App. 4(i); ME R USDCT Redacting Pleadings. For guidelines for filing confidential information in civil cases in the District of Maine, refer to ME R USDCT Confidentiality.

i. *Waiver of protection of identifiers.* A person waives the protection of FRCP 5.2(a) as to the person's own information by filing it without redaction and not under seal. FRCP 5.2(h).

F. Filing and Service Requirements

1. *Filing requirements*

   a. *Required filings.* Any paper after the complaint that is required to be served must be filed no later than a reasonable time after service. FRCP 5(d)(1).

   b. *DISTRICT OF MAINE: Place of filing.* Unless otherwise ordered by the court, papers shall be filed with the court at Bangor in cases filed and pending at Bangor, and at Portland in cases filed and pending at Portland. ME R USDCT Rule 5(a).

   c. *Nonelectronic filing.* A paper not filed electronically is filed by delivering it: (A) to the clerk; or (B) to a judge who agrees to accept it for filing, and who must then note the filing date on the paper and promptly send it to the clerk. FRCP 5(d)(2).

      i. *DISTRICT OF MAINE: Documents to be filed in paper.* The following documents shall be filed in paper, which may also be scanned into ECF by the clerk's office: (A) all handwritten pleadings; and (B) all pleadings and documents filed by pro se litigants who are incarcerated or who are not registered filing users in ECF. ME R USDCT App. 4(g)(8). Non-prisoner pro se litigants in civil actions may register with ECF or may file (and serve) all pleadings and other documents in paper. The clerk's office will scan into ECF any pleadings and documents filed on paper in accordance with ME R USDCT App. 4(g). ME R USDCT App. 4(o). For more information, refer to ME R USDCT App. 4(g).

   d. *Electronic filing*

      i. *DISTRICT OF MAINE: Authorization.* Unless exempt or otherwise ordered by the court, papers shall be filed and served electronically as required by the court's Administrative Procedures Governing the Filing and Service by Electronic Means, which is set forth in ME R USDCT App. 4. The provisions of the court's Administrative Procedures Governing the Filing and Service by Electronic Means (ME R USDCT App. 4) shall be applied and enforced as part of the Local Rules of the United States District Court for the District of Maine. ME R USDCT Rule 5(c).

      ii. *Filing by represented persons.* A person represented by an attorney must file electronically, unless nonelectronic filing is allowed by the court for good cause or is allowed or required by local rule. FRCP 5(d)(3)(A).

         • *DISTRICT OF MAINE.* An attorney may apply to the court for permission to file paper documents. ME R USDCT App. 4(a)(5).

      iii. *Filing by unrepresented persons.* A person not represented by an attorney: (i) may file electronically only if allowed by court order or by local rule; and (ii) may be required to file electronically only by court order, or by a local rule that includes reasonable exceptions. FRCP 5(d)(3)(B).

         • *DISTRICT OF MAINE.* Non-prisoner pro se litigants in civil actions may register with ECF or may file (and serve) all pleadings and other documents in paper. ME R USDCT App. 4(o). A non-prisoner who is a party to a civil action and who is not represented by an attorney may register to receive service electronically and to electronically transmit their documents to the court for filing in the ECF system. If during the course of the action the person retains an attorney who appears on the person's behalf, the clerk shall terminate the person's registration upon the attorney's appearance. ME R USDCT App. 4(b)(2).

      iv. *DISTRICT OF MAINE: Scope of electronic filing.* All documents submitted for filing in civil and criminal cases, regardless of case commencement date, except those documents specifically exempted in ME R USDCT App. 4(g), shall be filed electronically using the electronic case filing system (ECF). ME R USDCT App. 4(a)(1). For special filing requirements and exceptions, refer to ME R USDCT App. 4(g).

v. *DISTRICT OF MAINE: Consequences of electronic filing.* Electronic transmission of a document to the ECF system, together with the transmission of a Notice of Electronic Filing (NEF) from the court, constitutes filing of the document for all purposes of the Federal Rules of Civil Procedure. ME R USDCT App. 4(d)(1).

vi. *DISTRICT OF MAINE: Review of documents.* Documents filed with the clerk's office will normally be reviewed no later than the close of the next business day. It is the responsibility of the filing party to promptly notify the clerk's office via telephone of a matter that requires the immediate attention of a judicial officer. ME R USDCT App. 4(a)(4).

e. *DISTRICT OF MAINE: Facsimile filing.* No papers shall be submitted to the court by means of a facsimile machine without prior leave of the court. ME R USDCT Rule 5(c); ME R USDCT App. 4(m).

2. *Service requirements*

a. *Service; When required.* Unless the Federal Rules of Civil Procedure provide otherwise, each of the following papers must be served on every party: (A) an order stating that service is required; (B) a pleading filed after the original complaint, unless the court orders otherwise under FRCP 5(c) because there are numerous defendants; (C) a discovery paper required to be served on a party, unless the court orders otherwise; (D) a written motion, except one that may be heard ex parte; and (E) a written notice, appearance, demand, or offer of judgment, or any similar paper. FRCP 5(a)(1).

i. *If a party fails to appear.* No service is required on a party who is in default for failing to appear. But a pleading that asserts a new claim for relief against such a party must be served on that party under FRCP 4. FRCP 5(a)(2).

ii. *Seizing property.* If an action is begun by seizing property and no person is or need be named as a defendant, any service required before the filing of an appearance, answer, or claim must be made on the person who had custody or possession of the property when it was seized. FRCP 5(a)(3).

b. *Service; How made.* A paper is served under FRCP 5 by: (A) handing it to the person; (B) leaving it: (i) at the person's office with a clerk or other person in charge or, if no one is in charge, in a conspicuous place in the office; or (ii) if the person has no office or the office is closed, at the person's dwelling or usual place of abode with someone of suitable age and discretion who resides there; (C) mailing it to the person's last known address—in which event service is complete upon mailing; (D) leaving it with the court clerk if the person has no known address; (E) sending it to a registered user by filing it with the court's electronic-filing system or sending it by other electronic means that the person consented to in writing—in either of which events service is complete upon filing or sending, but is not effective if the filer or sender learns that it did not reach the person to be served; or (F) delivering it by any other means that the person consented to in writing—in which event service is complete when the person making service delivers it to the agency designated to make delivery. FRCP 5(b)(2).

i. *Serving an attorney.* If a party is represented by an attorney, service under FRCP 5 must be made on the attorney unless the court orders service on the party. FRCP 5(b)(1).

c. *DISTRICT OF MAINE: Service of electronically filed documents*

i. *Registered users.* Registration [as a filing user of the court's ECF system] constitutes consent to service of all documents by electronic means as provided in ME R USDCT App. 4. ME R USDCT App. 4(b)(4). Whenever a non-sealed pleading is filed electronically, the ECF system will automatically generate and send a Notice of Electronic Filing (NEF) to the filing user and registered users of record. The user filing the document should retain a paper or digital copy of the NEF, which shall serve as the court's date-stamp and proof of filing. ME R USDCT App. 4(e)(1).

- *Sealed documents.* Although the filing of sealed documents in civil cases produces an NEF, the document itself cannot be accessed and counsel shall be responsible for making service of the sealed documents. ME R USDCT App. 4(e)(2).

ii. *Non-registered users and pro se litigants.* Attorneys who have not yet registered as users with ECF and pro se litigants who have not registered with ECF shall be served a paper copy of any electronically filed pleading or other document in accordance with the provisions of FRCP 5. ME R USDCT App. 4(e)(3).

- *Registration of pro se litigants.* A non-prisoner who is a party to a civil action and who is not represented by an attorney may register to receive service electronically and to electronically transmit their documents to the court for filing in the ECF system. If during the course of the action the person retains an attorney who appears on the person's behalf, the clerk shall terminate the person's registration upon the attorney's appearance. ME R USDCT App. 4(b)(2).

d. *Serving numerous defendants.* If an action involves an unusually large number of defendants, the court may, on motion or on its own, order that: (A) defendants' pleadings and replies to them need not be served on other defendants; (B) any crossclaim, counterclaim, avoidance, or affirmative defense in those pleadings and replies to them will be treated as denied or avoided by all other parties; and (C) filing any such pleading and serving it on the plaintiff constitutes notice of the pleading to all parties. FRCP 5(c)(1).

      i. *Notifying parties.* A copy of every such order must be served on the parties as the court directs. FRCP 5(c)(2).

3. *DISTRICT OF MAINE: Filing and service of highly sensitive documents (HSDs).* For information on filing and serving highly sensitive documents (HSDs) in the District of Maine, refer to ME R USDCT General Order 21-5.

G. Hearings

1. *Hearing on certain FRCP 12 defenses before trial.* If a party so moves, any defense listed in FRCP 12(b)(1) through FRCP 12(b)(7)—whether made in a pleading or by motion—and a motion under FRCP 12(c) must be heard and decided before trial unless the court orders a deferral until trial. FRCP 12(i).

H. Forms

1. Official Federal Answer Forms

    a. Waiver of the service of summons. FRCP 4.

2. Federal Answer Forms

    a. Generally. 2B FEDFORMS § 8:10.

    b. Introduction to separate defenses. 2B FEDFORMS § 8:11.

    c. Presenting defenses. 2B FEDFORMS § 8:12.

    d. With counterclaim for interpleader. 2B FEDFORMS § 8:13.

    e. Denials and admissions. 2B FEDFORMS § 8:14.

    f. Denials, admissions and affirmative defenses. 2B FEDFORMS § 8:15.

    g. Separate answer of two defendants; Duty of fair representation. 2B FEDFORMS § 8:16.

    h. Separate answer of third defendant. 2B FEDFORMS § 8:17.

    i. Reciting paragraphs and subparagraphs of complaint; Account malpractice. 2B FEDFORMS § 8:18.

    j. One of multiple defendants. 2B FEDFORMS § 8:21.

    k. Pro se answer. 2B FEDFORMS § 8:22.50.

    l. Denial of particular averment. 2B FEDFORMS § 8:24.

    m. Admission of particular averment. 2B FEDFORMS § 8:25.

    n. Denial of all averments of paragraph. 2B FEDFORMS § 8:26.

    o. Admission of all averments of paragraph. 2B FEDFORMS § 8:27.

    p. Denial in part and admission in part of paragraph. 2B FEDFORMS § 8:28.

    q. General denial. 2B FEDFORMS § 8:29.

    r. Qualified general denial. 2B FEDFORMS § 8:30.

    s. Denial of knowledge or information sufficient to form a belief. 2B FEDFORMS § 8:31.

    t. Denial of jurisdictional allegations; Jurisdictional amount. 2B FEDFORMS § 8:32.

    u. Denial of jurisdictional allegations; Federal question. 2B FEDFORMS § 8:34.

    v. Denial of jurisdictional allegations; Diversity of citizenship. 2B FEDFORMS § 8:37.

    w. Contributory negligence. 2B FEDFORMS § 8:58.

    x. Fraud. 2B FEDFORMS § 8:74.

    y. Mistake. 2B FEDFORMS § 8:85.

    z. Statute of limitations. 2B FEDFORMS § 8:103.

I. Applicable Rules

1. *Federal rules*

    a. Summons. FRCP 4.

b. Serving and filing pleadings and other papers. FRCP 5.

c. Constitutional challenge to a statute; Notice, certification, and intervention. FRCP 5.1.

d. Privacy protection for filings made with the court. FRCP 5.2.

e. Computing and extending time; Time for motion papers. FRCP 6.

f. Pleadings allowed; Form of motions and other papers. FRCP 7.

g. Disclosure statement. FRCP 7.1.

h. General rules of pleading. FRCP 8.

i. Pleading special matters. FRCP 9.

j. Form of pleadings. FRCP 10.

k. Signing pleadings, motions, and other papers; Representations to the court; Sanctions. FRCP 11.

l. Defenses and objections; When and how presented; Motion for judgment on the pleadings; Consolidating motions; Waiving defenses; Pretrial hearing. FRCP 12.

m. Counterclaim and crossclaim. FRCP 13.

n. Third-party practice. FRCP 14.

o. Joinder of claims. FRCP 18.

p. Required joinder of parties. FRCP 19.

q. Permissive joinder of parties. FRCP 20.

r. Misjoinder and nonjoinder of parties. FRCP 21.

s. Right to a jury trial; Demand. FRCP 38.

t. Determining foreign law. FRCP 44.1.

2. *Local rules*

a. *DISTRICT OF MAINE*

i. Service and filing of pleadings and other papers. ME R USDCT Rule 5.

ii. Notice of constitutional question. ME R USDCT Rule 5.1.

iii. Time. ME R USDCT Rule 6.

iv. Corporate disclosure. ME R USDCT Rule 7.1.

v. Pleading special matters. ME R USDCT Rule 9.

vi. Form of pleadings, motions and other papers. ME R USDCT Rule 10.

vii. Demand for jury trial. ME R USDCT Rule 38.

viii. Attorneys; Appearances and withdrawals. ME R USDCT Rule 83.2.

ix. Alternative dispute resolution (ADR). ME R USDCT Rule 83.11.

x. Administrative procedures governing the filing and service by electronic means. ME R USDCT App. 4.

xi. Redacting pleadings. ME R USDCT Redacting Pleadings.

Pleadings
Amended Pleading

Document Last Updated July 2021

A. Checklist

(I) ❑ Matters to be considered by plaintiff or defendant

(a) ❑ Required documents

(1) ❑ Amended pleading

(b) ❑ Supplemental documents

    (1) ❑ Notice of constitutional question

    (2) ❑ Notice of issue concerning foreign law

(c) ❑ Timing

    (1) ❑ A party may amend its pleading once as a matter of course within: (A) twenty-one (21) days after serving it, or (B) if the pleading is one to which a responsive pleading is required, twenty-one (21) days after service of a responsive pleading or twenty-one (21) days after service of a motion under FRCP 12(b), FRCP 12(e), or FRCP 12(f), whichever is earlier

B. Timing

1. *Amended pleading*

    a. *Amending as a matter of course.* A party may amend its pleading once as a matter of course within: (A) twenty-one (21) days after serving it, or (B) if the pleading is one to which a responsive pleading is required, twenty-one (21) days after service of a responsive pleading or twenty-one (21) days after service of a motion under FRCP 12(b), FRCP 12(e), or FRCP 12(f), whichever is earlier. FRCP 15(a)(1).

    b. *Extension of time.* If the time for serving the responsive pleading is extended by a motion for enlargement of time under FRCP 6(b), or by a stipulation, the period for amending as of right also may be enlarged. FPP § 1480.

    c. *Other amendments.* In all other cases, a party may amend its pleading only with the opposing party's written consent or the court's leave. The court should freely give leave when justice so requires. FRCP 15(a)(2). Refer to the United States District Court for the District of Maine KeyRules Motion for Leave to Amend document for more information.

2. *Time to respond to an amended pleading.* Unless the court orders otherwise, any required response to an amended pleading must be made within the time remaining to respond to the original pleading or within fourteen (14) days after service of the amended pleading, whichever is later. FRCP 15(a)(3).

3. *Computation of time*

    a. *Computing time.* FRCP 6 applies in computing any time period specified in the Federal Rules of Civil Procedure, in any local rule or court order, or in any statute that does not specify a method of computing time. FRCP 6(a).

        i. *Period stated in days or a longer unit.* When the period is stated in days or a longer unit of time: (A) exclude the day of the event that triggers the period; (B) count every day, including intermediate Saturdays, Sundays, and legal holidays; and (C) include the last day of the period, but if the last day is a Saturday, Sunday, or legal holiday, the period continues to run until the end of the next day that is not a Saturday, Sunday, or legal holiday. FRCP 6(a)(1).

        ii. *Period stated in hours.* When the period is stated in hours: (A) begin counting immediately on the occurrence of the event that triggers the period; (B) count every hour, including hours during intermediate Saturdays, Sundays, and legal holidays; and (C) if the period would end on a Saturday, Sunday, or legal holiday, the period continues to run until the same time on the next day that is not a Saturday, Sunday, or legal holiday. FRCP 6(a)(2).

        iii. *Inaccessibility of the clerk's office.* Unless the court orders otherwise, if the clerk's office is inaccessible: (A) on the last day for filing under FRCP 6(a)(1), then the time for filing is extended to the first accessible day that is not a Saturday, Sunday, or legal holiday; or (B) during the last hour for filing under FRCP 6(a)(2), then the time for filing is extended to the same time on the first accessible day that is not a Saturday, Sunday, or legal holiday. FRCP 6(a)(3).

        iv. *"Last day" defined.* Unless a different time is set by a statute, local rule, or court order, the last day ends: (A) for electronic filing, at midnight in the court's time zone; and (B) for filing by other means, when the clerk's office is scheduled to close. FRCP 6(a)(4).

        v. *"Next day" defined.* The "next day" is determined by continuing to count forward when the period is measured after an event and backward when measured before an event. FRCP 6(a)(5).

        vi. *"Legal holiday" defined.* "Legal holiday" means: (A) the day set aside by statute for observing New Year's Day, Martin Luther King Jr.'s Birthday, Washington's Birthday, Memorial Day, Independence Day, Labor Day, Columbus Day, Veterans' Day, Thanksgiving Day, or Christmas Day; (B) any day declared a holiday by the President or Congress; and (C) for periods that are measured after an event, any other day declared a holiday by the state where the district court is located. FRCP 6(a)(6).

        vii. *DISTRICT OF MAINE: Applicability of FRCP 6.* FRCP 6 applies when computing any period of time stated in the Local Rules of the United States District Court for the District of Maine. ME R USDCT Rule 6(a).

b. *DISTRICT OF MAINE: Computation of electronic filing deadlines.* Filing documents electronically does not in any way alter any filing deadlines. All electronic transmissions of documents must be completed prior to midnight, Eastern Time, in order to be considered timely filed that day. Where a specific time of day deadline is set by court order or stipulation, the electronic filing must be completed by that time. ME R USDCT App. 4(f). A document filed electronically shall be deemed filed at the time and date stated on the Notice of Electronic Filing received from the court. ME R USDCT App. 4(d)(2).

   i. *Technical failures.* A filing user whose filing is made untimely as the result of a technical failure may seek appropriate relief from the court. ME R USDCT App. 4(n). A technical failure of the court's ECF system is deemed to have occurred when the court's ECF site cannot accept filings continuously or intermittently over the course of any period of time greater than one (1) hour. Known system outages will be posted on the court's website along with guidance on how to proceed, if applicable. ME R USDCT App. 4(n).

c. *Extending time.* When an act may or must be done within a specified time, the court may, for good cause, extend the time: (A) with or without motion or notice if the court acts, or if a request is made, before the original time or its extension expires; or (B) on motion made after the time has expired if the party failed to act because of excusable neglect. FRCP 6(b)(1). A court must not extend the time to act under FRCP 50(b), FRCP 50(d), FRCP 52(b), FRCP 59(b), FRCP 59(d), FRCP 59(e), and FRCP 60(b). FRCP 6(b)(2). Refer to the United States District Court for the District of Maine KeyRules Motion for Continuance/Extension of Time document for more information on extending time.

d. *Additional time after certain kinds of service.* When a party may or must act within a specified time after being served and service is made under FRCP 5(b)(2)(C) (by mail), FRCP 5(b)(2)(D) (by leaving with the clerk), or FRCP 5(b)(2)(F) (by other means consented to), three (3) days are added after the period would otherwise expire under FRCP 6(a). FRCP 6(d).

C. General Requirements

1. *Pleading, generally*

   a. *Pleadings allowed.* Only these pleadings are allowed: (1) a complaint; (2) an answer to a complaint; (3) an answer to a counterclaim designated as a counterclaim; (4) an answer to a crossclaim; (5) a third-party complaint; (6) an answer to a third-party complaint; and (7) if the court orders one, a reply to an answer. FRCP 7(a).

   b. *Pleading to be concise and direct.* Each allegation must be simple, concise, and direct. No technical form is required. FRCP 8(d)(1).

   c. *Alternative statements of a claim or defense.* A party may set out 2 or more statements of a claim or defense alternatively or hypothetically, either in a single count or defense or in separate ones. If a party makes alternative statements, the pleading is sufficient if any one of them is sufficient. FRCP 8(d)(2).

   d. *Inconsistent claims or defenses.* A party may state as many separate claims or defenses as it has, regardless of consistency. FRCP 8(d)(3).

   e. *Construing pleadings.* Pleadings must be construed so as to do justice. FRCP 8(e).

2. *Pleading special matters*

   a. *Capacity or authority to sue; Legal existence.* Except when required to show that the court has jurisdiction, a pleading need not allege: (A) a party's capacity to sue or be sued; (B) a party's authority to sue or be sued in a representative capacity; or (C) the legal existence of an organized association of persons that is made a party. FRCP 9(a)(1).

      i. *Raising those issues.* To raise any of those issues, a party must do so by a specific denial, which must state any supporting facts that are peculiarly within the party's knowledge. FRCP 9(a)(2).

   b. *Fraud or mistake; Conditions of mind.* In alleging fraud or mistake, a party must state with particularity the circumstances constituting fraud or mistake. Malice, intent, knowledge, and other conditions of a person's mind may be alleged generally. FRCP 9(b).

   c. *Conditions precedent.* In pleading conditions precedent, it suffices to allege generally that all conditions precedent have occurred or been performed. But when denying that a condition precedent has occurred or been performed, a party must do so with particularity. FRCP 9(c).

   d. *Official document or act.* In pleading an official document or official act, it suffices to allege that the document was legally issued or the act legally done. FRCP 9(d).

   e. *Judgment.* In pleading a judgment or decision of a domestic or foreign court, a judicial or quasi-judicial tribunal, or a board or officer, it suffices to plead the judgment or decision without showing jurisdiction to render it. FRCP 9(e).

f. *Time and place.* An allegation of time or place is material when testing the sufficiency of a pleading. FRCP 9(f).

g. *Special damages.* If an item of special damage is claimed, it must be specifically stated. FRCP 9(g).

h. *Admiralty or maritime claim*

   i. *How designated.* If a claim for relief is within the admiralty or maritime jurisdiction and also within the court's subject-matter jurisdiction on some other ground, the pleading may designate the claim as an admiralty or maritime claim for purposes of FRCP 14(c), FRCP 38(e), and FRCP 82 and the Supplemental Rules for Admiralty or Maritime Claims and Asset Forfeiture Actions. A claim cognizable only in the admiralty or maritime jurisdiction is an admiralty or maritime claim for those purposes, whether or not so designated. FRCP 9(h)(1).

   ii. *Designation for appeal.* A case that includes an admiralty or maritime claim within FRCP 9(h) is an admiralty case within 28 U.S.C.A. § 1292(a)(3). FRCP 9(h)(2).

3. *Amended pleading*

   a. *Amendments before trial.* The function of FRCP 15(a), which provides generally for the amendment of pleadings, is to enable a party to assert matters that were overlooked or were unknown at the time the party interposed the original complaint or answer. FPP § 1473; Smiga v. Dean Witter Reynolds, Inc., 766 F.2d 698, 703 (2d Cir. 1985).

      i. *Matters contained in amended pleading under FRCP 15(a).* Although FRCP 15(a) does not expressly state that an amendment must contain only matters that occurred within a particular time period, FRCP 15(d) provides that any "transaction, occurrence, or event that happened after the date of the pleading" should be set forth in a supplemental pleading. FPP § 1473. Thus, impliedly, an amended pleading, whether prepared with or without leave of court, only should relate to matters that have taken place prior to the date of the earlier pleading. FPP § 1473; Ford Motor Co. v. United States, 896 F. Supp. 1224, 1230 (Ct. Int'l Trade 1995).

      ii. *Amending as a matter of course.* The right to amend as of course is not restricted to any particular litigant or pleading. FPP § 1480. It is a right conferred on all of the parties to an action and thus extends to persons who were not original parties to the litigation, but are brought into the action by way of counterclaim, crossclaim, third-party claim, or defensive interpleader. FPP § 1480; Johnson v. Walsh, 65 F. Supp. 157 (W.D. Mo. 1946).

         • *Amending a complaint with multiple defendants.* When a number of defendants are involved in an action, some of whom have answered and some of whom have filed no responsive pleading, the plaintiff can amend as a matter of course as to those defendants who have not answered. FEDPROC § 62:261; Pallant v. Sinatra, 7 F.R.D. 293 (S.D.N.Y. 1945). On the other hand, a plaintiff may not file an amended complaint as of right against those defendants who have not yet answered, if the plaintiff has amended the complaint once already as a matter of course. FEDPROC § 62:261; Glaros v. Perse, 628 F.2d 679 (1st Cir. 1980).

      iii. *Amending with leave of court.* Refer to the United States District Court for the District of Maine KeyRules Motion for Leave to Amend document for information on amending the pleadings with leave of court.

      iv. *Types of amendments permitted under FRCP 15(a)*

         • *Cure a defective pleading.* Perhaps the most common use of FRCP 15(a) is by a party seeking to amend in order to cure a defective pleading. FPP § 1474.

         • *Correct insufficiently stated claims or defenses.* A more common use of FRCP 15(a) amendments is to correct insufficiently stated claims or defenses. Typically, amendments of this character involve either adding a necessary allegation in order to state a claim for relief or correcting a misnomer of a party to the action. FPP § 1474.

         • *Change nature or theory of claim or capacity of party.* Courts also have allowed a party to amend in order to change the nature or theory of the party's claim or the capacity in which the party is bringing the action. FPP § 1474.

         • *State additional claims or defenses or drop claims or defenses.* Plaintiffs and defendants also have been permitted to amend their pleadings to state additional claims, to assert additional defenses, or to drop claims or defenses. FPP § 1474; Weinberger v. Retail Credit Co., 498 F.2d 552, 554, n.4 (4th Cir. 1974).

         • *Increase amount of damages or elect a different remedy.* An FRCP 15(a) amendment also is appropriate for increasing the amount of damages sought, or for electing a different remedy than the one originally requested. FPP § 1474; McFadden v. Sanchez, 710 F.2d 907 (2d Cir. 1983).

         • *Add, substitute, or drop parties.* Finally, a party may make an FRCP 15(a) amendment to add, substitute, or drop parties to the action. FPP § 1474.

b. *Amendments during and after trial*

    i. *Based on an objection at trial.* If, at trial, a party objects that evidence is not within the issues raised in the pleadings, the court may permit the pleadings to be amended. The court should freely permit an amendment when doing so will aid in presenting the merits and the objecting party fails to satisfy the court that the evidence would prejudice that party's action or defense on the merits. The court may grant a continuance to enable the objecting party to meet the evidence. FRCP 15(b)(1).

    ii. *For issues tried by consent.* When an issue not raised by the pleadings is tried by the parties' express or implied consent, it must be treated in all respects as if raised in the pleadings. A party may move—at any time, even after judgment—to amend the pleadings to conform them to the evidence and to raise an unpleaded issue. But failure to amend does not affect the result of the trial of that issue. FRCP 15(b)(2).

    iii. Refer to the United States District Court for the District of Maine KeyRules Motion for Leave to Amend document for more information on moving to amend the pleadings.

c. *Relation back of amendments*

    i. *When an amendment relates back.* An amendment to a pleading relates back to the date of the original pleading when: (A) the law that provides the applicable statute of limitations allows relation back; (B) the amendment asserts a claim or defense that arose out of the conduct, transaction, or occurrence set out—or attempted to be set out—in the original pleading; or (C) the amendment changes the party or the naming of the party against whom a claim is asserted, if FRCP 15(c)(1)(B) is satisfied and if, within the period provided by FRCP 4(m) for serving the summons and complaint, the party to be brought in by amendment: (i) received such notice of the action that it will not be prejudiced in defending on the merits; and (ii) knew or should have known that the action would have been brought against it, but for a mistake concerning the proper party's identity. FRCP 15(c)(1).

    ii. *Notice to the United States.* When the United States or a United States officer or agency is added as a defendant by amendment, the notice requirements of FRCP 15(c)(1)(C)(i) and FRCP 15(c)(1)(C)(ii) are satisfied if, during the stated period, process was delivered or mailed to the United States attorney or the United States attorney's designee, to the Attorney General of the United States, or to the officer or agency. FRCP 15(c)(2).

d. *Effect of an amended pleading.* A pleading that has been amended under FRCP 15(a) supersedes the pleading it modifies and remains in effect throughout the action unless it subsequently is modified. FPP § 1476. Once an amended pleading is interposed, the original pleading no longer performs any function in the case and any subsequent motion made by an opposing party should be directed at the amended pleading. FPP § 1476; Ferdik v. Bonzelet, 963 F.2d 1258, 1262 (9th Cir. 1992), as amended (May 22, 1992); Davis v. TXO Prod. Corp., 929 F.2d 1515, 1517 (10th Cir. 1991).

4. *Amended complaint.* Refer to the United States District Court for the District of Maine KeyRules Complaint document for the requirements specific to the amended complaint.

5. *Amended answer.* Refer to the United States District Court for the District of Maine KeyRules Answer document for the requirements specific to the amended answer.

6. *Joinder*

a. *Joinder of claims.* A party asserting a claim, counterclaim, crossclaim, or third-party claim may join, as independent or alternative claims, as many claims as it has against an opposing party. FRCP 18(a).

    i. *Joinder of contingent claims.* A party may join two claims even though one of them is contingent on the disposition of the other; but the court may grant relief only in accordance with the parties' relative substantive rights. In particular, a plaintiff may state a claim for money and a claim to set aside a conveyance that is fraudulent as to that plaintiff, without first obtaining a judgment for the money. FRCP 18(b).

b. *Joinder of parties; Required*

    i. *Persons required to be joined if feasible; Required party.* A person who is subject to service of process and whose joinder will not deprive the court of subject-matter jurisdiction must be joined as a party if: (A) in that person's absence, the court cannot accord complete relief among existing parties; or (B) that person claims an interest relating to the subject of the action and is so situated that disposing of the action in the person's absence may: (i) as a practical matter impair or impede the person's ability to protect the interest; or (ii) leave an existing party subject to a substantial risk of incurring double, multiple, or otherwise inconsistent obligations because of the interest. FRCP 19(a)(1).

    ii. *Joinder of parties by court order.* If a person has not been joined as required, the court must order that the person be made a party. A person who refuses to join as a plaintiff may be made either a defendant or, in a proper case, an involuntary plaintiff. FRCP 19(a)(2).

    iii.   *Venue.* If a joined party objects to venue and the joinder would make venue improper, the court must dismiss that party. FRCP 19(a)(3).

    iv.   *When joinder of parties is not feasible.* If a person who is required to be joined if feasible cannot be joined, the court must determine whether, in equity and good conscience, the action should proceed among the existing parties or should be dismissed. FRCP 19(b). For a list of the factors for the court to consider in determining whether joinder of parties is feasible, refer to FRCP 19(b)(1) through FRCP 19(b)(4).

    v.   *Pleading the reasons for nonjoinder.* When asserting a claim for relief, a party must state: (1) the name, if known, of any person who is required to be joined if feasible but is not joined; and (2) the reasons for not joining that person. FRCP 19(c).

    vi.   *Exception for class actions.* FRCP 19 is subject to FRCP 23. FRCP 19(d). For information on class actions, refer to FRCP 23.

  c. *Joinder of parties; Permissible*

    i.   *Persons who may join or be joined*

- *Plaintiffs.* Persons may join in one action as plaintiffs if: (A) they assert any right to relief jointly, severally, or in the alternative with respect to or arising out of the same transaction, occurrence, or series of transactions or occurrences; and (B) any question of law or fact common to all plaintiffs will arise in the action. FRCP 20(a)(1).

- *Defendants.* Persons—as well as a vessel, cargo, or other property subject to admiralty process in rem—may be joined in one action as defendants if: (A) any right to relief is asserted against them jointly, severally, or in the alternative with respect to or arising out of the same transaction, occurrence, or series of transactions or occurrences; and (B) any question of law or fact common to all defendants will arise in the action. FRCP 20(a)(2).

- *Extent of relief.* Neither a plaintiff nor a defendant need be interested in obtaining or defending against all the relief demanded. The court may grant judgment to one or more plaintiffs according to their rights, and against one or more defendants according to their liabilities. FRCP 20(a)(3).

    ii.   *Protective measures.* The court may issue orders—including an order for separate trials—to protect a party against embarrassment, delay, expense, or other prejudice that arises from including a person against whom the party asserts no claim and who asserts no claim against the party. FRCP 20(b).

  d. *Misjoinder and nonjoinder of parties.* Misjoinder of parties is not a ground for dismissing an action. On motion or on its own, the court may at any time, on just terms, add or drop a party. The court may also sever any claim against a party. FRCP 21.

7. *Right to a jury trial; Demand*

  a. *Right preserved.* The right of trial by jury as declared by U.S.C.A. Const. Amend. VII, or as provided by a federal statute, is preserved to the parties inviolate. FRCP 38(a).

  b. *Demand.* On any issue triable of right by a jury, a party may demand a jury trial by: (1) serving the other parties with a written demand—which may be included in a pleading—no later than fourteen (14) days after the last pleading directed to the issue is served; and (2) filing the demand in accordance with FRCP 5(d). FRCP 38(b).

    i.   *DISTRICT OF MAINE: Removed actions.* A demand for jury trial in actions removed to the United States District Court for the District of Maine from the state courts shall be filed in accordance with the provisions of FRCP 81(c). ME R USDCT Rule 38.

  c. *Specifying issues.* In its demand, a party may specify the issues that it wishes to have tried by a jury; otherwise, it is considered to have demanded a jury trial on all the issues so triable. If the party has demanded a jury trial on only some issues, any other party may—within fourteen (14) days after being served with the demand or within a shorter time ordered by the court—serve a demand for a jury trial on any other or all factual issues triable by jury. FRCP 38(c).

  d. *Waiver; Withdrawal.* A party waives a jury trial unless its demand is properly served and filed. A proper demand may be withdrawn only if the parties consent. FRCP 38(d).

  e. *Admiralty and maritime claims.* The rules in FRCP 38 do not create a right to a jury trial on issues in a claim that is an admiralty or maritime claim under FRCP 9(h). FRCP 38(e).

8. *DISTRICT OF MAINE: Appearances.* An attorney's signature to a pleading shall constitute an appearance for the party filing the pleading. Otherwise, an attorney who wishes to participate in any manner in any action must file a formal written appearance identifying the party represented. An appearance whether by pleading or formal written appearance shall be signed by an attorney in his/her individual name and shall state his/her office address. ME R USDCT Rule 83.2(a). For more information, refer to ME R USDCT Rule 83.2.

9. *DISTRICT OF MAINE: Alternative dispute resolution (ADR).* Litigants are authorized and encouraged to employ, at their own expense, any available ADR process on which they can agree, including early neutral evaluation, settlement conferences, mediation, non-binding summary jury trial, corporate mini-trial, and arbitration proceedings. ME R USDCT Rule 83.11(a). For more information on ADR, refer to ME R USDCT Rule 83.11.

D. Documents

1. *Required documents*

   a. *Amended pleading.* Refer to the "C. General Requirements" section of this KeyRules document for information on the amended pleading.

      i. *Certificate of service.* No certificate of service is required when a paper is served by filing it with the court's electronic-filing system. When a paper that is required to be served is served by other means: (i) if the paper is filed, a certificate of service must be filed with it or within a reasonable time after service; and (ii) if the paper is not filed, a certificate of service need not be filed unless filing is required by court order or by local rule. FRCP 5(d)(1)(B).

2. *Supplemental documents*

   a. *Notice of constitutional question.* A party that files a pleading, written motion, or other paper drawing into question the constitutionality of a federal or state statute must promptly: (1) file a notice of constitutional question stating the question and identifying the paper that raises it, if: (A) a federal statute is questioned and the parties do not include the United States, one of its agencies, or one of its officers or employees in an official capacity; or (B) a state statute is questioned and the parties do not include the state, one of its agencies, or one of its officers or employees in an official capacity; and (2) serve the notice and paper on the Attorney General of the United States if a federal statute is questioned—or on the state attorney general if a state statute is questioned—either by certified or registered mail or by sending it to an electronic address designated by the attorney general for this purpose. FRCP 5.1(a).

      i. *DISTRICT OF MAINE.* To enable the court to comply with the provisions of 28 U.S.C.A. § 2403 and FRCP 24(c), in any action, suit or proceeding to which the United States or any agency, officer or employee thereof is not a party, any party who shall draw into question the constitutionality of any Act of Congress affecting the public interest shall forthwith so notify the clerk in writing, stating the title of the action, its docket number if any, and the Act of Congress in question. ME R USDCT Rule 5.1. To enable the court to comply with the provisions of 28 U.S.C.A. § 2403, in any action, suit or proceeding to which a state or any agency, officer or employee thereof is not a party, any party who shall draw in question the constitutionality of any statute of that state affecting the public interest shall forthwith so notify the clerk in writing, stating the title of the action, its docket number if any, and the statute of the state in question. ME R USDCT Rule 5.1.

      ii. *No forfeiture.* A party's failure to file and serve the notice, or the court's failure to certify, does not forfeit a constitutional claim or defense that is otherwise timely asserted. FRCP 5.1(d).

   b. *Notice of issue concerning foreign law.* A party who intends to raise an issue about a foreign country's law must give notice by a pleading or other writing. In determining foreign law, the court may consider any relevant material or source, including testimony, whether or not submitted by a party or admissible under the Federal Rules of Evidence. The court's determination must be treated as a ruling on a question of law. FRCP 44.1.

3. *Documents required for an amended complaint adding a new claim for relief or new party.* Refer to the United States District Court for the District of Maine KeyRules Complaint document for the documents for an amended complaint adding a new claim for relief or being filed and served against a new party.

E. Format

1. *Form of documents*

   a. *DISTRICT OF MAINE: Font size, line spacing, and paper size.* All such documents shall be typed in a font of no less than size twelve (12) point, and shall be double-spaced or printed on eight and one-half by eleven (8-1/2 x 11) inch paper. Footnotes shall be in a font of no less than size ten (10) point, and may be single spaced. ME R USDCT Rule 10.

b. *Caption.* Every pleading must have a caption with the court's name, a title, a file number, and an FRCP 7(a) designation. FRCP 10(a).

    i. *Names of parties.* The title of the complaint must name all the parties; the title of other pleadings, after naming the first party on each side, may refer generally to other parties. FRCP 10(a).

    ii. *DISTRICT OF MAINE: Additional caption requirements.* All pleadings, motions and other papers filed with the clerk or otherwise submitted to the court, except exhibits, shall bear the proper case number and shall contain on the first page a caption as described by FRCP 10(a) and immediately thereunder a designation of what the document is and the name of the party in whose behalf it is submitted. ME R USDCT Rule 10.

    iii. *DISTRICT OF MAINE: Three-judge district court.* To enable the court to comply with the provisions of 28 U.S.C.A. § 2284, in any action or proceeding which a party believes is required to be heard by a three-judge district court, the words "THREE-JUDGE DISTRICT COURT REQUESTED" or the equivalent shall be included directly beneath the designation of the pleadings. ME R USDCT Rule 9(a).

    iv. *DISTRICT OF MAINE: Injunctive relief.* If a pleading or motion seeks injunctive relief, in addition to the prayer for such relief, the words "INJUNCTIVE RELIEF SOUGHT" or the equivalent shall be included on the first page. ME R USDCT Rule 9(b).

    v. *DISTRICT OF MAINE: Demand for jury trial.* If a demand for jury trial is endorsed upon a pleading pursuant to FRCP 38(b), in addition to said endorsement the designation of the pleading shall include the words "AND DEMAND FOR JURY TRIAL" or the equivalent on the first page. ME R USDCT Rule 38.

c. *Claims or defenses*

    i. *Numbered paragraphs.* A party must state its claims or defenses in numbered paragraphs, each limited as far as practicable to a single set of circumstances. A later pleading may refer by number to a paragraph in an earlier pleading. FRCP 10(b).

    ii. *Separate statements.* If doing so would promote clarity, each claim founded on a separate transaction or occurrence—and each defense other than a denial—must be stated in a separate count or defense. FRCP 10(b).

d. *Adoption by reference.* A statement in a pleading may be adopted by reference elsewhere in the same pleading or in any other pleading or motion. FRCP 10(c).

    i. *Exhibits.* A copy of a written instrument that is an exhibit to a pleading is a part of the pleading for all purposes. FRCP 10(c).

e. *DISTRICT OF MAINE: Page numbering.* All pages shall be numbered at the bottom. ME R USDCT Rule 10.

f. *DISTRICT OF MAINE: Attachment of ancillary papers.* Ancillary papers shall be attached at the end of the document to which they relate. ME R USDCT Rule 10.

g. *Acceptance by the clerk.* The clerk must not refuse to file a paper solely because it is not in the form prescribed by the Federal Rules of Civil Procedure or by a local rule or practice. FRCP 5(d)(4).

2. *Form of electronic documents.* A paper filed electronically is a written paper for purposes of the Federal Rules of Civil Procedure. FRCP 5(d)(3)(D).

a. *DISTRICT OF MAINE: Document format.* The ECF system only accepts documents in a portable document format (PDF). Although there are two types of PDF documents—electronically converted PDF's and scanned PDF's—only electronically converted PDF's may be filed with the court using the ECF system, unless otherwise authorized by local rule or order. ME R USDCT App. 4. Any document or exhibit to be filed or submitted to the court shall not be password-protected or encrypted. ME R USDCT App. 4(g)(12).

    i. *Electronically converted PDFs.* Electronically converted PDF's are created from word processing documents (MS Word, WordPerfect, etc.) using Adobe Acrobat or similar software. They are text searchable and their file size is small. ME R USDCT App. 4. Software used to electronically convert documents to PDF which includes proprietary or advertisement information within the PDF document is prohibited. ME R USDCT App. 4.

    ii. *Scanned PDFs.* Scanned PDF's are created from paper documents run through an optical scanner. Scanned PDF's are not searchable and have a large file size. ME R USDCT App. 4.

b. *DISTRICT OF MAINE: Title.* All pleadings filed electronically shall be titled in accordance with the approved dictionary of civil or criminal events of the ECF system of the United States District Court for the District of Maine. ME R USDCT App. 4(d)(3).

c. *DISTRICT OF MAINE: Attachments.* Attachments to filings and exhibits must be filed in accordance with the court's

ECF User Manual, unless otherwise ordered by the court. ME R USDCT App. 4(j). When there are fifty (50) or fewer attachments to a pleading, the attachments must be filed by counsel electronically using ECF. When there are more than fifty (50) attachments, the attachments must be filed in one of the following ways: (A) using ECF, simply attach them to the pleading being filed; (B) using ECF, use the "Additional Attachments" menu item; (C) on paper; or (D) on a properly labeled three and one-half (3-1/2) inch floppy disk, CD or DVD. ME R USDCT App. 4(j)(2). Attachments filed on paper or on disk must contain a comprehensive index that clearly describes each document. ME R USDCT App. 4(j)(2).

    i. A filing user must submit as attachments only those excerpts of the referenced documents that are directly germane to the matter under consideration by the court. Excerpted material must be clearly and prominently identified as such. Users who file excerpts of documents do so without prejudice to their right to timely file additional excerpts or the complete document, as may be allowed by the court. Responding parties may timely file additional excerpts or the complete document that they believe are directly germane. ME R USDCT App. 4(j)(3).

    ii. Filers shall not attach as an exhibit any pleading or other paper already on file with the court in that case, but shall merely refer to that document. ME R USDCT App. 4(j)(4).

  d. *DISTRICT OF MAINE: Compliance with technical standards.* All documents filed by electronic means must comply with technical standards, if any, established by the Judicial Conference of the United States or by the United States District Court for the District of Maine. ME R USDCT App. 4(a)(3).

3. *Signing of pleadings, motions and other papers*

  a. *Signature.* Every pleading, written motion, and other paper must be signed by at least one attorney of record in the attorney's name—or by a party personally if the party is unrepresented. The paper must state the signer's address, e-mail address, and telephone number. FRCP 11(a).

    i. *No verification or accompanying affidavit required for pleadings.* Unless a rule or statute specifically states otherwise, a pleading need not be verified or accompanied by an affidavit. FRCP 11(a).

    ii. *Unsigned papers.* The court must strike an unsigned paper unless the omission is promptly corrected after being called to the attorney's or party's attention. FRCP 11(a).

  b. *Electronic signing.* A filing made through a person's electronic-filing account and authorized by that person, together with that person's name on a signature block, constitutes the person's signature. FRCP 5(d)(3)(C).

    i. *DISTRICT OF MAINE: Attorneys.* The user log-in and password together with a user's name on the signature block constitutes the attorney's signature pursuant to the Federal Rules of Civil Procedure and the Local Rules of the United States District Court for the District of Maine. All electronically filed documents must include a signature block and must set forth the attorney's name, address, telephone number and e-mail address. The name of the ECF user under whose log-in and password the document is submitted must be preceded by a "/s/" in the space where the signature would otherwise appear. ME R USDCT App. 4(h)(1).

    ii. *DISTRICT OF MAINE: Multiple signatures.* The filer of any document requiring more than one signature (e.g., pleadings filed by visiting lawyers, stipulations, joint status reports) must list thereon all the names of other signatories, preceded by a "/s/" in the space where the signatures would otherwise appear. By submitting such a document, the filing attorney certifies that each of the other signatories has expressly agreed to the form and substance of the document and that the filing attorney has their actual authority to submit the document electronically. ME R USDCT App. 4(h)(2). For more information, refer to ME R USDCT App. 4(h)(2).

    iii. *DISTRICT OF MAINE: Documents signed under oath.* Affidavits, declarations, verified complaints, or any other document signed under oath shall be filed electronically. The electronically filed version shall contain the typed name of the signatory, preceded by a "/s/" in the space where the signature would otherwise appear indicating that the paper document bears an original signature. ME R USDCT Rule 10; ME R USDCT App. 4(h)(3). For more information, refer to ME R USDCT Rule 10.

  c. *Representations to the court.* By presenting to the court a pleading, written motion, or other paper—whether by signing, filing, submitting, or later advocating it—an attorney or unrepresented party certifies that to the best of the person's knowledge, information, and belief, formed after an inquiry reasonable under the circumstances: (1) it is not being presented for any improper purpose, such as to harass, cause unnecessary delay, or needlessly increase the cost of litigation; (2) the claims, defenses, and other legal contentions are warranted by existing law or by a nonfrivolous argument for extending, modifying, or reversing existing law or for establishing new law; (3) the factual contentions have evidentiary support or, if specifically so identified, will likely have evidentiary support after a reasonable opportunity for further investigation or discovery; and (4) the denials of factual contentions are warranted on the evidence or, if specifically so identified, are reasonably based on belief or a lack of information. FRCP 11(b).

d. *Sanctions.* If, after notice and a reasonable opportunity to respond, the court determines that FRCP 11(b) has been violated, the court may impose an appropriate sanction on any attorney, law firm, or party that violated FRCP 11(b) or is responsible for the violation. FRCP 11(c)(1). Refer to the United States District Court for the District of Maine KeyRules Motion for Sanctions document for more information.

4. *Privacy protection for filings made with the court*

a. *Redacted filings.* Unless the court orders otherwise, in an electronic or paper filing with the court that contains an individual's Social Security number, taxpayer-identification number, or birth date, the name of an individual known to be a minor, or a financial-account number, a party or nonparty making the filing may include only: (1) the last four (4) digits of the Social Security number and taxpayer-identification number; (2) the year of the individual's birth; (3) the minor's initials; and (4) the last four (4) digits of the financial-account number. FRCP 5.2(a).

   i. *DISTRICT OF MAINE.* To address the privacy concerns created by the Internet access to court papers, unless otherwise ordered by the court, counsel shall modify certain personal data identifiers in pleadings and other papers as follows: (1) minors' names: use of the minors' initials only; (2) Social Security numbers: use of the last four (4) numbers only; (3) dates of birth: use of the year of birth only; [and] (4) financial account numbers: identify the type of account and the financial institution, but use only the last four (4) numbers of the account number. ME R USDCT Redacting Pleadings. Counsel should also use caution when filing papers that contain a person's medical records, employment history; financial information; and any proprietary or trade secret information. ME R USDCT Redacting Pleadings.

b. *Exemptions from the redaction requirement.* The redaction requirement does not apply to the following: (1) a financial-account number that identifies the property allegedly subject to forfeiture in a forfeiture proceeding; (2) the record of an administrative or agency proceeding; (3) the official record of a state-court proceeding; (4) the record of a court or tribunal, if that record was not subject to the redaction requirement when originally filed; (5) a filing covered by FRCP 5.2(c) or FRCP 5.2(d); and (6) a pro se filing in an action brought under 28 U.S.C.A. § 2241, 28 U.S.C.A. § 2254, or 28 U.S.C.A. § 2255. FRCP 5.2(b).

c. *Limitations on remote access to electronic files; Social Security appeals and immigration cases.* Unless the court orders otherwise, in an action for benefits under the Social Security Act, and in an action or proceeding relating to an order of removal, to relief from removal, or to immigration benefits or detention, access to an electronic file is authorized as follows: (1) the parties and their attorneys may have remote electronic access to any part of the case file, including the administrative record; (2) any other person may have electronic access to the full record at the courthouse, but may have remote electronic access only to: (A) the docket maintained by the court; and (B) an opinion, order, judgment, or other disposition of the court, but not any other part of the case file or the administrative record. FRCP 5.2(c).

d. *Filings made under seal.* The court may order that a filing be made under seal without redaction. The court may later unseal the filing or order the person who made the filing to file a redacted version for the public record. FRCP 5.2(d).

   i. *DISTRICT OF MAINE.* For information on filing sealed documents in the District of Maine, refer to ME R USDCT Rule 7A, ME R USDCT App. 4(p)(2), and ME R USDCT Sealed Filings.

e. *Protective orders.* For good cause, the court may by order in a case: (1) require redaction of additional information; or (2) limit or prohibit a nonparty's remote electronic access to a document filed with the court. FRCP 5.2(e).

f. *Option for additional unredacted filing under seal.* A person making a redacted filing may also file an unredacted copy under seal. The court must retain the unredacted copy as part of the record. FRCP 5.2(f).

   i. *DISTRICT OF MAINE.* A party wishing to file a document containing the personal data identifiers specified above may. . .file an unredacted document under seal. This document will be retained by the clerk's office as part of the record. ME R USDCT Redacting Pleadings. The court may, however, still require the party to file a redacted copy for the public file. ME R USDCT Redacting Pleadings.

g. *Option for filing a reference list.* A filing that contains redacted information may be filed together with a reference list that identifies each item of redacted information and specifies an appropriate identifier that uniquely corresponds to each item listed. The list must be filed under seal and may be amended as of right. Any reference in the case to a listed identifier will be construed to refer to the corresponding item of information. FRCP 5.2(g).

   i. *DISTRICT OF MAINE.* A party wishing to file a document containing the personal data identifiers specified above may. . .file a reference list under seal. The reference list shall contain the complete personal data identifier(s) and the redacted identifier(s) used in its (their) place in the filing. All references in the case to the redacted identifiers included in the reference list will be construed to refer to the corresponding complete identifier. The reference list must be filed under seal, and may be amended as of right. It shall be retained by the clerk's office as part of the record. ME R USDCT Redacting Pleadings. The court may, however, still require the party to file a redacted copy for the public file. ME R USDCT Redacting Pleadings.

h. *DISTRICT OF MAINE: Responsibility for redaction.* The clerk is not required to review documents filed with the court for compliance with FRCP 5.2. The responsibility to redact filings rests with counsel and the party or nonparty making the filing. ME R USDCT App. 4(i); ME R USDCT Redacting Pleadings. For guidelines for filing confidential information in civil cases in the District of Maine, refer to ME R USDCT Confidentiality.

i. *Waiver of protection of identifiers.* A person waives the protection of FRCP 5.2(a) as to the person's own information by filing it without redaction and not under seal. FRCP 5.2(h).

F. Filing and Service Requirements

1. *Filing requirements*

   a. *Required filings.* Any paper after the complaint that is required to be served must be filed no later than a reasonable time after service. FRCP 5(d)(1).

   b. *DISTRICT OF MAINE: Place of filing.* Unless otherwise ordered by the court, papers shall be filed with the court at Bangor in cases filed and pending at Bangor, and at Portland in cases filed and pending at Portland. ME R USDCT Rule 5(a).

   c. *Nonelectronic filing.* A paper not filed electronically is filed by delivering it: (A) to the clerk; or (B) to a judge who agrees to accept it for filing, and who must then note the filing date on the paper and promptly send it to the clerk. FRCP 5(d)(2).

      i. *DISTRICT OF MAINE: Documents to be filed in paper.* The following documents shall be filed in paper, which may also be scanned into ECF by the clerk's office: (A) all handwritten pleadings; and (B) all pleadings and documents filed by pro se litigants who are incarcerated or who are not registered filing users in ECF. ME R USDCT App. 4(g)(8). Non-prisoner pro se litigants in civil actions may register with ECF or may file (and serve) all pleadings and other documents in paper. The clerk's office will scan into ECF any pleadings and documents filed on paper in accordance with ME R USDCT App. 4(g). ME R USDCT App. 4(o). For more information, refer to ME R USDCT App. 4(g).

   d. *Electronic filing*

      i. *DISTRICT OF MAINE: Authorization.* Unless exempt or otherwise ordered by the court, papers shall be filed and served electronically as required by the court's Administrative Procedures Governing the Filing and Service by Electronic Means, which is set forth in ME R USDCT App. 4. The provisions of the court's Administrative Procedures Governing the Filing and Service by Electronic Means (ME R USDCT App. 4) shall be applied and enforced as part of the Local Rules of the United States District Court for the District of Maine. ME R USDCT Rule 5(c).

      ii. *Filing by represented persons.* A person represented by an attorney must file electronically, unless nonelectronic filing is allowed by the court for good cause or is allowed or required by local rule. FRCP 5(d)(3)(A).

         • *DISTRICT OF MAINE.* An attorney may apply to the court for permission to file paper documents. ME R USDCT App. 4(a)(5).

      iii. *Filing by unrepresented persons.* A person not represented by an attorney: (i) may file electronically only if allowed by court order or by local rule; and (ii) may be required to file electronically only by court order, or by a local rule that includes reasonable exceptions. FRCP 5(d)(3)(B).

         • *DISTRICT OF MAINE.* Non-prisoner pro se litigants in civil actions may register with ECF or may file (and serve) all pleadings and other documents in paper. ME R USDCT App. 4(o). A non-prisoner who is a party to a civil action and who is not represented by an attorney may register to receive service electronically and to electronically transmit their documents to the court for filing in the ECF system. If during the course of the action the person retains an attorney who appears on the person's behalf, the clerk shall terminate the person's registration upon the attorney's appearance. ME R USDCT App. 4(b)(2).

      iv. *DISTRICT OF MAINE: Scope of electronic filing.* All documents submitted for filing in civil and criminal cases, regardless of case commencement date, except those documents specifically exempted in ME R USDCT App. 4(g), shall be filed electronically using the electronic case filing system (ECF). ME R USDCT App. 4(a)(1). For special filing requirements and exceptions, refer to ME R USDCT App. 4(g).

v. *DISTRICT OF MAINE: Consequences of electronic filing.* Electronic transmission of a document to the ECF system, together with the transmission of a Notice of Electronic Filing (NEF) from the court, constitutes filing of the document for all purposes of the Federal Rules of Civil Procedure. ME R USDCT App. 4(d)(1).

vi. *DISTRICT OF MAINE: Review of documents.* Documents filed with the clerk's office will normally be reviewed no later than the close of the next business day. It is the responsibility of the filing party to promptly notify the clerk's office via telephone of a matter that requires the immediate attention of a judicial officer. ME R USDCT App. 4(a)(4).

e. *DISTRICT OF MAINE: Facsimile filing.* No papers shall be submitted to the court by means of a facsimile machine without prior leave of the court. ME R USDCT Rule 5(c); ME R USDCT App. 4(m).

2. *Service requirements*

a. *Service; When required.* Unless the Federal Rules of Civil Procedure provide otherwise, each of the following papers must be served on every party: (A) an order stating that service is required; (B) a pleading filed after the original complaint, unless the court orders otherwise under FRCP 5(c) because there are numerous defendants; (C) a discovery paper required to be served on a party, unless the court orders otherwise; (D) a written motion, except one that may be heard ex parte; and (E) a written notice, appearance, demand, or offer of judgment, or any similar paper. FRCP 5(a)(1).

i. *If a party fails to appear.* No service is required on a party who is in default for failing to appear. But a pleading that asserts a new claim for relief against such a party must be served on that party under FRCP 4. FRCP 5(a)(2).

ii. *Seizing property.* If an action is begun by seizing property and no person is or need be named as a defendant, any service required before the filing of an appearance, answer, or claim must be made on the person who had custody or possession of the property when it was seized. FRCP 5(a)(3).

b. *Service; How made.* A paper is served under FRCP 5 by: (A) handing it to the person; (B) leaving it: (i) at the person's office with a clerk or other person in charge or, if no one is in charge, in a conspicuous place in the office; or (ii) if the person has no office or the office is closed, at the person's dwelling or usual place of abode with someone of suitable age and discretion who resides there; (C) mailing it to the person's last known address—in which event service is complete upon mailing; (D) leaving it with the court clerk if the person has no known address; (E) sending it to a registered user by filing it with the court's electronic-filing system or sending it by other electronic means that the person consented to in writing—in either of which events service is complete upon filing or sending, but is not effective if the filer or sender learns that it did not reach the person to be served; or (F) delivering it by any other means that the person consented to in writing—in which event service is complete when the person making service delivers it to the agency designated to make delivery. FRCP 5(b)(2).

i. *Serving an attorney.* If a party is represented by an attorney, service under FRCP 5 must be made on the attorney unless the court orders service on the party. FRCP 5(b)(1).

c. *DISTRICT OF MAINE: Service of electronically filed documents*

i. *Registered users.* Registration [as a filing user of the court's ECF system] constitutes consent to service of all documents by electronic means as provided in ME R USDCT App. 4. ME R USDCT App. 4(b)(4). Whenever a non-sealed pleading is filed electronically, the ECF system will automatically generate and send a Notice of Electronic Filing (NEF) to the filing user and registered users of record. The user filing the document should retain a paper or digital copy of the NEF, which shall serve as the court's date-stamp and proof of filing. ME R USDCT App. 4(e)(1).

- *Sealed documents.* Although the filing of sealed documents in civil cases produces an NEF, the document itself cannot be accessed and counsel shall be responsible for making service of the sealed documents. ME R USDCT App. 4(e)(2).

ii. *Non-registered users and pro se litigants.* Attorneys who have not yet registered as users with ECF and pro se litigants who have not registered with ECF shall be served a paper copy of any electronically filed pleading or other document in accordance with the provisions of FRCP 5. ME R USDCT App. 4(e)(3).

- *Registration of pro se litigants.* A non-prisoner who is a party to a civil action and who is not represented by an attorney may register to receive service electronically and to electronically transmit their documents to the court for filing in the ECF system. If during the course of the action the person retains an attorney who appears on the person's behalf, the clerk shall terminate the person's registration upon the attorney's appearance. ME R USDCT App. 4(b)(2).

d. *Serving numerous defendants.* If an action involves an unusually large number of defendants, the court may, on motion or on its own, order that: (A) defendants' pleadings and replies to them need not be served on other defendants; (B) any crossclaim, counterclaim, avoidance, or affirmative defense in those pleadings and replies to them will be treated as denied or avoided by all other parties; and (C) filing any such pleading and serving it on the plaintiff constitutes notice of the pleading to all parties. FRCP 5(c)(1).

    i.   *Notifying parties.* A copy of every such order must be served on the parties as the court directs. FRCP 5(c)(2).

3. *Service requirements of an amended complaint asserting new or additional claims for relief.* The service of amended pleadings is generally governed by FRCP 5. Thus, except for an amended pleading against a defaulting party that does not assert new or additional claims for relief, an amended pleading must be served in accordance with FRCP 5. FEDPROC § 62:257; Int'l Controls Corp. v. Vesco, 556 F.2d 665 (2d Cir. 1977). However, while FRCP 5 permits service of an amended complaint on counsel, where the amended complaint contains an entirely different cause of action that could not have been properly served originally by the method used in serving the original complaint, the amended complaint must be served in accordance with the terms of FRCP 4. FEDPROC § 62:257; Lasch v. Antkies, 161 F. Supp. 851 (E.D. Pa. 1958). Refer to the United States District Court for the District of Maine KeyRules Complaint document for more information on serving the amended complaint in accordance with FRCP 4.

4. *DISTRICT OF MAINE: Filing and service of highly sensitive documents (HSDs).* For information on filing and serving highly sensitive documents (HSDs) in the District of Maine, refer to ME R USDCT General Order 21-5.

G. Hearings

1. *Hearings, generally.* Generally, there is no hearing contemplated in the federal statutes or rules for the amended pleading.

    a. *Amended answer; Hearing on certain FRCP 12 defenses before trial.* If a party so moves, any defense listed in FRCP 12(b)(1) through FRCP 12(b)(7)—whether made in a pleading or by motion—and a motion under FRCP 12(c) must be heard and decided before trial unless the court orders a deferral until trial. FRCP 12(i).

H. Forms

1. Federal Amended Pleading Forms

    a. Civil cover sheet. 2 FEDFORMS § 3:29.

    b. Notice of lawsuit and request for waiver of service of summons and waiver of summons. 2 FEDFORMS § 3:36.

    c. Complaint. 2 FEDFORMS § 7:14.

    d. Generally. 2B FEDFORMS § 8:10.

    e. Presenting defenses. 2B FEDFORMS § 8:12.

    f. Denials, admissions and affirmative defenses. 2B FEDFORMS § 8:15.

    g. Denial of particular averment. 2B FEDFORMS § 8:24.

    h. Admission of particular averment. 2B FEDFORMS § 8:25.

    i. Denial of all averments of paragraph. 2B FEDFORMS § 8:26.

    j. Admission of all averments of paragraph. 2B FEDFORMS § 8:27.

    k. Denial in part and admission in part of paragraph. 2B FEDFORMS § 8:28.

    l. Notice of amended complaint. 2C FEDFORMS § 14:10.

    m. Amendment to complaint. 2C FEDFORMS § 14:47.

    n. Amendment to complaint; Short version. 2C FEDFORMS § 14:48.

    o. Amendment to complaint; As of course. 2C FEDFORMS § 14:49.

    p. Notice; Of filing amended pleading as of course. AMJUR PP FEDPRAC § 162.

    q. Amendment; Of pleading as of course. AMJUR PP FEDPRAC § 163.

    r. Complaint; Single count. FEDPROF § 1A:171.

    s. Complaint; Multiple counts; With same jurisdictional basis. FEDPROF § 1A:172.

    t. Amendment of pleading; As matter of course. FEDPROF § 1A:332.

    u. Notice of filing amended pleading; Where amendment is matter of course. FEDPROF § 1A:333.

    v. Amendment of pleading; Particular clauses. FEDPROF § 1A:336.

    w. Amendment of pleading; Clause; Change in title of action. FEDPROF § 1A:337.

x. Amendment of pleading; Clause; To show amount in controversy. FEDPROF § 1A:339.

y. Amendment of pleading; Clause; To show diversity of citizenship. FEDPROF § 1A:340.

z. Amendment of pleading; Clause; Demand for relief. FEDPROF § 1A:341.

I. Applicable Rules

1. *Federal rules*

   a. Serving and filing pleadings and other papers. FRCP 5.

   b. Constitutional challenge to a statute; Notice, certification, and intervention. FRCP 5.1.

   c. Privacy protection for filings made with the court. FRCP 5.2.

   d. Computing and extending time; Time for motion papers. FRCP 6.

   e. Pleadings allowed; Form of motions and other papers. FRCP 7.

   f. General rules of pleading. FRCP 8.

   g. Pleading special matters. FRCP 9.

   h. Form of pleadings. FRCP 10.

   i. Signing pleadings, motions, and other papers; Representations to the court; Sanctions. FRCP 11.

   j. Defenses and objections; When and how presented; Motion for judgment on the pleadings; Consolidating motions; Waiving defenses; Pretrial hearing. FRCP 12.

   k. Amended and supplemental pleadings. FRCP 15.

   l. Joinder of claims. FRCP 18.

   m. Required joinder of parties. FRCP 19.

   n. Permissive joinder of parties. FRCP 20.

   o. Misjoinder and nonjoinder of parties. FRCP 21.

   p. Right to a jury trial; Demand. FRCP 38.

   q. Determining foreign law. FRCP 44.1.

2. *Local rules*

   a. *DISTRICT OF MAINE*

      i. Service and filing of pleadings and other papers. ME R USDCT Rule 5.

      ii. Notice of constitutional question. ME R USDCT Rule 5.1.

      iii. Time. ME R USDCT Rule 6.

      iv. Pleading special matters. ME R USDCT Rule 9.

      v. Form of pleadings, motions and other papers. ME R USDCT Rule 10.

      vi. Demand for jury trial. ME R USDCT Rule 38.

      vii. Attorneys; Appearances and withdrawals. ME R USDCT Rule 83.2.

      viii. Alternative dispute resolution (ADR). ME R USDCT Rule 83.11.

      ix. Administrative procedures governing the filing and service by electronic means. ME R USDCT App. 4.

      x. Redacting pleadings. ME R USDCT Redacting Pleadings.

Motions, Oppositions and Replies
Motion to Strike

Document Last Updated April 2021

A. Checklist

(I) ❑ Matters to be considered by moving party

    (a) ❑ Required documents

        (1) ❑ Notice of motion and motion

    (b) ❑ Supplemental documents

        (1) ❑ Deposition(s)

        (2) ❑ Notice of constitutional question

        (3) ❑ Nongovernmental corporate disclosure statement

        (4) ❑ DISTRICT OF MAINE: Additional supplemental documents

            (i) ❑ Proposed order

    (c) ❑ Timing

        (1) ❑ The court may act: on motion made by a party either before responding to the pleading or, if a response is not allowed, within twenty-one (21) days after being served with the pleading

        (2) ❑ A written motion and notice of the hearing must be served at least fourteen (14) days before the time specified for the hearing, with the following exceptions: (A) when the motion may be heard ex parte; (B) when the Federal Rules of Civil Procedure set a different time; or (C) when a court order—which a party may, for good cause, apply for ex parte—sets a different time

        (3) ❑ Any affidavit supporting a motion must be served with the motion

        (4) ❑ DISTRICT OF MAINE: Additional timing

            (i) ❑ Any affidavits and other documents setting forth or evidencing facts on which the motion is based must be filed with the motion

(II) ❑ Matters to be considered by opposing party

    (a) ❑ Required documents

        (1) ❑ Opposition

    (b) ❑ Supplemental documents

        (1) ❑ Deposition(s)

        (2) ❑ Notice of constitutional question

    (c) ❑ Timing

        (1) ❑ Except as FRCP 59(c) provides otherwise, any opposing affidavit must be served at least seven (7) days before the hearing, unless the court permits service at another time

        (2) ❑ DISTRICT OF MAINE: Additional timing

            (i) ❑ Unless within twenty-one (21) days after the filing of a motion the opposing party files written objection thereto, incorporating a memorandum of law, the opposing party shall be deemed to have waived objection

B. Timing

1. *Motion to strike.* The court may act: on motion made by a party either before responding to the pleading or, if a response is not allowed, within twenty-one (21) days after being served with the pleading. FRCP 12(f)(2).

2. *Timing of motions, generally*

    a. *Motion and notice of hearing.* A written motion and notice of the hearing must be served at least fourteen (14) days before the time specified for the hearing, with the following exceptions: (A) when the motion may be heard ex parte; (B) when the Federal Rules of Civil Procedure set a different time; or (C) when a court order—which a party may, for good cause, apply for ex parte—sets a different time. FRCP 6(c)(1).

b. *Supporting affidavit.* Any affidavit supporting a motion must be served with the motion. FRCP 6(c)(2).

c. *DISTRICT OF MAINE: Affidavits and other supporting documents.* Any affidavits and other documents setting forth or evidencing facts on which the motion is based must be filed with the motion. ME R USDCT Rule 7(a).

3. *Timing of opposing papers.* Except as FRCP 59(c) provides otherwise, any opposing affidavit must be served at least seven (7) days before the hearing, unless the court permits service at another time. FRCP 6(c)(2).

a. *DISTRICT OF MAINE.* Unless within twenty-one (21) days after the filing of a motion the opposing party files written objection thereto, incorporating a memorandum of law, the opposing party shall be deemed to have waived objection. ME R USDCT Rule 7(b). The deemed waiver imposed in ME R USDCT Rule 7(b) shall not apply to motions filed during trial. ME R USDCT Rule 7(b).

4. *Timing of reply papers.* Where the respondent files an answering affidavit setting up a new matter, the moving party ordinarily is allowed a reasonable time to file a reply affidavit since failure to deny the new matter by affidavit may operate as an admission of its truth. AMJUR MOTIONS § 25.

a. *DISTRICT OF MAINE.* Within fourteen (14) days of the filing of any objection to a motion, the moving party may file a reply memorandum. ME R USDCT Rule 7(c).

5. *Effect of FRCP 12 motion on the time to serve a responsive pleading.* Unless the court sets a different time, serving a motion under FRCP 12 alters the periods in FRCP 12(a) as follows: (A) if the court denies the motion or postpones its disposition until trial, the responsive pleading must be served within fourteen (14) days after notice of the court's action; or (B) if the court grants a motion for a more definite statement, the responsive pleading must be served within fourteen (14) days after the more definite statement is served. FRCP 12(a)(4).

6. *Computation of time*

a. *Computing time.* FRCP 6 applies in computing any time period specified in the Federal Rules of Civil Procedure, in any local rule or court order, or in any statute that does not specify a method of computing time. FRCP 6(a).

   i. *Period stated in days or a longer unit.* When the period is stated in days or a longer unit of time: (A) exclude the day of the event that triggers the period; (B) count every day, including intermediate Saturdays, Sundays, and legal holidays; and (C) include the last day of the period, but if the last day is a Saturday, Sunday, or legal holiday, the period continues to run until the end of the next day that is not a Saturday, Sunday, or legal holiday. FRCP 6(a)(1).

   ii. *Period stated in hours.* When the period is stated in hours: (A) begin counting immediately on the occurrence of the event that triggers the period; (B) count every hour, including hours during intermediate Saturdays, Sundays, and legal holidays; and (C) if the period would end on a Saturday, Sunday, or legal holiday, the period continues to run until the same time on the next day that is not a Saturday, Sunday, or legal holiday. FRCP 6(a)(2).

   iii. *Inaccessibility of the clerk's office.* Unless the court orders otherwise, if the clerk's office is inaccessible: (A) on the last day for filing under FRCP 6(a)(1), then the time for filing is extended to the first accessible day that is not a Saturday, Sunday, or legal holiday; or (B) during the last hour for filing under FRCP 6(a)(2), then the time for filing is extended to the same time on the first accessible day that is not a Saturday, Sunday, or legal holiday. FRCP 6(a)(3).

   iv. *"Last day" defined.* Unless a different time is set by a statute, local rule, or court order, the last day ends: (A) for electronic filing, at midnight in the court's time zone; and (B) for filing by other means, when the clerk's office is scheduled to close. FRCP 6(a)(4).

   v. *"Next day" defined.* The "next day" is determined by continuing to count forward when the period is measured after an event and backward when measured before an event. FRCP 6(a)(5).

   vi. *"Legal holiday" defined.* "Legal holiday" means: (A) the day set aside by statute for observing New Year's Day, Martin Luther King Jr.'s Birthday, Washington's Birthday, Memorial Day, Independence Day, Labor Day, Columbus Day, Veterans' Day, Thanksgiving Day, or Christmas Day; (B) any day declared a holiday by the President or Congress; and (C) for periods that are measured after an event, any other day declared a holiday by the state where the district court is located. FRCP 6(a)(6).

   vii. *DISTRICT OF MAINE: Applicability of FRCP 6.* FRCP 6 applies when computing any period of time stated in the Local Rules of the United States District Court for the District of Maine. ME R USDCT Rule 6(a).

b. *DISTRICT OF MAINE: Computation of electronic filing deadlines.* Filing documents electronically does not in any way alter any filing deadlines. All electronic transmissions of documents must be completed prior to midnight, Eastern Time, in order to be considered timely filed that day. Where a specific time of day deadline is set by court order

or stipulation, the electronic filing must be completed by that time. ME R USDCT App. 4(f). A document filed electronically shall be deemed filed at the time and date stated on the Notice of Electronic Filing received from the court. ME R USDCT App. 4(d)(2).

    i. *Technical failures.* A filing user whose filing is made untimely as the result of a technical failure may seek appropriate relief from the court. ME R USDCT App. 4(n). A technical failure of the court's ECF system is deemed to have occurred when the court's ECF site cannot accept filings continuously or intermittently over the course of any period of time greater than one (1) hour. Known system outages will be posted on the court's website along with guidance on how to proceed, if applicable. ME R USDCT App. 4(n).

  c. *Extending time.* When an act may or must be done within a specified time, the court may, for good cause, extend the time: (A) with or without motion or notice if the court acts, or if a request is made, before the original time or its extension expires; or (B) on motion made after the time has expired if the party failed to act because of excusable neglect. FRCP 6(b)(1). A court must not extend the time to act under FRCP 50(b), FRCP 50(d), FRCP 52(b), FRCP 59(b), FRCP 59(d), FRCP 59(e), and FRCP 60(b). FRCP 6(b)(2). Refer to the United States District Court for the District of Maine KeyRules Motion for Continuance/Extension of Time document for more information on extending time.

  d. *Additional time after certain kinds of service.* When a party may or must act within a specified time after being served and service is made under FRCP 5(b)(2)(C) (by mail), FRCP 5(b)(2)(D) (by leaving with the clerk), or FRCP 5(b)(2)(F) (by other means consented to), three (3) days are added after the period would otherwise expire under FRCP 6(a). FRCP 6(d).

C. General Requirements

1. *Motions, generally*

  a. *Motion requirements.* A request for a court order must be made by motion. The motion must: (A) be in writing unless made during a hearing or trial; (B) state with particularity the grounds for seeking the order; and (C) state the relief sought. FRCP 7(b)(1). The writing and particularity requirements are intended to ensure that the adverse parties are informed of and have a record of both the motion's pendency and the grounds on which the movant seeks an order. FPP § 1191; Feldberg v. Quechee Lakes Corp., 463 F.3d 195 (2d Cir. 2006).

    i. *Particularity requirement.* The particularity requirement [ensures] that the opposing parties will have notice of their opponent's contentions. FEDPROC § 62:358; Goodman v. 1973 26 Foot Trojan Vessel, Arkansas Registration No. AR1439SN, 859 F.2d 71 (8th Cir. 1988). That requirement ensures that notice of the basis for the motion is provided to the court and to the opposing party so as to avoid prejudice, provide the opponent with a meaningful opportunity to respond, and provide the court with enough information to process the motion correctly. FEDPROC § 62:358; Andreas v. Volkswagen of Am., Inc., 336 F.3d 789 (8th Cir. 2003).

- Reasonable specification of the grounds for a motion is sufficient. The particularity requirement for motions is satisfied when no party is prejudiced by a lack of particularity or when the court can comprehend the basis for the motion and deal with it fairly. However, where a movant fails to state even one ground for granting the motion in question, the movant has failed to meet the minimal standard of "reasonable specification." FEDPROC § 62:358; Martinez v. Trainor, 556 F.2d 818 (7th Cir. 1977).

- The court may excuse the failure to comply with the particularity requirement if it is inadvertent, and where no prejudice is shown by the opposing party. FEDPROC § 62:358.

  b. *Notice of motion.* A party interested in resisting the relief sought by a motion has a right to notice thereof, and an opportunity to be heard. AMJUR MOTIONS § 12.

    i. *Purpose.* In addition to statutory or court rule provisions requiring notice of a motion—the purpose of such a notice requirement having been said to be to prevent a party from being prejudicially surprised by a motion— principles of natural justice dictate that an adverse party generally must be given notice that a motion will be presented to the court. AMJUR MOTIONS § 12.

    ii. *Adequacy of notice.* The test of adequate notice generally turns on whether the other parties were afforded an adequate opportunity to prepare and respond to the issues to be raised in the proceeding. AMJUR MOTIONS § 12.

  c. *Single document containing motion and notice.* A single written document can satisfy the writing requirements both for a motion and for an FRCP 6(c)(1) notice. FRCP 7(Advisory Committee Notes).

2. *Motion to strike.* The court may strike from a pleading an insufficient defense or any redundant, immaterial, impertinent, or scandalous matter. The court may act: (1) on its own; or (2) on motion made by a party either before responding to the

pleading or, if a response is not allowed, within twenty-one (21) days after being served with the pleading. FRCP 12(f). FRCP 12(f) also is designed to reinforce the requirement in FRCP 8(e) that pleadings be simple, concise, and direct. However, as the cases make clear, it is neither an authorized nor a proper way to procure the dismissal of all or a part of a complaint, or a counterclaim, or to strike an opponent's affidavits. FPP § 1380.

a. *Practice on a motion to strike.* All well-pleaded facts are taken as admitted on a motion to strike but conclusions of law or conclusions drawn from the facts do not have to be treated in that fashion by the district judge. FPP § 1380. Both because striking a portion of a pleading is a drastic remedy and because it often is sought by the movant simply as a dilatory or [harassing] tactic, numerous judicial decisions make it clear that motions under FRCP 12(f) are viewed with disfavor by the federal courts and are infrequently granted. FPP § 1380.

b. *Striking an insufficient defense.* Only if a defense is insufficient as a matter of law will it be stricken. In other words, a defense may be stricken if, on the face of the pleadings, it is patently frivolous, or if it is clearly invalid as a matter of law. FEDPROC § 62:406. A defense will be stricken if it could not possibly prevent recovery by the plaintiff on its claim. FEDPROC § 62:407. In addition, a defense may be stricken if: the defense requires separate statements; the defense has been previously advanced and rejected; or the defense cannot be waived. FEDPROC § 62:407.

c. *Striking immaterial or impertinent matter.* Immaterial or impertinent matter will be stricken from a pleading if it is clear that it can have no possible bearing upon the subject matter of the litigation, and that its inclusion will prejudice the movant. If there is any doubt as to whether under any contingency the matter may raise an issue, the motion should be denied. FEDPROC § 62:409.

   i. *Immaterial matter defined.* "Immaterial matter," for purposes of FRCP 12(f), is matter which has no essential or important relationship to the claim for relief or the defenses being pleaded. FEDPROC § 62:408. A statement of unnecessary particulars in connection with and descriptive of that which is material may be stricken as immaterial matter. FEDPROC § 62:410.

   ii. *Impertinent matter defined.* "Impertinent matter," for purposes of FRCP 12(f), consists of statements that do not pertain, and are not necessary, to the issues in question. FEDPROC § 62:408.

d. *Striking redundant matter.* "Redundant matter," for purposes of FRCP 12(f), consists of allegations that constitute a needless repetition of other averments or which are wholly foreign to the issue to be decided. However, even if allegations are redundant, they need not be stricken if their presence in the pleading cannot prejudice the moving party. FEDPROC § 62:411.

   i. *Duplicative remedies.* Merely duplicative remedies do not necessarily make claims "redundant," within the meaning of FRCP 12(f), if the claims otherwise require proof of different elements, but a claim that merely recasts the same elements under the guise of a different theory may be stricken as redundant. FEDPROC § 62:411.

e. *Striking scandalous matter.* A matter is deemed scandalous, for purposes of FRCP 12(f), when it improperly casts a derogatory light on someone, usually a party to the action. Scandalous matter also consists of any unnecessary allegation which reflects cruelly upon the moral character of an individual, or states anything in repulsive language which detracts from the dignity of the court. To be scandalous, degrading charges must be irrelevant, or, if relevant, must go into in unnecessary detail. FEDPROC § 62:412.

   i. *When appropriate.* Allegations may be stricken as scandalous if the matter bears no possible relation to the controversy or may cause the objecting party prejudice. FEDPROC § 62:412. It is not enough that the matter offends the sensibilities of the objecting party if the challenged allegations describe acts or events that are relevant to the action. As a result, courts have permitted allegations to remain in the pleadings when they supported and were relevant to a claim for punitive damages. Nonetheless, the disfavored character of FRCP 12(f) is relaxed somewhat in the context of scandalous allegations and matter of this type often will be stricken from the pleadings in order to purge the court's files and protect the person who is the subject of the allegations. However, if the party seeking the elimination of the scandalous matter was the "first to hurl epithets," the district judge will deny the motion to strike, presumably applying something in the nature of a "clean hands" notion. FPP § 1382.

f. *Striking sham or false matter.* FRCP 12(f) does not authorize a motion to strike part or all of a pleading on the ground that it is sham, and the grounds for a motion to strike similarly do not include falsity of the matter alleged. FEDPROC § 62:413; PAE Gov't Servs., Inc. v. MPRI, Inc., 514 F.3d 856 (9th Cir. 2007). However, it has been said that a court will strike a pleading according to FRCP 12(f) when it appears beyond peradventure that it is a sham and false and that its allegations are devoid of factual basis. FEDPROC § 62:413.

g. *Striking conclusions of law.* Unwarranted conclusions of law may be stricken from a pleading pursuant to FRCP 12(f), but ordinarily an allegation is not subject to being stricken merely because it is a conclusion of law. To the contrary, the Federal Rules of Civil Procedure do not condemn conclusions of law, but rather encourage them as at times the clearest and simplest way of stating a claim for relief. Conclusions of law must be unwarranted enough to justify a motion to strike, such as when a plaintiff states causes of action under a federal statute which provides no explicit private right of action. FEDPROC § 62:414.

h. *Striking other particular matter.* Under FRCP 12(f), which permits a court to order stricken from any pleading any redundant, immaterial, impertinent, or scandalous matter, courts have the authority to strike a prayer for relief seeking damages that are not recoverable as a matter of law. A motion to strike may be used to remove an excessive or unauthorized claim for damages. Furthermore, a motion to strike a demand for punitive damages under FRCP 12(f) may be proper if such damages are clearly not collectible, such as in an ordinary breach of contract action. However, there are other ways to raise this issue, and in a particular case, one of these other methods may be more appropriate, such as a motion to dismiss for failure to state a claim pursuant to FRCP 12(b)(6). FEDPROC § 62:415.

i. *Form.* On a motion to strike portions of a pleading, the movant must indicate what paragraphs are being challenged in order to fulfill the particularity requirement; the movant cannot merely state the conclusion that the allegations are too indefinite and insufficient to state a claim or defense. FPP § 1192.

j. *Joining motions.* A motion under FRCP 12 may be joined with any other motion allowed by FRCP 12. FRCP 12(g)(1).

   i. *Limitation on further motions.* Except as provided in FRCP 12(h)(2) or FRCP 12(h)(3), a party that makes a motion under FRCP 12 must not make another motion under FRCP 12 raising a defense or objection that was available to the party but omitted from its earlier motion. FRCP 12(g)(2).

3. *Opposing papers.* The Federal Rules of Civil Procedure do not require any formal answer, return, or reply to a motion, except where the Federal Rules of Civil Procedure or local rules may require affidavits, memoranda, or other papers to be filed in opposition to a motion. Such papers are simply to apprise the court of such opposition and the grounds of that opposition. FEDPROC § 62:353.

a. *DISTRICT OF MAINE: Content of objections.* Any objections shall include citations and supporting authorities and affidavits and other documents setting forth or evidencing facts on which the objection is based. ME R USDCT Rule 7(b).

b. *Effect of failure to respond to motion.* Although in the absence of statutory provision or court rule, a motion ordinarily does not require a response or written answer, when a party files a motion and the opposing party fails to respond, the court may construe such failure to respond as nonopposition to the motion or an admission that the motion was meritorious. AMJUR MOTIONS § 28. The rule in some jurisdictions being that the failure to respond to a fact set forth in a motion is deemed an admission—and may grant the motion if the relief requested appears to be justified. AMJUR MOTIONS § 28.

c. *Assent or no opposition not determinative.* However, a motion will not be granted automatically simply because an "assent" or a notation of "no opposition" has been filed; federal judges frequently deny motions that have been assented to when it is thought that justice so dictates. FPP § 1190.

d. *Responsive pleading inappropriate as response to motion.* An attempt to answer or oppose a motion with a responsive pleading usually is not appropriate. FPP § 1190.

4. *Reply papers.* A moving party may be required or permitted to prepare papers in addition to its original motion papers. AMJUR MOTIONS § 25. Papers answering or replying to opposing papers may be appropriate, in the interests of justice, where it appears there is a substantial reason for allowing a reply. Thus, a court may accept reply papers where a party demonstrates that the papers to which it seeks to file a reply raise new issues that are material to the disposition of the question before the court, or where the court determines, sua sponte, that it wishes further briefing of an issue raised in those papers and orders the submission of additional papers. FEDPROC § 62:354.

a. *Function of reply papers.* The function of a reply affidavit or reply papers is to answer the arguments made in opposition to the position taken by the movant, not to raise new issues, arguments, or evidence, or change the nature of the primary motion. However, if the court permits new evidence with the reply papers, the other party should be given the opportunity to respond. Where the party opposing the motion has no opportunity to address the argument in writing, a court has the discretion to disregard arguments raised for the first time in a reply memorandum. Also, the view has been followed in some jurisdictions that as a matter of judicial economy, where there is no prejudice and where the issues could be raised simply by filing a motion to dismiss, the trial court has discretion to consider arguments raised for the first time in a reply memorandum, and that a trial court may grant a motion to strike issues raised for the first time in a reply memorandum. AMJUR MOTIONS § 26.

   i. *DISTRICT OF MAINE.* The moving party may file a reply memorandum. . .which shall be strictly confined to replying to new matter raised in the objection or opposing memorandum. ME R USDCT Rule 7(c).

5. *DISTRICT OF MAINE: Appearances.* An attorney's signature to a pleading shall constitute an appearance for the party filing the pleading. Otherwise, an attorney who wishes to participate in any manner in any action must file a formal written appearance identifying the party represented. An appearance whether by pleading or formal written appearance shall be signed by an attorney in his/her individual name and shall state his/her office address. ME R USDCT Rule 83.2(a). For more information, refer to ME R USDCT Rule 83.2.

6. *DISTRICT OF MAINE: Alternative dispute resolution (ADR).* Litigants are authorized and encouraged to employ, at their own expense, any available ADR process on which they can agree, including early neutral evaluation, settlement conferences, mediation, non-binding summary jury trial, corporate mini-trial, and arbitration proceedings. ME R USDCT Rule 83.11(a). For more information on ADR, refer to ME R USDCT Rule 83.11.

D. Documents

1. *Documents for moving party*

    a. *Required documents*

        i. *Notice of motion and motion.* Refer to the "C. General Requirements" section of this KeyRules document for information on the notice of motion and motion.

            - *DISTRICT OF MAINE: Memorandum of law.* Every motion shall incorporate a memorandum of law, including citations and supporting authorities. ME R USDCT Rule 7(a). Refer to the "E. Format" section of this KeyRules document for the form of memoranda of law.

            - *Certificate of service.* No certificate of service is required when a paper is served by filing it with the court's electronic-filing system. When a paper that is required to be served is served by other means: (i) if the paper is filed, a certificate of service must be filed with it or within a reasonable time after service; and (ii) if the paper is not filed, a certificate of service need not be filed unless filing is required by court order or by local rule. FRCP 5(d)(1)(B).

    b. *Supplemental documents*

        i. *Deposition(s).* Matter outside the pleadings normally is not considered on an FRCP 12(f) motion; for example, affidavits in support of or in opposition to the motion typically may not be used. FPP § 1380. Notwithstanding the general rule that matters outside the pleadings should ordinarily not be considered in passing upon a motion to strike under FRCP 12(f), a court may consider a deposition in deciding an FRCP 12(f) motion if the attorneys for both the plaintiff and the defendant, in their respective briefs, refer to the deposition and to the testimony contained therein. FEDPROC § 62:401.

            - *DISTRICT OF MAINE: Discovery transcripts or materials.* A party relying on discovery transcripts or materials in support of or in opposition to a motion shall file excerpts of such transcript or materials with the memorandum required by ME R USDCT Rule 7 as well as a list of specific citations to the parts on which the party relies. ME R USDCT Rule 26(c). Excerpts of depositions in support of or in opposition to a motion shall be filed electronically using ECF, unless otherwise permitted by the court. ME R USDCT App. 4(l)(3).

        ii. *Notice of constitutional question.* A party that files a pleading, written motion, or other paper drawing into question the constitutionality of a federal or state statute must promptly: (1) file a notice of constitutional question stating the question and identifying the paper that raises it, if: (A) a federal statute is questioned and the parties do not include the United States, one of its agencies, or one of its officers or employees in an official capacity; or (B) a state statute is questioned and the parties do not include the state, one of its agencies, or one of its officers or employees in an official capacity; and (2) serve the notice and paper on the Attorney General of the United States if a federal statute is questioned—or on the state attorney general if a state statute is questioned—either by certified or registered mail or by sending it to an electronic address designated by the attorney general for this purpose. FRCP 5.1(a).

            - *No forfeiture.* A party's failure to file and serve the notice, or the court's failure to certify, does not forfeit a constitutional claim or defense that is otherwise timely asserted. FRCP 5.1(d).

        iii. *Nongovernmental corporate disclosure statement.* A nongovernmental corporate party must file two (2) copies of a disclosure statement that: (1) identifies any parent corporation and any publicly held corporation owning ten percent (10%) or more of its stock; or (2) states that there is no such corporation. FRCP 7.1(a). A party must: (1) file the disclosure statement with its first appearance, pleading, petition, motion, response, or other request addressed to the court; and (2) promptly file a supplemental statement if any required information changes. FRCP 7.1(b).

            - *DISTRICT OF MAINE: Notice of interested parties.* To enable the court to evaluate possible disqualification or recusal, counsel for all non-governmental parties shall file with their first appearance a Notice of Interested Parties, which shall list all persons, associations of persons, firms, partnerships, limited liability companies, joint ventures, corporations (including parent or affiliated corporations, clearly identified as such), or any similar entities, owning ten percent (10%) or more of the named party. Counsel shall be under a continuing obligation to file an amended Notice if any material change occurs in the status of an Interested Party, such as through merger, acquisition, or new/additional membership. ME R USDCT Rule 7.1.

    iv. *DISTRICT OF MAINE: Additional supplemental documents*

- *Proposed order.* Proposed orders shall not be filed unless requested by the court. When requested by the court, proposed orders shall be filed by e-mail in word processing format. ME R USDCT App. 4(k)(1).

2. *Documents for opposing party*

  a. *Required documents*

    i. *Opposition.* Refer to the "C. General Requirements" section of this KeyRules document for information on the opposing papers.

- *DISTRICT OF MAINE: Memorandum of law.* Unless within twenty-one (21) days after the filing of a motion the opposing party files written objection thereto, incorporating a memorandum of law, the opposing party shall be deemed to have waived objection. ME R USDCT Rule 7(b).

- *Certificate of service.* No certificate of service is required when a paper is served by filing it with the court's electronic-filing system. When a paper that is required to be served is served by other means: (i) if the paper is filed, a certificate of service must be filed with it or within a reasonable time after service; and (ii) if the paper is not filed, a certificate of service need not be filed unless filing is required by court order or by local rule. FRCP 5(d)(1)(B).

  b. *Supplemental documents*

    i. *Deposition(s).* Matter outside the pleadings normally is not considered on an FRCP 12(f) motion; for example, affidavits in support of or in opposition to the motion typically may not be used. FPP § 1380. Notwithstanding the general rule that matters outside the pleadings should ordinarily not be considered in passing upon a motion to strike under FRCP 12(f), a court may consider a deposition in deciding an FRCP 12(f) motion if the attorneys for both the plaintiff and the defendant, in their respective briefs, refer to the deposition and to the testimony contained therein. FEDPROC § 62:401.

- *DISTRICT OF MAINE: Discovery transcripts or materials.* A party relying on discovery transcripts or materials in support of or in opposition to a motion shall file excerpts of such transcript or materials with the memorandum required by ME R USDCT Rule 7 as well as a list of specific citations to the parts on which the party relies. ME R USDCT Rule 26(c). Excerpts of depositions in support of or in opposition to a motion shall be filed electronically using ECF, unless otherwise permitted by the court. ME R USDCT App. 4(l)(3).

    ii. *Notice of constitutional question.* A party that files a pleading, written motion, or other paper drawing into question the constitutionality of a federal or state statute must promptly: (1) file a notice of constitutional question stating the question and identifying the paper that raises it, if: (A) a federal statute is questioned and the parties do not include the United States, one of its agencies, or one of its officers or employees in an official capacity; or (B) a state statute is questioned and the parties do not include the state, one of its agencies, or one of its officers or employees in an official capacity; and (2) serve the notice and paper on the Attorney General of the United States if a federal statute is questioned—or on the state attorney general if a state statute is questioned—either by certified or registered mail or by sending it to an electronic address designated by the attorney general for this purpose. FRCP 5.1(a).

- *No forfeiture.* A party's failure to file and serve the notice, or the court's failure to certify, does not forfeit a constitutional claim or defense that is otherwise timely asserted. FRCP 5.1(d).

E. Format

1. *Form of documents.* The rules governing captions and other matters of form in pleadings apply to motions and other papers. FRCP 7(b)(2).

  a. *DISTRICT OF MAINE: Font size, line spacing, and paper size.* All such documents shall be typed in a font of no less than size twelve (12) point, and shall be double-spaced or printed on eight and one-half by eleven (8-1/2 x 11) inch paper. Footnotes shall be in a font of no less than size ten (10) point, and may be single spaced. ME R USDCT Rule 10.

b. *Caption.* Every pleading must have a caption with the court's name, a title, a file number, and an FRCP 7(a) designation. FRCP 10(a).

    i. *Names of parties.* The title of the complaint must name all the parties; the title of other pleadings, after naming the first party on each side, may refer generally to other parties. FRCP 10(a).

    ii. *DISTRICT OF MAINE: Additional caption requirements.* All pleadings, motions and other papers filed with the clerk or otherwise submitted to the court, except exhibits, shall bear the proper case number and shall contain on the first page a caption as described by FRCP 10(a) and immediately thereunder a designation of what the document is and the name of the party in whose behalf it is submitted. ME R USDCT Rule 10.

c. *Claims or defenses*

    i. *Numbered paragraphs.* A party must state its claims or defenses in numbered paragraphs, each limited as far as practicable to a single set of circumstances. A later pleading may refer by number to a paragraph in an earlier pleading. FRCP 10(b).

    ii. *Separate statements.* If doing so would promote clarity, each claim founded on a separate transaction or occurrence—and each defense other than a denial—must be stated in a separate count or defense. FRCP 10(b).

d. *Adoption by reference.* A statement in a pleading may be adopted by reference elsewhere in the same pleading or in any other pleading or motion. FRCP 10(c).

    i. *Exhibits.* A copy of a written instrument that is an exhibit to a pleading is a part of the pleading for all purposes. FRCP 10(c).

e. *DISTRICT OF MAINE: Page numbering.* All pages shall be numbered at the bottom. ME R USDCT Rule 10.

f. *DISTRICT OF MAINE: Attachment of ancillary papers.* Ancillary papers shall be attached at the end of the document to which they relate. ME R USDCT Rule 10.

g. *Acceptance by the clerk.* The clerk must not refuse to file a paper solely because it is not in the form prescribed by the Federal Rules of Civil Procedure or by a local rule or practice. FRCP 5(d)(4).

2. *Form of electronic documents.* A paper filed electronically is a written paper for purposes of the Federal Rules of Civil Procedure. FRCP 5(d)(3)(D).

a. *DISTRICT OF MAINE: Document format.* The ECF system only accepts documents in a portable document format (PDF). Although there are two types of PDF documents—electronically converted PDF's and scanned PDF's—only electronically converted PDF's may be filed with the court using the ECF system, unless otherwise authorized by local rule or order. ME R USDCT App. 4. Any document or exhibit to be filed or submitted to the court shall not be password-protected or encrypted. ME R USDCT App. 4(g)(12).

    i. *Electronically converted PDFs.* Electronically converted PDF's are created from word processing documents (MS Word, WordPerfect, etc.) using Adobe Acrobat or similar software. They are text searchable and their file size is small. ME R USDCT App. 4. Software used to electronically convert documents to PDF which includes proprietary or advertisement information within the PDF document is prohibited. ME R USDCT App. 4.

    ii. *Scanned PDFs.* Scanned PDF's are created from paper documents run through an optical scanner. Scanned PDF's are not searchable and have a large file size. ME R USDCT App. 4.

b. *DISTRICT OF MAINE: Title.* All pleadings filed electronically shall be titled in accordance with the approved dictionary of civil or criminal events of the ECF system of the United States District Court for the District of Maine. ME R USDCT App. 4(d)(3).

c. *DISTRICT OF MAINE: Attachments.* Attachments to filings and exhibits must be filed in accordance with the court's ECF User Manual, unless otherwise ordered by the court. ME R USDCT App. 4(j). When there are fifty (50) or fewer attachments to a pleading, the attachments must be filed by counsel electronically using ECF. When there are more than fifty (50) attachments, the attachments must be filed in one of the following ways: (A) using ECF, simply attach them to the pleading being filed; (B) using ECF, use the "Additional Attachments" menu item; (C) on paper; or (D) on a properly labeled three and one-half (3-1/2) inch floppy disk, CD or DVD. ME R USDCT App. 4(j)(2). Attachments filed on paper or on disk must contain a comprehensive index that clearly describes each document. ME R USDCT App. 4(j)(2).

    i. A filing user must submit as attachments only those excerpts of the referenced documents that are directly germane to the matter under consideration by the court. Excerpted material must be clearly and prominently identified as such. Users who file excerpts of documents do so without prejudice to their right to timely file additional excerpts or the complete document, as may be allowed by the court. Responding parties may timely file additional excerpts or the complete document that they believe are directly germane. ME R USDCT App. 4(j)(3).

    ii.   Filers shall not attach as an exhibit any pleading or other paper already on file with the court in that case, but shall merely refer to that document. ME R USDCT App. 4(j)(4).

  d.   *DISTRICT OF MAINE: Compliance with technical standards.* All documents filed by electronic means must comply with technical standards, if any, established by the Judicial Conference of the United States or by the United States District Court for the District of Maine. ME R USDCT App. 4(a)(3).

3.   *DISTRICT OF MAINE: Form of memoranda of law.* All memoranda shall be typed, in a font of no less than size twelve (12) point, and shall be double-spaced on eight and one-half by eleven (8-1/2 x 11) inch paper or printed. Footnotes shall be in a font of no less than size ten (10) point, and may be single spaced. All pages shall be numbered at the bottom. ME R USDCT Rule 7(d).

  a.   *Page limitations.* No memorandum of law in support of or in opposition to a nondispositive motion shall exceed ten (10) pages. ME R USDCT Rule 7(d). No reply memorandum shall exceed seven (7) pages. ME R USDCT Rule 7(d); ME R USDCT Rule 7(c).

    i.   *Motion to exceed page limitation.* A motion to exceed the limitation of ME R USDCT Rule 7 shall be filed no later than three (3) business days in advance of the date for filing the memorandum to permit meaningful review by the court. A motion to exceed the page limitations shall not be filed simultaneously with a memorandum in excess of the limitations of ME R USDCT Rule 7. ME R USDCT Rule 7(d).

4.   *Signing of pleadings, motions and other papers*

  a.   *Signature.* Every pleading, written motion, and other paper must be signed by at least one attorney of record in the attorney's name—or by a party personally if the party is unrepresented. The paper must state the signer's address, e-mail address, and telephone number. FRCP 11(a).

    i.   *No verification or accompanying affidavit required for pleadings.* Unless a rule or statute specifically states otherwise, a pleading need not be verified or accompanied by an affidavit. FRCP 11(a).

    ii.   *Unsigned papers.* The court must strike an unsigned paper unless the omission is promptly corrected after being called to the attorney's or party's attention. FRCP 11(a).

  b.   *Electronic signing.* A filing made through a person's electronic-filing account and authorized by that person, together with that person's name on a signature block, constitutes the person's signature. FRCP 5(d)(3)(C).

    i.   *DISTRICT OF MAINE: Attorneys.* The user log-in and password together with a user's name on the signature block constitutes the attorney's signature pursuant to the Federal Rules of Civil Procedure and the Local Rules of the United States District Court for the District of Maine. All electronically filed documents must include a signature block and must set forth the attorney's name, address, telephone number and e-mail address. The name of the ECF user under whose log-in and password the document is submitted must be preceded by a "/s/" in the space where the signature would otherwise appear. ME R USDCT App. 4(h)(1).

    ii.   *DISTRICT OF MAINE: Multiple signatures.* The filer of any document requiring more than one signature (e.g., pleadings filed by visiting lawyers, stipulations, joint status reports) must list thereon all the names of other signatories, preceded by a "/s/" in the space where the signatures would otherwise appear. By submitting such a document, the filing attorney certifies that each of the other signatories has expressly agreed to the form and substance of the document and that the filing attorney has their actual authority to submit the document electronically. ME R USDCT App. 4(h)(2). For more information, refer to ME R USDCT App. 4(h)(2).

    iii.   *DISTRICT OF MAINE: Documents signed under oath.* Affidavits, declarations, verified complaints, or any other document signed under oath shall be filed electronically. The electronically filed version shall contain the typed name of the signatory, preceded by a "/s/" in the space where the signature would otherwise appear indicating that the paper document bears an original signature. ME R USDCT Rule 10; ME R USDCT App. 4(h)(3). For more information, refer to ME R USDCT Rule 10.

  c.   *Representations to the court.* By presenting to the court a pleading, written motion, or other paper—whether by signing, filing, submitting, or later advocating it—an attorney or unrepresented party certifies that to the best of the person's knowledge, information, and belief, formed after an inquiry reasonable under the circumstances: (1) it is not being presented for any improper purpose, such as to harass, cause unnecessary delay, or needlessly increase the cost of litigation; (2) the claims, defenses, and other legal contentions are warranted by existing law or by a nonfrivolous argument for extending, modifying, or reversing existing law or for establishing new law; (3) the factual contentions have evidentiary support or, if specifically so identified, will likely have evidentiary support after a reasonable opportunity for further investigation or discovery; and (4) the denials of factual contentions are warranted on the evidence or, if specifically so identified, are reasonably based on belief or a lack of information. FRCP 11(b).

d. *Sanctions.* If, after notice and a reasonable opportunity to respond, the court determines that FRCP 11(b) has been violated, the court may impose an appropriate sanction on any attorney, law firm, or party that violated FRCP 11(b) or is responsible for the violation. FRCP 11(c)(1). Refer to the United States District Court for the District of Maine KeyRules Motion for Sanctions document for more information.

5. *Privacy protection for filings made with the court*

a. *Redacted filings.* Unless the court orders otherwise, in an electronic or paper filing with the court that contains an individual's Social Security number, taxpayer-identification number, or birth date, the name of an individual known to be a minor, or a financial-account number, a party or nonparty making the filing may include only: (1) the last four (4) digits of the Social Security number and taxpayer-identification number; (2) the year of the individual's birth; (3) the minor's initials; and (4) the last four (4) digits of the financial-account number. FRCP 5.2(a).

   i. *DISTRICT OF MAINE.* To address the privacy concerns created by the Internet access to court papers, unless otherwise ordered by the court, counsel shall modify certain personal data identifiers in pleadings and other papers as follows: (1) minors' names: use of the minors' initials only; (2) Social Security numbers: use of the last four (4) numbers only; (3) dates of birth: use of the year of birth only; [and] (4) financial account numbers: identify the type of account and the financial institution, but use only the last four (4) numbers of the account number. ME R USDCT Redacting Pleadings. Counsel should also use caution when filing papers that contain a person's medical records, employment history; financial information; and any proprietary or trade secret information. ME R USDCT Redacting Pleadings.

b. *Exemptions from the redaction requirement.* The redaction requirement does not apply to the following: (1) a financial-account number that identifies the property allegedly subject to forfeiture in a forfeiture proceeding; (2) the record of an administrative or agency proceeding; (3) the official record of a state-court proceeding; (4) the record of a court or tribunal, if that record was not subject to the redaction requirement when originally filed; (5) a filing covered by FRCP 5.2(c) or FRCP 5.2(d); and (6) a pro se filing in an action brought under 28 U.S.C.A. § 2241, 28 U.S.C.A. § 2254, or 28 U.S.C.A. § 2255. FRCP 5.2(b).

c. *Limitations on remote access to electronic files; Social Security appeals and immigration cases.* Unless the court orders otherwise, in an action for benefits under the Social Security Act, and in an action or proceeding relating to an order of removal, to relief from removal, or to immigration benefits or detention, access to an electronic file is authorized as follows: (1) the parties and their attorneys may have remote electronic access to any part of the case file, including the administrative record; (2) any other person may have electronic access to the full record at the courthouse, but may have remote electronic access only to: (A) the docket maintained by the court; and (B) an opinion, order, judgment, or other disposition of the court, but not any other part of the case file or the administrative record. FRCP 5.2(c).

d. *Filings made under seal.* The court may order that a filing be made under seal without redaction. The court may later unseal the filing or order the person who made the filing to file a redacted version for the public record. FRCP 5.2(d).

   i. *DISTRICT OF MAINE.* For information on filing sealed documents in the District of Maine, refer to ME R USDCT Rule 7A, ME R USDCT App. 4(p)(2), and ME R USDCT Sealed Filings.

e. *Protective orders.* For good cause, the court may by order in a case: (1) require redaction of additional information; or (2) limit or prohibit a nonparty's remote electronic access to a document filed with the court. FRCP 5.2(e).

f. *Option for additional unredacted filing under seal.* A person making a redacted filing may also file an unredacted copy under seal. The court must retain the unredacted copy as part of the record. FRCP 5.2(f).

   i. *DISTRICT OF MAINE.* A party wishing to file a document containing the personal data identifiers specified above may. . .file an unredacted document under seal. This document will be retained by the clerk's office as part of the record. ME R USDCT Redacting Pleadings. The court may, however, still require the party to file a redacted copy for the public file. ME R USDCT Redacting Pleadings.

g. *Option for filing a reference list.* A filing that contains redacted information may be filed together with a reference list that identifies each item of redacted information and specifies an appropriate identifier that uniquely corresponds to each item listed. The list must be filed under seal and may be amended as of right. Any reference in the case to a listed identifier will be construed to refer to the corresponding item of information. FRCP 5.2(g).

   i. *DISTRICT OF MAINE.* A party wishing to file a document containing the personal data identifiers specified

above may. . .file a reference list under seal. The reference list shall contain the complete personal data identifier(s) and the redacted identifier(s) used in its (their) place in the filing. All references in the case to the redacted identifiers included in the reference list will be construed to refer to the corresponding complete identifier. The reference list must be filed under seal, and may be amended as of right. It shall be retained by the clerk's office as part of the record. ME R USDCT Redacting Pleadings. The court may, however, still require the party to file a redacted copy for the public file. ME R USDCT Redacting Pleadings.

h. *DISTRICT OF MAINE: Responsibility for redaction.* The clerk is not required to review documents filed with the court for compliance with FRCP 5.2. The responsibility to redact filings rests with counsel and the party or nonparty making the filing. ME R USDCT App. 4(i); ME R USDCT Redacting Pleadings. For guidelines for filing confidential information in civil cases in the District of Maine, refer to ME R USDCT Confidentiality.

i. *Waiver of protection of identifiers.* A person waives the protection of FRCP 5.2(a) as to the person's own information by filing it without redaction and not under seal. FRCP 5.2(h).

F. Filing and Service Requirements

1. *Filing requirements*

   a. *Required filings.* Any paper after the complaint that is required to be served must be filed no later than a reasonable time after service. FRCP 5(d)(1).

   b. *DISTRICT OF MAINE: Place of filing.* Unless otherwise ordered by the court, papers shall be filed with the court at Bangor in cases filed and pending at Bangor, and at Portland in cases filed and pending at Portland. ME R USDCT Rule 5(a).

   c. *Nonelectronic filing.* A paper not filed electronically is filed by delivering it: (A) to the clerk; or (B) to a judge who agrees to accept it for filing, and who must then note the filing date on the paper and promptly send it to the clerk. FRCP 5(d)(2).

      i. *DISTRICT OF MAINE: Documents to be filed in paper.* The following documents shall be filed in paper, which may also be scanned into ECF by the clerk's office: (A) all handwritten pleadings; and (B) all pleadings and documents filed by pro se litigants who are incarcerated or who are not registered filing users in ECF. ME R USDCT App. 4(g)(8). Non-prisoner pro se litigants in civil actions may register with ECF or may file (and serve) all pleadings and other documents in paper. The clerk's office will scan into ECF any pleadings and documents filed on paper in accordance with ME R USDCT App. 4(g). ME R USDCT App. 4(o). For more information, refer to ME R USDCT App. 4(g).

   d. *Electronic filing*

      i. *DISTRICT OF MAINE: Authorization.* Unless exempt or otherwise ordered by the court, papers shall be filed and served electronically as required by the court's Administrative Procedures Governing the Filing and Service by Electronic Means, which is set forth in ME R USDCT App. 4. The provisions of the court's Administrative Procedures Governing the Filing and Service by Electronic Means (ME R USDCT App. 4) shall be applied and enforced as part of the Local Rules of the United States District Court for the District of Maine. ME R USDCT Rule 5(c).

      ii. *Filing by represented persons.* A person represented by an attorney must file electronically, unless nonelectronic filing is allowed by the court for good cause or is allowed or required by local rule. FRCP 5(d)(3)(A).

         • *DISTRICT OF MAINE.* An attorney may apply to the court for permission to file paper documents. ME R USDCT App. 4(a)(5).

      iii. *Filing by unrepresented persons.* A person not represented by an attorney: (i) may file electronically only if allowed by court order or by local rule; and (ii) may be required to file electronically only by court order, or by a local rule that includes reasonable exceptions. FRCP 5(d)(3)(B).

         • *DISTRICT OF MAINE.* Non-prisoner pro se litigants in civil actions may register with ECF or may file (and serve) all pleadings and other documents in paper. ME R USDCT App. 4(o). A non-prisoner who is a party to a civil action and who is not represented by an attorney may register to receive service electronically and to electronically transmit their documents to the court for filing in the ECF system. If during the course of the action the person retains an attorney who appears on the person's behalf, the clerk shall terminate the person's registration upon the attorney's appearance. ME R USDCT App. 4(b)(2).

      iv. *DISTRICT OF MAINE: Scope of electronic filing.* All documents submitted for filing in civil and criminal cases, regardless of case commencement date, except those documents specifically exempted in ME R USDCT App.

4(g), shall be filed electronically using the electronic case filing system (ECF). ME R USDCT App. 4(a)(1). For special filing requirements and exceptions, refer to ME R USDCT App. 4(g).

v. *DISTRICT OF MAINE: Consequences of electronic filing.* Electronic transmission of a document to the ECF system, together with the transmission of a Notice of Electronic Filing (NEF) from the court, constitutes filing of the document for all purposes of the Federal Rules of Civil Procedure. ME R USDCT App. 4(d)(1).

vi. *DISTRICT OF MAINE: Review of documents.* Documents filed with the clerk's office will normally be reviewed no later than the close of the next business day. It is the responsibility of the filing party to promptly notify the clerk's office via telephone of a matter that requires the immediate attention of a judicial officer. ME R USDCT App. 4(a)(4).

e. *DISTRICT OF MAINE: Facsimile filing.* No papers shall be submitted to the court by means of a facsimile machine without prior leave of the court. ME R USDCT Rule 5(c); ME R USDCT App. 4(m).

2. *Service requirements*

a. *Service; When required.* Unless the Federal Rules of Civil Procedure provide otherwise, each of the following papers must be served on every party: (A) an order stating that service is required; (B) a pleading filed after the original complaint, unless the court orders otherwise under FRCP 5(c) because there are numerous defendants; (C) a discovery paper required to be served on a party, unless the court orders otherwise; (D) a written motion, except one that may be heard ex parte; and (E) a written notice, appearance, demand, or offer of judgment, or any similar paper. FRCP 5(a)(1).

i. *If a party fails to appear.* No service is required on a party who is in default for failing to appear. But a pleading that asserts a new claim for relief against such a party must be served on that party under FRCP 4. FRCP 5(a)(2).

ii. *Seizing property.* If an action is begun by seizing property and no person is or need be named as a defendant, any service required before the filing of an appearance, answer, or claim must be made on the person who had custody or possession of the property when it was seized. FRCP 5(a)(3).

b. *Service; How made.* A paper is served under FRCP 5 by: (A) handing it to the person; (B) leaving it: (i) at the person's office with a clerk or other person in charge or, if no one is in charge, in a conspicuous place in the office; or (ii) if the person has no office or the office is closed, at the person's dwelling or usual place of abode with someone of suitable age and discretion who resides there; (C) mailing it to the person's last known address—in which event service is complete upon mailing; (D) leaving it with the court clerk if the person has no known address; (E) sending it to a registered user by filing it with the court's electronic-filing system or sending it by other electronic means that the person consented to in writing—in either of which events service is complete upon filing or sending, but is not effective if the filer or sender learns that it did not reach the person to be served; or (F) delivering it by any other means that the person consented to in writing—in which event service is complete when the person making service delivers it to the agency designated to make delivery. FRCP 5(b)(2).

i. *Serving an attorney.* If a party is represented by an attorney, service under FRCP 5 must be made on the attorney unless the court orders service on the party. FRCP 5(b)(1).

c. *DISTRICT OF MAINE: Service of electronically filed documents*

i. *Registered users.* Registration [as a filing user of the court's ECF system] constitutes consent to service of all documents by electronic means as provided in ME R USDCT App. 4. ME R USDCT App. 4(b)(4). Whenever a non-sealed pleading is filed electronically, the ECF system will automatically generate and send a Notice of Electronic Filing (NEF) to the filing user and registered users of record. The user filing the document should retain a paper or digital copy of the NEF, which shall serve as the court's date-stamp and proof of filing. ME R USDCT App. 4(e)(1).

- *Sealed documents.* Although the filing of sealed documents in civil cases produces an NEF, the document itself cannot be accessed and counsel shall be responsible for making service of the sealed documents. ME R USDCT App. 4(e)(2).

ii. *Non-registered users and pro se litigants.* Attorneys who have not yet registered as users with ECF and pro se litigants who have not registered with ECF shall be served a paper copy of any electronically filed pleading or other document in accordance with the provisions of FRCP 5. ME R USDCT App. 4(e)(3).

- *Registration of pro se litigants.* A non-prisoner who is a party to a civil action and who is not represented by an attorney may register to receive service electronically and to electronically transmit their documents to the court for filing in the ECF system. If during the course of the action the person retains an attorney who appears on the person's behalf, the clerk shall terminate the person's registration upon the attorney's appearance. ME R USDCT App. 4(b)(2).

d. *Serving numerous defendants.* If an action involves an unusually large number of defendants, the court may, on motion or on its own, order that: (A) defendants' pleadings and replies to them need not be served on other defendants; (B) any crossclaim, counterclaim, avoidance, or affirmative defense in those pleadings and replies to them will be treated as denied or avoided by all other parties; and (C) filing any such pleading and serving it on the plaintiff constitutes notice of the pleading to all parties. FRCP 5(c)(1).

    i. *Notifying parties.* A copy of every such order must be served on the parties as the court directs. FRCP 5(c)(2).

3. *DISTRICT OF MAINE: Filing and service of highly sensitive documents (HSDs).* For information on filing and serving highly sensitive documents (HSDs) in the District of Maine, refer to ME R USDCT General Order 21-5.

G. Hearings

1. *Hearings, generally.* When a motion relies on facts outside the record, the court may hear the matter on affidavits or may hear it wholly or partly on oral testimony or on depositions. FRCP 43(c).

    a. *Oral argument.* Due process does not require that oral argument be permitted on a motion and, except as otherwise provided by local rule, the district court has discretion to determine whether it will decide the motion on the papers or hear argument by counsel (and perhaps receive evidence). FPP § 1190; F.D.I.C. v. Deglau, 207 F.3d 153 (3d Cir. 2000).

        i. *DISTRICT OF MAINE.* Unless otherwise required by federal rule or statute, all motions may be decided by the court without oral argument unless otherwise ordered by the court on its own motion or, in its discretion, upon request of counsel. ME R USDCT Rule 7(e).

    b. *Providing a regular schedule for oral hearings.* A court may establish regular times and places for oral hearings on motions. FRCP 78(a).

    c. *Providing for submission on briefs.* By rule or order, the court may provide for submitting and determining motions on briefs, without oral hearings. FRCP 78(b).

H. Forms

1. Federal Motion to Strike Forms

    a. Motion to strike insufficient affirmative defenses. 2C FEDFORMS § 11:151.

    b. Motion to strike insufficient defense in answer; Stating particular reason. 2C FEDFORMS § 11:153.

    c. Notice of motion and motion to strike insufficient affirmative defense. 2C FEDFORMS § 11:155.

    d. Motion to strike impertinence and scandal. 2C FEDFORMS § 11:157.

    e. Motion to strike impertinence and immateriality. 2C FEDFORMS § 11:158.

    f. Motion to strike redundancy and scandal. 2C FEDFORMS § 11:159.

    g. Motion to strike immaterial defense. 2C FEDFORMS § 11:160.

    h. Motion to strike for immateriality. 2C FEDFORMS § 11:161.

    i. Motion to strike counterclaim for lack of evidence. 2C FEDFORMS § 11:162.

    j. Motion; By plaintiff; To strike insufficient defense from answer. AMJUR PP FEDPRAC § 453.

    k. Motion; To strike redundant, immaterial, impertinent, or scandalous matter from pleading. AMJUR PP FEDPRAC § 454.

    l. Motion; To strike portions of complaint. AMJUR PP FEDPRAC § 456.

    m. Opposition; To motion. FEDPROF § 1B:175.

    n. Affidavit; Supporting or opposing motion. FEDPROF § 1B:176.

    o. Brief; Supporting or opposing motion. FEDPROF § 1B:177.

    p. Statement of points and authorities; Opposing motion. FEDPROF § 1B:178.

    q. Motion; To strike material outside statute of limitations. FEDPROF § 1B:199.

    r. Opposition to motion; Material not contained in pleading. FEDPROF § 1B:201.

    s. General form. GOLDLTGFMS § 20:8.

    t. General form; Federal form. GOLDLTGFMS § 20:10.

    u. Notice and motion to strike immaterial, redundant or scandalous matter. GOLDLTGFMS § 20:13.

v. Motion to strike complaint and dismiss action as to one defendant. GOLDLTGFMS § 20:14.

w. Defendant's motion to strike. GOLDLTGFMS § 20:16.

x. Defendant's motion to strike; Plaintiff's response. GOLDLTGFMS § 20:17.

y. Motion to strike answer. GOLDLTGFMS § 20:19.

z. Objections to motion to strike. GOLDLTGFMS § 20:20.

I. Applicable Rules

1. *Federal rules*

   a. Serving and filing pleadings and other papers. FRCP 5.

   b. Constitutional challenge to a statute; Notice, certification, and intervention. FRCP 5.1.

   c. Privacy protection for filings made with the court. FRCP 5.2.

   d. Computing and extending time; Time for motion papers. FRCP 6.

   e. Pleadings allowed; Form of motions and other papers. FRCP 7.

   f. Disclosure statement. FRCP 7.1.

   g. Form of pleadings. FRCP 10.

   h. Signing pleadings, motions, and other papers; Representations to the court; Sanctions. FRCP 11.

   i. Defenses and objections; When and how presented; Motion for judgment on the pleadings; Consolidating motions; Waiving defenses; Pretrial hearing. FRCP 12.

   j. Taking testimony. FRCP 43.

   k. Hearing motions; Submission on briefs. FRCP 78.

2. *Local rules*

   a. *DISTRICT OF MAINE*

      i. Service and filing of pleadings and other papers. ME R USDCT Rule 5.

      ii. Time. ME R USDCT Rule 6.

      iii. Motions and memoranda of law. ME R USDCT Rule 7.

      iv. Corporate disclosure. ME R USDCT Rule 7.1.

      v. Form of pleadings, motions and other papers. ME R USDCT Rule 10.

      vi. Discovery. ME R USDCT Rule 26.

      vii. Attorneys; Appearances and withdrawals. ME R USDCT Rule 83.2.

      viii. Alternative dispute resolution (ADR). ME R USDCT Rule 83.11.

      ix. Administrative procedures governing the filing and service by electronic means. ME R USDCT App. 4.

      x. Redacting pleadings. ME R USDCT Redacting Pleadings.

Motions, Oppositions and Replies
Motion to Dismiss for Improper Venue

Document Last Updated April 2021

A. Checklist

(I) ❑ Matters to be considered by moving party

    (a) ❑ Required documents

        (1) ❑ Notice of motion and motion

    (b) ❑ Supplemental documents

        (1) ❑ Supporting evidence

        (2) ❑ Notice of constitutional question

(3) ❑ Nongovernmental corporate disclosure statement

(4) ❑ DISTRICT OF MAINE: Additional supplemental documents

    (i) ❑ Proposed order

(c) ❑ Timing

    (1) ❑ Every defense to a claim for relief in any pleading must be asserted in the responsive pleading if one is required

    (2) ❑ A motion asserting any of the defenses in FRCP 12(b) must be made before pleading if a responsive pleading is allowed

    (3) ❑ If a pleading sets out a claim for relief that does not require a responsive pleading, an opposing party may assert at trial any defense to that claim

    (4) ❑ A written motion and notice of the hearing must be served at least fourteen (14) days before the time specified for the hearing, with the following exceptions: (A) when the motion may be heard ex parte; (B) when the Federal Rules of Civil Procedure set a different time; or (C) when a court order—which a party may, for good cause, apply for ex parte—sets a different time

    (5) ❑ Any affidavit supporting a motion must be served with the motion

    (6) ❑ DISTRICT OF MAINE: Additional timing

        (i) ❑ Any affidavits and other documents setting forth or evidencing facts on which the motion is based must be filed with the motion

(II) ❑ Matters to be considered by opposing party

(a) ❑ Required documents

    (1) ❑ Opposition

(b) ❑ Supplemental documents

    (1) ❑ Supporting evidence

    (2) ❑ Notice of constitutional question

(c) ❑ Timing

    (1) ❑ Except as FRCP 59(c) provides otherwise, any opposing affidavit must be served at least seven (7) days before the hearing, unless the court permits service at another time

    (2) ❑ DISTRICT OF MAINE: Additional timing

        (i) ❑ Unless within twenty-one (21) days after the filing of a motion the opposing party files written objection thereto, incorporating a memorandum of law, the opposing party shall be deemed to have waived objection

B. Timing

1. *Motion to dismiss for improper venue*

   a. *In a responsive pleading.* Every defense to a claim for relief in any pleading must be asserted in the responsive pleading if one is required. FRCP 12(b).

   b. *By motion.* A motion asserting any of the defenses in FRCP 12(b) must be made before pleading if a responsive pleading is allowed. FRCP 12(b). Although FRCP 12(b) encourages the responsive pleader to file a motion to dismiss before filing the answer, nothing in FRCP 12 prohibits the filing of a motion to dismiss with the answer. An untimely motion to dismiss may be considered if the defense asserted in the motion was previously raised in the responsive pleading. FEDPROC § 62:421.

   c. *At trial.* If a pleading sets out a claim for relief that does not require a responsive pleading, an opposing party may assert at trial any defense to that claim. FRCP 12(b).

2. *Timing of motions, generally*

   a. *Motion and notice of hearing.* A written motion and notice of the hearing must be served at least fourteen (14) days before the time specified for the hearing, with the following exceptions: (A) when the motion may be heard ex parte; (B) when the Federal Rules of Civil Procedure set a different time; or (C) when a court order—which a party may, for good cause, apply for ex parte—sets a different time. FRCP 6(c)(1).

b. *Supporting affidavit.* Any affidavit supporting a motion must be served with the motion. FRCP 6(c)(2).

c. *DISTRICT OF MAINE: Affidavits and other supporting documents.* Any affidavits and other documents setting forth or evidencing facts on which the motion is based must be filed with the motion. ME R USDCT Rule 7(a).

3. *Timing of opposing papers.* Except as FRCP 59(c) provides otherwise, any opposing affidavit must be served at least seven (7) days before the hearing, unless the court permits service at another time. FRCP 6(c)(2).

a. *DISTRICT OF MAINE.* Unless within twenty-one (21) days after the filing of a motion the opposing party files written objection thereto, incorporating a memorandum of law, the opposing party shall be deemed to have waived objection. ME R USDCT Rule 7(b). The deemed waiver imposed in ME R USDCT Rule 7(b) shall not apply to motions filed during trial. ME R USDCT Rule 7(b).

4. *Timing of reply papers.* Where the respondent files an answering affidavit setting up a new matter, the moving party ordinarily is allowed a reasonable time to file a reply affidavit since failure to deny the new matter by affidavit may operate as an admission of its truth. AMJUR MOTIONS § 25.

a. *DISTRICT OF MAINE.* Within fourteen (14) days of the filing of any objection to a motion, the moving party may file a reply memorandum. ME R USDCT Rule 7(c).

5. *Effect of FRCP 12 motion on the time to serve a responsive pleading.* Unless the court sets a different time, serving a motion under FRCP 12 alters the periods in FRCP 12(a) as follows: (A) if the court denies the motion or postpones its disposition until trial, the responsive pleading must be served within fourteen (14) days after notice of the court's action; or (B) if the court grants a motion for a more definite statement, the responsive pleading must be served within fourteen (14) days after the more definite statement is served. FRCP 12(a)(4).

6. *Computation of time*

a. *Computing time.* FRCP 6 applies in computing any time period specified in the Federal Rules of Civil Procedure, in any local rule or court order, or in any statute that does not specify a method of computing time. FRCP 6(a).

i. *Period stated in days or a longer unit.* When the period is stated in days or a longer unit of time: (A) exclude the day of the event that triggers the period; (B) count every day, including intermediate Saturdays, Sundays, and legal holidays; and (C) include the last day of the period, but if the last day is a Saturday, Sunday, or legal holiday, the period continues to run until the end of the next day that is not a Saturday, Sunday, or legal holiday. FRCP 6(a)(1).

ii. *Period stated in hours.* When the period is stated in hours: (A) begin counting immediately on the occurrence of the event that triggers the period; (B) count every hour, including hours during intermediate Saturdays, Sundays, and legal holidays; and (C) if the period would end on a Saturday, Sunday, or legal holiday, the period continues to run until the same time on the next day that is not a Saturday, Sunday, or legal holiday. FRCP 6(a)(2).

iii. *Inaccessibility of the clerk's office.* Unless the court orders otherwise, if the clerk's office is inaccessible: (A) on the last day for filing under FRCP 6(a)(1), then the time for filing is extended to the first accessible day that is not a Saturday, Sunday, or legal holiday; or (B) during the last hour for filing under FRCP 6(a)(2), then the time for filing is extended to the same time on the first accessible day that is not a Saturday, Sunday, or legal holiday. FRCP 6(a)(3).

iv. *"Last day" defined.* Unless a different time is set by a statute, local rule, or court order, the last day ends: (A) for electronic filing, at midnight in the court's time zone; and (B) for filing by other means, when the clerk's office is scheduled to close. FRCP 6(a)(4).

v. *"Next day" defined.* The "next day" is determined by continuing to count forward when the period is measured after an event and backward when measured before an event. FRCP 6(a)(5).

vi. *"Legal holiday" defined.* "Legal holiday" means: (A) the day set aside by statute for observing New Year's Day, Martin Luther King Jr.'s Birthday, Washington's Birthday, Memorial Day, Independence Day, Labor Day, Columbus Day, Veterans' Day, Thanksgiving Day, or Christmas Day; (B) any day declared a holiday by the President or Congress; and (C) for periods that are measured after an event, any other day declared a holiday by the state where the district court is located. FRCP 6(a)(6).

vii. *DISTRICT OF MAINE: Applicability of FRCP 6.* FRCP 6 applies when computing any period of time stated in the Local Rules of the United States District Court for the District of Maine. ME R USDCT Rule 6(a).

b. *DISTRICT OF MAINE: Computation of electronic filing deadlines.* Filing documents electronically does not in any way alter any filing deadlines. All electronic transmissions of documents must be completed prior to midnight, Eastern Time, in order to be considered timely filed that day. Where a specific time of day deadline is set by court order

or stipulation, the electronic filing must be completed by that time. ME R USDCT App. 4(f). A document filed electronically shall be deemed filed at the time and date stated on the Notice of Electronic Filing received from the court. ME R USDCT App. 4(d)(2).

  i. *Technical failures.* A filing user whose filing is made untimely as the result of a technical failure may seek appropriate relief from the court. ME R USDCT App. 4(n). A technical failure of the court's ECF system is deemed to have occurred when the court's ECF site cannot accept filings continuously or intermittently over the course of any period of time greater than one (1) hour. Known system outages will be posted on the court's website along with guidance on how to proceed, if applicable. ME R USDCT App. 4(n).

c. *Extending time.* When an act may or must be done within a specified time, the court may, for good cause, extend the time: (A) with or without motion or notice if the court acts, or if a request is made, before the original time or its extension expires; or (B) on motion made after the time has expired if the party failed to act because of excusable neglect. FRCP 6(b)(1). A court must not extend the time to act under FRCP 50(b), FRCP 50(d), FRCP 52(b), FRCP 59(b), FRCP 59(d), FRCP 59(e), and FRCP 60(b). FRCP 6(b)(2). Refer to the United States District Court for the District of Maine KeyRules Motion for Continuance/Extension of Time document for more information on extending time.

d. *Additional time after certain kinds of service.* When a party may or must act within a specified time after being served and service is made under FRCP 5(b)(2)(C) (by mail), FRCP 5(b)(2)(D) (by leaving with the clerk), or FRCP 5(b)(2)(F) (by other means consented to), three (3) days are added after the period would otherwise expire under FRCP 6(a). FRCP 6(d).

C. General Requirements

1. *Motions, generally*

  a. *Motion requirements.* A request for a court order must be made by motion. The motion must: (A) be in writing unless made during a hearing or trial; (B) state with particularity the grounds for seeking the order; and (C) state the relief sought. FRCP 7(b)(1). The writing and particularity requirements are intended to ensure that the adverse parties are informed of and have a record of both the motion's pendency and the grounds on which the movant seeks an order. FPP § 1191; Feldberg v. Quechee Lakes Corp., 463 F.3d 195 (2d Cir. 2006).

    i. *Particularity requirement.* The particularity requirement [ensures] that the opposing parties will have notice of their opponent's contentions. FEDPROC § 62:358; Goodman v. 1973 26 Foot Trojan Vessel, Arkansas Registration No. AR1439SN, 859 F.2d 71 (8th Cir. 1988). That requirement ensures that notice of the basis for the motion is provided to the court and to the opposing party so as to avoid prejudice, provide the opponent with a meaningful opportunity to respond, and provide the court with enough information to process the motion correctly. FEDPROC § 62:358; Andreas v. Volkswagen of Am., Inc., 336 F.3d 789 (8th Cir. 2003).

      • Reasonable specification of the grounds for a motion is sufficient. The particularity requirement for motions is satisfied when no party is prejudiced by a lack of particularity or when the court can comprehend the basis for the motion and deal with it fairly. However, where a movant fails to state even one ground for granting the motion in question, the movant has failed to meet the minimal standard of "reasonable specification." FEDPROC § 62:358; Martinez v. Trainor, 556 F.2d 818 (7th Cir. 1977).

      • The court may excuse the failure to comply with the particularity requirement if it is inadvertent, and where no prejudice is shown by the opposing party. FEDPROC § 62:358.

  b. *Notice of motion.* A party interested in resisting the relief sought by a motion has a right to notice thereof, and an opportunity to be heard. AMJUR MOTIONS § 12.

    i. *Purpose.* In addition to statutory or court rule provisions requiring notice of a motion—the purpose of such a notice requirement having been said to be to prevent a party from being prejudicially surprised by a motion— principles of natural justice dictate that an adverse party generally must be given notice that a motion will be presented to the court. AMJUR MOTIONS § 12.

    ii. *Adequacy of notice.* The test of adequate notice generally turns on whether the other parties were afforded an adequate opportunity to prepare and respond to the issues to be raised in the proceeding. AMJUR MOTIONS § 12.

  c. *Single document containing motion and notice.* A single written document can satisfy the writing requirements both for a motion and for an FRCP 6(c)(1) notice. FRCP 7(Advisory Committee Notes).

2. *Motion to dismiss for improper venue.* A party may assert the following defense by motion: improper venue. FRCP

12(b)(3). Objections to venue typically stem from a failure to adhere to the requirements specified in the general venue statute, 28 U.S.C.A. § 1391, or some other statutory venue provision. FPP § 1352.

a. *Forum selection clauses.* In recent years, however, there have been what appears to be an increasing number of venue motions based on the enforcement of forum selection clauses in contracts. FPP § 1352; Tropp v. Corp. of Lloyd's, 385 F. App'x 36, 37 (2d Cir. 2010).

   i. *Resolution of motions based on forum selection clauses.* The courts of appeal were previously split as to how to treat such motions, treating dismissal of the action as the proper remedy but divided as to whether dismissal was proper pursuant to FRCP 12(b)(3) or FRCP 12(b)(6) when it is based on one of these forum selection clauses rather than on noncompliance with a federal venue statute. FPP § 1352. The Supreme Court resolved this [split] in its 2013 decision Atlantic Marine Construction Co. Inc. v. United States District Court for the Western District of Texas by holding that the appropriate method for enforcing a valid forum-selection clause is the use of transfer to the contractually selected forum under 28 U.S.C.A. § 1404(a), provided the clause permits adjudication in a federal court. FPP § 1352; Atl. Marine Const. Co. Inc. v. U.S. Dist. Court for the W. Dist. of Texas, 571 U.S. 49, 134 S. Ct. 568, 187 L. Ed. 2d 487 (2013); Martinez v. Bloomberg LP, 740 F.3d 211, 216 (2d Cir. 2014).

   ii. *FRCP 12(b)(3) not appropriate method of enforcing forum selection clauses.* Forum-selection clauses cannot make venue "wrong" or "improper" within the meaning of 28 U.S.C.A. § 1406(a) or FRCP 12(b)(3), which is why FRCP 12(b)(3) is no longer an appropriate method for enforcing forum selection clauses. FPP § 1352; Atl. Marine Const. Co. Inc. v. U.S. Dist. Court for the W. Dist. of Texas, 571 U.S. 49, 134 S. Ct. 568, 187 L. Ed. 2d 487 (2013).

b. *Burden.* On a motion under FRCP 12(b)(3), facts must be shown that will defeat the plaintiff's assertion of venue. FPP § 1352; Pierce v. Shorty Small's of Branson Inc., 137 F.3d 1190 (10th Cir. 1998). Courts have not agreed as to which party has the burden of proof on a motion for improper venue. FEDPROC § 62:444.

   i. *On defendant.* A number of federal courts have concluded that the burden of doing so is on the defendant, since venue is a "personal privilege" that can be waived and a lack of venue should be established by the party asserting it. FPP § 1352; Myers v. Am. Dental Ass'n, 695 F.2d 716 (3d Cir. 1982).

   ii. *On plaintiff.* On the other hand, an equal (perhaps a larger) number of federal courts have imposed the burden on the plaintiff in keeping with the rule applied in the context of subject matter and personal jurisdiction defenses. FPP § 1352. The latter view seems correct inasmuch as it is the plaintiff's obligation to institute his action in a permissible forum, both in terms of jurisdiction and venue. FPP § 1352; Pierce v. Shorty Small's of Branson Inc., 137 F.3d 1190 (10th Cir. 1998).

      • If the court chooses to rely on pleadings and affidavits, the plaintiff need only make a prima facie showing of venue, but if the court holds an evidentiary hearing, the plaintiff must demonstrate venue by a preponderance of the evidence. FEDPROF § 1C:13; Gulf Ins. Co. v. Glasbrenner, 417 F.3d 353 (2d Cir. 2005).

c. *Form.* A motion to dismiss for lack of venue must be denied as insufficient where it is not apparent which venue provision the moving party wishes to invoke or, assuming that the general venue statute 28 U.S.C.A. § 1391 is contemplated, which paragraph is considered controlling. FEDPROC § 62:443.

d. *Practice on an FRCP 12(b)(3) motion.* All well-pleaded allegations in the complaint bearing on the venue question generally are taken as true, unless contradicted by the defendant's affidavits. A district court may examine facts outside the complaint to determine whether its venue is proper. FPP § 1352; Ambraco, Inc. v. Bossclip B.V., 570 F.3d 233 (5th Cir. 2009). And, as is consistent with practice in other contexts, such as construing the complaint, the court must draw all reasonable inferences and resolve all factual conflicts in favor of the plaintiff. FPP § 1352.

e. *Dismissal versus transfer.* The district court in a district in which a case is filed laying venue in the wrong division or district must dismiss the action or, if it is in the interest of justice to do so, transfer such action to any division or district in which it could have been brought. FEDPROC § 62:446.

   i. *Authority to transfer case.* A motion to dismiss for improper venue under FRCP 12(b)(3) no longer is necessary in order to object to an inconvenient forum. FPP § 1352. With the enactment of 28 U.S.C.A. § 1404(a) as part of the 1948 revision of the Judicial Code, the district courts now have authority to transfer any case to a more convenient forum if the transfer is in the interest of justice. FPP § 1352; Norwood v. Kirkpatrick, 349 U.S. 29, 75 S. Ct. 544, 99 L. Ed. 789 (1955). Consideration of a dismissal for improper venue must take into account 28 U.S.C.A. § 1406(a) as well as FRCP 12(b)(3). FEDPROC § 62:446.

      • The district court of a district in which is filed a case laying venue in the wrong division or district shall dismiss, or if it be in the interest of justice, transfer such case to any district or division in which it could have been brought. 28 U.S.C.A. § 1406(a).

- For the convenience of parties and witnesses, in the interest of justice, a district court may transfer any civil action to any other district or division where it might have been brought or to any district or division to which all parties have consented. 28 U.S.C.A. § 1404(a).

- Technically speaking, motions to transfer are made pursuant to a motion under 28 U.S.C.A. § 1404(a) rather than under FRCP 12(b)(3), although little, other than the possible application of the consolidation requirement in FRCP 12(g), turns on this distinction. FPP § 1352.

    ii. *Mitigating the harshness of dismissal.* Although dismissal was once the sole relief if an action was successfully challenged for improper venue or forum non conveniens, dismissal is a harsh remedy, so 28 U.S.C.A. § 1406(a) is intended to mitigate that harshness by permitting district courts to transfer such cases to the proper forum as an alternative to dismissing them. FEDPROC § 62:446.

  f. *Joining motions.* A motion under FRCP 12 may be joined with any other motion allowed by FRCP 12. FRCP 12(g)(1).

    i. *Limitation on further motions.* Except as provided in FRCP 12(h)(2) or FRCP 12(h)(3), a party that makes a motion under FRCP 12 must not make another motion under FRCP 12 raising a defense or objection that was available to the party but omitted from its earlier motion. FRCP 12(g)(2).

  g. *Waiving and preserving certain defenses.* No defense or objection is waived by joining it with one or more other defenses or objections in a responsive pleading or in a motion. FRCP 12(b).

    i. *Waiver by omission or failure to make or include motion.* A party waives any defense listed in FRCP 12(b)(2) through FRCP 12(b)(5) by:

- Omitting it from a motion in the circumstances described in FRCP 12(g)(2); or

- Failing to either: (i) make it by motion under FRCP 12; or (ii) include it in a responsive pleading or in an amendment allowed by FRCP 15(a)(1) as a matter of course. FRCP 12(h)(1).

    ii. *Waiver by consent.* The defendant also may waive the right to obtain a dismissal prior to trial either by express consent to be sued in a certain district or by some conduct that will be construed as implying consent. FPP § 1352.

3. *Venue, generally*

  a. *Applicability of 28 U.S.C.A. § 1391.* Except as otherwise provided by law: (1) 28 U.S.C.A. § 1391 shall govern the venue of all civil actions brought in district courts of the United States; and (2) the proper venue for a civil action shall be determined without regard to whether the action is local or transitory in nature. 28 U.S.C.A. § 1391(a).

  b. *Venue in general.* A civil action may be brought in: (1) a judicial district in which any defendant resides, if all defendants are residents of the state in which the district is located; (2) a judicial district in which a substantial part of the events or omissions giving rise to the claim occurred, or a substantial part of property that is the subject of the action is situated; or (3) if there is no district in which an action may otherwise be brought as provided in 28 U.S.C.A. § 1391, any judicial district in which any defendant is subject to the court's personal jurisdiction with respect to such action. 28 U.S.C.A. § 1391(b).

  c. *Residency.* For all venue purposes: (1) a natural person, including an alien lawfully admitted for permanent residence in the United States, shall be deemed to reside in the judicial district in which that person is domiciled; (2) an entity with the capacity to sue and be sued in its common name under applicable law, whether or not incorporated, shall be deemed to reside, if a defendant, in any judicial district in which such defendant is subject to the court's personal jurisdiction with respect to the civil action in question and, if a plaintiff, only in the judicial district in which it maintains its principal place of business; and (3) a defendant not resident in the United States may be sued in any judicial district, and the joinder of such a defendant shall be disregarded in determining where the action may be brought with respect to other defendants. 28 U.S.C.A. § 1391(c).

  d. *Residency of corporations in states with multiple districts.* For purposes of venue under this chapter (28 U.S.C.A. § 1390, et seq.), in a state which has more than one judicial district and in which a defendant that is a corporation is subject to personal jurisdiction at the time an action is commenced, such corporation shall be deemed to reside in any district in that state within which its contacts would be sufficient to subject it to personal jurisdiction if that district were a separate State, and, if there is no such district, the corporation shall be deemed to reside in the district within which it has the most significant contacts. 28 U.S.C.A. § 1391(d).

  e. *Actions where defendant is officer or employee of the United States.* A civil action in which a defendant is an officer or employee of the United States or any agency thereof acting in his official capacity or under color of legal authority, or an agency of the United States, or the United States, may, except as otherwise provided by law, be brought in any judicial district in which: (A) a defendant in the action resides, (B) a substantial part of the events or omissions giving rise to the claim occurred, or a substantial part of property that is the subject of the action is situated, or (C) the plaintiff resides if no real property is involved in the action. Additional persons may be joined as parties to any such action in accordance with the Federal Rules of Civil Procedure and with such other venue requirements as would be applicable if the United States or one of its officers, employees, or agencies were not a party. 28 U.S.C.A. § 1391(e)(1).

    i.   *Service.* The summons and complaint in such an action shall be served as provided by the Federal Rules of Civil Procedure except that the delivery of the summons and complaint to the officer or agency as required by the Federal Rules of Civil Procedure may be made by certified mail beyond the territorial limits of the district in which the action is brought. 28 U.S.C.A. § 1391(e)(2).

    f.   *Civil actions against a foreign state.* A civil action against a foreign state as defined in 28 U.S.C.A. § 1603(a) may be brought: (1) in any judicial district in which a substantial part of the events or omissions giving rise to the claim occurred, or a substantial part of property that is the subject of the action is situated; (2) in any judicial district in which the vessel or cargo of a foreign state is situated, if the claim is asserted under 28 U.S.C.A. § 1605(b); (3) in any judicial district in which the agency or instrumentality is licensed to do business or is doing business, if the action is brought against an agency or instrumentality of a foreign state as defined in 28 U.S.C.A. § 1603(b); or (4) in the United States District Court for the District of Columbia if the action is brought against a foreign state or political subdivision thereof. 28 U.S.C.A. § 1391(f).

    g.   *Multiparty, multiforum litigation.* A civil action in which jurisdiction of the district court is based upon 28 U.S.C.A. § 1369 may be brought in any district in which any defendant resides or in which a substantial part of the accident giving rise to the action took place. 28 U.S.C.A. § 1391(g).

4.   *Opposing papers.* The Federal Rules of Civil Procedure do not require any formal answer, return, or reply to a motion, except where the Federal Rules of Civil Procedure or local rules may require affidavits, memoranda, or other papers to be filed in opposition to a motion. Such papers are simply to apprise the court of such opposition and the grounds of that opposition. FEDPROC § 62:353.

    a.   *DISTRICT OF MAINE: Content of objections.* Any objections shall include citations and supporting authorities and affidavits and other documents setting forth or evidencing facts on which the objection is based. ME R USDCT Rule 7(b).

    b.   *Effect of failure to respond to motion.* Although in the absence of statutory provision or court rule, a motion ordinarily does not require a response or written answer, when a party files a motion and the opposing party fails to respond, the court may construe such failure to respond as nonopposition to the motion or an admission that the motion was meritorious. AMJUR MOTIONS § 28. The rule in some jurisdictions being that the failure to respond to a fact set forth in a motion is deemed an admission—and may grant the motion if the relief requested appears to be justified. AMJUR MOTIONS § 28.

    i.   *Unopposed motion to dismiss.* The circuits are split on whether a court may grant a motion to dismiss solely on the basis that the plaintiff did not file a response opposing the motion. FRCP-RC RULE 12.

    c.   *Assent or no opposition not determinative.* However, a motion will not be granted automatically simply because an "assent" or a notation of "no opposition" has been filed; federal judges frequently deny motions that have been assented to when it is thought that justice so dictates. FPP § 1190.

    d.   *Responsive pleading inappropriate as response to motion.* An attempt to answer or oppose a motion with a responsive pleading usually is not appropriate. FPP § 1190.

5.   *Reply papers.* A moving party may be required or permitted to prepare papers in addition to its original motion papers. AMJUR MOTIONS § 25. Papers answering or replying to opposing papers may be appropriate, in the interests of justice, where it appears there is a substantial reason for allowing a reply. Thus, a court may accept reply papers where a party demonstrates that the papers to which it seeks to file a reply raise new issues that are material to the disposition of the question before the court, or where the court determines, sua sponte, that it wishes further briefing of an issue raised in those papers and orders the submission of additional papers. FEDPROC § 62:354.

    a.   *Function of reply papers.* The function of a reply affidavit or reply papers is to answer the arguments made in opposition to the position taken by the movant, not to raise new issues, arguments, or evidence, or change the nature of the primary motion. However, if the court permits new evidence with the reply papers, the other party should be given the opportunity to respond. Where the party opposing the motion has no opportunity to address the argument in writing, a court has the discretion to disregard arguments raised for the first time in a reply memorandum. Also, the view has been followed in some jurisdictions that as a matter of judicial economy, where there is no prejudice and where the issues could be raised simply by filing a motion to dismiss, the trial court has discretion to consider arguments raised for the first time in a reply memorandum, and that a trial court may grant a motion to strike issues raised for the first time in a reply memorandum. AMJUR MOTIONS § 26.

    i. *DISTRICT OF MAINE.* The moving party may file a reply memorandum. . .which shall be strictly confined to replying to new matter raised in the objection or opposing memorandum. ME R USDCT Rule 7(c).

6. *DISTRICT OF MAINE: Appearances.* An attorney's signature to a pleading shall constitute an appearance for the party filing the pleading. Otherwise, an attorney who wishes to participate in any manner in any action must file a formal written appearance identifying the party represented. An appearance whether by pleading or formal written appearance shall be signed by an attorney in his/her individual name and shall state his/her office address. ME R USDCT Rule 83.2(a). For more information, refer to ME R USDCT Rule 83.2.

7. *DISTRICT OF MAINE: Alternative dispute resolution (ADR).* Litigants are authorized and encouraged to employ, at their own expense, any available ADR process on which they can agree, including early neutral evaluation, settlement conferences, mediation, non-binding summary jury trial, corporate mini-trial, and arbitration proceedings. ME R USDCT Rule 83.11(a). For more information on ADR, refer to ME R USDCT Rule 83.11.

D. Documents

1. *Documents for moving party*

    a. *Required documents*

        i. *Notice of motion and motion.* Refer to the "C. General Requirements" section of this KeyRules document for information on the notice of motion and motion.

          • *DISTRICT OF MAINE: Memorandum of law.* Every motion shall incorporate a memorandum of law, including citations and supporting authorities. ME R USDCT Rule 7(a). Refer to the "E. Format" section of this KeyRules document for the form of memoranda of law.

          • *Certificate of service.* No certificate of service is required when a paper is served by filing it with the court's electronic-filing system. When a paper that is required to be served is served by other means: (i) if the paper is filed, a certificate of service must be filed with it or within a reasonable time after service; and (ii) if the paper is not filed, a certificate of service need not be filed unless filing is required by court order or by local rule. FRCP 5(d)(1)(B).

    b. *Supplemental documents*

        i. *Supporting evidence.* When a motion relies on facts outside the record, the court may hear the matter on affidavits or may hear it wholly or partly on oral testimony or on depositions. FRCP 43(c).

          • *DISTRICT OF MAINE: Affidavits and other supporting documents.* Any affidavits and other documents setting forth or evidencing facts on which the motion is based must be filed with the motion. ME R USDCT Rule 7(a).

          • *DISTRICT OF MAINE: Discovery transcripts or materials.* A party relying on discovery transcripts or materials in support of or in opposition to a motion shall file excerpts of such transcript or materials with the memorandum required by ME R USDCT Rule 7 as well as a list of specific citations to the parts on which the party relies. ME R USDCT Rule 26(c). Excerpts of depositions in support of or in opposition to a motion shall be filed electronically using ECF, unless otherwise permitted by the court. ME R USDCT App. 4(l)(3).

        ii. *Notice of constitutional question.* A party that files a pleading, written motion, or other paper drawing into question the constitutionality of a federal or state statute must promptly: (1) file a notice of constitutional question stating the question and identifying the paper that raises it, if: (A) a federal statute is questioned and the parties do not include the United States, one of its agencies, or one of its officers or employees in an official capacity; or (B) a state statute is questioned and the parties do not include the state, one of its agencies, or one of its officers or employees in an official capacity; and (2) serve the notice and paper on the Attorney General of the United States if a federal statute is questioned—or on the state attorney general if a state statute is questioned—either by certified or registered mail or by sending it to an electronic address designated by the attorney general for this purpose. FRCP 5.1(a).

          • *No forfeiture.* A party's failure to file and serve the notice, or the court's failure to certify, does not forfeit a constitutional claim or defense that is otherwise timely asserted. FRCP 5.1(d).

        iii. *Nongovernmental corporate disclosure statement.* A nongovernmental corporate party must file two (2) copies of a disclosure statement that: (1) identifies any parent corporation and any publicly held corporation owning ten percent (10%) or more of its stock; or (2) states that there is no such corporation. FRCP 7.1(a). A party must: (1) file the disclosure statement with its first appearance, pleading, petition, motion, response, or other request addressed to the court; and (2) promptly file a supplemental statement if any required information changes. FRCP 7.1(b).

- *DISTRICT OF MAINE: Notice of interested parties.* To enable the court to evaluate possible disqualification or recusal, counsel for all non-governmental parties shall file with their first appearance a Notice of Interested Parties, which shall list all persons, associations of persons, firms, partnerships, limited liability companies, joint ventures, corporations (including parent or affiliated corporations, clearly identified as such), or any similar entities, owning ten percent (10%) or more of the named party. Counsel shall be under a continuing obligation to file an amended Notice if any material change occurs in the status of an Interested Party, such as through merger, acquisition, or new/additional membership. ME R USDCT Rule 7.1.

   iv. *DISTRICT OF MAINE: Additional supplemental documents*

- *Proposed order.* Proposed orders shall not be filed unless requested by the court. When requested by the court, proposed orders shall be filed by e-mail in word processing format. ME R USDCT App. 4(k)(1).

2. *Documents for opposing party*

  a. *Required documents*

    i. *Opposition.* Refer to the "C. General Requirements" section of this KeyRules document for information on the opposing papers.

- *DISTRICT OF MAINE: Memorandum of law.* Unless within twenty-one (21) days after the filing of a motion the opposing party files written objection thereto, incorporating a memorandum of law, the opposing party shall be deemed to have waived objection. ME R USDCT Rule 7(b).

- *Certificate of service.* No certificate of service is required when a paper is served by filing it with the court's electronic-filing system. When a paper that is required to be served is served by other means: (i) if the paper is filed, a certificate of service must be filed with it or within a reasonable time after service; and (ii) if the paper is not filed, a certificate of service need not be filed unless filing is required by court order or by local rule. FRCP 5(d)(1)(B).

  b. *Supplemental documents*

    i. *Supporting evidence.* When a motion relies on facts outside the record, the court may hear the matter on affidavits or may hear it wholly or partly on oral testimony or on depositions. FRCP 43(c).

- *DISTRICT OF MAINE: Affidavits and other supporting documents.* Any objections shall include. . .affidavits and other documents setting forth or evidencing facts on which the objection is based. ME R USDCT Rule 7(b).

- *DISTRICT OF MAINE: Discovery transcripts or materials.* A party relying on discovery transcripts or materials in support of or in opposition to a motion shall file excerpts of such transcript or materials with the memorandum required by ME R USDCT Rule 7 as well as a list of specific citations to the parts on which the party relies. ME R USDCT Rule 26(c). Excerpts of depositions in support of or in opposition to a motion shall be filed electronically using ECF, unless otherwise permitted by the court. ME R USDCT App. 4(l)(3).

    ii. *Notice of constitutional question.* A party that files a pleading, written motion, or other paper drawing into question the constitutionality of a federal or state statute must promptly: (1) file a notice of constitutional question stating the question and identifying the paper that raises it, if: (A) a federal statute is questioned and the parties do not include the United States, one of its agencies, or one of its officers or employees in an official capacity; or (B) a state statute is questioned and the parties do not include the state, one of its agencies, or one of its officers or employees in an official capacity; and (2) serve the notice and paper on the Attorney General of the United States if a federal statute is questioned—or on the state attorney general if a state statute is questioned—either by certified or registered mail or by sending it to an electronic address designated by the attorney general for this purpose. FRCP 5.1(a).

- *No forfeiture.* A party's failure to file and serve the notice, or the court's failure to certify, does not forfeit a constitutional claim or defense that is otherwise timely asserted. FRCP 5.1(d).

E. Format

1. *Form of documents.* The rules governing captions and other matters of form in pleadings apply to motions and other papers. FRCP 7(b)(2).

   a. *DISTRICT OF MAINE: Font size, line spacing, and paper size.* All such documents shall be typed in a font of no less than size twelve (12) point, and shall be double-spaced or printed on eight and one-half by eleven (8-1/2 x 11) inch paper. Footnotes shall be in a font of no less than size ten (10) point, and may be single spaced. ME R USDCT Rule 10.

   b. *Caption.* Every pleading must have a caption with the court's name, a title, a file number, and an FRCP 7(a) designation. FRCP 10(a).

      i. *Names of parties.* The title of the complaint must name all the parties; the title of other pleadings, after naming the first party on each side, may refer generally to other parties. FRCP 10(a).

      ii. *DISTRICT OF MAINE: Additional caption requirements.* All pleadings, motions and other papers filed with the clerk or otherwise submitted to the court, except exhibits, shall bear the proper case number and shall contain on the first page a caption as described by FRCP 10(a) and immediately thereunder a designation of what the document is and the name of the party in whose behalf it is submitted. ME R USDCT Rule 10.

   c. *Claims or defenses*

      i. *Numbered paragraphs.* A party must state its claims or defenses in numbered paragraphs, each limited as far as practicable to a single set of circumstances. A later pleading may refer by number to a paragraph in an earlier pleading. FRCP 10(b).

      ii. *Separate statements.* If doing so would promote clarity, each claim founded on a separate transaction or occurrence—and each defense other than a denial—must be stated in a separate count or defense. FRCP 10(b).

   d. *Adoption by reference.* A statement in a pleading may be adopted by reference elsewhere in the same pleading or in any other pleading or motion. FRCP 10(c).

      i. *Exhibits.* A copy of a written instrument that is an exhibit to a pleading is a part of the pleading for all purposes. FRCP 10(c).

   e. *DISTRICT OF MAINE: Page numbering.* All pages shall be numbered at the bottom. ME R USDCT Rule 10.

   f. *DISTRICT OF MAINE: Attachment of ancillary papers.* Ancillary papers shall be attached at the end of the document to which they relate. ME R USDCT Rule 10.

   g. *Acceptance by the clerk.* The clerk must not refuse to file a paper solely because it is not in the form prescribed by the Federal Rules of Civil Procedure or by a local rule or practice. FRCP 5(d)(4).

2. *Form of electronic documents.* A paper filed electronically is a written paper for purposes of the Federal Rules of Civil Procedure. FRCP 5(d)(3)(D).

   a. *DISTRICT OF MAINE: Document format.* The ECF system only accepts documents in a portable document format (PDF). Although there are two types of PDF documents—electronically converted PDF's and scanned PDF's—only electronically converted PDF's may be filed with the court using the ECF system, unless otherwise authorized by local rule or order. ME R USDCT App. 4. Any document or exhibit to be filed or submitted to the court shall not be password-protected or encrypted. ME R USDCT App. 4(g)(12).

      i. *Electronically converted PDFs.* Electronically converted PDF's are created from word processing documents (MS Word, WordPerfect, etc.) using Adobe Acrobat or similar software. They are text searchable and their file size is small. ME R USDCT App. 4. Software used to electronically convert documents to PDF which includes proprietary or advertisement information within the PDF document is prohibited. ME R USDCT App. 4.

      ii. *Scanned PDFs.* Scanned PDF's are created from paper documents run through an optical scanner. Scanned PDF's are not searchable and have a large file size. ME R USDCT App. 4.

   b. *DISTRICT OF MAINE: Title.* All pleadings filed electronically shall be titled in accordance with the approved dictionary of civil or criminal events of the ECF system of the United States District Court for the District of Maine. ME R USDCT App. 4(d)(3).

   c. *DISTRICT OF MAINE: Attachments.* Attachments to filings and exhibits must be filed in accordance with the court's ECF User Manual, unless otherwise ordered by the court. ME R USDCT App. 4(j). When there are fifty (50) or fewer attachments to a pleading, the attachments must be filed by counsel electronically using ECF. When there are more than fifty (50) attachments, the attachments must be filed in one of the following ways: (A) using ECF, simply attach them to the pleading being filed; (B) using ECF, use the "Additional Attachments" menu item; (C) on paper; or (D) on a properly labeled three and one-half (3-1/2) inch floppy disk, CD or DVD. ME R USDCT App. 4(j)(2). Attachments filed on paper or on disk must contain a comprehensive index that clearly describes each document. ME R USDCT App. 4(j)(2).

    i. A filing user must submit as attachments only those excerpts of the referenced documents that are directly germane to the matter under consideration by the court. Excerpted material must be clearly and prominently identified as such. Users who file excerpts of documents do so without prejudice to their right to timely file additional excerpts or the complete document, as may be allowed by the court. Responding parties may timely file additional excerpts or the complete document that they believe are directly germane. ME R USDCT App. 4(j)(3).

    ii. Filers shall not attach as an exhibit any pleading or other paper already on file with the court in that case, but shall merely refer to that document. ME R USDCT App. 4(j)(4).

  d. *DISTRICT OF MAINE: Compliance with technical standards.* All documents filed by electronic means must comply with technical standards, if any, established by the Judicial Conference of the United States or by the United States District Court for the District of Maine. ME R USDCT App. 4(a)(3).

3. *DISTRICT OF MAINE: Form of memoranda of law.* All memoranda shall be typed, in a font of no less than size twelve (12) point, and shall be double-spaced on eight and one-half by eleven (8-1/2 x 11) inch paper or printed. Footnotes shall be in a font of no less than size ten (10) point, and may be single spaced. All pages shall be numbered at the bottom. ME R USDCT Rule 7(d).

  a. *Page limitations.* No memorandum of law in support of or in opposition to a motion to dismiss, a motion for judgment on the pleadings, a motion for summary judgment or a motion for injunctive relief shall exceed twenty (20) pages. ME R USDCT Rule 7(d). No reply memorandum shall exceed seven (7) pages. ME R USDCT Rule 7(d); ME R USDCT Rule 7(c).

    i. *Motion to exceed page limitation.* A motion to exceed the limitation of ME R USDCT Rule 7 shall be filed no later than three (3) business days in advance of the date for filing the memorandum to permit meaningful review by the court. A motion to exceed the page limitations shall not be filed simultaneously with a memorandum in excess of the limitations of ME R USDCT Rule 7. ME R USDCT Rule 7(d).

4. *Signing of pleadings, motions and other papers*

  a. *Signature.* Every pleading, written motion, and other paper must be signed by at least one attorney of record in the attorney's name—or by a party personally if the party is unrepresented. The paper must state the signer's address, e-mail address, and telephone number. FRCP 11(a).

    i. *No verification or accompanying affidavit required for pleadings.* Unless a rule or statute specifically states otherwise, a pleading need not be verified or accompanied by an affidavit. FRCP 11(a).

    ii. *Unsigned papers.* The court must strike an unsigned paper unless the omission is promptly corrected after being called to the attorney's or party's attention. FRCP 11(a).

  b. *Electronic signing.* A filing made through a person's electronic-filing account and authorized by that person, together with that person's name on a signature block, constitutes the person's signature. FRCP 5(d)(3)(C).

    i. *DISTRICT OF MAINE: Attorneys.* The user log-in and password together with a user's name on the signature block constitutes the attorney's signature pursuant to the Federal Rules of Civil Procedure and the Local Rules of the United States District Court for the District of Maine. All electronically filed documents must include a signature block and must set forth the attorney's name, address, telephone number and e-mail address. The name of the ECF user under whose log-in and password the document is submitted must be preceded by a "/s/" in the space where the signature would otherwise appear. ME R USDCT App. 4(h)(1).

    ii. *DISTRICT OF MAINE: Multiple signatures.* The filer of any document requiring more than one signature (e.g., pleadings filed by visiting lawyers, stipulations, joint status reports) must list thereon all the names of other signatories, preceded by a "/s/" in the space where the signatures would otherwise appear. By submitting such a document, the filing attorney certifies that each of the other signatories has expressly agreed to the form and substance of the document and that the filing attorney has their actual authority to submit the document electronically. ME R USDCT App. 4(h)(2). For more information, refer to ME R USDCT App. 4(h)(2).

    iii. *DISTRICT OF MAINE: Documents signed under oath.* Affidavits, declarations, verified complaints, or any other document signed under oath shall be filed electronically. The electronically filed version shall contain the typed name of the signatory, preceded by a "/s/" in the space where the signature would otherwise appear

68

indicating that the paper document bears an original signature. ME R USDCT Rule 10; ME R USDCT App. 4(h)(3). For more information, refer to ME R USDCT Rule 10.

c. *Representations to the court.* By presenting to the court a pleading, written motion, or other paper—whether by signing, filing, submitting, or later advocating it—an attorney or unrepresented party certifies that to the best of the person's knowledge, information, and belief, formed after an inquiry reasonable under the circumstances: (1) it is not being presented for any improper purpose, such as to harass, cause unnecessary delay, or needlessly increase the cost of litigation; (2) the claims, defenses, and other legal contentions are warranted by existing law or by a nonfrivolous argument for extending, modifying, or reversing existing law or for establishing new law; (3) the factual contentions have evidentiary support or, if specifically so identified, will likely have evidentiary support after a reasonable opportunity for further investigation or discovery; and (4) the denials of factual contentions are warranted on the evidence or, if specifically so identified, are reasonably based on belief or a lack of information. FRCP 11(b).

d. *Sanctions.* If, after notice and a reasonable opportunity to respond, the court determines that FRCP 11(b) has been violated, the court may impose an appropriate sanction on any attorney, law firm, or party that violated FRCP 11(b) or is responsible for the violation. FRCP 11(c)(1). Refer to the United States District Court for the District of Maine KeyRules Motion for Sanctions document for more information.

5. *Privacy protection for filings made with the court*

a. *Redacted filings.* Unless the court orders otherwise, in an electronic or paper filing with the court that contains an individual's Social Security number, taxpayer-identification number, or birth date, the name of an individual known to be a minor, or a financial-account number, a party or nonparty making the filing may include only: (1) the last four (4) digits of the Social Security number and taxpayer-identification number; (2) the year of the individual's birth; (3) the minor's initials; and (4) the last four (4) digits of the financial-account number. FRCP 5.2(a).

   i. *DISTRICT OF MAINE.* To address the privacy concerns created by the Internet access to court papers, unless otherwise ordered by the court, counsel shall modify certain personal data identifiers in pleadings and other papers as follows: (1) minors' names: use of the minors' initials only; (2) Social Security numbers: use of the last four (4) numbers only; (3) dates of birth: use of the year of birth only; [and] (4) financial account numbers: identify the type of account and the financial institution, but use only the last four (4) numbers of the account number. ME R USDCT Redacting Pleadings. Counsel should also use caution when filing papers that contain a person's medical records, employment history; financial information; and any proprietary or trade secret information. ME R USDCT Redacting Pleadings.

b. *Exemptions from the redaction requirement.* The redaction requirement does not apply to the following: (1) a financial-account number that identifies the property allegedly subject to forfeiture in a forfeiture proceeding; (2) the record of an administrative or agency proceeding; (3) the official record of a state-court proceeding; (4) the record of a court or tribunal, if that record was not subject to the redaction requirement when originally filed; (5) a filing covered by FRCP 5.2(c) or FRCP 5.2(d); and (6) a pro se filing in an action brought under 28 U.S.C.A. § 2241, 28 U.S.C.A. § 2254, or 28 U.S.C.A. § 2255. FRCP 5.2(b).

c. *Limitations on remote access to electronic files; Social Security appeals and immigration cases.* Unless the court orders otherwise, in an action for benefits under the Social Security Act, and in an action or proceeding relating to an order of removal, to relief from removal, or to immigration benefits or detention, access to an electronic file is authorized as follows: (1) the parties and their attorneys may have remote electronic access to any part of the case file, including the administrative record; (2) any other person may have electronic access to the full record at the courthouse, but may have remote electronic access only to: (A) the docket maintained by the court; and (B) an opinion, order, judgment, or other disposition of the court, but not any other part of the case file or the administrative record. FRCP 5.2(c).

d. *Filings made under seal.* The court may order that a filing be made under seal without redaction. The court may later unseal the filing or order the person who made the filing to file a redacted version for the public record. FRCP 5.2(d).

   i. *DISTRICT OF MAINE.* For information on filing sealed documents in the District of Maine, refer to ME R USDCT Rule 7A, ME R USDCT App. 4(p)(2), and ME R USDCT Sealed Filings.

e. *Protective orders.* For good cause, the court may by order in a case: (1) require redaction of additional information; or (2) limit or prohibit a nonparty's remote electronic access to a document filed with the court. FRCP 5.2(e).

f. *Option for additional unredacted filing under seal.* A person making a redacted filing may also file an unredacted copy under seal. The court must retain the unredacted copy as part of the record. FRCP 5.2(f).

   i. *DISTRICT OF MAINE.* A party wishing to file a document containing the personal data identifiers specified

above may. . . .file an unredacted document under seal. This document will be retained by the clerk's office as part of the record. ME R USDCT Redacting Pleadings. The court may, however, still require the party to file a redacted copy for the public file. ME R USDCT Redacting Pleadings.

    g. *Option for filing a reference list.* A filing that contains redacted information may be filed together with a reference list that identifies each item of redacted information and specifies an appropriate identifier that uniquely corresponds to each item listed. The list must be filed under seal and may be amended as of right. Any reference in the case to a listed identifier will be construed to refer to the corresponding item of information. FRCP 5.2(g).

        i. *DISTRICT OF MAINE.* A party wishing to file a document containing the personal data identifiers specified above may. . . .file a reference list under seal. The reference list shall contain the complete personal data identifier(s) and the redacted identifier(s) used in its (their) place in the filing. All references in the case to the redacted identifiers included in the reference list will be construed to refer to the corresponding complete identifier. The reference list must be filed under seal, and may be amended as of right. It shall be retained by the clerk's office as part of the record. ME R USDCT Redacting Pleadings. The court may, however, still require the party to file a redacted copy for the public file. ME R USDCT Redacting Pleadings.

    h. *DISTRICT OF MAINE: Responsibility for redaction.* The clerk is not required to review documents filed with the court for compliance with FRCP 5.2. The responsibility to redact filings rests with counsel and the party or nonparty making the filing. ME R USDCT App. 4(i); ME R USDCT Redacting Pleadings. For guidelines for filing confidential information in civil cases in the District of Maine, refer to ME R USDCT Confidentiality.

    i. *Waiver of protection of identifiers.* A person waives the protection of FRCP 5.2(a) as to the person's own information by filing it without redaction and not under seal. FRCP 5.2(h).

F. Filing and Service Requirements

    1. *Filing requirements*

        a. *Required filings.* Any paper after the complaint that is required to be served must be filed no later than a reasonable time after service. FRCP 5(d)(1).

        b. *DISTRICT OF MAINE: Place of filing.* Unless otherwise ordered by the court, papers shall be filed with the court at Bangor in cases filed and pending at Bangor, and at Portland in cases filed and pending at Portland. ME R USDCT Rule 5(a).

        c. *Nonelectronic filing.* A paper not filed electronically is filed by delivering it: (A) to the clerk; or (B) to a judge who agrees to accept it for filing, and who must then note the filing date on the paper and promptly send it to the clerk. FRCP 5(d)(2).

            i. *DISTRICT OF MAINE: Documents to be filed in paper.* The following documents shall be filed in paper, which may also be scanned into ECF by the clerk's office: (A) all handwritten pleadings; and (B) all pleadings and documents filed by pro se litigants who are incarcerated or who are not registered filing users in ECF. ME R USDCT App. 4(g)(8). Non-prisoner pro se litigants in civil actions may register with ECF or may file (and serve) all pleadings and other documents in paper. The clerk's office will scan into ECF any pleadings and documents filed on paper in accordance with ME R USDCT App. 4(g). ME R USDCT App. 4(o). For more information, refer to ME R USDCT App. 4(g).

        d. *Electronic filing*

            i. *DISTRICT OF MAINE: Authorization.* Unless exempt or otherwise ordered by the court, papers shall be filed and served electronically as required by the court's Administrative Procedures Governing the Filing and Service by Electronic Means, which is set forth in ME R USDCT App. 4. The provisions of the court's Administrative Procedures Governing the Filing and Service by Electronic Means (ME R USDCT App. 4) shall be applied and enforced as part of the Local Rules of the United States District Court for the District of Maine. ME R USDCT Rule 5(c).

           ii. *Filing by represented persons.* A person represented by an attorney must file electronically, unless nonelectronic filing is allowed by the court for good cause or is allowed or required by local rule. FRCP 5(d)(3)(A).

              ● *DISTRICT OF MAINE.* An attorney may apply to the court for permission to file paper documents. ME R USDCT App. 4(a)(5).

           iii. *Filing by unrepresented persons.* A person not represented by an attorney: (i) may file electronically only if allowed by court order or by local rule; and (ii) may be required to file electronically only by court order, or by a local rule that includes reasonable exceptions. FRCP 5(d)(3)(B).

              ● *DISTRICT OF MAINE.* Non-prisoner pro se litigants in civil actions may register with ECF or may file (and serve) all pleadings and other documents in paper. ME R USDCT App. 4(o). A non-prisoner who is a party to a civil action and who is not represented by an attorney may register to receive service electronically and to electronically transmit their documents to the court for filing in the ECF system. If during the course of the action the person retains an attorney who appears on the person's behalf, the clerk shall terminate the person's registration upon the attorney's appearance. ME R USDCT App. 4(b)(2).

iv. *DISTRICT OF MAINE: Scope of electronic filing.* All documents submitted for filing in civil and criminal cases, regardless of case commencement date, except those documents specifically exempted in ME R USDCT App. 4(g), shall be filed electronically using the electronic case filing system (ECF). ME R USDCT App. 4(a)(1). For special filing requirements and exceptions, refer to ME R USDCT App. 4(g).

v. *DISTRICT OF MAINE: Consequences of electronic filing.* Electronic transmission of a document to the ECF system, together with the transmission of a Notice of Electronic Filing (NEF) from the court, constitutes filing of the document for all purposes of the Federal Rules of Civil Procedure. ME R USDCT App. 4(d)(1).

vi. *DISTRICT OF MAINE: Review of documents.* Documents filed with the clerk's office will normally be reviewed no later than the close of the next business day. It is the responsibility of the filing party to promptly notify the clerk's office via telephone of a matter that requires the immediate attention of a judicial officer. ME R USDCT App. 4(a)(4).

e. *DISTRICT OF MAINE: Facsimile filing.* No papers shall be submitted to the court by means of a facsimile machine without prior leave of the court. ME R USDCT Rule 5(c); ME R USDCT App. 4(m).

2. *Service requirements*

a. *Service; When required.* Unless the Federal Rules of Civil Procedure provide otherwise, each of the following papers must be served on every party: (A) an order stating that service is required; (B) a pleading filed after the original complaint, unless the court orders otherwise under FRCP 5(c) because there are numerous defendants; (C) a discovery paper required to be served on a party, unless the court orders otherwise; (D) a written motion, except one that may be heard ex parte; and (E) a written notice, appearance, demand, or offer of judgment, or any similar paper. FRCP 5(a)(1).

i. *If a party fails to appear.* No service is required on a party who is in default for failing to appear. But a pleading that asserts a new claim for relief against such a party must be served on that party under FRCP 4. FRCP 5(a)(2).

ii. *Seizing property.* If an action is begun by seizing property and no person is or need be named as a defendant, any service required before the filing of an appearance, answer, or claim must be made on the person who had custody or possession of the property when it was seized. FRCP 5(a)(3).

b. *Service; How made.* A paper is served under FRCP 5 by: (A) handing it to the person; (B) leaving it: (i) at the person's office with a clerk or other person in charge or, if no one is in charge, in a conspicuous place in the office; or (ii) if the person has no office or the office is closed, at the person's dwelling or usual place of abode with someone of suitable age and discretion who resides there; (C) mailing it to the person's last known address—in which event service is complete upon mailing; (D) leaving it with the court clerk if the person has no known address; (E) sending it to a registered user by filing it with the court's electronic-filing system or sending it by other electronic means that the person consented to in writing—in either of which events service is complete upon filing or sending, but is not effective if the filer or sender learns that it did not reach the person to be served; or (F) delivering it by any other means that the person consented to in writing—in which event service is complete when the person making service delivers it to the agency designated to make delivery. FRCP 5(b)(2).

i. *Serving an attorney.* If a party is represented by an attorney, service under FRCP 5 must be made on the attorney unless the court orders service on the party. FRCP 5(b)(1).

c. *DISTRICT OF MAINE: Service of electronically filed documents*

i. *Registered users.* Registration [as a filing user of the court's ECF system] constitutes consent to service of all documents by electronic means as provided in ME R USDCT App. 4. ME R USDCT App. 4(b)(4). Whenever a non-sealed pleading is filed electronically, the ECF system will automatically generate and send a Notice of Electronic Filing (NEF) to the filing user and registered users of record. The user filing the document should retain a paper or digital copy of the NEF, which shall serve as the court's date-stamp and proof of filing. ME R USDCT App. 4(e)(1).

- *Sealed documents.* Although the filing of sealed documents in civil cases produces an NEF, the document itself cannot be accessed and counsel shall be responsible for making service of the sealed documents. ME R USDCT App. 4(e)(2).

    ii. *Non-registered users and pro se litigants.* Attorneys who have not yet registered as users with ECF and pro se litigants who have not registered with ECF shall be served a paper copy of any electronically filed pleading or other document in accordance with the provisions of FRCP 5. ME R USDCT App. 4(e)(3).

- *Registration of pro se litigants.* A non-prisoner who is a party to a civil action and who is not represented by an attorney may register to receive service electronically and to electronically transmit their documents to the court for filing in the ECF system. If during the course of the action the person retains an attorney who appears on the person's behalf, the clerk shall terminate the person's registration upon the attorney's appearance. ME R USDCT App. 4(b)(2).

  d. *Serving numerous defendants.* If an action involves an unusually large number of defendants, the court may, on motion or on its own, order that: (A) defendants' pleadings and replies to them need not be served on other defendants; (B) any crossclaim, counterclaim, avoidance, or affirmative defense in those pleadings and replies to them will be treated as denied or avoided by all other parties; and (C) filing any such pleading and serving it on the plaintiff constitutes notice of the pleading to all parties. FRCP 5(c)(1).

    i. *Notifying parties.* A copy of every such order must be served on the parties as the court directs. FRCP 5(c)(2).

3. *DISTRICT OF MAINE: Filing and service of highly sensitive documents (HSDs).* For information on filing and serving highly sensitive documents (HSDs) in the District of Maine, refer to ME R USDCT General Order 21-5.

G. Hearings

1. *Hearings, generally.* When a motion relies on facts outside the record, the court may hear the matter on affidavits or may hear it wholly or partly on oral testimony or on depositions. FRCP 43(c).

  a. *Oral argument.* Due process does not require that oral argument be permitted on a motion and, except as otherwise provided by local rule, the district court has discretion to determine whether it will decide the motion on the papers or hear argument by counsel (and perhaps receive evidence). FPP § 1190; F.D.I.C. v. Deglau, 207 F.3d 153 (3d Cir. 2000).

    i. *DISTRICT OF MAINE.* Unless otherwise required by federal rule or statute, all motions may be decided by the court without oral argument unless otherwise ordered by the court on its own motion or, in its discretion, upon request of counsel. ME R USDCT Rule 7(e).

  b. *Providing a regular schedule for oral hearings.* A court may establish regular times and places for oral hearings on motions. FRCP 78(a).

  c. *Providing for submission on briefs.* By rule or order, the court may provide for submitting and determining motions on briefs, without oral hearings. FRCP 78(b).

2. *Hearing on certain FRCP 12 defenses before trial.* If a party so moves, any defense listed in FRCP 12(b)(1) through FRCP 12(b)(7)—whether made in a pleading or by motion—and a motion under FRCP 12(c) must be heard and decided before trial unless the court orders a deferral until trial. FRCP 12(i).

H. Forms

1. Federal Motion to Dismiss for Improper Venue Forms

  a. Motion; For dismissal or transfer of action on grounds of improper venue; Diversity case. FEDPROF § 1:71.

  b. Motion; For dismissal; Improper venue; Lack of personal jurisdiction. FEDPROF § 1:72.

  c. Defense; Improper venue; Defendant resident of another district. FEDPROF § 1A:292.

  d. Motion; General form. FEDPROF § 1B:171.

  e. Notice; Of motion. FEDPROF § 1B:172.

  f. Notice; Of motion; With costs of motion. FEDPROF § 1B:173.

  g. Notice; Of motion; Containing motion. FEDPROF § 1B:174.

  h. Opposition; To motion. FEDPROF § 1B:175.

  i. Affidavit; Supporting or opposing motion. FEDPROF § 1B:176.

  j. Brief; Supporting or opposing motion. FEDPROF § 1B:177.

  k. Statement of points and authorities; Opposing motion. FEDPROF § 1B:178.

  l. Motion to dismiss; Improper venue; Diversity action. FEDPROF § 1C:101.

  m. Motion to dismiss; Improper venue; Action not founded solely on diversity. FEDPROF § 1C:102.

n. Motion to dismiss; Improper venue; Corporate defendant not subject to personal jurisdiction in district. FEDPROF § 1C:103.

o. Motion to dismiss; Improper venue; Action of local nature. FEDPROF § 1C:104.

p. Motion; To dismiss or, alternatively, to transfer action; Improper venue. FEDPROF § 1C:105.

q. Affidavit; In support of motion to dismiss for improper venue; Corporate defendant not subject to personal jurisdiction in district. FEDPROF § 1C:106.

r. Motion; To dismiss action for improper venue. FEDPROF § 22:66.

s. Motion to dismiss complaint; General form. GOLDLTGFMS § 20:24.

t. Affidavit in support of motion to dismiss complaint. GOLDLTGFMS § 20:32.

u. Motion; Federal form. GOLDLTGFMS § 45:4.

v. Affidavit in support of motion; Improper venue. GOLDLTGFMS § 45:15.

I. Applicable Rules

1. *Federal rules*

   a. Venue generally. 28 U.S.C.A. § 1391.

   b. Serving and filing pleadings and other papers. FRCP 5.

   c. Constitutional challenge to a statute; Notice, certification, and intervention. FRCP 5.1.

   d. Privacy protection for filings made with the court. FRCP 5.2.

   e. Computing and extending time; Time for motion papers. FRCP 6.

   f. Pleadings allowed; Form of motions and other papers. FRCP 7.

   g. Disclosure statement. FRCP 7.1.

   h. Form of pleadings. FRCP 10.

   i. Signing pleadings, motions, and other papers; Representations to the court; Sanctions. FRCP 11.

   j. Defenses and objections; When and how presented; Motion for judgment on the pleadings; Consolidating motions; Waiving defenses; Pretrial hearing. FRCP 12.

   k. Taking testimony. FRCP 43.

   l. Hearing motions; Submission on briefs. FRCP 78.

2. *Local rules*

   a. *DISTRICT OF MAINE*

      i. Service and filing of pleadings and other papers. ME R USDCT Rule 5.

      ii. Time. ME R USDCT Rule 6.

      iii. Motions and memoranda of law. ME R USDCT Rule 7.

      iv. Corporate disclosure. ME R USDCT Rule 7.1.

      v. Form of pleadings, motions and other papers. ME R USDCT Rule 10.

      vi. Discovery. ME R USDCT Rule 26.

      vii. Attorneys; Appearances and withdrawals. ME R USDCT Rule 83.2.

      viii. Alternative dispute resolution (ADR). ME R USDCT Rule 83.11.

      ix. Administrative procedures governing the filing and service by electronic means. ME R USDCT App. 4.

      x. Redacting pleadings. ME R USDCT Redacting Pleadings.

Motions, Oppositions and Replies
Motion for Leave to Amend

Document Last Updated April 2021

A. Checklist

- (I) ❏ Matters to be considered by moving party
  - (a) ❏ Required documents
    - (1) ❏ Notice of motion and motion
    - (2) ❏ Proposed amended pleading
  - (b) ❏ Supplemental documents
    - (1) ❏ Supporting evidence
    - (2) ❏ Notice of constitutional question
    - (3) ❏ DISTRICT OF MAINE: Additional supplemental documents
      - (i) ❏ Proposed order
  - (c) ❏ Timing
    - (1) ❏ Unlike amendments as of course, amendments under FRCP 15(a)(2) may be made at any stage of the litigation
    - (2) ❏ A party may move—at any time, even after judgment—to amend the pleadings to conform them to the evidence and to raise an unpleaded issue
    - (3) ❏ A written motion and notice of the hearing must be served at least fourteen (14) days before the time specified for the hearing, with the following exceptions: (A) when the motion may be heard ex parte; (B) when the Federal Rules of Civil Procedure set a different time; or (C) when a court order—which a party may, for good cause, apply for ex parte—sets a different time
    - (4) ❏ Any affidavit supporting a motion must be served with the motion
    - (5) ❏ DISTRICT OF MAINE: Additional timing
      - (i) ❏ Any affidavits and other documents setting forth or evidencing facts on which the motion is based must be filed with the motion
- (II) ❏ Matters to be considered by opposing party
  - (a) ❏ Required documents
    - (1) ❏ Opposition
  - (b) ❏ Supplemental documents
    - (1) ❏ Supporting evidence
    - (2) ❏ Notice of constitutional question
  - (c) ❏ Timing
    - (1) ❏ Except as FRCP 59(c) provides otherwise, any opposing affidavit must be served at least seven (7) days before the hearing, unless the court permits service at another time
    - (2) ❏ DISTRICT OF MAINE: Additional timing
      - (i) ❏ Unless within twenty-one (21) days after the filing of a motion the opposing party files written objection thereto, incorporating a memorandum of law, the opposing party shall be deemed to have waived objection

B. Timing

1. *Motion for leave to amend.* Unlike amendments as of course, amendments under FRCP 15(a)(2) may be made at any stage of the litigation. FPP § 1484.

   a. *Amendments to conform to the evidence.* A party may move—at any time, even after judgment—to amend the pleadings to conform them to the evidence and to raise an unpleaded issue. FRCP 15(b)(2).

74

b. *Time to respond to an amended pleading.* Unless the court orders otherwise, any required response to an amended pleading must be made within the time remaining to respond to the original pleading or within fourteen (14) days after service of the amended pleading, whichever is later. FRCP 15(a)(3).

2. *Timing of motions, generally*

   a. *Motion and notice of hearing.* A written motion and notice of the hearing must be served at least fourteen (14) days before the time specified for the hearing, with the following exceptions: (A) when the motion may be heard ex parte; (B) when the Federal Rules of Civil Procedure set a different time; or (C) when a court order—which a party may, for good cause, apply for ex parte—sets a different time. FRCP 6(c)(1).

   b. *Supporting affidavit.* Any affidavit supporting a motion must be served with the motion. FRCP 6(c)(2).

   c. *DISTRICT OF MAINE: Affidavits and other supporting documents.* Any affidavits and other documents setting forth or evidencing facts on which the motion is based must be filed with the motion. ME R USDCT Rule 7(a).

3. *Timing of opposing papers.* Except as FRCP 59(c) provides otherwise, any opposing affidavit must be served at least seven (7) days before the hearing, unless the court permits service at another time. FRCP 6(c)(2).

   a. *DISTRICT OF MAINE.* Unless within twenty-one (21) days after the filing of a motion the opposing party files written objection thereto, incorporating a memorandum of law, the opposing party shall be deemed to have waived objection. ME R USDCT Rule 7(b). The deemed waiver imposed in ME R USDCT Rule 7(b) shall not apply to motions filed during trial. ME R USDCT Rule 7(b).

4. *Timing of reply papers.* Where the respondent files an answering affidavit setting up a new matter, the moving party ordinarily is allowed a reasonable time to file a reply affidavit since failure to deny the new matter by affidavit may operate as an admission of its truth. AMJUR MOTIONS § 25.

   a. *DISTRICT OF MAINE.* Within fourteen (14) days of the filing of any objection to a motion, the moving party may file a reply memorandum. ME R USDCT Rule 7(c).

5. *Computation of time*

   a. *Computing time.* FRCP 6 applies in computing any time period specified in the Federal Rules of Civil Procedure, in any local rule or court order, or in any statute that does not specify a method of computing time. FRCP 6(a).

      i. *Period stated in days or a longer unit.* When the period is stated in days or a longer unit of time: (A) exclude the day of the event that triggers the period; (B) count every day, including intermediate Saturdays, Sundays, and legal holidays; and (C) include the last day of the period, but if the last day is a Saturday, Sunday, or legal holiday, the period continues to run until the end of the next day that is not a Saturday, Sunday, or legal holiday. FRCP 6(a)(1).

      ii. *Period stated in hours.* When the period is stated in hours: (A) begin counting immediately on the occurrence of the event that triggers the period; (B) count every hour, including hours during intermediate Saturdays, Sundays, and legal holidays; and (C) if the period would end on a Saturday, Sunday, or legal holiday, the period continues to run until the same time on the next day that is not a Saturday, Sunday, or legal holiday. FRCP 6(a)(2).

      iii. *Inaccessibility of the clerk's office.* Unless the court orders otherwise, if the clerk's office is inaccessible: (A) on the last day for filing under FRCP 6(a)(1), then the time for filing is extended to the first accessible day that is not a Saturday, Sunday, or legal holiday; or (B) during the last hour for filing under FRCP 6(a)(2), then the time for filing is extended to the same time on the first accessible day that is not a Saturday, Sunday, or legal holiday. FRCP 6(a)(3).

      iv. *"Last day" defined.* Unless a different time is set by a statute, local rule, or court order, the last day ends: (A) for electronic filing, at midnight in the court's time zone; and (B) for filing by other means, when the clerk's office is scheduled to close. FRCP 6(a)(4).

      v. *"Next day" defined.* The "next day" is determined by continuing to count forward when the period is measured after an event and backward when measured before an event. FRCP 6(a)(5).

      vi. *"Legal holiday" defined.* "Legal holiday" means: (A) the day set aside by statute for observing New Year's Day, Martin Luther King Jr.'s Birthday, Washington's Birthday, Memorial Day, Independence Day, Labor Day, Columbus Day, Veterans' Day, Thanksgiving Day, or Christmas Day; (B) any day declared a holiday by the President or Congress; and (C) for periods that are measured after an event, any other day declared a holiday by the state where the district court is located. FRCP 6(a)(6).

      vii. *DISTRICT OF MAINE: Applicability of FRCP 6.* FRCP 6 applies when computing any period of time stated in the Local Rules of the United States District Court for the District of Maine. ME R USDCT Rule 6(a).

b. *DISTRICT OF MAINE: Computation of electronic filing deadlines.* Filing documents electronically does not in any way alter any filing deadlines. All electronic transmissions of documents must be completed prior to midnight, Eastern Time, in order to be considered timely filed that day. Where a specific time of day deadline is set by court order or stipulation, the electronic filing must be completed by that time. ME R USDCT App. 4(f). A document filed electronically shall be deemed filed at the time and date stated on the Notice of Electronic Filing received from the court. ME R USDCT App. 4(d)(2).

    i. *Technical failures.* A filing user whose filing is made untimely as the result of a technical failure may seek appropriate relief from the court. ME R USDCT App. 4(n). A technical failure of the court's ECF system is deemed to have occurred when the court's ECF site cannot accept filings continuously or intermittently over the course of any period of time greater than one (1) hour. Known system outages will be posted on the court's website along with guidance on how to proceed, if applicable. ME R USDCT App. 4(n).

c. *Extending time.* When an act may or must be done within a specified time, the court may, for good cause, extend the time: (A) with or without motion or notice if the court acts, or if a request is made, before the original time or its extension expires; or (B) on motion made after the time has expired if the party failed to act because of excusable neglect. FRCP 6(b)(1). A court must not extend the time to act under FRCP 50(b), FRCP 50(d), FRCP 52(b), FRCP 59(b), FRCP 59(d), FRCP 59(e), and FRCP 60(b). FRCP 6(b)(2). Refer to the United States District Court for the District of Maine KeyRules Motion for Continuance/Extension of Time document for more information on extending time.

d. *Additional time after certain kinds of service.* When a party may or must act within a specified time after being served and service is made under FRCP 5(b)(2)(C) (by mail), FRCP 5(b)(2)(D) (by leaving with the clerk), or FRCP 5(b)(2)(F) (by other means consented to), three (3) days are added after the period would otherwise expire under FRCP 6(a). FRCP 6(d).

C. General Requirements

1. *Motions, generally*

a. *Motion requirements.* A request for a court order must be made by motion. The motion must: (A) be in writing unless made during a hearing or trial; (B) state with particularity the grounds for seeking the order; and (C) state the relief sought. FRCP 7(b)(1). The writing and particularity requirements are intended to ensure that the adverse parties are informed of and have a record of both the motion's pendency and the grounds on which the movant seeks an order. FPP § 1191; Feldberg v. Quechee Lakes Corp., 463 F.3d 195 (2d Cir. 2006).

    i. *Particularity requirement.* The particularity requirement [ensures] that the opposing parties will have notice of their opponent's contentions. FEDPROC § 62:358; Goodman v. 1973 26 Foot Trojan Vessel, Arkansas Registration No. AR1439SN, 859 F.2d 71 (8th Cir. 1988). That requirement ensures that notice of the basis for the motion is provided to the court and to the opposing party so as to avoid prejudice, provide the opponent with a meaningful opportunity to respond, and provide the court with enough information to process the motion correctly. FEDPROC § 62:358; Andreas v. Volkswagen of Am., Inc., 336 F.3d 789 (8th Cir. 2003).

        • Reasonable specification of the grounds for a motion is sufficient. The particularity requirement for motions is satisfied when no party is prejudiced by a lack of particularity or when the court can comprehend the basis for the motion and deal with it fairly. However, where a movant fails to state even one ground for granting the motion in question, the movant has failed to meet the minimal standard of "reasonable specification." FEDPROC § 62:358; Martinez v. Trainor, 556 F.2d 818 (7th Cir. 1977).

        • The court may excuse the failure to comply with the particularity requirement if it is inadvertent, and where no prejudice is shown by the opposing party. FEDPROC § 62:358.

b. *Notice of motion.* A party interested in resisting the relief sought by a motion has a right to notice thereof, and an opportunity to be heard. AMJUR MOTIONS § 12.

    i. *Purpose.* In addition to statutory or court rule provisions requiring notice of a motion—the purpose of such a notice requirement having been said to be to prevent a party from being prejudicially surprised by a motion—principles of natural justice dictate that an adverse party generally must be given notice that a motion will be presented to the court. AMJUR MOTIONS § 12.

    ii. *Adequacy of notice.* The test of adequate notice generally turns on whether the other parties were afforded an adequate opportunity to prepare and respond to the issues to be raised in the proceeding. AMJUR MOTIONS § 12.

c. *Single document containing motion and notice.* A single written document can satisfy the writing requirements both for a motion and for an FRCP 6(c)(1) notice. FRCP 7(Advisory Committee Notes).

2. *Motion for leave to amend.* FRCP 15(a)(2) provides that after a party has amended a pleading once as of course or the time for amendments of that type has expired, a party may amend only by obtaining leave of the court or if the adverse party consents to it. FPP § 1484; In re Cessna Distributorship Antitrust Litig., 532 F.2d 64 (8th Cir. 1976). FRCP 15(a) does not set forth any specific procedure for obtaining leave to amend. Typically, it is sought by a motion addressed to the court's discretion. FPP § 1485.

    a. *Pleadings to be amended.* As in the case of amendments as of course under FRCP 15(a)(1), any of the pleadings enumerated in FRCP 7(a) may be amended with the court's leave and FRCP 15 does not restrict the purposes for which an amendment may be made or its character. FPP § 1484.

    b. *Prerequisites for leave to amend.* The only prerequisites are that the district court have jurisdiction over the case and an appeal must not be pending. FPP § 1484. If these two conditions are met, the court will proceed to examine the effect and the timing of the proposed amendments to determine whether they would prejudice the rights of any of the other parties to the suit. FPP § 1484; Nilsen v. City of Moss Point, Miss., 674 F.2d 379, 388 (5th Cir. 1982), on reh'g, 701 F.2d 556 (5th Cir. 1983).

    c. *When leave or consent is not obtained.* In general, if an amendment that cannot be made as of right is served without obtaining the court's leave or the opposing party's consent, it is without legal effect and any new matter it contains will not be considered unless the amendment is resubmitted for the court's approval. Some courts have held, however, that an untimely amended pleading served without judicial permission may be considered as properly introduced when leave to amend would have been granted had it been sought and when it does not appear that any of the parties will be prejudiced by allowing the change. FPP § 1484.

    d. *Form.* A motion to amend under FRCP 15(a), as is true of motions generally, is subject to the requirements of FRCP 7(b), and must set forth with particularity the relief or order requested and the grounds supporting the application. In order to satisfy these prerequisites a copy of the amendment should be submitted with the motion so that the court and the adverse party know the precise nature of the pleading changes being proposed. FPP § 1485.

    e. *Oral motion for leave to amend.* Leave to amend also may be requested in open court instead of by formal motion. Courts have held that an oral request to amend a pleading that is made before the court in the presence of opposing party's counsel may be sufficient if the adverse party is put on notice of the nature and purpose of the request and is given the same opportunity to present objections to the proposed amendment as would have occurred if a formal motion had been made. FPP § 1485.

    f. *Conditions imposed on leave to amend.* While FRCP 15(a) does not specifically authorize the district court to impose conditions on its granting of leave to amend, it is well settled that the court may impose such conditions to avoid or minimize any prejudice to the opposing party. FEDPROC § 62:270. Conditions frequently are imposed because the amending party knew of the facts sought to be asserted in the amendment but failed to assert such facts until later, to the prejudice of the opposing party. Conversely, the court may decline to impose conditions where the amendment was asserted with relative promptness. FEDPROC § 62:270.

      i. The moving party's refusal to comply with the conditions imposed by the court normally will result in a denial of the right to amend. FPP § 1486.

    g. *When leave to amend may be granted.* The Supreme Court, in its opinion in Foman v. Davis, enunciated the following general standard, which is to be employed under FRCP 15(a) by the district courts: If the underlying facts or circumstances relied upon by a plaintiff may be a proper subject of relief, he ought to be afforded an opportunity to test his claim on the merits. In the absence of any apparent or declared reason—such as undue delay, bad faith or dilatory motive on the part of the movant, repeated failure to cure deficiencies by amendments previously allowed, undue prejudice to the opposing party by virtue of allowance of the amendment, futility of amendment, etc.—the leave sought should, as the rules require, be "freely given." FPP § 1487; Foman v. Davis, 371 U.S. 178, 182, 83 S. Ct. 227, 230, 9 L. Ed. 2d 222 (1962).

3. *Amendments, generally*

    a. *Amendments before trial.* The function of FRCP 15(a), which provides generally for the amendment of pleadings, is to enable a party to assert matters that were overlooked or were unknown at the time the party interposed the original complaint or answer. FPP § 1473; Smiga v. Dean Witter Reynolds, Inc., 766 F.2d 698, 703 (2d Cir. 1985).

      i. *Matters contained in amended pleading under FRCP 15(a).* Although FRCP 15(a) does not expressly state that an amendment must contain only matters that occurred within a particular time period, FRCP 15(d) provides that any "transaction, occurrence, or event that happened after the date of the pleading" should be set forth in a supplemental pleading. FPP § 1473. Thus, impliedly, an amended pleading, whether prepared with or without leave of court, only should relate to matters that have taken place prior to the date of the earlier pleading. FPP § 1473; Ford Motor Co. v. United States, 896 F. Supp. 1224, 1230 (Ct. Int'l Trade 1995).

    ii.   *Amending as a matter of course.* A party may amend its pleading once as a matter of course within: (A) twenty-one (21) days after serving it, or (B) if the pleading is one to which a responsive pleading is required, twenty-one (21) days after service of a responsive pleading or twenty-one (21) days after service of a motion under FRCP 12(b), FRCP 12(e), or FRCP 12(f), whichever is earlier. FRCP 15(a)(1). Refer to the United States District Court for the District of Maine KeyRules Amended Pleading document for more information on amending as a matter of course.

    iii.   *Other amendments.* In all other cases, a party may amend its pleading only with the opposing party's written consent or the court's leave. The court should freely give leave when justice so requires. FRCP 15(a)(2).

    iv.   *Types of amendments permitted under FRCP 15(a)*

- *Cure a defective pleading.* Perhaps the most common use of FRCP 15(a) is by a party seeking to amend in order to cure a defective pleading. FPP § 1474.

- *Correct insufficiently stated claims or defenses.* A more common use of FRCP 15(a) amendments is to correct insufficiently stated claims or defenses. Typically, amendments of this character involve either adding a necessary allegation in order to state a claim for relief or correcting a misnomer of a party to the action. FPP § 1474.

- *Change nature or theory of claim or capacity of party.* Courts also have allowed a party to amend in order to change the nature or theory of the party's claim or the capacity in which the party is bringing the action. FPP § 1474.

- *State additional claims or defenses or drop claims or defenses.* Plaintiffs and defendants also have been permitted to amend their pleadings to state additional claims, to assert additional defenses, or to drop claims or defenses. FPP § 1474; Weinberger v. Retail Credit Co., 498 F.2d 552, 554, n.4 (4th Cir. 1974).

- *Increase amount of damages or elect a different remedy.* An FRCP 15(a) amendment also is appropriate for increasing the amount of damages sought, or for electing a different remedy than the one originally requested. FPP § 1474; McFadden v. Sanchez, 710 F.2d 907 (2d Cir. 1983).

- *Add, substitute, or drop parties.* Finally, a party may make an FRCP 15(a) amendment to add, substitute, or drop parties to the action. FPP § 1474.

  b. *Amendments during and after trial*

    i.   *Based on an objection at trial.* If, at trial, a party objects that evidence is not within the issues raised in the pleadings, the court may permit the pleadings to be amended. The court should freely permit an amendment when doing so will aid in presenting the merits and the objecting party fails to satisfy the court that the evidence would prejudice that party's action or defense on the merits. The court may grant a continuance to enable the objecting party to meet the evidence. FRCP 15(b)(1).

    ii.   *For issues tried by consent.* When an issue not raised by the pleadings is tried by the parties' express or implied consent, it must be treated in all respects as if raised in the pleadings. A party may move—at any time, even after judgment—to amend the pleadings to conform them to the evidence and to raise an unpleaded issue. But failure to amend does not affect the result of the trial of that issue. FRCP 15(b)(2).

  c. *Relation back of amendments*

    i.   *When an amendment relates back.* An amendment to a pleading relates back to the date of the original pleading when: (A) the law that provides the applicable statute of limitations allows relation back; (B) the amendment asserts a claim or defense that arose out of the conduct, transaction, or occurrence set out—or attempted to be set out—in the original pleading; or (C) the amendment changes the party or the naming of the party against whom a claim is asserted, if FRCP 15(c)(1)(B) is satisfied and if, within the period provided by FRCP 4(m) for serving the summons and complaint, the party to be brought in by amendment: (i) received such notice of the action that it will not be prejudiced in defending on the merits; and (ii) knew or should have known that the action would have been brought against it, but for a mistake concerning the proper party's identity. FRCP 15(c)(1).

    ii.   *Notice to the United States.* When the United States or a United States officer or agency is added as a defendant by amendment, the notice requirements of FRCP 15(c)(1)(C)(i) and FRCP 15(c)(1)(C)(ii) are satisfied if, during the stated period, process was delivered or mailed to the United States attorney or the United States attorney's designee, to the Attorney General of the United States, or to the officer or agency. FRCP 15(c)(2).

  d. *Effect of an amended pleading.* A pleading that has been amended under FRCP 15(a) supersedes the pleading it modifies and remains in effect throughout the action unless it subsequently is modified. FPP § 1476. Once an amended pleading is interposed, the original pleading no longer performs any function in the case and any subsequent motion made by an opposing party should be directed at the amended pleading. FPP § 1476; Ferdik v. Bonzelet, 963 F.2d 1258, 1262 (9th Cir. 1992), as amended (May 22, 1992); Davis v. TXO Prod. Corp., 929 F.2d 1515, 1517 (10th Cir. 1991).

4. *Opposing papers.* The Federal Rules of Civil Procedure do not require any formal answer, return, or reply to a motion, except where the Federal Rules of Civil Procedure or local rules may require affidavits, memoranda, or other papers to be filed in opposition to a motion. Such papers are simply to apprise the court of such opposition and the grounds of that opposition. FEDPROC § 62:353.

   a. *DISTRICT OF MAINE: Content of objections.* Any objections shall include citations and supporting authorities and affidavits and other documents setting forth or evidencing facts on which the objection is based. ME R USDCT Rule 7(b).

   b. *Effect of failure to respond to motion.* Although in the absence of statutory provision or court rule, a motion ordinarily does not require a response or written answer, when a party files a motion and the opposing party fails to respond, the court may construe such failure to respond as nonopposition to the motion or an admission that the motion was meritorious. AMJUR MOTIONS § 28. The rule in some jurisdictions being that the failure to respond to a fact set forth in a motion is deemed an admission—and may grant the motion if the relief requested appears to be justified. AMJUR MOTIONS § 28.

   c. *Assent or no opposition not determinative.* However, a motion will not be granted automatically simply because an "assent" or a notation of "no opposition" has been filed; federal judges frequently deny motions that have been assented to when it is thought that justice so dictates. FPP § 1190.

   d. *Responsive pleading inappropriate as response to motion.* An attempt to answer or oppose a motion with a responsive pleading usually is not appropriate. FPP § 1190.

5. *Reply papers.* A moving party may be required or permitted to prepare papers in addition to its original motion papers. AMJUR MOTIONS § 25. Papers answering or replying to opposing papers may be appropriate, in the interests of justice, where it appears there is a substantial reason for allowing a reply. Thus, a court may accept reply papers where a party demonstrates that the papers to which it seeks to file a reply raise new issues that are material to the disposition of the question before the court, or where the court determines, sua sponte, that it wishes further briefing of an issue raised in those papers and orders the submission of additional papers. FEDPROC § 62:354.

   a. *Function of reply papers.* The function of a reply affidavit or reply papers is to answer the arguments made in opposition to the position taken by the movant, not to raise new issues, arguments, or evidence, or change the nature of the primary motion. However, if the court permits new evidence with the reply papers, the other party should be given the opportunity to respond. Where the party opposing the motion has no opportunity to address the argument in writing, a court has the discretion to disregard arguments raised for the first time in a reply memorandum. Also, the view has been followed in some jurisdictions that as a matter of judicial economy, where there is no prejudice and where the issues could be raised simply by filing a motion to dismiss, the trial court has discretion to consider arguments raised for the first time in a reply memorandum, and that a trial court may grant a motion to strike issues raised for the first time in a reply memorandum. AMJUR MOTIONS § 26.

      i. *DISTRICT OF MAINE.* The moving party may file a reply memorandum. . .which shall be strictly confined to replying to new matter raised in the objection or opposing memorandum. ME R USDCT Rule 7(c).

6. *DISTRICT OF MAINE: Appearances.* An attorney's signature to a pleading shall constitute an appearance for the party filing the pleading. Otherwise, an attorney who wishes to participate in any manner in any action must file a formal written appearance identifying the party represented. An appearance whether by pleading or formal written appearance shall be signed by an attorney in his/her individual name and shall state his/her office address. ME R USDCT Rule 83.2(a). For more information, refer to ME R USDCT Rule 83.2.

7. *DISTRICT OF MAINE: Alternative dispute resolution (ADR).* Litigants are authorized and encouraged to employ, at their own expense, any available ADR process on which they can agree, including early neutral evaluation, settlement conferences, mediation, non-binding summary jury trial, corporate mini-trial, and arbitration proceedings. ME R USDCT Rule 83.11(a). For more information on ADR, refer to ME R USDCT Rule 83.11.

D. Documents

1. *Documents for moving party*

   a. *Required documents*

      i. *Notice of motion and motion.* Refer to the "C. General Requirements" section of this KeyRules document for information on the notice of motion and motion.

         - *DISTRICT OF MAINE: Memorandum of law.* Every motion shall incorporate a memorandum of law, including citations and supporting authorities. ME R USDCT Rule 7(a). Refer to the "E. Format" section of this KeyRules document for the form of memoranda of law.

         - *Certificate of service.* No certificate of service is required when a paper is served by filing it with the court's electronic-filing system. When a paper that is required to be served is served by other means: (i) if the paper is filed, a certificate of service must be filed with it or within a reasonable time after service; and (ii) if the paper is not filed, a certificate of service need not be filed unless filing is required by court order or by local rule. FRCP 5(d)(1)(B).

      ii. *Proposed amended pleading.* In order to satisfy [the prerequisites of FRCP 7(b)], a copy of the amendment should be submitted with the motion so that the court and the adverse party know the precise nature of the pleading changes being proposed. FPP § 1485. The amending party should submit a copy of the proposed amendment at least by the date of the hearing on the motion for leave to amend. FEDPROC § 62:268; Grombach v. Oerlikon Tool & Arms Corp. of America, 276 F.2d 155 (4th Cir. 1960). The documents accompanying the motion for leave to amend may be an appropriate substitute for a formally proposed amendment, if the documents sufficiently indicate the gist of the amendment. FEDPROC § 62:268.

   b. *Supplemental documents*

      i. *Supporting evidence.* When a motion relies on facts outside the record, the court may hear the matter on affidavits or may hear it wholly or partly on oral testimony or on depositions. FRCP 43(c).

         - *DISTRICT OF MAINE: Affidavits and other supporting documents.* Any affidavits and other documents setting forth or evidencing facts on which the motion is based must be filed with the motion. ME R USDCT Rule 7(a).

         - *DISTRICT OF MAINE: Discovery transcripts or materials.* A party relying on discovery transcripts or materials in support of or in opposition to a motion shall file excerpts of such transcript or materials with the memorandum required by ME R USDCT Rule 7 as well as a list of specific citations to the parts on which the party relies. ME R USDCT Rule 26(c). Excerpts of depositions in support of or in opposition to a motion shall be filed electronically using ECF, unless otherwise permitted by the court. ME R USDCT App. 4(l)(3).

      ii. *Notice of constitutional question.* A party that files a pleading, written motion, or other paper drawing into question the constitutionality of a federal or state statute must promptly: (1) file a notice of constitutional question stating the question and identifying the paper that raises it, if: (A) a federal statute is questioned and the parties do not include the United States, one of its agencies, or one of its officers or employees in an official capacity; or (B) a state statute is questioned and the parties do not include the state, one of its agencies, or one of its officers or employees in an official capacity; and (2) serve the notice and paper on the Attorney General of the United States if a federal statute is questioned—or on the state attorney general if a state statute is questioned—either by certified or registered mail or by sending it to an electronic address designated by the attorney general for this purpose. FRCP 5.1(a).

         - *No forfeiture.* A party's failure to file and serve the notice, or the court's failure to certify, does not forfeit a constitutional claim or defense that is otherwise timely asserted. FRCP 5.1(d).

      iii. *DISTRICT OF MAINE: Additional supplemental documents*

         - *Proposed order.* Proposed orders shall not be filed unless requested by the court. When requested by the court, proposed orders shall be filed by e-mail in word processing format. ME R USDCT App. 4(k)(1).

2. *Documents for opposing party*

   a. *Required documents*

      i. *Opposition.* Refer to the "C. General Requirements" section of this KeyRules document for information on the opposing papers.

         - *DISTRICT OF MAINE: Memorandum of law.* Unless within twenty-one (21) days after the filing of a

motion the opposing party files written objection thereto, incorporating a memorandum of law, the opposing party shall be deemed to have waived objection. ME R USDCT Rule 7(b).

- *Certificate of service.* No certificate of service is required when a paper is served by filing it with the court's electronic-filing system. When a paper that is required to be served is served by other means: (i) if the paper is filed, a certificate of service must be filed with it or within a reasonable time after service; and (ii) if the paper is not filed, a certificate of service need not be filed unless filing is required by court order or by local rule. FRCP 5(d)(1)(B).

b. *Supplemental documents*

   i. *Supporting evidence.* When a motion relies on facts outside the record, the court may hear the matter on affidavits or may hear it wholly or partly on oral testimony or on depositions. FRCP 43(c).

   - *DISTRICT OF MAINE: Affidavits and other supporting documents.* Any objections shall include. . .affidavits and other documents setting forth or evidencing facts on which the objection is based. ME R USDCT Rule 7(b).

   - *DISTRICT OF MAINE: Discovery transcripts or materials.* A party relying on discovery transcripts or materials in support of or in opposition to a motion shall file excerpts of such transcript or materials with the memorandum required by ME R USDCT Rule 7 as well as a list of specific citations to the parts on which the party relies. ME R USDCT Rule 26(c). Excerpts of depositions in support of or in opposition to a motion shall be filed electronically using ECF, unless otherwise permitted by the court. ME R USDCT App. 4(l)(3).

   ii. *Notice of constitutional question.* A party that files a pleading, written motion, or other paper drawing into question the constitutionality of a federal or state statute must promptly: (1) file a notice of constitutional question stating the question and identifying the paper that raises it, if: (A) a federal statute is questioned and the parties do not include the United States, one of its agencies, or one of its officers or employees in an official capacity; or (B) a state statute is questioned and the parties do not include the state, one of its agencies, or one of its officers or employees in an official capacity; and (2) serve the notice and paper on the Attorney General of the United States if a federal statute is questioned—or on the state attorney general if a state statute is questioned—either by certified or registered mail or by sending it to an electronic address designated by the attorney general for this purpose. FRCP 5.1(a).

   - *No forfeiture.* A party's failure to file and serve the notice, or the court's failure to certify, does not forfeit a constitutional claim or defense that is otherwise timely asserted. FRCP 5.1(d).

E. Format

1. *Form of documents.* The rules governing captions and other matters of form in pleadings apply to motions and other papers. FRCP 7(b)(2).

   a. *DISTRICT OF MAINE: Font size, line spacing, and paper size.* All such documents shall be typed in a font of no less than size twelve (12) point, and shall be double-spaced or printed on eight and one-half by eleven (8-1/2 x 11) inch paper. Footnotes shall be in a font of no less than size ten (10) point, and may be single spaced. ME R USDCT Rule 10.

   b. *Caption.* Every pleading must have a caption with the court's name, a title, a file number, and an FRCP 7(a) designation. FRCP 10(a).

   i. *Names of parties.* The title of the complaint must name all the parties; the title of other pleadings, after naming the first party on each side, may refer generally to other parties. FRCP 10(a).

   ii. *DISTRICT OF MAINE: Additional caption requirements.* All pleadings, motions and other papers filed with the clerk or otherwise submitted to the court, except exhibits, shall bear the proper case number and shall contain on the first page a caption as described by FRCP 10(a) and immediately thereunder a designation of what the document is and the name of the party in whose behalf it is submitted. ME R USDCT Rule 10.

   c. *Claims or defenses*

   i. *Numbered paragraphs.* A party must state its claims or defenses in numbered paragraphs, each limited as far as practicable to a single set of circumstances. A later pleading may refer by number to a paragraph in an earlier pleading. FRCP 10(b).

   ii. *Separate statements.* If doing so would promote clarity, each claim founded on a separate transaction or occurrence—and each defense other than a denial—must be stated in a separate count or defense. FRCP 10(b).

d. *Adoption by reference.* A statement in a pleading may be adopted by reference elsewhere in the same pleading or in any other pleading or motion. FRCP 10(c).

   i. *Exhibits.* A copy of a written instrument that is an exhibit to a pleading is a part of the pleading for all purposes. FRCP 10(c).

e. *DISTRICT OF MAINE: Page numbering.* All pages shall be numbered at the bottom. ME R USDCT Rule 10.

f. *DISTRICT OF MAINE: Attachment of ancillary papers.* Ancillary papers shall be attached at the end of the document to which they relate. ME R USDCT Rule 10.

g. *Acceptance by the clerk.* The clerk must not refuse to file a paper solely because it is not in the form prescribed by the Federal Rules of Civil Procedure or by a local rule or practice. FRCP 5(d)(4).

2. *Form of electronic documents.* A paper filed electronically is a written paper for purposes of the Federal Rules of Civil Procedure. FRCP 5(d)(3)(D).

   a. *DISTRICT OF MAINE: Document format.* The ECF system only accepts documents in a portable document format (PDF). Although there are two types of PDF documents—electronically converted PDF's and scanned PDF's—only electronically converted PDF's may be filed with the court using the ECF system, unless otherwise authorized by local rule or order. ME R USDCT App. 4. Any document or exhibit to be filed or submitted to the court shall not be password-protected or encrypted. ME R USDCT App. 4(g)(12).

      i. *Electronically converted PDFs.* Electronically converted PDF's are created from word processing documents (MS Word, WordPerfect, etc.) using Adobe Acrobat or similar software. They are text searchable and their file size is small. ME R USDCT App. 4. Software used to electronically convert documents to PDF which includes proprietary or advertisement information within the PDF document is prohibited. ME R USDCT App. 4.

      ii. *Scanned PDFs.* Scanned PDF's are created from paper documents run through an optical scanner. Scanned PDF's are not searchable and have a large file size. ME R USDCT App. 4.

   b. *DISTRICT OF MAINE: Title.* All pleadings filed electronically shall be titled in accordance with the approved dictionary of civil or criminal events of the ECF system of the United States District Court for the District of Maine. ME R USDCT App. 4(d)(3).

   c. *DISTRICT OF MAINE: Attachments.* Attachments to filings and exhibits must be filed in accordance with the court's ECF User Manual, unless otherwise ordered by the court. ME R USDCT App. 4(j). When there are fifty (50) or fewer attachments to a pleading, the attachments must be filed by counsel electronically using ECF. When there are more than fifty (50) attachments, the attachments must be filed in one of the following ways: (A) using ECF, simply attach them to the pleading being filed; (B) using ECF, use the "Additional Attachments" menu item; (C) on paper; or (D) on a properly labeled three and one-half (3-1/2) inch floppy disk, CD or DVD. ME R USDCT App. 4(j)(2). Attachments filed on paper or on disk must contain a comprehensive index that clearly describes each document. ME R USDCT App. 4(j)(2).

      i. A filing user must submit as attachments only those excerpts of the referenced documents that are directly germane to the matter under consideration by the court. Excerpted material must be clearly and prominently identified as such. Users who file excerpts of documents do so without prejudice to their right to timely file additional excerpts or the complete document, as may be allowed by the court. Responding parties may timely file additional excerpts or the complete document that they believe are directly germane. ME R USDCT App. 4(j)(3).

      ii. Filers shall not attach as an exhibit any pleading or other paper already on file with the court in that case, but shall merely refer to that document. ME R USDCT App. 4(j)(4).

   d. *DISTRICT OF MAINE: Compliance with technical standards.* All documents filed by electronic means must comply with technical standards, if any, established by the Judicial Conference of the United States or by the United States District Court for the District of Maine. ME R USDCT App. 4(a)(3).

3. *DISTRICT OF MAINE: Form of memoranda of law.* All memoranda shall be typed, in a font of no less than size twelve (12) point, and shall be double-spaced on eight and one-half by eleven (8-1/2 x 11) inch paper or printed. Footnotes shall be in a font of no less than size ten (10) point, and may be single spaced. All pages shall be numbered at the bottom. ME R USDCT Rule 7(d).

   a. *Page limitations.* No memorandum of law in support of or in opposition to a nondispositive motion shall exceed ten (10) pages. ME R USDCT Rule 7(d). No reply memorandum shall exceed seven (7) pages. ME R USDCT Rule 7(d); ME R USDCT Rule 7(c).

      i. *Motion to exceed page limitation.* A motion to exceed the limitation of ME R USDCT Rule 7 shall be filed no later than three (3) business days in advance of the date for filing the memorandum to permit meaningful review by the court. A motion to exceed the page limitations shall not be filed simultaneously with a memorandum in excess of the limitations of ME R USDCT Rule 7. ME R USDCT Rule 7(d).

4. *Signing of pleadings, motions and other papers*

   a. *Signature.* Every pleading, written motion, and other paper must be signed by at least one attorney of record in the attorney's name—or by a party personally if the party is unrepresented. The paper must state the signer's address, e-mail address, and telephone number. FRCP 11(a).

      i. *No verification or accompanying affidavit required for pleadings.* Unless a rule or statute specifically states otherwise, a pleading need not be verified or accompanied by an affidavit. FRCP 11(a).

      ii. *Unsigned papers.* The court must strike an unsigned paper unless the omission is promptly corrected after being called to the attorney's or party's attention. FRCP 11(a).

   b. *Electronic signing.* A filing made through a person's electronic-filing account and authorized by that person, together with that person's name on a signature block, constitutes the person's signature. FRCP 5(d)(3)(C).

      i. *DISTRICT OF MAINE: Attorneys.* The user log-in and password together with a user's name on the signature block constitutes the attorney's signature pursuant to the Federal Rules of Civil Procedure and the Local Rules of the United States District Court for the District of Maine. All electronically filed documents must include a signature block and must set forth the attorney's name, address, telephone number and e-mail address. The name of the ECF user under whose log-in and password the document is submitted must be preceded by a "/s/" in the space where the signature would otherwise appear. ME R USDCT App. 4(h)(1).

      ii. *DISTRICT OF MAINE: Multiple signatures.* The filer of any document requiring more than one signature (e.g., pleadings filed by visiting lawyers, stipulations, joint status reports) must list thereon all the names of other signatories, preceded by a "/s/" in the space where the signatures would otherwise appear. By submitting such a document, the filing attorney certifies that each of the other signatories has expressly agreed to the form and substance of the document and that the filing attorney has their actual authority to submit the document electronically. ME R USDCT App. 4(h)(2). For more information, refer to ME R USDCT App. 4(h)(2).

      iii. *DISTRICT OF MAINE: Documents signed under oath.* Affidavits, declarations, verified complaints, or any other document signed under oath shall be filed electronically. The electronically filed version shall contain the typed name of the signatory, preceded by a "/s/" in the space where the signature would otherwise appear indicating that the paper document bears an original signature. ME R USDCT Rule 10; ME R USDCT App. 4(h)(3). For more information, refer to ME R USDCT Rule 10.

   c. *Representations to the court.* By presenting to the court a pleading, written motion, or other paper—whether by signing, filing, submitting, or later advocating it—an attorney or unrepresented party certifies that to the best of the person's knowledge, information, and belief, formed after an inquiry reasonable under the circumstances: (1) it is not being presented for any improper purpose, such as to harass, cause unnecessary delay, or needlessly increase the cost of litigation; (2) the claims, defenses, and other legal contentions are warranted by existing law or by a nonfrivolous argument for extending, modifying, or reversing existing law or for establishing new law; (3) the factual contentions have evidentiary support or, if specifically so identified, will likely have evidentiary support after a reasonable opportunity for further investigation or discovery; and (4) the denials of factual contentions are warranted on the evidence or, if specifically so identified, are reasonably based on belief or a lack of information. FRCP 11(b).

   d. *Sanctions.* If, after notice and a reasonable opportunity to respond, the court determines that FRCP 11(b) has been violated, the court may impose an appropriate sanction on any attorney, law firm, or party that violated FRCP 11(b) or is responsible for the violation. FRCP 11(c)(1). Refer to the United States District Court for the District of Maine KeyRules Motion for Sanctions document for more information.

5. *Privacy protection for filings made with the court*

   a. *Redacted filings.* Unless the court orders otherwise, in an electronic or paper filing with the court that contains an individual's Social Security number, taxpayer-identification number, or birth date, the name of an individual known to be a minor, or a financial-account number, a party or nonparty making the filing may include only: (1) the last four (4) digits of the Social Security number and taxpayer-identification number; (2) the year of the individual's birth; (3) the minor's initials; and (4) the last four (4) digits of the financial-account number. FRCP 5.2(a).

      i. *DISTRICT OF MAINE.* To address the privacy concerns created by the Internet access to court papers, unless otherwise ordered by the court, counsel shall modify certain personal data identifiers in pleadings and other papers as follows: (1) minors' names: use of the minors' initials only; (2) Social Security numbers: use of the last

four (4) numbers only; (3) dates of birth: use of the year of birth only; [and] (4) financial account numbers: identify the type of account and the financial institution, but use only the last four (4) numbers of the account number. ME R USDCT Redacting Pleadings. Counsel should also use caution when filing papers that contain a person's medical records, employment history; financial information; and any proprietary or trade secret information. ME R USDCT Redacting Pleadings.

b. *Exemptions from the redaction requirement.* The redaction requirement does not apply to the following: (1) a financial-account number that identifies the property allegedly subject to forfeiture in a forfeiture proceeding; (2) the record of an administrative or agency proceeding; (3) the official record of a state-court proceeding; (4) the record of a court or tribunal, if that record was not subject to the redaction requirement when originally filed; (5) a filing covered by FRCP 5.2(c) or FRCP 5.2(d); and (6) a pro se filing in an action brought under 28 U.S.C.A. § 2241, 28 U.S.C.A. § 2254, or 28 U.S.C.A. § 2255. FRCP 5.2(b).

c. *Limitations on remote access to electronic files; Social Security appeals and immigration cases.* Unless the court orders otherwise, in an action for benefits under the Social Security Act, and in an action or proceeding relating to an order of removal, to relief from removal, or to immigration benefits or detention, access to an electronic file is authorized as follows: (1) the parties and their attorneys may have remote electronic access to any part of the case file, including the administrative record; (2) any other person may have electronic access to the full record at the courthouse, but may have remote electronic access only to: (A) the docket maintained by the court; and (B) an opinion, order, judgment, or other disposition of the court, but not any other part of the case file or the administrative record. FRCP 5.2(c).

d. *Filings made under seal.* The court may order that a filing be made under seal without redaction. The court may later unseal the filing or order the person who made the filing to file a redacted version for the public record. FRCP 5.2(d).

   i. *DISTRICT OF MAINE.* For information on filing sealed documents in the District of Maine, refer to ME R USDCT Rule 7A, ME R USDCT App. 4(p)(2), and ME R USDCT Sealed Filings.

e. *Protective orders.* For good cause, the court may by order in a case: (1) require redaction of additional information; or (2) limit or prohibit a nonparty's remote electronic access to a document filed with the court. FRCP 5.2(e).

f. *Option for additional unredacted filing under seal.* A person making a redacted filing may also file an unredacted copy under seal. The court must retain the unredacted copy as part of the record. FRCP 5.2(f).

   i. *DISTRICT OF MAINE.* A party wishing to file a document containing the personal data identifiers specified above may. . .file an unredacted document under seal. This document will be retained by the clerk's office as part of the record. ME R USDCT Redacting Pleadings. The court may, however, still require the party to file a redacted copy for the public file. ME R USDCT Redacting Pleadings.

g. *Option for filing a reference list.* A filing that contains redacted information may be filed together with a reference list that identifies each item of redacted information and specifies an appropriate identifier that uniquely corresponds to each item listed. The list must be filed under seal and may be amended as of right. Any reference in the case to a listed identifier will be construed to refer to the corresponding item of information. FRCP 5.2(g).

   i. *DISTRICT OF MAINE.* A party wishing to file a document containing the personal data identifiers specified above may. . .file a reference list under seal. The reference list shall contain the complete personal data identifier(s) and the redacted identifier(s) used in its (their) place in the filing. All references in the case to the redacted identifiers included in the reference list will be construed to refer to the corresponding complete identifier. The reference list must be filed under seal, and may be amended as of right. It shall be retained by the clerk's office as part of the record. ME R USDCT Redacting Pleadings. The court may, however, still require the party to file a redacted copy for the public file. ME R USDCT Redacting Pleadings.

h. *DISTRICT OF MAINE: Responsibility for redaction.* The clerk is not required to review documents filed with the court for compliance with FRCP 5.2. The responsibility to redact filings rests with counsel and the party or nonparty making the filing. ME R USDCT App. 4(i); ME R USDCT Redacting Pleadings. For guidelines for filing confidential information in civil cases in the District of Maine, refer to ME R USDCT Confidentiality.

i. *Waiver of protection of identifiers.* A person waives the protection of FRCP 5.2(a) as to the person's own information by filing it without redaction and not under seal. FRCP 5.2(h).

F. Filing and Service Requirements

1. *Filing requirements*

   a. *Required filings.* Any paper after the complaint that is required to be served must be filed no later than a reasonable time after service. FRCP 5(d)(1).

b. *DISTRICT OF MAINE: Place of filing.* Unless otherwise ordered by the court, papers shall be filed with the court at Bangor in cases filed and pending at Bangor, and at Portland in cases filed and pending at Portland. ME R USDCT Rule 5(a).

c. *Nonelectronic filing.* A paper not filed electronically is filed by delivering it: (A) to the clerk; or (B) to a judge who agrees to accept it for filing, and who must then note the filing date on the paper and promptly send it to the clerk. FRCP 5(d)(2).

    i. *DISTRICT OF MAINE: Documents to be filed in paper.* The following documents shall be filed in paper, which may also be scanned into ECF by the clerk's office: (A) all handwritten pleadings; and (B) all pleadings and documents filed by pro se litigants who are incarcerated or who are not registered filing users in ECF. ME R USDCT App. 4(g)(8). Non-prisoner pro se litigants in civil actions may register with ECF or may file (and serve) all pleadings and other documents in paper. The clerk's office will scan into ECF any pleadings and documents filed on paper in accordance with ME R USDCT App. 4(g). ME R USDCT App. 4(o). For more information, refer to ME R USDCT App. 4(g).

d. *Electronic filing*

    i. *DISTRICT OF MAINE: Authorization.* Unless exempt or otherwise ordered by the court, papers shall be filed and served electronically as required by the court's Administrative Procedures Governing the Filing and Service by Electronic Means, which is set forth in ME R USDCT App. 4. The provisions of the court's Administrative Procedures Governing the Filing and Service by Electronic Means (ME R USDCT App. 4) shall be applied and enforced as part of the Local Rules of the United States District Court for the District of Maine. ME R USDCT Rule 5(c).

    ii. *Filing by represented persons.* A person represented by an attorney must file electronically, unless nonelectronic filing is allowed by the court for good cause or is allowed or required by local rule. FRCP 5(d)(3)(A).

        • *DISTRICT OF MAINE.* An attorney may apply to the court for permission to file paper documents. ME R USDCT App. 4(a)(5).

    iii. *Filing by unrepresented persons.* A person not represented by an attorney: (i) may file electronically only if allowed by court order or by local rule; and (ii) may be required to file electronically only by court order, or by a local rule that includes reasonable exceptions. FRCP 5(d)(3)(B).

        • *DISTRICT OF MAINE.* Non-prisoner pro se litigants in civil actions may register with ECF or may file (and serve) all pleadings and other documents in paper. ME R USDCT App. 4(o). A non-prisoner who is a party to a civil action and who is not represented by an attorney may register to receive service electronically and to electronically transmit their documents to the court for filing in the ECF system. If during the course of the action the person retains an attorney who appears on the person's behalf, the clerk shall terminate the person's registration upon the attorney's appearance. ME R USDCT App. 4(b)(2).

    iv. *DISTRICT OF MAINE: Scope of electronic filing.* All documents submitted for filing in civil and criminal cases, regardless of case commencement date, except those documents specifically exempted in ME R USDCT App. 4(g), shall be filed electronically using the electronic case filing system (ECF). ME R USDCT App. 4(a)(1). For special filing requirements and exceptions, refer to ME R USDCT App. 4(g).

    v. *DISTRICT OF MAINE: Consequences of electronic filing.* Electronic transmission of a document to the ECF system, together with the transmission of a Notice of Electronic Filing (NEF) from the court, constitutes filing of the document for all purposes of the Federal Rules of Civil Procedure. ME R USDCT App. 4(d)(1).

    vi. *DISTRICT OF MAINE: Review of documents.* Documents filed with the clerk's office will normally be reviewed no later than the close of the next business day. It is the responsibility of the filing party to promptly notify the clerk's office via telephone of a matter that requires the immediate attention of a judicial officer. ME R USDCT App. 4(a)(4).

e. *DISTRICT OF MAINE: Facsimile filing.* No papers shall be submitted to the court by means of a facsimile machine without prior leave of the court. ME R USDCT Rule 5(c); ME R USDCT App. 4(m).

2. *Service requirements*

a. *Service; When required.* Unless the Federal Rules of Civil Procedure provide otherwise, each of the following papers must be served on every party: (A) an order stating that service is required; (B) a pleading filed after the original complaint, unless the court orders otherwise under FRCP 5(c) because there are numerous defendants; (C) a discovery paper required to be served on a party, unless the court orders otherwise; (D) a written motion, except one

that may be heard ex parte; and (E) a written notice, appearance, demand, or offer of judgment, or any similar paper. FRCP 5(a)(1).

    i. *If a party fails to appear.* No service is required on a party who is in default for failing to appear. But a pleading that asserts a new claim for relief against such a party must be served on that party under FRCP 4. FRCP 5(a)(2).

    ii. *Seizing property.* If an action is begun by seizing property and no person is or need be named as a defendant, any service required before the filing of an appearance, answer, or claim must be made on the person who had custody or possession of the property when it was seized. FRCP 5(a)(3).

  b. *Service; How made.* A paper is served under FRCP 5 by: (A) handing it to the person; (B) leaving it: (i) at the person's office with a clerk or other person in charge or, if no one is in charge, in a conspicuous place in the office; or (ii) if the person has no office or the office is closed, at the person's dwelling or usual place of abode with someone of suitable age and discretion who resides there; (C) mailing it to the person's last known address—in which event service is complete upon mailing; (D) leaving it with the court clerk if the person has no known address; (E) sending it to a registered user by filing it with the court's electronic-filing system or sending it by other electronic means that the person consented to in writing—in either of which events service is complete upon filing or sending, but is not effective if the filer or sender learns that it did not reach the person to be served; or (F) delivering it by any other means that the person consented to in writing—in which event service is complete when the person making service delivers it to the agency designated to make delivery. FRCP 5(b)(2).

    i. *Serving an attorney.* If a party is represented by an attorney, service under FRCP 5 must be made on the attorney unless the court orders service on the party. FRCP 5(b)(1).

  c. *DISTRICT OF MAINE: Service of electronically filed documents*

    i. *Registered users.* Registration [as a filing user of the court's ECF system] constitutes consent to service of all documents by electronic means as provided in ME R USDCT App. 4. ME R USDCT App. 4(b)(4). Whenever a non-sealed pleading is filed electronically, the ECF system will automatically generate and send a Notice of Electronic Filing (NEF) to the filing user and registered users of record. The user filing the document should retain a paper or digital copy of the NEF, which shall serve as the court's date-stamp and proof of filing. ME R USDCT App. 4(e)(1).

      • *Sealed documents.* Although the filing of sealed documents in civil cases produces an NEF, the document itself cannot be accessed and counsel shall be responsible for making service of the sealed documents. ME R USDCT App. 4(e)(2).

    ii. *Non-registered users and pro se litigants.* Attorneys who have not yet registered as users with ECF and pro se litigants who have not registered with ECF shall be served a paper copy of any electronically filed pleading or other document in accordance with the provisions of FRCP 5. ME R USDCT App. 4(e)(3).

      • *Registration of pro se litigants.* A non-prisoner who is a party to a civil action and who is not represented by an attorney may register to receive service electronically and to electronically transmit their documents to the court for filing in the ECF system. If during the course of the action the person retains an attorney who appears on the person's behalf, the clerk shall terminate the person's registration upon the attorney's appearance. ME R USDCT App. 4(b)(2).

  d. *Serving numerous defendants.* If an action involves an unusually large number of defendants, the court may, on motion or on its own, order that: (A) defendants' pleadings and replies to them need not be served on other defendants; (B) any crossclaim, counterclaim, avoidance, or affirmative defense in those pleadings and replies to them will be treated as denied or avoided by all other parties; and (C) filing any such pleading and serving it on the plaintiff constitutes notice of the pleading to all parties. FRCP 5(c)(1).

    i. *Notifying parties.* A copy of every such order must be served on the parties as the court directs. FRCP 5(c)(2).

3. *DISTRICT OF MAINE: Filing and service of highly sensitive documents (HSDs).* For information on filing and serving highly sensitive documents (HSDs) in the District of Maine, refer to ME R USDCT General Order 21-5.

G. Hearings

1. *Hearings, generally.* When a motion relies on facts outside the record, the court may hear the matter on affidavits or may hear it wholly or partly on oral testimony or on depositions. FRCP 43(c).

  a. *Oral argument.* Due process does not require that oral argument be permitted on a motion and, except as otherwise provided by local rule, the district court has discretion to determine whether it will decide the motion on the papers or hear argument by counsel (and perhaps receive evidence). FPP § 1190; F.D.I.C. v. Deglau, 207 F.3d 153 (3d Cir. 2000).

    i.   *DISTRICT OF MAINE.* Unless otherwise required by federal rule or statute, all motions may be decided by the court without oral argument unless otherwise ordered by the court on its own motion or, in its discretion, upon request of counsel. ME R USDCT Rule 7(e).

  b. *Providing a regular schedule for oral hearings.* A court may establish regular times and places for oral hearings on motions. FRCP 78(a).

  c. *Providing for submission on briefs.* By rule or order, the court may provide for submitting and determining motions on briefs, without oral hearings. FRCP 78(b).

H. Forms

1. Federal Motion for Leave to Amend Forms

  a. Leave to amend complaint; Attaching copy of amendment. 2C FEDFORMS § 14:18.

  b. Leave to amend complaint; Inserting amendment. 2C FEDFORMS § 14:19.

  c. Leave to amend complaint; Interlineation. 2C FEDFORMS § 14:20.

  d. Leave to amend complaint; Responding to motion to dismiss complaint. 2C FEDFORMS § 14:21.

  e. Leave to amend complaint; Close to trial. 2C FEDFORMS § 14:22.

  f. Leave to amend complaint; Adding new count. 2C FEDFORMS § 14:24.

  g. Leave to amend complaint; Asserting lack of knowledge of facts at time of original complaint. 2C FEDFORMS § 14:25.

  h. Leave to amend complaint; Seeking fourth amendment. 2C FEDFORMS § 14:26.

  i. Leave to amend complaint; Substituting plaintiff and dropping defendant. 2C FEDFORMS § 14:27.

  j. Leave to amend answer. 2C FEDFORMS § 14:30.

  k. Leave to amend answer; With leave endorsed. 2C FEDFORMS § 14:31.

  l. Leave to amend answer; Correcting errors, deleting and interlining. 2C FEDFORMS § 14:32.

  m. Leave to amend answer; Adding paragraph. 2C FEDFORMS § 14:33.

  n. Leave to amend answer; Adding defense. 2C FEDFORMS § 14:34.

  o. Leave to amend answer; During trial. 2C FEDFORMS § 14:35.

  p. Defendant's response to motion for leave to amend complaint a fourth time. 2C FEDFORMS § 14:36.

  q. Motion and notice; For leave to file amended pleading. FEDPROF § 1A:334.

  r. Motion; To amend pleading to conform to findings of master. FEDPROF § 1A:335.

  s. Affidavit; In support of motion for amendment of pleading. FEDPROF § 1A:342.

  t. Opposition; To motion. FEDPROF § 1B:175.

  u. Affidavit; Supporting or opposing motion. FEDPROF § 1B:176.

  v. Brief; Supporting or opposing motion. FEDPROF § 1B:177.

  w. Statement of points and authorities; Opposing motion. FEDPROF § 1B:178.

  x. Motion for leave to amend pleading. GOLDLTGFMS § 14:3.

  y. Motion to file second amended complaint on ground of newly discovered evidence. GOLDLTGFMS § 14:20.

  z. Motion for leave to file amended answer. GOLDLTGFMS § 14:22.

I. Applicable Rules

1. *Federal rules*

  a. Serving and filing pleadings and other papers. FRCP 5.

  b. Constitutional challenge to a statute; Notice, certification, and intervention. FRCP 5.1.

  c. Privacy protection for filings made with the court. FRCP 5.2.

  d. Computing and extending time; Time for motion papers. FRCP 6.

e. Pleadings allowed; Form of motions and other papers. FRCP 7.

f. Form of pleadings. FRCP 10.

g. Signing pleadings, motions, and other papers; Representations to the court; Sanctions. FRCP 11.

h. Amended and supplemental pleadings. FRCP 15.

i. Taking testimony. FRCP 43.

j. Hearing motions; Submission on briefs. FRCP 78.

2. *Local rules*

    a. *DISTRICT OF MAINE*

        i. Service and filing of pleadings and other papers. ME R USDCT Rule 5.

        ii. Time. ME R USDCT Rule 6.

        iii. Motions and memoranda of law. ME R USDCT Rule 7.

        iv. Form of pleadings, motions and other papers. ME R USDCT Rule 10.

        v. Discovery. ME R USDCT Rule 26.

        vi. Attorneys; Appearances and withdrawals. ME R USDCT Rule 83.2.

        vii. Alternative dispute resolution (ADR). ME R USDCT Rule 83.11.

        viii. Administrative procedures governing the filing and service by electronic means. ME R USDCT App. 4.

        ix. Redacting pleadings. ME R USDCT Redacting Pleadings.

Motions, Oppositions and Replies
Motion for Continuance/Extension of Time

Document Last Updated April 2021

A. Checklist

(I) ❑ Matters to be considered by moving party

    (a) ❑ Required documents

        (1) ❑ Notice of motion and motion

    (b) ❑ Supplemental documents

        (1) ❑ Supporting evidence

        (2) ❑ Notice of constitutional question

        (3) ❑ Nongovernmental corporate disclosure statement

        (4) ❑ DISTRICT OF MAINE: Additional supplemental documents

            (i) ❑ Proposed order

    (c) ❑ Timing

        (1) ❑ Motion for continuance: there are no specific timing requirements in the Federal Rules of Civil Procedure for moving for a continuance

        (2) ❑ Motion for extension of time: when an act may or must be done within a specified time, the court may, for good cause, extend the time: (A) with or without motion or notice if the court acts, or if a request is made, before the original time or its extension expires; or (B) on motion made after the time has expired if the party failed to act because of excusable neglect

        (3) ❑ A written motion and notice of the hearing must be served at least fourteen (14) days before the time specified for the hearing, with the following exceptions: (A) when the motion may be heard ex parte; (B) when the Federal Rules of Civil Procedure set a different time; or (C) when a court order—which a party may, for good cause, apply for ex parte—sets a different time

        (4) ❑ Any affidavit supporting a motion must be served with the motion

(5) ❑ DISTRICT OF MAINE: Additional timing

    (i) ❑ Any affidavits and other documents setting forth or evidencing facts on which the motion is based must be filed with the motion

(II) ❑ Matters to be considered by opposing party

  (a) ❑ Required documents

    (1) ❑ Opposition

  (b) ❑ Supplemental documents

    (1) ❑ Supporting evidence

    (2) ❑ Notice of constitutional question

  (c) ❑ Timing

    (1) ❑ Except as FRCP 59(c) provides otherwise, any opposing affidavit must be served at least seven (7) days before the hearing, unless the court permits service at another time

    (2) ❑ DISTRICT OF MAINE: Additional timing

      (i) ❑ Unless within twenty-one (21) days after the filing of a motion the opposing party files written objection thereto, incorporating a memorandum of law, the opposing party shall be deemed to have waived objection

B. Timing

1. *Motion for continuance.* There are no specific timing requirements in the Federal Rules of Civil Procedure for moving for a continuance.

2. *Motion for extension of time.* When an act may or must be done within a specified time, the court may, for good cause, extend the time: (A) with or without motion or notice if the court acts, or if a request is made, before the original time or its extension expires; or (B) on motion made after the time has expired if the party failed to act because of excusable neglect. FRCP 6(b)(1).

3. *Timing of motions, generally*

  a. *Motion and notice of hearing.* A written motion and notice of the hearing must be served at least fourteen (14) days before the time specified for the hearing, with the following exceptions: (A) when the motion may be heard ex parte; (B) when the Federal Rules of Civil Procedure set a different time; or (C) when a court order—which a party may, for good cause, apply for ex parte—sets a different time. FRCP 6(c)(1).

  b. *Supporting affidavit.* Any affidavit supporting a motion must be served with the motion. FRCP 6(c)(2).

  c. *DISTRICT OF MAINE: Affidavits and other supporting documents.* Any affidavits and other documents setting forth or evidencing facts on which the motion is based must be filed with the motion. ME R USDCT Rule 7(a).

4. *Timing of opposing papers.* Except as FRCP 59(c) provides otherwise, any opposing affidavit must be served at least seven (7) days before the hearing, unless the court permits service at another time. FRCP 6(c)(2).

  a. *DISTRICT OF MAINE.* Unless within twenty-one (21) days after the filing of a motion the opposing party files written objection thereto, incorporating a memorandum of law, the opposing party shall be deemed to have waived objection. ME R USDCT Rule 7(b). The deemed waiver imposed in ME R USDCT Rule 7(b) shall not apply to motions filed during trial. ME R USDCT Rule 7(b).

5. *Timing of reply papers.* Where the respondent files an answering affidavit setting up a new matter, the moving party ordinarily is allowed a reasonable time to file a reply affidavit since failure to deny the new matter by affidavit may operate as an admission of its truth. AMJUR MOTIONS § 25.

  a. *DISTRICT OF MAINE.* Within fourteen (14) days of the filing of any objection to a motion, the moving party may file a reply memorandum. ME R USDCT Rule 7(c).

6. *Computation of time*

  a. *Computing time.* FRCP 6 applies in computing any time period specified in the Federal Rules of Civil Procedure, in any local rule or court order, or in any statute that does not specify a method of computing time. FRCP 6(a).

    i. *Period stated in days or a longer unit.* When the period is stated in days or a longer unit of time: (A) exclude the day of the event that triggers the period; (B) count every day, including intermediate Saturdays, Sundays, and legal holidays; and (C) include the last day of the period, but if the last day is a Saturday, Sunday, or legal holiday,

the period continues to run until the end of the next day that is not a Saturday, Sunday, or legal holiday. FRCP 6(a)(1).

   ii. *Period stated in hours.* When the period is stated in hours: (A) begin counting immediately on the occurrence of the event that triggers the period; (B) count every hour, including hours during intermediate Saturdays, Sundays, and legal holidays; and (C) if the period would end on a Saturday, Sunday, or legal holiday, the period continues to run until the same time on the next day that is not a Saturday, Sunday, or legal holiday. FRCP 6(a)(2).

   iii. *Inaccessibility of the clerk's office.* Unless the court orders otherwise, if the clerk's office is inaccessible: (A) on the last day for filing under FRCP 6(a)(1), then the time for filing is extended to the first accessible day that is not a Saturday, Sunday, or legal holiday; or (B) during the last hour for filing under FRCP 6(a)(2), then the time for filing is extended to the same time on the first accessible day that is not a Saturday, Sunday, or legal holiday. FRCP 6(a)(3).

   iv. *"Last day" defined.* Unless a different time is set by a statute, local rule, or court order, the last day ends: (A) for electronic filing, at midnight in the court's time zone; and (B) for filing by other means, when the clerk's office is scheduled to close. FRCP 6(a)(4).

   v. *"Next day" defined.* The "next day" is determined by continuing to count forward when the period is measured after an event and backward when measured before an event. FRCP 6(a)(5).

   vi. *"Legal holiday" defined.* "Legal holiday" means: (A) the day set aside by statute for observing New Year's Day, Martin Luther King Jr.'s Birthday, Washington's Birthday, Memorial Day, Independence Day, Labor Day, Columbus Day, Veterans' Day, Thanksgiving Day, or Christmas Day; (B) any day declared a holiday by the President or Congress; and (C) for periods that are measured after an event, any other day declared a holiday by the state where the district court is located. FRCP 6(a)(6).

   vii. *DISTRICT OF MAINE: Applicability of FRCP 6.* FRCP 6 applies when computing any period of time stated in the Local Rules of the United States District Court for the District of Maine. ME R USDCT Rule 6(a).

  b. *DISTRICT OF MAINE: Computation of electronic filing deadlines.* Filing documents electronically does not in any way alter any filing deadlines. All electronic transmissions of documents must be completed prior to midnight, Eastern Time, in order to be considered timely filed that day. Where a specific time of day deadline is set by court order or stipulation, the electronic filing must be completed by that time. ME R USDCT App. 4(f). A document filed electronically shall be deemed filed at the time and date stated on the Notice of Electronic Filing received from the court. ME R USDCT App. 4(d)(2).

   i. *Technical failures.* A filing user whose filing is made untimely as the result of a technical failure may seek appropriate relief from the court. ME R USDCT App. 4(n). A technical failure of the court's ECF system is deemed to have occurred when the court's ECF site cannot accept filings continuously or intermittently over the course of any period of time greater than one (1) hour. Known system outages will be posted on the court's website along with guidance on how to proceed, if applicable. ME R USDCT App. 4(n).

  c. *Extending time.* Refer to the "C. General Requirements" section of this KeyRules document for information on extending time.

  d. *Additional time after certain kinds of service.* When a party may or must act within a specified time after being served and service is made under FRCP 5(b)(2)(C) (by mail), FRCP 5(b)(2)(D) (by leaving with the clerk), or FRCP 5(b)(2)(F) (by other means consented to), three (3) days are added after the period would otherwise expire under FRCP 6(a). FRCP 6(d).

C. General Requirements

  1. *Motions, generally*

   a. *Motion requirements.* A request for a court order must be made by motion. The motion must: (A) be in writing unless made during a hearing or trial; (B) state with particularity the grounds for seeking the order; and (C) state the relief sought. FRCP 7(b)(1). The writing and particularity requirements are intended to ensure that the adverse parties are informed of and have a record of both the motion's pendency and the grounds on which the movant seeks an order. FPP § 1191; Feldberg v. Quechee Lakes Corp., 463 F.3d 195 (2d Cir. 2006).

   i. *Particularity requirement.* The particularity requirement [ensures] that the opposing parties will have notice of their opponent's contentions. FEDPROC § 62:358; Goodman v. 1973 26 Foot Trojan Vessel, Arkansas Registration No. AR1439SN, 859 F.2d 71 (8th Cir. 1988). That requirement ensures that notice of the basis for the motion is provided to the court and to the opposing party so as to avoid prejudice, provide the opponent with a meaningful opportunity to respond, and provide the court with enough information to process the motion correctly. FEDPROC § 62:358; Andreas v. Volkswagen of Am., Inc., 336 F.3d 789 (8th Cir. 2003).

- Reasonable specification of the grounds for a motion is sufficient. The particularity requirement for motions is satisfied when no party is prejudiced by a lack of particularity or when the court can comprehend the basis for the motion and deal with it fairly. However, where a movant fails to state even one ground for granting the motion in question, the movant has failed to meet the minimal standard of "reasonable specification." FEDPROC § 62:358; Martinez v. Trainor, 556 F.2d 818 (7th Cir. 1977).

- The court may excuse the failure to comply with the particularity requirement if it is inadvertent, and where no prejudice is shown by the opposing party. FEDPROC § 62:358.

b. *Notice of motion.* A party interested in resisting the relief sought by a motion has a right to notice thereof, and an opportunity to be heard. AMJUR MOTIONS § 12.

   i. *Purpose.* In addition to statutory or court rule provisions requiring notice of a motion—the purpose of such a notice requirement having been said to be to prevent a party from being prejudicially surprised by a motion—principles of natural justice dictate that an adverse party generally must be given notice that a motion will be presented to the court. AMJUR MOTIONS § 12.

   ii. *Adequacy of notice.* The test of adequate notice generally turns on whether the other parties were afforded an adequate opportunity to prepare and respond to the issues to be raised in the proceeding. AMJUR MOTIONS § 12.

c. *Single document containing motion and notice.* A single written document can satisfy the writing requirements both for a motion and for an FRCP 6(c)(1) notice. FRCP 7(Advisory Committee Notes).

2. *Motion for continuance*

a. *Grounds for continuance.* The grounds upon which a continuance is sought may include the following: unpreparedness of a party; absence of a party; absence of counsel; absence of a witness or evidence; surprise and prejudice. FEDPROC § 77:29.

   i. *Unpreparedness of a party.* A party in a civil case may obtain a continuance on the ground he has not had reasonable and sufficient time to prepare the case for trial. The moving party has the burden to establish good cause for the motion. It is within the discretion of the court to determine whether a continuance is appropriate in these circumstances. In deciding the motion, the court may consider how long the trial has been scheduled, the moving party's explanation for being unprepared to try the case, the simplicity or complexity of the trial, including the number of expected witnesses or any unique aspects to the presentation of expected evidence, what actions did the moving party or counsel take to prepare the case for trial and preserve material evidence, whether the action is a bench or jury trial, and any indication the moving party has acted in bad faith or is consciously "gaming the system." Where the reason for unpreparedness is the withdraw of counsel shortly before or during trial, the court additionally will consider the reasons for the attorney's withdrawal, the time between withdraw and trial, and diligence by the moving party to secure competent substitute counsel. In circumstances in which the moving party could have adequately prepared, but did not do so because of inaction or dilatory conduct, the motion may be denied. FEDTRHB-CIV § 8:2.

   ii. *Absence of a party.* Since it is generally recognized that a party to a civil action ordinarily has a right to attend the trial, an illness severe enough to prevent a party from appearing in court is always a legitimate ground for asking for a continuance. FEDPROC § 77:30; Davis v. Operation Amigo, Inc., 378 F.2d 101 (10th Cir. 1967). However, the failure of the moving party to produce any competent medical evidence of the reasons and necessities for the party's unavailability will result in the denial of the continuance. FEDPROC § 77:30; Weisman v. Alleco, Inc., 925 F.2d 77 (4th Cir. 1991). Some courts, moreover, require a showing that the party has some particular contribution to make to the trial as a material witness or otherwise before granting a continuance due to the party's illness. FEDPROC § 77:30; Johnston v. Harris Cty. Flood Control Dist., 869 F.2d 1565 (5th Cir. 1989).

   iii. *Absence of counsel.* The courts have shown greater leniency when the illness of counsel is the ground for the continuance, especially where the case presents complex issues. FEDPROC § 77:31; Smith-Weik Mach. Corp. v. Murdock Mach. & Eng'g Co., 423 F.2d 842 (5th Cir. 1970). However, many courts do not favor the granting of a continuance where counsel is unavailable due to a claimed engagement elsewhere or where it is not clear that counsel's illness was genuine. FEDPROC § 77:31; Cmty. Nat. Life Ins. Co. v. Parker Square Sav. & Loan Ass'n, 406 F.2d 603 (10th Cir. 1969); Williams v. Johanns, 518 F. Supp. 2d 205 (D.D.C. 2007).

   iv. *Absence of a witness or evidence.* The moving party must show. . .that the witness's testimony would be competent and material and that there are no other witnesses who can establish the same facts. FEDPROC § 77:32; Krodel v. Houghtaling, 468 F.2d 887 (4th Cir. 1972); Vitarelle v. Long Island R. Co., 415 F.2d 302 (2d Cir. 1969).

    v. *Surprise and prejudice.* The action complained of should not be one which could have been anticipated by due diligence or of which the movant had actual notice. FEDPROC § 77:33; Commc'ns Maint., Inc. v. Motorola, Inc., 761 F.2d 1202 (7th Cir. 1985). Surprise and prejudice are often claimed as a result of the court allowing the other party to amend its pleadings under FRCP 15(b). FEDPROC § 77:29.

  b. *Factors considered in determining whether to grant a continuance.* Absent a controlling statute, the grant or denial of a continuance rests in the discretion of the trial judge, taking into consideration not only the facts of the particular case but also all of the demands on counsel's time and the court's. FEDPROC § 77:28; Star Fin. Servs., Inc. v. AASTAR Mortg. Corp., 89 F.3d 5 (1st Cir. 1996); Streber v. Hunter, 221 F.3d 701 (5th Cir. 2000). In determining whether to grant a continuance, the court will consider a variety of factors, including: good faith on the part of the moving party; due diligence of the moving party; the likelihood that the need prompting the request for a continuance will be met if the continuance is granted; inconvenience to the court and the nonmoving party, including the witnesses, if the continuance is granted; possible harm to the moving party if the continuance is denied; prior delays in the proceedings; the court's prior refusal to grant the opposing party a continuance; judicial economy. FEDPROC § 77:29; Amarin Plastics, Inc. v. Maryland Cup Corp., 946 F.2d 147 (1st Cir. 1991); Lewis v. Rawson, 564 F.3d 569 (2d Cir. 2009); United States v. 2.61 Acres of Land, More or Less, Situated in Mariposa Cty., State of Cal., 791 F.2d 666 (9th Cir. 1985); In re Homestore.com, Inc. Sec. Litig., 347 F. Supp. 2d 814 (C.D. Cal. 2004).

3. *Motion for extension of time*

  a. *Generally.* When an act may or must be done within a specified time, the court may, for good cause, extend the time: (A) with or without motion or notice if the court acts, or if a request is made, before the original time or its extension expires; or (B) on motion made after the time has expired if the party failed to act because of excusable neglect. FRCP 6(b)(1).

    i. *Exceptions.* A court must not extend the time to act under FRCP 50(b), FRCP 50(d), FRCP 52(b), FRCP 59(b), FRCP 59(d), FRCP 59(e), and FRCP 60(b). FRCP 6(b)(2). FRCP 6(b) does not require the district courts to extend a time period where the [extension] would contravene a local court rule and does not apply to periods of time that are definitely fixed by statute. FEDPROC § 77:4; Truncale v. Universal Pictures Co., 82 F. Supp. 576 (S.D.N.Y. 1949); Lusk v. Lyon Metal Prod., 9 F.R.D. 250 (W.D. Mo. 1949).

  b. *Extension of time under FRCP 6(b)(1)(A).* An application for extension of time under FRCP 6(b)(1)(A) normally will be granted in the absence of bad faith on the part of the party seeking relief or prejudice to the adverse party. FPP § 1165. Neither a formal motion for extension nor notice to the adverse party is expressly required by FRCP 6(b). FPP § 1165.

  c. *Extension of time under FRCP 6(b)(1)(B).* No relief may be granted under FRCP 6(b)(1)(B) after the expiration of the specified period, even though the failure to act may have been the result of excusable neglect, if no motion is made by the party who failed to act. FEDPROC § 77:3.

    i. *Excusable neglect.* Excusable neglect is intended and has proven to be quite elastic in its application. In essence it is an equitable concept that must take account of all relevant circumstances of the party's failure to act within the required time. FPP § 1165.

    ii. *Burden.* The burden is on the movant to establish that the failure to act in a timely manner was the result of excusable neglect. FEDPROC § 77:5. Common sense indicates that among the most important factors are the possibility of prejudice to the other parties, the length of the applicant's delay and its impact on the proceeding, the reason for the delay and whether it was within the control of the movant, and whether the movant has acted in good faith. FPP § 1165; Kettle Range Conservation Grp. v. U.S. Forest Serv., 8 F. App'x 729 (9th Cir. 2001). By far the most critical of these factors is the asserted reason for the mistake. FEDPROC § 77:5.

4. *Opposing papers.* The Federal Rules of Civil Procedure do not require any formal answer, return, or reply to a motion, except where the Federal Rules of Civil Procedure or local rules may require affidavits, memoranda, or other papers to be filed in opposition to a motion. Such papers are simply to apprise the court of such opposition and the grounds of that opposition. FEDPROC § 62:353.

  a. *DISTRICT OF MAINE: Content of objections.* Any objections shall include citations and supporting authorities and affidavits and other documents setting forth or evidencing facts on which the objection is based. ME R USDCT Rule 7(b).

  b. *Effect of failure to respond to motion.* Although in the absence of statutory provision or court rule, a motion ordinarily does not require a response or written answer, when a party files a motion and the opposing party fails to respond, the court may construe such failure to respond as nonopposition to the motion or an admission that the motion was meritorious. AMJUR MOTIONS § 28. The rule in some jurisdictions being that the failure to respond to a fact set forth in a motion is deemed an admission—and may grant the motion if the relief requested appears to be justified. AMJUR MOTIONS § 28.

    c. *Assent or no opposition not determinative.* However, a motion will not be granted automatically simply because an "assent" or a notation of "no opposition" has been filed; federal judges frequently deny motions that have been assented to when it is thought that justice so dictates. FPP § 1190.

    d. *Responsive pleading inappropriate as response to motion.* An attempt to answer or oppose a motion with a responsive pleading usually is not appropriate. FPP § 1190.

5. *Reply papers.* A moving party may be required or permitted to prepare papers in addition to its original motion papers. AMJUR MOTIONS § 25. Papers answering or replying to opposing papers may be appropriate, in the interests of justice, where it appears there is a substantial reason for allowing a reply. Thus, a court may accept reply papers where a party demonstrates that the papers to which it seeks to file a reply raise new issues that are material to the disposition of the question before the court, or where the court determines, sua sponte, that it wishes further briefing of an issue raised in those papers and orders the submission of additional papers. FEDPROC § 62:354.

    a. *Function of reply papers.* The function of a reply affidavit or reply papers is to answer the arguments made in opposition to the position taken by the movant, not to raise new issues, arguments, or evidence, or change the nature of the primary motion. However, if the court permits new evidence with the reply papers, the other party should be given the opportunity to respond. Where the party opposing the motion has no opportunity to address the argument in writing, a court has the discretion to disregard arguments raised for the first time in a reply memorandum. Also, the view has been followed in some jurisdictions that as a matter of judicial economy, where there is no prejudice and where the issues could be raised simply by filing a motion to dismiss, the trial court has discretion to consider arguments raised for the first time in a reply memorandum, and that a trial court may grant a motion to strike issues raised for the first time in a reply memorandum. AMJUR MOTIONS § 26.

        i. *DISTRICT OF MAINE.* The moving party may file a reply memorandum. . . .which shall be strictly confined to replying to new matter raised in the objection or opposing memorandum. ME R USDCT Rule 7(c).

6. *DISTRICT OF MAINE: Appearances.* An attorney's signature to a pleading shall constitute an appearance for the party filing the pleading. Otherwise, an attorney who wishes to participate in any manner in any action must file a formal written appearance identifying the party represented. An appearance whether by pleading or formal written appearance shall be signed by an attorney in his/her individual name and shall state his/her office address. ME R USDCT Rule 83.2(a). For more information, refer to ME R USDCT Rule 83.2.

7. *DISTRICT OF MAINE: Alternative dispute resolution (ADR).* Litigants are authorized and encouraged to employ, at their own expense, any available ADR process on which they can agree, including early neutral evaluation, settlement conferences, mediation, non-binding summary jury trial, corporate mini-trial, and arbitration proceedings. ME R USDCT Rule 83.11(a). For more information on ADR, refer to ME R USDCT Rule 83.11.

D. Documents

1. *Documents for moving party*

    a. *Required documents*

        i. *Notice of motion and motion.* Refer to the "C. General Requirements" section of this KeyRules document for information on the notice of motion and motion.

            • *DISTRICT OF MAINE: Memorandum of law.* Every motion shall incorporate a memorandum of law, including citations and supporting authorities. ME R USDCT Rule 7(a). Refer to the "E. Format" section of this KeyRules document for the form of memoranda of law.

            • *Certificate of service.* No certificate of service is required when a paper is served by filing it with the court's electronic-filing system. When a paper that is required to be served is served by other means: (i) if the paper is filed, a certificate of service must be filed with it or within a reasonable time after service; and (ii) if the paper is not filed, a certificate of service need not be filed unless filing is required by court order or by local rule. FRCP 5(d)(1)(B).

b. *Supplemental documents*

    i. *Supporting evidence.* When a motion relies on facts outside the record, the court may hear the matter on affidavits or may hear it wholly or partly on oral testimony or on depositions. FRCP 43(c).

        • *DISTRICT OF MAINE: Affidavits and other supporting documents.* Any affidavits and other documents setting forth or evidencing facts on which the motion is based must be filed with the motion. ME R USDCT Rule 7(a).

        • *DISTRICT OF MAINE: Discovery transcripts or materials.* A party relying on discovery transcripts or materials in support of or in opposition to a motion shall file excerpts of such transcript or materials with the memorandum required by ME R USDCT Rule 7 as well as a list of specific citations to the parts on which the party relies. ME R USDCT Rule 26(c). Excerpts of depositions in support of or in opposition to a motion shall be filed electronically using ECF, unless otherwise permitted by the court. ME R USDCT App. 4(l)(3).

    ii. *Notice of constitutional question.* A party that files a pleading, written motion, or other paper drawing into question the constitutionality of a federal or state statute must promptly: (1) file a notice of constitutional question stating the question and identifying the paper that raises it, if: (A) a federal statute is questioned and the parties do not include the United States, one of its agencies, or one of its officers or employees in an official capacity; or (B) a state statute is questioned and the parties do not include the state, one of its agencies, or one of its officers or employees in an official capacity; and (2) serve the notice and paper on the Attorney General of the United States if a federal statute is questioned—or on the state attorney general if a state statute is questioned—either by certified or registered mail or by sending it to an electronic address designated by the attorney general for this purpose. FRCP 5.1(a).

        • *No forfeiture.* A party's failure to file and serve the notice, or the court's failure to certify, does not forfeit a constitutional claim or defense that is otherwise timely asserted. FRCP 5.1(d).

    iii. *Nongovernmental corporate disclosure statement.* A nongovernmental corporate party must file two (2) copies of a disclosure statement that: (1) identifies any parent corporation and any publicly held corporation owning ten percent (10%) or more of its stock; or (2) states that there is no such corporation. FRCP 7.1(a). A party must: (1) file the disclosure statement with its first appearance, pleading, petition, motion, response, or other request addressed to the court; and (2) promptly file a supplemental statement if any required information changes. FRCP 7.1(b).

        • *DISTRICT OF MAINE: Notice of interested parties.* To enable the court to evaluate possible disqualification or recusal, counsel for all non-governmental parties shall file with their first appearance a Notice of Interested Parties, which shall list all persons, associations of persons, firms, partnerships, limited liability companies, joint ventures, corporations (including parent or affiliated corporations, clearly identified as such), or any similar entities, owning ten percent (10%) or more of the named party. Counsel shall be under a continuing obligation to file an amended Notice if any material change occurs in the status of an Interested Party, such as through merger, acquisition, or new/additional membership. ME R USDCT Rule 7.1.

    iv. *DISTRICT OF MAINE: Additional supplemental documents*

        • *Proposed order.* Proposed orders shall not be filed unless requested by the court. When requested by the court, proposed orders shall be filed by e-mail in word processing format. ME R USDCT App. 4(k)(1).

2. *Documents for opposing party*

  a. *Required documents*

    i. *Opposition.* Refer to the "C. General Requirements" section of this KeyRules document for information on the opposing papers.

        • *DISTRICT OF MAINE: Memorandum of law.* Unless within twenty-one (21) days after the filing of a motion the opposing party files written objection thereto, incorporating a memorandum of law, the opposing party shall be deemed to have waived objection. ME R USDCT Rule 7(b).

        • *Certificate of service.* No certificate of service is required when a paper is served by filing it with the court's electronic-filing system. When a paper that is required to be served is served by other means: (i) if the paper is filed, a certificate of service must be filed with it or within a reasonable time after service; and (ii) if the paper is not filed, a certificate of service need not be filed unless filing is required by court order or by local rule. FRCP 5(d)(1)(B).

b. *Supplemental documents*

    i. *Supporting evidence.* When a motion relies on facts outside the record, the court may hear the matter on affidavits or may hear it wholly or partly on oral testimony or on depositions. FRCP 43(c).

- *DISTRICT OF MAINE: Affidavits and other supporting documents.* Any objections shall include. . .affidavits and other documents setting forth or evidencing facts on which the objection is based. ME R USDCT Rule 7(b).

- *DISTRICT OF MAINE: Discovery transcripts or materials.* A party relying on discovery transcripts or materials in support of or in opposition to a motion shall file excerpts of such transcript or materials with the memorandum required by ME R USDCT Rule 7 as well as a list of specific citations to the parts on which the party relies. ME R USDCT Rule 26(c). Excerpts of depositions in support of or in opposition to a motion shall be filed electronically using ECF, unless otherwise permitted by the court. ME R USDCT App. 4(l)(3).

    ii. *Notice of constitutional question.* A party that files a pleading, written motion, or other paper drawing into question the constitutionality of a federal or state statute must promptly: (1) file a notice of constitutional question stating the question and identifying the paper that raises it, if: (A) a federal statute is questioned and the parties do not include the United States, one of its agencies, or one of its officers or employees in an official capacity; or (B) a state statute is questioned and the parties do not include the state, one of its agencies, or one of its officers or employees in an official capacity; and (2) serve the notice and paper on the Attorney General of the United States if a federal statute is questioned—or on the state attorney general if a state statute is questioned—either by certified or registered mail or by sending it to an electronic address designated by the attorney general for this purpose. FRCP 5.1(a).

- *No forfeiture.* A party's failure to file and serve the notice, or the court's failure to certify, does not forfeit a constitutional claim or defense that is otherwise timely asserted. FRCP 5.1(d).

E. Format

1. *Form of documents.* The rules governing captions and other matters of form in pleadings apply to motions and other papers. FRCP 7(b)(2).

    a. *DISTRICT OF MAINE: Font size, line spacing, and paper size.* All such documents shall be typed in a font of no less than size twelve (12) point, and shall be double-spaced or printed on eight and one-half by eleven (8-1/2 x 11) inch paper. Footnotes shall be in a font of no less than size ten (10) point, and may be single spaced. ME R USDCT Rule 10.

    b. *Caption.* Every pleading must have a caption with the court's name, a title, a file number, and an FRCP 7(a) designation. FRCP 10(a).

        i. *Names of parties.* The title of the complaint must name all the parties; the title of other pleadings, after naming the first party on each side, may refer generally to other parties. FRCP 10(a).

        ii. *DISTRICT OF MAINE: Additional caption requirements.* All pleadings, motions and other papers filed with the clerk or otherwise submitted to the court, except exhibits, shall bear the proper case number and shall contain on the first page a caption as described by FRCP 10(a) and immediately thereunder a designation of what the document is and the name of the party in whose behalf it is submitted. ME R USDCT Rule 10.

    c. *Claims or defenses*

        i. *Numbered paragraphs.* A party must state its claims or defenses in numbered paragraphs, each limited as far as practicable to a single set of circumstances. A later pleading may refer by number to a paragraph in an earlier pleading. FRCP 10(b).

        ii. *Separate statements.* If doing so would promote clarity, each claim founded on a separate transaction or occurrence—and each defense other than a denial—must be stated in a separate count or defense. FRCP 10(b).

    d. *Adoption by reference.* A statement in a pleading may be adopted by reference elsewhere in the same pleading or in any other pleading or motion. FRCP 10(c).

        i. *Exhibits.* A copy of a written instrument that is an exhibit to a pleading is a part of the pleading for all purposes. FRCP 10(c).

    e. *DISTRICT OF MAINE: Page numbering.* All pages shall be numbered at the bottom. ME R USDCT Rule 10.

    f. *DISTRICT OF MAINE: Attachment of ancillary papers.* Ancillary papers shall be attached at the end of the document to which they relate. ME R USDCT Rule 10.

g. *Acceptance by the clerk.* The clerk must not refuse to file a paper solely because it is not in the form prescribed by the Federal Rules of Civil Procedure or by a local rule or practice. FRCP 5(d)(4).

2. *Form of electronic documents.* A paper filed electronically is a written paper for purposes of the Federal Rules of Civil Procedure. FRCP 5(d)(3)(D).

    a. *DISTRICT OF MAINE: Document format.* The ECF system only accepts documents in a portable document format (PDF). Although there are two types of PDF documents—electronically converted PDF's and scanned PDF's—only electronically converted PDF's may be filed with the court using the ECF system, unless otherwise authorized by local rule or order. ME R USDCT App. 4. Any document or exhibit to be filed or submitted to the court shall not be password-protected or encrypted. ME R USDCT App. 4(g)(12).

        i. *Electronically converted PDFs.* Electronically converted PDF's are created from word processing documents (MS Word, WordPerfect, etc.) using Adobe Acrobat or similar software. They are text searchable and their file size is small. ME R USDCT App. 4. Software used to electronically convert documents to PDF which includes proprietary or advertisement information within the PDF document is prohibited. ME R USDCT App. 4.

        ii. *Scanned PDFs.* Scanned PDF's are created from paper documents run through an optical scanner. Scanned PDF's are not searchable and have a large file size. ME R USDCT App. 4.

    b. *DISTRICT OF MAINE: Title.* All pleadings filed electronically shall be titled in accordance with the approved dictionary of civil or criminal events of the ECF system of the United States District Court for the District of Maine. ME R USDCT App. 4(d)(3).

    c. *DISTRICT OF MAINE: Attachments.* Attachments to filings and exhibits must be filed in accordance with the court's ECF User Manual, unless otherwise ordered by the court. ME R USDCT App. 4(j). When there are fifty (50) or fewer attachments to a pleading, the attachments must be filed by counsel electronically using ECF. When there are more than fifty (50) attachments, the attachments must be filed in one of the following ways: (A) using ECF, simply attach them to the pleading being filed; (B) using ECF, use the "Additional Attachments" menu item; (C) on paper; or (D) on a properly labeled three and one-half (3-1/2) inch floppy disk, CD or DVD. ME R USDCT App. 4(j)(2). Attachments filed on paper or on disk must contain a comprehensive index that clearly describes each document. ME R USDCT App. 4(j)(2).

        i. A filing user must submit as attachments only those excerpts of the referenced documents that are directly germane to the matter under consideration by the court. Excerpted material must be clearly and prominently identified as such. Users who file excerpts of documents do so without prejudice to their right to timely file additional excerpts or the complete document, as may be allowed by the court. Responding parties may timely file additional excerpts or the complete document that they believe are directly germane. ME R USDCT App. 4(j)(3).

        ii. Filers shall not attach as an exhibit any pleading or other paper already on file with the court in that case, but shall merely refer to that document. ME R USDCT App. 4(j)(4).

    d. *DISTRICT OF MAINE: Compliance with technical standards.* All documents filed by electronic means must comply with technical standards, if any, established by the Judicial Conference of the United States or by the United States District Court for the District of Maine. ME R USDCT App. 4(a)(3).

3. *DISTRICT OF MAINE: Form of memoranda of law.* All memoranda shall be typed, in a font of no less than size twelve (12) point, and shall be double-spaced on eight and one-half by eleven (8-1/2 x 11) inch paper or printed. Footnotes shall be in a font of no less than size ten (10) point, and may be single spaced. All pages shall be numbered at the bottom. ME R USDCT Rule 7(d).

    a. *Page limitations.* No memorandum of law in support of or in opposition to a nondispositive motion shall exceed ten (10) pages. ME R USDCT Rule 7(d). No reply memorandum shall exceed seven (7) pages. ME R USDCT Rule 7(d); ME R USDCT Rule 7(c).

        i. *Motion to exceed page limitation.* A motion to exceed the limitation of ME R USDCT Rule 7 shall be filed no later than three (3) business days in advance of the date for filing the memorandum to permit meaningful review by the court. A motion to exceed the page limitations shall not be filed simultaneously with a memorandum in excess of the limitations of ME R USDCT Rule 7. ME R USDCT Rule 7(d).

4. *Signing of pleadings, motions and other papers*

    a. *Signature.* Every pleading, written motion, and other paper must be signed by at least one attorney of record in the

attorney's name—or by a party personally if the party is unrepresented. The paper must state the signer's address, e-mail address, and telephone number. FRCP 11(a).

    i. *No verification or accompanying affidavit required for pleadings.* Unless a rule or statute specifically states otherwise, a pleading need not be verified or accompanied by an affidavit. FRCP 11(a).

    ii. *Unsigned papers.* The court must strike an unsigned paper unless the omission is promptly corrected after being called to the attorney's or party's attention. FRCP 11(a).

b. *Electronic signing.* A filing made through a person's electronic-filing account and authorized by that person, together with that person's name on a signature block, constitutes the person's signature. FRCP 5(d)(3)(C).

    i. *DISTRICT OF MAINE: Attorneys.* The user log-in and password together with a user's name on the signature block constitutes the attorney's signature pursuant to the Federal Rules of Civil Procedure and the Local Rules of the United States District Court for the District of Maine. All electronically filed documents must include a signature block and must set forth the attorney's name, address, telephone number and e-mail address. The name of the ECF user under whose log-in and password the document is submitted must be preceded by a "/s/" in the space where the signature would otherwise appear. ME R USDCT App. 4(h)(1).

    ii. *DISTRICT OF MAINE: Multiple signatures.* The filer of any document requiring more than one signature (e.g., pleadings filed by visiting lawyers, stipulations, joint status reports) must list thereon all the names of other signatories, preceded by a "/s/" in the space where the signatures would otherwise appear. By submitting such a document, the filing attorney certifies that each of the other signatories has expressly agreed to the form and substance of the document and that the filing attorney has their actual authority to submit the document electronically. ME R USDCT App. 4(h)(2). For more information, refer to ME R USDCT App. 4(h)(2).

    iii. *DISTRICT OF MAINE: Documents signed under oath.* Affidavits, declarations, verified complaints, or any other document signed under oath shall be filed electronically. The electronically filed version shall contain the typed name of the signatory, preceded by a "/s/" in the space where the signature would otherwise appear indicating that the paper document bears an original signature. ME R USDCT Rule 10; ME R USDCT App. 4(h)(3). For more information, refer to ME R USDCT Rule 10.

c. *Representations to the court.* By presenting to the court a pleading, written motion, or other paper—whether by signing, filing, submitting, or later advocating it—an attorney or unrepresented party certifies that to the best of the person's knowledge, information, and belief, formed after an inquiry reasonable under the circumstances: (1) it is not being presented for any improper purpose, such as to harass, cause unnecessary delay, or needlessly increase the cost of litigation; (2) the claims, defenses, and other legal contentions are warranted by existing law or by a nonfrivolous argument for extending, modifying, or reversing existing law or for establishing new law; (3) the factual contentions have evidentiary support or, if specifically so identified, will likely have evidentiary support after a reasonable opportunity for further investigation or discovery; and (4) the denials of factual contentions are warranted on the evidence or, if specifically so identified, are reasonably based on belief or a lack of information. FRCP 11(b).

d. *Sanctions.* If, after notice and a reasonable opportunity to respond, the court determines that FRCP 11(b) has been violated, the court may impose an appropriate sanction on any attorney, law firm, or party that violated FRCP 11(b) or is responsible for the violation. FRCP 11(c)(1). Refer to the United States District Court for the District of Maine KeyRules Motion for Sanctions document for more information.

5. *Privacy protection for filings made with the court*

a. *Redacted filings.* Unless the court orders otherwise, in an electronic or paper filing with the court that contains an individual's Social Security number, taxpayer-identification number, or birth date, the name of an individual known to be a minor, or a financial-account number, a party or nonparty making the filing may include only: (1) the last four (4) digits of the Social Security number and taxpayer-identification number; (2) the year of the individual's birth; (3) the minor's initials; and (4) the last four (4) digits of the financial-account number. FRCP 5.2(a).

    i. *DISTRICT OF MAINE.* To address the privacy concerns created by the Internet access to court papers, unless otherwise ordered by the court, counsel shall modify certain personal data identifiers in pleadings and other papers as follows: (1) minors' names: use of the minors' initials only; (2) Social Security numbers: use of the last four (4) numbers only; (3) dates of birth: use of the year of birth only; [and] (4) financial account numbers: identify the type of account and the financial institution, but use only the last four (4) numbers of the account number. ME R USDCT Redacting Pleadings. Counsel should also use caution when filing papers that contain a person's medical records, employment history; financial information; and any proprietary or trade secret information. ME R USDCT Redacting Pleadings.

b. *Exemptions from the redaction requirement.* The redaction requirement does not apply to the following: (1) a

financial-account number that identifies the property allegedly subject to forfeiture in a forfeiture proceeding; (2) the record of an administrative or agency proceeding; (3) the official record of a state-court proceeding; (4) the record of a court or tribunal, if that record was not subject to the redaction requirement when originally filed; (5) a filing covered by FRCP 5.2(c) or FRCP 5.2(d); and (6) a pro se filing in an action brought under 28 U.S.C.A. § 2241, 28 U.S.C.A. § 2254, or 28 U.S.C.A. § 2255. FRCP 5.2(b).

    c.   *Limitations on remote access to electronic files; Social Security appeals and immigration cases.* Unless the court orders otherwise, in an action for benefits under the Social Security Act, and in an action or proceeding relating to an order of removal, to relief from removal, or to immigration benefits or detention, access to an electronic file is authorized as follows: (1) the parties and their attorneys may have remote electronic access to any part of the case file, including the administrative record; (2) any other person may have electronic access to the full record at the courthouse, but may have remote electronic access only to: (A) the docket maintained by the court; and (B) an opinion, order, judgment, or other disposition of the court, but not any other part of the case file or the administrative record. FRCP 5.2(c).

    d.   *Filings made under seal.* The court may order that a filing be made under seal without redaction. The court may later unseal the filing or order the person who made the filing to file a redacted version for the public record. FRCP 5.2(d).

        i.   *DISTRICT OF MAINE.* For information on filing sealed documents in the District of Maine, refer to ME R USDCT Rule 7A, ME R USDCT App. 4(p)(2), and ME R USDCT Sealed Filings.

    e.   *Protective orders.* For good cause, the court may by order in a case: (1) require redaction of additional information; or (2) limit or prohibit a nonparty's remote electronic access to a document filed with the court. FRCP 5.2(e).

    f.   *Option for additional unredacted filing under seal.* A person making a redacted filing may also file an unredacted copy under seal. The court must retain the unredacted copy as part of the record. FRCP 5.2(f).

        i.   *DISTRICT OF MAINE.* A party wishing to file a document containing the personal data identifiers specified above may. . .file an unredacted document under seal. This document will be retained by the clerk's office as part of the record. ME R USDCT Redacting Pleadings. The court may, however, still require the party to file a redacted copy for the public file. ME R USDCT Redacting Pleadings.

    g.   *Option for filing a reference list.* A filing that contains redacted information may be filed together with a reference list that identifies each item of redacted information and specifies an appropriate identifier that uniquely corresponds to each item listed. The list must be filed under seal and may be amended as of right. Any reference in the case to a listed identifier will be construed to refer to the corresponding item of information. FRCP 5.2(g).

        i.   *DISTRICT OF MAINE.* A party wishing to file a document containing the personal data identifiers specified above may. . .file a reference list under seal. The reference list shall contain the complete personal data identifier(s) and the redacted identifier(s) used in its (their) place in the filing. All references in the case to the redacted identifiers included in the reference list will be construed to refer to the corresponding complete identifier. The reference list must be filed under seal, and may be amended as of right. It shall be retained by the clerk's office as part of the record. ME R USDCT Redacting Pleadings. The court may, however, still require the party to file a redacted copy for the public file. ME R USDCT Redacting Pleadings.

    h.   *DISTRICT OF MAINE: Responsibility for redaction.* The clerk is not required to review documents filed with the court for compliance with FRCP 5.2. The responsibility to redact filings rests with counsel and the party or nonparty making the filing. ME R USDCT App. 4(i); ME R USDCT Redacting Pleadings. For guidelines for filing confidential information in civil cases in the District of Maine, refer to ME R USDCT Confidentiality.

    i.   *Waiver of protection of identifiers.* A person waives the protection of FRCP 5.2(a) as to the person's own information by filing it without redaction and not under seal. FRCP 5.2(h).

F. Filing and Service Requirements

    1.   *Filing requirements*

    a.   *Required filings.* Any paper after the complaint that is required to be served must be filed no later than a reasonable time after service. FRCP 5(d)(1).

    b.   *DISTRICT OF MAINE: Place of filing.* Unless otherwise ordered by the court, papers shall be filed with the court at Bangor in cases filed and pending at Bangor, and at Portland in cases filed and pending at Portland. ME R USDCT Rule 5(a).

    c.   *Nonelectronic filing.* A paper not filed electronically is filed by delivering it: (A) to the clerk; or (B) to a judge who

agrees to accept it for filing, and who must then note the filing date on the paper and promptly send it to the clerk. FRCP 5(d)(2).

    i. *DISTRICT OF MAINE: Documents to be filed in paper.* The following documents shall be filed in paper, which may also be scanned into ECF by the clerk's office: (A) all handwritten pleadings; and (B) all pleadings and documents filed by pro se litigants who are incarcerated or who are not registered filing users in ECF. ME R USDCT App. 4(g)(8). Non-prisoner pro se litigants in civil actions may register with ECF or may file (and serve) all pleadings and other documents in paper. The clerk's office will scan into ECF any pleadings and documents filed on paper in accordance with ME R USDCT App. 4(g). ME R USDCT App. 4(o). For more information, refer to ME R USDCT App. 4(g).

  d. *Electronic filing*

    i. *DISTRICT OF MAINE: Authorization.* Unless exempt or otherwise ordered by the court, papers shall be filed and served electronically as required by the court's Administrative Procedures Governing the Filing and Service by Electronic Means, which is set forth in ME R USDCT App. 4. The provisions of the court's Administrative Procedures Governing the Filing and Service by Electronic Means (ME R USDCT App. 4) shall be applied and enforced as part of the Local Rules of the United States District Court for the District of Maine. ME R USDCT Rule 5(c).

    ii. *Filing by represented persons.* A person represented by an attorney must file electronically, unless nonelectronic filing is allowed by the court for good cause or is allowed or required by local rule. FRCP 5(d)(3)(A).

       • *DISTRICT OF MAINE.* An attorney may apply to the court for permission to file paper documents. ME R USDCT App. 4(a)(5).

    iii. *Filing by unrepresented persons.* A person not represented by an attorney: (i) may file electronically only if allowed by court order or by local rule; and (ii) may be required to file electronically only by court order, or by a local rule that includes reasonable exceptions. FRCP 5(d)(3)(B).

       • *DISTRICT OF MAINE.* Non-prisoner pro se litigants in civil actions may register with ECF or may file (and serve) all pleadings and other documents in paper. ME R USDCT App. 4(o). A non-prisoner who is a party to a civil action and who is not represented by an attorney may register to receive service electronically and to electronically transmit their documents to the court for filing in the ECF system. If during the course of the action the person retains an attorney who appears on the person's behalf, the clerk shall terminate the person's registration upon the attorney's appearance. ME R USDCT App. 4(b)(2).

    iv. *DISTRICT OF MAINE: Scope of electronic filing.* All documents submitted for filing in civil and criminal cases, regardless of case commencement date, except those documents specifically exempted in ME R USDCT App. 4(g), shall be filed electronically using the electronic case filing system (ECF). ME R USDCT App. 4(a)(1). For special filing requirements and exceptions, refer to ME R USDCT App. 4(g).

    v. *DISTRICT OF MAINE: Consequences of electronic filing.* Electronic transmission of a document to the ECF system, together with the transmission of a Notice of Electronic Filing (NEF) from the court, constitutes filing of the document for all purposes of the Federal Rules of Civil Procedure. ME R USDCT App. 4(d)(1).

    vi. *DISTRICT OF MAINE: Review of documents.* Documents filed with the clerk's office will normally be reviewed no later than the close of the next business day. It is the responsibility of the filing party to promptly notify the clerk's office via telephone of a matter that requires the immediate attention of a judicial officer. ME R USDCT App. 4(a)(4).

  e. *DISTRICT OF MAINE: Facsimile filing.* No papers shall be submitted to the court by means of a facsimile machine without prior leave of the court. ME R USDCT Rule 5(c); ME R USDCT App. 4(m).

2. *Service requirements*

  a. *Service; When required.* Unless the Federal Rules of Civil Procedure provide otherwise, each of the following papers must be served on every party: (A) an order stating that service is required; (B) a pleading filed after the original complaint, unless the court orders otherwise under FRCP 5(c) because there are numerous defendants; (C) a discovery paper required to be served on a party, unless the court orders otherwise; (D) a written motion, except one that may be heard ex parte; and (E) a written notice, appearance, demand, or offer of judgment, or any similar paper. FRCP 5(a)(1).

    i. *If a party fails to appear.* No service is required on a party who is in default for failing to appear. But a pleading that asserts a new claim for relief against such a party must be served on that party under FRCP 4. FRCP 5(a)(2).

    ii. *Seizing property.* If an action is begun by seizing property and no person is or need be named as a defendant, any

service required before the filing of an appearance, answer, or claim must be made on the person who had custody or possession of the property when it was seized. FRCP 5(a)(3).

b. *Service; How made.* A paper is served under FRCP 5 by: (A) handing it to the person; (B) leaving it: (i) at the person's office with a clerk or other person in charge or, if no one is in charge, in a conspicuous place in the office; or (ii) if the person has no office or the office is closed, at the person's dwelling or usual place of abode with someone of suitable age and discretion who resides there; (C) mailing it to the person's last known address—in which event service is complete upon mailing; (D) leaving it with the court clerk if the person has no known address; (E) sending it to a registered user by filing it with the court's electronic-filing system or sending it by other electronic means that the person consented to in writing—in either of which events service is complete upon filing or sending, but is not effective if the filer or sender learns that it did not reach the person to be served; or (F) delivering it by any other means that the person consented to in writing—in which event service is complete when the person making service delivers it to the agency designated to make delivery. FRCP 5(b)(2).

    i. *Serving an attorney.* If a party is represented by an attorney, service under FRCP 5 must be made on the attorney unless the court orders service on the party. FRCP 5(b)(1).

c. *DISTRICT OF MAINE: Service of electronically filed documents*

    i. *Registered users.* Registration [as a filing user of the court's ECF system] constitutes consent to service of all documents by electronic means as provided in ME R USDCT App. 4. ME R USDCT App. 4(b)(4). Whenever a non-sealed pleading is filed electronically, the ECF system will automatically generate and send a Notice of Electronic Filing (NEF) to the filing user and registered users of record. The user filing the document should retain a paper or digital copy of the NEF, which shall serve as the court's date-stamp and proof of filing. ME R USDCT App. 4(e)(1).

        • *Sealed documents.* Although the filing of sealed documents in civil cases produces an NEF, the document itself cannot be accessed and counsel shall be responsible for making service of the sealed documents. ME R USDCT App. 4(e)(2).

    ii. *Non-registered users and pro se litigants.* Attorneys who have not yet registered as users with ECF and pro se litigants who have not registered with ECF shall be served a paper copy of any electronically filed pleading or other document in accordance with the provisions of FRCP 5. ME R USDCT App. 4(e)(3).

        • *Registration of pro se litigants.* A non-prisoner who is a party to a civil action and who is not represented by an attorney may register to receive service electronically and to electronically transmit their documents to the court for filing in the ECF system. If during the course of the action the person retains an attorney who appears on the person's behalf, the clerk shall terminate the person's registration upon the attorney's appearance. ME R USDCT App. 4(b)(2).

d. *Serving numerous defendants.* If an action involves an unusually large number of defendants, the court may, on motion or on its own, order that: (A) defendants' pleadings and replies to them need not be served on other defendants; (B) any crossclaim, counterclaim, avoidance, or affirmative defense in those pleadings and replies to them will be treated as denied or avoided by all other parties; and (C) filing any such pleading and serving it on the plaintiff constitutes notice of the pleading to all parties. FRCP 5(c)(1).

    i. *Notifying parties.* A copy of every such order must be served on the parties as the court directs. FRCP 5(c)(2).

3. *DISTRICT OF MAINE: Filing and service of highly sensitive documents (HSDs).* For information on filing and serving highly sensitive documents (HSDs) in the District of Maine, refer to ME R USDCT General Order 21-5.

G. Hearings

1. *Hearings, generally.* When a motion relies on facts outside the record, the court may hear the matter on affidavits or may hear it wholly or partly on oral testimony or on depositions. FRCP 43(c).

a. *Oral argument.* Due process does not require that oral argument be permitted on a motion and, except as otherwise provided by local rule, the district court has discretion to determine whether it will decide the motion on the papers or hear argument by counsel (and perhaps receive evidence). FPP § 1190; F.D.I.C. v. Deglau, 207 F.3d 153 (3d Cir. 2000).

    i. *DISTRICT OF MAINE.* Unless otherwise required by federal rule or statute, all motions may be decided by the court without oral argument unless otherwise ordered by the court on its own motion or, in its discretion, upon request of counsel. ME R USDCT Rule 7(e).

b. *Providing a regular schedule for oral hearings.* A court may establish regular times and places for oral hearings on motions. FRCP 78(a).

  c. *Providing for submission on briefs.* By rule or order, the court may provide for submitting and determining motions on briefs, without oral hearings. FRCP 78(b).

H. Forms

1. Federal Motion for Continuance/Extension of Time Forms

  a. Motion for enlargement of time. 2 FEDFORMS § 5:11.

  b. Motion for enlargement of time; By plaintiff. 2 FEDFORMS § 5:12.

  c. Motion for enlargement of time; To answer motion. 2 FEDFORMS § 5:14.

  d. Motion for continuance. 2 FEDFORMS § 5:36.

  e. Motion for continuance; Reciting supporting facts; New allegations in amended answer. 2 FEDFORMS § 5:37.

  f. Motion for continuance; Reciting supporting facts; Absence of witness. 2 FEDFORMS § 5:38.

  g. Motion for continuance; Reciting supporting facts; Absence of witness; Witness outside the country. 2 FEDFORMS § 5:39.

  h. Motion for continuance or in the alternative for change of venue; Hostility against defendant. 2 FEDFORMS § 5:40.

  i. Opposition in federal district court; To motion for continuance; On ground of additional time required to prepare for trial; No excusable neglect shown. AMJUR PP CONTIN § 79.

  j. Affidavit in opposition to motion for continuance; By plaintiff's attorney; Lack of due diligence in discovery of documents. AMJUR PP CONTIN § 80.

  k. Affidavit in opposition to motion for continuance; By plaintiff's attorney; Defendant's absent witness previously absent; Lack of due diligence in compelling attendance of witness. AMJUR PP CONTIN § 81.

  l. Affidavit in opposition to motion for continuance; By plaintiff; Admission that absent witness of defendant would testify according to affidavit. AMJUR PP CONTIN § 83.

  m. Affidavit in opposition to defendant's motion for continuance; By plaintiff's counsel; Testimony of absent witness merely cumulative. AMJUR PP CONTIN § 85.

  n. Notice; Of motion; Containing motion. FEDPROF § 1B:174.

  o. Brief; Supporting or opposing motion. FEDPROF § 1B:177.

  p. Opposition to motion; For continuance; No excusable neglect. FEDPROF § 1B:240.

  q. Affidavit; Opposing motion for continuance; Offer to stipulate to testimony of unavailable witness. FEDPROF § 1B:246.

  r. Reply to motion for extension of time. GOLDLTGFMS § 10:40.

  s. Motions; Extension of time to file jury demand. GOLDLTGFMS § 12:6.

  t. Motion for extension of time. GOLDLTGFMS § 25:38.

  u. Motion for extension of time to answer. GOLDLTGFMS § 26:13.

  v. Motion to extend time for serving answers. GOLDLTGFMS § 26:14.

  w. Motion for continuance. GOLDLTGFMS § 43:2.

  x. Motion for continuance; Lawyer unavailable. GOLDLTGFMS § 43:3.

  y. Motion for continuance; Witness unavailable. GOLDLTGFMS § 43:4.

  z. Motion for continuance; Party in military service. GOLDLTGFMS § 43:6.

I. Applicable Rules

1. *Federal rules*

  a. Serving and filing pleadings and other papers. FRCP 5.

  b. Constitutional challenge to a statute; Notice, certification, and intervention. FRCP 5.1.

  c. Privacy protection for filings made with the court. FRCP 5.2.

  d. Computing and extending time; Time for motion papers. FRCP 6.

  e. Pleadings allowed; Form of motions and other papers. FRCP 7.

    f.   Disclosure statement. FRCP 7.1.

    g.   Form of pleadings. FRCP 10.

    h.   Signing pleadings, motions, and other papers; Representations to the court; Sanctions. FRCP 11.

    i.   Taking testimony. FRCP 43.

    j.   Hearing motions; Submission on briefs. FRCP 78.

2. *Local rules*

    a. *DISTRICT OF MAINE*

        i.   Service and filing of pleadings and other papers. ME R USDCT Rule 5.

        ii.   Time. ME R USDCT Rule 6.

        iii.   Motions and memoranda of law. ME R USDCT Rule 7.

        iv.   Corporate disclosure. ME R USDCT Rule 7.1.

        v.   Form of pleadings, motions and other papers. ME R USDCT Rule 10.

        vi.   Discovery. ME R USDCT Rule 26.

        vii.   Attorneys; Appearances and withdrawals. ME R USDCT Rule 83.2.

        viii.   Alternative dispute resolution (ADR). ME R USDCT Rule 83.11.

        ix.   Administrative procedures governing the filing and service by electronic means. ME R USDCT App. 4.

        x.   Redacting pleadings. ME R USDCT Redacting Pleadings.

Motions, Oppositions and Replies
Motion for Summary Judgment

Document Last Updated April 2021

A. Checklist

(I) ❑ Matters to be considered by moving party

    (a) ❑ Required documents

        (1) ❑ Notice of motion and motion

        (2) ❑ DISTRICT OF MAINE: Additional required documents

            (i) ❑ Supporting statement of material facts and/or stipulated statement of material facts

    (b) ❑ Supplemental documents

        (1) ❑ Supporting evidence

        (2) ❑ Notice of constitutional question

        (3) ❑ Nongovernmental corporate disclosure statement

        (4) ❑ DISTRICT OF MAINE: Additional supplemental documents

            (i) ❑ Proposed order

    (c) ❑ Timing

        (1) ❑ Unless a different time is set by local rule or the court orders otherwise, a party may file a motion for summary judgment at any time until thirty (30) days after the close of all discovery

        (2) ❑ A written motion and notice of the hearing must be served at least fourteen (14) days before the time specified for the hearing, with the following exceptions: (A) when the motion may be heard ex parte; (B) when the Federal Rules of Civil Procedure set a different time; or (C) when a court order—which a party may, for good cause, apply for ex parte—sets a different time

        (3) ❑ Any affidavit supporting a motion must be served with the motion

    (4)   ❏ DISTRICT OF MAINE: Additional timing

        (i)   ❏ Any affidavits and other documents setting forth or evidencing facts on which the motion is based must be filed with the motion

(II) ❏ Matters to be considered by opposing party

    (a) ❏ Required documents

        (1) ❏ Opposition

        (2) ❏ DISTRICT OF MAINE: Additional required documents

            (i) ❏ Opposing statement of material facts

    (b) ❏ Supplemental documents

        (1) ❏ Supporting evidence

        (2) ❏ Notice of constitutional question

    (c) ❏ Timing

        (1) ❏ Except as FRCP 59(c) provides otherwise, any opposing affidavit must be served at least seven (7) days before the hearing, unless the court permits service at another time

        (2) ❏ DISTRICT OF MAINE: Additional timing

            (i) ❏ Unless within twenty-one (21) days after the filing of a motion the opposing party files written objection thereto, incorporating a memorandum of law, the opposing party shall be deemed to have waived objection

B. Timing

1. *Motion for summary judgment.* Unless a different time is set by local rule or the court orders otherwise, a party may file a motion for summary judgment at any time until thirty (30) days after the close of all discovery. FRCP 56(b).

2. *Timing of motions, generally*

    a. *Motion and notice of hearing.* A written motion and notice of the hearing must be served at least fourteen (14) days before the time specified for the hearing, with the following exceptions: (A) when the motion may be heard ex parte; (B) when the Federal Rules of Civil Procedure set a different time; or (C) when a court order—which a party may, for good cause, apply for ex parte—sets a different time. FRCP 6(c)(1).

    b. *Supporting affidavit.* Any affidavit supporting a motion must be served with the motion. FRCP 6(c)(2).

    c. *DISTRICT OF MAINE: Affidavits and other supporting documents.* Any affidavits and other documents setting forth or evidencing facts on which the motion is based must be filed with the motion. ME R USDCT Rule 7(a).

3. *Timing of opposing papers.* Except as FRCP 59(c) provides otherwise, any opposing affidavit must be served at least seven (7) days before the hearing, unless the court permits service at another time. FRCP 6(c)(2).

    a. *DISTRICT OF MAINE.* Unless within twenty-one (21) days after the filing of a motion the opposing party files written objection thereto, incorporating a memorandum of law, the opposing party shall be deemed to have waived objection. ME R USDCT Rule 7(b). The deemed waiver imposed in ME R USDCT Rule 7(b) shall not apply to motions filed during trial. ME R USDCT Rule 7(b).

4. *Timing of reply papers.* Where the respondent files an answering affidavit setting up a new matter, the moving party ordinarily is allowed a reasonable time to file a reply affidavit since failure to deny the new matter by affidavit may operate as an admission of its truth. AMJUR MOTIONS § 25.

    a. *DISTRICT OF MAINE.* Within fourteen (14) days of the filing of any objection to a motion, the moving party may file a reply memorandum. ME R USDCT Rule 7(c).

5. *Computation of time*

    a. *Computing time.* FRCP 6 applies in computing any time period specified in the Federal Rules of Civil Procedure, in any local rule or court order, or in any statute that does not specify a method of computing time. FRCP 6(a).

        i. *Period stated in days or a longer unit.* When the period is stated in days or a longer unit of time: (A) exclude the day of the event that triggers the period; (B) count every day, including intermediate Saturdays, Sundays, and legal holidays; and (C) include the last day of the period, but if the last day is a Saturday, Sunday, or legal holiday, the period continues to run until the end of the next day that is not a Saturday, Sunday, or legal holiday. FRCP 6(a)(1).

    ii.   *Period stated in hours.* When the period is stated in hours: (A) begin counting immediately on the occurrence of the event that triggers the period; (B) count every hour, including hours during intermediate Saturdays, Sundays, and legal holidays; and (C) if the period would end on a Saturday, Sunday, or legal holiday, the period continues to run until the same time on the next day that is not a Saturday, Sunday, or legal holiday. FRCP 6(a)(2).

    iii.   *Inaccessibility of the clerk's office.* Unless the court orders otherwise, if the clerk's office is inaccessible: (A) on the last day for filing under FRCP 6(a)(1), then the time for filing is extended to the first accessible day that is not a Saturday, Sunday, or legal holiday; or (B) during the last hour for filing under FRCP 6(a)(2), then the time for filing is extended to the same time on the first accessible day that is not a Saturday, Sunday, or legal holiday. FRCP 6(a)(3).

    iv.   *"Last day" defined.* Unless a different time is set by a statute, local rule, or court order, the last day ends: (A) for electronic filing, at midnight in the court's time zone; and (B) for filing by other means, when the clerk's office is scheduled to close. FRCP 6(a)(4).

    v.   *"Next day" defined.* The "next day" is determined by continuing to count forward when the period is measured after an event and backward when measured before an event. FRCP 6(a)(5).

    vi.   *"Legal holiday" defined.* "Legal holiday" means: (A) the day set aside by statute for observing New Year's Day, Martin Luther King Jr.'s Birthday, Washington's Birthday, Memorial Day, Independence Day, Labor Day, Columbus Day, Veterans' Day, Thanksgiving Day, or Christmas Day; (B) any day declared a holiday by the President or Congress; and (C) for periods that are measured after an event, any other day declared a holiday by the state where the district court is located. FRCP 6(a)(6).

    vii.   *DISTRICT OF MAINE: Applicability of FRCP 6.* FRCP 6 applies when computing any period of time stated in the Local Rules of the United States District Court for the District of Maine. ME R USDCT Rule 6(a).

  b.   *DISTRICT OF MAINE: Computation of electronic filing deadlines.* Filing documents electronically does not in any way alter any filing deadlines. All electronic transmissions of documents must be completed prior to midnight, Eastern Time, in order to be considered timely filed that day. Where a specific time of day deadline is set by court order or stipulation, the electronic filing must be completed by that time. ME R USDCT App. 4(f). A document filed electronically shall be deemed filed at the time and date stated on the Notice of Electronic Filing received from the court. ME R USDCT App. 4(d)(2).

    i.   *Technical failures.* A filing user whose filing is made untimely as the result of a technical failure may seek appropriate relief from the court. ME R USDCT App. 4(n). A technical failure of the court's ECF system is deemed to have occurred when the court's ECF site cannot accept filings continuously or intermittently over the course of any period of time greater than one (1) hour. Known system outages will be posted on the court's website along with guidance on how to proceed, if applicable. ME R USDCT App. 4(n).

  c.   *Extending time.* When an act may or must be done within a specified time, the court may, for good cause, extend the time: (A) with or without motion or notice if the court acts, or if a request is made, before the original time or its extension expires; or (B) on motion made after the time has expired if the party failed to act because of excusable neglect. FRCP 6(b)(1). A court must not extend the time to act under FRCP 50(b), FRCP 50(d), FRCP 52(b), FRCP 59(b), FRCP 59(d), FRCP 59(e), and FRCP 60(b). FRCP 6(b)(2). Refer to the United States District Court for the District of Maine KeyRules Motion for Continuance/Extension of Time document for more information on extending time.

  d.   *Additional time after certain kinds of service.* When a party may or must act within a specified time after being served and service is made under FRCP 5(b)(2)(C) (by mail), FRCP 5(b)(2)(D) (by leaving with the clerk), or FRCP 5(b)(2)(F) (by other means consented to), three (3) days are added after the period would otherwise expire under FRCP 6(a). FRCP 6(d).

C. General Requirements

1. *Motions, generally*

  a.   *Motion requirements.* A request for a court order must be made by motion. The motion must: (A) be in writing unless made during a hearing or trial; (B) state with particularity the grounds for seeking the order; and (C) state the relief sought. FRCP 7(b)(1). The writing and particularity requirements are intended to ensure that the adverse parties are informed of and have a record of both the motion's pendency and the grounds on which the movant seeks an order. FPP § 1191; Feldberg v. Quechee Lakes Corp., 463 F.3d 195 (2d Cir. 2006).

    i.   *Particularity requirement.* The particularity requirement [ensures] that the opposing parties will have notice of their opponent's contentions. FEDPROC § 62:358; Goodman v. 1973 26 Foot Trojan Vessel, Arkansas

Registration No. AR1439SN, 859 F.2d 71 (8th Cir. 1988). That requirement ensures that notice of the basis for the motion is provided to the court and to the opposing party so as to avoid prejudice, provide the opponent with a meaningful opportunity to respond, and provide the court with enough information to process the motion correctly. FEDPROC § 62:358; Andreas v. Volkswagen of Am., Inc., 336 F.3d 789 (8th Cir. 2003).

- Reasonable specification of the grounds for a motion is sufficient. The particularity requirement for motions is satisfied when no party is prejudiced by a lack of particularity or when the court can comprehend the basis for the motion and deal with it fairly. However, where a movant fails to state even one ground for granting the motion in question, the movant has failed to meet the minimal standard of "reasonable specification." FEDPROC § 62:358; Martinez v. Trainor, 556 F.2d 818 (7th Cir. 1977).

- The court may excuse the failure to comply with the particularity requirement if it is inadvertent, and where no prejudice is shown by the opposing party. FEDPROC § 62:358.

 b. *Notice of motion.* A party interested in resisting the relief sought by a motion has a right to notice thereof, and an opportunity to be heard. AMJUR MOTIONS § 12.

  i. *Purpose.* In addition to statutory or court rule provisions requiring notice of a motion—the purpose of such a notice requirement having been said to be to prevent a party from being prejudicially surprised by a motion—principles of natural justice dictate that an adverse party generally must be given notice that a motion will be presented to the court. AMJUR MOTIONS § 12.

  ii. *Adequacy of notice.* The test of adequate notice generally turns on whether the other parties were afforded an adequate opportunity to prepare and respond to the issues to be raised in the proceeding. AMJUR MOTIONS § 12.

 c. *Single document containing motion and notice.* A single written document can satisfy the writing requirements both for a motion and for an FRCP 6(c)(1) notice. FRCP 7(Advisory Committee Notes).

2. *DISTRICT OF MAINE: Pre-filing conference in standard track cases.* In all Standard Track cases, except those categories of cases listed in FRCP 26(a)(1)(B), a party intending to move for summary judgment shall file no later than seven (7) days after the close of discovery either (1) a joint motion setting forth a proposed schedule agreed to by all the parties and confirming that all of the parties agree that a pre-filing conference with a judicial officer would not be helpful, or (2) a notice of intent to move for summary judgment, and the need for a pre-filing conference with a judicial officer. ME R USDCT Rule 56(h).

 a. *By joint motion with proposed schedule.* The parties must jointly propose a schedule for briefing all proposed motions for summary judgment. ME R USDCT Rule 56(h)(1). The court may adopt or modify the jointly proposed schedule, or instead may set the matter for a pre-filing conference. ME R USDCT Rule 56(h)(1). The proposed schedule shall include:

  i. *Proposed page limits and deadlines for filing.* If the motion proposes to exceed the limits set forth in ME R USDCT Rule 7, the parties shall include a brief statement explaining why good cause exists for allowing extra time and/or pages. ME R USDCT Rule 56(h)(1)(A).

  ii. The estimated number of statements of material fact and the estimated number of additional statements by any party opposing the motion for summary judgment. ME R USDCT Rule 56(h)(1)(B).

  iii. Any stipulations to be filed. The parties shall generally describe any stipulated record or factual stipulations they propose to file and indicate whether stipulations of fact are made solely pursuant to ME R USDCT Rule 56(b). If any such stipulated filings will be made, the proposed schedule shall first set a deadline for this stipulated filing, which shall be at least five (5) calendar days before the deadline for filing the motion for summary judgment. ME R USDCT Rule 56(h)(1)(C).

  iv. Proposed page limits and deadlines for filing Daubert and/or Kumho motions, oppositions to Daubert and/or Kumho motions, and replies to oppositions to Daubert and/or Kumho motions. If the parties propose to exceed the time or page limits set forth in ME R USDCT Rule 7, the parties shall include a brief statement explaining why good cause exists for allowing extra time and/or pages. ME R USDCT Rule 56(h)(1)(D).

 b. *By notice.* Alternatively, absent agreement, the movant shall provide the court and all other parties to the action with written notice of the intent to seek summary judgment and the need for a pre-filing conference with a judicial officer. ME R USDCT Rule 56(h)(2).

 c. *Pre-filing conference.* At any pre-filing conference, the parties shall be prepared to discuss, and the judicial officer shall consider: (A) the issues to be addressed by a motion for summary judgment; (B) the length of any statement of material facts filed pursuant to ME R USDCT Rule 56(b) and ME R USDCT Rule 56(c); (C) the length of the memoranda filed pursuant to ME R USDCT Rule 7; (D) the time within which the motion for summary judgment shall be filed; (E) the use of a stipulated statement of material facts in addition to or in lieu of, separate statements of material fact; and (F) whether either party intends to file any Daubert and/or Kumho motions, and, if so, the issues to be addressed by such motions, the length of any memoranda of law to be filed pursuant to ME R USDCT Rule 7, and the time within which the Daubert and/or Kumho motions shall be filed. ME R USDCT Rule 56(h)(3). Following any pre-filing conference, the judicial officer shall issue an order reciting the action taken at the conference. ME R USDCT Rule 56(h)(3).

3. *Motion for summary judgment.* A party may move for summary judgment, identifying each claim or defense—or the part of each claim or defense—on which summary judgment is sought. The court shall grant summary judgment if the movant shows that there is no genuine dispute as to any material fact and the movant is entitled to judgment as a matter of law. The court should state on the record the reasons for granting or denying the motion. FRCP 56(a).

    a. *Burden of proof and presumptions*

        i. *Movant's burden.* It is well-settled that the party moving for summary judgment has the burden of demonstrating that the FRCP 56(c) test—"no genuine dispute as to any material fact"—is satisfied and that the movant is entitled to judgment as a matter of law. FPP § 2727; Adickes v. S. H. Kress & Co., 398 U.S. 144, 157, 90 S. Ct. 1598, 1608, 26 L. Ed. 2d 142 (1970).

            • The movant is held to a stringent standard. FPP § 2727. Before summary judgment will be granted it must be clear what the truth is and any doubt as to the existence of a genuine dispute of material fact will be resolved against the movant. FPP § 2727; Poller v. Columbia Broad. Sys., Inc., 368 U.S. 464, 82 S. Ct. 486, 7 L. Ed. 2d 458 (1962); Adickes v. S. H. Kress & Co., 398 U.S. 144, 90 S. Ct. 1598, 26 L. Ed. 2d 142 (1970).

            • Because the burden is on the movant, the evidence presented to the court always is construed in favor of the party opposing the motion and the opponent is given the benefit of all favorable inferences that can be drawn from it. FPP § 2727; Scott v. Harris, 550 U.S. 372, 127 S. Ct. 1769, 167 L. Ed. 2d 686 (2007).

            • Finally, facts asserted by the party opposing the motion, if supported by affidavits or other evidentiary material, are regarded as true. FPP § 2727; McLaughlin v. Liu, 849 F.2d 1205, 1208 (9th Cir. 1988).

        ii. *Opponent's burden.* If the summary-judgment movant makes out a prima facie case that would entitle him to a judgment as a matter of law if uncontroverted at trial, summary judgment will be granted unless the opposing party offers some competent evidence that could be presented at trial showing that there is a genuine dispute as to a material fact. FPP § 2727.2; Scott v. Harris, 550 U.S. 372, 127 S. Ct. 1769, 167 L. Ed. 2d 686 (2007). In this way the burden of producing evidence is shifted to the party opposing the motion. FPP § 2727.2; Celotex Corp. v. Catrett, 477 U.S. 317, 331, 106 S. Ct. 2548, 2557, 91 L. Ed. 2d 265 (1986).

            • The burden on the nonmoving party is not a heavy one; the nonmoving party simply is required to show specific facts, as opposed to general allegations, that present a genuine issue worthy of trial. FPP § 2727.2; Lujan v. Defs. of Wildlife, 504 U.S. 555, 112 S. Ct. 2130, 119 L. Ed. 2d 351 (1992).

            • A nonmoving party need neither match the moving party witness for witness nor persuade the court that the nonmoving party's case is convincing, but need only come forward with appropriate evidence demonstrating that a dispute of material fact is pending. FEDPROC § 62:589.

    b. *Failing to properly support or address a fact.* If a party fails to properly support an assertion of fact or fails to properly address another party's assertion of fact as required by FRCP 56(c), the court may: (1) give an opportunity to properly support or address the fact; (2) consider the fact undisputed for purposes of the motion; (3) grant summary judgment if the motion and supporting materials—including the facts considered undisputed—show that the movant is entitled to it; or (4) issue any other appropriate order. FRCP 56(e).

    c. *Judgment independent of the motion.* After giving notice and a reasonable time to respond, the court may: (1) grant summary judgment for a nonmovant; (2) grant the motion on grounds not raised by a party; or (3) consider summary judgment on its own after identifying for the parties material facts that may not be genuinely in dispute. FRCP 56(f).

    d. *Failing to grant all the requested relief.* If the court does not grant all the relief requested by the motion, it may enter an order stating any material fact—including an item of damages or other relief—that is not genuinely in dispute and treating the fact as established in the case. FRCP 56(g).

    e. *Affidavit or declaration submitted in bad faith.* If satisfied that an affidavit or declaration under FRCP 56 is submitted in bad faith or solely for delay, the court—after notice and a reasonable time to respond—may order the submitting party to pay the other party the reasonable expenses, including attorney's fees, it incurred as a result. An offending party or attorney may also be held in contempt or subjected to other appropriate sanctions. FRCP 56(h).

f. *DISTRICT OF MAINE: Facts admitted for purpose of summary judgment.* Facts deemed admitted solely for purposes of summary judgment shall not be deemed admitted for purposes other than determining whether summary judgment is appropriate. ME R USDCT Rule 56(g).

g. *Conversion of motions under FRCP 12(b)(6) and FRCP 12(c).* If, on a motion under FRCP 12(b)(6) or FRCP 12(c), matters outside the pleadings are presented to and not excluded by the court, the motion must be treated as one for summary judgment under FRCP 56. FRCP 12(d).

h. *DISTRICT OF MAINE: Compliance with ME R USDCT Rule 56.* In addition to the material required to be filed by ME R USDCT Rule 7, a motion for summary judgment and opposition thereto shall comply with the requirements of ME R USDCT Rule 56. ME R USDCT Rule 56(a).

4. *Opposing papers.* The Federal Rules of Civil Procedure do not require any formal answer, return, or reply to a motion, except where the Federal Rules of Civil Procedure or local rules may require affidavits, memoranda, or other papers to be filed in opposition to a motion. Such papers are simply to apprise the court of such opposition and the grounds of that opposition. FEDPROC § 62:353.

   a. *DISTRICT OF MAINE: Content of objections.* Any objections shall include citations and supporting authorities and affidavits and other documents setting forth or evidencing facts on which the objection is based. ME R USDCT Rule 7(b).

   b. *Effect of failure to respond to motion.* Although in the absence of statutory provision or court rule, a motion ordinarily does not require a response or written answer, when a party files a motion and the opposing party fails to respond, the court may construe such failure to respond as nonopposition to the motion or an admission that the motion was meritorious. AMJUR MOTIONS § 28. The rule in some jurisdictions being that the failure to respond to a fact set forth in a motion is deemed an admission—and may grant the motion if the relief requested appears to be justified. AMJUR MOTIONS § 28.

   c. *Assent or no opposition not determinative.* However, a motion will not be granted automatically simply because an "assent" or a notation of "no opposition" has been filed; federal judges frequently deny motions that have been assented to when it is thought that justice so dictates. FPP § 1190.

   d. *Responsive pleading inappropriate as response to motion.* An attempt to answer or oppose a motion with a responsive pleading usually is not appropriate. FPP § 1190.

   e. *Opposing a motion for summary judgment.* The party opposing summary judgment does not have a duty to present evidence in opposition to a motion under FRCP 56 in all circumstances. FPP § 2727.2; Jaroma v. Massey, 873 F.2d 17 (1st Cir. 1989).

      i. *When facts are unavailable to the nonmovant.* If a nonmovant shows by affidavit or declaration that, for specified reasons, it cannot present facts essential to justify its opposition, the court may: (1) defer considering the motion or deny it; (2) allow time to obtain affidavits or declarations or to take discovery; or (3) issue any other appropriate order. FRCP 56(d).

      ii. *DISTRICT OF MAINE: Motions to strike not allowed.* Motions to strike statements of fact are not allowed. If a party contends that an individual statement of fact should not be considered by the court, the party may include as part of the response that the statement of fact "should be stricken" with a brief statement of the reason(s) and the authority or record citation in support. Without prejudice to the determination of the request to strike the party shall admit, deny or qualify the statement as provided in ME R USDCT Rule 56. A party may respond to a request to strike either in the reply statement of material facts as provided in ME R USDCT Rule 56 or, if the request was made in a reply statement of material facts, by filing a response within fourteen (14) days. A response to a request to strike shall be strictly limited to a brief statement of the reason(s) why the statement of fact should be considered and the authority or record citation in support. ME R USDCT Rule 56(e).

      iii. *DISTRICT OF MAINE: Compliance with ME R USDCT Rule 56.* In addition to the material required to be filed by ME R USDCT Rule 7, a motion for summary judgment and opposition thereto shall comply with the requirements of ME R USDCT Rule 56. ME R USDCT Rule 56(a).

5. *Reply papers.* A moving party may be required or permitted to prepare papers in addition to its original motion papers. AMJUR MOTIONS § 25. Papers answering or replying to opposing papers may be appropriate, in the interests of justice, where it appears there is a substantial reason for allowing a reply. Thus, a court may accept reply papers where a party demonstrates that the papers to which it seeks to file a reply raise new issues that are material to the disposition of the question before the court, or where the court determines, sua sponte, that it wishes further briefing of an issue raised in those papers and orders the submission of additional papers. FEDPROC § 62:354.

   a. *Function of reply papers.* The function of a reply affidavit or reply papers is to answer the arguments made in opposition to the position taken by the movant, not to raise new issues, arguments, or evidence, or change the nature of the primary motion. However, if the court permits new evidence with the reply papers, the other party should be given the opportunity to respond. Where the party opposing the motion has no opportunity to address the argument in writing, a court has the discretion to disregard arguments raised for the first time in a reply memorandum. Also, the view has been followed in some jurisdictions that as a matter of judicial economy, where there is no prejudice and where the issues could be raised simply by filing a motion to dismiss, the trial court has discretion to consider arguments raised for the first time in a reply memorandum, and that a trial court may grant a motion to strike issues raised for the first time in a reply memorandum. AMJUR MOTIONS § 26.

    i. *DISTRICT OF MAINE.* The moving party may file a reply memorandum. . .which shall be strictly confined to replying to new matter raised in the objection or opposing memorandum. ME R USDCT Rule 7(c).

  b. *DISTRICT OF MAINE: Reply to opposition to motion for summary judgment*

    i. *Reply statement of material facts.* A party replying to the opposition to a motion for summary judgment shall submit with its reply a separate, short, and concise statement of material facts which shall be limited to any additional facts submitted by the opposing party. The reply statement shall admit, deny or qualify such additional facts by reference to the numbered paragraphs of the opposing party's statement of material facts and unless a fact is admitted, shall support each denial or qualification by a record citation as required by ME R USDCT Rule 56(f). Each such reply statement shall begin with the designation "Admitted," "Denied," or "Qualified" and, in the case of an admission, shall end with such designation. ME R USDCT Rule 56(d).

      • *Statement of facts deemed admitted unless properly controverted; Specific record of citations required.* Facts contained in a supporting or opposing statement of material facts, if supported by record citations as required by ME R USDCT Rule 56, shall be deemed admitted unless properly controverted. An assertion of fact set forth in a statement of material facts shall be followed by a citation to the specific page or paragraph of identified record material supporting the assertion. The court may disregard any statement of fact not supported by a specific citation to record material properly considered on summary judgment. The court shall have no independent duty to search or consider any part of the record not specifically referenced in the parties' separate statement of facts. ME R USDCT Rule 56(f).

    ii. *Motions to strike not allowed.* Motions to strike statements of fact are not allowed. If a party contends that an individual statement of fact should not be considered by the court, the party may include as part of the response that the statement of fact "should be stricken" with a brief statement of the reason(s) and the authority or record citation in support. Without prejudice to the determination of the request to strike the party shall admit, deny or qualify the statement as provided in ME R USDCT Rule 56. A party may respond to a request to strike either in the reply statement of material facts as provided in ME R USDCT Rule 56 or, if the request was made in a reply statement of material facts, by filing a response within fourteen (14) days. A response to a request to strike shall be strictly limited to a brief statement of the reason(s) why the statement of fact should be considered and the authority or record citation in support. ME R USDCT Rule 56(e).

6. *DISTRICT OF MAINE: Appearances.* An attorney's signature to a pleading shall constitute an appearance for the party filing the pleading. Otherwise, an attorney who wishes to participate in any manner in any action must file a formal written appearance identifying the party represented. An appearance whether by pleading or formal written appearance shall be signed by an attorney in his/her individual name and shall state his/her office address. ME R USDCT Rule 83.2(a). For more information, refer to ME R USDCT Rule 83.2.

7. *DISTRICT OF MAINE: Alternative dispute resolution (ADR).* Litigants are authorized and encouraged to employ, at their own expense, any available ADR process on which they can agree, including early neutral evaluation, settlement conferences, mediation, non-binding summary jury trial, corporate mini-trial, and arbitration proceedings. ME R USDCT Rule 83.11(a). For more information on ADR, refer to ME R USDCT Rule 83.11.

D. Documents

1. *Documents for moving party*

  a. *Required documents*

    i. *Notice of motion and motion.* Refer to the "C. General Requirements" section of this KeyRules document for information on the notice of motion and motion.

      • *DISTRICT OF MAINE: Memorandum of law.* Every motion shall incorporate a memorandum of law, including citations and supporting authorities. ME R USDCT Rule 7(a). Refer to the "E. Format" section of this KeyRules document for the form of memoranda of law.

- *Certificate of service.* No certificate of service is required when a paper is served by filing it with the court's electronic-filing system. When a paper that is required to be served is served by other means: (i) if the paper is filed, a certificate of service must be filed with it or within a reasonable time after service; and (ii) if the paper is not filed, a certificate of service need not be filed unless filing is required by court order or by local rule. FRCP 5(d)(1)(B).

ii. *DISTRICT OF MAINE: Additional required documents*

- *Supporting statement of material facts and/or stipulated statement of material facts.* A motion for summary judgment shall be supported by a separate, short, and concise statement of material facts, each set forth in a separately numbered paragraph(s), as to which the moving party contends there is no genuine issue of material fact to be tried. Each fact asserted in the statement shall be simply and directly stated in narrative without footnotes or tables and shall be supported by a record citation as required by ME R USDCT Rule 56(f). ME R USDCT Rule 56(b). Nothing in ME R USDCT Rule 56 precludes the parties from filing a stipulated statement of material facts as to all, or some, of the facts underlying a motion for summary judgment, or any opposition thereto. In the event the parties file a stipulated statement of material facts, such stipulated facts shall control and take precedence over any conflicting statement of fact filed by any party to the stipulation. ME R USDCT Rule 56(b). Facts contained in a supporting or opposing statement of material facts, if supported by record citations as required by ME R USDCT Rule 56, shall be deemed admitted unless properly controverted. An assertion of fact set forth in a statement of material facts shall be followed by a citation to the specific page or paragraph of identified record material supporting the assertion. The court may disregard any statement of fact not supported by a specific citation to record material properly considered on summary judgment. The court shall have no independent duty to search or consider any part of the record not specifically referenced in the parties' separate statement of facts. ME R USDCT Rule 56(f).

b. *Supplemental documents*

i. *Supporting evidence.* When a motion relies on facts outside the record, the court may hear the matter on affidavits or may hear it wholly or partly on oral testimony or on depositions. FRCP 43(c). A party asserting that a fact cannot be or is genuinely disputed must support the assertion by: (A) citing to particular parts of materials in the record, including depositions, documents, electronically stored information, affidavits or declarations, stipulations (including those made for purposes of the motion only), admissions, interrogatory answers, or other materials; or (B) showing that the materials cited do not establish the absence or presence of a genuine dispute, or that an adverse party cannot produce admissible evidence to support the fact. FRCP 56(c)(1). A party may object that the material cited to support or dispute a fact cannot be presented in a form that would be admissible in evidence. FRCP 56(c)(2). The court need consider only the cited materials, but it may consider other materials in the record. FRCP 56(c)(3). An affidavit or declaration used to support or oppose a motion must be made on personal knowledge, set out facts that would be admissible in evidence, and show that the affiant or declarant is competent to testify on the matters stated. FRCP 56(c)(4).

- *DISTRICT OF MAINE: Affidavits and other supporting documents.* Any affidavits and other documents setting forth or evidencing facts on which the motion is based must be filed with the motion. ME R USDCT Rule 7(a).

- *DISTRICT OF MAINE: Discovery transcripts or materials.* A party relying on discovery transcripts or materials in support of or in opposition to a motion shall file excerpts of such transcript or materials with the memorandum required by ME R USDCT Rule 7 as well as a list of specific citations to the parts on which the party relies. ME R USDCT Rule 26(c). Excerpts of depositions in support of or in opposition to a motion shall be filed electronically using ECF, unless otherwise permitted by the court. ME R USDCT App. 4(l)(3).

ii. *Notice of constitutional question.* A party that files a pleading, written motion, or other paper drawing into question the constitutionality of a federal or state statute must promptly: (1) file a notice of constitutional question stating the question and identifying the paper that raises it, if: (A) a federal statute is questioned and the parties do not include the United States, one of its agencies, or one of its officers or employees in an official capacity; or (B) a state statute is questioned and the parties do not include the state, one of its agencies, or one of its officers or employees in an official capacity; and (2) serve the notice and paper on the Attorney General of the United States if a federal statute is questioned—or on the state attorney general if a state statute is questioned—either by certified or registered mail or by sending it to an electronic address designated by the attorney general for this purpose. FRCP 5.1(a).

- *No forfeiture.* A party's failure to file and serve the notice, or the court's failure to certify, does not forfeit a constitutional claim or defense that is otherwise timely asserted. FRCP 5.1(d).

iii. *Nongovernmental corporate disclosure statement.* A nongovernmental corporate party must file two (2) copies of a disclosure statement that: (1) identifies any parent corporation and any publicly held corporation owning ten percent (10%) or more of its stock; or (2) states that there is no such corporation. FRCP 7.1(a). A party must: (1) file the disclosure statement with its first appearance, pleading, petition, motion, response, or other request addressed to the court; and (2) promptly file a supplemental statement if any required information changes. FRCP 7.1(b).

- *DISTRICT OF MAINE: Notice of interested parties.* To enable the court to evaluate possible disqualification or recusal, counsel for all non-governmental parties shall file with their first appearance a Notice of Interested Parties, which shall list all persons, associations of persons, firms, partnerships, limited liability companies, joint ventures, corporations (including parent or affiliated corporations, clearly identified as such), or any similar entities, owning ten percent (10%) or more of the named party. Counsel shall be under a continuing obligation to file an amended Notice if any material change occurs in the status of an Interested Party, such as through merger, acquisition, or new/additional membership. ME R USDCT Rule 7.1.

iv. *DISTRICT OF MAINE: Additional supplemental documents*

- *Proposed order.* Proposed orders shall not be filed unless requested by the court. When requested by the court, proposed orders shall be filed by e-mail in word processing format. ME R USDCT App. 4(k)(1).

2. *Documents for opposing party*

   a. *Required documents*

   i. *Opposition.* Refer to the "C. General Requirements" section of this KeyRules document for information on the opposing papers.

   - *DISTRICT OF MAINE: Memorandum of law.* Unless within twenty-one (21) days after the filing of a motion the opposing party files written objection thereto, incorporating a memorandum of law, the opposing party shall be deemed to have waived objection. ME R USDCT Rule 7(b).

   - *Certificate of service.* No certificate of service is required when a paper is served by filing it with the court's electronic-filing system. When a paper that is required to be served is served by other means: (i) if the paper is filed, a certificate of service must be filed with it or within a reasonable time after service; and (ii) if the paper is not filed, a certificate of service need not be filed unless filing is required by court order or by local rule. FRCP 5(d)(1)(B).

   ii. *DISTRICT OF MAINE: Additional required documents*

   - *Opposing statement of material facts.* A party opposing a motion for summary judgment shall submit with its opposition a separate, short, and concise statement of material facts. The opposing statement shall admit, deny or qualify the facts by reference to each numbered paragraph of the moving party's statement of material facts and unless a fact is admitted, shall support each denial or qualification by a record citation as required by ME R USDCT Rule 56. Each such statement shall begin with the designation "Admitted," "Denied," or "Qualified" and, in the case of an admission, shall end with such designation. The opposing statement may contain in a separately titled section additional facts, each set forth in a separately numbered paragraph and supported by a record citation as required by ME R USDCT Rule 56(f). ME R USDCT Rule 56(c). Facts contained in a supporting or opposing statement of material facts, if supported by record citations as required by ME R USDCT Rule 56, shall be deemed admitted unless properly controverted. An assertion of fact set forth in a statement of material facts shall be followed by a citation to the specific page or paragraph of identified record material supporting the assertion. The court may disregard any statement of fact not supported by a specific citation to record material properly considered on summary judgment. The court shall have no independent duty to search or consider any part of the record not specifically referenced in the parties' separate statement of facts. ME R USDCT Rule 56(f).

   b. *Supplemental documents*

   i. *Supporting evidence.* When a motion relies on facts outside the record, the court may hear the matter on affidavits or may hear it wholly or partly on oral testimony or on depositions. FRCP 43(c). A party asserting that a fact cannot be or is genuinely disputed must support the assertion by: (A) citing to particular parts of materials in the record, including depositions, documents, electronically stored information, affidavits or declarations, stipulations (including those made for purposes of the motion only), admissions, interrogatory answers, or other materials; or (B) showing that the materials cited do not establish the absence or presence of a genuine dispute, or that an adverse party cannot produce admissible evidence to support the fact. FRCP 56(c)(1). A party may object that the material cited to support or dispute a fact cannot be presented in a form that would be admissible in evidence. FRCP 56(c)(2). The court need consider only the cited materials, but it may consider other materials in the record. FRCP 56(c)(3). An affidavit or declaration used to support or oppose a motion must be made on personal knowledge, set out facts that would be admissible in evidence, and show that the affiant or declarant is competent to testify on the matters stated. FRCP 56(c)(4).

- *DISTRICT OF MAINE: Affidavits and other supporting documents.* Any objections shall include. . .affidavits and other documents setting forth or evidencing facts on which the objection is based. ME R USDCT Rule 7(b).

- *DISTRICT OF MAINE: Discovery transcripts or materials.* A party relying on discovery transcripts or materials in support of or in opposition to a motion shall file excerpts of such transcript or materials with the memorandum required by ME R USDCT Rule 7 as well as a list of specific citations to the parts on which the party relies. ME R USDCT Rule 26(c). Excerpts of depositions in support of or in opposition to a motion shall be filed electronically using ECF, unless otherwise permitted by the court. ME R USDCT App. 4(l)(3).

ii. *Notice of constitutional question.* A party that files a pleading, written motion, or other paper drawing into question the constitutionality of a federal or state statute must promptly: (1) file a notice of constitutional question stating the question and identifying the paper that raises it, if: (A) a federal statute is questioned and the parties do not include the United States, one of its agencies, or one of its officers or employees in an official capacity; or (B) a state statute is questioned and the parties do not include the state, one of its agencies, or one of its officers or employees in an official capacity; and (2) serve the notice and paper on the Attorney General of the United States if a federal statute is questioned—or on the state attorney general if a state statute is questioned—either by certified or registered mail or by sending it to an electronic address designated by the attorney general for this purpose. FRCP 5.1(a).

- *No forfeiture.* A party's failure to file and serve the notice, or the court's failure to certify, does not forfeit a constitutional claim or defense that is otherwise timely asserted. FRCP 5.1(d).

E. Format

1. *Form of documents.* The rules governing captions and other matters of form in pleadings apply to motions and other papers. FRCP 7(b)(2).

   a. *DISTRICT OF MAINE: Font size, line spacing, and paper size.* All such documents shall be typed in a font of no less than size twelve (12) point, and shall be double-spaced or printed on eight and one-half by eleven (8-1/2 x 11) inch paper. Footnotes shall be in a font of no less than size ten (10) point, and may be single spaced. ME R USDCT Rule 10.

   b. *Caption.* Every pleading must have a caption with the court's name, a title, a file number, and an FRCP 7(a) designation. FRCP 10(a).

      i. *Names of parties.* The title of the complaint must name all the parties; the title of other pleadings, after naming the first party on each side, may refer generally to other parties. FRCP 10(a).

      ii. *DISTRICT OF MAINE: Additional caption requirements.* All pleadings, motions and other papers filed with the clerk or otherwise submitted to the court, except exhibits, shall bear the proper case number and shall contain on the first page a caption as described by FRCP 10(a) and immediately thereunder a designation of what the document is and the name of the party in whose behalf it is submitted. ME R USDCT Rule 10.

   c. *Claims or defenses*

      i. *Numbered paragraphs.* A party must state its claims or defenses in numbered paragraphs, each limited as far as practicable to a single set of circumstances. A later pleading may refer by number to a paragraph in an earlier pleading. FRCP 10(b).

      ii. *Separate statements.* If doing so would promote clarity, each claim founded on a separate transaction or occurrence—and each defense other than a denial—must be stated in a separate count or defense. FRCP 10(b).

   d. *Adoption by reference.* A statement in a pleading may be adopted by reference elsewhere in the same pleading or in any other pleading or motion. FRCP 10(c).

      i. *Exhibits.* A copy of a written instrument that is an exhibit to a pleading is a part of the pleading for all purposes. FRCP 10(c).

   e. *DISTRICT OF MAINE: Page numbering.* All pages shall be numbered at the bottom. ME R USDCT Rule 10.

   f. *DISTRICT OF MAINE: Attachment of ancillary papers.* Ancillary papers shall be attached at the end of the document to which they relate. ME R USDCT Rule 10.

g. *Acceptance by the clerk.* The clerk must not refuse to file a paper solely because it is not in the form prescribed by the Federal Rules of Civil Procedure or by a local rule or practice. FRCP 5(d)(4).

2. *Form of electronic documents.* A paper filed electronically is a written paper for purposes of the Federal Rules of Civil Procedure. FRCP 5(d)(3)(D).

   a. *DISTRICT OF MAINE: Document format.* The ECF system only accepts documents in a portable document format (PDF). Although there are two types of PDF documents—electronically converted PDF's and scanned PDF's—only electronically converted PDF's may be filed with the court using the ECF system, unless otherwise authorized by local rule or order. ME R USDCT App. 4. Any document or exhibit to be filed or submitted to the court shall not be password-protected or encrypted. ME R USDCT App. 4(g)(12).

      i. *Electronically converted PDFs.* Electronically converted PDF's are created from word processing documents (MS Word, WordPerfect, etc.) using Adobe Acrobat or similar software. They are text searchable and their file size is small. ME R USDCT App. 4. Software used to electronically convert documents to PDF which includes proprietary or advertisement information within the PDF document is prohibited. ME R USDCT App. 4.

      ii. *Scanned PDFs.* Scanned PDF's are created from paper documents run through an optical scanner. Scanned PDF's are not searchable and have a large file size. ME R USDCT App. 4.

   b. *DISTRICT OF MAINE: Title.* All pleadings filed electronically shall be titled in accordance with the approved dictionary of civil or criminal events of the ECF system of the United States District Court for the District of Maine. ME R USDCT App. 4(d)(3).

   c. *DISTRICT OF MAINE: Attachments.* Attachments to filings and exhibits must be filed in accordance with the court's ECF User Manual, unless otherwise ordered by the court. ME R USDCT App. 4(j). When there are fifty (50) or fewer attachments to a pleading, the attachments must be filed by counsel electronically using ECF. When there are more than fifty (50) attachments, the attachments must be filed in one of the following ways: (A) using ECF, simply attach them to the pleading being filed; (B) using ECF, use the "Additional Attachments" menu item; (C) on paper; or (D) on a properly labeled three and one-half (3-1/2) inch floppy disk, CD or DVD. ME R USDCT App. 4(j)(2). Attachments filed on paper or on disk must contain a comprehensive index that clearly describes each document. ME R USDCT App. 4(j)(2).

      i. A filing user must submit as attachments only those excerpts of the referenced documents that are directly germane to the matter under consideration by the court. Excerpted material must be clearly and prominently identified as such. Users who file excerpts of documents do so without prejudice to their right to timely file additional excerpts or the complete document, as may be allowed by the court. Responding parties may timely file additional excerpts or the complete document that they believe are directly germane. ME R USDCT App. 4(j)(3).

      ii. Filers shall not attach as an exhibit any pleading or other paper already on file with the court in that case, but shall merely refer to that document. ME R USDCT App. 4(j)(4).

   d. *DISTRICT OF MAINE: Compliance with technical standards.* All documents filed by electronic means must comply with technical standards, if any, established by the Judicial Conference of the United States or by the United States District Court for the District of Maine. ME R USDCT App. 4(a)(3).

3. *DISTRICT OF MAINE: Form of memoranda of law.* All memoranda shall be typed, in a font of no less than size twelve (12) point, and shall be double-spaced on eight and one-half by eleven (8-1/2 x 11) inch paper or printed. Footnotes shall be in a font of no less than size ten (10) point, and may be single spaced. All pages shall be numbered at the bottom. ME R USDCT Rule 7(d).

   a. *Page limitations.* No memorandum of law in support of or in opposition to a motion to dismiss, a motion for judgment on the pleadings, a motion for summary judgment or a motion for injunctive relief shall exceed twenty (20) pages. ME R USDCT Rule 7(d). No reply memorandum shall exceed seven (7) pages. ME R USDCT Rule 7(d); ME R USDCT Rule 7(c).

      i. *Motion to exceed page limitation.* A motion to exceed the limitation of ME R USDCT Rule 7 shall be filed no later than three (3) business days in advance of the date for filing the memorandum to permit meaningful review by the court. A motion to exceed the page limitations shall not be filed simultaneously with a memorandum in excess of the limitations of ME R USDCT Rule 7. ME R USDCT Rule 7(d).

4. *Signing of pleadings, motions and other papers*

   a. *Signature.* Every pleading, written motion, and other paper must be signed by at least one attorney of record in the

attorney's name—or by a party personally if the party is unrepresented. The paper must state the signer's address, e-mail address, and telephone number. FRCP 11(a).

    i. *No verification or accompanying affidavit required for pleadings.* Unless a rule or statute specifically states otherwise, a pleading need not be verified or accompanied by an affidavit. FRCP 11(a).

    ii. *Unsigned papers.* The court must strike an unsigned paper unless the omission is promptly corrected after being called to the attorney's or party's attention. FRCP 11(a).

  b. *Electronic signing.* A filing made through a person's electronic-filing account and authorized by that person, together with that person's name on a signature block, constitutes the person's signature. FRCP 5(d)(3)(C).

    i. *DISTRICT OF MAINE: Attorneys.* The user log-in and password together with a user's name on the signature block constitutes the attorney's signature pursuant to the Federal Rules of Civil Procedure and the Local Rules of the United States District Court for the District of Maine. All electronically filed documents must include a signature block and must set forth the attorney's name, address, telephone number and e-mail address. The name of the ECF user under whose log-in and password the document is submitted must be preceded by a "/s/" in the space where the signature would otherwise appear. ME R USDCT App. 4(h)(1).

    ii. *DISTRICT OF MAINE: Multiple signatures.* The filer of any document requiring more than one signature (e.g., pleadings filed by visiting lawyers, stipulations, joint status reports) must list thereon all the names of other signatories, preceded by a "/s/" in the space where the signatures would otherwise appear. By submitting such a document, the filing attorney certifies that each of the other signatories has expressly agreed to the form and substance of the document and that the filing attorney has their actual authority to submit the document electronically. ME R USDCT App. 4(h)(2). For more information, refer to ME R USDCT App. 4(h)(2).

    iii. *DISTRICT OF MAINE: Documents signed under oath.* Affidavits, declarations, verified complaints, or any other document signed under oath shall be filed electronically. The electronically filed version shall contain the typed name of the signatory, preceded by a "/s/" in the space where the signature would otherwise appear indicating that the paper document bears an original signature. ME R USDCT Rule 10; ME R USDCT App. 4(h)(3). For more information, refer to ME R USDCT Rule 10.

  c. *Representations to the court.* By presenting to the court a pleading, written motion, or other paper—whether by signing, filing, submitting, or later advocating it—an attorney or unrepresented party certifies that to the best of the person's knowledge, information, and belief, formed after an inquiry reasonable under the circumstances: (1) it is not being presented for any improper purpose, such as to harass, cause unnecessary delay, or needlessly increase the cost of litigation; (2) the claims, defenses, and other legal contentions are warranted by existing law or by a nonfrivolous argument for extending, modifying, or reversing existing law or for establishing new law; (3) the factual contentions have evidentiary support or, if specifically so identified, will likely have evidentiary support after a reasonable opportunity for further investigation or discovery; and (4) the denials of factual contentions are warranted on the evidence or, if specifically so identified, are reasonably based on belief or a lack of information. FRCP 11(b).

  d. *Sanctions.* If, after notice and a reasonable opportunity to respond, the court determines that FRCP 11(b) has been violated, the court may impose an appropriate sanction on any attorney, law firm, or party that violated FRCP 11(b) or is responsible for the violation. FRCP 11(c)(1). Refer to the United States District Court for the District of Maine KeyRules Motion for Sanctions document for more information.

5. *Privacy protection for filings made with the court*

  a. *Redacted filings.* Unless the court orders otherwise, in an electronic or paper filing with the court that contains an individual's Social Security number, taxpayer-identification number, or birth date, the name of an individual known to be a minor, or a financial-account number, a party or nonparty making the filing may include only: (1) the last four (4) digits of the Social Security number and taxpayer-identification number; (2) the year of the individual's birth; (3) the minor's initials; and (4) the last four (4) digits of the financial-account number. FRCP 5.2(a).

    i. *DISTRICT OF MAINE.* To address the privacy concerns created by the Internet access to court papers, unless otherwise ordered by the court, counsel shall modify certain personal data identifiers in pleadings and other papers as follows: (1) minors' names: use of the minors' initials only; (2) Social Security numbers: use of the last four (4) numbers only; (3) dates of birth: use of the year of birth only; [and] (4) financial account numbers: identify the type of account and the financial institution, but use only the last four (4) numbers of the account number. ME R USDCT Redacting Pleadings. Counsel should also use caution when filing papers that contain a person's medical records, employment history; financial information; and any proprietary or trade secret information. ME R USDCT Redacting Pleadings.

  b. *Exemptions from the redaction requirement.* The redaction requirement does not apply to the following: (1) a

financial-account number that identifies the property allegedly subject to forfeiture in a forfeiture proceeding; (2) the record of an administrative or agency proceeding; (3) the official record of a state-court proceeding; (4) the record of a court or tribunal, if that record was not subject to the redaction requirement when originally filed; (5) a filing covered by FRCP 5.2(c) or FRCP 5.2(d); and (6) a pro se filing in an action brought under 28 U.S.C.A. § 2241, 28 U.S.C.A. § 2254, or 28 U.S.C.A. § 2255. FRCP 5.2(b).

    c. *Limitations on remote access to electronic files; Social Security appeals and immigration cases.* Unless the court orders otherwise, in an action for benefits under the Social Security Act, and in an action or proceeding relating to an order of removal, to relief from removal, or to immigration benefits or detention, access to an electronic file is authorized as follows: (1) the parties and their attorneys may have remote electronic access to any part of the case file, including the administrative record; (2) any other person may have electronic access to the full record at the courthouse, but may have remote electronic access only to: (A) the docket maintained by the court; and (B) an opinion, order, judgment, or other disposition of the court, but not any other part of the case file or the administrative record. FRCP 5.2(c).

    d. *Filings made under seal.* The court may order that a filing be made under seal without redaction. The court may later unseal the filing or order the person who made the filing to file a redacted version for the public record. FRCP 5.2(d).

        i. *DISTRICT OF MAINE.* For information on filing sealed documents in the District of Maine, refer to ME R USDCT Rule 7A, ME R USDCT App. 4(p)(2), and ME R USDCT Sealed Filings.

    e. *Protective orders.* For good cause, the court may by order in a case: (1) require redaction of additional information; or (2) limit or prohibit a nonparty's remote electronic access to a document filed with the court. FRCP 5.2(e).

    f. *Option for additional unredacted filing under seal.* A person making a redacted filing may also file an unredacted copy under seal. The court must retain the unredacted copy as part of the record. FRCP 5.2(f).

        i. *DISTRICT OF MAINE.* A party wishing to file a document containing the personal data identifiers specified above may. . .file an unredacted document under seal. This document will be retained by the clerk's office as part of the record. ME R USDCT Redacting Pleadings. The court may, however, still require the party to file a redacted copy for the public file. ME R USDCT Redacting Pleadings.

    g. *Option for filing a reference list.* A filing that contains redacted information may be filed together with a reference list that identifies each item of redacted information and specifies an appropriate identifier that uniquely corresponds to each item listed. The list must be filed under seal and may be amended as of right. Any reference in the case to a listed identifier will be construed to refer to the corresponding item of information. FRCP 5.2(g).

        i. *DISTRICT OF MAINE.* A party wishing to file a document containing the personal data identifiers specified above may. . .file a reference list under seal. The reference list shall contain the complete personal data identifier(s) and the redacted identifier(s) used in its (their) place in the filing. All references in the case to the redacted identifiers included in the reference list will be construed to refer to the corresponding complete identifier. The reference list must be filed under seal, and may be amended as of right. It shall be retained by the clerk's office as part of the record. ME R USDCT Redacting Pleadings. The court may, however, still require the party to file a redacted copy for the public file. ME R USDCT Redacting Pleadings.

    h. *DISTRICT OF MAINE: Responsibility for redaction.* The clerk is not required to review documents filed with the court for compliance with FRCP 5.2. The responsibility to redact filings rests with counsel and the party or nonparty making the filing. ME R USDCT App. 4(i); ME R USDCT Redacting Pleadings. For guidelines for filing confidential information in civil cases in the District of Maine, refer to ME R USDCT Confidentiality.

    i. *Waiver of protection of identifiers.* A person waives the protection of FRCP 5.2(a) as to the person's own information by filing it without redaction and not under seal. FRCP 5.2(h).

F. Filing and Service Requirements

    1. *Filing requirements*

    a. *Required filings.* Any paper after the complaint that is required to be served must be filed no later than a reasonable time after service. FRCP 5(d)(1).

    b. *DISTRICT OF MAINE: Place of filing.* Unless otherwise ordered by the court, papers shall be filed with the court at Bangor in cases filed and pending at Bangor, and at Portland in cases filed and pending at Portland. ME R USDCT Rule 5(a).

    c. *Nonelectronic filing.* A paper not filed electronically is filed by delivering it: (A) to the clerk; or (B) to a judge who

agrees to accept it for filing, and who must then note the filing date on the paper and promptly send it to the clerk. FRCP 5(d)(2).

    i. *DISTRICT OF MAINE: Documents to be filed in paper.* The following documents shall be filed in paper, which may also be scanned into ECF by the clerk's office: (A) all handwritten pleadings; and (B) all pleadings and documents filed by pro se litigants who are incarcerated or who are not registered filing users in ECF. ME R USDCT App. 4(g)(8). Non-prisoner pro se litigants in civil actions may register with ECF or may file (and serve) all pleadings and other documents in paper. The clerk's office will scan into ECF any pleadings and documents filed on paper in accordance with ME R USDCT App. 4(g). ME R USDCT App. 4(o). For more information, refer to ME R USDCT App. 4(g).

  d. *Electronic filing*

    i. *DISTRICT OF MAINE: Authorization.* Unless exempt or otherwise ordered by the court, papers shall be filed and served electronically as required by the court's Administrative Procedures Governing the Filing and Service by Electronic Means, which is set forth in ME R USDCT App. 4. The provisions of the court's Administrative Procedures Governing the Filing and Service by Electronic Means (ME R USDCT App. 4) shall be applied and enforced as part of the Local Rules of the United States District Court for the District of Maine. ME R USDCT Rule 5(c).

    ii. *Filing by represented persons.* A person represented by an attorney must file electronically, unless nonelectronic filing is allowed by the court for good cause or is allowed or required by local rule. FRCP 5(d)(3)(A).

       • *DISTRICT OF MAINE.* An attorney may apply to the court for permission to file paper documents. ME R USDCT App. 4(a)(5).

    iii. *Filing by unrepresented persons.* A person not represented by an attorney: (i) may file electronically only if allowed by court order or by local rule; and (ii) may be required to file electronically only by court order, or by a local rule that includes reasonable exceptions. FRCP 5(d)(3)(B).

       • *DISTRICT OF MAINE.* Non-prisoner pro se litigants in civil actions may register with ECF or may file (and serve) all pleadings and other documents in paper. ME R USDCT App. 4(o). A non-prisoner who is a party to a civil action and who is not represented by an attorney may register to receive service electronically and to electronically transmit their documents to the court for filing in the ECF system. If during the course of the action the person retains an attorney who appears on the person's behalf, the clerk shall terminate the person's registration upon the attorney's appearance. ME R USDCT App. 4(b)(2).

    iv. *DISTRICT OF MAINE: Scope of electronic filing.* All documents submitted for filing in civil and criminal cases, regardless of case commencement date, except those documents specifically exempted in ME R USDCT App. 4(g), shall be filed electronically using the electronic case filing system (ECF). ME R USDCT App. 4(a)(1). For special filing requirements and exceptions, refer to ME R USDCT App. 4(g).

    v. *DISTRICT OF MAINE: Consequences of electronic filing.* Electronic transmission of a document to the ECF system, together with the transmission of a Notice of Electronic Filing (NEF) from the court, constitutes filing of the document for all purposes of the Federal Rules of Civil Procedure. ME R USDCT App. 4(d)(1).

    vi. *DISTRICT OF MAINE: Review of documents.* Documents filed with the clerk's office will normally be reviewed no later than the close of the next business day. It is the responsibility of the filing party to promptly notify the clerk's office via telephone of a matter that requires the immediate attention of a judicial officer. ME R USDCT App. 4(a)(4).

  e. *DISTRICT OF MAINE: Facsimile filing.* No papers shall be submitted to the court by means of a facsimile machine without prior leave of the court. ME R USDCT Rule 5(c); ME R USDCT App. 4(m).

2. *Service requirements*

  a. *Service; When required.* Unless the Federal Rules of Civil Procedure provide otherwise, each of the following papers must be served on every party: (A) an order stating that service is required; (B) a pleading filed after the original complaint, unless the court orders otherwise under FRCP 5(c) because there are numerous defendants; (C) a discovery paper required to be served on a party, unless the court orders otherwise; (D) a written motion, except one that may be heard ex parte; and (E) a written notice, appearance, demand, or offer of judgment, or any similar paper. FRCP 5(a)(1).

    i. *If a party fails to appear.* No service is required on a party who is in default for failing to appear. But a pleading that asserts a new claim for relief against such a party must be served on that party under FRCP 4. FRCP 5(a)(2).

    ii. *Seizing property.* If an action is begun by seizing property and no person is or need be named as a defendant, any

service required before the filing of an appearance, answer, or claim must be made on the person who had custody or possession of the property when it was seized. FRCP 5(a)(3).

b. *Service; How made.* A paper is served under FRCP 5 by: (A) handing it to the person; (B) leaving it: (i) at the person's office with a clerk or other person in charge or, if no one is in charge, in a conspicuous place in the office; or (ii) if the person has no office or the office is closed, at the person's dwelling or usual place of abode with someone of suitable age and discretion who resides there; (C) mailing it to the person's last known address—in which event service is complete upon mailing; (D) leaving it with the court clerk if the person has no known address; (E) sending it to a registered user by filing it with the court's electronic-filing system or sending it by other electronic means that the person consented to in writing—in either of which events service is complete upon filing or sending, but is not effective if the filer or sender learns that it did not reach the person to be served; or (F) delivering it by any other means that the person consented to in writing—in which event service is complete when the person making service delivers it to the agency designated to make delivery. FRCP 5(b)(2).

   i. *Serving an attorney.* If a party is represented by an attorney, service under FRCP 5 must be made on the attorney unless the court orders service on the party. FRCP 5(b)(1).

c. *DISTRICT OF MAINE: Service of electronically filed documents*

   i. *Registered users.* Registration [as a filing user of the court's ECF system] constitutes consent to service of all documents by electronic means as provided in ME R USDCT App. 4. ME R USDCT App. 4(b)(4). Whenever a non-sealed pleading is filed electronically, the ECF system will automatically generate and send a Notice of Electronic Filing (NEF) to the filing user and registered users of record. The user filing the document should retain a paper or digital copy of the NEF, which shall serve as the court's date-stamp and proof of filing. ME R USDCT App. 4(e)(1).

   - *Sealed documents.* Although the filing of sealed documents in civil cases produces an NEF, the document itself cannot be accessed and counsel shall be responsible for making service of the sealed documents. ME R USDCT App. 4(e)(2).

   ii. *Non-registered users and pro se litigants.* Attorneys who have not yet registered as users with ECF and pro se litigants who have not registered with ECF shall be served a paper copy of any electronically filed pleading or other document in accordance with the provisions of FRCP 5. ME R USDCT App. 4(e)(3).

   - *Registration of pro se litigants.* A non-prisoner who is a party to a civil action and who is not represented by an attorney may register to receive service electronically and to electronically transmit their documents to the court for filing in the ECF system. If during the course of the action the person retains an attorney who appears on the person's behalf, the clerk shall terminate the person's registration upon the attorney's appearance. ME R USDCT App. 4(b)(2).

d. *Serving numerous defendants.* If an action involves an unusually large number of defendants, the court may, on motion or on its own, order that: (A) defendants' pleadings and replies to them need not be served on other defendants; (B) any crossclaim, counterclaim, avoidance, or affirmative defense in those pleadings and replies to them will be treated as denied or avoided by all other parties; and (C) filing any such pleading and serving it on the plaintiff constitutes notice of the pleading to all parties. FRCP 5(c)(1).

   i. *Notifying parties.* A copy of every such order must be served on the parties as the court directs. FRCP 5(c)(2).

3. *DISTRICT OF MAINE: Filing and service of highly sensitive documents (HSDs).* For information on filing and serving highly sensitive documents (HSDs) in the District of Maine, refer to ME R USDCT General Order 21-5.

G. Hearings

1. *Hearings, generally.* When a motion relies on facts outside the record, the court may hear the matter on affidavits or may hear it wholly or partly on oral testimony or on depositions. FRCP 43(c).

   a. *Oral argument.* Due process does not require that oral argument be permitted on a motion and, except as otherwise provided by local rule, the district court has discretion to determine whether it will decide the motion on the papers or hear argument by counsel (and perhaps receive evidence). FPP § 1190; F.D.I.C. v. Deglau, 207 F.3d 153 (3d Cir. 2000).

   i. *DISTRICT OF MAINE.* Unless otherwise required by federal rule or statute, all motions may be decided by the court without oral argument unless otherwise ordered by the court on its own motion or, in its discretion, upon request of counsel. ME R USDCT Rule 7(e).

   b. *Providing a regular schedule for oral hearings.* A court may establish regular times and places for oral hearings on motions. FRCP 78(a).

c. *Providing for submission on briefs.* By rule or order, the court may provide for submitting and determining motions on briefs, without oral hearings. FRCP 78(b).

2. *Hearing on motion for summary judgment.* FRCP 56 confers no right to an oral hearing on a summary judgment motion, nor is a hearing required by due process considerations. FEDPROC § 62:671; Forjan v. Leprino Foods, Inc., 209 F. App'x 8 (2d Cir. 2006).

    a. *Oral argument.* Oral argument on a motion for summary judgment may be considered ordinarily appropriate, so that as a general rule, a district court should grant a request for oral argument on all but frivolous summary judgment motions, or a nonmovant's request for oral argument must be granted unless summary judgment is also denied, according to some courts. FEDPROC § 62:672; Season-All Indus., Inc. v. Turkiye Sise Ve Cam Fabrikalari, A. S., 425 F.2d 34 (3d Cir. 1970); Houston v. Bryan, 725 F.2d 516 (9th Cir. 1984); Fernhoff v. Tahoe Reg'l Planning Agency, 803 F.2d 979 (9th Cir. 1986).

        i. *Waiver.* Oral argument on a summary judgment motion may be deemed waived where the opposing party does not request it. FEDPROC § 62:672; McCormack v. Citibank, N.A., 100 F.3d 532 (8th Cir. 1996).

H. Forms

1. Federal Motion for Summary Judgment Forms

    a. Motion and notice of motion for summary judgment. 4 FEDFORMS § 39:8.

    b. Motion by plaintiff for summary judgment. 4 FEDFORMS § 39:9.

    c. Motion by defendant for summary judgment. 4 FEDFORMS § 39:13.

    d. Motion by defendant for summary judgment by defendant; Claims of plaintiff and counterclaims of defendant. 4 FEDFORMS § 39:17.

    e. Motion by defendant for summary judgment; Interpleader against another claimant. 4 FEDFORMS § 39:18.

    f. Motion by defendant for summary judgment; Failure of plaintiff to produce evidence. 4 FEDFORMS § 39:19.

    g. Motion by defendant for summary judgment; Statute of limitations. 4 FEDFORMS § 39:20.

    h. Notice of motion for summary judgment. 4 FEDFORMS § 39:44.

    i. Affidavit in support of motion for summary judgment. 4 FEDFORMS § 39:73.

    j. Movant's contention there is no genuine dispute of material facts. 4 FEDFORMS § 39:76.

    k. Opposition to statement of undisputed material facts. 4 FEDFORMS § 39:77.

    l. Response to movant's contention there are no genuine disputes of material facts. 4 FEDFORMS § 39:78.

    m. Answer; To plaintiff's motion for summary judgment. AMJUR PP SUMMARY § 56.

    n. Affidavit opposing defendant's motion for summary judgment; By plaintiff. AMJUR PP SUMMARY § 64.

    o. Affidavit opposing motion for summary judgment; By party; Dispute as to issues of fact. AMJUR PP SUMMARY § 73.

    p. Affidavit opposing motion for summary judgment; By party; Inability to present facts. AMJUR PP SUMMARY § 74.

    q. Affidavit opposing motion for summary judgment; By party; Good defense to part of claim. AMJUR PP SUMMARY § 77.

    r. Statement of disputed and undisputed material facts; In opposition to motion for summary judgment. AMJUR PP SUMMARY § 89.

    s. Motion; For summary judgment; By claimant. FEDPROF § 1C:210.

    t. Motion; For summary judgment; By defending party. FEDPROF § 1C:214.

    u. Motion; By plaintiff; For partial summary judgment. FEDPROF § 1C:217.

    v. Notice of cross motion; For summary judgment; By defending party. FEDPROF § 1C:218.

    w. Statement of material facts; In support of summary judgment motion. FEDPROF § 1C:225.

    x. Statement in support of defendant's summary judgment motion; By codefendant. FEDPROF § 1C:226.

    y. Affidavit; Opposing claimant's motion for summary judgment; Witnesses unavailable. FEDPROF § 1C:230.

    z. Affidavit; Opposing part of claim. FEDPROF § 1C:231.

I. Applicable Rules

1. *Federal rules*

    a. Serving and filing pleadings and other papers. FRCP 5.

    b. Constitutional challenge to a statute; Notice, certification, and intervention. FRCP 5.1.

    c. Privacy protection for filings made with the court. FRCP 5.2.

    d. Computing and extending time; Time for motion papers. FRCP 6.

    e. Pleadings allowed; Form of motions and other papers. FRCP 7.

    f. Disclosure statement. FRCP 7.1.

    g. Form of pleadings. FRCP 10.

    h. Signing pleadings, motions, and other papers; Representations to the court; Sanctions. FRCP 11.

    i. Defenses and objections; When and how presented; Motion for judgment on the pleadings; Consolidating motions; Waiving defenses; Pretrial hearing. FRCP 12.

    j. Taking testimony. FRCP 43.

    k. Summary judgment. FRCP 56.

    l. Hearing motions; Submission on briefs. FRCP 78.

2. *Local rules*

    a. *DISTRICT OF MAINE*

        i. Service and filing of pleadings and other papers. ME R USDCT Rule 5.

        ii. Time. ME R USDCT Rule 6.

        iii. Motions and memoranda of law. ME R USDCT Rule 7.

        iv. Corporate disclosure. ME R USDCT Rule 7.1.

        v. Form of pleadings, motions and other papers. ME R USDCT Rule 10.

        vi. Discovery. ME R USDCT Rule 26.

        vii. Motions for summary judgment. ME R USDCT Rule 56.

        viii. Attorneys; Appearances and withdrawals. ME R USDCT Rule 83.2.

        ix. Alternative dispute resolution (ADR). ME R USDCT Rule 83.11.

        x. Administrative procedures governing the filing and service by electronic means. ME R USDCT App. 4.

        xi. Redacting pleadings. ME R USDCT Redacting Pleadings.

Motions, Oppositions and Replies
Motion for Sanctions

Document Last Updated April 2021

A. Checklist

(I) ❑ Matters to be considered by moving party

   (a) ❑ Required documents

      (1) ❑ Notice of motion and motion

   (b) ❑ Supplemental documents

      (1) ❑ Supporting evidence

      (2) ❑ Notice of constitutional question

      (3) ❑ Nongovernmental corporate disclosure statement

      (4) ❑ DISTRICT OF MAINE: Additional supplemental documents

         (i) ❑ Proposed order

(c) ❑ Timing

    (1) ❑ A party who is aware of an FRCP 11 violation should act promptly; however, motions for sanctions can be timely even when filed well after the original pleadings; it must not be filed or be presented to the court if the challenged paper, claim, defense, contention, or denial is withdrawn or appropriately corrected within twenty-one (21) days after service or within another time the court sets

    (2) ❑ A written motion and notice of the hearing must be served at least fourteen (14) days before the time specified for the hearing, with the following exceptions: (A) when the motion may be heard ex parte; (B) when the Federal Rules of Civil Procedure set a different time; or (C) when a court order—which a party may, for good cause, apply for ex parte—sets a different time

    (3) ❑ Any affidavit supporting a motion must be served with the motion

    (4) ❑ DISTRICT OF MAINE: Additional timing

        (i) ❑ Any affidavits and other documents setting forth or evidencing facts on which the motion is based must be filed with the motion

(II) ❑ Matters to be considered by opposing party

  (a) ❑ Required documents

    (1) ❑ Opposition

  (b) ❑ Supplemental documents

    (1) ❑ Supporting evidence

    (2) ❑ Notice of constitutional question

  (c) ❑ Timing

    (1) ❑ Except as FRCP 59(c) provides otherwise, any opposing affidavit must be served at least seven (7) days before the hearing, unless the court permits service at another time

    (2) ❑ DISTRICT OF MAINE: Additional timing

        (i) ❑ Unless within twenty-one (21) days after the filing of a motion the opposing party files written objection thereto, incorporating a memorandum of law, the opposing party shall be deemed to have waived objection

B. Timing

1. *Motion for sanctions.* The deterrent purpose of FRCP 11 can best be served by imposing sanctions at or near the time of the violation. FEDPROC § 62:775. Accordingly, a party who is aware of an FRCP 11 violation should act promptly. FEDPROC § 62:775; Oliveri v. Thompson, 803 F.2d 1265 (2d Cir. 1986). However, whether a case is well-grounded in fact will often not be evident until a plaintiff has been given a chance to conduct discovery. Therefore, motions for sanctions can be timely even when filed well after the original pleadings. FEDPROC § 62:775; Runfola & Assocs., Inc. v. Spectrum Reporting II, Inc., 88 F.3d 368 (6th Cir. 1996).

  a. *Safe harbor provision.* The motion must be served under FRCP 5, but it must not be filed or be presented to the court if the challenged paper, claim, defense, contention, or denial is withdrawn or appropriately corrected within twenty-one (21) days after service or within another time the court sets. FRCP 11(c)(2).

2. *Timing of motions, generally*

  a. *Motion and notice of hearing.* A written motion and notice of the hearing must be served at least fourteen (14) days before the time specified for the hearing, with the following exceptions: (A) when the motion may be heard ex parte; (B) when the Federal Rules of Civil Procedure set a different time; or (C) when a court order—which a party may, for good cause, apply for ex parte—sets a different time. FRCP 6(c)(1).

  b. *Supporting affidavit.* Any affidavit supporting a motion must be served with the motion. FRCP 6(c)(2).

  c. *DISTRICT OF MAINE: Affidavits and other supporting documents.* Any affidavits and other documents setting forth or evidencing facts on which the motion is based must be filed with the motion. ME R USDCT Rule 7(a).

3. *Timing of opposing papers.* Except as FRCP 59(c) provides otherwise, any opposing affidavit must be served at least seven (7) days before the hearing, unless the court permits service at another time. FRCP 6(c)(2).

  a. *DISTRICT OF MAINE.* Unless within twenty-one (21) days after the filing of a motion the opposing party files written objection thereto, incorporating a memorandum of law, the opposing party shall be deemed to have waived objection.

ME R USDCT Rule 7(b). The deemed waiver imposed in ME R USDCT Rule 7(b) shall not apply to motions filed during trial. ME R USDCT Rule 7(b).

4. *Timing of reply papers.* Where the respondent files an answering affidavit setting up a new matter, the moving party ordinarily is allowed a reasonable time to file a reply affidavit since failure to deny the new matter by affidavit may operate as an admission of its truth. AMJUR MOTIONS § 25.

   a. *DISTRICT OF MAINE.* Within fourteen (14) days of the filing of any objection to a motion, the moving party may file a reply memorandum. ME R USDCT Rule 7(c).

5. *Computation of time*

   a. *Computing time.* FRCP 6 applies in computing any time period specified in the Federal Rules of Civil Procedure, in any local rule or court order, or in any statute that does not specify a method of computing time. FRCP 6(a).

      i. *Period stated in days or a longer unit.* When the period is stated in days or a longer unit of time: (A) exclude the day of the event that triggers the period; (B) count every day, including intermediate Saturdays, Sundays, and legal holidays; and (C) include the last day of the period, but if the last day is a Saturday, Sunday, or legal holiday, the period continues to run until the end of the next day that is not a Saturday, Sunday, or legal holiday. FRCP 6(a)(1).

      ii. *Period stated in hours.* When the period is stated in hours: (A) begin counting immediately on the occurrence of the event that triggers the period; (B) count every hour, including hours during intermediate Saturdays, Sundays, and legal holidays; and (C) if the period would end on a Saturday, Sunday, or legal holiday, the period continues to run until the same time on the next day that is not a Saturday, Sunday, or legal holiday. FRCP 6(a)(2).

      iii. *Inaccessibility of the clerk's office.* Unless the court orders otherwise, if the clerk's office is inaccessible: (A) on the last day for filing under FRCP 6(a)(1), then the time for filing is extended to the first accessible day that is not a Saturday, Sunday, or legal holiday; or (B) during the last hour for filing under FRCP 6(a)(2), then the time for filing is extended to the same time on the first accessible day that is not a Saturday, Sunday, or legal holiday. FRCP 6(a)(3).

      iv. *"Last day" defined.* Unless a different time is set by a statute, local rule, or court order, the last day ends: (A) for electronic filing, at midnight in the court's time zone; and (B) for filing by other means, when the clerk's office is scheduled to close. FRCP 6(a)(4).

      v. *"Next day" defined.* The "next day" is determined by continuing to count forward when the period is measured after an event and backward when measured before an event. FRCP 6(a)(5).

      vi. *"Legal holiday" defined.* "Legal holiday" means: (A) the day set aside by statute for observing New Year's Day, Martin Luther King Jr.'s Birthday, Washington's Birthday, Memorial Day, Independence Day, Labor Day, Columbus Day, Veterans' Day, Thanksgiving Day, or Christmas Day; (B) any day declared a holiday by the President or Congress; and (C) for periods that are measured after an event, any other day declared a holiday by the state where the district court is located. FRCP 6(a)(6).

      vii. *DISTRICT OF MAINE: Applicability of FRCP 6.* FRCP 6 applies when computing any period of time stated in the Local Rules of the United States District Court for the District of Maine. ME R USDCT Rule 6(a).

   b. *DISTRICT OF MAINE: Computation of electronic filing deadlines.* Filing documents electronically does not in any way alter any filing deadlines. All electronic transmissions of documents must be completed prior to midnight, Eastern Time, in order to be considered timely filed that day. Where a specific time of day deadline is set by court order or stipulation, the electronic filing must be completed by that time. ME R USDCT App. 4(f). A document filed electronically shall be deemed filed at the time and date stated on the Notice of Electronic Filing received from the court. ME R USDCT App. 4(d)(2).

      i. *Technical failures.* A filing user whose filing is made untimely as the result of a technical failure may seek appropriate relief from the court. ME R USDCT App. 4(n). A technical failure of the court's ECF system is deemed to have occurred when the court's ECF site cannot accept filings continuously or intermittently over the course of any period of time greater than one (1) hour. Known system outages will be posted on the court's website along with guidance on how to proceed, if applicable. ME R USDCT App. 4(n).

   c. *Extending time.* When an act may or must be done within a specified time, the court may, for good cause, extend the time: (A) with or without motion or notice if the court acts, or if a request is made, before the original time or its extension expires; or (B) on motion made after the time has expired if the party failed to act because of excusable neglect. FRCP 6(b)(1). A court must not extend the time to act under FRCP 50(b), FRCP 50(d), FRCP 52(b), FRCP 59(b), FRCP 59(d), FRCP 59(e), and FRCP 60(b). FRCP 6(b)(2). Refer to the United States District Court for the

District of Maine KeyRules Motion for Continuance/Extension of Time document for more information on extending time.

d. *Additional time after certain kinds of service.* When a party may or must act within a specified time after being served and service is made under FRCP 5(b)(2)(C) (by mail), FRCP 5(b)(2)(D) (by leaving with the clerk), or FRCP 5(b)(2)(F) (by other means consented to), three (3) days are added after the period would otherwise expire under FRCP 6(a). FRCP 6(d).

C. General Requirements

1. *Motions, generally*

   a. *Motion requirements.* A request for a court order must be made by motion. The motion must: (A) be in writing unless made during a hearing or trial; (B) state with particularity the grounds for seeking the order; and (C) state the relief sought. FRCP 7(b)(1). The writing and particularity requirements are intended to ensure that the adverse parties are informed of and have a record of both the motion's pendency and the grounds on which the movant seeks an order. FPP § 1191; Feldberg v. Quechee Lakes Corp., 463 F.3d 195 (2d Cir. 2006).

      i. *Particularity requirement.* The particularity requirement [ensures] that the opposing parties will have notice of their opponent's contentions. FEDPROC § 62:358; Goodman v. 1973 26 Foot Trojan Vessel, Arkansas Registration No. AR1439SN, 859 F.2d 71 (8th Cir. 1988). That requirement ensures that notice of the basis for the motion is provided to the court and to the opposing party so as to avoid prejudice, provide the opponent with a meaningful opportunity to respond, and provide the court with enough information to process the motion correctly. FEDPROC § 62:358; Andreas v. Volkswagen of Am., Inc., 336 F.3d 789 (8th Cir. 2003).

      - Reasonable specification of the grounds for a motion is sufficient. The particularity requirement for motions is satisfied when no party is prejudiced by a lack of particularity or when the court can comprehend the basis for the motion and deal with it fairly. However, where a movant fails to state even one ground for granting the motion in question, the movant has failed to meet the minimal standard of "reasonable specification." FEDPROC § 62:358; Martinez v. Trainor, 556 F.2d 818 (7th Cir. 1977).

      - The court may excuse the failure to comply with the particularity requirement if it is inadvertent, and where no prejudice is shown by the opposing party. FEDPROC § 62:358.

   b. *Notice of motion.* A party interested in resisting the relief sought by a motion has a right to notice thereof, and an opportunity to be heard. AMJUR MOTIONS § 12.

      i. *Purpose.* In addition to statutory or court rule provisions requiring notice of a motion—the purpose of such a notice requirement having been said to be to prevent a party from being prejudicially surprised by a motion—principles of natural justice dictate that an adverse party generally must be given notice that a motion will be presented to the court. AMJUR MOTIONS § 12.

      ii. *Adequacy of notice.* The test of adequate notice generally turns on whether the other parties were afforded an adequate opportunity to prepare and respond to the issues to be raised in the proceeding. AMJUR MOTIONS § 12.

   c. *Single document containing motion and notice.* A single written document can satisfy the writing requirements both for a motion and for an FRCP 6(c)(1) notice. FRCP 7(Advisory Committee Notes).

2. *Motion for sanctions.* A motion for sanctions under FRCP 11 may be filed by either the plaintiff or the defendant. FEDPROC § 62:772. Only parties and other "participants" in an action have standing to seek sanctions, however. FEDPROC § 62:772; New York News, Inc. v. Kheel, 972 F.2d 482 (2d Cir. 1992).

   a. *Basis for motion for sanctions.* FRCP 11(c) authorizes sanctions for misconduct relating to representations to the court. These representations are based on misconduct relating to the presentation (whether by signing, filing, submitting, or later advocating) of a pleading, written motion, or other paper to the court. Improper conduct includes, but is not limited to: (1) the filing of a frivolous suit or document; (2) the filing of a document or lawsuit for an improper purpose; and (3) the filing of actions that needlessly increase the cost or length of litigation. LITGTORT § 20:7. Refer to the "E. Format" section of this KeyRules document for more information on representations to the court.

   b. *Informal notice.* In most cases. . . .counsel should be expected to give informal notice to the other party, whether in person or by a telephone call or letter, of a potential violation before proceeding to prepare and serve an FRCP 11 motion. FRCP 11(Advisory Committee Notes).

   c. *Safe harbor provision.* A motion for sanctions must be made separately from any other motion and must describe the specific conduct that allegedly violates FRCP 11(b). The motion must be served under FRCP 5, but it must not be filed or be presented to the court if the challenged paper, claim, defense, contention, or denial is withdrawn or appropriately corrected within twenty-one (21) days after service or within another time the court sets. If warranted, the court may award to the prevailing party the reasonable expenses, including attorney's fees, incurred for the motion. FRCP 11(c)(2). These provisions are intended to provide a type of "safe harbor" against motions under FRCP 11 in that a party will not be subject to sanctions on the basis of another party's motion unless, after receiving the motion, it refuses to withdraw that position or to acknowledge candidly that it does not currently have evidence to support a specified allegation. FRCP 11(Advisory Committee Notes).

d. *Imposition of sanctions.* If, after notice and a reasonable opportunity to respond, the court determines that FRCP 11(b) has been violated, the court may impose an appropriate sanction on any attorney, law firm, or party that violated FRCP 11(b) or is responsible for the violation. Absent exceptional circumstances, a law firm must be held jointly responsible for a violation committed by its partner, associate, or employee. FRCP 11(c)(1).

    i. *Government agencies and their counsel.* FRCP 11 applies to government agencies and their counsel as well as private parties. Thus, the United States is bound by FRCP 11 just as are private parties, and must have reasonable grounds to make allegations within its complaint or answer. FEDPROC § 62:767.

    ii. *Pro se litigants.* FRCP 11 applies to pro se litigants. FEDPROC § 62:769. Pro se litigants are held to a more lenient standard than professional counsel, with FRCP 11's application determined on a sliding scale according to the litigant's level of sophistication. FEDPROC § 62:769.

e. *Nature of a sanction.* A sanction imposed under FRCP 11 must be limited to what suffices to deter repetition of the conduct or comparable conduct by others similarly situated. The sanction may include nonmonetary directives; an order to pay a penalty into court; or, if imposed on motion and warranted for effective deterrence, an order directing payment to the movant of part or all of the reasonable attorney's fees and other expenses directly resulting from the violation. FRCP 11(c)(4).

f. *Counsel's liability for excessive costs.* Any attorney or other person admitted to conduct cases in any court of the United States or any Territory thereof who so multiplies the proceedings in any case unreasonably and vexatiously may be required by the court to satisfy personally the excess costs, expenses, and attorneys' fees reasonably incurred because of such conduct. 28 U.S.C.A. § 1927.

g. *Limitations on monetary sanctions.* The court must not impose a monetary sanction: (A) against a represented party for violating FRCP 11(b)(2); or (B) on its own, unless it issued the show-cause order under FRCP 11(c)(3) before voluntary dismissal or settlement of the claims made by or against the party that is, or whose attorneys are, to be sanctioned. FRCP 11(c)(5).

h. *Requirements for an order.* An order imposing a sanction must describe the sanctioned conduct and explain the basis for the sanction. FRCP 11(c)(6).

    i. *On the court's initiative.* On its own, the court may order an attorney, law firm, or party to show cause why conduct specifically described in the order has not violated FRCP 11(b). FRCP 11(c)(3).

3. *Opposing papers.* The Federal Rules of Civil Procedure do not require any formal answer, return, or reply to a motion, except where the Federal Rules of Civil Procedure or local rules may require affidavits, memoranda, or other papers to be filed in opposition to a motion. Such papers are simply to apprise the court of such opposition and the grounds of that opposition. FEDPROC § 62:353.

a. *DISTRICT OF MAINE: Content of objections.* Any objections shall include citations and supporting authorities and affidavits and other documents setting forth or evidencing facts on which the objection is based. ME R USDCT Rule 7(b).

b. *Effect of failure to respond to motion.* Although in the absence of statutory provision or court rule, a motion ordinarily does not require a response or written answer, when a party files a motion and the opposing party fails to respond, the court may construe such failure to respond as nonopposition to the motion or an admission that the motion was meritorious. AMJUR MOTIONS § 28. The rule in some jurisdictions being that the failure to respond to a fact set forth in a motion is deemed an admission—and may grant the motion if the relief requested appears to be justified. AMJUR MOTIONS § 28.

c. *Assent or no opposition not determinative.* However, a motion will not be granted automatically simply because an "assent" or a notation of "no opposition" has been filed; federal judges frequently deny motions that have been assented to when it is thought that justice so dictates. FPP § 1190.

d. *Responsive pleading inappropriate as response to motion.* An attempt to answer or oppose a motion with a responsive pleading usually is not appropriate. FPP § 1190.

4. *Reply papers.* A moving party may be required or permitted to prepare papers in addition to its original motion papers. AMJUR MOTIONS § 25. Papers answering or replying to opposing papers may be appropriate, in the interests of justice, where it appears there is a substantial reason for allowing a reply. Thus, a court may accept reply papers where a party demonstrates that the papers to which it seeks to file a reply raise new issues that are material to the disposition of the question before the court, or where the court determines, sua sponte, that it wishes further briefing of an issue raised in those papers and orders the submission of additional papers. FEDPROC § 62:354.

    a. *Function of reply papers.* The function of a reply affidavit or reply papers is to answer the arguments made in opposition to the position taken by the movant, not to raise new issues, arguments, or evidence, or change the nature of the primary motion. However, if the court permits new evidence with the reply papers, the other party should be given the opportunity to respond. Where the party opposing the motion has no opportunity to address the argument in writing, a court has the discretion to disregard arguments raised for the first time in a reply memorandum. Also, the view has been followed in some jurisdictions that as a matter of judicial economy, where there is no prejudice and where the issues could be raised simply by filing a motion to dismiss, the trial court has discretion to consider arguments raised for the first time in a reply memorandum, and that a trial court may grant a motion to strike issues raised for the first time in a reply memorandum. AMJUR MOTIONS § 26.

        i. *DISTRICT OF MAINE.* The moving party may file a reply memorandum. . .which shall be strictly confined to replying to new matter raised in the objection or opposing memorandum. ME R USDCT Rule 7(c).

5. *DISTRICT OF MAINE: Appearances.* An attorney's signature to a pleading shall constitute an appearance for the party filing the pleading. Otherwise, an attorney who wishes to participate in any manner in any action must file a formal written appearance identifying the party represented. An appearance whether by pleading or formal written appearance shall be signed by an attorney in his/her individual name and shall state his/her office address. ME R USDCT Rule 83.2(a). For more information, refer to ME R USDCT Rule 83.2.

6. *DISTRICT OF MAINE: Alternative dispute resolution (ADR).* Litigants are authorized and encouraged to employ, at their own expense, any available ADR process on which they can agree, including early neutral evaluation, settlement conferences, mediation, non-binding summary jury trial, corporate mini-trial, and arbitration proceedings. ME R USDCT Rule 83.11(a). For more information on ADR, refer to ME R USDCT Rule 83.11.

D. Documents

1. *Documents for moving party*

    a. *Required documents*

        i. *Notice of motion and motion.* Refer to the "C. General Requirements" section of this KeyRules document for information on the notice of motion and motion.

            - *DISTRICT OF MAINE: Memorandum of law.* Every motion shall incorporate a memorandum of law, including citations and supporting authorities. ME R USDCT Rule 7(a). Refer to the "E. Format" section of this KeyRules document for the form of memoranda of law.

            - *Certificate of service.* No certificate of service is required when a paper is served by filing it with the court's electronic-filing system. When a paper that is required to be served is served by other means: (i) if the paper is filed, a certificate of service must be filed with it or within a reasonable time after service; and (ii) if the paper is not filed, a certificate of service need not be filed unless filing is required by court order or by local rule. FRCP 5(d)(1)(B).

    b. *Supplemental documents*

        i. *Supporting evidence.* When a motion relies on facts outside the record, the court may hear the matter on affidavits or may hear it wholly or partly on oral testimony or on depositions. FRCP 43(c).

            - *DISTRICT OF MAINE: Affidavits and other supporting documents.* Any affidavits and other documents setting forth or evidencing facts on which the motion is based must be filed with the motion. ME R USDCT Rule 7(a).

            - *DISTRICT OF MAINE: Discovery transcripts or materials.* A party relying on discovery transcripts or materials in support of or in opposition to a motion shall file excerpts of such transcript or materials with the memorandum required by ME R USDCT Rule 7 as well as a list of specific citations to the parts on which the party relies. ME R USDCT Rule 26(c). Excerpts of depositions in support of or in opposition to a motion shall be filed electronically using ECF, unless otherwise permitted by the court. ME R USDCT App. 4(l)(3).

        ii. *Notice of constitutional question.* A party that files a pleading, written motion, or other paper drawing into question the constitutionality of a federal or state statute must promptly: (1) file a notice of constitutional question stating the question and identifying the paper that raises it, if: (A) a federal statute is questioned and the parties do not include the United States, one of its agencies, or one of its officers or employees in an official capacity; or (B) a state statute is questioned and the parties do not include the state, one of its agencies, or one of its officers or employees in an official capacity; and (2) serve the notice and paper on the Attorney General of the United States if a federal statute is questioned—or on the state attorney general if a state statute is questioned—either by certified or registered mail or by sending it to an electronic address designated by the attorney general for this purpose. FRCP 5.1(a).

- *No forfeiture.* A party's failure to file and serve the notice, or the court's failure to certify, does not forfeit a constitutional claim or defense that is otherwise timely asserted. FRCP 5.1(d).

iii. *Nongovernmental corporate disclosure statement.* A nongovernmental corporate party must file two (2) copies of a disclosure statement that: (1) identifies any parent corporation and any publicly held corporation owning ten percent (10%) or more of its stock; or (2) states that there is no such corporation. FRCP 7.1(a). A party must: (1) file the disclosure statement with its first appearance, pleading, petition, motion, response, or other request addressed to the court; and (2) promptly file a supplemental statement if any required information changes. FRCP 7.1(b).

- *DISTRICT OF MAINE: Notice of interested parties.* To enable the court to evaluate possible disqualification or recusal, counsel for all non-governmental parties shall file with their first appearance a Notice of Interested Parties, which shall list all persons, associations of persons, firms, partnerships, limited liability companies, joint ventures, corporations (including parent or affiliated corporations, clearly identified as such), or any similar entities, owning ten percent (10%) or more of the named party. Counsel shall be under a continuing obligation to file an amended Notice if any material change occurs in the status of an Interested Party, such as through merger, acquisition, or new/additional membership. ME R USDCT Rule 7.1.

iv. *DISTRICT OF MAINE: Additional supplemental documents*

- *Proposed order.* Proposed orders shall not be filed unless requested by the court. When requested by the court, proposed orders shall be filed by e-mail in word processing format. ME R USDCT App. 4(k)(1).

2. *Documents for opposing party*

  a. *Required documents*

   i. *Opposition.* Refer to the "C. General Requirements" section of this KeyRules document for information on the opposing papers.

   - *DISTRICT OF MAINE: Memorandum of law.* Unless within twenty-one (21) days after the filing of a motion the opposing party files written objection thereto, incorporating a memorandum of law, the opposing party shall be deemed to have waived objection. ME R USDCT Rule 7(b).

   - *Certificate of service.* No certificate of service is required when a paper is served by filing it with the court's electronic-filing system. When a paper that is required to be served is served by other means: (i) if the paper is filed, a certificate of service must be filed with it or within a reasonable time after service; and (ii) if the paper is not filed, a certificate of service need not be filed unless filing is required by court order or by local rule. FRCP 5(d)(1)(B).

  b. *Supplemental documents*

   i. *Supporting evidence.* When a motion relies on facts outside the record, the court may hear the matter on affidavits or may hear it wholly or partly on oral testimony or on depositions. FRCP 43(c).

   - *DISTRICT OF MAINE: Affidavits and other supporting documents.* Any objections shall include. . . .affidavits and other documents setting forth or evidencing facts on which the objection is based. ME R USDCT Rule 7(b).

   - *DISTRICT OF MAINE: Discovery transcripts or materials.* A party relying on discovery transcripts or materials in support of or in opposition to a motion shall file excerpts of such transcript or materials with the memorandum required by ME R USDCT Rule 7 as well as a list of specific citations to the parts on which the party relies. ME R USDCT Rule 26(c). Excerpts of depositions in support of or in opposition to a motion shall be filed electronically using ECF, unless otherwise permitted by the court. ME R USDCT App. 4(l)(3).

   ii. *Notice of constitutional question.* A party that files a pleading, written motion, or other paper drawing into question the constitutionality of a federal or state statute must promptly: (1) file a notice of constitutional question stating the question and identifying the paper that raises it, if: (A) a federal statute is questioned and the parties do not include the United States, one of its agencies, or one of its officers or employees in an official capacity; or (B) a state statute is questioned and the parties do not include the state, one of its agencies, or one of its officers or employees in an official capacity; and (2) serve the notice and paper on the Attorney General of the United States if a federal statute is questioned—or on the state attorney general if a state statute is questioned—either by certified or registered mail or by sending it to an electronic address designated by the attorney general for this purpose. FRCP 5.1(a).

- *No forfeiture.* A party's failure to file and serve the notice, or the court's failure to certify, does not forfeit a constitutional claim or defense that is otherwise timely asserted. FRCP 5.1(d).

E. Format

1. *Form of documents.* The rules governing captions and other matters of form in pleadings apply to motions and other papers. FRCP 7(b)(2).

   a. *DISTRICT OF MAINE: Font size, line spacing, and paper size.* All such documents shall be typed in a font of no less than size twelve (12) point, and shall be double-spaced or printed on eight and one-half by eleven (8-1/2 x 11) inch paper. Footnotes shall be in a font of no less than size ten (10) point, and may be single spaced. ME R USDCT Rule 10.

   b. *Caption.* Every pleading must have a caption with the court's name, a title, a file number, and an FRCP 7(a) designation. FRCP 10(a).

      i. *Names of parties.* The title of the complaint must name all the parties; the title of other pleadings, after naming the first party on each side, may refer generally to other parties. FRCP 10(a).

      ii. *DISTRICT OF MAINE: Additional caption requirements.* All pleadings, motions and other papers filed with the clerk or otherwise submitted to the court, except exhibits, shall bear the proper case number and shall contain on the first page a caption as described by FRCP 10(a) and immediately thereunder a designation of what the document is and the name of the party in whose behalf it is submitted. ME R USDCT Rule 10.

   c. *Claims or defenses*

      i. *Numbered paragraphs.* A party must state its claims or defenses in numbered paragraphs, each limited as far as practicable to a single set of circumstances. A later pleading may refer by number to a paragraph in an earlier pleading. FRCP 10(b).

      ii. *Separate statements.* If doing so would promote clarity, each claim founded on a separate transaction or occurrence—and each defense other than a denial—must be stated in a separate count or defense. FRCP 10(b).

   d. *Adoption by reference.* A statement in a pleading may be adopted by reference elsewhere in the same pleading or in any other pleading or motion. FRCP 10(c).

      i. *Exhibits.* A copy of a written instrument that is an exhibit to a pleading is a part of the pleading for all purposes. FRCP 10(c).

   e. *DISTRICT OF MAINE: Page numbering.* All pages shall be numbered at the bottom. ME R USDCT Rule 10.

   f. *DISTRICT OF MAINE: Attachment of ancillary papers.* Ancillary papers shall be attached at the end of the document to which they relate. ME R USDCT Rule 10.

   g. *Acceptance by the clerk.* The clerk must not refuse to file a paper solely because it is not in the form prescribed by the Federal Rules of Civil Procedure or by a local rule or practice. FRCP 5(d)(4).

2. *Form of electronic documents.* A paper filed electronically is a written paper for purposes of the Federal Rules of Civil Procedure. FRCP 5(d)(3)(D).

   a. *DISTRICT OF MAINE: Document format.* The ECF system only accepts documents in a portable document format (PDF). Although there are two types of PDF documents—electronically converted PDF's and scanned PDF's—only electronically converted PDF's may be filed with the court using the ECF system, unless otherwise authorized by local rule or order. ME R USDCT App. 4. Any document or exhibit to be filed or submitted to the court shall not be password-protected or encrypted. ME R USDCT App. 4(g)(12).

      i. *Electronically converted PDFs.* Electronically converted PDF's are created from word processing documents (MS Word, WordPerfect, etc.) using Adobe Acrobat or similar software. They are text searchable and their file size is small. ME R USDCT App. 4. Software used to electronically convert documents to PDF which includes proprietary or advertisement information within the PDF document is prohibited. ME R USDCT App. 4.

    ii. *Scanned PDFs.* Scanned PDF's are created from paper documents run through an optical scanner. Scanned PDF's are not searchable and have a large file size. ME R USDCT App. 4.

  b. *DISTRICT OF MAINE: Title.* All pleadings filed electronically shall be titled in accordance with the approved dictionary of civil or criminal events of the ECF system of the United States District Court for the District of Maine. ME R USDCT App. 4(d)(3).

  c. *DISTRICT OF MAINE: Attachments.* Attachments to filings and exhibits must be filed in accordance with the court's ECF User Manual, unless otherwise ordered by the court. ME R USDCT App. 4(j). When there are fifty (50) or fewer attachments to a pleading, the attachments must be filed by counsel electronically using ECF. When there are more than fifty (50) attachments, the attachments must be filed in one of the following ways: (A) using ECF, simply attach them to the pleading being filed; (B) using ECF, use the "Additional Attachments" menu item; (C) on paper; or (D) on a properly labeled three and one-half (3-1/2) inch floppy disk, CD or DVD. ME R USDCT App. 4(j)(2). Attachments filed on paper or on disk must contain a comprehensive index that clearly describes each document. ME R USDCT App. 4(j)(2).

    i. A filing user must submit as attachments only those excerpts of the referenced documents that are directly germane to the matter under consideration by the court. Excerpted material must be clearly and prominently identified as such. Users who file excerpts of documents do so without prejudice to their right to timely file additional excerpts or the complete document, as may be allowed by the court. Responding parties may timely file additional excerpts or the complete document that they believe are directly germane. ME R USDCT App. 4(j)(3).

    ii. Filers shall not attach as an exhibit any pleading or other paper already on file with the court in that case, but shall merely refer to that document. ME R USDCT App. 4(j)(4).

  d. *DISTRICT OF MAINE: Compliance with technical standards.* All documents filed by electronic means must comply with technical standards, if any, established by the Judicial Conference of the United States or by the United States District Court for the District of Maine. ME R USDCT App. 4(a)(3).

3. *DISTRICT OF MAINE: Form of memoranda of law.* All memoranda shall be typed, in a font of no less than size twelve (12) point, and shall be double-spaced on eight and one-half by eleven (8-1/2 x 11) inch paper or printed. Footnotes shall be in a font of no less than size ten (10) point, and may be single spaced. All pages shall be numbered at the bottom. ME R USDCT Rule 7(d).

  a. *Page limitations.* No memorandum of law in support of or in opposition to a nondispositive motion shall exceed ten (10) pages. ME R USDCT Rule 7(d). No reply memorandum shall exceed seven (7) pages. ME R USDCT Rule 7(d); ME R USDCT Rule 7(c).

    i. *Motion to exceed page limitation.* A motion to exceed the limitation of ME R USDCT Rule 7 shall be filed no later than three (3) business days in advance of the date for filing the memorandum to permit meaningful review by the court. A motion to exceed the page limitations shall not be filed simultaneously with a memorandum in excess of the limitations of ME R USDCT Rule 7. ME R USDCT Rule 7(d).

4. *Signing of pleadings, motions and other papers*

  a. *Signature.* Every pleading, written motion, and other paper must be signed by at least one attorney of record in the attorney's name—or by a party personally if the party is unrepresented. The paper must state the signer's address, e-mail address, and telephone number. FRCP 11(a).

    i. *No verification or accompanying affidavit required for pleadings.* Unless a rule or statute specifically states otherwise, a pleading need not be verified or accompanied by an affidavit. FRCP 11(a).

    ii. *Unsigned papers.* The court must strike an unsigned paper unless the omission is promptly corrected after being called to the attorney's or party's attention. FRCP 11(a).

  b. *Electronic signing.* A filing made through a person's electronic-filing account and authorized by that person, together with that person's name on a signature block, constitutes the person's signature. FRCP 5(d)(3)(C).

    i. *DISTRICT OF MAINE: Attorneys.* The user log-in and password together with a user's name on the signature block constitutes the attorney's signature pursuant to the Federal Rules of Civil Procedure and the Local Rules of the United States District Court for the District of Maine. All electronically filed documents must include a signature block and must set forth the attorney's name, address, telephone number and e-mail address. The name of the ECF user under whose log-in and password the document is submitted must be preceded by a "/s/" in the space where the signature would otherwise appear. ME R USDCT App. 4(h)(1).

    ii. *DISTRICT OF MAINE: Multiple signatures.* The filer of any document requiring more than one signature (e.g., pleadings filed by visiting lawyers, stipulations, joint status reports) must list thereon all the names of other signatories, preceded by a "/s/" in the space where the signatures would otherwise appear. By submitting such a document, the filing attorney certifies that each of the other signatories has expressly agreed to the form and substance of the document and that the filing attorney has their actual authority to submit the document electronically. ME R USDCT App. 4(h)(2). For more information, refer to ME R USDCT App. 4(h)(2).

    iii. *DISTRICT OF MAINE: Documents signed under oath.* Affidavits, declarations, verified complaints, or any other document signed under oath shall be filed electronically. The electronically filed version shall contain the typed name of the signatory, preceded by a "/s/" in the space where the signature would otherwise appear indicating that the paper document bears an original signature. ME R USDCT Rule 10; ME R USDCT App. 4(h)(3). For more information, refer to ME R USDCT Rule 10.

c. *Representations to the court.* By presenting to the court a pleading, written motion, or other paper—whether by signing, filing, submitting, or later advocating it—an attorney or unrepresented party certifies that to the best of the person's knowledge, information, and belief, formed after an inquiry reasonable under the circumstances: (1) it is not being presented for any improper purpose, such as to harass, cause unnecessary delay, or needlessly increase the cost of litigation; (2) the claims, defenses, and other legal contentions are warranted by existing law or by a nonfrivolous argument for extending, modifying, or reversing existing law or for establishing new law; (3) the factual contentions have evidentiary support or, if specifically so identified, will likely have evidentiary support after a reasonable opportunity for further investigation or discovery; and (4) the denials of factual contentions are warranted on the evidence or, if specifically so identified, are reasonably based on belief or a lack of information. FRCP 11(b).

d. *Sanctions.* Refer to the "C. General Requirements" section of this KeyRules document for information on sanctions.

5. *Privacy protection for filings made with the court*

a. *Redacted filings.* Unless the court orders otherwise, in an electronic or paper filing with the court that contains an individual's Social Security number, taxpayer-identification number, or birth date, the name of an individual known to be a minor, or a financial-account number, a party or nonparty making the filing may include only: (1) the last four (4) digits of the Social Security number and taxpayer-identification number; (2) the year of the individual's birth; (3) the minor's initials; and (4) the last four (4) digits of the financial-account number. FRCP 5.2(a).

    i. *DISTRICT OF MAINE.* To address the privacy concerns created by the Internet access to court papers, unless otherwise ordered by the court, counsel shall modify certain personal data identifiers in pleadings and other papers as follows: (1) minors' names: use of the minors' initials only; (2) Social Security numbers: use of the last four (4) numbers only; (3) dates of birth: use of the year of birth only; [and] (4) financial account numbers: identify the type of account and the financial institution, but use only the last four (4) numbers of the account number. ME R USDCT Redacting Pleadings. Counsel should also use caution when filing papers that contain a person's medical records, employment history; financial information; and any proprietary or trade secret information. ME R USDCT Redacting Pleadings.

b. *Exemptions from the redaction requirement.* The redaction requirement does not apply to the following: (1) a financial-account number that identifies the property allegedly subject to forfeiture in a forfeiture proceeding; (2) the record of an administrative or agency proceeding; (3) the official record of a state-court proceeding; (4) the record of a court or tribunal, if that record was not subject to the redaction requirement when originally filed; (5) a filing covered by FRCP 5.2(c) or FRCP 5.2(d); and (6) a pro se filing in an action brought under 28 U.S.C.A. § 2241, 28 U.S.C.A. § 2254, or 28 U.S.C.A. § 2255. FRCP 5.2(b).

c. *Limitations on remote access to electronic files; Social Security appeals and immigration cases.* Unless the court orders otherwise, in an action for benefits under the Social Security Act, and in an action or proceeding relating to an order of removal, to relief from removal, or to immigration benefits or detention, access to an electronic file is authorized as follows: (1) the parties and their attorneys may have remote electronic access to any part of the case file, including the administrative record; (2) any other person may have electronic access to the full record at the courthouse, but may have remote electronic access only to: (A) the docket maintained by the court; and (B) an opinion, order, judgment, or other disposition of the court, but not any other part of the case file or the administrative record. FRCP 5.2(c).

d. *Filings made under seal.* The court may order that a filing be made under seal without redaction. The court may later unseal the filing or order the person who made the filing to file a redacted version for the public record. FRCP 5.2(d).

    i. *DISTRICT OF MAINE.* For information on filing sealed documents in the District of Maine, refer to ME R USDCT Rule 7A, ME R USDCT App. 4(p)(2), and ME R USDCT Sealed Filings.

e. *Protective orders.* For good cause, the court may by order in a case: (1) require redaction of additional information; or (2) limit or prohibit a nonparty's remote electronic access to a document filed with the court. FRCP 5.2(e).

f. *Option for additional unredacted filing under seal.* A person making a redacted filing may also file an unredacted copy under seal. The court must retain the unredacted copy as part of the record. FRCP 5.2(f).

   i. *DISTRICT OF MAINE.* A party wishing to file a document containing the personal data identifiers specified above may. . .file an unredacted document under seal. This document will be retained by the clerk's office as part of the record. ME R USDCT Redacting Pleadings. The court may, however, still require the party to file a redacted copy for the public file. ME R USDCT Redacting Pleadings.

g. *Option for filing a reference list.* A filing that contains redacted information may be filed together with a reference list that identifies each item of redacted information and specifies an appropriate identifier that uniquely corresponds to each item listed. The list must be filed under seal and may be amended as of right. Any reference in the case to a listed identifier will be construed to refer to the corresponding item of information. FRCP 5.2(g).

   i. *DISTRICT OF MAINE.* A party wishing to file a document containing the personal data identifiers specified above may. . .file a reference list under seal. The reference list shall contain the complete personal data identifier(s) and the redacted identifier(s) used in its (their) place in the filing. All references in the case to the redacted identifiers included in the reference list will be construed to refer to the corresponding complete identifier. The reference list must be filed under seal, and may be amended as of right. It shall be retained by the clerk's office as part of the record. ME R USDCT Redacting Pleadings. The court may, however, still require the party to file a redacted copy for the public file. ME R USDCT Redacting Pleadings.

h. *DISTRICT OF MAINE: Responsibility for redaction.* The clerk is not required to review documents filed with the court for compliance with FRCP 5.2. The responsibility to redact filings rests with counsel and the party or nonparty making the filing. ME R USDCT App. 4(i); ME R USDCT Redacting Pleadings. For guidelines for filing confidential information in civil cases in the District of Maine, refer to ME R USDCT Confidentiality.

i. *Waiver of protection of identifiers.* A person waives the protection of FRCP 5.2(a) as to the person's own information by filing it without redaction and not under seal. FRCP 5.2(h).

F. Filing and Service Requirements

1. *Filing requirements*

   a. *Required filings.* Any paper after the complaint that is required to be served must be filed no later than a reasonable time after service. FRCP 5(d)(1).

   b. *DISTRICT OF MAINE: Place of filing.* Unless otherwise ordered by the court, papers shall be filed with the court at Bangor in cases filed and pending at Bangor, and at Portland in cases filed and pending at Portland. ME R USDCT Rule 5(a).

   c. *Nonelectronic filing.* A paper not filed electronically is filed by delivering it: (A) to the clerk; or (B) to a judge who agrees to accept it for filing, and who must then note the filing date on the paper and promptly send it to the clerk. FRCP 5(d)(2).

      i. *DISTRICT OF MAINE: Documents to be filed in paper.* The following documents shall be filed in paper, which may also be scanned into ECF by the clerk's office: (A) all handwritten pleadings; and (B) all pleadings and documents filed by pro se litigants who are incarcerated or who are not registered filing users in ECF. ME R USDCT App. 4(g)(8). Non-prisoner pro se litigants in civil actions may register with ECF or may file (and serve) all pleadings and other documents in paper. The clerk's office will scan into ECF any pleadings and documents filed on paper in accordance with ME R USDCT App. 4(g). ME R USDCT App. 4(o). For more information, refer to ME R USDCT App. 4(g).

   d. *Electronic filing*

      i. *DISTRICT OF MAINE: Authorization.* Unless exempt or otherwise ordered by the court, papers shall be filed and served electronically as required by the court's Administrative Procedures Governing the Filing and Service by Electronic Means, which is set forth in ME R USDCT App. 4. The provisions of the court's Administrative Procedures Governing the Filing and Service by Electronic Means (ME R USDCT App. 4) shall be applied and enforced as part of the Local Rules of the United States District Court for the District of Maine. ME R USDCT Rule 5(c).

      ii. *Filing by represented persons.* A person represented by an attorney must file electronically, unless nonelectronic filing is allowed by the court for good cause or is allowed or required by local rule. FRCP 5(d)(3)(A).

         • *DISTRICT OF MAINE.* An attorney may apply to the court for permission to file paper documents. ME R USDCT App. 4(a)(5).

iii. *Filing by unrepresented persons.* A person not represented by an attorney: (i) may file electronically only if allowed by court order or by local rule; and (ii) may be required to file electronically only by court order, or by a local rule that includes reasonable exceptions. FRCP 5(d)(3)(B).

- *DISTRICT OF MAINE.* Non-prisoner pro se litigants in civil actions may register with ECF or may file (and serve) all pleadings and other documents in paper. ME R USDCT App. 4(o). A non-prisoner who is a party to a civil action and who is not represented by an attorney may register to receive service electronically and to electronically transmit their documents to the court for filing in the ECF system. If during the course of the action the person retains an attorney who appears on the person's behalf, the clerk shall terminate the person's registration upon the attorney's appearance. ME R USDCT App. 4(b)(2).

iv. *DISTRICT OF MAINE: Scope of electronic filing.* All documents submitted for filing in civil and criminal cases, regardless of case commencement date, except those documents specifically exempted in ME R USDCT App. 4(g), shall be filed electronically using the electronic case filing system (ECF). ME R USDCT App. 4(a)(1). For special filing requirements and exceptions, refer to ME R USDCT App. 4(g).

v. *DISTRICT OF MAINE: Consequences of electronic filing.* Electronic transmission of a document to the ECF system, together with the transmission of a Notice of Electronic Filing (NEF) from the court, constitutes filing of the document for all purposes of the Federal Rules of Civil Procedure. ME R USDCT App. 4(d)(1).

vi. *DISTRICT OF MAINE: Review of documents.* Documents filed with the clerk's office will normally be reviewed no later than the close of the next business day. It is the responsibility of the filing party to promptly notify the clerk's office via telephone of a matter that requires the immediate attention of a judicial officer. ME R USDCT App. 4(a)(4).

e. *DISTRICT OF MAINE: Facsimile filing.* No papers shall be submitted to the court by means of a facsimile machine without prior leave of the court. ME R USDCT Rule 5(c); ME R USDCT App. 4(m).

2. *Service requirements*

a. *Service; When required.* Unless the Federal Rules of Civil Procedure provide otherwise, each of the following papers must be served on every party: (A) an order stating that service is required; (B) a pleading filed after the original complaint, unless the court orders otherwise under FRCP 5(c) because there are numerous defendants; (C) a discovery paper required to be served on a party, unless the court orders otherwise; (D) a written motion, except one that may be heard ex parte; and (E) a written notice, appearance, demand, or offer of judgment, or any similar paper. FRCP 5(a)(1).

i. *If a party fails to appear.* No service is required on a party who is in default for failing to appear. But a pleading that asserts a new claim for relief against such a party must be served on that party under FRCP 4. FRCP 5(a)(2).

ii. *Seizing property.* If an action is begun by seizing property and no person is or need be named as a defendant, any service required before the filing of an appearance, answer, or claim must be made on the person who had custody or possession of the property when it was seized. FRCP 5(a)(3).

b. *Service; How made.* A paper is served under FRCP 5 by: (A) handing it to the person; (B) leaving it: (i) at the person's office with a clerk or other person in charge or, if no one is in charge, in a conspicuous place in the office; or (ii) if the person has no office or the office is closed, at the person's dwelling or usual place of abode with someone of suitable age and discretion who resides there; (C) mailing it to the person's last known address—in which event service is complete upon mailing; (D) leaving it with the court clerk if the person has no known address; (E) sending it to a registered user by filing it with the court's electronic-filing system or sending it by other electronic means that the person consented to in writing—in either of which events service is complete upon filing or sending, but is not effective if the filer or sender learns that it did not reach the person to be served; or (F) delivering it by any other means that the person consented to in writing—in which event service is complete when the person making service delivers it to the agency designated to make delivery. FRCP 5(b)(2).

i. *Serving an attorney.* If a party is represented by an attorney, service under FRCP 5 must be made on the attorney unless the court orders service on the party. FRCP 5(b)(1).

c. *DISTRICT OF MAINE: Service of electronically filed documents*

i. *Registered users.* Registration [as a filing user of the court's ECF system] constitutes consent to service of all documents by electronic means as provided in ME R USDCT App. 4. ME R USDCT App. 4(b)(4). Whenever a non-sealed pleading is filed electronically, the ECF system will automatically generate and send a Notice of Electronic Filing (NEF) to the filing user and registered users of record. The user filing the document should retain a paper or digital copy of the NEF, which shall serve as the court's date-stamp and proof of filing. ME R USDCT App. 4(e)(1).

- *Sealed documents.* Although the filing of sealed documents in civil cases produces an NEF, the document itself cannot be accessed and counsel shall be responsible for making service of the sealed documents. ME R USDCT App. 4(e)(2).

ii. *Non-registered users and pro se litigants.* Attorneys who have not yet registered as users with ECF and pro se litigants who have not registered with ECF shall be served a paper copy of any electronically filed pleading or other document in accordance with the provisions of FRCP 5. ME R USDCT App. 4(e)(3).

- *Registration of pro se litigants.* A non-prisoner who is a party to a civil action and who is not represented by an attorney may register to receive service electronically and to electronically transmit their documents to the court for filing in the ECF system. If during the course of the action the person retains an attorney who appears on the person's behalf, the clerk shall terminate the person's registration upon the attorney's appearance. ME R USDCT App. 4(b)(2).

d. *Serving numerous defendants.* If an action involves an unusually large number of defendants, the court may, on motion or on its own, order that: (A) defendants' pleadings and replies to them need not be served on other defendants; (B) any crossclaim, counterclaim, avoidance, or affirmative defense in those pleadings and replies to them will be treated as denied or avoided by all other parties; and (C) filing any such pleading and serving it on the plaintiff constitutes notice of the pleading to all parties. FRCP 5(c)(1).

i. *Notifying parties.* A copy of every such order must be served on the parties as the court directs. FRCP 5(c)(2).

3. *DISTRICT OF MAINE: Filing and service of highly sensitive documents (HSDs).* For information on filing and serving highly sensitive documents (HSDs) in the District of Maine, refer to ME R USDCT General Order 21-5.

G. Hearings

1. *Hearings, generally.* When a motion relies on facts outside the record, the court may hear the matter on affidavits or may hear it wholly or partly on oral testimony or on depositions. FRCP 43(c).

a. *Oral argument.* Due process does not require that oral argument be permitted on a motion and, except as otherwise provided by local rule, the district court has discretion to determine whether it will decide the motion on the papers or hear argument by counsel (and perhaps receive evidence). FPP § 1190; F.D.I.C. v. Deglau, 207 F.3d 153 (3d Cir. 2000).

i. *DISTRICT OF MAINE.* Unless otherwise required by federal rule or statute, all motions may be decided by the court without oral argument unless otherwise ordered by the court on its own motion or, in its discretion, upon request of counsel. ME R USDCT Rule 7(e).

b. *Providing a regular schedule for oral hearings.* A court may establish regular times and places for oral hearings on motions. FRCP 78(a).

c. *Providing for submission on briefs.* By rule or order, the court may provide for submitting and determining motions on briefs, without oral hearings. FRCP 78(b).

H. Forms

1. Federal Motion for Sanctions Forms

a. Notice of motion for sanctions. 2C FEDFORMS § 10:74.

b. Notice of motion and motion for sanctions. 2C FEDFORMS § 10:75.

c. Notice of motion and motion for sanctions; Including motion for sanctions under FRCP 37(c). 2C FEDFORMS § 10:76.

d. Motion for sanctions; Including sanctions under FRCP 37(d). 2C FEDFORMS § 10:77.

e. Defendant's summary of attorney fees. 2C FEDFORMS § 10:78.

f. Motion; For order imposing sanctions pursuant to FRCP 11; Allegation; Notice of removal frivolous. AMJUR PP FEDPRAC § 375.

g. Motion; General form. FEDPROF § 1B:171.

h. Notice; Of motion. FEDPROF § 1B:172.

i. Notice; Of motion; With costs of motion. FEDPROF § 1B:173.

j.   Notice; Of motion; Containing motion. FEDPROF § 1B:174.

k.   Opposition; To motion. FEDPROF § 1B:175.

l.   Affidavit; Supporting or opposing motion. FEDPROF § 1B:176.

m.   Brief; Supporting or opposing motion. FEDPROF § 1B:177.

n.   Statement of points and authorities; Opposing motion. FEDPROF § 1B:178.

o.   Illustrative forms; FRCP 11; Notice and motion for sanctions. LITGTORT § 20:36.

p.   Illustrative forms; FRCP 11; Memorandum in support of motion. LITGTORT § 20:37.

q.   Illustrative forms; FRCP 11; Declaration in support of motion. LITGTORT § 20:38.

r.   Illustrative forms; FRCP 11 and 28 U.S.C.A. § 1927; Notice of motion and motion for sanctions. LITGTORT § 20:39.

s.   Illustrative forms; FRCP 11 and 28 U.S.C.A. § 1927; Brief in support of motion. LITGTORT § 20:40.

I. Applicable Rules

1.   *Federal rules*

a.   Counsel's liability for excessive costs. 28 U.S.C.A. § 1927.

b.   Serving and filing pleadings and other papers. FRCP 5.

c.   Constitutional challenge to a statute; Notice, certification, and intervention. FRCP 5.1.

d.   Privacy protection for filings made with the court. FRCP 5.2.

e.   Computing and extending time; Time for motion papers. FRCP 6.

f.   Pleadings allowed; Form of motions and other papers. FRCP 7.

g.   Disclosure statement. FRCP 7.1.

h.   Form of pleadings. FRCP 10.

i.   Signing pleadings, motions, and other papers; Representations to the court; Sanctions. FRCP 11.

j.   Taking testimony. FRCP 43.

k.   Hearing motions; Submission on briefs. FRCP 78.

2.   *Local rules*

a.   *DISTRICT OF MAINE*

i.   Service and filing of pleadings and other papers. ME R USDCT Rule 5.

ii.   Time. ME R USDCT Rule 6.

iii.   Motions and memoranda of law. ME R USDCT Rule 7.

iv.   Corporate disclosure. ME R USDCT Rule 7.1.

v.   Form of pleadings, motions and other papers. ME R USDCT Rule 10.

vi.   Discovery. ME R USDCT Rule 26.

vii.   Attorneys; Appearances and withdrawals. ME R USDCT Rule 83.2.

viii.   Alternative dispute resolution (ADR). ME R USDCT Rule 83.11.

ix.   Administrative procedures governing the filing and service by electronic means. ME R USDCT App. 4.

x.   Redacting pleadings. ME R USDCT Redacting Pleadings.

Motions, Oppositions and Replies
Motion to Compel Discovery

Document Last Updated April 2021

A. Checklist

(I) ❑ Matters to be considered by moving party

    (a) ❑ Required documents

        (1) ❑ Notice of motion and motion

    (b) ❑ Supplemental documents

        (1) ❑ Supporting evidence

        (2) ❑ Notice of constitutional question

        (3) ❑ DISTRICT OF MAINE: Additional supplemental documents

            (i) ❑ Proposed order

    (c) ❑ Timing

        (1) ❑ The Federal Rules of Civil Procedure do not contain any time limit for filing motions to compel discovery; rather, a motion must simply be submitted within a reasonable time; however, a motion to compel discovery is premature if it is filed before any request for discovery is made

        (2) ❑ A written motion and notice of the hearing must be served at least fourteen (14) days before the time specified for the hearing, with the following exceptions: (A) when the motion may be heard ex parte; (B) when the Federal Rules of Civil Procedure set a different time; or (C) when a court order—which a party may, for good cause, apply for ex parte—sets a different time

        (3) ❑ Any affidavit supporting a motion must be served with the motion

        (4) ❑ DISTRICT OF MAINE: Additional timing

            (i) ❑ Any affidavits and other documents setting forth or evidencing facts on which the motion is based must be filed with the motion

(II) ❑ Matters to be considered by opposing party

    (a) ❑ Required documents

        (1) ❑ Opposition

    (b) ❑ Supplemental documents

        (1) ❑ Supporting evidence

        (2) ❑ Notice of constitutional question

    (c) ❑ Timing

        (1) ❑ Except as FRCP 59(c) provides otherwise, any opposing affidavit must be served at least seven (7) days before the hearing, unless the court permits service at another time

        (2) ❑ DISTRICT OF MAINE: Additional timing

            (i) ❑ Unless within twenty-one (21) days after the filing of a motion the opposing party files written objection thereto, incorporating a memorandum of law, the opposing party shall be deemed to have waived objection

B. Timing

1. *Motion to compel discovery.* The Federal Rules of Civil Procedure do not contain any time limit for filing motions to compel discovery. Rather, a motion must simply be submitted within a reasonable time. FEDPROC § 26:729. However, a motion to compel discovery is premature if it is filed before any request for discovery is made. FEDPROC § 26:729; Bermudez v. Duenas, 936 F.2d 1064 (9th Cir. 1991).

2. *Timing of motions, generally*

    a. *Motion and notice of hearing.* A written motion and notice of the hearing must be served at least fourteen (14) days before the time specified for the hearing, with the following exceptions: (A) when the motion may be heard ex parte; (B) when the Federal Rules of Civil Procedure set a different time; or (C) when a court order—which a party may, for good cause, apply for ex parte—sets a different time. FRCP 6(c)(1).

b. *Supporting affidavit.* Any affidavit supporting a motion must be served with the motion. FRCP 6(c)(2).

c. *DISTRICT OF MAINE: Affidavits and other supporting documents.* Any affidavits and other documents setting forth or evidencing facts on which the motion is based must be filed with the motion. ME R USDCT Rule 7(a).

3. *Timing of opposing papers.* Except as FRCP 59(c) provides otherwise, any opposing affidavit must be served at least seven (7) days before the hearing, unless the court permits service at another time. FRCP 6(c)(2).

a. *DISTRICT OF MAINE.* Unless within twenty-one (21) days after the filing of a motion the opposing party files written objection thereto, incorporating a memorandum of law, the opposing party shall be deemed to have waived objection. ME R USDCT Rule 7(b). The deemed waiver imposed in ME R USDCT Rule 7(b) shall not apply to motions filed during trial. ME R USDCT Rule 7(b).

4. *Timing of reply papers.* Where the respondent files an answering affidavit setting up a new matter, the moving party ordinarily is allowed a reasonable time to file a reply affidavit since failure to deny the new matter by affidavit may operate as an admission of its truth. AMJUR MOTIONS § 25.

a. *DISTRICT OF MAINE.* Within fourteen (14) days of the filing of any objection to a motion, the moving party may file a reply memorandum. ME R USDCT Rule 7(c).

5. *Computation of time*

a. *Computing time.* FRCP 6 applies in computing any time period specified in the Federal Rules of Civil Procedure, in any local rule or court order, or in any statute that does not specify a method of computing time. FRCP 6(a).

   i. *Period stated in days or a longer unit.* When the period is stated in days or a longer unit of time: (A) exclude the day of the event that triggers the period; (B) count every day, including intermediate Saturdays, Sundays, and legal holidays; and (C) include the last day of the period, but if the last day is a Saturday, Sunday, or legal holiday, the period continues to run until the end of the next day that is not a Saturday, Sunday, or legal holiday. FRCP 6(a)(1).

   ii. *Period stated in hours.* When the period is stated in hours: (A) begin counting immediately on the occurrence of the event that triggers the period; (B) count every hour, including hours during intermediate Saturdays, Sundays, and legal holidays; and (C) if the period would end on a Saturday, Sunday, or legal holiday, the period continues to run until the same time on the next day that is not a Saturday, Sunday, or legal holiday. FRCP 6(a)(2).

   iii. *Inaccessibility of the clerk's office.* Unless the court orders otherwise, if the clerk's office is inaccessible: (A) on the last day for filing under FRCP 6(a)(1), then the time for filing is extended to the first accessible day that is not a Saturday, Sunday, or legal holiday; or (B) during the last hour for filing under FRCP 6(a)(2), then the time for filing is extended to the same time on the first accessible day that is not a Saturday, Sunday, or legal holiday. FRCP 6(a)(3).

   iv. *"Last day" defined.* Unless a different time is set by a statute, local rule, or court order, the last day ends: (A) for electronic filing, at midnight in the court's time zone; and (B) for filing by other means, when the clerk's office is scheduled to close. FRCP 6(a)(4).

   v. *"Next day" defined.* The "next day" is determined by continuing to count forward when the period is measured after an event and backward when measured before an event. FRCP 6(a)(5).

   vi. *"Legal holiday" defined.* "Legal holiday" means: (A) the day set aside by statute for observing New Year's Day, Martin Luther King Jr.'s Birthday, Washington's Birthday, Memorial Day, Independence Day, Labor Day, Columbus Day, Veterans' Day, Thanksgiving Day, or Christmas Day; (B) any day declared a holiday by the President or Congress; and (C) for periods that are measured after an event, any other day declared a holiday by the state where the district court is located. FRCP 6(a)(6).

   vii. *DISTRICT OF MAINE: Applicability of FRCP 6.* FRCP 6 applies when computing any period of time stated in the Local Rules of the United States District Court for the District of Maine. ME R USDCT Rule 6(a).

b. *DISTRICT OF MAINE: Computation of electronic filing deadlines.* Filing documents electronically does not in any way alter any filing deadlines. All electronic transmissions of documents must be completed prior to midnight, Eastern Time, in order to be considered timely filed that day. Where a specific time of day deadline is set by court order or stipulation, the electronic filing must be completed by that time. ME R USDCT App. 4(f). A document filed

electronically shall be deemed filed at the time and date stated on the Notice of Electronic Filing received from the court. ME R USDCT App. 4(d)(2).

 i. *Technical failures.* A filing user whose filing is made untimely as the result of a technical failure may seek appropriate relief from the court. ME R USDCT App. 4(n). A technical failure of the court's ECF system is deemed to have occurred when the court's ECF site cannot accept filings continuously or intermittently over the course of any period of time greater than one (1) hour. Known system outages will be posted on the court's website along with guidance on how to proceed, if applicable. ME R USDCT App. 4(n).

 c. *Extending time.* When an act may or must be done within a specified time, the court may, for good cause, extend the time: (A) with or without motion or notice if the court acts, or if a request is made, before the original time or its extension expires; or (B) on motion made after the time has expired if the party failed to act because of excusable neglect. FRCP 6(b)(1). A court must not extend the time to act under FRCP 50(b), FRCP 50(d), FRCP 52(b), FRCP 59(b), FRCP 59(d), FRCP 59(e), and FRCP 60(b). FRCP 6(b)(2). Refer to the United States District Court for the District of Maine KeyRules Motion for Continuance/Extension of Time document for more information on extending time.

 d. *Additional time after certain kinds of service.* When a party may or must act within a specified time after being served and service is made under FRCP 5(b)(2)(C) (by mail), FRCP 5(b)(2)(D) (by leaving with the clerk), or FRCP 5(b)(2)(F) (by other means consented to), three (3) days are added after the period would otherwise expire under FRCP 6(a). FRCP 6(d).

C. General Requirements

1. *Motions, generally*

 a. *Motion requirements.* A request for a court order must be made by motion. The motion must: (A) be in writing unless made during a hearing or trial; (B) state with particularity the grounds for seeking the order; and (C) state the relief sought. FRCP 7(b)(1). The writing and particularity requirements are intended to ensure that the adverse parties are informed of and have a record of both the motion's pendency and the grounds on which the movant seeks an order. FPP § 1191; Feldberg v. Quechee Lakes Corp., 463 F.3d 195 (2d Cir. 2006).

  i. *Particularity requirement.* The particularity requirement [ensures] that the opposing parties will have notice of their opponent's contentions. FEDPROC § 62:358; Goodman v. 1973 26 Foot Trojan Vessel, Arkansas Registration No. AR1439SN, 859 F.2d 71 (8th Cir. 1988). That requirement ensures that notice of the basis for the motion is provided to the court and to the opposing party so as to avoid prejudice, provide the opponent with a meaningful opportunity to respond, and provide the court with enough information to process the motion correctly. FEDPROC § 62:358; Andreas v. Volkswagen of Am., Inc., 336 F.3d 789 (8th Cir. 2003).

  • Reasonable specification of the grounds for a motion is sufficient. The particularity requirement for motions is satisfied when no party is prejudiced by a lack of particularity or when the court can comprehend the basis for the motion and deal with it fairly. However, where a movant fails to state even one ground for granting the motion in question, the movant has failed to meet the minimal standard of "reasonable specification." FEDPROC § 62:358; Martinez v. Trainor, 556 F.2d 818 (7th Cir. 1977).

  • The court may excuse the failure to comply with the particularity requirement if it is inadvertent, and where no prejudice is shown by the opposing party. FEDPROC § 62:358.

 b. *Notice of motion.* A party interested in resisting the relief sought by a motion has a right to notice thereof, and an opportunity to be heard. AMJUR MOTIONS § 12.

  i. *Purpose.* In addition to statutory or court rule provisions requiring notice of a motion—the purpose of such a notice requirement having been said to be to prevent a party from being prejudicially surprised by a motion—principles of natural justice dictate that an adverse party generally must be given notice that a motion will be presented to the court. AMJUR MOTIONS § 12.

  ii. *Adequacy of notice.* The test of adequate notice generally turns on whether the other parties were afforded an adequate opportunity to prepare and respond to the issues to be raised in the proceeding. AMJUR MOTIONS § 12.

 c. *Single document containing motion and notice.* A single written document can satisfy the writing requirements both for a motion and for an FRCP 6(c)(1) notice. FRCP 7(Advisory Committee Notes).

2. *DISTRICT OF MAINE: Procedure for discovery disputes*

 a. *Prior approval required.* No written discovery motions shall be filed without the prior approval of a judicial officer. ME R USDCT Rule 7(a); ME R USDCT Rule 26(b).

b. *Conference with opposing counsel.* A party with a discovery dispute must first confer with the opposing party in a good faith effort to resolve by agreement the issues in dispute. If that good faith effort is unsuccessful, the moving party shall file a Request for Hearing Re Discovery Dispute using the court's form seeking a prompt hearing with a judicial officer by telephone or in person. The party seeking the hearing shall confer with opposing counsel and agree on the relevant discovery materials that should be submitted to the court with the Request for Hearing. ME R USDCT Rule 26(b).

c. *Hearing on discovery dispute.* If the hearing is to be conducted by telephone, the clerk will inform counsel of the time and date of the hearing and it shall be the responsibility of the moving party to initiate the telephone call to chambers, unless the court, in its discretion, directs otherwise. The recording by counsel of telephone hearings with the court is prohibited, except with prior permission of the court. The court shall conduct the hearing on the record, but that record will not be officially transcribed except on specific request of counsel or the court. The request for a hearing with a judicial officer carries with it a professional representation by the lawyer that a conference has taken place and that he or she has made a good faith effort to resolve the dispute. The lawyers or unrepresented parties shall supply the judicial officer with the particular discovery materials (such as objectionable answers to interrogatories) that are needed to understand the dispute. ME R USDCT Rule 26(b).

d. *Filing of motion papers and supporting memoranda.* If the judicial officer decides that motion papers and supporting memoranda are needed to satisfactorily resolve the discovery dispute, such papers shall be filed in conformity with ME R USDCT Rule 7. Such motions shall (1) quote in full each interrogatory, question at deposition, request for admission or request for production to which the motion is addressed, or otherwise identify specifically and succinctly the discovery to which objection is taken or from which a protective order is sought; and (2) the response or objection and grounds therefor, if any, as stated by the opposing party. ME R USDCT Rule 26(b). Unless otherwise ordered by the court, the complete transcripts or discovery papers need not be filed with the court pursuant to ME R USDCT Rule 26(c) unless the motion cannot be fairly decided without reference to the complete original. ME R USDCT Rule 26(b).

3. *Motion to compel discovery.* On notice to other parties and all affected persons, a party may move for an order compelling disclosure or discovery. FRCP 37(a)(1). The moving party must affirmatively demonstrate that the opponent did not produce discoverable information. A party's suspicion that its opponent must have documents that it claims not to have is insufficient to warrant granting a motion to compel. FEDPROC § 26:726.

   a. *Appropriate court.* A motion for an order to a party must be made in the court where the action is pending. A motion for an order to a nonparty must be made in the court where the discovery is or will be taken. FRCP 37(a)(2).

   b. *Specific motions*

      i. *To compel disclosure.* If a party fails to make a disclosure required by FRCP 26(a), any other party may move to compel disclosure and for appropriate sanctions. FRCP 37(a)(3)(A). Refer to the United States District Court for the District of Maine KeyRules Motion for Discovery Sanctions document for more information on sanctions.

      ii. *To compel a discovery response.* A party seeking discovery may move for an order compelling an answer, designation, production, or inspection. This motion may be made if: (i) a deponent fails to answer a question asked under FRCP 30 or FRCP 31; (ii) a corporation or other entity fails to make a designation under FRCP 30(b)(6) or FRCP 31(a)(4); (iii) a party fails to answer an interrogatory submitted under FRCP 33; or (iv) a party fails to produce documents or fails to respond that inspection will be permitted—or fails to permit inspection—as requested under FRCP 34. FRCP 37(a)(3)(B).

      iii. *Related to a deposition.* When taking an oral deposition, the party asking a question may complete or adjourn the examination before moving for an order. FRCP 37(a)(3)(C).

      iv. *Evasive or incomplete disclosure, answer, or response.* For purposes of FRCP 37(a), an evasive or incomplete disclosure, answer, or response must be treated as a failure to disclose, answer, or respond. FRCP 37(a)(4).

   c. *Payment of expenses; Protective orders*

      i. *If the motion is granted (or disclosure or discovery is provided after filing).* If the motion is granted—or if the disclosure or requested discovery is provided after the motion was filed—the court must, after giving an opportunity to be heard, require the party or deponent whose conduct necessitated the motion, the party or attorney advising that conduct, or both to pay the movant's reasonable expenses incurred in making the motion, including attorney's fees. But the court must not order this payment if: (i) the movant filed the motion before attempting in good faith to obtain the disclosure or discovery without court action; (ii) the opposing party's nondisclosure, response, or objection was substantially justified; or (iii) other circumstances make an award of expenses unjust. FRCP 37(a)(5)(A).

ii. *If the motion is denied.* If the motion is denied, the court may issue any protective order authorized under FRCP 26(c) and must, after giving an opportunity to be heard, require the movant, the attorney filing the motion, or both to pay the party or deponent who opposed the motion its reasonable expenses incurred in opposing the motion, including attorney's fees. But the court must not order this payment if the motion was substantially justified or other circumstances make an award of expenses unjust. FRCP 37(a)(5)(B).

iii. *If the motion is granted in part and denied in part.* If the motion is granted in part and denied in part, the court may issue any protective order authorized under FRCP 26(c) and may, after giving an opportunity to be heard, apportion the reasonable expenses for the motion. FRCP 37(a)(5)(C).

4. *Opposing papers.* The Federal Rules of Civil Procedure do not require any formal answer, return, or reply to a motion, except where the Federal Rules of Civil Procedure or local rules may require affidavits, memoranda, or other papers to be filed in opposition to a motion. Such papers are simply to apprise the court of such opposition and the grounds of that opposition. FEDPROC § 62:353.

   a. *DISTRICT OF MAINE: Content of objections.* Any objections shall include citations and supporting authorities and affidavits and other documents setting forth or evidencing facts on which the objection is based. ME R USDCT Rule 7(b).

   b. *Effect of failure to respond to motion.* Although in the absence of statutory provision or court rule, a motion ordinarily does not require a response or written answer, when a party files a motion and the opposing party fails to respond, the court may construe such failure to respond as nonopposition to the motion or an admission that the motion was meritorious. AMJUR MOTIONS § 28. The rule in some jurisdictions being that the failure to respond to a fact set forth in a motion is deemed an admission—and may grant the motion if the relief requested appears to be justified. AMJUR MOTIONS § 28.

   c. *Assent or no opposition not determinative.* However, a motion will not be granted automatically simply because an "assent" or a notation of "no opposition" has been filed; federal judges frequently deny motions that have been assented to when it is thought that justice so dictates. FPP § 1190.

   d. *Responsive pleading inappropriate as response to motion.* An attempt to answer or oppose a motion with a responsive pleading usually is not appropriate. FPP § 1190.

5. *Reply papers.* A moving party may be required or permitted to prepare papers in addition to its original motion papers. AMJUR MOTIONS § 25. Papers answering or replying to opposing papers may be appropriate, in the interests of justice, where it appears there is a substantial reason for allowing a reply. Thus, a court may accept reply papers where a party demonstrates that the papers to which it seeks to file a reply raise new issues that are material to the disposition of the question before the court, or where the court determines, sua sponte, that it wishes further briefing of an issue raised in those papers and orders the submission of additional papers. FEDPROC § 62:354.

   a. *Function of reply papers.* The function of a reply affidavit or reply papers is to answer the arguments made in opposition to the position taken by the movant, not to raise new issues, arguments, or evidence, or change the nature of the primary motion. However, if the court permits new evidence with the reply papers, the other party should be given the opportunity to respond. Where the party opposing the motion has no opportunity to address the argument in writing, a court has the discretion to disregard arguments raised for the first time in a reply memorandum. Also, the view has been followed in some jurisdictions that as a matter of judicial economy, where there is no prejudice and where the issues could be raised simply by filing a motion to dismiss, the trial court has discretion to consider arguments raised for the first time in a reply memorandum, and that a trial court may grant a motion to strike issues raised for the first time in a reply memorandum. AMJUR MOTIONS § 26.

      i. *DISTRICT OF MAINE.* The moving party may file a reply memorandum. . . .which shall be strictly confined to replying to new matter raised in the objection or opposing memorandum. ME R USDCT Rule 7(c).

6. *DISTRICT OF MAINE: Appearances.* An attorney's signature to a pleading shall constitute an appearance for the party filing the pleading. Otherwise, an attorney who wishes to participate in any manner in any action must file a formal written appearance identifying the party represented. An appearance whether by pleading or formal written appearance shall be signed by an attorney in his/her individual name and shall state his/her office address. ME R USDCT Rule 83.2(a). For more information, refer to ME R USDCT Rule 83.2.

7. *DISTRICT OF MAINE: Alternative dispute resolution (ADR).* Litigants are authorized and encouraged to employ, at their own expense, any available ADR process on which they can agree, including early neutral evaluation, settlement conferences, mediation, non-binding summary jury trial, corporate mini-trial, and arbitration proceedings. ME R USDCT Rule 83.11(a). For more information on ADR, refer to ME R USDCT Rule 83.11.

D. Documents

1. *Documents for moving party*

   a. *Required documents*

      i. *Notice of motion and motion.* Refer to the "C. General Requirements" section of this KeyRules document for information on the notice of motion and motion.

         - *DISTRICT OF MAINE: Memorandum of law.* Every motion shall incorporate a memorandum of law, including citations and supporting authorities. ME R USDCT Rule 7(a). Refer to the "E. Format" section of this KeyRules document for the form of memoranda of law.

         - *Certificate of compliance.* The motion must include a certification that the movant has in good faith conferred or attempted to confer with the person or party failing to make disclosure or discovery in an effort to obtain it without court action. FRCP 37(a)(1).

         - *Certificate of service.* No certificate of service is required when a paper is served by filing it with the court's electronic-filing system. When a paper that is required to be served is served by other means: (i) if the paper is filed, a certificate of service must be filed with it or within a reasonable time after service; and (ii) if the paper is not filed, a certificate of service need not be filed unless filing is required by court order or by local rule. FRCP 5(d)(1)(B).

   b. *Supplemental documents*

      i. *Supporting evidence.* When a motion relies on facts outside the record, the court may hear the matter on affidavits or may hear it wholly or partly on oral testimony or on depositions. FRCP 43(c).

         - *DISTRICT OF MAINE: Affidavits and other supporting documents.* Any affidavits and other documents setting forth or evidencing facts on which the motion is based must be filed with the motion. ME R USDCT Rule 7(a).

         - *DISTRICT OF MAINE: Discovery transcripts or materials.* A party relying on discovery transcripts or materials in support of or in opposition to a motion shall file excerpts of such transcript or materials with the memorandum required by ME R USDCT Rule 7 as well as a list of specific citations to the parts on which the party relies. ME R USDCT Rule 26(c). Excerpts of depositions in support of or in opposition to a motion shall be filed electronically using ECF, unless otherwise permitted by the court. ME R USDCT App. 4(l)(3).

      ii. *Notice of constitutional question.* A party that files a pleading, written motion, or other paper drawing into question the constitutionality of a federal or state statute must promptly: (1) file a notice of constitutional question stating the question and identifying the paper that raises it, if: (A) a federal statute is questioned and the parties do not include the United States, one of its agencies, or one of its officers or employees in an official capacity; or (B) a state statute is questioned and the parties do not include the state, one of its agencies, or one of its officers or employees in an official capacity; and (2) serve the notice and paper on the Attorney General of the United States if a federal statute is questioned—or on the state attorney general if a state statute is questioned—either by certified or registered mail or by sending it to an electronic address designated by the attorney general for this purpose. FRCP 5.1(a).

         - *No forfeiture.* A party's failure to file and serve the notice, or the court's failure to certify, does not forfeit a constitutional claim or defense that is otherwise timely asserted. FRCP 5.1(d).

      iii. *DISTRICT OF MAINE: Additional supplemental documents*

         - *Proposed order.* Proposed orders shall not be filed unless requested by the court. When requested by the court, proposed orders shall be filed by e-mail in word processing format. ME R USDCT App. 4(k)(1).

2. *Documents for opposing party*

   a. *Required documents*

      i. *Opposition.* Refer to the "C. General Requirements" section of this KeyRules document for information on the opposing papers.

         - *DISTRICT OF MAINE: Memorandum of law.* Unless within twenty-one (21) days after the filing of a motion the opposing party files written objection thereto, incorporating a memorandum of law, the opposing party shall be deemed to have waived objection. ME R USDCT Rule 7(b).

         - *Certificate of service.* No certificate of service is required when a paper is served by filing it with the court's electronic-filing system. When a paper that is required to be served is served by other means: (i) if the paper is filed, a certificate of service must be filed with it or within a reasonable time after service; and (ii) if the paper is not filed, a certificate of service need not be filed unless filing is required by court order or by local rule. FRCP 5(d)(1)(B).

b. *Supplemental documents*

   i. *Supporting evidence.* When a motion relies on facts outside the record, the court may hear the matter on affidavits or may hear it wholly or partly on oral testimony or on depositions. FRCP 43(c).

   - *DISTRICT OF MAINE: Affidavits and other supporting documents.* Any objections shall include. . .affidavits and other documents setting forth or evidencing facts on which the objection is based. ME R USDCT Rule 7(b).

   - *DISTRICT OF MAINE: Discovery transcripts or materials.* A party relying on discovery transcripts or materials in support of or in opposition to a motion shall file excerpts of such transcript or materials with the memorandum required by ME R USDCT Rule 7 as well as a list of specific citations to the parts on which the party relies. ME R USDCT Rule 26(c). Excerpts of depositions in support of or in opposition to a motion shall be filed electronically using ECF, unless otherwise permitted by the court. ME R USDCT App. 4(l)(3).

   ii. *Notice of constitutional question.* A party that files a pleading, written motion, or other paper drawing into question the constitutionality of a federal or state statute must promptly: (1) file a notice of constitutional question stating the question and identifying the paper that raises it, if: (A) a federal statute is questioned and the parties do not include the United States, one of its agencies, or one of its officers or employees in an official capacity; or (B) a state statute is questioned and the parties do not include the state, one of its agencies, or one of its officers or employees in an official capacity; and (2) serve the notice and paper on the Attorney General of the United States if a federal statute is questioned—or on the state attorney general if a state statute is questioned—either by certified or registered mail or by sending it to an electronic address designated by the attorney general for this purpose. FRCP 5.1(a).

   - *No forfeiture.* A party's failure to file and serve the notice, or the court's failure to certify, does not forfeit a constitutional claim or defense that is otherwise timely asserted. FRCP 5.1(d).

E. Format

1. *Form of documents.* The rules governing captions and other matters of form in pleadings apply to motions and other papers. FRCP 7(b)(2).

   a. *DISTRICT OF MAINE: Font size, line spacing, and paper size.* All such documents shall be typed in a font of no less than size twelve (12) point, and shall be double-spaced or printed on eight and one-half by eleven (8-1/2 x 11) inch paper. Footnotes shall be in a font of no less than size ten (10) point, and may be single spaced. ME R USDCT Rule 10.

   b. *Caption.* Every pleading must have a caption with the court's name, a title, a file number, and an FRCP 7(a) designation. FRCP 10(a).

   i. *Names of parties.* The title of the complaint must name all the parties; the title of other pleadings, after naming the first party on each side, may refer generally to other parties. FRCP 10(a).

   ii. *DISTRICT OF MAINE: Additional caption requirements.* All pleadings, motions and other papers filed with the clerk or otherwise submitted to the court, except exhibits, shall bear the proper case number and shall contain on the first page a caption as described by FRCP 10(a) and immediately thereunder a designation of what the document is and the name of the party in whose behalf it is submitted. ME R USDCT Rule 10.

   c. *Claims or defenses*

   i. *Numbered paragraphs.* A party must state its claims or defenses in numbered paragraphs, each limited as far as practicable to a single set of circumstances. A later pleading may refer by number to a paragraph in an earlier pleading. FRCP 10(b).

   ii. *Separate statements.* If doing so would promote clarity, each claim founded on a separate transaction or occurrence—and each defense other than a denial—must be stated in a separate count or defense. FRCP 10(b).

   d. *Adoption by reference.* A statement in a pleading may be adopted by reference elsewhere in the same pleading or in any other pleading or motion. FRCP 10(c).

   i. *Exhibits.* A copy of a written instrument that is an exhibit to a pleading is a part of the pleading for all purposes. FRCP 10(c).

e. *DISTRICT OF MAINE: Page numbering.* All pages shall be numbered at the bottom. ME R USDCT Rule 10.

f. *DISTRICT OF MAINE: Attachment of ancillary papers.* Ancillary papers shall be attached at the end of the document to which they relate. ME R USDCT Rule 10.

g. *Acceptance by the clerk.* The clerk must not refuse to file a paper solely because it is not in the form prescribed by the Federal Rules of Civil Procedure or by a local rule or practice. FRCP 5(d)(4).

2. *Form of electronic documents.* A paper filed electronically is a written paper for purposes of the Federal Rules of Civil Procedure. FRCP 5(d)(3)(D).

   a. *DISTRICT OF MAINE: Document format.* The ECF system only accepts documents in a portable document format (PDF). Although there are two types of PDF documents—electronically converted PDF's and scanned PDF's—only electronically converted PDF's may be filed with the court using the ECF system, unless otherwise authorized by local rule or order. ME R USDCT App. 4. Any document or exhibit to be filed or submitted to the court shall not be password-protected or encrypted. ME R USDCT App. 4(g)(12).

      i. *Electronically converted PDFs.* Electronically converted PDF's are created from word processing documents (MS Word, WordPerfect, etc.) using Adobe Acrobat or similar software. They are text searchable and their file size is small. ME R USDCT App. 4. Software used to electronically convert documents to PDF which includes proprietary or advertisement information within the PDF document is prohibited. ME R USDCT App. 4.

      ii. *Scanned PDFs.* Scanned PDF's are created from paper documents run through an optical scanner. Scanned PDF's are not searchable and have a large file size. ME R USDCT App. 4.

   b. *DISTRICT OF MAINE: Title.* All pleadings filed electronically shall be titled in accordance with the approved dictionary of civil or criminal events of the ECF system of the United States District Court for the District of Maine. ME R USDCT App. 4(d)(3).

   c. *DISTRICT OF MAINE: Attachments.* Attachments to filings and exhibits must be filed in accordance with the court's ECF User Manual, unless otherwise ordered by the court. ME R USDCT App. 4(j). When there are fifty (50) or fewer attachments to a pleading, the attachments must be filed by counsel electronically using ECF. When there are more than fifty (50) attachments, the attachments must be filed in one of the following ways: (A) using ECF, simply attach them to the pleading being filed; (B) using ECF, use the "Additional Attachments" menu item; (C) on paper; or (D) on a properly labeled three and one-half (3-1/2) inch floppy disk, CD or DVD. ME R USDCT App. 4(j)(2). Attachments filed on paper or on disk must contain a comprehensive index that clearly describes each document. ME R USDCT App. 4(j)(2).

      i. A filing user must submit as attachments only those excerpts of the referenced documents that are directly germane to the matter under consideration by the court. Excerpted material must be clearly and prominently identified as such. Users who file excerpts of documents do so without prejudice to their right to timely file additional excerpts or the complete document, as may be allowed by the court. Responding parties may timely file additional excerpts or the complete document that they believe are directly germane. ME R USDCT App. 4(j)(3).

      ii. Filers shall not attach as an exhibit any pleading or other paper already on file with the court in that case, but shall merely refer to that document. ME R USDCT App. 4(j)(4).

   d. *DISTRICT OF MAINE: Compliance with technical standards.* All documents filed by electronic means must comply with technical standards, if any, established by the Judicial Conference of the United States or by the United States District Court for the District of Maine. ME R USDCT App. 4(a)(3).

3. *DISTRICT OF MAINE: Form of memoranda of law.* All memoranda shall be typed, in a font of no less than size twelve (12) point, and shall be double-spaced on eight and one-half by eleven (8-1/2 x 11) inch paper or printed. Footnotes shall be in a font of no less than size ten (10) point, and may be single spaced. All pages shall be numbered at the bottom. ME R USDCT Rule 7(d).

   a. *Page limitations.* No memorandum of law in support of or in opposition to a nondispositive motion shall exceed ten (10) pages. ME R USDCT Rule 7(d). No reply memorandum shall exceed seven (7) pages. ME R USDCT Rule 7(d); ME R USDCT Rule 7(c).

      i. *Motion to exceed page limitation.* A motion to exceed the limitation of ME R USDCT Rule 7 shall be filed no later than three (3) business days in advance of the date for filing the memorandum to permit meaningful review by the court. A motion to exceed the page limitations shall not be filed simultaneously with a memorandum in excess of the limitations of ME R USDCT Rule 7. ME R USDCT Rule 7(d).

4. *Signing disclosures and discovery requests, responses, and objections.* FRCP 11 does not apply to disclosures and discovery requests, responses, objections, and motions under FRCP 26 through FRCP 37. FRCP 11(d).

    a. *Signature required.* Every disclosure under FRCP 26(a)(1) or FRCP 26(a)(3) and every discovery request, response, or objection must be signed by at least one attorney of record in the attorney's own name—or by the party personally, if unrepresented—and must state the signer's address, e-mail address, and telephone number. FRCP 26(g)(1).

    b. *Electronic signing.* A filing made through a person's electronic-filing account and authorized by that person, together with that person's name on a signature block, constitutes the person's signature. FRCP 5(d)(3)(C).

        i. *DISTRICT OF MAINE: Attorneys.* The user log-in and password together with a user's name on the signature block constitutes the attorney's signature pursuant to the Federal Rules of Civil Procedure and the Local Rules of the United States District Court for the District of Maine. All electronically filed documents must include a signature block and must set forth the attorney's name, address, telephone number and e-mail address. The name of the ECF user under whose log-in and password the document is submitted must be preceded by a "/s/" in the space where the signature would otherwise appear. ME R USDCT App. 4(h)(1).

        ii. *DISTRICT OF MAINE: Multiple signatures.* The filer of any document requiring more than one signature (e.g., pleadings filed by visiting lawyers, stipulations, joint status reports) must list thereon all the names of other signatories, preceded by a "/s/" in the space where the signatures would otherwise appear. By submitting such a document, the filing attorney certifies that each of the other signatories has expressly agreed to the form and substance of the document and that the filing attorney has their actual authority to submit the document electronically. ME R USDCT App. 4(h)(2). For more information, refer to ME R USDCT App. 4(h)(2).

        iii. *DISTRICT OF MAINE: Documents signed under oath.* Affidavits, declarations, verified complaints, or any other document signed under oath shall be filed electronically. The electronically filed version shall contain the typed name of the signatory, preceded by a "/s/" in the space where the signature would otherwise appear indicating that the paper document bears an original signature. ME R USDCT Rule 10; ME R USDCT App. 4(h)(3). For more information, refer to ME R USDCT Rule 10.

    c. *Effect of signature.* By signing, an attorney or party certifies that to the best of the person's knowledge, information, and belief formed after a reasonable inquiry: (A) with respect to a disclosure, it is complete and correct as of the time it is made; and (B) with respect to a discovery request, response, or objection, it is: (i) consistent with the Federal Rules of Civil Procedure and warranted by existing law or by a nonfrivolous argument for extending, modifying, or reversing existing law, or for establishing new law; (ii) not interposed for any improper purpose, such as to harass, cause unnecessary delay, or needlessly increase the cost of litigation; and (iii) neither unreasonable nor unduly burdensome or expensive, considering the needs of the case, prior discovery in the case, the amount in controversy, and the importance of the issues at stake in the action. FRCP 26(g)(1).

    d. *Failure to sign.* Other parties have no duty to act on an unsigned disclosure, request, response, or objection until it is signed, and the court must strike it unless a signature is promptly supplied after the omission is called to the attorney's or party's attention. FRCP 26(g)(2).

    e. *Sanction for improper certification.* If a certification violates FRCP 26(g) without substantial justification, the court, on motion or on its own, must impose an appropriate sanction on the signer, the party on whose behalf the signer was acting, or both. The sanction may include an order to pay the reasonable expenses, including attorney's fees, caused by the violation. FRCP 26(g)(3). Refer to the United States District Court for the District of Maine KeyRules Motion for Discovery Sanctions document for more information.

5. *Privacy protection for filings made with the court*

    a. *Redacted filings.* Unless the court orders otherwise, in an electronic or paper filing with the court that contains an individual's Social Security number, taxpayer-identification number, or birth date, the name of an individual known to be a minor, or a financial-account number, a party or nonparty making the filing may include only: (1) the last four (4) digits of the Social Security number and taxpayer-identification number; (2) the year of the individual's birth; (3) the minor's initials; and (4) the last four (4) digits of the financial-account number. FRCP 5.2(a).

        i. *DISTRICT OF MAINE.* To address the privacy concerns created by the Internet access to court papers, unless otherwise ordered by the court, counsel shall modify certain personal data identifiers in pleadings and other papers as follows: (1) minors' names: use of the minors' initials only; (2) Social Security numbers: use of the last four (4) numbers only; (3) dates of birth: use of the year of birth only; [and] (4) financial account numbers: identify the type of account and the financial institution, but use only the last four (4) numbers of the account number. ME R USDCT Redacting Pleadings. Counsel should also use caution when filing papers that contain a person's medical records, employment history; financial information; and any proprietary or trade secret information. ME R USDCT Redacting Pleadings.

b. *Exemptions from the redaction requirement.* The redaction requirement does not apply to the following: (1) a financial-account number that identifies the property allegedly subject to forfeiture in a forfeiture proceeding; (2) the record of an administrative or agency proceeding; (3) the official record of a state-court proceeding; (4) the record of a court or tribunal, if that record was not subject to the redaction requirement when originally filed; (5) a filing covered by FRCP 5.2(c) or FRCP 5.2(d); and (6) a pro se filing in an action brought under 28 U.S.C.A. § 2241, 28 U.S.C.A. § 2254, or 28 U.S.C.A. § 2255. FRCP 5.2(b).

c. *Limitations on remote access to electronic files; Social Security appeals and immigration cases.* Unless the court orders otherwise, in an action for benefits under the Social Security Act, and in an action or proceeding relating to an order of removal, to relief from removal, or to immigration benefits or detention, access to an electronic file is authorized as follows: (1) the parties and their attorneys may have remote electronic access to any part of the case file, including the administrative record; (2) any other person may have electronic access to the full record at the courthouse, but may have remote electronic access only to: (A) the docket maintained by the court; and (B) an opinion, order, judgment, or other disposition of the court, but not any other part of the case file or the administrative record. FRCP 5.2(c).

d. *Filings made under seal.* The court may order that a filing be made under seal without redaction. The court may later unseal the filing or order the person who made the filing to file a redacted version for the public record. FRCP 5.2(d).

   i. *DISTRICT OF MAINE.* For information on filing sealed documents in the District of Maine, refer to ME R USDCT Rule 7A, ME R USDCT App. 4(p)(2), and ME R USDCT Sealed Filings.

e. *Protective orders.* For good cause, the court may by order in a case: (1) require redaction of additional information; or (2) limit or prohibit a nonparty's remote electronic access to a document filed with the court. FRCP 5.2(e).

f. *Option for additional unredacted filing under seal.* A person making a redacted filing may also file an unredacted copy under seal. The court must retain the unredacted copy as part of the record. FRCP 5.2(f).

   i. *DISTRICT OF MAINE.* A party wishing to file a document containing the personal data identifiers specified above may. . .file an unredacted document under seal. This document will be retained by the clerk's office as part of the record. ME R USDCT Redacting Pleadings. The court may, however, still require the party to file a redacted copy for the public file. ME R USDCT Redacting Pleadings.

g. *Option for filing a reference list.* A filing that contains redacted information may be filed together with a reference list that identifies each item of redacted information and specifies an appropriate identifier that uniquely corresponds to each item listed. The list must be filed under seal and may be amended as of right. Any reference in the case to a listed identifier will be construed to refer to the corresponding item of information. FRCP 5.2(g).

   i. *DISTRICT OF MAINE.* A party wishing to file a document containing the personal data identifiers specified above may. . .file a reference list under seal. The reference list shall contain the complete personal data identifier(s) and the redacted identifier(s) used in its (their) place in the filing. All references in the case to the redacted identifiers included in the reference list will be construed to refer to the corresponding complete identifier. The reference list must be filed under seal, and may be amended as of right. It shall be retained by the clerk's office as part of the record. ME R USDCT Redacting Pleadings. The court may, however, still require the party to file a redacted copy for the public file. ME R USDCT Redacting Pleadings.

h. *DISTRICT OF MAINE: Responsibility for redaction.* The clerk is not required to review documents filed with the court for compliance with FRCP 5.2. The responsibility to redact filings rests with counsel and the party or nonparty making the filing. ME R USDCT App. 4(i); ME R USDCT Redacting Pleadings. For guidelines for filing confidential information in civil cases in the District of Maine, refer to ME R USDCT Confidentiality.

i. *Waiver of protection of identifiers.* A person waives the protection of FRCP 5.2(a) as to the person's own information by filing it without redaction and not under seal. FRCP 5.2(h).

F. Filing and Service Requirements

1. *Filing requirements*

   a. *Required filings.* Any paper after the complaint that is required to be served must be filed no later than a reasonable time after service. FRCP 5(d)(1).

   b. *DISTRICT OF MAINE: Place of filing.* Unless otherwise ordered by the court, papers shall be filed with the court at Bangor in cases filed and pending at Bangor, and at Portland in cases filed and pending at Portland. ME R USDCT Rule 5(a).

   c. *Nonelectronic filing.* A paper not filed electronically is filed by delivering it: (A) to the clerk; or (B) to a judge who

agrees to accept it for filing, and who must then note the filing date on the paper and promptly send it to the clerk. FRCP 5(d)(2).

    i. **DISTRICT OF MAINE:** *Documents to be filed in paper.* The following documents shall be filed in paper, which may also be scanned into ECF by the clerk's office: (A) all handwritten pleadings; and (B) all pleadings and documents filed by pro se litigants who are incarcerated or who are not registered filing users in ECF. ME R USDCT App. 4(g)(8). Non-prisoner pro se litigants in civil actions may register with ECF or may file (and serve) all pleadings and other documents in paper. The clerk's office will scan into ECF any pleadings and documents filed on paper in accordance with ME R USDCT App. 4(g). ME R USDCT App. 4(o). For more information, refer to ME R USDCT App. 4(g).

  d. *Electronic filing*

    i. **DISTRICT OF MAINE:** *Authorization.* Unless exempt or otherwise ordered by the court, papers shall be filed and served electronically as required by the court's Administrative Procedures Governing the Filing and Service by Electronic Means, which is set forth in ME R USDCT App. 4. The provisions of the court's Administrative Procedures Governing the Filing and Service by Electronic Means (ME R USDCT App. 4) shall be applied and enforced as part of the Local Rules of the United States District Court for the District of Maine. ME R USDCT Rule 5(c).

    ii. *Filing by represented persons.* A person represented by an attorney must file electronically, unless nonelectronic filing is allowed by the court for good cause or is allowed or required by local rule. FRCP 5(d)(3)(A).

      • **DISTRICT OF MAINE.** An attorney may apply to the court for permission to file paper documents. ME R USDCT App. 4(a)(5).

    iii. *Filing by unrepresented persons.* A person not represented by an attorney: (i) may file electronically only if allowed by court order or by local rule; and (ii) may be required to file electronically only by court order, or by a local rule that includes reasonable exceptions. FRCP 5(d)(3)(B).

      • **DISTRICT OF MAINE.** Non-prisoner pro se litigants in civil actions may register with ECF or may file (and serve) all pleadings and other documents in paper. ME R USDCT App. 4(o). A non-prisoner who is a party to a civil action and who is not represented by an attorney may register to receive service electronically and to electronically transmit their documents to the court for filing in the ECF system. If during the course of the action the person retains an attorney who appears on the person's behalf, the clerk shall terminate the person's registration upon the attorney's appearance. ME R USDCT App. 4(b)(2).

    iv. **DISTRICT OF MAINE:** *Scope of electronic filing.* All documents submitted for filing in civil and criminal cases, regardless of case commencement date, except those documents specifically exempted in ME R USDCT App. 4(g), shall be filed electronically using the electronic case filing system (ECF). ME R USDCT App. 4(a)(1). For special filing requirements and exceptions, refer to ME R USDCT App. 4(g).

    v. **DISTRICT OF MAINE:** *Consequences of electronic filing.* Electronic transmission of a document to the ECF system, together with the transmission of a Notice of Electronic Filing (NEF) from the court, constitutes filing of the document for all purposes of the Federal Rules of Civil Procedure. ME R USDCT App. 4(d)(1).

    vi. **DISTRICT OF MAINE:** *Review of documents.* Documents filed with the clerk's office will normally be reviewed no later than the close of the next business day. It is the responsibility of the filing party to promptly notify the clerk's office via telephone of a matter that requires the immediate attention of a judicial officer. ME R USDCT App. 4(a)(4).

  e. **DISTRICT OF MAINE:** *Facsimile filing.* No papers shall be submitted to the court by means of a facsimile machine without prior leave of the court. ME R USDCT Rule 5(c); ME R USDCT App. 4(m).

2. *Service requirements*

  a. *Service; When required.* Unless the Federal Rules of Civil Procedure provide otherwise, each of the following papers must be served on every party: (A) an order stating that service is required; (B) a pleading filed after the original complaint, unless the court orders otherwise under FRCP 5(c) because there are numerous defendants; (C) a discovery paper required to be served on a party, unless the court orders otherwise; (D) a written motion, except one that may be heard ex parte; and (E) a written notice, appearance, demand, or offer of judgment, or any similar paper. FRCP 5(a)(1).

    i. *If a party fails to appear.* No service is required on a party who is in default for failing to appear. But a pleading that asserts a new claim for relief against such a party must be served on that party under FRCP 4. FRCP 5(a)(2).

    ii. *Seizing property.* If an action is begun by seizing property and no person is or need be named as a defendant, any

service required before the filing of an appearance, answer, or claim must be made on the person who had custody or possession of the property when it was seized. FRCP 5(a)(3).

b. *Service; How made.* A paper is served under FRCP 5 by: (A) handing it to the person; (B) leaving it: (i) at the person's office with a clerk or other person in charge or, if no one is in charge, in a conspicuous place in the office; or (ii) if the person has no office or the office is closed, at the person's dwelling or usual place of abode with someone of suitable age and discretion who resides there; (C) mailing it to the person's last known address—in which event service is complete upon mailing; (D) leaving it with the court clerk if the person has no known address; (E) sending it to a registered user by filing it with the court's electronic-filing system or sending it by other electronic means that the person consented to in writing—in either of which events service is complete upon filing or sending, but is not effective if the filer or sender learns that it did not reach the person to be served; or (F) delivering it by any other means that the person consented to in writing—in which event service is complete when the person making service delivers it to the agency designated to make delivery. FRCP 5(b)(2).

  i. *Serving an attorney.* If a party is represented by an attorney, service under FRCP 5 must be made on the attorney unless the court orders service on the party. FRCP 5(b)(1).

c. *DISTRICT OF MAINE: Service of electronically filed documents*

  i. *Registered users.* Registration [as a filing user of the court's ECF system] constitutes consent to service of all documents by electronic means as provided in ME R USDCT App. 4. ME R USDCT App. 4(b)(4). Whenever a non-sealed pleading is filed electronically, the ECF system will automatically generate and send a Notice of Electronic Filing (NEF) to the filing user and registered users of record. The user filing the document should retain a paper or digital copy of the NEF, which shall serve as the court's date-stamp and proof of filing. ME R USDCT App. 4(e)(1).

   • *Sealed documents.* Although the filing of sealed documents in civil cases produces an NEF, the document itself cannot be accessed and counsel shall be responsible for making service of the sealed documents. ME R USDCT App. 4(e)(2).

  ii. *Non-registered users and pro se litigants.* Attorneys who have not yet registered as users with ECF and pro se litigants who have not registered with ECF shall be served a paper copy of any electronically filed pleading or other document in accordance with the provisions of FRCP 5. ME R USDCT App. 4(e)(3).

   • *Registration of pro se litigants.* A non-prisoner who is a party to a civil action and who is not represented by an attorney may register to receive service electronically and to electronically transmit their documents to the court for filing in the ECF system. If during the course of the action the person retains an attorney who appears on the person's behalf, the clerk shall terminate the person's registration upon the attorney's appearance. ME R USDCT App. 4(b)(2).

d. *Serving numerous defendants.* If an action involves an unusually large number of defendants, the court may, on motion or on its own, order that: (A) defendants' pleadings and replies to them need not be served on other defendants; (B) any crossclaim, counterclaim, avoidance, or affirmative defense in those pleadings and replies to them will be treated as denied or avoided by all other parties; and (C) filing any such pleading and serving it on the plaintiff constitutes notice of the pleading to all parties. FRCP 5(c)(1).

  i. *Notifying parties.* A copy of every such order must be served on the parties as the court directs. FRCP 5(c)(2).

3. *DISTRICT OF MAINE: Filing and service of highly sensitive documents (HSDs).* For information on filing and serving highly sensitive documents (HSDs) in the District of Maine, refer to ME R USDCT General Order 21-5.

G. Hearings

1. *Hearings, generally.* When a motion relies on facts outside the record, the court may hear the matter on affidavits or may hear it wholly or partly on oral testimony or on depositions. FRCP 43(c).

a. *Oral argument.* Due process does not require that oral argument be permitted on a motion and, except as otherwise provided by local rule, the district court has discretion to determine whether it will decide the motion on the papers or hear argument by counsel (and perhaps receive evidence). FPP § 1190; F.D.I.C. v. Deglau, 207 F.3d 153 (3d Cir. 2000).

  i. *DISTRICT OF MAINE.* Unless otherwise required by federal rule or statute, all motions may be decided by the court without oral argument unless otherwise ordered by the court on its own motion or, in its discretion, upon request of counsel. ME R USDCT Rule 7(e).

b. *Providing a regular schedule for oral hearings.* A court may establish regular times and places for oral hearings on motions. FRCP 78(a).

c. *Providing for submission on briefs.* By rule or order, the court may provide for submitting and determining motions on briefs, without oral hearings. FRCP 78(b).

H. Forms

1. Federal Motion to Compel Discovery Forms

a. Notice of motion to compel party to answer deposition questions. 3B FEDFORMS § 27:17.

b. Motion to compel deposition, request for sanctions and request for expedited hearing. 3B FEDFORMS § 27:20.

c. Motion to compel answer to interrogatories. 3B FEDFORMS § 27:21.

d. Affidavit in support of motion. 3B FEDFORMS § 27:24.

e. Objection to motion for order requiring witness to answer oral questions on deposition. 3B FEDFORMS § 27:27.

f. Notice of motion; To compel required disclosure of names and addresses of witnesses and persons having knowledge of the claims involved; Civil proceeding. AMJUR PP DEPOSITION § 6.

g. Motion; To compel required disclosure of names and addresses of witnesses and persons having knowledge of the claims involved. AMJUR PP DEPOSITION § 7.

h. Motion; To compel answer to interrogatories; Complete failure to answer. AMJUR PP DEPOSITION § 403.

i. Affidavit; In opposition of motion to compel psychiatric or physical examinations; By attorney. AMJUR PP DEPOSITION § 645.

j. Motion; To compel further responses to interrogatories; Various grounds. AMJUR PP DEPOSITION § 713.

k. Affidavit; In support of motion to compel answers to interrogatories and to impose sanctions. AMJUR PP DEPOSITION § 715.

l. Opposition; To motion to compel electronic discovery; Federal class action. AMJUR PP DEPOSITION § 721.

m. Notice of motion; For order to compel compliance with request to permit entry on real property for inspection. AMJUR PP DEPOSITION § 733.

n. Motion; To compel production of documents; After rejected request; Request for sanctions. AMJUR PP DEPOSITION § 734.

o. Affidavit; In support of motion to compel production of documents; By attorney. AMJUR PP DEPOSITION § 736.

p. Motion; To compel doctor's production of medical records for trial. AMJUR PP DEPOSITION § 744.

q. Motion; To compel answers to outstanding discovery requests. FEDPROF § 23:44.

r. Motion; To compel required disclosure of names and addresses of witnesses and persons having knowledge of the claims involved. FEDPROF § 23:45.

s. Motion; To compel answer to questions asked on oral or written examination. FEDPROF § 23:214.

t. Motion; To compel further answers to questions asked on oral or written examination and to award expenses of motion. FEDPROF § 23:215.

u. Motion; To compel party to produce witness at deposition. FEDPROF § 23:216.

v. Affidavit; By opposing attorney; In opposition to motion to compel answers asked at deposition; Answers tend to incriminate. FEDPROF § 23:219.

w. Motion; To compel answer to interrogatories; Complete failure to answer. FEDPROF § 23:383.

x. Motion; To compel further responses to interrogatories; Various grounds. FEDPROF § 23:384.

y. Motion to compel discovery. GOLDLTGFMS § 21:2.

I. Applicable Rules

1. *Federal rules*

a. Serving and filing pleadings and other papers. FRCP 5.

b. Constitutional challenge to a statute; Notice, certification, and intervention. FRCP 5.1.

c. Privacy protection for filings made with the court. FRCP 5.2.

d. Computing and extending time; Time for motion papers. FRCP 6.

e. Pleadings allowed; Form of motions and other papers. FRCP 7.

144

    f.   Form of pleadings. FRCP 10.

    g.   Signing pleadings, motions, and other papers; Representations to the court; Sanctions. FRCP 11.

    h.   Duty to disclose; General provisions governing discovery. FRCP 26.

    i.   Failure to make disclosures or to cooperate in discovery; Sanctions. FRCP 37.

    j.   Taking testimony. FRCP 43.

    k.   Hearing motions; Submission on briefs. FRCP 78.

2. *Local rules*

    a.   *DISTRICT OF MAINE*

        i.   Service and filing of pleadings and other papers. ME R USDCT Rule 5.

        ii.   Time. ME R USDCT Rule 6.

        iii.   Motions and memoranda of law. ME R USDCT Rule 7.

        iv.   Form of pleadings, motions and other papers. ME R USDCT Rule 10.

        v.   Discovery. ME R USDCT Rule 26.

        vi.   Attorneys; Appearances and withdrawals. ME R USDCT Rule 83.2.

        vii.   Alternative dispute resolution (ADR). ME R USDCT Rule 83.11.

        viii.   Administrative procedures governing the filing and service by electronic means. ME R USDCT App. 4.

        ix.   Redacting pleadings. ME R USDCT Redacting Pleadings.

Motions, Oppositions and Replies
Motion for Protective Order

Document Last Updated April 2021

A. Checklist

(I) ❏ Matters to be considered by moving party

    (a) ❏ Required documents

        (1) ❏ Notice of motion and motion

    (b) ❏ Supplemental documents

        (1) ❏ Supporting evidence

        (2) ❏ Notice of constitutional question

        (3) ❏ Nongovernmental corporate disclosure statement

        (4) ❏ DISTRICT OF MAINE: Additional supplemental documents

            (i) ❏ Proposed order

    (c) ❏ Timing

        (1) ❏ The express language of FRCP 26(c) does not set out time limits within which a motion for a protective order must be made; yet the requirement that a motion be made within a reasonable time remains an implicit condition for obtaining a protective order; although a party or deponent is allowed a reasonable amount of time in which to apply for a protective order, a protective order, as a general rule, must be obtained before the date set for the discovery; a motion for a protective order must be made before or on the date the discovery is due

        (2) ❏ A written motion and notice of the hearing must be served at least fourteen (14) days before the time specified for the hearing, with the following exceptions: (A) when the motion may be heard ex parte; (B) when the Federal Rules of Civil Procedure set a different time; or (C) when a court order—which a party may, for good cause, apply for ex parte—sets a different time

        (3) ❏ Any affidavit supporting a motion must be served with the motion

(4) ❑ DISTRICT OF MAINE: Additional timing

    (i) ❑ Any affidavits and other documents setting forth or evidencing facts on which the motion is based must be filed with the motion

(II) ❑ Matters to be considered by opposing party

  (a) ❑ Required documents

    (1) ❑ Opposition

  (b) ❑ Supplemental documents

    (1) ❑ Supporting evidence

    (2) ❑ Notice of constitutional question

  (c) ❑ Timing

    (1) ❑ Except as FRCP 59(c) provides otherwise, any opposing affidavit must be served at least seven (7) days before the hearing, unless the court permits service at another time

    (2) ❑ DISTRICT OF MAINE: Additional timing

      (i) ❑ Unless within twenty-one (21) days after the filing of a motion the opposing party files written objection thereto, incorporating a memorandum of law, the opposing party shall be deemed to have waived objection

B. Timing

1. *Motion for protective order.* The express language of FRCP 26(c) does not set out time limits within which a motion for a protective order must be made; yet the requirement that a motion be made within a reasonable time remains an implicit condition for obtaining a protective order. FEDPROC § 26:289.

  a. *Reasonable time.* Although a party or deponent is allowed a reasonable amount of time in which to apply for a protective order, a protective order, as a general rule, must be obtained before the date set for the discovery. A motion for a protective order must be made before or on the date the discovery is due. FEDPROC § 26:289.

2. *Timing of motions, generally*

  a. *Motion and notice of hearing.* A written motion and notice of the hearing must be served at least fourteen (14) days before the time specified for the hearing, with the following exceptions: (A) when the motion may be heard ex parte; (B) when the Federal Rules of Civil Procedure set a different time; or (C) when a court order—which a party may, for good cause, apply for ex parte—sets a different time. FRCP 6(c)(1).

  b. *Supporting affidavit.* Any affidavit supporting a motion must be served with the motion. FRCP 6(c)(2).

  c. *DISTRICT OF MAINE: Affidavits and other supporting documents.* Any affidavits and other documents setting forth or evidencing facts on which the motion is based must be filed with the motion. ME R USDCT Rule 7(a).

3. *Timing of opposing papers.* Except as FRCP 59(c) provides otherwise, any opposing affidavit must be served at least seven (7) days before the hearing, unless the court permits service at another time. FRCP 6(c)(2).

  a. *DISTRICT OF MAINE.* Unless within twenty-one (21) days after the filing of a motion the opposing party files written objection thereto, incorporating a memorandum of law, the opposing party shall be deemed to have waived objection. ME R USDCT Rule 7(b). The deemed waiver imposed in ME R USDCT Rule 7(b) shall not apply to motions filed during trial. ME R USDCT Rule 7(b).

4. *Timing of reply papers.* Where the respondent files an answering affidavit setting up a new matter, the moving party ordinarily is allowed a reasonable time to file a reply affidavit since failure to deny the new matter by affidavit may operate as an admission of its truth. AMJUR MOTIONS § 25.

  a. *DISTRICT OF MAINE.* Within fourteen (14) days of the filing of any objection to a motion, the moving party may file a reply memorandum. ME R USDCT Rule 7(c).

5. *Computation of time*

  a. *Computing time.* FRCP 6 applies in computing any time period specified in the Federal Rules of Civil Procedure, in any local rule or court order, or in any statute that does not specify a method of computing time. FRCP 6(a).

    i. *Period stated in days or a longer unit.* When the period is stated in days or a longer unit of time: (A) exclude the day of the event that triggers the period; (B) count every day, including intermediate Saturdays, Sundays, and legal holidays; and (C) include the last day of the period, but if the last day is a Saturday, Sunday, or legal holiday,

the period continues to run until the end of the next day that is not a Saturday, Sunday, or legal holiday. FRCP 6(a)(1).

ii. *Period stated in hours.* When the period is stated in hours: (A) begin counting immediately on the occurrence of the event that triggers the period; (B) count every hour, including hours during intermediate Saturdays, Sundays, and legal holidays; and (C) if the period would end on a Saturday, Sunday, or legal holiday, the period continues to run until the same time on the next day that is not a Saturday, Sunday, or legal holiday. FRCP 6(a)(2).

iii. *Inaccessibility of the clerk's office.* Unless the court orders otherwise, if the clerk's office is inaccessible: (A) on the last day for filing under FRCP 6(a)(1), then the time for filing is extended to the first accessible day that is not a Saturday, Sunday, or legal holiday; or (B) during the last hour for filing under FRCP 6(a)(2), then the time for filing is extended to the same time on the first accessible day that is not a Saturday, Sunday, or legal holiday. FRCP 6(a)(3).

iv. *"Last day" defined.* Unless a different time is set by a statute, local rule, or court order, the last day ends: (A) for electronic filing, at midnight in the court's time zone; and (B) for filing by other means, when the clerk's office is scheduled to close. FRCP 6(a)(4).

v. *"Next day" defined.* The "next day" is determined by continuing to count forward when the period is measured after an event and backward when measured before an event. FRCP 6(a)(5).

vi. *"Legal holiday" defined.* "Legal holiday" means: (A) the day set aside by statute for observing New Year's Day, Martin Luther King Jr.'s Birthday, Washington's Birthday, Memorial Day, Independence Day, Labor Day, Columbus Day, Veterans' Day, Thanksgiving Day, or Christmas Day; (B) any day declared a holiday by the President or Congress; and (C) for periods that are measured after an event, any other day declared a holiday by the state where the district court is located. FRCP 6(a)(6).

vii. *DISTRICT OF MAINE: Applicability of FRCP 6.* FRCP 6 applies when computing any period of time stated in the Local Rules of the United States District Court for the District of Maine. ME R USDCT Rule 6(a).

b. *DISTRICT OF MAINE: Computation of electronic filing deadlines.* Filing documents electronically does not in any way alter any filing deadlines. All electronic transmissions of documents must be completed prior to midnight, Eastern Time, in order to be considered timely filed that day. Where a specific time of day deadline is set by court order or stipulation, the electronic filing must be completed by that time. ME R USDCT App. 4(f). A document filed electronically shall be deemed filed at the time and date stated on the Notice of Electronic Filing received from the court. ME R USDCT App. 4(d)(2).

i. *Technical failures.* A filing user whose filing is made untimely as the result of a technical failure may seek appropriate relief from the court. ME R USDCT App. 4(n). A technical failure of the court's ECF system is deemed to have occurred when the court's ECF site cannot accept filings continuously or intermittently over the course of any period of time greater than one (1) hour. Known system outages will be posted on the court's website along with guidance on how to proceed, if applicable. ME R USDCT App. 4(n).

c. *Extending time.* When an act may or must be done within a specified time, the court may, for good cause, extend the time: (A) with or without motion or notice if the court acts, or if a request is made, before the original time or its extension expires; or (B) on motion made after the time has expired if the party failed to act because of excusable neglect. FRCP 6(b)(1). A court must not extend the time to act under FRCP 50(b), FRCP 50(d), FRCP 52(b), FRCP 59(b), FRCP 59(d), FRCP 59(e), and FRCP 60(b). FRCP 6(b)(2). Refer to the United States District Court for the District of Maine KeyRules Motion for Continuance/Extension of Time document for more information on extending time.

d. *Additional time after certain kinds of service.* When a party may or must act within a specified time after being served and service is made under FRCP 5(b)(2)(C) (by mail), FRCP 5(b)(2)(D) (by leaving with the clerk), or FRCP 5(b)(2)(F) (by other means consented to), three (3) days are added after the period would otherwise expire under FRCP 6(a). FRCP 6(d).

C. General Requirements

1. *Motions, generally*

a. *Motion requirements.* A request for a court order must be made by motion. The motion must: (A) be in writing unless made during a hearing or trial; (B) state with particularity the grounds for seeking the order; and (C) state the relief sought. FRCP 7(b)(1). The writing and particularity requirements are intended to ensure that the adverse parties are informed of and have a record of both the motion's pendency and the grounds on which the movant seeks an order. FPP § 1191; Feldberg v. Quechee Lakes Corp., 463 F.3d 195 (2d Cir. 2006).

i. *Particularity requirement.* The particularity requirement [ensures] that the opposing parties will have notice of their opponent's contentions. FEDPROC § 62:358; Goodman v. 1973 26 Foot Trojan Vessel, Arkansas Registration No. AR1439SN, 859 F.2d 71 (8th Cir. 1988). That requirement ensures that notice of the basis for the motion is provided to the court and to the opposing party so as to avoid prejudice, provide the opponent with a meaningful opportunity to respond, and provide the court with enough information to process the motion correctly. FEDPROC § 62:358; Andreas v. Volkswagen of Am., Inc., 336 F.3d 789 (8th Cir. 2003).

- Reasonable specification of the grounds for a motion is sufficient. The particularity requirement for motions is satisfied when no party is prejudiced by a lack of particularity or when the court can comprehend the basis for the motion and deal with it fairly. However, where a movant fails to state even one ground for granting the motion in question, the movant has failed to meet the minimal standard of "reasonable specification." FEDPROC § 62:358; Martinez v. Trainor, 556 F.2d 818 (7th Cir. 1977).

- The court may excuse the failure to comply with the particularity requirement if it is inadvertent, and where no prejudice is shown by the opposing party. FEDPROC § 62:358.

b. *Notice of motion.* A party interested in resisting the relief sought by a motion has a right to notice thereof, and an opportunity to be heard. AMJUR MOTIONS § 12.

   i. *Purpose.* In addition to statutory or court rule provisions requiring notice of a motion—the purpose of such a notice requirement having been said to be to prevent a party from being prejudicially surprised by a motion—principles of natural justice dictate that an adverse party generally must be given notice that a motion will be presented to the court. AMJUR MOTIONS § 12.

   ii. *Adequacy of notice.* The test of adequate notice generally turns on whether the other parties were afforded an adequate opportunity to prepare and respond to the issues to be raised in the proceeding. AMJUR MOTIONS § 12.

c. *Single document containing motion and notice.* A single written document can satisfy the writing requirements both for a motion and for an FRCP 6(c)(1) notice. FRCP 7(Advisory Committee Notes).

2. *DISTRICT OF MAINE: Procedure for discovery disputes*

a. *Prior approval required.* No written discovery motions shall be filed without the prior approval of a judicial officer. ME R USDCT Rule 7(a); ME R USDCT Rule 26(b).

b. *Conference with opposing counsel.* A party with a discovery dispute must first confer with the opposing party in a good faith effort to resolve by agreement the issues in dispute. If that good faith effort is unsuccessful, the moving party shall file a Request for Hearing Re Discovery Dispute using the court's form seeking a prompt hearing with a judicial officer by telephone or in person. The party seeking the hearing shall confer with opposing counsel and agree on the relevant discovery materials that should be submitted to the court with the Request for Hearing. ME R USDCT Rule 26(b).

c. *Hearing on discovery dispute.* If the hearing is to be conducted by telephone, the clerk will inform counsel of the time and date of the hearing and it shall be the responsibility of the moving party to initiate the telephone call to chambers, unless the court, in its discretion, directs otherwise. The recording by counsel of telephone hearings with the court is prohibited, except with prior permission of the court. The court shall conduct the hearing on the record, but that record will not be officially transcribed except on specific request of counsel or the court. The request for a hearing with a judicial officer carries with it a professional representation by the lawyer that a conference has taken place and that he or she has made a good faith effort to resolve the dispute. The lawyers or unrepresented parties shall supply the judicial officer with the particular discovery materials (such as objectionable answers to interrogatories) that are needed to understand the dispute. ME R USDCT Rule 26(b).

d. *Filing of motion papers and supporting memoranda.* If the judicial officer decides that motion papers and supporting memoranda are needed to satisfactorily resolve the discovery dispute, such papers shall be filed in conformity with ME R USDCT Rule 7. Such motions shall (1) quote in full each interrogatory, question at deposition, request for admission or request for production to which the motion is addressed, or otherwise identify specifically and succinctly the discovery to which objection is taken or from which a protective order is sought; and (2) the response or objection and grounds therefor, if any, as stated by the opposing party. ME R USDCT Rule 26(b). Unless otherwise ordered by the court, the complete transcripts or discovery papers need not be filed with the court pursuant to ME R USDCT Rule 26(c) unless the motion cannot be fairly decided without reference to the complete original. ME R USDCT Rule 26(b).

3. *Motion for protective order.* A party or any person from whom discovery is sought may move for a protective order in the court where the action is pending—or as an alternative on matters relating to a deposition, in the court for the district where

the deposition will be taken. FRCP 26(c)(1). FRCP 26(c) was enacted as a safeguard for the protection of parties and witnesses in view of the broad discovery rights authorized by FRCP 26(b). FEDPROC § 26:260; United States v. Columbia Broad. Sys., Inc., 666 F.2d 364 (9th Cir. 1982).

a. *Grounds for protective orders.* The court may, for good cause, issue an order to protect a party or person from annoyance, embarrassment, oppression, or undue burden or expense, including one or more of the following: (A) forbidding the disclosure or discovery; (B) specifying terms, including time and place or the allocation of expenses, for the disclosure or discovery; (C) prescribing a discovery method other than the one selected by the party seeking discovery; (D) forbidding inquiry into certain matters, or limiting the scope of disclosure or discovery to certain matters; (E) designating the persons who may be present while the discovery is conducted; (F) requiring that a deposition be sealed and opened only on court order; (G) requiring that a trade secret or other confidential research, development, or commercial information not be revealed or be revealed only in a specified way; and (H) requiring that the parties simultaneously file specified documents or information in sealed envelopes, to be opened as the court directs. FRCP 26(c)(1).

b. *Third-party protection.* A party may not ask for an order to protect the rights of another party or a witness if that party or witness does not claim protection for himself, but a party may seek order if it believes its own interest is jeopardized by discovery sought from a third person. FPP § 2035.

c. *Burden.* The party seeking a protective order has the burden of demonstrating that good cause exists for issuance of the order. FEDPROC § 26:273. The good-cause requirement under FRCP 26(c), encompasses a standard of reasonableness. FEDPROC § 26:278.

    i. *Factual demonstration of injury.* The party requesting a protective order must demonstrate that failure to issue the order requested will work a clearly defined harm, and must make a specific demonstration of facts in support of the request as opposed to conclusory or speculative statements about the need for a protective order and the harm which will be suffered without one. FEDPROC § 26:276.

    ii. *Serious injury.* A party seeking a protective order under FRCP 26(c) must demonstrate that failure to issue the order requested will work a serious injury. FEDPROC § 26:277.

d. *Application of protective orders.* FRCP 26(c) provides no authority for the issuance of protective orders purporting to regulate the use of information or documents obtained through means other than discovery in the pending proceeding, and does not permit the district court to issue protective orders with respect to data obtained through means other than the court's discovery processes. FEDPROC § 26:265.

    i. *Information not discovered.* FRCP 26(c) does not give the court authority to prohibit disclosure of trade data which was compiled by counsel prior the commencing of a lawsuit. Similarly, material received by one party prior to commencement of an action (and therefore before initiation of any discovery and before a request for protective orders) cannot be made a legitimate part of the corpus of any protective order a court enters. FEDPROC § 26:265.

    ii. *Information discovered in other action.* The trial court lacks the discretion and power to issue a valid protective order to compel the return of documents obtained through discovery in a separate action. FEDPROC § 26:266.

e. *Ordering discovery.* If a motion for a protective order is wholly or partly denied, the court may, on just terms, order that any party or person provide or permit discovery. FRCP 26(c)(2).

f. *Awarding expenses.* FRCP 37(a)(5) applies to the award of expenses. FRCP 26(c)(3). Refer to the United States District Court for the District of Maine KeyRules Motion for Discovery Sanctions document for more information.

4. *Opposing papers.* The Federal Rules of Civil Procedure do not require any formal answer, return, or reply to a motion, except where the Federal Rules of Civil Procedure or local rules may require affidavits, memoranda, or other papers to be filed in opposition to a motion. Such papers are simply to apprise the court of such opposition and the grounds of that opposition. FEDPROC § 62:353.

a. *DISTRICT OF MAINE: Content of objections.* Any objections shall include citations and supporting authorities and affidavits and other documents setting forth or evidencing facts on which the objection is based. ME R USDCT Rule 7(b).

b. *Effect of failure to respond to motion.* Although in the absence of statutory provision or court rule, a motion ordinarily does not require a response or written answer, when a party files a motion and the opposing party fails to respond, the court may construe such failure to respond as nonopposition to the motion or an admission that the motion was meritorious. AMJUR MOTIONS § 28. The rule in some jurisdictions being that the failure to respond to a fact set forth in a motion is deemed an admission—and may grant the motion if the relief requested appears to be justified. AMJUR MOTIONS § 28.

c. *Assent or no opposition not determinative.* However, a motion will not be granted automatically simply because an "assent" or a notation of "no opposition" has been filed; federal judges frequently deny motions that have been assented to when it is thought that justice so dictates. FPP § 1190.

d. *Responsive pleading inappropriate as response to motion.* An attempt to answer or oppose a motion with a responsive pleading usually is not appropriate. FPP § 1190.

5. *Reply papers.* A moving party may be required or permitted to prepare papers in addition to its original motion papers. AMJUR MOTIONS § 25. Papers answering or replying to opposing papers may be appropriate, in the interests of justice, where it appears there is a substantial reason for allowing a reply. Thus, a court may accept reply papers where a party demonstrates that the papers to which it seeks to file a reply raise new issues that are material to the disposition of the question before the court, or where the court determines, sua sponte, that it wishes further briefing of an issue raised in those papers and orders the submission of additional papers. FEDPROC § 62:354.

a. *Function of reply papers.* The function of a reply affidavit or reply papers is to answer the arguments made in opposition to the position taken by the movant, not to raise new issues, arguments, or evidence, or change the nature of the primary motion. However, if the court permits new evidence with the reply papers, the other party should be given the opportunity to respond. Where the party opposing the motion has no opportunity to address the argument in writing, a court has the discretion to disregard arguments raised for the first time in a reply memorandum. Also, the view has been followed in some jurisdictions that as a matter of judicial economy, where there is no prejudice and where the issues could be raised simply by filing a motion to dismiss, the trial court has discretion to consider arguments raised for the first time in a reply memorandum, and that a trial court may grant a motion to strike issues raised for the first time in a reply memorandum. AMJUR MOTIONS § 26.

   i. *DISTRICT OF MAINE.* The moving party may file a reply memorandum. . .which shall be strictly confined to replying to new matter raised in the objection or opposing memorandum. ME R USDCT Rule 7(c).

6. *DISTRICT OF MAINE: Appearances.* An attorney's signature to a pleading shall constitute an appearance for the party filing the pleading. Otherwise, an attorney who wishes to participate in any manner in any action must file a formal written appearance identifying the party represented. An appearance whether by pleading or formal written appearance shall be signed by an attorney in his/her individual name and shall state his/her office address. ME R USDCT Rule 83.2(a). For more information, refer to ME R USDCT Rule 83.2.

7. *DISTRICT OF MAINE: Alternative dispute resolution (ADR).* Litigants are authorized and encouraged to employ, at their own expense, any available ADR process on which they can agree, including early neutral evaluation, settlement conferences, mediation, non-binding summary jury trial, corporate mini-trial, and arbitration proceedings. ME R USDCT Rule 83.11(a). For more information on ADR, refer to ME R USDCT Rule 83.11.

D. Documents

1. *Documents for moving party*

   a. *Required documents*

      i. *Notice of motion and motion.* Refer to the "C. General Requirements" section of this KeyRules document for information on the notice of motion and motion.

         - *DISTRICT OF MAINE: Memorandum of law.* Every motion shall incorporate a memorandum of law, including citations and supporting authorities. ME R USDCT Rule 7(a). Refer to the "E. Format" section of this KeyRules document for the form of memoranda of law.

         - *Certificate of service.* No certificate of service is required when a paper is served by filing it with the court's electronic-filing system. When a paper that is required to be served is served by other means: (i) if the paper is filed, a certificate of service must be filed with it or within a reasonable time after service; and (ii) if the paper is not filed, a certificate of service need not be filed unless filing is required by court order or by local rule. FRCP 5(d)(1)(B).

   b. *Supplemental documents*

      i. *Supporting evidence.* When a motion relies on facts outside the record, the court may hear the matter on affidavits or may hear it wholly or partly on oral testimony or on depositions. FRCP 43(c).

         - *DISTRICT OF MAINE: Affidavits and other supporting documents.* Any affidavits and other documents setting forth or evidencing facts on which the motion is based must be filed with the motion. ME R USDCT Rule 7(a).

         - *DISTRICT OF MAINE: Discovery transcripts or materials.* A party relying on discovery transcripts or materials in support of or in opposition to a motion shall file excerpts of such transcript or materials with the memorandum required by ME R USDCT Rule 7 as well as a list of specific citations to the parts on which the party relies. ME R USDCT Rule 26(c). Excerpts of depositions in support of or in opposition to a motion shall be filed electronically using ECF, unless otherwise permitted by the court. ME R USDCT App. 4(l)(3).

ii. *Notice of constitutional question.* A party that files a pleading, written motion, or other paper drawing into question the constitutionality of a federal or state statute must promptly: (1) file a notice of constitutional question stating the question and identifying the paper that raises it, if: (A) a federal statute is questioned and the parties do not include the United States, one of its agencies, or one of its officers or employees in an official capacity; or (B) a state statute is questioned and the parties do not include the state, one of its agencies, or one of its officers or employees in an official capacity; and (2) serve the notice and paper on the Attorney General of the United States if a federal statute is questioned—or on the state attorney general if a state statute is questioned—either by certified or registered mail or by sending it to an electronic address designated by the attorney general for this purpose. FRCP 5.1(a).

- *No forfeiture.* A party's failure to file and serve the notice, or the court's failure to certify, does not forfeit a constitutional claim or defense that is otherwise timely asserted. FRCP 5.1(d).

iii. *Nongovernmental corporate disclosure statement.* A nongovernmental corporate party must file two (2) copies of a disclosure statement that: (1) identifies any parent corporation and any publicly held corporation owning ten percent (10%) or more of its stock; or (2) states that there is no such corporation. FRCP 7.1(a). A party must: (1) file the disclosure statement with its first appearance, pleading, petition, motion, response, or other request addressed to the court; and (2) promptly file a supplemental statement if any required information changes. FRCP 7.1(b).

- *DISTRICT OF MAINE: Notice of interested parties.* To enable the court to evaluate possible disqualification or recusal, counsel for all non-governmental parties shall file with their first appearance a Notice of Interested Parties, which shall list all persons, associations of persons, firms, partnerships, limited liability companies, joint ventures, corporations (including parent or affiliated corporations, clearly identified as such), or any similar entities, owning ten percent (10%) or more of the named party. Counsel shall be under a continuing obligation to file an amended Notice if any material change occurs in the status of an Interested Party, such as through merger, acquisition, or new/additional membership. ME R USDCT Rule 7.1.

iv. *DISTRICT OF MAINE: Additional supplemental documents*

- *Proposed order.* Proposed orders shall not be filed unless requested by the court. When requested by the court, proposed orders shall be filed by e-mail in word processing format. ME R USDCT App. 4(k)(1). A party by motion or with the agreement of all parties may submit to the court a proposed order governing the production and use of confidential documents and information in the pending action. The proposed order shall conform to the Form Confidentiality Order set forth in ME R USDCT App. 2. Any proposed modification to the Form Confidentiality Order shall be identified with a short statement of the reason for each modification. ME R USDCT Rule 26(d).

2. *Documents for opposing party*

a. *Required documents*

i. *Opposition.* Refer to the "C. General Requirements" section of this KeyRules document for information on the opposing papers.

- *DISTRICT OF MAINE: Memorandum of law.* Unless within twenty-one (21) days after the filing of a motion the opposing party files written objection thereto, incorporating a memorandum of law, the opposing party shall be deemed to have waived objection. ME R USDCT Rule 7(b).

- *Certificate of service.* No certificate of service is required when a paper is served by filing it with the court's electronic-filing system. When a paper that is required to be served is served by other means: (i) if the paper is filed, a certificate of service must be filed with it or within a reasonable time after service; and (ii) if the paper is not filed, a certificate of service need not be filed unless filing is required by court order or by local rule. FRCP 5(d)(1)(B).

b. *Supplemental documents*

i. *Supporting evidence.* When a motion relies on facts outside the record, the court may hear the matter on affidavits or may hear it wholly or partly on oral testimony or on depositions. FRCP 43(c).

- *DISTRICT OF MAINE: Affidavits and other supporting documents.* Any objections shall include. . . .affidavits and other documents setting forth or evidencing facts on which the objection is based. ME R USDCT Rule 7(b).

- *DISTRICT OF MAINE: Discovery transcripts or materials.* A party relying on discovery transcripts or materials in support of or in opposition to a motion shall file excerpts of such transcript or materials with the memorandum required by ME R USDCT Rule 7 as well as a list of specific citations to the parts on which the party relies. ME R USDCT Rule 26(c). Excerpts of depositions in support of or in opposition to a motion shall be filed electronically using ECF, unless otherwise permitted by the court. ME R USDCT App. 4(l)(3).

    ii. *Notice of constitutional question.* A party that files a pleading, written motion, or other paper drawing into question the constitutionality of a federal or state statute must promptly: (1) file a notice of constitutional question stating the question and identifying the paper that raises it, if: (A) a federal statute is questioned and the parties do not include the United States, one of its agencies, or one of its officers or employees in an official capacity; or (B) a state statute is questioned and the parties do not include the state, one of its agencies, or one of its officers or employees in an official capacity; and (2) serve the notice and paper on the Attorney General of the United States if a federal statute is questioned—or on the state attorney general if a state statute is questioned—either by certified or registered mail or by sending it to an electronic address designated by the attorney general for this purpose. FRCP 5.1(a).

- *No forfeiture.* A party's failure to file and serve the notice, or the court's failure to certify, does not forfeit a constitutional claim or defense that is otherwise timely asserted. FRCP 5.1(d).

E. Format

1. *Form of documents.* The rules governing captions and other matters of form in pleadings apply to motions and other papers. FRCP 7(b)(2).

    a. *DISTRICT OF MAINE: Font size, line spacing, and paper size.* All such documents shall be typed in a font of no less than size twelve (12) point, and shall be double-spaced or printed on eight and one-half by eleven (8-1/2 x 11) inch paper. Footnotes shall be in a font of no less than size ten (10) point, and may be single spaced. ME R USDCT Rule 10.

    b. *Caption.* Every pleading must have a caption with the court's name, a title, a file number, and an FRCP 7(a) designation. FRCP 10(a).

        i. *Names of parties.* The title of the complaint must name all the parties; the title of other pleadings, after naming the first party on each side, may refer generally to other parties. FRCP 10(a).

        ii. *DISTRICT OF MAINE: Additional caption requirements.* All pleadings, motions and other papers filed with the clerk or otherwise submitted to the court, except exhibits, shall bear the proper case number and shall contain on the first page a caption as described by FRCP 10(a) and immediately thereunder a designation of what the document is and the name of the party in whose behalf it is submitted. ME R USDCT Rule 10.

    c. *Claims or defenses*

        i. *Numbered paragraphs.* A party must state its claims or defenses in numbered paragraphs, each limited as far as practicable to a single set of circumstances. A later pleading may refer by number to a paragraph in an earlier pleading. FRCP 10(b).

        ii. *Separate statements.* If doing so would promote clarity, each claim founded on a separate transaction or occurrence—and each defense other than a denial—must be stated in a separate count or defense. FRCP 10(b).

    d. *Adoption by reference.* A statement in a pleading may be adopted by reference elsewhere in the same pleading or in any other pleading or motion. FRCP 10(c).

        i. *Exhibits.* A copy of a written instrument that is an exhibit to a pleading is a part of the pleading for all purposes. FRCP 10(c).

    e. *DISTRICT OF MAINE: Page numbering.* All pages shall be numbered at the bottom. ME R USDCT Rule 10.

    f. *DISTRICT OF MAINE: Attachment of ancillary papers.* Ancillary papers shall be attached at the end of the document to which they relate. ME R USDCT Rule 10.

    g. *Acceptance by the clerk.* The clerk must not refuse to file a paper solely because it is not in the form prescribed by the Federal Rules of Civil Procedure or by a local rule or practice. FRCP 5(d)(4).

2. *Form of electronic documents.* A paper filed electronically is a written paper for purposes of the Federal Rules of Civil Procedure. FRCP 5(d)(3)(D).

    a. *DISTRICT OF MAINE: Document format.* The ECF system only accepts documents in a portable document format

(PDF). Although there are two types of PDF documents—electronically converted PDF's and scanned PDF's—only electronically converted PDF's may be filed with the court using the ECF system, unless otherwise authorized by local rule or order. ME R USDCT App. 4. Any document or exhibit to be filed or submitted to the court shall not be password-protected or encrypted. ME R USDCT App. 4(g)(12).

    i. *Electronically converted PDFs.* Electronically converted PDF's are created from word processing documents (MS Word, WordPerfect, etc.) using Adobe Acrobat or similar software. They are text searchable and their file size is small. ME R USDCT App. 4. Software used to electronically convert documents to PDF which includes proprietary or advertisement information within the PDF document is prohibited. ME R USDCT App. 4.

    ii. *Scanned PDFs.* Scanned PDF's are created from paper documents run through an optical scanner. Scanned PDF's are not searchable and have a large file size. ME R USDCT App. 4.

  b. *DISTRICT OF MAINE: Title.* All pleadings filed electronically shall be titled in accordance with the approved dictionary of civil or criminal events of the ECF system of the United States District Court for the District of Maine. ME R USDCT App. 4(d)(3).

  c. *DISTRICT OF MAINE: Attachments.* Attachments to filings and exhibits must be filed in accordance with the court's ECF User Manual, unless otherwise ordered by the court. ME R USDCT App. 4(j). When there are fifty (50) or fewer attachments to a pleading, the attachments must be filed by counsel electronically using ECF. When there are more than fifty (50) attachments, the attachments must be filed in one of the following ways: (A) using ECF, simply attach them to the pleading being filed; (B) using ECF, use the "Additional Attachments" menu item; (C) on paper; or (D) on a properly labeled three and one-half (3-1/2) inch floppy disk, CD or DVD. ME R USDCT App. 4(j)(2). Attachments filed on paper or on disk must contain a comprehensive index that clearly describes each document. ME R USDCT App. 4(j)(2).

    i. A filing user must submit as attachments only those excerpts of the referenced documents that are directly germane to the matter under consideration by the court. Excerpted material must be clearly and prominently identified as such. Users who file excerpts of documents do so without prejudice to their right to timely file additional excerpts or the complete document, as may be allowed by the court. Responding parties may timely file additional excerpts or the complete document that they believe are directly germane. ME R USDCT App. 4(j)(3).

    ii. Filers shall not attach as an exhibit any pleading or other paper already on file with the court in that case, but shall merely refer to that document. ME R USDCT App. 4(j)(4).

  d. *DISTRICT OF MAINE: Compliance with technical standards.* All documents filed by electronic means must comply with technical standards, if any, established by the Judicial Conference of the United States or by the United States District Court for the District of Maine. ME R USDCT App. 4(a)(3).

3. *DISTRICT OF MAINE: Form of memoranda of law.* All memoranda shall be typed, in a font of no less than size twelve (12) point, and shall be double-spaced on eight and one-half by eleven (8-1/2 x 11) inch paper or printed. Footnotes shall be in a font of no less than size ten (10) point, and may be single spaced. All pages shall be numbered at the bottom. ME R USDCT Rule 7(d).

  a. *Page limitations.* No memorandum of law in support of or in opposition to a nondispositive motion shall exceed ten (10) pages. ME R USDCT Rule 7(d). No reply memorandum shall exceed seven (7) pages. ME R USDCT Rule 7(d); ME R USDCT Rule 7(c).

    i. *Motion to exceed page limitation.* A motion to exceed the limitation of ME R USDCT Rule 7 shall be filed no later than three (3) business days in advance of the date for filing the memorandum to permit meaningful review by the court. A motion to exceed the page limitations shall not be filed simultaneously with a memorandum in excess of the limitations of ME R USDCT Rule 7. ME R USDCT Rule 7(d).

4. *Signing disclosures and discovery requests, responses, and objections.* FRCP 11 does not apply to disclosures and discovery requests, responses, objections, and motions under FRCP 26 through FRCP 37. FRCP 11(d).

  a. *Signature required.* Every disclosure under FRCP 26(a)(1) or FRCP 26(a)(3) and every discovery request, response, or objection must be signed by at least one attorney of record in the attorney's own name—or by the party personally, if unrepresented—and must state the signer's address, e-mail address, and telephone number. FRCP 26(g)(1).

  b. *Electronic signing.* A filing made through a person's electronic-filing account and authorized by that person, together with that person's name on a signature block, constitutes the person's signature. FRCP 5(d)(3)(C).

    i. *DISTRICT OF MAINE: Attorneys.* The user log-in and password together with a user's name on the signature block constitutes the attorney's signature pursuant to the Federal Rules of Civil Procedure and the Local Rules of the United States District Court for the District of Maine. All electronically filed documents must include a signature block and must set forth the attorney's name, address, telephone number and e-mail address. The name of the ECF user under whose log-in and password the document is submitted must be preceded by a "/s/" in the space where the signature would otherwise appear. ME R USDCT App. 4(h)(1).

    ii.   *DISTRICT OF MAINE: Multiple signatures.* The filer of any document requiring more than one signature (e.g., pleadings filed by visiting lawyers, stipulations, joint status reports) must list thereon all the names of other signatories, preceded by a "/s/" in the space where the signatures would otherwise appear. By submitting such a document, the filing attorney certifies that each of the other signatories has expressly agreed to the form and substance of the document and that the filing attorney has their actual authority to submit the document electronically. ME R USDCT App. 4(h)(2). For more information, refer to ME R USDCT App. 4(h)(2).

    iii.   *DISTRICT OF MAINE: Documents signed under oath.* Affidavits, declarations, verified complaints, or any other document signed under oath shall be filed electronically. The electronically filed version shall contain the typed name of the signatory, preceded by a "/s/" in the space where the signature would otherwise appear indicating that the paper document bears an original signature. ME R USDCT Rule 10; ME R USDCT App. 4(h)(3). For more information, refer to ME R USDCT Rule 10.

  c.   *Effect of signature.* By signing, an attorney or party certifies that to the best of the person's knowledge, information, and belief formed after a reasonable inquiry: (A) with respect to a disclosure, it is complete and correct as of the time it is made; and (B) with respect to a discovery request, response, or objection, it is: (i) consistent with the Federal Rules of Civil Procedure and warranted by existing law or by a nonfrivolous argument for extending, modifying, or reversing existing law, or for establishing new law; (ii) not interposed for any improper purpose, such as to harass, cause unnecessary delay, or needlessly increase the cost of litigation; and (iii) neither unreasonable nor unduly burdensome or expensive, considering the needs of the case, prior discovery in the case, the amount in controversy, and the importance of the issues at stake in the action. FRCP 26(g)(1).

  d.   *Failure to sign.* Other parties have no duty to act on an unsigned disclosure, request, response, or objection until it is signed, and the court must strike it unless a signature is promptly supplied after the omission is called to the attorney's or party's attention. FRCP 26(g)(2).

  e.   *Sanction for improper certification.* If a certification violates FRCP 26(g) without substantial justification, the court, on motion or on its own, must impose an appropriate sanction on the signer, the party on whose behalf the signer was acting, or both. The sanction may include an order to pay the reasonable expenses, including attorney's fees, caused by the violation. FRCP 26(g)(3). Refer to the United States District Court for the District of Maine KeyRules Motion for Discovery Sanctions document for more information.

5.   *Privacy protection for filings made with the court*

  a.   *Redacted filings.* Unless the court orders otherwise, in an electronic or paper filing with the court that contains an individual's Social Security number, taxpayer-identification number, or birth date, the name of an individual known to be a minor, or a financial-account number, a party or nonparty making the filing may include only: (1) the last four (4) digits of the Social Security number and taxpayer-identification number; (2) the year of the individual's birth; (3) the minor's initials; and (4) the last four (4) digits of the financial-account number. FRCP 5.2(a).

    i.   *DISTRICT OF MAINE.* To address the privacy concerns created by the Internet access to court papers, unless otherwise ordered by the court, counsel shall modify certain personal data identifiers in pleadings and other papers as follows: (1) minors' names: use of the minors' initials only; (2) Social Security numbers: use of the last four (4) numbers only; (3) dates of birth: use of the year of birth only; [and] (4) financial account numbers: identify the type of account and the financial institution, but use only the last four (4) numbers of the account number. ME R USDCT Redacting Pleadings. Counsel should also use caution when filing papers that contain a person's medical records, employment history; financial information; and any proprietary or trade secret information. ME R USDCT Redacting Pleadings.

  b.   *Exemptions from the redaction requirement.* The redaction requirement does not apply to the following: (1) a financial-account number that identifies the property allegedly subject to forfeiture in a forfeiture proceeding; (2) the record of an administrative or agency proceeding; (3) the official record of a state-court proceeding; (4) the record of a court or tribunal, if that record was not subject to the redaction requirement when originally filed; (5) a filing covered by FRCP 5.2(c) or FRCP 5.2(d); and (6) a pro se filing in an action brought under 28 U.S.C.A. § 2241, 28 U.S.C.A. § 2254, or 28 U.S.C.A. § 2255. FRCP 5.2(b).

  c.   *Limitations on remote access to electronic files; Social Security appeals and immigration cases.* Unless the court orders otherwise, in an action for benefits under the Social Security Act, and in an action or proceeding relating to an order of removal, to relief from removal, or to immigration benefits or detention, access to an electronic file is authorized as follows: (1) the parties and their attorneys may have remote electronic access to any part of the case file, including the administrative record; (2) any other person may have electronic access to the full record at the courthouse, but may have remote electronic access only to: (A) the docket maintained by the court; and (B) an opinion, order, judgment, or other disposition of the court, but not any other part of the case file or the administrative record. FRCP 5.2(c).

d. *Filings made under seal.* The court may order that a filing be made under seal without redaction. The court may later unseal the filing or order the person who made the filing to file a redacted version for the public record. FRCP 5.2(d).

    i. *DISTRICT OF MAINE.* For information on filing sealed documents in the District of Maine, refer to ME R USDCT Rule 7A, ME R USDCT App. 4(p)(2), and ME R USDCT Sealed Filings.

e. *Protective orders.* For good cause, the court may by order in a case: (1) require redaction of additional information; or (2) limit or prohibit a nonparty's remote electronic access to a document filed with the court. FRCP 5.2(e).

f. *Option for additional unredacted filing under seal.* A person making a redacted filing may also file an unredacted copy under seal. The court must retain the unredacted copy as part of the record. FRCP 5.2(f).

    i. *DISTRICT OF MAINE.* A party wishing to file a document containing the personal data identifiers specified above may. . .file an unredacted document under seal. This document will be retained by the clerk's office as part of the record. ME R USDCT Redacting Pleadings. The court may, however, still require the party to file a redacted copy for the public file. ME R USDCT Redacting Pleadings.

g. *Option for filing a reference list.* A filing that contains redacted information may be filed together with a reference list that identifies each item of redacted information and specifies an appropriate identifier that uniquely corresponds to each item listed. The list must be filed under seal and may be amended as of right. Any reference in the case to a listed identifier will be construed to refer to the corresponding item of information. FRCP 5.2(g).

    i. *DISTRICT OF MAINE.* A party wishing to file a document containing the personal data identifiers specified above may. . .file a reference list under seal. The reference list shall contain the complete personal data identifier(s) and the redacted identifier(s) used in its (their) place in the filing. All references in the case to the redacted identifiers included in the reference list will be construed to refer to the corresponding complete identifier. The reference list must be filed under seal, and may be amended as of right. It shall be retained by the clerk's office as part of the record. ME R USDCT Redacting Pleadings. The court may, however, still require the party to file a redacted copy for the public file. ME R USDCT Redacting Pleadings.

h. *DISTRICT OF MAINE: Responsibility for redaction.* The clerk is not required to review documents filed with the court for compliance with FRCP 5.2. The responsibility to redact filings rests with counsel and the party or nonparty making the filing. ME R USDCT App. 4(i); ME R USDCT Redacting Pleadings. For guidelines for filing confidential information in civil cases in the District of Maine, refer to ME R USDCT Confidentiality.

i. *Waiver of protection of identifiers.* A person waives the protection of FRCP 5.2(a) as to the person's own information by filing it without redaction and not under seal. FRCP 5.2(h).

F. Filing and Service Requirements

1. *Filing requirements*

    a. *Required filings.* Any paper after the complaint that is required to be served must be filed no later than a reasonable time after service. FRCP 5(d)(1).

    b. *DISTRICT OF MAINE: Place of filing.* Unless otherwise ordered by the court, papers shall be filed with the court at Bangor in cases filed and pending at Bangor, and at Portland in cases filed and pending at Portland. ME R USDCT Rule 5(a).

    c. *Nonelectronic filing.* A paper not filed electronically is filed by delivering it: (A) to the clerk; or (B) to a judge who agrees to accept it for filing, and who must then note the filing date on the paper and promptly send it to the clerk. FRCP 5(d)(2).

        i. *DISTRICT OF MAINE: Documents to be filed in paper.* The following documents shall be filed in paper, which may also be scanned into ECF by the clerk's office: (A) all handwritten pleadings; and (B) all pleadings and documents filed by pro se litigants who are incarcerated or who are not registered filing users in ECF. ME R USDCT App. 4(g)(8). Non-prisoner pro se litigants in civil actions may register with ECF or may file (and serve) all pleadings and other documents in paper. The clerk's office will scan into ECF any pleadings and documents filed on paper in accordance with ME R USDCT App. 4(g). ME R USDCT App. 4(o). For more information, refer to ME R USDCT App. 4(g).

d. *Electronic filing*

    i. *DISTRICT OF MAINE: Authorization.* Unless exempt or otherwise ordered by the court, papers shall be filed and served electronically as required by the court's Administrative Procedures Governing the Filing and Service by Electronic Means, which is set forth in ME R USDCT App. 4. The provisions of the court's Administrative Procedures Governing the Filing and Service by Electronic Means (ME R USDCT App. 4) shall be applied and enforced as part of the Local Rules of the United States District Court for the District of Maine. ME R USDCT Rule 5(c).

    ii. *Filing by represented persons.* A person represented by an attorney must file electronically, unless nonelectronic filing is allowed by the court for good cause or is allowed or required by local rule. FRCP 5(d)(3)(A).

- *DISTRICT OF MAINE.* An attorney may apply to the court for permission to file paper documents. ME R USDCT App. 4(a)(5).

    iii. *Filing by unrepresented persons.* A person not represented by an attorney: (i) may file electronically only if allowed by court order or by local rule; and (ii) may be required to file electronically only by court order, or by a local rule that includes reasonable exceptions. FRCP 5(d)(3)(B).

- *DISTRICT OF MAINE.* Non-prisoner pro se litigants in civil actions may register with ECF or may file (and serve) all pleadings and other documents in paper. ME R USDCT App. 4(o). A non-prisoner who is a party to a civil action and who is not represented by an attorney may register to receive service electronically and to electronically transmit their documents to the court for filing in the ECF system. If during the course of the action the person retains an attorney who appears on the person's behalf, the clerk shall terminate the person's registration upon the attorney's appearance. ME R USDCT App. 4(b)(2).

    iv. *DISTRICT OF MAINE: Scope of electronic filing.* All documents submitted for filing in civil and criminal cases, regardless of case commencement date, except those documents specifically exempted in ME R USDCT App. 4(g), shall be filed electronically using the electronic case filing system (ECF). ME R USDCT App. 4(a)(1). For special filing requirements and exceptions, refer to ME R USDCT App. 4(g).

    v. *DISTRICT OF MAINE: Consequences of electronic filing.* Electronic transmission of a document to the ECF system, together with the transmission of a Notice of Electronic Filing (NEF) from the court, constitutes filing of the document for all purposes of the Federal Rules of Civil Procedure. ME R USDCT App. 4(d)(1).

    vi. *DISTRICT OF MAINE: Review of documents.* Documents filed with the clerk's office will normally be reviewed no later than the close of the next business day. It is the responsibility of the filing party to promptly notify the clerk's office via telephone of a matter that requires the immediate attention of a judicial officer. ME R USDCT App. 4(a)(4).

e. *DISTRICT OF MAINE: Facsimile filing.* No papers shall be submitted to the court by means of a facsimile machine without prior leave of the court. ME R USDCT Rule 5(c); ME R USDCT App. 4(m).

2. *Service requirements*

a. *Service; When required.* Unless the Federal Rules of Civil Procedure provide otherwise, each of the following papers must be served on every party: (A) an order stating that service is required; (B) a pleading filed after the original complaint, unless the court orders otherwise under FRCP 5(c) because there are numerous defendants; (C) a discovery paper required to be served on a party, unless the court orders otherwise; (D) a written motion, except one that may be heard ex parte; and (E) a written notice, appearance, demand, or offer of judgment, or any similar paper. FRCP 5(a)(1).

    i. *If a party fails to appear.* No service is required on a party who is in default for failing to appear. But a pleading that asserts a new claim for relief against such a party must be served on that party under FRCP 4. FRCP 5(a)(2).

    ii. *Seizing property.* If an action is begun by seizing property and no person is or need be named as a defendant, any service required before the filing of an appearance, answer, or claim must be made on the person who had custody or possession of the property when it was seized. FRCP 5(a)(3).

b. *Service; How made.* A paper is served under FRCP 5 by: (A) handing it to the person; (B) leaving it: (i) at the person's office with a clerk or other person in charge or, if no one is in charge, in a conspicuous place in the office; or (ii) if the person has no office or the office is closed, at the person's dwelling or usual place of abode with someone of suitable age and discretion who resides there; (C) mailing it to the person's last known address—in which event service is complete upon mailing; (D) leaving it with the court clerk if the person has no known address; (E) sending it to a registered user by filing it with the court's electronic-filing system or sending it by other electronic means that the person consented to in writing—in either of which events service is complete upon filing or sending, but is not effective if the filer or sender learns that it did not reach the person to be served; or (F) delivering it by any other means that the person consented to in writing—in which event service is complete when the person making service delivers it to the agency designated to make delivery. FRCP 5(b)(2).

    i.   *Serving an attorney.* If a party is represented by an attorney, service under FRCP 5 must be made on the attorney unless the court orders service on the party. FRCP 5(b)(1).

  c. *DISTRICT OF MAINE: Service of electronically filed documents*

    i.   *Registered users.* Registration [as a filing user of the court's ECF system] constitutes consent to service of all documents by electronic means as provided in ME R USDCT App. 4. ME R USDCT App. 4(b)(4). Whenever a non-sealed pleading is filed electronically, the ECF system will automatically generate and send a Notice of Electronic Filing (NEF) to the filing user and registered users of record. The user filing the document should retain a paper or digital copy of the NEF, which shall serve as the court's date-stamp and proof of filing. ME R USDCT App. 4(e)(1).

       ● *Sealed documents.* Although the filing of sealed documents in civil cases produces an NEF, the document itself cannot be accessed and counsel shall be responsible for making service of the sealed documents. ME R USDCT App. 4(e)(2).

    ii. *Non-registered users and pro se litigants.* Attorneys who have not yet registered as users with ECF and pro se litigants who have not registered with ECF shall be served a paper copy of any electronically filed pleading or other document in accordance with the provisions of FRCP 5. ME R USDCT App. 4(e)(3).

       ● *Registration of pro se litigants.* A non-prisoner who is a party to a civil action and who is not represented by an attorney may register to receive service electronically and to electronically transmit their documents to the court for filing in the ECF system. If during the course of the action the person retains an attorney who appears on the person's behalf, the clerk shall terminate the person's registration upon the attorney's appearance. ME R USDCT App. 4(b)(2).

  d. *Serving numerous defendants.* If an action involves an unusually large number of defendants, the court may, on motion or on its own, order that: (A) defendants' pleadings and replies to them need not be served on other defendants; (B) any crossclaim, counterclaim, avoidance, or affirmative defense in those pleadings and replies to them will be treated as denied or avoided by all other parties; and (C) filing any such pleading and serving it on the plaintiff constitutes notice of the pleading to all parties. FRCP 5(c)(1).

    i.   *Notifying parties.* A copy of every such order must be served on the parties as the court directs. FRCP 5(c)(2).

3. *DISTRICT OF MAINE: Filing and service of highly sensitive documents (HSDs).* For information on filing and serving highly sensitive documents (HSDs) in the District of Maine, refer to ME R USDCT General Order 21-5.

G. Hearings

1. *Hearings, generally.* When a motion relies on facts outside the record, the court may hear the matter on affidavits or may hear it wholly or partly on oral testimony or on depositions. FRCP 43(c).

  a. *Oral argument.* Due process does not require that oral argument be permitted on a motion and, except as otherwise provided by local rule, the district court has discretion to determine whether it will decide the motion on the papers or hear argument by counsel (and perhaps receive evidence). FPP § 1190; F.D.I.C. v. Deglau, 207 F.3d 153 (3d Cir. 2000).

    i.   *DISTRICT OF MAINE.* Unless otherwise required by federal rule or statute, all motions may be decided by the court without oral argument unless otherwise ordered by the court on its own motion or, in its discretion, upon request of counsel. ME R USDCT Rule 7(e).

  b. *Providing a regular schedule for oral hearings.* A court may establish regular times and places for oral hearings on motions. FRCP 78(a).

  c. *Providing for submission on briefs.* By rule or order, the court may provide for submitting and determining motions on briefs, without oral hearings. FRCP 78(b).

H. Forms

1. Federal Motion for Protective Order Forms

  a. Motion for protective order limiting scope of oral examination; Privileged material. 3A FEDFORMS § 21:39.

  b. Notice of motion and motion for protective order. 3A FEDFORMS § 21:41.

  c. Notice of motion and motion for protective order; Prohibiting taking of deposition. 3A FEDFORMS § 21:42.

d. Notice of motion and motion for protective order; To quash notice of taking deposition or for continuance; Late taking of deposition. 3A FEDFORMS § 21:43.

e. Motion for protective order limiting scope of oral examination. 3A FEDFORMS § 21:55.

f. Motion for protective order limiting examination upon written questions. 3A FEDFORMS § 21:59.

g. Notice of motion; For protective order; Preventing deposition of consultant and production of documents; Federal class action. AMJUR PP DEPOSITION § 334.

h. Motion; For protective order pending court's order on motion to quash deposition notice of plaintiff. AMJUR PP DEPOSITION § 341.

i. Motion; For protective order; To prevent deposition of consultant and production of documents; Federal class action. AMJUR PP DEPOSITION § 343.

j. Opposition; By plaintiffs; To motion by defendants for protective order; Prevention of deposition of consultant and production of documents; Federal class action. AMJUR PP DEPOSITION § 370.

k. Declaration; By plaintiffs' attorney; In support of opposition to defendants' motion for protective order; Federal class action. AMJUR PP DEPOSITION § 371.

l. Notice of motion; For protective order; To vacate notice to produce documents. AMJUR PP DEPOSITION § 592.

m. Notice of motion; For protective order; To limit scope of inspection of premises; Premises liability action; Objection to scope of request. AMJUR PP DEPOSITION § 593.

n. Motion; For protective order; Staying proceedings on production requests; Pending ruling on movant's dispositive motion. AMJUR PP DEPOSITION § 594.

o. Motion; For protective order; Limiting requests for production; Additional protection of trade secrets. AMJUR PP DEPOSITION § 595.

p. Answer; To motion for protective order. FEDPROF § 23:203.

q. Motion; For protective order; Limiting interrogatories. FEDPROF § 23:381.

r. Motion; For protective order; Staying proceedings on production requests. FEDPROF § 23:432.

s. Motion; For protective order; Limiting requests for production. FEDPROF § 23:433.

t. Motion; For protective order staying proceedings on request for admissions. FEDPROF § 23:585.

u. Notice of motion for protective order. GOLDLTGFMS § 31:2.

v. Motion for protective order; Federal form. GOLDLTGFMS § 31:5.

w. Motion for protective order; Deposition not to be taken. GOLDLTGFMS § 31:6.

x. Motion for protective order; Retaking depositions. GOLDLTGFMS § 31:7.

y. Motion for protective order; Certain matters shall not be inquired into. GOLDLTGFMS § 31:8.

z. Motion for protective order; To limit scope of examination. GOLDLTGFMS § 31:10.

2. **Forms for the District of Maine**

a. Form confidentiality order. ME R USDCT App. 2.

I. Applicable Rules

1. *Federal rules*

a. Serving and filing pleadings and other papers. FRCP 5.

b. Constitutional challenge to a statute; Notice, certification, and intervention. FRCP 5.1.

c. Privacy protection for filings made with the court. FRCP 5.2.

d. Computing and extending time; Time for motion papers. FRCP 6.

e. Pleadings allowed; Form of motions and other papers. FRCP 7.

f. Disclosure statement. FRCP 7.1.

g. Form of pleadings. FRCP 10.

h. Signing pleadings, motions, and other papers; Representations to the court; Sanctions. FRCP 11.

i. Duty to disclose; General provisions governing discovery. FRCP 26.

j. Taking testimony. FRCP 43.

k. Hearing motions; Submission on briefs. FRCP 78.

2. *Local rules*

a. *DISTRICT OF MAINE*

i. Service and filing of pleadings and other papers. ME R USDCT Rule 5.

ii. Time. ME R USDCT Rule 6.

iii. Motions and memoranda of law. ME R USDCT Rule 7.

iv. Corporate disclosure. ME R USDCT Rule 7.1.

v. Form of pleadings, motions and other papers. ME R USDCT Rule 10.

vi. Discovery. ME R USDCT Rule 26.

vii. Attorneys; Appearances and withdrawals. ME R USDCT Rule 83.2.

viii. Alternative dispute resolution (ADR). ME R USDCT Rule 83.11.

ix. Administrative procedures governing the filing and service by electronic means. ME R USDCT App. 4.

x. Redacting pleadings. ME R USDCT Redacting Pleadings.

Motions, Oppositions and Replies
Motion for Discovery Sanctions

Document Last Updated April 2021

A. Checklist

(I) ❑ Matters to be considered by moving party

(a) ❑ Required documents

(1) ❑ Notice of motion and motion

(b) ❑ Supplemental documents

(1) ❑ Supporting evidence

(2) ❑ Notice of constitutional question

(3) ❑ DISTRICT OF MAINE: Additional supplemental documents

(i) ❑ Proposed order

(c) ❑ Timing

(1) ❑ There are no specific timing requirements in the Federal Rules of Civil Procedure for moving for discovery sanctions

(2) ❑ A written motion and notice of the hearing must be served at least fourteen (14) days before the time specified for the hearing, with the following exceptions: (A) when the motion may be heard ex parte; (B) when the Federal Rules of Civil Procedure set a different time; or (C) when a court order—which a party may, for good cause, apply for ex parte—sets a different time

(3) ❑ Any affidavit supporting a motion must be served with the motion

(4) ❑ DISTRICT OF MAINE: Additional timing

(i) ❑ Any affidavits and other documents setting forth or evidencing facts on which the motion is based must be filed with the motion

(II) ❑ Matters to be considered by opposing party

(a) ❑ Required documents

(1) ❑ Opposition

(b) ❑ Supplemental documents

    (1) ❑ Supporting evidence

    (2) ❑ Notice of constitutional question

(c) ❑ Timing

    (1) ❑ Except as FRCP 59(c) provides otherwise, any opposing affidavit must be served at least seven (7) days before the hearing, unless the court permits service at another time

    (2) ❑ DISTRICT OF MAINE: Additional timing

        (i) ❑ Unless within twenty-one (21) days after the filing of a motion the opposing party files written objection thereto, incorporating a memorandum of law, the opposing party shall be deemed to have waived objection

B. Timing

1. *Motion for discovery sanctions.* There are no specific timing requirements in the Federal Rules of Civil Procedure for moving for discovery sanctions.

2. *Timing of motions, generally*

    a. *Motion and notice of hearing.* A written motion and notice of the hearing must be served at least fourteen (14) days before the time specified for the hearing, with the following exceptions: (A) when the motion may be heard ex parte; (B) when the Federal Rules of Civil Procedure set a different time; or (C) when a court order—which a party may, for good cause, apply for ex parte—sets a different time. FRCP 6(c)(1).

    b. *Supporting affidavit.* Any affidavit supporting a motion must be served with the motion. FRCP 6(c)(2).

    c. *DISTRICT OF MAINE: Affidavits and other supporting documents.* Any affidavits and other documents setting forth or evidencing facts on which the motion is based must be filed with the motion. ME R USDCT Rule 7(a).

3. *Timing of opposing papers.* Except as FRCP 59(c) provides otherwise, any opposing affidavit must be served at least seven (7) days before the hearing, unless the court permits service at another time. FRCP 6(c)(2).

    a. *DISTRICT OF MAINE.* Unless within twenty-one (21) days after the filing of a motion the opposing party files written objection thereto, incorporating a memorandum of law, the opposing party shall be deemed to have waived objection. ME R USDCT Rule 7(b). The deemed waiver imposed in ME R USDCT Rule 7(b) shall not apply to motions filed during trial. ME R USDCT Rule 7(b).

4. *Timing of reply papers.* Where the respondent files an answering affidavit setting up a new matter, the moving party ordinarily is allowed a reasonable time to file a reply affidavit since failure to deny the new matter by affidavit may operate as an admission of its truth. AMJUR MOTIONS § 25.

    a. *DISTRICT OF MAINE.* Within fourteen (14) days of the filing of any objection to a motion, the moving party may file a reply memorandum. ME R USDCT Rule 7(c).

5. *Computation of time*

    a. *Computing time.* FRCP 6 applies in computing any time period specified in the Federal Rules of Civil Procedure, in any local rule or court order, or in any statute that does not specify a method of computing time. FRCP 6(a).

        i. *Period stated in days or a longer unit.* When the period is stated in days or a longer unit of time: (A) exclude the day of the event that triggers the period; (B) count every day, including intermediate Saturdays, Sundays, and legal holidays; and (C) include the last day of the period, but if the last day is a Saturday, Sunday, or legal holiday, the period continues to run until the end of the next day that is not a Saturday, Sunday, or legal holiday. FRCP 6(a)(1).

        ii. *Period stated in hours.* When the period is stated in hours: (A) begin counting immediately on the occurrence of the event that triggers the period; (B) count every hour, including hours during intermediate Saturdays, Sundays, and legal holidays; and (C) if the period would end on a Saturday, Sunday, or legal holiday, the period continues to run until the same time on the next day that is not a Saturday, Sunday, or legal holiday. FRCP 6(a)(2).

        iii. *Inaccessibility of the clerk's office.* Unless the court orders otherwise, if the clerk's office is inaccessible: (A) on the last day for filing under FRCP 6(a)(1), then the time for filing is extended to the first accessible day that is not a Saturday, Sunday, or legal holiday; or (B) during the last hour for filing under FRCP 6(a)(2), then the time for filing is extended to the same time on the first accessible day that is not a Saturday, Sunday, or legal holiday. FRCP 6(a)(3).

iv. *"Last day" defined.* Unless a different time is set by a statute, local rule, or court order, the last day ends: (A) for electronic filing, at midnight in the court's time zone; and (B) for filing by other means, when the clerk's office is scheduled to close. FRCP 6(a)(4).

v. *"Next day" defined.* The "next day" is determined by continuing to count forward when the period is measured after an event and backward when measured before an event. FRCP 6(a)(5).

vi. *"Legal holiday" defined.* "Legal holiday" means: (A) the day set aside by statute for observing New Year's Day, Martin Luther King Jr.'s Birthday, Washington's Birthday, Memorial Day, Independence Day, Labor Day, Columbus Day, Veterans' Day, Thanksgiving Day, or Christmas Day; (B) any day declared a holiday by the President or Congress; and (C) for periods that are measured after an event, any other day declared a holiday by the state where the district court is located. FRCP 6(a)(6).

vii. *DISTRICT OF MAINE: Applicability of FRCP 6.* FRCP 6 applies when computing any period of time stated in the Local Rules of the United States District Court for the District of Maine. ME R USDCT Rule 6(a).

b. *DISTRICT OF MAINE: Computation of electronic filing deadlines.* Filing documents electronically does not in any way alter any filing deadlines. All electronic transmissions of documents must be completed prior to midnight, Eastern Time, in order to be considered timely filed that day. Where a specific time of day deadline is set by court order or stipulation, the electronic filing must be completed by that time. ME R USDCT App. 4(f). A document filed electronically shall be deemed filed at the time and date stated on the Notice of Electronic Filing received from the court. ME R USDCT App. 4(d)(2).

i. *Technical failures.* A filing user whose filing is made untimely as the result of a technical failure may seek appropriate relief from the court. ME R USDCT App. 4(n). A technical failure of the court's ECF system is deemed to have occurred when the court's ECF site cannot accept filings continuously or intermittently over the course of any period of time greater than one (1) hour. Known system outages will be posted on the court's website along with guidance on how to proceed, if applicable. ME R USDCT App. 4(n).

c. *Extending time.* When an act may or must be done within a specified time, the court may, for good cause, extend the time: (A) with or without motion or notice if the court acts, or if a request is made, before the original time or its extension expires; or (B) on motion made after the time has expired if the party failed to act because of excusable neglect. FRCP 6(b)(1). A court must not extend the time to act under FRCP 50(b), FRCP 50(d), FRCP 52(b), FRCP 59(b), FRCP 59(d), FRCP 59(e), and FRCP 60(b). FRCP 6(b)(2). Refer to the United States District Court for the District of Maine KeyRules Motion for Continuance/Extension of Time document for more information on extending time.

d. *Additional time after certain kinds of service.* When a party may or must act within a specified time after being served and service is made under FRCP 5(b)(2)(C) (by mail), FRCP 5(b)(2)(D) (by leaving with the clerk), or FRCP 5(b)(2)(F) (by other means consented to), three (3) days are added after the period would otherwise expire under FRCP 6(a). FRCP 6(d).

C. General Requirements

1. *Motions, generally*

a. *Motion requirements.* A request for a court order must be made by motion. The motion must: (A) be in writing unless made during a hearing or trial; (B) state with particularity the grounds for seeking the order; and (C) state the relief sought. FRCP 7(b)(1). The writing and particularity requirements are intended to ensure that the adverse parties are informed of and have a record of both the motion's pendency and the grounds on which the movant seeks an order. FPP § 1191; Feldberg v. Quechee Lakes Corp., 463 F.3d 195 (2d Cir. 2006).

i. *Particularity requirement.* The particularity requirement [ensures] that the opposing parties will have notice of their opponent's contentions. FEDPROC § 62:358; Goodman v. 1973 26 Foot Trojan Vessel, Arkansas Registration No. AR1439SN, 859 F.2d 71 (8th Cir. 1988). That requirement ensures that notice of the basis for the motion is provided to the court and to the opposing party so as to avoid prejudice, provide the opponent with a meaningful opportunity to respond, and provide the court with enough information to process the motion correctly. FEDPROC § 62:358; Andreas v. Volkswagen of Am., Inc., 336 F.3d 789 (8th Cir. 2003).

- Reasonable specification of the grounds for a motion is sufficient. The particularity requirement for motions is satisfied when no party is prejudiced by a lack of particularity or when the court can comprehend the basis for the motion and deal with it fairly. However, where a movant fails to state even one ground for granting the motion in question, the movant has failed to meet the minimal standard of "reasonable specification." FEDPROC § 62:358; Martinez v. Trainor, 556 F.2d 818 (7th Cir. 1977).

- The court may excuse the failure to comply with the particularity requirement if it is inadvertent, and where no prejudice is shown by the opposing party. FEDPROC § 62:358.

b. *Notice of motion.* A party interested in resisting the relief sought by a motion has a right to notice thereof, and an opportunity to be heard. AMJUR MOTIONS § 12.

    i. *Purpose.* In addition to statutory or court rule provisions requiring notice of a motion—the purpose of such a notice requirement having been said to be to prevent a party from being prejudicially surprised by a motion—principles of natural justice dictate that an adverse party generally must be given notice that a motion will be presented to the court. AMJUR MOTIONS § 12.

    ii. *Adequacy of notice.* The test of adequate notice generally turns on whether the other parties were afforded an adequate opportunity to prepare and respond to the issues to be raised in the proceeding. AMJUR MOTIONS § 12.

c. *Single document containing motion and notice.* A single written document can satisfy the writing requirements both for a motion and for an FRCP 6(c)(1) notice. FRCP 7(Advisory Committee Notes).

2. *DISTRICT OF MAINE: Procedure for discovery disputes*

a. *Prior approval required.* No written discovery motions shall be filed without the prior approval of a judicial officer. ME R USDCT Rule 7(a); ME R USDCT Rule 26(b).

b. *Conference with opposing counsel.* A party with a discovery dispute must first confer with the opposing party in a good faith effort to resolve by agreement the issues in dispute. If that good faith effort is unsuccessful, the moving party shall file a Request for Hearing Re Discovery Dispute using the court's form seeking a prompt hearing with a judicial officer by telephone or in person. The party seeking the hearing shall confer with opposing counsel and agree on the relevant discovery materials that should be submitted to the court with the Request for Hearing. ME R USDCT Rule 26(b).

c. *Hearing on discovery dispute.* If the hearing is to be conducted by telephone, the clerk will inform counsel of the time and date of the hearing and it shall be the responsibility of the moving party to initiate the telephone call to chambers, unless the court, in its discretion, directs otherwise. The recording by counsel of telephone hearings with the court is prohibited, except with prior permission of the court. The court shall conduct the hearing on the record, but that record will not be officially transcribed except on specific request of counsel or the court. The request for a hearing with a judicial officer carries with it a professional representation by the lawyer that a conference has taken place and that he or she has made a good faith effort to resolve the dispute. The lawyers or unrepresented parties shall supply the judicial officer with the particular discovery materials (such as objectionable answers to interrogatories) that are needed to understand the dispute. ME R USDCT Rule 26(b).

d. *Filing of motion papers and supporting memoranda.* If the judicial officer decides that motion papers and supporting memoranda are needed to satisfactorily resolve the discovery dispute, such papers shall be filed in conformity with ME R USDCT Rule 7. Such motions shall (1) quote in full each interrogatory, question at deposition, request for admission or request for production to which the motion is addressed, or otherwise identify specifically and succinctly the discovery to which objection is taken or from which a protective order is sought; and (2) the response or objection and grounds therefor, if any, as stated by the opposing party. ME R USDCT Rule 26(b). Unless otherwise ordered by the court, the complete transcripts or discovery papers need not be filed with the court pursuant to ME R USDCT Rule 26(c) unless the motion cannot be fairly decided without reference to the complete original. ME R USDCT Rule 26(b).

3. *Motion for discovery sanctions*

a. *Sanctions, generally.* FRCP 37 is flexible. The court is directed to make such orders as are "just" and is not limited in any case of disregard of the discovery rules or court orders under them to a stereotyped response. The sanctions enumerated in FRCP 37 are not exclusive and arbitrary but flexible, selective, and plural. The district court may, within reason, use as many and as varied sanctions as are necessary to hold the scales of justice even. FPP § 2284.

    i. *Fixed limitation.* There is one fixed limitation that should be noted. A party may not be imprisoned or otherwise punished for contempt of court for failure to submit to a physical or mental examination, or for failure to produce a person in his or her custody or under his or her control for such an examination. FPP § 2284; Sibbach v. Wilson & Co., 312 U.S. 1, 312 U.S. 655, 61 S. Ct. 422, 85 L. Ed. 479 (1941).

    ii. *Court discretion.* Although FRCP 37 is very broad, and the courts have considerable discretion in imposing sanctions as authorized by FRCP 37, there are constitutional limits, stemming from the Due Process Clause of

U.S.C.A. Const. Amend. V and U.S.C.A. Const. Amend. XIV, on the imposition of sanctions. There are two principal facets of the due process issues:

- First, the court must ask whether there is a sufficient relationship between the discovery and the merits sought to be foreclosed by the sanction to legitimate depriving a party of the opportunity to litigate the merits. FPP § 2283.

- Second, before imposing a serious merits sanction the court should determine whether the party guilty of a failure to provide discovery was unable to comply with the discovery. FPP § 2283.

b. *Sanction for improper certification.* If a certification violates FRCP 26(g) without substantial justification, the court, on motion or on its own, must impose an appropriate sanction on the signer, the party on whose behalf the signer was acting, or both. The sanction may include an order to pay the reasonable expenses, including attorney's fees, caused by the violation. FRCP 26(g)(3).

c. *Motion to compel discovery; Payment of expenses; Protective orders*

   i. *If the motion is granted (or disclosure or discovery is provided after filing).* If the motion is granted—or if the disclosure or requested discovery is provided after the motion was filed—the court must, after giving an opportunity to be heard, require the party or deponent whose conduct necessitated the motion, the party or attorney advising that conduct, or both to pay the movant's reasonable expenses incurred in making the motion, including attorney's fees. But the court must not order this payment if: (i) the movant filed the motion before attempting in good faith to obtain the disclosure or discovery without court action; (ii) the opposing party's nondisclosure, response, or objection was substantially justified; or (iii) other circumstances make an award of expenses unjust. FRCP 37(a)(5)(A).

   ii. *If the motion is denied.* If the motion is denied, the court may issue any protective order authorized under FRCP 26(c) and must, after giving an opportunity to be heard, require the movant, the attorney filing the motion, or both to pay the party or deponent who opposed the motion its reasonable expenses incurred in opposing the motion, including attorney's fees. But the court must not order this payment if the motion was substantially justified or other circumstances make an award of expenses unjust. FRCP 37(a)(5)(B).

   iii. *If the motion is granted in part and denied in part.* If the motion is granted in part and denied in part, the court may issue any protective order authorized under FRCP 26(c) and may, after giving an opportunity to be heard, apportion the reasonable expenses for the motion. FRCP 37(a)(5)(C).

d. *Failure to comply with a court order*

   i. *Sanctions in the district where the deposition is taken.* If the court where the discovery is taken orders a deponent to be sworn or to answer a question and the deponent fails to obey, the failure may be treated as contempt of court. If a deposition-related motion is transferred to the court where the action is pending, and that court orders a deponent to be sworn or to answer a question and the deponent fails to obey, the failure may be treated as contempt of either the court where the discovery is taken or the court where the action is pending. FRCP 37(b)(1).

   ii. *Sanctions in the district where the action is pending; For not obeying a discovery order.* If a party or a party's officer, director, or managing agent—or a witness designated under FRCP 30(b)(6) or FRCP 31(a)(4)—fails to obey an order to provide or permit discovery, including an order under FRCP 26(f), FRCP 35, or FRCP 37(a), the court where the action is pending may issue further just orders. They may include the following: (i) directing that the matters embraced in the order or other designated facts be taken as established for purposes of the action, as the prevailing party claims; (ii) prohibiting the disobedient party from supporting or opposing designated claims or defenses, or from introducing designated matters in evidence; (iii) striking pleadings in whole or in part; (iv) staying further proceedings until the order is obeyed; (v) dismissing the action or proceeding in whole or in part; (vi) rendering a default judgment against the disobedient party; or (vii) treating as contempt of court the failure to obey any order except an order to submit to a physical or mental examination. FRCP 37(b)(2)(A).

   iii. *Sanctions in the district where the action is pending; For not producing a person for examination.* If a party fails to comply with an order under FRCP 35(a) requiring it to produce another person for examination, the court may issue any of the orders listed in FRCP 37(b)(2)(A)(i) through FRCP 37(b)(2)(A)(vi), unless the disobedient party shows that it cannot produce the other person. FRCP 37(b)(2)(B).

   iv. *Sanctions in the district where the action is pending; Payment of expenses.* Instead of or in addition to the orders in FRCP 37(b)(2)(A) and FRCP 37(b)(2)(B), the court must order the disobedient party, the attorney advising that party, or both to pay the reasonable expenses, including attorney's fees, caused by the failure, unless the failure was substantially justified or other circumstances make an award of expenses unjust. FRCP 37(b)(2)(C).

e. *Failure to disclose, to supplement an earlier response, or to admit*

    i. *Failure to disclose or supplement.* If a party fails to provide information or identify a witness as required by FRCP 26(a) or FRCP 26(e), the party is not allowed to use that information or witness to supply evidence on a motion, at a hearing, or at a trial, unless the failure was substantially justified or is harmless. In addition to or instead of this sanction, the court, on motion and after giving an opportunity to be heard: (A) may order payment of the reasonable expenses, including attorney's fees, caused by the failure; (B) may inform the jury of the party's failure; and (C) may impose other appropriate sanctions, including any of the orders listed in FRCP 37(b)(2)(A)(i) through FRCP 37(b)(2)(A)(vi). FRCP 37(c)(1).

    ii. *Failure to admit.* If a party fails to admit what is requested under FRCP 36 and if the requesting party later proves a document to be genuine or the matter true, the requesting party may move that the party who failed to admit pay the reasonable expenses, including attorney's fees, incurred in making that proof. The court must so order unless: (A) the request was held objectionable under FRCP 36(a); (B) the admission sought was of no substantial importance; (C) the party failing to admit had a reasonable ground to believe that it might prevail on the matter; or (D) there was other good reason for the failure to admit. FRCP 37(c)(2).

f. *Party's failure to attend its own deposition, serve answers to interrogatories, or respond to a request for inspection*

    i. *Motion; Grounds for sanctions.* The court where the action is pending may, on motion, order sanctions if: (i) a party or a party's officer, director, or managing agent—or a person designated under FRCP 30(b)(6) or FRCP 31(a)(4)—fails, after being served with proper notice, to appear for that person's deposition; or (ii) a party, after being properly served with interrogatories under FRCP 33 or a request for inspection under FRCP 34, fails to serve its answers, objections, or written response. FRCP 37(d)(1)(A).

    ii. *Unacceptable excuse for failing to act.* A failure described in FRCP 37(d)(1)(A) is not excused on the ground that the discovery sought was objectionable, unless the party failing to act has a pending motion for a protective order under FRCP 26(c). FRCP 37(d)(2).

    iii. *Types of sanctions.* Sanctions may include any of the orders listed in FRCP 37(b)(2)(A)(i) through FRCP 37(b)(2)(A)(vi). Instead of or in addition to these sanctions, the court must require the party failing to act, the attorney advising that party, or both to pay the reasonable expenses, including attorney's fees, caused by the failure, unless the failure was substantially justified or other circumstances make an award of expenses unjust. FRCP 37(d)(3).

g. *Failure to provide electronically stored information.* If electronically stored information that should have been preserved in the anticipation or conduct of litigation is lost because a party failed to take reasonable steps to preserve it, and it cannot be restored or replaced through additional discovery, the court: (1) upon finding prejudice to another party from loss of the information, may order measures no greater than necessary to cure the prejudice; or (2) only upon finding that the party acted with the intent to deprive another party of the information's use in the litigation may: (A) presume that the lost information was unfavorable to the party; (B) instruct the jury that it may or must presume the information was unfavorable to the party; or (C) dismiss the action or enter a default judgment. FRCP 37(e).

h. *Failure to participate in framing a discovery plan.* If a party or its attorney fails to participate in good faith in developing and submitting a proposed discovery plan as required by FRCP 26(f), the court may, after giving an opportunity to be heard, require that party or attorney to pay to any other party the reasonable expenses, including attorney's fees, caused by the failure. FRCP 37(f).

i. *Counsel's liability for excessive costs.* 28 U.S.C.A. § 1927 is a basis for sanctioning attorney misconduct in discovery proceedings, DISCPROFED § 22:3. Any attorney or other person admitted to conduct cases in any court of the United States or any Territory thereof who so multiplies the proceedings in any case unreasonably and vexatiously may be required by the court to satisfy personally the excess costs, expenses, and attorneys' fees reasonably incurred because of such conduct. 28 U.S.C.A. § 1927.

4. *Opposing papers.* The Federal Rules of Civil Procedure do not require any formal answer, return, or reply to a motion, except where the Federal Rules of Civil Procedure or local rules may require affidavits, memoranda, or other papers to be filed in opposition to a motion. Such papers are simply to apprise the court of such opposition and the grounds of that opposition. FEDPROC § 62:353.

    a. *DISTRICT OF MAINE: Content of objections.* Any objections shall include citations and supporting authorities and affidavits and other documents setting forth or evidencing facts on which the objection is based. ME R USDCT Rule 7(b).

    b. *Effect of failure to respond to motion.* Although in the absence of statutory provision or court rule, a motion ordinarily does not require a response or written answer, when a party files a motion and the opposing party fails to respond, the court may construe such failure to respond as nonopposition to the motion or an admission that the motion was meritorious. AMJUR MOTIONS § 28. The rule in some jurisdictions being that the failure to respond to a fact set forth in a motion is deemed an admission—and may grant the motion if the relief requested appears to be justified. AMJUR MOTIONS § 28.

    c. *Assent or no opposition not determinative.* However, a motion will not be granted automatically simply because an "assent" or a notation of "no opposition" has been filed; federal judges frequently deny motions that have been assented to when it is thought that justice so dictates. FPP § 1190.

    d. *Responsive pleading inappropriate as response to motion.* An attempt to answer or oppose a motion with a responsive pleading usually is not appropriate. FPP § 1190.

5. *Reply papers.* A moving party may be required or permitted to prepare papers in addition to its original motion papers. AMJUR MOTIONS § 25. Papers answering or replying to opposing papers may be appropriate, in the interests of justice, where it appears there is a substantial reason for allowing a reply. Thus, a court may accept reply papers where a party demonstrates that the papers to which it seeks to file a reply raise new issues that are material to the disposition of the question before the court, or where the court determines, sua sponte, that it wishes further briefing of an issue raised in those papers and orders the submission of additional papers. FEDPROC § 62:354.

    a. *Function of reply papers.* The function of a reply affidavit or reply papers is to answer the arguments made in opposition to the position taken by the movant, not to raise new issues, arguments, or evidence, or change the nature of the primary motion. However, if the court permits new evidence with the reply papers, the other party should be given the opportunity to respond. Where the party opposing the motion has no opportunity to address the argument in writing, a court has the discretion to disregard arguments raised for the first time in a reply memorandum. Also, the view has been followed in some jurisdictions that as a matter of judicial economy, where there is no prejudice and where the issues could be raised simply by filing a motion to dismiss, the trial court has discretion to consider arguments raised for the first time in a reply memorandum, and that a trial court may grant a motion to strike issues raised for the first time in a reply memorandum. AMJUR MOTIONS § 26.

        i. *DISTRICT OF MAINE.* The moving party may file a reply memorandum. . .which shall be strictly confined to replying to new matter raised in the objection or opposing memorandum. ME R USDCT Rule 7(c).

6. *DISTRICT OF MAINE: Appearances.* An attorney's signature to a pleading shall constitute an appearance for the party filing the pleading. Otherwise, an attorney who wishes to participate in any manner in any action must file a formal written appearance identifying the party represented. An appearance whether by pleading or formal written appearance shall be signed by an attorney in his/her individual name and shall state his/her office address. ME R USDCT Rule 83.2(a). For more information, refer to ME R USDCT Rule 83.2.

7. *DISTRICT OF MAINE: Alternative dispute resolution (ADR).* Litigants are authorized and encouraged to employ, at their own expense, any available ADR process on which they can agree, including early neutral evaluation, settlement conferences, mediation, non-binding summary jury trial, corporate mini-trial, and arbitration proceedings. ME R USDCT Rule 83.11(a). For more information on ADR, refer to ME R USDCT Rule 83.11.

D. Documents

1. *Documents for moving party*

    a. *Required documents*

        i. *Notice of motion and motion.* Refer to the "C. General Requirements" section of this KeyRules document for information on the notice of motion and motion.

            • *DISTRICT OF MAINE: Memorandum of law.* Every motion shall incorporate a memorandum of law, including citations and supporting authorities. ME R USDCT Rule 7(a). Refer to the "E. Format" section of this KeyRules document for the form of memoranda of law.

            • *Certificate of compliance.* A motion for sanctions for failing to answer or respond must include a certification that the movant has in good faith conferred or attempted to confer with the party failing to act in an effort to obtain the answer or response without court action. FRCP 37(d)(1)(B).

            • *Certificate of service.* No certificate of service is required when a paper is served by filing it with the court's electronic-filing system. When a paper that is required to be served is served by other means: (i) if the paper is filed, a certificate of service must be filed with it or within a reasonable time after service; and (ii) if the paper is not filed, a certificate of service need not be filed unless filing is required by court order or by local rule. FRCP 5(d)(1)(B).

b. *Supplemental documents*

  i. *Supporting evidence.* When a motion relies on facts outside the record, the court may hear the matter on affidavits or may hear it wholly or partly on oral testimony or on depositions. FRCP 43(c).

- *DISTRICT OF MAINE: Affidavits and other supporting documents.* Any affidavits and other documents setting forth or evidencing facts on which the motion is based must be filed with the motion. ME R USDCT Rule 7(a).

- *DISTRICT OF MAINE: Discovery transcripts or materials.* A party relying on discovery transcripts or materials in support of or in opposition to a motion shall file excerpts of such transcript or materials with the memorandum required by ME R USDCT Rule 7 as well as a list of specific citations to the parts on which the party relies. ME R USDCT Rule 26(c). Excerpts of depositions in support of or in opposition to a motion shall be filed electronically using ECF, unless otherwise permitted by the court. ME R USDCT App. 4(l)(3).

  ii. *Notice of constitutional question.* A party that files a pleading, written motion, or other paper drawing into question the constitutionality of a federal or state statute must promptly: (1) file a notice of constitutional question stating the question and identifying the paper that raises it, if: (A) a federal statute is questioned and the parties do not include the United States, one of its agencies, or one of its officers or employees in an official capacity; or (B) a state statute is questioned and the parties do not include the state, one of its agencies, or one of its officers or employees in an official capacity; and (2) serve the notice and paper on the Attorney General of the United States if a federal statute is questioned—or on the state attorney general if a state statute is questioned—either by certified or registered mail or by sending it to an electronic address designated by the attorney general for this purpose. FRCP 5.1(a).

- *No forfeiture.* A party's failure to file and serve the notice, or the court's failure to certify, does not forfeit a constitutional claim or defense that is otherwise timely asserted. FRCP 5.1(d).

  iii. *DISTRICT OF MAINE: Additional supplemental documents*

- *Proposed order.* Proposed orders shall not be filed unless requested by the court. When requested by the court, proposed orders shall be filed by e-mail in word processing format. ME R USDCT App. 4(k)(1).

2. *Documents for opposing party*

 a. *Required documents*

  i. *Opposition.* Refer to the "C. General Requirements" section of this KeyRules document for information on the opposing papers.

- *DISTRICT OF MAINE: Memorandum of law.* Unless within twenty-one (21) days after the filing of a motion the opposing party files written objection thereto, incorporating a memorandum of law, the opposing party shall be deemed to have waived objection. ME R USDCT Rule 7(b).

- *Certificate of service.* No certificate of service is required when a paper is served by filing it with the court's electronic-filing system. When a paper that is required to be served is served by other means: (i) if the paper is filed, a certificate of service must be filed with it or within a reasonable time after service; and (ii) if the paper is not filed, a certificate of service need not be filed unless filing is required by court order or by local rule. FRCP 5(d)(1)(B).

 b. *Supplemental documents*

  i. *Supporting evidence.* When a motion relies on facts outside the record, the court may hear the matter on affidavits or may hear it wholly or partly on oral testimony or on depositions. FRCP 43(c).

- *DISTRICT OF MAINE: Affidavits and other supporting documents.* Any objections shall include. . .affidavits and other documents setting forth or evidencing facts on which the objection is based. ME R USDCT Rule 7(b).

- *DISTRICT OF MAINE: Discovery transcripts or materials.* A party relying on discovery transcripts or materials in support of or in opposition to a motion shall file excerpts of such transcript or materials with the memorandum required by ME R USDCT Rule 7 as well as a list of specific citations to the parts on which the party relies. ME R USDCT Rule 26(c). Excerpts of depositions in support of or in opposition to a motion shall be filed electronically using ECF, unless otherwise permitted by the court. ME R USDCT App. 4(l)(3).

  ii. *Notice of constitutional question.* A party that files a pleading, written motion, or other paper drawing into question the constitutionality of a federal or state statute must promptly: (1) file a notice of constitutional question stating the question and identifying the paper that raises it, if: (A) a federal statute is questioned and the parties do not include the United States, one of its agencies, or one of its officers or employees in an official capacity; or (B) a state statute is questioned and the parties do not include the state, one of its agencies, or one of its officers or employees in an official capacity; and (2) serve the notice and paper on the Attorney General of the United States if a federal statute is questioned—or on the state attorney general if a state statute is questioned—either by certified or registered mail or by sending it to an electronic address designated by the attorney general for this purpose. FRCP 5.1(a).

- *No forfeiture.* A party's failure to file and serve the notice, or the court's failure to certify, does not forfeit a constitutional claim or defense that is otherwise timely asserted. FRCP 5.1(d).

E. Format

1. *Form of documents.* The rules governing captions and other matters of form in pleadings apply to motions and other papers. FRCP 7(b)(2).

   a. *DISTRICT OF MAINE: Font size, line spacing, and paper size.* All such documents shall be typed in a font of no less than size twelve (12) point, and shall be double-spaced or printed on eight and one-half by eleven (8-1/2 x 11) inch paper. Footnotes shall be in a font of no less than size ten (10) point, and may be single spaced. ME R USDCT Rule 10.

   b. *Caption.* Every pleading must have a caption with the court's name, a title, a file number, and an FRCP 7(a) designation. FRCP 10(a).

      i. *Names of parties.* The title of the complaint must name all the parties; the title of other pleadings, after naming the first party on each side, may refer generally to other parties. FRCP 10(a).

      ii. *DISTRICT OF MAINE: Additional caption requirements.* All pleadings, motions and other papers filed with the clerk or otherwise submitted to the court, except exhibits, shall bear the proper case number and shall contain on the first page a caption as described by FRCP 10(a) and immediately thereunder a designation of what the document is and the name of the party in whose behalf it is submitted. ME R USDCT Rule 10.

   c. *Claims or defenses*

      i. *Numbered paragraphs.* A party must state its claims or defenses in numbered paragraphs, each limited as far as practicable to a single set of circumstances. A later pleading may refer by number to a paragraph in an earlier pleading. FRCP 10(b).

      ii. *Separate statements.* If doing so would promote clarity, each claim founded on a separate transaction or occurrence—and each defense other than a denial—must be stated in a separate count or defense. FRCP 10(b).

   d. *Adoption by reference.* A statement in a pleading may be adopted by reference elsewhere in the same pleading or in any other pleading or motion. FRCP 10(c).

      i. *Exhibits.* A copy of a written instrument that is an exhibit to a pleading is a part of the pleading for all purposes. FRCP 10(c).

   e. *DISTRICT OF MAINE: Page numbering.* All pages shall be numbered at the bottom. ME R USDCT Rule 10.

   f. *DISTRICT OF MAINE: Attachment of ancillary papers.* Ancillary papers shall be attached at the end of the document to which they relate. ME R USDCT Rule 10.

   g. *Acceptance by the clerk.* The clerk must not refuse to file a paper solely because it is not in the form prescribed by the Federal Rules of Civil Procedure or by a local rule or practice. FRCP 5(d)(4).

2. *Form of electronic documents.* A paper filed electronically is a written paper for purposes of the Federal Rules of Civil Procedure. FRCP 5(d)(3)(D).

   a. *DISTRICT OF MAINE: Document format.* The ECF system only accepts documents in a portable document format (PDF). Although there are two types of PDF documents—electronically converted PDF's and scanned PDF's—only electronically converted PDF's may be filed with the court using the ECF system, unless otherwise authorized by local rule or order. ME R USDCT App. 4. Any document or exhibit to be filed or submitted to the court shall not be password-protected or encrypted. ME R USDCT App. 4(g)(12).

      i. *Electronically converted PDFs.* Electronically converted PDF's are created from word processing documents (MS Word, WordPerfect, etc.) using Adobe Acrobat or similar software. They are text searchable and their file size is small. ME R USDCT App. 4. Software used to electronically convert documents to PDF which includes proprietary or advertisement information within the PDF document is prohibited. ME R USDCT App. 4.

    ii.   *Scanned PDFs.* Scanned PDF's are created from paper documents run through an optical scanner. Scanned PDF's are not searchable and have a large file size. ME R USDCT App. 4.

  b. *DISTRICT OF MAINE: Title.* All pleadings filed electronically shall be titled in accordance with the approved dictionary of civil or criminal events of the ECF system of the United States District Court for the District of Maine. ME R USDCT App. 4(d)(3).

  c. *DISTRICT OF MAINE: Attachments.* Attachments to filings and exhibits must be filed in accordance with the court's ECF User Manual, unless otherwise ordered by the court. ME R USDCT App. 4(j). When there are fifty (50) or fewer attachments to a pleading, the attachments must be filed by counsel electronically using ECF. When there are more than fifty (50) attachments, the attachments must be filed in one of the following ways: (A) using ECF, simply attach them to the pleading being filed; (B) using ECF, use the "Additional Attachments" menu item; (C) on paper; or (D) on a properly labeled three and one-half (3-1/2) inch floppy disk, CD or DVD. ME R USDCT App. 4(j)(2). Attachments filed on paper or on disk must contain a comprehensive index that clearly describes each document. ME R USDCT App. 4(j)(2).

    i.   A filing user must submit as attachments only those excerpts of the referenced documents that are directly germane to the matter under consideration by the court. Excerpted material must be clearly and prominently identified as such. Users who file excerpts of documents do so without prejudice to their right to timely file additional excerpts or the complete document, as may be allowed by the court. Responding parties may timely file additional excerpts or the complete document that they believe are directly germane. ME R USDCT App. 4(j)(3).

    ii.   Filers shall not attach as an exhibit any pleading or other paper already on file with the court in that case, but shall merely refer to that document. ME R USDCT App. 4(j)(4).

  d. *DISTRICT OF MAINE: Compliance with technical standards.* All documents filed by electronic means must comply with technical standards, if any, established by the Judicial Conference of the United States or by the United States District Court for the District of Maine. ME R USDCT App. 4(a)(3).

3. *DISTRICT OF MAINE: Form of memoranda of law.* All memoranda shall be typed, in a font of no less than size twelve (12) point, and shall be double-spaced on eight and one-half by eleven (8-1/2 x 11) inch paper or printed. Footnotes shall be in a font of no less than size ten (10) point, and may be single spaced. All pages shall be numbered at the bottom. ME R USDCT Rule 7(d).

  a. *Page limitations.* No memorandum of law in support of or in opposition to a nondispositive motion shall exceed ten (10) pages. ME R USDCT Rule 7(d). No reply memorandum shall exceed seven (7) pages. ME R USDCT Rule 7(d); ME R USDCT Rule 7(c).

    i.   *Motion to exceed page limitation.* A motion to exceed the limitation of ME R USDCT Rule 7 shall be filed no later than three (3) business days in advance of the date for filing the memorandum to permit meaningful review by the court. A motion to exceed the page limitations shall not be filed simultaneously with a memorandum in excess of the limitations of ME R USDCT Rule 7. ME R USDCT Rule 7(d).

4. *Signing disclosures and discovery requests, responses, and objections.* FRCP 11 does not apply to disclosures and discovery requests, responses, objections, and motions under FRCP 26 through FRCP 37. FRCP 11(d).

  a. *Signature required.* Every disclosure under FRCP 26(a)(1) or FRCP 26(a)(3) and every discovery request, response, or objection must be signed by at least one attorney of record in the attorney's own name—or by the party personally, if unrepresented—and must state the signer's address, e-mail address, and telephone number. FRCP 26(g)(1).

  b. *Electronic signing.* A filing made through a person's electronic-filing account and authorized by that person, together with that person's name on a signature block, constitutes the person's signature. FRCP 5(d)(3)(C).

    i.   *DISTRICT OF MAINE: Attorneys.* The user log-in and password together with a user's name on the signature block constitutes the attorney's signature pursuant to the Federal Rules of Civil Procedure and the Local Rules of the United States District Court for the District of Maine. All electronically filed documents must include a signature block and must set forth the attorney's name, address, telephone number and e-mail address. The name of the ECF user under whose log-in and password the document is submitted must be preceded by a "/s/" in the space where the signature would otherwise appear. ME R USDCT App. 4(h)(1).

    ii.   *DISTRICT OF MAINE: Multiple signatures.* The filer of any document requiring more than one signature (e.g., pleadings filed by visiting lawyers, stipulations, joint status reports) must list thereon all the names of other signatories, preceded by a "/s/" in the space where the signatures would otherwise appear. By submitting such a document, the filing attorney certifies that each of the other signatories has expressly agreed to the form and substance of the document and that the filing attorney has their actual authority to submit the document electronically. ME R USDCT App. 4(h)(2). For more information, refer to ME R USDCT App. 4(h)(2).

 iii. *DISTRICT OF MAINE: Documents signed under oath.* Affidavits, declarations, verified complaints, or any other document signed under oath shall be filed electronically. The electronically filed version shall contain the typed name of the signatory, preceded by a "/s/" in the space where the signature would otherwise appear indicating that the paper document bears an original signature. ME R USDCT Rule 10; ME R USDCT App. 4(h)(3). For more information, refer to ME R USDCT Rule 10.

 c. *Effect of signature.* By signing, an attorney or party certifies that to the best of the person's knowledge, information, and belief formed after a reasonable inquiry: (A) with respect to a disclosure, it is complete and correct as of the time it is made; and (B) with respect to a discovery request, response, or objection, it is: (i) consistent with the Federal Rules of Civil Procedure and warranted by existing law or by a nonfrivolous argument for extending, modifying, or reversing existing law, or for establishing new law; (ii) not interposed for any improper purpose, such as to harass, cause unnecessary delay, or needlessly increase the cost of litigation; and (iii) neither unreasonable nor unduly burdensome or expensive, considering the needs of the case, prior discovery in the case, the amount in controversy, and the importance of the issues at stake in the action. FRCP 26(g)(1).

 d. *Failure to sign.* Other parties have no duty to act on an unsigned disclosure, request, response, or objection until it is signed, and the court must strike it unless a signature is promptly supplied after the omission is called to the attorney's or party's attention. FRCP 26(g)(2).

 e. *Sanction for improper certification.* Refer to the "C. General Requirements" section of this KeyRules document for information on the sanction for improper certification.

5. *Privacy protection for filings made with the court*

 a. *Redacted filings.* Unless the court orders otherwise, in an electronic or paper filing with the court that contains an individual's Social Security number, taxpayer-identification number, or birth date, the name of an individual known to be a minor, or a financial-account number, a party or nonparty making the filing may include only: (1) the last four (4) digits of the Social Security number and taxpayer-identification number; (2) the year of the individual's birth; (3) the minor's initials; and (4) the last four (4) digits of the financial-account number. FRCP 5.2(a).

  i. *DISTRICT OF MAINE.* To address the privacy concerns created by the Internet access to court papers, unless otherwise ordered by the court, counsel shall modify certain personal data identifiers in pleadings and other papers as follows: (1) minors' names: use of the minors' initials only; (2) Social Security numbers: use of the last four (4) numbers only; (3) dates of birth: use of the year of birth only; [and] (4) financial account numbers: identify the type of account and the financial institution, but use only the last four (4) numbers of the account number. ME R USDCT Redacting Pleadings. Counsel should also use caution when filing papers that contain a person's medical records, employment history; financial information; and any proprietary or trade secret information. ME R USDCT Redacting Pleadings.

 b. *Exemptions from the redaction requirement.* The redaction requirement does not apply to the following: (1) a financial-account number that identifies the property allegedly subject to forfeiture in a forfeiture proceeding; (2) the record of an administrative or agency proceeding; (3) the official record of a state-court proceeding; (4) the record of a court or tribunal, if that record was not subject to the redaction requirement when originally filed; (5) a filing covered by FRCP 5.2(c) or FRCP 5.2(d); and (6) a pro se filing in an action brought under 28 U.S.C.A. § 2241, 28 U.S.C.A. § 2254, or 28 U.S.C.A. § 2255. FRCP 5.2(b).

 c. *Limitations on remote access to electronic files; Social Security appeals and immigration cases.* Unless the court orders otherwise, in an action for benefits under the Social Security Act, and in an action or proceeding relating to an order of removal, to relief from removal, or to immigration benefits or detention, access to an electronic file is authorized as follows: (1) the parties and their attorneys may have remote electronic access to any part of the case file, including the administrative record; (2) any other person may have electronic access to the full record at the courthouse, but may have remote electronic access only to: (A) the docket maintained by the court; and (B) an opinion, order, judgment, or other disposition of the court, but not any other part of the case file or the administrative record. FRCP 5.2(c).

 d. *Filings made under seal.* The court may order that a filing be made under seal without redaction. The court may later unseal the filing or order the person who made the filing to file a redacted version for the public record. FRCP 5.2(d).

  i. *DISTRICT OF MAINE.* For information on filing sealed documents in the District of Maine, refer to ME R USDCT Rule 7A, ME R USDCT App. 4(p)(2), and ME R USDCT Sealed Filings.

 e. *Protective orders.* For good cause, the court may by order in a case: (1) require redaction of additional information; or (2) limit or prohibit a nonparty's remote electronic access to a document filed with the court. FRCP 5.2(e).

f. *Option for additional unredacted filing under seal.* A person making a redacted filing may also file an unredacted copy under seal. The court must retain the unredacted copy as part of the record. FRCP 5.2(f).

   i. *DISTRICT OF MAINE.* A party wishing to file a document containing the personal data identifiers specified above may. . .file an unredacted document under seal. This document will be retained by the clerk's office as part of the record. ME R USDCT Redacting Pleadings. The court may, however, still require the party to file a redacted copy for the public file. ME R USDCT Redacting Pleadings.

g. *Option for filing a reference list.* A filing that contains redacted information may be filed together with a reference list that identifies each item of redacted information and specifies an appropriate identifier that uniquely corresponds to each item listed. The list must be filed under seal and may be amended as of right. Any reference in the case to a listed identifier will be construed to refer to the corresponding item of information. FRCP 5.2(g).

   i. *DISTRICT OF MAINE.* A party wishing to file a document containing the personal data identifiers specified above may. . .file a reference list under seal. The reference list shall contain the complete personal data identifier(s) and the redacted identifier(s) used in its (their) place in the filing. All references in the case to the redacted identifiers included in the reference list will be construed to refer to the corresponding complete identifier. The reference list must be filed under seal, and may be amended as of right. It shall be retained by the clerk's office as part of the record. ME R USDCT Redacting Pleadings. The court may, however, still require the party to file a redacted copy for the public file. ME R USDCT Redacting Pleadings.

h. *DISTRICT OF MAINE: Responsibility for redaction.* The clerk is not required to review documents filed with the court for compliance with FRCP 5.2. The responsibility to redact filings rests with counsel and the party or nonparty making the filing. ME R USDCT App. 4(i); ME R USDCT Redacting Pleadings. For guidelines for filing confidential information in civil cases in the District of Maine, refer to ME R USDCT Confidentiality.

i. *Waiver of protection of identifiers.* A person waives the protection of FRCP 5.2(a) as to the person's own information by filing it without redaction and not under seal. FRCP 5.2(h).

F. Filing and Service Requirements

1. *Filing requirements*

a. *Required filings.* Any paper after the complaint that is required to be served must be filed no later than a reasonable time after service. FRCP 5(d)(1).

b. *DISTRICT OF MAINE: Place of filing.* Unless otherwise ordered by the court, papers shall be filed with the court at Bangor in cases filed and pending at Bangor, and at Portland in cases filed and pending at Portland. ME R USDCT Rule 5(a).

c. *Nonelectronic filing.* A paper not filed electronically is filed by delivering it: (A) to the clerk; or (B) to a judge who agrees to accept it for filing, and who must then note the filing date on the paper and promptly send it to the clerk. FRCP 5(d)(2).

   i. *DISTRICT OF MAINE: Documents to be filed in paper.* The following documents shall be filed in paper, which may also be scanned into ECF by the clerk's office: (A) all handwritten pleadings; and (B) all pleadings and documents filed by pro se litigants who are incarcerated or who are not registered filing users in ECF. ME R USDCT App. 4(g)(8). Non-prisoner pro se litigants in civil actions may register with ECF or may file (and serve) all pleadings and other documents in paper. The clerk's office will scan into ECF any pleadings and documents filed on paper in accordance with ME R USDCT App. 4(g). ME R USDCT App. 4(o). For more information, refer to ME R USDCT App. 4(g).

d. *Electronic filing*

   i. *DISTRICT OF MAINE: Authorization.* Unless exempt or otherwise ordered by the court, papers shall be filed and served electronically as required by the court's Administrative Procedures Governing the Filing and Service by Electronic Means, which is set forth in ME R USDCT App. 4. The provisions of the court's Administrative Procedures Governing the Filing and Service by Electronic Means (ME R USDCT App. 4) shall be applied and enforced as part of the Local Rules of the United States District Court for the District of Maine. ME R USDCT Rule 5(c).

   ii. *Filing by represented persons.* A person represented by an attorney must file electronically, unless nonelectronic filing is allowed by the court for good cause or is allowed or required by local rule. FRCP 5(d)(3)(A).

      • *DISTRICT OF MAINE.* An attorney may apply to the court for permission to file paper documents. ME R USDCT App. 4(a)(5).

iii. *Filing by unrepresented persons.* A person not represented by an attorney: (i) may file electronically only if allowed by court order or by local rule; and (ii) may be required to file electronically only by court order, or by a local rule that includes reasonable exceptions. FRCP 5(d)(3)(B).

- *DISTRICT OF MAINE.* Non-prisoner pro se litigants in civil actions may register with ECF or may file (and serve) all pleadings and other documents in paper. ME R USDCT App. 4(o). A non-prisoner who is a party to a civil action and who is not represented by an attorney may register to receive service electronically and to electronically transmit their documents to the court for filing in the ECF system. If during the course of the action the person retains an attorney who appears on the person's behalf, the clerk shall terminate the person's registration upon the attorney's appearance. ME R USDCT App. 4(b)(2).

iv. *DISTRICT OF MAINE: Scope of electronic filing.* All documents submitted for filing in civil and criminal cases, regardless of case commencement date, except those documents specifically exempted in ME R USDCT App. 4(g), shall be filed electronically using the electronic case filing system (ECF). ME R USDCT App. 4(a)(1). For special filing requirements and exceptions, refer to ME R USDCT App. 4(g).

v. *DISTRICT OF MAINE: Consequences of electronic filing.* Electronic transmission of a document to the ECF system, together with the transmission of a Notice of Electronic Filing (NEF) from the court, constitutes filing of the document for all purposes of the Federal Rules of Civil Procedure. ME R USDCT App. 4(d)(1).

vi. *DISTRICT OF MAINE: Review of documents.* Documents filed with the clerk's office will normally be reviewed no later than the close of the next business day. It is the responsibility of the filing party to promptly notify the clerk's office via telephone of a matter that requires the immediate attention of a judicial officer. ME R USDCT App. 4(a)(4).

e. *DISTRICT OF MAINE: Facsimile filing.* No papers shall be submitted to the court by means of a facsimile machine without prior leave of the court. ME R USDCT Rule 5(c); ME R USDCT App. 4(m).

2. *Service requirements*

a. *Service; When required.* Unless the Federal Rules of Civil Procedure provide otherwise, each of the following papers must be served on every party: (A) an order stating that service is required; (B) a pleading filed after the original complaint, unless the court orders otherwise under FRCP 5(c) because there are numerous defendants; (C) a discovery paper required to be served on a party, unless the court orders otherwise; (D) a written motion, except one that may be heard ex parte; and (E) a written notice, appearance, demand, or offer of judgment, or any similar paper. FRCP 5(a)(1).

i. *If a party fails to appear.* No service is required on a party who is in default for failing to appear. But a pleading that asserts a new claim for relief against such a party must be served on that party under FRCP 4. FRCP 5(a)(2).

ii. *Seizing property.* If an action is begun by seizing property and no person is or need be named as a defendant, any service required before the filing of an appearance, answer, or claim must be made on the person who had custody or possession of the property when it was seized. FRCP 5(a)(3).

b. *Service; How made.* A paper is served under FRCP 5 by: (A) handing it to the person; (B) leaving it: (i) at the person's office with a clerk or other person in charge or, if no one is in charge, in a conspicuous place in the office; or (ii) if the person has no office or the office is closed, at the person's dwelling or usual place of abode with someone of suitable age and discretion who resides there; (C) mailing it to the person's last known address—in which event service is complete upon mailing; (D) leaving it with the court clerk if the person has no known address; (E) sending it to a registered user by filing it with the court's electronic-filing system or sending it by other electronic means that the person consented to in writing—in either of which events service is complete upon filing or sending, but is not effective if the filer or sender learns that it did not reach the person to be served; or (F) delivering it by any other means that the person consented to in writing—in which event service is complete when the person making service delivers it to the agency designated to make delivery. FRCP 5(b)(2).

i. *Serving an attorney.* If a party is represented by an attorney, service under FRCP 5 must be made on the attorney unless the court orders service on the party. FRCP 5(b)(1).

c. *DISTRICT OF MAINE: Service of electronically filed documents*

i. *Registered users.* Registration [as a filing user of the court's ECF system] constitutes consent to service of all documents by electronic means as provided in ME R USDCT App. 4. ME R USDCT App. 4(b)(4). Whenever a non-sealed pleading is filed electronically, the ECF system will automatically generate and send a Notice of Electronic Filing (NEF) to the filing user and registered users of record. The user filing the document should retain a paper or digital copy of the NEF, which shall serve as the court's date-stamp and proof of filing. ME R USDCT App. 4(e)(1).

- *Sealed documents.* Although the filing of sealed documents in civil cases produces an NEF, the document itself cannot be accessed and counsel shall be responsible for making service of the sealed documents. ME R USDCT App. 4(e)(2).

    ii. *Non-registered users and pro se litigants.* Attorneys who have not yet registered as users with ECF and pro se litigants who have not registered with ECF shall be served a paper copy of any electronically filed pleading or other document in accordance with the provisions of FRCP 5. ME R USDCT App. 4(e)(3).

- *Registration of pro se litigants.* A non-prisoner who is a party to a civil action and who is not represented by an attorney may register to receive service electronically and to electronically transmit their documents to the court for filing in the ECF system. If during the course of the action the person retains an attorney who appears on the person's behalf, the clerk shall terminate the person's registration upon the attorney's appearance. ME R USDCT App. 4(b)(2).

    d. *Serving numerous defendants.* If an action involves an unusually large number of defendants, the court may, on motion or on its own, order that: (A) defendants' pleadings and replies to them need not be served on other defendants; (B) any crossclaim, counterclaim, avoidance, or affirmative defense in those pleadings and replies to them will be treated as denied or avoided by all other parties; and (C) filing any such pleading and serving it on the plaintiff constitutes notice of the pleading to all parties. FRCP 5(c)(1).

    i. *Notifying parties.* A copy of every such order must be served on the parties as the court directs. FRCP 5(c)(2).

3. *DISTRICT OF MAINE: Filing and service of highly sensitive documents (HSDs).* For information on filing and serving highly sensitive documents (HSDs) in the District of Maine, refer to ME R USDCT General Order 21-5.

G. Hearings

1. *Hearings, generally.* When a motion relies on facts outside the record, the court may hear the matter on affidavits or may hear it wholly or partly on oral testimony or on depositions. FRCP 43(c).

    a. *Oral argument.* Due process does not require that oral argument be permitted on a motion and, except as otherwise provided by local rule, the district court has discretion to determine whether it will decide the motion on the papers or hear argument by counsel (and perhaps receive evidence). FPP § 1190; F.D.I.C. v. Deglau, 207 F.3d 153 (3d Cir. 2000).

    i. *DISTRICT OF MAINE.* Unless otherwise required by federal rule or statute, all motions may be decided by the court without oral argument unless otherwise ordered by the court on its own motion or, in its discretion, upon request of counsel. ME R USDCT Rule 7(e).

    b. *Providing a regular schedule for oral hearings.* A court may establish regular times and places for oral hearings on motions. FRCP 78(a).

    c. *Providing for submission on briefs.* By rule or order, the court may provide for submitting and determining motions on briefs, without oral hearings. FRCP 78(b).

H. Forms

1. Federal Motion for Discovery Sanctions Forms

    a. Motion for contempt. 3B FEDFORMS § 27:43.

    b. Motion for sanctions for failure to appear at deposition. 3B FEDFORMS § 27:44.

    c. Motion that facts be taken as established for failure to answer questions upon deposition. 3B FEDFORMS § 27:45.

    d. Motion for order refusing to allow disobedient party to support or oppose designated claims or defenses. 3B FEDFORMS § 27:46.

    e. Motion for default judgment against defendant for failure to comply with order for production of documents. 3B FEDFORMS § 27:47.

    f. Motion for award of expenses incurred to prove matter opponent failed to admit under FRCP 36. 3B FEDFORMS § 27:48.

    g. Motion to strike answer or dismiss action for failure to comply with order requiring answer to interrogatories. 3B FEDFORMS § 27:51.

    h. Motion to dismiss for failure to comply with previous order requiring answer to interrogatories to party. 3B FEDFORMS § 27:54.

i. Motion; For order that facts be taken to be established, and/or prohibiting certain claims, defenses, or evidence in opposition thereto. FEDPROF § 23:618.

j. Affidavit; By attorney; In support of motion for order that facts be taken to be established, etc; Failure to produce documents for inspection. FEDPROF § 23:619.

k. Affidavit; By attorney; In support of motion for order that facts be taken to be established, etc; Failure to obey order to answer questions. FEDPROF § 23:620.

l. Motion; For order striking pleadings, and for default judgment or dismissal of action. FEDPROF § 23:623.

m. Affidavit; By attorney; In support of motion for default judgment for defendant's failure to obey discovery order. FEDPROF § 23:624.

n. Motion; By defendant; For dismissal of action and other sanctions; For failure to comply with orders to complete deposition. FEDPROF § 23:625.

o. Motion; By defendant; For dismissal of action or other sanctions; For failure and refusal to comply with order to produce documents. FEDPROF § 23:626.

p. Motion; By defendant; For dismissal with prejudice; Failure to answer interrogatories as ordered. FEDPROF § 23:627.

q. Motion; For order staying further proceedings until adverse party obeys order compelling discovery. FEDPROF § 23:628.

r. Affidavit; By attorney; Opposing motion for order striking pleading and directing entry of default judgment; Good-faith attempt to obey discovery order; Production of documents illegal under foreign law. FEDPROF § 23:629.

s. Motion; For sanctions for failure to comply with examination order. FEDPROF § 23:634.

t. Motion; For order finding person in contempt of court; Refusal, after order, to answer question. FEDPROF § 23:636.

u. Affidavit; By attorney; In support of motion for order finding party in contempt. FEDPROF § 23:637.

v. Affidavit; By plaintiff; In support of motion for order holding defendant in contempt of court; Defendant disobeyed order for production of documents. FEDPROF § 23:638.

w. Motion; For order compelling opposing party to pay expenses incurred in proving facts such party refused to admit. FEDPROF § 23:640.

x. Motion; For sanctions; Failure to attend own deposition, serve answers to interrogatories, or respond to request for inspection. FEDPROF § 23:642.

y. Motion; For order staying proceedings until required response to discovery request is made. FEDPROF § 23:643.

z. Affidavit; By attorney; In support of motion for sanctions; Failure to attend own deposition, serve answers to interrogatories, or respond to request for inspection. FEDPROF § 23:645.

I. Applicable Rules

1. *Federal rules*

   a. Counsel's liability for excessive costs. 28 U.S.C.A. § 1927.

   b. Serving and filing pleadings and other papers. FRCP 5.

   c. Constitutional challenge to a statute; Notice, certification, and intervention. FRCP 5.1.

   d. Privacy protection for filings made with the court. FRCP 5.2.

   e. Computing and extending time; Time for motion papers. FRCP 6.

   f. Pleadings allowed; Form of motions and other papers. FRCP 7.

   g. Form of pleadings. FRCP 10.

   h. Signing pleadings, motions, and other papers; Representations to the court; Sanctions. FRCP 11.

   i. Duty to disclose; General provisions governing discovery. FRCP 26.

   j. Failure to make disclosures or to cooperate in discovery; Sanctions. FRCP 37.

   k. Taking testimony. FRCP 43.

   l. Hearing motions; Submission on briefs. FRCP 78.

2. *Local rules*

   a. *DISTRICT OF MAINE*

      i. Service and filing of pleadings and other papers. ME R USDCT Rule 5.

      ii. Time. ME R USDCT Rule 6.

      iii. Motions and memoranda of law. ME R USDCT Rule 7.

      iv. Form of pleadings, motions and other papers. ME R USDCT Rule 10.

      v. Discovery. ME R USDCT Rule 26.

      vi. Attorneys; Appearances and withdrawals. ME R USDCT Rule 83.2.

      vii. Alternative dispute resolution (ADR). ME R USDCT Rule 83.11.

      viii. Administrative procedures governing the filing and service by electronic means. ME R USDCT App. 4.

      ix. Redacting pleadings. ME R USDCT Redacting Pleadings.

Motions, Oppositions and Replies
Motion for Preliminary Injunction

Document Last Updated April 2021

A. Checklist

(I) ❑ Matters to be considered by moving party

   (a) ❑ Required documents

      (1) ❑ Notice of motion and motion

      (2) ❑ Security

   (b) ❑ Supplemental documents

      (1) ❑ Supporting evidence

      (2) ❑ Notice of constitutional question

      (3) ❑ Nongovernmental corporate disclosure statement

      (4) ❑ DISTRICT OF MAINE: Additional supplemental documents

         (i) ❑ Proposed order

   (c) ❑ Timing

      (1) ❑ There are no specific timing requirements in the Federal Rules of Civil Procedure for moving for a preliminary injunction

      (2) ❑ FRCP 65 is silent about when notice must be given

      (3) ❑ A written motion and notice of the hearing must be served at least fourteen (14) days before the time specified for the hearing, with the following exceptions: (A) when the motion may be heard ex parte; (B) when the Federal Rules of Civil Procedure set a different time; or (C) when a court order—which a party may, for good cause, apply for ex parte—sets a different time

      (4) ❑ Any affidavit supporting a motion must be served with the motion

      (5) ❑ DISTRICT OF MAINE: Additional timing

         (i) ❑ Any affidavits and other documents setting forth or evidencing facts on which the motion is based must be filed with the motion

(II) ❑ Matters to be considered by opposing party

   (a) ❑ Required documents

      (1) ❑ Opposition

   (b) ❑ Supplemental documents

      (1) ❑ Supporting evidence

    (2) ❑ Notice of constitutional question

    (3) ❑ Nongovernmental corporate disclosure statement

(c) ❑ Timing

    (1) ❑ Except as FRCP 59(c) provides otherwise, any opposing affidavit must be served at least seven (7) days before the hearing, unless the court permits service at another time

    (2) ❑ DISTRICT OF MAINE: Additional timing

        (i) ❑ Unless within twenty-one (21) days after the filing of a motion the opposing party files written objection thereto, incorporating a memorandum of law, the opposing party shall be deemed to have waived objection

B. Timing

1. *Motion for preliminary injunction.* There are no specific timing requirements in the Federal Rules of Civil Procedure for moving for a preliminary injunction.

    a. *Notice.* FRCP 65 is silent about when notice must be given. FPP § 2949.

2. *Timing of motions, generally*

    a. *Motion and notice of hearing.* A written motion and notice of the hearing must be served at least fourteen (14) days before the time specified for the hearing, with the following exceptions: (A) when the motion may be heard ex parte; (B) when the Federal Rules of Civil Procedure set a different time; or (C) when a court order—which a party may, for good cause, apply for ex parte—sets a different time. FRCP 6(c)(1).

    b. *Supporting affidavit.* Any affidavit supporting a motion must be served with the motion. FRCP 6(c)(2).

    c. *DISTRICT OF MAINE: Affidavits and other supporting documents.* Any affidavits and other documents setting forth or evidencing facts on which the motion is based must be filed with the motion. ME R USDCT Rule 7(a).

3. *Timing of opposing papers.* Except as FRCP 59(c) provides otherwise, any opposing affidavit must be served at least seven (7) days before the hearing, unless the court permits service at another time. FRCP 6(c)(2).

    a. *DISTRICT OF MAINE.* Unless within twenty-one (21) days after the filing of a motion the opposing party files written objection thereto, incorporating a memorandum of law, the opposing party shall be deemed to have waived objection. ME R USDCT Rule 7(b). The deemed waiver imposed in ME R USDCT Rule 7(b) shall not apply to motions filed during trial. ME R USDCT Rule 7(b).

4. *Timing of reply papers.* Where the respondent files an answering affidavit setting up a new matter, the moving party ordinarily is allowed a reasonable time to file a reply affidavit since failure to deny the new matter by affidavit may operate as an admission of its truth. AMJUR MOTIONS § 25.

    a. *DISTRICT OF MAINE.* Within fourteen (14) days of the filing of any objection to a motion, the moving party may file a reply memorandum. ME R USDCT Rule 7(c).

5. *Computation of time*

    a. *Computing time.* FRCP 6 applies in computing any time period specified in the Federal Rules of Civil Procedure, in any local rule or court order, or in any statute that does not specify a method of computing time. FRCP 6(a).

        i. *Period stated in days or a longer unit.* When the period is stated in days or a longer unit of time: (A) exclude the day of the event that triggers the period; (B) count every day, including intermediate Saturdays, Sundays, and legal holidays; and (C) include the last day of the period, but if the last day is a Saturday, Sunday, or legal holiday, the period continues to run until the end of the next day that is not a Saturday, Sunday, or legal holiday. FRCP 6(a)(1).

        ii. *Period stated in hours.* When the period is stated in hours: (A) begin counting immediately on the occurrence of the event that triggers the period; (B) count every hour, including hours during intermediate Saturdays, Sundays, and legal holidays; and (C) if the period would end on a Saturday, Sunday, or legal holiday, the period continues to run until the same time on the next day that is not a Saturday, Sunday, or legal holiday. FRCP 6(a)(2).

        iii. *Inaccessibility of the clerk's office.* Unless the court orders otherwise, if the clerk's office is inaccessible: (A) on the last day for filing under FRCP 6(a)(1), then the time for filing is extended to the first accessible day that is not a Saturday, Sunday, or legal holiday; or (B) during the last hour for filing under FRCP 6(a)(2), then the time for filing is extended to the same time on the first accessible day that is not a Saturday, Sunday, or legal holiday. FRCP 6(a)(3).

iv. *"Last day" defined.* Unless a different time is set by a statute, local rule, or court order, the last day ends: (A) for electronic filing, at midnight in the court's time zone; and (B) for filing by other means, when the clerk's office is scheduled to close. FRCP 6(a)(4).

v. *"Next day" defined.* The "next day" is determined by continuing to count forward when the period is measured after an event and backward when measured before an event. FRCP 6(a)(5).

vi. *"Legal holiday" defined.* "Legal holiday" means: (A) the day set aside by statute for observing New Year's Day, Martin Luther King Jr.'s Birthday, Washington's Birthday, Memorial Day, Independence Day, Labor Day, Columbus Day, Veterans' Day, Thanksgiving Day, or Christmas Day; (B) any day declared a holiday by the President or Congress; and (C) for periods that are measured after an event, any other day declared a holiday by the state where the district court is located. FRCP 6(a)(6).

vii. *DISTRICT OF MAINE: Applicability of FRCP 6.* FRCP 6 applies when computing any period of time stated in the Local Rules of the United States District Court for the District of Maine. ME R USDCT Rule 6(a).

b. *DISTRICT OF MAINE: Computation of electronic filing deadlines.* Filing documents electronically does not in any way alter any filing deadlines. All electronic transmissions of documents must be completed prior to midnight, Eastern Time, in order to be considered timely filed that day. Where a specific time of day deadline is set by court order or stipulation, the electronic filing must be completed by that time. ME R USDCT App. 4(f). A document filed electronically shall be deemed filed at the time and date stated on the Notice of Electronic Filing received from the court. ME R USDCT App. 4(d)(2).

i. *Technical failures.* A filing user whose filing is made untimely as the result of a technical failure may seek appropriate relief from the court. ME R USDCT App. 4(n). A technical failure of the court's ECF system is deemed to have occurred when the court's ECF site cannot accept filings continuously or intermittently over the course of any period of time greater than one (1) hour. Known system outages will be posted on the court's website along with guidance on how to proceed, if applicable. ME R USDCT App. 4(n).

c. *Extending time.* When an act may or must be done within a specified time, the court may, for good cause, extend the time: (A) with or without motion or notice if the court acts, or if a request is made, before the original time or its extension expires; or (B) on motion made after the time has expired if the party failed to act because of excusable neglect. FRCP 6(b)(1). A court must not extend the time to act under FRCP 50(b), FRCP 50(d), FRCP 52(b), FRCP 59(b), FRCP 59(d), FRCP 59(e), and FRCP 60(b). FRCP 6(b)(2). Refer to the United States District Court for the District of Maine KeyRules Motion for Continuance/Extension of Time document for more information on extending time.

d. *Additional time after certain kinds of service.* When a party may or must act within a specified time after being served and service is made under FRCP 5(b)(2)(C) (by mail), FRCP 5(b)(2)(D) (by leaving with the clerk), or FRCP 5(b)(2)(F) (by other means consented to), three (3) days are added after the period would otherwise expire under FRCP 6(a). FRCP 6(d).

C. General Requirements

1. *Motions, generally*

a. *Motion requirements.* A request for a court order must be made by motion. The motion must: (A) be in writing unless made during a hearing or trial; (B) state with particularity the grounds for seeking the order; and (C) state the relief sought. FRCP 7(b)(1). The writing and particularity requirements are intended to ensure that the adverse parties are informed of and have a record of both the motion's pendency and the grounds on which the movant seeks an order. FPP § 1191; Feldberg v. Quechee Lakes Corp., 463 F.3d 195 (2d Cir. 2006).

i. *Particularity requirement.* The particularity requirement [ensures] that the opposing parties will have notice of their opponent's contentions. FEDPROC § 62:358; Goodman v. 1973 26 Foot Trojan Vessel, Arkansas Registration No. AR1439SN, 859 F.2d 71 (8th Cir. 1988). That requirement ensures that notice of the basis for the motion is provided to the court and to the opposing party so as to avoid prejudice, provide the opponent with a meaningful opportunity to respond, and provide the court with enough information to process the motion correctly. FEDPROC § 62:358; Andreas v. Volkswagen of Am., Inc., 336 F.3d 789 (8th Cir. 2003).

- Reasonable specification of the grounds for a motion is sufficient. The particularity requirement for motions is satisfied when no party is prejudiced by a lack of particularity or when the court can comprehend the basis for the motion and deal with it fairly. However, where a movant fails to state even one ground for granting the motion in question, the movant has failed to meet the minimal standard of "reasonable specification." FEDPROC § 62:358; Martinez v. Trainor, 556 F.2d 818 (7th Cir. 1977).

- The court may excuse the failure to comply with the particularity requirement if it is inadvertent, and where no prejudice is shown by the opposing party. FEDPROC § 62:358.

    b. *Notice of motion.* A party interested in resisting the relief sought by a motion has a right to notice thereof, and an opportunity to be heard. AMJUR MOTIONS § 12.

        i. *Purpose.* In addition to statutory or court rule provisions requiring notice of a motion—the purpose of such a notice requirement having been said to be to prevent a party from being prejudicially surprised by a motion—principles of natural justice dictate that an adverse party generally must be given notice that a motion will be presented to the court. AMJUR MOTIONS § 12.

        ii. *Adequacy of notice.* The test of adequate notice generally turns on whether the other parties were afforded an adequate opportunity to prepare and respond to the issues to be raised in the proceeding. AMJUR MOTIONS § 12.

    c. *Single document containing motion and notice.* A single written document can satisfy the writing requirements both for a motion and for an FRCP 6(c)(1) notice. FRCP 7(Advisory Committee Notes).

2. *Motion for preliminary injunction.* The appropriate procedure for requesting a preliminary injunction is by motion, although it also commonly is requested by an order to show cause. FPP § 2949; James Luterbach Const. Co. v. Adamkus, 781 F.2d 599, 603 (7th Cir. 1986); Studebaker Corp. v. Gittlin, 360 F.2d 692 (2d. Cir. 1966).

    a. *Preliminary injunction.* An interim grant of specific relief is a preliminary injunction that may be issued only on notice to the adverse party. FEDPROC § 47:53; Westar Energy, Inc. v. Lake, 552 F.3d 1215 (10th Cir. 2009). Defined broadly, a preliminary injunction is an injunction that is issued to protect plaintiff from irreparable injury and to preserve the court's power to render a meaningful decision after a trial on the merits. FPP § 2947; Evans v. Buchanan, 555 F.2d 373, 387 (3d Cir. 1977).

        i. *Disfavored injunctions.* There are three types of preliminary injunctions that are disfavored: (1) those that afford the moving party substantially all the relief it might recover after a full trial on the merits; (2) those that disturb the status quo; and (3) those that are mandatory as opposed to prohibitory. FEDPROC § 47:55; Prairie Band of Potawatomi Indians v. Pierce, 253 F.3d 1234 (10th Cir. 2001).

    b. *Notice.* The court may issue a preliminary injunction only on notice to the adverse party. FRCP 65(a)(1). Although FRCP 65(a)(1) does not define what constitutes proper notice, it has been held that providing a copy of the motion and a specification of the time and place of the hearing are adequate. FPP § 2949.

    c. *Security.* The court may issue a preliminary injunction or a temporary restraining order only if the movant gives security in an amount that the court considers proper to pay the costs and damages sustained by any party found to have been wrongfully enjoined or restrained. The United States, its officers, and its agencies are not required to give security. FRCP 65(c). The purpose of an injunction bond is to compensate the defendant, in the event that the defendant prevails on the merits, for the harm caused by an injunction entered before the final decision, and so it is required only for a temporary restraining order or a preliminary injunction, not for a permanent injunction. FEDPROC § 47:93. An injunction bond serves other functions as well; for instance, it generally limits the liability of the applicant and informs the applicant of the price that it can expect to pay if the injunction was wrongfully issued. FEDPROC § 47:93. For information on proceedings against a security provider, refer to FRCP 65.1.

        i. *DISTRICT OF MAINE.* For information on bonds and security in the District of Maine, refer to ME R USDCT Rule 65.1.

    d. *Preliminary injunction versus temporary restraining order.* Care should be taken to distinguish preliminary injunctions under FRCP 65(a) from temporary-restraining orders under FRCP 65(b). FPP § 2947.

        i. *Notice and duration.* [Temporary restraining orders] may be issued ex parte without an adversary hearing in order to prevent an immediate, irreparable injury and are of limited duration—they typically remain in effect for a maximum of twenty-eight (28) days. On the other hand, FRCP 65(a)(1) requires that notice be given to the opposing party before a preliminary injunction may be issued. FPP § 2947. Furthermore, a preliminary injunction normally lasts until the completion of the trial on the merits, unless it is dissolved earlier by court order or the consent of the parties. FPP § 2947. Therefore, its duration varies and is controlled by the nature of the situation in which it is utilized. FPP § 2947; Fundicao Tupy S.A. v. United States, 841 F.2d 1101, 1103 (Fed. Cir. 1988).

        ii. *Hearing.* Some type of a hearing also implicitly is required by FRCP 65(a)(2), which was added in 1966 and provides either for the consolidation of the trial on the merits with the preliminary injunction hearing or the inclusion in the trial record of any evidence received at the FRCP 65(a) hearing. FPP § 2947. Refer to the "G. Hearings" section of this KeyRules document for more information.

e. *Grounds for granting or denying a preliminary injunction.* The policies that bear on the propriety of granting a preliminary injunction rarely are discussed directly in the cases. Instead they are taken into account by the court considering a number of factors that have been found useful in deciding whether to grant or deny preliminary injunctions in particular cases. A formulation that has become popular in all kinds of cases, although it originally was devised in connection with stays of administrative orders, is that the four most important factors are: (1) the significance of the threat of irreparable harm to plaintiff if the injunction is not granted; (2) the state of the balance between this harm and the injury that granting the injunction would inflict on defendant; (3) the probability that plaintiff will succeed on the merits; and (4) the public interest. FPP § 2948; Pottgen v. Missouri State High Sch. Activities Ass'n, 40 F.3d 926 (8th Cir. 1994).

   i. *Irreparable harm.* Perhaps the single most important prerequisite for the issuance of a preliminary injunction is a demonstration that if it is not granted the applicant is likely to suffer irreparable harm before a decision on the merits can be rendered. Only when the threatened harm would impair the court's ability to grant an effective remedy is there really a need for preliminary relief. FPP § 2948.1. There must be a likelihood that irreparable harm will occur. Speculative injury is not sufficient; there must be more than an unfounded fear on the part of the applicant. Thus, a preliminary injunction will not be issued simply to prevent the possibility of some remote future injury. A presently existing actual threat must be shown. However, the injury need not have been inflicted when application is made or be certain to occur; a strong threat of irreparable injury before trial is an adequate basis. FPP § 2948.1.

   ii. *Balancing hardship to parties.* The second factor bearing on the court's exercise of its discretion as to whether to grant preliminary relief involves an evaluation of the severity of the impact on defendant should the temporary injunction be granted and the hardship that would occur to plaintiff if the injunction should be denied. FPP § 2948.2. Two factors that frequently are considered when balancing the hardship on the respective parties of the grant or denial of relief are whether a preliminary injunction would give plaintiff all or most of the relief to which plaintiff would be entitled if successful at trial and whether mandatory relief is being sought. FPP § 2948.2.

   iii. *Likelihood of prevailing on the merits.* The third factor that enters into the preliminary injunction calculus is the likelihood that plaintiff will prevail on the merits. This is relevant because the need for the court to act is, at least in part, a function of the validity of the applicant's claim. The courts use a bewildering variety of formulations of the need for showing some likelihood of success—the most common being that plaintiff must demonstrate a reasonable probability of success. But the verbal differences do not seem to reflect substantive disagreement. All courts agree that plaintiff must present a prima facie case but need not show a certainty of winning. FPP § 2948.3.

   iv. *Public interest.* The final major factor bearing on the court's discretion to issue or deny a preliminary injunction is the public interest. [Focusing] on this factor is another way of inquiring whether there are policy considerations that bear on whether the order should issue. Thus, when granting preliminary relief, courts frequently emphasize that the public interest will be furthered by the injunction. Conversely, preliminary relief will be denied if the court finds that the public interest would be injured were an injunction to be issued. If the court finds there is no public interest supporting preliminary relief, that conclusion also supports denial of any injunction, even if the public interest would not be harmed by one. FPP § 2948.4. Consequently, an evaluation of the public interest should be given considerable weight in determining whether a motion for a preliminary injunction should be granted. FPP § 2948.4; Yakus v. United States, 321 U.S. 414, 64 S. Ct. 660, 88 L. Ed. 834 (1944).

f. *Contents and scope of every injunction and restraining order*

   i. *Contents.* Every order granting an injunction and every restraining order must: (A) state the reasons why it issued; (B) state its terms specifically; and (C) describe in reasonable detail—and not by referring to the complaint or other document—the act or acts restrained or required. FRCP 65(d)(1).

   ii. *Persons bound.* The order binds only the following who receive actual notice of it by personal service or otherwise: (A) the parties; (B) the parties' officers, agents, servants, employees, and attorneys; and (C) other persons who are in active concert or participation with anyone described in FRCP 65(d)(2)(A) or FRCP 65(d)(2)(B). FRCP 65(d)(2).

g. *Other laws not modified.* FRCP 65 does not modify the following: (1) any federal statute relating to temporary restraining orders or preliminary injunctions in actions affecting employer and employee; (2) 28 U.S.C.A. § 2361, which relates to preliminary injunctions in actions of interpleader or in the nature of interpleader; or (3) 28 U.S.C.A. § 2284, which relates to actions that must be heard and decided by a three-judge district court. FRCP 65(e).

h. *Copyright impoundment.* FRCP 65 applies to copyright-impoundment proceedings. FRCP 65(f).

3. *Opposing papers.* The Federal Rules of Civil Procedure do not require any formal answer, return, or reply to a motion,

except where the Federal Rules of Civil Procedure or local rules may require affidavits, memoranda, or other papers to be filed in opposition to a motion. Such papers are simply to apprise the court of such opposition and the grounds of that opposition. FEDPROC § 62:353.

    a. *DISTRICT OF MAINE: Content of objections.* Any objections shall include citations and supporting authorities and affidavits and other documents setting forth or evidencing facts on which the objection is based. ME R USDCT Rule 7(b).

    b. *Effect of failure to respond to motion.* Although in the absence of statutory provision or court rule, a motion ordinarily does not require a response or written answer, when a party files a motion and the opposing party fails to respond, the court may construe such failure to respond as nonopposition to the motion or an admission that the motion was meritorious. AMJUR MOTIONS § 28. The rule in some jurisdictions being that the failure to respond to a fact set forth in a motion is deemed an admission—and may grant the motion if the relief requested appears to be justified. AMJUR MOTIONS § 28.

    c. *Assent or no opposition not determinative.* However, a motion will not be granted automatically simply because an "assent" or a notation of "no opposition" has been filed; federal judges frequently deny motions that have been assented to when it is thought that justice so dictates. FPP § 1190.

    d. *Responsive pleading inappropriate as response to motion.* An attempt to answer or oppose a motion with a responsive pleading usually is not appropriate. FPP § 1190.

4. *Reply papers.* A moving party may be required or permitted to prepare papers in addition to its original motion papers. AMJUR MOTIONS § 25. Papers answering or replying to opposing papers may be appropriate, in the interests of justice, where it appears there is a substantial reason for allowing a reply. Thus, a court may accept reply papers where a party demonstrates that the papers to which it seeks to file a reply raise new issues that are material to the disposition of the question before the court, or where the court determines, sua sponte, that it wishes further briefing of an issue raised in those papers and orders the submission of additional papers. FEDPROC § 62:354.

    a. *Function of reply papers.* The function of a reply affidavit or reply papers is to answer the arguments made in opposition to the position taken by the movant, not to raise new issues, arguments, or evidence, or change the nature of the primary motion. However, if the court permits new evidence with the reply papers, the other party should be given the opportunity to respond. Where the party opposing the motion has no opportunity to address the argument in writing, a court has the discretion to disregard arguments raised for the first time in a reply memorandum. Also, the view has been followed in some jurisdictions that as a matter of judicial economy, where there is no prejudice and where the issues could be raised simply by filing a motion to dismiss, the trial court has discretion to consider arguments raised for the first time in a reply memorandum, and that a trial court may grant a motion to strike issues raised for the first time in a reply memorandum. AMJUR MOTIONS § 26.

        i. *DISTRICT OF MAINE.* The moving party may file a reply memorandum. . . .which shall be strictly confined to replying to new matter raised in the objection or opposing memorandum. ME R USDCT Rule 7(c).

5. *DISTRICT OF MAINE: Appearances.* An attorney's signature to a pleading shall constitute an appearance for the party filing the pleading. Otherwise, an attorney who wishes to participate in any manner in any action must file a formal written appearance identifying the party represented. An appearance whether by pleading or formal written appearance shall be signed by an attorney in his/her individual name and shall state his/her office address. ME R USDCT Rule 83.2(a). For more information, refer to ME R USDCT Rule 83.2.

6. *DISTRICT OF MAINE: Alternative dispute resolution (ADR).* Litigants are authorized and encouraged to employ, at their own expense, any available ADR process on which they can agree, including early neutral evaluation, settlement conferences, mediation, non-binding summary jury trial, corporate mini-trial, and arbitration proceedings. ME R USDCT Rule 83.11(a). For more information on ADR, refer to ME R USDCT Rule 83.11.

D. Documents

1. *Documents for moving party*

    a. *Required documents*

        i. *Notice of motion and motion.* Refer to the "C. General Requirements" section of this KeyRules document for information on the notice of motion and motion.

          • *DISTRICT OF MAINE: Memorandum of law.* Every motion shall incorporate a memorandum of law, including citations and supporting authorities. ME R USDCT Rule 7(a). Refer to the "E. Format" section of this KeyRules document for the form of memoranda of law.

          • *Certificate of service.* No certificate of service is required when a paper is served by filing it with the court's electronic-filing system. When a paper that is required to be served is served by other means: (i) if the paper is filed, a certificate of service must be filed with it or within a reasonable time after service; and (ii) if the paper is not filed, a certificate of service need not be filed unless filing is required by court order or by local rule. FRCP 5(d)(1)(B).

    ii. *Security.* The court may issue a preliminary injunction or a temporary restraining order only if the movant gives security in an amount that the court considers proper to pay the costs and damages sustained by any party found to have been wrongfully enjoined or restrained. The United States, its officers, and its agencies are not required to give security. FRCP 65(c). Refer to the "C. General Requirements" section of this KeyRules document for more information.

  b. *Supplemental documents*

    i. *Supporting evidence.* When a motion relies on facts outside the record, the court may hear the matter on affidavits or may hear it wholly or partly on oral testimony or on depositions. FRCP 43(c). Evidence that goes beyond the unverified allegations of the pleadings and motion papers must be presented to support or oppose a motion for a preliminary injunction. Affidavits are appropriate on a preliminary-injunction motion and typically will be offered by both parties. FPP § 2949. All affidavits should state the facts supporting the litigant's position clearly and specifically. Preliminary injunctions frequently are denied if the affidavits are too vague or conclusory to demonstrate a clear right to relief under FRCP 65. FPP § 2949. In addition to affidavits, other written evidence may be admitted at an FRCP 65(a) hearing. For example, pleadings may be considered if they have been verified. FPP § 2949; K-2 Ski Co. v. Head Ski Co., 467 F.2d 1087 (9th Cir. 1972). Depositions also may be introduced. Indeed, because they typically are taken under oath and involve some degree of cross-examination, depositions are given at least as much weight as, if not more than, affidavits. FPP § 2949.

- *DISTRICT OF MAINE: Affidavits and other supporting documents.* Any affidavits and other documents setting forth or evidencing facts on which the motion is based must be filed with the motion. ME R USDCT Rule 7(a).

- *DISTRICT OF MAINE: Discovery transcripts or materials.* A party relying on discovery transcripts or materials in support of or in opposition to a motion shall file excerpts of such transcript or materials with the memorandum required by ME R USDCT Rule 7 as well as a list of specific citations to the parts on which the party relies. ME R USDCT Rule 26(c). Excerpts of depositions in support of or in opposition to a motion shall be filed electronically using ECF, unless otherwise permitted by the court. ME R USDCT App. 4(l)(3).

    ii. *Notice of constitutional question.* A party that files a pleading, written motion, or other paper drawing into question the constitutionality of a federal or state statute must promptly: (1) file a notice of constitutional question stating the question and identifying the paper that raises it, if: (A) a federal statute is questioned and the parties do not include the United States, one of its agencies, or one of its officers or employees in an official capacity; or (B) a state statute is questioned and the parties do not include the state, one of its agencies, or one of its officers or employees in an official capacity; and (2) serve the notice and paper on the Attorney General of the United States if a federal statute is questioned—or on the state attorney general if a state statute is questioned—either by certified or registered mail or by sending it to an electronic address designated by the attorney general for this purpose. FRCP 5.1(a).

- *No forfeiture.* A party's failure to file and serve the notice, or the court's failure to certify, does not forfeit a constitutional claim or defense that is otherwise timely asserted. FRCP 5.1(d).

    iii. *Nongovernmental corporate disclosure statement.* A nongovernmental corporate party must file two (2) copies of a disclosure statement that: (1) identifies any parent corporation and any publicly held corporation owning ten percent (10%) or more of its stock; or (2) states that there is no such corporation. FRCP 7.1(a). A party must: (1) file the disclosure statement with its first appearance, pleading, petition, motion, response, or other request addressed to the court; and (2) promptly file a supplemental statement if any required information changes. FRCP 7.1(b).

- *DISTRICT OF MAINE: Notice of interested parties.* To enable the court to evaluate possible disqualification or recusal, counsel for all non-governmental parties shall file with their first appearance a Notice of Interested Parties, which shall list all persons, associations of persons, firms, partnerships, limited liability companies, joint ventures, corporations (including parent or affiliated corporations, clearly identified as such), or any similar entities, owning ten percent (10%) or more of the named party. Counsel shall be under a continuing obligation to file an amended Notice if any material change occurs in the status of an Interested Party, such as through merger, acquisition, or new/additional membership. ME R USDCT Rule 7.1.

    iv. *DISTRICT OF MAINE: Additional supplemental documents*

- *Proposed order.* Proposed orders shall not be filed unless requested by the court. When requested by the court, proposed orders shall be filed by e-mail in word processing format. ME R USDCT App. 4(k)(1).

2. *Documents for opposing party*

  a. *Required documents*

    i. *Opposition.* Refer to the "C. General Requirements" section of this KeyRules document for information on the opposing papers.

- *DISTRICT OF MAINE: Memorandum of law.* Unless within twenty-one (21) days after the filing of a motion the opposing party files written objection thereto, incorporating a memorandum of law, the opposing party shall be deemed to have waived objection. ME R USDCT Rule 7(b).

- *Certificate of service.* No certificate of service is required when a paper is served by filing it with the court's electronic-filing system. When a paper that is required to be served is served by other means: (i) if the paper is filed, a certificate of service must be filed with it or within a reasonable time after service; and (ii) if the paper is not filed, a certificate of service need not be filed unless filing is required by court order or by local rule. FRCP 5(d)(1)(B).

  b. *Supplemental documents*

    i. *Supporting evidence.* When a motion relies on facts outside the record, the court may hear the matter on affidavits or may hear it wholly or partly on oral testimony or on depositions. FRCP 43(c). Evidence that goes beyond the unverified allegations of the pleadings and motion papers must be presented to support or oppose a motion for a preliminary injunction. Affidavits are appropriate on a preliminary-injunction motion and typically will be offered by both parties. FPP § 2949. All affidavits should state the facts supporting the litigant's position clearly and specifically. Preliminary injunctions frequently are denied if the affidavits are too vague or conclusory to demonstrate a clear right to relief under FRCP 65. FPP § 2949. In addition to affidavits, other written evidence may be admitted at an FRCP 65(a) hearing. For example, pleadings may be considered if they have been verified. FPP § 2949; K-2 Ski Co. v. Head Ski Co., 467 F.2d 1087 (9th Cir. 1972). Depositions also may be introduced. Indeed, because they typically are taken under oath and involve some degree of cross-examination, depositions are given at least as much weight as, if not more than, affidavits. FPP § 2949.

- *DISTRICT OF MAINE: Affidavits and other supporting documents.* Any objections shall include. . .affidavits and other documents setting forth or evidencing facts on which the objection is based. ME R USDCT Rule 7(b).

- *DISTRICT OF MAINE: Discovery transcripts or materials.* A party relying on discovery transcripts or materials in support of or in opposition to a motion shall file excerpts of such transcript or materials with the memorandum required by ME R USDCT Rule 7 as well as a list of specific citations to the parts on which the party relies. ME R USDCT Rule 26(c). Excerpts of depositions in support of or in opposition to a motion shall be filed electronically using ECF, unless otherwise permitted by the court. ME R USDCT App. 4(l)(3).

    ii. *Notice of constitutional question.* A party that files a pleading, written motion, or other paper drawing into question the constitutionality of a federal or state statute must promptly: (1) file a notice of constitutional question stating the question and identifying the paper that raises it, if: (A) a federal statute is questioned and the parties do not include the United States, one of its agencies, or one of its officers or employees in an official capacity; or (B) a state statute is questioned and the parties do not include the state, one of its agencies, or one of its officers or employees in an official capacity; and (2) serve the notice and paper on the Attorney General of the United States if a federal statute is questioned—or on the state attorney general if a state statute is questioned—either by certified or registered mail or by sending it to an electronic address designated by the attorney general for this purpose. FRCP 5.1(a).

- *No forfeiture.* A party's failure to file and serve the notice, or the court's failure to certify, does not forfeit a constitutional claim or defense that is otherwise timely asserted. FRCP 5.1(d).

   iii. *Nongovernmental corporate disclosure statement.* A nongovernmental corporate party must file two (2) copies of a disclosure statement that: (1) identifies any parent corporation and any publicly held corporation owning ten percent (10%) or more of its stock; or (2) states that there is no such corporation. FRCP 7.1(a). A party must: (1) file the disclosure statement with its first appearance, pleading, petition, motion, response, or other request addressed to the court; and (2) promptly file a supplemental statement if any required information changes. FRCP 7.1(b).

- *DISTRICT OF MAINE: Notice of interested parties.* To enable the court to evaluate possible disqualification or recusal, counsel for all non-governmental parties shall file with their first appearance a Notice of Interested Parties, which shall list all persons, associations of persons, firms, partnerships, limited liability companies, joint ventures, corporations (including parent or affiliated corporations, clearly identified as such), or any similar entities, owning ten percent (10%) or more of the named party. Counsel shall be under a continuing obligation to file an amended Notice if any material change occurs in the status of an Interested Party, such as through merger, acquisition, or new/additional membership. ME R USDCT Rule 7.1.

E. Format

1. *Form of documents.* The rules governing captions and other matters of form in pleadings apply to motions and other papers. FRCP 7(b)(2).

   a. *DISTRICT OF MAINE: Font size, line spacing, and paper size.* All such documents shall be typed in a font of no less than size twelve (12) point, and shall be double-spaced or printed on eight and one-half by eleven (8-1/2 x 11) inch paper. Footnotes shall be in a font of no less than size ten (10) point, and may be single spaced. ME R USDCT Rule 10.

   b. *Caption.* Every pleading must have a caption with the court's name, a title, a file number, and an FRCP 7(a) designation. FRCP 10(a).

      i. *Names of parties.* The title of the complaint must name all the parties; the title of other pleadings, after naming the first party on each side, may refer generally to other parties. FRCP 10(a).

      ii. *DISTRICT OF MAINE: Additional caption requirements.* All pleadings, motions and other papers filed with the clerk or otherwise submitted to the court, except exhibits, shall bear the proper case number and shall contain on the first page a caption as described by FRCP 10(a) and immediately thereunder a designation of what the document is and the name of the party in whose behalf it is submitted. ME R USDCT Rule 10.

      iii. *DISTRICT OF MAINE: Injunctive relief.* If a pleading or motion seeks injunctive relief, in addition to the prayer for such relief, the words "INJUNCTIVE RELIEF SOUGHT" or the equivalent shall be included on the first page. ME R USDCT Rule 9(b).

   c. *Claims or defenses*

      i. *Numbered paragraphs.* A party must state its claims or defenses in numbered paragraphs, each limited as far as practicable to a single set of circumstances. A later pleading may refer by number to a paragraph in an earlier pleading. FRCP 10(b).

      ii. *Separate statements.* If doing so would promote clarity, each claim founded on a separate transaction or occurrence—and each defense other than a denial—must be stated in a separate count or defense. FRCP 10(b).

   d. *Adoption by reference.* A statement in a pleading may be adopted by reference elsewhere in the same pleading or in any other pleading or motion. FRCP 10(c).

      i. *Exhibits.* A copy of a written instrument that is an exhibit to a pleading is a part of the pleading for all purposes. FRCP 10(c).

   e. *DISTRICT OF MAINE: Page numbering.* All pages shall be numbered at the bottom. ME R USDCT Rule 10.

   f. *DISTRICT OF MAINE: Attachment of ancillary papers.* Ancillary papers shall be attached at the end of the document to which they relate. ME R USDCT Rule 10.

   g. *Acceptance by the clerk.* The clerk must not refuse to file a paper solely because it is not in the form prescribed by the Federal Rules of Civil Procedure or by a local rule or practice. FRCP 5(d)(4).

2. *Form of electronic documents.* A paper filed electronically is a written paper for purposes of the Federal Rules of Civil Procedure. FRCP 5(d)(3)(D).

   a. *DISTRICT OF MAINE: Document format.* The ECF system only accepts documents in a portable document format (PDF). Although there are two types of PDF documents—electronically converted PDF's and scanned PDF's—only electronically converted PDF's may be filed with the court using the ECF system, unless otherwise authorized by local rule or order. ME R USDCT App. 4. Any document or exhibit to be filed or submitted to the court shall not be password-protected or encrypted. ME R USDCT App. 4(g)(12).

      i. *Electronically converted PDFs.* Electronically converted PDF's are created from word processing documents (MS Word, WordPerfect, etc.) using Adobe Acrobat or similar software. They are text searchable and their file size is small. ME R USDCT App. 4. Software used to electronically convert documents to PDF which includes proprietary or advertisement information within the PDF document is prohibited. ME R USDCT App. 4.

    ii.   *Scanned PDFs.* Scanned PDF's are created from paper documents run through an optical scanner. Scanned PDF's are not searchable and have a large file size. ME R USDCT App. 4.

  b. *DISTRICT OF MAINE: Title.* All pleadings filed electronically shall be titled in accordance with the approved dictionary of civil or criminal events of the ECF system of the United States District Court for the District of Maine. ME R USDCT App. 4(d)(3).

  c. *DISTRICT OF MAINE: Attachments.* Attachments to filings and exhibits must be filed in accordance with the court's ECF User Manual, unless otherwise ordered by the court. ME R USDCT App. 4(j). When there are fifty (50) or fewer attachments to a pleading, the attachments must be filed by counsel electronically using ECF. When there are more than fifty (50) attachments, the attachments must be filed in one of the following ways: (A) using ECF, simply attach them to the pleading being filed; (B) using ECF, use the "Additional Attachments" menu item; (C) on paper; or (D) on a properly labeled three and one-half (3-1/2) inch floppy disk, CD or DVD. ME R USDCT App. 4(j)(2). Attachments filed on paper or on disk must contain a comprehensive index that clearly describes each document. ME R USDCT App. 4(j)(2).

    i.   A filing user must submit as attachments only those excerpts of the referenced documents that are directly germane to the matter under consideration by the court. Excerpted material must be clearly and prominently identified as such. Users who file excerpts of documents do so without prejudice to their right to timely file additional excerpts or the complete document, as may be allowed by the court. Responding parties may timely file additional excerpts or the complete document that they believe are directly germane. ME R USDCT App. 4(j)(3).

    ii. Filers shall not attach as an exhibit any pleading or other paper already on file with the court in that case, but shall merely refer to that document. ME R USDCT App. 4(j)(4).

  d. *DISTRICT OF MAINE: Compliance with technical standards.* All documents filed by electronic means must comply with technical standards, if any, established by the Judicial Conference of the United States or by the United States District Court for the District of Maine. ME R USDCT App. 4(a)(3).

3. *DISTRICT OF MAINE: Form of memoranda of law.* All memoranda shall be typed, in a font of no less than size twelve (12) point, and shall be double-spaced on eight and one-half by eleven (8-1/2 x 11) inch paper or printed. Footnotes shall be in a font of no less than size ten (10) point, and may be single spaced. All pages shall be numbered at the bottom. ME R USDCT Rule 7(d).

  a. *Page limitations.* No memorandum of law in support of or in opposition to a motion to dismiss, a motion for judgment on the pleadings, a motion for summary judgment or a motion for injunctive relief shall exceed twenty (20) pages. ME R USDCT Rule 7(d). No reply memorandum shall exceed seven (7) pages. ME R USDCT Rule 7(d); ME R USDCT Rule 7(c).

    i.   *Motion to exceed page limitation.* A motion to exceed the limitation of ME R USDCT Rule 7 shall be filed no later than three (3) business days in advance of the date for filing the memorandum to permit meaningful review by the court. A motion to exceed the page limitations shall not be filed simultaneously with a memorandum in excess of the limitations of ME R USDCT Rule 7. ME R USDCT Rule 7(d).

4. *Signing of pleadings, motions and other papers*

  a. *Signature.* Every pleading, written motion, and other paper must be signed by at least one attorney of record in the attorney's name—or by a party personally if the party is unrepresented. The paper must state the signer's address, e-mail address, and telephone number. FRCP 11(a).

    i.   *No verification or accompanying affidavit required for pleadings.* Unless a rule or statute specifically states otherwise, a pleading need not be verified or accompanied by an affidavit. FRCP 11(a).

    ii. *Unsigned papers.* The court must strike an unsigned paper unless the omission is promptly corrected after being called to the attorney's or party's attention. FRCP 11(a).

  b. *Electronic signing.* A filing made through a person's electronic-filing account and authorized by that person, together with that person's name on a signature block, constitutes the person's signature. FRCP 5(d)(3)(C).

    i.   *DISTRICT OF MAINE: Attorneys.* The user log-in and password together with a user's name on the signature block constitutes the attorney's signature pursuant to the Federal Rules of Civil Procedure and the Local Rules of the United States District Court for the District of Maine. All electronically filed documents must include a signature block and must set forth the attorney's name, address, telephone number and e-mail address. The name of the ECF user under whose log-in and password the document is submitted must be preceded by a "/s/" in the space where the signature would otherwise appear. ME R USDCT App. 4(h)(1).

ii. *DISTRICT OF MAINE: Multiple signatures.* The filer of any document requiring more than one signature (e.g., pleadings filed by visiting lawyers, stipulations, joint status reports) must list thereon all the names of other signatories, preceded by a "/s/" in the space where the signatures would otherwise appear. By submitting such a document, the filing attorney certifies that each of the other signatories has expressly agreed to the form and substance of the document and that the filing attorney has their actual authority to submit the document electronically. ME R USDCT App. 4(h)(2). For more information, refer to ME R USDCT App. 4(h)(2).

iii. *DISTRICT OF MAINE: Documents signed under oath.* Affidavits, declarations, verified complaints, or any other document signed under oath shall be filed electronically. The electronically filed version shall contain the typed name of the signatory, preceded by a "/s/" in the space where the signature would otherwise appear indicating that the paper document bears an original signature. ME R USDCT Rule 10; ME R USDCT App. 4(h)(3). For more information, refer to ME R USDCT Rule 10.

c. *Representations to the court.* By presenting to the court a pleading, written motion, or other paper—whether by signing, filing, submitting, or later advocating it—an attorney or unrepresented party certifies that to the best of the person's knowledge, information, and belief, formed after an inquiry reasonable under the circumstances: (1) it is not being presented for any improper purpose, such as to harass, cause unnecessary delay, or needlessly increase the cost of litigation; (2) the claims, defenses, and other legal contentions are warranted by existing law or by a nonfrivolous argument for extending, modifying, or reversing existing law or for establishing new law; (3) the factual contentions have evidentiary support or, if specifically so identified, will likely have evidentiary support after a reasonable opportunity for further investigation or discovery; and (4) the denials of factual contentions are warranted on the evidence or, if specifically so identified, are reasonably based on belief or a lack of information. FRCP 11(b).

d. *Sanctions.* If, after notice and a reasonable opportunity to respond, the court determines that FRCP 11(b) has been violated, the court may impose an appropriate sanction on any attorney, law firm, or party that violated FRCP 11(b) or is responsible for the violation. FRCP 11(c)(1). Refer to the United States District Court for the District of Maine KeyRules Motion for Sanctions document for more information.

5. *Privacy protection for filings made with the court*

a. *Redacted filings.* Unless the court orders otherwise, in an electronic or paper filing with the court that contains an individual's Social Security number, taxpayer-identification number, or birth date, the name of an individual known to be a minor, or a financial-account number, a party or nonparty making the filing may include only: (1) the last four (4) digits of the Social Security number and taxpayer-identification number; (2) the year of the individual's birth; (3) the minor's initials; and (4) the last four (4) digits of the financial-account number. FRCP 5.2(a).

i. *DISTRICT OF MAINE.* To address the privacy concerns created by the Internet access to court papers, unless otherwise ordered by the court, counsel shall modify certain personal data identifiers in pleadings and other papers as follows: (1) minors' names: use of the minors' initials only; (2) Social Security numbers: use of the last four (4) numbers only; (3) dates of birth: use of the year of birth only; [and] (4) financial account numbers: identify the type of account and the financial institution, but use only the last four (4) numbers of the account number. ME R USDCT Redacting Pleadings. Counsel should also use caution when filing papers that contain a person's medical records, employment history; financial information; and any proprietary or trade secret information. ME R USDCT Redacting Pleadings.

b. *Exemptions from the redaction requirement.* The redaction requirement does not apply to the following: (1) a financial-account number that identifies the property allegedly subject to forfeiture in a forfeiture proceeding; (2) the record of an administrative or agency proceeding; (3) the official record of a state-court proceeding; (4) the record of a court or tribunal, if that record was not subject to the redaction requirement when originally filed; (5) a filing covered by FRCP 5.2(c) or FRCP 5.2(d); and (6) a pro se filing in an action brought under 28 U.S.C.A. § 2241, 28 U.S.C.A. § 2254, or 28 U.S.C.A. § 2255. FRCP 5.2(b).

c. *Limitations on remote access to electronic files; Social Security appeals and immigration cases.* Unless the court orders otherwise, in an action for benefits under the Social Security Act, and in an action or proceeding relating to an order of removal, to relief from removal, or to immigration benefits or detention, access to an electronic file is authorized as follows: (1) the parties and their attorneys may have remote electronic access to any part of the case file, including the administrative record; (2) any other person may have electronic access to the full record at the courthouse, but may have remote electronic access only to: (A) the docket maintained by the court; and (B) an opinion, order, judgment, or other disposition of the court, but not any other part of the case file or the administrative record. FRCP 5.2(c).

d. *Filings made under seal.* The court may order that a filing be made under seal without redaction. The court may later unseal the filing or order the person who made the filing to file a redacted version for the public record. FRCP 5.2(d).

    i. *DISTRICT OF MAINE.* For information on filing sealed documents in the District of Maine, refer to ME R USDCT Rule 7A, ME R USDCT App. 4(p)(2), and ME R USDCT Sealed Filings.

e. *Protective orders.* For good cause, the court may by order in a case: (1) require redaction of additional information; or (2) limit or prohibit a nonparty's remote electronic access to a document filed with the court. FRCP 5.2(e).

f. *Option for additional unredacted filing under seal.* A person making a redacted filing may also file an unredacted copy under seal. The court must retain the unredacted copy as part of the record. FRCP 5.2(f).

    i. *DISTRICT OF MAINE.* A party wishing to file a document containing the personal data identifiers specified above may. . .file an unredacted document under seal. This document will be retained by the clerk's office as part of the record. ME R USDCT Redacting Pleadings. The court may, however, still require the party to file a redacted copy for the public file. ME R USDCT Redacting Pleadings.

g. *Option for filing a reference list.* A filing that contains redacted information may be filed together with a reference list that identifies each item of redacted information and specifies an appropriate identifier that uniquely corresponds to each item listed. The list must be filed under seal and may be amended as of right. Any reference in the case to a listed identifier will be construed to refer to the corresponding item of information. FRCP 5.2(g).

    i. *DISTRICT OF MAINE.* A party wishing to file a document containing the personal data identifiers specified above may. . .file a reference list under seal. The reference list shall contain the complete personal data identifier(s) and the redacted identifier(s) used in its (their) place in the filing. All references in the case to the redacted identifiers included in the reference list will be construed to refer to the corresponding complete identifier. The reference list must be filed under seal, and may be amended as of right. It shall be retained by the clerk's office as part of the record. ME R USDCT Redacting Pleadings. The court may, however, still require the party to file a redacted copy for the public file. ME R USDCT Redacting Pleadings.

h. *DISTRICT OF MAINE: Responsibility for redaction.* The clerk is not required to review documents filed with the court for compliance with FRCP 5.2. The responsibility to redact filings rests with counsel and the party or nonparty making the filing. ME R USDCT App. 4(i); ME R USDCT Redacting Pleadings. For guidelines for filing confidential information in civil cases in the District of Maine, refer to ME R USDCT Confidentiality.

i. *Waiver of protection of identifiers.* A person waives the protection of FRCP 5.2(a) as to the person's own information by filing it without redaction and not under seal. FRCP 5.2(h).

F. Filing and Service Requirements

1. *Filing requirements*

    a. *Required filings.* Any paper after the complaint that is required to be served must be filed no later than a reasonable time after service. FRCP 5(d)(1).

    b. *DISTRICT OF MAINE: Place of filing.* Unless otherwise ordered by the court, papers shall be filed with the court at Bangor in cases filed and pending at Bangor, and at Portland in cases filed and pending at Portland. ME R USDCT Rule 5(a).

    c. *Nonelectronic filing.* A paper not filed electronically is filed by delivering it: (A) to the clerk; or (B) to a judge who agrees to accept it for filing, and who must then note the filing date on the paper and promptly send it to the clerk. FRCP 5(d)(2).

        i. *DISTRICT OF MAINE: Documents to be filed in paper.* The following documents shall be filed in paper, which may also be scanned into ECF by the clerk's office: (A) all handwritten pleadings; and (B) all pleadings and documents filed by pro se litigants who are incarcerated or who are not registered filing users in ECF. ME R USDCT App. 4(g)(8). Non-prisoner pro se litigants in civil actions may register with ECF or may file (and serve) all pleadings and other documents in paper. The clerk's office will scan into ECF any pleadings and documents filed on paper in accordance with ME R USDCT App. 4(g). ME R USDCT App. 4(o). For more information, refer to ME R USDCT App. 4(g).

    d. *Electronic filing*

        i. *DISTRICT OF MAINE: Authorization.* Unless exempt or otherwise ordered by the court, papers shall be filed and served electronically as required by the court's Administrative Procedures Governing the Filing and Service by Electronic Means, which is set forth in ME R USDCT App. 4. The provisions of the court's Administrative Procedures Governing the Filing and Service by Electronic Means (ME R USDCT App. 4) shall be applied and enforced as part of the Local Rules of the United States District Court for the District of Maine. ME R USDCT Rule 5(c).

    ii.   *Filing by represented persons.* A person represented by an attorney must file electronically, unless nonelectronic filing is allowed by the court for good cause or is allowed or required by local rule. FRCP 5(d)(3)(A).

        • *DISTRICT OF MAINE.* An attorney may apply to the court for permission to file paper documents. ME R USDCT App. 4(a)(5).

    iii. *Filing by unrepresented persons.* A person not represented by an attorney: (i) may file electronically only if allowed by court order or by local rule; and (ii) may be required to file electronically only by court order, or by a local rule that includes reasonable exceptions. FRCP 5(d)(3)(B).

        • *DISTRICT OF MAINE.* Non-prisoner pro se litigants in civil actions may register with ECF or may file (and serve) all pleadings and other documents in paper. ME R USDCT App. 4(o). A non-prisoner who is a party to a civil action and who is not represented by an attorney may register to receive service electronically and to electronically transmit their documents to the court for filing in the ECF system. If during the course of the action the person retains an attorney who appears on the person's behalf, the clerk shall terminate the person's registration upon the attorney's appearance. ME R USDCT App. 4(b)(2).

    iv. *DISTRICT OF MAINE: Scope of electronic filing.* All documents submitted for filing in civil and criminal cases, regardless of case commencement date, except those documents specifically exempted in ME R USDCT App. 4(g), shall be filed electronically using the electronic case filing system (ECF). ME R USDCT App. 4(a)(1). For special filing requirements and exceptions, refer to ME R USDCT App. 4(g).

    v. *DISTRICT OF MAINE: Consequences of electronic filing.* Electronic transmission of a document to the ECF system, together with the transmission of a Notice of Electronic Filing (NEF) from the court, constitutes filing of the document for all purposes of the Federal Rules of Civil Procedure. ME R USDCT App. 4(d)(1).

    vi. *DISTRICT OF MAINE: Review of documents.* Documents filed with the clerk's office will normally be reviewed no later than the close of the next business day. It is the responsibility of the filing party to promptly notify the clerk's office via telephone of a matter that requires the immediate attention of a judicial officer. ME R USDCT App. 4(a)(4).

    e. *DISTRICT OF MAINE: Facsimile filing.* No papers shall be submitted to the court by means of a facsimile machine without prior leave of the court. ME R USDCT Rule 5(c); ME R USDCT App. 4(m).

2. *Service requirements*

    a. *Service; When required.* Unless the Federal Rules of Civil Procedure provide otherwise, each of the following papers must be served on every party: (A) an order stating that service is required; (B) a pleading filed after the original complaint, unless the court orders otherwise under FRCP 5(c) because there are numerous defendants; (C) a discovery paper required to be served on a party, unless the court orders otherwise; (D) a written motion, except one that may be heard ex parte; and (E) a written notice, appearance, demand, or offer of judgment, or any similar paper. FRCP 5(a)(1).

    i. *If a party fails to appear.* No service is required on a party who is in default for failing to appear. But a pleading that asserts a new claim for relief against such a party must be served on that party under FRCP 4. FRCP 5(a)(2).

    ii. *Seizing property.* If an action is begun by seizing property and no person is or need be named as a defendant, any service required before the filing of an appearance, answer, or claim must be made on the person who had custody or possession of the property when it was seized. FRCP 5(a)(3).

    b. *Service; How made.* A paper is served under FRCP 5 by: (A) handing it to the person; (B) leaving it: (i) at the person's office with a clerk or other person in charge or, if no one is in charge, in a conspicuous place in the office; or (ii) if the person has no office or the office is closed, at the person's dwelling or usual place of abode with someone of suitable age and discretion who resides there; (C) mailing it to the person's last known address—in which event service is complete upon mailing; (D) leaving it with the court clerk if the person has no known address; (E) sending it to a registered user by filing it with the court's electronic-filing system or sending it by other electronic means that the person consented to in writing—in either of which events service is complete upon filing or sending, but is not effective if the filer or sender learns that it did not reach the person to be served; or (F) delivering it by any other means that the person consented to in writing—in which event service is complete when the person making service delivers it to the agency designated to make delivery. FRCP 5(b)(2).

    i. *Serving an attorney.* If a party is represented by an attorney, service under FRCP 5 must be made on the attorney unless the court orders service on the party. FRCP 5(b)(1).

    c. *DISTRICT OF MAINE: Service of electronically filed documents*

        i. *Registered users.* Registration [as a filing user of the court's ECF system] constitutes consent to service of all documents by electronic means as provided in ME R USDCT App. 4. ME R USDCT App. 4(b)(4). Whenever a non-sealed pleading is filed electronically, the ECF system will automatically generate and send a Notice of Electronic Filing (NEF) to the filing user and registered users of record. The user filing the document should retain a paper or digital copy of the NEF, which shall serve as the court's date-stamp and proof of filing. ME R USDCT App. 4(e)(1).

            • *Sealed documents.* Although the filing of sealed documents in civil cases produces an NEF, the document itself cannot be accessed and counsel shall be responsible for making service of the sealed documents. ME R USDCT App. 4(e)(2).

        ii. *Non-registered users and pro se litigants.* Attorneys who have not yet registered as users with ECF and pro se litigants who have not registered with ECF shall be served a paper copy of any electronically filed pleading or other document in accordance with the provisions of FRCP 5. ME R USDCT App. 4(e)(3).

            • *Registration of pro se litigants.* A non-prisoner who is a party to a civil action and who is not represented by an attorney may register to receive service electronically and to electronically transmit their documents to the court for filing in the ECF system. If during the course of the action the person retains an attorney who appears on the person's behalf, the clerk shall terminate the person's registration upon the attorney's appearance. ME R USDCT App. 4(b)(2).

    d. *Serving numerous defendants.* If an action involves an unusually large number of defendants, the court may, on motion or on its own, order that: (A) defendants' pleadings and replies to them need not be served on other defendants; (B) any crossclaim, counterclaim, avoidance, or affirmative defense in those pleadings and replies to them will be treated as denied or avoided by all other parties; and (C) filing any such pleading and serving it on the plaintiff constitutes notice of the pleading to all parties. FRCP 5(c)(1).

        i. *Notifying parties.* A copy of every such order must be served on the parties as the court directs. FRCP 5(c)(2).

3. *DISTRICT OF MAINE: Filing and service of highly sensitive documents (HSDs).* For information on filing and serving highly sensitive documents (HSDs) in the District of Maine, refer to ME R USDCT General Order 21-5.

G. Hearings

1. *Hearings, generally.* When a motion relies on facts outside the record, the court may hear the matter on affidavits or may hear it wholly or partly on oral testimony or on depositions. FRCP 43(c).

    a. *Oral argument.* Due process does not require that oral argument be permitted on a motion and, except as otherwise provided by local rule, the district court has discretion to determine whether it will decide the motion on the papers or hear argument by counsel (and perhaps receive evidence). FPP § 1190; F.D.I.C. v. Deglau, 207 F.3d 153 (3d Cir. 2000).

        i. *DISTRICT OF MAINE.* Unless otherwise required by federal rule or statute, all motions may be decided by the court without oral argument unless otherwise ordered by the court on its own motion or, in its discretion, upon request of counsel. ME R USDCT Rule 7(e).

    b. *Providing a regular schedule for oral hearings.* A court may establish regular times and places for oral hearings on motions. FRCP 78(a).

    c. *Providing for submission on briefs.* By rule or order, the court may provide for submitting and determining motions on briefs, without oral hearings. FRCP 78(b).

2. *Hearing on motion for preliminary injunction.*

    a. *Consolidating the hearing with the trial on the merits.* Before or after beginning the hearing on a motion for a preliminary injunction, the court may advance the trial on the merits and consolidate it with the hearing. Even when consolidation is not ordered, evidence that is received on the motion and that would be admissible at trial becomes part of the trial record and need not be repeated at trial. But the court must preserve any party's right to a jury trial. FRCP 65(a)(2).

    b. *Expediting the hearing after temporary restraining order is issued without notice.* If the order is issued without notice, the motion for a preliminary injunction must be set for hearing at the earliest possible time, taking precedence over all other matters except hearings on older matters of the same character. At the hearing, the party who obtained the order must proceed with the motion; if the party does not, the court must dissolve the order. FRCP 65(b)(3).

H. Forms

1. Federal Motion for Preliminary Injunction Forms

a. Motion for preliminary injunction. 4A FEDFORMS § 47:14.

b. Motion enjoining use of information acquired from employment with plaintiff. 4A FEDFORMS § 47:17.

c. Motion enjoining interference with public access. 4A FEDFORMS § 47:18.

d. Motion enjoining collection of tax assessment. 4A FEDFORMS § 47:19.

e. Motion enjoining conducting election or certifying representative. 4A FEDFORMS § 47:20.

f. Motion enjoining preventing plaintiff's acting as teacher. 4A FEDFORMS § 47:21.

g. Motion enjoining interference with plaintiff's enforcement of judgment in related case. 4A FEDFORMS § 47:22.

h. Motion for preliminary injunction in patent infringement action. 4A FEDFORMS § 47:23.

i. Motion for preliminary injunction on basis of prayer of complaint and for setting hearing on motion. 4A FEDFORMS § 47:24.

j. Notice of motion. 4A FEDFORMS § 47:39.

k. Notice of motion and motion. 4A FEDFORMS § 47:41.

l. Declaration; In support of motion for preliminary injunction. AMJUR PP INJUNCTION § 38.

m. Memorandum of points and authorities; In support of motion for preliminary injunction. AMJUR PP INJUNCTION § 39.

n. Notice; Motion for preliminary injunction. AMJUR PP INJUNCTION § 40.

o. Motion; For preliminary injunction. AMJUR PP INJUNCTION § 41.

p. Motion; For preliminary injunction; On pleadings and other papers without evidentiary hearing or oral argument. AMJUR PP INJUNCTION § 43.

q. Affidavit; In support of motion for preliminary injunction. AMJUR PP INJUNCTION § 52.

r. Bond; To obtain preliminary injunction. FEDPROF § 1:226.

s. Opposition; To motion. FEDPROF § 1B:175.

t. Brief; Supporting or opposing motion. FEDPROF § 1B:177.

u. Motion for temporary restraining order and preliminary injunction. GOLDLTGFMS § 13A:6.

v. Motion for preliminary injunction. GOLDLTGFMS § 13A:18.

w. Motion for preliminary injunction; Based upon pleadings and other papers without evidentiary hearing or oral argument. GOLDLTGFMS § 13A:19.

x. Motion for preliminary injunction; Supporting affidavit. GOLDLTGFMS § 13A:20.

y. Bond. GOLDLTGFMS § 19:2.

z. Bond; In support of injunction. GOLDLTGFMS § 19:3.

I. Applicable Rules

1. *Federal rules*

a. Serving and filing pleadings and other papers. FRCP 5.

b. Constitutional challenge to a statute; Notice, certification, and intervention. FRCP 5.1.

c. Privacy protection for filings made with the court. FRCP 5.2.

d. Computing and extending time; Time for motion papers. FRCP 6.

e. Pleadings allowed; Form of motions and other papers. FRCP 7.

f. Disclosure statement. FRCP 7.1.

g. Form of pleadings. FRCP 10.

h. Signing pleadings, motions, and other papers; Representations to the court; Sanctions. FRCP 11.

i. Taking testimony. FRCP 43.

    j.   Injunctions and restraining orders. FRCP 65.

    k.   Hearing motions; Submission on briefs. FRCP 78.

2. *Local rules*

    a. *DISTRICT OF MAINE*

        i.   Service and filing of pleadings and other papers. ME R USDCT Rule 5.

        ii.   Time. ME R USDCT Rule 6.

       iii.   Motions and memoranda of law. ME R USDCT Rule 7.

       iv.   Corporate disclosure. ME R USDCT Rule 7.1.

        v.   Pleading special matters. ME R USDCT Rule 9.

       vi.   Form of pleadings, motions and other papers. ME R USDCT Rule 10.

      vii.   Discovery. ME R USDCT Rule 26.

     viii.   Attorneys; Appearances and withdrawals. ME R USDCT Rule 83.2.

       ix.   Alternative dispute resolution (ADR). ME R USDCT Rule 83.11.

        x.   Administrative procedures governing the filing and service by electronic means. ME R USDCT App. 4.

       xi.   Redacting pleadings. ME R USDCT Redacting Pleadings.

Motions, Oppositions and Replies
Motion to Dismiss for Failure to State a Claim

Document Last Updated April 2021

A. Checklist

  (I) ❑ Matters to be considered by moving party

    (a) ❑ Required documents

        (1) ❑ Notice of motion and motion

    (b) ❑ Supplemental documents

        (1) ❑ Pleading being attacked

        (2) ❑ Notice of constitutional question

        (3) ❑ Nongovernmental corporate disclosure statement

        (4) ❑ DISTRICT OF MAINE: Additional supplemental documents

           (i) ❑ Proposed order

    (c) ❑ Timing

        (1) ❑ Failure to state a claim upon which relief can be granted may be raised: in any pleading allowed or ordered under FRCP 7(a); every defense to a claim for relief in any pleading must be asserted in the responsive pleading if one is required

        (2) ❑ A motion asserting any of the defenses in FRCP 12(b) must be made before pleading if a responsive pleading is allowed

        (3) ❑ Failure to state a claim upon which relief can be granted may be raised: by a motion under FRCP 12(c); after the pleadings are closed—but early enough not to delay trial—a party may move for judgment on the pleadings

        (4) ❑ Failure to state a claim upon which relief can be granted may be raised: at trial; if a pleading sets out a claim for relief that does not require a responsive pleading, an opposing party may assert at trial any defense to that claim

        (5) ❑ A written motion and notice of the hearing must be served at least fourteen (14) days before the time specified for the hearing, with the following exceptions: (A) when the motion may be heard ex parte; (B) when the Federal Rules of Civil Procedure set a different time; or (C) when a court order—which a party may, for good cause, apply for ex parte—sets a different time

(6) ❑ Any affidavit supporting a motion must be served with the motion

(7) ❑ DISTRICT OF MAINE: Additional timing

 (i) ❑ Any affidavits and other documents setting forth or evidencing facts on which the motion is based must be filed with the motion

(II) ❑ Matters to be considered by opposing party

 (a) ❑ Required documents

  (1) ❑ Opposition

 (b) ❑ Supplemental documents

  (1) ❑ Pleading being attacked

  (2) ❑ Notice of constitutional question

 (c) ❑ Timing

  (1) ❑ Except as FRCP 59(c) provides otherwise, any opposing affidavit must be served at least seven (7) days before the hearing, unless the court permits service at another time

  (2) ❑ DISTRICT OF MAINE: Additional timing

   (i) ❑ Unless within twenty-one (21) days after the filing of a motion the opposing party files written objection thereto, incorporating a memorandum of law, the opposing party shall be deemed to have waived objection

B. Timing

1. *Motion to dismiss for failure to state a claim*

 a. *In a pleading under FRCP 7(a).* Failure to state a claim upon which relief can be granted may be raised: in any pleading allowed or ordered under FRCP 7(a). FRCP 12(h)(2)(A).

  i. *In a responsive pleading.* Every defense to a claim for relief in any pleading must be asserted in the responsive pleading if one is required. FRCP 12(b).

 b. *By motion.* A motion asserting any of the defenses in FRCP 12(b) must be made before pleading if a responsive pleading is allowed. FRCP 12(b). Although FRCP 12(b) encourages the responsive pleader to file a motion to dismiss before filing the answer, nothing in FRCP 12 prohibits the filing of a motion to dismiss with the answer. An untimely motion to dismiss may be considered if the defense asserted in the motion was previously raised in the responsive pleading. FEDPROC § 62:421.

 c. *By motion under FRCP 12(c).* Failure to state a claim upon which relief can be granted may be raised: by a motion under FRCP 12(c). FRCP 12(h)(2)(B). After the pleadings are closed—but early enough not to delay trial—a party may move for judgment on the pleadings. FRCP 12(c).

 d. *At trial.* Failure to state a claim upon which relief can be granted may be raised: at trial. FRCP 12(h)(2)(C). If a pleading sets out a claim for relief that does not require a responsive pleading, an opposing party may assert at trial any defense to that claim. FRCP 12(b).

2. *Timing of motions, generally*

 a. *Motion and notice of hearing.* A written motion and notice of the hearing must be served at least fourteen (14) days before the time specified for the hearing, with the following exceptions: (A) when the motion may be heard ex parte; (B) when the Federal Rules of Civil Procedure set a different time; or (C) when a court order—which a party may, for good cause, apply for ex parte—sets a different time. FRCP 6(c)(1).

 b. *Supporting affidavit.* Any affidavit supporting a motion must be served with the motion. FRCP 6(c)(2).

 c. *DISTRICT OF MAINE: Affidavits and other supporting documents.* Any affidavits and other documents setting forth or evidencing facts on which the motion is based must be filed with the motion. ME R USDCT Rule 7(a).

3. *Timing of opposing papers.* Except as FRCP 59(c) provides otherwise, any opposing affidavit must be served at least seven (7) days before the hearing, unless the court permits service at another time. FRCP 6(c)(2).

 a. *DISTRICT OF MAINE.* Unless within twenty-one (21) days after the filing of a motion the opposing party files written objection thereto, incorporating a memorandum of law, the opposing party shall be deemed to have waived objection. ME R USDCT Rule 7(b). The deemed waiver imposed in ME R USDCT Rule 7(b) shall not apply to motions filed during trial. ME R USDCT Rule 7(b).

4. *Timing of reply papers.* Where the respondent files an answering affidavit setting up a new matter, the moving party ordinarily is allowed a reasonable time to file a reply affidavit since failure to deny the new matter by affidavit may operate as an admission of its truth. AMJUR MOTIONS § 25.

    a. *DISTRICT OF MAINE.* Within fourteen (14) days of the filing of any objection to a motion, the moving party may file a reply memorandum. ME R USDCT Rule 7(c).

5. *Effect of FRCP 12 motion on the time to serve a responsive pleading.* Unless the court sets a different time, serving a motion under FRCP 12 alters the periods in FRCP 12(a) as follows: (A) if the court denies the motion or postpones its disposition until trial, the responsive pleading must be served within fourteen (14) days after notice of the court's action; or (B) if the court grants a motion for a more definite statement, the responsive pleading must be served within fourteen (14) days after the more definite statement is served. FRCP 12(a)(4).

6. *Computation of time*

    a. *Computing time.* FRCP 6 applies in computing any time period specified in the Federal Rules of Civil Procedure, in any local rule or court order, or in any statute that does not specify a method of computing time. FRCP 6(a).

        i. *Period stated in days or a longer unit.* When the period is stated in days or a longer unit of time: (A) exclude the day of the event that triggers the period; (B) count every day, including intermediate Saturdays, Sundays, and legal holidays; and (C) include the last day of the period, but if the last day is a Saturday, Sunday, or legal holiday, the period continues to run until the end of the next day that is not a Saturday, Sunday, or legal holiday. FRCP 6(a)(1).

        ii. *Period stated in hours.* When the period is stated in hours: (A) begin counting immediately on the occurrence of the event that triggers the period; (B) count every hour, including hours during intermediate Saturdays, Sundays, and legal holidays; and (C) if the period would end on a Saturday, Sunday, or legal holiday, the period continues to run until the same time on the next day that is not a Saturday, Sunday, or legal holiday. FRCP 6(a)(2).

        iii. *Inaccessibility of the clerk's office.* Unless the court orders otherwise, if the clerk's office is inaccessible: (A) on the last day for filing under FRCP 6(a)(1), then the time for filing is extended to the first accessible day that is not a Saturday, Sunday, or legal holiday; or (B) during the last hour for filing under FRCP 6(a)(2), then the time for filing is extended to the same time on the first accessible day that is not a Saturday, Sunday, or legal holiday. FRCP 6(a)(3).

        iv. *"Last day" defined.* Unless a different time is set by a statute, local rule, or court order, the last day ends: (A) for electronic filing, at midnight in the court's time zone; and (B) for filing by other means, when the clerk's office is scheduled to close. FRCP 6(a)(4).

        v. *"Next day" defined.* The "next day" is determined by continuing to count forward when the period is measured after an event and backward when measured before an event. FRCP 6(a)(5).

        vi. *"Legal holiday" defined.* "Legal holiday" means: (A) the day set aside by statute for observing New Year's Day, Martin Luther King Jr.'s Birthday, Washington's Birthday, Memorial Day, Independence Day, Labor Day, Columbus Day, Veterans' Day, Thanksgiving Day, or Christmas Day; (B) any day declared a holiday by the President or Congress; and (C) for periods that are measured after an event, any other day declared a holiday by the state where the district court is located. FRCP 6(a)(6).

        vii. *DISTRICT OF MAINE: Applicability of FRCP 6.* FRCP 6 applies when computing any period of time stated in the Local Rules of the United States District Court for the District of Maine. ME R USDCT Rule 6(a).

    b. *DISTRICT OF MAINE: Computation of electronic filing deadlines.* Filing documents electronically does not in any way alter any filing deadlines. All electronic transmissions of documents must be completed prior to midnight, Eastern Time, in order to be considered timely filed that day. Where a specific time of day deadline is set by court order or stipulation, the electronic filing must be completed by that time. ME R USDCT App. 4(f). A document filed electronically shall be deemed filed at the time and date stated on the Notice of Electronic Filing received from the court. ME R USDCT App. 4(d)(2).

        i. *Technical failures.* A filing user whose filing is made untimely as the result of a technical failure may seek appropriate relief from the court. ME R USDCT App. 4(n). A technical failure of the court's ECF system is deemed to have occurred when the court's ECF site cannot accept filings continuously or intermittently over the course of any period of time greater than one (1) hour. Known system outages will be posted on the court's website along with guidance on how to proceed, if applicable. ME R USDCT App. 4(n).

    c. *Extending time.* When an act may or must be done within a specified time, the court may, for good cause, extend the time: (A) with or without motion or notice if the court acts, or if a request is made, before the original time or its extension expires; or (B) on motion made after the time has expired if the party failed to act because of excusable neglect. FRCP 6(b)(1). A court must not extend the time to act under FRCP 50(b), FRCP 50(d), FRCP 52(b), FRCP 59(b), FRCP 59(d), FRCP 59(e), and FRCP 60(b). FRCP 6(b)(2). Refer to the United States District Court for the District of Maine KeyRules Motion for Continuance/Extension of Time document for more information on extending time.

    d. *Additional time after certain kinds of service.* When a party may or must act within a specified time after being served and service is made under FRCP 5(b)(2)(C) (by mail), FRCP 5(b)(2)(D) (by leaving with the clerk), or FRCP 5(b)(2)(F) (by other means consented to), three (3) days are added after the period would otherwise expire under FRCP 6(a). FRCP 6(d).

C. General Requirements

1. *Motions, generally*

    a. *Motion requirements.* A request for a court order must be made by motion. The motion must: (A) be in writing unless made during a hearing or trial; (B) state with particularity the grounds for seeking the order; and (C) state the relief sought. FRCP 7(b)(1). The writing and particularity requirements are intended to ensure that the adverse parties are informed of and have a record of both the motion's pendency and the grounds on which the movant seeks an order. FPP § 1191; Feldberg v. Quechee Lakes Corp., 463 F.3d 195 (2d Cir. 2006).

        i. *Particularity requirement.* The particularity requirement [ensures] that the opposing parties will have notice of their opponent's contentions. FEDPROC § 62:358; Goodman v. 1973 26 Foot Trojan Vessel, Arkansas Registration No. AR1439SN, 859 F.2d 71 (8th Cir. 1988). That requirement ensures that notice of the basis for the motion is provided to the court and to the opposing party so as to avoid prejudice, provide the opponent with a meaningful opportunity to respond, and provide the court with enough information to process the motion correctly. FEDPROC § 62:358; Andreas v. Volkswagen of Am., Inc., 336 F.3d 789 (8th Cir. 2003).

          • Reasonable specification of the grounds for a motion is sufficient. The particularity requirement for motions is satisfied when no party is prejudiced by a lack of particularity or when the court can comprehend the basis for the motion and deal with it fairly. However, where a movant fails to state even one ground for granting the motion in question, the movant has failed to meet the minimal standard of "reasonable specification." FEDPROC § 62:358; Martinez v. Trainor, 556 F.2d 818 (7th Cir. 1977).

          • The court may excuse the failure to comply with the particularity requirement if it is inadvertent, and where no prejudice is shown by the opposing party. FEDPROC § 62:358.

    b. *Notice of motion.* A party interested in resisting the relief sought by a motion has a right to notice thereof, and an opportunity to be heard. AMJUR MOTIONS § 12.

        i. *Purpose.* In addition to statutory or court rule provisions requiring notice of a motion—the purpose of such a notice requirement having been said to be to prevent a party from being prejudicially surprised by a motion—principles of natural justice dictate that an adverse party generally must be given notice that a motion will be presented to the court. AMJUR MOTIONS § 12.

        ii. *Adequacy of notice.* The test of adequate notice generally turns on whether the other parties were afforded an adequate opportunity to prepare and respond to the issues to be raised in the proceeding. AMJUR MOTIONS § 12.

    c. *Single document containing motion and notice.* A single written document can satisfy the writing requirements both for a motion and for an FRCP 6(c)(1) notice. FRCP 7(Advisory Committee Notes).

2. *Motion to dismiss for failure to state a claim.* A party may assert the following defense by motion: failure to state a claim upon which relief can be granted. FRCP 12(b)(6). The motion under FRCP 12(b)(6) is available to test a claim for relief in any pleading, whether it be in the plaintiff's original complaint, a defendant's counterclaim, a defendant's crossclaim or counterclaim thereto, or a third-party claim or any other FRCP 14 claim. Most commonly, of course, an FRCP 12(b)(6) motion is directed against the plaintiff's complaint. FPP § 1356.

    a. *Applicable standard.* The FRCP 12(b)(6) motion is used to test the sufficiency of the complaint. FEDPROC § 62:455; Petruska v. Gannon Univ., 462 F.3d 294 (3d Cir. 2006). In this regard, the applicable standard is stated in FRCP 8(a)(2), which requires that a pleading setting forth a claim for relief contain a short and plain statement of the claim showing that the pleader is entitled to relief. Thus, a complaint must set forth sufficient information to suggest that there is some recognized legal theory upon which relief can be granted. FEDPROC § 62:455. Only when the plaintiff's complaint fails to meet this pleading standard—which has traditionally been understood to be a liberal standard but which the Supreme Court has recently interpreted to be more stringent—is it subject to dismissal under FRCP 12(b)(6). FPP § 1356.

    i.   *Greater particularity in complaint required.* In order to withstand a motion to dismiss filed under FRCP 12(b)(6) in response to claims understood to raise a high risk of abusive litigation, addressed by FRCP 9(b), a plaintiff must state factual allegations with greater particularity than that required by FRCP 8. FEDPROC § 62:464; Bell Atl. Corp. v. Twombly, 550 U.S. 544, 127 S. Ct. 1955, 167 L. Ed. 2d 929 (2007).

    ii. *Disfavored by the courts.* FRCP 12(b)(6) motions are looked on with disfavor by the courts, and are granted sparingly and with care. Dismissals for failure to state a claim are especially disfavored in cases where the complaint sets forth a novel legal theory that can best be assessed after factual development. FEDPROC § 62:458.

  b. *Construction of allegations of complaint (or other pleading).* In considering an FRCP 12(b)(6) motion to dismiss, the complaint is liberally construed and is viewed in the light most favorable to the plaintiff. FEDPROC § 62:461; Bell Atl. Corp. v. Twombly, 550 U.S. 544, 127 S. Ct. 1955, 167 L. Ed. 2d 929 (2007).

    i.   *Presumptions and inferences.* On a motion to dismiss, a federal court presumes that general allegations embrace those specific facts that are necessary to support the claim. FEDPROC § 62:461; Steel Co. v. Citizens for a Better Env't, 523 U.S. 83, 118 S. Ct. 1003, 140 L. Ed. 2d 210 (1998). In addition, the well-pleaded allegations of fact contained in the complaint and every inference fairly deducible therefrom are accepted as true for purposes of the motion, including facts alleged on information and belief. FEDPROC § 62:461; Bell Atl. Corp. v. Twombly, 550 U.S. 544, 127 S. Ct. 1955, 167 L. Ed. 2d 929 (2007); Tellabs, Inc. v. Makor Issues & Rights, Ltd., 551 U.S. 308, 127 S. Ct. 2499, 168 L. Ed. 2d 179 (2007).

       • However, the court will not accept as true the plaintiff's bare statements of opinions, conclusory allegations, including legal conclusion couched as a factual allegation, and unwarranted inferences of fact. FEDPROC § 62:461; Leopoldo Fontanillas, Inc. v. Luis Ayala Colon Sucesores, Inc., 283 F. Supp. 2d 579 (D.P.R. 2003); Hopkins v. Women's Div., Gen. Bd. of Glob. Ministries, 238 F. Supp. 2d 174 (D.D.C. 2002). Nor will the court accept as true facts which are legally impossible, facts which the court can take judicial notice of as being other than as alleged by the plaintiff, or facts which by the record or by a document attached to the complaint appear to be unfounded. FEDPROC § 62:461; Cohen v. United States, 129 F.2d 733 (8th Cir. 1942); Henthorn v. Dep't of Navy, 29 F.3d 682 (D.C. Cir. 1994).

  c. *Affirmative defenses.* It is generally agreed that affirmative defenses can be raised by an FRCP 12(b)(6) motion to dismiss. FEDPROC § 62:465; McCready v. eBay, Inc., 453 F.3d 882 (7th Cir. 2006). However, in order for these defenses to be raised on an FRCP 12(b)(6) motion to dismiss, the complaint must clearly show on its face that the affirmative defense is applicable and bars the action. FEDPROC § 62:465; In re Colonial Mortg. Bankers Corp., 324 F.3d 12 (1st Cir. 2003). Thus, FRCP 12(b)(6) motions may be used to raise the affirmative defenses of: statute of limitations; statute of frauds; res judicata; collateral estoppel; release; waiver; estoppel; sovereign immunity; qualified immunity; illegality; contributory negligence; and preemption. FEDPROC § 62:465.

  d. *Joining motions.* A motion under FRCP 12 may be joined with any other motion allowed by FRCP 12. FRCP 12(g)(1).

    i.   *Limitation on further motions.* Except as provided in FRCP 12(h)(2) or FRCP 12(h)(3), a party that makes a motion under FRCP 12 must not make another motion under FRCP 12 raising a defense or objection that was available to the party but omitted from its earlier motion. FRCP 12(g)(2).

  e. *Waiving and preserving certain defenses.* No defense or objection is waived by joining it with one or more other defenses or objections in a responsive pleading or in a motion. FRCP 12(b). Failure to state a claim upon which relief can be granted, to join a person required by FRCP 19(b), or to state a legal defense to a claim may be raised:

    i.   In any pleading allowed or ordered under FRCP 7(a);

    ii. By a motion under FRCP 12(c); or

    iii. At trial. FRCP 12(h)(2).

3. *Opposing papers.* The Federal Rules of Civil Procedure do not require any formal answer, return, or reply to a motion, except where the Federal Rules of Civil Procedure or local rules may require affidavits, memoranda, or other papers to be filed in opposition to a motion. Such papers are simply to apprise the court of such opposition and the grounds of that opposition. FEDPROC § 62:353.

  a. *DISTRICT OF MAINE: Content of objections.* Any objections shall include citations and supporting authorities and affidavits and other documents setting forth or evidencing facts on which the objection is based. ME R USDCT Rule 7(b).

b. *Effect of failure to respond to motion.* Although in the absence of statutory provision or court rule, a motion ordinarily does not require a response or written answer, when a party files a motion and the opposing party fails to respond, the court may construe such failure to respond as nonopposition to the motion or an admission that the motion was meritorious. AMJUR MOTIONS § 28. The rule in some jurisdictions being that the failure to respond to a fact set forth in a motion is deemed an admission—and may grant the motion if the relief requested appears to be justified. AMJUR MOTIONS § 28.

    i. *Unopposed motion to dismiss.* The circuits are split on whether a court may grant a motion to dismiss solely on the basis that the plaintiff did not file a response opposing the motion. FRCP-RC RULE 12.

        • Some circuits hold that FRCP 12(b)(6) motions can be granted solely because they are unopposed. FRCP-RC RULE 12; Fox v. Am. Airlines, Inc., 389 F.3d 1291, 1295 (D.C. Cir. 2004); Cohen v. Bd. of Trustees of the Univ. of the D.C., 819 F.3d 476, 483-484 (D.C. Cir. 2016). Other circuits hold that, while the plaintiff has forfeited its ability to present arguments for why the complaint is sufficient, the court still must assess the sufficiency of the complaint. FRCP-RC RULE 12.

c. *Assent or no opposition not determinative.* However, a motion will not be granted automatically simply because an "assent" or a notation of "no opposition" has been filed; federal judges frequently deny motions that have been assented to when it is thought that justice so dictates. FPP § 1190.

d. *Responsive pleading inappropriate as response to motion.* An attempt to answer or oppose a motion with a responsive pleading usually is not appropriate. FPP § 1190.

4. *Reply papers.* A moving party may be required or permitted to prepare papers in addition to its original motion papers. AMJUR MOTIONS § 25. Papers answering or replying to opposing papers may be appropriate, in the interests of justice, where it appears there is a substantial reason for allowing a reply. Thus, a court may accept reply papers where a party demonstrates that the papers to which it seeks to file a reply raise new issues that are material to the disposition of the question before the court, or where the court determines, sua sponte, that it wishes further briefing of an issue raised in those papers and orders the submission of additional papers. FEDPROC § 62:354.

a. *Function of reply papers.* The function of a reply affidavit or reply papers is to answer the arguments made in opposition to the position taken by the movant, not to raise new issues, arguments, or evidence, or change the nature of the primary motion. However, if the court permits new evidence with the reply papers, the other party should be given the opportunity to respond. Where the party opposing the motion has no opportunity to address the argument in writing, a court has the discretion to disregard arguments raised for the first time in a reply memorandum. Also, the view has been followed in some jurisdictions that as a matter of judicial economy, where there is no prejudice and where the issues could be raised simply by filing a motion to dismiss, the trial court has discretion to consider arguments raised for the first time in a reply memorandum, and that a trial court may grant a motion to strike issues raised for the first time in a reply memorandum. AMJUR MOTIONS § 26.

    i. *DISTRICT OF MAINE.* The moving party may file a reply memorandum. . .which shall be strictly confined to replying to new matter raised in the objection or opposing memorandum. ME R USDCT Rule 7(c).

5. *DISTRICT OF MAINE: Appearances.* An attorney's signature to a pleading shall constitute an appearance for the party filing the pleading. Otherwise, an attorney who wishes to participate in any manner in any action must file a formal written appearance identifying the party represented. An appearance whether by pleading or formal written appearance shall be signed by an attorney in his/her individual name and shall state his/her office address. ME R USDCT Rule 83.2(a). For more information, refer to ME R USDCT Rule 83.2.

6. *DISTRICT OF MAINE: Alternative dispute resolution (ADR).* Litigants are authorized and encouraged to employ, at their own expense, any available ADR process on which they can agree, including early neutral evaluation, settlement conferences, mediation, non-binding summary jury trial, corporate mini-trial, and arbitration proceedings. ME R USDCT Rule 83.11(a). For more information on ADR, refer to ME R USDCT Rule 83.11.

D. Documents

1. *Documents for moving party*

    a. *Required documents*

        i. *Notice of motion and motion.* Refer to the "C. General Requirements" section of this KeyRules document for information on the notice of motion and motion.

            • *DISTRICT OF MAINE: Memorandum of law.* Every motion shall incorporate a memorandum of law, including citations and supporting authorities. ME R USDCT Rule 7(a). Refer to the "E. Format" section of this KeyRules document for the form of memoranda of law.

- *Certificate of service.* No certificate of service is required when a paper is served by filing it with the court's electronic-filing system. When a paper that is required to be served is served by other means: (i) if the paper is filed, a certificate of service must be filed with it or within a reasonable time after service; and (ii) if the paper is not filed, a certificate of service need not be filed unless filing is required by court order or by local rule. FRCP 5(d)(1)(B).

b. *Supplemental documents*

    i. *Pleading being attacked.* As a general rule, the court may only consider the pleading which is attacked by an FRCP 12(b)(6) motion in determining its sufficiency. FEDPROC § 62:460; Armengau v. Cline, 7 F. App'x 336 (6th Cir. 2001). The plaintiff is not entitled to discovery to obtain information relevant to the motion, and the court is not permitted to look at matters outside the record. FEDPROC § 62:460; Cooperativa de Ahorro y Credito Aguada v. Kidder, Peabody & Co., 993 F.2d 269 (1st Cir. 1993). However, the court may consider documents which are attached to or submitted with the complaint, as well as legal arguments presented in memorandums or briefs and arguments of counsel. FEDPROC § 62:460; Tellabs, Inc. v. Makor Issues & Rights, Ltd., 551 U.S. 308, 127 S. Ct. 2499, 168 L. Ed. 2d 179 (2007); E.E.O.C. v. Ohio Edison Co., 7 F.3d 541 (6th Cir. 1993). Documents not attached to the complaint may also be considered if they are incorporated by reference, or their contents are alleged in the complaint, they are central to the claim, integral to or explicitly relied upon, their authenticity is undisputed, and their relevance is uncontested. FEDPROC § 62:460. If, on a motion under FRCP 12(b)(6) or FRCP 12(c), matters outside the pleadings are presented to and not excluded by the court, the motion must be treated as one for summary judgment under FRCP 56. All parties must be given a reasonable opportunity to present all the material that is pertinent to the motion. FRCP 12(d).

    ii. *Notice of constitutional question.* A party that files a pleading, written motion, or other paper drawing into question the constitutionality of a federal or state statute must promptly: (1) file a notice of constitutional question stating the question and identifying the paper that raises it, if: (A) a federal statute is questioned and the parties do not include the United States, one of its agencies, or one of its officers or employees in an official capacity; or (B) a state statute is questioned and the parties do not include the state, one of its agencies, or one of its officers or employees in an official capacity; and (2) serve the notice and paper on the Attorney General of the United States if a federal statute is questioned—or on the state attorney general if a state statute is questioned—either by certified or registered mail or by sending it to an electronic address designated by the attorney general for this purpose. FRCP 5.1(a).

- *No forfeiture.* A party's failure to file and serve the notice, or the court's failure to certify, does not forfeit a constitutional claim or defense that is otherwise timely asserted. FRCP 5.1(d).

    iii. *Nongovernmental corporate disclosure statement.* A nongovernmental corporate party must file two (2) copies of a disclosure statement that: (1) identifies any parent corporation and any publicly held corporation owning ten percent (10%) or more of its stock; or (2) states that there is no such corporation. FRCP 7.1(a). A party must: (1) file the disclosure statement with its first appearance, pleading, petition, motion, response, or other request addressed to the court; and (2) promptly file a supplemental statement if any required information changes. FRCP 7.1(b).

- *DISTRICT OF MAINE: Notice of interested parties.* To enable the court to evaluate possible disqualification or recusal, counsel for all non-governmental parties shall file with their first appearance a Notice of Interested Parties, which shall list all persons, associations of persons, firms, partnerships, limited liability companies, joint ventures, corporations (including parent or affiliated corporations, clearly identified as such), or any similar entities, owning ten percent (10%) or more of the named party. Counsel shall be under a continuing obligation to file an amended Notice if any material change occurs in the status of an Interested Party, such as through merger, acquisition, or new/additional membership. ME R USDCT Rule 7.1.

    iv. *DISTRICT OF MAINE: Additional supplemental documents*

- *Proposed order.* Proposed orders shall not be filed unless requested by the court. When requested by the court, proposed orders shall be filed by e-mail in word processing format. ME R USDCT App. 4(k)(1).

2. *Documents for opposing party*

a. *Required documents*

    i. *Opposition.* Refer to the "C. General Requirements" section of this KeyRules document for information on the opposing papers.

- *DISTRICT OF MAINE: Memorandum of law.* Unless within twenty-one (21) days after the filing of a

motion the opposing party files written objection thereto, incorporating a memorandum of law, the opposing party shall be deemed to have waived objection. ME R USDCT Rule 7(b).

- *Certificate of service.* No certificate of service is required when a paper is served by filing it with the court's electronic-filing system. When a paper that is required to be served is served by other means: (i) if the paper is filed, a certificate of service must be filed with it or within a reasonable time after service; and (ii) if the paper is not filed, a certificate of service need not be filed unless filing is required by court order or by local rule. FRCP 5(d)(1)(B).

  b. *Supplemental documents*

    i. *Pleading being attacked.* As a general rule, the court may only consider the pleading which is attacked by an FRCP 12(b)(6) motion in determining its sufficiency. FEDPROC § 62:460; Armengau v. Cline, 7 F. App'x 336 (6th Cir. 2001). The plaintiff is not entitled to discovery to obtain information relevant to the motion, and the court is not permitted to look at matters outside the record. FEDPROC § 62:460; Cooperativa de Ahorro y Credito Aguada v. Kidder, Peabody & Co., 993 F.2d 269 (1st Cir. 1993). However, the court may consider documents which are attached to or submitted with the complaint, as well as legal arguments presented in memorandums or briefs and arguments of counsel. FEDPROC § 62:460; Tellabs, Inc. v. Makor Issues & Rights, Ltd., 551 U.S. 308, 127 S. Ct. 2499, 168 L. Ed. 2d 179 (2007); E.E.O.C. v. Ohio Edison Co., 7 F.3d 541 (6th Cir. 1993). Documents not attached to the complaint may also be considered if they are incorporated by reference, or their contents are alleged in the complaint, they are central to the claim, integral to or explicitly relied upon, their authenticity is undisputed, and their relevance is uncontested. FEDPROC § 62:460. If, on a motion under FRCP 12(b)(6) or FRCP 12(c), matters outside the pleadings are presented to and not excluded by the court, the motion must be treated as one for summary judgment under FRCP 56. All parties must be given a reasonable opportunity to present all the material that is pertinent to the motion. FRCP 12(d).

    ii. *Notice of constitutional question.* A party that files a pleading, written motion, or other paper drawing into question the constitutionality of a federal or state statute must promptly: (1) file a notice of constitutional question stating the question and identifying the paper that raises it, if: (A) a federal statute is questioned and the parties do not include the United States, one of its agencies, or one of its officers or employees in an official capacity; or (B) a state statute is questioned and the parties do not include the state, one of its agencies, or one of its officers or employees in an official capacity; and (2) serve the notice and paper on the Attorney General of the United States if a federal statute is questioned—or on the state attorney general if a state statute is questioned—either by certified or registered mail or by sending it to an electronic address designated by the attorney general for this purpose. FRCP 5.1(a).

- *No forfeiture.* A party's failure to file and serve the notice, or the court's failure to certify, does not forfeit a constitutional claim or defense that is otherwise timely asserted. FRCP 5.1(d).

E. Format

1. *Form of documents.* The rules governing captions and other matters of form in pleadings apply to motions and other papers. FRCP 7(b)(2).

  a. *DISTRICT OF MAINE: Font size, line spacing, and paper size.* All such documents shall be typed in a font of no less than size twelve (12) point, and shall be double-spaced or printed on eight and one-half by eleven (8-1/2 x 11) inch paper. Footnotes shall be in a font of no less than size ten (10) point, and may be single spaced. ME R USDCT Rule 10.

  b. *Caption.* Every pleading must have a caption with the court's name, a title, a file number, and an FRCP 7(a) designation. FRCP 10(a).

    i. *Names of parties.* The title of the complaint must name all the parties; the title of other pleadings, after naming the first party on each side, may refer generally to other parties. FRCP 10(a).

    ii. *DISTRICT OF MAINE: Additional caption requirements.* All pleadings, motions and other papers filed with the clerk or otherwise submitted to the court, except exhibits, shall bear the proper case number and shall contain on the first page a caption as described by FRCP 10(a) and immediately thereunder a designation of what the document is and the name of the party in whose behalf it is submitted. ME R USDCT Rule 10.

  c. *Claims or defenses*

    i. *Numbered paragraphs.* A party must state its claims or defenses in numbered paragraphs, each limited as far as practicable to a single set of circumstances. A later pleading may refer by number to a paragraph in an earlier pleading. FRCP 10(b).

    ii. *Separate statements.* If doing so would promote clarity, each claim founded on a separate transaction or occurrence—and each defense other than a denial—must be stated in a separate count or defense. FRCP 10(b).

  d. *Adoption by reference.* A statement in a pleading may be adopted by reference elsewhere in the same pleading or in any other pleading or motion. FRCP 10(c).

    i. *Exhibits.* A copy of a written instrument that is an exhibit to a pleading is a part of the pleading for all purposes. FRCP 10(c).

  e. *DISTRICT OF MAINE: Page numbering.* All pages shall be numbered at the bottom. ME R USDCT Rule 10.

  f. *DISTRICT OF MAINE: Attachment of ancillary papers.* Ancillary papers shall be attached at the end of the document to which they relate. ME R USDCT Rule 10.

  g. *Acceptance by the clerk.* The clerk must not refuse to file a paper solely because it is not in the form prescribed by the Federal Rules of Civil Procedure or by a local rule or practice. FRCP 5(d)(4).

2. *Form of electronic documents.* A paper filed electronically is a written paper for purposes of the Federal Rules of Civil Procedure. FRCP 5(d)(3)(D).

  a. *DISTRICT OF MAINE: Document format.* The ECF system only accepts documents in a portable document format (PDF). Although there are two types of PDF documents—electronically converted PDF's and scanned PDF's—only electronically converted PDF's may be filed with the court using the ECF system, unless otherwise authorized by local rule or order. ME R USDCT App. 4. Any document or exhibit to be filed or submitted to the court shall not be password-protected or encrypted. ME R USDCT App. 4(g)(12).

    i. *Electronically converted PDFs.* Electronically converted PDF's are created from word processing documents (MS Word, WordPerfect, etc.) using Adobe Acrobat or similar software. They are text searchable and their file size is small. ME R USDCT App. 4. Software used to electronically convert documents to PDF which includes proprietary or advertisement information within the PDF document is prohibited. ME R USDCT App. 4.

    ii. *Scanned PDFs.* Scanned PDF's are created from paper documents run through an optical scanner. Scanned PDF's are not searchable and have a large file size. ME R USDCT App. 4.

  b. *DISTRICT OF MAINE: Title.* All pleadings filed electronically shall be titled in accordance with the approved dictionary of civil or criminal events of the ECF system of the United States District Court for the District of Maine. ME R USDCT App. 4(d)(3).

  c. *DISTRICT OF MAINE: Attachments.* Attachments to filings and exhibits must be filed in accordance with the court's ECF User Manual, unless otherwise ordered by the court. ME R USDCT App. 4(j). When there are fifty (50) or fewer attachments to a pleading, the attachments must be filed by counsel electronically using ECF. When there are more than fifty (50) attachments, the attachments must be filed in one of the following ways: (A) using ECF, simply attach them to the pleading being filed; (B) using ECF, use the "Additional Attachments" menu item; (C) on paper; or (D) on a properly labeled three and one-half (3-1/2) inch floppy disk, CD or DVD. ME R USDCT App. 4(j)(2). Attachments filed on paper or on disk must contain a comprehensive index that clearly describes each document. ME R USDCT App. 4(j)(2).

    i. A filing user must submit as attachments only those excerpts of the referenced documents that are directly germane to the matter under consideration by the court. Excerpted material must be clearly and prominently identified as such. Users who file excerpts of documents do so without prejudice to their right to timely file additional excerpts or the complete document, as may be allowed by the court. Responding parties may timely file additional excerpts or the complete document that they believe are directly germane. ME R USDCT App. 4(j)(3).

    ii. Filers shall not attach as an exhibit any pleading or other paper already on file with the court in that case, but shall merely refer to that document. ME R USDCT App. 4(j)(4).

  d. *DISTRICT OF MAINE: Compliance with technical standards.* All documents filed by electronic means must comply with technical standards, if any, established by the Judicial Conference of the United States or by the United States District Court for the District of Maine. ME R USDCT App. 4(a)(3).

3. *DISTRICT OF MAINE: Form of memoranda of law.* All memoranda shall be typed, in a font of no less than size twelve (12) point, and shall be double-spaced on eight and one-half by eleven (8-1/2 x 11) inch paper or printed. Footnotes shall be in a font of no less than size ten (10) point, and may be single spaced. All pages shall be numbered at the bottom. ME R USDCT Rule 7(d).

  a. *Page limitations.* No memorandum of law in support of or in opposition to a motion to dismiss, a motion for judgment on the pleadings, a motion for summary judgment or a motion for injunctive relief shall exceed twenty (20) pages. ME R USDCT Rule 7(d). No reply memorandum shall exceed seven (7) pages. ME R USDCT Rule 7(d); ME R USDCT Rule 7(c).

    i. *Motion to exceed page limitation.* A motion to exceed the limitation of ME R USDCT Rule 7 shall be filed no later than three (3) business days in advance of the date for filing the memorandum to permit meaningful review by the court. A motion to exceed the page limitations shall not be filed simultaneously with a memorandum in excess of the limitations of ME R USDCT Rule 7. ME R USDCT Rule 7(d).

4. *Signing of pleadings, motions and other papers*

    a. *Signature.* Every pleading, written motion, and other paper must be signed by at least one attorney of record in the attorney's name—or by a party personally if the party is unrepresented. The paper must state the signer's address, e-mail address, and telephone number. FRCP 11(a).

        i. *No verification or accompanying affidavit required for pleadings.* Unless a rule or statute specifically states otherwise, a pleading need not be verified or accompanied by an affidavit. FRCP 11(a).

        ii. *Unsigned papers.* The court must strike an unsigned paper unless the omission is promptly corrected after being called to the attorney's or party's attention. FRCP 11(a).

    b. *Electronic signing.* A filing made through a person's electronic-filing account and authorized by that person, together with that person's name on a signature block, constitutes the person's signature. FRCP 5(d)(3)(C).

        i. *DISTRICT OF MAINE: Attorneys.* The user log-in and password together with a user's name on the signature block constitutes the attorney's signature pursuant to the Federal Rules of Civil Procedure and the Local Rules of the United States District Court for the District of Maine. All electronically filed documents must include a signature block and must set forth the attorney's name, address, telephone number and e-mail address. The name of the ECF user under whose log-in and password the document is submitted must be preceded by a "/s/" in the space where the signature would otherwise appear. ME R USDCT App. 4(h)(1).

        ii. *DISTRICT OF MAINE: Multiple signatures.* The filer of any document requiring more than one signature (e.g., pleadings filed by visiting lawyers, stipulations, joint status reports) must list thereon all the names of other signatories, preceded by a "/s/" in the space where the signatures would otherwise appear. By submitting such a document, the filing attorney certifies that each of the other signatories has expressly agreed to the form and substance of the document and that the filing attorney has their actual authority to submit the document electronically. ME R USDCT App. 4(h)(2). For more information, refer to ME R USDCT App. 4(h)(2).

        iii. *DISTRICT OF MAINE: Documents signed under oath.* Affidavits, declarations, verified complaints, or any other document signed under oath shall be filed electronically. The electronically filed version shall contain the typed name of the signatory, preceded by a "/s/" in the space where the signature would otherwise appear indicating that the paper document bears an original signature. ME R USDCT Rule 10; ME R USDCT App. 4(h)(3). For more information, refer to ME R USDCT Rule 10.

    c. *Representations to the court.* By presenting to the court a pleading, written motion, or other paper—whether by signing, filing, submitting, or later advocating it—an attorney or unrepresented party certifies that to the best of the person's knowledge, information, and belief, formed after an inquiry reasonable under the circumstances: (1) it is not being presented for any improper purpose, such as to harass, cause unnecessary delay, or needlessly increase the cost of litigation; (2) the claims, defenses, and other legal contentions are warranted by existing law or by a nonfrivolous argument for extending, modifying, or reversing existing law or for establishing new law; (3) the factual contentions have evidentiary support or, if specifically so identified, will likely have evidentiary support after a reasonable opportunity for further investigation or discovery; and (4) the denials of factual contentions are warranted on the evidence or, if specifically so identified, are reasonably based on belief or a lack of information. FRCP 11(b).

    d. *Sanctions.* If, after notice and a reasonable opportunity to respond, the court determines that FRCP 11(b) has been violated, the court may impose an appropriate sanction on any attorney, law firm, or party that violated FRCP 11(b) or is responsible for the violation. FRCP 11(c)(1). Refer to the United States District Court for the District of Maine KeyRules Motion for Sanctions document for more information.

5. *Privacy protection for filings made with the court*

    a. *Redacted filings.* Unless the court orders otherwise, in an electronic or paper filing with the court that contains an individual's Social Security number, taxpayer-identification number, or birth date, the name of an individual known to be a minor, or a financial-account number, a party or nonparty making the filing may include only: (1) the last four

(4) digits of the Social Security number and taxpayer-identification number; (2) the year of the individual's birth; (3) the minor's initials; and (4) the last four (4) digits of the financial-account number. FRCP 5.2(a).

    i.   *DISTRICT OF MAINE.* To address the privacy concerns created by the Internet access to court papers, unless otherwise ordered by the court, counsel shall modify certain personal data identifiers in pleadings and other papers as follows: (1) minors' names: use of the minors' initials only; (2) Social Security numbers: use of the last four (4) numbers only; (3) dates of birth: use of the year of birth only; [and] (4) financial account numbers: identify the type of account and the financial institution, but use only the last four (4) numbers of the account number. ME R USDCT Redacting Pleadings. Counsel should also use caution when filing papers that contain a person's medical records, employment history; financial information; and any proprietary or trade secret information. ME R USDCT Redacting Pleadings.

b.   *Exemptions from the redaction requirement.* The redaction requirement does not apply to the following: (1) a financial-account number that identifies the property allegedly subject to forfeiture in a forfeiture proceeding; (2) the record of an administrative or agency proceeding; (3) the official record of a state-court proceeding; (4) the record of a court or tribunal, if that record was not subject to the redaction requirement when originally filed; (5) a filing covered by FRCP 5.2(c) or FRCP 5.2(d); and (6) a pro se filing in an action brought under 28 U.S.C.A. § 2241, 28 U.S.C.A. § 2254, or 28 U.S.C.A. § 2255. FRCP 5.2(b).

c.   *Limitations on remote access to electronic files; Social Security appeals and immigration cases.* Unless the court orders otherwise, in an action for benefits under the Social Security Act, and in an action or proceeding relating to an order of removal, to relief from removal, or to immigration benefits or detention, access to an electronic file is authorized as follows: (1) the parties and their attorneys may have remote electronic access to any part of the case file, including the administrative record; (2) any other person may have electronic access to the full record at the courthouse, but may have remote electronic access only to: (A) the docket maintained by the court; and (B) an opinion, order, judgment, or other disposition of the court, but not any other part of the case file or the administrative record. FRCP 5.2(c).

d.   *Filings made under seal.* The court may order that a filing be made under seal without redaction. The court may later unseal the filing or order the person who made the filing to file a redacted version for the public record. FRCP 5.2(d).

    i.   *DISTRICT OF MAINE.* For information on filing sealed documents in the District of Maine, refer to ME R USDCT Rule 7A, ME R USDCT App. 4(p)(2), and ME R USDCT Sealed Filings.

e.   *Protective orders.* For good cause, the court may by order in a case: (1) require redaction of additional information; or (2) limit or prohibit a nonparty's remote electronic access to a document filed with the court. FRCP 5.2(e).

f.   *Option for additional unredacted filing under seal.* A person making a redacted filing may also file an unredacted copy under seal. The court must retain the unredacted copy as part of the record. FRCP 5.2(f).

    i.   *DISTRICT OF MAINE.* A party wishing to file a document containing the personal data identifiers specified above may. . .file an unredacted document under seal. This document will be retained by the clerk's office as part of the record. ME R USDCT Redacting Pleadings. The court may, however, still require the party to file a redacted copy for the public file. ME R USDCT Redacting Pleadings.

g.   *Option for filing a reference list.* A filing that contains redacted information may be filed together with a reference list that identifies each item of redacted information and specifies an appropriate identifier that uniquely corresponds to each item listed. The list must be filed under seal and may be amended as of right. Any reference in the case to a listed identifier will be construed to refer to the corresponding item of information. FRCP 5.2(g).

    i.   *DISTRICT OF MAINE.* A party wishing to file a document containing the personal data identifiers specified above may. . .file a reference list under seal. The reference list shall contain the complete personal data identifier(s) and the redacted identifier(s) used in its (their) place in the filing. All references in the case to the redacted identifiers included in the reference list will be construed to refer to the corresponding complete identifier. The reference list must be filed under seal, and may be amended as of right. It shall be retained by the clerk's office as part of the record. ME R USDCT Redacting Pleadings. The court may, however, still require the party to file a redacted copy for the public file. ME R USDCT Redacting Pleadings.

h.   *DISTRICT OF MAINE: Responsibility for redaction.* The clerk is not required to review documents filed with the court for compliance with FRCP 5.2. The responsibility to redact filings rests with counsel and the party or nonparty making the filing. ME R USDCT App. 4(i); ME R USDCT Redacting Pleadings. For guidelines for filing confidential information in civil cases in the District of Maine, refer to ME R USDCT Confidentiality.

i.   *Waiver of protection of identifiers.* A person waives the protection of FRCP 5.2(a) as to the person's own information by filing it without redaction and not under seal. FRCP 5.2(h).

F. Filing and Service Requirements

1. *Filing requirements*

a. *Required filings.* Any paper after the complaint that is required to be served must be filed no later than a reasonable time after service. FRCP 5(d)(1).

b. *DISTRICT OF MAINE: Place of filing.* Unless otherwise ordered by the court, papers shall be filed with the court at Bangor in cases filed and pending at Bangor, and at Portland in cases filed and pending at Portland. ME R USDCT Rule 5(a).

c. *Nonelectronic filing.* A paper not filed electronically is filed by delivering it: (A) to the clerk; or (B) to a judge who agrees to accept it for filing, and who must then note the filing date on the paper and promptly send it to the clerk. FRCP 5(d)(2).

   i. *DISTRICT OF MAINE: Documents to be filed in paper.* The following documents shall be filed in paper, which may also be scanned into ECF by the clerk's office: (A) all handwritten pleadings; and (B) all pleadings and documents filed by pro se litigants who are incarcerated or who are not registered filing users in ECF. ME R USDCT App. 4(g)(8). Non-prisoner pro se litigants in civil actions may register with ECF or may file (and serve) all pleadings and other documents in paper. The clerk's office will scan into ECF any pleadings and documents filed on paper in accordance with ME R USDCT App. 4(g). ME R USDCT App. 4(o). For more information, refer to ME R USDCT App. 4(g).

d. *Electronic filing*

   i. *DISTRICT OF MAINE: Authorization.* Unless exempt or otherwise ordered by the court, papers shall be filed and served electronically as required by the court's Administrative Procedures Governing the Filing and Service by Electronic Means, which is set forth in ME R USDCT App. 4. The provisions of the court's Administrative Procedures Governing the Filing and Service by Electronic Means (ME R USDCT App. 4) shall be applied and enforced as part of the Local Rules of the United States District Court for the District of Maine. ME R USDCT Rule 5(c).

   ii. *Filing by represented persons.* A person represented by an attorney must file electronically, unless nonelectronic filing is allowed by the court for good cause or is allowed or required by local rule. FRCP 5(d)(3)(A).

     • *DISTRICT OF MAINE.* An attorney may apply to the court for permission to file paper documents. ME R USDCT App. 4(a)(5).

   iii. *Filing by unrepresented persons.* A person not represented by an attorney: (i) may file electronically only if allowed by court order or by local rule; and (ii) may be required to file electronically only by court order, or by a local rule that includes reasonable exceptions. FRCP 5(d)(3)(B).

     • *DISTRICT OF MAINE.* Non-prisoner pro se litigants in civil actions may register with ECF or may file (and serve) all pleadings and other documents in paper. ME R USDCT App. 4(o). A non-prisoner who is a party to a civil action and who is not represented by an attorney may register to receive service electronically and to electronically transmit their documents to the court for filing in the ECF system. If during the course of the action the person retains an attorney who appears on the person's behalf, the clerk shall terminate the person's registration upon the attorney's appearance. ME R USDCT App. 4(b)(2).

   iv. *DISTRICT OF MAINE: Scope of electronic filing.* All documents submitted for filing in civil and criminal cases, regardless of case commencement date, except those documents specifically exempted in ME R USDCT App. 4(g), shall be filed electronically using the electronic case filing system (ECF). ME R USDCT App. 4(a)(1). For special filing requirements and exceptions, refer to ME R USDCT App. 4(g).

   v. *DISTRICT OF MAINE: Consequences of electronic filing.* Electronic transmission of a document to the ECF system, together with the transmission of a Notice of Electronic Filing (NEF) from the court, constitutes filing of the document for all purposes of the Federal Rules of Civil Procedure. ME R USDCT App. 4(d)(1).

   vi. *DISTRICT OF MAINE: Review of documents.* Documents filed with the clerk's office will normally be reviewed no later than the close of the next business day. It is the responsibility of the filing party to promptly notify the clerk's office via telephone of a matter that requires the immediate attention of a judicial officer. ME R USDCT App. 4(a)(4).

e. *DISTRICT OF MAINE: Facsimile filing.* No papers shall be submitted to the court by means of a facsimile machine without prior leave of the court. ME R USDCT Rule 5(c); ME R USDCT App. 4(m).

2. *Service requirements*

a. *Service; When required.* Unless the Federal Rules of Civil Procedure provide otherwise, each of the following papers must be served on every party: (A) an order stating that service is required; (B) a pleading filed after the original complaint, unless the court orders otherwise under FRCP 5(c) because there are numerous defendants; (C) a discovery paper required to be served on a party, unless the court orders otherwise; (D) a written motion, except one that may be heard ex parte; and (E) a written notice, appearance, demand, or offer of judgment, or any similar paper. FRCP 5(a)(1).

    i. *If a party fails to appear.* No service is required on a party who is in default for failing to appear. But a pleading that asserts a new claim for relief against such a party must be served on that party under FRCP 4. FRCP 5(a)(2).

    ii. *Seizing property.* If an action is begun by seizing property and no person is or need be named as a defendant, any service required before the filing of an appearance, answer, or claim must be made on the person who had custody or possession of the property when it was seized. FRCP 5(a)(3).

b. *Service; How made.* A paper is served under FRCP 5 by: (A) handing it to the person; (B) leaving it: (i) at the person's office with a clerk or other person in charge or, if no one is in charge, in a conspicuous place in the office; or (ii) if the person has no office or the office is closed, at the person's dwelling or usual place of abode with someone of suitable age and discretion who resides there; (C) mailing it to the person's last known address—in which event service is complete upon mailing; (D) leaving it with the court clerk if the person has no known address; (E) sending it to a registered user by filing it with the court's electronic-filing system or sending it by other electronic means that the person consented to in writing—in either of which events service is complete upon filing or sending, but is not effective if the filer or sender learns that it did not reach the person to be served; or (F) delivering it by any other means that the person consented to in writing—in which event service is complete when the person making service delivers it to the agency designated to make delivery. FRCP 5(b)(2).

    i. *Serving an attorney.* If a party is represented by an attorney, service under FRCP 5 must be made on the attorney unless the court orders service on the party. FRCP 5(b)(1).

c. *DISTRICT OF MAINE: Service of electronically filed documents*

    i. *Registered users.* Registration [as a filing user of the court's ECF system] constitutes consent to service of all documents by electronic means as provided in ME R USDCT App. 4. ME R USDCT App. 4(b)(4). Whenever a non-sealed pleading is filed electronically, the ECF system will automatically generate and send a Notice of Electronic Filing (NEF) to the filing user and registered users of record. The user filing the document should retain a paper or digital copy of the NEF, which shall serve as the court's date-stamp and proof of filing. ME R USDCT App. 4(e)(1).

        • *Sealed documents.* Although the filing of sealed documents in civil cases produces an NEF, the document itself cannot be accessed and counsel shall be responsible for making service of the sealed documents. ME R USDCT App. 4(e)(2).

    ii. *Non-registered users and pro se litigants.* Attorneys who have not yet registered as users with ECF and pro se litigants who have not registered with ECF shall be served a paper copy of any electronically filed pleading or other document in accordance with the provisions of FRCP 5. ME R USDCT App. 4(e)(3).

        • *Registration of pro se litigants.* A non-prisoner who is a party to a civil action and who is not represented by an attorney may register to receive service electronically and to electronically transmit their documents to the court for filing in the ECF system. If during the course of the action the person retains an attorney who appears on the person's behalf, the clerk shall terminate the person's registration upon the attorney's appearance. ME R USDCT App. 4(b)(2).

d. *Serving numerous defendants.* If an action involves an unusually large number of defendants, the court may, on motion or on its own, order that: (A) defendants' pleadings and replies to them need not be served on other defendants; (B) any crossclaim, counterclaim, avoidance, or affirmative defense in those pleadings and replies to them will be treated as denied or avoided by all other parties; and (C) filing any such pleading and serving it on the plaintiff constitutes notice of the pleading to all parties. FRCP 5(c)(1).

    i. *Notifying parties.* A copy of every such order must be served on the parties as the court directs. FRCP 5(c)(2).

3. *DISTRICT OF MAINE: Filing and service of highly sensitive documents (HSDs).* For information on filing and serving highly sensitive documents (HSDs) in the District of Maine, refer to ME R USDCT General Order 21-5.

G. Hearings

1. *Hearings, generally.* When a motion relies on facts outside the record, the court may hear the matter on affidavits or may hear it wholly or partly on oral testimony or on depositions. FRCP 43(c).

a. *Oral argument.* Due process does not require that oral argument be permitted on a motion and, except as otherwise provided by local rule, the district court has discretion to determine whether it will decide the motion on the papers or hear argument by counsel (and perhaps receive evidence). FPP § 1190; F.D.I.C. v. Deglau, 207 F.3d 153 (3d Cir. 2000).

    i. *DISTRICT OF MAINE.* Unless otherwise required by federal rule or statute, all motions may be decided by the court without oral argument unless otherwise ordered by the court on its own motion or, in its discretion, upon request of counsel. ME R USDCT Rule 7(e).

  b. *Providing a regular schedule for oral hearings.* A court may establish regular times and places for oral hearings on motions. FRCP 78(a).

  c. *Providing for submission on briefs.* By rule or order, the court may provide for submitting and determining motions on briefs, without oral hearings. FRCP 78(b).

2. *Hearing on certain FRCP 12 defenses before trial.* If a party so moves, any defense listed in FRCP 12(b)(1) through FRCP 12(b)(7)—whether made in a pleading or by motion—and a motion under FRCP 12(c) must be heard and decided before trial unless the court orders a deferral until trial. FRCP 12(i).

H. Forms

1. Federal Motion to Dismiss for Failure to State a Claim Forms

  a. Failure to state a claim upon which relief can be granted. 2C FEDFORMS § 11:80.

  b. Failure to state a claim upon which relief can be granted; Long version. 2C FEDFORMS § 11:81.

  c. Failure to state a claim upon which relief can be granted; Dismissal of certain allegations. 2C FEDFORMS § 11:82.

  d. Failure to state a claim upon which relief can be granted; With supporting reasons. 2C FEDFORMS § 11:83.

  e. Failure to state a claim upon which relief can be granted; With supporting reasons; Plaintiff not the real party in interest. 2C FEDFORMS § 11:85.

  f. Failure to state a claim upon which relief can be granted; With supporting reasons; Failure to show implied contract. 2C FEDFORMS § 11:86.

  g. Failure to state a claim upon which relief can be granted; With supporting reasons; Issue not arbitrable. 2C FEDFORMS § 11:87.

  h. Failure to state a claim upon which relief can be granted; With supporting affidavits. 2C FEDFORMS § 11:88.

  i. Failure to state a claim upon which relief can be granted; In alternative for summary judgment. 2C FEDFORMS § 11:89.

  j. Notice in federal court; Motion for involuntary dismissal of action without prejudice; Complaint fails to state a claim on which relief can be granted. AMJUR PP DISMISSAL § 108.

  k. Motion; To dismiss; Failure to state a claim on which relief can be granted or facts sufficient to constitute cause of action. AMJUR PP LIMITATION § 100.

  l. Motion to dismiss; For failure to state a claim, improper service of process, improper venue, and want of jurisdiction. AMJUR PP MOTIONS § 42.

  m. Motion to dismiss; Failure to state sufficient claim; By one of several defendants. FEDPROF § 1C:108.

  n. Motion to dismiss; Failure to state sufficient claim; By third-party defendant. FEDPROF § 1C:109.

  o. Motion to dismiss; Failure to state sufficient claim after successive attempts. FEDPROF § 1C:110.

  p. Motion to dismiss; By individual defendants. FEDPROF § 1C:111.

  q. Motion to dismiss; By state agency. FEDPROF § 1C:112.

  r. Motion to dismiss counterclaim. FEDPROF § 1C:117.

  s. Allegation; In motion to dismiss; Res judicata. FEDPROF § 1C:119.

  t. Allegation; In motion to dismiss; Statute of limitations. FEDPROF § 1C:121.

  u. Allegation; In motion to dismiss; Strict liability claim barred by statute. FEDPROF § 1C:122.

  v. Allegation; In motion to dismiss; By United States; Absence of consent to suit. FEDPROF § 1C:124.

  w. Reply; To motion to dismiss for failure to state sufficient claim. FEDPROF § 1C:125.

  x. Motion to dismiss counterclaim. GOLDLTGFMS § 13:10.

    y. Motion to dismiss complaint; General form. GOLDLTGFMS § 20:24.

    z. Affidavit in support of motion to dismiss complaint. GOLDLTGFMS § 20:32.

I. Applicable Rules

1. *Federal rules*

    a. Serving and filing pleadings and other papers. FRCP 5.

    b. Constitutional challenge to a statute; Notice, certification, and intervention. FRCP 5.1.

    c. Privacy protection for filings made with the court. FRCP 5.2.

    d. Computing and extending time; Time for motion papers. FRCP 6.

    e. Pleadings allowed; Form of motions and other papers. FRCP 7.

    f. Disclosure statement. FRCP 7.1.

    g. Form of pleadings. FRCP 10.

    h. Signing pleadings, motions, and other papers; Representations to the court; Sanctions. FRCP 11.

    i. Defenses and objections; When and how presented; Motion for judgment on the pleadings; Consolidating motions; Waiving defenses; Pretrial hearing. FRCP 12.

    j. Taking testimony. FRCP 43.

    k. Hearing motions; Submission on briefs. FRCP 78.

2. *Local rules*

    a. *DISTRICT OF MAINE*

        i. Service and filing of pleadings and other papers. ME R USDCT Rule 5.

        ii. Time. ME R USDCT Rule 6.

        iii. Motions and memoranda of law. ME R USDCT Rule 7.

        iv. Corporate disclosure. ME R USDCT Rule 7.1.

        v. Form of pleadings, motions and other papers. ME R USDCT Rule 10.

        vi. Attorneys; Appearances and withdrawals. ME R USDCT Rule 83.2.

        vii. Alternative dispute resolution (ADR). ME R USDCT Rule 83.11.

        viii. Administrative procedures governing the filing and service by electronic means. ME R USDCT App. 4.

        ix. Redacting pleadings. ME R USDCT Redacting Pleadings.

Motions, Oppositions and Replies
Motion to Dismiss for Lack of Subject Matter Jurisdiction

Document Last Updated April 2021

A. Checklist

  (I) ❑ Matters to be considered by moving party

    (a) ❑ Required documents

      (1) ❑ Notice of motion and motion

    (b) ❑ Supplemental documents

      (1) ❑ Supporting evidence

      (2) ❑ Notice of constitutional question

      (3) ❑ Nongovernmental corporate disclosure statement

      (4) ❑ DISTRICT OF MAINE: Additional supplemental documents

        (i) ❑ Proposed order

    (c) ❑ Timing

        (1) ❑ The defense of lack of subject matter jurisdiction can be raised at any time

        (2) ❑ Every defense to a claim for relief in any pleading must be asserted in the responsive pleading if one is required

        (3) ❑ A motion asserting any of the defenses in FRCP 12(b) must be made before pleading if a responsive pleading is allowed

        (4) ❑ If a pleading sets out a claim for relief that does not require a responsive pleading, an opposing party may assert at trial any defense to that claim

        (5) ❑ A written motion and notice of the hearing must be served at least fourteen (14) days before the time specified for the hearing, with the following exceptions: (A) when the motion may be heard ex parte; (B) when the Federal Rules of Civil Procedure set a different time; or (C) when a court order—which a party may, for good cause, apply for ex parte—sets a different time

        (6) ❑ Any affidavit supporting a motion must be served with the motion

        (7) ❑ DISTRICT OF MAINE: Additional timing

            (i) ❑ Any affidavits and other documents setting forth or evidencing facts on which the motion is based must be filed with the motion

(II) ❑ Matters to be considered by opposing party

    (a) ❑ Required documents

        (1) ❑ Opposition

    (b) ❑ Supplemental documents

        (1) ❑ Supporting evidence

        (2) ❑ Notice of constitutional question

    (c) ❑ Timing

        (1) ❑ Except as FRCP 59(c) provides otherwise, any opposing affidavit must be served at least seven (7) days before the hearing, unless the court permits service at another time

        (2) ❑ DISTRICT OF MAINE: Additional timing

            (i) ❑ Unless within twenty-one (21) days after the filing of a motion the opposing party files written objection thereto, incorporating a memorandum of law, the opposing party shall be deemed to have waived objection

B. Timing

1. *Motion to dismiss for lack of subject matter jurisdiction.* [The defense of lack of subject matter jurisdiction] can be raised at any time. FEDPROC § 62:428.

    a. *In a responsive pleading.* Every defense to a claim for relief in any pleading must be asserted in the responsive pleading if one is required. FRCP 12(b).

    b. *By motion.* A motion asserting any of the defenses in FRCP 12(b) must be made before pleading if a responsive pleading is allowed. FRCP 12(b). Although FRCP 12(b) encourages the responsive pleader to file a motion to dismiss before filing the answer, nothing in FRCP 12 prohibits the filing of a motion to dismiss with the answer. An untimely motion to dismiss may be considered if the defense asserted in the motion was previously raised in the responsive pleading. FEDPROC § 62:421.

    c. *At trial.* If a pleading sets out a claim for relief that does not require a responsive pleading, an opposing party may assert at trial any defense to that claim. FRCP 12(b).

2. *Timing of motions, generally*

    a. *Motion and notice of hearing.* A written motion and notice of the hearing must be served at least fourteen (14) days before the time specified for the hearing, with the following exceptions: (A) when the motion may be heard ex parte; (B) when the Federal Rules of Civil Procedure set a different time; or (C) when a court order—which a party may, for good cause, apply for ex parte—sets a different time. FRCP 6(c)(1).

    b. *Supporting affidavit.* Any affidavit supporting a motion must be served with the motion. FRCP 6(c)(2).

    c.   *DISTRICT OF MAINE: Affidavits and other supporting documents.* Any affidavits and other documents setting forth or evidencing facts on which the motion is based must be filed with the motion. ME R USDCT Rule 7(a).

3. *Timing of opposing papers.* Except as FRCP 59(c) provides otherwise, any opposing affidavit must be served at least seven (7) days before the hearing, unless the court permits service at another time. FRCP 6(c)(2).

    a.   *DISTRICT OF MAINE.* Unless within twenty-one (21) days after the filing of a motion the opposing party files written objection thereto, incorporating a memorandum of law, the opposing party shall be deemed to have waived objection. ME R USDCT Rule 7(b). The deemed waiver imposed in ME R USDCT Rule 7(b) shall not apply to motions filed during trial. ME R USDCT Rule 7(b).

4. *Timing of reply papers.* Where the respondent files an answering affidavit setting up a new matter, the moving party ordinarily is allowed a reasonable time to file a reply affidavit since failure to deny the new matter by affidavit may operate as an admission of its truth. AMJUR MOTIONS § 25.

    a.   *DISTRICT OF MAINE.* Within fourteen (14) days of the filing of any objection to a motion, the moving party may file a reply memorandum. ME R USDCT Rule 7(c).

5. *Effect of FRCP 12 motion on the time to serve a responsive pleading.* Unless the court sets a different time, serving a motion under FRCP 12 alters the periods in FRCP 12(a) as follows: (A) if the court denies the motion or postpones its disposition until trial, the responsive pleading must be served within fourteen (14) days after notice of the court's action; or (B) if the court grants a motion for a more definite statement, the responsive pleading must be served within fourteen (14) days after the more definite statement is served. FRCP 12(a)(4).

6. *Computation of time*

    a.   *Computing time.* FRCP 6 applies in computing any time period specified in the Federal Rules of Civil Procedure, in any local rule or court order, or in any statute that does not specify a method of computing time. FRCP 6(a).

        i.   *Period stated in days or a longer unit.* When the period is stated in days or a longer unit of time: (A) exclude the day of the event that triggers the period; (B) count every day, including intermediate Saturdays, Sundays, and legal holidays; and (C) include the last day of the period, but if the last day is a Saturday, Sunday, or legal holiday, the period continues to run until the end of the next day that is not a Saturday, Sunday, or legal holiday. FRCP 6(a)(1).

        ii. *Period stated in hours.* When the period is stated in hours: (A) begin counting immediately on the occurrence of the event that triggers the period; (B) count every hour, including hours during intermediate Saturdays, Sundays, and legal holidays; and (C) if the period would end on a Saturday, Sunday, or legal holiday, the period continues to run until the same time on the next day that is not a Saturday, Sunday, or legal holiday. FRCP 6(a)(2).

        iii. *Inaccessibility of the clerk's office.* Unless the court orders otherwise, if the clerk's office is inaccessible: (A) on the last day for filing under FRCP 6(a)(1), then the time for filing is extended to the first accessible day that is not a Saturday, Sunday, or legal holiday; or (B) during the last hour for filing under FRCP 6(a)(2), then the time for filing is extended to the same time on the first accessible day that is not a Saturday, Sunday, or legal holiday. FRCP 6(a)(3).

        iv. *"Last day" defined.* Unless a different time is set by a statute, local rule, or court order, the last day ends: (A) for electronic filing, at midnight in the court's time zone; and (B) for filing by other means, when the clerk's office is scheduled to close. FRCP 6(a)(4).

        v. *"Next day" defined.* The "next day" is determined by continuing to count forward when the period is measured after an event and backward when measured before an event. FRCP 6(a)(5).

        vi. *"Legal holiday" defined.* "Legal holiday" means: (A) the day set aside by statute for observing New Year's Day, Martin Luther King Jr.'s Birthday, Washington's Birthday, Memorial Day, Independence Day, Labor Day, Columbus Day, Veterans' Day, Thanksgiving Day, or Christmas Day; (B) any day declared a holiday by the President or Congress; and (C) for periods that are measured after an event, any other day declared a holiday by the state where the district court is located. FRCP 6(a)(6).

        vii. *DISTRICT OF MAINE: Applicability of FRCP 6.* FRCP 6 applies when computing any period of time stated in the Local Rules of the United States District Court for the District of Maine. ME R USDCT Rule 6(a).

    b.   *DISTRICT OF MAINE: Computation of electronic filing deadlines.* Filing documents electronically does not in any way alter any filing deadlines. All electronic transmissions of documents must be completed prior to midnight, Eastern Time, in order to be considered timely filed that day. Where a specific time of day deadline is set by court order or stipulation, the electronic filing must be completed by that time. ME R USDCT App. 4(f). A document filed

electronically shall be deemed filed at the time and date stated on the Notice of Electronic Filing received from the court. ME R USDCT App. 4(d)(2).

    i. *Technical failures.* A filing user whose filing is made untimely as the result of a technical failure may seek appropriate relief from the court. ME R USDCT App. 4(n). A technical failure of the court's ECF system is deemed to have occurred when the court's ECF site cannot accept filings continuously or intermittently over the course of any period of time greater than one (1) hour. Known system outages will be posted on the court's website along with guidance on how to proceed, if applicable. ME R USDCT App. 4(n).

  c. *Extending time.* When an act may or must be done within a specified time, the court may, for good cause, extend the time: (A) with or without motion or notice if the court acts, or if a request is made, before the original time or its extension expires; or (B) on motion made after the time has expired if the party failed to act because of excusable neglect. FRCP 6(b)(1). A court must not extend the time to act under FRCP 50(b), FRCP 50(d), FRCP 52(b), FRCP 59(b), FRCP 59(d), FRCP 59(e), and FRCP 60(b). FRCP 6(b)(2). Refer to the United States District Court for the District of Maine KeyRules Motion for Continuance/Extension of Time document for more information on extending time.

  d. *Additional time after certain kinds of service.* When a party may or must act within a specified time after being served and service is made under FRCP 5(b)(2)(C) (by mail), FRCP 5(b)(2)(D) (by leaving with the clerk), or FRCP 5(b)(2)(F) (by other means consented to), three (3) days are added after the period would otherwise expire under FRCP 6(a). FRCP 6(d).

C. General Requirements

  1. *Motions, generally*

    a. *Motion requirements.* A request for a court order must be made by motion. The motion must: (A) be in writing unless made during a hearing or trial; (B) state with particularity the grounds for seeking the order; and (C) state the relief sought. FRCP 7(b)(1). The writing and particularity requirements are intended to ensure that the adverse parties are informed of and have a record of both the motion's pendency and the grounds on which the movant seeks an order. FPP § 1191; Feldberg v. Quechee Lakes Corp., 463 F.3d 195 (2d Cir. 2006).

      i. *Particularity requirement.* The particularity requirement [ensures] that the opposing parties will have notice of their opponent's contentions. FEDPROC § 62:358; Goodman v. 1973 26 Foot Trojan Vessel, Arkansas Registration No. AR1439SN, 859 F.2d 71 (8th Cir. 1988). That requirement ensures that notice of the basis for the motion is provided to the court and to the opposing party so as to avoid prejudice, provide the opponent with a meaningful opportunity to respond, and provide the court with enough information to process the motion correctly. FEDPROC § 62:358; Andreas v. Volkswagen of Am., Inc., 336 F.3d 789 (8th Cir. 2003).

        • Reasonable specification of the grounds for a motion is sufficient. The particularity requirement for motions is satisfied when no party is prejudiced by a lack of particularity or when the court can comprehend the basis for the motion and deal with it fairly. However, where a movant fails to state even one ground for granting the motion in question, the movant has failed to meet the minimal standard of "reasonable specification." FEDPROC § 62:358; Martinez v. Trainor, 556 F.2d 818 (7th Cir. 1977).

        • The court may excuse the failure to comply with the particularity requirement if it is inadvertent, and where no prejudice is shown by the opposing party. FEDPROC § 62:358.

    b. *Notice of motion.* A party interested in resisting the relief sought by a motion has a right to notice thereof, and an opportunity to be heard. AMJUR MOTIONS § 12.

      i. *Purpose.* In addition to statutory or court rule provisions requiring notice of a motion—the purpose of such a notice requirement having been said to be to prevent a party from being prejudicially surprised by a motion—principles of natural justice dictate that an adverse party generally must be given notice that a motion will be presented to the court. AMJUR MOTIONS § 12.

      ii. *Adequacy of notice.* The test of adequate notice generally turns on whether the other parties were afforded an adequate opportunity to prepare and respond to the issues to be raised in the proceeding. AMJUR MOTIONS § 12.

    c. *Single document containing motion and notice.* A single written document can satisfy the writing requirements both for a motion and for an FRCP 6(c)(1) notice. FRCP 7(Advisory Committee Notes).

  2. *Motion to dismiss for lack of subject matter jurisdiction.* A party may assert the following defense by motion: lack of subject-matter jurisdiction. FRCP 12(b)(1). The objection presented by a motion under FRCP 12(b)(1) challenging the court's subject matter jurisdiction is that the district judge has no authority or competence to hear and decide the case before

it. FPP § 1350. An FRCP 12(b)(1) motion most typically is employed when the movant believes that the claim asserted by the plaintiff does not involve a federal question, and there is no diversity of citizenship between the parties or, in a diversity of citizenship case, the amount in controversy does not exceed the required jurisdictional amount. FPP § 1350.

a. *Subject matter jurisdiction.* It always must be remembered that the federal courts are courts of limited jurisdiction and only can adjudicate those cases that fall within Article III of the Constitution (U.S.C.A. Const. Art. III § 1, et seq.) and a congressional authorization enacted thereunder. FPP § 1350.

    i. *Federal question.* The district courts shall have original jurisdiction of all civil actions arising under the Constitution, laws, or treaties of the United States. 28 U.S.C.A. § 1331.

    ii. *Diversity of citizenship; Amount in controversy.* The district courts shall have original jurisdiction of all civil actions where the matter in controversy exceeds the sum or value of seventy-five thousand dollars ($75,000), exclusive of interest and costs, and is between: (1) citizens of different states; (2) citizens of a state and citizens or subjects of a foreign state, except that the district courts shall not have original jurisdiction under 28 U.S.C.A. § 1332 of an action between citizens of a state and citizens or subjects of a foreign state who are lawfully admitted for permanent residence in the United States and are domiciled in the same state; (3) citizens of different states and in which citizens or subjects of a foreign state are additional parties; and (4) a foreign state, defined in 28 U.S.C.A. § 1603(a), as plaintiff and citizens of a state or of different states. 28 U.S.C.A. § 1332(a).

b. *Derivative jurisdiction.* Some courts have found that the derivative jurisdiction doctrine continues to apply to removal under 28 U.S.C.A. § 1442, and they have dismissed cases against the government, initially instituted in a state court, for lack of jurisdiction based on the doctrine. FPP § 1350.

c. *Types of FRCP 12(b)(1) motions.* There are two separate types of FRCP 12(b)(1) motions to dismiss for lack of subject-matter jurisdiction: the "facial attack" and the "factual attack." FEDPROC § 62:434.

    i. *Facial attack.* The facial attack is addressed to the sufficiency of the allegations of the complaint itself. FEDPROC § 62:434; Stalley ex rel. U.S. v. Orlando Reg'l Healthcare Sys., Inc., 524 F.3d 1229 (11th Cir. 2008). On such a motion, the court is merely required to determine whether the plaintiff has sufficiently alleged a basis of subject-matter jurisdiction. FEDPROC § 62:434; U.S. ex rel. Atkinson v. PA. Shipbuilding Co., 473 F.3d 506 (3d Cir. 2007).

    ii. *Factual attack.* A factual attack challenges the factual existence of subject-matter jurisdiction, irrespective of the pleadings, and matters outside the pleadings, such as testimony and affidavits, may be considered by the court. FEDPROC § 62:434; Kligman v. I.R.S., 272 F. App'x 166 (3d Cir. 2008); Paper, Allied-Indus., Chem. And Energy Workers Int'l Union v. Cont'l Carbon Co., 428 F.3d 1285 (10th Cir. 2005). The trial court in such a situation is free to weigh the evidence and satisfy itself as to the existence of its power to hear the case; therefore, no presumptive truthfulness attaches to the plaintiff's factual allegations. FEDPROC § 62:434; Land v. Dollar, 330 U.S. 731, 67 S. Ct. 1009, 91 L. Ed. 1209 (1947).

d. *Burden.* With the limited exception of the question whether the amount in controversy requirement in diversity of citizenship cases has been satisfied, the extensive case law on the subject makes clear that the burden of proof on an FRCP 12(b)(1) motion is on the party asserting that subject matter jurisdiction exists, which, of course, typically is the plaintiff. FPP § 1350; Thomson v. Gaskill, 315 U.S. 442, 62 S. Ct. 673, 86 L. Ed. 951 (1942). A plaintiff meets the burden of establishing subject-matter jurisdiction at the pleading stage by pleading sufficient allegations to show the proper basis for the court to assert subject-matter jurisdiction over the action. 2 FEDFORMS § 7:6.

    i. *Federal question.* If subject matter jurisdiction is based on the existence of a federal question, the pleader must show that he or she has alleged a claim for relief arising under federal law and that the claim is not frivolous. FPP § 1350; Baker v. Carr, 369 U.S. 186, 82 S. Ct. 691, 7 L. Ed. 2d 663 (1962).

    ii. *Diversity of citizenship.* If jurisdiction is based on diversity of citizenship, on the other hand, the pleader must show that real and complete diversity exists between all of the plaintiffs and all of the defendants, and also that the assertion that the claim exceeds the requisite jurisdictional amount in controversy is made in good faith. FPP § 1350; City of Indianapolis v. Chase Nat. Bank of City of New York, 314 U.S. 63, 62 S. Ct. 15, 86 L. Ed. 47 (1941). Satisfying this last requirement is a relatively simple task, however, because the claim is deemed to be made in good faith so long as it is not clear to a legal certainty that the claimant could not recover a judgment exceeding the statutorily mandated jurisdictional amount, a matter on which the party challenging the district court's jurisdiction has the burden. FPP § 1350.

e. *Joining motions.* A motion under FRCP 12 may be joined with any other motion allowed by FRCP 12. FRCP 12(g)(1). When the motion is based on more than one ground, the cases are legion stating that the district court should consider the FRCP 12(b)(1) challenge first because if it must dismiss the complaint for lack of subject matter jurisdiction, the accompanying defenses and objections become moot and do not need to be determined by the judge. FPP § 1350; Steel Co. v. Citizens for a Better Env't, 523 U.S. 83, 118 S. Ct. 1003, 140 L. Ed. 2d 210 (1998). However, there are a number of decisions in which the court has decided one or more defenses in addition to the subject matter jurisdiction question or simply assumed the existence of jurisdiction and gone on to decide another matter. FPP § 1350.

    i. *Limitation on further motions.* Except as provided in FRCP 12(h)(2) or FRCP 12(h)(3), a party that makes a motion under FRCP 12 must not make another motion under FRCP 12 raising a defense or objection that was available to the party but omitted from its earlier motion. FRCP 12(g)(2).

  f. *Waiving and preserving certain defenses.* No defense or objection is waived by joining it with one or more other defenses or objections in a responsive pleading or in a motion. FRCP 12(b). If the court determines at any time that it lacks subject-matter jurisdiction, the court must dismiss the action. FRCP 12(h)(3).

3. *Opposing papers.* The Federal Rules of Civil Procedure do not require any formal answer, return, or reply to a motion, except where the Federal Rules of Civil Procedure or local rules may require affidavits, memoranda, or other papers to be filed in opposition to a motion. Such papers are simply to apprise the court of such opposition and the grounds of that opposition. FEDPROC § 62:353.

  a. *DISTRICT OF MAINE: Content of objections.* Any objections shall include citations and supporting authorities and affidavits and other documents setting forth or evidencing facts on which the objection is based. ME R USDCT Rule 7(b).

  b. *Effect of failure to respond to motion.* Although in the absence of statutory provision or court rule, a motion ordinarily does not require a response or written answer, when a party files a motion and the opposing party fails to respond, the court may construe such failure to respond as nonopposition to the motion or an admission that the motion was meritorious. AMJUR MOTIONS § 28. The rule in some jurisdictions being that the failure to respond to a fact set forth in a motion is deemed an admission—and may grant the motion if the relief requested appears to be justified. AMJUR MOTIONS § 28.

    i. *Unopposed motion to dismiss.* The circuits are split on whether a court may grant a motion to dismiss solely on the basis that the plaintiff did not file a response opposing the motion. FRCP-RC RULE 12.

  c. *Assent or no opposition not determinative.* However, a motion will not be granted automatically simply because an "assent" or a notation of "no opposition" has been filed; federal judges frequently deny motions that have been assented to when it is thought that justice so dictates. FPP § 1190.

  d. *Responsive pleading inappropriate as response to motion.* An attempt to answer or oppose a motion with a responsive pleading usually is not appropriate. FPP § 1190.

4. *Reply papers.* A moving party may be required or permitted to prepare papers in addition to its original motion papers. AMJUR MOTIONS § 25. Papers answering or replying to opposing papers may be appropriate, in the interests of justice, where it appears there is a substantial reason for allowing a reply. Thus, a court may accept reply papers where a party demonstrates that the papers to which it seeks to file a reply raise new issues that are material to the disposition of the question before the court, or where the court determines, sua sponte, that it wishes further briefing of an issue raised in those papers and orders the submission of additional papers. FEDPROC § 62:354.

  a. *Function of reply papers.* The function of a reply affidavit or reply papers is to answer the arguments made in opposition to the position taken by the movant, not to raise new issues, arguments, or evidence, or change the nature of the primary motion. However, if the court permits new evidence with the reply papers, the other party should be given the opportunity to respond. Where the party opposing the motion has no opportunity to address the argument in writing, a court has the discretion to disregard arguments raised for the first time in a reply memorandum. Also, the view has been followed in some jurisdictions that as a matter of judicial economy, where there is no prejudice and where the issues could be raised simply by filing a motion to dismiss, the trial court has discretion to consider arguments raised for the first time in a reply memorandum, and that a trial court may grant a motion to strike issues raised for the first time in a reply memorandum. AMJUR MOTIONS § 26.

    i. *DISTRICT OF MAINE.* The moving party may file a reply memorandum. . .which shall be strictly confined to replying to new matter raised in the objection or opposing memorandum. ME R USDCT Rule 7(c).

5. *DISTRICT OF MAINE: Appearances.* An attorney's signature to a pleading shall constitute an appearance for the party filing the pleading. Otherwise, an attorney who wishes to participate in any manner in any action must file a formal written appearance identifying the party represented. An appearance whether by pleading or formal written appearance shall be signed by an attorney in his/her individual name and shall state his/her office address. ME R USDCT Rule 83.2(a). For more information, refer to ME R USDCT Rule 83.2.

6. *DISTRICT OF MAINE: Alternative dispute resolution (ADR).* Litigants are authorized and encouraged to employ, at their own expense, any available ADR process on which they can agree, including early neutral evaluation, settlement conferences, mediation, non-binding summary jury trial, corporate mini-trial, and arbitration proceedings. ME R USDCT Rule 83.11(a). For more information on ADR, refer to ME R USDCT Rule 83.11.

D. Documents

1. *Documents for moving party*

   a. *Required documents*

      i. *Notice of motion and motion.* Refer to the "C. General Requirements" section of this KeyRules document for information on the notice of motion and motion.

         • *DISTRICT OF MAINE: Memorandum of law.* Every motion shall incorporate a memorandum of law, including citations and supporting authorities. ME R USDCT Rule 7(a). Refer to the "E. Format" section of this KeyRules document for the form of memoranda of law.

         • *Certificate of service.* No certificate of service is required when a paper is served by filing it with the court's electronic-filing system. When a paper that is required to be served is served by other means: (i) if the paper is filed, a certificate of service must be filed with it or within a reasonable time after service; and (ii) if the paper is not filed, a certificate of service need not be filed unless filing is required by court order or by local rule. FRCP 5(d)(1)(B).

   b. *Supplemental documents*

      i. *Supporting evidence.* When a motion relies on facts outside the record, the court may hear the matter on affidavits or may hear it wholly or partly on oral testimony or on depositions. FRCP 43(c).

         • *DISTRICT OF MAINE: Affidavits and other supporting documents.* Any affidavits and other documents setting forth or evidencing facts on which the motion is based must be filed with the motion. ME R USDCT Rule 7(a).

         • *DISTRICT OF MAINE: Discovery transcripts or materials.* A party relying on discovery transcripts or materials in support of or in opposition to a motion shall file excerpts of such transcript or materials with the memorandum required by ME R USDCT Rule 7 as well as a list of specific citations to the parts on which the party relies. ME R USDCT Rule 26(c). Excerpts of depositions in support of or in opposition to a motion shall be filed electronically using ECF, unless otherwise permitted by the court. ME R USDCT App. 4(l)(3).

      ii. *Notice of constitutional question.* A party that files a pleading, written motion, or other paper drawing into question the constitutionality of a federal or state statute must promptly: (1) file a notice of constitutional question stating the question and identifying the paper that raises it, if: (A) a federal statute is questioned and the parties do not include the United States, one of its agencies, or one of its officers or employees in an official capacity; or (B) a state statute is questioned and the parties do not include the state, one of its agencies, or one of its officers or employees in an official capacity; and (2) serve the notice and paper on the Attorney General of the United States if a federal statute is questioned—or on the state attorney general if a state statute is questioned—either by certified or registered mail or by sending it to an electronic address designated by the attorney general for this purpose. FRCP 5.1(a).

         • *No forfeiture.* A party's failure to file and serve the notice, or the court's failure to certify, does not forfeit a constitutional claim or defense that is otherwise timely asserted. FRCP 5.1(d).

      iii. *Nongovernmental corporate disclosure statement.* A nongovernmental corporate party must file two (2) copies of a disclosure statement that: (1) identifies any parent corporation and any publicly held corporation owning ten percent (10%) or more of its stock; or (2) states that there is no such corporation. FRCP 7.1(a). A party must: (1) file the disclosure statement with its first appearance, pleading, petition, motion, response, or other request addressed to the court; and (2) promptly file a supplemental statement if any required information changes. FRCP 7.1(b).

         • *DISTRICT OF MAINE: Notice of interested parties.* To enable the court to evaluate possible disqualification or recusal, counsel for all non-governmental parties shall file with their first appearance a Notice of Interested Parties, which shall list all persons, associations of persons, firms, partnerships, limited liability companies, joint ventures, corporations (including parent or affiliated corporations, clearly identified as such), or any similar entities, owning ten percent (10%) or more of the named party. Counsel shall be under a continuing obligation to file an amended Notice if any material change occurs in the status of an Interested Party, such as through merger, acquisition, or new/additional membership. ME R USDCT Rule 7.1.

    iv. *DISTRICT OF MAINE: Additional supplemental documents*

- *Proposed order.* Proposed orders shall not be filed unless requested by the court. When requested by the court, proposed orders shall be filed by e-mail in word processing format. ME R USDCT App. 4(k)(1).

2. *Documents for opposing party*

   a. *Required documents*

    i. *Opposition.* Refer to the "C. General Requirements" section of this KeyRules document for information on the opposing papers.

- *DISTRICT OF MAINE: Memorandum of law.* Unless within twenty-one (21) days after the filing of a motion the opposing party files written objection thereto, incorporating a memorandum of law, the opposing party shall be deemed to have waived objection. ME R USDCT Rule 7(b).

- *Certificate of service.* No certificate of service is required when a paper is served by filing it with the court's electronic-filing system. When a paper that is required to be served is served by other means: (i) if the paper is filed, a certificate of service must be filed with it or within a reasonable time after service; and (ii) if the paper is not filed, a certificate of service need not be filed unless filing is required by court order or by local rule. FRCP 5(d)(1)(B).

   b. *Supplemental documents*

    i. *Supporting evidence.* When a motion relies on facts outside the record, the court may hear the matter on affidavits or may hear it wholly or partly on oral testimony or on depositions. FRCP 43(c).

- *DISTRICT OF MAINE: Affidavits and other supporting documents.* Any objections shall include. . .affidavits and other documents setting forth or evidencing facts on which the objection is based. ME R USDCT Rule 7(b).

- *DISTRICT OF MAINE: Discovery transcripts or materials.* A party relying on discovery transcripts or materials in support of or in opposition to a motion shall file excerpts of such transcript or materials with the memorandum required by ME R USDCT Rule 7 as well as a list of specific citations to the parts on which the party relies. ME R USDCT Rule 26(c). Excerpts of depositions in support of or in opposition to a motion shall be filed electronically using ECF, unless otherwise permitted by the court. ME R USDCT App. 4(l)(3).

    ii. *Notice of constitutional question.* A party that files a pleading, written motion, or other paper drawing into question the constitutionality of a federal or state statute must promptly: (1) file a notice of constitutional question stating the question and identifying the paper that raises it, if: (A) a federal statute is questioned and the parties do not include the United States, one of its agencies, or one of its officers or employees in an official capacity; or (B) a state statute is questioned and the parties do not include the state, one of its agencies, or one of its officers or employees in an official capacity; and (2) serve the notice and paper on the Attorney General of the United States if a federal statute is questioned—or on the state attorney general if a state statute is questioned—either by certified or registered mail or by sending it to an electronic address designated by the attorney general for this purpose. FRCP 5.1(a).

- *No forfeiture.* A party's failure to file and serve the notice, or the court's failure to certify, does not forfeit a constitutional claim or defense that is otherwise timely asserted. FRCP 5.1(d).

E. Format

1. *Form of documents.* The rules governing captions and other matters of form in pleadings apply to motions and other papers. FRCP 7(b)(2).

   a. *DISTRICT OF MAINE: Font size, line spacing, and paper size.* All such documents shall be typed in a font of no less than size twelve (12) point, and shall be double-spaced or printed on eight and one-half by eleven (8-1/2 x 11) inch paper. Footnotes shall be in a font of no less than size ten (10) point, and may be single spaced. ME R USDCT Rule 10.

   b. *Caption.* Every pleading must have a caption with the court's name, a title, a file number, and an FRCP 7(a) designation. FRCP 10(a).

    i. *Names of parties.* The title of the complaint must name all the parties; the title of other pleadings, after naming the first party on each side, may refer generally to other parties. FRCP 10(a).

    ii. *DISTRICT OF MAINE: Additional caption requirements.* All pleadings, motions and other papers filed with the clerk or otherwise submitted to the court, except exhibits, shall bear the proper case number and shall contain on the first page a caption as described by FRCP 10(a) and immediately thereunder a designation of what the document is and the name of the party in whose behalf it is submitted. ME R USDCT Rule 10.

c.   *Claims or defenses*

    i.   *Numbered paragraphs.* A party must state its claims or defenses in numbered paragraphs, each limited as far as practicable to a single set of circumstances. A later pleading may refer by number to a paragraph in an earlier pleading. FRCP 10(b).

    ii. *Separate statements.* If doing so would promote clarity, each claim founded on a separate transaction or occurrence—and each defense other than a denial—must be stated in a separate count or defense. FRCP 10(b).

d.   *Adoption by reference.* A statement in a pleading may be adopted by reference elsewhere in the same pleading or in any other pleading or motion. FRCP 10(c).

    i.   *Exhibits.* A copy of a written instrument that is an exhibit to a pleading is a part of the pleading for all purposes. FRCP 10(c).

e.   *DISTRICT OF MAINE: Page numbering.* All pages shall be numbered at the bottom. ME R USDCT Rule 10.

f.   *DISTRICT OF MAINE: Attachment of ancillary papers.* Ancillary papers shall be attached at the end of the document to which they relate. ME R USDCT Rule 10.

g.   *Acceptance by the clerk.* The clerk must not refuse to file a paper solely because it is not in the form prescribed by the Federal Rules of Civil Procedure or by a local rule or practice. FRCP 5(d)(4).

2.   *Form of electronic documents.* A paper filed electronically is a written paper for purposes of the Federal Rules of Civil Procedure. FRCP 5(d)(3)(D).

a.   *DISTRICT OF MAINE: Document format.* The ECF system only accepts documents in a portable document format (PDF). Although there are two types of PDF documents—electronically converted PDF's and scanned PDF's—only electronically converted PDF's may be filed with the court using the ECF system, unless otherwise authorized by local rule or order. ME R USDCT App. 4. Any document or exhibit to be filed or submitted to the court shall not be password-protected or encrypted. ME R USDCT App. 4(g)(12).

    i.   *Electronically converted PDFs.* Electronically converted PDF's are created from word processing documents (MS Word, WordPerfect, etc.) using Adobe Acrobat or similar software. They are text searchable and their file size is small. ME R USDCT App. 4. Software used to electronically convert documents to PDF which includes proprietary or advertisement information within the PDF document is prohibited. ME R USDCT App. 4.

    ii. *Scanned PDFs.* Scanned PDF's are created from paper documents run through an optical scanner. Scanned PDF's are not searchable and have a large file size. ME R USDCT App. 4.

b.   *DISTRICT OF MAINE: Title.* All pleadings filed electronically shall be titled in accordance with the approved dictionary of civil or criminal events of the ECF system of the United States District Court for the District of Maine. ME R USDCT App. 4(d)(3).

c.   *DISTRICT OF MAINE: Attachments.* Attachments to filings and exhibits must be filed in accordance with the court's ECF User Manual, unless otherwise ordered by the court. ME R USDCT App. 4(j). When there are fifty (50) or fewer attachments to a pleading, the attachments must be filed by counsel electronically using ECF. When there are more than fifty (50) attachments, the attachments must be filed in one of the following ways: (A) using ECF, simply attach them to the pleading being filed; (B) using ECF, use the "Additional Attachments" menu item; (C) on paper; or (D) on a properly labeled three and one-half (3-1/2) inch floppy disk, CD or DVD. ME R USDCT App. 4(j)(2). Attachments filed on paper or on disk must contain a comprehensive index that clearly describes each document. ME R USDCT App. 4(j)(2).

    i.   A filing user must submit as attachments only those excerpts of the referenced documents that are directly germane to the matter under consideration by the court. Excerpted material must be clearly and prominently identified as such. Users who file excerpts of documents do so without prejudice to their right to timely file additional excerpts or the complete document, as may be allowed by the court. Responding parties may timely file additional excerpts or the complete document that they believe are directly germane. ME R USDCT App. 4(j)(3).

    ii. Filers shall not attach as an exhibit any pleading or other paper already on file with the court in that case, but shall merely refer to that document. ME R USDCT App. 4(j)(4).

d.   *DISTRICT OF MAINE: Compliance with technical standards.* All documents filed by electronic means must comply with technical standards, if any, established by the Judicial Conference of the United States or by the United States District Court for the District of Maine. ME R USDCT App. 4(a)(3).

3. *DISTRICT OF MAINE: Form of memoranda of law.* All memoranda shall be typed, in a font of no less than size twelve (12) point, and shall be double-spaced on eight and one-half by eleven (8-1/2 x 11) inch paper or printed. Footnotes shall be in a font of no less than size ten (10) point, and may be single spaced. All pages shall be numbered at the bottom. ME R USDCT Rule 7(d).

   a. *Page limitations.* No memorandum of law in support of or in opposition to a motion to dismiss, a motion for judgment on the pleadings, a motion for summary judgment or a motion for injunctive relief shall exceed twenty (20) pages. ME R USDCT Rule 7(d). No reply memorandum shall exceed seven (7) pages. ME R USDCT Rule 7(d); ME R USDCT Rule 7(c).

      i. *Motion to exceed page limitation.* A motion to exceed the limitation of ME R USDCT Rule 7 shall be filed no later than three (3) business days in advance of the date for filing the memorandum to permit meaningful review by the court. A motion to exceed the page limitations shall not be filed simultaneously with a memorandum in excess of the limitations of ME R USDCT Rule 7. ME R USDCT Rule 7(d).

4. *Signing of pleadings, motions and other papers*

   a. *Signature.* Every pleading, written motion, and other paper must be signed by at least one attorney of record in the attorney's name—or by a party personally if the party is unrepresented. The paper must state the signer's address, e-mail address, and telephone number. FRCP 11(a).

      i. *No verification or accompanying affidavit required for pleadings.* Unless a rule or statute specifically states otherwise, a pleading need not be verified or accompanied by an affidavit. FRCP 11(a).

      ii. *Unsigned papers.* The court must strike an unsigned paper unless the omission is promptly corrected after being called to the attorney's or party's attention. FRCP 11(a).

   b. *Electronic signing.* A filing made through a person's electronic-filing account and authorized by that person, together with that person's name on a signature block, constitutes the person's signature. FRCP 5(d)(3)(C).

      i. *DISTRICT OF MAINE: Attorneys.* The user log-in and password together with a user's name on the signature block constitutes the attorney's signature pursuant to the Federal Rules of Civil Procedure and the Local Rules of the United States District Court for the District of Maine. All electronically filed documents must include a signature block and must set forth the attorney's name, address, telephone number and e-mail address. The name of the ECF user under whose log-in and password the document is submitted must be preceded by a "/s/" in the space where the signature would otherwise appear. ME R USDCT App. 4(h)(1).

      ii. *DISTRICT OF MAINE: Multiple signatures.* The filer of any document requiring more than one signature (e.g., pleadings filed by visiting lawyers, stipulations, joint status reports) must list thereon all the names of other signatories, preceded by a "/s/" in the space where the signatures would otherwise appear. By submitting such a document, the filing attorney certifies that each of the other signatories has expressly agreed to the form and substance of the document and that the filing attorney has their actual authority to submit the document electronically. ME R USDCT App. 4(h)(2). For more information, refer to ME R USDCT App. 4(h)(2).

      iii. *DISTRICT OF MAINE: Documents signed under oath.* Affidavits, declarations, verified complaints, or any other document signed under oath shall be filed electronically. The electronically filed version shall contain the typed name of the signatory, preceded by a "/s/" in the space where the signature would otherwise appear indicating that the paper document bears an original signature. ME R USDCT Rule 10; ME R USDCT App. 4(h)(3). For more information, refer to ME R USDCT Rule 10.

   c. *Representations to the court.* By presenting to the court a pleading, written motion, or other paper—whether by signing, filing, submitting, or later advocating it—an attorney or unrepresented party certifies that to the best of the person's knowledge, information, and belief, formed after an inquiry reasonable under the circumstances: (1) it is not being presented for any improper purpose, such as to harass, cause unnecessary delay, or needlessly increase the cost of litigation; (2) the claims, defenses, and other legal contentions are warranted by existing law or by a nonfrivolous argument for extending, modifying, or reversing existing law or for establishing new law; (3) the factual contentions have evidentiary support or, if specifically so identified, will likely have evidentiary support after a reasonable opportunity for further investigation or discovery; and (4) the denials of factual contentions are warranted on the evidence or, if specifically so identified, are reasonably based on belief or a lack of information. FRCP 11(b).

   d. *Sanctions.* If, after notice and a reasonable opportunity to respond, the court determines that FRCP 11(b) has been violated, the court may impose an appropriate sanction on any attorney, law firm, or party that violated FRCP 11(b) or is responsible for the violation. FRCP 11(c)(1). Refer to the United States District Court for the District of Maine KeyRules Motion for Sanctions document for more information.

5. *Privacy protection for filings made with the court*

a. *Redacted filings.* Unless the court orders otherwise, in an electronic or paper filing with the court that contains an individual's Social Security number, taxpayer-identification number, or birth date, the name of an individual known to be a minor, or a financial-account number, a party or nonparty making the filing may include only: (1) the last four (4) digits of the Social Security number and taxpayer-identification number; (2) the year of the individual's birth; (3) the minor's initials; and (4) the last four (4) digits of the financial-account number. FRCP 5.2(a).

   i. *DISTRICT OF MAINE.* To address the privacy concerns created by the Internet access to court papers, unless otherwise ordered by the court, counsel shall modify certain personal data identifiers in pleadings and other papers as follows: (1) minors' names: use of the minors' initials only; (2) Social Security numbers: use of the last four (4) numbers only; (3) dates of birth: use of the year of birth only; [and] (4) financial account numbers: identify the type of account and the financial institution, but use only the last four (4) numbers of the account number. ME R USDCT Redacting Pleadings. Counsel should also use caution when filing papers that contain a person's medical records, employment history; financial information; and any proprietary or trade secret information. ME R USDCT Redacting Pleadings.

b. *Exemptions from the redaction requirement.* The redaction requirement does not apply to the following: (1) a financial-account number that identifies the property allegedly subject to forfeiture in a forfeiture proceeding; (2) the record of an administrative or agency proceeding; (3) the official record of a state-court proceeding; (4) the record of a court or tribunal, if that record was not subject to the redaction requirement when originally filed; (5) a filing covered by FRCP 5.2(c) or FRCP 5.2(d); and (6) a pro se filing in an action brought under 28 U.S.C.A. § 2241, 28 U.S.C.A. § 2254, or 28 U.S.C.A. § 2255. FRCP 5.2(b).

c. *Limitations on remote access to electronic files; Social Security appeals and immigration cases.* Unless the court orders otherwise, in an action for benefits under the Social Security Act, and in an action or proceeding relating to an order of removal, to relief from removal, or to immigration benefits or detention, access to an electronic file is authorized as follows: (1) the parties and their attorneys may have remote electronic access to any part of the case file, including the administrative record; (2) any other person may have electronic access to the full record at the courthouse, but may have remote electronic access only to: (A) the docket maintained by the court; and (B) an opinion, order, judgment, or other disposition of the court, but not any other part of the case file or the administrative record. FRCP 5.2(c).

d. *Filings made under seal.* The court may order that a filing be made under seal without redaction. The court may later unseal the filing or order the person who made the filing to file a redacted version for the public record. FRCP 5.2(d).

   i. *DISTRICT OF MAINE.* For information on filing sealed documents in the District of Maine, refer to ME R USDCT Rule 7A, ME R USDCT App. 4(p)(2), and ME R USDCT Sealed Filings.

e. *Protective orders.* For good cause, the court may by order in a case: (1) require redaction of additional information; or (2) limit or prohibit a nonparty's remote electronic access to a document filed with the court. FRCP 5.2(e).

f. *Option for additional unredacted filing under seal.* A person making a redacted filing may also file an unredacted copy under seal. The court must retain the unredacted copy as part of the record. FRCP 5.2(f).

   i. *DISTRICT OF MAINE.* A party wishing to file a document containing the personal data identifiers specified above may. . .file an unredacted document under seal. This document will be retained by the clerk's office as part of the record. ME R USDCT Redacting Pleadings. The court may, however, still require the party to file a redacted copy for the public file. ME R USDCT Redacting Pleadings.

g. *Option for filing a reference list.* A filing that contains redacted information may be filed together with a reference list that identifies each item of redacted information and specifies an appropriate identifier that uniquely corresponds to each item listed. The list must be filed under seal and may be amended as of right. Any reference in the case to a listed identifier will be construed to refer to the corresponding item of information. FRCP 5.2(g).

   i. *DISTRICT OF MAINE.* A party wishing to file a document containing the personal data identifiers specified above may. . .file a reference list under seal. The reference list shall contain the complete personal data identifier(s) and the redacted identifier(s) used in its (their) place in the filing. All references in the case to the redacted identifiers included in the reference list will be construed to refer to the corresponding complete identifier. The reference list must be filed under seal, and may be amended as of right. It shall be retained by the clerk's office as part of the record. ME R USDCT Redacting Pleadings. The court may, however, still require the party to file a redacted copy for the public file. ME R USDCT Redacting Pleadings.

h. *DISTRICT OF MAINE: Responsibility for redaction.* The clerk is not required to review documents filed with the court for compliance with FRCP 5.2. The responsibility to redact filings rests with counsel and the party or nonparty making the filing. ME R USDCT App. 4(i); ME R USDCT Redacting Pleadings. For guidelines for filing confidential information in civil cases in the District of Maine, refer to ME R USDCT Confidentiality.

i. *Waiver of protection of identifiers.* A person waives the protection of FRCP 5.2(a) as to the person's own information by filing it without redaction and not under seal. FRCP 5.2(h).

F. Filing and Service Requirements

1. *Filing requirements*

   a. *Required filings.* Any paper after the complaint that is required to be served must be filed no later than a reasonable time after service. FRCP 5(d)(1).

   b. *DISTRICT OF MAINE: Place of filing.* Unless otherwise ordered by the court, papers shall be filed with the court at Bangor in cases filed and pending at Bangor, and at Portland in cases filed and pending at Portland. ME R USDCT Rule 5(a).

   c. *Nonelectronic filing.* A paper not filed electronically is filed by delivering it: (A) to the clerk; or (B) to a judge who agrees to accept it for filing, and who must then note the filing date on the paper and promptly send it to the clerk. FRCP 5(d)(2).

      i. *DISTRICT OF MAINE: Documents to be filed in paper.* The following documents shall be filed in paper, which may also be scanned into ECF by the clerk's office: (A) all handwritten pleadings; and (B) all pleadings and documents filed by pro se litigants who are incarcerated or who are not registered filing users in ECF. ME R USDCT App. 4(g)(8). Non-prisoner pro se litigants in civil actions may register with ECF or may file (and serve) all pleadings and other documents in paper. The clerk's office will scan into ECF any pleadings and documents filed on paper in accordance with ME R USDCT App. 4(g). ME R USDCT App. 4(o). For more information, refer to ME R USDCT App. 4(g).

   d. *Electronic filing*

      i. *DISTRICT OF MAINE: Authorization.* Unless exempt or otherwise ordered by the court, papers shall be filed and served electronically as required by the court's Administrative Procedures Governing the Filing and Service by Electronic Means, which is set forth in ME R USDCT App. 4. The provisions of the court's Administrative Procedures Governing the Filing and Service by Electronic Means (ME R USDCT App. 4) shall be applied and enforced as part of the Local Rules of the United States District Court for the District of Maine. ME R USDCT Rule 5(c).

      ii. *Filing by represented persons.* A person represented by an attorney must file electronically, unless nonelectronic filing is allowed by the court for good cause or is allowed or required by local rule. FRCP 5(d)(3)(A).

      - *DISTRICT OF MAINE.* An attorney may apply to the court for permission to file paper documents. ME R USDCT App. 4(a)(5).

      iii. *Filing by unrepresented persons.* A person not represented by an attorney: (i) may file electronically only if allowed by court order or by local rule; and (ii) may be required to file electronically only by court order, or by a local rule that includes reasonable exceptions. FRCP 5(d)(3)(B).

      - *DISTRICT OF MAINE.* Non-prisoner pro se litigants in civil actions may register with ECF or may file (and serve) all pleadings and other documents in paper. ME R USDCT App. 4(o). A non-prisoner who is a party to a civil action and who is not represented by an attorney may register to receive service electronically and to electronically transmit their documents to the court for filing in the ECF system. If during the course of the action the person retains an attorney who appears on the person's behalf, the clerk shall terminate the person's registration upon the attorney's appearance. ME R USDCT App. 4(b)(2).

      iv. *DISTRICT OF MAINE: Scope of electronic filing.* All documents submitted for filing in civil and criminal cases, regardless of case commencement date, except those documents specifically exempted in ME R USDCT App. 4(g), shall be filed electronically using the electronic case filing system (ECF). ME R USDCT App. 4(a)(1). For special filing requirements and exceptions, refer to ME R USDCT App. 4(g).

      v. *DISTRICT OF MAINE: Consequences of electronic filing.* Electronic transmission of a document to the ECF system, together with the transmission of a Notice of Electronic Filing (NEF) from the court, constitutes filing of the document for all purposes of the Federal Rules of Civil Procedure. ME R USDCT App. 4(d)(1).

      vi. *DISTRICT OF MAINE: Review of documents.* Documents filed with the clerk's office will normally be reviewed no later than the close of the next business day. It is the responsibility of the filing party to promptly notify the clerk's office via telephone of a matter that requires the immediate attention of a judicial officer. ME R USDCT App. 4(a)(4).

e. *DISTRICT OF MAINE: Facsimile filing.* No papers shall be submitted to the court by means of a facsimile machine without prior leave of the court. ME R USDCT Rule 5(c); ME R USDCT App. 4(m).

2. *Service requirements*

a. *Service; When required.* Unless the Federal Rules of Civil Procedure provide otherwise, each of the following papers must be served on every party: (A) an order stating that service is required; (B) a pleading filed after the original complaint, unless the court orders otherwise under FRCP 5(c) because there are numerous defendants; (C) a discovery paper required to be served on a party, unless the court orders otherwise; (D) a written motion, except one that may be heard ex parte; and (E) a written notice, appearance, demand, or offer of judgment, or any similar paper. FRCP 5(a)(1).

   i. *If a party fails to appear.* No service is required on a party who is in default for failing to appear. But a pleading that asserts a new claim for relief against such a party must be served on that party under FRCP 4. FRCP 5(a)(2).

   ii. *Seizing property.* If an action is begun by seizing property and no person is or need be named as a defendant, any service required before the filing of an appearance, answer, or claim must be made on the person who had custody or possession of the property when it was seized. FRCP 5(a)(3).

b. *Service; How made.* A paper is served under FRCP 5 by: (A) handing it to the person; (B) leaving it: (i) at the person's office with a clerk or other person in charge or, if no one is in charge, in a conspicuous place in the office; or (ii) if the person has no office or the office is closed, at the person's dwelling or usual place of abode with someone of suitable age and discretion who resides there; (C) mailing it to the person's last known address—in which event service is complete upon mailing; (D) leaving it with the court clerk if the person has no known address; (E) sending it to a registered user by filing it with the court's electronic-filing system or sending it by other electronic means that the person consented to in writing—in either of which events service is complete upon filing or sending, but is not effective if the filer or sender learns that it did not reach the person to be served; or (F) delivering it by any other means that the person consented to in writing—in which event service is complete when the person making service delivers it to the agency designated to make delivery. FRCP 5(b)(2).

   i. *Serving an attorney.* If a party is represented by an attorney, service under FRCP 5 must be made on the attorney unless the court orders service on the party. FRCP 5(b)(1).

c. *DISTRICT OF MAINE: Service of electronically filed documents*

   i. *Registered users.* Registration [as a filing user of the court's ECF system] constitutes consent to service of all documents by electronic means as provided in ME R USDCT App. 4. ME R USDCT App. 4(b)(4). Whenever a non-sealed pleading is filed electronically, the ECF system will automatically generate and send a Notice of Electronic Filing (NEF) to the filing user and registered users of record. The user filing the document should retain a paper or digital copy of the NEF, which shall serve as the court's date-stamp and proof of filing. ME R USDCT App. 4(e)(1).

   - *Sealed documents.* Although the filing of sealed documents in civil cases produces an NEF, the document itself cannot be accessed and counsel shall be responsible for making service of the sealed documents. ME R USDCT App. 4(e)(2).

   ii. *Non-registered users and pro se litigants.* Attorneys who have not yet registered as users with ECF and pro se litigants who have not registered with ECF shall be served a paper copy of any electronically filed pleading or other document in accordance with the provisions of FRCP 5. ME R USDCT App. 4(e)(3).

   - *Registration of pro se litigants.* A non-prisoner who is a party to a civil action and who is not represented by an attorney may register to receive service electronically and to electronically transmit their documents to the court for filing in the ECF system. If during the course of the action the person retains an attorney who appears on the person's behalf, the clerk shall terminate the person's registration upon the attorney's appearance. ME R USDCT App. 4(b)(2).

d. *Serving numerous defendants.* If an action involves an unusually large number of defendants, the court may, on motion or on its own, order that: (A) defendants' pleadings and replies to them need not be served on other defendants; (B) any crossclaim, counterclaim, avoidance, or affirmative defense in those pleadings and replies to them will be treated as denied or avoided by all other parties; and (C) filing any such pleading and serving it on the plaintiff constitutes notice of the pleading to all parties. FRCP 5(c)(1).

   i. *Notifying parties.* A copy of every such order must be served on the parties as the court directs. FRCP 5(c)(2).

3. *DISTRICT OF MAINE: Filing and service of highly sensitive documents (HSDs).* For information on filing and serving highly sensitive documents (HSDs) in the District of Maine, refer to ME R USDCT General Order 21-5.

G. Hearings

1. *Hearings, generally.* When a motion relies on facts outside the record, the court may hear the matter on affidavits or may hear it wholly or partly on oral testimony or on depositions. FRCP 43(c).

   a. *Oral argument.* Due process does not require that oral argument be permitted on a motion and, except as otherwise provided by local rule, the district court has discretion to determine whether it will decide the motion on the papers or hear argument by counsel (and perhaps receive evidence). FPP § 1190; F.D.I.C. v. Deglau, 207 F.3d 153 (3d Cir. 2000).

      i. *DISTRICT OF MAINE.* Unless otherwise required by federal rule or statute, all motions may be decided by the court without oral argument unless otherwise ordered by the court on its own motion or, in its discretion, upon request of counsel. ME R USDCT Rule 7(e).

   b. *Providing a regular schedule for oral hearings.* A court may establish regular times and places for oral hearings on motions. FRCP 78(a).

   c. *Providing for submission on briefs.* By rule or order, the court may provide for submitting and determining motions on briefs, without oral hearings. FRCP 78(b).

2. *Hearing on certain FRCP 12 defenses before trial.* If a party so moves, any defense listed in FRCP 12(b)(1) through FRCP 12(b)(7)—whether made in a pleading or by motion—and a motion under FRCP 12(c) must be heard and decided before trial unless the court orders a deferral until trial. FRCP 12(i).

3. *Hearing on motion to dismiss for lack of subject matter jurisdiction.* It may be error for a court to dismiss a case on the defendant's motion to dismiss for lack of subject-matter jurisdiction without first holding a hearing, as FRCP 12(b)(1) requires a preliminary hearing or hearing at trial to determine any disputed facts upon which the motion or opposition to it is predicated. However, where the defendant challenges the plaintiff's assertion of federal jurisdiction, and the plaintiff is afforded an opportunity to present facts in support of this jurisdictional contention by filing affidavits in opposition to the motion to dismiss, a court does not act improperly in ruling on the motion without conducting a hearing, where the plaintiff fails to request a hearing or to take advantage of all the other opportunities to present the facts. FEDPROC § 62:429.

H. Forms

1. Federal Motion to Dismiss for Lack of Subject Matter Jurisdiction Forms

   a. Motion to dismiss for lack of subject-matter jurisdiction. 2C FEDFORMS § 11:35.

   b. Motion to dismiss for lack of subject-matter jurisdiction; Want of diversity of citizenship because requisite diversity not alleged. 2C FEDFORMS § 11:37.

   c. Motion to dismiss for lack of subject-matter jurisdiction; Want of diversity on a factual basis and because requisite diversity not alleged. 2C FEDFORMS § 11:38.

   d. Motion to dismiss for lack of subject-matter jurisdiction; Want of diversity of citizenship because state of incorporation and principal place of business of defendant not as alleged. 2C FEDFORMS § 11:39.

   e. Motion to dismiss for lack of subject-matter jurisdiction; Want of diversity of citizenship because principal place of business of defendant not as alleged. 2C FEDFORMS § 11:40.

   f. Motion to dismiss for lack of subject-matter jurisdiction; Failure to comply with procedural requirements. 2C FEDFORMS § 11:41.

   g. Motion to dismiss for lack of subject-matter jurisdiction; Want of diversity upon realignment of parties according to interest. 2C FEDFORMS § 11:42.

   h. Motion to dismiss for lack of subject-matter jurisdiction; Want of federal question. 2C FEDFORMS § 11:43.

   i. Motion to dismiss for lack of subject-matter jurisdiction; Unsubstantial federal question. 2C FEDFORMS § 11:44.

   j. Motion to dismiss for lack of subject-matter jurisdiction; Want of amount in controversy. 2C FEDFORMS § 11:45.

   k. Motion to dismiss for lack of subject-matter jurisdiction; Want of amount in controversy; Insurance policy limits do not exceed required jurisdictional amount. 2C FEDFORMS § 11:46.

   l. Motion to dismiss for lack of subject-matter jurisdiction; Want of amount in controversy; Claim for damages in excess of jurisdictional amount not made in good faith. 2C FEDFORMS § 11:47.

   m. Motion to dismiss for lack of subject-matter jurisdiction; Want of amount in controversy; Made after judgment. 2C FEDFORMS § 11:48.

n. Motion to dismiss for lack of subject-matter jurisdiction; Want of consent by the United States to be sued. 2C FEDFORMS § 11:49.

o. Motion to dismiss for lack of subject-matter jurisdiction; Want of consent by United States to be sued; United States indispensable party. 2C FEDFORMS § 11:50.

p. Motion; To dismiss; Plaintiff and defendant citizens of same state when action filed. FEDPROF § 1C:72.

q. Motion to dismiss; Assignment to nonresident for purpose of invoking federal jurisdiction sham and ineffective to confer jurisdiction. FEDPROF § 1C:73.

r. Motion to dismiss; For lack of diversity in third-party complaint. FEDPROF § 1C:74.

s. Affidavit; In support of motion to dismiss for want of diversity of citizenship; Plaintiff and defendant citizens of same state on date action filed. FEDPROF § 1C:76.

t. Affidavit; In opposition to motion to dismiss for lack of diversity; Assignment of claim to plaintiff bona fide. FEDPROF § 1C:78.

u. Motion to dismiss; Insufficiency of amount in controversy. FEDPROF § 1C:81.

v. Motion to dismiss; Bad faith in claiming jurisdictional amount. FEDPROF § 1C:82.

w. Motion to dismiss; Lack of jurisdiction over subject matter, generally. FEDPROF § 1C:87.

x. Motion to dismiss; Absence of federal question. FEDPROF § 1C:88.

y. Motion to dismiss; Absence of federal question; Failure to exhaust state remedies. FEDPROF § 1C:89.

z. Affidavit; In opposition to motion to dismiss for absence of jurisdiction over subject matter. FEDPROF § 1C:90.

I. Applicable Rules

1. *Federal rules*

   a. Federal question. 28 U.S.C.A. § 1331.

   b. Diversity of citizenship; Amount in controversy; Costs. 28 U.S.C.A. § 1332.

   c. Serving and filing pleadings and other papers. FRCP 5.

   d. Constitutional challenge to a statute; Notice, certification, and intervention. FRCP 5.1.

   e. Privacy protection for filings made with the court. FRCP 5.2.

   f. Computing and extending time; Time for motion papers. FRCP 6.

   g. Pleadings allowed; Form of motions and other papers. FRCP 7.

   h. Disclosure statement. FRCP 7.1.

   i. Form of pleadings. FRCP 10.

   j. Signing pleadings, motions, and other papers; Representations to the court; Sanctions. FRCP 11.

   k. Defenses and objections; When and how presented; Motion for judgment on the pleadings; Consolidating motions; Waiving defenses; Pretrial hearing. FRCP 12.

   l. Taking testimony. FRCP 43.

   m. Hearing motions; Submission on briefs. FRCP 78.

2. *Local rules*

   a. *DISTRICT OF MAINE*

      i. Service and filing of pleadings and other papers. ME R USDCT Rule 5.

      ii. Time. ME R USDCT Rule 6.

      iii. Motions and memoranda of law. ME R USDCT Rule 7.

      iv. Corporate disclosure. ME R USDCT Rule 7.1.

      v. Form of pleadings, motions and other papers. ME R USDCT Rule 10.

      vi. Discovery. ME R USDCT Rule 26.

      vii. Attorneys; Appearances and withdrawals. ME R USDCT Rule 83.2.

      viii. Alternative dispute resolution (ADR). ME R USDCT Rule 83.11.

ix.   Administrative procedures governing the filing and service by electronic means. ME R USDCT App. 4.

x.   Redacting pleadings. ME R USDCT Redacting Pleadings.

Motions, Oppositions and Replies
Motion to Dismiss for Lack of Personal Jurisdiction

Document Last Updated April 2021

A. Checklist

(I)   ❏ Matters to be considered by moving party

   (a)   ❏ Required documents

      (1)   ❏ Notice of motion and motion

   (b)   ❏ Supplemental documents

      (1)   ❏ Supporting evidence

      (2)   ❏ Notice of constitutional question

      (3)   ❏ Nongovernmental corporate disclosure statement

      (4)   ❏ DISTRICT OF MAINE: Additional supplemental documents

         (i)   ❏ Proposed order

   (c)   ❏ Timing

      (1)   ❏ Every defense to a claim for relief in any pleading must be asserted in the responsive pleading if one is required

      (2)   ❏ A motion asserting any of the defenses in FRCP 12(b) must be made before pleading if a responsive pleading is allowed

      (3)   ❏ If a pleading sets out a claim for relief that does not require a responsive pleading, an opposing party may assert at trial any defense to that claim

      (4)   ❏ A written motion and notice of the hearing must be served at least fourteen (14) days before the time specified for the hearing, with the following exceptions: (A) when the motion may be heard ex parte; (B) when the Federal Rules of Civil Procedure set a different time; or (C) when a court order—which a party may, for good cause, apply for ex parte—sets a different time

      (5)   ❏ Any affidavit supporting a motion must be served with the motion

      (6)   ❏ DISTRICT OF MAINE: Additional timing

         (i)   ❏ Any affidavits and other documents setting forth or evidencing facts on which the motion is based must be filed with the motion

(II)   ❏ Matters to be considered by opposing party

   (a)   ❏ Required documents

      (1)   ❏ Opposition

   (b)   ❏ Supplemental documents

      (1)   ❏ Supporting evidence

      (2)   ❏ Notice of constitutional question

   (c)   ❏ Timing

      (1)   ❏ Except as FRCP 59(c) provides otherwise, any opposing affidavit must be served at least seven (7) days before the hearing, unless the court permits service at another time

      (2)   ❏ DISTRICT OF MAINE: Additional timing

         (i)   ❏ Unless within twenty-one (21) days after the filing of a motion the opposing party files written objection thereto, incorporating a memorandum of law, the opposing party shall be deemed to have waived objection

B. Timing

1. *Motion to dismiss for lack of personal jurisdiction*

   a. *In a responsive pleading.* Every defense to a claim for relief in any pleading must be asserted in the responsive pleading if one is required. FRCP 12(b).

   b. *By motion.* A motion asserting any of the defenses in FRCP 12(b) must be made before pleading if a responsive pleading is allowed. FRCP 12(b). Although FRCP 12(b) encourages the responsive pleader to file a motion to dismiss before filing the answer, nothing in FRCP 12 prohibits the filing of a motion to dismiss with the answer. An untimely motion to dismiss may be considered if the defense asserted in the motion was previously raised in the responsive pleading. FEDPROC § 62:421.

   c. *At trial.* If a pleading sets out a claim for relief that does not require a responsive pleading, an opposing party may assert at trial any defense to that claim. FRCP 12(b).

2. *Timing of motions, generally*

   a. *Motion and notice of hearing.* A written motion and notice of the hearing must be served at least fourteen (14) days before the time specified for the hearing, with the following exceptions: (A) when the motion may be heard ex parte; (B) when the Federal Rules of Civil Procedure set a different time; or (C) when a court order—which a party may, for good cause, apply for ex parte—sets a different time. FRCP 6(c)(1).

   b. *Supporting affidavit.* Any affidavit supporting a motion must be served with the motion. FRCP 6(c)(2).

   c. *DISTRICT OF MAINE: Affidavits and other supporting documents.* Any affidavits and other documents setting forth or evidencing facts on which the motion is based must be filed with the motion. ME R USDCT Rule 7(a).

3. *Timing of opposing papers.* Except as FRCP 59(c) provides otherwise, any opposing affidavit must be served at least seven (7) days before the hearing, unless the court permits service at another time. FRCP 6(c)(2).

   a. *DISTRICT OF MAINE.* Unless within twenty-one (21) days after the filing of a motion the opposing party files written objection thereto, incorporating a memorandum of law, the opposing party shall be deemed to have waived objection. ME R USDCT Rule 7(b). The deemed waiver imposed in ME R USDCT Rule 7(b) shall not apply to motions filed during trial. ME R USDCT Rule 7(b).

4. *Timing of reply papers.* Where the respondent files an answering affidavit setting up a new matter, the moving party ordinarily is allowed a reasonable time to file a reply affidavit since failure to deny the new matter by affidavit may operate as an admission of its truth. AMJUR MOTIONS § 25.

   a. *DISTRICT OF MAINE.* Within fourteen (14) days of the filing of any objection to a motion, the moving party may file a reply memorandum. ME R USDCT Rule 7(c).

5. *Effect of FRCP 12 motion on the time to serve a responsive pleading.* Unless the court sets a different time, serving a motion under FRCP 12 alters the periods in FRCP 12(a) as follows: (A) if the court denies the motion or postpones its disposition until trial, the responsive pleading must be served within fourteen (14) days after notice of the court's action; or (B) if the court grants a motion for a more definite statement, the responsive pleading must be served within fourteen (14) days after the more definite statement is served. FRCP 12(a)(4).

6. *Computation of time*

   a. *Computing time.* FRCP 6 applies in computing any time period specified in the Federal Rules of Civil Procedure, in any local rule or court order, or in any statute that does not specify a method of computing time. FRCP 6(a).

   i. *Period stated in days or a longer unit.* When the period is stated in days or a longer unit of time: (A) exclude the day of the event that triggers the period; (B) count every day, including intermediate Saturdays, Sundays, and legal holidays; and (C) include the last day of the period, but if the last day is a Saturday, Sunday, or legal holiday, the period continues to run until the end of the next day that is not a Saturday, Sunday, or legal holiday. FRCP 6(a)(1).

   ii. *Period stated in hours.* When the period is stated in hours: (A) begin counting immediately on the occurrence of the event that triggers the period; (B) count every hour, including hours during intermediate Saturdays, Sundays, and legal holidays; and (C) if the period would end on a Saturday, Sunday, or legal holiday, the period continues to run until the same time on the next day that is not a Saturday, Sunday, or legal holiday. FRCP 6(a)(2).

   iii. *Inaccessibility of the clerk's office.* Unless the court orders otherwise, if the clerk's office is inaccessible: (A) on the last day for filing under FRCP 6(a)(1), then the time for filing is extended to the first accessible day that is not a Saturday, Sunday, or legal holiday; or (B) during the last hour for filing under FRCP 6(a)(2), then the time for filing is extended to the same time on the first accessible day that is not a Saturday, Sunday, or legal holiday. FRCP 6(a)(3).

iv. *"Last day" defined.* Unless a different time is set by a statute, local rule, or court order, the last day ends: (A) for electronic filing, at midnight in the court's time zone; and (B) for filing by other means, when the clerk's office is scheduled to close. FRCP 6(a)(4).

v. *"Next day" defined.* The "next day" is determined by continuing to count forward when the period is measured after an event and backward when measured before an event. FRCP 6(a)(5).

vi. *"Legal holiday" defined.* "Legal holiday" means: (A) the day set aside by statute for observing New Year's Day, Martin Luther King Jr.'s Birthday, Washington's Birthday, Memorial Day, Independence Day, Labor Day, Columbus Day, Veterans' Day, Thanksgiving Day, or Christmas Day; (B) any day declared a holiday by the President or Congress; and (C) for periods that are measured after an event, any other day declared a holiday by the state where the district court is located. FRCP 6(a)(6).

vii. *DISTRICT OF MAINE: Applicability of FRCP 6.* FRCP 6 applies when computing any period of time stated in the Local Rules of the United States District Court for the District of Maine. ME R USDCT Rule 6(a).

b. *DISTRICT OF MAINE: Computation of electronic filing deadlines.* Filing documents electronically does not in any way alter any filing deadlines. All electronic transmissions of documents must be completed prior to midnight, Eastern Time, in order to be considered timely filed that day. Where a specific time of day deadline is set by court order or stipulation, the electronic filing must be completed by that time. ME R USDCT App. 4(f). A document filed electronically shall be deemed filed at the time and date stated on the Notice of Electronic Filing received from the court. ME R USDCT App. 4(d)(2).

i. *Technical failures.* A filing user whose filing is made untimely as the result of a technical failure may seek appropriate relief from the court. ME R USDCT App. 4(n). A technical failure of the court's ECF system is deemed to have occurred when the court's ECF site cannot accept filings continuously or intermittently over the course of any period of time greater than one (1) hour. Known system outages will be posted on the court's website along with guidance on how to proceed, if applicable. ME R USDCT App. 4(n).

c. *Extending time.* When an act may or must be done within a specified time, the court may, for good cause, extend the time: (A) with or without motion or notice if the court acts, or if a request is made, before the original time or its extension expires; or (B) on motion made after the time has expired if the party failed to act because of excusable neglect. FRCP 6(b)(1). A court must not extend the time to act under FRCP 50(b), FRCP 50(d), FRCP 52(b), FRCP 59(b), FRCP 59(d), FRCP 59(e), and FRCP 60(b). FRCP 6(b)(2). Refer to the United States District Court for the District of Maine KeyRules Motion for Continuance/Extension of Time document for more information on extending time.

d. *Additional time after certain kinds of service.* When a party may or must act within a specified time after being served and service is made under FRCP 5(b)(2)(C) (by mail), FRCP 5(b)(2)(D) (by leaving with the clerk), or FRCP 5(b)(2)(F) (by other means consented to), three (3) days are added after the period would otherwise expire under FRCP 6(a). FRCP 6(d).

C. General Requirements

1. *Motions, generally*

   a. *Motion requirements.* A request for a court order must be made by motion. The motion must: (A) be in writing unless made during a hearing or trial; (B) state with particularity the grounds for seeking the order; and (C) state the relief sought. FRCP 7(b)(1). The writing and particularity requirements are intended to ensure that the adverse parties are informed of and have a record of both the motion's pendency and the grounds on which the movant seeks an order. FPP § 1191; Feldberg v. Quechee Lakes Corp., 463 F.3d 195 (2d Cir. 2006).

      i. *Particularity requirement.* The particularity requirement [ensures] that the opposing parties will have notice of their opponent's contentions. FEDPROC § 62:358; Goodman v. 1973 26 Foot Trojan Vessel, Arkansas Registration No. AR1439SN, 859 F.2d 71 (8th Cir. 1988). That requirement ensures that notice of the basis for the motion is provided to the court and to the opposing party so as to avoid prejudice, provide the opponent with a meaningful opportunity to respond, and provide the court with enough information to process the motion correctly. FEDPROC § 62:358; Andreas v. Volkswagen of Am., Inc., 336 F.3d 789 (8th Cir. 2003).

         • Reasonable specification of the grounds for a motion is sufficient. The particularity requirement for motions is satisfied when no party is prejudiced by a lack of particularity or when the court can comprehend the basis for the motion and deal with it fairly. However, where a movant fails to state even one ground for granting the motion in question, the movant has failed to meet the minimal standard of "reasonable specification." FEDPROC § 62:358; Martinez v. Trainor, 556 F.2d 818 (7th Cir. 1977).

- The court may excuse the failure to comply with the particularity requirement if it is inadvertent, and where no prejudice is shown by the opposing party. FEDPROC § 62:358.

b. *Notice of motion.* A party interested in resisting the relief sought by a motion has a right to notice thereof, and an opportunity to be heard. AMJUR MOTIONS § 12.

   i. *Purpose.* In addition to statutory or court rule provisions requiring notice of a motion—the purpose of such a notice requirement having been said to be to prevent a party from being prejudicially surprised by a motion—principles of natural justice dictate that an adverse party generally must be given notice that a motion will be presented to the court. AMJUR MOTIONS § 12.

   ii. *Adequacy of notice.* The test of adequate notice generally turns on whether the other parties were afforded an adequate opportunity to prepare and respond to the issues to be raised in the proceeding. AMJUR MOTIONS § 12.

c. *Single document containing motion and notice.* A single written document can satisfy the writing requirements both for a motion and for an FRCP 6(c)(1) notice. FRCP 7(Advisory Committee Notes).

2. *Motion to dismiss for lack of personal jurisdiction.* A party may assert the following defense by motion: lack of personal jurisdiction. FRCP 12(b)(2). The most common use of the FRCP 12(b)(2) motion is to challenge the use of a state long-arm statute in a diversity action. FEDPROC § 62:439; Best Van Lines, Inc. v. Walker, 490 F.3d 239 (2d Cir. 2007). A dismissal pursuant to FRCP 12(b)(2) is proper where it appears that the assertion of jurisdiction over the defendant offends traditional notions of fair play and substantial justice—that is, where neither the defendant nor the controversy has a substantial enough connection with the forum state to make the exercise of jurisdiction reasonable. FEDPROC § 62:439; Neogen Corp. v. Neo Gen Screening, Inc., 282 F.3d 883 (6th Cir. 2002).

   a. *Personal jurisdiction, generally*

      i. *Due process limitations.* Due process requires that a court obtain jurisdiction over a defendant before it may adjudicate that defendant's personal rights. FEDPROC § 65:1; Omni Capital Int'l, Ltd. v. Rudolf Wolff & Co., Ltd., 484 U.S. 97, 108 S. Ct. 404, 98 L. Ed. 2d 415 (1987).

         - Originally, it was believed that a judgment in personam could only be entered against a defendant found and served within a state, but the increased flow of commerce between the states and the disuse of the writ of capias ad respondendum, which directed the sheriff to secure the defendant's appearance by taking the defendant into custody, in civil cases led to the liberalization of the concept of personal jurisdiction over nonresidents, and the flexible "minimum contacts" test is now followed. FEDPROC § 65:1.

         - Today the rule is that no binding judgment may be rendered against an individual or corporate defendant unless the defendant has sufficient contacts, ties, or relations with the jurisdiction. FEDPROC § 65:1; Burger King Corp. v. Rudzewicz, 471 U.S. 462, 105 S. Ct. 2174, 85 L. Ed. 2d 528 (1985); Int'l Shoe Co. v. State of Wash., Office of Unemployment Comp. & Placement, 326 U.S. 310, 66 S. Ct. 154, 90 L. Ed. 95 (1945).

         - Moreover, even if the defendant has sufficient contacts with the forum state to satisfy due process, a court nevertheless does not obtain personal jurisdiction over the defendant unless the defendant has notice sufficient to satisfy due process and, if such notice requires service of a summons, that there is authorization for the type and manner of service used. FEDPROC § 65:1; Omni Capital Int'l, Ltd. v. Rudolf Wolff & Co., Ltd., 484 U.S. 97, 108 S. Ct. 404, 98 L. Ed. 2d 415 (1987).

         - Personal jurisdiction is a prerequisite to the maintenance of an action and must exist even though subject matter jurisdiction and venue are proper. FEDPROC § 65:1; Bookout v. Beck, 354 F.2d 823 (9th Cir. 1965).

         - Personal jurisdiction over a nonresident defendant is appropriate under the Due Process Clause only where the defendant has sufficient minimum contacts with the forum state that are more than random, fortuitous, or attenuated contacts made by interacting with other persons affiliated with the state, such that summoning the defendant would not offend traditional notions of fair play and substantial justice. FEDPROC § 65:1; Pecoraro v. Sky Ranch for Boys, Inc., 340 F.3d 558 (8th Cir. 2003).

      ii. *Methods of obtaining jurisdiction over an individual.* There are four basic methods of obtaining jurisdiction over an individual:

         - Personal service within the jurisdiction. FEDPROC § 65:22.

221

- Service on a domiciliary of the forum state who is temporarily outside the jurisdiction, on the theory that the authority of a state over one of its citizens is not terminated by the mere fact of his absence. FEDPROC § 65:22; Milliken v. Meyer, 311 U.S. 457, 61 S. Ct. 339, 85 L. Ed. 278 (1940).

- Service on a nonresident who has sufficient contacts with the forum state, since the test of International Shoe is applicable to individuals. FEDPROC § 65:22; Kulko v. Superior Court of California In & For City & Cty. of San Francisco, 436 U.S. 84, 98 S. Ct. 1690, 56 L. Ed. 2d 132 (1978).

- Service on an agent who has been expressly appointed or appointed by operation of law, such as under a nonresident motorist statute. FEDPROC § 65:22; Nat'l Equip. Rental, Ltd. v. Szukhent, 375 U.S. 311, 84 S. Ct. 411, 11 L. Ed. 2d 354 (1964).

iii. *Territorial limits of effective service.* Serving a summons or filing a waiver of service establishes personal jurisdiction over a defendant: (A) who is subject to the jurisdiction of a court of general jurisdiction in the state where the district court is located; (B) who is a party joined under FRCP 14 or FRCP 19 and is served within a judicial district of the United States and not more than 100 miles from where the summons was issued; or (C) when authorized by a federal statute. FRCP 4(k)(1).

- *Federal claim outside state-court jurisdiction.* For a claim that arises under federal law, serving a summons or filing a waiver of service establishes personal jurisdiction over a defendant if: (A) the defendant is not subject to jurisdiction in any state's courts of general jurisdiction; and (B) exercising jurisdiction is consistent with the United States Constitution and laws. FRCP 4(k)(2).

b. *Motion based on lack of in rem or quasi-in-rem jurisdiction.* Although FRCP 12(b)(2) only refers to "lack of personal jurisdiction," the provision presumably is sufficiently elastic to embrace a defense or objection that the district court lacks in rem or quasi-in-rem jurisdiction, admittedly a subject that rarely arises in contemporary practice. FPP § 1351.

c. *Motion based on insufficient process or insufficient service of process.* FRCP 12(b)(2) motions to dismiss are frequently based on the failure to serve the defendant with process or a defective service of process, on the theory that if the defendant was not properly served with process, the court lacks personal jurisdiction over the defendant. FEDPROC § 62:440; Prokopiou v. Long Island R. Co., No. 06 CIV. 2558 KNF, 2007 WL 1098696 (S.D.N.Y. Apr. 9, 2007).

d. *Independent ground for dismissal.* Lack of overall reasonableness in the assertion of personal jurisdiction constitutes an independent ground for dismissal under FRCP 12(b)(2). FEDPROC § 62:442; Fed. Ins. Co. v. Lake Shore Inc., 886 F.2d 654 (4th Cir. 1989).

e. *Burden.* On the motion, the plaintiff bears the burden to establish the court's jurisdiction, which normally is not a heavy one, although the standard of proof may vary depending on the procedure used by the court in making its determination and whether the defendant is successful in rebutting the plaintiff's initial showing. Moreover, the Supreme Court has intimated that in the case of a challenge to the constitutional fairness and reasonableness of the chosen forum, the burden is on the defendant. FPP § 1351; Burger King Corp. v. Rudzewicz, 471 U.S. 462, 105 S. Ct. 2174, 85 L. Ed. 2d 528 (1985).

i. The most common formulation found in the judicial opinions is that the plaintiff bears the ultimate burden of demonstrating that the court's personal jurisdiction over the defendant exists by a preponderance of the evidence, but needs only make a prima facie showing when the district judge restricts her review of the FRCP 12(b)(2) motion solely to affidavits and other written evidence. FPP § 1351; Mullins v. TestAmerica, Inc., 564 F.3d 386 (5th Cir. 2009).

ii. In addition, for purposes of such a review, federal courts will, as they do on other motions under FRCP 12(b), take as true the allegations of the nonmoving party with regard to the jurisdictional issues and resolve all factual disputes in his or her favor. FPP § 1351.

f. *Motion denied.* A party who has unsuccessfully raised an objection under FRCP 12(b)(2) may proceed to trial on the merits without waiving the ability to renew the objection to the court's jurisdiction. FPP § 1351.

g. *Joining motions.* A motion under FRCP 12 may be joined with any other motion allowed by FRCP 12. FRCP 12(g)(1). As a general rule, when the court is confronted by a motion raising a combination of FRCP 12(b) defenses, it will pass on the jurisdictional issues before considering whether a claim was stated by the complaint. FPP § 1351.

i. *Limitation on further motions.* Except as provided in FRCP 12(h)(2) or FRCP 12(h)(3), a party that makes a motion under FRCP 12 must not make another motion under FRCP 12 raising a defense or objection that was available to the party but omitted from its earlier motion. FRCP 12(g)(2).

    h. *Waiving and preserving certain defenses.* No defense or objection is waived by joining it with one or more other defenses or objections in a responsive pleading or in a motion. FRCP 12(b).

      i. *Waiver by omission or failure to make or include motion.* A party waives any defense listed in FRCP 12(b)(2) through FRCP 12(b)(5) by:

- Omitting it from a motion in the circumstances described in FRCP 12(g)(2); or

- Failing to either: (i) make it by motion under FRCP 12; or (ii) include it in a responsive pleading or in an amendment allowed by FRCP 15(a)(1) as a matter of course. FRCP 12(h)(1).

      ii. *Waiver by consent or stipulation.* A valid consent or a stipulation that the court has jurisdiction prevents the successful assertion of an FRCP 12(b)(2) defense. FPP § 1351.

      iii. *Waiver by filing permissive counterclaim.* A defendant may be deemed to have waived an objection to personal jurisdiction if he or she files a permissive counterclaim under FRCP 13(b). FPP § 1351.

3. *Opposing papers.* The Federal Rules of Civil Procedure do not require any formal answer, return, or reply to a motion, except where the Federal Rules of Civil Procedure or local rules may require affidavits, memoranda, or other papers to be filed in opposition to a motion. Such papers are simply to apprise the court of such opposition and the grounds of that opposition. FEDPROC § 62:353.

    a. *DISTRICT OF MAINE: Content of objections.* Any objections shall include citations and supporting authorities and affidavits and other documents setting forth or evidencing facts on which the objection is based. ME R USDCT Rule 7(b).

    b. *Effect of failure to respond to motion.* Although in the absence of statutory provision or court rule, a motion ordinarily does not require a response or written answer, when a party files a motion and the opposing party fails to respond, the court may construe such failure to respond as nonopposition to the motion or an admission that the motion was meritorious. AMJUR MOTIONS § 28. The rule in some jurisdictions being that the failure to respond to a fact set forth in a motion is deemed an admission—and may grant the motion if the relief requested appears to be justified. AMJUR MOTIONS § 28.

      i. *Unopposed motion to dismiss.* The circuits are split on whether a court may grant a motion to dismiss solely on the basis that the plaintiff did not file a response opposing the motion. FRCP-RC RULE 12.

    c. *Assent or no opposition not determinative.* However, a motion will not be granted automatically simply because an "assent" or a notation of "no opposition" has been filed; federal judges frequently deny motions that have been assented to when it is thought that justice so dictates. FPP § 1190.

    d. *Responsive pleading inappropriate as response to motion.* An attempt to answer or oppose a motion with a responsive pleading usually is not appropriate. FPP § 1190.

4. *Reply papers.* A moving party may be required or permitted to prepare papers in addition to its original motion papers. AMJUR MOTIONS § 25. Papers answering or replying to opposing papers may be appropriate, in the interests of justice, where it appears there is a substantial reason for allowing a reply. Thus, a court may accept reply papers where a party demonstrates that the papers to which it seeks to file a reply raise new issues that are material to the disposition of the question before the court, or where the court determines, sua sponte, that it wishes further briefing of an issue raised in those papers and orders the submission of additional papers. FEDPROC § 62:354.

    a. *Function of reply papers.* The function of a reply affidavit or reply papers is to answer the arguments made in opposition to the position taken by the movant, not to raise new issues, arguments, or evidence, or change the nature of the primary motion. However, if the court permits new evidence with the reply papers, the other party should be given the opportunity to respond. Where the party opposing the motion has no opportunity to address the argument in writing, a court has the discretion to disregard arguments raised for the first time in a reply memorandum. Also, the view has been followed in some jurisdictions that as a matter of judicial economy, where there is no prejudice and where the issues could be raised simply by filing a motion to dismiss, the trial court has discretion to consider arguments raised for the first time in a reply memorandum, and that a trial court may grant a motion to strike issues raised for the first time in a reply memorandum. AMJUR MOTIONS § 26.

      i. *DISTRICT OF MAINE.* The moving party may file a reply memorandum. . .which shall be strictly confined to replying to new matter raised in the objection or opposing memorandum. ME R USDCT Rule 7(c).

5. *DISTRICT OF MAINE: Appearances.* An attorney's signature to a pleading shall constitute an appearance for the party filing the pleading. Otherwise, an attorney who wishes to participate in any manner in any action must file a formal written appearance identifying the party represented. An appearance whether by pleading or formal written appearance shall be

signed by an attorney in his/her individual name and shall state his/her office address. ME R USDCT Rule 83.2(a). For more information, refer to ME R USDCT Rule 83.2.

6. *DISTRICT OF MAINE: Alternative dispute resolution (ADR).* Litigants are authorized and encouraged to employ, at their own expense, any available ADR process on which they can agree, including early neutral evaluation, settlement conferences, mediation, non-binding summary jury trial, corporate mini-trial, and arbitration proceedings. ME R USDCT Rule 83.11(a). For more information on ADR, refer to ME R USDCT Rule 83.11.

D. Documents

1. *Documents for moving party*

   a. *Required documents*

      i. *Notice of motion and motion.* Refer to the "C. General Requirements" section of this KeyRules document for information on the notice of motion and motion.

         - *DISTRICT OF MAINE: Memorandum of law.* Every motion shall incorporate a memorandum of law, including citations and supporting authorities. ME R USDCT Rule 7(a). Refer to the "E. Format" section of this KeyRules document for the form of memoranda of law.

         - *Certificate of service.* No certificate of service is required when a paper is served by filing it with the court's electronic-filing system. When a paper that is required to be served is served by other means: (i) if the paper is filed, a certificate of service must be filed with it or within a reasonable time after service; and (ii) if the paper is not filed, a certificate of service need not be filed unless filing is required by court order or by local rule. FRCP 5(d)(1)(B).

   b. *Supplemental documents*

      i. *Supporting evidence.* When a motion relies on facts outside the record, the court may hear the matter on affidavits or may hear it wholly or partly on oral testimony or on depositions. FRCP 43(c).

         - *DISTRICT OF MAINE: Affidavits and other supporting documents.* Any affidavits and other documents setting forth or evidencing facts on which the motion is based must be filed with the motion. ME R USDCT Rule 7(a).

         - *DISTRICT OF MAINE: Discovery transcripts or materials.* A party relying on discovery transcripts or materials in support of or in opposition to a motion shall file excerpts of such transcript or materials with the memorandum required by ME R USDCT Rule 7 as well as a list of specific citations to the parts on which the party relies. ME R USDCT Rule 26(c). Excerpts of depositions in support of or in opposition to a motion shall be filed electronically using ECF, unless otherwise permitted by the court. ME R USDCT App. 4(l)(3).

      ii. *Notice of constitutional question.* A party that files a pleading, written motion, or other paper drawing into question the constitutionality of a federal or state statute must promptly: (1) file a notice of constitutional question stating the question and identifying the paper that raises it, if: (A) a federal statute is questioned and the parties do not include the United States, one of its agencies, or one of its officers or employees in an official capacity; or (B) a state statute is questioned and the parties do not include the state, one of its agencies, or one of its officers or employees in an official capacity; and (2) serve the notice and paper on the Attorney General of the United States if a federal statute is questioned—or on the state attorney general if a state statute is questioned—either by certified or registered mail or by sending it to an electronic address designated by the attorney general for this purpose. FRCP 5.1(a).

         - *No forfeiture.* A party's failure to file and serve the notice, or the court's failure to certify, does not forfeit a constitutional claim or defense that is otherwise timely asserted. FRCP 5.1(d).

      iii. *Nongovernmental corporate disclosure statement.* A nongovernmental corporate party must file two (2) copies of a disclosure statement that: (1) identifies any parent corporation and any publicly held corporation owning ten percent (10%) or more of its stock; or (2) states that there is no such corporation. FRCP 7.1(a). A party must: (1) file the disclosure statement with its first appearance, pleading, petition, motion, response, or other request addressed to the court; and (2) promptly file a supplemental statement if any required information changes. FRCP 7.1(b).

         - *DISTRICT OF MAINE: Notice of interested parties.* To enable the court to evaluate possible disqualification or recusal, counsel for all non-governmental parties shall file with their first appearance a Notice of Interested Parties, which shall list all persons, associations of persons, firms, partnerships, limited liability companies, joint ventures, corporations (including parent or affiliated corporations, clearly identified as such), or any similar entities, owning ten percent (10%) or more of the named party. Counsel shall be under a continuing obligation to file an amended Notice if any material change occurs in the status of an Interested Party, such as through merger, acquisition, or new/additional membership. ME R USDCT Rule 7.1.

    iv. *DISTRICT OF MAINE: Additional supplemental documents*

- *Proposed order.* Proposed orders shall not be filed unless requested by the court. When requested by the court, proposed orders shall be filed by e-mail in word processing format. ME R USDCT App. 4(k)(1).

  2. *Documents for opposing party*

    a. *Required documents*

      i. *Opposition.* Refer to the "C. General Requirements" section of this KeyRules document for information on the opposing papers.

- *DISTRICT OF MAINE: Memorandum of law.* Unless within twenty-one (21) days after the filing of a motion the opposing party files written objection thereto, incorporating a memorandum of law, the opposing party shall be deemed to have waived objection. ME R USDCT Rule 7(b).

- *Certificate of service.* No certificate of service is required when a paper is served by filing it with the court's electronic-filing system. When a paper that is required to be served is served by other means: (i) if the paper is filed, a certificate of service must be filed with it or within a reasonable time after service; and (ii) if the paper is not filed, a certificate of service need not be filed unless filing is required by court order or by local rule. FRCP 5(d)(1)(B).

    b. *Supplemental documents*

      i. *Supporting evidence.* When a motion relies on facts outside the record, the court may hear the matter on affidavits or may hear it wholly or partly on oral testimony or on depositions. FRCP 43(c).

- *DISTRICT OF MAINE: Affidavits and other supporting documents.* Any objections shall include. . .affidavits and other documents setting forth or evidencing facts on which the objection is based. ME R USDCT Rule 7(b).

- *DISTRICT OF MAINE: Discovery transcripts or materials.* A party relying on discovery transcripts or materials in support of or in opposition to a motion shall file excerpts of such transcript or materials with the memorandum required by ME R USDCT Rule 7 as well as a list of specific citations to the parts on which the party relies. ME R USDCT Rule 26(c). Excerpts of depositions in support of or in opposition to a motion shall be filed electronically using ECF, unless otherwise permitted by the court. ME R USDCT App. 4(l)(3).

      ii. *Notice of constitutional question.* A party that files a pleading, written motion, or other paper drawing into question the constitutionality of a federal or state statute must promptly: (1) file a notice of constitutional question stating the question and identifying the paper that raises it, if: (A) a federal statute is questioned and the parties do not include the United States, one of its agencies, or one of its officers or employees in an official capacity; or (B) a state statute is questioned and the parties do not include the state, one of its agencies, or one of its officers or employees in an official capacity; and (2) serve the notice and paper on the Attorney General of the United States if a federal statute is questioned—or on the state attorney general if a state statute is questioned—either by certified or registered mail or by sending it to an electronic address designated by the attorney general for this purpose. FRCP 5.1(a).

- *No forfeiture.* A party's failure to file and serve the notice, or the court's failure to certify, does not forfeit a constitutional claim or defense that is otherwise timely asserted. FRCP 5.1(d).

E. Format

  1. *Form of documents.* The rules governing captions and other matters of form in pleadings apply to motions and other papers. FRCP 7(b)(2).

    a. *DISTRICT OF MAINE: Font size, line spacing, and paper size.* All such documents shall be typed in a font of no less than size twelve (12) point, and shall be double-spaced or printed on eight and one-half by eleven (8-1/2 x 11) inch paper. Footnotes shall be in a font of no less than size ten (10) point, and may be single spaced. ME R USDCT Rule 10.

    b. *Caption.* Every pleading must have a caption with the court's name, a title, a file number, and an FRCP 7(a) designation. FRCP 10(a).

      i. *Names of parties.* The title of the complaint must name all the parties; the title of other pleadings, after naming the first party on each side, may refer generally to other parties. FRCP 10(a).

ii. *DISTRICT OF MAINE: Additional caption requirements.* All pleadings, motions and other papers filed with the clerk or otherwise submitted to the court, except exhibits, shall bear the proper case number and shall contain on the first page a caption as described by FRCP 10(a) and immediately thereunder a designation of what the document is and the name of the party in whose behalf it is submitted. ME R USDCT Rule 10.

c. *Claims or defenses*

i. *Numbered paragraphs.* A party must state its claims or defenses in numbered paragraphs, each limited as far as practicable to a single set of circumstances. A later pleading may refer by number to a paragraph in an earlier pleading. FRCP 10(b).

ii. *Separate statements.* If doing so would promote clarity, each claim founded on a separate transaction or occurrence—and each defense other than a denial—must be stated in a separate count or defense. FRCP 10(b).

d. *Adoption by reference.* A statement in a pleading may be adopted by reference elsewhere in the same pleading or in any other pleading or motion. FRCP 10(c).

i. *Exhibits.* A copy of a written instrument that is an exhibit to a pleading is a part of the pleading for all purposes. FRCP 10(c).

e. *DISTRICT OF MAINE: Page numbering.* All pages shall be numbered at the bottom. ME R USDCT Rule 10.

f. *DISTRICT OF MAINE: Attachment of ancillary papers.* Ancillary papers shall be attached at the end of the document to which they relate. ME R USDCT Rule 10.

g. *Acceptance by the clerk.* The clerk must not refuse to file a paper solely because it is not in the form prescribed by the Federal Rules of Civil Procedure or by a local rule or practice. FRCP 5(d)(4).

2. *Form of electronic documents.* A paper filed electronically is a written paper for purposes of the Federal Rules of Civil Procedure. FRCP 5(d)(3)(D).

a. *DISTRICT OF MAINE: Document format.* The ECF system only accepts documents in a portable document format (PDF). Although there are two types of PDF documents—electronically converted PDF's and scanned PDF's—only electronically converted PDF's may be filed with the court using the ECF system, unless otherwise authorized by local rule or order. ME R USDCT App. 4. Any document or exhibit to be filed or submitted to the court shall not be password-protected or encrypted. ME R USDCT App. 4(g)(12).

i. *Electronically converted PDFs.* Electronically converted PDF's are created from word processing documents (MS Word, WordPerfect, etc.) using Adobe Acrobat or similar software. They are text searchable and their file size is small. ME R USDCT App. 4. Software used to electronically convert documents to PDF which includes proprietary or advertisement information within the PDF document is prohibited. ME R USDCT App. 4.

ii. *Scanned PDFs.* Scanned PDF's are created from paper documents run through an optical scanner. Scanned PDF's are not searchable and have a large file size. ME R USDCT App. 4.

b. *DISTRICT OF MAINE: Title.* All pleadings filed electronically shall be titled in accordance with the approved dictionary of civil or criminal events of the ECF system of the United States District Court for the District of Maine. ME R USDCT App. 4(d)(3).

c. *DISTRICT OF MAINE: Attachments.* Attachments to filings and exhibits must be filed in accordance with the court's ECF User Manual, unless otherwise ordered by the court. ME R USDCT App. 4(j). When there are fifty (50) or fewer attachments to a pleading, the attachments must be filed by counsel electronically using ECF. When there are more than fifty (50) attachments, the attachments must be filed in one of the following ways: (A) using ECF, simply attach them to the pleading being filed; (B) using ECF, use the "Additional Attachments" menu item; (C) on paper; or (D) on a properly labeled three and one-half (3-1/2) inch floppy disk, CD or DVD. ME R USDCT App. 4(j)(2). Attachments filed on paper or on disk must contain a comprehensive index that clearly describes each document. ME R USDCT App. 4(j)(2).

i. A filing user must submit as attachments only those excerpts of the referenced documents that are directly germane to the matter under consideration by the court. Excerpted material must be clearly and prominently identified as such. Users who file excerpts of documents do so without prejudice to their right to timely file additional excerpts or the complete document, as may be allowed by the court. Responding parties may timely file additional excerpts or the complete document that they believe are directly germane. ME R USDCT App. 4(j)(3).

ii. Filers shall not attach as an exhibit any pleading or other paper already on file with the court in that case, but shall merely refer to that document. ME R USDCT App. 4(j)(4).

d. *DISTRICT OF MAINE: Compliance with technical standards.* All documents filed by electronic means must comply with technical standards, if any, established by the Judicial Conference of the United States or by the United States District Court for the District of Maine. ME R USDCT App. 4(a)(3).

3. *DISTRICT OF MAINE: Form of memoranda of law.* All memoranda shall be typed, in a font of no less than size twelve (12) point, and shall be double-spaced on eight and one-half by eleven (8-1/2 x 11) inch paper or printed. Footnotes shall be in a font of no less than size ten (10) point, and may be single spaced. All pages shall be numbered at the bottom. ME R USDCT Rule 7(d).

a. *Page limitations.* No memorandum of law in support of or in opposition to a motion to dismiss, a motion for judgment on the pleadings, a motion for summary judgment or a motion for injunctive relief shall exceed twenty (20) pages. ME R USDCT Rule 7(d). No reply memorandum shall exceed seven (7) pages. ME R USDCT Rule 7(d); ME R USDCT Rule 7(c).

i. *Motion to exceed page limitation.* A motion to exceed the limitation of ME R USDCT Rule 7 shall be filed no later than three (3) business days in advance of the date for filing the memorandum to permit meaningful review by the court. A motion to exceed the page limitations shall not be filed simultaneously with a memorandum in excess of the limitations of ME R USDCT Rule 7. ME R USDCT Rule 7(d).

4. *Signing of pleadings, motions and other papers*

a. *Signature.* Every pleading, written motion, and other paper must be signed by at least one attorney of record in the attorney's name—or by a party personally if the party is unrepresented. The paper must state the signer's address, e-mail address, and telephone number. FRCP 11(a).

i. *No verification or accompanying affidavit required for pleadings.* Unless a rule or statute specifically states otherwise, a pleading need not be verified or accompanied by an affidavit. FRCP 11(a).

ii. *Unsigned papers.* The court must strike an unsigned paper unless the omission is promptly corrected after being called to the attorney's or party's attention. FRCP 11(a).

b. *Electronic signing.* A filing made through a person's electronic-filing account and authorized by that person, together with that person's name on a signature block, constitutes the person's signature. FRCP 5(d)(3)(C).

i. *DISTRICT OF MAINE: Attorneys.* The user log-in and password together with a user's name on the signature block constitutes the attorney's signature pursuant to the Federal Rules of Civil Procedure and the Local Rules of the United States District Court for the District of Maine. All electronically filed documents must include a signature block and must set forth the attorney's name, address, telephone number and e-mail address. The name of the ECF user under whose log-in and password the document is submitted must be preceded by a "/s/" in the space where the signature would otherwise appear. ME R USDCT App. 4(h)(1).

ii. *DISTRICT OF MAINE: Multiple signatures.* The filer of any document requiring more than one signature (e.g., pleadings filed by visiting lawyers, stipulations, joint status reports) must list thereon all the names of other signatories, preceded by a "/s/" in the space where the signatures would otherwise appear. By submitting such a document, the filing attorney certifies that each of the other signatories has expressly agreed to the form and substance of the document and that the filing attorney has their actual authority to submit the document electronically. ME R USDCT App. 4(h)(2). For more information, refer to ME R USDCT App. 4(h)(2).

iii. *DISTRICT OF MAINE: Documents signed under oath.* Affidavits, declarations, verified complaints, or any other document signed under oath shall be filed electronically. The electronically filed version shall contain the typed name of the signatory, preceded by a "/s/" in the space where the signature would otherwise appear indicating that the paper document bears an original signature. ME R USDCT Rule 10; ME R USDCT App. 4(h)(3). For more information, refer to ME R USDCT Rule 10.

c. *Representations to the court.* By presenting to the court a pleading, written motion, or other paper—whether by signing, filing, submitting, or later advocating it—an attorney or unrepresented party certifies that to the best of the person's knowledge, information, and belief, formed after an inquiry reasonable under the circumstances: (1) it is not being presented for any improper purpose, such as to harass, cause unnecessary delay, or needlessly increase the cost of litigation; (2) the claims, defenses, and other legal contentions are warranted by existing law or by a nonfrivolous argument for extending, modifying, or reversing existing law or for establishing new law; (3) the factual contentions have evidentiary support or, if specifically so identified, will likely have evidentiary support after a reasonable opportunity for further investigation or discovery; and (4) the denials of factual contentions are warranted on the evidence or, if specifically so identified, are reasonably based on belief or a lack of information. FRCP 11(b).

d. *Sanctions.* If, after notice and a reasonable opportunity to respond, the court determines that FRCP 11(b) has been violated, the court may impose an appropriate sanction on any attorney, law firm, or party that violated FRCP 11(b) or is responsible for the violation. FRCP 11(c)(1). Refer to the United States District Court for the District of Maine KeyRules Motion for Sanctions document for more information.

5. *Privacy protection for filings made with the court*

a. *Redacted filings.* Unless the court orders otherwise, in an electronic or paper filing with the court that contains an individual's Social Security number, taxpayer-identification number, or birth date, the name of an individual known to be a minor, or a financial-account number, a party or nonparty making the filing may include only: (1) the last four (4) digits of the Social Security number and taxpayer-identification number; (2) the year of the individual's birth; (3) the minor's initials; and (4) the last four (4) digits of the financial-account number. FRCP 5.2(a).

    i. *DISTRICT OF MAINE.* To address the privacy concerns created by the Internet access to court papers, unless otherwise ordered by the court, counsel shall modify certain personal data identifiers in pleadings and other papers as follows: (1) minors' names: use of the minors' initials only; (2) Social Security numbers: use of the last four (4) numbers only; (3) dates of birth: use of the year of birth only; [and] (4) financial account numbers: identify the type of account and the financial institution, but use only the last four (4) numbers of the account number. ME R USDCT Redacting Pleadings. Counsel should also use caution when filing papers that contain a person's medical records, employment history; financial information; and any proprietary or trade secret information. ME R USDCT Redacting Pleadings.

b. *Exemptions from the redaction requirement.* The redaction requirement does not apply to the following: (1) a financial-account number that identifies the property allegedly subject to forfeiture in a forfeiture proceeding; (2) the record of an administrative or agency proceeding; (3) the official record of a state-court proceeding; (4) the record of a court or tribunal, if that record was not subject to the redaction requirement when originally filed; (5) a filing covered by FRCP 5.2(c) or FRCP 5.2(d); and (6) a pro se filing in an action brought under 28 U.S.C.A. § 2241, 28 U.S.C.A. § 2254, or 28 U.S.C.A. § 2255. FRCP 5.2(b).

c. *Limitations on remote access to electronic files; Social Security appeals and immigration cases.* Unless the court orders otherwise, in an action for benefits under the Social Security Act, and in an action or proceeding relating to an order of removal, to relief from removal, or to immigration benefits or detention, access to an electronic file is authorized as follows: (1) the parties and their attorneys may have remote electronic access to any part of the case file, including the administrative record; (2) any other person may have electronic access to the full record at the courthouse, but may have remote electronic access only to: (A) the docket maintained by the court; and (B) an opinion, order, judgment, or other disposition of the court, but not any other part of the case file or the administrative record. FRCP 5.2(c).

d. *Filings made under seal.* The court may order that a filing be made under seal without redaction. The court may later unseal the filing or order the person who made the filing to file a redacted version for the public record. FRCP 5.2(d).

    i. *DISTRICT OF MAINE.* For information on filing sealed documents in the District of Maine, refer to ME R USDCT Rule 7A, ME R USDCT App. 4(p)(2), and ME R USDCT Sealed Filings.

e. *Protective orders.* For good cause, the court may by order in a case: (1) require redaction of additional information; or (2) limit or prohibit a nonparty's remote electronic access to a document filed with the court. FRCP 5.2(e).

f. *Option for additional unredacted filing under seal.* A person making a redacted filing may also file an unredacted copy under seal. The court must retain the unredacted copy as part of the record. FRCP 5.2(f).

    i. *DISTRICT OF MAINE.* A party wishing to file a document containing the personal data identifiers specified above may. . .file an unredacted document under seal. This document will be retained by the clerk's office as part of the record. ME R USDCT Redacting Pleadings. The court may, however, still require the party to file a redacted copy for the public file. ME R USDCT Redacting Pleadings.

g. *Option for filing a reference list.* A filing that contains redacted information may be filed together with a reference list that identifies each item of redacted information and specifies an appropriate identifier that uniquely corresponds to each item listed. The list must be filed under seal and may be amended as of right. Any reference in the case to a listed identifier will be construed to refer to the corresponding item of information. FRCP 5.2(g).

    i. *DISTRICT OF MAINE.* A party wishing to file a document containing the personal data identifiers specified above may. . .file a reference list under seal. The reference list shall contain the complete personal data identifier(s) and the redacted identifier(s) used in its (their) place in the filing. All references in the case to the redacted identifiers included in the reference list will be construed to refer to the corresponding complete identifier. The reference list must be filed under seal, and may be amended as of right. It shall be retained by the clerk's office as part of the record. ME R USDCT Redacting Pleadings. The court may, however, still require the party to file a redacted copy for the public file. ME R USDCT Redacting Pleadings.

h. *DISTRICT OF MAINE: Responsibility for redaction.* The clerk is not required to review documents filed with the court for compliance with FRCP 5.2. The responsibility to redact filings rests with counsel and the party or nonparty making the filing. ME R USDCT App. 4(i); ME R USDCT Redacting Pleadings. For guidelines for filing confidential information in civil cases in the District of Maine, refer to ME R USDCT Confidentiality.

i. *Waiver of protection of identifiers.* A person waives the protection of FRCP 5.2(a) as to the person's own information by filing it without redaction and not under seal. FRCP 5.2(h).

F. Filing and Service Requirements

1. *Filing requirements*

   a. *Required filings.* Any paper after the complaint that is required to be served must be filed no later than a reasonable time after service. FRCP 5(d)(1).

   b. *DISTRICT OF MAINE: Place of filing.* Unless otherwise ordered by the court, papers shall be filed with the court at Bangor in cases filed and pending at Bangor, and at Portland in cases filed and pending at Portland. ME R USDCT Rule 5(a).

   c. *Nonelectronic filing.* A paper not filed electronically is filed by delivering it: (A) to the clerk; or (B) to a judge who agrees to accept it for filing, and who must then note the filing date on the paper and promptly send it to the clerk. FRCP 5(d)(2).

      i. *DISTRICT OF MAINE: Documents to be filed in paper.* The following documents shall be filed in paper, which may also be scanned into ECF by the clerk's office: (A) all handwritten pleadings; and (B) all pleadings and documents filed by pro se litigants who are incarcerated or who are not registered filing users in ECF. ME R USDCT App. 4(g)(8). Non-prisoner pro se litigants in civil actions may register with ECF or may file (and serve) all pleadings and other documents in paper. The clerk's office will scan into ECF any pleadings and documents filed on paper in accordance with ME R USDCT App. 4(g). ME R USDCT App. 4(o). For more information, refer to ME R USDCT App. 4(g).

   d. *Electronic filing*

      i. *DISTRICT OF MAINE: Authorization.* Unless exempt or otherwise ordered by the court, papers shall be filed and served electronically as required by the court's Administrative Procedures Governing the Filing and Service by Electronic Means, which is set forth in ME R USDCT App. 4. The provisions of the court's Administrative Procedures Governing the Filing and Service by Electronic Means (ME R USDCT App. 4) shall be applied and enforced as part of the Local Rules of the United States District Court for the District of Maine. ME R USDCT Rule 5(c).

      ii. *Filing by represented persons.* A person represented by an attorney must file electronically, unless nonelectronic filing is allowed by the court for good cause or is allowed or required by local rule. FRCP 5(d)(3)(A).

         - *DISTRICT OF MAINE.* An attorney may apply to the court for permission to file paper documents. ME R USDCT App. 4(a)(5).

      iii. *Filing by unrepresented persons.* A person not represented by an attorney: (i) may file electronically only if allowed by court order or by local rule; and (ii) may be required to file electronically only by court order, or by a local rule that includes reasonable exceptions. FRCP 5(d)(3)(B).

         - *DISTRICT OF MAINE.* Non-prisoner pro se litigants in civil actions may register with ECF or may file (and serve) all pleadings and other documents in paper. ME R USDCT App. 4(o). A non-prisoner who is a party to a civil action and who is not represented by an attorney may register to receive service electronically and to electronically transmit their documents to the court for filing in the ECF system. If during the course of the action the person retains an attorney who appears on the person's behalf, the clerk shall terminate the person's registration upon the attorney's appearance. ME R USDCT App. 4(b)(2).

      iv. *DISTRICT OF MAINE: Scope of electronic filing.* All documents submitted for filing in civil and criminal cases, regardless of case commencement date, except those documents specifically exempted in ME R USDCT App. 4(g), shall be filed electronically using the electronic case filing system (ECF). ME R USDCT App. 4(a)(1). For special filing requirements and exceptions, refer to ME R USDCT App. 4(g).

      v. *DISTRICT OF MAINE: Consequences of electronic filing.* Electronic transmission of a document to the ECF system, together with the transmission of a Notice of Electronic Filing (NEF) from the court, constitutes filing of the document for all purposes of the Federal Rules of Civil Procedure. ME R USDCT App. 4(d)(1).

vi. *DISTRICT OF MAINE: Review of documents.* Documents filed with the clerk's office will normally be reviewed no later than the close of the next business day. It is the responsibility of the filing party to promptly notify the clerk's office via telephone of a matter that requires the immediate attention of a judicial officer. ME R USDCT App. 4(a)(4).

e. *DISTRICT OF MAINE: Facsimile filing.* No papers shall be submitted to the court by means of a facsimile machine without prior leave of the court. ME R USDCT Rule 5(c); ME R USDCT App. 4(m).

2. *Service requirements*

a. *Service; When required.* Unless the Federal Rules of Civil Procedure provide otherwise, each of the following papers must be served on every party: (A) an order stating that service is required; (B) a pleading filed after the original complaint, unless the court orders otherwise under FRCP 5(c) because there are numerous defendants; (C) a discovery paper required to be served on a party, unless the court orders otherwise; (D) a written motion, except one that may be heard ex parte; and (E) a written notice, appearance, demand, or offer of judgment, or any similar paper. FRCP 5(a)(1).

   i. *If a party fails to appear.* No service is required on a party who is in default for failing to appear. But a pleading that asserts a new claim for relief against such a party must be served on that party under FRCP 4. FRCP 5(a)(2).

   ii. *Seizing property.* If an action is begun by seizing property and no person is or need be named as a defendant, any service required before the filing of an appearance, answer, or claim must be made on the person who had custody or possession of the property when it was seized. FRCP 5(a)(3).

b. *Service; How made.* A paper is served under FRCP 5 by: (A) handing it to the person; (B) leaving it: (i) at the person's office with a clerk or other person in charge or, if no one is in charge, in a conspicuous place in the office; or (ii) if the person has no office or the office is closed, at the person's dwelling or usual place of abode with someone of suitable age and discretion who resides there; (C) mailing it to the person's last known address—in which event service is complete upon mailing; (D) leaving it with the court clerk if the person has no known address; (E) sending it to a registered user by filing it with the court's electronic-filing system or sending it by other electronic means that the person consented to in writing—in either of which events service is complete upon filing or sending, but is not effective if the filer or sender learns that it did not reach the person to be served; or (F) delivering it by any other means that the person consented to in writing—in which event service is complete when the person making service delivers it to the agency designated to make delivery. FRCP 5(b)(2).

   i. *Serving an attorney.* If a party is represented by an attorney, service under FRCP 5 must be made on the attorney unless the court orders service on the party. FRCP 5(b)(1).

c. *DISTRICT OF MAINE: Service of electronically filed documents*

   i. *Registered users.* Registration [as a filing user of the court's ECF system] constitutes consent to service of all documents by electronic means as provided in ME R USDCT App. 4. ME R USDCT App. 4(b)(4). Whenever a non-sealed pleading is filed electronically, the ECF system will automatically generate and send a Notice of Electronic Filing (NEF) to the filing user and registered users of record. The user filing the document should retain a paper or digital copy of the NEF, which shall serve as the court's date-stamp and proof of filing. ME R USDCT App. 4(e)(1).

   - *Sealed documents.* Although the filing of sealed documents in civil cases produces an NEF, the document itself cannot be accessed and counsel shall be responsible for making service of the sealed documents. ME R USDCT App. 4(e)(2).

   ii. *Non-registered users and pro se litigants.* Attorneys who have not yet registered as users with ECF and pro se litigants who have not registered with ECF shall be served a paper copy of any electronically filed pleading or other document in accordance with the provisions of FRCP 5. ME R USDCT App. 4(e)(3).

   - *Registration of pro se litigants.* A non-prisoner who is a party to a civil action and who is not represented by an attorney may register to receive service electronically and to electronically transmit their documents to the court for filing in the ECF system. If during the course of the action the person retains an attorney who appears on the person's behalf, the clerk shall terminate the person's registration upon the attorney's appearance. ME R USDCT App. 4(b)(2).

d. *Serving numerous defendants.* If an action involves an unusually large number of defendants, the court may, on motion or on its own, order that: (A) defendants' pleadings and replies to them need not be served on other defendants; (B) any crossclaim, counterclaim, avoidance, or affirmative defense in those pleadings and replies to them will be treated as denied or avoided by all other parties; and (C) filing any such pleading and serving it on the plaintiff constitutes notice of the pleading to all parties. FRCP 5(c)(1).

    i.   *Notifying parties.* A copy of every such order must be served on the parties as the court directs. FRCP 5(c)(2).

3. *DISTRICT OF MAINE: Filing and service of highly sensitive documents (HSDs).* For information on filing and serving highly sensitive documents (HSDs) in the District of Maine, refer to ME R USDCT General Order 21-5.

G. Hearings

1. *Hearings, generally.* When a motion relies on facts outside the record, the court may hear the matter on affidavits or may hear it wholly or partly on oral testimony or on depositions. FRCP 43(c).

  a. *Oral argument.* Due process does not require that oral argument be permitted on a motion and, except as otherwise provided by local rule, the district court has discretion to determine whether it will decide the motion on the papers or hear argument by counsel (and perhaps receive evidence). FPP § 1190; F.D.I.C. v. Deglau, 207 F.3d 153 (3d Cir. 2000).

    i.   *DISTRICT OF MAINE.* Unless otherwise required by federal rule or statute, all motions may be decided by the court without oral argument unless otherwise ordered by the court on its own motion or, in its discretion, upon request of counsel. ME R USDCT Rule 7(e).

  b. *Providing a regular schedule for oral hearings.* A court may establish regular times and places for oral hearings on motions. FRCP 78(a).

  c. *Providing for submission on briefs.* By rule or order, the court may provide for submitting and determining motions on briefs, without oral hearings. FRCP 78(b).

2. *Hearing on certain FRCP 12 defenses before trial.* If a party so moves, any defense listed in FRCP 12(b)(1) through FRCP 12(b)(7)—whether made in a pleading or by motion—and a motion under FRCP 12(c) must be heard and decided before trial unless the court orders a deferral until trial. FRCP 12(i).

H. Forms

1. Federal Motion to Dismiss for Lack of Personal Jurisdiction Forms

  a. Motion to dismiss for lack of personal jurisdiction; Corporate defendant. 2C FEDFORMS § 11:52.

  b. Motion to dismiss for lack of personal jurisdiction; By corporate defendant; With citation. 2C FEDFORMS § 11:53.

  c. Motion to dismiss for lack of personal jurisdiction; By a foreign corporation. 2C FEDFORMS § 11:54.

  d. Motion to dismiss for lack of personal jurisdiction; For insufficiency of service. 2C FEDFORMS § 11:55.

  e. Motion to dismiss for lack of personal jurisdiction; Insufficiency of process and insufficiency of service of process. 2C FEDFORMS § 11:56.

  f. Motion and notice; To dismiss; Defendant not present within state where district court is located. AMJUR PP FEDPRAC § 501.

  g. Motion and notice; To dismiss; Lack of jurisdiction over person. AMJUR PP FEDPRAC § 502.

  h. Motion and notice; To dismiss; Lack of jurisdiction over person; Ineffective service of process on foreign state. AMJUR PP FEDPRAC § 503.

  i. Motion and notice; To dismiss; Lack of jurisdiction over person; Consul not agent of country represented for purpose of receiving service of process. AMJUR PP FEDPRAC § 504.

  j. Motion and notice; To dismiss; Lack of jurisdiction over corporate defendant. AMJUR PP FEDPRAC § 505.

  k. Motion and notice; To dismiss; International organization immune from suit. AMJUR PP FEDPRAC § 506.

  l. Motion and notice; To dismiss; Officer or employee of international organization acting within official capacity; Immune from suit. AMJUR PP FEDPRAC § 507.

  m. Motion and notice; To dismiss; Family member of member of foreign mission immune from suit. AMJUR PP FEDPRAC § 508.

  n. Motion and notice; To dismiss complaint or, in alternative, to quash service of summons; Lack of jurisdiction over corporate defendant. AMJUR PP FEDPRAC § 509.

  o. Motion to dismiss; Lack of personal jurisdiction; No minimum contacts. AMJUR PP FEDPRAC § 510.

  p. Declaration; For motion to dismiss for lack of personal jurisdiction; No minimum contacts. AMJUR PP FEDPRAC § 512.

q. Opposition; To motion. FEDPROF § 1B:175.

r. Affidavit; Supporting or opposing motion. FEDPROF § 1B:176.

s. Brief; Supporting or opposing motion. FEDPROF § 1B:177.

t. Statement of points and authorities; Opposing motion. FEDPROF § 1B:178.

u. Motion to dismiss; Lack of jurisdiction over person of defendant. FEDPROF § 1C:94.

v. Motion to dismiss; Lack of jurisdiction over person of defendant; Short form. FEDPROF § 1C:95.

w. Motion to dismiss; Lack of jurisdiction over person of defendant; Accident in foreign country and defendants have no contacts with forum state. FEDPROF § 1C:96.

x. Motion to dismiss; Lack of jurisdiction over corporate defendant. FEDPROF § 1C:97.

y. Motion; To dismiss complaint or, in the alternative, to quash service of summons; Lack of jurisdiction over corporate defendant. FEDPROF § 1C:98.

z. Motion to dismiss complaint; General form. GOLDLTGFMS § 20:24.

I. Applicable Rules

1. *Federal rules*

a. Summons. FRCP 4.

b. Serving and filing pleadings and other papers. FRCP 5.

c. Constitutional challenge to a statute; Notice, certification, and intervention. FRCP 5.1.

d. Privacy protection for filings made with the court. FRCP 5.2.

e. Computing and extending time; Time for motion papers. FRCP 6.

f. Pleadings allowed; Form of motions and other papers. FRCP 7.

g. Disclosure statement. FRCP 7.1.

h. Form of pleadings. FRCP 10.

i. Signing pleadings, motions, and other papers; Representations to the court; Sanctions. FRCP 11.

j. Defenses and objections; When and how presented; Motion for judgment on the pleadings; Consolidating motions; Waiving defenses; Pretrial hearing. FRCP 12.

k. Taking testimony. FRCP 43.

l. Hearing motions; Submission on briefs. FRCP 78.

2. *Local rules*

a. *DISTRICT OF MAINE*

   i. Service and filing of pleadings and other papers. ME R USDCT Rule 5.

   ii. Time. ME R USDCT Rule 6.

   iii. Motions and memoranda of law. ME R USDCT Rule 7.

   iv. Corporate disclosure. ME R USDCT Rule 7.1.

   v. Form of pleadings, motions and other papers. ME R USDCT Rule 10.

   vi. Discovery. ME R USDCT Rule 26.

   vii. Attorneys; Appearances and withdrawals. ME R USDCT Rule 83.2.

   viii. Alternative dispute resolution (ADR). ME R USDCT Rule 83.11.

   ix. Administrative procedures governing the filing and service by electronic means. ME R USDCT App. 4.

   x. Redacting pleadings. ME R USDCT Redacting Pleadings.

Motions, Oppositions and Replies
Motion for Judgment on the Pleadings

Document Last Updated April 2021

A. Checklist

(I) ❑ Matters to be considered by moving party

    (a) ❑ Required documents

        (1) ❑ Notice of motion and motion

    (b) ❑ Supplemental documents

        (1) ❑ Pleadings

        (2) ❑ Notice of constitutional question

        (3) ❑ Nongovernmental corporate disclosure statement

        (4) ❑ DISTRICT OF MAINE: Additional supplemental documents

            (i) ❑ Proposed order

    (c) ❑ Timing

        (1) ❑ After the pleadings are closed—but early enough not to delay trial—a party may move for judgment on the pleadings

        (2) ❑ A written motion and notice of the hearing must be served at least fourteen (14) days before the time specified for the hearing, with the following exceptions: (A) when the motion may be heard ex parte; (B) when the Federal Rules of Civil Procedure set a different time; or (C) when a court order—which a party may, for good cause, apply for ex parte—sets a different time

        (3) ❑ Any affidavit supporting a motion must be served with the motion

        (4) ❑ DISTRICT OF MAINE: Additional timing

            (i) ❑ Any affidavits and other documents setting forth or evidencing facts on which the motion is based must be filed with the motion

(II) ❑ Matters to be considered by opposing party

    (a) ❑ Required documents

        (1) ❑ Opposition

    (b) ❑ Supplemental documents

        (1) ❑ Pleadings

        (2) ❑ Notice of constitutional question

    (c) ❑ Timing

        (1) ❑ Except as FRCP 59(c) provides otherwise, any opposing affidavit must be served at least seven (7) days before the hearing, unless the court permits service at another time

        (2) ❑ DISTRICT OF MAINE: Additional timing

            (i) ❑ Unless within twenty-one (21) days after the filing of a motion the opposing party files written objection thereto, incorporating a memorandum of law, the opposing party shall be deemed to have waived objection

B. Timing

1. *Motion for judgment on the pleadings.* After the pleadings are closed—but early enough not to delay trial—a party may move for judgment on the pleadings. FRCP 12(c).

    a. *When pleadings are closed.* FRCP 7(a) provides that the pleadings are closed upon the filing of a complaint and an answer (absent a court-ordered reply), unless a counterclaim, crossclaim, or third-party claim is interposed, in which event the filing of an answer to a counterclaim, crossclaim answer, or third-party answer normally will mark the close of the pleadings. FPP § 1367.

b. *Timeliness and delay.* Ordinarily, a motion for judgment on the pleadings should be made promptly after the close of the pleadings. Generally, however, an FRCP 12(c) motion is considered timely if it is made early enough not to delay trial or cause prejudice to the non-movant. FPP § 1367.

2. *Timing of motions, generally*

a. *Motion and notice of hearing.* A written motion and notice of the hearing must be served at least fourteen (14) days before the time specified for the hearing, with the following exceptions: (A) when the motion may be heard ex parte; (B) when the Federal Rules of Civil Procedure set a different time; or (C) when a court order—which a party may, for good cause, apply for ex parte—sets a different time. FRCP 6(c)(1).

b. *Supporting affidavit.* Any affidavit supporting a motion must be served with the motion. FRCP 6(c)(2).

c. *DISTRICT OF MAINE: Affidavits and other supporting documents.* Any affidavits and other documents setting forth or evidencing facts on which the motion is based must be filed with the motion. ME R USDCT Rule 7(a).

3. *Timing of opposing papers.* Except as FRCP 59(c) provides otherwise, any opposing affidavit must be served at least seven (7) days before the hearing, unless the court permits service at another time. FRCP 6(c)(2).

a. *DISTRICT OF MAINE.* Unless within twenty-one (21) days after the filing of a motion the opposing party files written objection thereto, incorporating a memorandum of law, the opposing party shall be deemed to have waived objection. ME R USDCT Rule 7(b). The deemed waiver imposed in ME R USDCT Rule 7(b) shall not apply to motions filed during trial. ME R USDCT Rule 7(b).

4. *Timing of reply papers.* Where the respondent files an answering affidavit setting up a new matter, the moving party ordinarily is allowed a reasonable time to file a reply affidavit since failure to deny the new matter by affidavit may operate as an admission of its truth. AMJUR MOTIONS § 25.

a. *DISTRICT OF MAINE.* Within fourteen (14) days of the filing of any objection to a motion, the moving party may file a reply memorandum. ME R USDCT Rule 7(c).

5. *Effect of FRCP 12 motion on the time to serve a responsive pleading.* Unless the court sets a different time, serving a motion under FRCP 12 alters the periods in FRCP 12(a) as follows: (A) if the court denies the motion or postpones its disposition until trial, the responsive pleading must be served within fourteen (14) days after notice of the court's action; or (B) if the court grants a motion for a more definite statement, the responsive pleading must be served within fourteen (14) days after the more definite statement is served. FRCP 12(a)(4).

6. *Computation of time*

a. *Computing time.* FRCP 6 applies in computing any time period specified in the Federal Rules of Civil Procedure, in any local rule or court order, or in any statute that does not specify a method of computing time. FRCP 6(a).

   i. *Period stated in days or a longer unit.* When the period is stated in days or a longer unit of time: (A) exclude the day of the event that triggers the period; (B) count every day, including intermediate Saturdays, Sundays, and legal holidays; and (C) include the last day of the period, but if the last day is a Saturday, Sunday, or legal holiday, the period continues to run until the end of the next day that is not a Saturday, Sunday, or legal holiday. FRCP 6(a)(1).

   ii. *Period stated in hours.* When the period is stated in hours: (A) begin counting immediately on the occurrence of the event that triggers the period; (B) count every hour, including hours during intermediate Saturdays, Sundays, and legal holidays; and (C) if the period would end on a Saturday, Sunday, or legal holiday, the period continues to run until the same time on the next day that is not a Saturday, Sunday, or legal holiday. FRCP 6(a)(2).

   iii. *Inaccessibility of the clerk's office.* Unless the court orders otherwise, if the clerk's office is inaccessible: (A) on the last day for filing under FRCP 6(a)(1), then the time for filing is extended to the first accessible day that is not a Saturday, Sunday, or legal holiday; or (B) during the last hour for filing under FRCP 6(a)(2), then the time for filing is extended to the same time on the first accessible day that is not a Saturday, Sunday, or legal holiday. FRCP 6(a)(3).

   iv. *"Last day" defined.* Unless a different time is set by a statute, local rule, or court order, the last day ends: (A) for electronic filing, at midnight in the court's time zone; and (B) for filing by other means, when the clerk's office is scheduled to close. FRCP 6(a)(4).

   v. *"Next day" defined.* The "next day" is determined by continuing to count forward when the period is measured after an event and backward when measured before an event. FRCP 6(a)(5).

   vi. *"Legal holiday" defined.* "Legal holiday" means: (A) the day set aside by statute for observing New Year's Day,

Martin Luther King Jr.'s Birthday, Washington's Birthday, Memorial Day, Independence Day, Labor Day, Columbus Day, Veterans' Day, Thanksgiving Day, or Christmas Day; (B) any day declared a holiday by the President or Congress; and (C) for periods that are measured after an event, any other day declared a holiday by the state where the district court is located. FRCP 6(a)(6).

    vii.   *DISTRICT OF MAINE: Applicability of FRCP 6.* FRCP 6 applies when computing any period of time stated in the Local Rules of the United States District Court for the District of Maine. ME R USDCT Rule 6(a).

  b. *DISTRICT OF MAINE: Computation of electronic filing deadlines.* Filing documents electronically does not in any way alter any filing deadlines. All electronic transmissions of documents must be completed prior to midnight, Eastern Time, in order to be considered timely filed that day. Where a specific time of day deadline is set by court order or stipulation, the electronic filing must be completed by that time. ME R USDCT App. 4(f). A document filed electronically shall be deemed filed at the time and date stated on the Notice of Electronic Filing received from the court. ME R USDCT App. 4(d)(2).

    i. *Technical failures.* A filing user whose filing is made untimely as the result of a technical failure may seek appropriate relief from the court. ME R USDCT App. 4(n). A technical failure of the court's ECF system is deemed to have occurred when the court's ECF site cannot accept filings continuously or intermittently over the course of any period of time greater than one (1) hour. Known system outages will be posted on the court's website along with guidance on how to proceed, if applicable. ME R USDCT App. 4(n).

  c. *Extending time.* When an act may or must be done within a specified time, the court may, for good cause, extend the time: (A) with or without motion or notice if the court acts, or if a request is made, before the original time or its extension expires; or (B) on motion made after the time has expired if the party failed to act because of excusable neglect. FRCP 6(b)(1). A court must not extend the time to act under FRCP 50(b), FRCP 50(d), FRCP 52(b), FRCP 59(b), FRCP 59(d), FRCP 59(e), and FRCP 60(b). FRCP 6(b)(2). Refer to the United States District Court for the District of Maine KeyRules Motion for Continuance/Extension of Time document for more information on extending time.

  d. *Additional time after certain kinds of service.* When a party may or must act within a specified time after being served and service is made under FRCP 5(b)(2)(C) (by mail), FRCP 5(b)(2)(D) (by leaving with the clerk), or FRCP 5(b)(2)(F) (by other means consented to), three (3) days are added after the period would otherwise expire under FRCP 6(a). FRCP 6(d).

C. General Requirements

1. *Motions, generally*

  a. *Motion requirements.* A request for a court order must be made by motion. The motion must: (A) be in writing unless made during a hearing or trial; (B) state with particularity the grounds for seeking the order; and (C) state the relief sought. FRCP 7(b)(1). The writing and particularity requirements are intended to ensure that the adverse parties are informed of and have a record of both the motion's pendency and the grounds on which the movant seeks an order. FPP § 1191; Feldberg v. Quechee Lakes Corp., 463 F.3d 195 (2d Cir. 2006).

    i. *Particularity requirement.* The particularity requirement [ensures] that the opposing parties will have notice of their opponent's contentions. FEDPROC § 62:358; Goodman v. 1973 26 Foot Trojan Vessel, Arkansas Registration No. AR1439SN, 859 F.2d 71 (8th Cir. 1988). That requirement ensures that notice of the basis for the motion is provided to the court and to the opposing party so as to avoid prejudice, provide the opponent with a meaningful opportunity to respond, and provide the court with enough information to process the motion correctly. FEDPROC § 62:358; Andreas v. Volkswagen of Am., Inc., 336 F.3d 789 (8th Cir. 2003).

- Reasonable specification of the grounds for a motion is sufficient. The particularity requirement for motions is satisfied when no party is prejudiced by a lack of particularity or when the court can comprehend the basis for the motion and deal with it fairly. However, where a movant fails to state even one ground for granting the motion in question, the movant has failed to meet the minimal standard of "reasonable specification." FEDPROC § 62:358; Martinez v. Trainor, 556 F.2d 818 (7th Cir. 1977).

- The court may excuse the failure to comply with the particularity requirement if it is inadvertent, and where no prejudice is shown by the opposing party. FEDPROC § 62:358.

  b. *Notice of motion.* A party interested in resisting the relief sought by a motion has a right to notice thereof, and an opportunity to be heard. AMJUR MOTIONS § 12.

    i. *Purpose.* In addition to statutory or court rule provisions requiring notice of a motion—the purpose of such a notice requirement having been said to be to prevent a party from being prejudicially surprised by a motion—

principles of natural justice dictate that an adverse party generally must be given notice that a motion will be presented to the court. AMJUR MOTIONS § 12.

ii. *Adequacy of notice.* The test of adequate notice generally turns on whether the other parties were afforded an adequate opportunity to prepare and respond to the issues to be raised in the proceeding. AMJUR MOTIONS § 12.

c. *Single document containing motion and notice.* A single written document can satisfy the writing requirements both for a motion and for an FRCP 6(c)(1) notice. FRCP 7(Advisory Committee Notes).

2. *Motion for judgment on the pleadings.* After the pleadings are closed—but early enough not to delay trial—a party may move for judgment on the pleadings. FRCP 12(c).

  a. *Relationship to other motions*

    i. *Common law demurrer.* The motion for judgment on the pleadings under FRCP 12(c) has its historical roots in common law practice, which permitted either party, at any point in the proceeding, to demur to his opponent's pleading and secure a dismissal or final judgment on the basis of the pleadings. FPP § 1367.

      • The common law demurrer could be used to search the record and raise procedural defects, or it could be employed to resolve the substantive merits of the controversy as disclosed on the face of the pleadings. FPP § 1367.

      • In contrast to the common law practice, the FRCP 12(c) judgment on the pleadings procedure primarily is addressed to the latter function of disposing of cases on the basis of the underlying substantive merits of the parties' claims and defenses as they are revealed in the formal pleadings. FPP § 1367. The purpose of FRCP 12(c) is to save time and expense in cases where the ultimate issues of fact are not in dispute, and to prevent the piecemeal process of judicial determination which prevailed under the old common-law practice. FEDPROC § 62:560.

    ii. *Motions to dismiss.* While FRCP 12(b) motions to dismiss and FRCP 12(c) motions for judgment on the pleadings are to some extent merely interchangeable weapons in a party's arsenal of pretrial challenges, there are differences in the scope and effect of the two motions. An FRCP 12(b) motion to dismiss is directed solely toward the defects of the plaintiff's claim for relief, without concern for the merits of the controversy, while an FRCP 12(c) motion for judgment on the pleadings at least theoretically requires some scrutiny of the merits of the controversy. FEDPROC § 62:562.

    iii. *Motion to strike.* The FRCP 12(c) motion also should be contrasted with the motion to strike under FRCP 12(f). The latter motion permits either party to strike redundant, immaterial, impertinent, or scandalous matter from an adversary's pleading and may be used to challenge the sufficiency of defenses asserted by that adversary. The motion serves as a pruning device to eliminate objectionable matter from an opponent's pleadings and, unlike the FRCP 12(c) procedure, it is not directed at gaining a final judgment on the merits, although an FRCP 12(f) motion that succeeds in eliminating the defenses to the action may have that purpose and, in some cases, may have that effect. FPP § 1369.

      • If a plaintiff seeks to dispute the legal sufficiency of fewer than all of the defenses raised in the defendant's pleading, he should proceed under FRCP 12(f) rather than under FRCP 12(c) because the latter leads to the entry of a judgment. FPP § 1369.

    iv. *Motion for summary judgment.* In most circumstances a party will find it preferable to proceed under FRCP 56 rather than FRCP 12(c) for a variety of reasons. For example, the summary judgment procedure is available when the defendant fails to file an answer, whereas technically no relief would be available under FRCP 12(c) because the pleadings have not been closed. If a party believes that it will be necessary to introduce evidence outside the formal pleadings in order to demonstrate that no material issue of fact exists and he is clearly entitled to judgment, it is advisable to proceed directly under FRCP 56 rather than taking the circuitous route through FRCP 12(c). Moreover, the FRCP 12(c) path may present certain risks because the court, in its discretion, may refuse to permit the introduction of matters beyond the pleadings and insist on treating the motion as one under FRCP 12(c). FPP § 1369.

  b. *Bringing an FRCP 12(c) motion.* As numerous judicial opinions make clear, an FRCP 12(c) motion is designed to provide a means of disposing of cases when the material facts are not in dispute between the parties and a judgment on the merits can be achieved by focusing on the content of the competing pleadings, exhibits thereto, matters incorporated by reference in the pleadings, whatever is central or integral to the claim for relief or defense, and any facts of which the district court will take judicial notice. FPP § 1367; DiCarlo v. St. Mary Hosp., 530 F.3d 255 (3d Cir. 2008); Buddy Bean Lumber Co. v. Axis Surplus Ins. Co., 715 F.3d 695, 697 (8th Cir. 2013).

    i.   The motion for a judgment on the pleadings only has utility when all material allegations of fact are admitted or not controverted in the pleadings and only questions of law remain to be decided by the district court. FPP § 1367; Stafford v. Jewelers Mut. Ins. Co., 554 F. App'x 360, 370 (6th Cir. 2014).

c.   *Partial judgment on the pleadings.* Although not provided for by FRCP 12(c), a party may properly move for partial judgment on the pleadings to further the policy goal of the efficient resolution of actions when there are no material facts in dispute. This conclusion has been said to be buttressed by FRCP 56(a), which provides that a party may move for summary judgment, identifying each claim or defense—or the part of each claim or defense—on which summary judgment is sought. FEDPROC § 62:565.

d.   *Granting of a motion for judgment on the pleadings.* The federal courts have followed a fairly restrictive standard in ruling on motions for judgment on the pleadings. FPP § 1368. A motion for judgment on the pleadings is a motion for judgment on the merits, and should be granted only if no material issue of fact remains to be resolved and the movant establishes their entitlement to judgment as a matter of law. FEDPROC § 62:563; Great Plains Tr. Co. v. Morgan Stanley Dean Witter & Co., 313 F.3d 305 (5th Cir. 2002); Sikirica v. Nationwide Ins. Co., 416 F.3d 214 (3d Cir. 2005). A motion for a judgment on the pleadings must be sustained where the undisputed facts appearing in the pleadings, supplemented by any facts of which the court will take judicial notice, show that no relief can be granted. On a motion for judgment on the pleadings, dismissal can be based on either the lack of a cognizable legal theory or the absence of sufficient facts alleged under a cognizable legal theory. FEDPROC § 62:563.

    i.   A motion for judgment on the pleadings admits, for purposes of the motion, the truth of all well-pleaded facts in the pleadings of the opposing party, together with all fair inferences to be drawn therefrom, even where the defendant asserts, in the FRCP 12(c) motion, an FRCP 12(b)(6) defense of failure to state a claim upon which relief can be granted. FEDPROC § 62:564; In re World Trade Ctr. Disaster Site Litig., 521 F.3d 169 (2d Cir. 2008); Massachusetts Nurses Ass'n v. N. Adams Reg'l Hosp., 467 F.3d 27 (1st Cir. 2006). However, all allegations of the moving party which have been denied are taken as false. FEDPROC § 62:564; Volvo Const. Equip. N. Am., Inc. v. CLM Equip. Co., Inc., 386 F.3d 581 (4th Cir. 2004). In considering a motion for judgment on the pleadings, the trial court is thus required to view the facts presented in the pleadings and inferences to be drawn therefrom in the light most favorable to the nonmoving party. In this fashion the courts hope to [ensure] that the rights of the nonmoving party are decided as fully and fairly on an FRCP 12(c) motion as if there had been a trial. FEDPROC § 62:564.

    ii.   On a motion for judgment on the pleadings, the court may consider facts upon the basis of judicial notice. FEDPROC § 62:564; R.G. Fin. Corp. v. Vergara-Nunez, 446 F.3d 178 (1st Cir. 2006). However, a motion for judgment on the pleadings does not admit conclusions of law or unwarranted factual inferences. FEDPROC § 62:564; JPMorgan Chase Bank, N.A. v. Winget, 510 F.3d 577 (6th Cir. 2007).

e.   *Joining motions.* A motion under FRCP 12 may be joined with any other motion allowed by FRCP 12. FRCP 12(g)(1).

    i.   *Limitation on further motions.* Except as provided in FRCP 12(h)(2) or FRCP 12(h)(3), a party that makes a motion under FRCP 12 must not make another motion under FRCP 12 raising a defense or objection that was available to the party but omitted from its earlier motion. FRCP 12(g)(2).

3.   *Opposing papers.* The Federal Rules of Civil Procedure do not require any formal answer, return, or reply to a motion, except where the Federal Rules of Civil Procedure or local rules may require affidavits, memoranda, or other papers to be filed in opposition to a motion. Such papers are simply to apprise the court of such opposition and the grounds of that opposition. FEDPROC § 62:353.

a.   *DISTRICT OF MAINE: Content of objections.* Any objections shall include citations and supporting authorities and affidavits and other documents setting forth or evidencing facts on which the objection is based. ME R USDCT Rule 7(b).

b.   *Effect of failure to respond to motion.* Although in the absence of statutory provision or court rule, a motion ordinarily does not require a response or written answer, when a party files a motion and the opposing party fails to respond, the court may construe such failure to respond as nonopposition to the motion or an admission that the motion was meritorious. AMJUR MOTIONS § 28. The rule in some jurisdictions being that the failure to respond to a fact set forth in a motion is deemed an admission—and may grant the motion if the relief requested appears to be justified. AMJUR MOTIONS § 28.

c.   *Assent or no opposition not determinative.* However, a motion will not be granted automatically simply because an "assent" or a notation of "no opposition" has been filed; federal judges frequently deny motions that have been assented to when it is thought that justice so dictates. FPP § 1190.

d. *Responsive pleading inappropriate as response to motion.* An attempt to answer or oppose a motion with a responsive pleading usually is not appropriate. FPP § 1190.

4. *Reply papers.* A moving party may be required or permitted to prepare papers in addition to its original motion papers. AMJUR MOTIONS § 25. Papers answering or replying to opposing papers may be appropriate, in the interests of justice, where it appears there is a substantial reason for allowing a reply. Thus, a court may accept reply papers where a party demonstrates that the papers to which it seeks to file a reply raise new issues that are material to the disposition of the question before the court, or where the court determines, sua sponte, that it wishes further briefing of an issue raised in those papers and orders the submission of additional papers. FEDPROC § 62:354.

a. *Function of reply papers.* The function of a reply affidavit or reply papers is to answer the arguments made in opposition to the position taken by the movant, not to raise new issues, arguments, or evidence, or change the nature of the primary motion. However, if the court permits new evidence with the reply papers, the other party should be given the opportunity to respond. Where the party opposing the motion has no opportunity to address the argument in writing, a court has the discretion to disregard arguments raised for the first time in a reply memorandum. Also, the view has been followed in some jurisdictions that as a matter of judicial economy, where there is no prejudice and where the issues could be raised simply by filing a motion to dismiss, the trial court has discretion to consider arguments raised for the first time in a reply memorandum, and that a trial court may grant a motion to strike issues raised for the first time in a reply memorandum. AMJUR MOTIONS § 26.

i. *DISTRICT OF MAINE.* The moving party may file a reply memorandum. . .which shall be strictly confined to replying to new matter raised in the objection or opposing memorandum. ME R USDCT Rule 7(c).

5. *DISTRICT OF MAINE: Appearances.* An attorney's signature to a pleading shall constitute an appearance for the party filing the pleading. Otherwise, an attorney who wishes to participate in any manner in any action must file a formal written appearance identifying the party represented. An appearance whether by pleading or formal written appearance shall be signed by an attorney in his/her individual name and shall state his/her office address. ME R USDCT Rule 83.2(a). For more information, refer to ME R USDCT Rule 83.2.

6. *DISTRICT OF MAINE: Alternative dispute resolution (ADR).* Litigants are authorized and encouraged to employ, at their own expense, any available ADR process on which they can agree, including early neutral evaluation, settlement conferences, mediation, non-binding summary jury trial, corporate mini-trial, and arbitration proceedings. ME R USDCT Rule 83.11(a). For more information on ADR, refer to ME R USDCT Rule 83.11.

D. Documents

1. *Documents for moving party*

a. *Required documents*

i. *Notice of motion and motion.* Refer to the "C. General Requirements" section of this KeyRules document for information on the notice of motion and motion.

- *DISTRICT OF MAINE: Memorandum of law.* Every motion shall incorporate a memorandum of law, including citations and supporting authorities. ME R USDCT Rule 7(a). Refer to the "E. Format" section of this KeyRules document for the form of memoranda of law.

- *Certificate of service.* No certificate of service is required when a paper is served by filing it with the court's electronic-filing system. When a paper that is required to be served is served by other means: (i) if the paper is filed, a certificate of service must be filed with it or within a reasonable time after service; and (ii) if the paper is not filed, a certificate of service need not be filed unless filing is required by court order or by local rule. FRCP 5(d)(1)(B).

b. *Supplemental documents*

i. *Pleadings.* In considering a motion for judgment on the pleadings, the trial court is. . .required to view the facts presented in the pleadings and inferences to be drawn therefrom in the light most favorable to the nonmoving party. FEDPROC § 62:564. If, on a motion under FRCP 12(b)(6) or FRCP 12(c), matters outside the pleadings are presented to and not excluded by the court, the motion must be treated as one for summary judgment under FRCP 56. All parties must be given a reasonable opportunity to present all the material that is pertinent to the motion. FRCP 12(d).

ii. *Notice of constitutional question.* A party that files a pleading, written motion, or other paper drawing into question the constitutionality of a federal or state statute must promptly: (1) file a notice of constitutional question stating the question and identifying the paper that raises it, if: (A) a federal statute is questioned and the parties do not include the United States, one of its agencies, or one of its officers or employees in an official capacity; or (B) a state statute is questioned and the parties do not include the state, one of its agencies, or one of its officers or employees in an official capacity; and (2) serve the notice and paper on the Attorney General of the United States if a federal statute is questioned—or on the state attorney general if a state statute is questioned—either by certified or registered mail or by sending it to an electronic address designated by the attorney general for this purpose. FRCP 5.1(a).

- *No forfeiture.* A party's failure to file and serve the notice, or the court's failure to certify, does not forfeit a constitutional claim or defense that is otherwise timely asserted. FRCP 5.1(d).

iii. *Nongovernmental corporate disclosure statement.* A nongovernmental corporate party must file two (2) copies of a disclosure statement that: (1) identifies any parent corporation and any publicly held corporation owning ten percent (10%) or more of its stock; or (2) states that there is no such corporation. FRCP 7.1(a). A party must: (1) file the disclosure statement with its first appearance, pleading, petition, motion, response, or other request addressed to the court; and (2) promptly file a supplemental statement if any required information changes. FRCP 7.1(b).

- *DISTRICT OF MAINE: Notice of interested parties.* To enable the court to evaluate possible disqualification or recusal, counsel for all non-governmental parties shall file with their first appearance a Notice of Interested Parties, which shall list all persons, associations of persons, firms, partnerships, limited liability companies, joint ventures, corporations (including parent or affiliated corporations, clearly identified as such), or any similar entities, owning ten percent (10%) or more of the named party. Counsel shall be under a continuing obligation to file an amended Notice if any material change occurs in the status of an Interested Party, such as through merger, acquisition, or new/additional membership. ME R USDCT Rule 7.1.

iv. *DISTRICT OF MAINE: Additional supplemental documents*

- *Proposed order.* Proposed orders shall not be filed unless requested by the court. When requested by the court, proposed orders shall be filed by e-mail in word processing format. ME R USDCT App. 4(k)(1).

2. *Documents for opposing party*

a. *Required documents*

i. *Opposition.* Refer to the "C. General Requirements" section of this KeyRules document for information on the opposing papers.

- *DISTRICT OF MAINE: Memorandum of law.* Unless within twenty-one (21) days after the filing of a motion the opposing party files written objection thereto, incorporating a memorandum of law, the opposing party shall be deemed to have waived objection. ME R USDCT Rule 7(b).

- *Certificate of service.* No certificate of service is required when a paper is served by filing it with the court's electronic-filing system. When a paper that is required to be served is served by other means: (i) if the paper is filed, a certificate of service must be filed with it or within a reasonable time after service; and (ii) if the paper is not filed, a certificate of service need not be filed unless filing is required by court order or by local rule. FRCP 5(d)(1)(B).

b. *Supplemental documents*

i. *Pleadings.* In considering a motion for judgment on the pleadings, the trial court is. . . .required to view the facts presented in the pleadings and inferences to be drawn therefrom in the light most favorable to the nonmoving party. FEDPROC § 62:564. If, on a motion under FRCP 12(b)(6) or FRCP 12(c), matters outside the pleadings are presented to and not excluded by the court, the motion must be treated as one for summary judgment under FRCP 56. All parties must be given a reasonable opportunity to present all the material that is pertinent to the motion. FRCP 12(d).

ii. *Notice of constitutional question.* A party that files a pleading, written motion, or other paper drawing into question the constitutionality of a federal or state statute must promptly: (1) file a notice of constitutional question stating the question and identifying the paper that raises it, if: (A) a federal statute is questioned and the parties do not include the United States, one of its agencies, or one of its officers or employees in an official capacity; or (B) a state statute is questioned and the parties do not include the state, one of its agencies, or one of its officers or employees in an official capacity; and (2) serve the notice and paper on the Attorney General of the United States if a federal statute is questioned—or on the state attorney general if a state statute is questioned—either by certified or registered mail or by sending it to an electronic address designated by the attorney general for this purpose. FRCP 5.1(a).

- *No forfeiture.* A party's failure to file and serve the notice, or the court's failure to certify, does not forfeit a constitutional claim or defense that is otherwise timely asserted. FRCP 5.1(d).

E. Format

1. *Form of documents.* The rules governing captions and other matters of form in pleadings apply to motions and other papers. FRCP 7(b)(2).

   a. *DISTRICT OF MAINE: Font size, line spacing, and paper size.* All such documents shall be typed in a font of no less than size twelve (12) point, and shall be double-spaced or printed on eight and one-half by eleven (8-1/2 x 11) inch paper. Footnotes shall be in a font of no less than size ten (10) point, and may be single spaced. ME R USDCT Rule 10.

   b. *Caption.* Every pleading must have a caption with the court's name, a title, a file number, and an FRCP 7(a) designation. FRCP 10(a).

      i. *Names of parties.* The title of the complaint must name all the parties; the title of other pleadings, after naming the first party on each side, may refer generally to other parties. FRCP 10(a).

      ii. *DISTRICT OF MAINE: Additional caption requirements.* All pleadings, motions and other papers filed with the clerk or otherwise submitted to the court, except exhibits, shall bear the proper case number and shall contain on the first page a caption as described by FRCP 10(a) and immediately thereunder a designation of what the document is and the name of the party in whose behalf it is submitted. ME R USDCT Rule 10.

   c. *Claims or defenses*

      i. *Numbered paragraphs.* A party must state its claims or defenses in numbered paragraphs, each limited as far as practicable to a single set of circumstances. A later pleading may refer by number to a paragraph in an earlier pleading. FRCP 10(b).

      ii. *Separate statements.* If doing so would promote clarity, each claim founded on a separate transaction or occurrence—and each defense other than a denial—must be stated in a separate count or defense. FRCP 10(b).

   d. *Adoption by reference.* A statement in a pleading may be adopted by reference elsewhere in the same pleading or in any other pleading or motion. FRCP 10(c).

      i. *Exhibits.* A copy of a written instrument that is an exhibit to a pleading is a part of the pleading for all purposes. FRCP 10(c).

   e. *DISTRICT OF MAINE: Page numbering.* All pages shall be numbered at the bottom. ME R USDCT Rule 10.

   f. *DISTRICT OF MAINE: Attachment of ancillary papers.* Ancillary papers shall be attached at the end of the document to which they relate. ME R USDCT Rule 10.

   g. *Acceptance by the clerk.* The clerk must not refuse to file a paper solely because it is not in the form prescribed by the Federal Rules of Civil Procedure or by a local rule or practice. FRCP 5(d)(4).

2. *Form of electronic documents.* A paper filed electronically is a written paper for purposes of the Federal Rules of Civil Procedure. FRCP 5(d)(3)(D).

   a. *DISTRICT OF MAINE: Document format.* The ECF system only accepts documents in a portable document format (PDF). Although there are two types of PDF documents—electronically converted PDF's and scanned PDF's—only electronically converted PDF's may be filed with the court using the ECF system, unless otherwise authorized by local rule or order. ME R USDCT App. 4. Any document or exhibit to be filed or submitted to the court shall not be password-protected or encrypted. ME R USDCT App. 4(g)(12).

      i. *Electronically converted PDFs.* Electronically converted PDF's are created from word processing documents (MS Word, WordPerfect, etc.) using Adobe Acrobat or similar software. They are text searchable and their file size is small. ME R USDCT App. 4. Software used to electronically convert documents to PDF which includes proprietary or advertisement information within the PDF document is prohibited. ME R USDCT App. 4.

      ii. *Scanned PDFs.* Scanned PDF's are created from paper documents run through an optical scanner. Scanned PDF's are not searchable and have a large file size. ME R USDCT App. 4.

   b. *DISTRICT OF MAINE: Title.* All pleadings filed electronically shall be titled in accordance with the approved dictionary of civil or criminal events of the ECF system of the United States District Court for the District of Maine. ME R USDCT App. 4(d)(3).

   c. *DISTRICT OF MAINE: Attachments.* Attachments to filings and exhibits must be filed in accordance with the court's ECF User Manual, unless otherwise ordered by the court. ME R USDCT App. 4(j). When there are fifty (50) or fewer attachments to a pleading, the attachments must be filed by counsel electronically using ECF. When there are more than fifty (50) attachments, the attachments must be filed in one of the following ways: (A) using ECF, simply attach them to the pleading being filed; (B) using ECF, use the "Additional Attachments" menu item; (C) on paper; or (D) on a properly labeled three and one-half (3-1/2) inch floppy disk, CD or DVD. ME R USDCT App. 4(j)(2). Attachments filed on paper or on disk must contain a comprehensive index that clearly describes each document. ME R USDCT App. 4(j)(2).

i. A filing user must submit as attachments only those excerpts of the referenced documents that are directly germane to the matter under consideration by the court. Excerpted material must be clearly and prominently identified as such. Users who file excerpts of documents do so without prejudice to their right to timely file additional excerpts or the complete document, as may be allowed by the court. Responding parties may timely file additional excerpts or the complete document that they believe are directly germane. ME R USDCT App. 4(j)(3).

ii. Filers shall not attach as an exhibit any pleading or other paper already on file with the court in that case, but shall merely refer to that document. ME R USDCT App. 4(j)(4).

d. *DISTRICT OF MAINE: Compliance with technical standards.* All documents filed by electronic means must comply with technical standards, if any, established by the Judicial Conference of the United States or by the United States District Court for the District of Maine. ME R USDCT App. 4(a)(3).

3. *DISTRICT OF MAINE: Form of memoranda of law.* All memoranda shall be typed, in a font of no less than size twelve (12) point, and shall be double-spaced on eight and one-half by eleven (8-1/2 x 11) inch paper or printed. Footnotes shall be in a font of no less than size ten (10) point, and may be single spaced. All pages shall be numbered at the bottom. ME R USDCT Rule 7(d).

a. *Page limitations.* No memorandum of law in support of or in opposition to a motion to dismiss, a motion for judgment on the pleadings, a motion for summary judgment or a motion for injunctive relief shall exceed twenty (20) pages. ME R USDCT Rule 7(d). No reply memorandum shall exceed seven (7) pages. ME R USDCT Rule 7(d); ME R USDCT Rule 7(c).

i. *Motion to exceed page limitation.* A motion to exceed the limitation of ME R USDCT Rule 7 shall be filed no later than three (3) business days in advance of the date for filing the memorandum to permit meaningful review by the court. A motion to exceed the page limitations shall not be filed simultaneously with a memorandum in excess of the limitations of ME R USDCT Rule 7. ME R USDCT Rule 7(d).

4. *Signing of pleadings, motions and other papers*

a. *Signature.* Every pleading, written motion, and other paper must be signed by at least one attorney of record in the attorney's name—or by a party personally if the party is unrepresented. The paper must state the signer's address, e-mail address, and telephone number. FRCP 11(a).

i. *No verification or accompanying affidavit required for pleadings.* Unless a rule or statute specifically states otherwise, a pleading need not be verified or accompanied by an affidavit. FRCP 11(a).

ii. *Unsigned papers.* The court must strike an unsigned paper unless the omission is promptly corrected after being called to the attorney's or party's attention. FRCP 11(a).

b. *Electronic signing.* A filing made through a person's electronic-filing account and authorized by that person, together with that person's name on a signature block, constitutes the person's signature. FRCP 5(d)(3)(C).

i. *DISTRICT OF MAINE: Attorneys.* The user log-in and password together with a user's name on the signature block constitutes the attorney's signature pursuant to the Federal Rules of Civil Procedure and the Local Rules of the United States District Court for the District of Maine. All electronically filed documents must include a signature block and must set forth the attorney's name, address, telephone number and e-mail address. The name of the ECF user under whose log-in and password the document is submitted must be preceded by a "/s/" in the space where the signature would otherwise appear. ME R USDCT App. 4(h)(1).

ii. *DISTRICT OF MAINE: Multiple signatures.* The filer of any document requiring more than one signature (e.g., pleadings filed by visiting lawyers, stipulations, joint status reports) must list thereon all the names of other signatories, preceded by a "/s/" in the space where the signatures would otherwise appear. By submitting such a document, the filing attorney certifies that each of the other signatories has expressly agreed to the form and substance of the document and that the filing attorney has their actual authority to submit the document electronically. ME R USDCT App. 4(h)(2). For more information, refer to ME R USDCT App. 4(h)(2).

iii. *DISTRICT OF MAINE: Documents signed under oath.* Affidavits, declarations, verified complaints, or any other document signed under oath shall be filed electronically. The electronically filed version shall contain the typed name of the signatory, preceded by a "/s/" in the space where the signature would otherwise appear indicating that the paper document bears an original signature. ME R USDCT Rule 10; ME R USDCT App. 4(h)(3). For more information, refer to ME R USDCT Rule 10.

c. *Representations to the court.* By presenting to the court a pleading, written motion, or other paper—whether by signing, filing, submitting, or later advocating it—an attorney or unrepresented party certifies that to the best of the person's knowledge, information, and belief, formed after an inquiry reasonable under the circumstances: (1) it is not being presented for any improper purpose, such as to harass, cause unnecessary delay, or needlessly increase the cost of litigation; (2) the claims, defenses, and other legal contentions are warranted by existing law or by a nonfrivolous argument for extending, modifying, or reversing existing law or for establishing new law; (3) the factual contentions have evidentiary support or, if specifically so identified, will likely have evidentiary support after a reasonable opportunity for further investigation or discovery; and (4) the denials of factual contentions are warranted on the evidence or, if specifically so identified, are reasonably based on belief or a lack of information. FRCP 11(b).

d. *Sanctions.* If, after notice and a reasonable opportunity to respond, the court determines that FRCP 11(b) has been violated, the court may impose an appropriate sanction on any attorney, law firm, or party that violated FRCP 11(b) or is responsible for the violation. FRCP 11(c)(1). Refer to the United States District Court for the District of Maine KeyRules Motion for Sanctions document for more information.

5. *Privacy protection for filings made with the court*

a. *Redacted filings.* Unless the court orders otherwise, in an electronic or paper filing with the court that contains an individual's Social Security number, taxpayer-identification number, or birth date, the name of an individual known to be a minor, or a financial-account number, a party or nonparty making the filing may include only: (1) the last four (4) digits of the Social Security number and taxpayer-identification number; (2) the year of the individual's birth; (3) the minor's initials; and (4) the last four (4) digits of the financial-account number. FRCP 5.2(a).

  i. *DISTRICT OF MAINE.* To address the privacy concerns created by the Internet access to court papers, unless otherwise ordered by the court, counsel shall modify certain personal data identifiers in pleadings and other papers as follows: (1) minors' names: use of the minors' initials only; (2) Social Security numbers: use of the last four (4) numbers only; (3) dates of birth: use of the year of birth only; [and] (4) financial account numbers: identify the type of account and the financial institution, but use only the last four (4) numbers of the account number. ME R USDCT Redacting Pleadings. Counsel should also use caution when filing papers that contain a person's medical records, employment history; financial information; and any proprietary or trade secret information. ME R USDCT Redacting Pleadings.

b. *Exemptions from the redaction requirement.* The redaction requirement does not apply to the following: (1) a financial-account number that identifies the property allegedly subject to forfeiture in a forfeiture proceeding; (2) the record of an administrative or agency proceeding; (3) the official record of a state-court proceeding; (4) the record of a court or tribunal, if that record was not subject to the redaction requirement when originally filed; (5) a filing covered by FRCP 5.2(c) or FRCP 5.2(d); and (6) a pro se filing in an action brought under 28 U.S.C.A. § 2241, 28 U.S.C.A. § 2254, or 28 U.S.C.A. § 2255. FRCP 5.2(b).

c. *Limitations on remote access to electronic files; Social Security appeals and immigration cases.* Unless the court orders otherwise, in an action for benefits under the Social Security Act, and in an action or proceeding relating to an order of removal, to relief from removal, or to immigration benefits or detention, access to an electronic file is authorized as follows: (1) the parties and their attorneys may have remote electronic access to any part of the case file, including the administrative record; (2) any other person may have electronic access to the full record at the courthouse, but may have remote electronic access only to: (A) the docket maintained by the court; and (B) an opinion, order, judgment, or other disposition of the court, but not any other part of the case file or the administrative record. FRCP 5.2(c).

d. *Filings made under seal.* The court may order that a filing be made under seal without redaction. The court may later unseal the filing or order the person who made the filing to file a redacted version for the public record. FRCP 5.2(d).

  i. *DISTRICT OF MAINE.* For information on filing sealed documents in the District of Maine, refer to ME R USDCT Rule 7A, ME R USDCT App. 4(p)(2), and ME R USDCT Sealed Filings.

e. *Protective orders.* For good cause, the court may by order in a case: (1) require redaction of additional information; or (2) limit or prohibit a nonparty's remote electronic access to a document filed with the court. FRCP 5.2(e).

f. *Option for additional unredacted filing under seal.* A person making a redacted filing may also file an unredacted copy under seal. The court must retain the unredacted copy as part of the record. FRCP 5.2(f).

  i. *DISTRICT OF MAINE.* A party wishing to file a document containing the personal data identifiers specified

above may. . .file an unredacted document under seal. This document will be retained by the clerk's office as part of the record. ME R USDCT Redacting Pleadings. The court may, however, still require the party to file a redacted copy for the public file. ME R USDCT Redacting Pleadings.

g. *Option for filing a reference list.* A filing that contains redacted information may be filed together with a reference list that identifies each item of redacted information and specifies an appropriate identifier that uniquely corresponds to each item listed. The list must be filed under seal and may be amended as of right. Any reference in the case to a listed identifier will be construed to refer to the corresponding item of information. FRCP 5.2(g).

    i. *DISTRICT OF MAINE.* A party wishing to file a document containing the personal data identifiers specified above may. . .file a reference list under seal. The reference list shall contain the complete personal data identifier(s) and the redacted identifier(s) used in its (their) place in the filing. All references in the case to the redacted identifiers included in the reference list will be construed to refer to the corresponding complete identifier. The reference list must be filed under seal, and may be amended as of right. It shall be retained by the clerk's office as part of the record. ME R USDCT Redacting Pleadings. The court may, however, still require the party to file a redacted copy for the public file. ME R USDCT Redacting Pleadings.

h. *DISTRICT OF MAINE: Responsibility for redaction.* The clerk is not required to review documents filed with the court for compliance with FRCP 5.2. The responsibility to redact filings rests with counsel and the party or nonparty making the filing. ME R USDCT App. 4(i); ME R USDCT Redacting Pleadings. For guidelines for filing confidential information in civil cases in the District of Maine, refer to ME R USDCT Confidentiality.

i. *Waiver of protection of identifiers.* A person waives the protection of FRCP 5.2(a) as to the person's own information by filing it without redaction and not under seal. FRCP 5.2(h).

F. Filing and Service Requirements

1. *Filing requirements*

a. *Required filings.* Any paper after the complaint that is required to be served must be filed no later than a reasonable time after service. FRCP 5(d)(1).

b. *DISTRICT OF MAINE: Place of filing.* Unless otherwise ordered by the court, papers shall be filed with the court at Bangor in cases filed and pending at Bangor, and at Portland in cases filed and pending at Portland. ME R USDCT Rule 5(a).

c. *Nonelectronic filing.* A paper not filed electronically is filed by delivering it: (A) to the clerk; or (B) to a judge who agrees to accept it for filing, and who must then note the filing date on the paper and promptly send it to the clerk. FRCP 5(d)(2).

    i. *DISTRICT OF MAINE: Documents to be filed in paper.* The following documents shall be filed in paper, which may also be scanned into ECF by the clerk's office: (A) all handwritten pleadings; and (B) all pleadings and documents filed by pro se litigants who are incarcerated or who are not registered filing users in ECF. ME R USDCT App. 4(g)(8). Non-prisoner pro se litigants in civil actions may register with ECF or may file (and serve) all pleadings and other documents in paper. The clerk's office will scan into ECF any pleadings and documents filed on paper in accordance with ME R USDCT App. 4(g). ME R USDCT App. 4(o). For more information, refer to ME R USDCT App. 4(g).

d. *Electronic filing*

    i. *DISTRICT OF MAINE: Authorization.* Unless exempt or otherwise ordered by the court, papers shall be filed and served electronically as required by the court's Administrative Procedures Governing the Filing and Service by Electronic Means, which is set forth in ME R USDCT App. 4. The provisions of the court's Administrative Procedures Governing the Filing and Service by Electronic Means (ME R USDCT App. 4) shall be applied and enforced as part of the Local Rules of the United States District Court for the District of Maine. ME R USDCT Rule 5(c).

    ii. *Filing by represented persons.* A person represented by an attorney must file electronically, unless nonelectronic filing is allowed by the court for good cause or is allowed or required by local rule. FRCP 5(d)(3)(A).

       • *DISTRICT OF MAINE.* An attorney may apply to the court for permission to file paper documents. ME R USDCT App. 4(a)(5).

    iii. *Filing by unrepresented persons.* A person not represented by an attorney: (i) may file electronically only if allowed by court order or by local rule; and (ii) may be required to file electronically only by court order, or by a local rule that includes reasonable exceptions. FRCP 5(d)(3)(B).

       • *DISTRICT OF MAINE.* Non-prisoner pro se litigants in civil actions may register with ECF or may file (and serve) all pleadings and other documents in paper. ME R USDCT App. 4(o). A non-prisoner who is a party to a civil action and who is not represented by an attorney may register to receive service electronically and to electronically transmit their documents to the court for filing in the ECF system. If during the course of the action the person retains an attorney who appears on the person's behalf, the clerk shall terminate the person's registration upon the attorney's appearance. ME R USDCT App. 4(b)(2).

iv. *DISTRICT OF MAINE: Scope of electronic filing.* All documents submitted for filing in civil and criminal cases, regardless of case commencement date, except those documents specifically exempted in ME R USDCT App. 4(g), shall be filed electronically using the electronic case filing system (ECF). ME R USDCT App. 4(a)(1). For special filing requirements and exceptions, refer to ME R USDCT App. 4(g).

v. *DISTRICT OF MAINE: Consequences of electronic filing.* Electronic transmission of a document to the ECF system, together with the transmission of a Notice of Electronic Filing (NEF) from the court, constitutes filing of the document for all purposes of the Federal Rules of Civil Procedure. ME R USDCT App. 4(d)(1).

vi. *DISTRICT OF MAINE: Review of documents.* Documents filed with the clerk's office will normally be reviewed no later than the close of the next business day. It is the responsibility of the filing party to promptly notify the clerk's office via telephone of a matter that requires the immediate attention of a judicial officer. ME R USDCT App. 4(a)(4).

e. *DISTRICT OF MAINE: Facsimile filing.* No papers shall be submitted to the court by means of a facsimile machine without prior leave of the court. ME R USDCT Rule 5(c); ME R USDCT App. 4(m).

2. *Service requirements*

a. *Service; When required.* Unless the Federal Rules of Civil Procedure provide otherwise, each of the following papers must be served on every party: (A) an order stating that service is required; (B) a pleading filed after the original complaint, unless the court orders otherwise under FRCP 5(c) because there are numerous defendants; (C) a discovery paper required to be served on a party, unless the court orders otherwise; (D) a written motion, except one that may be heard ex parte; and (E) a written notice, appearance, demand, or offer of judgment, or any similar paper. FRCP 5(a)(1).

i. *If a party fails to appear.* No service is required on a party who is in default for failing to appear. But a pleading that asserts a new claim for relief against such a party must be served on that party under FRCP 4. FRCP 5(a)(2).

ii. *Seizing property.* If an action is begun by seizing property and no person is or need be named as a defendant, any service required before the filing of an appearance, answer, or claim must be made on the person who had custody or possession of the property when it was seized. FRCP 5(a)(3).

b. *Service; How made.* A paper is served under FRCP 5 by: (A) handing it to the person; (B) leaving it: (i) at the person's office with a clerk or other person in charge or, if no one is in charge, in a conspicuous place in the office; or (ii) if the person has no office or the office is closed, at the person's dwelling or usual place of abode with someone of suitable age and discretion who resides there; (C) mailing it to the person's last known address—in which event service is complete upon mailing; (D) leaving it with the court clerk if the person has no known address; (E) sending it to a registered user by filing it with the court's electronic-filing system or sending it by other electronic means that the person consented to in writing—in either of which events service is complete upon filing or sending, but is not effective if the filer or sender learns that it did not reach the person to be served; or (F) delivering it by any other means that the person consented to in writing—in which event service is complete when the person making service delivers it to the agency designated to make delivery. FRCP 5(b)(2).

i. *Serving an attorney.* If a party is represented by an attorney, service under FRCP 5 must be made on the attorney unless the court orders service on the party. FRCP 5(b)(1).

c. *DISTRICT OF MAINE: Service of electronically filed documents*

i. *Registered users.* Registration [as a filing user of the court's ECF system] constitutes consent to service of all documents by electronic means as provided in ME R USDCT App. 4. ME R USDCT App. 4(b)(4). Whenever a non-sealed pleading is filed electronically, the ECF system will automatically generate and send a Notice of Electronic Filing (NEF) to the filing user and registered users of record. The user filing the document should retain a paper or digital copy of the NEF, which shall serve as the court's date-stamp and proof of filing. ME R USDCT App. 4(e)(1).

- *Sealed documents.* Although the filing of sealed documents in civil cases produces an NEF, the document itself cannot be accessed and counsel shall be responsible for making service of the sealed documents. ME R USDCT App. 4(e)(2).

  ii. *Non-registered users and pro se litigants.* Attorneys who have not yet registered as users with ECF and pro se litigants who have not registered with ECF shall be served a paper copy of any electronically filed pleading or other document in accordance with the provisions of FRCP 5. ME R USDCT App. 4(e)(3).

   • *Registration of pro se litigants.* A non-prisoner who is a party to a civil action and who is not represented by an attorney may register to receive service electronically and to electronically transmit their documents to the court for filing in the ECF system. If during the course of the action the person retains an attorney who appears on the person's behalf, the clerk shall terminate the person's registration upon the attorney's appearance. ME R USDCT App. 4(b)(2).

 d. *Serving numerous defendants.* If an action involves an unusually large number of defendants, the court may, on motion or on its own, order that: (A) defendants' pleadings and replies to them need not be served on other defendants; (B) any crossclaim, counterclaim, avoidance, or affirmative defense in those pleadings and replies to them will be treated as denied or avoided by all other parties; and (C) filing any such pleading and serving it on the plaintiff constitutes notice of the pleading to all parties. FRCP 5(c)(1).

  i. *Notifying parties.* A copy of every such order must be served on the parties as the court directs. FRCP 5(c)(2).

 3. *DISTRICT OF MAINE: Filing and service of highly sensitive documents (HSDs).* For information on filing and serving highly sensitive documents (HSDs) in the District of Maine, refer to ME R USDCT General Order 21-5.

G. Hearings

 1. *Hearings, generally.* When a motion relies on facts outside the record, the court may hear the matter on affidavits or may hear it wholly or partly on oral testimony or on depositions. FRCP 43(c).

 a. *Oral argument.* Due process does not require that oral argument be permitted on a motion and, except as otherwise provided by local rule, the district court has discretion to determine whether it will decide the motion on the papers or hear argument by counsel (and perhaps receive evidence). FPP § 1190; F.D.I.C. v. Deglau, 207 F.3d 153 (3d Cir. 2000).

  i. *DISTRICT OF MAINE.* Unless otherwise required by federal rule or statute, all motions may be decided by the court without oral argument unless otherwise ordered by the court on its own motion or, in its discretion, upon request of counsel. ME R USDCT Rule 7(e).

 b. *Providing a regular schedule for oral hearings.* A court may establish regular times and places for oral hearings on motions. FRCP 78(a).

 c. *Providing for submission on briefs.* By rule or order, the court may provide for submitting and determining motions on briefs, without oral hearings. FRCP 78(b).

 2. *Hearing on certain FRCP 12 defenses before trial.* If a party so moves, any defense listed in FRCP 12(b)(1) through FRCP 12(b)(7)—whether made in a pleading or by motion—and a motion under FRCP 12(c) must be heard and decided before trial unless the court orders a deferral until trial. FRCP 12(i).

H. Forms

1. Federal Motion for Judgment on the Pleadings Forms

 a. Motion for judgment on the pleadings. 2C FEDFORMS § 11:131.

 b. Motion for judgment on the pleadings; Alternate wording. 2C FEDFORMS § 11:132.

 c. Motion for judgment on the pleadings; Long version. 2C FEDFORMS § 11:133.

 d. Motion for judgment on the pleadings; Several grounds. 2C FEDFORMS § 11:134.

 e. Notice of motion and motion for judgment on the pleadings. 2C FEDFORMS § 11:135.

 f. Notice of motion for judgment on the pleadings (partial) or for partial summary judgment. 2C FEDFORMS § 11:136.

 g. Order granting judgment on the pleadings. 2C FEDFORMS § 11:137.

 h. Order granting judgment on the pleadings; Motion by plaintiff. 2C FEDFORMS § 11:138.

 i. Judgment on the pleadings. 2C FEDFORMS § 11:139.

 j. Motion and notice; For judgment on pleadings. AMJUR PP FEDPRAC § 551.

 k. Countermotion and notice; For judgment on pleadings; By defendants. AMJUR PP FEDPRAC § 552.

 l. Order; For judgment on pleadings; In favor of plaintiff. AMJUR PP FEDPRAC § 553.

 m. Order; For judgment on pleadings; In favor of defendant. AMJUR PP FEDPRAC § 554.

n. Motion; General form. FEDPROF § 1B:171.

o. Notice; Of motion. FEDPROF § 1B:172.

p. Notice; Of motion; With costs of motion. FEDPROF § 1B:173.

q. Notice; Of motion; Containing motion. FEDPROF § 1B:174.

r. Opposition; To motion. FEDPROF § 1B:175.

s. Affidavit; Supporting or opposing motion. FEDPROF § 1B:176.

t. Brief; Supporting or opposing motion. FEDPROF § 1B:177.

u. Statement of points and authorities; Opposing motion. FEDPROF § 1B:178.

v. Motion; For judgment on the pleadings. FEDPROF § 1C:206.

w. Order; For judgment on the pleadings; In favor of plaintiff. FEDPROF § 1C:208.

x. Order; For judgment on the pleadings; In favor of defendant. FEDPROF § 1C:209.

y. Motion for judgment on pleadings; Plaintiff. GOLDLTGFMS § 20:38.

z. Motion for judgment on pleadings; Defendant. GOLDLTGFMS § 20:39.

I. Applicable Rules

1. *Federal rules*

   a. Serving and filing pleadings and other papers. FRCP 5.

   b. Constitutional challenge to a statute; Notice, certification, and intervention. FRCP 5.1.

   c. Privacy protection for filings made with the court. FRCP 5.2.

   d. Computing and extending time; Time for motion papers. FRCP 6.

   e. Pleadings allowed; Form of motions and other papers. FRCP 7.

   f. Disclosure statement. FRCP 7.1.

   g. Form of pleadings. FRCP 10.

   h. Signing pleadings, motions, and other papers; Representations to the court; Sanctions. FRCP 11.

   i. Defenses and objections; When and how presented; Motion for judgment on the pleadings; Consolidating motions; Waiving defenses; Pretrial hearing. FRCP 12.

   j. Taking testimony. FRCP 43.

   k. Hearing motions; Submission on briefs. FRCP 78.

2. *Local rules*

   a. *DISTRICT OF MAINE*

      i. Service and filing of pleadings and other papers. ME R USDCT Rule 5.

      ii. Time. ME R USDCT Rule 6.

      iii. Motions and memoranda of law. ME R USDCT Rule 7.

      iv. Corporate disclosure. ME R USDCT Rule 7.1.

      v. Form of pleadings, motions and other papers. ME R USDCT Rule 10.

      vi. Attorneys; Appearances and withdrawals. ME R USDCT Rule 83.2.

      vii. Alternative dispute resolution (ADR). ME R USDCT Rule 83.11.

      viii. Administrative procedures governing the filing and service by electronic means. ME R USDCT App. 4.

      ix. Redacting pleadings. ME R USDCT Redacting Pleadings.

246

Motions, Oppositions and Replies
Motion for More Definite Statement

Document Last Updated April 2021

A. Checklist

(I) ❑ Matters to be considered by moving party

    (a) ❑ Required documents

        (1) ❑ Notice of motion and motion

    (b) ❑ Supplemental documents

        (1) ❑ Supporting evidence

        (2) ❑ Notice of constitutional question

        (3) ❑ Nongovernmental corporate disclosure statement

        (4) ❑ DISTRICT OF MAINE: Additional supplemental documents

            (i) ❑ Proposed order

    (c) ❑ Timing

        (1) ❑ The motion must be made before filing a responsive pleading

        (2) ❑ A written motion and notice of the hearing must be served at least fourteen (14) days before the time specified for the hearing, with the following exceptions: (A) when the motion may be heard ex parte; (B) when the Federal Rules of Civil Procedure set a different time; or (C) when a court order—which a party may, for good cause, apply for ex parte—sets a different time

        (3) ❑ Any affidavit supporting a motion must be served with the motion

        (4) ❑ DISTRICT OF MAINE: Additional timing

            (i) ❑ Any affidavits and other documents setting forth or evidencing facts on which the motion is based must be filed with the motion

(II) ❑ Matters to be considered by opposing party

    (a) ❑ Required documents

        (1) ❑ Opposition

    (b) ❑ Supplemental documents

        (1) ❑ Supporting evidence

        (2) ❑ Notice of constitutional question

    (c) ❑ Timing

        (1) ❑ Except as FRCP 59(c) provides otherwise, any opposing affidavit must be served at least seven (7) days before the hearing, unless the court permits service at another time

        (2) ❑ DISTRICT OF MAINE: Additional timing

            (i) ❑ Unless within twenty-one (21) days after the filing of a motion the opposing party files written objection thereto, incorporating a memorandum of law, the opposing party shall be deemed to have waived objection

B. Timing

1. *Motion for more definite statement.* The motion must be made before filing a responsive pleading. FRCP 12(e). Thus, a motion for a more definite statement must be made before an answer. FEDPROC § 62:380.

2. *Timing of motions, generally*

    a. *Motion and notice of hearing.* A written motion and notice of the hearing must be served at least fourteen (14) days before the time specified for the hearing, with the following exceptions: (A) when the motion may be heard ex parte; (B) when the Federal Rules of Civil Procedure set a different time; or (C) when a court order—which a party may, for good cause, apply for ex parte—sets a different time. FRCP 6(c)(1).

247

    b.   *Supporting affidavit.* Any affidavit supporting a motion must be served with the motion. FRCP 6(c)(2).

    c.   *DISTRICT OF MAINE: Affidavits and other supporting documents.* Any affidavits and other documents setting forth or evidencing facts on which the motion is based must be filed with the motion. ME R USDCT Rule 7(a).

3.   *Timing of opposing papers.* Except as FRCP 59(c) provides otherwise, any opposing affidavit must be served at least seven (7) days before the hearing, unless the court permits service at another time. FRCP 6(c)(2).

    a.   *DISTRICT OF MAINE.* Unless within twenty-one (21) days after the filing of a motion the opposing party files written objection thereto, incorporating a memorandum of law, the opposing party shall be deemed to have waived objection. ME R USDCT Rule 7(b). The deemed waiver imposed in ME R USDCT Rule 7(b) shall not apply to motions filed during trial. ME R USDCT Rule 7(b).

4.   *Timing of reply papers.* Where the respondent files an answering affidavit setting up a new matter, the moving party ordinarily is allowed a reasonable time to file a reply affidavit since failure to deny the new matter by affidavit may operate as an admission of its truth. AMJUR MOTIONS § 25.

    a.   *DISTRICT OF MAINE.* Within fourteen (14) days of the filing of any objection to a motion, the moving party may file a reply memorandum. ME R USDCT Rule 7(c).

5.   *Effect of FRCP 12 motion on the time to serve a responsive pleading.* Unless the court sets a different time, serving a motion under FRCP 12 alters the periods in FRCP 12(a) as follows: (A) if the court denies the motion or postpones its disposition until trial, the responsive pleading must be served within fourteen (14) days after notice of the court's action; or (B) if the court grants a motion for a more definite statement, the responsive pleading must be served within fourteen (14) days after the more definite statement is served. FRCP 12(a)(4).

6.   *Computation of time*

    a.   *Computing time.* FRCP 6 applies in computing any time period specified in the Federal Rules of Civil Procedure, in any local rule or court order, or in any statute that does not specify a method of computing time. FRCP 6(a).

        i.   *Period stated in days or a longer unit.* When the period is stated in days or a longer unit of time: (A) exclude the day of the event that triggers the period; (B) count every day, including intermediate Saturdays, Sundays, and legal holidays; and (C) include the last day of the period, but if the last day is a Saturday, Sunday, or legal holiday, the period continues to run until the end of the next day that is not a Saturday, Sunday, or legal holiday. FRCP 6(a)(1).

        ii.   *Period stated in hours.* When the period is stated in hours: (A) begin counting immediately on the occurrence of the event that triggers the period; (B) count every hour, including hours during intermediate Saturdays, Sundays, and legal holidays; and (C) if the period would end on a Saturday, Sunday, or legal holiday, the period continues to run until the same time on the next day that is not a Saturday, Sunday, or legal holiday. FRCP 6(a)(2).

        iii.   *Inaccessibility of the clerk's office.* Unless the court orders otherwise, if the clerk's office is inaccessible: (A) on the last day for filing under FRCP 6(a)(1), then the time for filing is extended to the first accessible day that is not a Saturday, Sunday, or legal holiday; or (B) during the last hour for filing under FRCP 6(a)(2), then the time for filing is extended to the same time on the first accessible day that is not a Saturday, Sunday, or legal holiday. FRCP 6(a)(3).

        iv.   *"Last day" defined.* Unless a different time is set by a statute, local rule, or court order, the last day ends: (A) for electronic filing, at midnight in the court's time zone; and (B) for filing by other means, when the clerk's office is scheduled to close. FRCP 6(a)(4).

        v.   *"Next day" defined.* The "next day" is determined by continuing to count forward when the period is measured after an event and backward when measured before an event. FRCP 6(a)(5).

        vi.   *"Legal holiday" defined.* "Legal holiday" means: (A) the day set aside by statute for observing New Year's Day, Martin Luther King Jr.'s Birthday, Washington's Birthday, Memorial Day, Independence Day, Labor Day, Columbus Day, Veterans' Day, Thanksgiving Day, or Christmas Day; (B) any day declared a holiday by the President or Congress; and (C) for periods that are measured after an event, any other day declared a holiday by the state where the district court is located. FRCP 6(a)(6).

        vii.   *DISTRICT OF MAINE: Applicability of FRCP 6.* FRCP 6 applies when computing any period of time stated in the Local Rules of the United States District Court for the District of Maine. ME R USDCT Rule 6(a).

    b.   *DISTRICT OF MAINE: Computation of electronic filing deadlines.* Filing documents electronically does not in any way alter any filing deadlines. All electronic transmissions of documents must be completed prior to midnight, Eastern Time, in order to be considered timely filed that day. Where a specific time of day deadline is set by court order

or stipulation, the electronic filing must be completed by that time. ME R USDCT App. 4(f). A document filed electronically shall be deemed filed at the time and date stated on the Notice of Electronic Filing received from the court. ME R USDCT App. 4(d)(2).

    i. *Technical failures.* A filing user whose filing is made untimely as the result of a technical failure may seek appropriate relief from the court. ME R USDCT App. 4(n). A technical failure of the court's ECF system is deemed to have occurred when the court's ECF site cannot accept filings continuously or intermittently over the course of any period of time greater than one (1) hour. Known system outages will be posted on the court's website along with guidance on how to proceed, if applicable. ME R USDCT App. 4(n).

  c. *Extending time.* When an act may or must be done within a specified time, the court may, for good cause, extend the time: (A) with or without motion or notice if the court acts, or if a request is made, before the original time or its extension expires; or (B) on motion made after the time has expired if the party failed to act because of excusable neglect. FRCP 6(b)(1). A court must not extend the time to act under FRCP 50(b), FRCP 50(d), FRCP 52(b), FRCP 59(b), FRCP 59(d), FRCP 59(e), and FRCP 60(b). FRCP 6(b)(2). Refer to the United States District Court for the District of Maine KeyRules Motion for Continuance/Extension of Time document for more information on extending time.

  d. *Additional time after certain kinds of service.* When a party may or must act within a specified time after being served and service is made under FRCP 5(b)(2)(C) (by mail), FRCP 5(b)(2)(D) (by leaving with the clerk), or FRCP 5(b)(2)(F) (by other means consented to), three (3) days are added after the period would otherwise expire under FRCP 6(a). FRCP 6(d).

C. General Requirements

1. *Motions, generally*

  a. *Motion requirements.* A request for a court order must be made by motion. The motion must: (A) be in writing unless made during a hearing or trial; (B) state with particularity the grounds for seeking the order; and (C) state the relief sought. FRCP 7(b)(1). The writing and particularity requirements are intended to ensure that the adverse parties are informed of and have a record of both the motion's pendency and the grounds on which the movant seeks an order. FPP § 1191; Feldberg v. Quechee Lakes Corp., 463 F.3d 195 (2d Cir. 2006).

    i. *Particularity requirement.* The particularity requirement [ensures] that the opposing parties will have notice of their opponent's contentions. FEDPROC § 62:358; Goodman v. 1973 26 Foot Trojan Vessel, Arkansas Registration No. AR1439SN, 859 F.2d 71 (8th Cir. 1988). That requirement ensures that notice of the basis for the motion is provided to the court and to the opposing party so as to avoid prejudice, provide the opponent with a meaningful opportunity to respond, and provide the court with enough information to process the motion correctly. FEDPROC § 62:358; Andreas v. Volkswagen of Am., Inc., 336 F.3d 789 (8th Cir. 2003).

- Reasonable specification of the grounds for a motion is sufficient. The particularity requirement for motions is satisfied when no party is prejudiced by a lack of particularity or when the court can comprehend the basis for the motion and deal with it fairly. However, where a movant fails to state even one ground for granting the motion in question, the movant has failed to meet the minimal standard of "reasonable specification." FEDPROC § 62:358; Martinez v. Trainor, 556 F.2d 818 (7th Cir. 1977).

- The court may excuse the failure to comply with the particularity requirement if it is inadvertent, and where no prejudice is shown by the opposing party. FEDPROC § 62:358.

  b. *Notice of motion.* A party interested in resisting the relief sought by a motion has a right to notice thereof, and an opportunity to be heard. AMJUR MOTIONS § 12.

    i. *Purpose.* In addition to statutory or court rule provisions requiring notice of a motion—the purpose of such a notice requirement having been said to be to prevent a party from being prejudicially surprised by a motion—principles of natural justice dictate that an adverse party generally must be given notice that a motion will be presented to the court. AMJUR MOTIONS § 12.

    ii. *Adequacy of notice.* The test of adequate notice generally turns on whether the other parties were afforded an adequate opportunity to prepare and respond to the issues to be raised in the proceeding. AMJUR MOTIONS § 12.

  c. *Single document containing motion and notice.* A single written document can satisfy the writing requirements both for a motion and for an FRCP 6(c)(1) notice. FRCP 7(Advisory Committee Notes).

2. *Motion for more definite statement.* A party may move for a more definite statement of a pleading to which a responsive pleading is allowed but which is so vague or ambiguous that the party cannot reasonably prepare a response. FRCP 12(e).

A motion for a more definite statement under FRCP 12(e) is inappropriate where a responsive pleading is not required or permitted. FEDPROC § 62:379.

a. *Contents.* The motion must be made before filing a responsive pleading and must point out the defects complained of and the details desired. FRCP 12(e). A motion for a more definite statement must point out the defects complained of and the details desired, should offer discussion or legal analysis in support of the FRCP 12(e) claim, and will be denied where the motion fails to satisfy this requirement. FEDPROC § 62:381.

    i. *Identification of deficiencies of pleading.* Regardless of whether the plaintiff or the defendant moves under FRCP 12(e), she must identify the deficiencies in the pleading believed to be objectionable, point out the details she desires to have pleaded in a more intelligible form, and assert her inability to prepare a responsive pleading. These requirements are designed to enable the district judge to test the propriety of the motion and formulate an appropriate order in the light of its limited purpose of enabling the framing of a responsive pleading. FPP § 1378.

    ii. *Particularization or excessive amount of information not required.* Since FRCP 12(e) must be construed in light of the federal rules relating to liberal pleading, a motion for a more definite statement need not particularize the requested information in great detail and should not request an excessive amount of information. Indeed, if the movant does ask for too much, his motion may be denied on the ground that evidentiary matter is being sought. FPP § 1378.

b. *Burden.* Most federal courts cast the burden of establishing the need for a more definite statement on the movant. Whether he will succeed in discharging that burden depends on such factors as the availability of information from other sources that may clear up the pleading for the movant and a coparty's ability to answer. FPP § 1378.

c. *Motion disfavored.* Motions for a more definite statement are not favored by the courts, and thus, are rarely granted, since pleadings in the federal courts are only required to fairly notify the opposing party of the nature of the claim, and since there are ample provisions for discovery under FRCP 26 to FRCP 37 as well as for pretrial procedure under FRCP 16. Generally, motions for more definite statement are disfavored because of their dilatory effect on the progress of litigation, and the preferred course is to encourage the use of discovery procedures to apprise the parties of the factual basis of the claims made in the pleadings. FEDPROC § 62:382.

    i. *Discretion of court.* A motion for a more definite statement pursuant to FRCP 12(e) is addressed to the discretion of the court. Whether the motion should be granted or denied depends primarily on the facts of each individual case. FEDPROC § 62:382.

d. *Joining motions.* A motion under FRCP 12 may be joined with any other motion allowed by FRCP 12. FRCP 12(g)(1).

    i. *Limitation on further motions.* Except as provided in FRCP 12(h)(2) or FRCP 12(h)(3), a party that makes a motion under FRCP 12 must not make another motion under FRCP 12 raising a defense or objection that was available to the party but omitted from its earlier motion. FRCP 12(g)(2). Because FRCP 12(g) provides for the waiver of an FRCP 12 defense or objection only if it "was available to the party," if a movant legitimately is unable to assert other defenses at the time a motion is made under FRCP 12(e), the movant will not be penalized when she actually does interpose a second motion under FRCP 12. FPP § 1378.

e. *General standard for granting motion.* The general standard for granting a motion for a more definite statement is set forth in FRCP 12(e) itself, which provides that a party may move for a more definite statement if a pleading to which a responsive pleading is allowed is so vague or ambiguous that the party cannot reasonably prepare a response. The clear trend of judicial decisions is to deny motions for a more definite statement unless the complaint is so excessively vague and ambiguous as to prejudice the defendant seriously in attempting to answer it. The burden is on the movant to demonstrate that the complaint is so vague or ambiguous that they cannot respond, even with a simple denial, in good faith or without prejudice to itself. FEDPROC § 62:383.

f. *Compliance and enforcement of order.* If the court orders a more definite statement and the order is not obeyed within fourteen (14) days after notice of the order or within the time the court sets, the court may strike the pleading or issue any other appropriate order. FRCP 12(e).

3. *Opposing papers.* The Federal Rules of Civil Procedure do not require any formal answer, return, or reply to a motion, except where the Federal Rules of Civil Procedure or local rules may require affidavits, memoranda, or other papers to be filed in opposition to a motion. Such papers are simply to apprise the court of such opposition and the grounds of that opposition. FEDPROC § 62:353.

a. *DISTRICT OF MAINE: Content of objections.* Any objections shall include citations and supporting authorities and affidavits and other documents setting forth or evidencing facts on which the objection is based. ME R USDCT Rule 7(b).

b. *Effect of failure to respond to motion.* Although in the absence of statutory provision or court rule, a motion ordinarily does not require a response or written answer, when a party files a motion and the opposing party fails to respond, the court may construe such failure to respond as nonopposition to the motion or an admission that the motion was meritorious. AMJUR MOTIONS § 28. The rule in some jurisdictions being that the failure to respond to a fact set forth in a motion is deemed an admission—and may grant the motion if the relief requested appears to be justified. AMJUR MOTIONS § 28.

c. *Assent or no opposition not determinative.* However, a motion will not be granted automatically simply because an "assent" or a notation of "no opposition" has been filed; federal judges frequently deny motions that have been assented to when it is thought that justice so dictates. FPP § 1190.

d. *Responsive pleading inappropriate as response to motion.* An attempt to answer or oppose a motion with a responsive pleading usually is not appropriate. FPP § 1190.

4. *Reply papers.* A moving party may be required or permitted to prepare papers in addition to its original motion papers. AMJUR MOTIONS § 25. Papers answering or replying to opposing papers may be appropriate, in the interests of justice, where it appears there is a substantial reason for allowing a reply. Thus, a court may accept reply papers where a party demonstrates that the papers to which it seeks to file a reply raise new issues that are material to the disposition of the question before the court, or where the court determines, sua sponte, that it wishes further briefing of an issue raised in those papers and orders the submission of additional papers. FEDPROC § 62:354.

a. *Function of reply papers.* The function of a reply affidavit or reply papers is to answer the arguments made in opposition to the position taken by the movant, not to raise new issues, arguments, or evidence, or change the nature of the primary motion. However, if the court permits new evidence with the reply papers, the other party should be given the opportunity to respond. Where the party opposing the motion has no opportunity to address the argument in writing, a court has the discretion to disregard arguments raised for the first time in a reply memorandum. Also, the view has been followed in some jurisdictions that as a matter of judicial economy, where there is no prejudice and where the issues could be raised simply by filing a motion to dismiss, the trial court has discretion to consider arguments raised for the first time in a reply memorandum, and that a trial court may grant a motion to strike issues raised for the first time in a reply memorandum. AMJUR MOTIONS § 26.

   i. *DISTRICT OF MAINE.* The moving party may file a reply memorandum. . .which shall be strictly confined to replying to new matter raised in the objection or opposing memorandum. ME R USDCT Rule 7(c).

5. *DISTRICT OF MAINE: Appearances.* An attorney's signature to a pleading shall constitute an appearance for the party filing the pleading. Otherwise, an attorney who wishes to participate in any manner in any action must file a formal written appearance identifying the party represented. An appearance whether by pleading or formal written appearance shall be signed by an attorney in his/her individual name and shall state his/her office address. ME R USDCT Rule 83.2(a). For more information, refer to ME R USDCT Rule 83.2.

6. *DISTRICT OF MAINE: Alternative dispute resolution (ADR).* Litigants are authorized and encouraged to employ, at their own expense, any available ADR process on which they can agree, including early neutral evaluation, settlement conferences, mediation, non-binding summary jury trial, corporate mini-trial, and arbitration proceedings. ME R USDCT Rule 83.11(a). For more information on ADR, refer to ME R USDCT Rule 83.11.

D. Documents

1. *Documents for moving party*

   a. *Required documents*

      i. *Notice of motion and motion.* Refer to the "C. General Requirements" section of this KeyRules document for information on the notice of motion and motion.

         • *DISTRICT OF MAINE: Memorandum of law.* Every motion shall incorporate a memorandum of law, including citations and supporting authorities. ME R USDCT Rule 7(a). Refer to the "E. Format" section of this KeyRules document for the form of memoranda of law.

         • *Certificate of service.* No certificate of service is required when a paper is served by filing it with the court's electronic-filing system. When a paper that is required to be served is served by other means: (i) if the paper is filed, a certificate of service must be filed with it or within a reasonable time after service; and (ii) if the paper is not filed, a certificate of service need not be filed unless filing is required by court order or by local rule. FRCP 5(d)(1)(B).

   b. *Supplemental documents*

      i. *Supporting evidence.* When a motion relies on facts outside the record, the court may hear the matter on affidavits or may hear it wholly or partly on oral testimony or on depositions. FRCP 43(c). Good practice for a party seeking relief under FRCP 12(e) is to support the motion by an affidavit showing the necessity for a more definite statement. FEDPROC § 62:381. Courts differ in their attitude toward the use of affidavits on an FRCP 12(e) motion. Some insist on affidavits delineating the ways in which the pleading should be made more definite; others feel that affidavits would be helpful but do not insist upon them; and a few courts, usually when a more definite statement obviously is appropriate, do not seem to require supporting affidavits. FPP § 1378.

- *DISTRICT OF MAINE: Affidavits and other supporting documents.* Any affidavits and other documents setting forth or evidencing facts on which the motion is based must be filed with the motion. ME R USDCT Rule 7(a).

- *DISTRICT OF MAINE: Discovery transcripts or materials.* A party relying on discovery transcripts or materials in support of or in opposition to a motion shall file excerpts of such transcript or materials with the memorandum required by ME R USDCT Rule 7 as well as a list of specific citations to the parts on which the party relies. ME R USDCT Rule 26(c). Excerpts of depositions in support of or in opposition to a motion shall be filed electronically using ECF, unless otherwise permitted by the court. ME R USDCT App. 4(l)(3).

ii. *Notice of constitutional question.* A party that files a pleading, written motion, or other paper drawing into question the constitutionality of a federal or state statute must promptly: (1) file a notice of constitutional question stating the question and identifying the paper that raises it, if: (A) a federal statute is questioned and the parties do not include the United States, one of its agencies, or one of its officers or employees in an official capacity; or (B) a state statute is questioned and the parties do not include the state, one of its agencies, or one of its officers or employees in an official capacity; and (2) serve the notice and paper on the Attorney General of the United States if a federal statute is questioned—or on the state attorney general if a state statute is questioned—either by certified or registered mail or by sending it to an electronic address designated by the attorney general for this purpose. FRCP 5.1(a).

- *No forfeiture.* A party's failure to file and serve the notice, or the court's failure to certify, does not forfeit a constitutional claim or defense that is otherwise timely asserted. FRCP 5.1(d).

iii. *Nongovernmental corporate disclosure statement.* A nongovernmental corporate party must file two (2) copies of a disclosure statement that: (1) identifies any parent corporation and any publicly held corporation owning ten percent (10%) or more of its stock; or (2) states that there is no such corporation. FRCP 7.1(a). A party must: (1) file the disclosure statement with its first appearance, pleading, petition, motion, response, or other request addressed to the court; and (2) promptly file a supplemental statement if any required information changes. FRCP 7.1(b).

- *DISTRICT OF MAINE: Notice of interested parties.* To enable the court to evaluate possible disqualification or recusal, counsel for all non-governmental parties shall file with their first appearance a Notice of Interested Parties, which shall list all persons, associations of persons, firms, partnerships, limited liability companies, joint ventures, corporations (including parent or affiliated corporations, clearly identified as such), or any similar entities, owning ten percent (10%) or more of the named party. Counsel shall be under a continuing obligation to file an amended Notice if any material change occurs in the status of an Interested Party, such as through merger, acquisition, or new/additional membership. ME R USDCT Rule 7.1.

iv. *DISTRICT OF MAINE: Additional supplemental documents*

- *Proposed order.* Proposed orders shall not be filed unless requested by the court. When requested by the court, proposed orders shall be filed by e-mail in word processing format. ME R USDCT App. 4(k)(1).

2. *Documents for opposing party*

   a. *Required documents*

      i. *Opposition.* Refer to the "C. General Requirements" section of this KeyRules document for information on the opposing papers.

      - *DISTRICT OF MAINE: Memorandum of law.* Unless within twenty-one (21) days after the filing of a motion the opposing party files written objection thereto, incorporating a memorandum of law, the opposing party shall be deemed to have waived objection. ME R USDCT Rule 7(b).

      - *Certificate of service.* No certificate of service is required when a paper is served by filing it with the court's electronic-filing system. When a paper that is required to be served is served by other means: (i) if the paper is filed, a certificate of service must be filed with it or within a reasonable time after service; and (ii) if the paper is not filed, a certificate of service need not be filed unless filing is required by court order or by local rule. FRCP 5(d)(1)(B).

b. *Supplemental documents*

    i. *Supporting evidence.* When a motion relies on facts outside the record, the court may hear the matter on affidavits or may hear it wholly or partly on oral testimony or on depositions. FRCP 43(c).

- *DISTRICT OF MAINE: Affidavits and other supporting documents.* Any objections shall include. . .affidavits and other documents setting forth or evidencing facts on which the objection is based. ME R USDCT Rule 7(b).

- *DISTRICT OF MAINE: Discovery transcripts or materials.* A party relying on discovery transcripts or materials in support of or in opposition to a motion shall file excerpts of such transcript or materials with the memorandum required by ME R USDCT Rule 7 as well as a list of specific citations to the parts on which the party relies. ME R USDCT Rule 26(c). Excerpts of depositions in support of or in opposition to a motion shall be filed electronically using ECF, unless otherwise permitted by the court. ME R USDCT App. 4(I)(3).

    ii. *Notice of constitutional question.* A party that files a pleading, written motion, or other paper drawing into question the constitutionality of a federal or state statute must promptly: (1) file a notice of constitutional question stating the question and identifying the paper that raises it, if: (A) a federal statute is questioned and the parties do not include the United States, one of its agencies, or one of its officers or employees in an official capacity; or (B) a state statute is questioned and the parties do not include the state, one of its agencies, or one of its officers or employees in an official capacity; and (2) serve the notice and paper on the Attorney General of the United States if a federal statute is questioned—or on the state attorney general if a state statute is questioned—either by certified or registered mail or by sending it to an electronic address designated by the attorney general for this purpose. FRCP 5.1(a).

- *No forfeiture.* A party's failure to file and serve the notice, or the court's failure to certify, does not forfeit a constitutional claim or defense that is otherwise timely asserted. FRCP 5.1(d).

E. Format

1. *Form of documents.* The rules governing captions and other matters of form in pleadings apply to motions and other papers. FRCP 7(b)(2).

    a. *DISTRICT OF MAINE: Font size, line spacing, and paper size.* All such documents shall be typed in a font of no less than size twelve (12) point, and shall be double-spaced or printed on eight and one-half by eleven (8-1/2 x 11) inch paper. Footnotes shall be in a font of no less than size ten (10) point, and may be single spaced. ME R USDCT Rule 10.

    b. *Caption.* Every pleading must have a caption with the court's name, a title, a file number, and an FRCP 7(a) designation. FRCP 10(a).

        i. *Names of parties.* The title of the complaint must name all the parties; the title of other pleadings, after naming the first party on each side, may refer generally to other parties. FRCP 10(a).

        ii. *DISTRICT OF MAINE: Additional caption requirements.* All pleadings, motions and other papers filed with the clerk or otherwise submitted to the court, except exhibits, shall bear the proper case number and shall contain on the first page a caption as described by FRCP 10(a) and immediately thereunder a designation of what the document is and the name of the party in whose behalf it is submitted. ME R USDCT Rule 10.

    c. *Claims or defenses*

        i. *Numbered paragraphs.* A party must state its claims or defenses in numbered paragraphs, each limited as far as practicable to a single set of circumstances. A later pleading may refer by number to a paragraph in an earlier pleading. FRCP 10(b).

        ii. *Separate statements.* If doing so would promote clarity, each claim founded on a separate transaction or occurrence—and each defense other than a denial—must be stated in a separate count or defense. FRCP 10(b).

    d. *Adoption by reference.* A statement in a pleading may be adopted by reference elsewhere in the same pleading or in any other pleading or motion. FRCP 10(c).

        i. *Exhibits.* A copy of a written instrument that is an exhibit to a pleading is a part of the pleading for all purposes. FRCP 10(c).

    e. *DISTRICT OF MAINE: Page numbering.* All pages shall be numbered at the bottom. ME R USDCT Rule 10.

    f. *DISTRICT OF MAINE: Attachment of ancillary papers.* Ancillary papers shall be attached at the end of the document to which they relate. ME R USDCT Rule 10.

g. *Acceptance by the clerk.* The clerk must not refuse to file a paper solely because it is not in the form prescribed by the Federal Rules of Civil Procedure or by a local rule or practice. FRCP 5(d)(4).

2. *Form of electronic documents.* A paper filed electronically is a written paper for purposes of the Federal Rules of Civil Procedure. FRCP 5(d)(3)(D).

   a. *DISTRICT OF MAINE: Document format.* The ECF system only accepts documents in a portable document format (PDF). Although there are two types of PDF documents—electronically converted PDF's and scanned PDF's—only electronically converted PDF's may be filed with the court using the ECF system, unless otherwise authorized by local rule or order. ME R USDCT App. 4. Any document or exhibit to be filed or submitted to the court shall not be password-protected or encrypted. ME R USDCT App. 4(g)(12).

      i. *Electronically converted PDFs.* Electronically converted PDF's are created from word processing documents (MS Word, WordPerfect, etc.) using Adobe Acrobat or similar software. They are text searchable and their file size is small. ME R USDCT App. 4. Software used to electronically convert documents to PDF which includes proprietary or advertisement information within the PDF document is prohibited. ME R USDCT App. 4.

      ii. *Scanned PDFs.* Scanned PDF's are created from paper documents run through an optical scanner. Scanned PDF's are not searchable and have a large file size. ME R USDCT App. 4.

   b. *DISTRICT OF MAINE: Title.* All pleadings filed electronically shall be titled in accordance with the approved dictionary of civil or criminal events of the ECF system of the United States District Court for the District of Maine. ME R USDCT App. 4(d)(3).

   c. *DISTRICT OF MAINE: Attachments.* Attachments to filings and exhibits must be filed in accordance with the court's ECF User Manual, unless otherwise ordered by the court. ME R USDCT App. 4(j). When there are fifty (50) or fewer attachments to a pleading, the attachments must be filed by counsel electronically using ECF. When there are more than fifty (50) attachments, the attachments must be filed in one of the following ways: (A) using ECF, simply attach them to the pleading being filed; (B) using ECF, use the "Additional Attachments" menu item; (C) on paper; or (D) on a properly labeled three and one-half (3-1/2) inch floppy disk, CD or DVD. ME R USDCT App. 4(j)(2). Attachments filed on paper or on disk must contain a comprehensive index that clearly describes each document. ME R USDCT App. 4(j)(2).

      i. A filing user must submit as attachments only those excerpts of the referenced documents that are directly germane to the matter under consideration by the court. Excerpted material must be clearly and prominently identified as such. Users who file excerpts of documents do so without prejudice to their right to timely file additional excerpts or the complete document, as may be allowed by the court. Responding parties may timely file additional excerpts or the complete document that they believe are directly germane. ME R USDCT App. 4(j)(3).

      ii. Filers shall not attach as an exhibit any pleading or other paper already on file with the court in that case, but shall merely refer to that document. ME R USDCT App. 4(j)(4).

   d. *DISTRICT OF MAINE: Compliance with technical standards.* All documents filed by electronic means must comply with technical standards, if any, established by the Judicial Conference of the United States or by the United States District Court for the District of Maine. ME R USDCT App. 4(a)(3).

3. *DISTRICT OF MAINE: Form of memoranda of law.* All memoranda shall be typed, in a font of no less than size twelve (12) point, and shall be double-spaced on eight and one-half by eleven (8-1/2 x 11) inch paper or printed. Footnotes shall be in a font of no less than size ten (10) point, and may be single spaced. All pages shall be numbered at the bottom. ME R USDCT Rule 7(d).

   a. *Page limitations.* No memorandum of law in support of or in opposition to a nondispositive motion shall exceed ten (10) pages. ME R USDCT Rule 7(d). No reply memorandum shall exceed seven (7) pages. ME R USDCT Rule 7(d); ME R USDCT Rule 7(c).

      i. *Motion to exceed page limitation.* A motion to exceed the limitation of ME R USDCT Rule 7 shall be filed no later than three (3) business days in advance of the date for filing the memorandum to permit meaningful review by the court. A motion to exceed the page limitations shall not be filed simultaneously with a memorandum in excess of the limitations of ME R USDCT Rule 7. ME R USDCT Rule 7(d).

4. *Signing of pleadings, motions and other papers*

   a. *Signature.* Every pleading, written motion, and other paper must be signed by at least one attorney of record in the

attorney's name—or by a party personally if the party is unrepresented. The paper must state the signer's address, e-mail address, and telephone number. FRCP 11(a).

    i.   *No verification or accompanying affidavit required for pleadings.* Unless a rule or statute specifically states otherwise, a pleading need not be verified or accompanied by an affidavit. FRCP 11(a).

    ii.   *Unsigned papers.* The court must strike an unsigned paper unless the omission is promptly corrected after being called to the attorney's or party's attention. FRCP 11(a).

  b. *Electronic signing.* A filing made through a person's electronic-filing account and authorized by that person, together with that person's name on a signature block, constitutes the person's signature. FRCP 5(d)(3)(C).

    i.   *DISTRICT OF MAINE: Attorneys.* The user log-in and password together with a user's name on the signature block constitutes the attorney's signature pursuant to the Federal Rules of Civil Procedure and the Local Rules of the United States District Court for the District of Maine. All electronically filed documents must include a signature block and must set forth the attorney's name, address, telephone number and e-mail address. The name of the ECF user under whose log-in and password the document is submitted must be preceded by a "/s/" in the space where the signature would otherwise appear. ME R USDCT App. 4(h)(1).

    ii.   *DISTRICT OF MAINE: Multiple signatures.* The filer of any document requiring more than one signature (e.g., pleadings filed by visiting lawyers, stipulations, joint status reports) must list thereon all the names of other signatories, preceded by a "/s/" in the space where the signatures would otherwise appear. By submitting such a document, the filing attorney certifies that each of the other signatories has expressly agreed to the form and substance of the document and that the filing attorney has their actual authority to submit the document electronically. ME R USDCT App. 4(h)(2). For more information, refer to ME R USDCT App. 4(h)(2).

    iii.   *DISTRICT OF MAINE: Documents signed under oath.* Affidavits, declarations, verified complaints, or any other document signed under oath shall be filed electronically. The electronically filed version shall contain the typed name of the signatory, preceded by a "/s/" in the space where the signature would otherwise appear indicating that the paper document bears an original signature. ME R USDCT Rule 10; ME R USDCT App. 4(h)(3). For more information, refer to ME R USDCT Rule 10.

  c. *Representations to the court.* By presenting to the court a pleading, written motion, or other paper—whether by signing, filing, submitting, or later advocating it—an attorney or unrepresented party certifies that to the best of the person's knowledge, information, and belief, formed after an inquiry reasonable under the circumstances: (1) it is not being presented for any improper purpose, such as to harass, cause unnecessary delay, or needlessly increase the cost of litigation; (2) the claims, defenses, and other legal contentions are warranted by existing law or by a nonfrivolous argument for extending, modifying, or reversing existing law or for establishing new law; (3) the factual contentions have evidentiary support or, if specifically so identified, will likely have evidentiary support after a reasonable opportunity for further investigation or discovery; and (4) the denials of factual contentions are warranted on the evidence or, if specifically so identified, are reasonably based on belief or a lack of information. FRCP 11(b).

  d. *Sanctions.* If, after notice and a reasonable opportunity to respond, the court determines that FRCP 11(b) has been violated, the court may impose an appropriate sanction on any attorney, law firm, or party that violated FRCP 11(b) or is responsible for the violation. FRCP 11(c)(1). Refer to the United States District Court for the District of Maine KeyRules Motion for Sanctions document for more information.

5. *Privacy protection for filings made with the court*

  a. *Redacted filings.* Unless the court orders otherwise, in an electronic or paper filing with the court that contains an individual's Social Security number, taxpayer-identification number, or birth date, the name of an individual known to be a minor, or a financial-account number, a party or nonparty making the filing may include only: (1) the last four (4) digits of the Social Security number and taxpayer-identification number; (2) the year of the individual's birth; (3) the minor's initials; and (4) the last four (4) digits of the financial-account number. FRCP 5.2(a).

    i.   *DISTRICT OF MAINE.* To address the privacy concerns created by the Internet access to court papers, unless otherwise ordered by the court, counsel shall modify certain personal data identifiers in pleadings and other papers as follows: (1) minors' names: use of the minors' initials only; (2) Social Security numbers: use of the last four (4) numbers only; (3) dates of birth: use of the year of birth only; [and] (4) financial account numbers: identify the type of account and the financial institution, but use only the last four (4) numbers of the account number. ME R USDCT Redacting Pleadings. Counsel should also use caution when filing papers that contain a person's medical records, employment history; financial information; and any proprietary or trade secret information. ME R USDCT Redacting Pleadings.

  b. *Exemptions from the redaction requirement.* The redaction requirement does not apply to the following: (1) a

financial-account number that identifies the property allegedly subject to forfeiture in a forfeiture proceeding; (2) the record of an administrative or agency proceeding; (3) the official record of a state-court proceeding; (4) the record of a court or tribunal, if that record was not subject to the redaction requirement when originally filed; (5) a filing covered by FRCP 5.2(c) or FRCP 5.2(d); and (6) a pro se filing in an action brought under 28 U.S.C.A. § 2241, 28 U.S.C.A. § 2254, or 28 U.S.C.A. § 2255. FRCP 5.2(b).

c. *Limitations on remote access to electronic files; Social Security appeals and immigration cases.* Unless the court orders otherwise, in an action for benefits under the Social Security Act, and in an action or proceeding relating to an order of removal, to relief from removal, or to immigration benefits or detention, access to an electronic file is authorized as follows: (1) the parties and their attorneys may have remote electronic access to any part of the case file, including the administrative record; (2) any other person may have electronic access to the full record at the courthouse, but may have remote electronic access only to: (A) the docket maintained by the court; and (B) an opinion, order, judgment, or other disposition of the court, but not any other part of the case file or the administrative record. FRCP 5.2(c).

d. *Filings made under seal.* The court may order that a filing be made under seal without redaction. The court may later unseal the filing or order the person who made the filing to file a redacted version for the public record. FRCP 5.2(d).

   i. *DISTRICT OF MAINE.* For information on filing sealed documents in the District of Maine, refer to ME R USDCT Rule 7A, ME R USDCT App. 4(p)(2), and ME R USDCT Sealed Filings.

e. *Protective orders.* For good cause, the court may by order in a case: (1) require redaction of additional information; or (2) limit or prohibit a nonparty's remote electronic access to a document filed with the court. FRCP 5.2(e).

f. *Option for additional unredacted filing under seal.* A person making a redacted filing may also file an unredacted copy under seal. The court must retain the unredacted copy as part of the record. FRCP 5.2(f).

   i. *DISTRICT OF MAINE.* A party wishing to file a document containing the personal data identifiers specified above may. . .file an unredacted document under seal. This document will be retained by the clerk's office as part of the record. ME R USDCT Redacting Pleadings. The court may, however, still require the party to file a redacted copy for the public file. ME R USDCT Redacting Pleadings.

g. *Option for filing a reference list.* A filing that contains redacted information may be filed together with a reference list that identifies each item of redacted information and specifies an appropriate identifier that uniquely corresponds to each item listed. The list must be filed under seal and may be amended as of right. Any reference in the case to a listed identifier will be construed to refer to the corresponding item of information. FRCP 5.2(g).

   i. *DISTRICT OF MAINE.* A party wishing to file a document containing the personal data identifiers specified above may. . .file a reference list under seal. The reference list shall contain the complete personal data identifier(s) and the redacted identifier(s) used in its (their) place in the filing. All references in the case to the redacted identifiers included in the reference list will be construed to refer to the corresponding complete identifier. The reference list must be filed under seal, and may be amended as of right. It shall be retained by the clerk's office as part of the record. ME R USDCT Redacting Pleadings. The court may, however, still require the party to file a redacted copy for the public file. ME R USDCT Redacting Pleadings.

h. *DISTRICT OF MAINE: Responsibility for redaction.* The clerk is not required to review documents filed with the court for compliance with FRCP 5.2. The responsibility to redact filings rests with counsel and the party or nonparty making the filing. ME R USDCT App. 4(i); ME R USDCT Redacting Pleadings. For guidelines for filing confidential information in civil cases in the District of Maine, refer to ME R USDCT Confidentiality.

i. *Waiver of protection of identifiers.* A person waives the protection of FRCP 5.2(a) as to the person's own information by filing it without redaction and not under seal. FRCP 5.2(h).

F. Filing and Service Requirements

1. *Filing requirements*

a. *Required filings.* Any paper after the complaint that is required to be served must be filed no later than a reasonable time after service. FRCP 5(d)(1).

b. *DISTRICT OF MAINE: Place of filing.* Unless otherwise ordered by the court, papers shall be filed with the court at Bangor in cases filed and pending at Bangor, and at Portland in cases filed and pending at Portland. ME R USDCT Rule 5(a).

c. *Nonelectronic filing.* A paper not filed electronically is filed by delivering it: (A) to the clerk; or (B) to a judge who

agrees to accept it for filing, and who must then note the filing date on the paper and promptly send it to the clerk. FRCP 5(d)(2).

    i. *DISTRICT OF MAINE: Documents to be filed in paper.* The following documents shall be filed in paper, which may also be scanned into ECF by the clerk's office: (A) all handwritten pleadings; and (B) all pleadings and documents filed by pro se litigants who are incarcerated or who are not registered filing users in ECF. ME R USDCT App. 4(g)(8). Non-prisoner pro se litigants in civil actions may register with ECF or may file (and serve) all pleadings and other documents in paper. The clerk's office will scan into ECF any pleadings and documents filed on paper in accordance with ME R USDCT App. 4(g). ME R USDCT App. 4(o). For more information, refer to ME R USDCT App. 4(g).

d. *Electronic filing*

    i. *DISTRICT OF MAINE: Authorization.* Unless exempt or otherwise ordered by the court, papers shall be filed and served electronically as required by the court's Administrative Procedures Governing the Filing and Service by Electronic Means, which is set forth in ME R USDCT App. 4. The provisions of the court's Administrative Procedures Governing the Filing and Service by Electronic Means (ME R USDCT App. 4) shall be applied and enforced as part of the Local Rules of the United States District Court for the District of Maine. ME R USDCT Rule 5(c).

    ii. *Filing by represented persons.* A person represented by an attorney must file electronically, unless nonelectronic filing is allowed by the court for good cause or is allowed or required by local rule. FRCP 5(d)(3)(A).

      • *DISTRICT OF MAINE.* An attorney may apply to the court for permission to file paper documents. ME R USDCT App. 4(a)(5).

    iii. *Filing by unrepresented persons.* A person not represented by an attorney: (i) may file electronically only if allowed by court order or by local rule; and (ii) may be required to file electronically only by court order, or by a local rule that includes reasonable exceptions. FRCP 5(d)(3)(B).

      • *DISTRICT OF MAINE.* Non-prisoner pro se litigants in civil actions may register with ECF or may file (and serve) all pleadings and other documents in paper. ME R USDCT App. 4(o). A non-prisoner who is a party to a civil action and who is not represented by an attorney may register to receive service electronically and to electronically transmit their documents to the court for filing in the ECF system. If during the course of the action the person retains an attorney who appears on the person's behalf, the clerk shall terminate the person's registration upon the attorney's appearance. ME R USDCT App. 4(b)(2).

    iv. *DISTRICT OF MAINE: Scope of electronic filing.* All documents submitted for filing in civil and criminal cases, regardless of case commencement date, except those documents specifically exempted in ME R USDCT App. 4(g), shall be filed electronically using the electronic case filing system (ECF). ME R USDCT App. 4(a)(1). For special filing requirements and exceptions, refer to ME R USDCT App. 4(g).

    v. *DISTRICT OF MAINE: Consequences of electronic filing.* Electronic transmission of a document to the ECF system, together with the transmission of a Notice of Electronic Filing (NEF) from the court, constitutes filing of the document for all purposes of the Federal Rules of Civil Procedure. ME R USDCT App. 4(d)(1).

    vi. *DISTRICT OF MAINE: Review of documents.* Documents filed with the clerk's office will normally be reviewed no later than the close of the next business day. It is the responsibility of the filing party to promptly notify the clerk's office via telephone of a matter that requires the immediate attention of a judicial officer. ME R USDCT App. 4(a)(4).

e. *DISTRICT OF MAINE: Facsimile filing.* No papers shall be submitted to the court by means of a facsimile machine without prior leave of the court. ME R USDCT Rule 5(c); ME R USDCT App. 4(m).

2. *Service requirements*

a. *Service; When required.* Unless the Federal Rules of Civil Procedure provide otherwise, each of the following papers must be served on every party: (A) an order stating that service is required; (B) a pleading filed after the original complaint, unless the court orders otherwise under FRCP 5(c) because there are numerous defendants; (C) a discovery paper required to be served on a party, unless the court orders otherwise; (D) a written motion, except one that may be heard ex parte; and (E) a written notice, appearance, demand, or offer of judgment, or any similar paper. FRCP 5(a)(1).

    i. *If a party fails to appear.* No service is required on a party who is in default for failing to appear. But a pleading that asserts a new claim for relief against such a party must be served on that party under FRCP 4. FRCP 5(a)(2).

    ii. *Seizing property.* If an action is begun by seizing property and no person is or need be named as a defendant, any

service required before the filing of an appearance, answer, or claim must be made on the person who had custody or possession of the property when it was seized. FRCP 5(a)(3).

b. *Service; How made.* A paper is served under FRCP 5 by: (A) handing it to the person; (B) leaving it: (i) at the person's office with a clerk or other person in charge or, if no one is in charge, in a conspicuous place in the office; or (ii) if the person has no office or the office is closed, at the person's dwelling or usual place of abode with someone of suitable age and discretion who resides there; (C) mailing it to the person's last known address—in which event service is complete upon mailing; (D) leaving it with the court clerk if the person has no known address; (E) sending it to a registered user by filing it with the court's electronic-filing system or sending it by other electronic means that the person consented to in writing—in either of which events service is complete upon filing or sending, but is not effective if the filer or sender learns that it did not reach the person to be served; or (F) delivering it by any other means that the person consented to in writing—in which event service is complete when the person making service delivers it to the agency designated to make delivery. FRCP 5(b)(2).

    i. *Serving an attorney.* If a party is represented by an attorney, service under FRCP 5 must be made on the attorney unless the court orders service on the party. FRCP 5(b)(1).

c. *DISTRICT OF MAINE: Service of electronically filed documents*

    i. *Registered users.* Registration [as a filing user of the court's ECF system] constitutes consent to service of all documents by electronic means as provided in ME R USDCT App. 4. ME R USDCT App. 4(b)(4). Whenever a non-sealed pleading is filed electronically, the ECF system will automatically generate and send a Notice of Electronic Filing (NEF) to the filing user and registered users of record. The user filing the document should retain a paper or digital copy of the NEF, which shall serve as the court's date-stamp and proof of filing. ME R USDCT App. 4(e)(1).

        • *Sealed documents.* Although the filing of sealed documents in civil cases produces an NEF, the document itself cannot be accessed and counsel shall be responsible for making service of the sealed documents. ME R USDCT App. 4(e)(2).

    ii. *Non-registered users and pro se litigants.* Attorneys who have not yet registered as users with ECF and pro se litigants who have not registered with ECF shall be served a paper copy of any electronically filed pleading or other document in accordance with the provisions of FRCP 5. ME R USDCT App. 4(e)(3).

        • *Registration of pro se litigants.* A non-prisoner who is a party to a civil action and who is not represented by an attorney may register to receive service electronically and to electronically transmit their documents to the court for filing in the ECF system. If during the course of the action the person retains an attorney who appears on the person's behalf, the clerk shall terminate the person's registration upon the attorney's appearance. ME R USDCT App. 4(b)(2).

d. *Serving numerous defendants.* If an action involves an unusually large number of defendants, the court may, on motion or on its own, order that: (A) defendants' pleadings and replies to them need not be served on other defendants; (B) any crossclaim, counterclaim, avoidance, or affirmative defense in those pleadings and replies to them will be treated as denied or avoided by all other parties; and (C) filing any such pleading and serving it on the plaintiff constitutes notice of the pleading to all parties. FRCP 5(c)(1).

    i. *Notifying parties.* A copy of every such order must be served on the parties as the court directs. FRCP 5(c)(2).

3. *DISTRICT OF MAINE: Filing and service of highly sensitive documents (HSDs).* For information on filing and serving highly sensitive documents (HSDs) in the District of Maine, refer to ME R USDCT General Order 21-5.

G. Hearings

1. *Hearings, generally.* When a motion relies on facts outside the record, the court may hear the matter on affidavits or may hear it wholly or partly on oral testimony or on depositions. FRCP 43(c).

a. *Oral argument.* Due process does not require that oral argument be permitted on a motion and, except as otherwise provided by local rule, the district court has discretion to determine whether it will decide the motion on the papers or hear argument by counsel (and perhaps receive evidence). FPP § 1190; F.D.I.C. v. Deglau, 207 F.3d 153 (3d Cir. 2000).

    i. *DISTRICT OF MAINE.* Unless otherwise required by federal rule or statute, all motions may be decided by the court without oral argument unless otherwise ordered by the court on its own motion or, in its discretion, upon request of counsel. ME R USDCT Rule 7(e).

b. *Providing a regular schedule for oral hearings.* A court may establish regular times and places for oral hearings on motions. FRCP 78(a).

    c.   *Providing for submission on briefs.* By rule or order, the court may provide for submitting and determining motions on briefs, without oral hearings. FRCP 78(b).

H. Forms

1. Federal Motion for More Definite Statement Forms

    a.   Motion for more definite statement. 2C FEDFORMS § 11:144.

    b.   Motion for more definite statement; Describing allegations requiring more definite statement. 2C FEDFORMS § 11:145.

    c.   Motion for more definite statement; Damages. 2C FEDFORMS § 11:146.

    d.   Motion for more definite statement; Patent case. 2C FEDFORMS § 11:147.

    e.   Compliance with order for more definite statement of complaint. 2C FEDFORMS § 11:149.

    f.   Motion to strike complaint upon failure of plaintiff to furnish more definite statement ordered by the court. 2C FEDFORMS § 11:150.

    g.   Motion; To strike pleading for failure to comply with order for more definite statement. AMJUR PP FEDPRAC § 455.

    h.   Notice of motion; To strike complaint and dismiss action for failure to furnish more definite statement. AMJUR PP FEDPRAC § 457.

    i.   Motion and notice; For more definite statement; General form. AMJUR PP FEDPRAC § 560.

    j.   Motion and notice; To strike complaint and to dismiss action for failure of plaintiff to furnish more definite statement in compliance with order. AMJUR PP FEDPRAC § 561.

    k.   Motion; By multiple defendants; For more definite statement. AMJUR PP FEDPRAC § 562.

    l.   More definite statement. AMJUR PP FEDPRAC § 565.

    m.   Motion; For more definite statement as to date of transaction alleged in complaint. AMJUR PP FEDPRAC § 1426.

    n.   Motion; For more definite statement concerning jurisdictional amount. AMJUR PP FEDPRAC § 1448.

    o.   Notice; Of motion; Containing motion. FEDPROF § 1B:174.

    p.   Opposition; To motion. FEDPROF § 1B:175.

    q.   Affidavit; Supporting or opposing motion. FEDPROF § 1B:176.

    r.   Brief; Supporting or opposing motion. FEDPROF § 1B:177.

    s.   Statement of points and authorities; Opposing motion. FEDPROF § 1B:178.

    t.   Motion; For more definite statement. FEDPROF § 1B:207.

    u.   Motion; By plaintiff; For more definite statement. FEDPROF § 1B:208.

    v.   Motion; By defendant; For more definite statement. FEDPROF § 1B:209.

    w.   Motion; By defendant; For more definite statement; By trustee. FEDPROF § 1B:211.

    x.   Motion; By multiple defendants; For more definite statement. FEDPROF § 1B:212.

    y.   Response; By plaintiff; To motion for more definite statement. FEDPROF § 1B:213.

    z.   Notice and motion for more definite statement. GOLDLTGFMS § 20:6.

I. Applicable Rules

1. *Federal rules*

    a.   Serving and filing pleadings and other papers. FRCP 5.

    b.   Constitutional challenge to a statute; Notice, certification, and intervention. FRCP 5.1.

    c.   Privacy protection for filings made with the court. FRCP 5.2.

    d.   Computing and extending time; Time for motion papers. FRCP 6.

    e.   Pleadings allowed; Form of motions and other papers. FRCP 7.

    f.   Disclosure statement. FRCP 7.1.

    g.   Form of pleadings. FRCP 10.

h. Signing pleadings, motions, and other papers; Representations to the court; Sanctions. FRCP 11.

i. Defenses and objections; When and how presented; Motion for judgment on the pleadings; Consolidating motions; Waiving defenses; Pretrial hearing. FRCP 12.

j. Taking testimony. FRCP 43.

k. Hearing motions; Submission on briefs. FRCP 78.

2. *Local rules*

a. *DISTRICT OF MAINE*

i. Service and filing of pleadings and other papers. ME R USDCT Rule 5.

ii. Time. ME R USDCT Rule 6.

iii. Motions and memoranda of law. ME R USDCT Rule 7.

iv. Corporate disclosure. ME R USDCT Rule 7.1.

v. Form of pleadings, motions and other papers. ME R USDCT Rule 10.

vi. Discovery. ME R USDCT Rule 26.

vii. Attorneys; Appearances and withdrawals. ME R USDCT Rule 83.2.

viii. Alternative dispute resolution (ADR). ME R USDCT Rule 83.11.

ix. Administrative procedures governing the filing and service by electronic means. ME R USDCT App. 4.

x. Redacting pleadings. ME R USDCT Redacting Pleadings.

Motions, Oppositions and Replies
Motion for Post-Trial Relief

Document Last Updated April 2021

A. Checklist

(I) ❑ Matters to be considered by moving party

  (a) ❑ Required documents

    (1) ❑ Notice of motion and motion

  (b) ❑ Supplemental documents

    (1) ❑ Supporting evidence

    (2) ❑ Notice of constitutional question

    (3) ❑ DISTRICT OF MAINE: Additional supplemental documents

      (i) ❑ Proposed order

  (c) ❑ Timing

    (1) ❑ Motion for new trial: a motion for a new trial must be filed no later than twenty-eight (28) days after the entry of judgment; when a motion for a new trial is based on affidavits, they must be filed with the motion

    (2) ❑ Motion to alter or amend judgment: a motion to alter or amend a judgment must be filed no later than twenty-eight (28) days after the entry of the judgment

    (3) ❑ Motion for relief from judgment: clerical mistakes and errors of oversight or omission may be corrected at any time; a motion under FRCP 60(b) must be made within a reasonable time—and for reasons under FRCP 60(b)(1), FRCP 60(b)(2), and FRCP 60(b)(3) no more than a year after the entry of the judgment or order or the date of the proceeding

    (4) ❑ A written motion and notice of the hearing must be served at least fourteen (14) days before the time specified for the hearing, with the following exceptions: (A) when the motion may be heard ex parte; (B) when the Federal Rules of Civil Procedure set a different time; or (C) when a court order—which a party may, for good cause, apply for ex parte—sets a different time

    (5) ❑ Any affidavit supporting a motion must be served with the motion

(6) ❑ DISTRICT OF MAINE: Additional timing

    (i) ❑ Any affidavits and other documents setting forth or evidencing facts on which the motion is based must be filed with the motion

(II) ❑ Matters to be considered by opposing party

  (a) ❑ Required documents

    (1) ❑ Opposition

  (b) ❑ Supplemental documents

    (1) ❑ Supporting evidence

    (2) ❑ Notice of constitutional question

  (c) ❑ Timing

    (1) ❑ Except as FRCP 59(c) provides otherwise, any opposing affidavit must be served at least seven (7) days before the hearing, unless the court permits service at another time; the opposing party has fourteen (14) days after being served to file opposing affidavits [in support of a motion for new trial]

    (2) ❑ DISTRICT OF MAINE: Additional timing

      (i) ❑ Unless within twenty-one (21) days after the filing of a motion the opposing party files written objection thereto, incorporating a memorandum of law, the opposing party shall be deemed to have waived objection

B. Timing

1. *Motion for post-trial relief*

  a. *Motion for new trial.* A motion for a new trial must be filed no later than twenty-eight (28) days after the entry of judgment. FRCP 59(b). A motion for a new trial on the ground of newly discovered evidence is subject to the same time limit as any other motion under FRCP 59 and must be made within twenty-eight (28) days after entry of judgment. However, under FRCP 60(b)(2) a party may move for relief from the judgment on this ground within a year of the entry of the judgment. FPP § 2808. The same standard applies for establishing this ground for relief, whether the motion is under FRCP 59 or FRCP 60(b)(2). FPP § 2808; WMS Gaming, Inc. v. Int'l Game Tech., 184 F.3d 1339, 1361 n.10 (Fed. Cir. 1999).

    i. *Supporting affidavit.* When a motion for a new trial is based on affidavits, they must be filed with the motion. FRCP 59(c).

  b. *Motion to alter or amend judgment.* A motion to alter or amend a judgment must be filed no later than twenty-eight (28) days after the entry of the judgment. FRCP 59(e).

  c. *Motion for relief from judgment*

    i. *Correction of clerical mistakes, oversights and omissions in judgment, order, or proceeding.* Clerical mistakes and errors of oversight or omission may be corrected at any time. FPP § 2855.

    ii. *Relief from judgment, order, or proceeding.* A motion under FRCP 60(b) must be made within a reasonable time—and for reasons under FRCP 60(b)(1), FRCP 60(b)(2), and FRCP 60(b)(3) no more than a year after the entry of the judgment or order or the date of the proceeding. FRCP 60(c)(1).

      • *Exception for motions under FRCP 60(b)(4).* The time limitations applicable generally to FRCP 60(b) motions ordinarily [do not] apply to motions seeking relief for voidness, and the moving party need not show diligence in seeking to overturn the judgment or a meritorious defense. FEDPROC § 51:149.

2. *Timing of motions, generally*

  a. *Motion and notice of hearing.* A written motion and notice of the hearing must be served at least fourteen (14) days before the time specified for the hearing, with the following exceptions: (A) when the motion may be heard ex parte; (B) when the Federal Rules of Civil Procedure set a different time; or (C) when a court order—which a party may, for good cause, apply for ex parte—sets a different time. FRCP 6(c)(1).

  b. *Supporting affidavit.* Any affidavit supporting a motion must be served with the motion. FRCP 6(c)(2).

  c. *DISTRICT OF MAINE: Affidavits and other supporting documents.* Any affidavits and other documents setting forth or evidencing facts on which the motion is based must be filed with the motion. ME R USDCT Rule 7(a).

3. *Timing of opposing papers.* Except as FRCP 59(c) provides otherwise, any opposing affidavit must be served at least seven

(7) days before the hearing, unless the court permits service at another time. FRCP 6(c)(2). The opposing party has fourteen (14) days after being served to file opposing affidavits [in support of a motion for new trial]. FRCP 59(c).

a. *DISTRICT OF MAINE.* Unless within twenty-one (21) days after the filing of a motion the opposing party files written objection thereto, incorporating a memorandum of law, the opposing party shall be deemed to have waived objection. ME R USDCT Rule 7(b). The deemed waiver imposed in ME R USDCT Rule 7(b) shall not apply to motions filed during trial. ME R USDCT Rule 7(b).

4. *Timing of reply papers.* Where the respondent files an answering affidavit setting up a new matter, the moving party ordinarily is allowed a reasonable time to file a reply affidavit since failure to deny the new matter by affidavit may operate as an admission of its truth. AMJUR MOTIONS § 25.

a. *Reply affidavits in support of motion for new trial.* The court may permit reply affidavits. FRCP 59(c).

b. *DISTRICT OF MAINE.* Within fourteen (14) days of the filing of any objection to a motion, the moving party may file a reply memorandum. ME R USDCT Rule 7(c).

5. *Computation of time*

a. *Computing time.* FRCP 6 applies in computing any time period specified in the Federal Rules of Civil Procedure, in any local rule or court order, or in any statute that does not specify a method of computing time. FRCP 6(a).

   i. *Period stated in days or a longer unit.* When the period is stated in days or a longer unit of time: (A) exclude the day of the event that triggers the period; (B) count every day, including intermediate Saturdays, Sundays, and legal holidays; and (C) include the last day of the period, but if the last day is a Saturday, Sunday, or legal holiday, the period continues to run until the end of the next day that is not a Saturday, Sunday, or legal holiday. FRCP 6(a)(1).

   ii. *Period stated in hours.* When the period is stated in hours: (A) begin counting immediately on the occurrence of the event that triggers the period; (B) count every hour, including hours during intermediate Saturdays, Sundays, and legal holidays; and (C) if the period would end on a Saturday, Sunday, or legal holiday, the period continues to run until the same time on the next day that is not a Saturday, Sunday, or legal holiday. FRCP 6(a)(2).

   iii. *Inaccessibility of the clerk's office.* Unless the court orders otherwise, if the clerk's office is inaccessible: (A) on the last day for filing under FRCP 6(a)(1), then the time for filing is extended to the first accessible day that is not a Saturday, Sunday, or legal holiday; or (B) during the last hour for filing under FRCP 6(a)(2), then the time for filing is extended to the same time on the first accessible day that is not a Saturday, Sunday, or legal holiday. FRCP 6(a)(3).

   iv. *"Last day" defined.* Unless a different time is set by a statute, local rule, or court order, the last day ends: (A) for electronic filing, at midnight in the court's time zone; and (B) for filing by other means, when the clerk's office is scheduled to close. FRCP 6(a)(4).

   v. *"Next day" defined.* The "next day" is determined by continuing to count forward when the period is measured after an event and backward when measured before an event. FRCP 6(a)(5).

   vi. *"Legal holiday" defined.* "Legal holiday" means: (A) the day set aside by statute for observing New Year's Day, Martin Luther King Jr.'s Birthday, Washington's Birthday, Memorial Day, Independence Day, Labor Day, Columbus Day, Veterans' Day, Thanksgiving Day, or Christmas Day; (B) any day declared a holiday by the President or Congress; and (C) for periods that are measured after an event, any other day declared a holiday by the state where the district court is located. FRCP 6(a)(6).

   vii. *DISTRICT OF MAINE: Applicability of FRCP 6.* FRCP 6 applies when computing any period of time stated in the Local Rules of the United States District Court for the District of Maine. ME R USDCT Rule 6(a).

b. *DISTRICT OF MAINE: Computation of electronic filing deadlines.* Filing documents electronically does not in any way alter any filing deadlines. All electronic transmissions of documents must be completed prior to midnight, Eastern Time, in order to be considered timely filed that day. Where a specific time of day deadline is set by court order or stipulation, the electronic filing must be completed by that time. ME R USDCT App. 4(f). A document filed electronically shall be deemed filed at the time and date stated on the Notice of Electronic Filing received from the court. ME R USDCT App. 4(d)(2).

   i. *Technical failures.* A filing user whose filing is made untimely as the result of a technical failure may seek appropriate relief from the court. ME R USDCT App. 4(n). A technical failure of the court's ECF system is deemed to have occurred when the court's ECF site cannot accept filings continuously or intermittently over the course of any period of time greater than one (1) hour. Known system outages will be posted on the court's website along with guidance on how to proceed, if applicable. ME R USDCT App. 4(n).

c. *Extending time.* When an act may or must be done within a specified time, the court may, for good cause, extend the time: (A) with or without motion or notice if the court acts, or if a request is made, before the original time or its extension expires; or (B) on motion made after the time has expired if the party failed to act because of excusable neglect. FRCP 6(b)(1). A court must not extend the time to act under FRCP 50(b), FRCP 50(d), FRCP 52(b), FRCP 59(b), FRCP 59(d), FRCP 59(e), and FRCP 60(b). FRCP 6(b)(2). Refer to the United States District Court for the District of Maine KeyRules Motion for Continuance/Extension of Time document for more information on extending time.

d. *Additional time after certain kinds of service.* When a party may or must act within a specified time after being served and service is made under FRCP 5(b)(2)(C) (by mail), FRCP 5(b)(2)(D) (by leaving with the clerk), or FRCP 5(b)(2)(F) (by other means consented to), three (3) days are added after the period would otherwise expire under FRCP 6(a). FRCP 6(d).

C. General Requirements

1. *Motions, generally*

   a. *Motion requirements.* A request for a court order must be made by motion. The motion must: (A) be in writing unless made during a hearing or trial; (B) state with particularity the grounds for seeking the order; and (C) state the relief sought. FRCP 7(b)(1). The writing and particularity requirements are intended to ensure that the adverse parties are informed of and have a record of both the motion's pendency and the grounds on which the movant seeks an order. FPP § 1191; Feldberg v. Quechee Lakes Corp., 463 F.3d 195 (2d Cir. 2006).

      i. *Particularity requirement.* The particularity requirement [ensures] that the opposing parties will have notice of their opponent's contentions. FEDPROC § 62:358; Goodman v. 1973 26 Foot Trojan Vessel, Arkansas Registration No. AR1439SN, 859 F.2d 71 (8th Cir. 1988). That requirement ensures that notice of the basis for the motion is provided to the court and to the opposing party so as to avoid prejudice, provide the opponent with a meaningful opportunity to respond, and provide the court with enough information to process the motion correctly. FEDPROC § 62:358; Andreas v. Volkswagen of Am., Inc., 336 F.3d 789 (8th Cir. 2003).

         • Reasonable specification of the grounds for a motion is sufficient. The particularity requirement for motions is satisfied when no party is prejudiced by a lack of particularity or when the court can comprehend the basis for the motion and deal with it fairly. However, where a movant fails to state even one ground for granting the motion in question, the movant has failed to meet the minimal standard of "reasonable specification." FEDPROC § 62:358; Martinez v. Trainor, 556 F.2d 818 (7th Cir. 1977).

         • The court may excuse the failure to comply with the particularity requirement if it is inadvertent, and where no prejudice is shown by the opposing party. FEDPROC § 62:358.

   b. *Notice of motion.* A party interested in resisting the relief sought by a motion has a right to notice thereof, and an opportunity to be heard. AMJUR MOTIONS § 12.

      i. *Purpose.* In addition to statutory or court rule provisions requiring notice of a motion—the purpose of such a notice requirement having been said to be to prevent a party from being prejudicially surprised by a motion—principles of natural justice dictate that an adverse party generally must be given notice that a motion will be presented to the court. AMJUR MOTIONS § 12.

      ii. *Adequacy of notice.* The test of adequate notice generally turns on whether the other parties were afforded an adequate opportunity to prepare and respond to the issues to be raised in the proceeding. AMJUR MOTIONS § 12.

   c. *Single document containing motion and notice.* A single written document can satisfy the writing requirements both for a motion and for an FRCP 6(c)(1) notice. FRCP 7(Advisory Committee Notes).

2. *Motion for post-trial relief*

   a. *Motion for new trial.* FRCP 59 gives the trial judge ample power to prevent what the judge considers to be a miscarriage of justice. It is the judge's right, and indeed duty, to order a new trial if it is deemed in the interest of justice to do so. FPP § 2803; Juneau Square Corp. v. First Wisconsin Nat. Bank of Milwaukee, 624 F.2d 798, 807 (7th Cir. 1980).

      i. *Grounds for new trial.* The court may, on motion, grant a new trial on all or some of the issues—and to any party—as follows: (A) after a jury trial, for any reason for which a new trial has heretofore been granted in an action at law in federal court; or (B) after a nonjury trial, for any reason for which a rehearing has heretofore been granted in a suit in equity in federal court. FRCP 59(a)(1). Any error of law, if prejudicial, is a good ground for a new trial. The other grounds most commonly raised. . .are that the verdict is against the weight of the evidence, that the verdict is too large or too small, that there is newly discovered evidence, that conduct of counsel or of the court has tainted the verdict, or that there has been misconduct affecting the jury. FPP § 2805.

- *Weight of the evidence.* The power of a federal judge to grant a new trial on the ground that the verdict was against the weight of the evidence is clear. FPP § 2806; Byrd v. Blue Ridge Rural Elec. Co-op., Inc., 356 U.S. 525, 540, 78 S. Ct. 893, 902, 2 L. Ed. 2d 953 (1958); Montgomery Ward & Co. v. Duncan, 311 U.S. 243, 251, 61 S. Ct. 189, 194, 85 L. Ed. 147 (1940). On a motion for a new trial—unlike a motion for a judgment as a matter of law—the judge may set aside the verdict even though there is substantial evidence to support it. FPP § 2806; ATD Corp. v. Lydall, Inc., 159 F.3d 534, 549 (Fed. Cir. 1998). The judge is not required to take that view of the evidence most favorable to the verdict-winner. FPP § 2806; Bates v. Hensley, 414 F.2d 1006, 1011 (8th Cir. 1969). The mere fact that the evidence is in conflict is not enough to set aside the verdict, however. Indeed the more sharply the evidence conflicts, the more reluctant the judge should be to substitute his judgment for that of the jury. FPP § 2806; Dawson v. Wal-Mart Stores, Inc., 978 F.2d 205 (5th Cir. 1992); Williams v. City of Valdosta, 689 F.2d 964, 974 (11th Cir. 1982). But on a motion for a new trial on the ground that the verdict is against the weight of the evidence, the judge is free to weigh the evidence. FPP § 2806; Uniloc USA, Inc. v. Microsoft Corp., 632 F.3d 1292 (Fed. Cir. 2011). Indeed, it has been said that the granting of a new trial on the ground that the verdict is against the weight of the evidence "involves an element of discretion which goes further than the mere sufficiency of the evidence. It embraces all the reasons which inhere in the integrity of the jury system itself." FPP § 2806; Tidewater Oil Co. v. Waller, 302 F.2d 638, 643 (10th Cir. 1962).

- *Size of the verdict.* A motion under FRCP 59 is an appropriate means to challenge the size of the verdict. The court always may grant relief if the verdict is excessive or inadequate as a matter of law, but this is not the limit of the court's power. FPP § 2807. It also may grant a new trial if the size of the verdict is against the weight of the evidence. FPP § 2807; Sprague v. Boston & Maine Corp., 769 F.2d 26, 28 (1st Cir. 1985). If the court finds that a verdict is unreasonably high, it may condition denial of the motion for a new trial on plaintiff's consent to a remittitur. FPP § 2807. If the verdict is too low, it may not provide for an additur as an alternative to a new trial. FPP § 2807; Dimick v. Schiedt, 293 U.S. 474, 55 S. Ct. 296, 79 L. Ed. 603 (1935).

- *Newly discovered evidence.* Newly discovered evidence must be of facts existing at the time of trial. FPP § 2808; Alicea v. Machete Music, 744 F.3d 773, 781 (1st Cir. 2014). The moving party must have been excusably ignorant of the facts despite using due diligence to learn about them. FPP § 2808; United States v. 41 Cases, More or Less, 420 F.2d 1126 (5th Cir. 1970); Huff v. Metro. Life Ins. Co., 675 F.2d 119 (6th Cir. 1982). If the facts were known to the party and no excusable ignorance can be shown, a new-trial motion will not be granted. Failure to show due diligence also generally will result in the denial of the motion. FPP § 2808. However, it has been held that a new trial may be granted even though proper diligence was not used if this is necessary to prevent a manifest miscarriage of justice. FPP § 2808; Ferrell v. Trailmobile, Inc., 223 F.2d 697 (5th Cir. 1955).

- *Conduct of counsel and judge.* If a verdict has been unfairly influenced by the misconduct of counsel, a new trial should be granted. Misconduct of counsel that may necessitate a new trial may involve things such as improper comments or arguments to the jury, including presenting arguments about evidence not properly before the court. FPP § 2809. Improper conduct by the trial judge also is a ground for a new trial. Motions raising this ground happily are rare and a new trial is not required if the judge's behavior has not made the trial unfair. The moving party must meet a heavy burden to prevail on the ground of judicial misconduct. FPP § 2809.

- *Misconduct affecting jury.* A common ground for a motion for a new trial is that the jury, or members of it, has not performed in the fashion expected of juries. FPP § 2810. Because of the limitations on the use of testimony by the jurors and because a new trial is required in any event only if conduct affecting the jury has been harmful to the losing party, most motions for a new trial on this ground are denied. It is ground for a new trial if a juror was prejudiced from the start but claims that a juror did not disclose all that he should at voir dire usually fail, unless it can be found that the information omitted would have supported a challenge for cause. Motions for a new trial asserting that the jury did not deliberate for a sufficient length of time also usually fail. FPP § 2810.

ii. *Partial new trial.* FRCP 59(a) provides that a new trial may be granted "on all or some of the issues—and to any party—. . . ." Thus it recognizes the court's power to grant a partial new trial. FPP § 2814. If a partial new trial is granted, those portions of the first judgment not set aside become part of the judgment entered following the jury verdict at the new trial. Thus, the end result is a single judgment. FPP § 2814.

iii. *Further action after a nonjury trial.* After a nonjury trial, the court may, on motion for a new trial, open the judgment if one has been entered, take additional testimony, amend findings of fact and conclusions of law or make new ones, and direct the entry of a new judgment. FRCP 59(a)(2).

iv. *New trial on the court's initiate or for reasons not in the motion.* No later than twenty-eight (28) days after the entry of judgment, the court, on its own, may order a new trial for any reason that would justify granting one on a party's motion. After giving the parties notice and an opportunity to be heard, the court may grant a timely motion for a new trial for a reason not stated in the motion. In either event, the court must specify the reasons in its order. FRCP 59(d).

b. *Motion to alter or amend judgment.* FRCP 59(e) authorizes a motion to alter or amend a judgment after its entry. FRCP 59(e) also has been interpreted as permitting a motion to vacate a judgment rather than merely amend it. FPP § 2810.1.

i. *Types of motions covered under FRCP 59(e).* FRCP 59(e) covers a broad range of motions, and the only real limitation on the type of the motion permitted is that it must request a substantive alteration of the judgment, not merely the correction of a clerical error, or relief of a type wholly collateral to the judgment. FPP § 2810.1; Osterneck v. Ernst & Whinney, 489 U.S. 169, 109 S. Ct. 987, 103 L. Ed. 2d 146 (1989). The type of relief requested in postjudgment motions for attorney's fees and costs, for instance, is considered collateral unless it is specifically addressed in the judgment, and thus these motions generally do not fall under FRCP 59(e). FPP § 2810.1; Hastert v. Illinois State Bd. of Election Comm'rs, 28 F.3d 1430, 1438 n.8 (7th Cir. 1993), as amended on reh'g (June 1, 1994). FRCP 59(e) does, however, include motions for reconsideration. FPP § 2810.1; United States v. $23,000 in U.S. Currency, 356 F.3d 157, 165 n.9 (1st Cir. 2004). A motion under FRCP 59(e) also is appropriate if the court in the original judgment has failed to give relief on a certain claim on which it has found that the party is entitled to relief. Finally, the motion may be used to request an amendment of the judgment to provide for prejudgment interest. The court may not, however, give relief under FRCP 59(e) if this would defeat a party's right to jury trial on an issue. FPP § 2810.1.

ii. *Grounds for granting an FRCP 59(e) motion.* There are four basic grounds upon which an FRCP 59(e) motion may be granted. FPP § 2810.1; F.D.I.C. v. World Univ. Inc., 978 F.2d 10 (1st Cir. 1992). First, the movant may demonstrate that the motion is necessary to correct manifest errors of law or fact upon which the judgment is based. Of course, the corollary principle applies and the movant's failure to show any manifest error may result in the motion's denial. FPP § 2810.1. Second, the motion may be granted so that the moving party may present newly discovered or previously unavailable evidence. FPP § 2810.1; GenCorp, Inc. v. Am. Int'l Underwriters, 178 F.3d 804, 834 (6th Cir. 1999). Third, the motion will be granted if necessary to prevent manifest injustice. Serious misconduct of counsel may justify relief under this theory. Fourth, an FRCP 59(e) motion may be justified by an intervening change in controlling law. FPP § 2810.1.

iii. *Limitations on an FRCP 59(e) motion.* The FRCP 59(e) motion may not be used to relitigate old matters, or to raise arguments or present evidence that could have been raised prior to the entry of judgment. Also, amendment of the judgment will be denied if it would serve no useful purpose. In practice, because of the narrow purposes for which they are intended, FRCP 59(e) motions typically are denied. FPP § 2810.1.

c. *Motion for relief from judgment*

i. *Corrections based on clerical mistakes; Oversights and omissions.* The court may correct a clerical mistake or a mistake arising from oversight or omission whenever one is found in a judgment, order, or other part of the record. The court may do so on motion or on its own, with or without notice. But after an appeal has been docketed in the appellate court and while it is pending, such a mistake may be corrected only with the appellate court's leave. FRCP 60(a).

- *Correctable mistakes.* A motion under FRCP 60(a) only can be used to make the judgment or record speak the truth and cannot be used to make it say something other than what originally was pronounced. FPP § 2854. FRCP 60(a) is not a vehicle for relitigating matters that already have been litigated and decided, nor to change what has been deliberately done. FPP § 2854. The mistake correctable under FRCP 60(a) need not be committed by the clerk or the court; FRCP 60(a) may be utilized to correct mistakes by the parties as well. FPP § 2854.

- *Substantive changes.* When the change sought is substantive in nature, such as a change in the calculation of interest not originally intended, the addition of an amount to a judgment to compensate for depreciation in stock awarded, or the broadening of a summary-judgment motion to dismiss all claims, relief is not appropriate under FRCP 60(a). FPP § 2854. Errors of a more substantial nature are to be corrected by a motion under FRCP 59(e) or FRCP 60(b). FPP § 2854.

ii. *Relief from judgment, order, or proceeding.* Relief under FRCP 60(b) ordinarily is obtained by motion in the court that rendered the judgment. FPP § 2865.

- *Grounds for relief from a final judgment, order, or proceeding.* On motion and just terms, the court may relieve a party or its legal representative from a final judgment, order, or proceeding for the following reasons: (1) mistake, inadvertence, surprise, or excusable neglect; (2) newly discovered evidence that, with reasonable diligence, could not have been discovered in time to move for a new trial under FRCP 59(b); (3) fraud (whether previously called intrinsic or extrinsic), misrepresentation, or misconduct by an opposing party; (4) the judgment is void; (5) the judgment has been satisfied, released or discharged; it is based on an earlier judgment that has been reversed or vacated; or applying it prospectively is no longer equitable; or (6) any other reason that justifies relief. FRCP 60(b).

- *Mistake, inadvertence, surprise, or excusable neglect.* Although FRCP 60(b)(1) speaks only of mistake, inadvertence, surprise, or excusable neglect, a defendant must prove the existence of a meritorious defense as a prerequisite to obtaining relief on these grounds. FEDPROC § 51:131; Augusta Fiberglass Coatings, Inc. v. Fodor Contracting Corp., 843 F.2d 808 (4th Cir. 1988). In all averments of fraud or mistake, the circumstances constituting fraud or mistake must be stated with particularity. This requirement applies with respect to averments of mistake in motion papers under FRCP 60(b)(1). FEDPROC § 51:138. In assessing whether conduct is excusable, several factors must be taken into account, including: (1) the danger of prejudice to the nonmoving party; (2) the length of the delay and its potential impact on judicial proceedings; (3) whether the movant acted in good faith; and (4) the reason for the delay, including whether it was within the reasonable control of the movant. FEDPROC § 51:132; Nara v. Frank, 488 F.3d 187 (3d Cir. 2007), as amended (June 12, 2007).

- *Newly discovered evidence.* The standards for relief from a judgment on the basis of newly discovered evidence are, in summary: (1) the motion must involve legally admissible "evidence" in some technical sense, rather than just factual information of some variety; (2) the evidence must have been in existence at the time of the trial or consists of facts existing at the time of trial; (3) the evidence must be newly discovered since the trial; (4) the evidence must not have been discoverable by the exercise of due diligence in time for use at the trial or to move for a new trial; (5) the evidence must be material and not merely cumulative or impeaching; and (6) the evidence must be such that, if received, it will probably produce a different result. FEDPROC § 51:140.

- *Fraud, misrepresentation, or other misconduct of opposing party.* Many other cases support the propositions that the burden of proof of fraud is on the moving party and that fraud must be established by clear and convincing evidence. Further, the fraud must have prevented the moving party from fully and fairly presenting his case. It also must be chargeable to an adverse party; the moving party cannot get relief because of the party's own fraud. FPP § 2860. There is some disagreement about the meaning of "fraud" or "misconduct" in this context. One view is that the moving party must show that the adverse party committed a deliberate act that adversely impacted the fairness of the relevant legal proceeding in question. FEDPROC § 51:144; Jordan v. Paccar, Inc., 97 F.3d 1452 (6th Cir. 1996). The prevailing view is broader, however, and allows a motion for relief to be granted regardless of whether the adverse party acted with an evil, nefarious, malicious, innocent, or careless purpose. FEDPROC § 51:144.

- *Void judgment.* A judgment is not void merely because it is erroneous. It is void only if the court that rendered it lacked jurisdiction of the subject matter, or of the parties, or if it acted in a manner inconsistent with due process of law. Of course, although a challenge on one of those three grounds can be made under FRCP 60(b)(4), if the court finds that there was subject-matter or personal jurisdiction, or that no due-process violation has occurred, the motion will be denied. FPP § 2862.

- *Judgment satisfied or no longer equitable.* The significant portion of FRCP 60(b)(5) is the final ground, allowing relief if it is no longer equitable for the judgment to be applied prospectively. FPP § 2863. In order to obtain relief on these grounds, the judgment itself must have prospective application and such application must be inequitable due to a change in circumstances since the judgment was rendered. FEDPROC § 51:156. The mere possibility that a judgment has some future effect does not mean that it is "prospective," for purposes of applying FRCP 60(b)(5), because virtually every court order causes at least some reverberations into the future and has some prospective effect; the essential inquiry into the prospective nature of a judgment revolves around whether it is executory, or involves the supervision of changing conduct or conditions. FEDPROC § 51:157; Kalamazoo River Study Grp. v. Rockwell Int'l Corp., 355 F.3d 574 (6th Cir. 2004). The court's duty when confronted with such a motion is not to examine the correctness of the existing decree at the time it was entered, or even whether it is needed today, but to determine whether, assuming it was needed when entered, intervening changes have eliminated that need. FEDPROC § 51:158; Swift & Co. v. United States, 367 U.S. 909, 81 S. Ct. 1918, 6 L. Ed. 2d 1249 (1961).

- *Any other reason justifying relief.* The broad power granted by FRCP 60(b)(6) is not for the purpose of relieving a party from free, calculated, and deliberate choices the party has made. A party remains under a duty to take legal steps to protect his own interests. FPP § 2864. [Case law] certainly seemed to establish that FRCP 60(b)(6) and the first five clauses are mutually exclusive and that relief cannot be had under FRCP 60(b)(6) if it would have been available under the earlier clauses. FPP § 2864.

- *Effect of motion.* The motion does not affect the judgment's finality or suspend its operation. FRCP 60(c)(2).

- *Other powers to grant relief.* FRCP 60 does not limit a court's power to: (1) entertain an independent action to relieve a party from a judgment, order, or proceeding; (2) grant relief under 28 U.S.C.A. § 1655 to a defendant who was not personally notified of the action; or (3) set aside a judgment for fraud on the court. FRCP 60(d).

    iii. *Bills and writs abolished.* The following are abolished: bills of review, bills in the nature of bills of review, and writs of coram nobis, coram vobis, and audita querela. FRCP 60(e).

3. *Opposing papers.* The Federal Rules of Civil Procedure do not require any formal answer, return, or reply to a motion, except where the Federal Rules of Civil Procedure or local rules may require affidavits, memoranda, or other papers to be filed in opposition to a motion. Such papers are simply to apprise the court of such opposition and the grounds of that opposition. FEDPROC § 62:353.

    a. *DISTRICT OF MAINE: Content of objections.* Any objections shall include citations and supporting authorities and affidavits and other documents setting forth or evidencing facts on which the objection is based. ME R USDCT Rule 7(b).

    b. *Effect of failure to respond to motion.* Although in the absence of statutory provision or court rule, a motion ordinarily does not require a response or written answer, when a party files a motion and the opposing party fails to respond, the court may construe such failure to respond as nonopposition to the motion or an admission that the motion was meritorious. AMJUR MOTIONS § 28. The rule in some jurisdictions being that the failure to respond to a fact set forth in a motion is deemed an admission—and may grant the motion if the relief requested appears to be justified. AMJUR MOTIONS § 28.

    c. *Assent or no opposition not determinative.* However, a motion will not be granted automatically simply because an "assent" or a notation of "no opposition" has been filed; federal judges frequently deny motions that have been assented to when it is thought that justice so dictates. FPP § 1190.

    d. *Responsive pleading inappropriate as response to motion.* An attempt to answer or oppose a motion with a responsive pleading usually is not appropriate. FPP § 1190.

4. *Reply papers.* A moving party may be required or permitted to prepare papers in addition to its original motion papers. AMJUR MOTIONS § 25. Papers answering or replying to opposing papers may be appropriate, in the interests of justice, where it appears there is a substantial reason for allowing a reply. Thus, a court may accept reply papers where a party demonstrates that the papers to which it seeks to file a reply raise new issues that are material to the disposition of the question before the court, or where the court determines, sua sponte, that it wishes further briefing of an issue raised in those papers and orders the submission of additional papers. FEDPROC § 62:354.

    a. *Function of reply papers.* The function of a reply affidavit or reply papers is to answer the arguments made in opposition to the position taken by the movant, not to raise new issues, arguments, or evidence, or change the nature of the primary motion. However, if the court permits new evidence with the reply papers, the other party should be given the opportunity to respond. Where the party opposing the motion has no opportunity to address the argument in writing, a court has the discretion to disregard arguments raised for the first time in a reply memorandum. Also, the view has been followed in some jurisdictions that as a matter of judicial economy, where there is no prejudice and where the issues could be raised simply by filing a motion to dismiss, the trial court has discretion to consider arguments raised for the first time in a reply memorandum, and that a trial court may grant a motion to strike issues raised for the first time in a reply memorandum. AMJUR MOTIONS § 26.

    i. *DISTRICT OF MAINE.* The moving party may file a reply memorandum. . .which shall be strictly confined to replying to new matter raised in the objection or opposing memorandum. ME R USDCT Rule 7(c).

5. *DISTRICT OF MAINE: Appearances.* An attorney's signature to a pleading shall constitute an appearance for the party filing the pleading. Otherwise, an attorney who wishes to participate in any manner in any action must file a formal written

appearance identifying the party represented. An appearance whether by pleading or formal written appearance shall be signed by an attorney in his/her individual name and shall state his/her office address. ME R USDCT Rule 83.2(a). For more information, refer to ME R USDCT Rule 83.2.

6. *DISTRICT OF MAINE: Alternative dispute resolution (ADR)*. Litigants are authorized and encouraged to employ, at their own expense, any available ADR process on which they can agree, including early neutral evaluation, settlement conferences, mediation, non-binding summary jury trial, corporate mini-trial, and arbitration proceedings. ME R USDCT Rule 83.11(a). For more information on ADR, refer to ME R USDCT Rule 83.11.

D. Documents

1. *Documents for moving party*

   a. *Required documents*

      i. *Notice of motion and motion.* Refer to the "C. General Requirements" section of this KeyRules document for information on the notice of motion and motion.

      - *DISTRICT OF MAINE: Memorandum of law.* Every motion shall incorporate a memorandum of law, including citations and supporting authorities. ME R USDCT Rule 7(a). Refer to the "E. Format" section of this KeyRules document for the form of memoranda of law.

      - *Certificate of service.* No certificate of service is required when a paper is served by filing it with the court's electronic-filing system. When a paper that is required to be served is served by other means: (i) if the paper is filed, a certificate of service must be filed with it or within a reasonable time after service; and (ii) if the paper is not filed, a certificate of service need not be filed unless filing is required by court order or by local rule. FRCP 5(d)(1)(B).

   b. *Supplemental documents*

      i. *Supporting evidence.* When a motion relies on facts outside the record, the court may hear the matter on affidavits or may hear it wholly or partly on oral testimony or on depositions. FRCP 43(c).

      - *DISTRICT OF MAINE: Affidavits and other supporting documents.* Any affidavits and other documents setting forth or evidencing facts on which the motion is based must be filed with the motion. ME R USDCT Rule 7(a).

      - *DISTRICT OF MAINE: Discovery transcripts or materials.* A party relying on discovery transcripts or materials in support of or in opposition to a motion shall file excerpts of such transcript or materials with the memorandum required by ME R USDCT Rule 7 as well as a list of specific citations to the parts on which the party relies. ME R USDCT Rule 26(c). Excerpts of depositions in support of or in opposition to a motion shall be filed electronically using ECF, unless otherwise permitted by the court. ME R USDCT App. 4(l)(3).

      ii. *Notice of constitutional question.* A party that files a pleading, written motion, or other paper drawing into question the constitutionality of a federal or state statute must promptly: (1) file a notice of constitutional question stating the question and identifying the paper that raises it, if: (A) a federal statute is questioned and the parties do not include the United States, one of its agencies, or one of its officers or employees in an official capacity; or (B) a state statute is questioned and the parties do not include the state, one of its agencies, or one of its officers or employees in an official capacity; and (2) serve the notice and paper on the Attorney General of the United States if a federal statute is questioned—or on the state attorney general if a state statute is questioned—either by certified or registered mail or by sending it to an electronic address designated by the attorney general for this purpose. FRCP 5.1(a).

      - *No forfeiture.* A party's failure to file and serve the notice, or the court's failure to certify, does not forfeit a constitutional claim or defense that is otherwise timely asserted. FRCP 5.1(d).

      iii. *DISTRICT OF MAINE: Additional supplemental documents*

      - *Proposed order.* Proposed orders shall not be filed unless requested by the court. When requested by the court, proposed orders shall be filed by e-mail in word processing format. ME R USDCT App. 4(k)(1).

2. *Documents for opposing party*

   a. *Required documents*

      i. *Opposition.* Refer to the "C. General Requirements" section of this KeyRules document for information on the opposing papers.

      - *DISTRICT OF MAINE: Memorandum of law.* Unless within twenty-one (21) days after the filing of a

motion the opposing party files written objection thereto, incorporating a memorandum of law, the opposing party shall be deemed to have waived objection. ME R USDCT Rule 7(b).

- *Certificate of service.* No certificate of service is required when a paper is served by filing it with the court's electronic-filing system. When a paper that is required to be served is served by other means: (i) if the paper is filed, a certificate of service must be filed with it or within a reasonable time after service; and (ii) if the paper is not filed, a certificate of service need not be filed unless filing is required by court order or by local rule. FRCP 5(d)(1)(B).

b. *Supplemental documents*

i. *Supporting evidence.* When a motion relies on facts outside the record, the court may hear the matter on affidavits or may hear it wholly or partly on oral testimony or on depositions. FRCP 43(c).

- *DISTRICT OF MAINE: Affidavits and other supporting documents.* Any objections shall include. . .affidavits and other documents setting forth or evidencing facts on which the objection is based. ME R USDCT Rule 7(b).

- *DISTRICT OF MAINE: Discovery transcripts or materials.* A party relying on discovery transcripts or materials in support of or in opposition to a motion shall file excerpts of such transcript or materials with the memorandum required by ME R USDCT Rule 7 as well as a list of specific citations to the parts on which the party relies. ME R USDCT Rule 26(c). Excerpts of depositions in support of or in opposition to a motion shall be filed electronically using ECF, unless otherwise permitted by the court. ME R USDCT App. 4(l)(3).

ii. *Notice of constitutional question.* A party that files a pleading, written motion, or other paper drawing into question the constitutionality of a federal or state statute must promptly: (1) file a notice of constitutional question stating the question and identifying the paper that raises it, if: (A) a federal statute is questioned and the parties do not include the United States, one of its agencies, or one of its officers or employees in an official capacity; or (B) a state statute is questioned and the parties do not include the state, one of its agencies, or one of its officers or employees in an official capacity; and (2) serve the notice and paper on the Attorney General of the United States if a federal statute is questioned—or on the state attorney general if a state statute is questioned—either by certified or registered mail or by sending it to an electronic address designated by the attorney general for this purpose. FRCP 5.1(a).

- *No forfeiture.* A party's failure to file and serve the notice, or the court's failure to certify, does not forfeit a constitutional claim or defense that is otherwise timely asserted. FRCP 5.1(d).

E. Format

1. *Form of documents.* The rules governing captions and other matters of form in pleadings apply to motions and other papers. FRCP 7(b)(2).

a. *DISTRICT OF MAINE: Font size, line spacing, and paper size.* All such documents shall be typed in a font of no less than size twelve (12) point, and shall be double-spaced or printed on eight and one-half by eleven (8-1/2 x 11) inch paper. Footnotes shall be in a font of no less than size ten (10) point, and may be single spaced. ME R USDCT Rule 10.

b. *Caption.* Every pleading must have a caption with the court's name, a title, a file number, and an FRCP 7(a) designation. FRCP 10(a).

i. *Names of parties.* The title of the complaint must name all the parties; the title of other pleadings, after naming the first party on each side, may refer generally to other parties. FRCP 10(a).

ii. *DISTRICT OF MAINE: Additional caption requirements.* All pleadings, motions and other papers filed with the clerk or otherwise submitted to the court, except exhibits, shall bear the proper case number and shall contain on the first page a caption as described by FRCP 10(a) and immediately thereunder a designation of what the document is and the name of the party in whose behalf it is submitted. ME R USDCT Rule 10.

c. *Claims or defenses*

i. *Numbered paragraphs.* A party must state its claims or defenses in numbered paragraphs, each limited as far as practicable to a single set of circumstances. A later pleading may refer by number to a paragraph in an earlier pleading. FRCP 10(b).

ii. *Separate statements.* If doing so would promote clarity, each claim founded on a separate transaction or occurrence—and each defense other than a denial—must be stated in a separate count or defense. FRCP 10(b).

    d. *Adoption by reference.* A statement in a pleading may be adopted by reference elsewhere in the same pleading or in any other pleading or motion. FRCP 10(c).

        i. *Exhibits.* A copy of a written instrument that is an exhibit to a pleading is a part of the pleading for all purposes. FRCP 10(c).

    e. *DISTRICT OF MAINE: Page numbering.* All pages shall be numbered at the bottom. ME R USDCT Rule 10.

    f. *DISTRICT OF MAINE: Attachment of ancillary papers.* Ancillary papers shall be attached at the end of the document to which they relate. ME R USDCT Rule 10.

    g. *Acceptance by the clerk.* The clerk must not refuse to file a paper solely because it is not in the form prescribed by the Federal Rules of Civil Procedure or by a local rule or practice. FRCP 5(d)(4).

2. *Form of electronic documents.* A paper filed electronically is a written paper for purposes of the Federal Rules of Civil Procedure. FRCP 5(d)(3)(D).

    a. *DISTRICT OF MAINE: Document format.* The ECF system only accepts documents in a portable document format (PDF). Although there are two types of PDF documents—electronically converted PDF's and scanned PDF's—only electronically converted PDF's may be filed with the court using the ECF system, unless otherwise authorized by local rule or order. ME R USDCT App. 4. Any document or exhibit to be filed or submitted to the court shall not be password-protected or encrypted. ME R USDCT App. 4(g)(12).

        i. *Electronically converted PDFs.* Electronically converted PDF's are created from word processing documents (MS Word, WordPerfect, etc.) using Adobe Acrobat or similar software. They are text searchable and their file size is small. ME R USDCT App. 4. Software used to electronically convert documents to PDF which includes proprietary or advertisement information within the PDF document is prohibited. ME R USDCT App. 4.

        ii. *Scanned PDFs.* Scanned PDF's are created from paper documents run through an optical scanner. Scanned PDF's are not searchable and have a large file size. ME R USDCT App. 4.

    b. *DISTRICT OF MAINE: Title.* All pleadings filed electronically shall be titled in accordance with the approved dictionary of civil or criminal events of the ECF system of the United States District Court for the District of Maine. ME R USDCT App. 4(d)(3).

    c. *DISTRICT OF MAINE: Attachments.* Attachments to filings and exhibits must be filed in accordance with the court's ECF User Manual, unless otherwise ordered by the court. ME R USDCT App. 4(j). When there are fifty (50) or fewer attachments to a pleading, the attachments must be filed by counsel electronically using ECF. When there are more than fifty (50) attachments, the attachments must be filed in one of the following ways: (A) using ECF, simply attach them to the pleading being filed; (B) using ECF, use the "Additional Attachments" menu item; (C) on paper; or (D) on a properly labeled three and one-half (3-1/2) inch floppy disk, CD or DVD. ME R USDCT App. 4(j)(2). Attachments filed on paper or on disk must contain a comprehensive index that clearly describes each document. ME R USDCT App. 4(j)(2).

        i. A filing user must submit as attachments only those excerpts of the referenced documents that are directly germane to the matter under consideration by the court. Excerpted material must be clearly and prominently identified as such. Users who file excerpts of documents do so without prejudice to their right to timely file additional excerpts or the complete document, as may be allowed by the court. Responding parties may timely file additional excerpts or the complete document that they believe are directly germane. ME R USDCT App. 4(j)(3).

        ii. Filers shall not attach as an exhibit any pleading or other paper already on file with the court in that case, but shall merely refer to that document. ME R USDCT App. 4(j)(4).

    d. *DISTRICT OF MAINE: Compliance with technical standards.* All documents filed by electronic means must comply with technical standards, if any, established by the Judicial Conference of the United States or by the United States District Court for the District of Maine. ME R USDCT App. 4(a)(3).

3. *DISTRICT OF MAINE: Form of memoranda of law.* All memoranda shall be typed, in a font of no less than size twelve (12) point, and shall be double-spaced on eight and one-half by eleven (8-1/2 x 11) inch paper or printed. Footnotes shall be in a font of no less than size ten (10) point, and may be single spaced. All pages shall be numbered at the bottom. ME R USDCT Rule 7(d).

    a. *Page limitations.* No memorandum of law in support of or in opposition to a nondispositive motion shall exceed ten (10) pages. ME R USDCT Rule 7(d). No reply memorandum shall exceed seven (7) pages. ME R USDCT Rule 7(d); ME R USDCT Rule 7(c).

        i. *Motion to exceed page limitation.* A motion to exceed the limitation of ME R USDCT Rule 7 shall be filed no later than three (3) business days in advance of the date for filing the memorandum to permit meaningful review by the court. A motion to exceed the page limitations shall not be filed simultaneously with a memorandum in excess of the limitations of ME R USDCT Rule 7. ME R USDCT Rule 7(d).

4. *Signing of pleadings, motions and other papers*

    a. *Signature.* Every pleading, written motion, and other paper must be signed by at least one attorney of record in the attorney's name—or by a party personally if the party is unrepresented. The paper must state the signer's address, e-mail address, and telephone number. FRCP 11(a).

        i. *No verification or accompanying affidavit required for pleadings.* Unless a rule or statute specifically states otherwise, a pleading need not be verified or accompanied by an affidavit. FRCP 11(a).

        ii. *Unsigned papers.* The court must strike an unsigned paper unless the omission is promptly corrected after being called to the attorney's or party's attention. FRCP 11(a).

    b. *Electronic signing.* A filing made through a person's electronic-filing account and authorized by that person, together with that person's name on a signature block, constitutes the person's signature. FRCP 5(d)(3)(C).

        i. *DISTRICT OF MAINE: Attorneys.* The user log-in and password together with a user's name on the signature block constitutes the attorney's signature pursuant to the Federal Rules of Civil Procedure and the Local Rules of the United States District Court for the District of Maine. All electronically filed documents must include a signature block and must set forth the attorney's name, address, telephone number and e-mail address. The name of the ECF user under whose log-in and password the document is submitted must be preceded by a "/s/" in the space where the signature would otherwise appear. ME R USDCT App. 4(h)(1).

        ii. *DISTRICT OF MAINE: Multiple signatures.* The filer of any document requiring more than one signature (e.g., pleadings filed by visiting lawyers, stipulations, joint status reports) must list thereon all the names of other signatories, preceded by a "/s/" in the space where the signatures would otherwise appear. By submitting such a document, the filing attorney certifies that each of the other signatories has expressly agreed to the form and substance of the document and that the filing attorney has their actual authority to submit the document electronically. ME R USDCT App. 4(h)(2). For more information, refer to ME R USDCT App. 4(h)(2).

        iii. *DISTRICT OF MAINE: Documents signed under oath.* Affidavits, declarations, verified complaints, or any other document signed under oath shall be filed electronically. The electronically filed version shall contain the typed name of the signatory, preceded by a "/s/" in the space where the signature would otherwise appear indicating that the paper document bears an original signature. ME R USDCT Rule 10; ME R USDCT App. 4(h)(3). For more information, refer to ME R USDCT Rule 10.

    c. *Representations to the court.* By presenting to the court a pleading, written motion, or other paper—whether by signing, filing, submitting, or later advocating it—an attorney or unrepresented party certifies that to the best of the person's knowledge, information, and belief, formed after an inquiry reasonable under the circumstances: (1) it is not being presented for any improper purpose, such as to harass, cause unnecessary delay, or needlessly increase the cost of litigation; (2) the claims, defenses, and other legal contentions are warranted by existing law or by a nonfrivolous argument for extending, modifying, or reversing existing law or for establishing new law; (3) the factual contentions have evidentiary support or, if specifically so identified, will likely have evidentiary support after a reasonable opportunity for further investigation or discovery; and (4) the denials of factual contentions are warranted on the evidence or, if specifically so identified, are reasonably based on belief or a lack of information. FRCP 11(b).

    d. *Sanctions.* If, after notice and a reasonable opportunity to respond, the court determines that FRCP 11(b) has been violated, the court may impose an appropriate sanction on any attorney, law firm, or party that violated FRCP 11(b) or is responsible for the violation. FRCP 11(c)(1). Refer to the United States District Court for the District of Maine KeyRules Motion for Sanctions document for more information.

5. *Privacy protection for filings made with the court*

    a. *Redacted filings.* Unless the court orders otherwise, in an electronic or paper filing with the court that contains an individual's Social Security number, taxpayer-identification number, or birth date, the name of an individual known to be a minor, or a financial-account number, a party or nonparty making the filing may include only: (1) the last four (4) digits of the Social Security number and taxpayer-identification number; (2) the year of the individual's birth; (3) the minor's initials; and (4) the last four (4) digits of the financial-account number. FRCP 5.2(a).

        i. *DISTRICT OF MAINE.* To address the privacy concerns created by the Internet access to court papers, unless otherwise ordered by the court, counsel shall modify certain personal data identifiers in pleadings and other papers as follows: (1) minors' names: use of the minors' initials only; (2) Social Security numbers: use of the last

four (4) numbers only; (3) dates of birth: use of the year of birth only; [and] (4) financial account numbers: identify the type of account and the financial institution, but use only the last four (4) numbers of the account number. ME R USDCT Redacting Pleadings. Counsel should also use caution when filing papers that contain a person's medical records, employment history; financial information; and any proprietary or trade secret information. ME R USDCT Redacting Pleadings.

b. *Exemptions from the redaction requirement.* The redaction requirement does not apply to the following: (1) a financial-account number that identifies the property allegedly subject to forfeiture in a forfeiture proceeding; (2) the record of an administrative or agency proceeding; (3) the official record of a state-court proceeding; (4) the record of a court or tribunal, if that record was not subject to the redaction requirement when originally filed; (5) a filing covered by FRCP 5.2(c) or FRCP 5.2(d); and (6) a pro se filing in an action brought under 28 U.S.C.A. § 2241, 28 U.S.C.A. § 2254, or 28 U.S.C.A. § 2255. FRCP 5.2(b).

c. *Limitations on remote access to electronic files; Social Security appeals and immigration cases.* Unless the court orders otherwise, in an action for benefits under the Social Security Act, and in an action or proceeding relating to an order of removal, to relief from removal, or to immigration benefits or detention, access to an electronic file is authorized as follows: (1) the parties and their attorneys may have remote electronic access to any part of the case file, including the administrative record; (2) any other person may have electronic access to the full record at the courthouse, but may have remote electronic access only to: (A) the docket maintained by the court; and (B) an opinion, order, judgment, or other disposition of the court, but not any other part of the case file or the administrative record. FRCP 5.2(c).

d. *Filings made under seal.* The court may order that a filing be made under seal without redaction. The court may later unseal the filing or order the person who made the filing to file a redacted version for the public record. FRCP 5.2(d).

    i. *DISTRICT OF MAINE.* For information on filing sealed documents in the District of Maine, refer to ME R USDCT Rule 7A, ME R USDCT App. 4(p)(2), and ME R USDCT Sealed Filings.

e. *Protective orders.* For good cause, the court may by order in a case: (1) require redaction of additional information; or (2) limit or prohibit a nonparty's remote electronic access to a document filed with the court. FRCP 5.2(e).

f. *Option for additional unredacted filing under seal.* A person making a redacted filing may also file an unredacted copy under seal. The court must retain the unredacted copy as part of the record. FRCP 5.2(f).

    i. *DISTRICT OF MAINE.* A party wishing to file a document containing the personal data identifiers specified above may. . .file an unredacted document under seal. This document will be retained by the clerk's office as part of the record. ME R USDCT Redacting Pleadings. The court may, however, still require the party to file a redacted copy for the public file. ME R USDCT Redacting Pleadings.

g. *Option for filing a reference list.* A filing that contains redacted information may be filed together with a reference list that identifies each item of redacted information and specifies an appropriate identifier that uniquely corresponds to each item listed. The list must be filed under seal and may be amended as of right. Any reference in the case to a listed identifier will be construed to refer to the corresponding item of information. FRCP 5.2(g).

    i. *DISTRICT OF MAINE.* A party wishing to file a document containing the personal data identifiers specified above may. . .file a reference list under seal. The reference list shall contain the complete personal data identifier(s) and the redacted identifier(s) used in its (their) place in the filing. All references in the case to the redacted identifiers included in the reference list will be construed to refer to the corresponding complete identifier. The reference list must be filed under seal, and may be amended as of right. It shall be retained by the clerk's office as part of the record. ME R USDCT Redacting Pleadings. The court may, however, still require the party to file a redacted copy for the public file. ME R USDCT Redacting Pleadings.

h. *DISTRICT OF MAINE: Responsibility for redaction.* The clerk is not required to review documents filed with the court for compliance with FRCP 5.2. The responsibility to redact filings rests with counsel and the party or nonparty making the filing. ME R USDCT App. 4(i); ME R USDCT Redacting Pleadings. For guidelines for filing confidential information in civil cases in the District of Maine, refer to ME R USDCT Confidentiality.

i. *Waiver of protection of identifiers.* A person waives the protection of FRCP 5.2(a) as to the person's own information by filing it without redaction and not under seal. FRCP 5.2(h).

F. Filing and Service Requirements

1. *Filing requirements*

    a. *Required filings.* Any paper after the complaint that is required to be served must be filed no later than a reasonable time after service. FRCP 5(d)(1).

b. *DISTRICT OF MAINE: Place of filing.* Unless otherwise ordered by the court, papers shall be filed with the court at Bangor in cases filed and pending at Bangor, and at Portland in cases filed and pending at Portland. ME R USDCT Rule 5(a).

c. *Nonelectronic filing.* A paper not filed electronically is filed by delivering it: (A) to the clerk; or (B) to a judge who agrees to accept it for filing, and who must then note the filing date on the paper and promptly send it to the clerk. FRCP 5(d)(2).

   i. *DISTRICT OF MAINE: Documents to be filed in paper.* The following documents shall be filed in paper, which may also be scanned into ECF by the clerk's office: (A) all handwritten pleadings; and (B) all pleadings and documents filed by pro se litigants who are incarcerated or who are not registered filing users in ECF. ME R USDCT App. 4(g)(8). Non-prisoner pro se litigants in civil actions may register with ECF or may file (and serve) all pleadings and other documents in paper. The clerk's office will scan into ECF any pleadings and documents filed on paper in accordance with ME R USDCT App. 4(g). ME R USDCT App. 4(o). For more information, refer to ME R USDCT App. 4(g).

d. *Electronic filing*

   i. *DISTRICT OF MAINE: Authorization.* Unless exempt or otherwise ordered by the court, papers shall be filed and served electronically as required by the court's Administrative Procedures Governing the Filing and Service by Electronic Means, which is set forth in ME R USDCT App. 4. The provisions of the court's Administrative Procedures Governing the Filing and Service by Electronic Means (ME R USDCT App. 4) shall be applied and enforced as part of the Local Rules of the United States District Court for the District of Maine. ME R USDCT Rule 5(c).

   ii. *Filing by represented persons.* A person represented by an attorney must file electronically, unless nonelectronic filing is allowed by the court for good cause or is allowed or required by local rule. FRCP 5(d)(3)(A).

      • *DISTRICT OF MAINE.* An attorney may apply to the court for permission to file paper documents. ME R USDCT App. 4(a)(5).

   iii. *Filing by unrepresented persons.* A person not represented by an attorney: (i) may file electronically only if allowed by court order or by local rule; and (ii) may be required to file electronically only by court order, or by a local rule that includes reasonable exceptions. FRCP 5(d)(3)(B).

      • *DISTRICT OF MAINE.* Non-prisoner pro se litigants in civil actions may register with ECF or may file (and serve) all pleadings and other documents in paper. ME R USDCT App. 4(o). A non-prisoner who is a party to a civil action and who is not represented by an attorney may register to receive service electronically and to electronically transmit their documents to the court for filing in the ECF system. If during the course of the action the person retains an attorney who appears on the person's behalf, the clerk shall terminate the person's registration upon the attorney's appearance. ME R USDCT App. 4(b)(2).

   iv. *DISTRICT OF MAINE: Scope of electronic filing.* All documents submitted for filing in civil and criminal cases, regardless of case commencement date, except those documents specifically exempted in ME R USDCT App. 4(g), shall be filed electronically using the electronic case filing system (ECF). ME R USDCT App. 4(a)(1). For special filing requirements and exceptions, refer to ME R USDCT App. 4(g).

   v. *DISTRICT OF MAINE: Consequences of electronic filing.* Electronic transmission of a document to the ECF system, together with the transmission of a Notice of Electronic Filing (NEF) from the court, constitutes filing of the document for all purposes of the Federal Rules of Civil Procedure. ME R USDCT App. 4(d)(1).

   vi. *DISTRICT OF MAINE: Review of documents.* Documents filed with the clerk's office will normally be reviewed no later than the close of the next business day. It is the responsibility of the filing party to promptly notify the clerk's office via telephone of a matter that requires the immediate attention of a judicial officer. ME R USDCT App. 4(a)(4).

e. *DISTRICT OF MAINE: Facsimile filing.* No papers shall be submitted to the court by means of a facsimile machine without prior leave of the court. ME R USDCT Rule 5(c); ME R USDCT App. 4(m).

2. *Service requirements*

a. *Service; When required.* Unless the Federal Rules of Civil Procedure provide otherwise, each of the following papers must be served on every party: (A) an order stating that service is required; (B) a pleading filed after the original complaint, unless the court orders otherwise under FRCP 5(c) because there are numerous defendants; (C) a discovery paper required to be served on a party, unless the court orders otherwise; (D) a written motion, except one

that may be heard ex parte; and (E) a written notice, appearance, demand, or offer of judgment, or any similar paper. FRCP 5(a)(1).

  i. *If a party fails to appear.* No service is required on a party who is in default for failing to appear. But a pleading that asserts a new claim for relief against such a party must be served on that party under FRCP 4. FRCP 5(a)(2).

  ii. *Seizing property.* If an action is begun by seizing property and no person is or need be named as a defendant, any service required before the filing of an appearance, answer, or claim must be made on the person who had custody or possession of the property when it was seized. FRCP 5(a)(3).

 b. *Service; How made.* A paper is served under FRCP 5 by: (A) handing it to the person; (B) leaving it: (i) at the person's office with a clerk or other person in charge or, if no one is in charge, in a conspicuous place in the office; or (ii) if the person has no office or the office is closed, at the person's dwelling or usual place of abode with someone of suitable age and discretion who resides there; (C) mailing it to the person's last known address—in which event service is complete upon mailing; (D) leaving it with the court clerk if the person has no known address; (E) sending it to a registered user by filing it with the court's electronic-filing system or sending it by other electronic means that the person consented to in writing—in either of which events service is complete upon filing or sending, but is not effective if the filer or sender learns that it did not reach the person to be served; or (F) delivering it by any other means that the person consented to in writing—in which event service is complete when the person making service delivers it to the agency designated to make delivery. FRCP 5(b)(2).

  i. *Serving an attorney.* If a party is represented by an attorney, service under FRCP 5 must be made on the attorney unless the court orders service on the party. FRCP 5(b)(1).

 c. *DISTRICT OF MAINE: Service of electronically filed documents*

  i. *Registered users.* Registration [as a filing user of the court's ECF system] constitutes consent to service of all documents by electronic means as provided in ME R USDCT App. 4. ME R USDCT App. 4(b)(4). Whenever a non-sealed pleading is filed electronically, the ECF system will automatically generate and send a Notice of Electronic Filing (NEF) to the filing user and registered users of record. The user filing the document should retain a paper or digital copy of the NEF, which shall serve as the court's date-stamp and proof of filing. ME R USDCT App. 4(e)(1).

   • *Sealed documents.* Although the filing of sealed documents in civil cases produces an NEF, the document itself cannot be accessed and counsel shall be responsible for making service of the sealed documents. ME R USDCT App. 4(e)(2).

  ii. *Non-registered users and pro se litigants.* Attorneys who have not yet registered as users with ECF and pro se litigants who have not registered with ECF shall be served a paper copy of any electronically filed pleading or other document in accordance with the provisions of FRCP 5. ME R USDCT App. 4(e)(3).

   • *Registration of pro se litigants.* A non-prisoner who is a party to a civil action and who is not represented by an attorney may register to receive service electronically and to electronically transmit their documents to the court for filing in the ECF system. If during the course of the action the person retains an attorney who appears on the person's behalf, the clerk shall terminate the person's registration upon the attorney's appearance. ME R USDCT App. 4(b)(2).

 d. *Serving numerous defendants.* If an action involves an unusually large number of defendants, the court may, on motion or on its own, order that: (A) defendants' pleadings and replies to them need not be served on other defendants; (B) any crossclaim, counterclaim, avoidance, or affirmative defense in those pleadings and replies to them will be treated as denied or avoided by all other parties; and (C) filing any such pleading and serving it on the plaintiff constitutes notice of the pleading to all parties. FRCP 5(c)(1).

  i. *Notifying parties.* A copy of every such order must be served on the parties as the court directs. FRCP 5(c)(2).

 3. *DISTRICT OF MAINE: Filing and service of highly sensitive documents (HSDs).* For information on filing and serving highly sensitive documents (HSDs) in the District of Maine, refer to ME R USDCT General Order 21-5.

G. Hearings

 1. *Hearings, generally.* When a motion relies on facts outside the record, the court may hear the matter on affidavits or may hear it wholly or partly on oral testimony or on depositions. FRCP 43(c).

 a. *Oral argument.* Due process does not require that oral argument be permitted on a motion and, except as otherwise provided by local rule, the district court has discretion to determine whether it will decide the motion on the papers or hear argument by counsel (and perhaps receive evidence). FPP § 1190; F.D.I.C. v. Deglau, 207 F.3d 153 (3d Cir. 2000).

    i.   *DISTRICT OF MAINE.* Unless otherwise required by federal rule or statute, all motions may be decided by the court without oral argument unless otherwise ordered by the court on its own motion or, in its discretion, upon request of counsel. ME R USDCT Rule 7(e).

  b. *Providing a regular schedule for oral hearings.* A court may establish regular times and places for oral hearings on motions. FRCP 78(a).

  c. *Providing for submission on briefs.* By rule or order, the court may provide for submitting and determining motions on briefs, without oral hearings. FRCP 78(b).

H. Forms

1. Federal Motion for Post-Trial Relief Forms

  a. Motion for new trial. 4 FEDFORMS § 42:10.

  b. Motion for new trial with statement of grounds. 4 FEDFORMS § 42:11.

  c. Motion for partial new trial. 4 FEDFORMS § 42:14.

  d. Affidavit in support of motion. 4 FEDFORMS § 42:30.

  e. Motion for new trial in nonjury action. 4 FEDFORMS § 42:43.

  f. Motion for new trial or to amend findings and judgment. 4 FEDFORMS § 42:47.

  g. Motion for new trial or to amend judgment. 4 FEDFORMS § 42:50.

  h. Motion for new trial and amendment of findings. 4 FEDFORMS § 42:51.

  i. Motion to amend judgment. 4 FEDFORMS § 42:56.

  j. Notice of motion to amend judgment by correcting amount. 4 FEDFORMS § 42:57.

  k. Motion to correct clerical error. 4 FEDFORMS § 43:13.

  l. Motion to vacate judgment. 4 FEDFORMS § 43:21.

  m. Motion to vacate consent decree on ground of excusable neglect, mistake or surprise. 4 FEDFORMS § 43:23.

  n. Affidavit to vacate judgment; Excusable neglect, mistake, inadvertence or surprise. 4 FEDFORMS § 43:25.

  o. Notice of motion; To amend or correct judgment. AMJUR PP JUDGMENTS § 38.

  p. Motion for additur or new trial; Plaintiff awarded only medical bills without consideration of pain and suffering; No-fault automobile insurances. AMJUR PP JUDGMENTS § 47.

  q. Motion for judgment; In federal court; By plaintiff; In accordance with motion for directed verdict or for new trial. AMJUR PP JUDGMENTS § 257.

  r. Motion for judgment; By defendant; In accordance with motion for directed verdict or for new trial; In federal court. AMJUR PP JUDGMENTS § 258.

  s. Notice of motion; To vacate judgment. AMJUR PP JUDGMENTS § 344.

  t. Motion; Correction of clerical mistake in judgment. FEDPROF § 1E:117.

  u. Motion; For relief from judgment; General form. FEDPROF § 1E:118.

  v. Motion; For relief from judgment; Newly discovered evidence. FEDPROF § 1E:119.

  w. Affidavit; Supporting motion for relief from judgment; Newly discovered evidence. FEDPROF § 1E:123.

  x. Motion for new trial; General form. GOLDLTGFMS § 61:3.

  y. Motion to vacate judgment; General form. GOLDLTGFMS § 63:2.

  z. Motion to vacate judgment; Date of discovery of facts. GOLDLTGFMS § 63:3.

I. Applicable Rules

1. *Federal rules*

  a. Serving and filing pleadings and other papers. FRCP 5.

  b. Constitutional challenge to a statute; Notice, certification, and intervention. FRCP 5.1.

c. Privacy protection for filings made with the court. FRCP 5.2.

d. Computing and extending time; Time for motion papers. FRCP 6.

e. Pleadings allowed; Form of motions and other papers. FRCP 7.

f. Form of pleadings. FRCP 10.

g. Signing pleadings, motions, and other papers; Representations to the court; Sanctions. FRCP 11.

h. Taking testimony. FRCP 43.

i. New trial; Altering or amending a judgment. FRCP 59.

j. Relief from a judgment or order. FRCP 60.

k. Hearing motions; Submission on briefs. FRCP 78.

2. *Local rules*

a. *DISTRICT OF MAINE*

i. Service and filing of pleadings and other papers. ME R USDCT Rule 5.

ii. Time. ME R USDCT Rule 6.

iii. Motions and memoranda of law. ME R USDCT Rule 7.

iv. Form of pleadings, motions and other papers. ME R USDCT Rule 10.

v. Discovery. ME R USDCT Rule 26.

vi. Attorneys; Appearances and withdrawals. ME R USDCT Rule 83.2.

vii. Alternative dispute resolution (ADR). ME R USDCT Rule 83.11.

viii. Administrative procedures governing the filing and service by electronic means. ME R USDCT App. 4.

ix. Redacting pleadings. ME R USDCT Redacting Pleadings.

Requests, Notices and Applications
Interrogatories

Document Last Updated July 2021

A. Checklist

(I) ❑ Matters to be considered by requesting party

    (a) ❑ Required documents

        (1) ❑ Interrogatories

    (b) ❑ Supplemental documents

        (1) ❑ Certificate of service

    (c) ❑ Timing

        (1) ❑ A party may not seek discovery from any source before the parties have conferred as required by FRCP 26(f), except in a proceeding exempted from initial disclosure under FRCP 26(a)(1)(B), or when authorized by the Federal Rules of Civil Procedure, by stipulation, or by court order

(II) ❑ Matters to be considered by responding party

    (a) ❑ Required documents

        (1) ❑ Response to interrogatories

    (b) ❑ Supplemental documents

        (1) ❑ Certificate of service

    (c) ❑ Timing

        (1) ❑ The responding party must serve its answers and any objections within thirty (30) days after being served with the interrogatories

B. Timing

1. *Interrogatories.* FRCP 33(a) contains no limit on when interrogatories may first be served. FPP § 2170. FRCP 33 is also silent on how late in a case interrogatories may be served. But FRCP 16(b)(3)(A) provides that the scheduling order in the case "must limit the time to. . .complete discovery." Although the scheduling order requirement does not apply to cases exempted by local rule, ordinarily there should be a scheduling order that sets a discovery cutoff. FPP § 2170.

2. *Commencement of discovery.* A party may not seek discovery from any source before the parties have conferred as required by FRCP 26(f), except in a proceeding exempted from initial disclosure under FRCP 26(a)(1)(B), or when authorized by the Federal Rules of Civil Procedure, by stipulation, or by court order. FRCP 26(d)(1).

3. *DISTRICT OF MAINE: Completion of discovery in standard track cases.* In standard track cases, discovery shall ordinarily be completed within five (5) months. ME R USDCT Rule 16.1(b)(2).

4. *Computation of time*

    a. *Computing time.* FRCP 6 applies in computing any time period specified in the Federal Rules of Civil Procedure, in any local rule or court order, or in any statute that does not specify a method of computing time. FRCP 6(a).

        i. *Period stated in days or a longer unit.* When the period is stated in days or a longer unit of time: (A) exclude the day of the event that triggers the period; (B) count every day, including intermediate Saturdays, Sundays, and legal holidays; and (C) include the last day of the period, but if the last day is a Saturday, Sunday, or legal holiday, the period continues to run until the end of the next day that is not a Saturday, Sunday, or legal holiday. FRCP 6(a)(1).

        ii. *Period stated in hours.* When the period is stated in hours: (A) begin counting immediately on the occurrence of the event that triggers the period; (B) count every hour, including hours during intermediate Saturdays, Sundays, and legal holidays; and (C) if the period would end on a Saturday, Sunday, or legal holiday, the period continues to run until the same time on the next day that is not a Saturday, Sunday, or legal holiday. FRCP 6(a)(2).

        iii. *Inaccessibility of the clerk's office.* Unless the court orders otherwise, if the clerk's office is inaccessible: (A) on the last day for filing under FRCP 6(a)(1), then the time for filing is extended to the first accessible day that is not a Saturday, Sunday, or legal holiday; or (B) during the last hour for filing under FRCP 6(a)(2), then the time for filing is extended to the same time on the first accessible day that is not a Saturday, Sunday, or legal holiday. FRCP 6(a)(3).

        iv. *"Last day" defined.* Unless a different time is set by a statute, local rule, or court order, the last day ends: (A) for electronic filing, at midnight in the court's time zone; and (B) for filing by other means, when the clerk's office is scheduled to close. FRCP 6(a)(4).

        v. *"Next day" defined.* The "next day" is determined by continuing to count forward when the period is measured after an event and backward when measured before an event. FRCP 6(a)(5).

        vi. *"Legal holiday" defined.* "Legal holiday" means: (A) the day set aside by statute for observing New Year's Day, Martin Luther King Jr.'s Birthday, Washington's Birthday, Memorial Day, Independence Day, Labor Day, Columbus Day, Veterans' Day, Thanksgiving Day, or Christmas Day; (B) any day declared a holiday by the President or Congress; and (C) for periods that are measured after an event, any other day declared a holiday by the state where the district court is located. FRCP 6(a)(6).

        vii. *DISTRICT OF MAINE: Applicability of FRCP 6.* FRCP 6 applies when computing any period of time stated in the Local Rules of the United States District Court for the District of Maine. ME R USDCT Rule 6(a).

    b. *Extending time.* When an act may or must be done within a specified time, the court may, for good cause, extend the time: (A) with or without motion or notice if the court acts, or if a request is made, before the original time or its extension expires; or (B) on motion made after the time has expired if the party failed to act because of excusable neglect. FRCP 6(b)(1). A court must not extend the time to act under FRCP 50(b), FRCP 50(d), FRCP 52(b), FRCP 59(b), FRCP 59(d), FRCP 59(e), and FRCP 60(b). FRCP 6(b)(2). Refer to the United States District Court for the District of Maine KeyRules Motion for Continuance/Extension of Time document for more information on extending time.

    c. *Additional time after certain kinds of service.* When a party may or must act within a specified time after being served and service is made under FRCP 5(b)(2)(C) (by mail), FRCP 5(b)(2)(D) (by leaving with the clerk), or FRCP 5(b)(2)(F) (by other means consented to), three (3) days are added after the period would otherwise expire under FRCP 6(a). FRCP 6(d).

C. General Requirements

1. *General provisions governing discovery*

   a. *Discovery scope and limits*

   i. *Scope in general.* Unless otherwise limited by court order, the scope of discovery is as follows: Parties may obtain discovery regarding any nonprivileged matter that is relevant to any party's claim or defense and proportional to the needs of the case, considering the importance of the issues at stake in the action, the amount in controversy, the parties' relative access to relevant information, the parties' resources, the importance of the discovery in resolving the issues, and whether the burden or expense of the proposed discovery outweighs its likely benefit. Information within this scope of discovery need not be admissible in evidence to be discoverable. FRCP 26(b)(1).

   ii. *Limitations on frequency and extent*

   - *When permitted.* By order, the court may alter the limits in the Federal Rules of Civil Procedure on the number of depositions and interrogatories or on the length of depositions under FRCP 30. By order or local rule, the court may also limit the number of requests under FRCP 36. FRCP 26(b)(2)(A).

   - *Specific limitations on electronically stored information.* A party need not provide discovery of electronically stored information from sources that the party identifies as not reasonably accessible because of undue burden or cost. On motion to compel discovery or for a protective order, the party from whom discovery is sought must show that the information is not reasonably accessible because of undue burden or cost. If that showing is made, the court may nonetheless order discovery from such sources if the requesting party shows good cause, considering the limitations of FRCP 26(b)(2)(C). The court may specify conditions for the discovery. FRCP 26(b)(2)(B).

   - *When required.* On motion or on its own, the court must limit the frequency or extent of discovery otherwise allowed by the Federal Rules of Civil Procedure or by local rule if it determines that: (i) the discovery sought is unreasonably cumulative or duplicative, or can be obtained from some other source that is more convenient, less burdensome, or less expensive; (ii) the party seeking discovery has had ample opportunity to obtain the information by discovery in the action; or (iii) the proposed discovery is outside the scope permitted by FRCP 26(b)(1). FRCP 26(b)(2)(C).

   iii. *Trial preparation; Materials*

   - *Documents and tangible things.* Ordinarily, a party may not discover documents and tangible things that are prepared in anticipation of litigation or for trial by or for another party or its representative (including the other party's attorney, consultant, surety, indemnitor, insurer, or agent). But, subject to FRCP 26(b)(4), those materials may be discovered if: (i) they are otherwise discoverable under FRCP 26(b)(1); and (ii) the party shows that it has substantial need for the materials to prepare its case and cannot, without undue hardship, obtain their substantial equivalent by other means. FRCP 26(b)(3)(A).

   - *Protection against disclosure.* If the court orders discovery of those materials, it must protect against disclosure of the mental impressions, conclusions, opinions, or legal theories of a party's attorney or other representative concerning the litigation. FRCP 26(b)(3)(B).

   - *Previous statement.* Any party or other person may, on request and without the required showing, obtain the person's own previous statement about the action or its subject matter. If the request is refused, the person may move for a court order, and FRCP 37(a)(5) applies to the award of expenses. A previous statement is either: (i) a written statement that the person has signed or otherwise adopted or approved; or (ii) a contemporaneous stenographic, mechanical, electrical, or other recording—or a transcription of it—that recites substantially verbatim the person's oral statement. FRCP 26(b)(3)(C).

   iv. *Trial preparation; Experts*

   - *Deposition of an expert who may testify.* A party may depose any person who has been identified as an expert whose opinions may be presented at trial. If FRCP 26(a)(2)(B) requires a report from the expert, the deposition may be conducted only after the report is provided. FRCP 26(b)(4)(A).

   - *Trial-preparation protection for draft reports or disclosures.* FRCP 26(b)(3)(A) and FRCP 26(b)(3)(B) protect drafts of any report or disclosure required under FRCP 26(a)(2), regardless of the form in which the draft is recorded. FRCP 26(b)(4)(B).

   - *Trial-preparation protection for communications between a party's attorney and expert witnesses.* FRCP

26(b)(3)(A) and FRCP 26(b)(3)(B) protect communications between the party's attorney and any witness required to provide a report under FRCP 26(a)(2)(B), regardless of the form of the communications, except to the extent that the communications: (i) relate to compensation for the expert's study or testimony; (ii) identify facts or data that the party's attorney provided and that the expert considered in forming the opinions to be expressed; or (iii) identify assumptions that the party's attorney provided and that the expert relied on in forming the opinions to be expressed. FRCP 26(b)(4)(C).

- *Expert employed only for trial preparation.* Ordinarily, a party may not, by interrogatories or deposition, discover facts known or opinions held by an expert who has been retained or specially employed by another party in anticipation of litigation or to prepare for trial and who is not expected to be called as a witness at trial. But a party may do so only: (i) as provided in FRCP 35(b); or (ii) on showing exceptional circumstances under which it is impracticable for the party to obtain facts or opinions on the same subject by other means. FRCP 26(b)(4)(D).

- *Payment.* Unless manifest injustice would result, the court must require that the party seeking discovery: (i) pay the expert a reasonable fee for time spent in responding to discovery under FRCP 26(b)(4)(A) or FRCP 26(b)(4)(D); and (ii) for discovery under FRCP 26(b)(4)(D), also pay the other party a fair portion of the fees and expenses it reasonably incurred in obtaining the expert's facts and opinions. FRCP 26(b)(4)(E).

v. *Claiming privilege or protecting trial-preparation materials*

- *Information withheld.* When a party withholds information otherwise discoverable by claiming that the information is privileged or subject to protection as trial-preparation material, the party must: (i) expressly make the claim; and (ii) describe the nature of the documents, communications, or tangible things not produced or disclosed—and do so in a manner that, without revealing information itself privileged or protected, will enable other parties to assess the claim. FRCP 26(b)(5)(A).

- *Information produced.* If information produced in discovery is subject to a claim of privilege or of protection as trial-preparation material, the party making the claim may notify any party that received the information of the claim and the basis for it. After being notified, a party must promptly return, sequester, or destroy the specified information and any copies it has; must not use or disclose the information until the claim is resolved; must take reasonable steps to retrieve the information if the party disclosed it before being notified; and may promptly present the information to the court under seal for a determination of the claim. The producing party must preserve the information until the claim is resolved. FRCP 26(b)(5)(B).

b. *Protective orders.* A party or any person from whom discovery is sought may move for a protective order in the court where the action is pending—or as an alternative on matters relating to a deposition, in the court for the district where the deposition will be taken. FRCP 26(c)(1). Refer to the United States District Court for the District of Maine KeyRules Motion for Protective Order document for more information.

i. *DISTRICT OF MAINE: Confidentiality order.* A party by motion or with the agreement of all parties may submit to the court a proposed order governing the production and use of confidential documents and information in the pending action. The proposed order shall conform to the Form Confidentiality Order set forth in ME R USDCT App. 2. Any proposed modification to the Form Confidentiality Order shall be identified with a short statement of the reason for each modification. ME R USDCT Rule 26(d).

c. *Sequence of discovery.* Unless the parties stipulate or the court orders otherwise for the parties' and witnesses' convenience and in the interests of justice: (A) methods of discovery may be used in any sequence; and (B) discovery by one party does not require any other party to delay its discovery. FRCP 26(d)(3).

2. *Interrogatories*

a. *Scope.* An interrogatory may relate to any matter that may be inquired into under FRCP 26(b). An interrogatory is not objectionable merely because it asks for an opinion or contention that relates to fact or the application of law to fact, but the court may order that the interrogatory need not be answered until designated discovery is complete, or until a pretrial conference or some other time. FRCP 33(a)(2).

b. *Parties subject to interrogatories.* Depositions may be taken of any person but interrogatories are limited to parties to the litigation. FPP § 2171. Interrogatories may not be directed to the attorney for a party. They must be addressed to the party, who is then required to give all information known to it or its attorney. FPP § 2171; Hickman v. Taylor, 329 U.S. 495, 504, 67 S. Ct. 385, 390, 91 L. Ed. 451 (1947). For more information, refer to FPP § 2171.

c. *Number.* Unless otherwise stipulated or ordered by the court, a party may serve on any other party no more than twenty-five (25) written interrogatories, including all discrete subparts. Leave to serve additional interrogatories may be granted to the extent consistent with FRCP 26(b)(1) and FRCP 26(b)(2). FRCP 33(a)(1).

d. *Form*. Ideally an interrogatory should be a single direct question phrased in a fashion that will inform the other party what is requested. In fact the courts have given parties considerable latitude in framing interrogatories. Rather general language has been permitted so long as the interrogatory gives the other party a reasonably clear indication of the information to be included in its answer. FPP § 2168.

   i. *Use of definitions*. There is no prohibition against the use of definitions in interrogatories, and definitions may be helpful in clarifying the meaning of obscure terms or avoiding repetitions in a long set of interrogatories. FPP § 2168.

   ii. *Use of standardized form interrogatories*. There have been mixed reactions to the use of standardized form interrogatories. They have been referred to opprobriously as "canned sets of interrogatories of the shotgun variety" and it has been said that their indiscriminate use is an "undesirable practice." FPP § 2168.

e. *Motion to compel*. The party submitting the interrogatories must attempt to confer with the responding party in an effort to secure the information without court action and, if that fails, move for an order under FRCP 37(a) compelling answers. FPP § 2182. Refer to the United States District Court for the District of Maine KeyRules Motion to Compel Discovery document for more information.

3. *Sanctions for failure to cooperate in discovery*. The court where the action is pending may, on motion, order sanctions if a party, after being properly served with interrogatories under FRCP 33 or a request for inspection under FRCP 34, fails to serve its answers, objections, or written response. FRCP 37(d)(1)(A)(ii). If a motion to compel is granted, the court must, after giving an opportunity to be heard, require the party or deponent whose conduct necessitated the motion, the party or attorney advising that conduct, or both to pay the movant's reasonable expenses incurred in making the motion, including attorney's fees. But the court must not order this payment if the opposing party's nondisclosure, response, or objection was substantially justified. FRCP 37(a)(5)(A)(ii). Refer to the United States District Court for the District of Maine KeyRules Motion for Discovery Sanctions document for more information.

4. *Stipulations about discovery procedure*. Unless the court orders otherwise, the parties may stipulate that: (a) a deposition may be taken before any person, at any time or place, on any notice, and in the manner specified—in which event it may be used in the same way as any other deposition; and (b) other procedures governing or limiting discovery be modified—but a stipulation extending the time for any form of discovery must have court approval if it would interfere with the time set for completing discovery, for hearing a motion, or for trial. FRCP 29.

5. *DISTRICT OF MAINE: Appearances*. An attorney's signature to a pleading shall constitute an appearance for the party filing the pleading. Otherwise, an attorney who wishes to participate in any manner in any action must file a formal written appearance identifying the party represented. An appearance whether by pleading or formal written appearance shall be signed by an attorney in his/her individual name and shall state his/her office address. ME R USDCT Rule 83.2(a). For more information, refer to ME R USDCT Rule 83.2.

6. *DISTRICT OF MAINE: Alternative dispute resolution (ADR)*. Litigants are authorized and encouraged to employ, at their own expense, any available ADR process on which they can agree, including early neutral evaluation, settlement conferences, mediation, non-binding summary jury trial, corporate mini-trial, and arbitration proceedings. ME R USDCT Rule 83.11(a). For more information on ADR, refer to ME R USDCT Rule 83.11.

D. Documents

1. *Required documents*

   a. *Interrogatories*. Refer to the "C. General Requirements" section of this KeyRules document for information on interrogatories.

2. *Supplemental documents*

   a. *Certificate of service*. No certificate of service is required when a paper is served by filing it with the court's electronic-filing system. When a paper that is required to be served is served by other means: (i) if the paper is filed, a certificate of service must be filed with it or within a reasonable time after service; and (ii) if the paper is not filed, a certificate of service need not be filed unless filing is required by court order or by local rule. FRCP 5(d)(1)(B).

E. Format

1. *Form of documents*. The rules governing captions and other matters of form in pleadings apply to motions and other papers. FRCP 7(b)(2).

   a. *DISTRICT OF MAINE: Font size, line spacing, and paper size*. All such documents shall be typed in a font of no less than size twelve (12) point, and shall be double-spaced or printed on eight and one-half by eleven (8-1/2 x 11) inch paper. Footnotes shall be in a font of no less than size ten (10) point, and may be single spaced. ME R USDCT Rule 10.

b. *Caption.* Every pleading must have a caption with the court's name, a title, a file number, and an FRCP 7(a) designation. FRCP 10(a).

    i. *Names of parties.* The title of the complaint must name all the parties; the title of other pleadings, after naming the first party on each side, may refer generally to other parties. FRCP 10(a).

    ii. *DISTRICT OF MAINE: Additional caption requirements.* All pleadings, motions and other papers filed with the clerk or otherwise submitted to the court, except exhibits, shall bear the proper case number and shall contain on the first page a caption as described by FRCP 10(a) and immediately thereunder a designation of what the document is and the name of the party in whose behalf it is submitted. ME R USDCT Rule 10.

c. *Claims or defenses*

    i. *Numbered paragraphs.* A party must state its claims or defenses in numbered paragraphs, each limited as far as practicable to a single set of circumstances. A later pleading may refer by number to a paragraph in an earlier pleading. FRCP 10(b).

    ii. *Separate statements.* If doing so would promote clarity, each claim founded on a separate transaction or occurrence—and each defense other than a denial—must be stated in a separate count or defense. FRCP 10(b).

d. *Adoption by reference.* A statement in a pleading may be adopted by reference elsewhere in the same pleading or in any other pleading or motion. FRCP 10(c).

    i. *Exhibits.* A copy of a written instrument that is an exhibit to a pleading is a part of the pleading for all purposes. FRCP 10(c).

e. *DISTRICT OF MAINE: Page numbering.* All pages shall be numbered at the bottom. ME R USDCT Rule 10.

f. *DISTRICT OF MAINE: Attachment of ancillary papers.* Ancillary papers shall be attached at the end of the document to which they relate. ME R USDCT Rule 10.

g. *Acceptance by the clerk.* The clerk must not refuse to file a paper solely because it is not in the form prescribed by the Federal Rules of Civil Procedure or by a local rule or practice. FRCP 5(d)(4).

2. *Signing disclosures and discovery requests, responses, and objections.* FRCP 11 does not apply to disclosures and discovery requests, responses, objections, and motions under FRCP 26 through FRCP 37. FRCP 11(d).

a. *Signature required.* Every disclosure under FRCP 26(a)(1) or FRCP 26(a)(3) and every discovery request, response, or objection must be signed by at least one attorney of record in the attorney's own name—or by the party personally, if unrepresented—and must state the signer's address, e-mail address, and telephone number. FRCP 26(g)(1).

b. *Effect of signature.* By signing, an attorney or party certifies that to the best of the person's knowledge, information, and belief formed after a reasonable inquiry: (A) with respect to a disclosure, it is complete and correct as of the time it is made; and (B) with respect to a discovery request, response, or objection, it is: (i) consistent with the Federal Rules of Civil Procedure and warranted by existing law or by a nonfrivolous argument for extending, modifying, or reversing existing law, or for establishing new law; (ii) not interposed for any improper purpose, such as to harass, cause unnecessary delay, or needlessly increase the cost of litigation; and (iii) neither unreasonable nor unduly burdensome or expensive, considering the needs of the case, prior discovery in the case, the amount in controversy, and the importance of the issues at stake in the action. FRCP 26(g)(1).

c. *Failure to sign.* Other parties have no duty to act on an unsigned disclosure, request, response, or objection until it is signed, and the court must strike it unless a signature is promptly supplied after the omission is called to the attorney's or party's attention. FRCP 26(g)(2).

d. *Sanction for improper certification.* If a certification violates FRCP 26(g) without substantial justification, the court, on motion or on its own, must impose an appropriate sanction on the signer, the party on whose behalf the signer was acting, or both. The sanction may include an order to pay the reasonable expenses, including attorney's fees, caused by the violation. FRCP 26(g)(3). Refer to the United States District Court for the District of Maine KeyRules Motion for Discovery Sanctions document for more information.

3. *Privacy protection for filings made with the court*

a. *Redacted filings.* Unless the court orders otherwise, in an electronic or paper filing with the court that contains an individual's Social Security number, taxpayer-identification number, or birth date, the name of an individual known to be a minor, or a financial-account number, a party or nonparty making the filing may include only: (1) the last four (4) digits of the Social Security number and taxpayer-identification number; (2) the year of the individual's birth; (3) the minor's initials; and (4) the last four (4) digits of the financial-account number. FRCP 5.2(a).

    i. *DISTRICT OF MAINE.* To address the privacy concerns created by the Internet access to court papers, unless otherwise ordered by the court, counsel shall modify certain personal data identifiers in pleadings and other papers as follows: (1) minors' names: use of the minors' initials only; (2) Social Security numbers: use of the last four (4) numbers only; (3) dates of birth: use of the year of birth only; [and] (4) financial account numbers: identify the type of account and the financial institution, but use only the last four (4) numbers of the account number. ME R USDCT Redacting Pleadings. Counsel should also use caution when filing papers that contain a person's medical records, employment history; financial information; and any proprietary or trade secret information. ME R USDCT Redacting Pleadings.

b. *Exemptions from the redaction requirement.* The redaction requirement does not apply to the following: (1) a financial-account number that identifies the property allegedly subject to forfeiture in a forfeiture proceeding; (2) the record of an administrative or agency proceeding; (3) the official record of a state-court proceeding; (4) the record of a court or tribunal, if that record was not subject to the redaction requirement when originally filed; (5) a filing covered by FRCP 5.2(c) or FRCP 5.2(d); and (6) a pro se filing in an action brought under 28 U.S.C.A. § 2241, 28 U.S.C.A. § 2254, or 28 U.S.C.A. § 2255. FRCP 5.2(b).

c. *Limitations on remote access to electronic files; Social Security appeals and immigration cases.* Unless the court orders otherwise, in an action for benefits under the Social Security Act, and in an action or proceeding relating to an order of removal, to relief from removal, or to immigration benefits or detention, access to an electronic file is authorized as follows: (1) the parties and their attorneys may have remote electronic access to any part of the case file, including the administrative record; (2) any other person may have electronic access to the full record at the courthouse, but may have remote electronic access only to: (A) the docket maintained by the court; and (B) an opinion, order, judgment, or other disposition of the court, but not any other part of the case file or the administrative record. FRCP 5.2(c).

d. *Filings made under seal.* The court may order that a filing be made under seal without redaction. The court may later unseal the filing or order the person who made the filing to file a redacted version for the public record. FRCP 5.2(d).

   i. *DISTRICT OF MAINE.* For information on filing sealed documents in the District of Maine, refer to ME R USDCT Rule 7A, ME R USDCT App. 4(p)(2), and ME R USDCT Sealed Filings.

e. *Protective orders.* For good cause, the court may by order in a case: (1) require redaction of additional information; or (2) limit or prohibit a nonparty's remote electronic access to a document filed with the court. FRCP 5.2(e).

f. *Option for additional unredacted filing under seal.* A person making a redacted filing may also file an unredacted copy under seal. The court must retain the unredacted copy as part of the record. FRCP 5.2(f).

   i. *DISTRICT OF MAINE.* A party wishing to file a document containing the personal data identifiers specified above may. . .file an unredacted document under seal. This document will be retained by the clerk's office as part of the record. ME R USDCT Redacting Pleadings. The court may, however, still require the party to file a redacted copy for the public file. ME R USDCT Redacting Pleadings.

g. *Option for filing a reference list.* A filing that contains redacted information may be filed together with a reference list that identifies each item of redacted information and specifies an appropriate identifier that uniquely corresponds to each item listed. The list must be filed under seal and may be amended as of right. Any reference in the case to a listed identifier will be construed to refer to the corresponding item of information. FRCP 5.2(g).

   i. *DISTRICT OF MAINE.* A party wishing to file a document containing the personal data identifiers specified above may. . .file a reference list under seal. The reference list shall contain the complete personal data identifier(s) and the redacted identifier(s) used in its (their) place in the filing. All references in the case to the redacted identifiers included in the reference list will be construed to refer to the corresponding complete identifier. The reference list must be filed under seal, and may be amended as of right. It shall be retained by the clerk's office as part of the record. ME R USDCT Redacting Pleadings. The court may, however, still require the party to file a redacted copy for the public file. ME R USDCT Redacting Pleadings.

h. *DISTRICT OF MAINE: Responsibility for redaction.* The clerk is not required to review documents filed with the court for compliance with FRCP 5.2. The responsibility to redact filings rests with counsel and the party or nonparty making the filing. ME R USDCT App. 4(i); ME R USDCT Redacting Pleadings. For guidelines for filing confidential information in civil cases in the District of Maine, refer to ME R USDCT Confidentiality.

i. *Waiver of protection of identifiers.* A person waives the protection of FRCP 5.2(a) as to the person's own information by filing it without redaction and not under seal. FRCP 5.2(h).

F. Filing and Service Requirements

1. *Filing requirements*

   a. *Required filings.* Any paper after the complaint that is required to be served must be filed no later than a reasonable time after service. But disclosures under FRCP 26(a)(1) or FRCP 26(a)(2) and the following discovery requests and responses must not be filed until they are used in the proceeding or the court orders filing: depositions, interrogatories, requests for documents or tangible things or to permit entry onto land, and requests for admission. FRCP 5(d)(1)(A). Refer to the United States District Court for the District of Maine KeyRules pleading and motion documents for information on filing with the court.

    i.   *DISTRICT OF MAINE.* Unless otherwise ordered by the court, depositions upon oral examination and interrogatories, requests for documents, requests for admissions, and answers and responses thereto and disclosures made under FRCP 26(a)(1) through FRCP 26(a)(3) and pursuant to scheduling orders issued by the court, shall be served upon other parties but shall not be filed with the court. ME R USDCT Rule 5(b); ME R USDCT Rule 26(a).

2.   *Service requirements*

    a.   *Service; When required.* Unless the Federal Rules of Civil Procedure provide otherwise, each of the following papers must be served on every party: (A) an order stating that service is required; (B) a pleading filed after the original complaint, unless the court orders otherwise under FRCP 5(c) because there are numerous defendants; (C) a discovery paper required to be served on a party, unless the court orders otherwise; (D) a written motion, except one that may be heard ex parte; and (E) a written notice, appearance, demand, or offer of judgment, or any similar paper. FRCP 5(a)(1).

        i.   *If a party fails to appear.* No service is required on a party who is in default for failing to appear. But a pleading that asserts a new claim for relief against such a party must be served on that party under FRCP 4. FRCP 5(a)(2).

        ii.   *Seizing property.* If an action is begun by seizing property and no person is or need be named as a defendant, any service required before the filing of an appearance, answer, or claim must be made on the person who had custody or possession of the property when it was seized. FRCP 5(a)(3).

    b.   *Service; How made.* A paper is served under FRCP 5 by: (A) handing it to the person; (B) leaving it: (i) at the person's office with a clerk or other person in charge or, if no one is in charge, in a conspicuous place in the office; or (ii) if the person has no office or the office is closed, at the person's dwelling or usual place of abode with someone of suitable age and discretion who resides there; (C) mailing it to the person's last known address—in which event service is complete upon mailing; (D) leaving it with the court clerk if the person has no known address; (E) sending it to a registered user by filing it with the court's electronic-filing system or sending it by other electronic means that the person consented to in writing—in either of which events service is complete upon filing or sending, but is not effective if the filer or sender learns that it did not reach the person to be served; or (F) delivering it by any other means that the person consented to in writing—in which event service is complete when the person making service delivers it to the agency designated to make delivery. FRCP 5(b)(2).

        i.   *Serving an attorney.* If a party is represented by an attorney, service under FRCP 5 must be made on the attorney unless the court orders service on the party. FRCP 5(b)(1).

3.   *DISTRICT OF MAINE: Preservation of original discovery.* The party that has served notice of a deposition or has served discovery papers shall be responsible for preserving and for [ensuring] the integrity of original transcripts and discovery papers for use by the court. ME R USDCT Rule 5(b); ME R USDCT Rule 26(a).

G. Hearings

1.   There is no hearing contemplated in the federal statutes or rules for interrogatories.

H. Forms

1. Federal Interrogatories Forms

    a.   Interrogatories; Short form. 3A FEDFORMS § 24:18.

    b.   Interrogatories; Emphasis on notice. 3A FEDFORMS § 24:19.

    c.   Interrogatories by plaintiff; To corporation. 3A FEDFORMS § 24:20.

    d.   Interrogatories by plaintiff; Complete set. 3A FEDFORMS § 24:21.

    e.   Interrogatories by plaintiff; Requesting identification of documents and production under FRCP 34. 3A FEDFORMS § 24:22.

    f.   Interrogatories by plaintiff; With definition of terms used and instructions for answering. 3A FEDFORMS § 24:23.

    g.   Interrogatories by plaintiff; Employment discrimination case. 3A FEDFORMS § 24:24.

    h.   Interrogatories by defendant. 3A FEDFORMS § 24:25.

i.   Interrogatories by defendant; Complete set; Accident. 3A FEDFORMS § 24:26.

j.   Interrogatories by defendant; Complete set; Railroad. 3A FEDFORMS § 24:27.

k.   Interrogatories by defendant; Complete set; Patent. 3A FEDFORMS § 24:28.

l.   Interrogatories by defendant; Complete set; Automobile accident. 3A FEDFORMS § 24:29.

m.   Interrogatories by defendant; Follow-up interrogatories to plaintiff after lapse of time since first set of interrogatories or deposition. 3A FEDFORMS § 24:30.

n.   Certificate of service of interrogatories. 3A FEDFORMS § 24:32.

o.   Introductory statement; Interrogatories to individual. AMJUR PP DEPOSITION § 405.

p.   Introductory statement; Interrogatories to corporation. AMJUR PP DEPOSITION § 406.

q.   Interrogatories; Outline form. FEDPROF § 23:343.

r.   Interrogatories; To defendant; Trademark action. FEDPROF § 23:355.

s.   Interrogatories; With request for documents; To defendant; Collection of royalties. FEDPROF § 23:356.

t.   Interrogatories; To defendant; Copyright infringement. FEDPROF § 23:358.

u.   Interrogatories; To plaintiff; Products liability. FEDPROF § 23:360.

v.   Interrogatories; To plaintiff; Personal injury. FEDPROF § 23:361.

w.   Interrogatories; To defendant; Premises liability. FEDPROF § 23:364.

x.   Interrogatories; To defendant; Medical malpractice. FEDPROF § 23:365.

y.   General forms; Standard interrogatories. GOLDLTGFMS § 26:28.

z.   General forms; Civil cases. GOLDLTGFMS § 26:29.

I. Applicable Rules

1. *Federal rules*

   a.   Serving and filing pleadings and other papers. FRCP 5.

   b.   Privacy protection for filings made with the court. FRCP 5.2.

   c.   Computing and extending time; Time for motion papers. FRCP 6.

   d.   Pleadings allowed; Form of motions and other papers. FRCP 7.

   e.   Form of pleadings. FRCP 10.

   f.   Signing pleadings, motions, and other papers; Representations to the court; Sanctions. FRCP 11.

   g.   Duty to disclose; General provisions governing discovery. FRCP 26.

   h.   Stipulations about discovery procedure. FRCP 29.

   i.   Interrogatories to parties. FRCP 33.

   j.   Failure to make disclosures or to cooperate in discovery; Sanctions. FRCP 37.

2. *Local rules*

   a.   *DISTRICT OF MAINE*

      i.   Service and filing of pleadings and other papers. ME R USDCT Rule 5.

      ii.   Time. ME R USDCT Rule 6.

      iii. Form of pleadings, motions and other papers. ME R USDCT Rule 10.

      iv.   Case management tracks. ME R USDCT Rule 16.1.

      v.   Discovery. ME R USDCT Rule 26.

      vi.   Attorneys; Appearances and withdrawals. ME R USDCT Rule 83.2.

      vii. Alternative dispute resolution (ADR). ME R USDCT Rule 83.11.

      viii. Administrative procedures governing the filing and service by electronic means. ME R USDCT App. 4.

      ix.   Redacting pleadings. ME R USDCT Redacting Pleadings.

Requests, Notices and Applications
Response to Interrogatories

Document Last Updated July 2021

A. Checklist

- (I) ❑ Matters to be considered by requesting party
    - (a) ❑ Required documents
        - (1) ❑ Interrogatories
    - (b) ❑ Supplemental documents
        - (1) ❑ Certificate of service
    - (c) ❑ Timing
        - (1) ❑ A party may not seek discovery from any source before the parties have conferred as required by FRCP 26(f), except in a proceeding exempted from initial disclosure under FRCP 26(a)(1)(B), or when authorized by the Federal Rules of Civil Procedure, by stipulation, or by court order
- (II) ❑ Matters to be considered by responding party
    - (a) ❑ Required documents
        - (1) ❑ Response to interrogatories
    - (b) ❑ Supplemental documents
        - (1) ❑ Certificate of service
    - (c) ❑ Timing
        - (1) ❑ The responding party must serve its answers and any objections within thirty (30) days after being served with the interrogatories

B. Timing

1. *Response to interrogatories.* The responding party must serve its answers and any objections within thirty (30) days after being served with the interrogatories. A shorter or longer time may be stipulated to under FRCP 29 or be ordered by the court. FRCP 33(b)(2).

2. *DISTRICT OF MAINE: Completion of discovery in standard track cases.* In standard track cases, discovery shall ordinarily be completed within five (5) months. ME R USDCT Rule 16.1(b)(2).

3. *Computation of time*

    a. *Computing time.* FRCP 6 applies in computing any time period specified in the Federal Rules of Civil Procedure, in any local rule or court order, or in any statute that does not specify a method of computing time. FRCP 6(a).

    i. *Period stated in days or a longer unit.* When the period is stated in days or a longer unit of time: (A) exclude the day of the event that triggers the period; (B) count every day, including intermediate Saturdays, Sundays, and legal holidays; and (C) include the last day of the period, but if the last day is a Saturday, Sunday, or legal holiday, the period continues to run until the end of the next day that is not a Saturday, Sunday, or legal holiday. FRCP 6(a)(1).

    ii. *Period stated in hours.* When the period is stated in hours: (A) begin counting immediately on the occurrence of the event that triggers the period; (B) count every hour, including hours during intermediate Saturdays, Sundays, and legal holidays; and (C) if the period would end on a Saturday, Sunday, or legal holiday, the period continues to run until the same time on the next day that is not a Saturday, Sunday, or legal holiday. FRCP 6(a)(2).

    iii. *Inaccessibility of the clerk's office.* Unless the court orders otherwise, if the clerk's office is inaccessible: (A) on the last day for filing under FRCP 6(a)(1), then the time for filing is extended to the first accessible day that is not a Saturday, Sunday, or legal holiday; or (B) during the last hour for filing under FRCP 6(a)(2), then the time for filing is extended to the same time on the first accessible day that is not a Saturday, Sunday, or legal holiday. FRCP 6(a)(3).

    iv. *"Last day" defined.* Unless a different time is set by a statute, local rule, or court order, the last day ends: (A) for electronic filing, at midnight in the court's time zone; and (B) for filing by other means, when the clerk's office is scheduled to close. FRCP 6(a)(4).

v. *"Next day" defined.* The "next day" is determined by continuing to count forward when the period is measured after an event and backward when measured before an event. FRCP 6(a)(5).

vi. *"Legal holiday" defined.* "Legal holiday" means: (A) the day set aside by statute for observing New Year's Day, Martin Luther King Jr.'s Birthday, Washington's Birthday, Memorial Day, Independence Day, Labor Day, Columbus Day, Veterans' Day, Thanksgiving Day, or Christmas Day; (B) any day declared a holiday by the President or Congress; and (C) for periods that are measured after an event, any other day declared a holiday by the state where the district court is located. FRCP 6(a)(6).

vii. *DISTRICT OF MAINE: Applicability of FRCP 6.* FRCP 6 applies when computing any period of time stated in the Local Rules of the United States District Court for the District of Maine. ME R USDCT Rule 6(a).

b. *Extending time.* When an act may or must be done within a specified time, the court may, for good cause, extend the time: (A) with or without motion or notice if the court acts, or if a request is made, before the original time or its extension expires; or (B) on motion made after the time has expired if the party failed to act because of excusable neglect. FRCP 6(b)(1). A court must not extend the time to act under FRCP 50(b), FRCP 50(d), FRCP 52(b), FRCP 59(b), FRCP 59(d), FRCP 59(e), and FRCP 60(b). FRCP 6(b)(2). Refer to the United States District Court for the District of Maine KeyRules Motion for Continuance/Extension of Time document for more information on extending time.

c. *Additional time after certain kinds of service.* When a party may or must act within a specified time after being served and service is made under FRCP 5(b)(2)(C) (by mail), FRCP 5(b)(2)(D) (by leaving with the clerk), or FRCP 5(b)(2)(F) (by other means consented to), three (3) days are added after the period would otherwise expire under FRCP 6(a). FRCP 6(d).

C. General Requirements

1. *General provisions governing discovery*

   a. *Discovery scope and limits*

      i. *Scope in general.* Unless otherwise limited by court order, the scope of discovery is as follows: Parties may obtain discovery regarding any nonprivileged matter that is relevant to any party's claim or defense and proportional to the needs of the case, considering the importance of the issues at stake in the action, the amount in controversy, the parties' relative access to relevant information, the parties' resources, the importance of the discovery in resolving the issues, and whether the burden or expense of the proposed discovery outweighs its likely benefit. Information within this scope of discovery need not be admissible in evidence to be discoverable. FRCP 26(b)(1).

      ii. *Limitations on frequency and extent*

         • *When permitted.* By order, the court may alter the limits in the Federal Rules of Civil Procedure on the number of depositions and interrogatories or on the length of depositions under FRCP 30. By order or local rule, the court may also limit the number of requests under FRCP 36. FRCP 26(b)(2)(A).

         • *Specific limitations on electronically stored information.* A party need not provide discovery of electronically stored information from sources that the party identifies as not reasonably accessible because of undue burden or cost. On motion to compel discovery or for a protective order, the party from whom discovery is sought must show that the information is not reasonably accessible because of undue burden or cost. If that showing is made, the court may nonetheless order discovery from such sources if the requesting party shows good cause, considering the limitations of FRCP 26(b)(2)(C). The court may specify conditions for the discovery. FRCP 26(b)(2)(B).

         • *When required.* On motion or on its own, the court must limit the frequency or extent of discovery otherwise allowed by the Federal Rules of Civil Procedure or by local rule if it determines that: (i) the discovery sought is unreasonably cumulative or duplicative, or can be obtained from some other source that is more convenient, less burdensome, or less expensive; (ii) the party seeking discovery has had ample opportunity to obtain the information by discovery in the action; or (iii) the proposed discovery is outside the scope permitted by FRCP 26(b)(1). FRCP 26(b)(2)(C).

      iii. *Trial preparation; Materials*

         • *Documents and tangible things.* Ordinarily, a party may not discover documents and tangible things that are prepared in anticipation of litigation or for trial by or for another party or its representative (including the other party's attorney, consultant, surety, indemnitor, insurer, or agent). But, subject to FRCP 26(b)(4), those materials may be discovered if: (i) they are otherwise discoverable under FRCP 26(b)(1); and (ii) the party shows that it has substantial need for the materials to prepare its case and cannot, without undue hardship, obtain their substantial equivalent by other means. FRCP 26(b)(3)(A).

- *Protection against disclosure.* If the court orders discovery of those materials, it must protect against disclosure of the mental impressions, conclusions, opinions, or legal theories of a party's attorney or other representative concerning the litigation. FRCP 26(b)(3)(B).

- *Previous statement.* Any party or other person may, on request and without the required showing, obtain the person's own previous statement about the action or its subject matter. If the request is refused, the person may move for a court order, and FRCP 37(a)(5) applies to the award of expenses. A previous statement is either: (i) a written statement that the person has signed or otherwise adopted or approved; or (ii) a contemporaneous stenographic, mechanical, electrical, or other recording—or a transcription of it—that recites substantially verbatim the person's oral statement. FRCP 26(b)(3)(C).

iv. *Trial preparation; Experts*

- *Deposition of an expert who may testify.* A party may depose any person who has been identified as an expert whose opinions may be presented at trial. If FRCP 26(a)(2)(B) requires a report from the expert, the deposition may be conducted only after the report is provided. FRCP 26(b)(4)(A).

- *Trial-preparation protection for draft reports or disclosures.* FRCP 26(b)(3)(A) and FRCP 26(b)(3)(B) protect drafts of any report or disclosure required under FRCP 26(a)(2), regardless of the form in which the draft is recorded. FRCP 26(b)(4)(B).

- *Trial-preparation protection for communications between a party's attorney and expert witnesses.* FRCP 26(b)(3)(A) and FRCP 26(b)(3)(B) protect communications between the party's attorney and any witness required to provide a report under FRCP 26(a)(2)(B), regardless of the form of the communications, except to the extent that the communications: (i) relate to compensation for the expert's study or testimony; (ii) identify facts or data that the party's attorney provided and that the expert considered in forming the opinions to be expressed; or (iii) identify assumptions that the party's attorney provided and that the expert relied on in forming the opinions to be expressed. FRCP 26(b)(4)(C).

- *Expert employed only for trial preparation.* Ordinarily, a party may not, by interrogatories or deposition, discover facts known or opinions held by an expert who has been retained or specially employed by another party in anticipation of litigation or to prepare for trial and who is not expected to be called as a witness at trial. But a party may do so only: (i) as provided in FRCP 35(b); or (ii) on showing exceptional circumstances under which it is impracticable for the party to obtain facts or opinions on the same subject by other means. FRCP 26(b)(4)(D).

- *Payment.* Unless manifest injustice would result, the court must require that the party seeking discovery: (i) pay the expert a reasonable fee for time spent in responding to discovery under FRCP 26(b)(4)(A) or FRCP 26(b)(4)(D); and (ii) for discovery under FRCP 26(b)(4)(D), also pay the other party a fair portion of the fees and expenses it reasonably incurred in obtaining the expert's facts and opinions. FRCP 26(b)(4)(E).

v. *Claiming privilege or protecting trial-preparation materials*

- *Information withheld.* When a party withholds information otherwise discoverable by claiming that the information is privileged or subject to protection as trial-preparation material, the party must: (i) expressly make the claim; and (ii) describe the nature of the documents, communications, or tangible things not produced or disclosed—and do so in a manner that, without revealing information itself privileged or protected, will enable other parties to assess the claim. FRCP 26(b)(5)(A).

- *Information produced.* If information produced in discovery is subject to a claim of privilege or of protection as trial-preparation material, the party making the claim may notify any party that received the information of the claim and the basis for it. After being notified, a party must promptly return, sequester, or destroy the specified information and any copies it has; must not use or disclose the information until the claim is resolved; must take reasonable steps to retrieve the information if the party disclosed it before being notified; and may promptly present the information to the court under seal for a determination of the claim. The producing party must preserve the information until the claim is resolved. FRCP 26(b)(5)(B).

b. *Protective orders.* A party or any person from whom discovery is sought may move for a protective order in the court where the action is pending—or as an alternative on matters relating to a deposition, in the court for the district where the deposition will be taken. FRCP 26(c)(1). Refer to the United States District Court for the District of Maine KeyRules Motion for Protective Order document for more information.

i. *DISTRICT OF MAINE: Confidentiality order.* A party by motion or with the agreement of all parties may submit to the court a proposed order governing the production and use of confidential documents and information in the pending action. The proposed order shall conform to the Form Confidentiality Order set forth in ME R USDCT App. 2. Any proposed modification to the Form Confidentiality Order shall be identified with a short statement of the reason for each modification. ME R USDCT Rule 26(d).

c. *Sequence of discovery.* Unless the parties stipulate or the court orders otherwise for the parties' and witnesses' convenience and in the interests of justice: (A) methods of discovery may be used in any sequence; and (B) discovery by one party does not require any other party to delay its discovery. FRCP 26(d)(3).

2. *Response to interrogatories*

   a. *Answers and objections*

      i. *Responding party.* The interrogatories must be answered: (A) by the party to whom they are directed; or (B) if that party is a public or private corporation, a partnership, an association, or a governmental agency, by any officer or agent, who must furnish the information available to the party. FRCP 33(b)(1). It is improper for the party's attorney to answer them, though undoubtedly the common practice is for the attorney to prepare the answers and have the party swear to them. FPP § 2172.

      ii. *DISTRICT OF MAINE: Repeat interrogatory before response.* Answers and objections to interrogatories shall set forth in full, immediately preceding the answer or objection, the interrogatory to which answer or objection is being made. ME R USDCT Rule 33.

      iii. *Answering each interrogatory.* Each interrogatory must, to the extent it is not objected to, be answered separately and fully in writing under oath. FRCP 33(b)(3). It has been said that interrogatories should be answered directly and without evasion in accordance with information that the answering party possesses after due inquiry. FPP § 2177.

      iv. *Objections.* The grounds for objecting to an interrogatory must be stated with specificity. Any ground not stated in a timely objection is waived unless the court, for good cause, excuses the failure. FRCP 33(b)(4).

        • *Grounds for objections.* Interrogatories may be objected to on the ground that they are not within the scope of discovery as defined in FRCP 26(b), either because they seek information not relevant to the subject matter of the action, or information that is privileged, or information that is protected by the work-product rule and for which the requisite showing has not been made, or information of experts that is not discoverable. FPP § 2174. But this does not exhaust the grounds on which objection can be made. FPP § 2174.

      v. *Qualifying answers.* If the party to whom the interrogatory is addressed thinks that there is uncertainty in the meaning of the interrogatory, it may qualify its answer if need be. FPP § 2168.

   b. *Use.* An answer to an interrogatory may be used to the extent allowed by the Federal Rules of Evidence. FRCP 33(c).

   c. *Option to produce business records.* If the answer to an interrogatory may be determined by examining, auditing, compiling, abstracting, or summarizing a party's business records (including electronically stored information), and if the burden of deriving or ascertaining the answer will be substantially the same for either party, the responding party may answer by: (1) specifying the records that must be reviewed, in sufficient detail to enable the interrogating party to locate and identify them as readily as the responding party could; and (2) giving the interrogating party a reasonable opportunity to examine and audit the records and to make copies, compilations, abstracts, or summaries. FRCP 33(d).

3. *Supplementing disclosures and responses.* A party who has made a disclosure under FRCP 26(a)—or who has responded to an interrogatory, request for production, or request for admission—must supplement or correct its disclosure or response: (A) in a timely manner if the party learns that in some material respect the disclosure or response is incomplete or incorrect, and if the additional or corrective information has not otherwise been made known to the other parties during the discovery process or in writing; or (B) as ordered by the court. FRCP 26(e)(1).

4. *Sanctions for failure to cooperate in discovery.* The court where the action is pending may, on motion, order sanctions if a party, after being properly served with interrogatories under FRCP 33 or a request for inspection under FRCP 34, fails to serve its answers, objections, or written response. FRCP 37(d)(1)(A)(ii). If a motion to compel is granted, the court must, after giving an opportunity to be heard, require the party or deponent whose conduct necessitated the motion, the party or attorney advising that conduct, or both to pay the movant's reasonable expenses incurred in making the motion, including attorney's fees. But the court must not order this payment if the opposing party's nondisclosure, response, or objection was substantially justified. FRCP 37(a)(5)(A)(ii). Refer to the United States District Court for the District of Maine KeyRules Motion for Discovery Sanctions document for more information.

5. *Stipulations about discovery procedure.* Unless the court orders otherwise, the parties may stipulate that: (a) a deposition

may be taken before any person, at any time or place, on any notice, and in the manner specified—in which event it may be used in the same way as any other deposition; and (b) other procedures governing or limiting discovery be modified—but a stipulation extending the time for any form of discovery must have court approval if it would interfere with the time set for completing discovery, for hearing a motion, or for trial. FRCP 29.

6. *DISTRICT OF MAINE: Appearances.* An attorney's signature to a pleading shall constitute an appearance for the party filing the pleading. Otherwise, an attorney who wishes to participate in any manner in any action must file a formal written appearance identifying the party represented. An appearance whether by pleading or formal written appearance shall be signed by an attorney in his/her individual name and shall state his/her office address. ME R USDCT Rule 83.2(a). For more information, refer to ME R USDCT Rule 83.2.

7. *DISTRICT OF MAINE: Alternative dispute resolution (ADR).* Litigants are authorized and encouraged to employ, at their own expense, any available ADR process on which they can agree, including early neutral evaluation, settlement conferences, mediation, non-binding summary jury trial, corporate mini-trial, and arbitration proceedings. ME R USDCT Rule 83.11(a). For more information on ADR, refer to ME R USDCT Rule 83.11.

D. Documents

1. *Required documents*

   a. *Response to interrogatories.* Refer to the "C. General Requirements" section of this KeyRules document for information on the response to interrogatories.

2. *Supplemental documents*

   a. *Certificate of service.* No certificate of service is required when a paper is served by filing it with the court's electronic-filing system. When a paper that is required to be served is served by other means: (i) if the paper is filed, a certificate of service must be filed with it or within a reasonable time after service; and (ii) if the paper is not filed, a certificate of service need not be filed unless filing is required by court order or by local rule. FRCP 5(d)(1)(B).

E. Format

1. *Form of documents.* The rules governing captions and other matters of form in pleadings apply to motions and other papers. FRCP 7(b)(2).

   a. *DISTRICT OF MAINE: Font size, line spacing, and paper size.* All such documents shall be typed in a font of no less than size twelve (12) point, and shall be double-spaced or printed on eight and one-half by eleven (8-1/2 x 11) inch paper. Footnotes shall be in a font of no less than size ten (10) point, and may be single spaced. ME R USDCT Rule 10.

   b. *Caption.* Every pleading must have a caption with the court's name, a title, a file number, and an FRCP 7(a) designation. FRCP 10(a).

      i. *Names of parties.* The title of the complaint must name all the parties; the title of other pleadings, after naming the first party on each side, may refer generally to other parties. FRCP 10(a).

      ii. *DISTRICT OF MAINE: Additional caption requirements.* All pleadings, motions and other papers filed with the clerk or otherwise submitted to the court, except exhibits, shall bear the proper case number and shall contain on the first page a caption as described by FRCP 10(a) and immediately thereunder a designation of what the document is and the name of the party in whose behalf it is submitted. ME R USDCT Rule 10.

   c. *Claims or defenses*

      i. *Numbered paragraphs.* A party must state its claims or defenses in numbered paragraphs, each limited as far as practicable to a single set of circumstances. A later pleading may refer by number to a paragraph in an earlier pleading. FRCP 10(b).

      ii. *Separate statements.* If doing so would promote clarity, each claim founded on a separate transaction or occurrence—and each defense other than a denial—must be stated in a separate count or defense. FRCP 10(b).

   d. *Adoption by reference.* A statement in a pleading may be adopted by reference elsewhere in the same pleading or in any other pleading or motion. FRCP 10(c).

      i. *Exhibits.* A copy of a written instrument that is an exhibit to a pleading is a part of the pleading for all purposes. FRCP 10(c).

   e. *DISTRICT OF MAINE: Page numbering.* All pages shall be numbered at the bottom. ME R USDCT Rule 10.

   f. *DISTRICT OF MAINE: Attachment of ancillary papers.* Ancillary papers shall be attached at the end of the document to which they relate. ME R USDCT Rule 10.

g. *Acceptance by the clerk.* The clerk must not refuse to file a paper solely because it is not in the form prescribed by the Federal Rules of Civil Procedure or by a local rule or practice. FRCP 5(d)(4).

2. *Signing disclosures and discovery requests, responses, and objections.* FRCP 11 does not apply to disclosures and discovery requests, responses, objections, and motions under FRCP 26 through FRCP 37. FRCP 11(d).

a. *Signature required.* Every disclosure under FRCP 26(a)(1) or FRCP 26(a)(3) and every discovery request, response, or objection must be signed by at least one attorney of record in the attorney's own name—or by the party personally, if unrepresented—and must state the signer's address, e-mail address, and telephone number. FRCP 26(g)(1).

   i. *Signature on answers or objections.* The person who makes the answers must sign them, and the attorney who objects must sign any objections. FRCP 33(b)(5).

b. *Effect of signature.* By signing, an attorney or party certifies that to the best of the person's knowledge, information, and belief formed after a reasonable inquiry: (A) with respect to a disclosure, it is complete and correct as of the time it is made; and (B) with respect to a discovery request, response, or objection, it is: (i) consistent with the Federal Rules of Civil Procedure and warranted by existing law or by a nonfrivolous argument for extending, modifying, or reversing existing law, or for establishing new law; (ii) not interposed for any improper purpose, such as to harass, cause unnecessary delay, or needlessly increase the cost of litigation; and (iii) neither unreasonable nor unduly burdensome or expensive, considering the needs of the case, prior discovery in the case, the amount in controversy, and the importance of the issues at stake in the action. FRCP 26(g)(1).

c. *Failure to sign.* Other parties have no duty to act on an unsigned disclosure, request, response, or objection until it is signed, and the court must strike it unless a signature is promptly supplied after the omission is called to the attorney's or party's attention. FRCP 26(g)(2).

d. *Sanction for improper certification.* If a certification violates FRCP 26(g) without substantial justification, the court, on motion or on its own, must impose an appropriate sanction on the signer, the party on whose behalf the signer was acting, or both. The sanction may include an order to pay the reasonable expenses, including attorney's fees, caused by the violation. FRCP 26(g)(3). Refer to the United States District Court for the District of Maine KeyRules Motion for Discovery Sanctions document for more information.

3. *Privacy protection for filings made with the court*

a. *Redacted filings.* Unless the court orders otherwise, in an electronic or paper filing with the court that contains an individual's Social Security number, taxpayer-identification number, or birth date, the name of an individual known to be a minor, or a financial-account number, a party or nonparty making the filing may include only: (1) the last four (4) digits of the Social Security number and taxpayer-identification number; (2) the year of the individual's birth; (3) the minor's initials; and (4) the last four (4) digits of the financial-account number. FRCP 5.2(a).

   i. *DISTRICT OF MAINE.* To address the privacy concerns created by the Internet access to court papers, unless otherwise ordered by the court, counsel shall modify certain personal data identifiers in pleadings and other papers as follows: (1) minors' names: use of the minors' initials only; (2) Social Security numbers: use of the last four (4) numbers only; (3) dates of birth: use of the year of birth only; [and] (4) financial account numbers: identify the type of account and the financial institution, but use only the last four (4) numbers of the account number. ME R USDCT Redacting Pleadings. Counsel should also use caution when filing papers that contain a person's medical records, employment history; financial information; and any proprietary or trade secret information. ME R USDCT Redacting Pleadings.

b. *Exemptions from the redaction requirement.* The redaction requirement does not apply to the following: (1) a financial-account number that identifies the property allegedly subject to forfeiture in a forfeiture proceeding; (2) the record of an administrative or agency proceeding; (3) the official record of a state-court proceeding; (4) the record of a court or tribunal, if that record was not subject to the redaction requirement when originally filed; (5) a filing covered by FRCP 5.2(c) or FRCP 5.2(d); and (6) a pro se filing in an action brought under 28 U.S.C.A. § 2241, 28 U.S.C.A. § 2254, or 28 U.S.C.A. § 2255. FRCP 5.2(b).

c. *Limitations on remote access to electronic files; Social Security appeals and immigration cases.* Unless the court orders otherwise, in an action for benefits under the Social Security Act, and in an action or proceeding relating to an order of removal, to relief from removal, or to immigration benefits or detention, access to an electronic file is authorized as follows: (1) the parties and their attorneys may have remote electronic access to any part of the case file, including the administrative record; (2) any other person may have electronic access to the full record at the courthouse, but may have remote electronic access only to: (A) the docket maintained by the court; and (B) an opinion, order, judgment, or other disposition of the court, but not any other part of the case file or the administrative record. FRCP 5.2(c).

d. *Filings made under seal.* The court may order that a filing be made under seal without redaction. The court may later unseal the filing or order the person who made the filing to file a redacted version for the public record. FRCP 5.2(d).

   i. *DISTRICT OF MAINE.* For information on filing sealed documents in the District of Maine, refer to ME R USDCT Rule 7A, ME R USDCT App. 4(p)(2), and ME R USDCT Sealed Filings.

e. *Protective orders.* For good cause, the court may by order in a case: (1) require redaction of additional information; or (2) limit or prohibit a nonparty's remote electronic access to a document filed with the court. FRCP 5.2(e).

f. *Option for additional unredacted filing under seal.* A person making a redacted filing may also file an unredacted copy under seal. The court must retain the unredacted copy as part of the record. FRCP 5.2(f).

   i. *DISTRICT OF MAINE.* A party wishing to file a document containing the personal data identifiers specified above may. . .file an unredacted document under seal. This document will be retained by the clerk's office as part of the record. ME R USDCT Redacting Pleadings. The court may, however, still require the party to file a redacted copy for the public file. ME R USDCT Redacting Pleadings.

g. *Option for filing a reference list.* A filing that contains redacted information may be filed together with a reference list that identifies each item of redacted information and specifies an appropriate identifier that uniquely corresponds to each item listed. The list must be filed under seal and may be amended as of right. Any reference in the case to a listed identifier will be construed to refer to the corresponding item of information. FRCP 5.2(g).

   i. *DISTRICT OF MAINE.* A party wishing to file a document containing the personal data identifiers specified above may. . .file a reference list under seal. The reference list shall contain the complete personal data identifier(s) and the redacted identifier(s) used in its (their) place in the filing. All references in the case to the redacted identifiers included in the reference list will be construed to refer to the corresponding complete identifier. The reference list must be filed under seal, and may be amended as of right. It shall be retained by the clerk's office as part of the record. ME R USDCT Redacting Pleadings. The court may, however, still require the party to file a redacted copy for the public file. ME R USDCT Redacting Pleadings.

h. *DISTRICT OF MAINE: Responsibility for redaction.* The clerk is not required to review documents filed with the court for compliance with FRCP 5.2. The responsibility to redact filings rests with counsel and the party or nonparty making the filing. ME R USDCT App. 4(i); ME R USDCT Redacting Pleadings. For guidelines for filing confidential information in civil cases in the District of Maine, refer to ME R USDCT Confidentiality.

i. *Waiver of protection of identifiers.* A person waives the protection of FRCP 5.2(a) as to the person's own information by filing it without redaction and not under seal. FRCP 5.2(h).

F. Filing and Service Requirements

1. *Filing requirements*

   a. *Required filings.* Any paper after the complaint that is required to be served must be filed no later than a reasonable time after service. But disclosures under FRCP 26(a)(1) or FRCP 26(a)(2) and the following discovery requests and responses must not be filed until they are used in the proceeding or the court orders filing: depositions, interrogatories, requests for documents or tangible things or to permit entry onto land, and requests for admission. FRCP 5(d)(1)(A). Refer to the United States District Court for the District of Maine KeyRules pleading and motion documents for information on filing with the court.

      i. *DISTRICT OF MAINE.* Unless otherwise ordered by the court, depositions upon oral examination and interrogatories, requests for documents, requests for admissions, and answers and responses thereto and disclosures made under FRCP 26(a)(1) through FRCP 26(a)(3) and pursuant to scheduling orders issued by the court, shall be served upon other parties but shall not be filed with the court. ME R USDCT Rule 5(b); ME R USDCT Rule 26(a).

2. *Service requirements*

   a. *Service; When required.* Unless the Federal Rules of Civil Procedure provide otherwise, each of the following papers must be served on every party: (A) an order stating that service is required; (B) a pleading filed after the original complaint, unless the court orders otherwise under FRCP 5(c) because there are numerous defendants; (C) a discovery paper required to be served on a party, unless the court orders otherwise; (D) a written motion, except one that may be heard ex parte; and (E) a written notice, appearance, demand, or offer of judgment, or any similar paper. FRCP 5(a)(1).

      i. *If a party fails to appear.* No service is required on a party who is in default for failing to appear. But a pleading that asserts a new claim for relief against such a party must be served on that party under FRCP 4. FRCP 5(a)(2).

  ii. *Seizing property.* If an action is begun by seizing property and no person is or need be named as a defendant, any service required before the filing of an appearance, answer, or claim must be made on the person who had custody or possession of the property when it was seized. FRCP 5(a)(3).

 b. *Service; How made.* A paper is served under FRCP 5 by: (A) handing it to the person; (B) leaving it: (i) at the person's office with a clerk or other person in charge or, if no one is in charge, in a conspicuous place in the office; or (ii) if the person has no office or the office is closed, at the person's dwelling or usual place of abode with someone of suitable age and discretion who resides there; (C) mailing it to the person's last known address—in which event service is complete upon mailing; (D) leaving it with the court clerk if the person has no known address; (E) sending it to a registered user by filing it with the court's electronic-filing system or sending it by other electronic means that the person consented to in writing—in either of which events service is complete upon filing or sending, but is not effective if the filer or sender learns that it did not reach the person to be served; or (F) delivering it by any other means that the person consented to in writing—in which event service is complete when the person making service delivers it to the agency designated to make delivery. FRCP 5(b)(2).

  i. *Serving an attorney.* If a party is represented by an attorney, service under FRCP 5 must be made on the attorney unless the court orders service on the party. FRCP 5(b)(1).

 3. *DISTRICT OF MAINE: Preservation of original discovery.* The party that has served notice of a deposition or has served discovery papers shall be responsible for preserving and for [ensuring] the integrity of original transcripts and discovery papers for use by the court. ME R USDCT Rule 5(b); ME R USDCT Rule 26(a).

G. Hearings

 1. There is no hearing contemplated in the federal statutes or rules for responses to interrogatories.

H. Forms

1. Federal Response to Interrogatories Forms

 a. Answers to interrogatories. 3A FEDFORMS § 24:34.

 b. Answers to interrogatories; Complete set. 3A FEDFORMS § 24:35.

 c. Amendments to answers to interrogatories. 3A FEDFORMS § 24:36.

 d. Supplemental answer to plaintiff's interrogatories. 3A FEDFORMS § 24:37.

 e. Second supplemental answer to plaintiff's interrogatories. 3A FEDFORMS § 24:38.

 f. Supplementation of response to interrogatory. 3A FEDFORMS § 24:39.

 g. Answers by individual. 3A FEDFORMS § 24:41.

 h. Answers by corporation. 3A FEDFORMS § 24:42.

 i. Declaration; Answers by individual. 3A FEDFORMS § 24:43.

 j. Declaration; Answers by corporation. 3A FEDFORMS § 24:44.

 k. Objections to interrogatories. 3A FEDFORMS § 24:45.

 l. Objections to interrogatories; Defendant's objections. 3A FEDFORMS § 24:46.

 m. Objections to interrogatories; Corporate merger. 3A FEDFORMS § 24:47.

 n. Objections to interrogatories; With answers. 3A FEDFORMS § 24:48.

 o. Statement in answer as to interrogatory to which objection made. 3A FEDFORMS § 24:49.

 p. Introductory statement; Answer to interrogatories. AMJUR PP DEPOSITION § 407.

 q. Answers to interrogatories; Illustrative form. AMJUR PP DEPOSITION § 408.

 r. Response to interrogatories; Illustrative form. AMJUR PP DEPOSITION § 409.

 s. Verification; By defendant; Of answers to interrogatories. AMJUR PP DEPOSITION § 410.

 t. Answers; To interrogatories; Outline form. FEDPROF § 23:352.

 u. Answers; To interrogatories; By two defendants; Outline form. FEDPROF § 23:353.

 v. Objections to interrogatories; Illustrative grounds. FEDPROF § 23:375.

 w. Answer to interrogatories. GOLDLTGFMS § 26:75.

 x. Answer to interrogatories; Pursuant to civil procedure rules. GOLDLTGFMS § 26:76.

y.   Answer to interrogatories; Corporate information as basis for answers. GOLDLTGFMS § 26:77.

z.   Answer to interrogatories; Objecting. GOLDLTGFMS § 26:79.

I. Applicable Rules

1. *Federal rules*

a.   Serving and filing pleadings and other papers. FRCP 5.

b.   Privacy protection for filings made with the court. FRCP 5.2.

c.   Computing and extending time; Time for motion papers. FRCP 6.

d.   Pleadings allowed; Form of motions and other papers. FRCP 7.

e.   Form of pleadings. FRCP 10.

f.   Signing pleadings, motions, and other papers; Representations to the court; Sanctions. FRCP 11.

g.   Duty to disclose; General provisions governing discovery. FRCP 26.

h.   Stipulations about discovery procedure. FRCP 29.

i.   Interrogatories to parties. FRCP 33.

j.   Failure to make disclosures or to cooperate in discovery; Sanctions. FRCP 37.

2. *Local rules*

a.   *DISTRICT OF MAINE*

i.   Service and filing of pleadings and other papers. ME R USDCT Rule 5.

ii.   Time. ME R USDCT Rule 6.

iii.   Form of pleadings, motions and other papers. ME R USDCT Rule 10.

iv.   Case management tracks. ME R USDCT Rule 16.1.

v.   Discovery. ME R USDCT Rule 26.

vi.   Interrogatories. ME R USDCT Rule 33.

vii.   Attorneys; Appearances and withdrawals. ME R USDCT Rule 83.2.

viii.   Alternative dispute resolution (ADR). ME R USDCT Rule 83.11.

ix.   Administrative procedures governing the filing and service by electronic means. ME R USDCT App. 4.

x.   Redacting pleadings. ME R USDCT Redacting Pleadings.

Requests, Notices and Applications
Request for Production of Documents

Document Last Updated July 2021

A. Checklist

(I) ❑ Matters to be considered by requesting party

(a) ❑ Required documents

(1) ❑ Request for production of documents

(b) ❑ Supplemental documents

(1) ❑ Subpoena

(2) ❑ Certificate of service

(c) ❑ Timing

(1) ❑ More than twenty-one (21) days after the summons and complaint are served on a party, a request under FRCP 34 may be delivered: (i) to that party by any other party, and (ii) by that party to any plaintiff or to any other party that has been served

(2) ❑ A party may not seek discovery from any source before the parties have conferred as required by FRCP 26(f),

except in a proceeding exempted from initial disclosure under FRCP 26(a)(1)(B), or when authorized by the Federal Rules of Civil Procedure, by stipulation, or by court order

(II) ❑ Matters to be considered by responding party

    (a) ❑ Required documents

        (1) ❑ Response to request for production of documents

    (b) ❑ Supplemental documents

        (1) ❑ Certificate of service

    (c) ❑ Timing

        (1) ❑ The party to whom the request is directed must respond in writing within thirty (30) days after being served or—if the request was delivered under FRCP 26(d)(2)—within thirty (30) days after the parties' first FRCP 26(f) conference

B. Timing

1. *Request for production of documents.* Generally, a party may not seek discovery from any source before the parties have conferred as required by FRCP 26(f), except in a proceeding exempted from initial disclosure or when authorized by the Federal Rules of Civil Procedure, by stipulation, or by court order. FEDPROC § 26:586. Discovery under FRCP 34 should ordinarily precede the trial, and a court may refuse to permit discovery shortly before the trial date. FEDPROC § 26:586.

    a. *Early FRCP 34 requests*

        i. *Time to deliver.* More than twenty-one (21) days after the summons and complaint are served on a party, a request under FRCP 34 may be delivered: (i) to that party by any other party, and (ii) by that party to any plaintiff or to any other party that has been served. FRCP 26(d)(2)(A).

        ii. *When considered served.* The request is considered to have been served at the first FRCP 26(f) conference. FRCP 26(d)(2)(B).

2. *Commencement of discovery.* A party may not seek discovery from any source before the parties have conferred as required by FRCP 26(f), except in a proceeding exempted from initial disclosure under FRCP 26(a)(1)(B), or when authorized by the Federal Rules of Civil Procedure, by stipulation, or by court order. FRCP 26(d)(1).

3. *DISTRICT OF MAINE: Completion of discovery in standard track cases.* In standard track cases, discovery shall ordinarily be completed within five (5) months. ME R USDCT Rule 16.1(b)(2).

4. *Computation of time*

    a. *Computing time.* FRCP 6 applies in computing any time period specified in the Federal Rules of Civil Procedure, in any local rule or court order, or in any statute that does not specify a method of computing time. FRCP 6(a).

        i. *Period stated in days or a longer unit.* When the period is stated in days or a longer unit of time: (A) exclude the day of the event that triggers the period; (B) count every day, including intermediate Saturdays, Sundays, and legal holidays; and (C) include the last day of the period, but if the last day is a Saturday, Sunday, or legal holiday, the period continues to run until the end of the next day that is not a Saturday, Sunday, or legal holiday. FRCP 6(a)(1).

        ii. *Period stated in hours.* When the period is stated in hours: (A) begin counting immediately on the occurrence of the event that triggers the period; (B) count every hour, including hours during intermediate Saturdays, Sundays, and legal holidays; and (C) if the period would end on a Saturday, Sunday, or legal holiday, the period continues to run until the same time on the next day that is not a Saturday, Sunday, or legal holiday. FRCP 6(a)(2).

        iii. *Inaccessibility of the clerk's office.* Unless the court orders otherwise, if the clerk's office is inaccessible: (A) on the last day for filing under FRCP 6(a)(1), then the time for filing is extended to the first accessible day that is not a Saturday, Sunday, or legal holiday; or (B) during the last hour for filing under FRCP 6(a)(2), then the time for filing is extended to the same time on the first accessible day that is not a Saturday, Sunday, or legal holiday. FRCP 6(a)(3).

        iv. *"Last day" defined.* Unless a different time is set by a statute, local rule, or court order, the last day ends: (A) for electronic filing, at midnight in the court's time zone; and (B) for filing by other means, when the clerk's office is scheduled to close. FRCP 6(a)(4).

        v. *"Next day" defined.* The "next day" is determined by continuing to count forward when the period is measured after an event and backward when measured before an event. FRCP 6(a)(5).

vi. *"Legal holiday" defined.* "Legal holiday" means: (A) the day set aside by statute for observing New Year's Day, Martin Luther King Jr.'s Birthday, Washington's Birthday, Memorial Day, Independence Day, Labor Day, Columbus Day, Veterans' Day, Thanksgiving Day, or Christmas Day; (B) any day declared a holiday by the President or Congress; and (C) for periods that are measured after an event, any other day declared a holiday by the state where the district court is located. FRCP 6(a)(6).

vii. *DISTRICT OF MAINE: Applicability of FRCP 6.* FRCP 6 applies when computing any period of time stated in the Local Rules of the United States District Court for the District of Maine. ME R USDCT Rule 6(a).

b. *Extending time.* When an act may or must be done within a specified time, the court may, for good cause, extend the time: (A) with or without motion or notice if the court acts, or if a request is made, before the original time or its extension expires; or (B) on motion made after the time has expired if the party failed to act because of excusable neglect. FRCP 6(b)(1). A court must not extend the time to act under FRCP 50(b), FRCP 50(d), FRCP 52(b), FRCP 59(b), FRCP 59(d), FRCP 59(e), and FRCP 60(b). FRCP 6(b)(2). Refer to the United States District Court for the District of Maine KeyRules Motion for Continuance/Extension of Time document for more information on extending time.

c. *Additional time after certain kinds of service.* When a party may or must act within a specified time after being served and service is made under FRCP 5(b)(2)(C) (by mail), FRCP 5(b)(2)(D) (by leaving with the clerk), or FRCP 5(b)(2)(F) (by other means consented to), three (3) days are added after the period would otherwise expire under FRCP 6(a). FRCP 6(d).

C. General Requirements

1. *General provisions governing discovery*

a. *Discovery scope and limits*

i. *Scope in general.* Unless otherwise limited by court order, the scope of discovery is as follows: Parties may obtain discovery regarding any nonprivileged matter that is relevant to any party's claim or defense and proportional to the needs of the case, considering the importance of the issues at stake in the action, the amount in controversy, the parties' relative access to relevant information, the parties' resources, the importance of the discovery in resolving the issues, and whether the burden or expense of the proposed discovery outweighs its likely benefit. Information within this scope of discovery need not be admissible in evidence to be discoverable. FRCP 26(b)(1).

ii. *Limitations on frequency and extent*

- *When permitted.* By order, the court may alter the limits in the Federal Rules of Civil Procedure on the number of depositions and interrogatories or on the length of depositions under FRCP 30. By order or local rule, the court may also limit the number of requests under FRCP 36. FRCP 26(b)(2)(A).

- *Specific limitations on electronically stored information.* A party need not provide discovery of electronically stored information from sources that the party identifies as not reasonably accessible because of undue burden or cost. On motion to compel discovery or for a protective order, the party from whom discovery is sought must show that the information is not reasonably accessible because of undue burden or cost. If that showing is made, the court may nonetheless order discovery from such sources if the requesting party shows good cause, considering the limitations of FRCP 26(b)(2)(C). The court may specify conditions for the discovery. FRCP 26(b)(2)(B).

- *When required.* On motion or on its own, the court must limit the frequency or extent of discovery otherwise allowed by the Federal Rules of Civil Procedure or by local rule if it determines that: (i) the discovery sought is unreasonably cumulative or duplicative, or can be obtained from some other source that is more convenient, less burdensome, or less expensive; (ii) the party seeking discovery has had ample opportunity to obtain the information by discovery in the action; or (iii) the proposed discovery is outside the scope permitted by FRCP 26(b)(1). FRCP 26(b)(2)(C).

iii. *Trial preparation; Materials*

- *Documents and tangible things.* Ordinarily, a party may not discover documents and tangible things that are prepared in anticipation of litigation or for trial by or for another party or its representative (including the other party's attorney, consultant, surety, indemnitor, insurer, or agent). But, subject to FRCP 26(b)(4), those materials may be discovered if: (i) they are otherwise discoverable under FRCP 26(b)(1); and (ii) the party shows that it has substantial need for the materials to prepare its case and cannot, without undue hardship, obtain their substantial equivalent by other means. FRCP 26(b)(3)(A).

- *Protection against disclosure.* If the court orders discovery of those materials, it must protect against disclosure of the mental impressions, conclusions, opinions, or legal theories of a party's attorney or other representative concerning the litigation. FRCP 26(b)(3)(B).

- *Previous statement.* Any party or other person may, on request and without the required showing, obtain the person's own previous statement about the action or its subject matter. If the request is refused, the person may move for a court order, and FRCP 37(a)(5) applies to the award of expenses. A previous statement is either: (i) a written statement that the person has signed or otherwise adopted or approved; or (ii) a contemporaneous stenographic, mechanical, electrical, or other recording—or a transcription of it—that recites substantially verbatim the person's oral statement. FRCP 26(b)(3)(C).

iv. *Trial preparation; Experts*

- *Deposition of an expert who may testify.* A party may depose any person who has been identified as an expert whose opinions may be presented at trial. If FRCP 26(a)(2)(B) requires a report from the expert, the deposition may be conducted only after the report is provided. FRCP 26(b)(4)(A).

- *Trial-preparation protection for draft reports or disclosures.* FRCP 26(b)(3)(A) and FRCP 26(b)(3)(B) protect drafts of any report or disclosure required under FRCP 26(a)(2), regardless of the form in which the draft is recorded. FRCP 26(b)(4)(B).

- *Trial-preparation protection for communications between a party's attorney and expert witnesses.* FRCP 26(b)(3)(A) and FRCP 26(b)(3)(B) protect communications between the party's attorney and any witness required to provide a report under FRCP 26(a)(2)(B), regardless of the form of the communications, except to the extent that the communications: (i) relate to compensation for the expert's study or testimony; (ii) identify facts or data that the party's attorney provided and that the expert considered in forming the opinions to be expressed; or (iii) identify assumptions that the party's attorney provided and that the expert relied on in forming the opinions to be expressed. FRCP 26(b)(4)(C).

- *Expert employed only for trial preparation.* Ordinarily, a party may not, by interrogatories or deposition, discover facts known or opinions held by an expert who has been retained or specially employed by another party in anticipation of litigation or to prepare for trial and who is not expected to be called as a witness at trial. But a party may do so only: (i) as provided in FRCP 35(b); or (ii) on showing exceptional circumstances under which it is impracticable for the party to obtain facts or opinions on the same subject by other means. FRCP 26(b)(4)(D).

- *Payment.* Unless manifest injustice would result, the court must require that the party seeking discovery: (i) pay the expert a reasonable fee for time spent in responding to discovery under FRCP 26(b)(4)(A) or FRCP 26(b)(4)(D); and (ii) for discovery under FRCP 26(b)(4)(D), also pay the other party a fair portion of the fees and expenses it reasonably incurred in obtaining the expert's facts and opinions. FRCP 26(b)(4)(E).

v. *Claiming privilege or protecting trial-preparation materials*

- *Information withheld.* When a party withholds information otherwise discoverable by claiming that the information is privileged or subject to protection as trial-preparation material, the party must: (i) expressly make the claim; and (ii) describe the nature of the documents, communications, or tangible things not produced or disclosed—and do so in a manner that, without revealing information itself privileged or protected, will enable other parties to assess the claim. FRCP 26(b)(5)(A).

- *Information produced.* If information produced in discovery is subject to a claim of privilege or of protection as trial-preparation material, the party making the claim may notify any party that received the information of the claim and the basis for it. After being notified, a party must promptly return, sequester, or destroy the specified information and any copies it has; must not use or disclose the information until the claim is resolved; must take reasonable steps to retrieve the information if the party disclosed it before being notified; and may promptly present the information to the court under seal for a determination of the claim. The producing party must preserve the information until the claim is resolved. FRCP 26(b)(5)(B).

b. *Protective orders.* A party or any person from whom discovery is sought may move for a protective order in the court where the action is pending—or as an alternative on matters relating to a deposition, in the court for the district where the deposition will be taken. FRCP 26(c)(1). Refer to the United States District Court for the District of Maine KeyRules Motion for Protective Order document for more information.

i. *DISTRICT OF MAINE: Confidentiality order.* A party by motion or with the agreement of all parties may submit to the court a proposed order governing the production and use of confidential documents and information in the pending action. The proposed order shall conform to the Form Confidentiality Order set forth in ME R USDCT App. 2. Any proposed modification to the Form Confidentiality Order shall be identified with a short statement of the reason for each modification. ME R USDCT Rule 26(d).

c. *Sequence of discovery.* Unless the parties stipulate or the court orders otherwise for the parties' and witnesses' convenience and in the interests of justice: (A) methods of discovery may be used in any sequence; and (B) discovery by one party does not require any other party to delay its discovery. FRCP 26(d)(3).

2. *Request for production of documents*

a. *Scope.* A party may serve on any other party a request within the scope of FRCP 26(b): (1) to produce and permit the requesting party or its representative to inspect, copy, test, or sample the following items in the responding party's possession, custody, or control: (A) any designated documents or electronically stored information—including writings, drawings, graphs, charts, photographs, sound recordings, images, and other data or data compilations—stored in any medium from which information can be obtained either directly or, if necessary, after translation by the responding party into a reasonably usable form; or (B) any designated tangible things; or (2) to permit entry onto designated land or other property possessed or controlled by the responding party, so that the requesting party may inspect, measure, survey, photograph, test, or sample the property or any designated object or operation on it. FRCP 34(a).

b. *Contents of the request.* The request: (A) must describe with reasonable particularity each item or category of items to be inspected; (B) must specify a reasonable time, place, and manner for the inspection and for performing the related acts; and (C) may specify the form or forms in which electronically stored information is to be produced. FRCP 34(b)(1).

   i. *Description of items.* Although the phrase "reasonable particularity" eludes precise definition and depends on the facts and circumstances in each case, at least two tests have been suggested. The first test is whether the request places a party on "reasonable notice" of what is called for and what is not so that a reasonable person would know what documents or things are called for. The second is whether the request gives a court enough information to enable it to rule intelligently on objections. The reasonable-particularity requirement may be adjusted depending on the stage of discovery and how much specificity can be expected at that point. FEDPROC § 26:588.

c. *Other authority on production and inspection*

   i. *Freedom of Information Act (FOIA).* Although the Freedom of Information Act (FOIA) is fundamentally designed to inform the public about agency action, and not to benefit private litigants, Congress has not acted upon proposals to forbid or limit the use of the FOIA for discovery purposes. FEDPROC § 26:559; Nat'l Presto Indus., Inc., 218 Ct. Cl. 696 (1978). However, a FOIA request may not be used to supplement civil discovery under FRCP 34, as in the case where information is privileged and therefore outside the scope of civil discovery. FEDPROC § 26:559; United States v. Weber Aircraft Corp., 465 U.S. 792, 104 S. Ct. 1488, 79 L. Ed. 2d 814 (1984).

   ii. *Hague Convention.* Under the Hague Convention, a party seeking evidence abroad must obtain and send a letter of request to the central authority of the country in which the evidence is sought, requesting service of the request on the desired person or entity; if the request complies with the Convention, the central authority will then obtain the desired evidence. FEDPROC § 26:560. [Editor's note: the Hague Convention can be found at T.I.A.S. No. 6638 and is also available in the appendix to FRCP 4].

d. *Motion to compel.* If a party who has been requested to permit discovery under FRCP 34 makes no response to the request, or if its response objects to all or part of the requested discovery, or if it otherwise fails to permit discovery as requested, the party who submitted the request, if it still wishes the discovery that has been refused, may move under FRCP 37(a) for an order compelling inspection in accordance with the request. FPP § 2214. Refer to the United States District Court for the District of Maine KeyRules Motion to Compel Discovery document for more information.

3. *Sanctions for failure to cooperate in discovery.* The court where the action is pending may, on motion, order sanctions if a party, after being properly served with interrogatories under FRCP 33 or a request for inspection under FRCP 34, fails to serve its answers, objections, or written response. FRCP 37(d)(1)(A)(ii). If a motion to compel is granted, the court must, after giving an opportunity to be heard, require the party or deponent whose conduct necessitated the motion, the party or attorney advising that conduct, or both to pay the movant's reasonable expenses incurred in making the motion, including attorney's fees. But the court must not order this payment if the opposing party's nondisclosure, response, or objection was substantially justified. FRCP 37(a)(5)(A)(ii). Refer to the United States District Court for the District of Maine KeyRules Motion for Discovery Sanctions document for more information.

4. *Stipulations about discovery procedure.* Unless the court orders otherwise, the parties may stipulate that: (a) a deposition may be taken before any person, at any time or place, on any notice, and in the manner specified—in which event it may be used in the same way as any other deposition; and (b) other procedures governing or limiting discovery be modified—but a stipulation extending the time for any form of discovery must have court approval if it would interfere with the time set for completing discovery, for hearing a motion, or for trial. FRCP 29.

5. *DISTRICT OF MAINE: Appearances.* An attorney's signature to a pleading shall constitute an appearance for the party filing the pleading. Otherwise, an attorney who wishes to participate in any manner in any action must file a formal written appearance identifying the party represented. An appearance whether by pleading or formal written appearance shall be signed by an attorney in his/her individual name and shall state his/her office address. ME R USDCT Rule 83.2(a). For more information, refer to ME R USDCT Rule 83.2.

6. *DISTRICT OF MAINE: Alternative dispute resolution (ADR).* Litigants are authorized and encouraged to employ, at their own expense, any available ADR process on which they can agree, including early neutral evaluation, settlement conferences, mediation, non-binding summary jury trial, corporate mini-trial, and arbitration proceedings. ME R USDCT Rule 83.11(a). For more information on ADR, refer to ME R USDCT Rule 83.11.

D. Documents

1. *Required documents*

   a. *Request for production of documents.* Refer to the "C. General Requirements" section of this KeyRules document for information on the request for production of documents.

2. *Supplemental documents*

   a. *Subpoena.* As provided in FRCP 45, a nonparty may be compelled to produce documents and tangible things or to permit an inspection. FRCP 34(c). For information on the form and contents of the subpoena, refer to FRCP 45.

   b. *Certificate of service.* No certificate of service is required when a paper is served by filing it with the court's electronic-filing system. When a paper that is required to be served is served by other means: (i) if the paper is filed, a certificate of service must be filed with it or within a reasonable time after service; and (ii) if the paper is not filed, a certificate of service need not be filed unless filing is required by court order or by local rule. FRCP 5(d)(1)(B).

E. Format

1. *Form of documents.* The rules governing captions and other matters of form in pleadings apply to motions and other papers. FRCP 7(b)(2).

   a. *DISTRICT OF MAINE: Font size, line spacing, and paper size.* All such documents shall be typed in a font of no less than size twelve (12) point, and shall be double-spaced or printed on eight and one-half by eleven (8-1/2 x 11) inch paper. Footnotes shall be in a font of no less than size ten (10) point, and may be single spaced. ME R USDCT Rule 10.

   b. *Caption.* Every pleading must have a caption with the court's name, a title, a file number, and an FRCP 7(a) designation. FRCP 10(a).

      i. *Names of parties.* The title of the complaint must name all the parties; the title of other pleadings, after naming the first party on each side, may refer generally to other parties. FRCP 10(a).

      ii. *DISTRICT OF MAINE: Additional caption requirements.* All pleadings, motions and other papers filed with the clerk or otherwise submitted to the court, except exhibits, shall bear the proper case number and shall contain on the first page a caption as described by FRCP 10(a) and immediately thereunder a designation of what the document is and the name of the party in whose behalf it is submitted. ME R USDCT Rule 10.

   c. *Claims or defenses*

      i. *Numbered paragraphs.* A party must state its claims or defenses in numbered paragraphs, each limited as far as practicable to a single set of circumstances. A later pleading may refer by number to a paragraph in an earlier pleading. FRCP 10(b).

      ii. *Separate statements.* If doing so would promote clarity, each claim founded on a separate transaction or occurrence—and each defense other than a denial—must be stated in a separate count or defense. FRCP 10(b).

   d. *Adoption by reference.* A statement in a pleading may be adopted by reference elsewhere in the same pleading or in any other pleading or motion. FRCP 10(c).

      i. *Exhibits.* A copy of a written instrument that is an exhibit to a pleading is a part of the pleading for all purposes. FRCP 10(c).

e. *DISTRICT OF MAINE: Page numbering.* All pages shall be numbered at the bottom. ME R USDCT Rule 10.

f. *DISTRICT OF MAINE: Attachment of ancillary papers.* Ancillary papers shall be attached at the end of the document to which they relate. ME R USDCT Rule 10.

g. *Acceptance by the clerk.* The clerk must not refuse to file a paper solely because it is not in the form prescribed by the Federal Rules of Civil Procedure or by a local rule or practice. FRCP 5(d)(4).

2. *Signing disclosures and discovery requests, responses, and objections.* FRCP 11 does not apply to disclosures and discovery requests, responses, objections, and motions under FRCP 26 through FRCP 37. FRCP 11(d).

   a. *Signature required.* Every disclosure under FRCP 26(a)(1) or FRCP 26(a)(3) and every discovery request, response, or objection must be signed by at least one attorney of record in the attorney's own name—or by the party personally, if unrepresented—and must state the signer's address, e-mail address, and telephone number. FRCP 26(g)(1).

      i. *Signature on request.* Though FRCP 34 does not say so, it is sufficient if the request is signed by the attorney for the party seeking discovery. FPP § 2212.

   b. *Effect of signature.* By signing, an attorney or party certifies that to the best of the person's knowledge, information, and belief formed after a reasonable inquiry: (A) with respect to a disclosure, it is complete and correct as of the time it is made; and (B) with respect to a discovery request, response, or objection, it is: (i) consistent with the Federal Rules of Civil Procedure and warranted by existing law or by a nonfrivolous argument for extending, modifying, or reversing existing law, or for establishing new law; (ii) not interposed for any improper purpose, such as to harass, cause unnecessary delay, or needlessly increase the cost of litigation; and (iii) neither unreasonable nor unduly burdensome or expensive, considering the needs of the case, prior discovery in the case, the amount in controversy, and the importance of the issues at stake in the action. FRCP 26(g)(1).

   c. *Failure to sign.* Other parties have no duty to act on an unsigned disclosure, request, response, or objection until it is signed, and the court must strike it unless a signature is promptly supplied after the omission is called to the attorney's or party's attention. FRCP 26(g)(2).

   d. *Sanction for improper certification.* If a certification violates FRCP 26(g) without substantial justification, the court, on motion or on its own, must impose an appropriate sanction on the signer, the party on whose behalf the signer was acting, or both. The sanction may include an order to pay the reasonable expenses, including attorney's fees, caused by the violation. FRCP 26(g)(3). Refer to the United States District Court for the District of Maine KeyRules Motion for Discovery Sanctions document for more information.

3. *Privacy protection for filings made with the court*

   a. *Redacted filings.* Unless the court orders otherwise, in an electronic or paper filing with the court that contains an individual's Social Security number, taxpayer-identification number, or birth date, the name of an individual known to be a minor, or a financial-account number, a party or nonparty making the filing may include only: (1) the last four (4) digits of the Social Security number and taxpayer-identification number; (2) the year of the individual's birth; (3) the minor's initials; and (4) the last four (4) digits of the financial-account number. FRCP 5.2(a).

      i. *DISTRICT OF MAINE.* To address the privacy concerns created by the Internet access to court papers, unless otherwise ordered by the court, counsel shall modify certain personal data identifiers in pleadings and other papers as follows: (1) minors' names: use of the minors' initials only; (2) Social Security numbers: use of the last four (4) numbers only; (3) dates of birth: use of the year of birth only; [and] (4) financial account numbers: identify the type of account and the financial institution, but use only the last four (4) numbers of the account number. ME R USDCT Redacting Pleadings. Counsel should also use caution when filing papers that contain a person's medical records, employment history, financial information, and any proprietary or trade secret information. ME R USDCT Redacting Pleadings.

   b. *Exemptions from the redaction requirement.* The redaction requirement does not apply to the following: (1) a financial-account number that identifies the property allegedly subject to forfeiture in a forfeiture proceeding; (2) the record of an administrative or agency proceeding; (3) the official record of a state-court proceeding; (4) the record of a court or tribunal, if that record was not subject to the redaction requirement when originally filed; (5) a filing covered by FRCP 5.2(c) or FRCP 5.2(d); and (6) a pro se filing in an action brought under 28 U.S.C.A. § 2241, 28 U.S.C.A. § 2254, or 28 U.S.C.A. § 2255. FRCP 5.2(b).

   c. *Limitations on remote access to electronic files; Social Security appeals and immigration cases.* Unless the court orders otherwise, in an action for benefits under the Social Security Act, and in an action or proceeding relating to an order of removal, to relief from removal, or to immigration benefits or detention, access to an electronic file is authorized as follows: (1) the parties and their attorneys may have remote electronic access to any part of the case file, including the administrative record; (2) any other person may have electronic access to the full record at the courthouse, but may have remote electronic access only to: (A) the docket maintained by the court; and (B) an opinion, order, judgment, or other disposition of the court, but not any other part of the case file or the administrative record. FRCP 5.2(c).

d. *Filings made under seal.* The court may order that a filing be made under seal without redaction. The court may later unseal the filing or order the person who made the filing to file a redacted version for the public record. FRCP 5.2(d).

   i. *DISTRICT OF MAINE.* For information on filing sealed documents in the District of Maine, refer to ME R USDCT Rule 7A, ME R USDCT App. 4(p)(2), and ME R USDCT Sealed Filings.

e. *Protective orders.* For good cause, the court may by order in a case: (1) require redaction of additional information; or (2) limit or prohibit a nonparty's remote electronic access to a document filed with the court. FRCP 5.2(e).

f. *Option for additional unredacted filing under seal.* A person making a redacted filing may also file an unredacted copy under seal. The court must retain the unredacted copy as part of the record. FRCP 5.2(f).

   i. *DISTRICT OF MAINE.* A party wishing to file a document containing the personal data identifiers specified above may. . .file an unredacted document under seal. This document will be retained by the clerk's office as part of the record. ME R USDCT Redacting Pleadings. The court may, however, still require the party to file a redacted copy for the public file. ME R USDCT Redacting Pleadings.

g. *Option for filing a reference list.* A filing that contains redacted information may be filed together with a reference list that identifies each item of redacted information and specifies an appropriate identifier that uniquely corresponds to each item listed. The list must be filed under seal and may be amended as of right. Any reference in the case to a listed identifier will be construed to refer to the corresponding item of information. FRCP 5.2(g).

   i. *DISTRICT OF MAINE.* A party wishing to file a document containing the personal data identifiers specified above may. . .file a reference list under seal. The reference list shall contain the complete personal data identifier(s) and the redacted identifier(s) used in its (their) place in the filing. All references in the case to the redacted identifiers included in the reference list will be construed to refer to the corresponding complete identifier. The reference list must be filed under seal, and may be amended as of right. It shall be retained by the clerk's office as part of the record. ME R USDCT Redacting Pleadings. The court may, however, still require the party to file a redacted copy for the public file. ME R USDCT Redacting Pleadings.

h. *DISTRICT OF MAINE: Responsibility for redaction.* The clerk is not required to review documents filed with the court for compliance with FRCP 5.2. The responsibility to redact filings rests with counsel and the party or nonparty making the filing. ME R USDCT App. 4(i); ME R USDCT Redacting Pleadings. For guidelines for filing confidential information in civil cases in the District of Maine, refer to ME R USDCT Confidentiality.

i. *Waiver of protection of identifiers.* A person waives the protection of FRCP 5.2(a) as to the person's own information by filing it without redaction and not under seal. FRCP 5.2(h).

F. Filing and Service Requirements

1. *Filing requirements*

   a. *Required filings.* Any paper after the complaint that is required to be served must be filed no later than a reasonable time after service. But disclosures under FRCP 26(a)(1) or FRCP 26(a)(2) and the following discovery requests and responses must not be filed until they are used in the proceeding or the court orders filing: depositions, interrogatories, requests for documents or tangible things or to permit entry onto land, and requests for admission. FRCP 5(d)(1)(A). Refer to the United States District Court for the District of Maine KeyRules pleading and motion documents for information on filing with the court.

      i. *DISTRICT OF MAINE.* Unless otherwise ordered by the court, depositions upon oral examination and interrogatories, requests for documents, requests for admissions, and answers and responses thereto and disclosures made under FRCP 26(a)(1) through FRCP 26(a)(3) and pursuant to scheduling orders issued by the court, shall be served upon other parties but shall not be filed with the court. ME R USDCT Rule 5(b); ME R USDCT Rule 26(a).

2. *Service requirements*

   a. *Service; When required.* Unless the Federal Rules of Civil Procedure provide otherwise, each of the following papers must be served on every party: (A) an order stating that service is required; (B) a pleading filed after the original complaint, unless the court orders otherwise under FRCP 5(c) because there are numerous defendants; (C) a discovery paper required to be served on a party, unless the court orders otherwise; (D) a written motion, except one

that may be heard ex parte; and (E) a written notice, appearance, demand, or offer of judgment, or any similar paper. FRCP 5(a)(1).

    i.   *If a party fails to appear.* No service is required on a party who is in default for failing to appear. But a pleading that asserts a new claim for relief against such a party must be served on that party under FRCP 4. FRCP 5(a)(2).

    ii. *Seizing property.* If an action is begun by seizing property and no person is or need be named as a defendant, any service required before the filing of an appearance, answer, or claim must be made on the person who had custody or possession of the property when it was seized. FRCP 5(a)(3).

  b. *Service; How made.* A paper is served under FRCP 5 by: (A) handing it to the person; (B) leaving it: (i) at the person's office with a clerk or other person in charge or, if no one is in charge, in a conspicuous place in the office; or (ii) if the person has no office or the office is closed, at the person's dwelling or usual place of abode with someone of suitable age and discretion who resides there; (C) mailing it to the person's last known address—in which event service is complete upon mailing; (D) leaving it with the court clerk if the person has no known address; (E) sending it to a registered user by filing it with the court's electronic-filing system or sending it by other electronic means that the person consented to in writing—in either of which events service is complete upon filing or sending, but is not effective if the filer or sender learns that it did not reach the person to be served; or (F) delivering it by any other means that the person consented to in writing—in which event service is complete when the person making service delivers it to the agency designated to make delivery. FRCP 5(b)(2).

    i.   *Serving an attorney.* If a party is represented by an attorney, service under FRCP 5 must be made on the attorney unless the court orders service on the party. FRCP 5(b)(1).

3. *DISTRICT OF MAINE: Preservation of original discovery.* The party that has served notice of a deposition or has served discovery papers shall be responsible for preserving and for [ensuring] the integrity of original transcripts and discovery papers for use by the court. ME R USDCT Rule 5(b); ME R USDCT Rule 26(a).

G. Hearings

1. There is no hearing contemplated in the federal statutes or rules for requests for production of documents.

H. Forms

1. Federal Request for Production of Documents Forms

  a. Request for production, inspection and copying of documents, and inspection and photographing of things and real property. 3A FEDFORMS § 25:17.

  b. Request for production of documents; Electronically stored information. 3A FEDFORMS § 25:18.

  c. Request for production of documents; Business records. 3A FEDFORMS § 25:19.

  d. Request for production of documents; Patent case. 3A FEDFORMS § 25:20.

  e. Request for production of documents; Government records and regulations. 3A FEDFORMS § 25:21.

  f. Request for production of documents; Government personnel files, memoranda, minutes of meetings, and statistics. 3A FEDFORMS § 25:22.

  g. Request for production of documents; Documents to be identified in physically separate but accompanying interrogatories under FRCP 33. 3A FEDFORMS § 25:23.

  h. Request for production of documents; Employment discrimination. 3A FEDFORMS § 25:24.

  i. Request; Production of documents for inspection and copying. AMJUR PP DEPOSITION § 498.

  j. Request; Production of documents, records, and objects, under FRCP 34. FEDPROF § 23:403.

  k. Request; Production of documents for inspection and copying. FEDPROF § 23:404.

  l. Request; Production of documents for inspection and copying; Business records. FEDPROF § 23:405.

  m. Request; Production of objects for inspection and sampling. FEDPROF § 23:406.

  n. Request; Production of documents for inspection and copying; Government records and files. FEDPROF § 23:407.

  o. Request; Production of documents and things; Patent proceeding. FEDPROF § 23:408.

  p. Request; Production of documents and things; Trademark action. FEDPROF § 23:409.

  q. Request; Production of documents; Trademark action; Likelihood of confusion. FEDPROF § 23:410.

  r. Request; Production of documents; Automobile negligence. FEDPROF § 23:411.

s. Request; Production of documents; Premises liability. FEDPROF § 23:412.

t. Request; Production of documents for inspection and copying; Wrongful death due to forklift accident. FEDPROF § 23:413.

u. Request; Production of documents; Products liability. FEDPROF § 23:414.

v. Request; Production of documents; Collection of tariff. FEDPROF § 23:415.

w. Request; Production of medical records. FEDPROF § 23:416.

x. Request; Production of employment records. FEDPROF § 23:417.

y. Request; Production of education records. FEDPROF § 23:418.

z. Request; Production of decedent's records. FEDPROF § 23:419.

I. Applicable Rules

1. *Federal rules*

   a. Serving and filing pleadings and other papers. FRCP 5.

   b. Privacy protection for filings made with the court. FRCP 5.2.

   c. Computing and extending time; Time for motion papers. FRCP 6.

   d. Pleadings allowed; Form of motions and other papers. FRCP 7.

   e. Form of pleadings. FRCP 10.

   f. Signing pleadings, motions, and other papers; Representations to the court; Sanctions. FRCP 11.

   g. Duty to disclose; General provisions governing discovery. FRCP 26.

   h. Stipulations about discovery procedure. FRCP 29.

   i. Producing documents, electronically stored information, and tangible things, or entering onto land, for inspection and other purposes. FRCP 34.

   j. Failure to make disclosures or to cooperate in discovery; Sanctions. FRCP 37.

2. *Local rules*

   a. *DISTRICT OF MAINE*

      i. Service and filing of pleadings and other papers. ME R USDCT Rule 5.

      ii. Time. ME R USDCT Rule 6.

      iii. Form of pleadings, motions and other papers. ME R USDCT Rule 10.

      iv. Case management tracks. ME R USDCT Rule 16.1.

      v. Discovery. ME R USDCT Rule 26.

      vi. Attorneys; Appearances and withdrawals. ME R USDCT Rule 83.2.

      vii. Alternative dispute resolution (ADR). ME R USDCT Rule 83.11.

      viii. Administrative procedures governing the filing and service by electronic means. ME R USDCT App. 4.

      ix. Redacting pleadings. ME R USDCT Redacting Pleadings.

Requests, Notices and Applications
Response to Request for Production of Documents

Document Last Updated July 2021

A. Checklist

(I) ❑ Matters to be considered by requesting party

   (a) ❑ Required documents

      (1) ❑ Request for production of documents

302

    (b) ❑ Supplemental documents

        (1) ❑ Subpoena

        (2) ❑ Certificate of service

    (c) ❑ Timing

        (1) ❑ More than twenty-one (21) days after the summons and complaint are served on a party, a request under FRCP 34 may be delivered: (i) to that party by any other party, and (ii) by that party to any plaintiff or to any other party that has been served

        (2) ❑ A party may not seek discovery from any source before the parties have conferred as required by FRCP 26(f), except in a proceeding exempted from initial disclosure under FRCP 26(a)(1)(B), or when authorized by the Federal Rules of Civil Procedure, by stipulation, or by court order

(II) ❑ Matters to be considered by responding party

    (a) ❑ Required documents

        (1) ❑ Response to request for production of documents

    (b) ❑ Supplemental documents

        (1) ❑ Certificate of service

    (c) ❑ Timing

        (1) ❑ The party to whom the request is directed must respond in writing within thirty (30) days after being served or—if the request was delivered under FRCP 26(d)(2)—within thirty (30) days after the parties' first FRCP 26(f) conference

B. Timing

1. *Response to request for production of documents.* The party to whom the request is directed must respond in writing within thirty (30) days after being served or—if the request was delivered under FRCP 26(d)(2)—within thirty (30) days after the parties' first FRCP 26(f) conference. A shorter or longer time may be stipulated to under FRCP 29 or be ordered by the court. FRCP 34(b)(2)(A).

2. *DISTRICT OF MAINE: Completion of discovery in standard track cases.* In standard track cases, discovery shall ordinarily be completed within five (5) months. ME R USDCT Rule 16.1(b)(2).

3. *Computation of time*

    a. *Computing time.* FRCP 6 applies in computing any time period specified in the Federal Rules of Civil Procedure, in any local rule or court order, or in any statute that does not specify a method of computing time. FRCP 6(a).

        i. *Period stated in days or a longer unit.* When the period is stated in days or a longer unit of time: (A) exclude the day of the event that triggers the period; (B) count every day, including intermediate Saturdays, Sundays, and legal holidays; and (C) include the last day of the period, but if the last day is a Saturday, Sunday, or legal holiday, the period continues to run until the end of the next day that is not a Saturday, Sunday, or legal holiday. FRCP 6(a)(1).

        ii. *Period stated in hours.* When the period is stated in hours: (A) begin counting immediately on the occurrence of the event that triggers the period; (B) count every hour, including hours during intermediate Saturdays, Sundays, and legal holidays; and (C) if the period would end on a Saturday, Sunday, or legal holiday, the period continues to run until the same time on the next day that is not a Saturday, Sunday, or legal holiday. FRCP 6(a)(2).

        iii. *Inaccessibility of the clerk's office.* Unless the court orders otherwise, if the clerk's office is inaccessible: (A) on the last day for filing under FRCP 6(a)(1), then the time for filing is extended to the first accessible day that is not a Saturday, Sunday, or legal holiday; or (B) during the last hour for filing under FRCP 6(a)(2), then the time for filing is extended to the same time on the first accessible day that is not a Saturday, Sunday, or legal holiday. FRCP 6(a)(3).

        iv. *"Last day" defined.* Unless a different time is set by a statute, local rule, or court order, the last day ends: (A) for electronic filing, at midnight in the court's time zone; and (B) for filing by other means, when the clerk's office is scheduled to close. FRCP 6(a)(4).

        v. *"Next day" defined.* The "next day" is determined by continuing to count forward when the period is measured after an event and backward when measured before an event. FRCP 6(a)(5).

        vi. *"Legal holiday" defined.* "Legal holiday" means: (A) the day set aside by statute for observing New Year's Day,

Martin Luther King Jr.'s Birthday, Washington's Birthday, Memorial Day, Independence Day, Labor Day, Columbus Day, Veterans' Day, Thanksgiving Day, or Christmas Day; (B) any day declared a holiday by the President or Congress; and (C) for periods that are measured after an event, any other day declared a holiday by the state where the district court is located. FRCP 6(a)(6).

    vii. *DISTRICT OF MAINE: Applicability of FRCP 6.* FRCP 6 applies when computing any period of time stated in the Local Rules of the United States District Court for the District of Maine. ME R USDCT Rule 6(a).

  b. *Extending time.* When an act may or must be done within a specified time, the court may, for good cause, extend the time: (A) with or without motion or notice if the court acts, or if a request is made, before the original time or its extension expires; or (B) on motion made after the time has expired if the party failed to act because of excusable neglect. FRCP 6(b)(1). A court must not extend the time to act under FRCP 50(b), FRCP 50(d), FRCP 52(b), FRCP 59(b), FRCP 59(d), FRCP 59(e), and FRCP 60(b). FRCP 6(b)(2). Refer to the United States District Court for the District of Maine KeyRules Motion for Continuance/Extension of Time document for more information on extending time.

  c. *Additional time after certain kinds of service.* When a party may or must act within a specified time after being served and service is made under FRCP 5(b)(2)(C) (by mail), FRCP 5(b)(2)(D) (by leaving with the clerk), or FRCP 5(b)(2)(F) (by other means consented to), three (3) days are added after the period would otherwise expire under FRCP 6(a). FRCP 6(d).

C. General Requirements

1. *General provisions governing discovery*

  a. *Discovery scope and limits*

    i. *Scope in general.* Unless otherwise limited by court order, the scope of discovery is as follows: Parties may obtain discovery regarding any nonprivileged matter that is relevant to any party's claim or defense and proportional to the needs of the case, considering the importance of the issues at stake in the action, the amount in controversy, the parties' relative access to relevant information, the parties' resources, the importance of the discovery in resolving the issues, and whether the burden or expense of the proposed discovery outweighs its likely benefit. Information within this scope of discovery need not be admissible in evidence to be discoverable. FRCP 26(b)(1).

    ii. *Limitations on frequency and extent*

- *When permitted.* By order, the court may alter the limits in the Federal Rules of Civil Procedure on the number of depositions and interrogatories or on the length of depositions under FRCP 30. By order or local rule, the court may also limit the number of requests under FRCP 36. FRCP 26(b)(2)(A).

- *Specific limitations on electronically stored information.* A party need not provide discovery of electronically stored information from sources that the party identifies as not reasonably accessible because of undue burden or cost. On motion to compel discovery or for a protective order, the party from whom discovery is sought must show that the information is not reasonably accessible because of undue burden or cost. If that showing is made, the court may nonetheless order discovery from such sources if the requesting party shows good cause, considering the limitations of FRCP 26(b)(2)(C). The court may specify conditions for the discovery. FRCP 26(b)(2)(B).

- *When required.* On motion or on its own, the court must limit the frequency or extent of discovery otherwise allowed by the Federal Rules of Civil Procedure or by local rule if it determines that: (i) the discovery sought is unreasonably cumulative or duplicative, or can be obtained from some other source that is more convenient, less burdensome, or less expensive; (ii) the party seeking discovery has had ample opportunity to obtain the information by discovery in the action; or (iii) the proposed discovery is outside the scope permitted by FRCP 26(b)(1). FRCP 26(b)(2)(C).

    iii. *Trial preparation; Materials*

- *Documents and tangible things.* Ordinarily, a party may not discover documents and tangible things that are prepared in anticipation of litigation or for trial by or for another party or its representative (including the other party's attorney, consultant, surety, indemnitor, insurer, or agent). But, subject to FRCP 26(b)(4), those materials may be discovered if: (i) they are otherwise discoverable under FRCP 26(b)(1); and (ii) the party shows that it has substantial need for the materials to prepare its case and cannot, without undue hardship, obtain their substantial equivalent by other means. FRCP 26(b)(3)(A).

- *Protection against disclosure.* If the court orders discovery of those materials, it must protect against disclosure of the mental impressions, conclusions, opinions, or legal theories of a party's attorney or other representative concerning the litigation. FRCP 26(b)(3)(B).

- *Previous statement.* Any party or other person may, on request and without the required showing, obtain the person's own previous statement about the action or its subject matter. If the request is refused, the person may move for a court order, and FRCP 37(a)(5) applies to the award of expenses. A previous statement is either: (i) a written statement that the person has signed or otherwise adopted or approved; or (ii) a contemporaneous stenographic, mechanical, electrical, or other recording—or a transcription of it—that recites substantially verbatim the person's oral statement. FRCP 26(b)(3)(C).

iv. *Trial preparation; Experts*

- *Deposition of an expert who may testify.* A party may depose any person who has been identified as an expert whose opinions may be presented at trial. If FRCP 26(a)(2)(B) requires a report from the expert, the deposition may be conducted only after the report is provided. FRCP 26(b)(4)(A).

- *Trial-preparation protection for draft reports or disclosures.* FRCP 26(b)(3)(A) and FRCP 26(b)(3)(B) protect drafts of any report or disclosure required under FRCP 26(a)(2), regardless of the form in which the draft is recorded. FRCP 26(b)(4)(B).

- *Trial-preparation protection for communications between a party's attorney and expert witnesses.* FRCP 26(b)(3)(A) and FRCP 26(b)(3)(B) protect communications between the party's attorney and any witness required to provide a report under FRCP 26(a)(2)(B), regardless of the form of the communications, except to the extent that the communications: (i) relate to compensation for the expert's study or testimony; (ii) identify facts or data that the party's attorney provided and that the expert considered in forming the opinions to be expressed; or (iii) identify assumptions that the party's attorney provided and that the expert relied on in forming the opinions to be expressed. FRCP 26(b)(4)(C).

- *Expert employed only for trial preparation.* Ordinarily, a party may not, by interrogatories or deposition, discover facts known or opinions held by an expert who has been retained or specially employed by another party in anticipation of litigation or to prepare for trial and who is not expected to be called as a witness at trial. But a party may do so only: (i) as provided in FRCP 35(b); or (ii) on showing exceptional circumstances under which it is impracticable for the party to obtain facts or opinions on the same subject by other means. FRCP 26(b)(4)(D).

- *Payment.* Unless manifest injustice would result, the court must require that the party seeking discovery: (i) pay the expert a reasonable fee for time spent in responding to discovery under FRCP 26(b)(4)(A) or FRCP 26(b)(4)(D); and (ii) for discovery under FRCP 26(b)(4)(D), also pay the other party a fair portion of the fees and expenses it reasonably incurred in obtaining the expert's facts and opinions. FRCP 26(b)(4)(E).

v. *Claiming privilege or protecting trial-preparation materials*

- *Information withheld.* When a party withholds information otherwise discoverable by claiming that the information is privileged or subject to protection as trial-preparation material, the party must: (i) expressly make the claim; and (ii) describe the nature of the documents, communications, or tangible things not produced or disclosed—and do so in a manner that, without revealing information itself privileged or protected, will enable other parties to assess the claim. FRCP 26(b)(5)(A).

- *Information produced.* If information produced in discovery is subject to a claim of privilege or of protection as trial-preparation material, the party making the claim may notify any party that received the information of the claim and the basis for it. After being notified, a party must promptly return, sequester, or destroy the specified information and any copies it has; must not use or disclose the information until the claim is resolved; must take reasonable steps to retrieve the information if the party disclosed it before being notified; and may promptly present the information to the court under seal for a determination of the claim. The producing party must preserve the information until the claim is resolved. FRCP 26(b)(5)(B).

b. *Protective orders.* A party or any person from whom discovery is sought may move for a protective order in the court where the action is pending—or as an alternative on matters relating to a deposition, in the court for the district where the deposition will be taken. FRCP 26(c)(1). Refer to the United States District Court for the District of Maine KeyRules Motion for Protective Order document for more information.

i. *DISTRICT OF MAINE: Confidentiality order.* A party by motion or with the agreement of all parties may submit to the court a proposed order governing the production and use of confidential documents and information in the pending action. The proposed order shall conform to the Form Confidentiality Order set forth in ME R USDCT

App. 2. Any proposed modification to the Form Confidentiality Order shall be identified with a short statement of the reason for each modification. ME R USDCT Rule 26(d).

c. *Sequence of discovery.* Unless the parties stipulate or the court orders otherwise for the parties' and witnesses' convenience and in the interests of justice: (A) methods of discovery may be used in any sequence; and (B) discovery by one party does not require any other party to delay its discovery. FRCP 26(d)(3).

2. *Response to request for production of documents*

a. *Responding to each item.* For each item or category, the response must either state that inspection and related activities will be permitted as requested or state with specificity the grounds for objecting to the request, including the reasons. The responding party may state that it will produce copies of documents or of electronically stored information instead of permitting inspection. The production must then be completed no later than the time for inspection specified in the request or another reasonable time specified in the response. FRCP 34(b)(2)(B).

b. *Objections.* An objection must state whether any responsive materials are being withheld on the basis of that objection. An objection to part of a request must specify the part and permit inspection of the rest. FRCP 34(b)(2)(C).

i. *Insufficient objections.* A response which raises no objection, but simply indicates that the information requested is "unknown" and that the records sought are "not maintained," is evasive and insufficient. FEDPROC § 26:601.

ii. *Waiver.* A party may waive its objections to a request for production by failing to object in a timely and effective manner. FEDPROC § 26:598.

c. *Responding to a request for production of electronically stored information.* The response may state an objection to a requested form for producing electronically stored information. If the responding party objects to a requested form—or if no form was specified in the request—the party must state the form or forms it intends to use. FRCP 34(b)(2)(D).

d. *Producing the documents or electronically stored information.* Unless otherwise stipulated or ordered by the court, these procedures apply to producing documents or electronically stored information: (i) a party must produce documents as they are kept in the usual course of business or must organize and label them to correspond to the categories in the request; (ii) if a request does not specify a form for producing electronically stored information, a party must produce it in a form or forms in which it is ordinarily maintained or in a reasonably usable form or forms; and (iii) a party need not produce the same electronically stored information in more than one form. FRCP 34(b)(2)(E).

e. *Documents and things in possession, custody, or control.* FRCP 34 provides. . .that discovery may be had of documents and things that are in the "possession, custody, or control" of a party. FPP § 2210. The concept of "control" is very important in applying FRCP 34, but the application of this concept is often highly fact-specific. Inspection can be had if the party to whom the request is made has the legal right to obtain the document, even though in fact it has no copy. FPP § 2210.

i. *Production of documents and things belonging to a third-party or beyond the jurisdiction of the court.* A party may be required to produce documents and things that it possesses even though they belong to a third person who is not a party to the action. FPP § 2210; Societe Internationale Pour Participations Industrielles Et Commerciales, S. A. v. Rogers, 357 U.S. 197, 78 S. Ct. 1087, 2 L. Ed. 2d 1255 (1958). And if a party has possession, custody, or control, it must produce documents and things even though the documents and things are themselves beyond the jurisdiction of the court. FPP § 2210.

ii. *Documents or things that do not exist.* If a document or thing does not exist, it cannot be in the possession, custody, or control of a party and therefore cannot be produced for inspection. FEDPROC § 26:577.

iii. *Lack of control as an objection.* Finally, lack of control may be considered an objection to the discovery request and, like any such objection, it may be waived. FPP § 2210.

f. *Documents made available to all parties.* Documents made available to one party to a suit must be made available to all parties. FEDPROC § 26:591.

g. *Attorney's duty to ensure compliance.* An attorney representing a party in connection with a request for the production and inspection of documents pursuant to FRCP 34 has an obligation to verify that the client has produced the documents requested, and a further obligation to [ensure] that records are kept indicating which documents have been produced. Failure to comply with these duties has been characterized as careless and inexcusable and has resulted in the imposition of sanctions. FEDPROC § 26:593.

3. *Supplementing disclosures and responses.* A party who has made a disclosure under FRCP 26(a)—or who has responded

306

to an interrogatory, request for production, or request for admission—must supplement or correct its disclosure or response: (A) in a timely manner if the party learns that in some material respect the disclosure or response is incomplete or incorrect, and if the additional or corrective information has not otherwise been made known to the other parties during the discovery process or in writing; or (B) as ordered by the court. FRCP 26(e)(1).

4. *Sanctions for failure to cooperate in discovery.* The court where the action is pending may, on motion, order sanctions if a party, after being properly served with interrogatories under FRCP 33 or a request for inspection under FRCP 34, fails to serve its answers, objections, or written response. FRCP 37(d)(1)(A)(ii). If a motion to compel is granted, the court must, after giving an opportunity to be heard, require the party or deponent whose conduct necessitated the motion, the party or attorney advising that conduct, or both to pay the movant's reasonable expenses incurred in making the motion, including attorney's fees. But the court must not order this payment if the opposing party's nondisclosure, response, or objection was substantially justified. FRCP 37(a)(5)(A)(ii). Refer to the United States District Court for the District of Maine KeyRules Motion for Discovery Sanctions document for more information.

5. *Stipulations about discovery procedure.* Unless the court orders otherwise, the parties may stipulate that: (a) a deposition may be taken before any person, at any time or place, on any notice, and in the manner specified—in which event it may be used in the same way as any other deposition; and (b) other procedures governing or limiting discovery be modified—but a stipulation extending the time for any form of discovery must have court approval if it would interfere with the time set for completing discovery, for hearing a motion, or for trial. FRCP 29.

6. *DISTRICT OF MAINE: Appearances.* An attorney's signature to a pleading shall constitute an appearance for the party filing the pleading. Otherwise, an attorney who wishes to participate in any manner in any action must file a formal written appearance identifying the party represented. An appearance whether by pleading or formal written appearance shall be signed by an attorney in his/her individual name and shall state his/her office address. ME R USDCT Rule 83.2(a). For more information, refer to ME R USDCT Rule 83.2.

7. *DISTRICT OF MAINE: Alternative dispute resolution (ADR).* Litigants are authorized and encouraged to employ, at their own expense, any available ADR process on which they can agree, including early neutral evaluation, settlement conferences, mediation, non-binding summary jury trial, corporate mini-trial, and arbitration proceedings. ME R USDCT Rule 83.11(a). For more information on ADR, refer to ME R USDCT Rule 83.11.

D. Documents

1. *Required documents*

   a. *Response to request for production of documents.* Refer to the "C. General Requirements" section of this KeyRules document for information on the response to request for production of documents.

2. *Supplemental documents*

   a. *Certificate of service.* No certificate of service is required when a paper is served by filing it with the court's electronic-filing system. When a paper that is required to be served is served by other means: (i) if the paper is filed, a certificate of service must be filed with it or within a reasonable time after service; and (ii) if the paper is not filed, a certificate of service need not be filed unless filing is required by court order or by local rule. FRCP 5(d)(1)(B).

E. Format

1. *Form of documents.* The rules governing captions and other matters of form in pleadings apply to motions and other papers. FRCP 7(b)(2).

   a. *DISTRICT OF MAINE: Font size, line spacing, and paper size.* All such documents shall be typed in a font of no less than size twelve (12) point, and shall be double-spaced or printed on eight and one-half by eleven (8-1/2 x 11) inch paper. Footnotes shall be in a font of no less than size ten (10) point, and may be single spaced. ME R USDCT Rule 10.

   b. *Caption.* Every pleading must have a caption with the court's name, a title, a file number, and an FRCP 7(a) designation. FRCP 10(a).

      i. *Names of parties.* The title of the complaint must name all the parties; the title of other pleadings, after naming the first party on each side, may refer generally to other parties. FRCP 10(a).

      ii. *DISTRICT OF MAINE: Additional caption requirements.* All pleadings, motions and other papers filed with the clerk or otherwise submitted to the court, except exhibits, shall bear the proper case number and shall contain on the first page a caption as described by FRCP 10(a) and immediately thereunder a designation of what the document is and the name of the party in whose behalf it is submitted. ME R USDCT Rule 10.

   c. *Claims or defenses*

      i. *Numbered paragraphs.* A party must state its claims or defenses in numbered paragraphs, each limited as far as practicable to a single set of circumstances. A later pleading may refer by number to a paragraph in an earlier pleading. FRCP 10(b).

    ii. *Separate statements.* If doing so would promote clarity, each claim founded on a separate transaction or occurrence—and each defense other than a denial—must be stated in a separate count or defense. FRCP 10(b).

  d. *Adoption by reference.* A statement in a pleading may be adopted by reference elsewhere in the same pleading or in any other pleading or motion. FRCP 10(c).

    i. *Exhibits.* A copy of a written instrument that is an exhibit to a pleading is a part of the pleading for all purposes. FRCP 10(c).

  e. *DISTRICT OF MAINE: Page numbering.* All pages shall be numbered at the bottom. ME R USDCT Rule 10.

  f. *DISTRICT OF MAINE: Attachment of ancillary papers.* Ancillary papers shall be attached at the end of the document to which they relate. ME R USDCT Rule 10.

  g. *Acceptance by the clerk.* The clerk must not refuse to file a paper solely because it is not in the form prescribed by the Federal Rules of Civil Procedure or by a local rule or practice. FRCP 5(d)(4).

2. *Signing disclosures and discovery requests, responses, and objections.* FRCP 11 does not apply to disclosures and discovery requests, responses, objections, and motions under FRCP 26 through FRCP 37. FRCP 11(d).

  a. *Signature required.* Every disclosure under FRCP 26(a)(1) or FRCP 26(a)(3) and every discovery request, response, or objection must be signed by at least one attorney of record in the attorney's own name—or by the party personally, if unrepresented—and must state the signer's address, e-mail address, and telephone number. FRCP 26(g)(1).

  b. *Effect of signature.* By signing, an attorney or party certifies that to the best of the person's knowledge, information, and belief formed after a reasonable inquiry: (A) with respect to a disclosure, it is complete and correct as of the time it is made; and (B) with respect to a discovery request, response, or objection, it is: (i) consistent with the Federal Rules of Civil Procedure and warranted by existing law or by a nonfrivolous argument for extending, modifying, or reversing existing law, or for establishing new law; (ii) not interposed for any improper purpose, such as to harass, cause unnecessary delay, or needlessly increase the cost of litigation; and (iii) neither unreasonable nor unduly burdensome or expensive, considering the needs of the case, prior discovery in the case, the amount in controversy, and the importance of the issues at stake in the action. FRCP 26(g)(1).

  c. *Failure to sign.* Other parties have no duty to act on an unsigned disclosure, request, response, or objection until it is signed, and the court must strike it unless a signature is promptly supplied after the omission is called to the attorney's or party's attention. FRCP 26(g)(2).

  d. *Sanction for improper certification.* If a certification violates FRCP 26(g) without substantial justification, the court, on motion or on its own, must impose an appropriate sanction on the signer, the party on whose behalf the signer was acting, or both. The sanction may include an order to pay the reasonable expenses, including attorney's fees, caused by the violation. FRCP 26(g)(3). Refer to the United States District Court for the District of Maine KeyRules Motion for Discovery Sanctions document for more information.

3. *Privacy protection for filings made with the court*

  a. *Redacted filings.* Unless the court orders otherwise, in an electronic or paper filing with the court that contains an individual's Social Security number, taxpayer-identification number, or birth date, the name of an individual known to be a minor, or a financial-account number, a party or nonparty making the filing may include only: (1) the last four (4) digits of the Social Security number and taxpayer-identification number; (2) the year of the individual's birth; (3) the minor's initials; and (4) the last four (4) digits of the financial-account number. FRCP 5.2(a).

    i. *DISTRICT OF MAINE.* To address the privacy concerns created by the Internet access to court papers, unless otherwise ordered by the court, counsel shall modify certain personal data identifiers in pleadings and other papers as follows: (1) minors' names: use of the minors' initials only; (2) Social Security numbers: use of the last four (4) numbers only; (3) dates of birth: use of the year of birth only; [and] (4) financial account numbers: identify the type of account and the financial institution, but use only the last four (4) numbers of the account number. ME R USDCT Redacting Pleadings. Counsel should also use caution when filing papers that contain a person's medical records, employment history; financial information; and any proprietary or trade secret information. ME R USDCT Redacting Pleadings.

  b. *Exemptions from the redaction requirement.* The redaction requirement does not apply to the following: (1) a financial-account number that identifies the property allegedly subject to forfeiture in a forfeiture proceeding; (2) the record of an administrative or agency proceeding; (3) the official record of a state-court proceeding; (4) the record of a court or tribunal, if that record was not subject to the redaction requirement when originally filed; (5) a filing covered by FRCP 5.2(c) or FRCP 5.2(d); and (6) a pro se filing in an action brought under 28 U.S.C.A. § 2241, 28 U.S.C.A. § 2254, or 28 U.S.C.A. § 2255. FRCP 5.2(b).

c. *Limitations on remote access to electronic files; Social Security appeals and immigration cases.* Unless the court orders otherwise, in an action for benefits under the Social Security Act, and in an action or proceeding relating to an order of removal, to relief from removal, or to immigration benefits or detention, access to an electronic file is authorized as follows: (1) the parties and their attorneys may have remote electronic access to any part of the case file, including the administrative record; (2) any other person may have electronic access to the full record at the courthouse, but may have remote electronic access only to: (A) the docket maintained by the court; and (B) an opinion, order, judgment, or other disposition of the court, but not any other part of the case file or the administrative record. FRCP 5.2(c).

d. *Filings made under seal.* The court may order that a filing be made under seal without redaction. The court may later unseal the filing or order the person who made the filing to file a redacted version for the public record. FRCP 5.2(d).

   i. *DISTRICT OF MAINE.* For information on filing sealed documents in the District of Maine, refer to ME R USDCT Rule 7A, ME R USDCT App. 4(p)(2), and ME R USDCT Sealed Filings.

e. *Protective orders.* For good cause, the court may by order in a case: (1) require redaction of additional information; or (2) limit or prohibit a nonparty's remote electronic access to a document filed with the court. FRCP 5.2(e).

f. *Option for additional unredacted filing under seal.* A person making a redacted filing may also file an unredacted copy under seal. The court must retain the unredacted copy as part of the record. FRCP 5.2(f).

   i. *DISTRICT OF MAINE.* A party wishing to file a document containing the personal data identifiers specified above may. . .file an unredacted document under seal. This document will be retained by the clerk's office as part of the record. ME R USDCT Redacting Pleadings. The court may, however, still require the party to file a redacted copy for the public file. ME R USDCT Redacting Pleadings.

g. *Option for filing a reference list.* A filing that contains redacted information may be filed together with a reference list that identifies each item of redacted information and specifies an appropriate identifier that uniquely corresponds to each item listed. The list must be filed under seal and may be amended as of right. Any reference in the case to a listed identifier will be construed to refer to the corresponding item of information. FRCP 5.2(g).

   i. *DISTRICT OF MAINE.* A party wishing to file a document containing the personal data identifiers specified above may. . .file a reference list under seal. The reference list shall contain the complete personal data identifier(s) and the redacted identifier(s) used in its (their) place in the filing. All references in the case to the redacted identifiers included in the reference list will be construed to refer to the corresponding complete identifier. The reference list must be filed under seal, and may be amended as of right. It shall be retained by the clerk's office as part of the record. ME R USDCT Redacting Pleadings. The court may, however, still require the party to file a redacted copy for the public file. ME R USDCT Redacting Pleadings.

h. *DISTRICT OF MAINE: Responsibility for redaction.* The clerk is not required to review documents filed with the court for compliance with FRCP 5.2. The responsibility to redact filings rests with counsel and the party or nonparty making the filing. ME R USDCT App. 4(i); ME R USDCT Redacting Pleadings. For guidelines for filing confidential information in civil cases in the District of Maine, refer to ME R USDCT Confidentiality.

i. *Waiver of protection of identifiers.* A person waives the protection of FRCP 5.2(a) as to the person's own information by filing it without redaction and not under seal. FRCP 5.2(h).

F. Filing and Service Requirements

1. *Filing requirements*

   a. *Required filings.* Any paper after the complaint that is required to be served must be filed no later than a reasonable time after service. But disclosures under FRCP 26(a)(1) or FRCP 26(a)(2) and the following discovery requests and responses must not be filed until they are used in the proceeding or the court orders filing: depositions, interrogatories, requests for documents or tangible things or to permit entry onto land, and requests for admission. FRCP 5(d)(1)(A). Refer to the United States District Court for the District of Maine KeyRules pleading and motion documents for information on filing with the court.

      i. *DISTRICT OF MAINE.* Unless otherwise ordered by the court, depositions upon oral examination and interrogatories, requests for documents, requests for admissions, and answers and responses thereto and disclosures made under FRCP 26(a)(1) through FRCP 26(a)(3) and pursuant to scheduling orders issued by the court, shall be served upon other parties but shall not be filed with the court. ME R USDCT Rule 5(b); ME R USDCT Rule 26(a).

2. *Service requirements.* The response must be served on all the parties to the action, unless the court otherwise orders, rather than only on the requesting party. FPP § 2213.

    a. *Service; When required.* Unless the Federal Rules of Civil Procedure provide otherwise, each of the following papers must be served on every party: (A) an order stating that service is required; (B) a pleading filed after the original complaint, unless the court orders otherwise under FRCP 5(c) because there are numerous defendants; (C) a discovery paper required to be served on a party, unless the court orders otherwise; (D) a written motion, except one that may be heard ex parte; and (E) a written notice, appearance, demand, or offer of judgment, or any similar paper. FRCP 5(a)(1).

        i. *If a party fails to appear.* No service is required on a party who is in default for failing to appear. But a pleading that asserts a new claim for relief against such a party must be served on that party under FRCP 4. FRCP 5(a)(2).

        ii. *Seizing property.* If an action is begun by seizing property and no person is or need be named as a defendant, any service required before the filing of an appearance, answer, or claim must be made on the person who had custody or possession of the property when it was seized. FRCP 5(a)(3).

    b. *Service; How made.* A paper is served under FRCP 5 by: (A) handing it to the person; (B) leaving it: (i) at the person's office with a clerk or other person in charge or, if no one is in charge, in a conspicuous place in the office; or (ii) if the person has no office or the office is closed, at the person's dwelling or usual place of abode with someone of suitable age and discretion who resides there; (C) mailing it to the person's last known address—in which event service is complete upon mailing; (D) leaving it with the court clerk if the person has no known address; (E) sending it to a registered user by filing it with the court's electronic-filing system or sending it by other electronic means that the person consented to in writing—in either of which events service is complete upon filing or sending, but is not effective if the filer or sender learns that it did not reach the person to be served; or (F) delivering it by any other means that the person consented to in writing—in which event service is complete when the person making service delivers it to the agency designated to make delivery. FRCP 5(b)(2).

        i. *Serving an attorney.* If a party is represented by an attorney, service under FRCP 5 must be made on the attorney unless the court orders service on the party. FRCP 5(b)(1).

3. *DISTRICT OF MAINE: Preservation of original discovery.* The party that has served notice of a deposition or has served discovery papers shall be responsible for preserving and for [ensuring] the integrity of original transcripts and discovery papers for use by the court. ME R USDCT Rule 5(b); ME R USDCT Rule 26(a).

G. Hearings

1. There is no hearing contemplated in the federal statutes or rules for responses to requests for production of documents.

H. Forms

1. Federal Response to Request for Production of Documents Forms

    a. Response to request for production. 3A FEDFORMS § 25:26.

    b. Response to request for production of documents; Government personnel files, memoranda, minutes of meetings, and statistics. 3A FEDFORMS § 25:27.

    c. Response; To request for production of documents and other items. AMJUR PP DEPOSITION § 523.

    d. Response; To request for production and inspection of documents and other items. AMJUR PP DEPOSITION § 524.

    e. Verification; By defendant; Of response to request for production of documents and other items. AMJUR PP DEPOSITION § 525.

    f. Response; To request for inspection. AMJUR PP DEPOSITION § 526.

    g. Response; To request for production of documents; Objection; Documents not within objecting party's possession. AMJUR PP DEPOSITION § 597.

    h. Response; To request for production of documents; Objection; Documents within attorney-client privilege. AMJUR PP DEPOSITION § 598.

    i. Response; To request for production of documents prepared in anticipation of litigation; Objection; Requestor may easily obtain information elsewhere. AMJUR PP DEPOSITION § 599.

    j. Response; To request for production of documents and things. FEDPROF § 23:423.

    k. Response; To request for production of documents; With various objections. FEDPROF § 23:424.

    l. Response to request for production of documents and things; Government records. FEDPROF § 23:425.

m. Objection; To request for production of documents; Documents not within objecting party's possession. FEDPROF § 23:426.

n. Objection; To request for production of documents; Documents within attorney-client privilege. FEDPROF § 23:427.

o. Objection; To request for production of documents prepared in anticipation of litigation; Requestor may easily obtain information elsewhere. FEDPROF § 23:428.

p. Objection; To request for production of documents; Documents do not exist. FEDPROF § 23:429.

q. First notice for production; Response. GOLDLTGFMS § 28:30.

I. Applicable Rules

1. *Federal rules*

   a. Serving and filing pleadings and other papers. FRCP 5.

   b. Privacy protection for filings made with the court. FRCP 5.2.

   c. Computing and extending time; Time for motion papers. FRCP 6.

   d. Pleadings allowed; Form of motions and other papers. FRCP 7.

   e. Form of pleadings. FRCP 10.

   f. Signing pleadings, motions, and other papers; Representations to the court; Sanctions. FRCP 11.

   g. Duty to disclose; General provisions governing discovery. FRCP 26.

   h. Stipulations about discovery procedure. FRCP 29.

   i. Producing documents, electronically stored information, and tangible things, or entering onto land, for inspection and other purposes. FRCP 34.

   j. Failure to make disclosures or to cooperate in discovery; Sanctions. FRCP 37.

2. *Local rules*

   a. *DISTRICT OF MAINE*

      i. Service and filing of pleadings and other papers. ME R USDCT Rule 5.

      ii. Time. ME R USDCT Rule 6.

      iii. Form of pleadings, motions and other papers. ME R USDCT Rule 10.

      iv. Case management tracks. ME R USDCT Rule 16.1.

      v. Discovery. ME R USDCT Rule 26.

      vi. Attorneys; Appearances and withdrawals. ME R USDCT Rule 83.2.

      vii. Alternative dispute resolution (ADR). ME R USDCT Rule 83.11.

      viii. Administrative procedures governing the filing and service by electronic means. ME R USDCT App. 4.

      ix. Redacting pleadings. ME R USDCT Redacting Pleadings.

Requests, Notices and Applications
Request for Admissions

Document Last Updated July 2021

A. Checklist

(I) ❑ Matters to be considered by requesting party

   (a) ❑ Required documents

      (1) ❑ Request for admissions

   (b) ❑ Supplemental documents

      (1) ❑ Document(s)

      (2) ❑ Certificate of service

    (c) ❑ Timing

        (1) ❑ A party may not seek discovery from any source before the parties have conferred as required by FRCP 26(f), except in a proceeding exempted from initial disclosure under FRCP 26(a)(1)(B), or when authorized by the Federal Rules of Civil Procedure, by stipulation, or by court order

(II) ❑ Matters to be considered by responding party

    (a) ❑ Required documents

        (1) ❑ Response to request for admissions

    (b) ❑ Supplemental documents

        (1) ❑ Certificate of service

    (c) ❑ Timing

        (1) ❑ A matter is admitted unless, within thirty (30) days after being served, the party to whom the request is directed serves on the requesting party a written answer or objection addressed to the matter and signed by the party or its attorney

B. Timing

1. *Request for admissions.* A party may not seek discovery through requests for admission before the parties have conferred as required by FRCP 26(f), except in a proceeding exempted from initial disclosure or when authorized by the Federal Rules of Civil Procedure, by stipulation, or by court order. FEDPROC § 26:657.

2. *Commencement of discovery.* A party may not seek discovery from any source before the parties have conferred as required by FRCP 26(f), except in a proceeding exempted from initial disclosure under FRCP 26(a)(1)(B), or when authorized by the Federal Rules of Civil Procedure, by stipulation, or by court order. FRCP 26(d)(1).

3. *DISTRICT OF MAINE: Completion of discovery in standard track cases.* In standard track cases, discovery shall ordinarily be completed within five (5) months. ME R USDCT Rule 16.1(b)(2).

4. *Computation of time*

    a. *Computing time.* FRCP 6 applies in computing any time period specified in the Federal Rules of Civil Procedure, in any local rule or court order, or in any statute that does not specify a method of computing time. FRCP 6(a).

        i. *Period stated in days or a longer unit.* When the period is stated in days or a longer unit of time: (A) exclude the day of the event that triggers the period; (B) count every day, including intermediate Saturdays, Sundays, and legal holidays; and (C) include the last day of the period, but if the last day is a Saturday, Sunday, or legal holiday, the period continues to run until the end of the next day that is not a Saturday, Sunday, or legal holiday. FRCP 6(a)(1).

        ii. *Period stated in hours.* When the period is stated in hours: (A) begin counting immediately on the occurrence of the event that triggers the period; (B) count every hour, including hours during intermediate Saturdays, Sundays, and legal holidays; and (C) if the period would end on a Saturday, Sunday, or legal holiday, the period continues to run until the same time on the next day that is not a Saturday, Sunday, or legal holiday. FRCP 6(a)(2).

        iii. *Inaccessibility of the clerk's office.* Unless the court orders otherwise, if the clerk's office is inaccessible: (A) on the last day for filing under FRCP 6(a)(1), then the time for filing is extended to the first accessible day that is not a Saturday, Sunday, or legal holiday; or (B) during the last hour for filing under FRCP 6(a)(2), then the time for filing is extended to the same time on the first accessible day that is not a Saturday, Sunday, or legal holiday. FRCP 6(a)(3).

        iv. *"Last day" defined.* Unless a different time is set by a statute, local rule, or court order, the last day ends: (A) for electronic filing, at midnight in the court's time zone; and (B) for filing by other means, when the clerk's office is scheduled to close. FRCP 6(a)(4).

        v. *"Next day" defined.* The "next day" is determined by continuing to count forward when the period is measured after an event and backward when measured before an event. FRCP 6(a)(5).

        vi. *"Legal holiday" defined.* "Legal holiday" means: (A) the day set aside by statute for observing New Year's Day, Martin Luther King Jr.'s Birthday, Washington's Birthday, Memorial Day, Independence Day, Labor Day, Columbus Day, Veterans' Day, Thanksgiving Day, or Christmas Day; (B) any day declared a holiday by the President or Congress; and (C) for periods that are measured after an event, any other day declared a holiday by the state where the district court is located. FRCP 6(a)(6).

vii. *DISTRICT OF MAINE: Applicability of FRCP 6.* FRCP 6 applies when computing any period of time stated in the Local Rules of the United States District Court for the District of Maine. ME R USDCT Rule 6(a).

b. *Extending time.* When an act may or must be done within a specified time, the court may, for good cause, extend the time: (A) with or without motion or notice if the court acts, or if a request is made, before the original time or its extension expires; or (B) on motion made after the time has expired if the party failed to act because of excusable neglect. FRCP 6(b)(1). A court must not extend the time to act under FRCP 50(b), FRCP 50(d), FRCP 52(b), FRCP 59(b), FRCP 59(d), FRCP 59(e), and FRCP 60(b). FRCP 6(b)(2). Refer to the United States District Court for the District of Maine KeyRules Motion for Continuance/Extension of Time document for more information on extending time.

c. *Additional time after certain kinds of service.* When a party may or must act within a specified time after being served and service is made under FRCP 5(b)(2)(C) (by mail), FRCP 5(b)(2)(D) (by leaving with the clerk), or FRCP 5(b)(2)(F) (by other means consented to), three (3) days are added after the period would otherwise expire under FRCP 6(a). FRCP 6(d).

C. General Requirements

1. *General provisions governing discovery*

   a. *Discovery scope and limits*

      i. *Scope in general.* Unless otherwise limited by court order, the scope of discovery is as follows: Parties may obtain discovery regarding any nonprivileged matter that is relevant to any party's claim or defense and proportional to the needs of the case, considering the importance of the issues at stake in the action, the amount in controversy, the parties' relative access to relevant information, the parties' resources, the importance of the discovery in resolving the issues, and whether the burden or expense of the proposed discovery outweighs its likely benefit. Information within this scope of discovery need not be admissible in evidence to be discoverable. FRCP 26(b)(1).

      ii. *Limitations on frequency and extent*

         • *When permitted.* By order, the court may alter the limits in the Federal Rules of Civil Procedure on the number of depositions and interrogatories or on the length of depositions under FRCP 30. By order or local rule, the court may also limit the number of requests under FRCP 36. FRCP 26(b)(2)(A).

         • *Specific limitations on electronically stored information.* A party need not provide discovery of electronically stored information from sources that the party identifies as not reasonably accessible because of undue burden or cost. On motion to compel discovery or for a protective order, the party from whom discovery is sought must show that the information is not reasonably accessible because of undue burden or cost. If that showing is made, the court may nonetheless order discovery from such sources if the requesting party shows good cause, considering the limitations of FRCP 26(b)(2)(C). The court may specify conditions for the discovery. FRCP 26(b)(2)(B).

         • *When required.* On motion or on its own, the court must limit the frequency or extent of discovery otherwise allowed by the Federal Rules of Civil Procedure or by local rule if it determines that: (i) the discovery sought is unreasonably cumulative or duplicative, or can be obtained from some other source that is more convenient, less burdensome, or less expensive; (ii) the party seeking discovery has had ample opportunity to obtain the information by discovery in the action; or (iii) the proposed discovery is outside the scope permitted by FRCP 26(b)(1). FRCP 26(b)(2)(C).

      iii. *Trial preparation; Materials*

         • *Documents and tangible things.* Ordinarily, a party may not discover documents and tangible things that are prepared in anticipation of litigation or for trial by or for another party or its representative (including the other party's attorney, consultant, surety, indemnitor, insurer, or agent). But, subject to FRCP 26(b)(4), those materials may be discovered if: (i) they are otherwise discoverable under FRCP 26(b)(1); and (ii) the party shows that it has substantial need for the materials to prepare its case and cannot, without undue hardship, obtain their substantial equivalent by other means. FRCP 26(b)(3)(A).

         • *Protection against disclosure.* If the court orders discovery of those materials, it must protect against disclosure of the mental impressions, conclusions, opinions, or legal theories of a party's attorney or other representative concerning the litigation. FRCP 26(b)(3)(B).

         • *Previous statement.* Any party or other person may, on request and without the required showing, obtain the person's own previous statement about the action or its subject matter. If the request is refused, the person may move for a court order, and FRCP 37(a)(5) applies to the award of expenses. A previous statement is either: (i) a written statement that the person has signed or otherwise adopted or approved; or (ii) a contemporaneous stenographic, mechanical, electrical, or other recording—or a transcription of it—that recites substantially verbatim the person's oral statement. FRCP 26(b)(3)(C).

iv. *Trial preparation; Experts*

- *Deposition of an expert who may testify.* A party may depose any person who has been identified as an expert whose opinions may be presented at trial. If FRCP 26(a)(2)(B) requires a report from the expert, the deposition may be conducted only after the report is provided. FRCP 26(b)(4)(A).

- *Trial-preparation protection for draft reports or disclosures.* FRCP 26(b)(3)(A) and FRCP 26(b)(3)(B) protect drafts of any report or disclosure required under FRCP 26(a)(2), regardless of the form in which the draft is recorded. FRCP 26(b)(4)(B).

- *Trial-preparation protection for communications between a party's attorney and expert witnesses.* FRCP 26(b)(3)(A) and FRCP 26(b)(3)(B) protect communications between the party's attorney and any witness required to provide a report under FRCP 26(a)(2)(B), regardless of the form of the communications, except to the extent that the communications: (i) relate to compensation for the expert's study or testimony; (ii) identify facts or data that the party's attorney provided and that the expert considered in forming the opinions to be expressed; or (iii) identify assumptions that the party's attorney provided and that the expert relied on in forming the opinions to be expressed. FRCP 26(b)(4)(C).

- *Expert employed only for trial preparation.* Ordinarily, a party may not, by interrogatories or deposition, discover facts known or opinions held by an expert who has been retained or specially employed by another party in anticipation of litigation or to prepare for trial and who is not expected to be called as a witness at trial. But a party may do so only: (i) as provided in FRCP 35(b); or (ii) on showing exceptional circumstances under which it is impracticable for the party to obtain facts or opinions on the same subject by other means. FRCP 26(b)(4)(D).

- *Payment.* Unless manifest injustice would result, the court must require that the party seeking discovery: (i) pay the expert a reasonable fee for time spent in responding to discovery under FRCP 26(b)(4)(A) or FRCP 26(b)(4)(D); and (ii) for discovery under FRCP 26(b)(4)(D), also pay the other party a fair portion of the fees and expenses it reasonably incurred in obtaining the expert's facts and opinions. FRCP 26(b)(4)(E).

v. *Claiming privilege or protecting trial-preparation materials*

- *Information withheld.* When a party withholds information otherwise discoverable by claiming that the information is privileged or subject to protection as trial-preparation material, the party must: (i) expressly make the claim; and (ii) describe the nature of the documents, communications, or tangible things not produced or disclosed—and do so in a manner that, without revealing information itself privileged or protected, will enable other parties to assess the claim. FRCP 26(b)(5)(A).

- *Information produced.* If information produced in discovery is subject to a claim of privilege or of protection as trial-preparation material, the party making the claim may notify any party that received the information of the claim and the basis for it. After being notified, a party must promptly return, sequester, or destroy the specified information and any copies it has; must not use or disclose the information until the claim is resolved; must take reasonable steps to retrieve the information if the party disclosed it before being notified; and may promptly present the information to the court under seal for a determination of the claim. The producing party must preserve the information until the claim is resolved. FRCP 26(b)(5)(B).

b. *Protective orders.* A party or any person from whom discovery is sought may move for a protective order in the court where the action is pending—or as an alternative on matters relating to a deposition, in the court for the district where the deposition will be taken. FRCP 26(c)(1). Refer to the United States District Court for the District of Maine KeyRules Motion for Protective Order document for more information.

   i. *DISTRICT OF MAINE: Confidentiality order.* A party by motion or with the agreement of all parties may submit to the court a proposed order governing the production and use of confidential documents and information in the pending action. The proposed order shall conform to the Form Confidentiality Order set forth in ME R USDCT App. 2. Any proposed modification to the Form Confidentiality Order shall be identified with a short statement of the reason for each modification. ME R USDCT Rule 26(d).

c. *Sequence of discovery.* Unless the parties stipulate or the court orders otherwise for the parties' and witnesses' convenience and in the interests of justice: (A) methods of discovery may be used in any sequence; and (B) discovery by one party does not require any other party to delay its discovery. FRCP 26(d)(3).

2. *Request for admissions*

    a. *Scope.* A party may serve on any other party a written request to admit, for purposes of the pending action only, the truth of any matters within the scope of FRCP 26(b)(1) relating to: (A) facts, the application of law to fact, or opinions about either; and (B) the genuineness of any described documents. FRCP 36(a)(1). A party may serve a request for admission even though the party has the burden of proving the matters asserted therein because FRCP 36 permits requests for admission to address claims of the party seeking discovery, and generally, the party asserting a claim bears the burden of proof thereon. FEDPROC § 26:666.

    b. *Number.* FRCP 36 does not limit a party to a single request, or set of requests, for admissions. But FRCP 26(b)(2)(A) authorizes courts to limit the number of requests by order or local rule. In addition, the court has power to protect a party from harassment by repeated requests for admissions, but will not bar such repeated requests when the circumstances of the case justify them. Even a second request about the same fact or the genuineness of the same document is permissible if circumstances warrant a renewed request. FPP § 2258.

    c. *Form.* Each matter must be separately stated. FRCP 36(a)(2). The party called upon to respond should not be required to go through a document and assume the responsibility of determining what facts it is being requested to admit. FPP § 2258. Each request for an admission should be phrased simply and directly so that it can be admitted or denied without explanation. FPP § 2258; United Coal Companies v. Powell Const. Co., 839 F.2d 958, 968 (3d Cir. 1988). A request for an admission need not state the source of information about the matter for which the request is made. FPP § 2258.

    d. *Effect of an admission; Withdrawing or amending it.* A matter admitted under FRCP 36 is conclusively established unless the court, on motion, permits the admission to be withdrawn or amended. Subject to FRCP 16(e), the court may permit withdrawal or amendment if it would promote the presentation of the merits of the action and if the court is not persuaded that it would prejudice the requesting party in maintaining or defending the action on the merits. An admission under FRCP 36 is not an admission for any other purpose and cannot be used against the party in any other proceeding. FRCP 36(b).

    e. *Motion to compel.* The motion to compel discovery provided by FRCP 37(a) does not apply to a failure to respond to a request for admissions. The automatic admission from a failure to respond is a sufficient remedy for the party who made the request. If, however, a request is objected to, or the requesting party thinks that a response to a request is insufficient, it may move under FRCP 36(a)(6) to determine the sufficiency of the answers or objections. FPP § 2265.

    f. *Motion regarding the sufficiency of an answer or objection.* The requesting party may move to determine the sufficiency of an answer or objection. Unless the court finds an objection justified, it must order that an answer be served. On finding that an answer does not comply with FRCP 36, the court may order either that the matter is admitted or that an amended answer be served. The court may defer its final decision until a pretrial conference or a specified time before trial. FRCP 37(a)(5) applies to an award of expenses. FRCP 36(a)(6). Refer to the United States District Court for the District of Maine KeyRules Motion for Discovery Sanctions document for more information on sanctions.

3. *Sanctions for failure to cooperate in discovery.* The pattern of sanctions for FRCP 36 is somewhat different from that for the other discovery rules. The most important sanctions are two: a failure to respond to a request is deemed an admission of the matter to which the request is directed; and a party who, without good reason, refuses to admit a matter will be required to pay the costs incurred in proving that matter. FPP § 2265. If a party fails to admit what is requested under FRCP 36 and if the requesting party later proves a document to be genuine or the matter true, the requesting party may move that the party who failed to admit pay the reasonable expenses, including attorney's fees, incurred in making that proof. The court must so order unless: (A) the request was held objectionable under FRCP 36(a); (B) the admission sought was of no substantial importance; (C) the party failing to admit had a reasonable ground to believe that it might prevail on the matter; or (D) there was other good reason for the failure to admit. FRCP 37(c)(2). Refer to the United States District Court for the District of Maine KeyRules Motion for Discovery Sanctions document for more information on sanctions.

4. *Stipulations about discovery procedure.* Unless the court orders otherwise, the parties may stipulate that: (a) a deposition may be taken before any person, at any time or place, on any notice, and in the manner specified—in which event it may be used in the same way as any other deposition; and (b) other procedures governing or limiting discovery be modified—but a stipulation extending the time for any form of discovery must have court approval if it would interfere with the time set for completing discovery, for hearing a motion, or for trial. FRCP 29.

5. *DISTRICT OF MAINE: Appearances.* An attorney's signature to a pleading shall constitute an appearance for the party filing the pleading. Otherwise, an attorney who wishes to participate in any manner in any action must file a formal written appearance identifying the party represented. An appearance whether by pleading or formal written appearance shall be

signed by an attorney in his/her individual name and shall state his/her office address. ME R USDCT Rule 83.2(a). For more information, refer to ME R USDCT Rule 83.2.

6. *DISTRICT OF MAINE: Alternative dispute resolution (ADR).* Litigants are authorized and encouraged to employ, at their own expense, any available ADR process on which they can agree, including early neutral evaluation, settlement conferences, mediation, non-binding summary jury trial, corporate mini-trial, and arbitration proceedings. ME R USDCT Rule 83.11(a). For more information on ADR, refer to ME R USDCT Rule 83.11.

D. Documents

1. *Required documents*

   a. *Request for admissions.* Refer to the "C. General Requirements" section of this KeyRules document for information on the request for admissions.

2. *Supplemental documents*

   a. *Document(s).* A request to admit the genuineness of a document must be accompanied by a copy of the document unless it is, or has been, otherwise furnished or made available for inspection and copying. FRCP 36(a)(2).

   b. *Certificate of service.* No certificate of service is required when a paper is served by filing it with the court's electronic-filing system. When a paper that is required to be served is served by other means: (i) if the paper is filed, a certificate of service must be filed with it or within a reasonable time after service; and (ii) if the paper is not filed, a certificate of service need not be filed unless filing is required by court order or by local rule. FRCP 5(d)(1)(B).

E. Format

1. *Form of documents.* The rules governing captions and other matters of form in pleadings apply to motions and other papers. FRCP 7(b)(2).

   a. *DISTRICT OF MAINE: Font size, line spacing, and paper size.* All such documents shall be typed in a font of no less than size twelve (12) point, and shall be double-spaced or printed on eight and one-half by eleven (8-1/2 x 11) inch paper. Footnotes shall be in a font of no less than size ten (10) point, and may be single spaced. ME R USDCT Rule 10.

   b. *Caption.* Every pleading must have a caption with the court's name, a title, a file number, and an FRCP 7(a) designation. FRCP 10(a).

      i. *Names of parties.* The title of the complaint must name all the parties; the title of other pleadings, after naming the first party on each side, may refer generally to other parties. FRCP 10(a).

      ii. *DISTRICT OF MAINE: Additional caption requirements.* All pleadings, motions and other papers filed with the clerk or otherwise submitted to the court, except exhibits, shall bear the proper case number and shall contain on the first page a caption as described by FRCP 10(a) and immediately thereunder a designation of what the document is and the name of the party in whose behalf it is submitted. ME R USDCT Rule 10.

   c. *Claims or defenses*

      i. *Numbered paragraphs.* A party must state its claims or defenses in numbered paragraphs, each limited as far as practicable to a single set of circumstances. A later pleading may refer by number to a paragraph in an earlier pleading. FRCP 10(b).

      ii. *Separate statements.* If doing so would promote clarity, each claim founded on a separate transaction or occurrence—and each defense other than a denial—must be stated in a separate count or defense. FRCP 10(b).

   d. *Adoption by reference.* A statement in a pleading may be adopted by reference elsewhere in the same pleading or in any other pleading or motion. FRCP 10(c).

      i. *Exhibits.* A copy of a written instrument that is an exhibit to a pleading is a part of the pleading for all purposes. FRCP 10(c).

   e. *DISTRICT OF MAINE: Page numbering.* All pages shall be numbered at the bottom. ME R USDCT Rule 10.

   f. *DISTRICT OF MAINE: Attachment of ancillary papers.* Ancillary papers shall be attached at the end of the document to which they relate. ME R USDCT Rule 10.

   g. *Acceptance by the clerk.* The clerk must not refuse to file a paper solely because it is not in the form prescribed by the Federal Rules of Civil Procedure or by a local rule or practice. FRCP 5(d)(4).

2. *Signing disclosures and discovery requests, responses, and objections.* FRCP 11 does not apply to disclosures and discovery requests, responses, objections, and motions under FRCP 26 through FRCP 37. FRCP 11(d).

   a. *Signature required.* Every disclosure under FRCP 26(a)(1) or FRCP 26(a)(3) and every discovery request, response, or objection must be signed by at least one attorney of record in the attorney's own name—or by the party personally, if unrepresented—and must state the signer's address, e-mail address, and telephone number. FRCP 26(g)(1).

b. *Effect of signature.* By signing, an attorney or party certifies that to the best of the person's knowledge, information, and belief formed after a reasonable inquiry: (A) with respect to a disclosure, it is complete and correct as of the time it is made; and (B) with respect to a discovery request, response, or objection, it is: (i) consistent with the Federal Rules of Civil Procedure and warranted by existing law or by a nonfrivolous argument for extending, modifying, or reversing existing law, or for establishing new law; (ii) not interposed for any improper purpose, such as to harass, cause unnecessary delay, or needlessly increase the cost of litigation; and (iii) neither unreasonable nor unduly burdensome or expensive, considering the needs of the case, prior discovery in the case, the amount in controversy, and the importance of the issues at stake in the action. FRCP 26(g)(1).

c. *Failure to sign.* Other parties have no duty to act on an unsigned disclosure, request, response, or objection until it is signed, and the court must strike it unless a signature is promptly supplied after the omission is called to the attorney's or party's attention. FRCP 26(g)(2).

d. *Sanction for improper certification.* If a certification violates FRCP 26(g) without substantial justification, the court, on motion or on its own, must impose an appropriate sanction on the signer, the party on whose behalf the signer was acting, or both. The sanction may include an order to pay the reasonable expenses, including attorney's fees, caused by the violation. FRCP 26(g)(3). Refer to the United States District Court for the District of Maine KeyRules Motion for Discovery Sanctions document for more information.

3. *Privacy protection for filings made with the court*

a. *Redacted filings.* Unless the court orders otherwise, in an electronic or paper filing with the court that contains an individual's Social Security number, taxpayer-identification number, or birth date, the name of an individual known to be a minor, or a financial-account number, a party or nonparty making the filing may include only: (1) the last four (4) digits of the Social Security number and taxpayer-identification number; (2) the year of the individual's birth; (3) the minor's initials; and (4) the last four (4) digits of the financial-account number. FRCP 5.2(a).

   i. *DISTRICT OF MAINE.* To address the privacy concerns created by the Internet access to court papers, unless otherwise ordered by the court, counsel shall modify certain personal data identifiers in pleadings and other papers as follows: (1) minors' names: use of the minors' initials only; (2) Social Security numbers: use of the last four (4) numbers only; (3) dates of birth: use of the year of birth only; [and] (4) financial account numbers: identify the type of account and the financial institution, but use only the last four (4) numbers of the account number. ME R USDCT Redacting Pleadings. Counsel should also use caution when filing papers that contain a person's medical records, employment history; financial information; and any proprietary or trade secret information. ME R USDCT Redacting Pleadings.

b. *Exemptions from the redaction requirement.* The redaction requirement does not apply to the following: (1) a financial-account number that identifies the property allegedly subject to forfeiture in a forfeiture proceeding; (2) the record of an administrative or agency proceeding; (3) the official record of a state-court proceeding; (4) the record of a court or tribunal, if that record was not subject to the redaction requirement when originally filed; (5) a filing covered by FRCP 5.2(c) or FRCP 5.2(d); and (6) a pro se filing in an action brought under 28 U.S.C.A. § 2241, 28 U.S.C.A. § 2254, or 28 U.S.C.A. § 2255. FRCP 5.2(b).

c. *Limitations on remote access to electronic files; Social Security appeals and immigration cases.* Unless the court orders otherwise, in an action for benefits under the Social Security Act, and in an action or proceeding relating to an order of removal, to relief from removal, or to immigration benefits or detention, access to an electronic file is authorized as follows: (1) the parties and their attorneys may have remote electronic access to any part of the case file, including the administrative record; (2) any other person may have electronic access to the full record at the courthouse, but may have remote electronic access only to: (A) the docket maintained by the court; and (B) an opinion, order, judgment, or other disposition of the court, but not any other part of the case file or the administrative record. FRCP 5.2(c).

d. *Filings made under seal.* The court may order that a filing be made under seal without redaction. The court may later unseal the filing or order the person who made the filing to file a redacted version for the public record. FRCP 5.2(d).

   i. *DISTRICT OF MAINE.* For information on filing sealed documents in the District of Maine, refer to ME R USDCT Rule 7A, ME R USDCT App. 4(p)(2), and ME R USDCT Sealed Filings.

e. *Protective orders.* For good cause, the court may by order in a case: (1) require redaction of additional information; or (2) limit or prohibit a nonparty's remote electronic access to a document filed with the court. FRCP 5.2(e).

f. *Option for additional unredacted filing under seal.* A person making a redacted filing may also file an unredacted copy under seal. The court must retain the unredacted copy as part of the record. FRCP 5.2(f).

   i. *DISTRICT OF MAINE.* A party wishing to file a document containing the personal data identifiers specified above may. . .file an unredacted document under seal. This document will be retained by the clerk's office as part of the record. ME R USDCT Redacting Pleadings. The court may, however, still require the party to file a redacted copy for the public file. ME R USDCT Redacting Pleadings.

g. *Option for filing a reference list.* A filing that contains redacted information may be filed together with a reference list that identifies each item of redacted information and specifies an appropriate identifier that uniquely corresponds to each item listed. The list must be filed under seal and may be amended as of right. Any reference in the case to a listed identifier will be construed to refer to the corresponding item of information. FRCP 5.2(g).

   i. *DISTRICT OF MAINE.* A party wishing to file a document containing the personal data identifiers specified above may. . .file a reference list under seal. The reference list shall contain the complete personal data identifier(s) and the redacted identifier(s) used in its (their) place in the filing. All references in the case to the redacted identifiers included in the reference list will be construed to refer to the corresponding complete identifier. The reference list must be filed under seal, and may be amended as of right. It shall be retained by the clerk's office as part of the record. ME R USDCT Redacting Pleadings. The court may, however, still require the party to file a redacted copy for the public file. ME R USDCT Redacting Pleadings.

h. *DISTRICT OF MAINE: Responsibility for redaction.* The clerk is not required to review documents filed with the court for compliance with FRCP 5.2. The responsibility to redact filings rests with counsel and the party or nonparty making the filing. ME R USDCT App. 4(i); ME R USDCT Redacting Pleadings. For guidelines for filing confidential information in civil cases in the District of Maine, refer to ME R USDCT Confidentiality.

i. *Waiver of protection of identifiers.* A person waives the protection of FRCP 5.2(a) as to the person's own information by filing it without redaction and not under seal. FRCP 5.2(h).

F. Filing and Service Requirements

1. *Filing requirements*

   a. *Required filings.* Any paper after the complaint that is required to be served must be filed no later than a reasonable time after service. But disclosures under FRCP 26(a)(1) or FRCP 26(a)(2) and the following discovery requests and responses must not be filed until they are used in the proceeding or the court orders filing: depositions, interrogatories, requests for documents or tangible things or to permit entry onto land, and requests for admission. FRCP 5(d)(1)(A). Refer to the United States District Court for the District of Maine KeyRules pleading and motion documents for information on filing with the court.

      i. *DISTRICT OF MAINE.* Unless otherwise ordered by the court, depositions upon oral examination and interrogatories, requests for documents, requests for admissions, and answers and responses thereto and disclosures made under FRCP 26(a)(1) through FRCP 26(a)(3) and pursuant to scheduling orders issued by the court, shall be served upon other parties but shall not be filed with the court. ME R USDCT Rule 5(b); ME R USDCT Rule 26(a).

2. *Service requirements.* [A request for an admission] must be served on the party from whom the admission is requested and, unless the court has otherwise ordered, a copy of the request must be served on every other party. FPP § 2258.

   a. *Service; When required.* Unless the Federal Rules of Civil Procedure provide otherwise, each of the following papers must be served on every party: (A) an order stating that service is required; (B) a pleading filed after the original complaint, unless the court orders otherwise under FRCP 5(c) because there are numerous defendants; (C) a discovery paper required to be served on a party, unless the court orders otherwise; (D) a written motion, except one that may be heard ex parte; and (E) a written notice, appearance, demand, or offer of judgment, or any similar paper. FRCP 5(a)(1).

      i. *If a party fails to appear.* No service is required on a party who is in default for failing to appear. But a pleading that asserts a new claim for relief against such a party must be served on that party under FRCP 4. FRCP 5(a)(2).

      ii. *Seizing property.* If an action is begun by seizing property and no person is or need be named as a defendant, any service required before the filing of an appearance, answer, or claim must be made on the person who had custody or possession of the property when it was seized. FRCP 5(a)(3).

   b. *Service; How made.* A paper is served under FRCP 5 by: (A) handing it to the person; (B) leaving it: (i) at the person's office with a clerk or other person in charge or, if no one is in charge, in a conspicuous place in the office; or (ii) if the person has no office or the office is closed, at the person's dwelling or usual place of abode with someone of suitable age and discretion who resides there; (C) mailing it to the person's last known address—in which event service is complete upon mailing; (D) leaving it with the court clerk if the person has no known address; (E) sending it to a registered user by filing it with the court's electronic-filing system or sending it by other electronic means that the person consented to in writing—in either of which events service is complete upon filing or sending, but is not effective if the filer or sender learns that it did not reach the person to be served; or (F) delivering it by any other means that the person consented to in writing—in which event service is complete when the person making service delivers it to the agency designated to make delivery. FRCP 5(b)(2).

    i. *Serving an attorney.* If a party is represented by an attorney, service under FRCP 5 must be made on the attorney unless the court orders service on the party. FRCP 5(b)(1).

3. *DISTRICT OF MAINE: Preservation of original discovery.* The party that has served notice of a deposition or has served discovery papers shall be responsible for preserving and for [ensuring] the integrity of original transcripts and discovery papers for use by the court. ME R USDCT Rule 5(b); ME R USDCT Rule 26(a).

G. Hearings

1. There is no hearing contemplated in the federal statutes or rules for requests for admissions.

H. Forms

1. Federal Request for Admissions Forms

    a. Plaintiff's request for admission. 3B FEDFORMS § 26:60.

    b. Plaintiff's request for admission; Specific examples. 3B FEDFORMS § 26:61.

    c. Plaintiff's request for admission; Statements in documents. 3B FEDFORMS § 26:62.

    d. Plaintiff's request for admission; Statements in documents; Letter to defendant. 3B FEDFORMS § 26:63.

    e. Plaintiff's request for admission; Specific facts. 3B FEDFORMS § 26:64.

    f. Plaintiff's request for admission; Specific facts; Presentation of checks. 3B FEDFORMS § 26:65.

    g. Plaintiff's request for admission; Specific documents and facts. 3B FEDFORMS § 26:66.

    h. Plaintiff's request for admission; Specific documents and facts; Short version. 3B FEDFORMS § 26:67.

    i. Plaintiff's request for admission; True copies, filing and operational effect of government documents. 3B FED-FORMS § 26:68.

    j. Plaintiff's request for additional admission. 3B FEDFORMS § 26:69.

    k. Defendant's request for admission of genuineness; Specific document. 3B FEDFORMS § 26:70.

    l. Defendant's request for admission of genuineness; Specific document; Copy attached. 3B FEDFORMS § 26:71.

    m. Defendant's request for admission of genuineness; Specific document; Attached letters. 3B FEDFORMS § 26:72.

    n. Defendant's request for admission; Truth of statement. 3B FEDFORMS § 26:73.

    o. Request; For admission of facts and genuineness of documents. AMJUR PP DEPOSITION § 674.

    p. Request for admissions under FRCP 36. FEDPROF § 23:555.

    q. Request for admissions; General form. FEDPROF § 23:556.

    r. Request for admissions; Action to collect royalties. FEDPROF § 23:557.

    s. Request for admissions; Trademark action. FEDPROF § 23:558.

    t. Request for admissions; Automobile negligence action. FEDPROF § 23:559.

    u. Request for admissions; Motor vehicle action. FEDPROF § 23:560.

    v. Request for admissions; Premises liability action. FEDPROF § 23:561.

    w. Request for admissions; Products liability action. FEDPROF § 23:562.

    x. Request for admissions; Medical malpractice action. FEDPROF § 23:563.

    y. Request for admissions; Genuineness of documents. FEDPROF § 23:564.

    z. Request for admissions; Wrongful death due to forklift accident. FEDPROF § 23:565.

I. Applicable Rules

1. *Federal rules*

    a. Serving and filing pleadings and other papers. FRCP 5.

    b. Privacy protection for filings made with the court. FRCP 5.2.

    c. Computing and extending time; Time for motion papers. FRCP 6.

    d. Pleadings allowed; Form of motions and other papers. FRCP 7.

    e. Form of pleadings. FRCP 10.

    f. Signing pleadings, motions, and other papers; Representations to the court; Sanctions. FRCP 11.

    g. Duty to disclose; General provisions governing discovery. FRCP 26.

    h. Stipulations about discovery procedure. FRCP 29.

    i. Requests for admission. FRCP 36.

    j. Failure to make disclosures or to cooperate in discovery; Sanctions. FRCP 37.

2. *Local rules*

    a. *DISTRICT OF MAINE*

        i.   Service and filing of pleadings and other papers. ME R USDCT Rule 5.

        ii. Time. ME R USDCT Rule 6.

        iii. Form of pleadings, motions and other papers. ME R USDCT Rule 10.

        iv. Case management tracks. ME R USDCT Rule 16.1.

        v.   Discovery. ME R USDCT Rule 26.

        vi. Attorneys; Appearances and withdrawals. ME R USDCT Rule 83.2.

        vii. Alternative dispute resolution (ADR). ME R USDCT Rule 83.11.

        viii. Administrative procedures governing the filing and service by electronic means. ME R USDCT App. 4.

        ix. Redacting pleadings. ME R USDCT Redacting Pleadings.

Requests, Notices and Applications
Response to Request for Admissions

Document Last Updated July 2021

A. Checklist

(I) ❑ Matters to be considered by requesting party

   (a) ❑ Required documents

      (1) ❑ Request for admissions

   (b) ❑ Supplemental documents

      (1) ❑ Document(s)

      (2) ❑ Certificate of service

   (c) ❑ Timing

      (1) ❑ A party may not seek discovery from any source before the parties have conferred as required by FRCP 26(f), except in a proceeding exempted from initial disclosure under FRCP 26(a)(1)(B), or when authorized by the Federal Rules of Civil Procedure, by stipulation, or by court order

(II) ❑ Matters to be considered by responding party

   (a) ❑ Required documents

      (1) ❑ Response to request for admissions

(b) ❑ Supplemental documents

(1) ❑ Certificate of service

(c) ❑ Timing

(1) ❑ A matter is admitted unless, within thirty (30) days after being served, the party to whom the request is directed serves on the requesting party a written answer or objection addressed to the matter and signed by the party or its attorney

B. Timing

1. *Response to request for admissions.* A matter is admitted unless, within thirty (30) days after being served, the party to whom the request is directed serves on the requesting party a written answer or objection addressed to the matter and signed by the party or its attorney. A shorter or longer time for responding may be stipulated to under FRCP 29 or be ordered by the court. FRCP 36(a)(3).

2. *DISTRICT OF MAINE: Completion of discovery in standard track cases.* In standard track cases, discovery shall ordinarily be completed within five (5) months. ME R USDCT Rule 16.1(b)(2).

3. *Computation of time*

   a. *Computing time.* FRCP 6 applies in computing any time period specified in the Federal Rules of Civil Procedure, in any local rule or court order, or in any statute that does not specify a method of computing time. FRCP 6(a).

      i. *Period stated in days or a longer unit.* When the period is stated in days or a longer unit of time: (A) exclude the day of the event that triggers the period; (B) count every day, including intermediate Saturdays, Sundays, and legal holidays; and (C) include the last day of the period, but if the last day is a Saturday, Sunday, or legal holiday, the period continues to run until the end of the next day that is not a Saturday, Sunday, or legal holiday. FRCP 6(a)(1).

      ii. *Period stated in hours.* When the period is stated in hours: (A) begin counting immediately on the occurrence of the event that triggers the period; (B) count every hour, including hours during intermediate Saturdays, Sundays, and legal holidays; and (C) if the period would end on a Saturday, Sunday, or legal holiday, the period continues to run until the same time on the next day that is not a Saturday, Sunday, or legal holiday. FRCP 6(a)(2).

      iii. *Inaccessibility of the clerk's office.* Unless the court orders otherwise, if the clerk's office is inaccessible: (A) on the last day for filing under FRCP 6(a)(1), then the time for filing is extended to the first accessible day that is not a Saturday, Sunday, or legal holiday; or (B) during the last hour for filing under FRCP 6(a)(2), then the time for filing is extended to the same time on the first accessible day that is not a Saturday, Sunday, or legal holiday. FRCP 6(a)(3).

      iv. *"Last day" defined.* Unless a different time is set by a statute, local rule, or court order, the last day ends: (A) for electronic filing, at midnight in the court's time zone; and (B) for filing by other means, when the clerk's office is scheduled to close. FRCP 6(a)(4).

      v. *"Next day" defined.* The "next day" is determined by continuing to count forward when the period is measured after an event and backward when measured before an event. FRCP 6(a)(5).

      vi. *"Legal holiday" defined.* "Legal holiday" means: (A) the day set aside by statute for observing New Year's Day, Martin Luther King Jr.'s Birthday, Washington's Birthday, Memorial Day, Independence Day, Labor Day, Columbus Day, Veterans' Day, Thanksgiving Day, or Christmas Day; (B) any day declared a holiday by the President or Congress; and (C) for periods that are measured after an event, any other day declared a holiday by the state where the district court is located. FRCP 6(a)(6).

      vii. *DISTRICT OF MAINE: Applicability of FRCP 6.* FRCP 6 applies when computing any period of time stated in the Local Rules of the United States District Court for the District of Maine. ME R USDCT Rule 6(a).

   b. *Extending time.* When an act may or must be done within a specified time, the court may, for good cause, extend the time: (A) with or without motion or notice if the court acts, or if a request is made, before the original time or its extension expires; or (B) on motion made after the time has expired if the party failed to act because of excusable neglect. FRCP 6(b)(1). A court must not extend the time to act under FRCP 50(b), FRCP 50(d), FRCP 52(b), FRCP 59(b), FRCP 59(d), FRCP 59(e), and FRCP 60(b). FRCP 6(b)(2). Refer to the United States District Court for the District of Maine KeyRules Motion for Continuance/Extension of Time document for more information on extending time.

   c. *Additional time after certain kinds of service.* When a party may or must act within a specified time after being served and service is made under FRCP 5(b)(2)(C) (by mail), FRCP 5(b)(2)(D) (by leaving with the clerk), or FRCP 5(b)(2)(F) (by other means consented to), three (3) days are added after the period would otherwise expire under FRCP 6(a). FRCP 6(d).

C. General Requirements

1. *General provisions governing discovery*

   a. *Discovery scope and limits*

      i. *Scope in general.* Unless otherwise limited by court order, the scope of discovery is as follows: Parties may obtain discovery regarding any nonprivileged matter that is relevant to any party's claim or defense and proportional to the needs of the case, considering the importance of the issues at stake in the action, the amount in controversy, the parties' relative access to relevant information, the parties' resources, the importance of the discovery in resolving the issues, and whether the burden or expense of the proposed discovery outweighs its likely benefit. Information within this scope of discovery need not be admissible in evidence to be discoverable. FRCP 26(b)(1).

      ii. *Limitations on frequency and extent*

      - *When permitted.* By order, the court may alter the limits in the Federal Rules of Civil Procedure on the number of depositions and interrogatories or on the length of depositions under FRCP 30. By order or local rule, the court may also limit the number of requests under FRCP 36. FRCP 26(b)(2)(A).

      - *Specific limitations on electronically stored information.* A party need not provide discovery of electronically stored information from sources that the party identifies as not reasonably accessible because of undue burden or cost. On motion to compel discovery or for a protective order, the party from whom discovery is sought must show that the information is not reasonably accessible because of undue burden or cost. If that showing is made, the court may nonetheless order discovery from such sources if the requesting party shows good cause, considering the limitations of FRCP 26(b)(2)(C). The court may specify conditions for the discovery. FRCP 26(b)(2)(B).

      - *When required.* On motion or on its own, the court must limit the frequency or extent of discovery otherwise allowed by the Federal Rules of Civil Procedure or by local rule if it determines that: (i) the discovery sought is unreasonably cumulative or duplicative, or can be obtained from some other source that is more convenient, less burdensome, or less expensive; (ii) the party seeking discovery has had ample opportunity to obtain the information by discovery in the action; or (iii) the proposed discovery is outside the scope permitted by FRCP 26(b)(1). FRCP 26(b)(2)(C).

      iii. *Trial preparation; Materials*

      - *Documents and tangible things.* Ordinarily, a party may not discover documents and tangible things that are prepared in anticipation of litigation or for trial by or for another party or its representative (including the other party's attorney, consultant, surety, indemnitor, insurer, or agent). But, subject to FRCP 26(b)(4), those materials may be discovered if: (i) they are otherwise discoverable under FRCP 26(b)(1); and (ii) the party shows that it has substantial need for the materials to prepare its case and cannot, without undue hardship, obtain their substantial equivalent by other means. FRCP 26(b)(3)(A).

      - *Protection against disclosure.* If the court orders discovery of those materials, it must protect against disclosure of the mental impressions, conclusions, opinions, or legal theories of a party's attorney or other representative concerning the litigation. FRCP 26(b)(3)(B).

      - *Previous statement.* Any party or other person may, on request and without the required showing, obtain the person's own previous statement about the action or its subject matter. If the request is refused, the person may move for a court order, and FRCP 37(a)(5) applies to the award of expenses. A previous statement is either: (i) a written statement that the person has signed or otherwise adopted or approved; or (ii) a contemporaneous stenographic, mechanical, electrical, or other recording—or a transcription of it—that recites substantially verbatim the person's oral statement. FRCP 26(b)(3)(C).

      iv. *Trial preparation; Experts*

      - *Deposition of an expert who may testify.* A party may depose any person who has been identified as an expert whose opinions may be presented at trial. If FRCP 26(a)(2)(B) requires a report from the expert, the deposition may be conducted only after the report is provided. FRCP 26(b)(4)(A).

      - *Trial-preparation protection for draft reports or disclosures.* FRCP 26(b)(3)(A) and FRCP 26(b)(3)(B) protect drafts of any report or disclosure required under FRCP 26(a)(2), regardless of the form in which the draft is recorded. FRCP 26(b)(4)(B).

- *Trial-preparation protection for communications between a party's attorney and expert witnesses.* FRCP 26(b)(3)(A) and FRCP 26(b)(3)(B) protect communications between the party's attorney and any witness required to provide a report under FRCP 26(a)(2)(B), regardless of the form of the communications, except to the extent that the communications: (i) relate to compensation for the expert's study or testimony; (ii) identify facts or data that the party's attorney provided and that the expert considered in forming the opinions to be expressed; or (iii) identify assumptions that the party's attorney provided and that the expert relied on in forming the opinions to be expressed. FRCP 26(b)(4)(C).

- *Expert employed only for trial preparation.* Ordinarily, a party may not, by interrogatories or deposition, discover facts known or opinions held by an expert who has been retained or specially employed by another party in anticipation of litigation or to prepare for trial and who is not expected to be called as a witness at trial. But a party may do so only: (i) as provided in FRCP 35(b); or (ii) on showing exceptional circumstances under which it is impracticable for the party to obtain facts or opinions on the same subject by other means. FRCP 26(b)(4)(D).

- *Payment.* Unless manifest injustice would result, the court must require that the party seeking discovery: (i) pay the expert a reasonable fee for time spent in responding to discovery under FRCP 26(b)(4)(A) or FRCP 26(b)(4)(D); and (ii) for discovery under FRCP 26(b)(4)(D), also pay the other party a fair portion of the fees and expenses it reasonably incurred in obtaining the expert's facts and opinions. FRCP 26(b)(4)(E).

   v. *Claiming privilege or protecting trial-preparation materials*

- *Information withheld.* When a party withholds information otherwise discoverable by claiming that the information is privileged or subject to protection as trial-preparation material, the party must: (i) expressly make the claim; and (ii) describe the nature of the documents, communications, or tangible things not produced or disclosed—and do so in a manner that, without revealing information itself privileged or protected, will enable other parties to assess the claim. FRCP 26(b)(5)(A).

- *Information produced.* If information produced in discovery is subject to a claim of privilege or of protection as trial-preparation material, the party making the claim may notify any party that received the information of the claim and the basis for it. After being notified, a party must promptly return, sequester, or destroy the specified information and any copies it has; must not use or disclose the information until the claim is resolved; must take reasonable steps to retrieve the information if the party disclosed it before being notified; and may promptly present the information to the court under seal for a determination of the claim. The producing party must preserve the information until the claim is resolved. FRCP 26(b)(5)(B).

  b. *Protective orders.* A party or any person from whom discovery is sought may move for a protective order in the court where the action is pending—or as an alternative on matters relating to a deposition, in the court for the district where the deposition will be taken. FRCP 26(c)(1). Refer to the United States District Court for the District of Maine KeyRules Motion for Protective Order document for more information.

    i. *DISTRICT OF MAINE: Confidentiality order.* A party by motion or with the agreement of all parties may submit to the court a proposed order governing the production and use of confidential documents and information in the pending action. The proposed order shall conform to the Form Confidentiality Order set forth in ME R USDCT App. 2. Any proposed modification to the Form Confidentiality Order shall be identified with a short statement of the reason for each modification. ME R USDCT Rule 26(d).

  c. *Sequence of discovery.* Unless the parties stipulate or the court orders otherwise for the parties' and witnesses' convenience and in the interests of justice: (A) methods of discovery may be used in any sequence; and (B) discovery by one party does not require any other party to delay its discovery. FRCP 26(d)(3).

2. *Response to request for admissions*

  a. *Form.* The response to a request for admissions must be in writing and signed by the party or its attorney. FPP § 2259. The response should be a single document, in which the various requests are listed in order and an admission, a denial, an objection, or a statement of inability to admit or deny made to each of the requests as is appropriate. FPP § 2259.

  b. *Answer.* If a matter is not admitted, the answer must specifically deny it or state in detail why the answering party cannot truthfully admit or deny it. FRCP 36(a)(4).

    i. *Denial.* A denial must fairly respond to the substance of the matter; and when good faith requires that a party qualify an answer or deny only a part of a matter, the answer must specify the part admitted and qualify or deny the rest. FRCP 36(a)(4). It is expected that denials will be forthright, specific, and unconditional. If a response is thought insufficient as a denial, the court may treat it as an admission. FPP § 2260.

    ii.   *Lack of knowledge or information.* The answering party may assert lack of knowledge or information as a reason for failing to admit or deny only if the party states that it has made reasonable inquiry and that the information it knows or can readily obtain is insufficient to enable it to admit or deny. FRCP 36(a)(4). A general statement that it can neither admit nor deny, unaccompanied by reasons, will be held an insufficient response, and the court may either take the matter as admitted or order a further answer. FPP § 2261.

  c. *Objections.* Objections must be made in writing within the time allowed for answering the request. If some requests are to be answered and others objected to, the answers and objections should be contained in a single document. FPP § 2262. The grounds for objecting to a request must be stated. A party must not object solely on the ground that the request presents a genuine issue for trial. FRCP 36(a)(5). Failure to object to a request waives the objection. FPP § 2262.

  d. *Motion regarding the sufficiency of an answer or objection.* The requesting party may move to determine the sufficiency of an answer or objection. Unless the court finds an objection justified, it must order that an answer be served. On finding that an answer does not comply with FRCP 36, the court may order either that the matter is admitted or that an amended answer be served. The court may defer its final decision until a pretrial conference or a specified time before trial. FRCP 37(a)(5) applies to an award of expenses. FRCP 36(a)(6). Refer to the United States District Court for the District of Maine KeyRules Motion for Discovery Sanctions document for more information on sanctions.

  e. *Effect of an admission; Withdrawing or amending it.* A matter admitted under FRCP 36 is conclusively established unless the court, on motion, permits the admission to be withdrawn or amended. Subject to FRCP 16(e), the court may permit withdrawal or amendment if it would promote the presentation of the merits of the action and if the court is not persuaded that it would prejudice the requesting party in maintaining or defending the action on the merits. An admission under FRCP 36 is not an admission for any other purpose and cannot be used against the party in any other proceeding. FRCP 36(b).

3. *Supplementing disclosures and responses.* A party who has made a disclosure under FRCP 26(a)—or who has responded to an interrogatory, request for production, or request for admission—must supplement or correct its disclosure or response: (A) in a timely manner if the party learns that in some material respect the disclosure or response is incomplete or incorrect, and if the additional or corrective information has not otherwise been made known to the other parties during the discovery process or in writing; or (B) as ordered by the court. FRCP 26(e)(1).

4. *Sanctions for failure to cooperate in discovery.* The pattern of sanctions for FRCP 36 is somewhat different from that for the other discovery rules. The most important sanctions are two: a failure to respond to a request is deemed an admission of the matter to which the request is directed; and a party who, without good reason, refuses to admit a matter will be required to pay the costs incurred in proving that matter. FPP § 2265. If a party fails to admit what is requested under FRCP 36 and if the requesting party later proves a document to be genuine or the matter true, the requesting party may move that the party who failed to admit pay the reasonable expenses, including attorney's fees, incurred in making that proof. The court must so order unless: (A) the request was held objectionable under FRCP 36(a); (B) the admission sought was of no substantial importance; (C) the party failing to admit had a reasonable ground to believe that it might prevail on the matter; or (D) there was other good reason for the failure to admit. FRCP 37(c)(2). Refer to the United States District Court for the District of Maine KeyRules Motion for Discovery Sanctions document for more information on sanctions.

5. *Stipulations about discovery procedure.* Unless the court orders otherwise, the parties may stipulate that: (a) a deposition may be taken before any person, at any time or place, on any notice, and in the manner specified—in which event it may be used in the same way as any other deposition; and (b) other procedures governing or limiting discovery be modified—but a stipulation extending the time for any form of discovery must have court approval if it would interfere with the time set for completing discovery, for hearing a motion, or for trial. FRCP 29.

6. *DISTRICT OF MAINE: Appearances.* An attorney's signature to a pleading shall constitute an appearance for the party filing the pleading. Otherwise, an attorney who wishes to participate in any manner in any action must file a formal written appearance identifying the party represented. An appearance whether by pleading or formal written appearance shall be signed by an attorney in his/her individual name and shall state his/her office address. ME R USDCT Rule 83.2(a). For more information, refer to ME R USDCT Rule 83.2.

7. *DISTRICT OF MAINE: Alternative dispute resolution (ADR).* Litigants are authorized and encouraged to employ, at their own expense, any available ADR process on which they can agree, including early neutral evaluation, settlement conferences, mediation, non-binding summary jury trial, corporate mini-trial, and arbitration proceedings. ME R USDCT Rule 83.11(a). For more information on ADR, refer to ME R USDCT Rule 83.11.

D. Documents

1. *Required documents*

    a. *Response to request for admissions.* Refer to the "C. General Requirements" section of this KeyRules document for information on the response to request for admissions.

2. *Supplemental documents*

    a. *Certificate of service.* No certificate of service is required when a paper is served by filing it with the court's electronic-filing system. When a paper that is required to be served is served by other means: (i) if the paper is filed, a certificate of service must be filed with it or within a reasonable time after service; and (ii) if the paper is not filed, a certificate of service need not be filed unless filing is required by court order or by local rule. FRCP 5(d)(1)(B).

E. Format

1. *Form of documents.* The rules governing captions and other matters of form in pleadings apply to motions and other papers. FRCP 7(b)(2).

    a. *DISTRICT OF MAINE: Font size, line spacing, and paper size.* All such documents shall be typed in a font of no less than size twelve (12) point, and shall be double-spaced or printed on eight and one-half by eleven (8-1/2 x 11) inch paper. Footnotes shall be in a font of no less than size ten (10) point, and may be single spaced. ME R USDCT Rule 10.

    b. *Caption.* Every pleading must have a caption with the court's name, a title, a file number, and an FRCP 7(a) designation. FRCP 10(a).

        i. *Names of parties.* The title of the complaint must name all the parties; the title of other pleadings, after naming the first party on each side, may refer generally to other parties. FRCP 10(a).

        ii. *DISTRICT OF MAINE: Additional caption requirements.* All pleadings, motions and other papers filed with the clerk or otherwise submitted to the court, except exhibits, shall bear the proper case number and shall contain on the first page a caption as described by FRCP 10(a) and immediately thereunder a designation of what the document is and the name of the party in whose behalf it is submitted. ME R USDCT Rule 10.

    c. *Claims or defenses*

        i. *Numbered paragraphs.* A party must state its claims or defenses in numbered paragraphs, each limited as far as practicable to a single set of circumstances. A later pleading may refer by number to a paragraph in an earlier pleading. FRCP 10(b).

        ii. *Separate statements.* If doing so would promote clarity, each claim founded on a separate transaction or occurrence—and each defense other than a denial—must be stated in a separate count or defense. FRCP 10(b).

    d. *Adoption by reference.* A statement in a pleading may be adopted by reference elsewhere in the same pleading or in any other pleading or motion. FRCP 10(c).

        i. *Exhibits.* A copy of a written instrument that is an exhibit to a pleading is a part of the pleading for all purposes. FRCP 10(c).

    e. *DISTRICT OF MAINE: Page numbering.* All pages shall be numbered at the bottom. ME R USDCT Rule 10.

    f. *DISTRICT OF MAINE: Attachment of ancillary papers.* Ancillary papers shall be attached at the end of the document to which they relate. ME R USDCT Rule 10.

    g. *Acceptance by the clerk.* The clerk must not refuse to file a paper solely because it is not in the form prescribed by the Federal Rules of Civil Procedure or by a local rule or practice. FRCP 5(d)(4).

2. *Signing disclosures and discovery requests, responses, and objections.* FRCP 11 does not apply to disclosures and discovery requests, responses, objections, and motions under FRCP 26 through FRCP 37. FRCP 11(d).

    a. *Signature required.* Every disclosure under FRCP 26(a)(1) or FRCP 26(a)(3) and every discovery request, response, or objection must be signed by at least one attorney of record in the attorney's own name—or by the party personally, if unrepresented—and must state the signer's address, e-mail address, and telephone number. FRCP 26(g)(1).

        i. *Signature on response.* The response to a request for admissions must be in writing and signed by the party or its attorney. FPP § 2259.

    b. *Effect of signature.* By signing, an attorney or party certifies that to the best of the person's knowledge, information, and belief formed after a reasonable inquiry: (A) with respect to a disclosure, it is complete and correct as of the time it is made; and (B) with respect to a discovery request, response, or objection, it is: (i) consistent with the Federal

Rules of Civil Procedure and warranted by existing law or by a nonfrivolous argument for extending, modifying, or reversing existing law, or for establishing new law; (ii) not interposed for any improper purpose, such as to harass, cause unnecessary delay, or needlessly increase the cost of litigation; and (iii) neither unreasonable nor unduly burdensome or expensive, considering the needs of the case, prior discovery in the case, the amount in controversy, and the importance of the issues at stake in the action. FRCP 26(g)(1).

c. *Failure to sign.* Other parties have no duty to act on an unsigned disclosure, request, response, or objection until it is signed, and the court must strike it unless a signature is promptly supplied after the omission is called to the attorney's or party's attention. FRCP 26(g)(2).

d. *Sanction for improper certification.* If a certification violates FRCP 26(g) without substantial justification, the court, on motion or on its own, must impose an appropriate sanction on the signer, the party on whose behalf the signer was acting, or both. The sanction may include an order to pay the reasonable expenses, including attorney's fees, caused by the violation. FRCP 26(g)(3). Refer to the United States District Court for the District of Maine KeyRules Motion for Discovery Sanctions document for more information.

3. *Privacy protection for filings made with the court*

a. *Redacted filings.* Unless the court orders otherwise, in an electronic or paper filing with the court that contains an individual's Social Security number, taxpayer-identification number, or birth date, the name of an individual known to be a minor, or a financial-account number, a party or nonparty making the filing may include only: (1) the last four (4) digits of the Social Security number and taxpayer-identification number; (2) the year of the individual's birth; (3) the minor's initials; and (4) the last four (4) digits of the financial-account number. FRCP 5.2(a).

   i. *DISTRICT OF MAINE.* To address the privacy concerns created by the Internet access to court papers, unless otherwise ordered by the court, counsel shall modify certain personal data identifiers in pleadings and other papers as follows: (1) minors' names: use of the minors' initials only; (2) Social Security numbers: use of the last four (4) numbers only; (3) dates of birth: use of the year of birth only; [and] (4) financial account numbers: identify the type of account and the financial institution, but use only the last four (4) numbers of the account number. ME R USDCT Redacting Pleadings. Counsel should also use caution when filing papers that contain a person's medical records, employment history; financial information; and any proprietary or trade secret information. ME R USDCT Redacting Pleadings.

b. *Exemptions from the redaction requirement.* The redaction requirement does not apply to the following: (1) a financial-account number that identifies the property allegedly subject to forfeiture in a forfeiture proceeding; (2) the record of an administrative or agency proceeding; (3) the official record of a state-court proceeding; (4) the record of a court or tribunal, if that record was not subject to the redaction requirement when originally filed; (5) a filing covered by FRCP 5.2(c) or FRCP 5.2(d); and (6) a pro se filing in an action brought under 28 U.S.C.A. § 2241, 28 U.S.C.A. § 2254, or 28 U.S.C.A. § 2255. FRCP 5.2(b).

c. *Limitations on remote access to electronic files; Social Security appeals and immigration cases.* Unless the court orders otherwise, in an action for benefits under the Social Security Act, and in an action or proceeding relating to an order of removal, to relief from removal, or to immigration benefits or detention, access to an electronic file is authorized as follows: (1) the parties and their attorneys may have remote electronic access to any part of the case file, including the administrative record; (2) any other person may have electronic access to the full record at the courthouse, but may have remote electronic access only to: (A) the docket maintained by the court; and (B) an opinion, order, judgment, or other disposition of the court, but not any other part of the case file or the administrative record. FRCP 5.2(c).

d. *Filings made under seal.* The court may order that a filing be made under seal without redaction. The court may later unseal the filing or order the person who made the filing to file a redacted version for the public record. FRCP 5.2(d).

   i. *DISTRICT OF MAINE.* For information on filing sealed documents in the District of Maine, refer to ME R USDCT Rule 7A, ME R USDCT App. 4(p)(2), and ME R USDCT Sealed Filings.

e. *Protective orders.* For good cause, the court may by order in a case: (1) require redaction of additional information; or (2) limit or prohibit a nonparty's remote electronic access to a document filed with the court. FRCP 5.2(e).

f. *Option for additional unredacted filing under seal.* A person making a redacted filing may also file an unredacted copy under seal. The court must retain the unredacted copy as part of the record. FRCP 5.2(f).

   i. *DISTRICT OF MAINE.* A party wishing to file a document containing the personal data identifiers specified above may. . .file an unredacted document under seal. This document will be retained by the clerk's office as part of the record. ME R USDCT Redacting Pleadings. The court may, however, still require the party to file a redacted copy for the public file. ME R USDCT Redacting Pleadings.

g. *Option for filing a reference list.* A filing that contains redacted information may be filed together with a reference list that identifies each item of redacted information and specifies an appropriate identifier that uniquely corresponds to each item listed. The list must be filed under seal and may be amended as of right. Any reference in the case to a listed identifier will be construed to refer to the corresponding item of information. FRCP 5.2(g).

   i. *DISTRICT OF MAINE.* A party wishing to file a document containing the personal data identifiers specified above may. . .file a reference list under seal. The reference list shall contain the complete personal data identifier(s) and the redacted identifier(s) used in its (their) place in the filing. All references in the case to the redacted identifiers included in the reference list will be construed to refer to the corresponding complete identifier. The reference list must be filed under seal, and may be amended as of right. It shall be retained by the clerk's office as part of the record. ME R USDCT Redacting Pleadings. The court may, however, still require the party to file a redacted copy for the public file. ME R USDCT Redacting Pleadings.

h. *DISTRICT OF MAINE: Responsibility for redaction.* The clerk is not required to review documents filed with the court for compliance with FRCP 5.2. The responsibility to redact filings rests with counsel and the party or nonparty making the filing. ME R USDCT App. 4(i); ME R USDCT Redacting Pleadings. For guidelines for filing confidential information in civil cases in the District of Maine, refer to ME R USDCT Confidentiality.

i. *Waiver of protection of identifiers.* A person waives the protection of FRCP 5.2(a) as to the person's own information by filing it without redaction and not under seal. FRCP 5.2(h).

F. Filing and Service Requirements

1. *Filing requirements*

   a. *Required filings.* Any paper after the complaint that is required to be served must be filed no later than a reasonable time after service. But disclosures under FRCP 26(a)(1) or FRCP 26(a)(2) and the following discovery requests and responses must not be filed until they are used in the proceeding or the court orders filing: depositions, interrogatories, requests for documents or tangible things or to permit entry onto land, and requests for admission. FRCP 5(d)(1)(A). Refer to the United States District Court for the District of Maine KeyRules pleading and motion documents for information on filing with the court.

      i. *DISTRICT OF MAINE.* Unless otherwise ordered by the court, depositions upon oral examination and interrogatories, requests for documents, requests for admissions, and answers and responses thereto and disclosures made under FRCP 26(a)(1) through FRCP 26(a)(3) and pursuant to scheduling orders issued by the court, shall be served upon other parties but shall not be filed with the court. ME R USDCT Rule 5(b); ME R USDCT Rule 26(a).

2. *Service requirements.* A copy of the response must be served upon the party making the request. A copy of the response must also be served on all other parties to the action unless the court has ordered to the contrary. FPP § 2259.

   a. *Service; When required.* Unless the Federal Rules of Civil Procedure provide otherwise, each of the following papers must be served on every party: (A) an order stating that service is required; (B) a pleading filed after the original complaint, unless the court orders otherwise under FRCP 5(c) because there are numerous defendants; (C) a discovery paper required to be served on a party, unless the court orders otherwise; (D) a written motion, except one that may be heard ex parte; and (E) a written notice, appearance, demand, or offer of judgment, or any similar paper. FRCP 5(a)(1).

      i. *If a party fails to appear.* No service is required on a party who is in default for failing to appear. But a pleading that asserts a new claim for relief against such a party must be served on that party under FRCP 4. FRCP 5(a)(2).

      ii. *Seizing property.* If an action is begun by seizing property and no person is or need be named as a defendant, any service required before the filing of an appearance, answer, or claim must be made on the person who had custody or possession of the property when it was seized. FRCP 5(a)(3).

   b. *Service; How made.* A paper is served under FRCP 5 by: (A) handing it to the person; (B) leaving it: (i) at the person's office with a clerk or other person in charge or, if no one is in charge, in a conspicuous place in the office; or (ii) if the person has no office or the office is closed, at the person's dwelling or usual place of abode with someone of suitable age and discretion who resides there; (C) mailing it to the person's last known address—in which event service is complete upon mailing; (D) leaving it with the court clerk if the person has no known address; (E) sending it to a registered user by filing it with the court's electronic-filing system or sending it by other electronic means that the person consented to in writing—in either of which events service is complete upon filing or sending, but is not effective if the filer or sender learns that it did not reach the person to be served; or (F) delivering it by any other means that the person consented to in writing—in which event service is complete when the person making service delivers it to the agency designated to make delivery. FRCP 5(b)(2).

    i. *Serving an attorney.* If a party is represented by an attorney, service under FRCP 5 must be made on the attorney unless the court orders service on the party. FRCP 5(b)(1).

3. *DISTRICT OF MAINE: Preservation of original discovery.* The party that has served notice of a deposition or has served discovery papers shall be responsible for preserving and for [ensuring] the integrity of original transcripts and discovery papers for use by the court. ME R USDCT Rule 5(b); ME R USDCT Rule 26(a).

G. Hearings

1. There is no hearing contemplated in the federal statutes or rules for responses to requests for admissions.

H. Forms

1. Federal Response to Request for Admissions Forms

    a. Response to request for admission. 3B FEDFORMS § 26:74.

    b. Response to request for admission; Admissions, qualified admissions, denials. 3B FEDFORMS § 26:75.

    c. Response to request for admission; Denials and admissions of specific facts and explanatory statement of inability to admit or deny. 3B FEDFORMS § 26:76.

    d. Response to request for admission; Denials and admissions of specific facts and explanatory statement of inability to admit or deny; Statement. 3B FEDFORMS § 26:77.

    e. Objections to requests for admissions. 3B FEDFORMS § 26:78.

    f. Objections to request for admissions; Privileged. 3B FEDFORMS § 26:79.

    g. Amended response to request for admission. 3B FEDFORMS § 26:80.

    h. Response; To request for admission of facts. AMJUR PP DEPOSITION § 684.

    i. Response; To request for admission of facts; With verification. AMJUR PP DEPOSITION § 685.

    j. Reply; To request for admissions of fact and genuineness of documents; Refusal to answer on ground of privilege. AMJUR PP DEPOSITION § 686.

    k. Answer; To demand for admissions; Admission or denial not required under governing statute or rule. AMJUR PP DEPOSITION § 687.

    l. Reply; Objection to request for admissions; Irrelevancy and immateriality; Answer already made in response to interrogatories. AMJUR PP DEPOSITION § 688.

    m. Answer; To request for admissions; General form. FEDPROF § 23:571.

    n. Answer; To request for admissions; Insurance claim. FEDPROF § 23:572.

    o. Objections; To request for admissions. FEDPROF § 23:573.

    p. Objections to request. GOLDLTGFMS § 30:12.

    q. Reply to request for admissions. GOLDLTGFMS § 30:15.

    r. Response to request; General form. GOLDLTGFMS § 30:16.

    s. Response to request; Denials. GOLDLTGFMS § 30:17.

    t. Response to request; Admission of genuineness of document. GOLDLTGFMS § 30:18.

    u. Response to request; Admission of facts. GOLDLTGFMS § 30:19.

    v. Reply and objections to request for admissions. GOLDLTGFMS § 30:20.

I. Applicable Rules

1. *Federal rules*

    a. Serving and filing pleadings and other papers. FRCP 5.

    b. Privacy protection for filings made with the court. FRCP 5.2.

    c. Computing and extending time; Time for motion papers. FRCP 6.

    d. Pleadings allowed; Form of motions and other papers. FRCP 7.

e. Form of pleadings. FRCP 10.

f. Signing pleadings, motions, and other papers; Representations to the court; Sanctions. FRCP 11.

g. Duty to disclose; General provisions governing discovery. FRCP 26.

h. Stipulations about discovery procedure. FRCP 29.

i. Requests for admission. FRCP 36.

j. Failure to make disclosures or to cooperate in discovery; Sanctions. FRCP 37.

2. *Local rules*

a. *DISTRICT OF MAINE*

i. Service and filing of pleadings and other papers. ME R USDCT Rule 5.

ii. Time. ME R USDCT Rule 6.

iii. Form of pleadings, motions and other papers. ME R USDCT Rule 10.

iv. Case management tracks. ME R USDCT Rule 16.1.

v. Discovery. ME R USDCT Rule 26.

vi. Attorneys; Appearances and withdrawals. ME R USDCT Rule 83.2.

vii. Alternative dispute resolution (ADR). ME R USDCT Rule 83.11.

viii. Administrative procedures governing the filing and service by electronic means. ME R USDCT App. 4.

ix. Redacting pleadings. ME R USDCT Redacting Pleadings.

Requests, Notices and Applications
Notice of Deposition

Document Last Updated July 2021

A. Checklist

(I) ❑ Matters to be considered by deposing party for depositions by oral examination

    (a) ❑ Required documents

        (1) ❑ Notice of deposition

    (b) ❑ Supplemental documents

        (1) ❑ Subpoena

        (2) ❑ Subpoena duces tecum

        (3) ❑ Request for production of documents

        (4) ❑ Certificate of service

    (c) ❑ Timing

        (1) ❑ A party may, by oral questions, depose any person, including a party, without leave of court except as provided in FRCP 30(a)(2)

        (2) ❑ A party must obtain leave of court, and the court must grant leave to the extent consistent with FRCP 26(b)(1) and FRCP 26(b)(2): (A) if the parties have not stipulated to the deposition and: (i) the deposition would result in more than ten (10) depositions being taken under FRCP 30 or FRCP 31 by the plaintiffs, or by the defendants, or by the third-party defendants; (ii) the deponent has already been deposed in the case; or (iii) the party seeks to take the deposition before the time specified in FRCP 26(d), unless the party certifies in the notice, with supporting facts, that the deponent is expected to leave the United States and be unavailable for examination in this country after that time; or (B) if the deponent is confined in prison

        (3) ❑ A party who wants to depose a person by oral questions must give reasonable written notice to every other party

(II) ❑ Matters to be considered by deposing party for depositions by written questions

    (a) ❑ Required documents

        (1) ❑ Notice of deposition

        (2) ❑ Written questions

    (b) ❑ Supplemental documents

        (1) ❑ Subpoena

        (2) ❑ Certificate of service

    (c) ❑ Timing

        (1) ❑ A party may, by written questions, depose any person, including a party, without leave of court except as provided in FRCP 31(a)(2)

        (2) ❑ A party must obtain leave of court, and the court must grant leave to the extent consistent with FRCP 26(b)(1) and FRCP 26(b)(2): (A) if the parties have not stipulated to the deposition and: (i) the deposition would result in more than ten (10) depositions being taken under FRCP 31 or FRCP 30 by the plaintiffs, or by the defendants, or by the third-party defendants; (ii) the deponent has already been deposed in the case; or (iii) the party seeks to take a deposition before the time specified in FRCP 26(d); or (B) if the deponent is confined in prison

        (3) ❑ A party who wants to depose a person by written questions must serve them on every other party, with a notice

B. Timing

1. *Depositions by oral examination*

    a. *Without leave.* A party may, by oral questions, depose any person, including a party, without leave of court except as provided in FRCP 30(a)(2). FRCP 30(a)(1).

    b. *With leave.* A party must obtain leave of court, and the court must grant leave to the extent consistent with FRCP 26(b)(1) and FRCP 26(b)(2): (A) if the parties have not stipulated to the deposition and: (i) the deposition would result in more than ten (10) depositions being taken under FRCP 30 or FRCP 31 by the plaintiffs, or by the defendants, or by the third-party defendants; (ii) the deponent has already been deposed in the case; or (iii) the party seeks to take the deposition before the time specified in FRCP 26(d), unless the party certifies in the notice, with supporting facts, that the deponent is expected to leave the United States and be unavailable for examination in this country after that time; or (B) if the deponent is confined in prison. FRCP 30(a)(2).

    c. *Notice of deposition.* A party who wants to depose a person by oral questions must give reasonable written notice to every other party. FRCP 30(b)(1).

2. *Depositions by written questions*

    a. *Without leave.* A party may, by written questions, depose any person, including a party, without leave of court except as provided in FRCP 31(a)(2). FRCP 31(a)(1).

    b. *With leave.* A party must obtain leave of court, and the court must grant leave to the extent consistent with FRCP 26(b)(1) and FRCP 26(b)(2): (A) if the parties have not stipulated to the deposition and: (i) the deposition would result in more than ten (10) depositions being taken under FRCP 31 or FRCP 30 by the plaintiffs, or by the defendants, or by the third-party defendants; (ii) the deponent has already been deposed in the case; or (iii) the party seeks to take a deposition before the time specified in FRCP 26(d); or (B) if the deponent is confined in prison. FRCP 31(a)(2).

    c. *Notice of deposition with written questions.* A party who wants to depose a person by written questions must serve them on every other party, with a notice. FRCP 31(a)(3). Refer to the "C. General Requirements" section of this KeyRules document for the contents of the notice.

    d. *Questions from other parties.* Any questions to the deponent from other parties must be served on all parties as follows: cross-questions, within fourteen (14) days after being served with the notice and direct questions; redirect questions, within seven (7) days after being served with cross-questions; and recross-questions, within seven (7) days after being served with redirect questions. The court may, for good cause, extend or shorten these times. FRCP 31(a)(5).

3. *Commencement of discovery.* A party may not seek discovery from any source before the parties have conferred as required by FRCP 26(f), except in a proceeding exempted from initial disclosure under FRCP 26(a)(1)(B), or when authorized by the Federal Rules of Civil Procedure, by stipulation, or by court order. FRCP 26(d)(1).

4. *DISTRICT OF MAINE: Completion of discovery in standard track cases.* In standard track cases, discovery shall ordinarily be completed within five (5) months. ME R USDCT Rule 16.1(b)(2).

5. *Computation of time*

 a. *Computing time.* FRCP 6 applies in computing any time period specified in the Federal Rules of Civil Procedure, in any local rule or court order, or in any statute that does not specify a method of computing time. FRCP 6(a).

 i. *Period stated in days or a longer unit.* When the period is stated in days or a longer unit of time: (A) exclude the day of the event that triggers the period; (B) count every day, including intermediate Saturdays, Sundays, and legal holidays; and (C) include the last day of the period, but if the last day is a Saturday, Sunday, or legal holiday, the period continues to run until the end of the next day that is not a Saturday, Sunday, or legal holiday. FRCP 6(a)(1).

 ii. *Period stated in hours.* When the period is stated in hours: (A) begin counting immediately on the occurrence of the event that triggers the period; (B) count every hour, including hours during intermediate Saturdays, Sundays, and legal holidays; and (C) if the period would end on a Saturday, Sunday, or legal holiday, the period continues to run until the same time on the next day that is not a Saturday, Sunday, or legal holiday. FRCP 6(a)(2).

 iii. *Inaccessibility of the clerk's office.* Unless the court orders otherwise, if the clerk's office is inaccessible: (A) on the last day for filing under FRCP 6(a)(1), then the time for filing is extended to the first accessible day that is not a Saturday, Sunday, or legal holiday; or (B) during the last hour for filing under FRCP 6(a)(2), then the time for filing is extended to the same time on the first accessible day that is not a Saturday, Sunday, or legal holiday. FRCP 6(a)(3).

 iv. *"Last day" defined.* Unless a different time is set by a statute, local rule, or court order, the last day ends: (A) for electronic filing, at midnight in the court's time zone; and (B) for filing by other means, when the clerk's office is scheduled to close. FRCP 6(a)(4).

 v. *"Next day" defined.* The "next day" is determined by continuing to count forward when the period is measured after an event and backward when measured before an event. FRCP 6(a)(5).

 vi. *"Legal holiday" defined.* "Legal holiday" means: (A) the day set aside by statute for observing New Year's Day, Martin Luther King Jr.'s Birthday, Washington's Birthday, Memorial Day, Independence Day, Labor Day, Columbus Day, Veterans' Day, Thanksgiving Day, or Christmas Day; (B) any day declared a holiday by the President or Congress; and (C) for periods that are measured after an event, any other day declared a holiday by the state where the district court is located. FRCP 6(a)(6).

 vii. *DISTRICT OF MAINE: Applicability of FRCP 6.* FRCP 6 applies when computing any period of time stated in the Local Rules of the United States District Court for the District of Maine. ME R USDCT Rule 6(a).

 b. *Extending time.* When an act may or must be done within a specified time, the court may, for good cause, extend the time: (A) with or without motion or notice if the court acts, or if a request is made, before the original time or its extension expires; or (B) on motion made after the time has expired if the party failed to act because of excusable neglect. FRCP 6(b)(1). A court must not extend the time to act under FRCP 50(b), FRCP 50(d), FRCP 52(b), FRCP 59(b), FRCP 59(d), FRCP 59(e), and FRCP 60(b). FRCP 6(b)(2). Refer to the United States District Court for the District of Maine KeyRules Motion for Continuance/Extension of Time document for more information on extending time.

 c. *Additional time after certain kinds of service.* When a party may or must act within a specified time after being served and service is made under FRCP 5(b)(2)(C) (by mail), FRCP 5(b)(2)(D) (by leaving with the clerk), or FRCP 5(b)(2)(F) (by other means consented to), three (3) days are added after the period would otherwise expire under FRCP 6(a). FRCP 6(d).

C. General Requirements

1. *General provisions governing discovery*

 a. *Discovery scope and limits*

 i. *Scope in general.* Unless otherwise limited by court order, the scope of discovery is as follows: Parties may obtain discovery regarding any nonprivileged matter that is relevant to any party's claim or defense and proportional to the needs of the case, considering the importance of the issues at stake in the action, the amount in controversy, the parties' relative access to relevant information, the parties' resources, the importance of the discovery in resolving the issues, and whether the burden or expense of the proposed discovery outweighs its likely benefit. Information within this scope of discovery need not be admissible in evidence to be discoverable. FRCP 26(b)(1).

ii. *Limitations on frequency and extent*

- *When permitted.* By order, the court may alter the limits in the Federal Rules of Civil Procedure on the number of depositions and interrogatories or on the length of depositions under FRCP 30. By order or local rule, the court may also limit the number of requests under FRCP 36. FRCP 26(b)(2)(A).

- *Specific limitations on electronically stored information.* A party need not provide discovery of electronically stored information from sources that the party identifies as not reasonably accessible because of undue burden or cost. On motion to compel discovery or for a protective order, the party from whom discovery is sought must show that the information is not reasonably accessible because of undue burden or cost. If that showing is made, the court may nonetheless order discovery from such sources if the requesting party shows good cause, considering the limitations of FRCP 26(b)(2)(C). The court may specify conditions for the discovery. FRCP 26(b)(2)(B).

- *When required.* On motion or on its own, the court must limit the frequency or extent of discovery otherwise allowed by the Federal Rules of Civil Procedure or by local rule if it determines that: (i) the discovery sought is unreasonably cumulative or duplicative, or can be obtained from some other source that is more convenient, less burdensome, or less expensive; (ii) the party seeking discovery has had ample opportunity to obtain the information by discovery in the action; or (iii) the proposed discovery is outside the scope permitted by FRCP 26(b)(1). FRCP 26(b)(2)(C).

iii. *Trial preparation; Materials*

- *Documents and tangible things.* Ordinarily, a party may not discover documents and tangible things that are prepared in anticipation of litigation or for trial by or for another party or its representative (including the other party's attorney, consultant, surety, indemnitor, insurer, or agent). But, subject to FRCP 26(b)(4), those materials may be discovered if: (i) they are otherwise discoverable under FRCP 26(b)(1); and (ii) the party shows that it has substantial need for the materials to prepare its case and cannot, without undue hardship, obtain their substantial equivalent by other means. FRCP 26(b)(3)(A).

- *Protection against disclosure.* If the court orders discovery of those materials, it must protect against disclosure of the mental impressions, conclusions, opinions, or legal theories of a party's attorney or other representative concerning the litigation. FRCP 26(b)(3)(B).

- *Previous statement.* Any party or other person may, on request and without the required showing, obtain the person's own previous statement about the action or its subject matter. If the request is refused, the person may move for a court order, and FRCP 37(a)(5) applies to the award of expenses. A previous statement is either: (i) a written statement that the person has signed or otherwise adopted or approved; or (ii) a contemporaneous stenographic, mechanical, electrical, or other recording—or a transcription of it—that recites substantially verbatim the person's oral statement. FRCP 26(b)(3)(C).

iv. *Trial preparation; Experts*

- *Deposition of an expert who may testify.* A party may depose any person who has been identified as an expert whose opinions may be presented at trial. If FRCP 26(a)(2)(B) requires a report from the expert, the deposition may be conducted only after the report is provided. FRCP 26(b)(4)(A).

- *Trial-preparation protection for draft reports or disclosures.* FRCP 26(b)(3)(A) and FRCP 26(b)(3)(B) protect drafts of any report or disclosure required under FRCP 26(a)(2), regardless of the form in which the draft is recorded. FRCP 26(b)(4)(B).

- *Trial-preparation protection for communications between a party's attorney and expert witnesses.* FRCP 26(b)(3)(A) and FRCP 26(b)(3)(B) protect communications between the party's attorney and any witness required to provide a report under FRCP 26(a)(2)(B), regardless of the form of the communications, except to the extent that the communications: (i) relate to compensation for the expert's study or testimony; (ii) identify facts or data that the party's attorney provided and that the expert considered in forming the opinions to be expressed; or (iii) identify assumptions that the party's attorney provided and that the expert relied on in forming the opinions to be expressed. FRCP 26(b)(4)(C).

- *Expert employed only for trial preparation.* Ordinarily, a party may not, by interrogatories or deposition, discover facts known or opinions held by an expert who has been retained or specially employed by another party in anticipation of litigation or to prepare for trial and who is not expected to be called as a witness at trial. But a party may do so only: (i) as provided in FRCP 35(b); or (ii) on showing exceptional circumstances under which it is impracticable for the party to obtain facts or opinions on the same subject by other means. FRCP 26(b)(4)(D).

- *Payment.* Unless manifest injustice would result, the court must require that the party seeking discovery: (i) pay the expert a reasonable fee for time spent in responding to discovery under FRCP 26(b)(4)(A) or FRCP 26(b)(4)(D); and (ii) for discovery under FRCP 26(b)(4)(D), also pay the other party a fair portion of the fees and expenses it reasonably incurred in obtaining the expert's facts and opinions. FRCP 26(b)(4)(E).

v. *Claiming privilege or protecting trial-preparation materials*

- *Information withheld.* When a party withholds information otherwise discoverable by claiming that the information is privileged or subject to protection as trial-preparation material, the party must: (i) expressly make the claim; and (ii) describe the nature of the documents, communications, or tangible things not produced or disclosed—and do so in a manner that, without revealing information itself privileged or protected, will enable other parties to assess the claim. FRCP 26(b)(5)(A).

- *Information produced.* If information produced in discovery is subject to a claim of privilege or of protection as trial-preparation material, the party making the claim may notify any party that received the information of the claim and the basis for it. After being notified, a party must promptly return, sequester, or destroy the specified information and any copies it has; must not use or disclose the information until the claim is resolved; must take reasonable steps to retrieve the information if the party disclosed it before being notified; and may promptly present the information to the court under seal for a determination of the claim. The producing party must preserve the information until the claim is resolved. FRCP 26(b)(5)(B).

b. *Protective orders.* A party or any person from whom discovery is sought may move for a protective order in the court where the action is pending—or as an alternative on matters relating to a deposition, in the court for the district where the deposition will be taken. FRCP 26(c)(1). Refer to the United States District Court for the District of Maine KeyRules Motion for Protective Order document for more information.

    i. *DISTRICT OF MAINE: Confidentiality order.* A party by motion or with the agreement of all parties may submit to the court a proposed order governing the production and use of confidential documents and information in the pending action. The proposed order shall conform to the Form Confidentiality Order set forth in ME R USDCT App. 2. Any proposed modification to the Form Confidentiality Order shall be identified with a short statement of the reason for each modification. ME R USDCT Rule 26(d).

c. *Sequence of discovery.* Unless the parties stipulate or the court orders otherwise for the parties' and witnesses' convenience and in the interests of justice: (A) methods of discovery may be used in any sequence; and (B) discovery by one party does not require any other party to delay its discovery. FRCP 26(d)(3).

2. *Persons before whom depositions may be taken*

a. *Within the United States.* Within the United States or a territory or insular possession subject to United States jurisdiction, a deposition must be taken before: (A) an officer authorized to administer oaths either by federal law or by the law in the place of examination; or (B) a person appointed by the court where the action is pending to administer oaths and take testimony. FRCP 28(a)(1).

    i. *Definition of "officer".* The term "officer" in FRCP 30, FRCP 31, and FRCP 32 includes a person appointed by the court under FRCP 28 or designated by the parties under FRCP 29(a). FRCP 28(a)(2).

b. *In a foreign country.* A deposition may be taken in a foreign country: (A) under an applicable treaty or convention; (B) under a letter of request, whether or not captioned a "letter rogatory"; (C) on notice, before a person authorized to administer oaths either by federal law or by the law in the place of examination; or (D) before a person commissioned by the court to administer any necessary oath and take testimony. FRCP 28(b)(1).

    i. *Issuing a letter of request or a commission.* A letter of request, a commission, or both may be issued: (A) on appropriate terms after an application and notice of it; and (B) without a showing that taking the deposition in another manner is impracticable or inconvenient. FRCP 28(b)(2).

    ii. *Form of a request, notice, or commission.* When a letter of request or any other device is used according to a treaty or convention, it must be captioned in the form prescribed by that treaty or convention. A letter of request may be addressed "To the Appropriate Authority in [name of country]." A deposition notice or a commission must designate by name or descriptive title the person before whom the deposition is to be taken. FRCP 28(b)(3).

    iii. *Letter of request; Admitting evidence.* Evidence obtained in response to a letter of request need not be excluded merely because it is not a verbatim transcript, because the testimony was not taken under oath, or because of any similar departure from the requirements for depositions taken within the United States. FRCP 28(b)(4).

c. *Disqualification.* A deposition must not be taken before a person who is any party's relative, employee, or attorney; who is related to or employed by any party's attorney; or who is financially interested in the action. FRCP 28(c).

3. *Depositions by oral examination*

a. *Notice of the deposition.* A party who wants to depose a person by oral questions must give reasonable written notice to every other party. The notice must state the time and place of the deposition and, if known, the deponent's name and address. If the name is unknown, the notice must provide a general description sufficient to identify the person or the particular class or group to which the person belongs. FRCP 30(b)(1).

  i. *Notice or subpoena directed to an organization.* In its notice or subpoena, a party may name as the deponent a public or private corporation, a partnership, an association, a governmental agency, or other entity and must describe with reasonable particularity the matters for examination. The named organization must designate one or more officers, directors, or managing agents, or designate other persons who consent to testify on its behalf; and it may set out the matters on which each person designated will testify. Before or promptly after the notice or subpoena is served, the serving party and the organization must confer in good faith about the matters for examination. A subpoena must advise a nonparty organization of its duty to confer with the serving party and to designate each person who will testify. The persons designated must testify about information known or reasonably available to the organization. FRCP 30(b)(6) does not preclude a deposition by any other procedure allowed by the Federal Rules of Civil Procedure. FRCP 30(b)(6).

b. *Method of recording*

  i. *Method stated in the notice.* The party who notices the deposition must state in the notice the method for recording the testimony. Unless the court orders otherwise, testimony may be recorded by audio, audiovisual, or stenographic means. The noticing party bears the recording costs. Any party may arrange to transcribe a deposition. FRCP 30(b)(3)(A).

  ii. *Additional method.* With prior notice to the deponent and other parties, any party may designate another method for recording the testimony in addition to that specified in the original notice. That party bears the expense of the additional record or transcript unless the court orders otherwise. FRCP 30(b)(3)(B).

c. *By remote means.* The parties may stipulate—or the court may on motion order—that a deposition be taken by telephone or other remote means. For the purpose of FRCP 30 and FRCP 28(a), FRCP 37(a)(2), and FRCP 37(b)(1), the deposition takes place where the deponent answers the questions. FRCP 30(b)(4).

d. *Officer's duties*

  i. *Before the deposition.* Unless the parties stipulate otherwise, a deposition must be conducted before an officer appointed or designated under FRCP 28. The officer must begin the deposition with an on-the-record statement that includes: (i) the officer's name and business address; (ii) the date, time, and place of the deposition; (iii) the deponent's name; (iv) the officer's administration of the oath or affirmation to the deponent; and (v) the identity of all persons present. FRCP 30(b)(5)(A).

  ii. *Conducting the deposition; Avoiding distortion.* If the deposition is recorded non-stenographically, the officer must repeat the items in FRCP 30(b)(5)(A)(i) through FRCP 30(b)(5)(A)(iii) at the beginning of each unit of the recording medium. The deponent's and attorneys' appearance or demeanor must not be distorted through recording techniques. FRCP 30(b)(5)(B).

  iii. *After the deposition.* At the end of a deposition, the officer must state on the record that the deposition is complete and must set out any stipulations made by the attorneys about custody of the transcript or recording and of the exhibits, or about any other pertinent matters. FRCP 30(b)(5)(C).

e. *Examination and cross-examination.* The examination and cross-examination of a deponent proceed as they would at trial under the Federal Rules of Evidence, except FRE 103 and FRE 615. FRCP 30(c)(1).

  i. *Record of the examination.* After putting the deponent under oath or affirmation, the officer must record the testimony by the method designated under FRCP 30(b)(3)(A). The testimony must be recorded by the officer personally or by a person acting in the presence and under the direction of the officer. FRCP 30(c)(1).

    • *DISTRICT OF MAINE: Video deposition.* In a video deposition, the camera shall focus from a single stationary position on the witness and any exhibits utilized by the witness, unless the parties otherwise agree or the court enters an order under ME R USDCT Rule 26(b). ME R USDCT Rule 30.

  ii. *Objections.* An objection at the time of the examination—whether to evidence, to a party's conduct, to the officer's qualifications, to the manner of taking the deposition, or to any other aspect of the deposition—must be noted on the record, but the examination still proceeds; the testimony is taken subject to any objection. An objection must be stated concisely in a nonargumentative and nonsuggestive manner. A person may instruct a deponent not to answer only when necessary to preserve a privilege, to enforce a limitation ordered by the court, or to present a motion under FRCP 30(d)(3). FRCP 30(c)(2).

iii. *Participating through written questions.* Instead of participating in the oral examination, a party may serve written questions in a sealed envelope on the party noticing the deposition, who must deliver them to the officer. The officer must ask the deponent those questions and record the answers verbatim. FRCP 30(c)(3).

f. *Duration.* Unless otherwise stipulated or ordered by the court, a deposition is limited to one (1) day of seven (7) hours. The court must allow additional time consistent with FRCP 26(b)(1) and FRCP 26(b)(2) if needed to fairly examine the deponent or if the deponent, another person, or any other circumstance impedes or delays the examination. FRCP 30(d)(1).

g. *Sanctions.* The court may impose an appropriate sanction—including the reasonable expenses and attorney's fees incurred by any party—on a person who impedes, delays, or frustrates the fair examination of the deponent. FRCP 30(d)(2). Refer to the United States District Court for the District of Maine KeyRules Motion for Discovery Sanctions document for more information on sanctions.

h. *Motion to terminate or limit.* At any time during a deposition, the deponent or a party may move to terminate or limit it on the ground that it is being conducted in bad faith or in a manner that unreasonably annoys, embarrasses, or oppresses the deponent or party. The motion may be filed in the court where the action is pending or the deposition is being taken. If the objecting deponent or party so demands, the deposition must be suspended for the time necessary to obtain an order. FRCP 30(d)(3)(A).

   i. *Order.* The court may order that the deposition be terminated or may limit its scope and manner as provided in FRCP 26(c). If terminated, the deposition may be resumed only by order of the court where the action is pending. FRCP 30(d)(3)(B).

   ii. *Award of expenses.* FRCP 37(a)(5) applies to the award of expenses. FRCP 30(d)(3)(C). Refer to the United States District Court for the District of Maine KeyRules Motion for Discovery Sanctions document for more information on sanctions.

i. *Review by the witness; Statement of changes.* On request by the deponent or a party before the deposition is completed, the deponent must be allowed thirty (30) days after being notified by the officer that the transcript or recording is available in which: (A) to review the transcript or recording; and (B) if there are changes in form or substance, to sign a statement listing the changes and the reasons for making them. FRCP 30(e)(1).

   i. *Changes indicated in the officer's certificate.* The officer must note in the certificate prescribed by FRCP 30(f)(1) whether a review was requested and, if so, must attach any changes the deponent makes during the thirty (30) day period. FRCP 30(e)(2).

j. *Certification and delivery.* The officer must certify in writing that the witness was duly sworn and that the deposition accurately records the witness's testimony. The certificate must accompany the record of the deposition. Unless the court orders otherwise, the officer must seal the deposition in an envelope or package bearing the title of the action and marked "Deposition of [witness's name]" and must promptly send it to the attorney who arranged for the transcript or recording. The attorney must store it under conditions that will protect it against loss, destruction, tampering, or deterioration. FRCP 30(f)(1).

k. *Documents and tangible things.* Documents and tangible things produced for inspection during a deposition must, on a party's request, be marked for identification and attached to the deposition. Any party may inspect and copy them. But if the person who produced them wants to keep the originals, the person may: (i) offer copies to be marked, attached to the deposition, and then used as originals—after giving all parties a fair opportunity to verify the copies by comparing them with the originals; or (ii) give all parties a fair opportunity to inspect and copy the originals after they are marked—in which event the originals may be used as if attached to the deposition. FRCP 30(f)(2)(A).

   i. *Order regarding the originals.* Any party may move for an order that the originals be attached to the deposition pending final disposition of the case. FRCP 30(f)(2)(B).

l. *Copies of the transcript or recording.* Unless otherwise stipulated or ordered by the court, the officer must retain the stenographic notes of a deposition taken stenographically or a copy of the recording of a deposition taken by another method. When paid reasonable charges, the officer must furnish a copy of the transcript or recording to any party or the deponent. FRCP 30(f)(3).

m. *Failure to attend a deposition or serve a subpoena; Expenses.* A party who, expecting a deposition to be taken, attends in person or by an attorney may recover reasonable expenses for attending, including attorney's fees, if the noticing party failed to: (1) attend and proceed with the deposition; or (2) serve a subpoena on a nonparty deponent, who consequently did not attend. FRCP 30(g). Refer to the United States District Court for the District of Maine KeyRules Motion for Discovery Sanctions document for more information on sanctions.

4. *Depositions by written questions*

   a. *Notice of deposition.* A party who wants to depose a person by written questions must serve them on every other party, with a notice stating, if known, the deponent's name and address. If the name is unknown, the notice must provide a general description sufficient to identify the person or the particular class or group to which the person belongs. The notice must also state the name or descriptive title and the address of the officer before whom the deposition will be taken. FRCP 31(a)(3).

   b. *Questions directed to an organization.* A public or private corporation, a partnership, an association, or a governmental agency may be deposed by written questions in accordance with FRCP 30(b)(6). FRCP 31(a)(4).

   c. *Delivery to the officer; Officer's duties.* The party who noticed the deposition must deliver to the officer a copy of all the questions served and of the notice. The officer must promptly proceed in the manner provided in FRCP 30(c), FRCP 30(e), and FRCP 30(f) to: (1) take the deponent's testimony in response to the questions; (2) prepare and certify the deposition; and (3) send it to the party, attaching a copy of the questions and of the notice. FRCP 31(b).

   d. *Notice of completion.* The party who noticed the deposition must notify all other parties when it is completed. FRCP 31(c)(1).

5. *Depositions to perpetuate testimony.* For information on depositions to perpetuate testimony, refer to FRCP 27.

6. *Stipulations about discovery procedure.* Unless the court orders otherwise, the parties may stipulate that: (a) a deposition may be taken before any person, at any time or place, on any notice, and in the manner specified—in which event it may be used in the same way as any other deposition; and (b) other procedures governing or limiting discovery be modified—but a stipulation extending the time for any form of discovery must have court approval if it would interfere with the time set for completing discovery, for hearing a motion, or for trial. FRCP 29.

7. *DISTRICT OF MAINE: Appearances.* An attorney's signature to a pleading shall constitute an appearance for the party filing the pleading. Otherwise, an attorney who wishes to participate in any manner in any action must file a formal written appearance identifying the party represented. An appearance whether by pleading or formal written appearance shall be signed by an attorney in his/her individual name and shall state his/her office address. ME R USDCT Rule 83.2(a). For more information, refer to ME R USDCT Rule 83.2.

8. *DISTRICT OF MAINE: Alternative dispute resolution (ADR).* Litigants are authorized and encouraged to employ, at their own expense, any available ADR process on which they can agree, including early neutral evaluation, settlement conferences, mediation, non-binding summary jury trial, corporate mini-trial, and arbitration proceedings. ME R USDCT Rule 83.11(a). For more information on ADR, refer to ME R USDCT Rule 83.11.

D. Documents

1. *Depositions by oral examination*

   a. *Required documents*

      i. *Notice of deposition.* Refer to the "C. General Requirements" section of this KeyRules document for information on the notice of deposition.

   b. *Supplemental documents*

      i. *Subpoena.* The deponent's attendance may be compelled by subpoena under FRCP 45. FRCP 30(a)(1). For more information on subpoenas, refer to FRCP 45.

      ii. *Subpoena duces tecum.* If a subpoena duces tecum is to be served on the deponent, the materials designated for production, as set out in the subpoena, must be listed in the notice or in an attachment. FRCP 30(b)(2). For more information on subpoenas duces tecum, refer to FRCP 45.

      iii. *Request for production of documents.* The notice to a party deponent may be accompanied by a request under FRCP 34 to produce documents and tangible things at the deposition. FRCP 30(b)(2). Refer to the United States District Court for the District of Maine KeyRules Request for Production of Documents document for more information.

      iv. *Certificate of service.* No certificate of service is required when a paper is served by filing it with the court's electronic-filing system. When a paper that is required to be served is served by other means: (i) if the paper is filed, a certificate of service must be filed with it or within a reasonable time after service; and (ii) if the paper is not filed, a certificate of service need not be filed unless filing is required by court order or by local rule. FRCP 5(d)(1)(B).

2. *Depositions by written questions*

    a. *Required documents*

        i. *Notice of deposition.* Refer to the "C. General Requirements" section of this KeyRules document for information on the notice of deposition.

        ii. *Written questions.* A party who wants to depose a person by written questions must serve them on every other party, with a notice. FRCP 31(a)(3).

    b. *Supplemental documents*

        i. *Subpoena.* The deponent's attendance may be compelled by subpoena under FRCP 45. FRCP 31(a)(1). For more information on subpoenas, refer to FRCP 45.

        ii. *Certificate of service.* No certificate of service is required when a paper is served by filing it with the court's electronic-filing system. When a paper that is required to be served is served by other means: (i) if the paper is filed, a certificate of service must be filed with it or within a reasonable time after service; and (ii) if the paper is not filed, a certificate of service need not be filed unless filing is required by court order or by local rule. FRCP 5(d)(1)(B).

E. Format

1. *Form of documents.* The rules governing captions and other matters of form in pleadings apply to motions and other papers. FRCP 7(b)(2).

    a. *DISTRICT OF MAINE: Font size, line spacing, and paper size.* All such documents shall be typed in a font of no less than size twelve (12) point, and shall be double-spaced or printed on eight and one-half by eleven (8-1/2 x 11) inch paper. Footnotes shall be in a font of no less than size ten (10) point, and may be single spaced. ME R USDCT Rule 10.

    b. *Caption.* Every pleading must have a caption with the court's name, a title, a file number, and an FRCP 7(a) designation. FRCP 10(a).

        i. *Names of parties.* The title of the complaint must name all the parties; the title of other pleadings, after naming the first party on each side, may refer generally to other parties. FRCP 10(a).

        ii. *DISTRICT OF MAINE: Additional caption requirements.* All pleadings, motions and other papers filed with the clerk or otherwise submitted to the court, except exhibits, shall bear the proper case number and shall contain on the first page a caption as described by FRCP 10(a) and immediately thereunder a designation of what the document is and the name of the party in whose behalf it is submitted. ME R USDCT Rule 10.

    c. *Claims or defenses*

        i. *Numbered paragraphs.* A party must state its claims or defenses in numbered paragraphs, each limited as far as practicable to a single set of circumstances. A later pleading may refer by number to a paragraph in an earlier pleading. FRCP 10(b).

        ii. *Separate statements.* If doing so would promote clarity, each claim founded on a separate transaction or occurrence—and each defense other than a denial—must be stated in a separate count or defense. FRCP 10(b).

    d. *Adoption by reference.* A statement in a pleading may be adopted by reference elsewhere in the same pleading or in any other pleading or motion. FRCP 10(c).

        i. *Exhibits.* A copy of a written instrument that is an exhibit to a pleading is a part of the pleading for all purposes. FRCP 10(c).

    e. *DISTRICT OF MAINE: Page numbering.* All pages shall be numbered at the bottom. ME R USDCT Rule 10.

    f. *DISTRICT OF MAINE: Attachment of ancillary papers.* Ancillary papers shall be attached at the end of the document to which they relate. ME R USDCT Rule 10.

    g. *Acceptance by the clerk.* The clerk must not refuse to file a paper solely because it is not in the form prescribed by the Federal Rules of Civil Procedure or by a local rule or practice. FRCP 5(d)(4).

2. *Signing disclosures and discovery requests, responses, and objections.* FRCP 11 does not apply to disclosures and discovery requests, responses, objections, and motions under FRCP 26 through FRCP 37. FRCP 11(d).

    a. *Signature required.* Every disclosure under FRCP 26(a)(1) or FRCP 26(a)(3) and every discovery request, response, or objection must be signed by at least one attorney of record in the attorney's own name—or by the party personally, if unrepresented—and must state the signer's address, e-mail address, and telephone number. FRCP 26(g)(1).

b. *Effect of signature.* By signing, an attorney or party certifies that to the best of the person's knowledge, information, and belief formed after a reasonable inquiry: (A) with respect to a disclosure, it is complete and correct as of the time it is made; and (B) with respect to a discovery request, response, or objection, it is: (i) consistent with the Federal Rules of Civil Procedure and warranted by existing law or by a nonfrivolous argument for extending, modifying, or reversing existing law, or for establishing new law; (ii) not interposed for any improper purpose, such as to harass, cause unnecessary delay, or needlessly increase the cost of litigation; and (iii) neither unreasonable nor unduly burdensome or expensive, considering the needs of the case, prior discovery in the case, the amount in controversy, and the importance of the issues at stake in the action. FRCP 26(g)(1).

c. *Failure to sign.* Other parties have no duty to act on an unsigned disclosure, request, response, or objection until it is signed, and the court must strike it unless a signature is promptly supplied after the omission is called to the attorney's or party's attention. FRCP 26(g)(2).

d. *Sanction for improper certification.* If a certification violates FRCP 26(g) without substantial justification, the court, on motion or on its own, must impose an appropriate sanction on the signer, the party on whose behalf the signer was acting, or both. The sanction may include an order to pay the reasonable expenses, including attorney's fees, caused by the violation. FRCP 26(g)(3). Refer to the United States District Court for the District of Maine KeyRules Motion for Discovery Sanctions document for more information.

3. *Privacy protection for filings made with the court*

a. *Redacted filings.* Unless the court orders otherwise, in an electronic or paper filing with the court that contains an individual's Social Security number, taxpayer-identification number, or birth date, the name of an individual known to be a minor, or a financial-account number, a party or nonparty making the filing may include only: (1) the last four (4) digits of the Social Security number and taxpayer-identification number; (2) the year of the individual's birth; (3) the minor's initials; and (4) the last four (4) digits of the financial-account number. FRCP 5.2(a).

   i. *DISTRICT OF MAINE.* To address the privacy concerns created by the Internet access to court papers, unless otherwise ordered by the court, counsel shall modify certain personal data identifiers in pleadings and other papers as follows: (1) minors' names: use of the minors' initials only; (2) Social Security numbers: use of the last four (4) numbers only; (3) dates of birth: use of the year of birth only; [and] (4) financial account numbers: identify the type of account and the financial institution, but use only the last four (4) numbers of the account number. ME R USDCT Redacting Pleadings. Counsel should also use caution when filing papers that contain a person's medical records, employment history; financial information; and any proprietary or trade secret information. ME R USDCT Redacting Pleadings.

b. *Exemptions from the redaction requirement.* The redaction requirement does not apply to the following: (1) a financial-account number that identifies the property allegedly subject to forfeiture in a forfeiture proceeding; (2) the record of an administrative or agency proceeding; (3) the official record of a state-court proceeding; (4) the record of a court or tribunal, if that record was not subject to the redaction requirement when originally filed; (5) a filing covered by FRCP 5.2(c) or FRCP 5.2(d); and (6) a pro se filing in an action brought under 28 U.S.C.A. § 2241, 28 U.S.C.A. § 2254, or 28 U.S.C.A. § 2255. FRCP 5.2(b).

c. *Limitations on remote access to electronic files; Social Security appeals and immigration cases.* Unless the court orders otherwise, in an action for benefits under the Social Security Act, and in an action or proceeding relating to an order of removal, to relief from removal, or to immigration benefits or detention, access to an electronic file is authorized as follows: (1) the parties and their attorneys may have remote electronic access to any part of the case file, including the administrative record; (2) any other person may have electronic access to the full record at the courthouse, but may have remote electronic access only to: (A) the docket maintained by the court; and (B) an opinion, order, judgment, or other disposition of the court, but not any other part of the case file or the administrative record. FRCP 5.2(c).

d. *Filings made under seal.* The court may order that a filing be made under seal without redaction. The court may later unseal the filing or order the person who made the filing to file a redacted version for the public record. FRCP 5.2(d).

   i. *DISTRICT OF MAINE.* For information on filing sealed documents in the District of Maine, refer to ME R USDCT Rule 7A, ME R USDCT App. 4(p)(2), and ME R USDCT Sealed Filings.

e. *Protective orders.* For good cause, the court may by order in a case: (1) require redaction of additional information; or (2) limit or prohibit a nonparty's remote electronic access to a document filed with the court. FRCP 5.2(e).

f. *Option for additional unredacted filing under seal.* A person making a redacted filing may also file an unredacted copy under seal. The court must retain the unredacted copy as part of the record. FRCP 5.2(f).

   i. *DISTRICT OF MAINE.* A party wishing to file a document containing the personal data identifiers specified

above may. . .file an unredacted document under seal. This document will be retained by the clerk's office as part of the record. ME R USDCT Redacting Pleadings. The court may, however, still require the party to file a redacted copy for the public file. ME R USDCT Redacting Pleadings.

g. *Option for filing a reference list.* A filing that contains redacted information may be filed together with a reference list that identifies each item of redacted information and specifies an appropriate identifier that uniquely corresponds to each item listed. The list must be filed under seal and may be amended as of right. Any reference in the case to a listed identifier will be construed to refer to the corresponding item of information. FRCP 5.2(g).

    i. *DISTRICT OF MAINE.* A party wishing to file a document containing the personal data identifiers specified above may. . .file a reference list under seal. The reference list shall contain the complete personal data identifier(s) and the redacted identifier(s) used in its (their) place in the filing. All references in the case to the redacted identifiers included in the reference list will be construed to refer to the corresponding complete identifier. The reference list must be filed under seal, and may be amended as of right. It shall be retained by the clerk's office as part of the record. ME R USDCT Redacting Pleadings. The court may, however, still require the party to file a redacted copy for the public file. ME R USDCT Redacting Pleadings.

h. *DISTRICT OF MAINE: Responsibility for redaction.* The clerk is not required to review documents filed with the court for compliance with FRCP 5.2. The responsibility to redact filings rests with counsel and the party or nonparty making the filing. ME R USDCT App. 4(i); ME R USDCT Redacting Pleadings. For guidelines for filing confidential information in civil cases in the District of Maine, refer to ME R USDCT Confidentiality.

i. *Waiver of protection of identifiers.* A person waives the protection of FRCP 5.2(a) as to the person's own information by filing it without redaction and not under seal. FRCP 5.2(h).

F. Filing and Service Requirements

1. *Filing requirements*

    a. *Required filings.* Any paper after the complaint that is required to be served must be filed no later than a reasonable time after service. But disclosures under FRCP 26(a)(1) or FRCP 26(a)(2) and the following discovery requests and responses must not be filed until they are used in the proceeding or the court orders filing: depositions, interrogatories, requests for documents or tangible things or to permit entry onto land, and requests for admission. FRCP 5(d)(1)(A). Refer to the United States District Court for the District of Maine KeyRules pleading and motion documents for information on filing with the court.

        i. *DISTRICT OF MAINE.* Unless otherwise ordered by the court, depositions upon oral examination and interrogatories, requests for documents, requests for admissions, and answers and responses thereto and disclosures made under FRCP 26(a)(1) through FRCP 26(a)(3) and pursuant to scheduling orders issued by the court, shall be served upon other parties but shall not be filed with the court. ME R USDCT Rule 5(b); ME R USDCT Rule 26(a).

    b. *Notice of filing*

        i. *Depositions by oral examination.* A party who files the deposition must promptly notify all other parties of the filing. FRCP 30(f)(4).

        ii. *Depositions by written questions.* A party who files the deposition must promptly notify all other parties of the filing. FRCP 31(c)(2).

2. *Service requirements*

    a. *Service; When required.* Unless the Federal Rules of Civil Procedure provide otherwise, each of the following papers must be served on every party: (A) an order stating that service is required; (B) a pleading filed after the original complaint, unless the court orders otherwise under FRCP 5(c) because there are numerous defendants; (C) a discovery paper required to be served on a party, unless the court orders otherwise; (D) a written motion, except one that may be heard ex parte; and (E) a written notice, appearance, demand, or offer of judgment, or any similar paper. FRCP 5(a)(1).

        i. *If a party fails to appear.* No service is required on a party who is in default for failing to appear. But a pleading that asserts a new claim for relief against such a party must be served on that party under FRCP 4. FRCP 5(a)(2).

        ii. *Seizing property.* If an action is begun by seizing property and no person is or need be named as a defendant, any service required before the filing of an appearance, answer, or claim must be made on the person who had custody or possession of the property when it was seized. FRCP 5(a)(3).

    b. *Service; How made.* A paper is served under FRCP 5 by: (A) handing it to the person; (B) leaving it: (i) at the person's office with a clerk or other person in charge or, if no one is in charge, in a conspicuous place in the office; or (ii) if the person has no office or the office is closed, at the person's dwelling or usual place of abode with someone of suitable age and discretion who resides there; (C) mailing it to the person's last known address—in which event service is complete upon mailing; (D) leaving it with the court clerk if the person has no known address; (E) sending it to a registered user by filing it with the court's electronic-filing system or sending it by other electronic means that the person consented to in writing—in either of which events service is complete upon filing or sending, but is not effective if the filer or sender learns that it did not reach the person to be served; or (F) delivering it by any other means that the person consented to in writing—in which event service is complete when the person making service delivers it to the agency designated to make delivery. FRCP 5(b)(2).

    i.   *Serving an attorney.* If a party is represented by an attorney, service under FRCP 5 must be made on the attorney unless the court orders service on the party. FRCP 5(b)(1).

3.   *DISTRICT OF MAINE: Preservation of original discovery.* The party that has served notice of a deposition or has served discovery papers shall be responsible for preserving and for [ensuring] the integrity of original transcripts and discovery papers for use by the court. ME R USDCT Rule 5(b); ME R USDCT Rule 26(a).

G. Hearings

1.   There is no hearing contemplated in the federal statutes or rules for the notice of deposition.

H. Forms

1. Federal Notice of Deposition Forms

    a.   Notice to take deposition to perpetuate testimony. 3A FEDFORMS § 22:14.

    b.   Notice of taking of deposition to perpetuate testimony pending appeal. 3A FEDFORMS § 22:20.

    c.   Notice of taking deposition upon oral examination. 3A FEDFORMS § 23:72.

    d.   Notice of taking deposition upon oral examination; Party. 3A FEDFORMS § 23:73.

    e.   Notice of taking deposition upon oral examination; Naming and describing person not a party. 3A FEDFORMS § 23:74.

    f.   Notice of taking deposition upon oral examination; Describing deponents whose names are unknown. 3A FEDFORMS § 23:75.

    g.   Notice of taking deposition upon oral examination; Pursuant to order granting leave to take deposition. 3A FEDFORMS § 23:76.

    h.   Notice of taking of deposition of party with notice to produce documents. 3A FEDFORMS § 23:77.

    i.   Notice of taking of deposition of witness; Including designation of materials in related subpoena duces tecum. 3A FEDFORMS § 23:78.

    j.   Notice of taking of deposition of witness; Including reference to materials designated in attached subpoena. 3A FEDFORMS § 23:79.

    k.   Notice of taking deposition upon written questions served with notice. 3A FEDFORMS § 23:99.

    l.   Questions to be attached to notice or served with it. 3A FEDFORMS § 23:100.

    m.   Notice of return and filing of deposition taken upon written questions. 3A FEDFORMS § 23:106.

    n.   Notice; Taking of deposition on oral examination. FEDPROF § 23:142.

    o.   Notice; Taking of deposition on oral examination; Patent proceedings. FEDPROF § 23:143.

    p.   Notice; Taking of deposition on oral examination; Corporate officer. FEDPROF § 23:144.

    q.   Notice; Taking of deposition on oral examination; Corporate officers to be designated by corporation. FEDPROF § 23:145.

    r.   Notice; Taking of deposition on written questions. FEDPROF § 23:146.

    s.   Notice; Taking of deposition on oral examination or on written questions; Pursuant to court order. FEDPROF § 23:147.

    t.   Notice; In connection with deposition on written questions; Of cross, redirect, or recross questions. FEDPROF § 23:148.

    u.   Attachment to notice; Taking of deposition on written questions; Questions to be propounded. FEDPROF § 23:149.

v. Attachment to notice; Cross, redirect, or recross questions to be propounded. FEDPROF § 23:150.

w. Notice; To party taking deposition; Written questions submitted in lieu of participation in oral examination. FEDPROF § 23:151.

x. Notice of taking deposition; Expert witness; Request for production of supporting documents. FEDPROF § 23:157.

y. Subpoena; To testify at taking of deposition and to produce documents or things (form AO 88). FEDPROF § 23:158.

z. Provision in subpoena; Advice to nonparty organization of its duty to designate witness. FEDPROF § 23:161.

I. Applicable Rules

1. *Federal rules*

   a. Serving and filing pleadings and other papers. FRCP 5.

   b. Privacy protection for filings made with the court. FRCP 5.2.

   c. Computing and extending time; Time for motion papers. FRCP 6.

   d. Pleadings allowed; Form of motions and other papers. FRCP 7.

   e. Form of pleadings. FRCP 10.

   f. Signing pleadings, motions, and other papers; Representations to the court; Sanctions. FRCP 11.

   g. Duty to disclose; General provisions governing discovery. FRCP 26.

   h. Persons before whom depositions may be taken. FRCP 28.

   i. Stipulations about discovery procedure. FRCP 29.

   j. Depositions by oral examination. FRCP 30.

   k. Depositions by written questions. FRCP 31.

   l. Failure to make disclosures or to cooperate in discovery; Sanctions. FRCP 37.

2. *Local rules*

   a. *DISTRICT OF MAINE*

      i. Service and filing of pleadings and other papers. ME R USDCT Rule 5.

      ii. Time. ME R USDCT Rule 6.

      iii. Form of pleadings, motions and other papers. ME R USDCT Rule 10.

      iv. Case management tracks. ME R USDCT Rule 16.1.

      v. Discovery. ME R USDCT Rule 26.

      vi. Depositions. ME R USDCT Rule 30.

      vii. Attorneys; Appearances and withdrawals. ME R USDCT Rule 83.2.

      viii. Alternative dispute resolution (ADR). ME R USDCT Rule 83.11.

      ix. Administrative procedures governing the filing and service by electronic means. ME R USDCT App. 4.

      x. Redacting pleadings. ME R USDCT Redacting Pleadings.

Requests, Notices and Applications
Application for Temporary Restraining Order

Document Last Updated July 2021

A. Checklist

(I) ❑ Matters to be considered by party applying with notice

    (a) ❑ Required documents

        (1) ❑ Notice of motion and motion

        (2) ❑ Security

(b) ❏ Supplemental documents

    (1) ❏ Supporting evidence

    (2) ❏ Notice of constitutional question

    (3) ❏ Nongovernmental corporate disclosure statement

    (4) ❏ DISTRICT OF MAINE: Additional supplemental documents

        (i) ❏ Proposed order

(c) ❏ Timing

    (1) ❏ There are no specific timing requirements in the Federal Rules of Civil Procedure for applying for a temporary restraining order with notice

    (2) ❏ A written motion and notice of the hearing must be served at least fourteen (14) days before the time specified for the hearing, with the following exceptions: (A) when the motion may be heard ex parte; (B) when the Federal Rules of Civil Procedure set a different time; or (C) when a court order—which a party may, for good cause, apply for ex parte—sets a different time

    (3) ❏ Any affidavit supporting a motion must be served with the motion

    (4) ❏ DISTRICT OF MAINE: Additional timing

        (i) ❏ Any affidavits and other documents setting forth or evidencing facts on which the motion is based must be filed with the motion

(II) ❏ Matters to be considered by party applying ex parte (without notice)

  (a) ❏ Required documents

    (1) ❏ Motion

    (2) ❏ Affidavit or verified complaint

    (3) ❏ Certificate of attorney's efforts to give notice

    (4) ❏ Security

  (b) ❏ Supplemental documents

    (1) ❏ Supporting evidence

    (2) ❏ Notice of constitutional question

    (3) ❏ Nongovernmental corporate disclosure statement

    (4) ❏ DISTRICT OF MAINE: Additional supplemental documents

        (i) ❏ Proposed order

  (c) ❏ Timing

    (1) ❏ There are no specific timing requirements in the Federal Rules of Civil Procedure for applying for a temporary restraining order ex parte (without notice)

    (2) ❏ DISTRICT OF MAINE: Additional timing

        (i) ❏ Any affidavits and other documents setting forth or evidencing facts on which the motion is based must be filed with the motion

B. Timing

1. *Application for temporary restraining order*

    a. *With notice.* There are no specific timing requirements in the Federal Rules of Civil Procedure for applying for a temporary restraining order with notice.

    b. *Ex parte (without notice).* There are no specific timing requirements in the Federal Rules of Civil Procedure for applying for a temporary restraining order ex parte (without notice).

2. *Motion to dissolve or modify.* On two (2) days' notice to the party who obtained the order without notice—or on shorter notice set by the court—the adverse party may appear and move to dissolve or modify the order. The court must then hear and decide the motion as promptly as justice requires. FRCP 65(b)(4).

3. *Timing of motions, generally*

    a. *Motion and notice of hearing.* A written motion and notice of the hearing must be served at least fourteen (14) days before the time specified for the hearing, with the following exceptions: (A) when the motion may be heard ex parte; (B) when the Federal Rules of Civil Procedure set a different time; or (C) when a court order—which a party may, for good cause, apply for ex parte—sets a different time. FRCP 6(c)(1).

    b. *Supporting affidavit.* Any affidavit supporting a motion must be served with the motion. FRCP 6(c)(2).

    c. *DISTRICT OF MAINE: Affidavits and other supporting documents.* Any affidavits and other documents setting forth or evidencing facts on which the motion is based must be filed with the motion. ME R USDCT Rule 7(a).

4. *Computation of time*

    a. *Computing time.* FRCP 6 applies in computing any time period specified in the Federal Rules of Civil Procedure, in any local rule or court order, or in any statute that does not specify a method of computing time. FRCP 6(a).

        i. *Period stated in days or a longer unit.* When the period is stated in days or a longer unit of time: (A) exclude the day of the event that triggers the period; (B) count every day, including intermediate Saturdays, Sundays, and legal holidays; and (C) include the last day of the period, but if the last day is a Saturday, Sunday, or legal holiday, the period continues to run until the end of the next day that is not a Saturday, Sunday, or legal holiday. FRCP 6(a)(1).

        ii. *Period stated in hours.* When the period is stated in hours: (A) begin counting immediately on the occurrence of the event that triggers the period; (B) count every hour, including hours during intermediate Saturdays, Sundays, and legal holidays; and (C) if the period would end on a Saturday, Sunday, or legal holiday, the period continues to run until the same time on the next day that is not a Saturday, Sunday, or legal holiday. FRCP 6(a)(2).

        iii. *Inaccessibility of the clerk's office.* Unless the court orders otherwise, if the clerk's office is inaccessible: (A) on the last day for filing under FRCP 6(a)(1), then the time for filing is extended to the first accessible day that is not a Saturday, Sunday, or legal holiday; or (B) during the last hour for filing under FRCP 6(a)(2), then the time for filing is extended to the same time on the first accessible day that is not a Saturday, Sunday, or legal holiday. FRCP 6(a)(3).

        iv. *"Last day" defined.* Unless a different time is set by a statute, local rule, or court order, the last day ends: (A) for electronic filing, at midnight in the court's time zone; and (B) for filing by other means, when the clerk's office is scheduled to close. FRCP 6(a)(4).

        v. *"Next day" defined.* The "next day" is determined by continuing to count forward when the period is measured after an event and backward when measured before an event. FRCP 6(a)(5).

        vi. *"Legal holiday" defined.* "Legal holiday" means: (A) the day set aside by statute for observing New Year's Day, Martin Luther King Jr.'s Birthday, Washington's Birthday, Memorial Day, Independence Day, Labor Day, Columbus Day, Veterans' Day, Thanksgiving Day, or Christmas Day; (B) any day declared a holiday by the President or Congress; and (C) for periods that are measured after an event, any other day declared a holiday by the state where the district court is located. FRCP 6(a)(6).

        vii. *DISTRICT OF MAINE: Applicability of FRCP 6.* FRCP 6 applies when computing any period of time stated in the Local Rules of the United States District Court for the District of Maine. ME R USDCT Rule 6(a).

    b. *DISTRICT OF MAINE: Computation of electronic filing deadlines.* Filing documents electronically does not in any way alter any filing deadlines. All electronic transmissions of documents must be completed prior to midnight, Eastern Time, in order to be considered timely filed that day. Where a specific time of day deadline is set by court order or stipulation, the electronic filing must be completed by that time. ME R USDCT App. 4(f). A document filed electronically shall be deemed filed at the time and date stated on the Notice of Electronic Filing received from the court. ME R USDCT App. 4(d)(2).

        i. *Technical failures.* A filing user whose filing is made untimely as the result of a technical failure may seek appropriate relief from the court. ME R USDCT App. 4(n). A technical failure of the court's ECF system is deemed to have occurred when the court's ECF site cannot accept filings continuously or intermittently over the course of any period of time greater than one (1) hour. Known system outages will be posted on the court's website along with guidance on how to proceed, if applicable. ME R USDCT App. 4(n).

    c. *Extending time.* When an act may or must be done within a specified time, the court may, for good cause, extend the time: (A) with or without motion or notice if the court acts, or if a request is made, before the original time or its extension expires; or (B) on motion made after the time has expired if the party failed to act because of excusable neglect. FRCP 6(b)(1). A court must not extend the time to act under FRCP 50(b), FRCP 50(d), FRCP 52(b), FRCP 59(b), FRCP 59(d), FRCP 59(e), and FRCP 60(b). FRCP 6(b)(2). Refer to the United States District Court for the District of Maine KeyRules Motion for Continuance/Extension of Time document for more information on extending time.

d.   *Additional time after certain kinds of service.* When a party may or must act within a specified time after being served and service is made under FRCP 5(b)(2)(C) (by mail), FRCP 5(b)(2)(D) (by leaving with the clerk), or FRCP 5(b)(2)(F) (by other means consented to), three (3) days are added after the period would otherwise expire under FRCP 6(a). FRCP 6(d).

C. General Requirements

1.   *Motions, generally*

a.   *Motion requirements.* A request for a court order must be made by motion. The motion must: (A) be in writing unless made during a hearing or trial; (B) state with particularity the grounds for seeking the order; and (C) state the relief sought. FRCP 7(b)(1). The writing and particularity requirements are intended to ensure that the adverse parties are informed of and have a record of both the motion's pendency and the grounds on which the movant seeks an order. FPP § 1191; Feldberg v. Quechee Lakes Corp., 463 F.3d 195 (2d Cir. 2006).

   i.   *Particularity requirement.* The particularity requirement [ensures] that the opposing parties will have notice of their opponent's contentions. FEDPROC § 62:358; Goodman v. 1973 26 Foot Trojan Vessel, Arkansas Registration No. AR1439SN, 859 F.2d 71 (8th Cir. 1988). That requirement ensures that notice of the basis for the motion is provided to the court and to the opposing party so as to avoid prejudice, provide the opponent with a meaningful opportunity to respond, and provide the court with enough information to process the motion correctly. FEDPROC § 62:358; Andreas v. Volkswagen of Am., Inc., 336 F.3d 789 (8th Cir. 2003).

   •   Reasonable specification of the grounds for a motion is sufficient. The particularity requirement for motions is satisfied when no party is prejudiced by a lack of particularity or when the court can comprehend the basis for the motion and deal with it fairly. However, where a movant fails to state even one ground for granting the motion in question, the movant has failed to meet the minimal standard of "reasonable specification." FEDPROC § 62:358; Martinez v. Trainor, 556 F.2d 818 (7th Cir. 1977).

   •   The court may excuse the failure to comply with the particularity requirement if it is inadvertent, and where no prejudice is shown by the opposing party. FEDPROC § 62:358.

b.   *Notice of motion.* A party interested in resisting the relief sought by a motion has a right to notice thereof, and an opportunity to be heard. AMJUR MOTIONS § 12.

   i.   *Purpose.* In addition to statutory or court rule provisions requiring notice of a motion—the purpose of such a notice requirement having been said to be to prevent a party from being prejudicially surprised by a motion—principles of natural justice dictate that an adverse party generally must be given notice that a motion will be presented to the court. AMJUR MOTIONS § 12.

   ii. *Adequacy of notice.* The test of adequate notice generally turns on whether the other parties were afforded an adequate opportunity to prepare and respond to the issues to be raised in the proceeding. AMJUR MOTIONS § 12.

c.   *Single document containing motion and notice.* A single written document can satisfy the writing requirements both for a motion and for an FRCP 6(c)(1) notice. FRCP 7(Advisory Committee Notes).

2.   *Application for temporary restraining order.* Applicants for injunctive relief occasionally are faced with the possibility that irreparable injury will occur before the hearing for a preliminary injunction required by FRCP 65(a) can be held. In that event a temporary restraining order may be available under FRCP 65(b). FPP § 2951. The order is designed to preserve the status quo until there is an opportunity to hold a hearing on the application for a preliminary injunction and may be issued with or without notice to the adverse party. FPP § 2951; Granny Goose Foods, Inc. v. Bhd. of Teamsters & Auto Truck Drivers Local No. 70 of Alameda Cty., 415 U.S. 423, 94 S. Ct. 1113, 39 L. Ed. 2d 435 (1974).

a.   *Issuing with notice.* When the opposing party actually receives notice of the application for a restraining order, the procedure that is followed does not differ functionally from that on an application for a preliminary injunction and the proceeding is not subject to any special requirements. FPP § 2951; Dilworth v. Riner, 343 F.2d 226 (5th Cir. 1965).

   i.   *Duration.* By its terms FRCP 65(b) only governs restraining orders issued without notice or a hearing. But. . .it has been argued that its provisions, at least with regard to the duration of a restraining order, apply even to an order granted when notice has been given to the adverse party but there has been no hearing. FPP § 2951.

b. *Issuing without notice*

   i. *When available.* The court may issue a temporary restraining order without written or oral notice to the adverse party or its attorney only if: (A) specific facts in an affidavit or a verified complaint clearly show that immediate and irreparable injury, loss, or damage will result to the movant before the adverse party can be heard in opposition; and (B) the movant's attorney certifies in writing any efforts made to give notice and the reasons why it should not be required. FRCP 65(b)(1).

   ii. *Contents.* Every temporary restraining order issued without notice must state the date and hour it was issued; describe the injury and state why it is irreparable; state why the order was issued without notice; and be promptly filed in the clerk's office and entered in the record. FRCP 65(b)(2).

   iii. *Expiration.* The order expires at the time after entry—not to exceed fourteen (14) days—that the court sets, unless before that time the court, for good cause, extends it for a like period or the adverse party consents to a longer extension. The reasons for an extension must be entered in the record. FRCP 65(b)(2).

c. *Temporary restraining order versus preliminary injunction.* A temporary restraining order differs from a preliminary injunction, the core reasons being that a temporary restraining order is of limited duration and it may issue without notice to the opposing party before the adverse party can be heard in opposition. FEDPROC § 47:80.

d. *Factors considered.* As in the case of an application for a preliminary injunction, four factors must be considered in determining whether a temporary restraining order is to be granted, which are whether the moving party has established: (1) a substantial likelihood of success on the merits; (2) that irreparable injury will be suffered if the relief is not granted; (3) that the threatened injury outweighs the harm the relief would inflict on the nonmoving party; and (4) that entry of the relief would serve the public interest. FEDPROC § 47:84; Schiavo ex rel. Schindler v. Schiavo, 403 F.3d 1223 (11th Cir. 2005).

   i. *Balancing of factors.* No one factor, taken individually, is necessarily dispositive in determining whether to grant a temporary restraining order or preliminary injunction; weakness of the showing regarding one factor may be overborne by the strength of the others. FEDPROC § 47:84.

   ii. *Showing required.* Although the factors for consideration in determining whether to grant emergency injunctive relief are not applied mechanically, a movant must establish the existence of both of the first two factors of likelihood of success on the merits of the case and whether plaintiff will suffer irreparable harm absent injunctive relief, in order to be entitled to a preliminary injunction or a temporary restraining order. In each case, however, all of the factors must be considered to determine whether on balance they weigh toward granting relief. FEDPROC § 47:84.

      • In the context of a temporary restraining order, it is particularly important for the moving party to demonstrate a substantial likelihood of success on the merits, because otherwise, there would be no justification for the court's intrusion into the ordinary processes of administration and judicial review. FEDPROC § 47:84.

   iii. Refer to the United States District Court for the District of Maine KeyRules Motion for Preliminary Injunction document for more information on the factors considered in moving for a preliminary injunction.

e. *Burden.* As with a preliminary injunction, the burden is on the moving party to establish that relief is appropriate. FEDPROC § 47:84.

f. *Security.* The court may issue a preliminary injunction or a temporary restraining order only if the movant gives security in an amount that the court considers proper to pay the costs and damages sustained by any party found to have been wrongfully enjoined or restrained. The United States, its officers, and its agencies are not required to give security. FRCP 65(c). The purpose of an injunction bond is to compensate the defendant, in the event that the defendant prevails on the merits, for the harm caused by an injunction entered before the final decision, and so it is required only for a temporary restraining order or a preliminary injunction, not for a permanent injunction. FEDPROC § 47:93. An injunction bond serves other functions as well; for instance, it generally limits the liability of the applicant and informs the applicant of the price that it can expect to pay if the injunction was wrongfully issued. FEDPROC § 47:93. For information on proceedings against a security provider, refer to FRCP 65.1.

   i. *DISTRICT OF MAINE.* For information on bonds and security in the District of Maine, refer to ME R USDCT Rule 65.1.

g. *Contents and scope of every injunction and restraining order*

   i. *Contents.* Every order granting an injunction and every restraining order must: (A) state the reasons why it issued; (B) state its terms specifically; and (C) describe in reasonable detail—and not by referring to the complaint or other document—the act or acts restrained or required. FRCP 65(d)(1).

ii. *Persons bound.* The order binds only the following who receive actual notice of it by personal service or otherwise: (A) the parties; (B) the parties' officers, agents, servants, employees, and attorneys; and (C) other persons who are in active concert or participation with anyone described in FRCP 65(d)(2)(A) or FRCP 65(d)(2)(B). FRCP 65(d)(2).

h. *Other laws not modified.* FRCP 65 does not modify the following: (1) any federal statute relating to temporary restraining orders or preliminary injunctions in actions affecting employer and employee; (2) 28 U.S.C.A. § 2361, which relates to preliminary injunctions in actions of interpleader or in the nature of interpleader; or (3) 28 U.S.C.A. § 2284, which relates to actions that must be heard and decided by a three-judge district court. FRCP 65(e).

i. *Copyright impoundment.* FRCP 65 applies to copyright-impoundment proceedings. FRCP 65(f).

3. *DISTRICT OF MAINE: Appearances.* An attorney's signature to a pleading shall constitute an appearance for the party filing the pleading. Otherwise, an attorney who wishes to participate in any manner in any action must file a formal written appearance identifying the party represented. An appearance whether by pleading or formal written appearance shall be signed by an attorney in his/her individual name and shall state his/her office address. ME R USDCT Rule 83.2(a). For more information, refer to ME R USDCT Rule 83.2.

4. *DISTRICT OF MAINE: Alternative dispute resolution (ADR).* Litigants are authorized and encouraged to employ, at their own expense, any available ADR process on which they can agree, including early neutral evaluation, settlement conferences, mediation, non-binding summary jury trial, corporate mini-trial, and arbitration proceedings. ME R USDCT Rule 83.11(a). For more information on ADR, refer to ME R USDCT Rule 83.11.

D. Documents

1. *Application for temporary restraining order (with notice)*

   a. *Required documents*

      i. *Notice of motion and motion.* Refer to the "C. General Requirements" section of this KeyRules document for information on the notice of motion and motion.

         • *DISTRICT OF MAINE: Memorandum of law.* Every motion shall incorporate a memorandum of law, including citations and supporting authorities. ME R USDCT Rule 7(a). Refer to the "E. Format" section of this KeyRules document for the form of memoranda of law.

         • *Certificate of service.* No certificate of service is required when a paper is served by filing it with the court's electronic-filing system. When a paper that is required to be served is served by other means: (i) if the paper is filed, a certificate of service must be filed with it or within a reasonable time after service; and (ii) if the paper is not filed, a certificate of service need not be filed unless filing is required by court order or by local rule. FRCP 5(d)(1)(B).

      ii. *Security.* The court may issue a preliminary injunction or a temporary restraining order only if the movant gives security in an amount that the court considers proper to pay the costs and damages sustained by any party found to have been wrongfully enjoined or restrained. The United States, its officers, and its agencies are not required to give security. FRCP 65(c). Refer to the "C. General Requirements" section of this KeyRules document for more information.

   b. *Supplemental documents*

      i. *Supporting evidence.* When a motion relies on facts outside the record, the court may hear the matter on affidavits or may hear it wholly or partly on oral testimony or on depositions. FRCP 43(c).

         • *DISTRICT OF MAINE: Affidavits and other supporting documents.* Any affidavits and other documents setting forth or evidencing facts on which the motion is based must be filed with the motion. ME R USDCT Rule 7(a).

         • *DISTRICT OF MAINE: Discovery transcripts or materials.* A party relying on discovery transcripts or materials in support of or in opposition to a motion shall file excerpts of such transcript or materials with the memorandum required by ME R USDCT Rule 7 as well as a list of specific citations to the parts on which the party relies. ME R USDCT Rule 26(c). Excerpts of depositions in support of or in opposition to a motion shall be filed electronically using ECF, unless otherwise permitted by the court. ME R USDCT App. 4(l)(3).

      ii. *Notice of constitutional question.* A party that files a pleading, written motion, or other paper drawing into question the constitutionality of a federal or state statute must promptly: (1) file a notice of constitutional question stating the question and identifying the paper that raises it, if: (A) a federal statute is questioned and the parties do not include the United States, one of its agencies, or one of its officers or employees in an official capacity; or (B) a state statute is questioned and the parties do not include the state, one of its agencies, or one of its officers or employees in an official capacity; and (2) serve the notice and paper on the Attorney General of the United States if a federal statute is questioned—or on the state attorney general if a state statute is questioned—either by certified or registered mail or by sending it to an electronic address designated by the attorney general for this purpose. FRCP 5.1(a).

- *No forfeiture.* A party's failure to file and serve the notice, or the court's failure to certify, does not forfeit a constitutional claim or defense that is otherwise timely asserted. FRCP 5.1(d).

iii. *Nongovernmental corporate disclosure statement.* A nongovernmental corporate party must file two (2) copies of a disclosure statement that: (1) identifies any parent corporation and any publicly held corporation owning ten percent (10%) or more of its stock; or (2) states that there is no such corporation. FRCP 7.1(a). A party must: (1) file the disclosure statement with its first appearance, pleading, petition, motion, response, or other request addressed to the court; and (2) promptly file a supplemental statement if any required information changes. FRCP 7.1(b).

- *DISTRICT OF MAINE: Notice of interested parties.* To enable the court to evaluate possible disqualification or recusal, counsel for all non-governmental parties shall file with their first appearance a Notice of Interested Parties, which shall list all persons, associations of persons, firms, partnerships, limited liability companies, joint ventures, corporations (including parent or affiliated corporations, clearly identified as such), or any similar entities, owning ten percent (10%) or more of the named party. Counsel shall be under a continuing obligation to file an amended Notice if any material change occurs in the status of an Interested Party, such as through merger, acquisition, or new/additional membership. ME R USDCT Rule 7.1.

iv. *DISTRICT OF MAINE: Additional supplemental documents*

- *Proposed order.* Proposed orders shall not be filed unless requested by the court. When requested by the court, proposed orders shall be filed by e-mail in word processing format. ME R USDCT App. 4(k)(1).

2. *Application for temporary restraining order (without notice, or "ex parte")*

a. *Required documents*

i. *Motion.* Refer to the "C. General Requirements" section of this KeyRules document for information on the motion.

- *DISTRICT OF MAINE: Memorandum of law.* Every motion shall incorporate a memorandum of law, including citations and supporting authorities. ME R USDCT Rule 7(a). Refer to the "E. Format" section of this KeyRules document for the form of memoranda of law.

ii. *Affidavit or verified complaint.* The applicant for an ex parte restraining order must present to the court, in an affidavit or a verified complaint, facts that clearly show irreparable injury. Both an affidavit and a verified complaint are not required, and neither technically is necessary if notice has been given to the adverse party and the case for a restraining order can be demonstrated in some other appropriate fashion. FPP § 2952.

iii. *Certificate of attorney's efforts to give notice.* The applicant's attorney must certify in writing any efforts made to give notice and the reasons why it should not be required. This provision has been interpreted as a recognition of the fact that informal notice and a hastily arranged hearing are better than no notice or hearing at all. A temporary restraining order may be denied if proper efforts were not made to notify the defendant. FEDPROC § 47:81.

iv. *Security.* The court may issue a preliminary injunction or a temporary restraining order only if the movant gives security in an amount that the court considers proper to pay the costs and damages sustained by any party found to have been wrongfully enjoined or restrained. The United States, its officers, and its agencies are not required to give security. FRCP 65(c). Refer to the "C. General Requirements" section of this KeyRules document for more information.

b. *Supplemental documents*

i. *Supporting evidence.* When a motion relies on facts outside the record, the court may hear the matter on affidavits or may hear it wholly or partly on oral testimony or on depositions. FRCP 43(c).

- *DISTRICT OF MAINE: Affidavits and other supporting documents.* Any affidavits and other documents setting forth or evidencing facts on which the motion is based must be filed with the motion. ME R USDCT Rule 7(a).

- *DISTRICT OF MAINE: Discovery transcripts or materials.* A party relying on discovery transcripts or materials in support of or in opposition to a motion shall file excerpts of such transcript or materials with the memorandum required by ME R USDCT Rule 7 as well as a list of specific citations to the parts on which the party relies. ME R USDCT Rule 26(c). Excerpts of depositions in support of or in opposition to a motion shall be filed electronically using ECF, unless otherwise permitted by the court. ME R USDCT App. 4(l)(3).

ii. *Notice of constitutional question.* A party that files a pleading, written motion, or other paper drawing into question the constitutionality of a federal or state statute must promptly: (1) file a notice of constitutional question stating the question and identifying the paper that raises it, if: (A) a federal statute is questioned and the parties do not include the United States, one of its agencies, or one of its officers or employees in an official capacity; or (B) a state statute is questioned and the parties do not include the state, one of its agencies, or one of its officers or employees in an official capacity; and (2) serve the notice and paper on the Attorney General of the United States if a federal statute is questioned—or on the state attorney general if a state statute is questioned—either by certified or registered mail or by sending it to an electronic address designated by the attorney general for this purpose. FRCP 5.1(a).

- *No forfeiture.* A party's failure to file and serve the notice, or the court's failure to certify, does not forfeit a constitutional claim or defense that is otherwise timely asserted. FRCP 5.1(d).

iii. *Nongovernmental corporate disclosure statement.* A nongovernmental corporate party must file two (2) copies of a disclosure statement that: (1) identifies any parent corporation and any publicly held corporation owning ten percent (10%) or more of its stock; or (2) states that there is no such corporation. FRCP 7.1(a). A party must: (1) file the disclosure statement with its first appearance, pleading, petition, motion, response, or other request addressed to the court; and (2) promptly file a supplemental statement if any required information changes. FRCP 7.1(b).

- *DISTRICT OF MAINE: Notice of interested parties.* To enable the court to evaluate possible disqualification or recusal, counsel for all non-governmental parties shall file with their first appearance a Notice of Interested Parties, which shall list all persons, associations of persons, firms, partnerships, limited liability companies, joint ventures, corporations (including parent or affiliated corporations, clearly identified as such), or any similar entities, owning ten percent (10%) or more of the named party. Counsel shall be under a continuing obligation to file an amended Notice if any material change occurs in the status of an Interested Party, such as through merger, acquisition, or new/additional membership. ME R USDCT Rule 7.1.

iv. *DISTRICT OF MAINE: Additional supplemental documents*

- *Proposed order.* Proposed orders shall not be filed unless requested by the court. When requested by the court, proposed orders shall be filed by e-mail in word processing format. ME R USDCT App. 4(k)(1).

E. Format

1. *Form of documents.* The rules governing captions and other matters of form in pleadings apply to motions and other papers. FRCP 7(b)(2).

   a. *DISTRICT OF MAINE: Font size, line spacing, and paper size.* All such documents shall be typed in a font of no less than size twelve (12) point, and shall be double-spaced or printed on eight and one-half by eleven (8-1/2 x 11) inch paper. Footnotes shall be in a font of no less than size ten (10) point, and may be single spaced. ME R USDCT Rule 10.

   b. *Caption.* Every pleading must have a caption with the court's name, a title, a file number, and an FRCP 7(a) designation. FRCP 10(a).

   i. *Names of parties.* The title of the complaint must name all the parties; the title of other pleadings, after naming the first party on each side, may refer generally to other parties. FRCP 10(a).

   ii. *DISTRICT OF MAINE: Additional caption requirements.* All pleadings, motions and other papers filed with the clerk or otherwise submitted to the court, except exhibits, shall bear the proper case number and shall contain on the first page a caption as described by FRCP 10(a) and immediately thereunder a designation of what the document is and the name of the party in whose behalf it is submitted. ME R USDCT Rule 10.

   iii. *DISTRICT OF MAINE: Injunctive relief.* If a pleading or motion seeks injunctive relief, in addition to the prayer for such relief, the words "INJUNCTIVE RELIEF SOUGHT" or the equivalent shall be included on the first page. ME R USDCT Rule 9(b).

   c. *Claims or defenses*

   i. *Numbered paragraphs.* A party must state its claims or defenses in numbered paragraphs, each limited as far as practicable to a single set of circumstances. A later pleading may refer by number to a paragraph in an earlier pleading. FRCP 10(b).

    ii. *Separate statements.* If doing so would promote clarity, each claim founded on a separate transaction or occurrence—and each defense other than a denial—must be stated in a separate count or defense. FRCP 10(b).

  d. *Adoption by reference.* A statement in a pleading may be adopted by reference elsewhere in the same pleading or in any other pleading or motion. FRCP 10(c).

    i. *Exhibits.* A copy of a written instrument that is an exhibit to a pleading is a part of the pleading for all purposes. FRCP 10(c).

  e. *DISTRICT OF MAINE: Page numbering.* All pages shall be numbered at the bottom. ME R USDCT Rule 10.

  f. *DISTRICT OF MAINE: Attachment of ancillary papers.* Ancillary papers shall be attached at the end of the document to which they relate. ME R USDCT Rule 10.

  g. *Acceptance by the clerk.* The clerk must not refuse to file a paper solely because it is not in the form prescribed by the Federal Rules of Civil Procedure or by a local rule or practice. FRCP 5(d)(4).

2. *Form of electronic documents.* A paper filed electronically is a written paper for purposes of the Federal Rules of Civil Procedure. FRCP 5(d)(3)(D).

  a. *DISTRICT OF MAINE: Document format.* The ECF system only accepts documents in a portable document format (PDF). Although there are two types of PDF documents—electronically converted PDF's and scanned PDF's—only electronically converted PDF's may be filed with the court using the ECF system, unless otherwise authorized by local rule or order. ME R USDCT App. 4. Any document or exhibit to be filed or submitted to the court shall not be password-protected or encrypted. ME R USDCT App. 4(g)(12).

    i. *Electronically converted PDFs.* Electronically converted PDF's are created from word processing documents (MS Word, WordPerfect, etc.) using Adobe Acrobat or similar software. They are text searchable and their file size is small. ME R USDCT App. 4. Software used to electronically convert documents to PDF which includes proprietary or advertisement information within the PDF document is prohibited. ME R USDCT App. 4.

    ii. *Scanned PDFs.* Scanned PDF's are created from paper documents run through an optical scanner. Scanned PDF's are not searchable and have a large file size. ME R USDCT App. 4.

  b. *DISTRICT OF MAINE: Title.* All pleadings filed electronically shall be titled in accordance with the approved dictionary of civil or criminal events of the ECF system of the United States District Court for the District of Maine. ME R USDCT App. 4(d)(3).

  c. *DISTRICT OF MAINE: Attachments.* Attachments to filings and exhibits must be filed in accordance with the court's ECF User Manual, unless otherwise ordered by the court. ME R USDCT App. 4(j). When there are fifty (50) or fewer attachments to a pleading, the attachments must be filed by counsel electronically using ECF. When there are more than fifty (50) attachments, the attachments must be filed in one of the following ways: (A) using ECF, simply attach them to the pleading being filed; (B) using ECF, use the "Additional Attachments" menu item; (C) on paper; or (D) on a properly labeled three and one-half (3-1/2) inch floppy disk, CD or DVD. ME R USDCT App. 4(j)(2). Attachments filed on paper or on disk must contain a comprehensive index that clearly describes each document. ME R USDCT App. 4(j)(2).

    i. A filing user must submit as attachments only those excerpts of the referenced documents that are directly germane to the matter under consideration by the court. Excerpted material must be clearly and prominently identified as such. Users who file excerpts of documents do so without prejudice to their right to timely file additional excerpts or the complete document, as may be allowed by the court. Responding parties may timely file additional excerpts or the complete document that they believe are directly germane. ME R USDCT App. 4(j)(3).

    ii. Filers shall not attach as an exhibit any pleading or other paper already on file with the court in that case, but shall merely refer to that document. ME R USDCT App. 4(j)(4).

  d. *DISTRICT OF MAINE: Compliance with technical standards.* All documents filed by electronic means must comply with technical standards, if any, established by the Judicial Conference of the United States or by the United States District Court for the District of Maine. ME R USDCT App. 4(a)(3).

3. *DISTRICT OF MAINE: Form of memoranda of law.* All memoranda shall be typed, in a font of no less than size twelve (12) point, and shall be double-spaced on eight and one-half by eleven (8-1/2 x 11) inch paper or printed. Footnotes shall be in

a font of no less than size ten (10) point, and may be single spaced. All pages shall be numbered at the bottom. ME R USDCT Rule 7(d).

a. *Page limitations.* No memorandum of law in support of or in opposition to a motion to dismiss, a motion for judgment on the pleadings, a motion for summary judgment or a motion for injunctive relief shall exceed twenty (20) pages. ME R USDCT Rule 7(d). No reply memorandum shall exceed seven (7) pages. ME R USDCT Rule 7(d); ME R USDCT Rule 7(c).

    i. *Motion to exceed page limitation.* A motion to exceed the limitation of ME R USDCT Rule 7 shall be filed no later than three (3) business days in advance of the date for filing the memorandum to permit meaningful review by the court. A motion to exceed the page limitations shall not be filed simultaneously with a memorandum in excess of the limitations of ME R USDCT Rule 7. ME R USDCT Rule 7(d).

4. *Signing of pleadings, motions and other papers*

a. *Signature.* Every pleading, written motion, and other paper must be signed by at least one attorney of record in the attorney's name—or by a party personally if the party is unrepresented. The paper must state the signer's address, e-mail address, and telephone number. FRCP 11(a).

    i. *No verification or accompanying affidavit required for pleadings.* Unless a rule or statute specifically states otherwise, a pleading need not be verified or accompanied by an affidavit. FRCP 11(a).

    ii. *Unsigned papers.* The court must strike an unsigned paper unless the omission is promptly corrected after being called to the attorney's or party's attention. FRCP 11(a).

b. *Electronic signing.* A filing made through a person's electronic-filing account and authorized by that person, together with that person's name on a signature block, constitutes the person's signature. FRCP 5(d)(3)(C).

    i. *DISTRICT OF MAINE: Attorneys.* The user log-in and password together with a user's name on the signature block constitutes the attorney's signature pursuant to the Federal Rules of Civil Procedure and the Local Rules of the United States District Court for the District of Maine. All electronically filed documents must include a signature block and must set forth the attorney's name, address, telephone number and e-mail address. The name of the ECF user under whose log-in and password the document is submitted must be preceded by a "/s/" in the space where the signature would otherwise appear. ME R USDCT App. 4(h)(1).

    ii. *DISTRICT OF MAINE: Multiple signatures.* The filer of any document requiring more than one signature (e.g., pleadings filed by visiting lawyers, stipulations, joint status reports) must list thereon all the names of other signatories, preceded by a "/s/" in the space where the signatures would otherwise appear. By submitting such a document, the filing attorney certifies that each of the other signatories has expressly agreed to the form and substance of the document and that the filing attorney has their actual authority to submit the document electronically. ME R USDCT App. 4(h)(2). For more information, refer to ME R USDCT App. 4(h)(2).

    iii. *DISTRICT OF MAINE: Documents signed under oath.* Affidavits, declarations, verified complaints, or any other document signed under oath shall be filed electronically. The electronically filed version shall contain the typed name of the signatory, preceded by a "/s/" in the space where the signature would otherwise appear indicating that the paper document bears an original signature. ME R USDCT Rule 10; ME R USDCT App. 4(h)(3). For more information, refer to ME R USDCT Rule 10.

c. *Representations to the court.* By presenting to the court a pleading, written motion, or other paper—whether by signing, filing, submitting, or later advocating it—an attorney or unrepresented party certifies that to the best of the person's knowledge, information, and belief, formed after an inquiry reasonable under the circumstances: (1) it is not being presented for any improper purpose, such as to harass, cause unnecessary delay, or needlessly increase the cost of litigation; (2) the claims, defenses, and other legal contentions are warranted by existing law or by a nonfrivolous argument for extending, modifying, or reversing existing law or for establishing new law; (3) the factual contentions have evidentiary support or, if specifically so identified, will likely have evidentiary support after a reasonable opportunity for further investigation or discovery; and (4) the denials of factual contentions are warranted on the evidence or, if specifically so identified, are reasonably based on belief or a lack of information. FRCP 11(b).

d. *Sanctions.* If, after notice and a reasonable opportunity to respond, the court determines that FRCP 11(b) has been violated, the court may impose an appropriate sanction on any attorney, law firm, or party that violated FRCP 11(b) or is responsible for the violation. FRCP 11(c)(1). Refer to the United States District Court for the District of Maine KeyRules Motion for Sanctions document for more information.

5. *Privacy protection for filings made with the court*

a. *Redacted filings.* Unless the court orders otherwise, in an electronic or paper filing with the court that contains an individual's Social Security number, taxpayer-identification number, or birth date, the name of an individual known to be a minor, or a financial-account number, a party or nonparty making the filing may include only: (1) the last four (4) digits of the Social Security number and taxpayer-identification number; (2) the year of the individual's birth; (3) the minor's initials; and (4) the last four (4) digits of the financial-account number. FRCP 5.2(a).

    i.   *DISTRICT OF MAINE.* To address the privacy concerns created by the Internet access to court papers, unless otherwise ordered by the court, counsel shall modify certain personal data identifiers in pleadings and other papers as follows: (1) minors' names: use of the minors' initials only; (2) Social Security numbers: use of the last four (4) numbers only; (3) dates of birth: use of the year of birth only; [and] (4) financial account numbers: identify the type of account and the financial institution, but use only the last four (4) numbers of the account number. ME R USDCT Redacting Pleadings. Counsel should also use caution when filing papers that contain a person's medical records, employment history; financial information; and any proprietary or trade secret information. ME R USDCT Redacting Pleadings.

b.   *Exemptions from the redaction requirement.* The redaction requirement does not apply to the following: (1) a financial-account number that identifies the property allegedly subject to forfeiture in a forfeiture proceeding; (2) the record of an administrative or agency proceeding; (3) the official record of a state-court proceeding; (4) the record of a court or tribunal, if that record was not subject to the redaction requirement when originally filed; (5) a filing covered by FRCP 5.2(c) or FRCP 5.2(d); and (6) a pro se filing in an action brought under 28 U.S.C.A. § 2241, 28 U.S.C.A. § 2254, or 28 U.S.C.A. § 2255. FRCP 5.2(b).

c.   *Limitations on remote access to electronic files; Social Security appeals and immigration cases.* Unless the court orders otherwise, in an action for benefits under the Social Security Act, and in an action or proceeding relating to an order of removal, to relief from removal, or to immigration benefits or detention, access to an electronic file is authorized as follows: (1) the parties and their attorneys may have remote electronic access to any part of the case file, including the administrative record; (2) any other person may have electronic access to the full record at the courthouse, but may have remote electronic access only to: (A) the docket maintained by the court; and (B) an opinion, order, judgment, or other disposition of the court, but not any other part of the case file or the administrative record. FRCP 5.2(c).

d.   *Filings made under seal.* The court may order that a filing be made under seal without redaction. The court may later unseal the filing or order the person who made the filing to file a redacted version for the public record. FRCP 5.2(d).

    i.   *DISTRICT OF MAINE.* For information on filing sealed documents in the District of Maine, refer to ME R USDCT Rule 7A, ME R USDCT App. 4(p)(2), and ME R USDCT Sealed Filings.

e.   *Protective orders.* For good cause, the court may by order in a case: (1) require redaction of additional information; or (2) limit or prohibit a nonparty's remote electronic access to a document filed with the court. FRCP 5.2(e).

f.   *Option for additional unredacted filing under seal.* A person making a redacted filing may also file an unredacted copy under seal. The court must retain the unredacted copy as part of the record. FRCP 5.2(f).

    i.   *DISTRICT OF MAINE.* A party wishing to file a document containing the personal data identifiers specified above may. . .file an unredacted document under seal. This document will be retained by the clerk's office as part of the record. ME R USDCT Redacting Pleadings. The court may, however, still require the party to file a redacted copy for the public file. ME R USDCT Redacting Pleadings.

g.   *Option for filing a reference list.* A filing that contains redacted information may be filed together with a reference list that identifies each item of redacted information and specifies an appropriate identifier that uniquely corresponds to each item listed. The list must be filed under seal and may be amended as of right. Any reference in the case to a listed identifier will be construed to refer to the corresponding item of information. FRCP 5.2(g).

    i.   *DISTRICT OF MAINE.* A party wishing to file a document containing the personal data identifiers specified above may. . .file a reference list under seal. The reference list shall contain the complete personal data identifier(s) and the redacted identifier(s) used in its (their) place in the filing. All references in the case to the redacted identifiers included in the reference list will be construed to refer to the corresponding complete identifier. The reference list must be filed under seal, and may be amended as of right. It shall be retained by the clerk's office as part of the record. ME R USDCT Redacting Pleadings. The court may, however, still require the party to file a redacted copy for the public file. ME R USDCT Redacting Pleadings.

h.   *DISTRICT OF MAINE: Responsibility for redaction.* The clerk is not required to review documents filed with the court for compliance with FRCP 5.2. The responsibility to redact filings rests with counsel and the party or nonparty making the filing. ME R USDCT App. 4(i); ME R USDCT Redacting Pleadings. For guidelines for filing confidential information in civil cases in the District of Maine, refer to ME R USDCT Confidentiality.

i. *Waiver of protection of identifiers.* A person waives the protection of FRCP 5.2(a) as to the person's own information by filing it without redaction and not under seal. FRCP 5.2(h).

F. Filing and Service Requirements

1. *Filing requirements*

   a. *Required filings.* Any paper after the complaint that is required to be served must be filed no later than a reasonable time after service. FRCP 5(d)(1).

   b. *DISTRICT OF MAINE: Place of filing.* Unless otherwise ordered by the court, papers shall be filed with the court at Bangor in cases filed and pending at Bangor, and at Portland in cases filed and pending at Portland. ME R USDCT Rule 5(a).

   c. *Nonelectronic filing.* A paper not filed electronically is filed by delivering it: (A) to the clerk; or (B) to a judge who agrees to accept it for filing, and who must then note the filing date on the paper and promptly send it to the clerk. FRCP 5(d)(2).

      i. *DISTRICT OF MAINE: Documents to be filed in paper.* The following documents shall be filed in paper, which may also be scanned into ECF by the clerk's office: (A) all handwritten pleadings; and (B) all pleadings and documents filed by pro se litigants who are incarcerated or who are not registered filing users in ECF. ME R USDCT App. 4(g)(8). Non-prisoner pro se litigants in civil actions may register with ECF or may file (and serve) all pleadings and other documents in paper. The clerk's office will scan into ECF any pleadings and documents filed on paper in accordance with ME R USDCT App. 4(g). ME R USDCT App. 4(o). For more information, refer to ME R USDCT App. 4(g).

   d. *Electronic filing*

      i. *DISTRICT OF MAINE: Authorization.* Unless exempt or otherwise ordered by the court, papers shall be filed and served electronically as required by the court's Administrative Procedures Governing the Filing and Service by Electronic Means, which is set forth in ME R USDCT App. 4. The provisions of the court's Administrative Procedures Governing the Filing and Service by Electronic Means (ME R USDCT App. 4) shall be applied and enforced as part of the Local Rules of the United States District Court for the District of Maine. ME R USDCT Rule 5(c).

      ii. *Filing by represented persons.* A person represented by an attorney must file electronically, unless nonelectronic filing is allowed by the court for good cause or is allowed or required by local rule. FRCP 5(d)(3)(A).

         • *DISTRICT OF MAINE.* An attorney may apply to the court for permission to file paper documents. ME R USDCT App. 4(a)(5).

      iii. *Filing by unrepresented persons.* A person not represented by an attorney: (i) may file electronically only if allowed by court order or by local rule; and (ii) may be required to file electronically only by court order, or by a local rule that includes reasonable exceptions. FRCP 5(d)(3)(B).

         • *DISTRICT OF MAINE.* Non-prisoner pro se litigants in civil actions may register with ECF or may file (and serve) all pleadings and other documents in paper. ME R USDCT App. 4(o). A non-prisoner who is a party to a civil action and who is not represented by an attorney may register to receive service electronically and to electronically transmit their documents to the court for filing in the ECF system. If during the course of the action the person retains an attorney who appears on the person's behalf, the clerk shall terminate the person's registration upon the attorney's appearance. ME R USDCT App. 4(b)(2).

      iv. *DISTRICT OF MAINE: Scope of electronic filing.* All documents submitted for filing in civil and criminal cases, regardless of case commencement date, except those documents specifically exempted in ME R USDCT App. 4(g), shall be filed electronically using the electronic case filing system (ECF). ME R USDCT App. 4(a)(1). For special filing requirements and exceptions, refer to ME R USDCT App. 4(g).

      v. *DISTRICT OF MAINE: Consequences of electronic filing.* Electronic transmission of a document to the ECF system, together with the transmission of a Notice of Electronic Filing (NEF) from the court, constitutes filing of the document for all purposes of the Federal Rules of Civil Procedure. ME R USDCT App. 4(d)(1).

      vi. *DISTRICT OF MAINE: Review of documents.* Documents filed with the clerk's office will normally be reviewed no later than the close of the next business day. It is the responsibility of the filing party to promptly notify the clerk's office via telephone of a matter that requires the immediate attention of a judicial officer. ME R USDCT App. 4(a)(4).

   e. *DISTRICT OF MAINE: Facsimile filing.* No papers shall be submitted to the court by means of a facsimile machine without prior leave of the court. ME R USDCT Rule 5(c); ME R USDCT App. 4(m).

2. *Service requirements*

a. *Service; When required.* Unless the Federal Rules of Civil Procedure provide otherwise, each of the following papers must be served on every party: (A) an order stating that service is required; (B) a pleading filed after the original complaint, unless the court orders otherwise under FRCP 5(c) because there are numerous defendants; (C) a discovery paper required to be served on a party, unless the court orders otherwise; (D) a written motion, except one that may be heard ex parte; and (E) a written notice, appearance, demand, or offer of judgment, or any similar paper. FRCP 5(a)(1).

i. *If a party fails to appear.* No service is required on a party who is in default for failing to appear. But a pleading that asserts a new claim for relief against such a party must be served on that party under FRCP 4. FRCP 5(a)(2).

ii. *Seizing property.* If an action is begun by seizing property and no person is or need be named as a defendant, any service required before the filing of an appearance, answer, or claim must be made on the person who had custody or possession of the property when it was seized. FRCP 5(a)(3).

b. *Service; How made.* A paper is served under FRCP 5 by: (A) handing it to the person; (B) leaving it: (i) at the person's office with a clerk or other person in charge or, if no one is in charge, in a conspicuous place in the office; or (ii) if the person has no office or the office is closed, at the person's dwelling or usual place of abode with someone of suitable age and discretion who resides there; (C) mailing it to the person's last known address—in which event service is complete upon mailing; (D) leaving it with the court clerk if the person has no known address; (E) sending it to a registered user by filing it with the court's electronic-filing system or sending it by other electronic means that the person consented to in writing—in either of which events service is complete upon filing or sending, but is not effective if the filer or sender learns that it did not reach the person to be served; or (F) delivering it by any other means that the person consented to in writing—in which event service is complete when the person making service delivers it to the agency designated to make delivery. FRCP 5(b)(2).

i. *Serving an attorney.* If a party is represented by an attorney, service under FRCP 5 must be made on the attorney unless the court orders service on the party. FRCP 5(b)(1).

c. *DISTRICT OF MAINE: Service of electronically filed documents*

i. *Registered users.* Registration [as a filing user of the court's ECF system] constitutes consent to service of all documents by electronic means as provided in ME R USDCT App. 4. ME R USDCT App. 4(b)(4). Whenever a non-sealed pleading is filed electronically, the ECF system will automatically generate and send a Notice of Electronic Filing (NEF) to the filing user and registered users of record. The user filing the document should retain a paper or digital copy of the NEF, which shall serve as the court's date-stamp and proof of filing. ME R USDCT App. 4(e)(1).

- *Sealed documents.* Although the filing of sealed documents in civil cases produces an NEF, the document itself cannot be accessed and counsel shall be responsible for making service of the sealed documents. ME R USDCT App. 4(e)(2).

ii. *Non-registered users and pro se litigants.* Attorneys who have not yet registered as users with ECF and pro se litigants who have not registered with ECF shall be served a paper copy of any electronically filed pleading or other document in accordance with the provisions of FRCP 5. ME R USDCT App. 4(e)(3).

- *Registration of pro se litigants.* A non-prisoner who is a party to a civil action and who is not represented by an attorney may register to receive service electronically and to electronically transmit their documents to the court for filing in the ECF system. If during the course of the action the person retains an attorney who appears on the person's behalf, the clerk shall terminate the person's registration upon the attorney's appearance. ME R USDCT App. 4(b)(2).

d. *Serving numerous defendants.* If an action involves an unusually large number of defendants, the court may, on motion or on its own, order that: (A) defendants' pleadings and replies to them need not be served on other defendants; (B) any crossclaim, counterclaim, avoidance, or affirmative defense in those pleadings and replies to them will be treated as denied or avoided by all other parties; and (C) filing any such pleading and serving it on the plaintiff constitutes notice of the pleading to all parties. FRCP 5(c)(1).

i. *Notifying parties.* A copy of every such order must be served on the parties as the court directs. FRCP 5(c)(2).

3. *DISTRICT OF MAINE: Filing and service of highly sensitive documents (HSDs).* For information on filing and serving highly sensitive documents (HSDs) in the District of Maine, refer to ME R USDCT General Order 21-5.

G. Hearings

1. *Hearings, generally.* When a motion relies on facts outside the record, the court may hear the matter on affidavits or may hear it wholly or partly on oral testimony or on depositions. FRCP 43(c).

   a. *Oral argument.* Due process does not require that oral argument be permitted on a motion and, except as otherwise provided by local rule, the district court has discretion to determine whether it will decide the motion on the papers or hear argument by counsel (and perhaps receive evidence). FPP § 1190; F.D.I.C. v. Deglau, 207 F.3d 153 (3d Cir. 2000).

      i. *DISTRICT OF MAINE.* Unless otherwise required by federal rule or statute, all motions may be decided by the court without oral argument unless otherwise ordered by the court on its own motion or, in its discretion, upon request of counsel. ME R USDCT Rule 7(e).

   b. *Providing a regular schedule for oral hearings.* A court may establish regular times and places for oral hearings on motions. FRCP 78(a).

   c. *Providing for submission on briefs.* By rule or order, the court may provide for submitting and determining motions on briefs, without oral hearings. FRCP 78(b).

2. *Hearing on motion for preliminary injunction after ex parte temporary restraining order is issued.* If the order is issued without notice, the motion for a preliminary injunction must be set for hearing at the earliest possible time, taking precedence over all other matters except hearings on older matters of the same character. At the hearing, the party who obtained the order must proceed with the motion; if the party does not, the court must dissolve the order. FRCP 65(b)(3). Refer to the United States District Court for the District of Maine KeyRules Motion for Preliminary Injunction document for more information on the hearing on the motion for preliminary injunction.

H. Forms

1. Federal Application for Temporary Restraining Order Forms

   a. Motion for temporary restraining order. 4A FEDFORMS § 47:75.

   b. Motion for temporary restraining order; Enforcement of statute. 4A FEDFORMS § 47:76.

   c. Motion for temporary restraining order; Restraining attorney. 4A FEDFORMS § 47:77.

   d. Motion for temporary restraining order; Restraining defendant from refusing to admit plaintiffs to school. 4A FEDFORMS § 47:78.

   e. Motion for temporary restraining order; Requesting expedited hearing; Athletic eligibility. 4A FEDFORMS § 47:79.

   f. Motion for temporary restraining order; Without notice. 4A FEDFORMS § 47:80.

   g. Motion for temporary restraining order; Without notice; Reciting attempts to give notice. 4A FEDFORMS § 47:81.

   h. Motion for temporary restraining order; Without notice; Encumbering property. 4A FEDFORMS § 47:82.

   i. Certificate of attorney's efforts to give notice; School board. 4A FEDFORMS § 47:83.

   j. Certificate of attorney's efforts to give notice; Telephone call to opposing counsel. 4A FEDFORMS § 47:84.

   k. Certificate of attorney's efforts to give notice; Hand-delivered to attorney. 4A FEDFORMS § 47:85.

   l. Motion to extend temporary restraining order and for amendment of order. 4A FEDFORMS § 47:86.

   m. Motion to dissolve or modify temporary restraining order. 4A FEDFORMS § 47:87.

   n. Motion to dissolve temporary restraining order; Material change in circumstances. 4A FEDFORMS § 47:88.

   o. Motion to dissolve temporary restraining order; Various grounds. 4A FEDFORMS § 47:89.

   p. Motion to dissolve temporary restraining order and dismiss complaint. 4A FEDFORMS § 47:93.

   q. Ex parte motion; For temporary restraining order and order to show cause; Interference with property rights. AMJUR PP INJUNCTION § 42.

   r. Affidavit; In support of ex parte motion for temporary restraining order. AMJUR PP INJUNCTION § 48.

   s. Certificate of attorney; In support of ex parte motion for temporary restraining order. AMJUR PP INJUNCTION § 50.

   t. Affidavit; In support of ex parte motion for temporary restraining order; Interference with property rights. AMJUR PP INJUNCTION § 51.

   u. Motion for temporary restraining order and preliminary injunction. GOLDLTGFMS § 13A:6.

v. Motion for temporary restraining order; General form. GOLDLTGFMS § 13A:11.

w. Motion for temporary restraining order; Ex parte application. GOLDLTGFMS § 13A:12.

x. Motion for temporary restraining order; Ex parte application; Supporting affidavit by party. GOLDLTGFMS § 13A:13.

y. Motion for temporary restraining order; Ex parte application; Supporting affidavit by party; Copyright infringement. GOLDLTGFMS § 13A:14.

z. Motion for temporary restraining order; Ex parte application; Certificate by counsel. GOLDLTGFMS § 13A:15.

I. Applicable Rules

1. *Federal rules*

   a. Serving and filing pleadings and other papers. FRCP 5.

   b. Constitutional challenge to a statute; Notice, certification, and intervention. FRCP 5.1.

   c. Privacy protection for filings made with the court. FRCP 5.2.

   d. Computing and extending time; Time for motion papers. FRCP 6.

   e. Pleadings allowed; Form of motions and other papers. FRCP 7.

   f. Disclosure statement. FRCP 7.1.

   g. Form of pleadings. FRCP 10.

   h. Signing pleadings, motions, and other papers; Representations to the court; Sanctions. FRCP 11.

   i. Taking testimony. FRCP 43.

   j. Injunctions and restraining orders. FRCP 65.

   k. Hearing motions; Submission on briefs. FRCP 78.

2. *Local rules*

   a. *DISTRICT OF MAINE*

      i. Service and filing of pleadings and other papers. ME R USDCT Rule 5.

      ii. Time. ME R USDCT Rule 6.

      iii. Motions and memoranda of law. ME R USDCT Rule 7.

      iv. Corporate disclosure. ME R USDCT Rule 7.1.

      v. Pleading special matters. ME R USDCT Rule 9.

      vi. Form of pleadings, motions and other papers. ME R USDCT Rule 10.

      vii. Discovery. ME R USDCT Rule 26.

      viii. Attorneys; Appearances and withdrawals. ME R USDCT Rule 83.2.

      ix. Alternative dispute resolution (ADR). ME R USDCT Rule 83.11.

      x. Administrative procedures governing the filing and service by electronic means. ME R USDCT App. 4.

      xi. Redacting pleadings. ME R USDCT Redacting Pleadings.

Requests, Notices and Applications
Pretrial Conferences, Scheduling, Management

Document Last Updated July 2021

A. Checklist

(I) ❑ Matters to be considered by parties for the pretrial conference

   (a) ❑ Documents to consider

      (1) ❑ Pretrial memorandum or statement

(b) ❑ Timing

    (1) ❑ The court determines at what stage in the action to hold a pretrial conference

(II) ❑ Matters to be considered by parties for the scheduling conference

  (a) ❑ Documents to consider

    (1) ❑ Request for scheduling conference

    (2) ❑ DISTRICT OF MAINE: Additional documents to consider

      (i) ❑ Joint proposed discovery and motion plan

  (b) ❑ Timing

    (1) ❑ If a scheduling conference is called, it is important to recognize that, unlike the ordinary pretrial conference, the scheduling conference occurs before the substantive issues have been defined and is directed toward organizing the processing of the action by setting deadlines for the completion of the various pretrial phases

    (2) ❑ DISTRICT OF MAINE: Additional timing

      (i) ❑ [In standard track cases,] the court may require counsel to file a joint proposed discovery and motion plan prior to the scheduling conference

      (ii) ❑ [In complex track cases,] not less than two (2) business days before the conference the lawyers shall file a joint proposed discovery and motion plan and any proposal for ADR

(III) ❑ Matters to be considered by parties for the final pretrial conference

  (a) ❑ Required documents

    (1) ❑ DISTRICT OF MAINE: Additional required documents

      (i) ❑ Pretrial memorandum

  (b) ❑ Timing

    (1) ❑ DISTRICT OF MAINE: Additional timing

      (i) ❑ A final pretrial conference shall be held as close to the time of trial as reasonable under the circumstances

      (ii) ❑ Not later than five (5) business days prior to the final pretrial conference, each party shall file with the court and serve on every other party a pretrial memorandum

(IV) ❑ Matters to be considered by parties for the discovery planning conference

  (a) ❑ Required documents

    (1) ❑ Written report outlining proposed discovery plan

  (b) ❑ Timing

    (1) ❑ Except in a proceeding exempted from initial disclosure under FRCP 26(a)(1)(B) or when the court orders otherwise, the parties must confer as soon as practicable—and in any event at least twenty-one (21) days before a scheduling conference is to be held or a scheduling order is due under FRCP 16(b)

    (2) ❑ Within fourteen (14) days after the conference, the attorneys of record are responsible for submitting a written report outlining the plan

B. Timing

1. *Pretrial conferences, generally.* The court determines at what stage in the action to hold a pretrial conference. When only one conference is involved, the most favored practice seems to be to wait until after the case has been prepared for trial. FPP § 1524. Although there rarely will be any need to hold a conference in a relatively simple case until after the preliminary motions have been disposed of, the only inherently logical limitation on the court's discretion as to when to hold a conference is that it should not be held before all the necessary and indispensable parties are served. FPP § 1524.

2. *Scheduling conference.* If a scheduling conference is called, it is important to recognize that, unlike the ordinary pretrial conference, the scheduling conference occurs before the substantive issues have been defined and is directed toward organizing the processing of the action by setting deadlines for the completion of the various pretrial phases. FPP § 1522.1.

  a. *DISTRICT OF MAINE: Joint proposed discovery and motion plan.* [In standard track cases,] the court may require counsel to file a joint proposed discovery and motion plan prior to the scheduling conference. ME R USDCT Rule 16.3(b)(4). [In complex track cases,] not less than two (2) business days before the conference the lawyers shall file a joint proposed discovery and motion plan and any proposal for ADR. ME R USDCT Rule 16.3(c)(3).

3. *DISTRICT OF MAINE: Final pretrial conference.* A final pretrial conference shall be held as close to the time of trial as reasonable under the circumstances. The clerk shall notify counsel of the time and place by mailing to them a written notice. ME R USDCT Rule 16.4(a).

    a. *Pretrial memorandum.* Not later than five (5) business days prior to the final pretrial conference, each party shall file with the court and serve on every other party a pretrial memorandum. ME R USDCT Rule 16.4(b). Refer to the "C. General Requirements" section of this KeyRules document for more information.

4. *Discovery planning conference.* Except in a proceeding exempted from initial disclosure under FRCP 26(a)(1)(B) or when the court orders otherwise, the parties must confer as soon as practicable—and in any event at least twenty-one (21) days before a scheduling conference is to be held or a scheduling order is due under FRCP 16(b). FRCP 26(f)(1).

    a. *Submission of written report outlining proposed discovery plan.* The attorneys of record and all unrepresented parties that have appeared in the case are jointly responsible for arranging the conference, for attempting in good faith to agree on the proposed discovery plan, and for submitting to the court within fourteen (14) days after the conference a written report outlining the plan. FRCP 26(f)(2).

    b. *Expedited schedule.* If necessary to comply with its expedited schedule for FRCP 16(b) conferences, a court may by local rule: (A) require the parties' conference to occur less than twenty-one (21) days before the scheduling conference is held or a scheduling order is due under FRCP 16(b); and (B) require the written report outlining the discovery plan to be filed less than fourteen (14) days after the parties' conference, or excuse the parties from submitting a written report and permit them to report orally on their discovery plan at the FRCP 16(b) conference. FRCP 26(f)(4).

5. *Computation of time*

    a. *Computing time.* FRCP 6 applies in computing any time period specified in the Federal Rules of Civil Procedure, in any local rule or court order, or in any statute that does not specify a method of computing time. FRCP 6(a).

        i. *Period stated in days or a longer unit.* When the period is stated in days or a longer unit of time: (A) exclude the day of the event that triggers the period; (B) count every day, including intermediate Saturdays, Sundays, and legal holidays; and (C) include the last day of the period, but if the last day is a Saturday, Sunday, or legal holiday, the period continues to run until the end of the next day that is not a Saturday, Sunday, or legal holiday. FRCP 6(a)(1).

        ii. *Period stated in hours.* When the period is stated in hours: (A) begin counting immediately on the occurrence of the event that triggers the period; (B) count every hour, including hours during intermediate Saturdays, Sundays, and legal holidays; and (C) if the period would end on a Saturday, Sunday, or legal holiday, the period continues to run until the same time on the next day that is not a Saturday, Sunday, or legal holiday. FRCP 6(a)(2).

        iii. *Inaccessibility of the clerk's office.* Unless the court orders otherwise, if the clerk's office is inaccessible: (A) on the last day for filing under FRCP 6(a)(1), then the time for filing is extended to the first accessible day that is not a Saturday, Sunday, or legal holiday; or (B) during the last hour for filing under FRCP 6(a)(2), then the time for filing is extended to the same time on the first accessible day that is not a Saturday, Sunday, or legal holiday. FRCP 6(a)(3).

        iv. *"Last day" defined.* Unless a different time is set by a statute, local rule, or court order, the last day ends: (A) for electronic filing, at midnight in the court's time zone; and (B) for filing by other means, when the clerk's office is scheduled to close. FRCP 6(a)(4).

        v. *"Next day" defined.* The "next day" is determined by continuing to count forward when the period is measured after an event and backward when measured before an event. FRCP 6(a)(5).

        vi. *"Legal holiday" defined.* "Legal holiday" means: (A) the day set aside by statute for observing New Year's Day, Martin Luther King Jr.'s Birthday, Washington's Birthday, Memorial Day, Independence Day, Labor Day, Columbus Day, Veterans' Day, Thanksgiving Day, or Christmas Day; (B) any day declared a holiday by the President or Congress; and (C) for periods that are measured after an event, any other day declared a holiday by the state where the district court is located. FRCP 6(a)(6).

        vii. *DISTRICT OF MAINE: Applicability of FRCP 6.* FRCP 6 applies when computing any period of time stated in the Local Rules of the United States District Court for the District of Maine. ME R USDCT Rule 6(a).

    b. *DISTRICT OF MAINE: Computation of electronic filing deadlines.* Filing documents electronically does not in any way alter any filing deadlines. All electronic transmissions of documents must be completed prior to midnight, Eastern Time, in order to be considered timely filed that day. Where a specific time of day deadline is set by court order or stipulation, the electronic filing must be completed by that time. ME R USDCT App. 4(f). A document filed

electronically shall be deemed filed at the time and date stated on the Notice of Electronic Filing received from the court. ME R USDCT App. 4(d)(2).

i. *Technical failures.* A filing user whose filing is made untimely as the result of a technical failure may seek appropriate relief from the court. ME R USDCT App. 4(n). A technical failure of the court's ECF system is deemed to have occurred when the court's ECF site cannot accept filings continuously or intermittently over the course of any period of time greater than one (1) hour. Known system outages will be posted on the court's website along with guidance on how to proceed, if applicable. ME R USDCT App. 4(n).

c. *Extending time.* When an act may or must be done within a specified time, the court may, for good cause, extend the time: (A) with or without motion or notice if the court acts, or if a request is made, before the original time or its extension expires; or (B) on motion made after the time has expired if the party failed to act because of excusable neglect. FRCP 6(b)(1). A court must not extend the time to act under FRCP 50(b), FRCP 50(d), FRCP 52(b), FRCP 59(b), FRCP 59(d), FRCP 59(e), and FRCP 60(b). FRCP 6(b)(2). Refer to the United States District Court for the District of Maine KeyRules Motion for Continuance/Extension of Time document for more information on extending time.

d. *Additional time after certain kinds of service.* When a party may or must act within a specified time after being served and service is made under FRCP 5(b)(2)(C) (by mail), FRCP 5(b)(2)(D) (by leaving with the clerk), or FRCP 5(b)(2)(F) (by other means consented to), three (3) days are added after the period would otherwise expire under FRCP 6(a). FRCP 6(d).

C. General Requirements

1. *Pretrial conferences, generally*

    a. *Purposes of a pretrial conference.* FRCP 16 provides an important mechanism for carrying out one of the basic policies of the [Federal Rules of Civil Procedure]—the determination of disputes on their merits rather than on the basis of procedural niceties or tactical advantage. FPP § 1522. In any action, the court may order the attorneys and any unrepresented parties to appear for one or more pretrial conferences for such purposes as: (1) expediting disposition of the action; (2) establishing early and continuing control so that the case will not be protracted because of lack of management; (3) discouraging wasteful pretrial activities; (4) improving the quality of the trial through more thorough preparation; and (5) facilitating settlement. FRCP 16(a).

    b. *When appropriate.* FRCP 16 specifically provides that the court "may order the attorneys and any unrepresented parties to appear for one or more pretrial conferences." This language makes it clear that the utilization of the pretrial conference procedure lies within the discretion of the district court both as a matter of general policy and in terms of whether and when the rule should be invoked in a particular case. FPP § 1523; Mizwicki v. Helwig, 196 F.3d 828 (7th Cir. 1999). There is no requirement that any pretrial conferences be held or not held in certain types of actions. FPP § 1523.

    c. *Attendance at a pretrial conference.* A represented party must authorize at least one of its attorneys to make stipulations and admissions about all matters that can reasonably be anticipated for discussion at a pretrial conference. If appropriate, the court may require that a party or its representative be present or reasonably available by other means to consider possible settlement. FRCP 16(c)(1).

    d. *Matters for consideration at a pretrial conference.* At any pretrial conference, the court may consider and take appropriate action on the following matters: (A) formulating and simplifying the issues, and eliminating frivolous claims or defenses; (B) amending the pleadings if necessary or desirable; (C) obtaining admissions and stipulations about facts and documents to avoid unnecessary proof, and ruling in advance on the admissibility of evidence; (D) avoiding unnecessary proof and cumulative evidence, and limiting the use of testimony under FRE 702; (E) determining the appropriateness and timing of summary adjudication under FRCP 56; (F) controlling and scheduling discovery, including orders affecting disclosures and discovery under FRCP 26 and FRCP 29 through FRCP 37; (G) identifying witnesses and documents, scheduling the filing and exchange of any pretrial briefs, and setting dates for further conferences and for trial; (H) referring matters to a magistrate judge or a master; (I) settling the case and using special procedures to assist in resolving the dispute when authorized by statute or local rule; (J) determining the form and content of the pretrial order; (K) disposing of pending motions; (L) adopting special procedures for managing potentially difficult or protracted actions that may involve complex issues, multiple parties, difficult legal questions, or unusual proof problems; (M) ordering a separate trial under FRCP 42(b) of a claim, counterclaim, crossclaim, third-party claim, or particular issue; (N) ordering the presentation of evidence early in the trial on a manageable issue that might, on the evidence, be the basis for a judgment as a matter of law under FRCP 50(a) or a judgment on partial findings under FRCP 52(c); (O) establishing a reasonable limit on the time allowed to present evidence; and (P) facilitating in other ways the just, speedy, and inexpensive disposition of the action. FRCP 16(c)(2). For a preliminary pretrial checklist, refer to GOLDLTGFMS § 34:3.

e. *Pretrial orders.* After any conference under FRCP 16, the court should issue an order reciting the action taken. This order controls the course of the action unless the court modifies it. FRCP 16(d).

f. *Sanctions.* On motion or on its own, the court may issue any just orders, including those authorized by FRCP 37(b)(2)(A)(ii) through FRCP 37(b)(2)(A)(vii), if a party or its attorney: (A) fails to appear at a scheduling or other pretrial conference; (B) is substantially unprepared to participate—or does not participate in good faith—in the conference; or (C) fails to obey a scheduling or other pretrial order. FRCP 16(f)(1).

    i. *Imposing fees and costs.* Instead of or in addition to any other sanction, the court must order the party, its attorney, or both to pay the reasonable expenses—including attorney's fees—incurred because of any noncompliance with FRCP 16, unless the noncompliance was substantially justified or other circumstances make an award of expenses unjust. FRCP 16(f)(2).

2. *Scheduling conference.* A scheduling conference may be requested by the judge or by the parties, but it is not mandatory. FPP § 1522.1.

    a. *DISTRICT OF MAINE: Management track procedures.* Each case shall be assigned to a track by the clerk based on the initial pleading. The court may on its own initiative, or upon good cause shown by a party, change the track assignment of any case. ME R USDCT Rule 16.1(c). Each civil case shall be assigned to one of the following tracks: (1) Administrative; (2) Standard; (3) Complex; (4) Prisoner Civil Rights; (5) Individuals With Disabilities Education Act; [or] (6) Employee Retirement Income Security Act. ME R USDCT Rule 16.1(a). For the definitions of the tracks, refer to ME R USDCT Rule 16.1(b).

       i. *Standard track.* The case management of all cases on the standard track shall be governed by the scheduling order. ME R USDCT Rule 16.3(b)(1).

- *Telephone conference.* When a scheduling conference is requested, it may be conducted by telephone at the discretion of the judicial officer. In those instances, the clerk will inform the lawyers or unrepresented parties of the date and time of the conference. It shall be the responsibility of the party who requested the conference to initiate the telephone conference call to chambers. ME R USDCT Rule 16.3(b)(2).

- *Counsel discussion before the conference.* Prior to the requested scheduling conference, the lawyers must confer and discuss the following topics: voluntary exchange of information and discovery; a discovery plan; the various alternative dispute resolution options; consenting to trial before the magistrate judge; the legal issues in the case; a plan for raising and disposing of serious and legitimate dispositive motions; settlement; and stipulations. ME R USDCT Rule 16.3(b)(3).

- *Agenda for the conference.* The agenda for the scheduling conference shall include the following topics: narrowing the case to its essential issues; sequencing and limiting discovery and motion practice; settlement; ADR options; and consent to trial before the magistrate judge. ME R USDCT Rule 16.3(b)(5).

- *Matters considered at the conference.* During the conference the judicial officer shall explore the advisability and utility of ADR, ascertaining actual discovery needs and costs and imposing discovery limits and deadlines. ME R USDCT Rule 16.3(b)(6).

       ii. *Complex track.* Promptly after the pleadings are complete an initial scheduling conference will be held before a judicial officer. ME R USDCT Rule 16.3(c)(1). Unless the parties otherwise agree, the settlement conference in a nonjury case will be conducted by a judicial officer other than the one who will preside at trial. ME R USDCT Rule 16.3(c)(7).

- *Telephone conference.* If the conference is to be conducted by telephone, the clerk will inform the lawyers or unrepresented parties of the time and date of the conference and it shall be the responsibility of the plaintiff to initiate the telephone conference call to chambers. ME R USDCT Rule 16.3(c)(1).

- *Counsel discussion before the conference.* Prior to the conference the lawyers must meet face-to-face unless they are more than 30 miles apart and in that event by telephone and discuss the following issues: voluntary exchange of information and discovery; a discovery plan; the various kinds of alternative dispute resolution; consenting to trial by the magistrate judge; the legal issues in the case; a plan for raising and disposing of serious and legitimate dispositive motions; settlement; and stipulations. ME R USDCT Rule 16.3(c)(2).

- *Agenda for the conference.* The agenda for the initial conference shall include the following topics: narrowing the case to its essential issues; sequencing and limiting discovery and motion practice; a trial date; all legal issues; settlement; ADR options; consenting to trial before the magistrate judge; and the date of the next conference. ME R USDCT Rule 16.3(c)(4).

- *Matters considered at the conference.* During the conference the judicial officer shall explore the advisability and utility of ADR, ascertaining the actual discovery needs and costs and imposing discovery limits and deadlines. ME R USDCT Rule 16.3(c)(5). During the initial conference the judicial officer will ordinarily schedule further settlement discussions as part of the next conference and will determine whether clients or client representatives should be required to attend the next conference. The attendance of the clients (in person or by being available by telephone) will usually be required. ME R USDCT Rule 16.3(c)(6).

- *Additional conferences.* Additional case management and settlement conferences will be scheduled at the discretion of the judicial officer. The judicial officer will regularly hold case management conferences (either in person or by telephone) in those cases in which there is substantial discovery. At each such conference, the lawyers shall be prepared to discuss in a detailed manner the settlement status of the case, ongoing and projected litigation costs, ADR options, and avoidance of unnecessary motion practice. ME R USDCT Rule 16.3(c)(8).

iii. For the management track procedures of the remaining tracks, refer to ME R USDCT Rule 16.3.

b. *Scheduling order.* Except in categories of actions exempted by local rule, the district judge—or a magistrate judge when authorized by local rule—must issue a scheduling order: (A) after receiving the parties' report under FRCP 26(f); or (B) after consulting with the parties' attorneys and any unrepresented parties at a scheduling conference. FRCP 16(b)(1).

i. *DISTRICT OF MAINE: Applicable cases.* A proposed scheduling order shall issue in all cases except Social Security disability cases, habeas corpus petitions, bankruptcy appeals, and any other case or category of cases as a judicial officer may order. ME R USDCT Rule 16.2(a).

ii. *Required contents of the order.* The scheduling order must limit the time to join other parties, amend the pleadings, complete discovery, and file motions. FRCP 16(b)(3)(A).

- *DISTRICT OF MAINE: Track designation.* The proposed scheduling order shall identify the case management track to which the case is assigned. ME R USDCT Rule 16.2(b).

- *DISTRICT OF MAINE: Additional contents for administrative track cases.* The proposed scheduling order in administrative track cases shall establish the deadline (1) to join other parties and to amend the pleadings; and (2) to file motions. The order shall also direct the parties to exchange written settlement papers by dates certain and it shall identify the month in which the case shall be ready for trial. ME R USDCT Rule 16.2(c)(1).

- *DISTRICT OF MAINE: Additional contents for standard track cases.* The proposed scheduling order in standard track cases shall establish the deadline (1) for initial disclosures pursuant to FRCP 26(a)(1); (2) to join other parties and to amend the pleadings; (3) to file motions; (4) to disclose experts and complete discovery; and (5) to complete other pretrial preparation. The order shall also direct the parties to exchange written settlement papers by dates certain and it shall identify the month in which the case shall be ready for trial. ME R USDCT Rule 16.2(c)(2).

- *DISTRICT OF MAINE: Additional contents for prisoner civil rights track cases.* The proposed scheduling order in prisoner civil rights track cases shall establish the deadline (1) to join other parties and to amend the pleadings; (2) to file motions; (3) to complete discovery; and (4) to complete other pretrial preparation. This order shall also direct the parties to exchange written settlement papers by dates certain and it shall identify the month in which the case shall be ready for trial. ME R USDCT Rule 16.2(c)(3).

- *DISTRICT OF MAINE: Additional contents for ERISA track cases.* The proposed scheduling order in ERISA track cases shall establish the deadline (1) for establishing the administrative record; (2) for filing motions to modify the administrative record and/or for discovery; (3) for amendment of the pleadings and joinder of parties; and (4) for filing motions for judgment on the record for judicial review. ME R USDCT Rule 16.2(c)(4).

iii. *Permitted contents of the order.* The scheduling order may: (i) modify the timing of disclosures under FRCP 26(a) and FRCP 26(e)(1); (ii) modify the extent of discovery; (iii) provide for disclosure, discovery, or preservation of electronically stored information; (iv) include any agreements the parties reach for asserting claims of privilege or of protection as trial-preparation material after information is produced, including agreements reached under FRE 502; (v) direct that before moving for an order relating to discovery, the movant must request a conference with the court; (vi) set dates for pretrial conferences and for trial; and (vii) include other appropriate matters. FRCP 16(b)(3)(B).

c. *Time to issue.* The judge must issue the scheduling order as soon as practicable, but unless the judge finds good cause for delay, the judge must issue it within the earlier of ninety (90) days after any defendant has been served with the complaint or sixty (60) days after any defendant has appeared. FRCP 16(b)(2).

    i. *DISTRICT OF MAINE.* The proposed scheduling order in administrative, standard track, prisoner civil rights track, and ERISA cases shall issue immediately upon the appearance of defendant(s) but in no event more than ninety (90) days after defendant has been served with the complaint or sixty (60) days after any defendant has appeared unless the judge finds good cause for delay. The scheduling order in complex cases shall issue after an initial conference with counsel at which discovery, motion practice, ADR and other matters will be discussed. The scheduling order in IDEA track cases shall issue after an initial conference with counsel at which the administrative record, additional evidence, if any, motion practice, and other matters will be discussed. ME R USDCT Rule 16.2(d).

d. *DISTRICT OF MAINE: Objections to proposed scheduling order.* Unless a party files an objection to the proposed scheduling order within twenty-one (21) days of its filing, fourteen (14) days in ERISA track cases, the proposed order shall thereupon become the Scheduling Order of the court as required by FRCP 16(b). A party wishing to alter any deadline or any discovery limitation of a scheduling order must file a detailed explanation of the reasons for each requested alteration with the objection or request a scheduling conference with a judicial officer, or both. A conference, if deemed necessary by the court, will be scheduled promptly. ME R USDCT Rule 16.2(e).

e. *Modifying a schedule.* A schedule may be modified only for good cause and with the judge's consent. FRCP 16(b)(4).

3. *Final pretrial conference.* The court may hold a final pretrial conference to formulate a trial plan, including a plan to facilitate the admission of evidence. FRCP 16(e).

a. *DISTRICT OF MAINE: Preparation for the conference*

    i. *Filing of pretrial memorandum.* Not later than five (5) business days prior to the final pretrial conference, each party shall file with the court and serve on every other party a pretrial memorandum, which normally need not exceed five (5) pages in length, containing the following information: (1) a brief factual statement of the party's claim or defense, as the case may be, including an itemized statement of any damages claimed; (2) a brief statement of the party's contentions with respect to any controverted points of law, including evidentiary questions, together with supporting authority; (3) proposed stipulations concerning matters which are not in substantial dispute and to facts and documents which will avoid unnecessary proof; (4) the names and addresses of all witnesses the party intends to call at trial, other than those to be used for impeachment and rebuttal, but in the absence of stipulation, the disclosure of a witness shall not constitute a representation that the witness will be produced or called at trial; (5) any proposed use of case-specific juror questionnaires and (6) a list of the documents and things the party intends to offer as exhibits at trial. ME R USDCT Rule 16.4(b).

    ii. *Discussion of items in pretrial memorandum.* Each party shall be prepared at the pretrial conference to discuss the issues set forth in ME R USDCT Rule 16.4(b)(1) through ME R USDCT Rule 16.4(b)(5), to exchange or to agree to exchange medical reports, hospital records, and other documents, to make a representation concerning settlement as set forth in ME R USDCT Rule 16.4 and to discuss fully all aspects of the case. ME R USDCT Rule 16.4(b).

    iii. *Settlement discussions.* The parties, through their lawyers, shall be prepared to fully engage in meaningful settlement discussions at the conference. If the case will be tried by the judge without a jury, a different judicial officer will conduct the settlement discussions. ME R USDCT Rule 16.4(g). A judicial officer may direct that a separate settlement conference be held with party representatives present in person. ME R USDCT Rule 16.4(g).

b. *Timing and attendance.* The conference must be held as close to the start of trial as is reasonable, and must be attended by at least one attorney who will conduct the trial for each party and by any unrepresented party. FRCP 16(e).

    i. *DISTRICT OF MAINE.* A final pretrial conference shall be held as close to the time of trial as reasonable under the circumstances. The clerk shall notify counsel of the time and place by mailing to them a written notice. ME R USDCT Rule 16.4(a). Unless excused for good cause, each party shall be represented at the final pretrial conference by counsel who is to conduct the trial on behalf of such party, who shall be thoroughly familiar with ME R USDCT Rule 16.4 and with the case. ME R USDCT Rule 16.4(c).

c. *DISTRICT OF MAINE: Conduct of conference.* A final pretrial conference may be conducted by the trial judge or any other judicial officer. ME R USDCT Rule 16.4(a). The court will consider at the final pretrial conference the pleadings and papers then on file; all motions and other proceedings then pending; and any other matters referred to in ME R USDCT Rule 16.4 or in FRCP 16 which may be applicable. ME R USDCT Rule 16.4(c).

    i.   Counsel shall be required to make a representation to the court at the final pretrial conference that counsel has made a recommendation to the client in respect to settlement and that the client has acted on such recommendation. Counsel's inability to make such representations shall be grounds for imposition of sanctions. ME R USDCT Rule 16.4(c).

d.   *DISTRICT OF MAINE: Final pretrial order.* Either at or following the final pretrial conference, the court shall make a final pretrial order, which shall recite the action taken at the conference, and such order shall control the subsequent course of the action, unless modified by the court to prevent manifest injustice. Unless otherwise ordered, any objections to the final pretrial order must be made within fourteen (14) days after receipt by counsel of a copy thereof. Any discussion at the conference relating to settlement shall not be a part of the final pretrial order. The final pretrial order deadlines shall be such that they do not come into play until after the last settlement conference has been held and it appears that trial is unavoidable. In any case where there is a pending dispositive motion, one item on the final pretrial conference agenda shall be whether the provisions and deadlines of the final pretrial order should be stayed until the motion is resolved. The judicial officer presiding at the final pretrial conference shall tailor the order to the individual case and consider whether certain provisions of the final pretrial order should be waived. (For example, in a simple automobile negligence personal injury case it may not be necessary to list exhibits or summaries of witness testimony. In such cases trial briefs and draft jury instructions may also be unnecessary.) The number of copies of documents to be filed shall be limited. In a jury case, the original set of exhibits is ordinarily sufficient and should not be filed with the clerk before trial. In a nonjury case, one extra set of exhibits for the judge to review in advance of the trial shall be filed as set forth in the final pretrial order. ME R USDCT Rule 16.4(d).

e.   *Modification of final pretrial order.* The court may modify the order issued after a final pretrial conference only to prevent manifest injustice. FRCP 16(e).

f.   *DISTRICT OF MAINE: Sanctions.* If a party fails to comply with the requirements of FRCP 16 or ME R USDCT Rule 16.4, the court may impose such penalties and sanctions as are just, including those set forth in FRCP 16(f). ME R USDCT Rule 16.4(e).

g.   *DISTRICT OF MAINE: Special circumstances.* The court may provide for a special pretrial procedure in any case when special circumstances warrant. ME R USDCT Rule 16.4(f).

4.   *Discovery planning conference*

a.   *Conference content.* In conferring, the parties must consider the nature and basis of their claims and defenses and the possibilities for promptly settling or resolving the case; make or arrange for the disclosures required by FRCP 26(a)(1); discuss any issues about preserving discoverable information; and develop a proposed discovery plan. FRCP 26(f)(2).

b.   *Parties' responsibilities.* The attorneys of record and all unrepresented parties that have appeared in the case are jointly responsible for arranging the conference, for attempting in good faith to agree on the proposed discovery plan, and for submitting to the court within fourteen (14) days after the conference a written report outlining the plan. The court may order the parties or attorneys to attend the conference in person. FRCP 26(f)(2).

c.   *Discovery plan.* A discovery plan must state the parties' views and proposals on: (A) what changes should be made in the timing, form, or requirement for disclosures under FRCP 26(a), including a statement of when initial disclosures were made or will be made; (B) the subjects on which discovery may be needed, when discovery should be completed, and whether discovery should be conducted in phases or be limited to or focused on particular issues; (C) any issues about disclosure, discovery, or preservation of electronically stored information, including the form or forms in which it should be produced; (D) any issues about claims of privilege or of protection as trial-preparation materials, including—if the parties agree on a procedure to assert these claims after production—whether to ask the court to include their agreement in an order under FRE 502; (E) what changes should be made in the limitations on discovery imposed under the Federal Rules of Civil Procedure or by local rule, and what other limitations should be imposed; and (F) any other orders that the court should issue under FRCP 26(c) or under FRCP 16(b) and FRCP 26(c). FRCP 26(f)(3).

d.   *Sanctions.* If a party or its attorney fails to participate in good faith in developing and submitting a proposed discovery plan as required by FRCP 26(f), the court may, after giving an opportunity to be heard, require that party or attorney to pay to any other party the reasonable expenses, including attorney's fees, caused by the failure. FRCP 37(f).

5.   *DISTRICT OF MAINE: Appearances.* An attorney's signature to a pleading shall constitute an appearance for the party

filing the pleading. Otherwise, an attorney who wishes to participate in any manner in any action must file a formal written appearance identifying the party represented. An appearance whether by pleading or formal written appearance shall be signed by an attorney in his/her individual name and shall state his/her office address. ME R USDCT Rule 83.2(a). For more information, refer to ME R USDCT Rule 83.2.

6. *DISTRICT OF MAINE: Alternative dispute resolution (ADR).* Litigants are authorized and encouraged to employ, at their own expense, any available ADR process on which they can agree, including early neutral evaluation, settlement conferences, mediation, non-binding summary jury trial, corporate mini-trial, and arbitration proceedings. ME R USDCT Rule 83.11(a). For more information on ADR, refer to ME R USDCT Rule 83.11.

D. Documents

1. *Pretrial conference*

   a. *Documents to consider*

   i. *Pretrial memorandum or statement.* Even though it is not specifically mentioned in FRCP 16, most courts require the attorney for each side to file a pretrial memorandum or statement prior to the conference, which, if adopted by the court, may be binding at trial. FPP § 1524. The purpose of the memorandum is to reveal the lawyer's theory of the case and the issues counsel believes are in contention in order to aid the court in determining what matters should be considered at the conference itself. FPP § 1524; Manbeck v. Ostrowski, 384 F.2d 970 (D.C. Cir. 1967).

2. *Scheduling conference*

   a. *Documents to consider*

   i. *Request for scheduling conference.* A scheduling conference may be requested by the judge or by the parties, but it is not mandatory. FPP § 1522.1.

   ii. *DISTRICT OF MAINE: Additional documents to consider*

   • *Joint proposed discovery and motion plan.* [In standard track cases,] the court may require counsel to file a joint proposed discovery and motion plan prior to the scheduling conference. ME R USDCT Rule 16.3(b)(4). [In complex track cases,] not less than two (2) business days before the conference the lawyers shall file a joint proposed discovery and motion plan and any proposal for ADR. ME R USDCT Rule 16.3(c)(3).

3. *Final pretrial conference*

   a. *Required documents*

   i. *DISTRICT OF MAINE: Additional required documents*

   • *Pretrial memorandum.* Not later than five (5) business days prior to the final pretrial conference, each party shall file with the court and serve on every other party a pretrial memorandum. ME R USDCT Rule 16.4(b). Refer to the "C. General Requirements" section of this KeyRules document for the contents of the pretrial memorandum.

4. *Discovery planning conference*

   a. *Required documents*

   i. *Written report outlining proposed discovery plan.* Refer to the "C. General Requirements" section of this KeyRules document for information on the parties' responsibilities for submitting a written report outlining the proposed discovery plan.

E. Format

1. *Form of documents.* The rules governing captions and other matters of form in pleadings apply to motions and other papers. FRCP 7(b)(2).

   a. *DISTRICT OF MAINE: Font size, line spacing, and paper size.* All such documents shall be typed in a font of no less than size twelve (12) point, and shall be double-spaced or printed on eight and one-half by eleven (8-1/2 x 11) inch paper. Footnotes shall be in a font of no less than size ten (10) point, and may be single spaced. ME R USDCT Rule 10.

   b. *Caption.* Every pleading must have a caption with the court's name, a title, a file number, and an FRCP 7(a) designation. FRCP 10(a).

   i. *Names of parties.* The title of the complaint must name all the parties; the title of other pleadings, after naming the first party on each side, may refer generally to other parties. FRCP 10(a).

    ii.   *DISTRICT OF MAINE: Additional caption requirements.* All pleadings, motions and other papers filed with the clerk or otherwise submitted to the court, except exhibits, shall bear the proper case number and shall contain on the first page a caption as described by FRCP 10(a) and immediately thereunder a designation of what the document is and the name of the party in whose behalf it is submitted. ME R USDCT Rule 10.

  c. *Claims or defenses*

    i.   *Numbered paragraphs.* A party must state its claims or defenses in numbered paragraphs, each limited as far as practicable to a single set of circumstances. A later pleading may refer by number to a paragraph in an earlier pleading. FRCP 10(b).

    ii.   *Separate statements.* If doing so would promote clarity, each claim founded on a separate transaction or occurrence—and each defense other than a denial—must be stated in a separate count or defense. FRCP 10(b).

  d. *Adoption by reference.* A statement in a pleading may be adopted by reference elsewhere in the same pleading or in any other pleading or motion. FRCP 10(c).

    i.   *Exhibits.* A copy of a written instrument that is an exhibit to a pleading is a part of the pleading for all purposes. FRCP 10(c).

  e. *DISTRICT OF MAINE: Page numbering.* All pages shall be numbered at the bottom. ME R USDCT Rule 10.

  f. *DISTRICT OF MAINE: Attachment of ancillary papers.* Ancillary papers shall be attached at the end of the document to which they relate. ME R USDCT Rule 10.

  g. *Acceptance by the clerk.* The clerk must not refuse to file a paper solely because it is not in the form prescribed by the Federal Rules of Civil Procedure or by a local rule or practice. FRCP 5(d)(4).

2. *Form of electronic documents.* A paper filed electronically is a written paper for purposes of the Federal Rules of Civil Procedure. FRCP 5(d)(3)(D).

  a. *DISTRICT OF MAINE: Document format.* The ECF system only accepts documents in a portable document format (PDF). Although there are two types of PDF documents—electronically converted PDF's and scanned PDF's—only electronically converted PDF's may be filed with the court using the ECF system, unless otherwise authorized by local rule or order. ME R USDCT App. 4. Any document or exhibit to be filed or submitted to the court shall not be password-protected or encrypted. ME R USDCT App. 4(g)(12).

    i.   *Electronically converted PDFs.* Electronically converted PDF's are created from word processing documents (MS Word, WordPerfect, etc.) using Adobe Acrobat or similar software. They are text searchable and their file size is small. ME R USDCT App. 4. Software used to electronically convert documents to PDF which includes proprietary or advertisement information within the PDF document is prohibited. ME R USDCT App. 4.

    ii.   *Scanned PDFs.* Scanned PDF's are created from paper documents run through an optical scanner. Scanned PDF's are not searchable and have a large file size. ME R USDCT App. 4.

  b. *DISTRICT OF MAINE: Title.* All pleadings filed electronically shall be titled in accordance with the approved dictionary of civil or criminal events of the ECF system of the United States District Court for the District of Maine. ME R USDCT App. 4(d)(3).

  c. *DISTRICT OF MAINE: Attachments.* Attachments to filings and exhibits must be filed in accordance with the court's ECF User Manual, unless otherwise ordered by the court. ME R USDCT App. 4(j). When there are fifty (50) or fewer attachments to a pleading, the attachments must be filed by counsel electronically using ECF. When there are more than fifty (50) attachments, the attachments must be filed in one of the following ways: (A) using ECF, simply attach them to the pleading being filed; (B) using ECF, use the "Additional Attachments" menu item; (C) on paper; or (D) on a properly labeled three and one-half (3-1/2) inch floppy disk, CD or DVD. ME R USDCT App. 4(j)(2). Attachments filed on paper or on disk must contain a comprehensive index that clearly describes each document. ME R USDCT App. 4(j)(2).

    i.   A filing user must submit as attachments only those excerpts of the referenced documents that are directly germane to the matter under consideration by the court. Excerpted material must be clearly and prominently identified as such. Users who file excerpts of documents do so without prejudice to their right to timely file additional excerpts or the complete document, as may be allowed by the court. Responding parties may timely file additional excerpts or the complete document that they believe are directly germane. ME R USDCT App. 4(j)(3).

    ii.   Filers shall not attach as an exhibit any pleading or other paper already on file with the court in that case, but shall merely refer to that document. ME R USDCT App. 4(j)(4).

    d.   *DISTRICT OF MAINE: Compliance with technical standards.* All documents filed by electronic means must comply with technical standards, if any, established by the Judicial Conference of the United States or by the United States District Court for the District of Maine. ME R USDCT App. 4(a)(3).

3.   *Signing of pleadings, motions and other papers*

    a.   *Signature.* Every pleading, written motion, and other paper must be signed by at least one attorney of record in the attorney's name—or by a party personally if the party is unrepresented. The paper must state the signer's address, e-mail address, and telephone number. FRCP 11(a).

        i.   *No verification or accompanying affidavit required for pleadings.* Unless a rule or statute specifically states otherwise, a pleading need not be verified or accompanied by an affidavit. FRCP 11(a).

        ii.   *Unsigned papers.* The court must strike an unsigned paper unless the omission is promptly corrected after being called to the attorney's or party's attention. FRCP 11(a).

    b.   *Electronic signing.* A filing made through a person's electronic-filing account and authorized by that person, together with that person's name on a signature block, constitutes the person's signature. FRCP 5(d)(3)(C).

        i.   *DISTRICT OF MAINE: Attorneys.* The user log-in and password together with a user's name on the signature block constitutes the attorney's signature pursuant to the Federal Rules of Civil Procedure and the Local Rules of the United States District Court for the District of Maine. All electronically filed documents must include a signature block and must set forth the attorney's name, address, telephone number and e-mail address. The name of the ECF user under whose log-in and password the document is submitted must be preceded by a "/s/" in the space where the signature would otherwise appear. ME R USDCT App. 4(h)(1).

        ii.   *DISTRICT OF MAINE: Multiple signatures.* The filer of any document requiring more than one signature (e.g., pleadings filed by visiting lawyers, stipulations, joint status reports) must list thereon all the names of other signatories, preceded by a "/s/" in the space where the signatures would otherwise appear. By submitting such a document, the filing attorney certifies that each of the other signatories has expressly agreed to the form and substance of the document and that the filing attorney has their actual authority to submit the document electronically. ME R USDCT App. 4(h)(2). For more information, refer to ME R USDCT App. 4(h)(2).

        iii.   *DISTRICT OF MAINE: Documents signed under oath.* Affidavits, declarations, verified complaints, or any other document signed under oath shall be filed electronically. The electronically filed version shall contain the typed name of the signatory, preceded by a "/s/" in the space where the signature would otherwise appear indicating that the paper document bears an original signature. ME R USDCT Rule 10; ME R USDCT App. 4(h)(3). For more information, refer to ME R USDCT Rule 10.

    c.   *Representations to the court.* By presenting to the court a pleading, written motion, or other paper—whether by signing, filing, submitting, or later advocating it—an attorney or unrepresented party certifies that to the best of the person's knowledge, information, and belief, formed after an inquiry reasonable under the circumstances: (1) it is not being presented for any improper purpose, such as to harass, cause unnecessary delay, or needlessly increase the cost of litigation; (2) the claims, defenses, and other legal contentions are warranted by existing law or by a nonfrivolous argument for extending, modifying, or reversing existing law or for establishing new law; (3) the factual contentions have evidentiary support or, if specifically so identified, will likely have evidentiary support after a reasonable opportunity for further investigation or discovery; and (4) the denials of factual contentions are warranted on the evidence or, if specifically so identified, are reasonably based on belief or a lack of information. FRCP 11(b).

    d.   *Sanctions.* If, after notice and a reasonable opportunity to respond, the court determines that FRCP 11(b) has been violated, the court may impose an appropriate sanction on any attorney, law firm, or party that violated FRCP 11(b) or is responsible for the violation. FRCP 11(c)(1). Refer to the United States District Court for the District of Maine KeyRules Motion for Sanctions document for more information.

4.   *Privacy protection for filings made with the court*

    a.   *Redacted filings.* Unless the court orders otherwise, in an electronic or paper filing with the court that contains an individual's Social Security number, taxpayer-identification number, or birth date, the name of an individual known to be a minor, or a financial-account number, a party or nonparty making the filing may include only: (1) the last four (4) digits of the Social Security number and taxpayer-identification number; (2) the year of the individual's birth; (3) the minor's initials; and (4) the last four (4) digits of the financial-account number. FRCP 5.2(a).

        i.   *DISTRICT OF MAINE.* To address the privacy concerns created by the Internet access to court papers, unless otherwise ordered by the court, counsel shall modify certain personal data identifiers in pleadings and other papers as follows: (1) minors' names: use of the minors' initials only; (2) Social Security numbers: use of the last

four (4) numbers only; (3) dates of birth: use of the year of birth only; [and] (4) financial account numbers: identify the type of account and the financial institution, but use only the last four (4) numbers of the account number. ME R USDCT Redacting Pleadings. Counsel should also use caution when filing papers that contain a person's medical records, employment history; financial information; and any proprietary or trade secret information. ME R USDCT Redacting Pleadings.

b. *Exemptions from the redaction requirement.* The redaction requirement does not apply to the following: (1) a financial-account number that identifies the property allegedly subject to forfeiture in a forfeiture proceeding; (2) the record of an administrative or agency proceeding; (3) the official record of a state-court proceeding; (4) the record of a court or tribunal, if that record was not subject to the redaction requirement when originally filed; (5) a filing covered by FRCP 5.2(c) or FRCP 5.2(d); and (6) a pro se filing in an action brought under 28 U.S.C.A. § 2241, 28 U.S.C.A. § 2254, or 28 U.S.C.A. § 2255. FRCP 5.2(b).

c. *Limitations on remote access to electronic files; Social Security appeals and immigration cases.* Unless the court orders otherwise, in an action for benefits under the Social Security Act, and in an action or proceeding relating to an order of removal, to relief from removal, or to immigration benefits or detention, access to an electronic file is authorized as follows: (1) the parties and their attorneys may have remote electronic access to any part of the case file, including the administrative record; (2) any other person may have electronic access to the full record at the courthouse, but may have remote electronic access only to: (A) the docket maintained by the court; and (B) an opinion, order, judgment, or other disposition of the court, but not any other part of the case file or the administrative record. FRCP 5.2(c).

d. *Filings made under seal.* The court may order that a filing be made under seal without redaction. The court may later unseal the filing or order the person who made the filing to file a redacted version for the public record. FRCP 5.2(d).

    i. *DISTRICT OF MAINE.* For information on filing sealed documents in the District of Maine, refer to ME R USDCT Rule 7A, ME R USDCT App. 4(p)(2), and ME R USDCT Sealed Filings.

e. *Protective orders.* For good cause, the court may by order in a case: (1) require redaction of additional information; or (2) limit or prohibit a nonparty's remote electronic access to a document filed with the court. FRCP 5.2(e).

f. *Option for additional unredacted filing under seal.* A person making a redacted filing may also file an unredacted copy under seal. The court must retain the unredacted copy as part of the record. FRCP 5.2(f).

    i. *DISTRICT OF MAINE.* A party wishing to file a document containing the personal data identifiers specified above may. . .file an unredacted document under seal. This document will be retained by the clerk's office as part of the record. ME R USDCT Redacting Pleadings. The court may, however, still require the party to file a redacted copy for the public file. ME R USDCT Redacting Pleadings.

g. *Option for filing a reference list.* A filing that contains redacted information may be filed together with a reference list that identifies each item of redacted information and specifies an appropriate identifier that uniquely corresponds to each item listed. The list must be filed under seal and may be amended as of right. Any reference in the case to a listed identifier will be construed to refer to the corresponding item of information. FRCP 5.2(g).

    i. *DISTRICT OF MAINE.* A party wishing to file a document containing the personal data identifiers specified above may. . .file a reference list under seal. The reference list shall contain the complete personal data identifier(s) and the redacted identifier(s) used in its (their) place in the filing. All references in the case to the redacted identifiers included in the reference list will be construed to refer to the corresponding complete identifier. The reference list must be filed under seal, and may be amended as of right. It shall be retained by the clerk's office as part of the record. ME R USDCT Redacting Pleadings. The court may, however, still require the party to file a redacted copy for the public file. ME R USDCT Redacting Pleadings.

h. *DISTRICT OF MAINE: Responsibility for redaction.* The clerk is not required to review documents filed with the court for compliance with FRCP 5.2. The responsibility to redact filings rests with counsel and the party or nonparty making the filing. ME R USDCT App. 4(i); ME R USDCT Redacting Pleadings. For guidelines for filing confidential information in civil cases in the District of Maine, refer to ME R USDCT Confidentiality.

i. *Waiver of protection of identifiers.* A person waives the protection of FRCP 5.2(a) as to the person's own information by filing it without redaction and not under seal. FRCP 5.2(h).

F. Filing and Service Requirements

1. *Filing requirements*

a. *Required filings.* Any paper after the complaint that is required to be served must be filed no later than a reasonable time after service. FRCP 5(d)(1).

b. *DISTRICT OF MAINE: Place of filing.* Unless otherwise ordered by the court, papers shall be filed with the court at Bangor in cases filed and pending at Bangor, and at Portland in cases filed and pending at Portland. ME R USDCT Rule 5(a).

c. *Nonelectronic filing.* A paper not filed electronically is filed by delivering it: (A) to the clerk; or (B) to a judge who agrees to accept it for filing, and who must then note the filing date on the paper and promptly send it to the clerk. FRCP 5(d)(2).

   i. *DISTRICT OF MAINE: Documents to be filed in paper.* The following documents shall be filed in paper, which may also be scanned into ECF by the clerk's office: (A) all handwritten pleadings; and (B) all pleadings and documents filed by pro se litigants who are incarcerated or who are not registered filing users in ECF. ME R USDCT App. 4(g)(8). Non-prisoner pro se litigants in civil actions may register with ECF or may file (and serve) all pleadings and other documents in paper. The clerk's office will scan into ECF any pleadings and documents filed on paper in accordance with ME R USDCT App. 4(g). ME R USDCT App. 4(o). For more information, refer to ME R USDCT App. 4(g).

d. *Electronic filing*

   i. *DISTRICT OF MAINE: Authorization.* Unless exempt or otherwise ordered by the court, papers shall be filed and served electronically as required by the court's Administrative Procedures Governing the Filing and Service by Electronic Means, which is set forth in ME R USDCT App. 4. The provisions of the court's Administrative Procedures Governing the Filing and Service by Electronic Means (ME R USDCT App. 4) shall be applied and enforced as part of the Local Rules of the United States District Court for the District of Maine. ME R USDCT Rule 5(c).

   ii. *Filing by represented persons.* A person represented by an attorney must file electronically, unless nonelectronic filing is allowed by the court for good cause or is allowed or required by local rule. FRCP 5(d)(3)(A).

   - *DISTRICT OF MAINE.* An attorney may apply to the court for permission to file paper documents. ME R USDCT App. 4(a)(5).

   iii. *Filing by unrepresented persons.* A person not represented by an attorney: (i) may file electronically only if allowed by court order or by local rule; and (ii) may be required to file electronically only by court order, or by a local rule that includes reasonable exceptions. FRCP 5(d)(3)(B).

   - *DISTRICT OF MAINE.* Non-prisoner pro se litigants in civil actions may register with ECF or may file (and serve) all pleadings and other documents in paper. ME R USDCT App. 4(o). A non-prisoner who is a party to a civil action and who is not represented by an attorney may register to receive service electronically and to electronically transmit their documents to the court for filing in the ECF system. If during the course of the action the person retains an attorney who appears on the person's behalf, the clerk shall terminate the person's registration upon the attorney's appearance. ME R USDCT App. 4(b)(2).

   iv. *DISTRICT OF MAINE: Scope of electronic filing.* All documents submitted for filing in civil and criminal cases, regardless of case commencement date, except those documents specifically exempted in ME R USDCT App. 4(g), shall be filed electronically using the electronic case filing system (ECF). ME R USDCT App. 4(a)(1). For special filing requirements and exceptions, refer to ME R USDCT App. 4(g).

   v. *DISTRICT OF MAINE: Consequences of electronic filing.* Electronic transmission of a document to the ECF system, together with the transmission of a Notice of Electronic Filing (NEF) from the court, constitutes filing of the document for all purposes of the Federal Rules of Civil Procedure. ME R USDCT App. 4(d)(1).

   vi. *DISTRICT OF MAINE: Review of documents.* Documents filed with the clerk's office will normally be reviewed no later than the close of the next business day. It is the responsibility of the filing party to promptly notify the clerk's office via telephone of a matter that requires the immediate attention of a judicial officer. ME R USDCT App. 4(a)(4).

e. *DISTRICT OF MAINE: Facsimile filing.* No papers shall be submitted to the court by means of a facsimile machine without prior leave of the court. ME R USDCT Rule 5(c); ME R USDCT App. 4(m).

2. *Service requirements*

   a. *Service; When required.* Unless the Federal Rules of Civil Procedure provide otherwise, each of the following papers must be served on every party: (A) an order stating that service is required; (B) a pleading filed after the original complaint, unless the court orders otherwise under FRCP 5(c) because there are numerous defendants; (C) a discovery paper required to be served on a party, unless the court orders otherwise; (D) a written motion, except one

that may be heard ex parte; and (E) a written notice, appearance, demand, or offer of judgment, or any similar paper. FRCP 5(a)(1).

    i. *If a party fails to appear.* No service is required on a party who is in default for failing to appear. But a pleading that asserts a new claim for relief against such a party must be served on that party under FRCP 4. FRCP 5(a)(2).

    ii. *Seizing property.* If an action is begun by seizing property and no person is or need be named as a defendant, any service required before the filing of an appearance, answer, or claim must be made on the person who had custody or possession of the property when it was seized. FRCP 5(a)(3).

  b. *Service; How made.* A paper is served under FRCP 5 by: (A) handing it to the person; (B) leaving it: (i) at the person's office with a clerk or other person in charge or, if no one is in charge, in a conspicuous place in the office; or (ii) if the person has no office or the office is closed, at the person's dwelling or usual place of abode with someone of suitable age and discretion who resides there; (C) mailing it to the person's last known address—in which event service is complete upon mailing; (D) leaving it with the court clerk if the person has no known address; (E) sending it to a registered user by filing it with the court's electronic-filing system or sending it by other electronic means that the person consented to in writing—in either of which events service is complete upon filing or sending, but is not effective if the filer or sender learns that it did not reach the person to be served; or (F) delivering it by any other means that the person consented to in writing—in which event service is complete when the person making service delivers it to the agency designated to make delivery. FRCP 5(b)(2).

    i. *Serving an attorney.* If a party is represented by an attorney, service under FRCP 5 must be made on the attorney unless the court orders service on the party. FRCP 5(b)(1).

  c. *DISTRICT OF MAINE: Service of electronically filed documents*

    i. *Registered users.* Registration [as a filing user of the court's ECF system] constitutes consent to service of all documents by electronic means as provided in ME R USDCT App. 4. ME R USDCT App. 4(b)(4). Whenever a non-sealed pleading is filed electronically, the ECF system will automatically generate and send a Notice of Electronic Filing (NEF) to the filing user and registered users of record. The user filing the document should retain a paper or digital copy of the NEF, which shall serve as the court's date-stamp and proof of filing. ME R USDCT App. 4(e)(1).

      • *Sealed documents.* Although the filing of sealed documents in civil cases produces an NEF, the document itself cannot be accessed and counsel shall be responsible for making service of the sealed documents. ME R USDCT App. 4(e)(2).

    ii. *Non-registered users and pro se litigants.* Attorneys who have not yet registered as users with ECF and pro se litigants who have not registered with ECF shall be served a paper copy of any electronically filed pleading or other document in accordance with the provisions of FRCP 5. ME R USDCT App. 4(e)(3).

      • *Registration of pro se litigants.* A non-prisoner who is a party to a civil action and who is not represented by an attorney may register to receive service electronically and to electronically transmit their documents to the court for filing in the ECF system. If during the course of the action the person retains an attorney who appears on the person's behalf, the clerk shall terminate the person's registration upon the attorney's appearance. ME R USDCT App. 4(b)(2).

  d. *Serving numerous defendants.* If an action involves an unusually large number of defendants, the court may, on motion or on its own, order that: (A) defendants' pleadings and replies to them need not be served on other defendants; (B) any crossclaim, counterclaim, avoidance, or affirmative defense in those pleadings and replies to them will be treated as denied or avoided by all other parties; and (C) filing any such pleading and serving it on the plaintiff constitutes notice of the pleading to all parties. FRCP 5(c)(1).

    i. *Notifying parties.* A copy of every such order must be served on the parties as the court directs. FRCP 5(c)(2).

3. *DISTRICT OF MAINE: Filing and service of highly sensitive documents (HSDs).* For information on filing and serving highly sensitive documents (HSDs) in the District of Maine, refer to ME R USDCT General Order 21-5.

G. Hearings

1. Refer to the "C. General Requirements" section of this KeyRules document for information on pretrial conferences, scheduling conferences, and discovery planning conferences.

H. Forms

1. Federal Pretrial Conferences, Scheduling, Management Forms

  a. Plaintiff's informal summary of status of case to court before pretrial conference in complex case. 2C FEDFORMS § 15:31.

b.   Joint pretrial report. 2C FEDFORMS § 15:32.

c.   Joint statement of undisputed facts. 2C FEDFORMS § 15:33.

d.   Joint statement of disputed facts. 2C FEDFORMS § 15:34.

e.   Joint report of counsel prior to pretrial conference. 2C FEDFORMS § 15:35.

f.   Plaintiff's list of exhibits to be offered at trial. 2C FEDFORMS § 15:38.

g.   Defendant's list of prospective witnesses. 2C FEDFORMS § 15:39.

h.   Designation of witnesses whom plaintiff intends to call at trial pursuant to pretrial conference oral stipulation. 2C FEDFORMS § 15:40.

i.   Defendant's list of prospective exhibits. 2C FEDFORMS § 15:42.

j.   Report of parties' planning meeting. 3A FEDFORMS § 21:93.

k.   Report of parties' discovery conference. 3A FEDFORMS § 21:94.

l.   Report of parties' discovery conference; Outline structure. 3A FEDFORMS § 21:95.

m.   Joint scheduling report. 3A FEDFORMS § 21:96.

n.   Stipulation and order regarding discovery conference discussions. 3A FEDFORMS § 21:97.

o.   Pretrial statement; By plaintiff; Automobile collision involving corporate defendant. FEDPROF § 1C:295.

p.   Pretrial statement; By defendant; Automobile collision. FEDPROF § 1C:296.

q.   Pretrial statement; By parties jointly; Automobile collision. FEDPROF § 1C:297.

r.   Pretrial statement; Provision; Waiver of abandoned claims or defenses. FEDPROF § 1C:298.

s.   Status report. GOLDLTGFMS § 34:2.

t.   Pretrial memorandum. GOLDLTGFMS § 34:4.

u.   Pretrial memorandum; Plaintiff. GOLDLTGFMS § 34:5.

v.   Pretrial memorandum; Defendant. GOLDLTGFMS § 34:6.

w.   Pretrial memorandum; Short form. GOLDLTGFMS § 34:7.

x.   Pretrial memorandum; Civil action. GOLDLTGFMS § 34:8.

y.   Pretrial memorandum; Worker's compensation case. GOLDLTGFMS § 34:9.

I. Applicable Rules

1. *Federal rules*

   a.   Serving and filing pleadings and other papers. FRCP 5.

   b.   Privacy protection for filings made with the court. FRCP 5.2.

   c.   Computing and extending time; Time for motion papers. FRCP 6.

   d.   Pleadings allowed; Form of motions and other papers. FRCP 7.

   e.   Form of pleadings. FRCP 10.

   f.   Signing pleadings, motions, and other papers; Representations to the court; Sanctions. FRCP 11.

   g.   Pretrial conferences; Scheduling; Management. FRCP 16.

   h.   Duty to disclose; General provisions governing discovery. FRCP 26.

   i.   Failure to make disclosures or to cooperate in discovery; Sanctions. FRCP 37.

2. *Local rules*

   a.   *DISTRICT OF MAINE*

      i.   Service and filing of pleadings and other papers. ME R USDCT Rule 5.

      ii.   Time. ME R USDCT Rule 6.

      iii.   Form of pleadings, motions and other papers. ME R USDCT Rule 10.

      iv.   Case management tracks. ME R USDCT Rule 16.1.

v.   Scheduling order. ME R USDCT Rule 16.2.

vi.   Management track procedures. ME R USDCT Rule 16.3.

vii. Final pretrial conference and order. ME R USDCT Rule 16.4.

viii. Attorneys; Appearances and withdrawals. ME R USDCT Rule 83.2.

ix.   Alternative dispute resolution (ADR). ME R USDCT Rule 83.11.

x.   Administrative procedures governing the filing and service by electronic means. ME R USDCT App. 4.

xi.   Redacting pleadings. ME R USDCT Redacting Pleadings.

Appendix - Related Court Documents

Complaint

2020 WL 6260626 (D.Me.)

<table>
<tr><td>

Westlaw Query>>

To find more Complaint filings on Westlaw: access Maine Trial Court Documents (from the Home page, click Trial Court Documents, then Maine), click the Advanced Search link, select Complaint, and click Search. Use the Jurisdiction filter on the left to narrow results to Federal.

</td></tr>
</table>

United States District Court, D. Maine.

Max LINN, Plaintiff,

v.

BLUEWATER MEDIA, LLC and Andrew Latimer, Defendants.

No. 1:20-cv-00391-DBH.

October 23, 2020.

Complaint and Demand for Jury Trial

George J. Marcus, Esq., John H. Doyle, Esq., Marcus | Clegg, 16 Middle Street, Unit 501, Portland, ME 04101, (207) 828-8000, for plaintiff Max Linn.

PARTIES

1. Plaintiff Max Linn ("*Linn*" or "*Plaintiff*") is an individual residing in Bar Harbor, Maine.

2. Defendant Bluewater Media, LLC ("*Bluewater*") is a Florida limited liability company, whose principal office is located in Clearwater, Florida.

3. Defendant Andrew Latimer ("*Latimer*", and together with Bluewater, the "*Defendants*") is an individual who, on information and belief, resides in Saint Petersburg, Florida. On information and belief, Latimer owns Bluewater and serves as its Chief Executive Officer. At all relevant times, Latimer was in control of, and directed, the operations of Bluewater in his capacity as owner and CEO of the same.

JURISDICTION AND VENUE

4. This Court has jurisdiction pursuant to 28 U.S.C. § 1332(a)(1) because of diversity of citizenship between Plaintiff and Defendants. The amount in controversy exceeds $75,000 as specified by 28 U.S.C. § 1332(a).

5. Venue is proper pursuant to 28 U.S.C. § 1391(b) because a substantial part of the events or omissions giving rise to the causes of action described herein occurred in Maine.

FACTS

6. Linn is an independent candidate for the office of United States Senator for the State of Maine and in connection with the conduct of his campaign for such office, on January 8, 2020, Linn caused to be registered with the Federal Elections Commission his official campaign committee, Max Linn for Senate 2020 (the "Campaign Committee").

7. Linn has financed his campaign, to a substantial degree, by loaning personal funds to the Campaign Committee, to be used by the Campaign Committee for campaign expenses.

8. On or about June, 2020, Linn contacted Defendants to inquire about services Defendants could provide to assist Linn's campaign, and Defendants subsequently agreed to provide certain services.

9. On June 18, 2020, Latimer emailed to Linn a draft plan, entitled "Max Linn for Senate – The Independent Plan" (hereinafter, the

"Plan"), pursuant to which Defendants would provide services to Linn's campaign, including, among other things: website development; advertising production; media ad purchases on radio, television and social media; a campaign-branded recreational vehicle; and personnel (the "Services"). The Plan is attached hereto as *Exhibit A.*

10. Further details with regards to the manner, method, timing, and particular costs of provision of Services were discussed and agreed to verbally and by electronic communications between Linn and Latimer.

11. On July 13, 2020, the Campaign Committee paid Bluewater $75,000 by wire transfer as a deposit to commence the Services.

12. On or about August 14, 2020, Bluewater delivered to the Campaign Committee its Invoice # 6539 in the amount of $80,000 dollars, ostensibly for prepaid media, campaign management, production support, and web development costs. On August 20, 2020, the Campaign Committee paid Invoice # 6539 by delivering Bluewater two checks drawn on the Campaign Committee's account in the total amount of $80,000.

13. On or about August 18, 2020, Bluewater delivered to the Campaign Committee its Invoice # 6563 in the amount of $200,000 dollars, ostensibly for prepaid media. On August 31, 2020, the Campaign Committee paid Invoice # 6563 by delivering Bluewater a wire transfer in the amount of $200,000.

14. In addition, Latimer directed that certain expenses, that were contemplated to be paid by Bluewater and invoiced to the Campaign Committee in the same manner as the other Services, be paid directly by debit card from the Campaign Committee's account and the sum of approximately $25,000 was paid in this manner.

15. Following inquiry by the Campaign Committee regarding these direct payments by the Campaign Committee, on September 22, 2020, Bluewater refunded to the Campaign Committee $25,000 by wire transfer.

16. In sum, after crediting the amount refunded by Bluewater, the Campaign Committee paid Bluewater a total of $330,000 (the "Amount Paid") for the Services.

17. From the Amount Paid, Bluewater purchased computers, camera equipment, and software (the "Equipment") for the campaign, which Equipment Bluewater then shipped from Maine to itself in Florida at the campaign's expense. In total, including the costs to ship the Equipment to Florida, Bluewater applied $39,669.22 of the Amount Paid to the Equipment.

18. On information and belief, this Equipment, purchased entirely with funds paid by the Campaign Committee, remains in the possession of Bluewater.

19. From the Amount Paid, Bluewater alleges it expended $68,100 to pay individuals (the "Personnel") to perform some of the Services, but has not accounted for the services rendered by these individuals, nor the proper amount payable for their services. Further, Plaintiff believes the cost of such Personnel should not have exceeded $15,000, leaving a difference of $53,100.

20. Linn and Latimer agreed that Personnel would assist the campaign through the date of the election, November 3, 2020, but at the direction of the Defendants, the Personnel discontinued service, to the extent they provided any, on or about August 27, 2020.

21. From the Amount Paid, Bluewater alleges it expended $213,318.04 on television and radio advertisements (the "Advertisements"), but has not provided to Linn or the Campaign Committee records showing that this amount was actually paid to run the Advertisements. Linn and the Campaign Committee believe less than this amount was actually spent on Advertisements.

22. Assuming arguendo, that all amounts Bluewater invoiced are appropriate, by Bluewater's own accounting the Campaign Committee over-paid Bluewater by $4,454.04, which amount Bluewater has not returned.

23. Bluewater additionally utilized the Campaign Committee's bank debit card on August 5, 2020, to make payments totaling $1,166.29 to B&H Photography and Video (the "B&H Payment") and has not provided to Linn or the Campaign Committee an invoice regarding this purchase, nor has Bluewater delivered to Linn or the Campaign Committee whatever items were purchased (the "B&H Equipment"). On information and belief, Bluewater retains possession of these items.

24. Linn has lent to the Campaign Committee $465,000, and on October 22, 2020, in exchange for Linn's discharge of indebtedness in an amount up to the amount of the claim against Defendants, the Campaign Committee assigned to Linn all claims it may have against the Defendants with regards to the above-referenced subject matter.

COUNT I

Conversion

25. Linn restates and realleges the allegations made in the preceding paragraphs of this Complaint as if fully set forth herein.

26. The Campaign Committee at all relevant times owned and had the right to possess the Equipment and the B&H Equipment and has now assigned its rights with respect to the same to Linn.

27. Defendants' wrongfully converted to their own possession and purposes the Equipment, the B&H Equipment, and portions of the Amount Paid.

28. As a direct and proximate result of Defendants' conversion, Linn has been damaged in an amount, not less than $40,835.51, the actual amount to be determined at trial.

COUNT II

Breach of Contract

29. Linn restates and realleges the allegations made in the preceding paragraphs of this Complaint as if fully set forth herein.

30. Plaintiff and Defendants entered into a binding, enforceable contract for the provision by Defendants of the Services as described in the Plan and further elaborated in verbal discussions between Linn and Latimer (the "Contract").

31. Bluewater and Latimer breached that Contract by failing to provide the Services as specified and by over-charging for the Services.

32. As a direct and proximate result of Latimer's and Bluewater's breach of the Contract, Linn has been damaged in an amount, not less than $75,000, the actual amount to be determined at trial, which is in addition to the claims described in Count I.

COUNT III

Unjust Enrichment

33. Linn restates and realleges the allegations made in the preceding paragraphs of this Complaint as if fully set forth herein.

34. The Campaign Committee conferred a valuable benefit on Bluewater and Latimer by remitting the Amount Paid.

35. Bluewater and Latimer realized the benefit of the Amount Paid, and the Equipment and the B&H Equipment that it continues to retain, without providing commensurate Services or reimbursement for that value to the Campaign Committee.

36. Defendants' acceptance and retention of the value of the Amount Paid, the B&H Equipment, and the Equipment without full provision of Services or reimbursement for that value to the Campaign Committee is unjust and inequitable, and Defendants have been unjustly enriched thereby in an amount, exceeding $75,000, to be determined at trial.

PRAYER FOR RELIEF

WHEREFORE, Plaintiff, respectfully requests that the Court enter an order:

(a) Finding that Defendants converted the Equipment, the B&H Equipment, and portions of the Amounts Paid as set forth herein;

(b) Finding that Defendants breached the Contract as set forth herein;

(c) Finding that Defendants were unjustly enriched as set forth herein and ordering restitution;

(d) Granting judgment in favor of Plaintiff and against Latimer and Bluewater jointly and severally for the full amount of Plaintiff's damages, to be proven at trial; and

(e) Granting such other and further relief as the Court deems just and proper.

Plaintiff demands a trial by jury.

Dated: October 23, 2020

/s/ George J. Marcus

George J. Marcus, Esq.

John H. Doyle, Esq.

Attorneys for Plaintiff Max Linn

MARCUS | CLEGG

16 Middle Street, Unit 501

Portland, ME 04101

(207) 828-8000

Answer

2020 WL 8993153 (D.Me.)

Westlaw Query>>

To find more Answer filings on Westlaw: access Maine Trial Court Documents (from the Home page, click Trial Court Documents, then Maine), click the Advanced Search link, select Answer and Counterclaim, and click Search. Use the Jurisdiction filter on the left to narrow results to Federal.

United States District Court, D. Maine.

Catherine DUDLEY, Plaintiff,

v.

HUDSON SPECIALTY INSURANCE COMPANY, Defendant.

No. 2:20-CV-00334-GZS.

October 26, 2020.

Answer, Counterclaim, and Jury Claim of Defendant Hudson Specialty Insurance Company to Plaintiff's Complaint

Hudson Specialty Insurance Company, By its attorney, John G. Wheatley, Bar # 4262, Melick & Porter, LLP, One Liberty Square, Boston, Massachusetts 02109, Telephone: (617) 523-6200, Facsimile: (617) 523-8130, jwheatley@melicklaw.com.

The defendant, Hudson Specialty Insurance Company ("defendant" or "Hudson"), hereby makes this its answer to the plaintiff's complaint.

JURISDICTION AND VENUE

1. Paragraph 1 of the complaint contains a legal conclusion to which no response is required.

2. Paragraph 2 of the complaint contains a legal conclusion to which no response is required.

PARTIES

3. The defendant is presently without knowledge or information sufficient to form a belief as to the truth of the allegations contained in this paragraph and calls upon the plaintiff to prove same.

4. Admitted.

FACTUAL ALLEGATIONS

5. The defendant is presently without knowledge or information sufficient to form a belief as to the truth of the allegations contained in this paragraph and calls upon the plaintiff to prove same.

6. The defendant is presently without knowledge or information sufficient to form a belief as to the truth of the allegations contained in this paragraph and calls upon the plaintiff to prove same.

7. The defendant is presently without knowledge or information sufficient to form a belief as to the truth of the allegations contained in this paragraph, including sub-parts a. through g., and calls upon the plaintiff to prove same.

8. Admitted.

9. The defendant admits that it issued a commercial general liability insurance policy to Michel Kanyambo and Speciose Mahirwe, policy number HBD 10028800, for the policy period of September 14, 2017, to September 14, 2018. The defendant denies any remaining allegations contained in paragraph 9.

10. The defendant responds that the policy speaks for itself.

11. The defendant responds that the policy speaks for itself.

374

12. Admitted.

13. Paragraph 13 of the complaint contains a legal conclusion to which no response is required.

14. Denied.

15. Denied.

16. The defendant is presently without knowledge or information sufficient to form a belief as to the truth of the allegations contained in this paragraph and calls upon the plaintiff to prove same.

17. The defendant admits that such a request was made, but denies that it was made timely or properly.

18. The defendant admits that it did not defend the subject lawsuit against Michel Kanyambo and Speciose Mahirwe, but denies any further allegations or characterizations by the plaintiff.

19. The defendant is presently without knowledge or information sufficient to form a belief as to the truth of the allegations contained in this paragraph and calls upon the plaintiff to prove same.

20. The defendant is presently without knowledge or information sufficient to form a belief as to the truth of the allegations contained in this paragraph and calls upon the plaintiff to prove same.

21. The defendant is presently without knowledge or information sufficient to form a belief as to the truth of the allegations contained in this paragraph and calls upon the plaintiff to prove same.

22. Paragraph 22 of the complaint contains a conclusion of law to which no response is required. To the extent a response is deemed required, the defendant denies any factual allegations contained in paragraph 22.

23. Paragraph 23 of the complaint contains a conclusion of law to which no response is required. To the extent a response is deemed required, the defendant denies any factual allegations contained in paragraph 23.

24. Paragraph 24 of the complaint contains a conclusion of law to which no response is required. To the extent a response is deemed required, the defendant denies any factual allegations contained in paragraph 24.

25. Paragraph 25 of the complaint contains a conclusion of law to which no response is required. To the extent a response is deemed required, the defendant denies any factual allegations contained in paragraph 25.

26. The defendant is presently without knowledge or information sufficient to form a belief as to the truth of the allegations contained in this paragraph and calls upon the plaintiff to prove same.

27. The defendant is presently without knowledge or information sufficient to form a belief as to the truth of the allegations contained in this paragraph and calls upon the plaintiff to prove same.

28. The defendant is presently without knowledge or information sufficient to form a belief as to the truth of the allegations contained in this paragraph and calls upon the plaintiff to prove same.

COUNT I

(REACH AND APPLY)

29. The defendant incorporates herein by reference its answers to paragraphs 1 through 28, and makes them its answer to paragraph 29.

30. Denied.

WHEREFORE, the defendant demands that the plaintiff's complaint against it be dismissed and that judgment enter for the defendant, together with an award of its costs.

COUNT II

(BREACH OF CONTRACT)

31. The defendant incorporates herein by reference its answers to paragraphs 1 through 28, and makes them its answer to paragraph 31.

32. Denied.

33. Denied.

34. Denied.

35. Denied.

36. Denied.

WHEREFORE, the defendant demands that the plaintiff's complaint against it be dismissed and that judgment enter for the defendant, together with an award of its costs.

AFFIRMATIVE DEFENSES

FIRST DEFENSE

And further answering, the defendant says that the complaint should be dismissed pursuant to Fed. R. Civ. P. 12(b)(6) for failure to state a claim upon which relief can be granted.

SECOND DEFENSE

And further answering, the defendant states that the policy referenced in the plaintiff's complaint was not in effect on the date of the loss.

THIRD DEFENSE

And further answering, the defendant states that the plaintiff's claims and damages are not covered due to failure to comply with the terms and conditions of the insurance contract.

FOURTH DEFENSE

And further answering, the defendant states that the plaintiff's complaint should be dismissed insofar as and to the extent that the plaintiff lacks standing to pursue her claims.

FIFTH DEFENSE

And further answering, the defendant states that the plaintiff's complaint should be dismissed due to insufficient and untimely notice of the underlying accident, injury, claim and/or lawsuit.

SIXTH DEFENSE

And further answering, the defendant says that, by their words, deeds, actions and inactions, the plaintiff is estopped from recovery against the defendant.

SEVENTH DEFENSE

And further answering, the defendant states that the plaintiff's claim is barred by lack of contractual relationship, lack of privity, and failure of consideration.

EIGHTH DEFENSE

And further answering, the defendant states that the plaintiff's claim is barred due to failure to comply with the cooperation and notice provisions of the insurance policy.

NINTH DEFENSE

And further answering, the defendant states that the plaintiff's complaint should be dismissed as part of the relief sought by the defendant's counterclaim against the plaintiff, which is incorporated herein by reference.

COUNTERCLAIM OF DEFENDANT DECLARATORY JUDGMENT

Nature of the Action

By this counterclaim, the defendant seeks a declaratory judgment that it is not responsible for the plaintiff's alleged judgment against Michel Kanyambo and Speciose Mahirwe ("Underlying Defendants"), because the plaintiff's judgment arose out of a claim against the Underlying Defendants that did not fall within the insurance policy issued by the defendant.

Facts Applicable to All Counts

1.   The Underlying Defendants were named party-defendants in an underlying claim brought by Catherine Dudley in Androscoggin County Superior Court, identified generally as *Catherine Dudley v. Michel Kanyambo et al.*, CV-19-172 (the "Underlying Claim").

2.   In the Underlying Claim, the plaintiff alleged that she was injured on September 23, 2018, as a result of a fall while on property owned by the Underlying Defendants, located at 5-7 Howard Street in Lewiston, Maine.

3.   Hudson provided a commercial general liability insurance policy to the Underlying Defendants, pursuant to policy number HBD 10028800, effective 09/14/2017 to 09/14/2018 (the "Policy").

4.   On July 31, 2018, Hudson offered a renewal insurance policy to the Underlying Defendants to succeed the commercial general liability policy that was set to expire on September 14, 2018.

5.   The Underlying Defendants did not accept the renewal policy offered and quoted by Hudson.

6.   On information and belief, the Underlying Defendants instead sought and obtained insurance coverage from Certain Underwriters at Lloyds, London.

7.   As a result, the insurance coverage provided under Hudson insurance policy number HBD 10028800 expired on September 14, 2018.

8.   The Policy affords coverage only for covered losses that occur during the policy period.

9.   The Underlying Claim is for bodily injury that occurred outside of the policy period.

10.   As a condition to coverage, the Policy requires the insured to notify Hudson "as soon as practicable of an 'occurrence' or an offense which may result in a claim." Once suit is filed, the Policy requires the insured to notify Hudson as soon as practicable and to immediately provide Hudson with copies of all legal papers received in connection with the suit.

11.   The Policy provides that legal expenses incurred without Hudson's consent are made at the insured's own expense.

12.   While the Underlying Claim was pending, Hudson issued a loss report to the Underlying Defendants at the request of their insurance agent. Neither the Underlying Defendants nor their insurance agent notified Hudson of the Underlying Claim at the time they requested the loss report or at any time prior thereto.

13.   The Underlying Defendants did not notify Hudson of the Underlying Claim until at least seven or eight months after suit was filed.

COUNT I

(Declaratory Judgment - 14 M.R.S. § 5951 et seq.)

14.   Hudson restates and incorporates herein the allegations of paragraphs 1 through 13.

15.   An actual controversy has arisen between Hudson and the plaintiff as to whether Hudson is responsible for the judgment against the Underlying Defendants, pursuant to the Policy.

16.   Specifically, but without limitation, a controversy is presented as to whether:

a.   Hudson is responsible for the Underlying Claim, when the subject accident and alleged injury at issue did not occur within the policy period;

b.   Hudson owed defense coverage to the Underlying Defendants and, if so, whether it is responsible for litigation costs incurred without Hudson's knowledge or consent; and

c.   Hudson received sufficient and timely notice of the Underlying Claim as a condition to coverage under the Policy.

17.   Hudson therefore seeks, pursuant to 14 M.R.S. § 5951 et seq., to obtain a binding judicial declaration concerning Hudson's rights and responsibilities with respect to the plaintiff's alleged underlying judgment against the Underlying Defendants, under the terms of the Policy.

Wherefore, Hudson Specialty Insurance Company requests relief in accordance with the foregoing, to include a binding declaration that the defendant is not responsible for the plaintiff's judgment against Michel Kanyambo and Speciose Mahirwe, and award it its costs as well as any other relief this Honorable Court deems fit.

JURY CLAIM

THE DEFENDANT/PLAINTIFF-IN-COUNTERCLAIM HEREBY MAKES A CLAIM FOR A TRIAL BY JURY.

HUDSON SPECIALTY INSURANCE COMPANY,

By its attorney,

/s/ John G. Wheatley

John G. Wheatley, Bar # 4262

Melick & Porter, LLP

One Liberty Square

Boston, Massachusetts 02109

Telephone: (617) 523-6200

Facsimile: (617) 523-8130

jwheatley@melicklaw.com

Dated: October 26, 2020

Amended Pleading

2021 WL 1431179 (D.Me.)

United States District Court, D. Maine.

Barbara O'HEARN, Plaintiff,

v.

Certain Underwriters at LLOYD'S, London,

and

PATRONS OXFORD INSURANCE COMPANY,

and

KENNEBUNK, Kennebunkport & Wells Water District,
Defendants.

No. 2:20-cv-00331-NT.

January 29, 2021.

Plaintiff's First Amended Complaint

Robert W. Weaver, Robert W. Weaver, Esq., Maine Bar No. 4892, Irwin & Morris, 60 Pineland Drive, Suite 202 Auburn Hall, New Gloucester, ME 04260, (207) 699-5106, rweaver@irwinmorris.com, for Plaintiff, Barbara O'Hearn.

Complaint and Demand for Jury Trial

NOW COMES Plaintiff, Barbara O'Hearn, by and through undersigned counsel, and Complains against the Defendants as follows:

THE PARTIES

1. Plaintiff, Barbara O'Hearn, is an individual who resides in the Town of Cambridge, County of Washington, in the State of New York.

2. Upon information and belief, Defendant, Certain Underwriters at Lloyd's, London (hereinafter "Lloyd's"), Subscribing to Policy No. NEF-01545, are the insurers of real property located at 356 Atlantic Avenue in the Town of Wells, County of York, State of Maine, which is owned by Plaintiff. The policy was issued by New England Flood Insurance which is believed to be a servicer of the policy and which has a principal place of business located at 22 Deer Street, Suite 400 in the City of Portsmouth, County of Rockingham, State of New Hampshire.

3. Upon information and belief, Defendant Patrons Oxford Insurance Company (hereinafter "Patrons Insurance") is an insurance company licensed by the Maine Bureau of Insurance to provide insurance products in the State of Maine, and identified by license number PCD7, with its principal place of business in the City of Portland, County of Cumberland, State of Maine.

4. Upon information and belief, Defendant Kennebunk, Kennebunkport & Wells Water District is a quasi-municipal water utility that serves the Towns of Kennebunk, Kennebunkport, Wells, Ogunquit, Arundel and portions of Biddeford and York, with a principal place of business located at 92 Main Street in the Town of Kennebunk, County of York, State of Maine.

JURISDICTIONAL STATEMENT

5. This Court has original jurisdiction over all claims herein pursuant to 28 U.S.C. Section 1332 because Plaintiff is an individual residing in the State of New York; Defendant Lloyd's issued its insurance policy through New England Flood Insurance which has a principal place of business located in the State of New Hampshire; Defendant Patron's Oxford is an insurance company with its primary place of business in the State of Maine; and Defendant Kennebunk, Kennebunkport & Wells Water District's principal place of business is in the State of Maine; furthermore, the matter in controversy exceeds the sum of $75,000.00.

VENUE

6. Venue is proper with this Court pursuant to 28 U.S.C. Section 1391(a) and Rule 3(b) of the rules of the United States District Court for the District of Maine in that all aspects of the acts at issue occurred in York County, State of Maine.

JURY DEMAND

7. Plaintiff demands a jury trial on all relevant issues of fact.

STATEMENT OF FACTS

8. At all times relevant hereto, Plaintiff Barbara O'Hearn, owned property located at 356 Atlantic Avenue in Wells, Maine.

9. At all times relevant hereto, Plaintiff's property located at 356 Atlantic Avenue in Wells, Maine was insured pursuant to a flood insurance policy with Defendant Lloyd's, serviced by New England Flood Insurance, specifically policy number NEF-01545.

10. At all times relevant hereto, Plaintiff's property located at 356 Atlantic Avenue in Wells, Maine was insured pursuant to a homeowners' policy with Defendant Patrons Oxford; specifically, policy number HOM 557091.

11. On or about September 20, 2019, a water main owned, operated and maintained by Defendant Kennebunk, Kennebunkport and Wells Water District broke, causing the release of a substantial amount of water onto Plaintiff's property. The water flowed onto Plaintiff's property and brought with it mud, sand and silt that flooded Plaintiff's basement apartment; damaging Plaintiff's home and personal property therein (hereinafter "the loss").

12. Plaintiff's neighbors called 9-1-1 to report the break in the water main, describing the water escaping the main with such force that it looked like a geyser. The force of the escaping water broke apart the road and started rushing downhill towards Plaintiff's property.

13. After local emergency personnel responded to the 9-1-1 call, employees or agents of Defendant Kennebunk, Kennebunkport and Wells Water District arrived on the scene of the water main break.

14. The employees or agents from Defendant Kennebunk, Kennebunkport and Wells Water District proceeded to dig up the road to gain access to the broken water main. One of the employees or agents stated to Plaintiff's neighbor that the water district should have installed a new main the last time the road was ripped up because the pipes and mains were very old. The employee or agent of Defendant Kennebunk, Kennebunkport and Wells Water District also stated that the water district knew they'd have problems due to the old pipes and water mains.

15. On or about September 27, 2019, Defendant Patrons Oxford notified Plaintiff that it was denying coverage of her claimed damages from the water loss, stating that damage from surface water was not covered pursuant to her homeowners' policy.

16. On or about January 8, 2020, Defendant Lloyd's rejected Plaintiff's Proof of Loss, which estimated damages of approximately $89,330.91 to her home, based, in part, on a dispute as to the amount of damages. Defendant Lloyd's, through its claims administrator Vanguard, issued a partial payment of $15,061.70 to Plaintiff, representing its undisputed amount of damages to Plaintiff's home attributable to the loss.

17. Since filing her Proof of Loss for damage to her home, Plaintiff has incurred additional costs to repair the damage caused by the loss.

COUNT I

(Declaratory Judgment-Patrons Oxford Insurance Company)

18. Plaintiff incorporates by reference paragraphs 1-17 above as if fully stated herein.

19. The policy exclusion relied upon by Defendant Patrons Oxford in its denial of Plaintiff's claim for insurance proceeds pursuant to her homeowners' policy are ambiguous and should be strictly construed in favor of Plaintiff and for coverage of the loss.

20. Proper interpretation of the homeowners' policy provides coverage for the property damage suffered by Plaintiff on or about September 20, 2019.

21. An actual controversy exists between Plaintiff, on the one hand, and Defendant, Patrons Oxford on the other hand, and by the terms and provisions of Rule 57 of the Federal Rules of Civil Procedure and 28 U.S.C. §§ 2201 and 2202, this Court is invested with the power to declare the rights and liabilities of the parties hereto and to grant such relief as it deems necessary and proper.

WHEREFORE, Plaintiff, respectfully requests this Honorable Court to declare and adjudge that Plaintiff's claim is covered and payable pursuant to the Patrons' Oxford homeowners' policy and that Defendant's denial of her claim is wrongful and in breach of Defendant's contractual obligations and grant any other relief that this Honorable Court deems just and equitable under the circumstances, including the award of costs and attorney's fees.

COUNT II

(Breach of Contract-Patrons Oxford Insurance Company)

22. Plaintiff incorporates by reference paragraphs 1-17 above as if fully stated herein.

23. At all relevant times alleged herein, Plaintiff and Defendant Patrons Oxford were subject to a valid and effective insurance contract as set forth above.

24. Pursuant to the terms of the insurance contract, Plaintiff was to pay a premium for coverage in exchange for the insurance coverage provided in the homeowners' policy.

25. Plaintiff complied with the terms of the insurance contract and made a valid claim for damages to her property pursuant to the insurance contract.

26. Defendant failed to make payment to Plaintiff pursuant to the contract and thereby materially breached the contract, causing damages to Plaintiff.

WHEREFORE, Plaintiff demands judgment against Defendant Patrons Oxford Insurance Company in an amount to reasonably and fairly compensate her for all damages, plus attorney's fees, costs, and interest, and any such other damages as this Honorable Court may deem just.

COUNT III

(Breach of Contract-Certain Underwriters at Lloyd's, London)

27. Plaintiff incorporates by reference paragraphs 1-17 above as if fully stated herein.

28. At all relevant times alleged herein, Plaintiff and Defendant Lloyd's were subject to a valid and effective insurance contract as set forth above.

29. Pursuant to the terms of the insurance contract, Plaintiff was to pay a premium for coverage in exchange for the insurance coverage provided in the flood insurance policy.

30. Plaintiff complied with the terms of the insurance contract and made a valid claim for damages to her property pursuant to the insurance contract.

31. Defendant failed to make payment for the full amount of the loss to Plaintiff pursuant to the contract and thereby materially breached the contract, causing damages to Plaintiff.

WHEREFORE, Plaintiff demands judgment against Defendant Certain Underwriters at Lloyd's, London in an amount to reasonably and fairly compensate her for all damages, plus attorney's fees, costs, and interest, and any such other damages as this Honorable Court may deem just.

COUNT IV

(Breach of Good Faith and Fair Dealing-Certain Underwriters at Lloyd's, London)

32. Plaintiff incorporates by references paragraphs 1-17 and 28-31 above as if fully stated herein.

33. Defendant Lloyd's, as the insurer, owed Plaintiff, as an insured, an implied duty of good faith and fair dealing.

34. Defendant Lloyd's breached the implied duty of good faith and fair dealing when it failed to pay the full value of the claim made for damages covered under the flood insurance policy when the value of the claim became reasonably known through estimates provided by Plaintiff.

WHEREFORE, Plaintiff demands judgment against Defendant Certain Underwriters at Lloyd's, London in an amount to reasonably and fairly compensate her for all damages, including consequential damages, plus attorney's fees, costs, and interest, and any such other damages as this Honorable Court may deem just.

COUNT V

(Unfair Claims Settlement Practices, 24-A M.R.S.A. § 2436-A Certain Underwriters at Lloyd's, London)

35. Plaintiff incorporates by reference paragraphs 1-17 and 28-34 above as if fully stated herein.

36. Pursuant to 24-A M.R.S.A. § 2436-A, an insurer may not, without just cause, fail to effectuate prompt, fair and equitable settlement of claims submitted on which liability is reasonably clear.

37. As set forth above, Defendant Lloyd's does not dispute liability in this matter, nor has it disputed coverage.

38. Defendant Lloyd's failure to effectuate a prompt, fair and equitable settlement of Plaintiff's claims constitutes an unfair settlement practice.

WHEREFORE, Plaintiff demands judgment against Defendant Certain Underwriters at Lloyd's, London in an amount to reasonably and fairly compensate her for all damages, plus attorney's fees, costs, and interest pursuant to 24-A M.R.S.A. § 2436-A.

COUNT VI

(Negligence-Kennebunk, Kennebunkport and Wells Water District)

39. Plaintiff incorporates by reference paragraphs 1-17 above as if fully stated herein.

40. Defendant Kennebunk, Kennebunkport and Wells Water District owed a duty of ordinary care to operate and maintain its water mains so they would not malfunction and cause damage to others.

41. Defendant Kennebunk, Kennebunkport and Wells Water District owed a heightened duty of care to Plaintiff due to the customer relationship between the two parties.

42. Defendant was negligent in its operation and maintenance of its water main, causing the water main to break and release water onto Plaintiff's property. Specifically, Defendant was negligent in not replacing old pipes and water mains that it knew needed to be replaced in order to prevent bursting and leaking.

43. As a direct and proximate cause of Defendant's negligence as outlined above, Plaintiff sustained damage to her real and personal property.

WHEREFORE, Plaintiff demands judgment against Defendant Kennebunk, Kennebunkport and Wells Water District in an amount to reasonably and fairly compensate her for all damages, plus attorney's fees, costs, and interest, and any such other damages as this Honorable Court may deem just.

Dated at New Gloucester, Maine this 29th day of January, 2021.

/S/ Robert W. Weaver

Robert W. Weaver, Esq., Maine Bar No. 4892

Attorney for Plaintiff, Barbara O'Hearn

Irwin & Morris

60 Pineland Drive, Suite 202 Auburn Hall

New Gloucester, ME 04260

(207) 699-5106

rweaver@irwinmorris.com

Motion to Strike

2016 WL 9021506 (D.Me.)

United States District Court, D. Maine.

COAST TO COAST ENGINEERING SERVICES, INC., Plaintiff,

v.

Robert ROOP, Defendant.

No. 2:16-cv-54-DBH.

December 27, 2016.

Motion to Strike or Dismiss Defendants' Counterclaims

Timothy J. Bryant, Esq., Benjamin S. Piper, Esq., Preti Flaherty Beliveau & Pachios, LLP, One City Center, P.O. Box 9546, Portland, ME 04112-9546, Tel: (207) 791-3000, tbryant@preti.com, bpiper@preti.com, for Coast to Coast Engineering Services, Inc.

Plaintiff Coast to Coast Engineering Services, Inc. (d/b/a Criterium Engineers) ("Criterium"), by and through undersigned counsel, moves pursuant to F.R. Civ. P. 12(f) and 12(b)(6) to strike or dismiss Defendants Robert Roop and Lockatong Engineering, Inc.'s ("Lockatong") (collectively "Defendants") newly filed counterclaims (ECF No. 52) (the "Amended Counterclaims"). The Amended Counterclaims, filed forty-five minutes before the Final Pretrial Conference, assert new factual allegations and a new cause of action against Criterium. Whereas Mr. Roop's original Counterclaims had sought only a declaration that he was not in breach of the Settlement Agreement at issue in this action, he and Lockatong now assert a claim for breach of contract against Criterium. These counterclaims were filed months after the deadline to amend the pleadings and after the close of discovery. The Defendants did not seek leave to amend their pleadings. There is no reason Mr. Roop could not have sought leave to file the Amended Counterclaims in a timely manner. Permitting the Amended Counterclaims after the Defendants' undue delay would prejudice Criterium, require additional, discovery, and delay trial of this matter. Moreover, the Amended Counterclaims are futile as they fail to state a claim upon which relief can be granted.

BACKGROUND

Mr. Roop founded Lockatong in 2001. Roop Dep. Tr. 7/27/16 16:22-17:1.[1] That same year he became a franchisee of Criterium and ran his franchise through Lockatong. *Id.* 17:2-4; 20:14-18. He is the sole owner of Lockatong. *Id.* 20:23-24:1. On March 13, 2015, Mr. Roop and Lockatong entered into the Release and Settlement Agreement (the "Settlement Agreement") at issue in this action. Mr. Roop and Lockatong were represented by the same counsel in negotiating and executing the Settlement Agreement and in this action.

On February 3, 2016, Criterium filed the Complaint (ECF No. 1) in this action against Mr. Roop for failure to return materials as required by the Settlement Agreement. Criterium's counsel informed Mr. Roop's counsel shortly thereafter that it did not file suit against Lockatong in the first instance because it could not be sure that the unreturned materials that had been sent to Mr. Roop had been stored or otherwise possessed by Lockatong. He further stated that Criterium intended to add Lockatong as a party if it learned during discovery that Lockatong possessed materials required to be returned under the Settlement Agreement. Criterium's counsel informed the Court of the same during a June 2016 discovery conference.

---

1. Mr. Roop's deposition transcript is currently on file with the Court.

On April 12, 2016, Mr. Roop filed his Answer, Affirmative Defenses, and Counterclaims (ECF No. 3). The Counterclaims asserted just one count, seeking a declaratory judgment stating that (a) the Settlement Agreement should be made publicly available, Criterium having waived contractual entitlement to confidentiality; (b) Mr. Roop is in compliance with his obligations under the Settlement Agreement; (c) the Settlement Agreement makes no mention of the Criterium Document to which Mr. Roop had access while he serve in executive positions at Criterium and that he does not have such documents and confirmed as much to Criterium's counsel; (d) the Settlement Agreement does not require Mr. Roop to provide sworn affidavits on demand; (e) Mr. Roop is the substantially prevailing party under the Settlement Agreement in this action, entitling him to fees and costs; and (f) any other declarations reasonably required to provide clarity to the parties in relation to their respective rights and obligations under the Settlement Agreement. *See* Counterclaims ¶¶ 48-51. The Counterclaims did not assert a count for breach of contract, nor did the lone count seek a declaration that Criterium had breached the Settlement Agreement. *Id.*

The parties commenced discovery, through which Criterium learned that materials sent to Mr. Roop by Criterium had been stored in Lockatong's office and on its computer equipment and had not been returned to Criterium. On September 22, 2016, in accordance with its prior representations, Criterium moved to amend its Complaint to add Lockatong as a defendant and add factual allegations regarding facts learned during discovery. The Proposed Amended Complaint did not add any new counts or change they theory of breach. At that point there were nearly two months remaining in the discovery period. The deadline to amend the pleadings expired on September 23, 2016 (ECF No. 20). Mr. Roop did not seek leave to amend its pleadings by that date; nor has he done so since.

On November 23, 2016, the Court granted Criterium's motion to amend its pleadings (ECF No. 39). On December 2, 2016, Criterium filed three motions *in limine*, which among other things sought exclusion of evidence beyond the scope of Mr. Roop's Counterclaims (ECF Nos. 44-46). Criterium filed its First Amended Complaint on December 7, 2016. At 1:14 PM on December 7, 46 minutes before the Final Pretrial Conference, Mr. Roop and Lockatong filed their Answer to the Amended Complaint, Affirmative Defenses, and Counterclaims (ECF No. 52). The Amended Counterclaims assert a claim for breach of contract against Criterium and seek a judgment for breach of contract and damages. They further add factual allegations concerning Criterium's alleged breach of the Settlement Agreement that had not been included in the original Counterclaims. For example, they allege for the first time that Criterium breached non-disclosure obligations under Section 9 of the Settlement Agreement, Am. Countercl. ¶¶51-52, breached Section 1 by seeking to impose additional obligations on the Defendants, Am. Countercl. ¶¶ 53-56, and failed to properly de-index the "criterium-lockatong.com" website, Am. Countercl. ¶ 59.

Criterium's counsel informed the Court during the pretrial conference that Criterium intended to seek dismissal of the Counterclaims because they impermissibly inserted new issues into the trial after the close of discovery.

LEGAL STANDARD

A request to amend pleadings "will be treated differently depending on its timing and the context in which it is filed." *Steir v. Girls Scouts of the USA*, 383 F.3d 7, 11-12 (1st Cir. 2004). After the defendant has filed a responsive pleading, a pleading may only be amended with the opposing party's written consent or the court's leave. Fed. R. Civ. P. 15(a)(2). Leave of court or consent is required where a party wishes to assert new counterclaims in response to an amended complaint. *Bern v. Unlimited, Inc. v. Burton Corp.*, 25 F. Supp.3d 170, 177, 179 (D. Mass. 2014). "While leave to amend 'shall be freely given when justice so requires,' Fed.R.Civ.P. 15(a), parties seeking the benefit of the rule's liberality have an obligation to exercise due diligence; unseemly delay, in combination with other factors, may warrant denial of a suggested amendment." *Quaker State Oil Ref. Corp. v. Garrity Oil Co.*, 884 F.2d 1510, 1517 (1st Cir. 1989). "Reasons for denying leave include undue delay in filing the motion, bad faith or dilatory motive, repeated failure to cure deficiencies, undue prejudice to the opposing party, and futility of amendment." *United States ex rel Gagne v. City of Worcester*, 565 F.3d 40, 48 (1st Cir. 2009).

"When leave to amend a pleading is sought after the scheduling order's deadline for doing so has passed, the party seeking leave must demonstrate either good cause for its failure to do so before the deadline or excusable neglect." *Ergo Licensing, LLC v. Carefusion 303, Inc.*, No. CIV. 08-259-P-S, 2010 WL 373660, at *1 (D. Me. Feb. 2, 2010) (citing Fed.R.Civ.P. 16(b)(4); *O'Connell v. Hyatt Hotels of Puerto Rico*, 357 F.3d 152, 154–55 (1st Cir. 2004)). To show excusable neglect, a party must "offer a convincing explanation as to why the neglect was excusable," which must include "intervening circumstances beyond the party's control." *Nansamba v. North Shore Medical Center, Inc.*, 727 F.3d 33, 38-39 (1st Cir. 2013) (quoting *Cintron-Lorenzo v. Departamento de Asuntos del Consumidor*, 312 F.3d 522, 527 (1st Cir. 2002); *Pioneer Inv. Servs. Co. v. Brunswick Assocs. Ltd. P'ship*, 507 U.S. 380, 388, 113 S. Ct. 1489 (1993)). If the party seeking leave to amend does not contend that its delay was due to excusable neglect, the party must show that the deadline could not reasonably be met despite its diligence. *Id.* "Particularly disfavored are motions to amend whose timing prejudices the opposing party by requiring a re-opening of discovery with additional costs, a significant postponement of the trial, and a likely major alteration in trial tactics and strategy." *Perry v. Tinkham*, No. 1:12-cv-00229-GZS, 2014 WL 5765417, at *4 (D. Me. Nov. 5, 2014) (quoting *Steir v. Girl Scouts of the USA*, 383 F.3d 7, 12 (1st Cir. 2004) (internal quotation marks omitted)).

ARGUMENT

I. There was no good cause or excusable neglect justifying the delayed filing of the Amended Counterclaims.

Applying the foregoing standards to the circumstances here, the Court should exercise its discretion to strike or dismiss the Amended Counterclaims. After the close of discovery and while the parties were preparing for trial, the Defendants asserted new factual and legal theories for the first time. There is no reason these issues could not have been pleaded earlier. Because Criterium did not have the opportunity or the motivation to explore these theories during discovery, it would be prejudiced by the introduction of these issues into the case.

The deadline for the parties to amend their pleadings was September 23, 2016. Mr. Roop and Lockatong were aware since September 22 of the contents of Criterium's proposed First Amended Complaint, yet Mr. Roop did not seek leave to amend in the nearly eleven weeks between September 22 and December 7. It was only after Criterium filed its motions *in limine* that the Defendants sought to expand the scope of issues in this case—and thereby combat the motions *in limine*—by amending their counterclaims

Criterium's Amended Complaint did not alter the scope of the case in a manner that compelled or invited the Amended Counterclaims. The Amended Complaint is based on the same course of conduct as the original—the failure to return documents as required by the Settlement Agreement. It contains the same single breach of contract cause of action. The changes in the Amended Counterclaims do not in any way reflect the changes in the Amended Complaint. There is no reason Mr. Roop could not have sought leave to file the Amended Counterclaims before Criterium filed its Amended Complaint.

While the Amended Complaint added Lockatong as a defendant, that addition does not justify the Amended Counterclaims or excuse the Defendants' delay. That Mr. Roop is a party to the Amended Counterclaims indisputably establishes that they could have been filed before the addition of Lockatong as a Defendant. Moreover, there is no practical distinction between Mr. Roop and Lockatong for purposes of the Amended Counterclaims. As discussed above, Mr. Roop is the sole owner of Lockatong and he operated his Criterium franchise through Lockatong. Both Mr. Roop and Lockatong were represented by the same counsel in the negotiation and execution of the Settlement Agreement and in this action.

Furthermore, there are no contractual rights or obligations asserted in the Amended Counterclaims that run to Lockatong and not to Mr. Roop. Nor are there factual allegations that are unique to Lockatong. Indeed, the Amended Complaint adds certain allegations that are unique to *Mr. Roop*. For example, the portions of Section 9 of the Settlement Agreement pertaining to communications with franchisees apply to Roop only, not Lockatong. Thus, Lockatong does not even have standing to assert the so-called "Criterium Form Breaches" asserted for the first time in the Amended Counterclaims. *See* Amended Counterclaims ¶¶ 53-56. Similarly, Defendants specified for the first time in their Opposition to Motion in Limine to Exclude Evidence Concerning Certain Actions and Omissions Related to the Criterium-Lockatong.com Domain and Criterium Office Listing Website ("Opp'n to Mot. in Limine") (ECF No. 64) that they rely on Section 15.1 of the Roop-Criterium Franchise Agreement in alleging that Criterium interfered with their rights to deidentify. *Compare* Opp'n to Mot. in Limine at 2-3 *with* Amended Counterclaims ¶¶ 57-60. The Roop-Criterium Franchise Agreement is between Mr. Roop and Criterium only, not Lockatong. Thus, Lockatong has no standing to assert claims based on that agreement. Finally, the Defendants admit that Criterium only asked Mr. Roop, not Lockatong, to sign an affidavit. Amended Counterclaims ¶¶ 26-30. If Mr. Roop wished to enforce the rights and obligations asserted in the Amended Counterclaims, he could have sought leave to do so before the deadline to amend the pleadings, in which case Lockatong could have responded to the Amended Complaint without changing the theories of the case.

As it stands, Criterium would require additional discovery to address the Amended Counterclaims. The Amended Counterclaims for the first time assert a claim for breach of contract and unspecified damages. While the original Counterclaims alluded to breaches by Criterium—without seeking relief therefor—the factual theories upon which the alleged breaches are based are far broader in the Amended Counterclaims. For example, the Amended Counterclaims allege for the first time breaches based on disclosures in violation of Section 9, seeking to expand the terms of Section 9, and failing to deindex the criterium.lockatong.com website. Amended Counterclaims ¶¶ 51-56, 59. Basic fairness would require that Criterium be entitled to discovery to explore these theories of breach. To the extent other theories of breach were asserted in the original Counterclaims, Criterium should still be entitled to discovery on those theories because it did not previously have the same motivation to explore those theories: during discovery Mr. Roop sought only a declaration that he was not in breach; he did not seek damages for a breach by Criterium.

The further discovery necessary to address the Amended Counterclaims would almost certainly delay trial, which is currently set for February 27, 2017. This delay is unnecessarily brought about by Mr. Roop's failure to seek leave to amend in accordance with the scheduling order. Rather than subject Criterium to this cost and delay and add additional time and complexity to the trial (for alleged breaches for which no harm has been alleged, as discussed below) the Court should strike or dismiss the Amended Counterclaims. This is justified by the lack of diligence in seeking leave to amend and the resulting prejudice. *See Perry v. Tinkham*, No. 1:12-cv-00229-GZS, 2014 WL 5765417, at *4-5 (D. Me. Nov. 5, 2014) (disallowing motion to amend filed after the deadline to amend the pleadings where the motion to amend could have been filed earlier); *Ergo Licensing, LLC v. Carefusion 303, Inc.*, No.

CIV. 08-259-P-S, 2010 WL 373660, at *1 (D. Me. Feb. 2, 2010) (denying motion to amend counterclaim when the motion for leave to amend was filed 19 days after the deadline to do so); *Quaker State Oil Ref. Corp. v. Garrity Oil Co.*, 884 F.2d 1510, 1517–18 (1st Cir. 1989) (upholding denial of leave to add a counterclaim even where two months remained in discovery, because there was no satisfactory explanation for the delay and granting leave would prejudice the opposing party).

II. The Amended Counterclaims are futile.

Criterium further respectfully requests dismissal of the Counterclaims for their failure to state a claim. Whether this request is construed as a motion to dismiss for failure to state a claim or an objection to a motion for leave to amend pleadings based on futility, the standard is the same. *Adorno v. Crowley Towing & Trans. Co.*, 443 F.3d 122, 126 (1st Cir. 2006). The claimant must plead enough facts to state a claim for relief that is plausible on its face. *Bell Atlantic Corp. v. Twombly*, 550 U.S. 544, 555 (2007). "A claim has facial plausibility when the [claimant] pleads factual content that allows the court to draw the reasonable inference that the defendant is liable for the misconduct alleged." *Ashcroft v. Iqbal*, 556 U.S. 662, 678 (2009). Such inferences should be drawn from the factual content of the pleading, ignoring conclusory allegations. *Ocasio-Hernandez v. Fortuno-Burset*, 640 F.3d 1, 12 (1st Cir. 2011).

Most of the alleged breaches by Criterium facially deficient because they are not grounded in the Settlement Agreement. The Defendants' allegations concerning the criterium-lockatong.com domain and Criterium-Lockatong's appearance on Criterium's office listing page are not linked to any contractual provision. On this point, Criterium incorporates by reference the arguments made in its Motion in Limine to Exclude Testimony of Tom Hall (ECF No. 44) and its Motion in Limine to Exclude Evidence Concerning Certain Actions and Omissions Related to the Criterium-Lockatong.com Domain and Criterium Office Listing Webpage (ECF No. 45). Criterium adds that the Amended Counterclaims nowhere identify any contractual basis for the "de-identification process" it cites as the basis for these allegations. *See* Amended Counterclaims ¶¶ 32, 57-59, 68. As discussed above, Defendants specified for the first time in response to one of Criterium's motions in limine that it relies on Section 15.1 of the Roop-Criterium Franchise Agreement in alleging that Criterium interfered with the obligation to deidentify. The language Section 15.1 places obligations on Mr. Roop alone. It states that any action by Criterium to assist in the deidentification process is discretionary and may be done at Roop's expense. Because Section 15.1 placed no obligations whatsoever on Criterium, it cannot serve as the basis for a breach of contract claim against Criterium.

Moreover, By repeatedly requesting during the course of these proceedings that the Court void the confidentiality of the Settlement Agreement, the Defendants have waived their allegations concerning violations of the Settlement Agreement's non-disclosure provisions. *See* Defendant's Objection to Plaintiff's Motion for Leave to File First Amended Complaint (ECF No. 24) at 7, 9; Defendant's Pretrial Memorandum (ECF No. 41) at 4. Even if the Defendants had not waived these provisions, the alleged disclosures are pleaded in a conclusory manner that fails to specify the disclosures or state why they violate Section 9 of the Settlement Agreement. Moreover, the portions of Section 9 of the Settlement Agreement pertaining to communications with franchisees pertains to Roop only, not Lockatong. Thus, the addition of Lockatong provides no basis for the Defendants to assert the so-called "Criterium Form Breaches" for the first time. *Cf.* Amended Counterclaims ¶¶ 53-56.

Further, the Amended Counterclaims are futile and should be dismissed because they do not allege any harm from the alleged breaches of contract. "[A]ctual injury or damage is an element of . . . breach of contract claims." *In re. Hannaford Bros Co. Customer Data Sec. Breach Litig.*, 2010 ME 93, ¶ 8, 4 A.3d 492, 495. The Defendants, therefore, were required to plead damages in order to state a claim for relief. *See Foley v. Wells Fargo Bank, N.A.*, 772 F.3d 63, 77 (1st Cir. 2014) ("Even though Foley sufficiently pleaded a breach of contract, we recognize that he also need have adequately pleaded damages."); *Sullivan v. Bank of N.Y. Mellon Corp.*, 91 F. Supp. 3d 154, 163-64 (D. Mass. 2015) (dismissing breach of contract claim where the plaintiffs failed to allege any harm).

The only harm the Defendants have conceivably alleged are their costs in this action. Those costs were not caused by Criterium's alleged breaches. They result from Criterium's bringing this action in an effort to enforce the Settlement Agreement. Criterium's bringing this action cannot be construed as a breach of contract because the Settlement Agreement contains enforcement and fee-shifting provisions. Because the contract provides that parties may sue to enforce its terms and provides for compensation to the prevailing party, Criterium's enforcement actions are within the terms of the Settlement Agreement. The Defendants may try to prevail on Criterium's claims and demonstrate their entitlement to attorneys' fees under the Settlement Agreement. Such a recovery is not contingent on their bringing other claims for which they have not suffered harm. On the contrary, their doing so only artificially inflates the attorneys' fees by expanding the scope and complexity of this case.

Because the Amended Counterclaims allege breaches of duties not contemplated by the Settlement Agreement, and because the Amended Counterclaims allege no harm caused by those alleged breaches, they are futile and should be dismissed or stricken.

CONCLUSION

Because the Amended Counterclaims should have and could have been filed earlier and allowing them now would prejudice trial, and because the Amended Counterclaims are futile, Criterium respectfully requests that the Amended cken or, in the alternative, dismissed with prejudice.

ber 27, 2016

ly submitted,

Benjamin S. Piper

Timothy J. Bryant, Esq.

Benjamin S. Piper, Esq.

Attorneys for *Coast to Coast Engineering Services, Inc.*

PRETI FLAHERTY BELIVEAU & PACHIOS, LLP

One City Center, P.O. Box 9546

Portland, ME 04112-9546

Tel: (207) 791-3000

tbryant@preti.com

bpiper@preti.com

Motion to Dismiss for Improper Venue

2021 WL 2008424 (D.Me.)

United States District Court, D. Maine.

MMT INC,

v.

HYDRO INTERNATIONAL INC, et al.

No. 1:21-cv-00027-JJM-LDA.

February 5, 2021.

Defendants' Motion to Dismiss for Improper Venue and Lack of Personal Jurisdiction, or, in the Alternative, to Transfer to the District of Maine

James R. Oswald, Bar No. 5727, Adler Pollock & Sheehan P.C., One Citizens Plaza, 8th Floor, Providence, RI 02903, (401) 274-7200, joswald@apslaw.com.

Daniel J. Mitchell, pro hac vice, Edward J. Sackman, pro hac vice, Bernstein Shur, 100 Middle St, PO Box 9729, Portland, ME 04104-5029, (207) 774-1200, dmitchell@bernsteunshur.com, nsackman@bernsteinshur.com, for defendants.

Defendants HIL Technologies, Inc., Hydro International, Inc., and Hydro International, plc (collectively, "Defendants" or "Hydro International")[1], by and through undersigned counsel, hereby move this Court pursuant to Fed. R. Civ. P. 12(b)(3), and 28 U.S.C. § 1406, for an Order dismissing Plaintiff MMT, Inc. d/b/a StormTree's ("Plaintiff" or "StormTree") Verified Complaint for improper venue. In the alternative, Defendants move this Court for an Order transferring this case to the only district where all of StormTree's claims may be heard in a single proceeding: the United States District Court for the District of Maine. Defendants further move pursuant to Fed. R. Civ. P. 12(b)(2) to dismiss StormTree's federal claims for lack of personal jurisdiction. If the federal claims are dismissed, the Court will no longer have subject matter jurisdiction over the remaining state law claims.

FACTS RELEVANT TO MOTION TO DISMISS OR TO TRANSFER[2]

This case arises from a dispute regarding two stormwater treatment products: Plaintiff's "StormTree" offering and Defendants' "StormScape" system. *See, e.g.,* Verif. Compl. at ¶¶ 60-75. Both products make use of a subterranean structure surrounding a tree to filter stormwater before it permeates the surrounding soil. *See id.* at ¶¶ 11, 34-39, 42-44. Plaintiff alleges that StormScape uses

---

1. Plaintiff has misidentified Hydro International, Inc., as no such entity exists. *See* Exhibit A, Declaration of David J. Mongeau (hereinafter, "Ex. A"), at ¶ 7. Hydro International, plc, which Plaintiff alleges is a United Kingdom private limited company with a principal place of business in Clevedon, United Kingdom, *see* Verified Complaint ("Verif. Compl.") at ¶ 3, was a company based in the United Kingdom and was the former corporate parent company of Hydro International. Ex. A at ¶ 8. Due to a reorganization a few years ago, Hydro International plc no longer exists, and does not own and is not affiliated with Hydro International. *Id.* For the purposes of this motion, however, these named Defendants are included in the collective description.

2. Defendants principally draw the facts cited herein from the Verified Complaint, reserving all rights to challenge such facts at the appropriate time. In addition, Defendants rely upon a verified declaration by David J. Mongeau. Defendants may appropriately do so because, unlike a motion to dismiss for failure to state a claim, "[w]hen confronted with a motion to dismiss for improper venue, the court may consider both the complaint and evidence outside the complaint." *T-Jat Sys. 2006 Ltd. v. Expedia, Inc. (DE)*, No. 16-cv-581-RGA, 2019 WL 351252, at *3 (D. Del. Jan. 29, 2019) (citation omitted).

technology that infringes on two of StormTree's patents. *See id.* at ¶¶ 60-75 (Counts II and III). In addition, it claims that StormScape used confidential information Defendants obtained after signing a non-disclosure agreement (the "NDA"), ostensibly in furtherance of investigating a potential business relationship with StormTree, but in actuality to learn non-public information about StormTree's technology. *Id.* at ¶¶ 23-33, 53-59 (Count I). StormTree further alleges that Hydro International's StormScape product infringes upon its trademark rights because it is confusingly similar to StormTree. *Id.* at ¶¶ 45-48, 76-83 (Count IV). StormTree also asserts a state law claim alleging misappropriation of unspecified trade secrets. *Id.* at ¶¶ 84-87 (Count V). Finally, it asserts a state law fraud claim alleging that Defendants induced StormTree to enter the NDA by representing that they were interested in a business relationship when in fact Defendants just sought to attain StormTree's confidential information. *Id.* at ¶¶ 88-93 (Count VI).

Defendants contest each and every one of these allegations, but for purposes of this motion focus upon the procedural defects in Plaintiff's suit. Critically, none of the Defendants reside in Rhode Island. Specifically, Hydro International, Inc. is alleged to be incorporated in Delaware, with a principal place of business in Portland, Maine. Verif. Compl. at ¶ 2. HIL Technologies, Inc. is incorporated in Maine and has its principal place of business in Portland, Maine. Ex. A at ¶¶ 4, 6; *see also* Verif. Compl. at ¶ 2. Defendant Hydro International, plc is alleged to be a United Kingdom private liability company with a principal place of business in Clevedon, United Kingdom. Verif. Compl. at ¶ 3.[3] For all the time periods discussed by Plaintiff in the Verified Complaint, Defendants' business, including their sales of products, has been transacted through their headquarters office in Portland, Maine. Ex. A at ¶ 9. Defendants' business records also are maintained at the Maine headquarters. *Id.* Defendants' key personnel, including those involved in the development and sale of its products, also are based out of the Maine headquarters. *Id.* at ¶ 10. Defendants never have had an office in Rhode Island, they never have maintained any personnel in Rhode Island, and they do not employ any residents of Rhode Island. *Id.*

Defendants have no sales in Rhode Island of any of the stormwater treatment products described in the Verified Complaint, including the Hydro "Bioinfiltrator" or StormScape products, nor have they sold any other biofiltration stormwater treatment products in Rhode Island. *Id.* at ¶ 11. Moreover, Defendants do not market the subject products in this district. *Id.* Defendants have not made any direct attempts to sell such products in Rhode Island, nor have they ever been present in Rhode Island for the purpose of trying to sell such products to any customer. *Id.*

On January 14, 2021, Plaintiff commenced the present action, seeking damages and injunctive relief for, *inter alia*, patent and trademark infringement, as well as asserting claims for breach of the NDA, state law trade secrets misappropriation, and fraud. Plaintiff also seeks a temporary restraining order. *See* Docket Entry Nos. 1-2. Plaintiff alleges in summary fashion that "[v]enue is proper in this District pursuant to 28 U.S.C. §§ 1391(b) and 1400(b)." Verif. Compl. at ¶ 9.

For the reasons that follow, this Court should dismiss this matter for improper venue and, in the case of the federal claims, lack of personal jurisdiction. If the federal claims are dismissed, the Court will no longer have subject matter jurisdiction because the only remaining source of such jurisdiction is the federal diversity statute, and Plaintiff has failed to plead or even address the $75,000 amount-in-controversy requirement. *See* 28 U.S.C. § 1332(a). Alternatively, the Court should transfer this matter to the United States District Court for the District of Maine. *See* 28 U.S.C. § 1406(a).

ARGUMENT

I. Venue is Improper

This case implicates two venue statutes. The general venue statute provides that venue is proper in the federal court in which the defendant resides, or in which a substantial part of the events giving rise to suit took place, or, if there is no other forum in which the action may otherwise be brought, any judicial district in which any defendant is subject to personal jurisdiction. *See* 28 U.S.C. § 1391(b). In cases arising from patent infringement, a different statute applies: 28 U.S.C. § 1400(b). That provision requires that the defendant either reside in the district or have committed infringing acts in the district *and* have a regular and established place of business there. *See* id.

"[T]he purpose of statutorily specified venue is [typically] to protect the *defendant* against the risk that a plaintiff will select an unfair or inconvenient place of trial." *Leroy v. Great W. United Corp.*, 443 U.S. 173, 183-84 (1979) (emphasis in original). Neither the provisions of Section 1400(b) nor Section 1391(b) permit venue in the District of Rhode Island based on the facts alleged by Plaintiff. Plaintiff does not—and cannot—allege that Defendants are incorporated in this district, or that they have a regular and established place of business here. Nor has Plaintiff alleged that a substantial part of the events or omissions giving rise to its claims occurred in this district. With respect to the patent claims, Plaintiff fails to allege that Defendants committed infringing acts in this

---

3. As discussed *supra*, the only Defendant identified by Plaintiff that exists as an entity is HIL Technology, Inc., a Maine Corporation. Ex. A at ¶¶ 4, 6-8. However, for the purposes of this motion, Defendants will treat as true Plaintiff's allegations as to the existence of Hydro International, Inc. and Hydro International, plc, which does not alter Defendants' arguments.

district and that they have a regular and established place of business here. Because neither Section 1400(b) nor Section 1391(b) provides a basis for venue in this Court, the action must be dismissed.

A. Legal Standard

When addressing a motion to dismiss for improper venue under Federal Rule of Civil Procedure 12(b)(3), allegations in a plaintiff's complaint may *prima facie* establish that venue is proper. *Banque de la Mediterranee-France, S.A. v. Thergen, Inc.*, 780 F. Supp. 92, 94 (D. R.I. 1992). However, when venue is challenged, the plaintiff bears the burden to show that "venue is proper in the judicial district in which the action has been brought." *Id.*; *see* Fed. R. Civ. P. 12(b)(3); *see also Cordis Corp. v. Cardiac Pacemakers*, 599 F.2d 1085, 1086 (1st Cir. 1979).

A district court lacking proper venue has the discretion either to dismiss or, in the interest of justice, transfer the case to an appropriate district where this defect is avoided. *See* 28 U.S.C. § 1406(a);[4] *see also Goldlawr, Inc. v. Heiman*, 369 U.S. 463, 466 (1962); *Konica Minolta, Inc. v. ICR Co.*, No. 15-1446 (SRC)(CLW), 2015 WL 9308252, at *5 (D.N.J. Dec. 22, 2015).

B. Plaintiff's Patent Infringement Claims Should be Dismissed for Improper Venue

Counts II and III of the Verified Complaint contain claims for patent infringement, and, looking at the Verified Complaint as a whole, these claims clearly are its main focus. *See, e.g.*, Verif. Compl. at 1 (opening the Verified Complaint with the statement that StormTree brings this action "for patent infringement, trademark infringement, and ancillary State law claims. . ."); *see also* ¶¶ 11, 34-39, 42-44, 60-75. In patent infringement cases, an action "may be brought in the judicial district where the defendant resides, or where the defendant has committed acts of infringement and has a regular and established place of business." 28 U.S.C. § 1400(b). As applied to domestic corporations, "reside[nce]" in Section 1400(b) refers only to the State of incorporation. *See TC Heartland LLC v. Kraft Foods Group Brands LLC*, 137 S. Ct. 1514, 1521 (2017); *see also SCVNGR, Inc. v. DailyGobble, Inc.*, 2017 WL 11556738, at *1 (D.R.I. Dec. 27, 2017) (McConnell, J.) (applying patent venue statute to dismiss and transfer patent action against out-of-state defendant). The "regular and established place of business standard requires more than the minimum contacts necessary for establishing personal jurisdiction or for satisfying the doing business standard of the general venue provision." *In re Cray Inc.*, 871 F.3d 1355, 1361 (Fed. Cir. 2017) (citing 28 U.S.C. § 1391(c)).

Here, none of the Defendants is incorporated in Rhode Island or has a place of business in Rhode Island. Defendant Hydro International, Inc. is alleged by Plaintiff to be incorporated in Delaware, with a principal place of business in Portland, Maine; Defendant HIL Technologies, Inc. is incorporated in Maine and has its principal place of business in Portland, Maine; and Defendant Hydro International, plc is alleged by Plaintiff to be a United Kingdom private liability company with a principal place of business in Clevedon, United Kingdom. *See* Verif. Compl. at ¶¶ 2-3. Accordingly, no defendant resides in Rhode Island. *See TC Heartland*, 137 S. Ct. at 1521. Moreover, Defendants are not alleged by Plaintiff to have *any* place of business, let alone a "regular and established place of business" in Rhode Island. *See Cray*, 871 F.3d at 1362-63 (discussing what constitutes a "regular and established place of business," including a physical, geographical location in the district from which business is carried out, steady business activity, and permanence in the district). Defendants have no physical location in Rhode Island from which they conduct business and have no presence in this market, let alone a permanent or "established" one. *See id.*; Ex. A at ¶¶ 10-11.

Thus, Plaintiff has failed to show—because it cannot show—that venue is proper in this district under 28 U.S.C. § 1400(b). Accordingly, Defendants respectfully request that this Court dismiss Plaintiff's patent infringement claims (Counts II and III of the Verified Complaint) on this basis, or alternatively, transfer these claims to the United States District Court for the District of Maine, as discussed in Section IV, below.[5] In addition, as discussed below, Plaintiff's remaining claims also should be dismissed or transferred because venue is improper.

---

4. The relevant provision states that the "district court of a district in which is filed a case laying venue in the wrong division or district shall dismiss, or if it be in the interest of justice, transfer such case to any district or division in which it could have been brought." 28 U.S.C. § 1406(a).

5. Even if this Court finds proper venue over other claims alleged in the Verified Complaint, it should decline to exercise "pendent venue" over the patent infringement claims, which are Plaintiff's primary claims. Courts that have addressed this issue following *TC Heartland LLC v. Kraft Foods Group Brands LLC*, 137 S. Ct. 1514, 1521 (2017), have found that there is no "pendent" venue over a patent infringement claim unless there is "original" venue over a separate patent infringement claim under Section 1400(b). *See, e.g.*, *ARP Wave, LLC v. Salpeter*, 364 F. Supp. 3d 990, 998 (D. Minn. 2019) (refusing to apply the pendent-venue doctrine to a patent infringement claim); *Metuchen Pharm. LLC v. Empower Pharm. LLC*, Civ. A. No. 18-11406 (JLL), 2018 WL 5669151, at *4 (D.N.J. Nov. 1, 2018) (same); *Nat'l Products, Inc. v. Arkon Res., Inc.*, Case No. C15-1984JLR, 2018 WL 1457254, at *7 (W.D. Wash. Mar.

C. Venue Also is Improper on Plaintiff's Trademark Infringement Claim

Venue for trademark infringement claims is governed by the general federal venue statute, 28 U.S.C. § 1391(b), which provides that a civil action may be brought in:

(1) a judicial district in which any defendant resides, if all defendants are residents of the State in which the district is located;

(2) a judicial district in which a substantial part of the events or omissions giving rise to the claim occurred, or a substantial part of property that is the subject of the action is situated; or

(3) if there is no district in which an action may otherwise be brought as provided in this section, any judicial district in which any defendant is subject to the court's personal jurisdiction with respect to such action.

28 U.S.C. § 1391(b)(1)-(3). If a case does not satisfy one of these three categories, then venue is improper and the case "must be dismissed or transferred under 28 U.S.C. § 1406(a)." *DeBarros v. Frank*, 2020 WL 5570005, at *8 (D.R.I. Sept. 17, 2020), *report and recommendation adopted*, 2021 WL 165096 (D.R.I. Jan. 19, 2021). Here, none of these provisions permit venue for Plaintiff's trademark infringement claim (Count IV) in the District of Rhode Island based on the facts alleged by Plaintiff.

Defendants are not residents of Rhode Island, as Plaintiff concedes. *See* Verif. Compl. ¶¶ 2-3; Ex. A at ¶¶ 4, 6-8, 10. Therefore, venue in this district based on Section 1391(b)(1) is not appropriate. Moreover, the Verified Complaint is devoid of any allegations which show that a substantial part of the events underlying the trademark infringement claim took place in Rhode Island. *See Astro-Med, Inc. v. Nihon Kohden Am., Inc.*, 591 F.3d 1, 12 (1st Cir. 2009) (Rhode Island is proper venue if "substantial part of the events . . . giving rise to the claim occurred" there based on a holistic view of entire sequence). Rather, Plaintiff's allegations surrounding the trademark infringement claim relate to activities that took place entirely outside of Rhode Island. *See* Verif. Compl. ¶¶ 45-46 (alleging that in May and June of 2020, Defendants filed an application for the StormScape trademark registration and promoted it on the internet). The key individuals involved in the alleged creation, manufacture, marketing, promotion, distribution, and facilitation of the StormScape product were located in Maine. Ex. A. at ¶¶ 10, 12-13. Additionally, Defendants earn no compensation or profit from sales of the products in question in this district. Ex. A. at ¶ 11. Because the trademark infringement claims lack the requisite connection to this forum, venue based on Section 1391(b)(2) is inappropriate. *See, e.g., Benedict v. Folsted*, C.A. No. 18-242 WES, 2018 WL 3491697, at *3 (D.R.I. July 20, 2018) (holding that when a defendant is not a resident of Rhode Island and the plaintiff does not allege that events giving rise to the claim occurred in Rhode Island, venue does not lie in this district).

Lastly, in light of the above, there is a proper federal venue in which this case may have otherwise been brought: the District of Maine. Defendant HIL Technology, Inc. is a Maine Corporation, and the material events or omissions giving rise to the trademark claim occurred in Maine. *See, e.g.,* Verif. Compl. at ¶¶ 45-46; Ex. A at ¶¶ 4, 12-13.; *see also* 28 U.S.C. § 1391(b)(2). With the District of Maine available as a proper venue, there is no need to resort to 28 U.S.C. § 1391(b)(3) to determine if venue would be appropriate in another district.

Because Defendants are not residents of Rhode Island and the basis for Plaintiff's trademark infringement claim arises in Maine, and because there is an available alternative forum—the United States District Court for the District of Maine—to hear Plaintiff's action, venue of the Plaintiff's trademark infringement claim is improper in this Court under 28 U.S.C. § 1391(b). Accordingly, Defendants respectfully request that this Court dismiss the trademark infringement claim in Count IV of the Verified Complaint, or alternatively, transfer this claim to the United States District Court for the District of Maine.

D. Venue is Improper on Plaintiff's Remaining State Law Claims

For all of the same reasons, venue is improper under Section 1391(b) on Plaintiff's remaining state law claims (Count I – Breach of Nondisclosure Agreement; Count V – Misappropriation of Trade Secrets; and Count VI – Fraud). Again, neither the Defendants nor any of their employees reside in Rhode Island. *See* Verif. Compl. at ¶¶ 2-3; Ex. A. at ¶ 10. Defendants never sold products in Rhode Island using the allegedly confidential information obtained from Plaintiff. Ex. A. at ¶ 11. No substantial part of the acts or omissions giving rise to the state law claims occurred in Rhode Island, and accordingly, venue is improper in this district. *See Benedict v. Folsted*, 2018 WL 3491697, at *3.[6]

23, 2018) (same); *Jenny Yoo Collection, Inc. v. Watters Design Inc.*, 16-CV-2205 (VSB), 2017 WL 4997838, at *7 (S.D.N.Y. Oct. 20, 2017) (same). Thus, this Court should not exercise pendent venue over Plaintiff's patent claims.

6. It is anticipated that Plaintiff will argue that the NDA renders venue proper in this district because it states that "the Parties irrevocably submit to the non-exclusive jurisdiction of the Courts of the State of Rhode Island." Exhibit C to Verified Complaint at ¶ 10. By its own terms, however, that language would only apply if Plaintiff had brought suit in Rhode Island state court, and not federal court as Plaintiff has done here.

II. This Court Lacks Personal Jurisdiction Over Defendants with Respect to Plaintiff's Claims Based on Federal Law

A. Legal Standard

"It is axiomatic that, to hear a case, a court must have personal jurisdiction over the parties, that is, the power to require the parties to obey its decrees." *Hannon v. Beard*, 524 F.3d 275, 279 (1st Cir. 2008) (quotation omitted). It is "presumed that a cause lies outside [the federal courts'] limited jurisdiction, and the burden of establishing the contrary rests upon the party asserting jurisdiction." *Kokkonen* v. *Guardian Life Ins. Co. of Am.*, 511 U.S. 375, 377 (1994) (citations omitted). A court is without authority to adjudicate an action if it lacks personal jurisdiction over the defendant. *Carreras v. PMG Collins, LLC*, 660 F.3d 549, 552 (1st Cir. 2011). On a motion to dismiss for lack of personal jurisdiction under Fed. R. Civ. P. 12(b)(2), it is the plaintiff's burden to prove that jurisdiction exists. *Mass. Sch. of Law at Andover, Inc. v. Am. Bar Ass'n*, 142 F.3d 26, 34 (1st Cir. 1998).

The First Circuit has set forth the standard for ruling on motions to dismiss for lack of personal jurisdiction. "The standard for deciding such motions is commonly referred to as the '*prima facie*' standard." *Microfibres, Inc. v. McDevitt-Askew*, 20 F. Supp. 2d 316, 319 (D.R.I. 1998) (citing *Boit v. Gar–Tec Products, Inc.*, 967 F.2d 671, 675 (1st Cir. 1992)). This requires the court to consider only whether the plaintiff has proffered evidence that is sufficient to support findings of all facts essential to personal jurisdiction. *Id.* "To meet its burden, the plaintiff must establish sufficient facts to support a prima facie case authorizing personal jurisdiction over the defendant under both the forum's long-arm statute and the due process clause of the Constitution." *Id.* (citing *U.S.S. Yachts, Inc. v. Ocean Yachts, Inc.*, 894 F.2d 9, 11 (1st Cir. 1990)) (quotation marks omitted). To make such a showing, a plaintiff "cannot rely solely on conclusory averments, but must adduce evidence of specific facts." *Kuan Chen v. United States Sports Academy, Inc.*, 956 F.3d 45, 54 (1st Cir. 2020) (quotation marks omitted).

B. This Court Lacks General or Specific Jurisdiction with Respect to Plaintiff's Claims for Patent and Trademark Infringement

Whether addressing a diversity case or a federal question case, "a plaintiff must satisfy both the forum state's long-arm statute and the Due Process Clause of the Fourteenth Amendment" to establish personal jurisdiction. *Baskin-Robbins Franchising LLC v. Alpenrose Dairy, Inc.*, 825 F.3d 28, 34 & n.2 (1st Cir. 2016); *see also Microfibres*, 20 F.Supp.2d at 320. Because Rhode Island's long-arm statute is coextensive with the Due Process Clause, the Fourteenth Amendment controls. *See Microfibres*, 20 F.Supp.2d at 320 (citing *Levinger v. Matthew Stuart & Co., Inc.*, 676 F. Supp. 437, 439 (D.R.I. 1988)).

There are two ways of establishing personal jurisdiction: general or specific. *See Cossaboon v. Me. Med. Ctr.*, 600 F.3d 25, 31 (1st Cir. 2010). Plaintiff can establish neither in this case with respect to its patent and trademark infringement claims (Counts II, III, and IV of the Verified Complaint). Accordingly, these claims should be dismissed pursuant to Fed. R. Civ. P. 12(b)(2).

1. Defendants Have Had No "Continuous and Systematic Contacts" with Rhode Island to Establish General Jurisdiction

In order for a court to have general jurisdiction over a defendant, a plaintiff bears the burden of establishing that the defendant has had "continuous and systematic contacts" with the forum. *See Microfibres*, 20 F. Supp. 2d at 320. "Substantial contacts alone are not enough." *Id.* As discussed above, Defendants clearly did not have continuous and systematic contacts with Rhode Island; in fact, they had virtually no contacts at all. *See* Ex. A at ¶¶ 10-11. In fact, Plaintiff's only allegation pertaining to Defendants' "contacts" with Rhode Island is based on the "tortious injury caused by them to Plaintiff in Rhode Island." *See* Verif. Compl. at ¶ 7. Defendants' contacts with Rhode Island essentially were nonexistent, therefore, the doctrine of general jurisdiction does not apply.

2. Plaintiff Has Not Established Specific Jurisdiction Over Defendants with Regard to Its Patent and Trademark Infringement Claims

Likewise, specific jurisdiction over Defendants is lacking in this case. The United States Court of Appeals for the First Circuit has established a three-prong test to determine whether a court has specific jurisdiction over a defendant.

First, the claim underlying the litigation must directly arise out of, or relate to, the defendant's forum-state activities. Second, the defendant's in-state contacts must represent a purposeful availment of the privilege of conducting activities in the forum state, thereby invoking the benefits and protections of that state's laws and making the defendant's involuntary presence before the state's court foreseeable. Third, the exercise of jurisdiction must . . . be reasonable.

Copia Commc'ns, LLC v. AMResorts, L.P., 812 F.3d 1, 4 (1st Cir. 2016) (quotation marks omitted).

a. Relatedness

"Relatedness is the divining rod that separates specific jurisdiction cases from general jurisdiction cases." *Ticketmaster-New York, Inc. v. Alioto*, 26 F.3d 201, 208 (1st Cir. 1994). It "ensures that the element of causation remains in the forefront of the due process investigation." *Id*. In this case, Plaintiff has not pleaded any facts showing that its patent and trademark infringement claims "arise out of, or relate to, [Defendants'] forum-state activities." *Copia Commc'ns*, 812 F.3d at 4 (quotation marks omitted). The alleged facts relate only to events that took place outside of Rhode Island. Plaintiff's claims concern purported infringing products; however, there are no sales of the allegedly infringing products in this jurisdiction, and the products were not marketed in this jurisdiction. Ex. A. at ¶ 11. The element of relatedness is not met. On this basis alone the Court may find that there is no specific jurisdiction over Defendants with respect to these claims.

b. Purposeful Availment

There are "two cornerstones" of purposeful availment: foreseeability and voluntariness. *Ticketmaster*, 26 F.3d at 207-08. A defendant's contacts "must be deliberate and not based on the unilateral actions of another party." *Bluetarp Fin. Inc. v. Matrix Const. Co., Inc.*, 709 F.3d 72, 82 (1st Cir. 2013). Purposeful availment thus equates to a "rough quid pro quo: when a defendant deliberately targets its behavior toward the society or economy of a particular forum, the forum should have the power to subject the defendant to judgment regarding that behavior." *Carreras v. PMG Collins, LLC*, 660 F.3d 549, 555 (1st Cir. 2011). Thus, "random, fortuitous, or attenuated contacts" do not amount to purposeful availment. *Id*. Rather, personal jurisdiction requires that the forum-related contacts "must be of such a nature that the defendant can reasonably foresee being haled into court there." *Id*.

Plaintiff has simply not met its burden to establish that Defendants purposefully availed themselves of this forum. Defendants have no presence in Rhode Island and have not interjected themselves into the local economy as market participants. Defendants do not market in Rhode Island, have no sales in Rhode Island, and thus generate no revenue from Rhode Island. Ex. A. at ¶ 11. Under these facts, it cannot be said that Defendants could have reasonably foreseen that they would be subject to jurisdiction here. *See Cossaboon*, 600 F.3d at 36.

c. Reasonableness

The Supreme Court has "long insisted that the concept of reasonableness must inform a properly performed minimum contacts analysis." *Ticketmaster*, 26 F.3d at 209. Thus, even if "purposefully generated contacts exist, courts must consider a panoply of other factors which bear on the fairness of subjecting a nonresident to the authority of a foreign tribunal." *Id*. (quoting *United Elec., Radio and Mach. Workers of Am. v. 163 Pleasant Street Corp.*, 960 F.2d 1080, 1088 (1st Cir. 1992)). The Supreme Court has identified five reasonableness factors, commonly referred to as "Gestalt" factors:

> (1) the defendant's burden in appearing, (2) the forum state's interest in adjudicating the dispute, (3) the plaintiff's interest in obtaining convenient and effective relief, (4) the judicial system's interest in obtaining the most effective resolution of the controversy, and (5) the common interests of all sovereigns in promoting substantive social policies.

Ticketmaster, 26 F.3d at 209. These factors are employed by the First Circuit to help ensure that a court achieves substantial justice in the exercise of its jurisdiction. *Sawtelle v. Farrell*, 70 F.3d 1381, 1394 (1st Cir. 1995).

Here, in light of Plaintiff's failure to satisfy the first two prongs of specific jurisdiction, it becomes unnecessary to decide whether interests of justice would be served by applying that jurisdiction. *See Microfibres*, 20 F. Supp. 2d at 321 (citing *Sawtelle*, 70 F.3d at 1394) (noting that failure to demonstrate the necessary minimum contacts eliminates the need to reach the issue of reasonableness). Accordingly, the doctrine of specific jurisdiction has no application here.

In this case, the Plaintiff has not pointed to *any* contacts Defendants had with Rhode Island, let alone contacts that are connected to Plaintiff's patent and trademark infringement claims set forth in Counts II, III, and IV of the Verified Complaint. Accordingly, this Court lacks both general and specific personal jurisdiction over Defendants with respect to these claims, and Defendants respectfully request their dismissal.

III. This Court Lacks Subject Matter Jurisdiction Over Plaintiff's Claims Based on State Law

Because Plaintiff's claims based on federal law must be dismissed for the reasons set forth above, there is no basis to exercise pendent subject matter jurisdiction over the state law claims, and they must qualify for jurisdiction on their own. *See* 28 U.S.C. § 1367. As to Plaintiff's claims based on state law (Count I – Breach of Nondisclosure Agreement; Count V – Misappropriation of Trade Secrets; and Count VI – Fraud), Plaintiff seeks to ground this Court's subject matter jurisdiction in diversity. *See* Verif. Compl. at ¶ 6 (citing 28 U.S.C. § 1332 as a basis for subject matter jurisdiction). However, Plaintiff's jurisdictional allegations are patently insufficient to invoke diversity jurisdiction. While it does appear that there is diversity of citizenship among the parties, the Verified Complaint is devoid of any allegations establishing that the amount in controversy in this case exceeds the $75,000 jurisdictional threshold.

A. Legal Standard

The federal district courts "shall have original jurisdiction of all civil actions where the matter in controversy exceeds the sum or value of $75,000, exclusive of interest and costs, and is between . . . citizens of different states." 28 U.S.C. § 1332(a)(1). A party invoking diversity jurisdiction carries the burden to establish that the minimum amount in controversy has been met. *See Abdel-Aleem v. OPK Biotech LLC*, 665 F.3d 38, 41 (1st Cir. 2012). Lack of subject matter jurisdiction is an affirmative defense that a defendant may assert in a motion to dismiss. *See Flaquer v. Bevilacqua*, 2009 WL 1873799, at *2 (D.R.I. June 29, 2009).

B. Plaintiff Has Failed to Plead the Requisite Amount in Controversy with Respect to Its State Law Claims

With Plaintiff's federal claims against Defendants eliminated, the Court's subject matter jurisdiction over Plaintiff's state law claims, if any, could only be based on diversity jurisdiction under 28 U.S.C. § 1332(a). With regard to that provision's amount-in-controversy requirement, a plaintiff's "general allegation of damages that meet the amount requirement suffices unless questioned by the opposing party or the court." *Abdel-Aleem*, 665 F.3d at 41-42 (quotation marks omitted). Once the opposing party has questioned the amount—as Defendants do here— the burden shifts to the party seeking to invoke jurisdiction to allege "with sufficient particularity facts indicating that it is not a legal certainty that the claim involves less than the jurisdictional amount." *Id.* (quotation marks omitted). Here, however, Plaintiff has made no allegation *whatsoever* that its damages with respect to its state law claims exceed the amount in controversy minimum, nor can it satisfy its burden with sufficient particularity.

Although "the First Circuit has not yet articulated the defendant's burden of proving the amount in controversy where the plaintiff has not claimed a specific amount of damages in the pleadings," *Ise v. Harborside Rhode Island Ltd. P'ship*, 875 F. Supp. 2d 107, 108 (D.R.I. 2012), it is clear to a legal certainty that the claims here involve less than the jurisdictional amount. Although it may be true that Plaintiff seeks "exemplary damages," "prejudgment interest," and "costs [and] attorneys' fees" for its claims brought under state law—*see* Verif. Compl. at 26—Plaintiff never articulates the damages that might flow from these secondary forms of relief. Absent any theory or even passing reference to the amount in controversy, none of these claimed damages would "bring damages within shouting distance of the amount in controversy requirement." *Ise*, 875 F. Supp. 2d at 107.

Because Plaintiff has not plausibly alleged an amount in controversy more than $75,000, this Court lacks subject matter jurisdiction over Plaintiff's claims based on state law. Accordingly, Defendants respectfully request that Counts I, V, and VI of the Verified Complaint be dismissed.

IV. Transfer to the Maine Federal District Court is in the Interest of Justice

For all the reasons discussed *supra*, venue and jurisdiction are improper in this district. Pursuant to 28 U.S.C. § 1406, when venue is improper, the Court "shall dismiss, or if it be in the interest of justice, transfer such case to any district or division in which it could have been brought." 28 U.S.C. § 1406(a). If, on finding that venue in this District is improper, this Court finds it "in the interest of justice" to transfer this case, Defendants respectfully request a transfer to the District of Maine—the district where they reside, where a substantial part of the events giving rise to suit allegedly took place, and where venue is proper. *See* 28 U.S.C. § 1406(a); *DailyGobble*, 2017 WL 11556738, at *1.

CONCLUSION

For all of the foregoing reasons, Defendants respectfully request that this Court dismiss Plaintiff's Verified Complaint. Alternatively, if the Court believes that outright dismissal is inappropriate, Defendants request that it transfer this case to the United States District Court for the District of Maine.

Dated: February 5, 2021

Respectfully submitted,

/s/ James R. Oswald

James R. Oswald, Bar No. 5727

ADLER POLLOCK & SHEEHAN P.C.

One Citizens Plaza, 8th Floor

Providence, RI 02903

(401) 274-7200

joswald@apslaw.com

/s/ Daniel J. Mitchell

Daniel J. Mitchell, *pro hac vice*

Edward J. Sackman, *pro hac vice*

BERNSTEIN SHUR

100 Middle St

PO Box 9729

Portland, ME 04104-5029

(207) 774-1200

dmitchell@bernsteunshur.com

nsackman@bernsteinshur.com

Attorneys for Defendants

Motion for Summary Judgment

2020 WL 8993137 (D.Me.)

United States District Court, D. Maine.

Douglas BURKA, M.D., an Individual residing in the State of Maryland, Plaintiff,

v.

GARRISON PROPERTY AND CASUALTY INSURANCE COMPANY, and United Services Automobile Association Insurance Company, foreign insurers doing business in the State of Maine, Defendants.

No. 2:20-cv-00172-DBH.

September 16, 2020.

Defendants' Motion for Summary Judgment Pursuant to Fed. R. Civ. P. 56

Garrison Property and Casualty Company and United Services Automobile Association Insurance Company, By Their Attorneys, Getman, Schulthess, Steere & Poulin, P.A., Elizabeth L. Hurley, Esq., ME Bar #005838, 1838 Elm Street, Manchester, NH 03104, (603) 634-4300, ehurley@gssp-lawyers.com.

NOW COME the Defendants, Garrison Property and Casualty Insurance Company ("Garrison") and United Services Automobile Association Insurance Company ("USAA"), by and through their counsel, Getman, Schulthess, Steere & Poulin, P.A., and pursuant to Fed. R. Civ. P. 56, move for entry of summary judgment in their favor as to all claims in the above-captioned matter for the following reasons:

1.   In this litigation the plaintiff, Douglas Burka, seeks a ruling that he is entitled to reimbursement from the defendants, Garrison and USAA (collectively "USAA/Garrison"), for litigation costs and attorneys' fees incurred in the defense of two lawsuits that were filed against him.

2.   One of the lawsuits was filed by Douglas Burka's former wife, Allison Burka ("Allison"), in Cumberland County Superior Court, State of Maine. *Allison Burka v. Douglas Burka*, Cumberland County Superior Court, No. 16-CV-20 ("the Maine Lawsuit"). In that lawsuit, Allison alleged that Douglas Burka engaged in emotionally abusive and controlling conduct, obtained unauthorized access to her medical records in Maine, obtained unauthorized access to her online accounts while she was a resident of Maine and invaded her privacy in the couple's home in Maine.

3.   The second lawsuit was filed by Allison (under her maiden name Cayne) and her parents, Howard N. Cayne and Caroline K. Cayne, against both Douglas Burka and his father, Steven A. Burka, M.D., in the Montgomery County Circuit Court, State of Maryland. *Howard N. Cayne, Caroline K. Cayne and Allison Cayne v. Steven A. Burka, M.D. and Douglas Burka, M.D.*, Montgomery County Circuit Court, No. 415273-V ("the Maryland Lawsuit"). In this lawsuit, the plaintiffs alleged that the defendants knowingly obtained their medical records under false pretenses and through deception and knowingly disclosed their medical records without authorization. They alleged that the defendants' conduct constituted criminal violations of Maryland law and the federal Health Insurance Portability and Accountability Act (HIPAA). The plaintiffs claimed that the defendants acted with evil motive, ill will and intent to injure them.

4.   During the relevant time period, Douglas Burka was the named insured under a Dwelling Policy, a Homeowner Policy and a Renters Policy issued to him in Maine by USAA/Garrison and a Renters policy issued to him by USAA/Garrison in Maryland. USAA/Garrison denied any duty to defend or indemnify Douglas Burka in the two lawsuits based on several policy provisions and exclusions.

5.   Douglas Burka claims that he incurred more than $700,000 in legal fees, together with credit card interest. He is seeking over $1,000,000 in damages, including interest, against USAA/Garrison based on alleged Breach of Contract (Count I), Breach of 24 M.R.S.A. § 2436 (Count II) and Breach of 24 M.R.S.A. § 2436-A (Count III).

6.   The Complaint filed by Douglas Burka against USAA/Garrison does not set forth any factual basis for claiming that he was entitled to a defense under any of the policies and does not cite any policy provisions under which coverage should have been provided. Instead, Douglas Burka relies exclusively on a September 18, 2019 letter sent to him by USAA/Garrison long after the two lawsuits were settled and all defense costs had already been incurred.

7.   The parties have agreed that the Maine Dwelling Policy, Maine Homeowner Policy and Maryland Renters Policy do not afford coverage for the claims, and that the only policy at issue in this dispute is the Maine Renters Policy. Thus, the sole issue before the Court is whether USAA/Garrison had a duty to defend Douglas Burka in the Maine Lawsuit and/or Maryland Lawsuit under the Maine Renters Policy.

8.   Summary judgment should be granted when "there is no genuine dispute as to any material fact and the movant is entitled to judgment as a matter of law." Fed. R. Civ. P. 56(a).

9.   In Maine, whether an insurer owes a duty to defend is a question of law. *City of South Portland v. Maine Municipal Assoc. Property & Casualty Pool*, 158 A.3d 11, 13 (Me. 2017). In order to determine whether there is a duty to defend, the Court must compare the insurance policy with the complaint against the insured to determine whether there is "any legal or factual basis that could potentially be developed at trial and result in an award of damages covered by the terms of the policy." *Id*. at 14, *quoting Harlor v. Amica Mutual Ins. Co.*, 150 A.3d 793, 797 (Me. 2016).

10.   "While broad, the duty to defend is not without limits." *True North Maine, Inc. v. Liberty Mutual Ins. Co.*, 2019 U.S. Dist. LEXIS 25767, *9, 2019 WL 691772 (D. Me. Feb. 19, 2019). "[T]he Maine Supreme Judicial Court's directive against 'conjur[ing] the duty to defend from speculation or supposition' hints at a concern that its broad doctrine is susceptible to over-extension." *Medical Mutual Ins. Co. v. Burka*, 899 F.3d at 72, *quoting Barnie's Bar & Grill, Inc. v. United States Liability Ins. Co.*, 2016 ME 181, 152 A.3d 613, 615 (2016). "Put simply, the obligation to resolve doubts in favor of the insured does not mean that courts should make generalized assumptions in favor of coverage." *Id*.

11.   This Court should grant summary judgment in favor of USAA/Garrison because (1) the Maine Renters policy did not afford coverage for the claims asserted by the plaintiffs in the two lawsuits for the reasons set forth in the accompanying Memorandum of Law and, therefore, there was no duty to defend; and (2) the September 18, 2019 letter sent by USAA/Garrison after the case was settled and all litigation expenses had been incurred does not give rise to an obligation to reimburse Douglas Burka for those expenses where there was no duty to provide coverage under the policies.

12.   Since USAA/Garrison did not have a duty to defend, there was no breach of contract (Count I), nor was there any unfair claims settlement practice in violation of 24 M.R.S.A. § 2436 (Count II) or interest owed on overdue payments under 24 M.R.S.A. § 2436-A (Count III).

13.   A supporting Memorandum of Law accompanies this Motion in accordance with the requirements of Local Rule 7(a).

14.   Due to the dispositive nature of this motion, concurrence of opposing counsel has not been requested.

WHEREFORE, the Defendants, Garrison Property and Casualty Insurance Company and United Services Automobile Association Insurance Company, respectfully request that this Honorable Court:

   A.   Grant summary judgment in their favor as to Counts I, II, and III;

   B.   Schedule a hearing to address the Motion for Summary Judgment; and

   C.   Grant such other relief as may be just and equitable.

Dated: September 15, 2020

Respectfully submitted,

GARRISON PROPERTY AND CASUALTY COMPANY and UNITED SERVICES AUTOMOBILE ASSOCIATION INSURANCE COMPANY

By Their Attorneys,

Getman, Schulthess, Steere & Poulin, P.A.

By: */s/ Elizabeth L. Hurley*

Elizabeth L. Hurley, Esq.

ME Bar #005838

1838 Elm Street

Manchester, NH 03104

(603) 634-4300

ehurley@gssp-lawyers.com

Motion for Sanctions

2018 WL 3104356 (D.Me.)

United States District Court, D. Maine.

Alan J. PERRY, Nina E. Perry and Laura A. Perry, Plaintiffs,

v.

Juliet ALEXANDER, Individually and as Trustee of Jupiter Maine Realty Trust and Peter Tinkham, Individually and as Trustee of Jupiter Realty Trust and as Trustee of Samantha Louise Tinkham Irrevocable Special Needs Trust, Defendants.

No. 15-310-GZS.

February 15, 2018.

Plaintiffs' Motion to Enforce Settlement Agreement and for Sanctions

Christopher C. Dinan, for plaintiff Alan Perry.

Edward L. Dilworth III, for plaintiffs Laura Perry and Nina Perry.

The Court determined in its January 19, 2018 Order that there was a settlement in this matter and denied the motions for sanctions each party filed when the settlement was not concluded. Since the Order, the Defendants have again refused to sign the release and deed to the Weld cottage that would allow the settlement to be effected. The Defendants, as such, have again repudiated the settlement.

Given the Court's finding and the Defendants' repudiation, the only realistic options for the Plaintiffs are to seek to enforce the agreement (by motion or by separate action) or move to reopen the proceedings by placing it on a trial list. Plaintiffs Alan Perry, Nina Perry and Laura Perry move for an Order which will enforce settlement and effectuate the terms of the agreement. *See Dankese v. Defense Logistics Agency*, 693 F.2d 13 (1st Cir. 1982). First, Plaintiffs ask this Court for an Order which establishes that the Universal Settlement Agreement and Release of All Claims previously signed by Plaintiffs is deemed fully and properly executed by the Defendants -- even though Defendants have refused to sign it. Second, Plaintiffs ask that the Order state that the quitclaim deed (attached) releasing all interest of the Defendants in the Weld cottage to Laura A. Perry is deemed signed by Defendants and that it shall be deemed sufficient for recording by the Franklin County Registry of Deeds. Third, Plaintiffs seek all costs and attorney fees they have incurred from the time of Defendants' initial breach in August of 2017 until there is a final judgment in both the 2012 and 2015 cases, as those were both to have concluded pursuant to the settlement agreement. Such fees should be directed to be paid by Arbella Insurance Company and be offset from the $80,000 that Arbella is to pay Defendants in the settlement. This includes a request for all attorney fees and costs that may be incurred in any appeal of those cases. Such an Order is appropriate not only due to Defendants' breach, but is also appropriate so that Defendants are aware of the stakes if they, as threatened, appeal any aspect of these cases.

PROCEDURAL HISTORY POST-ORDER

On January 19, 2018, the Court issued an Order denying the parties' cross-motions for sanctions and finding that the parties had entered into a "valid, binding agreement to resolve their claims against each other and conclude this matter" on July 26, 2017. *See Order*, Doc. No. 238, p. 11. In response, Plaintiff Alan Perry's attorney contacted Defendants in an effort to effectuate the agreement. On January 25, 2018, Attorney Christopher Dinan sent the following correspondence to the Defendant (by email and USPS):

Dear Ms. Alexander and Mr. Tinkham,

I assume you are now in receipt of the recent Order denying all Motions for Sanctions and concluding that the case is settled. Attached to the emailed version of this letter and enclosed with the mailed version is the Release that the Plaintiffs in this matter signed.

Please advise if you are willing to sign this and any necessary, related documents to complete the settlement. If you are, I will determine if the insurers remain willing to abide by its terms.

If you do not let us know your position by February 2, 2018, we will assume that you are unwilling to proceed with the settlement and will file an appropriate motion with the court. I will look forward to hearing from you promptly. In responding, please use e-mail so there is no unnecessary delay or confusion by slow mail delivery.

See Doc. No. 240-1 and attached Affidavit of Christopher C. Dinan.

Defendants filed what they called a "Motion for Judicial Aid in Settlement" which was docketed on January 22, 2018. *See* Doc. No. 239-1. In that Motion, Defendants assert that they need "funds" to pay for an attorney in the declaratory judgment action brought by ALPS Insurance and pending in this court. Of course, that matter was also to have been dismissed if the Defendants completed the settlement in this matter. Ultimately, Defendants appear to be asking the court to enforce the monetary side of the settlement while disregarding all other pertinent material terms. It goes without saying that this suggestion is unacceptable to Plaintiffs, and inconsistent with the settlement that the court has determined was reached.

On January 31, 2018, Defendants filed a letter along with a series of documents, apparently in response to Attorney Dinan's email. The Defendants' filing included Attorney Dinan's email to Defendants (Doc. No. 204-1), emails between Defendants and their attorney concerning settlement (Doc. No. 240-2), Defendants redacted and signed agreement (Doc. No. 240-3), "Appellants' Response to Appellees' Resurrected Motion to Dismiss" (Doc. No. 240-4), and the envelope (Doc. No. 240-5). Defendants' redacted and revised version of the release makes clear that Defendants have no intention of abiding by the Order issued by this Court.

In its January 19, 2018 Order, the Court reviewed the evidence presented at the October 27, 2017 hearing and determined that there had been a binding and enforceable settlement and that the material terms included: (1) a payment of $80,000 to Defendants; (2) a payment of $80,000 to Plaintiffs; (3) Plaintiff Laura Perry would own the cottage in Weld, Maine; (4) Plaintiffs would provide Defendants with information concerning the death of Auburn Perry, Sr.; (5) Plaintiffs would make a good faith effort to return to Defendants certain items given by Samantha Tinkham to Auburn Perry, Sr.; (6) there would be a mutual release of all claims in this litigation; (7) Defendants would release any claims they might have against the Estate of Auburn Perry, Sr.; and (8) Defendants would release any prospective claims they might have against the Estate of Laura Perry upon her passing. *See Order*, Doc. No. 238, p. 11-12.

ARGUMENT

I. ENFORCEMENT OF THE SETTLEMENT

There is no longer a question concerning whether the parties entered into a binding settlement agreement in July of 2017. This Court determined that as of July 26, 2017, the parties entered into a binding and enforceable agreement. In addition, the Court specifically defined which material terms were part of that settlement. Because the Plaintiffs cannot implement the terms of the settlement absent a signed release and a signed quitclaim deed, Defendants' refusal constitutes repudiation.

The Plaintiffs' primary concern is enforcement of that settlement when Defendants refuse to sign either the release that represents the crux of the agreement or the deed to the Weld cottage. Defendants' actions have made clear that they will not sign. The only "agreement" that they have signed eliminates the bulk of the settlement's material terms. The manner in which the Defendants have approached this issue reflects no consideration of the Plaintiffs' position, of the Court's findings, or of the devastating impact that their failure to participate on October 27, 2017 had on their position.

In the "agreement" that they signed, Defendants refuse to acknowledge that the 2012 case and the 2015 case were both settled and represent that they only agree to release what they deem "triable" claims in the 2015 case. Defendants redacted any mention of the 2012 case from the release. Defendants also removed the terms releasing their claims against the estates of Auburn Perry, Sr. and Laura Perry. In addition, Defendants redacted the provision concerning Laura Perry's ownership of the Weld Cottage. These and all other "revisions" do not represent the bargained-for exchange that was negotiated by the parties in July of 2017.

The First Circuit has held that "a party to a settlement agreement may seek to enforce the agreement's terms when the other party refuses to comply. Where . . . the settlement collapses before the original suit is dismissed, the party seeking enforcement may file a motion with the trial court." *Fid. & Guar. Ins. Co. v. Star Equip. Corp.*, 541 F.3d 1, 5 (1st Cir. 2008). Moreover, it is well within the court's authority to enforce an agreement through the entry of judgment incorporating the terms previously agreed to by the parties. *See Muther v. Broad Cove Shore Ass'n*, 2009 ME 37, ¶ 8, 968 A.2d 539. The Plaintiffs ask the Court to do just that.

In other to protect themselves from future litigation, Plaintiffs ask this Court to issue an order enforcing the material terms of the settlement agreement. In particular, Plaintiffs seek an Order declaring the release shall be treated as if signed by both parties. This will protect Plaintiffs, among other things, from future litigation concerning the estates of Auburn Perry, Sr. and Laura Perry as well as relitigation of any claims which were brought or could have been brought in the 2012 or 2015 cases. Moreover, in order to ensure the Weld cottage is properly transferred to Laura Perry, Plaintiffs request the order state that the quitclaim deed shall be treated for all intents and purposes, including for recording, as if signed by Defendants.

II. REQUEST FOR SANCTIONS

The federal district court has inherent power to impose attorney fees as a sanction when a party shows bad faith by hampering the enforcement of a court order. *See Chambers v. NASCO, Inc.*, 501 U.S. 32, 46 (1991). "The mildest [form of sanctions] is an order to reimburse the opposing party for expenses caused by the failure to cooperate. ...Harshest of all are orders of dismissal and default judgment." *Cine Forty-Second Street Theatre Corp. v. Allied Artists Pictures Corp.*, 602 F.2d 1062, 1066 (2nd Cir. 1979). *See also In re Emanuel*, 422 B.R. 453, 464 (Bankr. S.D.N.Y. 2010) (an award for reasonable attorneys' fees and expenses incurred "is the mildest form of sanctions").

While this Court has rejected the parties' dueling motions for sanctions previously, the Plaintiffs previously sought only the harshest of sanctions. They now seek the mildest form of sanctions -- fees. All of the steps that were taken concerning the Plaintiffs' Motion for Sanctions were necessary to the pending Motion to Enforce. The evidentiary hearing and the conferences concerning status and evidence all related to a determination of whether there was a settlement, which is an element of all the motions before the Court. In short, the Plaintiffs' fees since the end of July are caused by the Defendants' breach of their settlement agreement.

Maine's Law Court has held that the imposition of attorney fees may be awarded as a sanction when a litigant has acted with significant bad faith. *Linscott v. Foy*, 1998 ME 206, ¶ 17, 716 A.2d 1017. For example, in *Linscott v. Foy*, the Law Court found that the trial court did not abuse its discretion by awarding attorney fees as a sanction when the trial court found, after an evidentiary hearing, that Foy failed to perform his part of the agreement. It entered judgment in favor of Linscott and directed Foy to close the transaction in accordance with the terms of the agreement. *Id.* Foy did not comply with the court's order and refused to transfer the stock. *Id.* ¶ 5. In addition, Foy filed two lawsuits in different jurisdictions seeking to upend the settlement agreement. Id ¶ 6.

In finding that Foy's actions were "unquestionably egregious," the Court awarded Linscott attorney fees as a sanction against Foy. *Id.* ¶ 18. The Court reasoned that because Foy repeatedly refused to comply with a final order of the court, filed various frivolous motions in other courts, and failed to execute the releases contemplated by the settlement agreement to end the "expensive and time-consuming litigation," attorney fees were an appropriate sanction. *Id.* The court noted that it had "no difficulty concluding that these actions were undertaken in bad faith and were abusive of the court and the other parties, thereby providing the court with authority to consider imposition of attorney fees." *Id.* ¶ 19. And, finally, the court concluded that the appropriate award of attorney fees should include all fees and costs that would not have been generated but for Foy's refusal to comply with the court's order. *Id.*

Here, Defendants' conduct has also been egregious, not only in its post-settlement conduct but throughout the litigation. The Defendants refused in August, 2017 to sign the settlement agreement drafted by their counsel. They then refused to participate in the evidentiary hearing, asking that the court adopt a special procedure to review their submissions without the participations of the Plaintiffs. After the court determined that there was a settlement, they again refused to complete documentation of the settlement, instead filing materials with the court that were inconsistent with the status of the case and the procedural rules. They repeatedly use mocking language such as "80 large" and insult the process by crossing off huge swaths of the settlement agreement.

Due to the Defendants' actions, Plaintiffs have been denied the resolution for which they bargained, and have expended a significant amount of money litigating the enforceability of the settlement just to obtain that for which they originally bargained. But for Defendants' conduct, those costs and fees would not have been generated and all cases would have been dismissed by Labor Day, 2017.

Since the Defendants reneged on the settlement in early August of 2017, there have been 55 docket entries in this case. Defendants authorized their counsel to notify the Court that a settlement had been reached between the parties and then refused to sign the release giving effect to that settlement. This left Plaintiffs with few choices, other than to litigate further in some fashion. Plaintiffs subsequently filed a Motion for Sanctions which depended on a determination that there had been a settlement, which required a testimonial hearing, for which Plaintiffs had to subpoena two out-of-state attorneys who each traveled one hundred miles or more to attend -- a hearing that Defendants refused to attend but hand-delivered documents for the court's review *while the Plaintiffs were inside the courtroom presenting evidence to support the enforceability of the agreement*. Defendants then filed their fourth interlocutory appeal on the Court's Order denying their Request to Appoint Counsel, which frustratingly remains pending despite Plaintiffs' multiple filings, including a Motion to Dismiss. The Defendants' conduct is a match for the conduct in *Linscott* which was found to be egregious, and sufficient for the sanction of fees and costs.

In sum, the Plaintiffs ask this Court to sanction the Defendants by requiring they pay the attorney fees and other costs incurred by Plaintiffs from August 2017 to present. The Court has the inherent power to issue such a sanction due to the egregiousness of

Defendants' repeated contumacious conduct. It is unjust to require Plaintiffs to suffer the financial consequences of Defendants' continued misconduct. Therefore, Plaintiffs ask this Court to so sanction the Defendants and direct that such fees and costs be paid by Arbella Insurance from the funds set aside to Defendants. Only in this fashion can Plaintiffs avoid the necessity of separately filing for trustee process or pursuing attachment of Defendants' real estate holdings.

For the same reasons, Plaintiffs ask this Court to include in its order a provision requiring Defendants to pay any fees or costs incurred by Plaintiffs if the Defendants decide to appeal. Given Defendants' history in this litigation and in others, Plaintiffs anticipate an appeal upon this court's final ruling. Plaintiffs will incur additional expenses responding to this appeal and the numerous motions that will undoubtedly follow, all of which would not have occurred if Defendants completed the settlement to which they agreed. In an effort to deter such conduct and to be certain Defendants are aware of the stakes if they appeal, Plaintiffs ask this Court to prospectively award attorney fees and costs for any appeal or subsequent motions filed by Defendants.

CONCLUSION

For the foregoing reasons, Plaintiffs ask for this Court's assistance in implementing the settlement. Plaintiffs request a comprehensive order which can be used to foreclose further litigation by Defendants as to the issues addressed by the settlement agreement. Moreover, Plaintiffs seek an Order that will allow the transfer of the Weld property to Laura Perry pursuant to the agreement, despite the Defendants' refusal to sign the deed consistent with the agreement they made. Plaintiffs ask the Court to declare the quitclaim deed be deemed to be signed by the Defendants such that Laura Perry may appropriately record the deed. Finally, Plaintiffs ask this Court to award them attorney fees and costs incurred enforcing this settlement,[1] including the likely appeals to be filed by Defendants, as a sanction against Defendants for their breach of the settlement agreement and repeated abuse of the court system.

Dated: February 15, 2018

/s/ Christopher C. Dinan

Christopher C. Dinan

Attorney for Plaintiff Alan Perry

Dated: February 15, 2018

/s/ Edward L. Dilworth III

Edward L. Dilworth III

Attorney for Plaintiffs Laura Perry and Nina Perry

---

1. Plaintiffs will file a fee affidavit/application upon the Court's request or when judgment is final, whichever is sooner.

Motion to Compel Discovery

2010 WL 5889070 (D.Me.)

Westlaw Query>>

To find more Motion to Compel Discovery filings on Westlaw: access Maine Trial Court Documents (from the Home page, click Trial Court Documents, then Maine), click the Advanced Search link, select Motion to Compel, and click Search. Use the Jurisdiction filter on the left to narrow results to Federal.

United States District Court, D. Maine.

FRONTIER COMMUNICATIONS CORPORATION, Plaintiff,

v.

BARRETT PAVING MATERIALS, INC., et al., Defendants.

No. 1:07-cv-00113-GZS.

March 29, 2010.

Plaintiff Frontier Communications Corporation's Motion to Compel Discovery

Martha C. Gaythwaite, Friedman Gaythwaite Wolf & Leavitt, Six City Center, P.O. Box 4726, Portland, ME 04112-4726, (207) 761-0900, Of Counsel: John S. Hahn, Jay C. Johnson, Mayer Brown LLP, 1909 K Street, NW, Washington, DC 20006-1101, (202) 263-3000.

Pursuant to the Federal Rules of Civil Procedure, the Local Rules of this Court and the Magistrate's March 17, 2010 Order, Plaintiff Frontier Communications Corporation ("Frontier") respectfully files this motion to compel Defendant UGI Utilities, Inc. ("UGI") to respond to certain discovery requests in this litigation.

INTRODUCTION

This motion has become necessary for two reasons. First, although UGI at various times has asserted that it produced "all" of the documents in its possession that it considers responsive, it recently produced additional documents that were "inadvertently omitted" from its prior productions. These omissions, combined with the age and nature of the documents at issue, justify tailored discovery into UGI's document storage and handling practices. UGI's document production methodology is a black box--even to its own counsel--and without some discovery, there can be no assurance that UGI's production is complete.

Second, UGI has argued that its summary judgment motion in this case should be granted because it has won summary judgment in other cases that involved comparable allegations. Yet UGI has objected to all discovery requests regarding these "similar" cases, flatly refusing to produce documents or answer interrogatories. This refusal is inconsistent with UGI's reliance on the fact that it has prevailed in other cases involving ownership and operation of manufactured gas plants. If UGI's victories matter here, then the facts underlying those victories are also relevant for discovery purposes.

BACKGROUND

Almost one year ago, in compliance with a court-imposed deadline for submitting "early dispositive motions," Defendant CenterPoint Energy Resources filed a motion for summary judgment premised on some of the same legal theories now being advanced by UGI. The Court granted that motion last September. *See* Docket No. 164. The next day, the Magistrate ordered that a years-long stay of discovery should be lifted. *See* Docket No. 165 at 14.

Weeks later, UGI filed its own summary judgment motion. *See* Docket No. 172. Although UGI's motion was not filed before the deadline for early dispositive motions, and it had not participated in any discovery in this case, UGI claimed that it already had produced all relevant documents in its possession. Nevertheless, Frontier sent interrogatories and requests for the production of documents to UGI on November 25, 2009. *See* Docket No. 188 at 2 n.2. Frontier had to file its opposition to UGI's summary judgment motion without the benefit of taking any discovery in this case. *See* Docket No. 183 (filed Dec. 8, 2009).

In response to Frontier's discovery, UGI apparently "discovered some additional documents" that it had "inadvertently omitted" from previous productions. *Id.*; *see also* UGI's Responses to Plaintiff's Request for Production (attached as Ex. A) at 2. UGI also refused to answer numerous interrogatories and requests for production that it claimed were "not reasonably calculated to lead to admissible evidence." Ex. A at 2, 3, 7-10; UGI's Answers to Plaintiff's First Set of Interrogatories (attached as Ex. B) at 10, 21-24. Most of these discovery requests seek information or documents related to other cases in which UGI had been accused of operating a manufactured gas plant under circumstances similar to the case at bar.

During a conference with the Magistrate, Frontier was given permission to file a motion to compel UGI to respond to those discovery requests that may be relevant to its summary judgment opposition. *See* Docket No. 205.

On March 25, 2010, UGI provided Frontier with a "certification" outlining its efforts to look for documents responsive to Frontier's discovery requests. Thereafter counsel for Frontier and UGI exchanged emails and participated in conference calls in an effort to resolve their discovery dispute. Despite those efforts, the parties have not been able to resolve the discovery dispute.

ARGUMENT

In the First Circuit, "[t]he scope of discovery is broad, and to be discoverable, information need only appear to be reasonably calculated to lead to the discovery of admissible evidence." *Remexcel Managerial Consultants, Inc. v. Arelquin*, 583 F.3d 45, 52 (1st Cir. 2009) (internal quotations marks and citations omitted). A party that refuses to produce information that is discoverable under this standard may be compelled to comply with proper discovery requests. *See* Fed. R. Civ. P. 37(a)(3)(B).

A. Frontier should be permitted to conduct tailored discovery of UGI's document production procedures.

The documents at issue in this case consist primarily of corporate records dating to the 1920s and 30s. Approximately seven years ago, UGI produced initial batches of responsive documents during the earliest stages of a prior, related case (02-cv-0183). When moving for summary judgment in this case last year, it claimed that "[i]n March 2003, UGI produced (and subsequently supplemented) *all documents in its possession* referring to [Bangor Gas Light Company]," the former owner of the manufactured gas plant here at issue. *See* Docket No. 172 at 2 n.4 (emphasis added). That representation proved inaccurate, however, when Frontier served its initial round of document requests in the present case.

UGI's responses to Frontier's document requests state in several places that "[u]pon further review," it "discovered" documents that were *not* turned over to Frontier in March 2003 or in any supplemental production in the prior case. Ex. A at 2. UGI further acknowledged in its summary judgment reply brief that it "inadvertently omitted" a number of "additional documents" from its original productions. Docket No. 188 at 2 n2. In an effort to clarify the scope and completeness of its document production, UGI's outside counsel transmitted a "certification" letter to Frontier's outside counsel on March 25, 2010. *See* Ex. C (Letter from E. Tupper Kinder to Martha Gaythwaite (Mar. 25, 2010)).

The certification letter provided by UGI's counsel does not shed any additional light on the company's document search and retrieval process. Instead of providing details about the document search process, the letter simply asserts that UGI reviewed "all historical and other records . . . that could conceivably contain reference to the Bangor Gas Light Company or its operations . . . ." *Id.* at 1. Neither does the letter explain how some documents were "inadvertently omitted" from this original search and the resulting 2003 document production. *Id.* at 2. Consequently, the "certification" made by UGI's counsel contains no information that would give Frontier any comfort regarding the completeness of UGI's document production.

In follow up communications in an effort to resolve the discovery dispute, and better understand the certification letter, Frontier learned that UGI simply looked for documents that mentioned the word Bangor or Bangor MGP. However, for reasons that remain unclear, the "inadvertently omitted" documents were not initially produced even though they refer to Bangor. When asked for an explanation, UGI stated that, "consistency probably suggested that any annual report that mentioned Bangor should be produced." March 29, 2010 email Communication from Attorney Kinder. Since UGI had claimed that it had searched for all documents that mentioned Bangor or the Bangor MGP, this reference to consistency is a confusing *non sequitur*.

B. UGI's production criteria excludes potentially responsive documents.

The substance of UGI's document production also falls short of the legal standard for responsiveness. UGI's response to Frontier's document requests is carefully worded. Never does UGI state that it has produced all responsive documents. Rather, it describes the production of documents that "contain reference to the Bangor Gas Light Company or the Bangor MGP." Ex. A at 2, 3, 4; *see* Docket No. 188 at 2 n.2. UGI apparently made no effort to produce documents responsive to Frontier's requests that did not explicitly mention Bangor Gas Light Company or the Bangor MGP. So, for example, if there are documents in UGI's archives that "relate to" the Bangor Gas Light Company (Frontier's third document request in Ex. A), but do not explicitly mention the company's name, they apparently were not produced.

UGI's certification letter adds to the confusion. Contrary to the narrow statements in UGI's discovery responses, the letter's second sentence represents that UGI has produced "all documents known to be in UGI's possession that relate to the Bangor Gas Light Company or its operations . . . ." Ex. C at 1. But when Frontier's counsel pressed this point during a recent call with UGI's outside counsel, the latter conceded that, to his knowledge, the only documents produced were those that explicitly mentioned Bangor Gas Light Company or the Bangor manufactured gas plant.

At this point, the only way to ensure the completeness of UGI's document production is to give Frontier an opportunity to explore exactly what efforts UGI made to find responsive documents. Again, this could be achieved with a tailored deposition of relevant UGI personnel familiar with decisions made during the production process. Frontier could use this deposition to gain an understanding of how the documents recently produced were inadvertently omitted, and more important, whether other relevant documents may also have been omitted.

C. American Gas Minutes

UGI apparently has minutes of American Gas that it has not produced because those minutes do not specifically contain the word Bangor. There should be no serious dispute that the minutes of American Gas might contain relevant and admissible information even if they do not contain the word "Bangor". Requests to produce these minutes are reasonably calculated to obtain information about the operations of American Gas and the way in which it viewed its subsidiaries and their MGP operations. UGI's self-serving claim that the documents are not being produced because they are not relevant is not a sufficient basis for withholding documents especially where, as here, UGI has admitted that it only reviewed the records for the word "Bangor."

D. Requests for information concerning "similar" cases are reasonably calculated to lead to the discovery of admissible evidence.

UGI's responses to Frontier's discovery requests repeatedly object to all interrogatories and requests that would in any way involve production of information related to prior disputes in which UGI was accused of owning or operating a manufactured gas plant. *See* Ex. A, Responses 1, 2, 6, 7, 8, 9; Ex. B, Responses 7, 16, 17, 18, 19. UGI acknowledges that "[o]ver the course of its history beginning in 1882, UGI was associated with a large number of manufactured gas plant facilities." Ex. B at 21. UGI also has pointed out in its summary judgment papers that this history of "associating" with manufactured gas plant facilities has led to accusations "similar" to the ones Frontier is making--that UGI owned or operated these plants. Docket No. 172 at 2. More than that, UGI emphasized that it has "won summary judgment" in these "similar" cases, and that those judgments were affirmed on appeal. *Id*. This point is not presented as a legal argument, but rather an argument based on the similarity of the cases.

If UGI intends to argue for summary judgment here based on that the fact it has "won" other, "similar" cases, then information related to those cases is relevant to counter UGI's argument. UGI, perhaps recognizing this, suggests in its reply that it is not relying on the fact of its victories, but rather on "application of the principles set forth in the governing case, *United States v. Bestfoods*, 524 U.S. 51 (1998), to similar CERCLA claims . . . ." Docket 188 at 3. But UGI cannot un-ring the bell. Its repeated references to prior cases involving other manufactured gas plant sites are plainly meant to do more than cite the legal propositions present in those cases. UGI is drawing factual parallels between those cases and this one, and the only way to test the validity of those parallels is to compel UGI to respond to Frontier's requests for discovery.

Separate and apart from the fact that UGI has tried to use cases involving other MGP operations in support of its summary judgment request, Frontier's Interrogatories and Requests for Production concerning other MGP plants are reasonably calculated to lead to the discovery of admissible evidence. Frontier expects that these records will show that American Gas exercised a degree of control over the Bangor facility that was different in scope and degree than the control it exercised over other MGP plants. For example, Frontier's principal expert, Dr. George Baker, has reviewed the documents that have already been produced and has concluded that the documents demonstrate a disregard of the separate corporate identity and evidence an extraordinary degree of control over the Bangor Gas Light Company.[1] Dr. Baker also found corporate irregularities in the records that have been produced. To the extent that American Gas treated its other subsidiaries differently than it treated the Bangor Gas Light Company, it provides additional proof in support of Dr. Baker's opinions. The documents that UGI is withholding are reasonably calculated to lead to the discovery of admissible evidence and should be produced.

CONCLUSION

For the reasons stated above, UGI should be compelled to make available a knowledgeable document custodian for a deposition, and to respond to Requests for Production 1, 2, 6, 7, 8 and 9 and Interrogatories 7, 16, 17, 18 and 19.

Dated: March 29, 2010

Respectfully submitted,

/s/ Martha C. Gaythwaite

---

1. A copy of Dr. Baker's expert witness designation is submitted with this Motion to Compel and marked Exhibit D.

Martha C. Gaythwaite

Friedman Gaythwaite Wolf & Leavitt

Six City Center

P.O. Box 4726

Portland, ME 04112-4726

(207) 761-0900

Of Counsel:

John S. Hahn

Jay C. Johnson

Mayer Brown LLP

1909 K Street, NW

Washington, DC 20006-1101

(202) 263-3000

Motion for Protective Order

2012 WL 10703537 (D.Me.)

United States District Court, D. Maine.

Daniel R. GOLDENSON, Suzanne K. Goldenson, SKG Partners, L.P., and SKG General Corp., Plaintiffs,

v.

John L. STEFFENS, Gregory P. Ho, Spring Mountain Capital GP, LLC, Spring Mountain Capital, LP, and Spring Mountain Capital, LLC, Defendants.

No. 10-CV-440 (JAW).

February 28, 2012.

Defendants' Motion for a Protective Order Relating to Plaintiffs' Second Request for the Production of Documents and Things

Verrill Dana LLP, James T. Kilbreth, P.O. Box 586, Portland, ME 04112, Telephone: (207) 774-4000, Spears & Imes LLP, David Spears (pro hac vice), Michelle Skinner (pro hac vice), Spears & Imes LLP, 51 Madison Avenue, New York, New York 10010, Telephone: (212) 213-6996, for defendants.

EXPEDITED BRIEFING AND PROTECTION REQUESTED

On February 9, 2012, Defendants received Plaintiffs' Second Request For The Production of Documents and Things ("Second Request"), returnable within 30 days. *See* Ex. A. In Request Nos. 1-10 and 12 (out of 13 total Requests), Plaintiffs seek documents that relate solely to their uncharged misallocation theory of wrongdoing.[1] Defendants hereby move for a protective order relieving them of any obligation to produce documents responsive to those Requests.

The misallocation theory is nowhere set out, described, or referred to, directly or indirectly, in Plaintiffs' First Amended Complaint ("Complaint"). Further, Plaintiffs consciously chose not to add such a theory, or claims based on it, to their pleadings during the period prescribed by the Court's Scheduling Order for amendments to pleadings. Therefore, Plaintiffs cannot pursue such a theory in discovery or in any other phase of this proceeding, particularly under the present circumstances, where Plaintiffs seek to use the misallocation theory and their Second Request to delay this proceeding indefinitely. The Court is respectfully requested to order that Defendants are not required to respond to Requests 1-10 and 12 from Plaintiffs' Second Request.

I. BACKGROUND

Plaintiffs' Complaint sets out an investment fraud theory of wrongdoing exclusively, and all eleven of the Complaint's causes of action, as well as the theory of damages set out in the Complaint, dovetail with that single theory. *See* Defendants' Opposition To Plaintiffs' Motion To Extend Time To Take The Deposition Of Party Defendants Steffens And Ho, dated February 27, 2012 ("Docket

---

1. At the February 3, 2012 hearing and in the February 6, 2012 Order, the Court denied Plaintiffs' motion to compel the production of certain documents that Plaintiffs sought in support of their misallocation theory, on the ground that those documents were not called for by the First Request. Plaintiffs' Second Request appears to be a renewal and gross expansion of their efforts to obtain documents of the type the Court denied them previously.

No. 87"), pp. 3-5. The eight paragraphs of the "Summary Of The Allegations" section of the Complaint very clearly outline Plaintiffs' fraud theory against Defendants, which relates to Plaintiffs' investments in Ezra Merkin's Ascot Partners, L.P., both indirectly through an investment in Defendants' QP I Fund and directly through separate investments with Merkin. They state that Plaintiffs made investments in reliance on misstatements and omissions by Defendants; and that when the Madoff fraud was revealed in December 2008, Plaintiffs suffered losses on those investments. The allegations set out in the body of the Complaint are fully consistent with the summary.

Yet over time Plaintiffs have increasingly sought to rely on a new and uncharged theory of wrongdoing -- that Madoff-related losses suffered by other Spring Mountain funds and investors were misallocated to QP I investors, including Plaintiffs. Plaintiffs first described their misallocation theory at a November 28, 2011 discovery hearing.[2] Plaintiffs elaborated on the new theory in their motion for enlargement of time for designation of Plaintiffs' experts, dated December 22, 2011 ("Docket No. 69"). There, Plaintiffs described one of their proposed experts as "an expert forensic financial analyst regarding the books and records of the Defendants and related parties and their treatment of certain financial transactions relevant to the Plaintiffs' investments." Id. p. 2. Plaintiffs stated that they had requested "financial reports from Spring Mountain concerning the Plaintiffs' investments in Spring Mountain and Ascot," but had not received any reports "generated later than 2006," making an analysis by the forensics expert "impossible." Id. p. 3 n.4. Plaintiffs added:

This is important in view of the Plaintiffs' contention that these Defendants purposefully misallocated and mischaracterized purported Madoff fraud-related losses and "market losses" in December of 2008 in order [to] favor certain Spring Mountain funds and investors at the expense of others, including the Goldensons.

Id.

In Defendants' Response, dated January 4, 2012 ("Docket No. 73"), Defendants challenged Plaintiffs' embrace of the misallocation theory, pointing out that the Complaint nowhere alleged such a theory and that Plaintiffs were impermissibly seeking to amend the Complaint to add a new theory of liability. Id. pp. 5-6. Plaintiffs' Reply, dated January 11, 2012 ("Docket No. 74"), countered that Plaintiffs were not required to "plead evidence" or to plead "fraud with complete insight." Id. p. 2. Plaintiffs also claimed that their misallocation theory is described in paragraphs 93, 108, 127, 148, and 158 of the Complaint. Id. pp. 2-3. Plaintiffs cited those same paragraphs at the February 3 hearing when Defendants challenged them again on the misallocation theory.

In Plaintiffs' recently filed motion for protection and for sanctions, dated February 19, 2012 ("Docket No. 85"), they refined the misallocation theory as follows:

... that the Defendants 1) attributed losses to QP 1 [sic] investors that other funds and investors in fact sustained; and 2) misrepresented the actual extent of the Madoff-related losses that the QP 1 [sic] Fund suffered ... in statements upon which those investors relied in reporting investment income and losses to federal and state tax authorities and to the Securities Investor Protection Corporation.

Id. p. 4.

II. ARGUMENT

A. The Misallocation Theory Is Not Set Out In The Complaint

The Complaint sets out an investment fraud theory of wrongdoing -- that Defendants made misstatements and omissions to Plaintiffs regarding the QP I Fund and Ascot Partners, L.P.; that Plaintiffs relied on those misstatements and omissions and made an investment in the QP I Fund in 2002 and multiple direct investments in Ascot Partners, L.P. through Merkin in 2002 and 2006; and that Plaintiffs suffered investment losses when Madoff's fraud was revealed and it turned out that all of the assets of Ascot Partners, L.P. were held by Madoff. Plaintiffs allege eleven causes of action, each of which is based on this investment fraud theory. The Complaint does not contain a word about Plaintiffs' newly-coined misallocation theory: there are no factual allegations relating to such a theory, no cause of action based on such a theory, and no related injury or damages described.

The paragraphs of the Complaint in which Plaintiffs claim to see the misallocation theory described provide no support for Plaintiffs' argument. See ¶¶ 93-95, 108, 127(I), 148, 158. Rather, those paragraphs allege only that Defendants misreported to QP I investors that the extent of that Fund's losses associated with the Madoff fraud was limited to the Fund's investments in two Merkin funds, Ascot Partners, L.P. and Gabriel Capital, L.P., when in fact the QP I Fund was also an investor in the Cerberus hedge fund, which had an indirect exposure to Madoff. Notably, those paragraphs do not allege that Defendants "attributed losses to QP I investors that

---

2. November 28 was the next business day after the deadline set by the Scheduling Order for amending the pleadings. Thus, Plaintiffs had this theory clearly in mind at a time when they could have amended the Complaint to include it. That they did not do so confirms that the misallocation theory is merely a device for seeking to achieve delay.

other [Spring Mountain] funds and investors in fact sustained," or that Defendants "misrepresented the actual extent of the Madoff-related losses that the QP I fund suffered" in federal and state tax reporting documents provided to QP I investors and tax authorities and in claims filed with SIPC. *See* Docket No. 85.

Nor can Plaintiffs' misallocation theory be considered "evidence" in support of their fraud theory of wrongdoing. *See* Docket No. 74 p. 2 (Plaintiffs arguing that misallocation theory not required to be alleged in Complaint because Plaintiffs not required to "plead evidence" or "plead fraud with insight"). The misallocation theory pertains solely to events that could only have occurred in the period after Madoff's fraud was revealed, and it does not relate in any way to misstatements or omissions by Defendants that led Plaintiffs to make the subject investments or remain in those investments. Moreover, it has nothing whatsoever to do with investment fraud, but rather represents a separate and distinct theory of wrongdoing that sounds in defalcation or wrongful taking.

B. As Plaintiffs Well Know, The Misallocation Theory Is Contrary To Incontestable Facts About How Spring Mountain Ran Its Business

In addition to not being alleged, Plaintiffs' misallocation theory is absurd on its face for reasons that Plaintiffs are fully aware of. During that period of time when Plaintiffs presumably would say the supposed misallocation occurred -- early 2009 and/or later -- Defendants relied on an independent third-party Administrator to receive and review periodic account statements from submanagers of the QP I Fund;[3] to calculate an overall net asset value for each QP I investor based on the combining of values from those separate account statements; and to prepare and send an individualized account statement to each QP I investor setting out, among other things, that investor's present total net asset value in the QP I Fund.[4] *See* Ex. B (Declaration of Lucianne Painter, dated February 27, 2012); *see, e.g.*, Exs. C and D (two separate account statements for Plaintiffs' investment in QP I).[5] Spring Mountain began to rely on an outside Administrator to perform those ministerial tasks in 2003, and from 2007 to the present, the Administrator has been Citigroup. *See* Ex. B ¶ 2.

An inspection of Exhibits C and D demonstrates that Plaintiffs must have known from the beginning that their misallocation theory is completely at odds with the existence and role of the Administrator. Exhibit C is the QP I account statement sent to Plaintiffs for the period ended October 31, 2008, barely one month before the December 8 revelation of Madoff's fraud. At the top right of the page, the investor who receives the statement is directed to "make inquiries" regarding the statement to a named Citigroup employee, whose telephone number and email address are provided. Even worse, Exhibit D, which is a QP I account statement received by Plaintiffs in 2011, not only contains the same direction at the top right of the first page, but also sets out the following information on a second page:

> This statement is provided by Citi solely in its capacity as administrator for the Fund.... The statement is based on information received from third parties such as broker-dealers, counterparties and custodians engaged by the Fund and independent pricing vendors or other third parties approved by the Fund, and, as required, from the Fund or its Investment Manager. In the case of a Fund that is a fund of funds, the statement is based on information received from the administrators of the underlying funds. In computing the Fund's net asset value, Citi relies exclusively on values for the Fund's portfolio investments provided by such sources.

In sum, Defendants could not have misallocated losses from other Spring Mountain funds or investors to the QP I Fund because, as Plaintiffs are fully aware, Defendants did not calculate the values of the respective investments held by QP I or the net asset values for individual QP I investors, but rather relied on Citigroup to calculate those values and communicate them to the investors.

C. Even Assuming *Arguendo* That A Misallocation Could Have Occurred, Its Significance For Plaintiffs Would Be Minimal

By its express terms, Plaintiffs' misallocation theory would apply only to their investment in the QP I Fund, and not to their separate direct investments in Ascot Partners, L.P. Plaintiffs invested a total of $2 million in the QP I Fund. To date, they have received redemptions and distributions of $2,386,810.41, and the value of their remaining investment in the Fund, which has not yet become liquid, is approximately $471,838.29. The combination of what they have already received and the value of what they have not

---

3. The outside hedge funds that QP I invested in, like Ascot Partners and Cerberus, were referred to as submanagers.

4. As Plaintiffs note in their Complaint, the periodic reports they received as QP I investors "provided no information whatsoever about the individual underlying Portfolio Funds in which [the QP I Fund] had invested." *See* ¶ 65.

5. Defendants have redacted all financial information in Exhibits C and D in order to avoid disclosing information that Plaintiffs designated as confidential when they produced Exhibit C. Both of these documents were received by Plaintiffs contemporaneously with the dates on them.

received is $2,855,646.[6] The total Madoff-related losses to the QP I Fund from its investments in Ascot Partners, L.P. and Gabriel Capital, L.P. was $9,106,052. Plaintiffs' pro rata portion of that loss, based on their percentage ownership interest in the QP I Fund when those losses were experienced and taken into account by the Administrator, is estimated to be approximately $262,000. *See* Ex. E (Second Declaration of Lucianne Painter, dated February 28, 2012).

Thus, Plaintiffs are alleging that some portion of the $262,000 decrease in value of their interest in the QP I Fund associated with losses in Ascot and Gabriel actually represents Madoff-related losses incurred by other Spring Mountain funds and investors that were misallocated to Plaintiffs as QP I investors. Assuming *arguendo* that there could have been such a misallocation, how much of that $262,000 could be attributable to the misallocation? Five percent ($13,100)? Ten percent ($26,200)? Fifty percent ($131,000)? Plaintiffs are claiming investment losses of millions of dollars -- almost all of it from their separate direct investments in Ascot Partners, L.P. through Merkin, and not from their relatively small indirect investment in Ascot Partners through the QP I Fund -- and whatever quantum their expert could conceivably "establish" for any misallocation by Defendants would be a tiny percentage of Plaintiffs' claimed damages overall. Indeed, it would even be considerably less than Defendants have spent defending against Plaintiffs' desperate attempts to prolong discovery by waging an all-out war to obtain documents relating to the misallocation theory.

D. Requests 1-10 and 12 Are Impermissible Because They Relate Exclusively To The Misallocation Theory

The Second Request expands ten-fold the universe of Spring Mountain funds as to which Plaintiffs are seeking documents. While the First Request defined "Spring Mountain" to mean only the entities named as Defendants and the QP I Fund, *see* Ex. F Def. 14, the Second Request defines Spring Mountain to also include 10 additional funds, *see* Ex. A Def. 21.[7] Other Definitions in the Second Request also greatly expand its reach beyond that of the First Request. *See, e.g.*, Ex. A Defs. 2, 5, 6, 13, 14, 19. Obviously, Plaintiffs' demands for a large number of documents relating to Spring Mountain funds other than the QP I Fund relate exclusively to Plaintiffs' effort to establish that Madoff-related losses from those other funds were misallocated to themselves as QP I Fund investors.

In addition, individual Requests in the Second Request obviously relate solely to Plaintiffs' misallocation theory.

- Request Nos. 1 and 2 call for certain valuation documents for all Spring Mountain funds for the period January 1, 2007 through December 31, 2009; this is the period for which Plaintiffs say they need "before and after snapshots" so as to quantify the misallocation.

- Request No. 3 calls for documents showing all investments made by any Spring Mountain fund in any Merkin fund from 2001 to the present, and vice versa; investments by other Spring Mountain funds in Merkin funds could only be relevant to an analysis of whether losses by the other Spring Mountain funds were misallocated to QP I.

- Request Nos. 4 and 5 call for documents relating to transfers of assets between any Spring Mountain fund and any other Spring Mountain fund, or between any Spring Mountain fund and any Merkin fund, between September 1, 2008 and January 31, 2009; this is the period during which any misallocation would have occurred, and transfers between funds only could relate to misallocation.

- Request No. 6 calls for all communications between any Spring Mountain fund and any Merkin fund, from September 1, 2001 to the present; this time period covers the time when any misallocation would have occurred, and the reference to all Spring Mountain funds could only relate to misallocation.

- Request No. 7 calls for all communications between Spring Mountain and its auditors and/or the Administrator for the Spring Mountain funds concerning the reporting or accounting treatment of Madoff-related losses by any fund.

- Request No. 8 calls for all returns and forms filed with the IRS by any Spring Mountain fund for the years 2005 through 2011; this is clearly directed toward Plaintiffs' most recent articulation of the misallocation theory as including the creation by Defendants of false tax documents to be provided to investors and tax authorities; also, the date range extends more than one year after the period of time addressed in the Complaint.

- Request No. 9 calls for individual tax returns for Steffens and Ho for 2007 through 2011; this is directed toward the same prong of the most recent articulation of the misallocation theory; also, the date range extends more than one year after the period of time addressed in the Complaint.

- Request No. 10 calls for communications sent to investors in any Spring Mountain fund concerning Madoff; these would

---

6. All of these numbers are "net" of the QP I Fund's losses associated with its investment in Ascot Partners, L.P. and Gabriel Capital, L.P., or any other submanager that suffered Madoff-related losses.

7. Definition 21 also expands the definition of Spring Mountain to include "all Spring Mountain principals, partners, employees, consultants and independent contractors."

...er the revelation of Madoff's fraud in December 2008, and they could only relate to losses by the other ...ion of those losses.

...12 calls for all documents concerning communications between Spring Mountain and either the SIPA Trustee ...ation of Madoff's firm, the Receiver for Ascot Partners, L.P., and/or the Receiver for Gabriel, between December ...and the present; these relate to losses claimed for individual funds.

...ion to the fact that all of these Requests relate exclusively to the invalid misallocation theory, the burden they would impose on ...efendants in terms of resources and time is enormous. Given the very minimal impact that the misallocation theory could have -- even theoretically -- on Plaintiffs' damages, the burden to Defendants swamps the potential significance of the requested documents to Plaintiffs. Further, for Plaintiffs to have served this egregiously broad and burdensome Second Request such a short time before the discovery cutoff, and then insist that they cannot take the individual Defendants' depositions until it is complied with, confirms that they are not proceeding in good faith and have no purpose other than delay.

III.   CONCLUSION

For all of the reasons set forth above, Defendants respectfully move for a protective order relieving Defendants of the obligation to respond to Request Nos. 1-10 and 12 of Plaintiffs' Second Request.

*****

Defendants further request that this motion be decided on the basis of expedited briefing.

Dated: February 28, 2012

VERRILL DANA LLP

By: */s/ James T. Kilbreth*

James T. Kilbreth

P.O. Box 586

Portland, ME 04112

Telephone: (207) 774-4000

Attorneys for Defendants

SPEARS & IMES LLP

By: */s/ Michelle Skinner*

David Spears (*pro hac vice*)

Michelle Skinner (*pro hac vice*)

Spears & Imes LLP

51 Madison Avenue

New York, New York 10010

Telephone: (212) 213-6996

Motion for Preliminary Injunction

2020 WL 7249934 (D.Me.)

Westlaw Query>>

To find more Motion for Preliminary Injunction filings on Westlaw: access Maine Trial Court Documents (from the Home page, click Trial Court Documents, then Maine), click the Advanced Search link, select Motion for Preliminary Injunction, and click Search. Use the Jurisdiction filter on the left to narrow results to Federal.

United States District Court, D. Maine.

Michael MCKENZIE, Individually and Doing Business as American Image Art, an Unincorporated Dba, Plaintiff,

v.

James W. BRANNAN, as Personal Representative of the Estate of Robert Indiana, et Al, Defendants.

No. 2:20-cv-00262-JAW.

August 14, 2020.

Plaintiff's Motion for Preliminary Injunction with Supporting Memorandum of Law

John J.E. Markham, II (Maine BBO No. 2674), Bridget A. Zerner (pro Hac Vice - MA 669468), Markham & Read, 908 Maine Street, Waldoboro, Maine 04572, Tel: (207) 790-8049, One Commercial Wharf West, Boston, Massachusetts 02110, Tel: (617) 523-6329, Fax: (617)742-8604, jmarkham@markhamread.com, bzerner@markhamread.com.

Pursuant to Rule 65, Fed. R. Civ. P. and Local Rule 7(a), Plaintiff Michael McKenzie ("McKenzie"), individually and doing business as American Image Art ("AIA" or sometimes "American Image"), moves this Court to preliminarily enjoin Defendant James W. Brannan, sued herein as the personal representative of The Estate of Robert Indiana (the "Indiana Estate"), from proceeding with an arbitration now pending in New York until this case is resolved. The matters being arbitrated in New York have been settled by a written agreement reached in Portland, Maine on November 26, 2019, called a "Binding Term Sheet" which resolved the issues being arbitrated and also specifically agreed that "[t]he arbitration between the Estate and AIA [McKenzie] pending in the AAA will be dismissed with prejudice." This case simply seeks to enforce that Binding Term Sheet, both its substance and its promise to dismiss the New York arbitration, a very costly and now unnecessary proceeding as shown below.

The Indiana Estate, for its part, claims the Binding Term Sheet is no longer binding. The Estate also seeks to have the question of whether it is binding decided by the arbitrators sitting in New York. *See*, Indiana Estate's Motion to Compel Arbitration and to Stay Proceedings. (Dkt. No. 15) In McKenzie's Opposition to that motion, filed separately, and also below, we show that this Court, not the arbitrators in New York, should by law resolve whether the Binding Term Sheet remains binding. There has never been an agreement between the parties that the provisions of the Binding Term Sheet are subject to arbitration and without such an agreement the arbitrators are without authority to decide anything about the Binding Term Sheet.

Summary of Grounds Supporting this Motion

As shown in more detail further below, (1) the Binding Term Sheet is a specifically enforceable contract both as to its substantive terms and also as to its agreement to dismiss the New York arbitration, (2) if the New York arbitration continues, it will cause irreparable harm to McKenzie because it puts at risk irreplaceable rights provided him in the Binding Term Sheet; (3) McKenzie is likely to succeed on the merits of the claim made in this case, which is the specific enforcement of the Binding Term Sheet; (4) the balance of hardships favors granting the injunction herein sought because the hardship is much greater on McKenzie if the arbitration continues than it would be on the Indiana Estate if it is stayed until this case is resolved; and (5) the public interest favors the injunction herein sought because (i) public policy favors enforcing settlements over any later-felt buyer's remorse of one party to a settlement and (ii) enforcing the Binding Term Sheet will save the Estate substantial sums of money that instead of being spent on the New York arbitration will go to a Maine charity located on Vinalhaven, Maine.

The facts stated below are supported by both the Verified Complaint and by a Declaration of Michael McKenzie sworn to August 13, 2020, annexed hereto.[1]

FACTS

Plaintiff McKenzie and the Vinalhaven-Based Artist Named Robert Indiana

McKenzie is a long-time art publisher. (Dkt. No. 1, Verified Complaint, ¶18) In the mid-1970s, McKenzie started collaborating with artist Robert Indiana who was part of the American "pop art" movement of the 1960s and who created many notable and acclaimed works of art, including his famous LOVE creation, *Id.*, para 12, and depicted here:

This LOVE artwork was first displayed on a Museum of Modern Art Christmas card in 1965. In 1970, it became the sculpture depicted above, and was made more famous after being used on a United States postal stamp distributed in 1973. (*Id.*)

Plaintiff Michael McKenzie, a longtime art publisher and collaborator, created the iconic HOPE artwork and approached Indiana to collaborate by making color variations of that art, which Indiana did, exemplified by the artwork depicted below (*Id.*, at ¶14):

In 1976, Indiana moved to Vinalhaven, Maine where he lived in isolation while still creating his art until his death on May 19, 2018. (*Id.*, ¶12) Both the above-depicted LOVE and HOPE have become world renowned works of art. With these as the centerpieces of Indiana's artwork, his sculptures, prints, and silkscreens continued to be created until his death in 2018.[2]

In 2008, Indiana and McKenzie entered into an "Agreement for Art Editions", (Verified Complaint ¶¶13-14 and Dkt. Nos. 12-1 and 15-2), herein referred to as the "HOPE Agreement" under which McKenzie was to produce art with Indiana. It worked quite well for the ten years it ran until Indiana died in May 2018:

> I worked with Robert Indiana personally under this HOPE agreement (as amended) from 2008 until his death on May 19, 2018 and our publishing work under this Agreement made millions of dollars for Robert Indiana. Specifically, over that time period, my work with him netted over $10.3 million in payments made to him during that time.

(McKenzie Declaration, Exhibit A hereto, ¶3)

Because of the commercial success of his artwork, Indiana amassed a fortune. The Knox County Maine probate court records relating to his estate, filed as *Estate of Robert Indiana aka Robert Earle Clark* (Knox No. 2018-014), shows an "Interim Probate Account" for the period of May 25, 2018 through October 1, 2019 stating assets having a net value of $89,738,458.38. (*See*, Exhibit A to the Verified Complaint, filed as Dkt. No. 1-1)

In his will, Indiana, who died without known heirs, bequeathed his entire estate, less debts and claims, to Star of Hope Foundation, a Maine licensed charity operating from Vinalhaven, Maine. (Verified Complaint, Dkt. No. 1, ¶ 17) The Star of Hope is based in Vinalhaven, Maine and operates from the Star of Hope Lodge, an old and elegant structure which is now under renovation and which is to become the centerpiece of the charity:

> The Star of Hope is based in Vinalhaven, Maine and operates from the Star of Hope Lodge, an old and elegant structure which is now under renovation and which is to become the centerpiece of the charity's mission, namely, to promote education of the visual arts through various means including Vinalhaven-based exhibitions, and a museum, artist-in-residence programs, and other outreach endeavors. All of these activities will have a very significant and positive effect on the Vinalhaven community, both commercially and culturally, given the world-wide popularity and respect for the Robert Indiana artwork and its ability to attract people to Vinalhaven from all over the world.

(*Id.*)

Disputes Involving McKenzie and the Indiana Estate

After the death of Robert Indiana in 2018, a dispute arose between McKenzie and the Indiana Estate relating to the production contract which had been entered into between Indiana and McKenzie and which has been in effect since 2008. This dispute resulted in claims that were initially asserted as crossclaims in federal court in New York in an action entitled *Morgan Art Foundation*

---

1. On preliminary injunction motions, a verified complaint is "treated as the functional equivalent of an affidavit." *See, Sheinkopf v. Stone*, 927 F.2d 1259, 1262 (1st Cir.1991); *Kelly Services, Inc. v. Greene*, 535 F. Supp. 2d 180, 182 (D. Me. 2008). This motion presents both.

2. His artwork has been featured in permanent collections of important museums such as the Museum of Modern Art and the Whitney Museum of American Art in New York, the National Gallery of Art, and the Smithsonian Museum of American Art in Washington, D.C., among others. (*Id.* ¶ 15)

Limited v. Michael McKenzie, American Image Art, and James W. Brannan As Personal Representative of The Estate of Robert Indiana, et al., 2018-cv-04438 (S.D.N.Y.) By Order of October 9, 2018, based on the joint motion of the Indiana Estate and McKenzie, the judge in that case referred those crossclaims to arbitration in New York under the AAA as had been provided for in the contract between Indiana and McKenzie. (Verified Complaint ¶ 20-22, Ex. C at Dkt. No. 1-3)

That arbitration was subsequently commenced and has a planned schedule which is very complex, labor intensive and quite costly, with a reasonable estimate being in the millions of dollars. (*Id.*, ¶¶ 22 - 24) The Maine Attorney General thereafter intervened in Maine. He did so because the Indiana Estate is being probated here, the only beneficiary of the Indiana Estate is a Maine-based public charity, the Star of Hope, and also because he was concerned[3] that the mounting fees in the New York litigation were costing the Estate significant sums of money which would be left to the Vinalhaven charity if not spent on litigation.[4] The Attorney General thus persuaded the parties (the Indiana Estate and McKenzie) to enter into binding mediation. (Verified Complaint ¶¶ 22-25)

The Mediation Resulted in a Binding Term Sheet

The mediation was held in Portland, Maine on November 25 and 26, 2019. It resulted in a "Binding Term Sheet" executed by the parties on November 26, 2019. (*Id.* ¶ 26) The Binding Term Sheet (found at Verified Complaint, Exhibit E, filed at Dkt. No. 7-1) is comprehensive, resolving all disputes between the parties relating to past and future relations involving the Indiana artwork and its production. It also provides:

> This agreement is subject to normal and customary terms of settlement, including confidentiality and non-disparagement. *This term sheet is intended to be binding* and will be replaced by a more formal Settlement Agreement and Production Agreement. Payments, releases, dismissals and other consideration under this term sheet will be made after a more formal Settlement Agreement and Releases and Production Agreement are executed.

(*Id.*)(emphasis added)

As is relates to the New York arbitration, the Binding Term Sheet specifically states:

> The arbitration between the Estate and AIA [McKenzie] pending in the AAA will be dismissed with prejudice.

(Term Sheet at Dkt. No. 7-3) Indeed, after execution of the Binding Term Sheet, the Indiana Estate's lawyers informed the New York Arbitration Panel as follows:

> We are pleased to report that the parties have signed a term sheet that resolves all claims and counterclaims in this action.

(*See*, Email of Estate Counsel, November 29, 2019) (Exhibit F to Verified Complaint, found at Dkt. No. 1-6) McKenzie agrees with that characterization and it is the reading of the Binding Term Sheet. However, while the parties initially attempted to incorporate the binding terms into a more formal settlement agreement, as required by the Binding Term Sheet, that has not occurred. McKenzie contends that the failure to do so is because the Indiana Estate has attempted to walk away from the substantive provisions of the Binding Term Sheet rather than filling in the "normal and customary terms of settlement" quoted above and as required by the Binding Term Sheet. Accordingly, on July 27, 2020, McKenzie filed this action seeking a declaratory judgment that the Binding Term Sheet is indeed binding, that it is subject to specific enforcement, and that it should be specifically enforced, including its provision requiring the parties to dismiss the costly New York arbitration. It also seeks an order directing the parties to stay the New York Arbitration until this declaratory judgment action can be heard and determined which McKenzie will press to have done on an expedited basis.[5]

This motion now seeks to preliminarily enjoin the New York arbitration until this Court can rule on the rest of the relief sought by

---

3. Pursuant to Maine Revised Statutes, Title 5, § 194. Frey, the Maine Attorney General, has supervisory and protective authority over non-profit organizations operating in Maine, including the Star of Hope. He has filed a challenge to the large legal fees and personal representative fees billed the Estate. *See*, McKenzie Declaration and **Exhibit A** where the filings of the Attorney General are attached.

4. The legal costs to the Estate, being probated in the Rockland, Maine Probate Court, total $3,284,636.59 for the period of time from May 2018 through October 2019. (*See*, Verified Complaint, Exhibit A at Dkt. No. 1-1, the Estate's Interim Probate Account, as of December 2, 2019, at Schedule B thereto.) The fees charged by the personal representative through that same period are another $550,000. (*Id.*) However, most of the work in the arbitration has not even been commenced as the Arbitration Schedule shows. (*See*, Arbitration Schedule at Verified Complaint, Exhibit D, Dkt. No. 1-4) and given that intricate and time-consuming schedule, the contemplated activity will continue to consume millions of dollars if the arbitration proceeds.

5. As will be shown in more detail in McKenzie's Opposition to the Estate's Motion to send the question of the arbitrability of the Binding Term Sheet to the New York arbitrators to decide, the Binding Term Sheet is a separate agreement from the Indiana/McKenzie HOPE production agreement that authorized the New York arbitration. Unlike that earlier HOPE Agreement, the

this action. As of now, McKenzie and the Indiana Estate have "jointly agreed to a temporary stay of the arbitration proceedings." *See*, Indiana Estate's Motion to Compel Arbitration (at Dkt. No 15, p. 5) until October 31, 2020 and as of this filing have a joint request into the AAA Panel (Dkt. No 15-6) seeking that delay in order to attempt to get a ruling from this Court on this motion and the related motion of the Indiana Estate to stay this action and refer the matter of the enforceability of the Binding Term Sheet back to the AAA Panel in New York so that it can be determined there and not in this Court. The AAA Panel has not decided the joint request for a short delay, stating that it is skeptical that this case can be decided quickly. (*See*, Email from AAA Panel, 8/8/2020, annexed hereto as **Exhibit B**)

ARGUMENT

I. The Preliminary Injunction Standard Is Well-Defined

"A district court faced with a motion for a preliminary injunction must weigh four factors: (1) the plaintiff's likelihood of success on the merits; (2) the potential for irreparable harm in the absence of an injunction; (3) whether issuing an injunction will burden the defendants less than denying an injunction would burden the plaintiffs; and (4) the effect, if any, on the public interest." *Swarovski Aktiengesellschaft v. Building No. 19, Inc.*, 704 F.3d 44, 48 (1st Cir. 2013) (internal quotation marks and citations omitted). Though each factor is important, "[t]he *sine qua non* of this four-part inquiry is likelihood of success on the merits: if the moving party cannot demonstrate that he is likely to succeed in his quest, the remaining factors become matters of idle curiosity." Id., quoting *New Comm Wireless Servs., Inc. v. SprintCom, Inc.*, 287 F.3d 1, 9 (1st Cir. 2002).

II. McKenzie Has a Strong Likelihood of Success on the Merits

A. Maine Law Governs All Issues Relating to the Binding Term Sheet

This is a diversity action and therefore the law of the forum state (Maine), including its conflict of law rule, governs the construction and enforceability of the Binding Term Sheet. *See, Commercial Union Ins. Co. v. Walbrook Ins. Co.*, 41 F.3d 764, 772 (1st Cir. 1994). The conflict of law rule in Maine follows the Restatement (Second) of Conflicts of Laws and the "most significant contacts and relationships approach in determining choice of law." *Long v. Fairbank Farms Reconstruction Corp.*, 199-201 (D. Me. 2011)(Singal, J)(citations omitted). "Under this standard, the state that has the more significant contacts and the more substantial relationships to the occurrence and the parties should enjoy the application of its laws." *Id.*; *see also, Auto Europe, LLC v. Connecticut Indem. Co.*, 321 F.3d 60, 65 (1st Cir. 2003). The Restatement directs that in determining which state has the most significant contacts, courts should consider: (a) the place of contracting, (b) the place of negotiation of the contract, (c) the place of performance, (d) the location of the subject matter of the contract, and (e) the places of incorporation and business of the parties. *Id.*; Restatement § 188(2) (1971).

Under these factors, Maine substantive law governs the interpretation of the Binding Term Sheet. As McKenzie shows in his Declaration at paragraph 15, the mediation was performed in and resulted in a Binding Term Sheet executed in Portland, Maine. The Indiana Estate is being probated in Rockland, Maine by Defendant Brannan, who resides there and the only beneficiary of the Estate is the Star of Hope Foundation, located in Vinalhaven, and will receive the assets of the Estate once probate is concluded. Moreover, a substantial part of the artwork production process under the Binding Term Sheet is to be performed in Maine and the proceeds of artwork sales sent to Maine will have a substantial impact on the Estate/Star of Hope in Maine. *See*, McKenzie Dec., ¶15. Maine thus has a much greater interest in the performance of the contract than New York.

B. McKenzie Can Enforce the Binding Term Sheet Because the Parties Manifested an Intent (Explicitly Stated) to Be Bound by Its Terms

A "party to a settlement agreement may seek to enforce the agreement's terms when the other party refuses to comply." *Fid. & Guar.*

_____

Binding Term Sheet does not have an arbitration clause and thus the New York arbitration panel does not have jurisdiction to decide the underlying question posed in this action, namely, whether the Binding Term Sheet is specifically enforceable. *See, Applied Energetics, Inc. v. NewOak Capital Markets, LLC*, 645 F.3d 522, 526 (2d Cir. 2011)(reversing order compelling arbitration where subsequent agreement superseded and precluded arbitration noting that where the parties dispute whether an obligation to arbitrate exists, the presumption in favor of arbitration does not apply) Here, the Binding Term Sheet not only does not agree to arbitration, it provides that the existing arbitration commenced under the earlier HOPE Agreement should be dismissed. *See, Porzig v. Dresdner, Kleinwort, Benson, N.A. LLC*, 497 F.3d 133, 140 (2d Cir. 2007) ("The authority of the arbitral panel is established only through the contract between the parties who have subjected themselves to arbitration, and a panel may not exceed the power granted to it by the parties in the contract.")

Ins. Co. v. Star Equip. Corp., 541 F.3d 1, 5 (1st Cir. 2008)(enforcing settlement agreement despite one party's "subjective belief that the agreement was not final"); *see also*, *Concordia Partners, LLC v. Ward*, 2:12-CV-138-GZS, 2014 WL 3378663, at *1 (D. Me. July 9, 2014) (Singal, J.) "A compromise agreement, fairly arrived at, is an enforceable contract both under Maine law and general doctrine." *Penobscot Indian Nation v. Key Bank of Maine*, 112 F.3d 538, 557 (1st Cir. 1997) citing *Warner v. Rossignol*, 513 F.2d 678, 682 (1st Cir.1975); *see also*, *Phillips v. Fuller*, 541 A.2d 629, 629 n. 1 (Me.1988) (recognizing that claim can be asserted for a breach of a settlement agreement); *A.L. Brown Constr. Co., Inc. v. McGuire*, 495 A.2d 794, 798 (Me.1985) (finding settlement agreement to be an enforceable contract). "Settlement agreements are analyzed as contracts, and the existence of a binding settlement is a question of fact." *2301 Cong. Realty, LLC v. Wise Bus. Forms, Inc.*, 106 A.3d 1131, 1133-34 (Me. 2014)(internal citations omitted) For a settlement agreement to be binding, the parties must have mutually intended "to be bound by terms sufficiently definite to enforce." Id.[6]

Here, the parties reached an agreement to specific terms as to a new "Production Agreement" to permit McKenzie the exclusive right to publish and sell certain authorized artwork. (Dkt. No. 7-1, Binding Term Sheet) The settlement agreement set out the specific terms including: the duration of the contract, the works to be produced and sold, the percentage of gross proceeds to be paid to the Estate, the specific control of artwork, information rights retained by the Estate, assignability, handling of an autopen machine, a process for assessing authenticity of artwork, percentage apportionment of funds held in escrow by the Rosenbaum Conservatory to the parties, handling of artwork held by the Rosenbaum Conservatory Galleries, and McKenzie's ability to produce non-Indiana artwork. (*Id.*, pp. 1-3) The agreement also provides for specific mutual releases of claims against the parties McKenzie and the Estate and its representative and other parties, calls unreservedly for the dismissal with prejudice of the arbitration between the Estate and McKenzie which is the New York arbitration where these same issues were being litigated, and an agreement that the Estate will provide indemnity and defense of McKenzie in the pending SDNY case against Morgan. (*Id.*, p. 3) The agreement also specifically states:

> This term sheet is intended to be binding. and will be replaced by a more formal Settlement Agreement and Production Agreement. Payments, releases, dismissals and other consideration under this term sheet will be made after a more formal Settlement Agreement and Releases and Production Agreement are executed.

(*Id.*, p. 3) Both McKenzie and the Estate (Brannan) executed the agreement on November 26, 2019. (*Id.*, pp. 4-5) The Binding Term Sheet, executed by the parties, thus establishes:

> ... a legally binding agreement [because] the parties...mutually assented to be bound by all of its material terms; the assent [is] reflected and manifested in the contract, either expressly or impliedly; and the contract [is] sufficiently definite to enable the court to determine its exact meaning and fix exactly the legal liability of the parties.

See, Roy v. Danis, 553 A.2d 663, 664 (Me. 1989). Moreover, after the parties executed the Term Sheet, counsel for the Estate reported to the Arbitration Panel just three days after the conclusion of mediation, as follows:

> We are pleased to report that the parties have signed a term sheet that resolves all claims and counterclaims in this action.

(Dkt. No. 1-6, Exhibit F to Verified Complaint, Email of Estate Counsel, November 29, 2019.) *Compare*, *Concordia Partners, LLC v. Ward*, 2:12-CV-138-GZS, 2014 WL 3378663, at *8 (D. Me. July 9, 2014)(After report to court of settlement, "the Court cannot countenance a later attempt to recharacterize clear representations that this case was settled into mere requests for more time to negotiate a settlement. Quite simply, counsel and the parties are bound by representations made to the Court, particularly when the record shows—as this record does—that extensive, thoughtful negotiation preceded those representations."); *Forrest Associates v. Passamaquoddy Tribe*, 760 A.2d 1041, 1043 (Me. 2000)(Authorized statements made by the agent to a third person are considered admissions of the principal.) *See also*, *Forcelli, supra.*, 972 N.Y.S.2d at 573 ("A party will be bound by the acts of its agent in settlement negotiations and an agreement will be binding where the agent has either actual or apparent authority.")

The fact that there is a provision requiring reducing the Binding Term Sheet to a more formal document does not mean that an enforceable agreement was not reached by the Binding Term Sheet itself. "The absence of a formalized contract does not affect the binding nature of a potential contract if the parties intended to close the contract prior to a formal writing." *Michaud v. Nexxlinx of Maine, Inc.*, 1:13-CV-270-JDL, 2015 WL 728497, at *6 (D. Me. Feb. 19, 2015) (citing Maine law) In *Michaud*, a settlement agreement reached through emails and letters of counsel was enforced where the parties agreed on the material terms of an amount of financial payment and non-monetary terms but later the plaintiff refused to sign the final settlement document. The plaintiff

---

6. McKenzie notes that while Maine law should apply under the choice-of-law analysis, even if New York law was applied, there is no conflict, and the settlement agreement would be enforced. *See, e.g.*, *Forcelli v. Gelco Corp.*, 972 N.Y.S.2d 570, 573 (N.Y. App. Div. 2d Dept. 2013) [internal citations omitted]: "Stipulations of settlement are judicially favored, will not lightly be set aside, and 'are to be enforced with rigor and without a searching examination into their substance' as long as they are 'clear, final and the product of mutual accord.'"

argued that the settlement was unenforceable because the parties did not agree on the specific language for the non-monetary terms. The Court held the agreement was enforceable explaining:

> Defendants' settlement, contained in the March 6 letter, included "a confidentiality provision, a non-disparagement provision, and a no-contact provision." Insofar as Defendants advised Attorney Baber that they would "require" the inclusion of the "provisions," the "provisions" constitute material terms to the agreement. The fact that the parties did not agree on the exact language regarding the "provisions" does not render the settlement agreement unenforceable. The settlement agreement, as with any contract, is subject to a reasonable interpretation of its terms. *See, e.g., Fitzgerald v. Hutchins*, 2009 ME 115, ¶ 18, 983 A.2d 382, 389 (rejecting argument that there was no agreement to pay a "commission" where the parties did not agree on the amount of the commission, and explaining that the law will supply a reasonable rate of commission) ... [additional case citations omitted] ... Without such a rule of law, a party would be able to cite the absence of an agreement on specific language on even the most basic terms typically included in a settlement agreement (*e.g.*, release of claims) as justification for the party's refusal to execute a settlement to which the party clearly agreed.

Michaud, 1:13-CV-270-JDL, 2015 WL 728497, at *7 (Nivison, MJ. adopted by Levy, J.)

In *Eastwick v. Cate St. Capital, Inc.*, 171 A.3d 1152, 1154-55 (Me. 2017), modified(Nov. 30, 2017), the parties mediated an employment dispute and signed a memorandum of understanding ("MOU") that set out the specific terms such as the termination of the employment contract and payment of consideration as well as provisions for an exchange of releases in "standard terms" covering all claims between the parties and requiring confidentiality. Thereafter, disputes arose between the parties in drafting the final settlement and release documents. The Supreme Judicial Court affirmed the lower court finding that the MOU was anintegrated, binding settlement agreement finding that the purpose of the MOU was tomemorialize their settlement, it left no remaining issues that required further mediation, and indicated finality even though it provided for use of the mediator thereafter to resolve any disputes that arose in the drafting or execution of the settlement in order to make the settlement final.

Similarly, in *Muther v. Broad Cove Shore Ass'n*, 968 A.2d 539 (Me. 2009), the parties engaged in a judicially assisted settlement conference for over seven hours, notified the court of a settlement agreement, and counsel read the detailed terms of the agreement into the record, with counsel making corrections, clarifications, and additions as necessary. *Id.*, at 540-41. Each party then affirmed on the record, in response to inquiries from the court, that the recital was a fair and accurate representation of that agreement. *Id.*, at 541. The parties also agreed that the settlement would be reduced to a stipulated judgment for judicial signature at a later date but thereafter the defendant refused to sign a draft of the stipulated judgment proposed by plaintiffs, arguing that it contained terms that were materially different from those understood the day ofthe settlement conference. *Id.* Subsequent attempts to agree on the terms of a stipulated judgment failed. *Id.* The Court held that the "the transcript of the settlement agreement, without more, conclusively establishes the existence of a binding settlement agreement as a matter of law, and subsequent disputes that arose while attempting to reduce the settlement to a stipulated judgment did not affect the authority of the court to enforce the agreement through the entry of a judgment incorporating the terms previously stipulated to by the parties." *Id.*, at 542.

In our case, one very clear provision of the Binding Term Sheet is that the New York arbitration should be dismissed and there is absolutely nothing further to negotiate on that point.

C. This Court Should Enjoin the Estate from Proceeding with the Arbitration Because the Dispute Has Been Resolved by a Binding Settlement Agreement

This Court has the authority to enjoin a party from proceeding with an arbitration. *See,Societe Generale de Surveillance, S.A. v. Raytheon European Mgmt. & Sys. Co.*, 643 F.2d 863, 868 (1st Cir. 1981) (holding that the power to "enjoin a party from arbitrating" is "concomitantof the power to compel arbitration"). Following *Societe Generale de Surveillance, S.A.*, courts inthis Circuit routinely stay arbitrations. *See, e.g., John Hancock Life Ins. Co. (USA) v. Leisher*,CV 15-13539-RGS, Dkt. 20, Electronic Order (D. Mass. Apr. 11, 2016) (ordering that arbitrationprocess was to be stayed until the court resolved whether the settlement agreement was valid andbinding)*; Fantastic Sams Franchise Corp. v. FSRO Ass'n, Ltd.*, 824 F. Supp. 2d 221, 225 (D.Mass. 2011) (granting plaintiff's motion to stay arbitration based on contractual language thatclass-wide arbitration was prohibited), *aff'd*, 683 F.3d 18 (1st Cir. 2012); *AGP Indus. SA,(PERU) v. JPS Elastromerics Corp.*, 511 F. Supp. 2d 212, 215 (D. Mass. 2007) (permanently staying arbitration, finding no agreement to arbitrate); *A.T. Cross Co. v. Royal Selangor(s) PTE, Ltd.*, 217 F. Supp. 2d 229, 237 (D.R.I. 2002) (granting motion to stay arbitration); *see also, In re American Express Financial Advisors Security Litigation*, 672 F.3d 113, 143 (2d Cir. 2011) (holding that plaintiffs were bound by a settlement agreement in a class action, and were enjoined from "arbitrating their Released Claims before FINRA arbitrators.")

Specifically, this Court should enjoin the Defendants from proceeding with arbitration and decide the enforceability of the Binding Term Sheet, both its substantive provisions stating the new agreement between McKenzie and the Estate, and the provision to dismiss the arbitration. The First Circuit has recently made clear that this dispute - arbitrability and the enforcement of the settlement agreement's termination of the New York arbitration - is for this Court to decide. In *Biller v. S-H OpCo Greenwich Bay Manor, LLC*, 961 F.3d 502, 509-10 (1st Cir. 2020), the First Circuit held that where an arbitration clause "does not supply clear and unmistakable evidence" that the parties agreed to have an arbitrator decide the "gateway" question of "arbitrability," such as whether the parties have agreed to arbitrate or whether their agreement covers a particular controversy, it is for the court, not the arbitrator, to decide in the first instance. Furthermore, "[w]hen the arbitration-resister "specifically challenges the enforceability of the arbitration clause itself" (again, unless another provision clearly delegated the issue to the arbitrator) the court must decide that challenge before it can compel arbitration. *Id.*, at 512 citing *Granite Rock Co. v. Intl. Broth. of Teamsters*, 561 U.S. 287, 301 (2010). A "claim that two parties later agreed to extinguish their arbitration pledge (specifically) is for the courts to decide." *Id.*, at 514. Defendant should be enjoined from continuing the arbitration until this Court resolves these issues. *See, id.; see also, Bd. of Trustees of Trucking Employees of N. Jersey Welfare Fund, Inc. - Pension Fund v. Centra*, 983 F.2d 495, 506-07 (3d Cir. 1992) (where pension fund brought suit pursuant to Multiemployer Pension Plan Amendments Act (MPPAA) to collect withdrawal payments from company that allegedly controlled participating employer at time of its withdrawal from fund and district court ordered resolution by arbitrator of dispute concerning enforceability of alleged settlement of withdrawal of liability claims, appeals court held that question of whether employer had breached settlement agreement was one for court, not arbitrator, because question did not fall within the exhaustive list of arbitrable issues outlined in MPPAA and remanded to district court accordingly).

While the parties' contract disputes under the preceding agreement were in arbitration pursuant to the arbitration clause in the preceding agreement (Dkt. No. 1-2, Ex. B), the Binding Term Sheet terminates and explicitly states that it replaces the preceding contract, the HOPE Agreement (with the arbitration clause) and specifically provides for dismissal with prejudice of the New York arbitration authorized by that agreement's arbitration clause. *See, Applied Energetics, Inc. v. NewOak Capital Markets, LLC*, 645 F.3d 522, 525 (2d Cir. 2011) (contracting parties are free to revoke an earlier agreement to arbitrate by executing a subsequent agreement the terms of which plainly preclude arbitration).

Based on the strong likelihood of success on the merits and this Court's authority to enjoin the Estate from continuing the pending arbitration until this action is resolved, this motion should be granted. The remaining factors also weigh in favor of the injunction herein sought.

III. McKenzie Will Suffer Irreparable Harm

Plaintiffs would suffer irreparable harm if forced to arbitrate and incur the associated costs after the matter was already settled. *Compare, Graham v. Smith*, 292 F. Supp. 2d 153, 159-60 (D. Me. 2003) citing *PaineWebber Inc. v. Hartmann*, 921 F.2d 507, 515 (3d Cir.1990) ("we think it is obvious that the harm to a party could be *per se* irreparable if a court were to abdicate its responsibility to determine the scope of an arbitrator's jurisdiction and, instead, were to compel the party, who has not agreed to do so, to submit to an arbitrator's own determination of his authority.") and citing, *in accord McLaughlin Gormley King Co. v. Terminix Int'l. Co.*, 105 F.3d 1192, 1194 (8th Cir.1997) ("If a court has concluded that a dispute is non-arbitrable, prior cases uniformly hold that the party urging arbitration may be enjoined from pursuing what would now be a futile arbitration, even if the threatened irreparable injury to the other party is only the cost of defending the arbitration and having the court set aside any unfavorable award."); *and Raytheon Engineers & Constructors, Inc. v. SMS Schloemann-Sieman Akiengesellschaft*, 99 C 7771, 2000 WL 420866, *3, (N.D.Ill. March 16, 2000) ("forcing a party to arbitrate a dispute that it has not agreed to arbitrate is irreparable harm.").

Additionally, McKenzie risks losing the benefits conferred by the Binding Term Sheet, namely losing an irretrievable part of the market for the particular artwork involved and thus the right to control McKenzie's part of the brand as provided in the Binding Term Sheet - a loss that cannot be simply converted to money damages. *Compare, Ludington v. LaFreniere*, 704 A.2d 875 (Me. 1998) (Specific performance is a substitute for the legal remedy of compensation whenever, in the discretion of the court, "the legal remedy is inadequate or impracticable.")

IV. The Balance of Hardships Favors Issuing this Preliminary Injunction

The enforceability of the settlement agreement can be resolved fairly quickly as it involves a single written contract (the Binding Term Sheet) and well-established contract law to be applied to its written terms. Presently, the arbitration is scheduled to run through May of 2021, with a hearing to be held in March 2021, although the parties were recently instructed by the arbitration panel to submit a revised pre-hearing schedule. (*See*, AAA Panel Emails to Counsel, **Exhibits B and C** hereto) A stay until this issue is decided still leaves adequate time to pursue arbitration should it be needed. No harm would come if this matter could not be resolved by May 2021 because the arbitration deadlines can be extended for good cause, a threshold that is certainly met by this action. (*See*, Dkt. No. 1-4, AAA Procedural and Scheduling Order, ¶ 12 (b)) The irreparable harm to be suffered by McKenzie if the costly arbitration proceedings are pursued simultaneously to and contrary to this proceeding which should enforce the settlement as shown above outweighs the harm from a delay in the arbitration proceedings.

V. The Public Interest is Served by Enjoining Arbitration for McKenzie to Seek Enforcement of the Settlement

The public interest in promoting and enforcing settlements without more favors granting an injunction. *See, Fid. & Guar. Ins. Co. v. Star Equip. Corp.*, 541 F.3d 1, 5 (1st Cir. 2008) ("Settlement agreements enjoy great favor with the courts as a preferred alternative to costly, time-consuming litigation."); *see also, Marmet Health Care Ctr., Inc. v. Brown*, 565 U.S. 530, 533 (2012) (federal law "reflects an emphatic federal policy in favor of arbitral dispute resolution.") Affirmance of such binding agreements furthers private resolution of civil disputes with attendant savings of judicial time for matters not resolvable this way and agreements made in mediation should not be jettisoned once made based on afterthoughts. The sanctity of enforceability of these agreements, once made, furthers the viability of the court-saving ADR methods. *See, Louis Berger Group, Inc. v. State Bank of India*, 802 F. Supp. 2d 482, 490 (S.D.N.Y. 2011) ("Stays are particularly appropriate where they promote judicial economy, avoidance of confusion and possible inconsistent results")

Moreover, as explained above, Robert Indiana died without known heirs and in his will bequeathed his entire estate, less debts and claims, to Star of Hope, a Maine charity in Vinalhaven. Enjoining the expensive New York arbitration while McKenzie seeks enforcement of the Binding Term Sheet is in the public interest as it preserves the Estate's assets that wouldotherwise go to the benefit of the charity and thus to the benefit of the Vinalhaven communityrather than continuing to be spent on ongoing, very costly arbitration. Minimizing legal fees thatwould instead benefit a Vinalhaven charity was the reason the mediation resulting in the Binding Term Sheet was commenced. Spending what would be charitable funds on lawyers in this arbitration is particularly against public policy since as the lawyers for the Estate told the arbitrators in New York, after the Binding Term Sheet was executed in Portland:

We are pleased to report that the parties have signed a term sheet that resolves all claims and counterclaims in this action.

(*See*, Email of Estate Counsel, November 29, 2019, Exhibit F to Verified Complaint, found at Dkt. No. 1-6) Litigating again and at great cost what has already been resolved is the worst kind of waste and the precise justification for public policy favoring enforcement of settlement agreements.

CONCLUSION

For each of the foregoing reasons, this Court should preliminarily enjoin the Estate from proceeding with the pending arbitration in New York.

Pursuant to Local Rule 7(e), Plaintiff McKenzie requests oral argument.

Dated: August 14, 2020

Respectfully submitted,

/s/ *John J.E. Markham, II*

John J.E. Markham, II (Maine BBO No. 2674)

/s/ *Bridget A. Zerner*

Bridget A. Zerner (*Pro Hac Vice* - MA 669468)

MARKHAM & READ

908 Maine Street

Waldoboro, Maine 04572

Tel: (207) 790-8049

One Commercial Wharf West

Boston, Massachusetts 02110

Tel: (617) 523-6329

Fax: (617)742-8604

jmarkham@markhamread.com

bzerner@markhamread.com

Motion to Dismiss for Failure to State a Claim

2020 WL 6707461 (D.Me.)

United States District Court, D. Maine.

Annie ZHAO, individually and on behalf of all others similarly situated, Plaintiff,

v.

CIEE, INC.,

and

COUNCIL ON INTERNATIONAL EDUCATIONAL EXCHANGE, INC., Defendants.

No. 2:20-cv-00240-LEW.

July 10, 2020.

Defendants CIEE, Inc. and Council on International Educational Exchange, Inc.'s Motion to Dismiss Purusuant to Fed. R. Civ. P. 12(b)(6)

Robert J. Keach, Esq., Chad W. Higgins, Esq., Patrick I. Marass, Esq., Zachary B. Brandwein, Esq., Bernstein Shur, 100 Middle Street; PO Box 9729, Portland, ME 04104-5029, 207-774-1200, rkeach@bernsteinshur.com, chiggins@bernsteinshur.com, pmarass@bernsteinshur.com, zbrandwein@bernsteinshur.com, for defendants, CIEE, Inc. and Council on International Educational Exchange, Inc.

Defendants CIEE, Inc. and the Council on International Educational Exchange, Inc. (collectively, "CIEE"), respectfully submit this Motion to Dismiss pursuant to Federal Rule of Civil Procedure 12(b)(6). CIEE requests the Court dismiss all claims against it in this lawsuit.

INTRODUCTION AND FACTUAL BACKGROUND

CIEE is the country's oldest and largest study abroad and intercultural exchange non-profit organization. Complaint (ECF Doc. 1-3) ("Compl.") ¶ 17. Its mission is "[t]o help people gain understanding, acquire knowledge, and develop skills for living in a globally interdependent and culturally diverse world by offering the most comprehensive, relevant, and valuable exchange programs available." *Id.* ¶ 18.

Plaintiff Annie Zhao ("Plaintiff") contracted with CIEE to attend a Spring 2020 study abroad program at the University of Amsterdam in the Netherlands. *Id.* ¶ 6. Plaintiff's study abroad program, and most of CIEE's other Spring 2020 programs, began in late January. *Id.* ¶ 39.

On March 11, 2020, the World Health Organization declared the novel coronavirus a pandemic. *Id.* ¶ 55. Also, on March 11, 2020, the United States Centers for Disease Control and Prevention ("CDC") issued a Level 3 Travel Warning for Europe, a Level 2 Travel Warning for the world, and the United States Department of State ("U.S. State Department") issued a Level 3 global travel advisory. *Id.* ¶ 56. Regrettably—but out of concern for the health of its students— on March 12, 2020, CIEE issued notification of its intent to suspend the study abroad portion of Plaintiff's program. *Id.* ¶ 57. The next day, the President of the United States declared the novel coronavirus pandemic a national emergency. *Id.* ¶ 59. CIEE suspended the on-site portions of it study-abroad programs on March 15, 2020. *Id.* ¶ 60. In his message to students, CIEE President and CEO James P. Pellow stated that the "expanding global disruption caused by the spread of COVID-19" precipitated CIEE's decision that "study abroad programs will be suspended [. . .]."

Id. As Plaintiff acknowledges, "CIEE undeniably made the right decision [. . .]." *Id.* ¶ 1. CIEE transitioned Plaintiff's program—and others it was forced to suspend—into online and distance-learning classes. *Id.* ¶¶ 65, 67. It did so to ensure students could "earn their originally anticipated academic credits." *Id.* ¶ 65.

Plaintiff's Complaint alleges that CIEE's suspension of its study abroad programs in the face of an unprecedented global health crisis was a breach of its contractual obligations. *See* Compl. Count I. The Complaint concedes that the Plaintiff and putative class members "entered into the same or substantially similar, binding contracts with [CIEE]." *Id.* ¶ 95. Throughout, the Complaint invokes the parties' contract. *Id.* ¶¶ 69-71 (repeatedly employing the phrase: "CIEE's no-refund policy [. . .] breaches its contractual obligation [. . .]"); *id.* ¶ 79 ("constituted a material breach of CIEE's contractual obligations to its student participants"). Yet, Plaintiff never fully cites relevant provisions of the contract, nor does she include the contract with the Complaint. *See generally* Compl. Reading the agreed-to terms in the parties' agreement demonstrates that it unambiguously bars Plaintiff's claims and the claims of her putative class.

As set forth in the Complaint, Plaintiff, and other participants in CIEE's programs agreed to "substantially identical contracts with" CIEE. Compl. ¶¶ 85C, 92-93, 95-98. This contract was the CIEE Program Participant Contract and Forum and Methodology for Dispute Resolution Agreement ("Participant Contract"). Compl. ¶¶ 5, 15; *see* Declaration of Deborah Cronin, Ex. B, attached hereto as *Exhibit 1* ("Dec. Cronin"). At the top of the first page, the Participant Contract unambiguously states:

> **This form is important. It includes terms and conditions and releases CIEE from liability. All participants MUST sign this form.**
>
> I understand and agree that this agreement shall constitute a binding contract between the undersigned and "CIEE." "CIEE" is defined to include: the Council on International Educational Exchange, Inc., its owners, directors, officers, employees and affiliates.

(Emphasis in original.) In signing the Participant Contract, all participants, including the Plaintiff, certified and agreed to adhere to the CIEE Terms and Conditions ("Terms and Conditions"). Dec. Cronin, Ex. A. The Terms and Conditions provide in relevant part:

> If an emergency requires that a program be canceled following the program start date and prior to the end of an academic term, CIEE will make reasonable efforts to make alternative arrangements in order to allow students to complete their academic work, but cannot guarantee that full or partial credit will be obtained. If alternative arrangements cannot be made, CIEE will make reasonable efforts to collect documentation of student work completed to date. CIEE will share this information with the home institutions of students enrolled in the program so they will be able to evaluate, per home institution policies, whether to grant their students any, full, or partial credit for work completed.

Id. Ex. A.

The Terms and Conditions apply to CIEE's "Fall 2019, January 2020, Spring 2020, and Summer 2020 programs and supersede any other published policies pertaining to these terms." *Id.* They also provide that "in the case of conflict among [CIEE's policies], the CIEE Participant Contract and Forum and Methodology for Dispute Resolution Agreement, inclusive of these Terms & Conditions, first applies." *Id.*

All participants in CIEE programs—including the Plaintiff—also acknowledged and agreed to the following relevant provisions of the Participant Contract:

> I understand that I am responsible for CIEE program fees as published at http://www.ciee.org/study-abroad/ for my program and term(s) of study, as well as any associated fees as billed to me by my home institution. I also understand and agree that CIEE does not give refunds (or partial refunds) for unused services that are included as part of the program fee.

Id. Ex. B, ¶ 10.

> Without limitation, CIEE is not responsible for any injury, loss, or damage to person or property, death, delay, or inconvenience in connection with the provision of any goods or services occasioned by or resulting from, but not limited to, acts of God, force majeure, acts of government [. . .] epidemics or the threat thereof, disease, lack of access to or quality of medical care, difficulty in evacuation in case of a medical or other emergency, or for any other cause beyond the direct control of CIEE. CIEE is not responsible in any manner for claims predicated upon participants arriving on site prior to the program start date or departing subsequent to the program end date.

Id. Ex. B, ¶ 18.

> I understand that perceived or actual epidemics (such as, but not limited to, H1N1, Ebola, SARS, bird flu, or Zika) can delay, disrupt, interrupt or cancel programs. I agree to assume all risk of any such problems which could result from any such occurrences.

Id. Ex. B, ¶ 19.

> I understand that perceived or actual events (such as, but not limited to, political turmoil / unrest, economic collapse,

environmental issues, natural disasters, pandemics, epidemics, university strikes, terrorist events, governmental travel warnings, and many other events outside CIEE's control, such as those described in Paragraphs 18-19, 21-22) can delay, disrupt, interrupt or cancel programs. I agree to hold harmless CIEE from any such actual or perceived events.

Id. Ex. B, ¶ 23.

The Terms and Conditions and the Participant Contract bar Counts I and II of Plaintiff's Complaint.

LEGAL STANDARD

To survive a motion to dismiss pursuant to Federal Rule of Civil Procedure 12(b)(6), the Plaintiff must plead facts sufficient to establish every element of the claim. *Ashcroft v. Iqbal*, 556 U.S. 662, 678 (2009). Her allegations "must be enough to raise a right to relief above the speculative level." *Bell Atl. Corp. v. Twombly*, 550 U.S. 544, 555 (2007). The Plaintiff's Complaint must provide "more than labels and conclusions, and a formulaic recitation of the elements of a cause of action will not do." *Id.* Although this Court must accept the Complaint's factual allegations as true, it is "not bound to credit 'bald assertions, unsupportable conclusions, and opprobrious epithets.'" *Brower v. ADT LLC*, No. 2:15-CV-00337-JAW, 2016 WL 4919884, at *7 (D. Me. Sept. 14, 2016) (Woodcock, J.) (quoting *Campagna v. Mass. Dep't of Envtl. Prot.*, 334 F.3d 150, 155 (1st Cir. 2003)). Determining whether the Complaint, "states a plausible claim for relief" is "a context-specific task that requires [this Court] to draw on its judicial experience and common sense." *Id.* at 679. If the facts alleged, taken as true, do not "state a claim to relief that is plausible on its face," the Plaintiff's Complaint must be dismissed. *Id.* at 678 (quoting *Twombly*, 550 U.S. at 570).

Additionally, "when 'a complaint's factual allegations are expressly linked to—and admittedly depend upon—a document (the authenticity of which is not challenged),' then the court can review it upon a motion to dismiss." *Alt. Energy, Inc. v. St. Paul Fire & Marine Ins. Co.*, 267 F.3d 30, 34 (1st Cir. 2001) (quoting *Beddall v. State St. Bank & Trust Co.*, 137 F.3d 12, 17 (1st Cir. 1998). Plaintiff's Complaint repeatedly references CIEE's contract with participants, upon which all her claims rest. *See* Compl. ¶¶ 69-71, 79, 85C, 92-93, 95-98. Accordingly, including the Terms and Conditions and the Participant Contract with this Motion does not constitute an introduction of matters outside the pleadings. *See Tellabs, Inc. v. Makor Issues & Rights, Ltd.*, 551 U.S. 308, 322 (2007) (holding "courts must consider the complaint in its entirety, as well as other sources courts ordinarily examine when ruling on Rule 12(b)(6) motions to dismiss, in particular, documents incorporated into the complaint by reference [. . .]"); *see also Diva's Inc. v. City of Bangor*, 411 F.3d 30, 38 (1st Cir. 2005) (denying appellant's argument that the district court erred when considering a document upon which the complaint depended when it was attached to the defendant's motion to dismiss, and holding it was proper for the district court to review it when deciding a Rule 12(b)(6) motion). The Terms and Conditions and the Participant Contract are integral to the Plaintiff's Complaint and Plaintiff does not—nor could she—contest the authenticity of the Terms and Conditions and Participant Contract on which she bases her Complaint. *Alt. Energy, Inc.*, 267 F.3d at 34. Accordingly, this Court can evaluate these documents within the context of this Rule 12(b)(6) Motion.[1]

ARGUMENT

I. Plaintiff Failed to State a Claim for Breach of Contract and Any Claims Arising from the Novel Coronavirus are Otherwise Barred.

Under Maine law, "the elements of breach of contract are: (1) breach of a material contract term; (2) causation; and (3) damages." *Brower*, 2016 WL 4919884 at *11 (quoting *Me. Energy Recovery Co. v. United Steel Structures, Inc.*, 1999 ME 31, ¶ 7, 724 A.2d

---

1. If, however, the Court deems otherwise, it should treat this Motion as one for summary judgment under Rule 56. *See* Fed. R. Civ. P. 12(d). In which case, summary judgment is proper "if the pleadings, depositions, answers to interrogatories, and admissions on file, together with the affidavits, if any, show that there is no genuine issue as to any material fact and that the moving party is entitled to judgment as a matter of law." Fed. R. Civ. P. 56. Only disputes over facts that might affect the outcome of the suit under the governing law will properly preclude the entry of summary judgment. *Anderson v. Liberty Lobby, Inc.*, 477 U.S. 242, 248 (1986). In addition, the evidence of the non-moving party is to be believed and all justifiable inferences are to be drawn in the non-moving party's favor. *Anderson*, 477 U.S. at 252 (citing *Adickes v. S.H. Kress & Co.*, 398 U.S. 144, 158–59 (1970)). Plaintiff's Complaint fails under either standard. As outlined in this Motion, the Terms and Conditions and Participant Contract unambiguously indicate that CIEE is entitled to judgment on both counts in the Complaint as a matter of law. *See* id.; Fed. R. Civ. P. 56.

1248.[2] Count I of Plaintiff's Complaint fails to state a cognizable claim for breach of contract because the language of the Terms and Conditions and Participant Contract demonstrate CIEE has not breached a material term.

A. Plaintiff failed to state a claim for breach of contract because CIEE fully performed its obligations pursuant to the Terms and Conditions when it transitioned its study abroad programs into online learning classes

The Terms and Conditions and Participant Contract are unambiguous, and their interpretation is a question of law that this Court can properly determine in a Rule 12(b)(6) motion. *See Brower*, 2016 WL 4919884 at *8 ("Under Maine law, determining whether or not a contract is ambiguous is a question of law," and if "a contract is unambiguous, its interpretation is also a question of law." (alterations and quotation marks omitted); *see also Am. Prot. Ins. Co. v. Acadia Ins. Co.*, 2003 ME 6, ¶ 11, 814 A.2d 989; *Fowler v. Boise Cascade Corp.*, 948 F.2d 49, 54 (1st Cir. 1991). Although Plaintiff declined to attach the Terms and Conditions and the Participant Contract to the Complaint, these documents must be considered in their entirety, their language and provisions afforded their plain meaning, and construed in a way that does not render them meaningless. *Am. Prot. Ins. Co.*, 2003 ME at ¶ 12. Even crediting the Complaint's factual allegations as true, Plaintiff has failed to state a claim for breach of contract.

The Complaint quotes a portion of paragraph 14 of the Participant Contract when it argues that "CIEE's no-refund policy for its cancelled Spring 2020 programs [. . .] breaches the term of its contract with participants, which provides, among other things: 'In the unlikely event that a program is cancelled (due to low enrollment or any other reason), CIEE will refund all payments received but will have no further liability to participant."[3] Compl. ¶ 72. Plaintiff also alleges that "CIEE's offer to substitute online classes [. . .] was not agreed to in any contract with program participants." *Id.* ¶ 99. Plaintiff's arguments ignore the plain language of the parties' contractual agreements and they seek to distort the Terms and Conditions and the Participant Contract to render them meaningless. *Am. Prot. Ins. Co.*, 2003 ME at ¶ 12.

The Terms and Conditions supersede the cited provision in paragraph 14 of the Participant Contract. Cronin Dec. Ex. A. ("The Terms and Conditions as outlined below pertain to the . . . . Spring 2020 . . . program [] and supersede any other published policies pertaining to these terms." Furthermore, it provides in relevant part:

> If an emergency requires that a program be canceled following the program start date and prior to the end of an academic term, CIEE will make reasonable efforts to make alternative arrangements in order to allow students to complete their academic work, but cannot guarantee that full or partial credit will be obtained.

Id.

Here, CIEE suspended Plaintiff's Amsterdam program following the program start date in January 2020 but prior to the end of the academic term. Compl. ¶¶ 57, 60. It did so appropriately— as Plaintiff acknowledged—due to the novel coronavirus, which, the U.S. CDC and the U.S. State Department both recognized as an unprecedented public health emergency. *Id.* ¶¶ 1, 56. The Complaint's own allegations demonstrate CIEE transitioned the programs to online and distance-learning classes, so students— including Plaintiff—could complete their academic work. *Id.* ¶¶ 60, 65, 67.

The Terms and Conditions control CIEE's obligations—which are to "make reasonable efforts to make alternative arrangements in order to allow students to complete their academic work." These are exactly the terms to which the Plaintiff and every CIEE program participant— including all members of the putative class—agreed. CIEE satisfied these obligations. Plaintiff's allegations that CIEE breached its contractual obligations because it "canceled" its programs and transitioned students to online learning fails as a matter of law. Accordingly, Plaintiff has failed to state a claim for breach of contract and this Court should dismiss Count I of her Complaint with prejudice.

B. The Participant Contract's plain and repeated language bars Count I and Count II of Plaintiff's Complaint

Moreover, the plain language of the Participant Contract's numerous provisions demonstrates the parties' mutual intent to hold CIEE harmless for losses associated with the novel coronavirus pandemic. These provisions alone make dismissal of Plaintiff's Complaint appropriate. *See Brower*, 2016 WL 4919884 at *11. In *Brower*, the parties' contract contained a provision exculpating the defendant from liability. *Id.* That contract provided in relevant part, "you agree that we . . . . are exempt from liability for any loss, damage, injury, or other consequence arising directly or indirectly from the services we perform or the systems we provide under this

---

2. Paragraph 33 of the Participant Contract provides that any dispute or claim which refers or relates to this contract, any literature related to the Program, or the Program itself, shall be [. . .] subject to substantive and procedural Maine law." Cronin Dec. Ex. B ¶ 33.

3. Although the Complaint quotes this language, which comes from paragraph 14 of the Participant Contract, Plaintiff failed to cite to that provision and declined to attach the Terms and Conditions or Participant Contract itself to the Complaint.

contract." *Id*. The Court dismissed the plaintiff's contract claim pursuant to a Rule 12(b)(6) motion and added that even if the defendant had breached the contract, the "exculpatory and limited liability clauses would compel the Court to dismiss [plaintiff's] breach of contract claims." *Id*. Here, like in *Brower*, even crediting the Complaint's allegations as true, the exculpatory provisions of the Participant Contract preclude Plaintiff's claims against CIEE.

First, the very beginning of the Particpant Contract explained that it was a "binding contract between the undersigned and 'CIEE'" and articulated in bold lettering that "**This form is important. It includes terms and conditions and releases CIEE from liability.**" Cronin Dec. Ex. B (emphasis in original).

Second, in paragraph 10 of the Participant Contract, Plaintiff—and members of the putative class—stated they understood and agreed "that CIEE does not give refunds (or partial refunds) for unused services that are included as part of the program fee." Cronin Dec. Ex. B ¶ 10. Plaintiff— and all members of the putative class—expressly acknowledged in the Participant Contract that they were not entitled to a refund from CIEE. *See Maine Mun. Employees Health Tr. v. Maloney*, 2004 ME 51, ¶ 6, 846 A.2d 336 ("Because [defendant] had no [contractual] duty to reimburse [plaintiff], the District Court properly dismissed [plaintiff's] breach of contract claim.").

Third, in paragraphs 18, 19, and 23 of the Participant Contact, Plaintiff and members of the putative class agreed that CIEE would not be liable for breach of contract if an unprecedented emergency—such as the novel coronavirus—disrupted their study abroad programs. Paragraph 18 provides: "Without limitation, CIEE is not responsible for any injury, loss, or damage to person or property, death, delay, or inconvenience in connection with the provision of any goods or services occasioned by or resulting from, but not limited to, acts of God, force majeure, acts of government [. . .] epidemics or the threat thereof, [and] disease [. . .]." Cronin Dec. Ex. B ¶ 18. Paragraph 19 provides that Plaintiff and members of the putative class agreed to "assume all risk of any such problems which could result from," "perceived or actual epidemics (such as, but not limited to, H1N1, Ebola, SARS, bird flu, or Zika)" which could "delay, disrupt, interrupt or cancel programs." *Id*. ¶ 19. Likewise, in paragraph 23 of the Participant Contract, the Plaintiff—and members of the putative class—agreed "to hold harmless CIEE" from "perceived or actual events (such as, but not limited to, [. . .] natural disasters, pandemics, epidemics, [. . .], governmental travel warnings, and many other events outside CIEE's control, such as those described in Paragraphs 18-19, 21-22)," which could "delay, disrupt, interrupt or cancel programs." *Id*. ¶ 23. *See E.H. Ashley & Co. v. Wells Fargo Alarm Servs.*, 907 F.2d 1274, 1276 (1st Cir. 1990) (affirming summary judgment for the defendant on a contract claim where the contract contained a limitation of liability waiving and releasing plaintiff's right to recover).

Pursuant to these plain terms, the Plaintiff—and members of the putative class—assumed all risk of loss associated with the novel coronavirus pandemic. They explicitly agreed to hold CIEE harmless. The Plaintiff's Complaint simply ignores these provisions. Although it should not, even if this Court were to assume CIEE breached the parties' agreement, the repeated exculpatory provisions in the Participant Contract bar both counts of the Complaint. This Court has enforced similar unambiguous contractual provisions when granting a Rule 12(b)(6) motion, *see Brower*, 2016 WL 4919884 at *11, as should be done here.

II The Existence of the Terms and Conditions and the Participant Contract Preclude the Plaintiff's Ability to Recover on Count II of the Complaint.

Count II of Plaintiff's Complaint is subject to dismissal for the reasons stated above. That there exist Terms and Conditions and the Participant Contract, to which Plaintiff acknowledges she agreed, also bar her equitable unjust enrichment claim. *Paffhausen v. Balano*, 1998 ME 47, ¶ 6, 708 A.2d 269. Unjust enrichment is a theory of equitable recovery for the value of a benefit retained and is only available in the absence of an express contract. *Id*. The Law Court has explained that an unjust enrichment claim "presupposes the absence of a contractual relationship between the parties." *York Cty. v. PropertyInfo Corp., Inc.*, 2019 ME 12, ¶ 26, 200 A.3d 803. The existence of a contract, therefore, precludes recovery for unjust enrichment under Maine Law. *See* id. ("Here, there is no dispute that [plaintiff] and [defendant] entered into an express contract, and that relationship precludes the availability of any recovery in equity for unjust enrichment.")

In this case, the Complaint's own allegations establish CIEE entered "substantially similar" express contracts with Plaintiff and all putative class members. Compl. ¶¶ 5, 6, 15, 85C, 92-93, 95-98. The existence of that contract, which Plaintiff acknowledges exists and governs the relationship between the parties, precludes Plaintiff's unjust enrichment claim. *See* id. Further, as detailed above, CIEE did not breach the Terms and Conditions or the Participant Contract. Regardless, their very existence precludes—as a matter of law—Plaintiff's unjust enrichment claim. Plaintiff, accordingly, has failed to state a cognizable claim for unjust enrichment and this Court should dismiss Count II.

CONCLUSION

For all the foregoing reasons, this Court should dismiss Plaintiff's claims against Defendants CIEE, Inc. and the Council on International Education Exchange, Inc. pursuant to Federal Rule of Civil Procedure 12(b)(6).

Dated: July 10, 2020

Respectfully Submitted,

/s/ Chad W. Higgins

Robert J. Keach, Esq.

Chad W. Higgins, Esq.

Patrick I. Marass, Esq.

Zachary B. Brandwein, Esq.

BERNSTEIN SHUR

100 Middle Street; PO Box 9729

Portland, ME 04104-5029

207-774-1200

rkeach@bernsteinshur.com

chiggins@bernsteinshur.com

pmarass@bernsteinshur.com

zbrandwein@bernsteinshur.com

Attorneys for Defendants

CIEE, Inc. and Council on International

Educational Exchange, Inc.

Motion to Dismiss for Lack of Subject Matter Jurisdiction

2019 WL 7667614 (D.Me.)

Westlaw Query>>

To find more Motion to Dismiss for Lack of Subject Matter Jurisdiction filings on Westlaw: access Maine Trial Court Documents (from the Home page, click Trial Court Documents, then Maine), click the Advanced Search link, select Motion to Dismiss for Lack of Jurisdiction, and click Search. Use the Jurisdiction filter on the left to narrow results to Federal.

United States District Court, D. Maine.

FEDEQ DV004 LLC and FEDEQ DV005 LLC, Plaintiffs,

v.

CITY OF PORTLAND and Jon Jennings, Defendants.

No. 2:19-cv-00382-JAW.

December 9, 2019.

Defendants' Motion to Dismiss for Lack of Subject Matter Jurisdiction, or in the Alternative, Motion for More Definite Statement to Show Subject Matter Jurisdiction under 28 U.S.C. § 1332

Russell B. Pierce, Jr., Esq., Norman, Hanson & DeTroy, LLC, Two Canal Plaza, P.O. Box 4600, Portland, ME 04112-4600, (207) 774-7000, rpierce@nhdlaw.com, for defendant Jon Jennings and the City of Portland.

NOW COME Defendants City of Portland and Jon Jennings, and pursuant to Rule 12(b)(1) of the Federal Rules of Civil Procedure and 28 U.S.C. § 1332, hereby move that the Plaintiffs reveal the state citizenship of each and every member of the plaintiff limited liability companies, for the purpose of showing complete diversity of citizenship and jurisdiction under 28 U.S.C. § 1332. *D.B. Zwirn Special Opportunities Fund, L.P. v. Mehrotra*, 661 F.3d 124, 125 (1st Cir. 2011) (per curiam) ("[T]he citizenship of a limited liability company 'is determined by the citizenship of all of its members.' ") (quoting *Pramco, LLC ex rel. CFSC Consortium, LLC v. San Juan Bay Marina, Inc.*, 435 F.3d 51, 54 (1st Cir. 2006)); *Duncan v. O'Shea*, 2019 WL 1320043, *4 (D. Me. March 22, 2019).

In the alternative, Defendants move for an order to show cause why this case should not be dismissed for lack of subject matter jurisdiction, based upon information and belief that a principal of one or both of the plaintiffs - i.e., Patrick Venne - is domiciled as a citizen of the State of Maine, therefore defeating complete diversity of citizenship among the parties and requiring dismissal for lack of subject matter jurisdiction. 28 U.S.C. § 1332(a).

I. Relevant Procedural Posture

This action was commenced against the City of Portland and City Manager, Jon Jennings, on or about August 16, 2019. The Plaintiffs are identified as two limited liability companies, FEDEQ DV004 LLC and FEDEQ DV005 LLC. Complaint (ECF Doc. # 1) at opening paragraph and ¶ 3 (referring to Plaintiffs as "Federated 04" and "Federated 05") (hereafter "Complaint"). The pleadings state that these two plaintiff entities appear to be successors-in-interest to other limited liability companies (see Complaint at page 1, "INTRODUCTION") and "are single purpose Florida limited liability companies formed for the purpose of owning and developing real property which have their principal place of business in and are principally controlled and managed by a common individual residing in, Miami-Dade County, Florida." Complaint at ¶ 3.

This is all the Complaint reveals relating to Plaintiffs' citizenship, on the issue of complete diversity, 28 U.S.C. § 1332. The City of Portland is of course alleged to be "a municipal corporation and the largest city in the State of Maine," and Defending Jennings is alleged to be "a natural person upon information and belief residing in the City of Portland, County of Cumberland, State of Maine."

Complaint (ECF Doc. # 1) at ¶¶ 3, 4.[1] The City of Portland filed an amended answer and counterclaims for breach of contract, admitting these allegations in substance (with the exception of the domiciliary allegation directed to Jennings, albeit Jennings does aver herein as the current City Manager of Portland that he is a citizen of the State of Maine). Amended Answer ¶¶ 4 & 5 (ECF Doc. # 19). Jennings responded to the Complaint by moving to dismiss the one state tort claim asserted against him in a final Count of the Complaint. *See* ECF Docs. ## 13, 26. The Plaintiffs have moved to dismiss the City of Portland's counterclaims, asserting failure to state a claim; the City opposes that motion, with a deadline of December 20, 2019 for response. See ECF Docs. ## 31, 41. Those motions remain pending and unresolved (Defendant Jennings' reply memorandum in support of one of the motions to dismiss, ECF Doc. # 26, is due on December 17, 2019).

The Court issued an amended scheduling order on October 9, 2019, to which both sides objected: Plaintiffs seek to expand the standard order's discovery limitations; Defendants seek a stay of discovery pending resolution of the Jennings motion to dismiss (and the Plaintiffs' motion to dismiss counterclaims). A hearing is scheduled on this issue for December 10, 2019. ECF Docket No. 32. The Amended Scheduling Order noted "Diversity" as the basis for subject matter jurisdiction. ECF Doc. # 17 at page 1.

On December 4, 2019, undersigned counsel Russell B. Pierce, Jr. - who is on record representing Defendant Jennings - also entered an appearance as counsel for Defendant City of Portland. The City's then-counsel of record, John Wall, moved to withdraw on December 5, 2019, with withdrawal granted on December 6, 2019.[2]

II. Legal Argument

The undersigned has brought the present motion as soon as possible, upon realizing on more in depth review of the matter, following his entry of appearance on December 4, 2019, that there may be an issue regarding complete diversity of citizenship in this case. Specifically, the Complaint alleges only state law claims: "injunctive and declaratory relief, contractual rescission on the basis of breach of the implied covenant of good faith and fair dealing and fraudulent inducement, and for breach of contract damages exceeding $75,000 exclusive of interest, costs and attorneys' fees, and with respect to Mr. Jennings for tortious interference with contractual relationship." Complaint ¶ 1. The Complaint contains an ambiguous reference to the "federal question" jurisdictional statute, 28 U.S.C. § 1331. Complaint ¶ 2. But nowhere on the face of the Complaint does it appear that a claim arising under federal question jurisdiction is present. Although the same jurisdictional allegation alleges 28 U.S.C. § 1367, governing supplemental jurisdiction over state law claims, supplemental jurisdiction under section 1367 only applies "in any civil action in which the district courts have original jurisdiction." 28 U.S.C. § 1367(a). This Court does not have original jurisdiction over this case, as a matter containing only state law causes of action between citizens, unless the Plaintiffs can establish diversity jurisdiction under section 1332.

Although it is not relevant to the present background or analysis, the City of Portland denied the general jurisdictional allegation in its Amended Answer. ECF Doc. # 19 at ¶ 2. Parties of course cannot waive subject matter jurisdiction, nor confer it by agreement or by stipulation in the pleadings. *Bissell v. Breakers By-the-Sea*, 7 F. Supp. 2d 60, 63 (D. Me. 1998) ("The mantra is that federal courts are courts of 'limited' jurisdiction, and that parties cannot create jurisdiction by simply 'conferring' it on the court.") (citations omitted). *See, e.g, Hearts with Haiti v. Kendrick*, 192 F. Supp. 3d 181 (D. Me. 2016), *aff'd*, 856 F.3d 1 (1st Cir. 2017). "Once challenged, the party invoking diversity jurisdiction must prove domicile by a preponderance of the evidence. The key point of inquiry is whether diversity of citizenship existed at the time the suit was filed; subsequent events may bear on the sincerity of a professed intention to remain but are not part of the primary calculus." *Garcia Perez v. Santaella*, 364 F.3d 348, 350-51 (1st Cir. 2004) (citations omitted).

The second indicator of a potential issue was the undersigned's review of a set of Plaintiffs' Rule 26(a)(1) Initial Disclosures, which Plaintiffs had served despite the parties' respective objections to the amended scheduling order. In that disclosure, Plaintiffs list as a person with knowledge of facts in the case, Patrick Venne of 462 Capisic Street, Portland, ME 04102. Mr. Venne is described in the disclosure as General Counsel for Plaintiffs and related entities, a former project executive for Plaintiffs and related parties, "and

---

1. As a municipal corporation, the City of Portland has its principal place of business in Portland, Maine, thus making it a citizen of Maine. *See* 28 U.S.C. § 1332(c)(1); *see also Shenker v. City of Lawrence*, 601 F. Supp. 2d 356, 357 (D. Mass. 2009) (municipality of City of Lawrence in Massachusetts is deemed a citizen of Massachusetts for purposes of diversity jurisdiction).

2. The issues in this motion are completely unrelated in any fashion to this change in counsel of record. The only indirect relationship, as stated herein, is that it was by virtue of his entry of appearance for the City of Portland, that on the morning of December 6, 2019 the undersigned first became cognizant of the need to examine diversity jurisdiction more closely than the current Complaint allegations allowed.

current principal in project underlying dispute." Mr. Venne has submitted a declaration to this Court (ECF Doc. # 33-1), reflecting that he is an attorney licensed to practice law in the State of Maine, and is admitted to practice in this Court.[3]

Related to this second indication of an issue on jurisdiction, and noted as significant by the undersigned for the first time on December 6, 2019, was the Corporate Disclosure and Notice of Interested Parties filed by the Plaintiff-entities under Local Rule 7.1 and Fed. R. Civ. P. 7.1. Because parties are required only to list persons "owning 10% or more of the named party," under Local Rule 7.1, there still remains an issue as to whether Mr. Venne's status as a "current principal" in one or both of the Plaintiff-entities defeats complete diversity of citizenship. Complete diversity would be defeated by his domicile in Maine and his status as a potential member of one or both of these entities (or as a member in an LLC or similar entity holding a membership interest in one or both of the Plaintiffs). Indeed there is further implication in the Plaintiff's Corporate Disclosure that there are in fact other persons who have ownership interests in one or both Plaintiff LLCs, but that the interest may be "less than 10% thereof" so the identity of the person or persons are currently undisclosed for purposes of that filing. *See* Corporate Disclosure Statement ¶¶ 4, 6 (ECF Doc. # 3).

At the very least, the Plaintiffs' Complaint in this matter is deficient on its face in alleging subject matter jurisdiction in this Court. There are no federal claims in the Complaint "arising under the Constitution, laws, or treaties of the United States" so as to justify the Complaint's citation to federal question jurisdiction under section 1331. *See* Complaint ¶ 2. Plaintiffs' own description of their causes of action (Complaint ¶ 1), references only state law causes of action and the amount-in-controversy of $75,000, contained in the diversity jurisdiction statute, 28 U.S.C. § 1332(a).

Assuming therefore that Plaintiffs seek to invoke diversity jurisdiction, the citizenship of both Plaintiffs - as limited liability companies - will be "determined by the citizenship of all of [their] members." *D.B. Zwirn Special Opportunities Fund, L.P. v. Mehrotra*, 661 F.3d 124, 125 (1st Cir. 2011) (per curiam) (quoting *Pramco, LLC ex rel. CFSC Consortium, LLC v. San Juan Bay Marina, Inc.*, 435 F.3d 51, 54 (1st Cir. 2006). This state of annual registration (Florida) or state of principal place of business are not relevant to the citizenship of limited liability companies. *See id*. It is not enough that there be disclosure of only a majority of interests. The requirement is that "all of its members" be completely diverse in citizenship from all Defendants. *See Harris Management Inc. v. Coulombe*, 2014 WL 4723096 (D. Me. September 23, 2014). "In cases involving multiple plaintiffs or defendants, the presence of but one nondiverse party divests the district court of original jurisdiction over the entire action." *Id*. (quoting *In re Olympic Mills Corp.*, 477 F.3d 1, 6 (1st Cir. 2007)). And, if in turn any interest in a limited liability company is held by another limited liability company or other similar entity - such as the trust in issue in *Harris Management* - those entities' citizenships are analyzed in turn with respect to the citizenship of all their members and respectively imputed to the plaintiff. *Id*.

While the parties might have a preference for this Court to decide this matter, that preference alone cannot overcome the requisites for subject matter jurisdiction. When a plaintiff is a limited liability company, it is required of the plaintiff to plead (and prove by a preponderance, if challenged) the complete membership interests of all its members and each of their state citizenships. The present Complaint fails to do so. Further, Mr. Venne's involvement and his characterization as a "current principal" - as well as suggestions in the Corporate Disclosure Statement supporting an inference that there are other less-than-10% interests in one or both of the plaintiff LLCs - call for further inquiry. Defendants therefore request a mandatory more definite statement from the Plaintiffs to show subject matter jurisdiction under 28 U.S.C. § 1332; or in the alternative, Defendants move this Court for an order to show cause why this matter should not be dismissed for lack of subject matter jurisdiction.

Furthermore, because of the threshold, critical significance of this subject matter jurisdiction issue, if necessary Defendants request a stay on any further briefing deadlines, pending resolution of the subject matter jurisdiction issues. We recognize that there may be a possibility that this jurisdictional issue is addressed promptly to the satisfaction of the parties and the Court, to allow us to resume fairly expeditiously the current track of completing the briefing on pending motions to dismiss. However, given the above indicia and the facial defectiveness of Plaintiffs' pleadings relating to invoking the diversity jurisdiction of this Court, if the issues require more detailed analysis or argument, as a threshold subject matter jurisdiction issue it should be the first and paramount focus at this early juncture of proceedings. Again, the undersigned represents to this Court that his awareness of this potential issue began on December 6, 2019, when he first became involved with greater focus on the claims by and between Plaintiffs and the City of Portland, having entered his appearance on December 4, 2019. This motion was brought as promptly as possible upon discernment and awareness of the potential for lack of subject matter jurisdiction, or the need for further disclosure from the Plaintiffs before the Court can be satisfied of its subject matter jurisdiction.

Dated: December 9, 2019

/s/ Russell B. Pierce, Jr.

Russell B. Pierce, Jr., Esq.

---

3. Mr. Venne had previously entered an appearance as counsel of record for the Plaintiffs on October 9, 2019, listing his Portland Maine address. ECF Doc. # 16. His motion to withdraw as attorney of record was granted on December 6, 2019. ECF Docket No. 42.

Attorney for Defendant Jon Jennings and the City of Portland

Norman, Hanson & DeTroy, LLC

Two Canal Plaza, P.O. Box 4600

Portland, ME 04112-4600

(207) 774-7000

rpierce@nhdlaw.com

Motion to Dismiss for Lack of Personal Jurisdiction

2020 WL 8993140 (D.Me.)

United States District Court, D. Maine.

Nathan GODFRIED, Plaintiff,

v.

FORD MOTOR COMPANY, Defendant.

No. 1:19-cv-00372.

November 3, 2020.

Memorandum of Law in Support of Defendant Ford Motor Company's Motion to Dismiss for Lack of Personal Jurisdiction

The Defendant, Ford Motor Company, By its Attorneys, Campbell Conroy & O'Neil, P.C., James M. Campbell, Bar #2567, jmcampbell@campbell-trial-lawyers.com, Michelle I. Schaffer, Bar #2307, mschaffer@campbell-trial-lawyers.com, One Constitution Wharf, Suite 310, Boston, MA 02129, T: (617) 241-3000.

This Court lacks personal jurisdiction over Ford Motor Company (Ford) in this matter. General jurisdiction is lacking as Ford is a Delaware corporation with a principal place of business in Michigan and; therefore, it is not "essentially at home" in Maine. Further, there is no causal nexus between Ford's contacts in Maine and Plaintiff's cause of action such that specific jurisdiction is not authorized by the Due Process Clause. Accordingly, Ford's motion to dismiss pursuant to Fed. R. Civ. P. 12(b)(2) should be granted.

I.   FACTUAL BACKGROUND AND PROCEDURAL HISTORY

This case arises out of an accident which occurred on or about August 18, 2013 on Route 2 in Penobscot County, Maine. (*See* Exhibit A, Complaint, at ¶ 4). On that date, non-party Frank Cochran allegedly was transporting "a Rear Attached Mower Series 501 Component 14-92 which had a serial number 53828" ("rear attached mower series 501"), manufactured "sometime between January 1955 and December of 1966." (*Id*. at ¶ 3). As Mr. Cochran was transporting the rear attached mower series 501 on Route 2, it purportedly dropped from an upright position to a deployed position and struck Plaintiff who was riding his bicycle in the breakdown/bicycle lane. (*Id*. at ¶¶ 5-6). Plaintiff alleges that as a result of the accident, he sustained serious and permanent injuries, including an above-the-knee left leg amputation. (*Id*. at ¶ 6). Plaintiff asserts strict liability claims against Ford, alleging the rear attached mower series 501 was defective because (1) the method of securing the rear attached mower series 501 in an upright position was subject to predictable failure and (2) the rear attached mower series 501 failed to include multiple methods to secure it in an upright position. (Exhibit A, Complaint, at ¶¶ 11-12).

The Complaint, however, does not allege that this Court has personal jurisdiction over Ford. (*See* Exhibit A, Complaint, at ¶¶ 7-9). Instead, the Complaint alleges only that this Court has jurisdiction over the ***subject matter*** of the action (*id*. at ¶ 7), and that venue is properly laid in the District of Maine. (*Id*. at ¶ 8). The Complaint does not allege that Ford engaged in any conduct in Maine relevant to Plaintiff's Complaint, asserting only that Ford "is a Delaware corporation which ***does business*** in Maine." (*See id*. at ¶ 2 (emphasis added)).

II.   ARGUMENT

"It is basic law that a court must have personal jurisdiction over the parties to hear a case, that is, the power to require the parties to obey its decrees." *United States v. Swiss Am. Bank, Ltd.*, 274 F.3d 610, 617 (1st Cir. 2001) (internal quotation marks and citation omitted). A district court sitting in diversity, as in this case, exercises personal jurisdiction equal to that of a court of general jurisdiction in the State in which it sits. Fed. R. Civ. P. 4(k)(1)(A); *Am. Express Int'l., Inc. v. Mendez-Capellan*, 889 F.2d 1175, 1178

(1st Cir. 1989). Maine's long-arm statute allows the exercise of personal jurisdiction to the extent permitted under the United States Constitution. 14 M.R.S.A. § 704-A(1); *Harlow v. Children's Hosp.*, 432 F.3d 50, 57 (1st Cir. 2005); *Nowak v. Tak How Invs., Ltd.*, 94 F.3d 708, 712 (1st Cir. 1996). Thus, to exercise jurisdiction over Ford, the Court must determine whether under the Due Process Clause, Ford has "certain minimum contacts with . . . [Maine] such that maintenance of the suit does not offend traditional notions of fair play and substantial justice." *Int'l Shoe Co. v. Washington*, 326 U.S. 310, 316 (1945).

There are two types of personal jurisdiction--general and specific--and the Court must possess one of the two types before a case may proceed. *Daimler A.G. v. Bauman*, 571 U.S. 117, 126-33 (2014). A defendant is subject to general personal jurisdiction when it has "continuous and systematic contacts" sufficient to render the non-resident defendant "essentially at home in the forum state, ... *i.e.* comparable to a domestic enterprise in that State." *Id.* at 113 n.11; *Goodyear Dunlop Tires Operations, S.A. v. Brown*, 564 U.S. 915, 919 (2011).

Specific personal jurisdiction exists over a defendant when "there is a demonstrable nexus between a plaintiff's claims and a defendant's forum-based activities." *Swiss Am. Bank*, 274 F.3d at 618 (quoting *Mass. Sch. of Law at Andover, Inc. v. Am. Bar Ass'n*, 142 F.3d 26, 34 (1st Cir. 1998)). Thus, the question is whether the non-resident defendant has purposefully directed its activities at a resident of the forum and the injury arises from or is related to those activities. *See, e.g., Phillips Exeter Acad. v. Howard Phillips Fund, Inc.*, 196 F.3d 284, 289 (1st Cir. 1999).

Once a defendant challenges the court's personal jurisdiction, the plaintiff bears the burden of proving by a preponderance of the evidence that jurisdiction is proper. *Astro-Med, Inc. v. Nihon Kohden Am., Inc.*, 591 F.3d 1, 8 (1st Cir. 2009); *Daynard v. Ness, Motley, Loadholt, Richardson & Poole, P.A.*, 290 F.3d 42, 50 (1st Cir. 2002). The most commonly used method of determining a motion to dismiss for lack of personal jurisdiction, commonly referred to as the *prima facie* standard, "is for the district court to consider only whether the plaintiff has proffered evidence that, if credited, is enough to support findings of all facts essential to personal jurisdiction." *Boit v. Gar-Tec Products, Inc.*, 967 F.2d 671, 675 (1st Cir. 1992). To defeat a motion to dismiss under this standard, "the plaintiff must make the showing as to every fact required to satisfy 'both the forum's long-arm statute and the due process clause of the Constitution.' " *Id.*; *see also A Corp. v. All Am. Plumbing, Inc.*, 812 F.3d 54, 58 (1st Cir. 2016). The *prima facie* showing of personal jurisdiction must be based on evidence of specific facts set forth in the record. *Kowalski v. Doherty, Wallace, Pillsbury & Murphy*, 787 F.2d 7, 9 (1st Cir. 1986). The plaintiff may not rely on unsupported allegations in their pleadings alone to make a *prima facie* showing of personal jurisdiction, but rather, " 'must go beyond the pleadings and make affirmative proof.' " *Boit*, 967 F.2d at 675 (quoting *Chlebda v. H.E. Fortna & Bro. Inc.*, 609 F.2d 1022, 1024 (1st Cir. 1979)).

A.   *Plaintiff Cannot Establish General Jurisdiction over Ford.*

The United States Supreme Court's decision in *Daimler* forecloses this Court's exercise of general jurisdiction over Ford. *Daimler* held that general jurisdiction exists only where the defendant's "affiliations with the State are so 'continuous and systematic' as to render [it] essentially at home in the forum state." *Daimler*, 571 U.S. at 119 (quoting *Goodyear*, 564 U.S. at 919). With respect to a corporation, affiliations with the forum state meet that requirement in the corporation's place of incorporation and its principal place of business. *Id.* at 137. In an "**exceptional** case,"[1] a corporation's operations in a state other than its formal place of incorporation or principal place of business may be so substantial as to render the corporation at home in that state. *Id.* at 139 n.19 (emphasis added).

Daimler and *Goodyear*, however, "make clear that even a company's engagement in substantial, continuous, and systematic course of business is alone insufficient to render it at home in a forum." *Sonera Holding B.V. v. Cukurova Holding A.S.*, 750 F.3d 221, 226 (2d Cir. 2014) (internal quotation marks omitted). Because general jurisdiction permits claims against an out-of-state defendant on any matter without regard to the connection of the claims to the forum, the burden to establish general jurisdiction is a "more stringent" one. *In re Roman Catholic Diocese of Albany, N.Y., Inc.*, 745 F.3d 30, 38 (2d Cir. 2017). Thus, it is "incredibly difficult" to establish general jurisdiction over a defendant in any forum other than the corporation's place of incorporation or principal place of business. *Monkton Ins. Servs., Ltd. v. Ritter*, 768 F.3d 429, 432 (5th Cir. 2014).

Plaintiff does not establish a *prima facie* case of general personal jurisdiction over Ford. His Complaint alleges that Ford "is a Delaware corporation which does business in Maine." (Exhibit A, Complaint, at ¶ 2; *see also* Exhibit B, Affidavit of Erich Kemnitz, at ¶ 6). There is no allegation that Ford is "at home" in Maine; nor could there be. "A corporation that operates in many places can scarcely be deemed at home in all of them." *Daimler*, 571 U.S. at 139 n.20. Determining that a corporation is "at home" simply because it does business in a state would be "unacceptably grasping." *Id.* at 138.

While Plaintiff has included rote allegations of contacts by Ford with Maine, the Supreme Court specifically rejected "substantial,

---

1. As an example of such an "exceptional" case, the Supreme Court pointed to *Perkins v. Benguet Consol. Mining Co.*, 342 U.S. 437 (1952), where a Philippine company had temporarily made Ohio its principal place of business. *Daimler*, 571 U.S. at 129. In contrast, here, Plaintiff does not even try to make a showing in his Complaint that Ford has made its home in Maine.

continuous, and systematic course of business" as sufficient to exercise general jurisdiction over a corporation, let alone merely doing business. *Id.* Numerous state and federal courts have explicitly held that Ford is not subject to general jurisdiction in each state in which it "does business." *See e.g., Pitts v. Ford Motor Co.*, 127 F. Supp. 3d 676, 683 (S.D. Miss. 2015) (finding Ford's contacts with Mississippi "demonstrate that Ford is at most 'doing business' in Mississippi, and those contacts do not reveal activities that are so 'continuous and systematic' as to render Ford 'at home' in Mississippi"); *Magill v. Ford Motor Co.*, 379 P.3d 1033, 1039 (Colo. 2016) (finding the trial court erred by exercising general jurisdiction over Ford because "Ford is incorporated in Delaware and has its principal place of business in Michigan" and plaintiff failed to demonstrate Ford is "essentially at home" in Colorado"); *Brown v. Ford Motor Co.*, 347 F. Supp. 3d 1347, 1350 (N.D. Ga. 2018) (finding no exceptional circumstances present to render Ford at home in Georgia); *Erwin v. Ford Motor Co.*, No. 8:16-cv-1322-T-24 AEP, 2016 U.S. Dist. LEXIS 185960, 2016 WL 7655398, at *9 (M.D. Fla. Aug. 31, 2016) (holding that Ford was not subject to general jurisdiction in Florida despite multiple business contacts and legal contacts with the state).

Thus, because no exceptional circumstances exist here and Ford is not "at home" in Maine, Plaintiff cannot show that Ford is subject to general jurisdiction in Maine.

B. *Plaintiff Cannot Establish Specific Jurisdiction over Ford.*

Plaintiff also cannot establish specific jurisdiction over Ford because his claims are not related to Ford's contacts with Maine. "The inquiry whether a forum State may assert specific jurisdiction over a nonresident defendant focuses on the relationship among the defendant, the forum, and the litigation." *Walden v. Fiore*, 571 U.S. 277, 283-84 (2014); *see also id.* (finding that the district court lacked specific jurisdiction where no part of the defendant's course of conduct relating to the plaintiff's injury occurred in the forum state). Specific jurisdiction requires that the "corporation's in-state activity is 'continuous and systematic' and *that activity gave rise to the episode-in-suit.*" *Goodyear*, 564 U.S. at 923 (emphasis in original) (quoting *Int'l Shoe Co.*, 326 U.S. at 317); *see also Bristol-Myers Squibb v. Super. Ct. of Cal.*, 137 S. Ct. 1773, 1780 (2017) ("[T]here must be an affiliation between the forum and the underlying controversy, principally, [an] activity or occurrence that takes place in the forum State and is therefore subject to the State's regulation.").

The First Circuit has adopted the following framework to determine whether specific jurisdiction can be exercised over a non-resident defendant:

> [P]laintiffs seeking to establish that the court has specific personal jurisdiction over a defendant must show that: (1) their claim directly arises out of or relates to the defendant's forum-state activities; (2) the defendant's contacts with the forum state represent a purposeful availment of conducting activities in that state, thus invoking the benefits and protections of that state's laws and rendering the defendant's involuntary presence in that state's courts foreseeable; and (3) the exercise of jurisdiction is ultimately reasonable.

Scottsdale Capital Advisors Corp. v. The Deal, LLC, 887 F.3d 17, 20 (1st Cir. 2018); *see also Copia Commc'ns, LLC v. AMResorts, L.P.*, 812 F.3d 1, 4 (1st Cir. 2016). "Failure to make any one of these showings dooms any effort to establish specific personal jurisdiction." *Scottsdale Capital Advisors*, 887 F.3d at 20.

In determining whether a plaintiff's claim "directly arises out of" or "relates to" a defendant's contacts with the forum state, the district court must "probe the causal nexus between the defendant's contacts and the plaintiff's cause of action." *Phillips Exeter Acady.*, 196 F.3d at 289; *see also Adelson v. Hananel ("Adelson II")*, 652 F.3d 75, 81 (1st Cir. 2011). Here, Plaintiff cannot establish personal jurisdiction because his cause of action is unrelated to Ford's contacts with the forum state. Plaintiff asserts boilerplate allegations that Ford "does business" within Maine, but there is no nexus between Plaintiff's allegations of a purportedly defectively designed rear attached mower series 501 and Ford's "business" in Maine. Plaintiff has not established that the rear attached mower series 501 was designed or fabricated in Maine; nor has Plaintiff established that the rear attached mower series 501--manufactured approximately 47 to 58 years prior to the accident--was first sold in Maine. (Exhibit B, Affidavit of Erich Kemnitz, at ¶ 7). Thus, Plaintiff cannot present evidence that Ford's in-state conduct in Maine "form[s] an 'important, or [at least] material, element of proof in the plaintiff's case.'" *Negron-Torres v. Verizon Communs., Inc.*, 478 F.3d 19, 25 (1st Cir. 2007).

The fact that Plaintiff was injured in Maine does not establish specific jurisdiction either, because "injury to a forum resident is not a sufficient connection to the forum." *Walden*, 571 U.S. at 290. "The proper question is not where the plaintiff experienced a particular injury or effect but whether the defendant's conduct connects him to the forum in a meaningful way." *Id.*; *see also Pitts*, 127 F. Supp. 3d at 686 ("[t]he mere fact that Plaintiffs were injured in Mississippi does not, by itself, create specific jurisdiction over Ford in Mississippi").

Plaintiff's injuries do not arise in any way from conduct Ford committed in Maine or purposefully directed toward Maine. Accordingly, the three-step test for determining whether specific personal jurisdiction exists cannot be satisfied, and the Due Process Clause prohibits this Court from exercising specific personal jurisdiction over Ford under these circumstances.

III. CONCLUSION

For all of the foregoing reasons, Defendant Ford Motor Company respectfully requests that this Court grant its motion and dismiss Plaintiff's Complaint against Ford for lack of personal jurisdiction pursuant to Federal Rule of Civil Procedure 12(b)(2).

DATED: November 3, 2020

Respectfully submitted

The Defendant,

FORD MOTOR COMPANY

By its Attorneys,

CAMPBELL CONROY & O'NEIL, P.C.

/s/ Michelle I. Schaffer

James M. Campbell, Bar #2567

jmcampbell@campbell-trial-lawyers.com

Michelle I. Schaffer, Bar #2307

mschaffer@campbell-trial-lawyers.com

One Constitution Wharf, Suite 310

Boston, MA 02129

T: (617) 241-3000

Motion for Judgment on the Pleadings

2020 WL 6336267 (D.Me.)

United States District Court, D. Maine.

Angela MUSTO, Plaintiff,

v.

LIBERTY INSURANCE CORPORATION, d/b/a Liberty Mutual, Defendant.

No. 1:20-cv-00188-GZS.

July 14, 2020.

Memorandum of Law in Support of Defendant, Liberty Mutual's, Motion for Judgment on the Pleadings Pursuant to Fed. R. Civ. P. 12(c)

Defendant, Liberty Mutual, By its attorneys, Tierney M. Chadwick, Esq. Bar No. 005755, Sloane and Walsh, LLP, One Boston Place, 201 Washington Street, Suite 1600, Boston, MA 02108, (617) 523-6010, tchadwick@sloanewalsh.com.

NOW COMES the Defendant, Liberty Mutual Corporation d/b/a Liberty Mutual ("Liberty Mutual"), and by and through its undersigned counsel, hereby submits this Memorandum of Law in support of its Motion for Judgment on the Pleadings under Fed. R. Civ. P. 12 (c). It support of its Motion, Liberty Mutual states as follows:

1. Plaintiff's claim for Breach of Contract (Count I) fails as a matter of law because (1) she concedes that the only dispute between to the parties was a dispute over the amount of loss, (2) she chose to demand appraisal, (3) an appraisal award issued that "set the amount of loss," and (4) Liberty Mutual has issued all payments owed pursuant to that award;

2. Plaintiff's claim for violation of 24-M.R.S.A § 2436-A (Count II) fails because in support of such claims she merely mirrors the language of the statute without providing any factual allegations to "plausibly suggest" violation of the statute; and

3. Plaintiff's claim for statutory attorneys' fees (Count III) fails because her other counts fail to state a claim.

For the reasons explained more fully below in this memorandum, Liberty Mutual respectfully requests that this Honorable Court grant its Motion for Judgment on the Pleadings.

I. *FACTUAL BACKGROUND*

This matter arises from an alleged smoke loss from a power failure at Plaintiff's property located at 64 Grant Road in Litchfield, Maine (the "Property") that occurred on or about February 20, 2019. At the time of the loss, the Property was insured under a Liberty Mutual Homeowner's Policy, policy number H3721815048370, effective dates September 1, 2018 through September 1, 2019 (the "Policy"). (*See Homeowner's Policy*, attached hereto as *Exhibit 1*.)[1] On or about February 25, 2019, Liberty Mutual received

---

1. Ms. Musto's 2018 to 2019 homeowner's policy is attached as Exhibit 1 and the appraisal award is attached as Exhibit 2. Given Liberty Mutual's reliance upon these documents in drafting the allegations of its Counterclaim Complaint against Ms. Musto, the Court's consideration of them is appropriate in the Rule 12(c) context. *Trans-Spec v. Caterpillar*, 524 F.3d 315, 321 (1st Cir. 2008); *Shaw v. Digital Equip. Corp.*, 82 F.3d 1194, 1220 (1st Cir. 1996) (stating a court "may properly consider the relevant entirety of a document integral to or explicitly relied upon in the complaint, even though not attached to the complaint, without converting the motion into one for summary judgment"), citing *Watterson v. Page*, 987 F.2d 1, 3-4 (1st Cir. 1993).

notification that a loss occurred at the Property and Liberty Mutual promptly assigned Paul Davis Restoration ("PDR") to inspect the property. *See* Declaratory Judgment Cmplt. at ¶ 8.

Plaintiff's Complaint is explicit that the sole grounds for her Breach of Contract claim is her allegation that "Liberty Mutual has breached its contractual obligations to Plaintiff under the subject policy by refusing to fully reimburse Plaintiff for her damages caused by the covered loss of February 20, 2019." *See* Complaint at ¶22. Indeed, Plaintiff's Complaint concedes that "Liberty Mutual has acknowledged coverage for the loss of February 20, 2019 under its policy...." *Id.* at ¶ 20.

Accordingly, where the only dispute between the parties as to this loss was the "amount of loss," that dispute is resolved by submitting the claim to appraisal. Specifically, the Policy states:

SECTION I - CONDITIONS

6. Appraisal. If you and we fail to agree on the amount of loss, either may demand an appraisal of the loss. In this event, each party will choose a competent appraiser within 20 days after receiving a written request from the other. The two appraisers will choose an umpire. If they cannot agree upon an umpire within 15 days, you or we may request that the choice be made by a judge of a court of record in the state where the "residence" premises" is located. The appraisers will separately set the amount of loss. *If the appraisers submit a written report of an agreement to us, the amount agreed upon will be the amount of loss.* If they fail to agree, they will submit their differences to the umpire. A decision agreed to by any two will set the amount of loss.

Ex. 1 at pg. 19 (emphasis supplied).

Likewise, the statutorily required Standard fire policy contains the following language with respect to appraisal:

Appraisal. In case the insured and this Company shall fail to agree as to the actual cash value or the amount of loss, then, on the written demand of either, each shall select a competent and disinterested appraiser and notify the other of the appraiser selected within twenty days of such demand. The appraisers shall first select a competent and disinterested umpire; and failing for fifteen days to agree upon such umpire, then, on request of the insured or this Company, such umpire shall be selected by a judge of a court of record in the state in which the property covered is located. The appraisers shall then appraise the loss, stating separately actual cash value and loss to each item; and, failing to agree, shall submit their differences, only, to the umpire. *An award in writing, so itemized, of any two when filed with this Company shall determine the amount of actual cash value and loss.* Each appraiser shall be paid by the party selecting that appraiser and the expenses of appraisal and umpire shall be paid by the parties equally.

Me. Rev. Stat. tit. 24-A, § 3002 (emphasis supplied).

Here, the parties submitted to the appraisal process and received an award signed by two appraisers that established the amount of the loss. Specifically, on or about June 5, 2019, Mr. Harvey, Plaintiff's former public adjuster, emailed a complaint and demand for appraisal of Plaintiff's claim. *Counterclaim* at ¶ 20. Mr. Harvey named Brian Condon as Plaintiff's appraiser. *Id.* On or about June 18, 2019, Liberty Mutual, through counsel, responded to Plaintiff's demand for appraisal and named William Reynolds as its appraiser. *Id.*

On or about October 10, 2019, Liberty Mutual, through counsel, sent a letter to the appraisal panel: Mr. Condon, Mr. Reynolds, and the agreed-upon umpire, Chris Wharff. *Id.* at ¶ 24. The correspondence requested a site inspection and hearing so that the parties may submit evidence to the appraisers. *Id.* An appraisal inspection was scheduled to go forward on November 6, 2019; however, it was canceled by Plaintiff's appraiser on the morning of the inspection as a mere 2-3 hours before it was scheduled to begin. *Id.* at ¶ 25.

Plaintiff objected to the appraisal process on multiple grounds, including allegations that Liberty Mutual's appraiser's, William Reynolds, was not a "disinterested person." *Id.* at ¶ 28. However, Plaintiff has never identified any information, either in her pre-suit correspondence or in her Complaint, to support these allegations. *Id.* Liberty Mutual requested on two occasions, through correspondence dated December 10, 2019 and January 27, 2020, that Plaintiff provide the grounds on which she relied upon to allege Mr. Reynolds is "not disinterested," but Plaintiff failed to do so. *Id.* at ¶ 29.

On or about February 18, 2020, Mr. Wharff executed an appraisal award, agreed to by Mr. Reynolds which established the value of the claim as follows:

Building replacement cost value:	$20,500
Contents replacement cost value:	$8,700
Combined depreciation:	($3,750)
Combined actual cash value:	$24,450

Id. at ¶ 30; *Appraisal Award*, attached hereto as *Exhibit 4*.

Upon receipt of this award, Liberty Mutual issued two checks in light of the appraisal award; one check for Coverage A - Dwelling, less deductible and prior payments, and the other check for Coverage C - Contents, less prior payments. *Id*. at ¶ 32. Liberty Mutual promptly issued the payments and Mr. Edwards confirmed receipt on March 24, 2020. *Id*. Plaintiff has not alleged, and has not informed Liberty Mutual, that she has performed any of the repair work at the building, and accordingly no payment is presently owed for the recoverable depreciation. Accordingly, Liberty Mutual has paid all amounts owed to Plaintiff with respect to her Coverage A - Building claim and her Coverage C - Contents claim.

With respect to Plaintiff's claim for "additional living expenses" under Coverage D of the Policy, Liberty Mutual also advised Mr. Harvey that Liberty Mutual will permit up to two weeks of additional living expenses during the actual cleaning of the Property. *Id*. Notably, the Policy requires that costs be "incurred" by Musto before she is entitled to payment for additional living expenses. *See Ex. 1* at p. 35. Plaintiff has not alleged, nor provided any information to Liberty Mutual demonstrating, that she has incurred any costs with respect to her additional living expenses.

II. *ARGUMENT*

A. *STANDARD OF REVIEW.*

Under Federal Rule of Civil Procedure 12(c), the court may grant judgment on the pleadings when the nonmoving party can prove that there are no facts in support of a claim that would entitle it to relief. *Rivera-Gomez v. de Castro*, 843 F.2d 631, 635 (1st Cir. 1988).

> [B]ecause rendition of judgment in such an abrupt fashion represents an extremely early assessment of the merits of the case, the trial court must accept all of the nonmovant's well-pleaded factual averments as true and draw all reasonable inferences in [its] favor.... [T]he court may not grant a defendant's Rule 12(c) motion "unless it appears beyond doubt that the plaintiff can prove no set of facts in support of [its] claim which would entitle [it] to relief."

Id. "Motions for judgment on the pleadings are ordinarily accorded the same treatment as motions to dismiss." *Aponte-Torres v. Univ. of P. R.*, 445 F.3d 50, 54 (1st Cir.2006) (*citing Collier v. City of Chicopee*, 158 F.3d 601, 602 (1st Cir.1998)). "There is, of course, a modest difference between Rule 12(c) and Rule 12(b)(6) motions. A Rule 12(c) motion, unlike a Rule 12(b)(6) motion, implicates the pleadings as a whole." *Id*. at 55 (*citing* 5C Charles Alan Wright & Arthur R. Miller, Federal Practice and Procedure § 1368 (3d ed.2004)).

As with a motion to dismiss, in order to survive a motion for judgment on the pleadings, "a complaint must contain sufficient factual matter, accepted as true, to 'state a claim to relief that is plausible on its face.' " *See Ashcroft v. Iqbal*, 556 U.S. 662, 678 (2009) (quoting *Bell Atlantic Corp. v. Twombly*, 550 U.S. 544, 570 (2007)); *see also Twombly*, 550 U.S. at 555 (stating that a complaint must provide more than "a formulaic recitation of the elements of a cause of action"). What is required at the pleading stage are factual "allegations plausibly suggesting (not merely consistent with)" an entitlement to relief, in order to "reflect[] the threshold requirement of [Fed.R.Civ.P.] 8(a)(2) that the 'plain statement' possess enough heft to 'sho[w]' that the pleader is entitled to relief.' " *Twombly*, 550 U.S. at 557. However, the court's acceptance of the allegations in a complaint is limited to allegations of facts; the court is "not bound to accept as true a legal conclusion couched as a factual allegation." *Iqbal*, 556 U.S. at 678 (*quoting Twombly*, 550 U.S. at 555).

Therefore, Plaintiff must plead sufficient "factual content [to] allow the court to draw the reasonable inference that the defendant is liable for the misconduct alleged." *Id*. The notice pleading standard adopted in Rule 8 does not require the complaint to contain "detailed factual allegations," but it must have more than "naked assertion[s] devoid of further factual enhancement." *Id*. (internal quotation marks omitted).

Judgment is warranted so long as there are no genuine issues of material fact. *Lovell v. One Bancorp*, 690 F.Supp. 1090, 1096 (D.Me. 1988). In examining the facts, the court "must accept all of the nonmoving party's well-pleaded factual averments as true and draw all reasonable inferences in [its] favor." *Feliciano v. State of R.I.*, 160 F.3d 780, 788 (1st Cir. 1998).

B. *PLAINTIFF'S CLAIM FOR BREACH OF CONTRACT (COUNT I) FAILS AS A MATTER OF LAW BECAUSE (1) SHE CONCEDES THAT THE ONLY DISPUTE BETWEEN TO THE PARTIES WAS A DISPUTE OVER THE AMOUNT OF LOSS, (2) SHE CHOSE TO DEMAND APPRAISAL, (3) AN APPRAISAL AWARD ISSUED THAT "SET THE AMOUNT OF LOSS," AND (4) LIBERTY MUTUAL HAS ISSUED ALL PAYMENTS OWED PURSUANT TO THAT AWARD.*

As noted above, Plaintiff's Complaint is explicit that the sole grounds for her Breach of Contract claim is her allegation that "Liberty Mutual has breached its contractual obligations to Plaintiff under the subject policy by refusing to fully reimburse Plaintiff for her damages caused by the covered loss of February 20, 2019." *See* Complaint at ¶22. Liberty Mutual did not deny coverage to Plaintiff, rather the dispute with respect to the insurance claim was limited to the parties' disagreement as to the value of the claim. *Id*. at ¶20.

To state a claim for breach of contract, Plaintiff must allege facts "plausibly suggesting" "that the defendant breached a material term of the contract, and that the breach caused the plaintiff to suffer damages." *Tobin v. Barter*, 89 A. 23d 1088, 1091-92 (Me. 2014).

Here, Plaintiff has identified no specific term of the Policy that she alleged Liberty Mutual breached, and she cannot make such allegation, as no breach of the Policy has occurred. A cause of action for breach of contract arises at the time of the breach. *Palermo v. Aetna Cas. & Sur. Co.*, 606 A.2d 797, 798 (Me. 1992). Accordingly, a breach does not occur until the insurer denies coverage and/or refuses payment. *Id.* at 799; *citing Allstate Ins Co. v. Spinelli*, 443 A.2d 1286, 1287 (Del. 1982) ("We hold that such a cause of action does not accrue ... until the insurer denies coverage and notifies the insured of rejection."). Here, neither occurred. Rather, the Plaintiff chose to demand appraisal after a dispute over valuation occurred. The parties proceeded to appraisal, where an award was signed by two appraisers, and Liberty Mutual issued payment consistent with the award.

The appraisal award issued by the appraisal panel is binding and Liberty Mutual's payment of that amount satisfies Liberty Mutual's obligations with respect to Plaintiff's claim. (*Ex. 4*). As noted above, Plaintiff's Policy provides, in pertinent part, "[a] decision agreed to by any two will set the amount of loss." (*Ex. 1*). An appraisal award set by any two appraisers is presumed binding. *See* Me. Rev. St., tit. 24-A, § 3002; *Rolfe v. Patrons' Androscoggin Mut. Fire Ins. Co.*, 105 Me. 58, 58 (1908). Accordingly, here, where Plaintiff chose to demand appraisal, a binding appraisal award was issued, and Liberty Mutual made payment consistent with that award, Plaintiff has failed to state a claim upon which relief can be granted.

C. PLAINTIFF'S CLAIM FOR VIOLATION OF 24-A M.R.S.A. § 2436-A FAILS BECAUSE IN SUPPORT OF SUCH CLAIMS SHE MERELY MIRRORED THE LANGUAGE OF THE STATUTE WITHOUT PROVIDING ANY FACTUAL ALLEGATIONS TO "PLAUSIBLY SUGGEST" VIOLATION OF THE STATUTE.

Plaintiff's claim for violation of 24-A M.R.S.A. § 2436-A fails because Plaintiff's has not alleged facts which "plausibly suggest" that Liberty Mutual violated that statute. *Twombly, supra.*

The Unfair Claims Settlement Practices statute, 24-A M.R.S.A. § 2436-A, allows insureds to collect statutory interest and attorneys' fees in certain instances of improper actions by an insurer. Specifically, the Unfair Claims Settlement Practices statute provides, in pertinent part:

1. Civil actions. A person injured by any of the following actions taken by that person's own insurer may bring a civil action and recover damages, together with costs and disbursements, reasonable attorney's fees and interest on damages at the rate of 1 1/2% per month:

   A. Knowingly misrepresenting to an insured pertinent facts or policy provisions relating to coverage at issue;

   B. Failing to acknowledge and review claims, which may include payment or denial of a claim, within a reasonable time following receipt of written notice by the insurer of a claim by an insured arising under a policy;

   C. Threatening to appeal from an arbitration award in favor of an insured for the sole purpose of compelling the insured to accept a settlement less than the arbitration award;

   D. Failing to affirm or deny coverage, reserving any appropriate defenses, within a reasonable time after having completed its investigation related to a claim; or

   E. Without just cause, failing to effectuate prompt, fair and equitable settlement of claims submitted in which liability has become reasonably clear.

See 24-A M.R.S.A. § 2436-A.

Plaintiff's Complaint essentially does exactly what is forbidden in the pleading stage under the requirements of *Iqbal* and *Twombly* - in support of her allegations that Liberty violated the Unfair Claims Practice Statute, she merely mirrors the language of the statute itself without providing factual allegations to "plausibly suggest" violations of that statute or make. *See and compare* 24-A M.R.S.A. § 2436-A(B) & (D) with Complaint at ¶¶ 26-28.

First, Plaintiff alleges that "Liberty Mutual has failed to respond to Plaintiff's claim in a reasonable manner, even though Defendant Liberty Mutual's liability to Plaintiff under Plaintiff's homeowner policy is absolutely clear." *See* Complaint at ¶27. However, Plaintiff provides *no allegations whatsoever*, regarding actual delays of which she is complaining. *See* Complaint. The only date mentioned in the Complaint is February 20, 2019, the date of loss. The reasons for this are clear. Plaintiff reported the loss to Liberty Mutual on February 25, 2019, and within two days of the loss being reported to Liberty Mutual it had conducted an investigation and issued payment to Plaintiff. *See* Counterclaim at ¶¶8-10. Liberty Mutual thereafter promptly issued a reservation of rights letter regarding the pellet stove, later accepted coverage for the pellet stove and timely adjusted the loss. *See* Counterclaim at ¶¶11-33. Plaintiff cannot sustain a claim for violation of 24-A M.R.S.A. § 2436-A(B) by simply parroting the language of the statute. *Twombly.* She must provide *some* factual allegation which supports such a claim, which she cannot do here.

Second, Plaintiff alleges that "Liberty Mutual unreasonably and without proper justification denied coverage and refused to honor Plaintiff's claim for full reimbursement under the terms and provisions of the Liberty Mutual Policy." *See* Complaint at ¶28. The first portion of this allegation is belied by the Plaintiff's own allegations. As noted above, Plaintiff's Complaint *concedes* that "Liberty Mutual has acknowledged coverage for the loss of February 20, 2019 under its policy... ." *Id.* at ¶ 20. There was no denial of coverage to Plaintiff, even under Plaintiff's allegation. The second portion of the allegation, to wit that Liberty Mutual did not provide "full reimbursement," fails for the same reason her breach of contract claim fails. The Policy and relevant statute establish that the appraisal award "will set the amount of loss." (*Ex. 1*). Here, the appraisal award set the amount of loss, Liberty paid the amount of the award that is owed, and Plaintiff has not alleged or informed Liberty Mutual that she has incurred any further costs, e.g. recoverable depreciation or additional living expenses, which may be owed.

Third, Plaintiff alleges that Liberty Mutual violated 24-A M.R.S.A. § 2436-A by "attempt[ing] to impose an appraisal process that does not comply with the terms and provisions of the Liberty Mutual policy and that is contrary to Maine law" and "utilizing an appraiser who, on information and belief, is not independent and has an established relationship with Defendant Liberty Mutual." *See* Complaint at ¶¶ 29-30. Neither of those allegations support a claim for violation of 24-A M.R.S.A. § 2436-A on their face.

Plaintiff has provided no allegation suggesting or even attempting to explain how the appraisal process did not "comply with the terms and provisions of the Liberty Mutual policy" or was "contrary to Maine law." In fact, up until paragraphs 29 and 30 of the Complaint, Plaintiff fails to make any allegations that the appraisal even *occurred* presumably because she is aware that her choice to demand appraisal, and Liberty Mutual's compliance with her demand and payment of the award defeats her Breach of Contract claim.

Likewise, her claim that Liberty Mutual's chosen appraiser was not "independent" fails as an initial matter because neither the Policy nor the statute requires an appraiser to be "independent," *see Ex. 1* at pg. 19 (requiring that appraiser be "competent"); Me. Rev. Stat. tit. 24-A, § 3002 (requiring that appraiser be "competent and disinterested"), and the allegation of Mr. Reynolds supposed lack of independence does not violate any clause of M.R.S.A. § 2436-A. Substantively, this allegation fails because it is, once again, not supported by any factual allegation "plausibly suggesting" that it could give rise to a violation of the statute. *Twombly, supra.* Plaintiff merely states that it is so on "information and belief," without any support thereof. Liberty Mutual has sought such information from Plaintiff for months pre-suit, and seeks the basis for such allegation now, but none has been given.

D. *PLAINTIFF'S CLAIM FOR STATUTORY ATTORNEYS' FEES (COUNT III) FAILS BECAUSE HER OTHER COUNTS FAIL TO STATE A CLAIM.*

As detailed above, Plaintiff failed to state any claim upon which relief can be granted. For that reason, Plaintiff is not entitled to attorney's fees with respect to this action.

Plaintiff alleges a common law claim for attorney's fees with respect to this action. The case cited in Plaintiff's complaint, *Foremost Insurance Company v. Levesque*, stands for the proposition that if a carrier brings an action against an insured with respect to its duties to defend and indemnify, and subsequently is unsuccessful, its insured may be entitled to attorney's fees spent to defend the action. 2007 Me. 96, 926 A.2d 1185, 1190 (Me. 2007). Specifically, the Court noted, "[w]hen an insured prevails after incurring legal fees to defend a suit brought by its insurer, policy reasons support the allowance of attorney fees to the insured." *Id.*

These facts are not present in the instant action. Here, Liberty Mutual did not deny Plaintiff's claim in any part and it has promptly paid all undisputed monies as they have arisen, including issuance of the appraisal award. Additionally, Liberty Mutual did not bring this action against Plaintiff, nor did it demand appraisal. Due to the fact that Plaintiff failed to state a claim upon which relief may be granted with respect to Counts I and II, Plaintiff has ultimately failed to state a claim upon which relief may be granted with respect to attorney's fees.

III. *CONCLUSION*

For the reasons stated above, the Defendant, Liberty Mutual, respectfully requests that this Honorable Court grant its Motion for Judgment on the Pleadings.

Respectfully submitted,

Dated July ___, 2020

Defendant,

Liberty Mutual,

By its attorneys,

Tierney M. Chadwick, Esq. Bar No. 005755

Sloane and Walsh, LLP

One Boston Place

201 Washington Street, Suite 1600

Boston, MA 02108

(617) 523-6010

tchadwick@sloanewalsh.com

Motion for More Definite Statement

2015 WL 10058677 (D.Me.)

United States District Court, D. Maine.

UNITED OHIO INSURANCE CO., Plaintiff,

v.

Jan FISH, Defendant,

v.

James CAMPBELL,

and

Ann Flagg CAMPBELL, Parties-in-Interest.

No. 2:15-cv-245-JDL.

August 28, 2015.

Motion to Dismiss for Failure to State a Claim and Motion for a More Definite Statement

Timothy C. Woodcock, Esq., Eaton Peabody, 80 Exchange Street, P.O. Box 1210, Bangor, ME 04402-1210, (207) 947-0111, twoodcock@eatonpeabody.com, for defendant.

NOW COMES, Defendant, Jan Fish, by and through her attorney, Timothy C. Woodcock, Esq., and moves in the alternative pursuant to Rule 12(b)(6) and 12(e) of the Federal Rules of Civil Procedure for Failure to State a Claim and for a more Definite Statement of the basis for the request for Declaratory Judgment of Plaintiff, United Ohio Insurance Company, on the grounds set forth below.

I. *BACKGROUND*

Pending is a Complaint dated June 16, 2015 seeking declaratory relief filed by Plaintiff, United Ohio Insurance Company ("United Ohio"). Defendant, Jan Fish, waived formal service of process and Defendant's Answer to the Complaint is due on August 31, 2015.

United Ohio has alleged, correctly, that Jan Fish is an insured. *Complaint* at ¶ 9. It has further alleged, correctly, that Jan Fish is a defendant in the case of *James Campbell and Ann Flagg Campbell v. Jan Fish*, CV-15-0030, now pending in State Superior Court for Knox County. *Id.* at ¶¶ 7-8.

United Ohio acknowledged that Defendant Fish provided United Ohio with notice of the Campbells' complaint and that United Ohio is, at present, providing a defense. *Id.* at ¶¶ 10-11. United Ohio denies, however, that it owes Defendant Fish either a duty to defend her against the Campbells' claims or a duty to indemnify her for any damages that may be awarded against her. *Id.* at ¶ 12. United Ohio included with its Complaint the Campbells' Superior Court Complaint and the United Ohio Policy. *Id.* at ¶¶ 8-9. Beyond its bare assertion that it owed Defendant Fish neither defense nor indemnification, United Ohio's Complaint did not reveal why it was so contending.

This Court may take judicial notice that by pleading dated July 23, 2015, Defendant Fish's attorney filed an Answer on her behalf, responding to the Campbell's allegations and raising certain affirmative defenses.

II. *MAINE LAW ON DETERMINATION OF DUTY TO DEFEND*

It should be noted at the outset, that Plaintiff has predicated Article III jurisdiction solely on diversity of citizenship. *Complaint* at ¶ 4. The issues raised by gravamen of United Ohio's Complaint involve no federal question. They arise out of and are governed exclusively by Maine law; in particular, Maine law governing insurers' duties to defend and indemnify. Accordingly, the sufficiency of United Ohio's Declaratory Judgment Complaint both for Rule 12(b)(6) and Rule 12(e) purposes must be determined by Maine law governing this field in general and the particular insurer—insured relationship at hand.

The Maine Law Court has described that relationship as "special". *Foremost Insurance Co. v. Levesque ("Foremost I"),* 2000 ME 96, ¶ 10, 926 A.2d 1145, 1188, citing *Gibson v. Farm Family Insurance Co.,* 673 A.2d 1350, 1354 (Me. 1996).

Among the factors determining this relationship is that the language and terms of insurance policies is standardized throughout the insurance industry. *Massachusetts Bay Insurance Co. v. Ferraiolo Construction Co.,* 584 A.2d 608, 609 (Me. 1990). As a result, "[t]he insured can only negotiate particular standard riders or exclusions." *Ibid.* For those reasons, the terms of insurance policies are construed "most strongly against the insurer." *Ibid.*

Consistent with this unequal relationship, the Law Court has set forth very particular steps that an insurance carrier, upon learning that an insured has been sued, must take to determine whether it owes the insured a duty to defend. The Law Court has also developed specific standards that an insurer must apply to these steps.

In determining whether it has a duty to defend, the analysis that the insurance carrier must apply is straightforward and unambiguous. It must simply compare the allegations in the complaint against the insured with the terms of the insurance policy. *Vigna v. Allstate,* 686 A.2d 599 (Me. 1996). In doing so, "[a]ny ambiguity must be resolved in favor of a duty to defend." *Massachusetts Bay Insurance Co. v. Ferraiolo Construction Co.,* 584 A.2d at 609; accord, *Gibson v. Farm Family Insurance Co.,* 673 A.2d at 1352, citing, *Union Mutual Fire Insurance Co. v. Town of Topsham,* 441 A.2d 1012, 1015 (Me. 1982).

The Law Court has admonished insurers that "[a]n insured is not at the mercy of the notice pleading of the third party to establish his own insurer's duty to defend." *Gibson v. Farm Family,* 673 A.2d at 1352, citing, *J.A.J., Inc. v. Aetna Casualty & Surety Co.,* 429 A.2d 806, 808 (Me. 1987). Thus, "[i]f, comparing an insurance policy with an underlying complaint there is **any** legal or factual basis that **could** obligate an insurer to indemnify, then the insured is entitled to a defense." *Maine Bonding & Casualty Co. v. Douglas Dynamics, Inc.,* 594 A.2d. 1079, 1080 (Me. 1991) (emphases supplied), quoting, *State Farm Mutual Insurance Co. v. Bragg,* 589 A.2d 35, 36 (Me. 1991). Indeed, as the Law Court has explained, "[e]ven if a complaint is insufficient to withstand a motion to dismiss, it may still give rise to a duty to defend if it states that that could potentially fall within the insurance coverage." *Maine Bonding & Casualty v. Douglas Dynamics,* 594 A.2d at 1080, citing *Lavoie v. Dorchester Mutual Fire Insurance Co.,* 560 A.2d 570, 571 (Me. 1986).

Recognizing that claims against their insureds will inevitably involve adjudication of contested facts, the Law Court has emphasized that, in comparing the complaint to the insurance policy, insurance carriers **must** provide a defense, "[i]f there is **any** legal or factual basis that could be developed at trial, which would obligate the insurer to pay under the policy. . ." *Maine Mutual Fire Insurance Co. v. Gervais,* 1999 ME 134 ¶ 8, 745 A.2d 360, 362-363 (emphasis supplied).

Although it should go without saying, it bears emphasis at this point that the analytical process and relevant standards for determining an insurer's duty to defend an insured are affirmative obligations **on the insurer.** These are steps that the **insurer *must*** take in order to determine whether, in the first instance, it has a duty to defend. Putting a fine point on these requirements, the Law Court has cautioned insurers, "[i]n applying the comparison test, we seek to discourage mini-trials on the duty to defend." *Maine Bonding & Casualty v. Douglas Dynamics,* 594 A.2d at 1080-1081. Therefore, "[i]f there is any legal or factual basis that could be developed at trial, which would obligate the insurer to pay under the policy, the insured is entitled to a defense." *Maine Mutual Fire Insurance Co. v. Gervais,* 1999 ME at ¶ 8, 745 A.2d at 362-363; see also, 24-A MRS § 2436(1)(D).

III. *UNITED OHIO'S COMPLAINT WARRANTS DISMISSAL*

Rule 8 of the Federal Rules of Civil Procedure requires that each complaint set forth "a short and plain statement of the claim showing that the pleader is entitled to relief" and provides further that "each allegation must be simple, concise, and, direct." Fed. R. Civ. P. 8(a)(2).

Leading Supreme Court decisions setting the standards for reviewing a complaint for compliance with Rule 8 are *Ashcroft v. Iqbal,* 556 U.S. 544 (2009) and *Bell Atlantic v. Twombly,* 550 U.S. 544 (2007). These decisions were applied by the First Circuit Court of Appeals in *Schatz v. Republican State Leadership Committee,* 669 F.3d 50 (1st Cir. 2012). In *Schatz,* the First Circuit set forth the "proper" way to assess whether a complaint has complied with Rule 8. "Step one: isolate and ignore statements in the complaint that simply offer legal labels and conclusions or merely rehash cause-of-action elements" *Id.* at 55. "Step two: take the complaint's well pled (*i.e.,* non-conclusory non-speculative) facts as true, drawing all reasonable inferences in the pleader's favor, and see if they plausibly narrate a claim for relief." *Ibid*; accord, *Pan Am Systems, Inc. v. Hardenbergh,* 871 F.Supp. 3d 6, 11 (D. Me. 2012).

Held to these standards, United Ohio's Complaint fails completely. Paragraphs 1 through 11 set forth preliminary allegations that are merely predicates for United Ohio's contention that it has neither a duty to defend nor a duty to indemnify. At Paragraph 12, United Ohio baldly and without further explanation or illumination alleges that, "UOIC, however, has no duty to defend Jan Fish in the Campbell lawsuit, and has no duty to defend her in the event that there is a judgment entered in Campbell's (sic) favor in the Campbell lawsuit." *Complaint* at ¶ 12. On its face, this allegation does nothing more than "simply offer legal labels and conclusions. . ." It cannot, therefore, by itself meet the standards required by Rule 8. Moreover, Paragraph 12 of the Complaint is the **only** point at which United Ohio actually sets forth the bases for its request for declaratory relief. Id., passim.

The paucity of United Ohio's allegations is particularly striking as annexed to the Complaint are United Ohio's 103 page policy with Janet Fish and the entirety of the Campbells' six page, four count complaint. Clearly, United Ohio has concluded that none of the allegations or requests for relief in the Campbells' complaint trigger its duty to defend; yet, nowhere in its Declaratory Judgment Complaint does United Ohio even hint as to why this is so. Moreover, United Ohio can hardly deny that it possesses this information. Thus, even by the general standards governing Rule 8, United Ohio's Complaint fails. The insufficiency of the Complaint becomes more apparent still when held against the mandatory steps that Maine law requires of insurers.

In particular, at no point does United Ohio allege that, as required, it compared the Campbell's complaint to Defendant Fish's policy; at no point does it allege that no legal or factual basis that could be developed at trial which would obligate it to pay under the policy. See, *Maine Mutual Fire Insurance Co. v. Gervais*, 1999 ME at ¶ 8, 745 A.2d at 362-363. Yet, as the Law Court has made clear, an insurer **must** make this very determination **before** it deny an insured a duty to defend.[1]

United Ohio's failure to assert these points, necessarily raises the question as to whether, as required, it has actually performed this comparative analysis and, if so, whether it applied the correct standards to the task. Put another way, nothing in United Ohio's Complaint provides a sufficient basis on which to rest those conclusions.

Although it would not save United Ohio's deficient Complaint, a Reservation of Rights Letter might have dispelled some of the mystery that now enshrouds the Complaint. In the ordinary course an insurance carrier presented with a complaint against an insured would conduct the complaint-policy comparison required by the Law Court and, if that comparison raised questions about its duties to defend or indemnify or both, it would write a Reservation of Rights Letter to the insured. In that letter, the insurer would detail the reasons why it is reserving its rights as to defense and indemnification. See, Windt. A., Insurance Claims and Disputes (4th ed.), §2:7, p. 69.

By letter dated May 27, 2015, United Ohio notified Defendant Fish that it was denying that it was obligated to provide a defense or indemnification with respect to the Campbell's claims. See, *Attachment 1*. However, United Ohio's Reservation of Rights Letter, like United Ohio's Declaratory Judgment Complaint, provided no hint as to why it had reached those conclusions. *Id.*

This is not a case, therefore, in which United Ohio's failure to plead that it complied with the Law Court's analytical preconditions, but a thorough Reservation of Rights Letter demonstrates that, in fact, it did so. Rather, the records United Ohio has generated—the Reservation of Rights Letter and the Declaratory Judgment Complaint are so vague and conclusory that they shed no light on why United Ohio has concluded that, should the Campbells litigate their claims against Defendant Fish to judgment, they could not prove any legal or factual points that would be covered under the policy.[2]

Beyond the legal necessity for United Ohio's adherence to the comparative review mandated by the Law Court, there is a practical necessity as well. United Ohio generated the policy here at issue and was the master of its terms. See, *Massachusetts Bay Insurance Co. v. Ferraiolo Construction Co.*, 584 A.2d at 609. Moreover, United Ohio is a member of the insurance industry, whereas Defendant Fish is a layperson; a mere citizen.

Presumably, United Ohio knows why it issued its Reservation of Rights Letter to Defendant Fish; it knows why it concluded that the Campbell's complaint, as pled, does not trigger its duty to defend or its duty to indemnify. Given those assumptions and given the Law Court's affirmative directives to all insurers in situations such as this, United Ohio may not maintain this declaratory judgment action without revealing the results of its comparison of the Campbells' complaint with the terms of Defendant Fish's policy.

IV. *UNITED OHIO SHOULD FILE A MORE DEFINITE STATEMENT*

Motions for a More Definite Statement are provided for in Rule 12(e) of the Federal Rules of Civil Procedure which authorizes such

---

1. Defendant Fish acknowledges that United Ohio is currently providing Defendant with a defense. For purposes of determining whether the instant Complaint for Declaratory Judgment is sufficient, however, that fact is irrelevant. The determinative fact is that at this very early juncture in the case of *Campbell v. Fish*, United Ohio is seeking the judgment of this Court that it has no duty to defend.

2. By letter dated June 16, 2015, counsel for United Ohio set forth theories on which United Ohio could rest a denial of defense or indemnification, but that letter was clearly not the equivalent of a Reservation of Rights Letter and is not competent to serve in lieu of such a letter.

motions where the initial pleading is "so vague or ambiguous that the party cannot reasonably prepare a response." *Rule 12(e)*, F.R. Civ. Pro. This Court has explained that, "[i]t is accepted. . . 'that a Motion for a More Definite Statement is granted sparingly since it is not to be used as a substitute for discovery in trial preparation. . .but it to be used only when a pleading is too general.'" *Ames v. Department of Marine Resources,* 256 F.R.D. 22, 26 (Me. 2009), quoting in part, *Town of Hooksett School District v. W.R. Grace & Co.,* 617 F. Supp. 126, 125 (D.N.H. 1984). Such motions are intended to "strike at unintelligibility rather than a lack of detail in the complaint." *Id.* at 26-27, citing *Cox v. Maine Maritime Academy,* 122 F.R.D. 115, 116 (D. Me. 1988).

In commenting on Rule 12(e) motions, a learned treatise has noted that in considering them federal courts which have guarded against "shift[ing] the burden of fact elicitation from the discovery phase back to the pleadings, with a resulting delay in joinder of the issue and resolution on the merits." Wright and Miller, Federal Practice and Procedure, § 1376, p. 222. Acknowledging the value in this approach, that same authority has also cautioned federal courts against "using this approach too cavalierly." *Id.* at 325. The treatise went on to observe that, "[i]f details are necessary in order to make a vague complaint intelligible, the fact that the details also subject to the discovery process should not preclude their production under Rule 12(e)." *Ibid.* On this point, the treatise identified "a possible exception to the generally restrictive attitude toward Rule 12(e) motions [which] involves compelling a more definite statement of matter relating to possible threshold defenses to the claim for relief." *Id.* at p. 333.

As with the foregoing discussion in support of Defendant's Motion to Dismiss, a review of United Ohio's Complaint shows that it reveals nothing about why United Ohio is contending that it does not owe its insured a defense to the Campbell's claims. Under Rule 12(e), it should be required to allege at least **one** particular basis on which the Complaint is premised.

V. *UNITED OHIO'S COMPLAINT FAILS TO COMPLY WITH RULE 1*

Rule 1 of the Federal Rules of Civil Procedure provides in pertinent part that all the rules, both individually and collectively, "should be construed and administered to secure the just, speedy, and, inexpensive determination of every action and proceeding." F. R. Civ. Pro., Rule 1.

In this case, where the Plaintiff has a special contractual relationship with the Defendant, where the Plaintiff and only the Plaintiff knows why it is contending that it does not owe a duty to defend nor a duty to indemnify, and where the Plaintiff's has failed to disclose either in its Complaint why it has reached those conclusions and maintains them as legal contentions, it would not comport with the spirit and intent of Rule 1 to permit the Plaintiff to proceed without clearly setting forth the basis for its complaint. Although the foregoing discussion demonstrates that United Ohio's Complaint does not meet the standards required by Rule 8 and Rule 12(b)(6) and 12(e), Rule 1 reinforces those rules and provides its own rationale for the relief Defendant requests herein.

VI. *SUMMARY*

United Ohio's Declaratory Judgment Complaint fails to meet the standards Rule 8 provides for pleadings and, therefore, its Complaint should be dismissed pursuant to Rule 12(b)(6). United Ohio's Complaint also fails to meet the Rule 8 standards and, therefore, United Ohio should be required to file a more definite statement. Finally, under the circumstances of this case, Plaintiff's opaque Complaint fails to comport with the letter and spirit of Rule 1 of the Rules of Civil Procedure.

WHEREFORE, Defendant, Jan Fish, moves, in the alternative that United Ohio's Complaint be dismissed or that this Court order United Ohio to supplement its Complaint with sufficient specificity to fully comply with the standards of Rule 8 and with the legal duties imposed upon United Ohio, as an insurer, under Maine law.

Dated at Bangor, Maine, this 28th day of August, 2015.

DEFENDANT, JAN FISH

s/ Timothy C. Woodcock

Timothy C. Woodcock, Esq.

EATON PEABODY

80 Exchange Street

P.O. Box 1210

Bangor, ME 04402-1210

(207) 947-0111

twoodcock@eatonpeabody.com

Attorneys for Defendant

Application for Temporary Restraining Order

2018 WL 6424369 (D.Me.)

Westlaw Query>>

To find more Application for Temporary Restraining Order filings on Westlaw: access Maine Trial Court Documents (from the Home page, click Trial Court Documents, then Maine), click the Advanced Search link, select Motion for TRO, and click Search. Use the Jurisdiction filter on the left to narrow results to Federal.

United States District Court, D. Maine.

SYMETRA LIFE INSURANCE COMPANY, Plaintiff,

v.

Guy Raymond EMERSON, Defendant.

No. 2:18-cv-00492-JDL.

December 4, 2018.

Plaintiff's Motion for Emergency Ex Parte Temporary Restraining Order and Preliminary Injunction with Incorporated Memorandum of Law

Geraldine G. Sanchez, Bar No. 8050, Roach Hewitt Ruprecht Sanchez & Bischoff PC, 66 Pearl Street, Suite 200, Portland, Maine 04101, 207-747-4870, Email: gsanchez@roachhewitt.com; John Whitaker, WSBA No. 28,868, (Pro Hac Vice pending), Christensen O'Connor Johnson Kindness PLLC, 1201 Third Avenue, Suite 3600, Seattle, WA 98101-3029, 206.682.8100, Email: john.whitaker@cojk.com, litdoc@cojk.com, for plaintiff, Symetra Life Insurance Company.

INJUNCTIVE RELIEF SOUGHT

Plaintiff Symetra Life Insurance Company ("Symetra") hereby moves, pursuant to Federal Rule of Civil Procedure 65, this Court for an emergency *ex parte* temporary restraining order (TRO) and preliminary injunction. This motion is supported by Symetra's Verified Complaint (the "Complaint" or "VC"), filed herewith. The requested relief is necessary because Defendant Guy Emerson is conducting an online assault on numerous individuals employed by Symetra and their families, including minor children. Indeed, Emerson has even invited depraved behavior directed at the daughters of at least one Symetra employee. In addition, Emerson's improper use of Symetra's trademarks and copyrighted-images is calculated to confuse the public in a manner that cannot be remediated with monetary damages.

REQUEST FOR EX PARTE RELIEF

Plaintiff requests that the Court issue a TRO without written or oral notice to Emerson because, as set forth in the Verified Complaint, Symetra will suffer immediate and irreparable injury, loss, or damage if Emerson is heard in opposition. Specifically, when Plaintiff has demanded that Emerson immediately cease the conduct complained off (including without limitation, calls to the public to ridicule, harass and defame the Plaintiff, its agents, employees, officers, directors and their respective families), Emerson in fact escalated his conduct and Symetra in good faith believes this conduct will further escalate if he has notice of the request for a TRO. *See, e.g,* Complaint, ¶¶42-46. As a result of this, Symetra's counsel certifies to this Court that notice should not be given to Emerson.

FACTS

A. Background on Symetra

Headquartered in Bellevue, Washington, Symetra Financial Corporation is a diversified financial services company with $42.9 billion in assets, approximately 2.5 million customers, and over 1,600 employees nationwide. (VC, ¶5). Symetra is a wholly owned subsidiary of Symetra Financial Corporation. (*Id.*) Symetra has been a trusted component of the insurance industry for more than 50 years. (VC, ¶6). Over that time, Symetra has developed substantial goodwill and an exceptional reputation in the industry. (*Id.*)

Symetra has offered various insurance products to its customers using the SYMETRA LIFE INSURANCE COMPANY mark for many years. (VC, ¶8). This mark has come to have significant meaning in the industry for quality service and honesty. In addition, Symetra owns U.S. Federal registration serial number 3127698 for the SYMETRA mark, which registration is valid and incontestable. (VC, ¶¶6, 7).

Symetra maintains a web site, https://www.symetra.com, on which it advertises its services and provides biographical information about the leadership team of Symetra. (VC, ¶9). On Symetra's web site are several images that depict certain members of the leadership team. The images on the Symetra web site are controlled by Symetra, which has exclusive rights to the use and display of those images. (*Id.*) Symetra's employees depend and rely upon Symetra to provide a professional and safe work environment. (VC, ¶10).

B. Background on Guy Emerson

Emerson is a disability claimant under his former employer's Life and Disability Plan with Symetra Life Insurance Company. (VC, ¶11). As a plan participant, Emerson submitted a claim for long term disability to Symetra which has been administering his claim, apparently to Emerson's dissatisfaction. (*Id.*) However, rather than avail himself of the appropriate mechanisms for addressing his claim, Emerson instead chose to embark on a campaign of terror and intimidation intended to force Symetra to acquiesce to Emerson's claim. *See, e.g.*, Complaint at ¶¶12-45).

C. Emerson's Outrageous Conduct

Without the knowledge or authorization of Symetra, Emerson registered the "symetralifeinsurancecompany.com" domain name (the Infringing Domain) for his own benefit and use. (VC, ¶12). Emerson registered the Infringing Domain using Symetra's registered and common-law marks with full knowledge of Symetra's exclusive rights in those marks and without any colorable claim of authorization by Symetra. (VC, ¶¶12-15).

Emerson began extensive research into the names and personal information of several officers, directors, and employees of Symetra. (VC, ¶¶16-17). He amassed a substantial amount of personally identifiable information from numerous sources. Those sources necessarily included publicly accessible sources. (*Id.*) Additionally, he may have accessed protected computing systems either without authorization or by exceeding the authorized access of those protected computing systems to retrieve personally identifiable information about various officers, directors, and employees of Symetra. (VC, ¶18). Even more troubling, Emerson also conducted extensive research into the names and personal information of the *family members* of several Symetra officers, directors, and employees. (VC, ¶¶19-21).

Emerson also made unauthorized copies of numerous copyright-protected images from the Symetra web site and other sites, such as social and professional networking sites. (VC, ¶¶22-23). Those images generally included pictures of various officers, directors, and employees of Symetra. Emerson's use of those images is in violation of any authorization endorsed by any of those sites. Accordingly, Emerson's copying and display of those images is unauthorized. (*Id.*)

Emerson launched a web site (the "Offending Website") hosted at the Infringing Domain. (VC, ¶¶24-26). A copy of the Offending Website is attached to the Complaint in this action as Exhibit A, which was filed under seal to protect the many individuals, some of whom are minor children, identified on it. On the Offending Website, Emerson published the personally identifiable information about numerous officers, directors, and employees of Symetra. (VC, ¶¶25-26). In addition, Emerson also published the personally identifiable information of many family members, some of whom are minor children, who have nothing at all to do with any dispute between Emerson and Symetra. (*Id.*)

Emerson structured and designed the Offending Website so as to confuse the public into the belief that the Offending Website is in fact affiliated with Symetra. (VC, ¶27).The Offending Website even includes a copyright notice falsely identifying Symetra as the owner. (*Id.*) The Offending Website includes numerous statements about the services of Symetra which are false and demeaning of Symetra's services. (VC, ¶28).

In one example, the Offending Website includes the following quotation which is falsely attributed to Symetra's Chief Executive Officer:

> Well of course we engage in bad faith tactics like delaying and denying our policy holders [*sic*] valid claims. How do you think me [*sic*], my key executive officers, and my board members stay so damn rich. [*sic*]

(VC, ¶29). In another example, the Offending Website includes the following quotation which is falsely attributed to one of Symetra's board members:

> I swear I knew nothing about Symetra delaying and denying policy holders [sic] valid claims, or defrauding their customers, and I really don't care, so long as the checks keep coming.

(VC, ¶30). In another example, the Offending Website falsely states that Symetra's Motto is "DELAY-DENY-DEFRAUD." (VC, ¶31). The Offending Website also falsely states that "SYMETRA IS NOTORIOUS FOR DELAYING, DENYING AND DE-

FRAUDING ITS POLICY HOLDERS." (VC, ¶32). In another example, the Offending Website falsely states that Symetra is "NOT VETERAN FREINDLY [*sic*]." (VC, ¶33). In yet another example, the Offending Website falsely states that Symetra's policy holders "don't receive anything, or very little[,] from Symetra when [] risk materializes into an injury." (VC, ¶34).

The Offending Website is also rife with invitations to the public to harass and victimize all of the named individuals. (VC, ¶35). The Offending Website not only invites harassing conduct against the named officers, directors, and employees of Symetra, it also invites harassing conduct against the family members, some of whom are minor children. (*Id.*)

In one example, the Offending Website invites and encourages members of the public to harass various employees of Symetra for the apparent purpose of forcing Symetra to capitulate to Emerson's demands, as shown in this passage taken from the Offending Website:

> If a Symetra Claims Representative is delaying, denying, engaging in bad faith tactics, or committing outright fraud to avoid paying your valid insurance claim, call them, e-mail them, or pay them a visit at home. If you don't have their home address, home phone number, or e-mail address, contact me and I will find them for you.

(VC, ¶36). In some instances, the Offending Website incites, encourages, or at least invites violent, depraved, or menacing conduct against the *children* of Symetra employees. In one example, the Offending Website includes the following text (edited to protect the privacy of children):

> If [Symetra Employee] is delaying, or denying your valid insurance claim feel free to stop by her home to discuss your claim with her. If [Symetra Employee] is not home when you arrive, I'm sure that her daughter [First Child], or her daughter [Second Child], would be more than willing to keep you company until she arrives home.

(VC, ¶37). The foregoing passage is a thinly veiled invitation to depraved members of the public to harass or visit violence upon the family members of various Symetra employees. As a direct result of Emerson's veiled threats and conduct, several of the family members of Symetra's employees have suffered severe emotional distress, including fears of being accosted, assaulted, injured, or worse as a result of Emerson's Offending Site. (VC, ¶¶38-39). Several affected individuals were forced to take down or otherwise restrict access to their online social web sites out of a fear of harassment or violence due to Emerson's depraved conduct. (VC, ¶¶40-41).

After Symetra approached Emerson to remove the offensive content, rather than comply and avoid this action, he instead stepped up his outrageous conduct by including even more defamatory and inciteful content. (VC, ¶42). Emerson mocked Symetra by publishing additional inflammatory and harassing content directed at employees of Symetra, including images misappropriated from various sites captioned with defamatory and insulting statements. (*Id.*)

Emerson's conduct demonstrates that his intent is to try and force Symetra into capitulating with demands he has placed on Symetra or allow its employees and their families to suffer ridicule, embarrassment, harassment, or even violence. (VC, ¶43). That conduct demonstrates an extortionate intent and objective. (*Id.*) It also demonstrates that he is actively pursuing more and more egregious methods and tactics to try and heighten the damage being suffered by Symetra.

Emerson's outrageous conduct is having a detrimental impact on Symetra's ability to provide its employees with the safe and professional work environment that they deserve and that Symetra strives to provide. *See, e.g.*, VC, ¶41.

ARGUMENT

A. The Legal Standard for Obtaining a Temporary Restraining Order and a Preliminary Injunction

Symetra is seeking a temporary restraining order and preliminary injunction to enjoin any further damage to Symetra's goodwill and business reputation, and hopefully prevent any potential physical harm to Symetra's employees or their children. The same four factor test applies to temporary restraining orders and preliminary injunctions and each supports Symetra's request: (1) Symetra is likely to succeed on the merits; (2) Symetra will suffer irreparable harm absent the injunction; (3) the harm to Symetra outweighs any harm to Emerson; and (4) the injunction does not adversely affect the public interest. See *Latin Am. Music Co. v. Cardenas Fernandez & Assoc., Inc.*, 2 Fed. Appx. 40, 42, 42 n.2 (1st Cir. 2001).

B. There Is a Substantial Likelihood that Symetra Will Prevail on Its Claims.

Symetra has a substantial likelihood that it will prevail on its claims in this matter. Emerson's outrageous conduct is indefensible and has no rational defense. Emerson acted with full knowledge of Symetra's use of, and statutory and common law rights to, Symetra's trademarks and without regard to the likelihood of confusion by the public created by Emerson's activities.

The Infringing Domain is identical to Symetra's common law trademark of SYMETRA LIFE INSURANCE COMPANY. The Infringing Domain fully incorporates exactly the same mark as Symetra's Federally registered trademark. Emerson's actions demonstrate an intentional, willful, and malicious intent to trade on the goodwill associated with Symetra's trademark to the great and irreparable injury of Symetra.

The false, misleading, and defamatory statements on the Offending Website, falsely attributed to officers of Symetra, have caused and will continue to cause irreparable harm to the reputation and goodwill of Symetra. In addition, Emerson's attempt to present a sheen of authenticity to the Offending Website has confused existing or potential customers of Symetra that the Offending Website is in fact affiliated with Symetra. Conversely, Emerson has no legitimate defense to the confusion he has caused and is fomenting. Accordingly, Symetra is highly likely to prevail on its trademark claims.

Even more egregious and indefensible is Emerson's defamatory conduct. Emerson's publications on the Offending Website are hereinafter referred to as the "False and Defamatory Statements."

- The False and Defamatory Statements falsely accuse Symetra of knowingly endorsing fraudulent and deceptive business practices.
- The False and Defamatory Statements were published without privilege and were published with actual malice.
- The False and Defamatory Statements are defamatory *per se* and damages to Symetra are presumed as a matter of law.
- The False and Defamatory Statements are libelous on their face in that they are defamatory without the necessity of explanatory matter or other extrinsic facts, and or they impute criminal conduct to Symetra.
- Emerson published the False and Defamatory Statements without conducting a reasonable investigation.
- Emerson published the False and Defamatory Statements without any reliable or credible sources or information.
- Because Emerson published the False and Defamatory Statements with both Constitutional and common law malice, Symetra is entitled to an award of punitive damages to punish him for his wrongdoing and deter him from repeating such heinous conduct in the future against others.

Most worrisome of all are Emerson's veiled threats of physical violence against the *children* of certain of Symetra's employees. Emerson's call for depraved members of the public to visit the unattended daughters of certain Symetra employees is indefensible. Such conduct and threats cannot be tolerated and can never have any legitimate justification.

Emerson's conduct is willful and demonstrates an entire want of care that raises a conscious indifference to consequences. Accordingly, Symetra is likely to prevail on its defamation claims.

C. Symetra Will Suffer Irreparable Harm If the Injunction Is Denied.

It is highly likely that Symetra, its employees, and the family members of those employees will suffer irreparable harm if the requested injunction is denied. At a minimum, the goodwill and business reputation of Symetra will continue to suffer substantial harm based on Emerson's false allegations that Symetra engages in systemic fraud and bad faith. Symetra has spent many decades building up the goodwill that it has, and Emerson's actions threaten to undermine decades of effort and goodwill by publishing unsubstantiated and false charges of fraud. Reputations are hard to build buy easy to destroy. Money damages are insufficient to remedy the harm to Symetra's goodwill and business reputation. In addition, the potential for physical harm, as invited by Emerson, is an irreparable harm on its face.

D. The Harm to Symetra Outweighs Any Harm to Emerson.

The balancing of harms weighs heavily in favor of granting this injunction. As noted, there is an ongoing substantial harm to Symetra's business reputation and goodwill due to the false and misleading statements being published by Emerson. In addition, there is a real threat that some depraved member of the public will act on Emerson's invitation to accost the daughters of one of Symetra's employees while they are home alone. That danger alone outweighs any conceivable harm to Emerson.

Conversely, entry of the requested injunction will cause no harm whatsoever on Emerson. Enjoining Emerson from publishing defamatory and inciteful statements on a web site is effectively no harm at all. Defamatory statements and calls to violence enjoy no First Amendment protections. Nor will Emerson's defamatory and inciteful conduct accomplish his apparently intended goal of forcing Symetra to pay out a claim that it has denied. Indeed, Emerson's efforts in that regard are not only futile, they have necessitated the filing of this action. Accordingly, it is even in Emerson's best interests for the Court to enter this injunction to ameliorate any further harm to either Symetra or Emerson.

Finally, entry of this injunction has no bearing on the course of Emerson's disability claim. Any dispute between Emerson and Symetra regarding the status of any claim by Emerson will be resolved in accordance with application policies and procedures governing the provision of insurance services. Accordingly, entry of this injunction will have no impact whatsoever on any disability compensation to which Emerson may or may not be due.

E. Granting the Injunction Will Not Disserve the Public Interest.

The interest of the public will in fact be better served by entry of the requested injunction. There is no colorable argument that the public is better served by allowing Emerson to persist in his attacks on Symetra's employees and their families.

CONCLUSION

For the foregoing reasons, Symetra respectfully asks that the Court enter a Temporary Restraining Order and Preliminary Injunction as follows:

A. Emerson, and 1all other persons acting for, with, by, through or under authority of Emerson, or in concert or participation with Emerson, and each of them, be enjoined from:

a. using any trademark, name, logo, design, or source designation of any kind on or in connection with any online presence that is a copy, reproduction, colorable imitation, or simulation of, or confusingly similar to any of Symetra's trademarks, trade dresses, names, or logos;

b. using any trademark, name, logo, design, or source designation of any kind on or in connection with any online presence that is likely to cause confusion, mistake, deception, or public misunderstanding that such goods or services are sponsored or authorized by Symetra, or are in any way connected or related to Symetra;

c. any further public *ad hominem* comments relating to any Symetra agent, employee, officer, or director or the family of any such agent, employee, officer, or director;

d. any further publication of any personally identifiable information pertaining to any Symetra agent, employee, officer, or director or the family of any such agent, employee, officer, or director.

B. Emerson be ordered to take down and refrain from reestablishing any online presence that includes or refers to any personally identifiable information of any Symetra agent, officer, director, employee or any family member of the same.

C. The web site currently maintained at the "symetralifeinsurancecompany.com" domain be ordered taken down and that its contents not be republished at any other publicly accessible location.

D. Such other and further relief as the Court deems just and proper.

Dated this 4th day of December, 2018.

Respectfully submitted,

/s/ Geraldine G. Sanchez

Geraldine G. Sanchez, Bar No. 8050

Roach Hewitt Ruprecht Sanchez & Bischoff PC

66 Pearl Street, Suite 200

Portland, Maine 04101

207-747-4870

Email: gsanchez@roachhewitt.com

/s/ John Whitaker

John Whitaker, WSBA No. 28,868

(Pro Hac Vice pending)

CHRISTENSEN O'CONNOR JOHNSON KINDNESS PLLC

1201 Third Avenue, Suite 3600

Seattle, WA 98101-3029

206.682.8100

Email: john.whitaker@cojk.com

litdoc@cojk.com

ATTORNEYS FOR PLAINTIFF

SYMETRA LIFE INSURANCE COMPANY

Table of Laws and Rules

UNITED STATES CONSTITUTION

UNITED STATES CODE ANNOTATED

FEDERAL RULES OF CIVIL PROCEDURE

FEDERAL RULES OF CIVIL PROCEDURE—Continued

FEDERAL RULES OF CIVIL PROCEDURE—Continued

FEDERAL RULES OF CIVIL PROCEDURE—Continued

FEDERAL RULES OF CIVIL PROCEDURE—Continued

FEDERAL RULES OF CIVIL PROCEDURE—Continued

RULES OF THE U.S. DISTRICT COURT FOR THE DISTRICT OF MAINE—Continued

Table of Cases